A Companion to Medieval English Literature and Culture c.1350–c.1500

Blackwell Companions to Literature and Culture

This series offers comprehensive, newly written surveys of key periods and movements and certain major authors, in English literary culture and history. Extensive volumes provide new perspectives and positions on contexts and on canonical and post-canonical texts, orientating the beginning student in new fields of study and providing the experienced undergraduate and new graduate with current and new directions, as pioneered and developed by leading scholars in the field.

Published Recently

45.	*A Companion to Shakespeare's Sonnets*	Edited by Michael Schoenfeldt
46.	*A Companion to Satire*	Edited by Ruben Quintero
47.	*A Companion to William Faulkner*	Edited by Richard C. Moreland
48.	*A Companion to the History of the Book*	Edited by Simon Eliot and Jonathan Rose
49.	*A Companion to Emily Dickinson*	Edited by Martha Nell Smith and Mary Loeffelholz
50.	*A Companion to Digital Literary Studies*	Edited by Ray Siemens and Susan Schreibman
51.	*A Companion to Charles Dickens*	Edited by David Paroissien
52.	*A Companion to James Joyce*	Edited by Richard Brown
53.	*A Companion to Latin American Literature and Culture*	Edited by Sara Castro-Klaren
54.	*A Companion to the History of the English Language*	Edited by Haruko Momma and Michael Matto
55.	*A Companion to Henry James*	Edited by Greg Zacharias
56.	*A Companion to the British and Irish Short* Story	Edited by Cheryl Alexander Malcolm and David Malcolm
57.	*A Companion to Jane Austen*	Edited by Claudia L. Johnson and Clara Tuite
58.	*A Companion to the Arthurian Literature*	Edited by Helen Fulton
59.	*A Companion to the Modern American Novel: 1900–1950*	Edited by John T. Matthews
60.	*A Companion to the Global Renaissance*	Edited by Jyotsna G. Singh
61.	*A Companion to Thomas Hardy*	Edited by Keith Wilson
62.	*A Companion to T. S. Eliot*	Edited by David E. Chinitz
63.	*A Companion to Samuel Beckett*	Edited by S. E. Gontarski
64.	*A Companion to Twentieth-Century U.S. Fiction*	Edited by David Seed

For more information on the Blackwell Companions to Literature and Culture series, please visit www.wiley.com

A COMPANION TO

MEDIEVAL ENGLISH LITERATURE AND CULTURE C.1350–C.1500

EDITED BY **PETER BROWN**

WILEY-BLACKWELL
A John Wiley & Sons, Ltd., Publication

This paperback edition first published 2009

Edition history: Blackwell Publishing Ltd (hardback, 2007)

Blackwell Publishing was acquired by John Wiley & Sons in February 2007. Blackwell's publishing program has been merged with Wiley's global Scientific, Technical, and Medical business to form Wiley-Blackwell.

Registered Office
John Wiley & Sons Ltd, The Atrium, Southern Gate, Chichester, West Sussex, PO19 8SQ, United Kingdom

Editorial Offices
350 Main Street, Malden, MA 02148-5020, USA
9600 Garsington Road, Oxford, OX4 2DQ, UK
The Atrium, Southern Gate, Chichester, West Sussex, PO19 8SQ, UK

For details of our global editorial offices, for customer services, and for information about how to apply for permission to reuse the copyright material in this book please see our website at www.wiley.com/wiley-blackwell.

Library of Congress Cataloging-in-Publication Data
A companion to medieval English literature and culture, c.1350–c.1500 / edited by Peter Brown.
p. cm.—(Blackwell companions to literature and culture ; 42)
Includes bibliographical references and index.
ISBN: 978-1-4051-9552-2: (pbk)
ISBN: 978-0-6312-1973-6 (hbk, alk. paper)
1. English literature—Middle English, 1100–1500—History and criticism. 2. Great Britain—History—1066–1687. 3. Great Britain—Intellectual life—1066–1485. I. Brown, Peter, 1948– II. Series.
PR255.C653 2006
820.92001—dc22
2005034700

A catalogue record for this book is available from the British Library.

Set in 11/13pt Garamond 3 by SPI Publisher Services, Pondicherry, India
Printed in Singapore

1 2009

Contents

Illustrations

Notes on Contributors

Kathleen Ashley is Professor of English at the University of Southern Maine. She has published on cultural performance, hagiography and autobiography, including a co-authored book, *Writing Faith* (1999) and a co-edited volume, *Autobiography and Postmodernism* (1994).

Denise Baker is Professor of English and Associate Dean at the University of North Carolina at Greensboro. She is the author of *Julian of Norwich's Showings: From Vision to Book* and editor of *Inscribing the Hundred Years' War in French and English Cultures* and the Norton Critical Edition of *The Showings of Julian of Norwich.* She has published essays on Chaucer, Gower, Langland and the Middle English mystics.

Christopher Baswell is Professor of English at UCLA. He is author of *Virgil in Medieval England* (1995), and co-editor of *The Longman Anthology of British Literature*, volume IA: *The Middle Ages* (2002).

Catherine Batt is a Senior Lecturer in the School of English, University of Leeds. Her publications include *Essays on Thomas Hoccleve* (as editor and contributor, 1996) and *Malory's* Morte Darthur: *Remaking Arthurian Tradition* (2002). She is working on a translation of Henry, Duke of Lancaster's devotional treatise, *Le Livre de Seyntz Medicines.*

Santha Bhattacharji is a Senior College Lecturer in English at Keble College, Oxford. Publications include *God is an Earthquake: The Spirituality of Margery Kempe* (1997), and the new *DNB* entry for Julian of Norwich.

Julia Boffey is Professor of Medieval Studies at Queen Mary, University of London. Recent publications include *Fifteenth-Century Dream Visions* and, with A. S. G. Edwards, *A New Index of Middle English Verse.*

Montgomery Bohna teaches medieval and early modern British history at the University of Pittsburgh. He has published articles on Cade's Revolt of 1450 and the Lincolnshire Rebellion of 1470.

Mishtooni Bose is Christopher Tower Official Student in Medieval Poetry in English at Christ Church, Oxford. Her most recent publication is 'Vernacular Philosophy and the Making of Orthodoxy in the Fifteenth Century', *New Medieval Literatures* 7 (2005). This is part of a larger study of responses to heresy in late medieval England.

Peter Brown is Professor of Medieval English Literature at the University of Kent. Other edited publications include *A Blackwell Companion to Chaucer* (Blackwell, 2000) and *Reading Dreams: The Interpretation of Dreams from Chaucer to Shakespeare* (1999). He has recently completed a monograph on Chaucer and *perspectiva.*

Ardis Butterfield is Reader in English at University College London. Her recent publications include *Poetry and Music in Medieval France from Jean Renart to Guillaume de Machaut* (2002) and an edited collection of essays on *Chaucer and the City* (2002), as well as articles on Machaut, Gautier de Coinci, Anglo-Norman fabliaux, Gower and Chaucer. She is completing a book on Chaucer and literary relations between England and France in the Hundred Years War.

A. S. G. Edwards is Professor of Textual Studies at De Montfort University, Leicester. He has written on aspects of manuscript production and circulation in later medieval English texts. His *New Index of Middle English Verse* (with Julia Boffey) was published in 2005.

Ruth Evans is a Professor in the Department of English Studies, University of Stirling. She is co-editor (with Sarah Salih and Anke Bernau) of *Medieval Virginities* (2003) and (with Jocelyn Wogan-Browne, Nicholas Watson and Andrew Taylor) of *The Idea of the Vernacular* (1999). She is completing a monograph on Chaucer and memory.

R. James Goldstein, Professor of English at Auburn University, Alabama, is the author of *The Matter of Scotland: Historical Narrative in Medieval Scotland* (1993) and essays on Middle Scots, Chaucer and Langland.

Richard Firth Green teaches at the Ohio State University. He has written *Poets and Princepleasers: Literature and the English Court in the Late Middle Ages* (1980) and *A Crisis of Truth: Literature and Law in Ricardian England* (1999).

Darryll Grantley is Senior Lecturer in Drama at the University of Kent. His research interests extend over both medieval and early modern drama; his publications include *Wit's Pilgrimage: Drama and the Social Impact of Education in Early Modern England* (2000) and *English Dramatic Interludes 1300–1580* (2004).

Rosemary Greentree, a Research Fellow in the Department of English, University of Adelaide, has written *Reader, Teller and Teacher: The Narrator of Robert Henryson's* Moral Fables and a bibliography of *The Middle English Lyric and Short Poem*, and co-edited a bibliography of the *Miller's*, *Reeve's* and *Cook's Tales.*

Kevin Gustafson is an Assistant Professor of English at the University of Texas at Arlington. His publications include articles on medieval and sixteenth-century English literature, and his edition and translation of *Cleanness* is forthcoming from Broadview Press.

Thomas Hahn has written about Latin literature of the Middle Ages, popular writing in England (romances and Robin Hood), Chaucer and his contemporaries, and medieval and early modern racial and geopolitical notions of identity (especially with regard to India and the New World), as these have circulated through text and image. He teaches English at the University of Rochester, New York.

Nick Havely is Senior Lecturer in the Department of English and Related Literature at the University of York and is author of a number of books and articles on Chaucer, Dante and Anglo-Italian literary contacts from the Middle Ages onwards. He has recently been awarded a Leverhulme Research Fellowship for a project on Dante in the English-speaking world from the fourteenth century to the present.

Geraldine Heng is Director of Medieval Studies and Associate Professor of English at the University of Texas at Austin, and the author of *Empire of Magic: Medieval Romance and the Politics of Cultural Fantasy* (2003).

E. A. Jones is Senior Lecturer in English Medieval Literature and Culture at the University of Exeter. He has published on devotional compilations, and on hermits and anchorites.

Richard Kaeuper (University of Rochester, New York) has written on government finance, law and public order, and chivalry (stressing use of literary sources).

Stephen Kelly is a Lecturer in English at Queen's University, Belfast. He is author of *Langland's Social Poetics: Re-imagining the Cultures of* Piers Plowman (forthcoming) and, with John Thompson and Ryan Perry, *Making Histories: The Middle English Prose 'Brut' and the Bibliographical Imagination* (forthcoming). *Imagining the Book*, co-edited with John Thompson, appeared in 2005.

Pamela King has recently left her post as Head of School at St Martin's College, Lancaster, to take up the Chair in Medieval Studies at the University of Bristol. Her principal publications are on medieval English theatre, literature and art. She is author of *The York Cycle and the Worship of the City* (2006).

Catherine La Farge is Lecturer at the National University of Ireland, Galway. She has written on gender issues in Chaucer and Malory, conversation in Malory, and issues of colonization in medieval travel writing.

Carol M. Meale is Senior Research Fellow, University of Bristol. Among other work she has edited *Readings in Medieval English Romance* (1994) and *Women and Literature in Britain 1150–1500*, 2nd edn (1996).

Mark Miller is Associate Professor of English at the University of Chicago. He is the author of *Philosophical Chaucer: Love, Sex, and Agency in the* Canterbury Tales (2004). His current project is a book on moral psychology in late medieval England.

Donka Minkova is Professor of English Language at UCLA. Her publications include *The History of Final Vowels in English* (1991), *English Words: History and Structure* (with Robert Stockwell, 2001), and *Alliteration and Sound Change in Early English* (2003). She has also co-edited with Robert Stockwell *Studies in the History of the English Language: A Millennial Perspective* (2002) and with Theresa Tinkle *Chaucer and the Challenges of Medievalism* (2003).

J. Allan Mitchell is Assistant Professor of English at the University of Victoria, Canada. He is the author of *Ethics and Exemplary Narrative in Chaucer and Gower* (2004) and is currently preparing an edition of Lydgate's *Temple of Glas* for the Middle English Texts Series.

Nicholas Perkins is a Fellow of St Hugh's College, Oxford, and University Lecturer in English. He is the author of *Hoccleve's 'Regiment of Princes': Counsel and Constraint* (2001), and articles on early and late Middle English writing.

Helen Phillips is Senior Lecturer in English Literature at Cardiff University, Wales. Her recent publications include *Introduction to the Canterbury Tales: Reading, Fiction, Context* (2000), an edited collection of essays, *Robin Hood: Medieval and Post-Medieval* (2005), and articles on medieval and nineteenth-century literature.

Raluca L. Radulescu is Lecturer in Medieval Literature in the English Department at the University of Wales, Bangor. Her publications include a monograph, *The Gentry Context for Malory's* Morte Darthur (2003), edited collections of essays on Malory, gentry culture and the *Brut* chronicle, and a number of articles on medieval literature and historical writing.

David Raybin is Professor of English at Eastern Illinois University and editor of *The Chaucer Review*. His publications include *Closure in the Canterbury Tales: The Role of the Parson's Tale*, edited with Linda Tarte Holley (2001) and *Rebels and Rivals: The Contestive*

Spirit in the Canterbury Tales, edited with Susanna Greer Fein and Peter C. Braeger (1991).

Sarah Rees Jones is a Senior Lecturer in History at the Centre for Medieval Studies, University of York. She is the author of articles on the topography of medieval York, Thomas More's *Utopia*, Margery Kempe, the regulation of labour, and the English urban household. She has edited a number of collections of essays on later medieval urban society and culture.

S. H. Rigby is Professor of Medieval Social and Economic History at the University of Manchester. His publications include *Marxism and History*, *English Society in the Later Middle Ages* and *Chaucer in Context*, and he is the editor of *A Companion to Britain in the Later Middle Ages*.

Dana M. Symons is an Assistant Professor at Simon Fraser University, BC, Canada. She has edited a volume in the Middle English Texts Series, *Chaucerian Dream Visions and Complaints*, and has published on medieval romance.

Meg Twycross is Professor Emeritus of English Medieval Studies at Lancaster University, and editor of the journal *Medieval English Theatre*. Her latest major publication (with Sarah Carpenter) is *Masks and Masking in Medieval and Early Tudor England* (2002).

Barry Windeatt is Professor of English at the University of Cambridge and a Fellow of Emmanuel College. His research focuses on the imaginative literature, visual culture and contemplative traditions of medieval England in a European context.

Laura Wright is a Senior Lecturer in English Language at the University of Cambridge and a Fellow of Lucy Cavendish College. She is editor of *The Development of Standard English, 1300–1800: Theories, Descriptions, Conflicts* (2000). Her areas of interest are the history of the English language and in particular the history of the London dialect.

Acknowledgements

My thanks are due first to Andrew McNeillie, who suggested that I take on the editing of this Companion. He has remained interested in its welfare in spite of many other commitments. My editorial labours have also been eased by other, generous contributions of professional skill and encouragement. At Blackwell Publishing Emma Bennett, Jenny Hunt, Karen Wilson and Astrid Wind have been models of patience and providers of helpful advice; Glynis Baguley has combined the roles of copy editor and project manager with wit and flair; and at the University of Kent Templeman Library Angela Faunch and Dot Turner have maintained their good humour despite many outlandish requests for the delivery of esoteric documents. The following people kindly helped me to find some of this book's contributors: John Burrow, Chris Cannon, Rita Copeland, Sheila Delany, Hoyt Duggan, Roger Ellis, Judith Ferster, Louise Fradenburg, Robin Frame, Simon Gaunt, Kantik Ghosh, Vincent Gillespie, Jeremy Goldberg, Nicky Hallett, Anne Hudson, Sarah McNamer, Derek Pearsall, Tony Spearing and Paul Strohm. Finally, I gratefully acknowledge the research leave, provided by the University of Kent, which enabled me to bring this project to completion

Canterbury
May 2006

Quotations from writings by Geoffrey Chaucer are from *The Riverside Chaucer*, ed. Larry D. Benson, 3rd edn (Boston: Houghton Mifflin, 1987).

Quotations from the Bible are from the English translation of the Latin Vulgate, otherwise known as the Douay–Rheims version.

Abbreviations

CYT	Canon's Yeoman's Tale
DNB	*Oxford Dictionary of National Biography*, ed. H. C. G. Matthew and Brian Harrison, new edn, 60 vols (Oxford: Oxford University Press, 2004)
EETS	Early English Text Society
es	extra series
FrankT	Franklin's Tale
FrT	Friar's Tale
GP	General Prologue
IMEV	Carleton Brown and Rossell Hope Robbins, *Index of Middle English Verse* (New York: Columbia University Press for the Index Society, 1943)
KnT	Knight's Tale
LGW	*Legend of Good Women*
ManT	Manciple's Tale
ME	Middle English
MED	*Middle English Dictionary*, ed. Hans Kurath, Sherman M. Kuhn and Robert E. Lewis, 12 vols (Ann Arbor: University of Michigan Press, 1954–2001)
MilP	Miller's Prologue
MilT	Miller's Tale
MkT	Monk's Tale
MLT	Man of Law's Tale
OED	*The Oxford English Dictionary*, 2nd edn, prepared by J. A. Simpson and E. S. C. Weiner, 20 vols (Oxford: Clarendon Press, 1989)
os	original series
PardP	Pardoner's Prologue
PardT	Pardoner's Tale
ParsP	Parson's Prologue
PhyT	Physician's Tale

PL	*Patrologia Latina: Patrologiae cursus completus . . . series Latina (prima)*, ed. J.-P. Migne, 221 vols (Paris: 1844–64)
REED	*Records of Early English Drama* (Toronto: University of Toronto Press, 1979–)
RvT	Reeve's Tale
SIMEV	Rossell Hope Robbins and John L. Cutler, *Supplement to the Index of Middle English Verse* (Lexington: University of Kentucky Press, 1965)
SNT	Second Nun's Tale
SqT	Squire's Tale
ss	supplementary series
STC	Pollard, A. W. and Redgrave, G. R. (eds), *A Short-Title Catalogue of Books Printed in England, Scotland and Ireland and of English Books Printed Abroad 1475–1640*, rev. W. A. Jackson, F. S. Ferguson, and K. F. Pantzer, 3 vols (London: Bibliographical Society, 1976–91).
SumT	Summoner's Tale
TEAMS	The Consortium for the Teaching of the Middle Ages
TC	*Troilus and Criseyde*
WBP	Wife of Bath's Prologue
WBT	Wife of Bath's Tale

Introduction

A volume such as this would have been impossible ten years ago. Then, the accent in late medieval English literature was on the 'literary'. Geoffrey Chaucer was in the foreground, shadowed by William Langland and the *Gawain* poet. The fifteenth century was dominated by Thomas Malory's *Morte Darthur* and the mystery plays, which often seemed like the last gasp of the old order before Humanism and the Reformation destroyed it for good. Medievalists occasionally made forays into critical theory – if only to demonstrate that St Augustine had anticipated Jacques Lacan – and into neighbouring disciplines, especially history, but by and large they gave the impression that the traditional approaches to the traditional canon gave them plenty to do.

That insularity has now gone. The category of 'literature' has broadened and deepened to include other kinds of writing, especially of the religious variety. Of course, religious writing has always been an unavoidable component of medieval literature more generally, insofar as it occurs in the works of canonical authors. But the centrality of religious writing – of which there is an enormous amount as yet under-studied – is now more generally acknowledged as a means of coming to terms with distinctive and influential structures of thought, feeling and representation. Manuals of religious instruction, devotional treatises and mystical writing have been subject to the same kind of scrutiny once reserved for, say, the *Canterbury Tales*. A major impetus for this redirection of focus has been the recognition that the ideas of John Wyclif and his Lollard followers, who placed a high value on literacy, texts, translation and interpretation (especially of the Bible), are crucial to an understanding of the more general status, circulation and meaning of late medieval writing. Furthermore, the polemical works produced by Wycliffites, and the measures taken to counteract them, take us to the heart of religious and political ideology and controversy, offering fascinating and complex objects of study, and providing insights into questions of authority, translation and censorship.

At the same time, more general processes of literary production have become a key interest: the ways in which manuscripts and early printed books were made, how texts circulated, who commissioned, owned and read them, how literacy interfaced with orality, all impact on the interpretations available to readers in the twenty-first century. Within networks of production and reception, women are now seen as having had functions and roles at once distinctive from and equivalent to those enjoyed by men. The same is true of authorship itself. In recent years, the writings of Margery Kempe and Julian of Norwich, in particular, have been subject to intense analysis and debate – a process that is beginning to provide some redress for the previous emphasis on male authorship.

New approaches and new texts have brought into play a wide range of theoretical positions, but critical theory is no longer treated as a thing apart; rather, it is a tool to be integrated with the acts of close reading and interpretation. If a particular approach has become dominant, it is the one (existing in manifold versions and applications) that insists on the vital importance of cultural contexts. Those contexts might be religious, or concern social hierarchy or urban life, or extend to the ways in which late medieval society itself constructed narratives of its own experiences in, say, the form of chronicles. More widely still, the contextualizing framework might include the way in which an entire culture reacts to, engages with and represents the values of another, be they those of continental Europe or of ethnic groups often perceived as threats, such as Jews and Saracens. Whatever the context it is not used – as it formerly might have been – as backdrop, but as one side of a dialogue in which the other interlocutor is the text itself.

A consequence of the changes in focus and perception outlined above is that the timeline of late medieval English literature now looks different. Many more interesting developments are happening in the fifteenth century than was formerly thought to be the case. The medieval and later periods do not now look so fragmented and discontinuous: for one thing, proto-Reformation ideas are shaping literature a century or more before the event. And the framing of cause and effect has become more generous, less narrow: to understand attitudes to the East as they surface in late medieval romance it is necessary to look at earlier experiences of crusade; to follow through the implications and potential of morality drama we need to look at sixteenth-century examples.

A Rumpelstiltskin absent from late medieval English literary studies for ten years would nevertheless find in the present volume some familiar features: it incorporates, as necessary, traditional literary history, and insists on the importance of understanding key linguistic principles of dialect and pronunciation. The newly awakened critic, perhaps after ten years too bleary-eyed to stamp his foot in chagrin, would notice the continuing use of Chaucer as a touchstone for the work of other writers, but would have to recognize that, if not belittled, he is embedded within a much wider framework of literary and cultural activities than formerly. Moreover, those writers once represented primarily as his disciples, notably Thomas Hoccleve, John Gower, John Lydgate and Robert Henryson, are now given much greater prominence on account of their individual merits. Rumpelstiltskin would have to acknowledge, if ruefully, that much excellent new work has been done, however much remains to be done.

A number of factors account for the 'new map' of late medieval English literature. Several are common to the discipline as a whole: the embedding of theory within critical practice; a more catholic sense of what constitutes literature; the disestablishment of a traditional canon; a recognition of the importance of cultural contexts; an interest in the application of postcolonialist approaches to other periods of literature. Some factors special to the study of medieval literature are the outcome of tendencies that have been long in the making but which have now borne fruit. A number have been helped by small but regular and focused conferences, and the publication of their proceedings, as in the cases of manuscript and early book studies, translation and mysticism. Others are the culmination of work by influential scholars who have argued persuasively and consistently for the importance of particular cultural contexts (Lollardy, for example) or for particular approaches (say, through social history). The end result is a field of study which at the present juncture is particularly progressive, open and interactive. No longer is late medieval English literature a series of fragmented minority activities. Instead, as the present volume shows, there is a strong sense of shared interests and common endeavour – seasoned, as always, by a healthy pinch of controversy.[1]

So much for developments within the study of late medieval English literature. How have they affected perceptions of the development of the literature itself? Two authoritative works, recently published and regularly cited in the following chapters, offer their own narratives. The one provided by David Wallace, editor of *The Cambridge History of Medieval Literature* (1999), covers the period 1066 to 1547 with thirty-one essays from different contributors, and is designed as a sequential account of changing literary cultures. It is an account that contrasts with received orthodoxies. Its span puts the 'bottleneck' of the late fourteenth century into a much broader perspective; and it opposes the idea – prominent in the earlier *Cambridge History of English Literature* – that the evolution of literature is tied to the development of national identity. Instead, Wallace's volume aims to defamiliarize present-day assumptions, resist a grand narrative, and capture instead 'some sense of the strangeness, the unlikeliness, the historical peculiarity, of medieval compositional processes' (xiv).

Medieval English literature suggests a multiplicity of possible narratives, not least of which is one that questions the very idea of an 'English' literature without reference to the literatures of Wales, Scotland and Ireland. Similarly, the category of literature itself is not to be confined – as it has been by older critical practice – to works of genius and artistic excellence, but should be broad and inclusive. As far as possible, a medieval text should not be viewed in the isolated and distorting frameworks of modern print production, but instead as a part of a process that brings into play the manuscript culture and social system within which it appeared. That system was Christian, and it is pointless to pretend that medieval literature is a conceptual sphere distinct from the religious one. Thus, the study of the culture of the past, in its fullest sense, provides the best means of understanding the literary compositions produced within it:

> Medieval literature cannot be understood (does not survive) except as part of transmissive processes – moving through the hands of copyists, owners, readers and institutional authorities – that form part of other and greater histories (social, political, religious and economic). (Wallace: xxi)

By contrast, James Simpson in his single-authored *Reform and Cultural Revolution* (2002) – the second volume of the Oxford English Literary History – shows no compunction about creating an overarching schema to explain developments in the history of English literature from 1350 to 1547. For him, the period displays a 'narrative of diminishing liberties' (1), which is the consequence of two distinct but competing tendencies. The 'revolution' enacted by Henry VIII imposed a homogeneity on jurisdiction, religious practice and political life that expressed itself in ideals of unity and novelty – values that were readily internalized in forms of literary expression. Prior to this, the motive force of cultural life, which is to say the dominant feature in literary practice, was reform. Simpson is thus standing on their heads two *idées reçues*: first, that late medieval English literature is essentially static in its modes, genres and ideologies; second, that the sixteenth century is a moment of cultural liberation. Simpson admits that other explanatory frameworks are possible, notably one that sees the shift from manuscript to print as the means whereby literature and language were centralized, but his main concern is to demonstrate the validity of his thesis in relation to a number of key modes and themes.

For instance, in the case of 'the comic' (the subject of an entire chapter), Simpson considers the literary expression of two ethical systems. One is limited to the chivalric class and is providential (an underlying patterning of fate ensures that knights win through by virtue of their status); the other is not limited to any class, and is prudential, one that 'can be practised by anyone with the wit to perceive possible futures' (257). Romance – which is comic in the sense that many romance narratives have happy endings – belongs predominantly to the first system, and yet romance often contains a critique of that system or, as Simpson might say, the means of its own reform. This view runs counter to that of sixteenth-century commentators, who saw the reform of chivalry, from brutal practice to civilizing influence, as an achievement of their own day. In fact, medieval romances habitually bring into question and test the very principles on which their protagonists operate – if only to reassert the validity of those principles. They expose honour to shame, and demonstrate that individual identity depends upon affiliation with a larger social group, and indeed with that group's interactions with other social forces. Repeatedly, those other forces are mercantile and female, and in this lies the key to understanding the ways in which medieval romance tends to urge a re-examination of chivalry: it speaks to the women and merchants – excluded as they were from chivalric status – precisely because they were the target audiences of many of the more popular Middle English romances. Chaucer, for his part, mounted his own critique of romance. For example, he juxtaposed it with fabliau – a type of tale in which the victor is the most prudential person, that is, the most adept manipulator of a given situation. But when Caxton edited Sir Thomas Malory's romances for printing as the *Morte Darthur* (1485), his changes were 'in keeping with the Tudor centralization of chivalry' (292).

Both Wallace and Simpson have received their shares of plaudits and brickbats. Wallace has been thought too pluralist in his willingness to entertain a wide spectrum of competing narratives that might explain the development of late medieval English literature, with the result that his 'history' is fragmented and incoherent.[2] Simpson, by contrast, is open to the charge of being reductive, of subsuming the variety of late medieval writing and the different developmental dynamics of its genres in a single explanatory thesis. The effect can be a distortion or misrepresentations of certain kinds of development in order to save the appearances of the broader narrative.[3] The present book does not attempt a general intervention in either side of the debate, although its orientation is more towards Wallace than Simpson. However, some individual contributors do take positions in relation to one or the other approach, and since both histories are important and durable points of reference, it has been appropriate to take due account of them here.

The overall concept of the present volume, and the topics identified for most of its chapters, was the work of its begetter, Nicholas Havely. I am indebted to him for devising a scheme that has proved resilient but flexible. It has undergone some revision as chapters have been commissioned, and a few new topics have been added. In particular, the organization of the contributions is now quite different from that originally envisaged. The structure is that of a funnel. The book begins with sections that have the broadest circumference, and continues with others that have gradually diminishing frames of reference. The subject matter narrows until the final, and longest, section, deals at length with individual texts. But even a chapter offering the widest possible conspectus brings its ideas to bear on specific literary examples. Conversely, discussion of individual works frequently raises themes that are considered more fully in earlier contributions. The chapters are thus interactive and at the end of each the reader is directed to others that deal with related topics. Each contributor is a specialist in his or her field, and has been encouraged to write in an authoritative but accessible way that will set the reader thinking, open up horizons of meaning, and provide models of interpretative technique. The result is a compendious volume, full of original material and dependable judgements, that will enliven the study, discussion and research of late medieval English literature for many years to come.

Notes

1 Stephen G. Nicholls, 'Writing the New Middle Ages', *PMLA* 120 (2005), 422–41.

2 See John Burrow's review in *Speculum* 76 (2001), 243–5 and the colloquium in *Studies in the Age of Chaucer* 23 (2001), 471–519, with contributions by Christine Chism, Theresa Coletti, Fiona Somerset, Sarah Stanbury, Anne Savage and David Wallace.

3 David Aers and Sarah Beckwith (eds), 'Reform and Cultural Revolution: Writing English Literary History, 1350–1547', special issue of the *Journal of Medieval and Early Modern Studies* 35 (2005), 3–119, with contributions by David Wallace, Derek Pearsall, Richard K. Emmerson, Bruce Holsinger, Thomas Betteridge and James Simpson.

PART I
Overviews

1
Critical Approaches

David Raybin

Critical theory at the beginning of the twenty-first century has refocused the historicizing of late medieval English literature and culture. A new wave of manuscript studies is bringing deeper understanding of the surviving physical evidence, of early book culture, of reception, and of the trilingual character of late medieval English literature. Feminist analysis and gender-based studies continue to expand our sense of the scope of the history available to be examined. Religious studies, such as those of the Lollard movement or the cultures of orthodoxy and dissent, are refining our understanding of the age's spiritual climate. The scholarship of intertextuality – especially of how earlier writers influenced Chaucer and his contemporaries, and of how Chaucer and Langland influenced fifteenth-century authors – has articulated important continuities between the periods now labelled *medieval* and *early modern*. Studies of popular culture interrogate the historical basis of legend. And philologists old and new are allowing us to see how verbal play and nuance may reveal a writer's stance on pivotal spiritual and political debates. In studies of the past decade, a few emphases are prominent: *Multilingualism and Vernacularity* – what does it mean that writers choose to write in English instead of (or along with) courtly French and learned Latin, and how far may one distinguish London English from concurrent dialects? *Englishness* – what is the new 'England' that writers define in terms of language and geography? *Literary and Social Affinities* – with what circles do writers associate and how do audience concerns create meaning? *Violence and the Other* – against what cultures, classes, beliefs and behaviours do medieval English writers define themselves, and why does violence figure so prominently in this definition through difference? Such strategies as Marxist criticism, psychoanalytic criticism, and deconstruction continue to be practised, but to a large extent their values have been assimilated into the general critical vocabulary.

By the phrase *critical theory* I mean here not only the abstract discourse that scholars use to describe their strategies, but more importantly the *practice* that informs the discipline and the studies to which I will refer. Paul Strohm distinguishes 'engaged or "practical" theory' from its 'hypothetical opposite – "pure" theory, uncorrected or unchastened by sustained contact with a particular text' (Strohm 2000: xi). Abstract theorists have opened exciting avenues for textual analysis, providing common vocabularies for such analysis. However, in the context of the present volume, which is defined by its concern for the 'particular text', my focus will be less on how writers define their methods than on their practical performance of those methods.

Anthologies

The ways in which editors construct anthologies provide a good baseline for understanding how theoretical reorientations shift our perspectives on earlier texts. The choices made by the anthologists tell large groups of people what they should read, and although editors do not always argue overtly for their choices, a theoretical stance is usually implicit in the selections. Derek Pearsall explains that a comprehensive anthology must include 'larger samples of what is best [in the writing of a period] and smaller samples of what is more representative' and that for reader as well as anthologist 'the two criteria are constantly in operational conflict and in question' (Pearsall 1999: xv). I will look at how three anthologies resolve the conflict.

The most widely read anthology, the book that introduces most North American students to English medieval literature, is the *Norton Anthology of English Literature*, now in its seventh edition.[1] The selections representing 'Middle English Literature in the Fourteenth and Fifteenth Centuries' are: *Sir Gawain and the Green Knight*; a hefty chunk of Geoffrey Chaucer (including the General Prologue and four tales); some *Piers Plowman*; selections from Julian of Norwich, Margery Kempe, Thomas Malory and Robert Henryson; three plays; and eleven anonymous lyrics. Although *Norton* is noted for its extensive historical introductions, the texts themselves exhibit a focus on the poetry traditionally rated 'best', along with a sampling of prose, drama, and writings by women. The critical judgement implicit in the *Norton Anthology* asserts that while texts by women must be acknowledged, relatively little else has changed in what we ought to read.

The *Longman Anthology of British Literature*, currently in its second edition, is *Norton*'s chief competitor.[2] Its 'The Middle Ages' section includes everything in *Norton* save *Everyman* and *Noah* (for which *Mankind* and the York *Crucifixion* are substituted) with quite a few additions. Some additions amplify the *Norton* offerings: more Chaucer and a larger sampling of *Piers Plowman*, Julian and Kempe. Other additions insert new perspectives: the political dimension of non-literary works on the Rising of 1381 and 'vernacular religion and repression'; the multicultural voices in insular works from Scotland and Wales; a deepened recognition of fifteenth-century culture as reflected in selections from John Lydgate and Christine de Pizan. Collectively, the additions enact an ambivalent editorial reflection upon the traditional canon. The inclusion of Welsh works (in translation), poetry in Middle Scots, and texts of English political opposition effectively expands the definition of what represents *British* literature and includes more of 'what is more representative', while the expansion of the Chaucer offerings indicates an editorial commitment to featuring Chaucer as the dominant writer of the age. Notably, neither the *Longman* nor the *Norton* anthology includes either *Pearl* or Chaucer's most spiritual poetry (Man of Law's Tale, Clerk's Tale, Prioress's Tale, Second Nun's Tale). When it comes to what we are supposed to read, we are clearly to favour texts representing forces of religious dissent or secular humour over texts representing spiritual practices we might view as too traditionally medieval.

A more substantial rethinking of what we should read is offered in Derek Pearsall's *Chaucer to Spenser: An Anthology of Writings in English 1375–1575*. The editor's theoretical stance is articulated in two decisions. First, the volume's scope, manifested in its title, restructures a student's encounter with Chaucer by asserting a continuity between fourteenth- and sixteenth-century English literature. Second, the volume's individual selections reflect a theory of inclusiveness that juxtaposes aesthetically significant literary texts with texts having less literary appeal but which provide a historicized context for reading.

Pearsall seeks to manifest the 'common cultural tradition' that binds together the *Parliament of Fowls* and the *Shepherd's Calendar* because he fears that Chaucer, 'Taught so frequently now as the sole representative of English writing before Shakespeare . . . is in danger of being read and learnt about in a vacuum' (Pearsall 1999: xv). Many proponents of the term *early modern* assume that a vast wasteland separates Tudor literature, appreciated as introducing the modern world, and medieval literature, disparaged as an immature other that briefly flourished with Chaucer. In highlighting fifteenth-century traditions that both reflect the rich heritage of Chaucer and his contemporaries and anticipate the accomplishment of Spenser and his, Pearsall contests the notion of rupture: 'every text looks both backward and forward', with continuities being 'as well worth stressing as changes' (Pearsall 1999: xv–xvi). His selections simultaneously assert the excellence of Chaucer and his contemporaries (the large space given to Chaucer underpins the volume), direct a reader to appreciate the merits of a wide range of fifteenth-century writers, and allow one to see the themes and generic choices linking many sixteenth-century writers to their predecessors. The cumulative effect of the volume is to present a few writers (Chaucer and eight others) as principal conversants in a broader literary discussion that belies the notion of a discontinuous or valueless fifteenth century.

The Triumph of History

In the same year (1999) that *Chaucer to Spenser* challenged the *Norton* idea of what we should read, the creators of the massive *Cambridge History of Medieval English Literature*, privileging its title's 'history' over its 'literature', took the complementary step of promoting a historicism oriented towards anthropology as *the* proper method for selecting and reading texts, which are to be chosen on criteria other than simple literary merit. Proselytizers for a particular theoretical perspective often argue the whys of their choices. Editor David Wallace and his collaborators contend that history is necessary to literary understanding and, further, that literary texts are neither more valuable than, nor easily distinguishable from, other texts. To appreciate Wallace's perspective, one may turn to a collection of essays entitled *Bodies and Disciplines: Intersections of Literature and History in Fifteenth-century England* that he edited with historian Barbara A. Hanawalt. In their introduction, the editors boast of how combining new subjects of study with improved theoretical constructs has made fifteenth-century English studies 'one of the most dynamic growth areas in both literary and historical scholarship':

> This may be, in part, because the fourteenth century has been overworked, but it may also be that medievalists, now somewhat more theory-literate, are better equipped to address the challenges of this difficult period. The extraordinary range of subject matters in this volume . . . attests to the emergence of a new fifteenth-century England. The Wars of the Roses, Caxton and Malory – subjects that loom large in traditional accounts of the period – play a negligible role in this volume. Rather, the essayists direct our attention to the smaller, local dramas that occupied many and various segments of the population. (Hanawalt and Wallace 1996: x)

Indeed, although the majority of the contributors to *Bodies and Disciplines* are affiliated with programmes in English literary studies, the essays focus primarily on facets of local, institutional and corporeal history. Civil and ecclesiastical court records, guild ordinances and household books are brought to bear upon both written and enacted texts as the authors demonstrate how 'the freedoms and constraints endured and enjoyed by different bodies, or the same body at different moments', may be 'considered as part of greater social strategies' (xi). The fifteenth century becomes an exciting area for literary study precisely because its written texts, presumed to lack the aesthetic qualities offered by Chaucer or the *Gawain* poet, lend themselves to the kinds of socio-cultural analysis favoured by new historicism.

The attitude that situates literature as adjunct to history permeates the interpretation of English medieval literary history promulgated in the *Cambridge History*. Literary subjects that have traditionally formed the core of such a history receive limited attention, while subjects more congenial to non-literary historical analysis are accentuated. The titles of the volume's large sections and their chapters offer a succinct representation of Wallace's theoretical design. *Writing in the British Isles* includes chapters entitled 'Writing in Wales', 'Writing in Ireland', 'Writing in Scotland, 1058–1560', 'Writing history in England' and 'London texts and literate practice', effectively ignoring the existence of English-language literary texts. *Institutional Productions* includes chapters on 'Monastic productions', 'The friars and medieval English literature', 'Classroom and confession', '*Vox populi* and the literature of 1381' and 'Englishing the Bible, 1066–1549'. An interest in the collective will thus obscures questions of aesthetics and design posed by single authorship. The chapters in *After the Black Death*, the literary heart of the volume, acknowledge individual authorship but reject the traditional notion of a Ricardian literary renaissance centred upon three magnificent poets. Indeed, the *Pearl*-

poet is not afforded a chapter and receives mention only in passing.[3] The volume's final section, *Before the Reformation*, consists of chapters that highlight the institutional conflicts that opposed traditional and dissident religion and politics. Where the older model of literary history, like the standard anthology, prizes aesthetically or technically admirable literary texts, the *Cambridge History* privileges social structures, events and themes.

It is evident that *Chaucer to Spenser* and the *Cambridge History* are founded upon distinct theoretical stances: Pearsall champions a *literary* history that documents the ebb and flow of creative achievement linking greater and lesser Ricardian, fifteenth-century and Tudor poets; Wallace favours a *cultural* history that contextualizes the texts – all texts with non-literary ones often privileged – produced by medieval and Tudor writers as reflections of their conflicted societies. This gap notwithstanding, the volumes share a perspective that defines almost all substantial studies of medieval literature published in the last decade. Whether a scholar looks at written texts or enacted texts, whether her interests lie in politics or poetry, drama or faith, whether he is intrigued by a text's ideology or enthused by its aesthetic, the critic's principal task is to enhance scholarly understanding of the relationship of the text to the ever more broadly conceived historical context in which it appeared. In the remainder of this chapter I will discuss some of the areas in which practical theorists address this hunger to historicize and some of the ways in which their efforts have advanced understanding of the late Middle Ages in England.

Multilingualism and Vernacularity

The circumstances of late medieval England have attracted exciting new thinking about how, in practice, languages interact and evolve, and how, in consequence, one properly approaches texts whose linguistic identity is either mixed or insecure.[4] The interest may relate to the fact that at the beginning of the twenty-first century such conditions are current; as Tony Hunt notes in comparing contemporary to medieval culture, 'outside a few western societies with a strong sense of language identity and near-universal literacy, conditions which obviously did not obtain in medieval Britain, *multi*lingualism is the norm' (in Trotter 2000: 131). To think seriously about the multilingual character of late medieval Britain poses a vigorous challenge to the age-old assumption that the way linguistic things worked out was inevitable. The traditional view is that English triumphed easily and necessarily over French and Latin to become the dominant language of both literature and common speech, with Chaucer playing an important role in the literary arena. Arrests to this view have emerged in three main areas. First, the records show that the ascendancy of English as the language of learned and aristocratic discourse came late, while French and Latin were used widely throughout the fourteenth century and well into the fifteenth. Second, English was itself a much less homogeneous language than the standard explanation assumes, as myriad regional dialects joined with Welsh and Middle Scots to create a linguistic map in which London's Middle

English was one of many coexisting forms. The appearance in 1986 of *A Linguistic Atlas of Late Mediaeval English* (ed. A. McIntosh, M. L. Samuels and M. Benskin, 4 vols. Aberdeen: Aberdeen University Press) has enabled the identification of these regional English dialects and the better pinpointing of textual and scribal provenance. Third, the swelling of Chaucer's English vocabulary reflects the way language generally expanded in his era. Christopher Cannon has shown that Chaucer introduced new words at a steady pace throughout his literary career, using many of them only once, and that Chaucer's behaviour in this regard was both typical of his literary-minded predecessors and contemporaries and natural in a trilingual society (Cannon 1998: 90, 129–30).

These challenges to imagining an English-language Middle Ages correlate with a broad range of theoretical advances. Reception studies demand that texts be examined in the context of their production, distribution and audience. Marxist studies resist the notion that an individual can institute broad change. New historical studies privilege cultural studies over the study of individual texts, insist that we interrogate the bases of our cultural assumptions, and distinguish our standards from those of a culture under examination. Postcolonial studies (one of the least developed and most promising areas of study)[5] expose the practice of equating a hegemonic cultural group with the local culture that it dominates. As D. A. Trotter says,

> The study of the linguistic situation of medieval Britain . . . requires . . . a determined refusal to hide behind the artificial barriers of either allegedly separate languages, or (perhaps above all) conveniently separated disciplines, each hermetically sealed against the dangers of contamination from adjacent fields of enquiry, and each buttressed by its own traditions or (less charitably) insulated by its own uncritical and self-preserving conceptions. (Trotter 2000: 1)

A happy result of this problematic is that large-scale collaborative projects have been created to rethink why multilingualism matters. Trotter's *Multilingualism in Later Medieval Britain* unites linguists from six nations for a dialogue on (1) multilingual *contact* (the environments in which English interacted with Welsh, Latin and Anglo-Norman); (2) linguistic *mixing* – that is, the functionality of macaronic texts in the business world, the rules governing intratextual code-switching, and the appropriation of phrasal verb structures in literary and non-literary texts; and (3) the general permeability of language use in what was a thoroughly multilingual culture. This area of newly theorized research is thus conceived in a vein similar to the *Cambridge History*, where the results combine the work of specialists not only in the languages of England – Old English, Middle English, Latin and Anglo-Norman – but also in those of Wales, Ireland and Scotland.

Coming to recognize the multilingual character of medieval English culture has also enabled manuscript studies to flourish. Another example of collaborative research exists in an international project that exemplifies directions in which such studies are moving. London, British Library MS Harley 2253 has long been valued for the secular and political lyrics that mark it as possibly 'the most important single MS of Middle English poetry'.[6] Had this unique manuscript not survived, scholars might reasonably surmise that few lyrics on subjects other than religion were composed in Middle English prior to Chaucer. G. L. Brook's edition of *The Harley Lyrics* (1948; 3rd edn 1964) clusters the more famous poems into a manageable volume, but by isolating the lyrics from their manuscript context, Brook obscured the fact that 'In manuscript the English poems are *not* gathered in one place: they appear intermittently across seventy pages, and mixed in with them are forty-odd items' (Fein 2000: 5). The codex's highly varied items are written in Middle English, Latin and Anglo-Norman, so that to study the Middle English lyrics in the context of their presentation (determined by the principal scribe's selections and organizational choices) and probable reception requires thinking, like the scribe, trilingually. Susanna Fein's *Studies in the Harley Manuscript* is a collection of sixteen specialist essays that examine this manuscript in terms of its scribes, contents, social contexts and languages. Theories informing projects like this one base themselves on the evidence of the book as a unique archaeological object with verbal content, created at a precise point in time for a specific purpose and a specific audience. As is being increasingly recognized, work on individual manuscripts, on the codicological activity of specific regions or by specific persons, on the identities of readers, patrons and scribes, and on networks of transmission and reception, all promise to reveal larger historical patterns by which we may restructure our knowledge. As it is almost always the case that medieval English books hold texts in more than one language (and even when they don't we may wonder why), what they may tell us about multilingual contact remains a field of great current interest.

Englishness

If late medieval English was not simply the language created and used by Chaucer and the Chancery scribes, and if the largest of the British isles was a space where French and Latin mixed with the various native dialects, then what does 'England' mean, and what distinguishes a literature as 'English'?[7] A number of recent books, responding to various theoretical pressures, have examined different aspects of this subject. Helen Cooney opens her collection, *Nation, Court and Culture*, with a chapter in which Pearsall rejects the idea of a distinctly English late medieval consciousness and thus sets a standard against which the arguments for 'Englishness' in the remainder of the volume may be measured. Pearsall's argument is that, notwithstanding Chaucer's famous evocation of 'Engelond' in the opening of the *Canterbury Tales*, neither he nor his contemporaries nor his fifteenth-century successors thought of England as a definable insular nation or of 'Englishness' as a distinguishing natural consciousness. To the contrary, Chaucer, John Gower, William Langland, the *Gawain* poet, Lydgate, Thomas Hoccleve, Malory, William Caxton, John Shirley and their aristocratic and royal patrons all 'were fluent in French and steeped in French culture'; and even as Henry V, the most strenuous advocate for the use of English, was writing in this language 'to announce the victory at Agincourt' to 'the mayor and aldermen of London', he was 'writing in French to his brothers' (in Cooney 2001: 22, 19).

The remainder of *Nation, Court and Culture* responds, obliquely, to Pearsall's argument. Thinking in terms of 'geopolitical theory', John Scattergood finds in the nationalistic poem 'The Libelle of Englyshe Polycye' a 'concern with borders and their preservation' that is 'based on a knowledgeable analysis of European economics and trade' and contemplates a common Anglo-Irish interest (in Cooney 2001: 49, 44–5). Exploring ideas of nationhood in manuscript collections from across the fifteenth century, Phillipa Hardman shows movement from a deep concern with Englishness to an 'uncomplicated, even sentimental sense of England signal[ling] that among the community of readers . . . the anxieties of the previous hundred years were felt to be laid to rest' (in Cooney 2001: 69). Other contributors get at the idea of fifteenth-century Englishness by addressing its apprehensions in terms of the particular historical circumstances in which literature was produced. Whether one wrote political verse for the Lancastrian court or composed in such less public genres as *dit amoureux*, complaint, allegory and carol, we find what Cooney categorizes as 'writers clinging anxiously and with some tenacity to the old certitudes and conventions surrounding the concepts of nation and court' (2001: 14). Over the course of the century English writers might have grown more secure in their national identity, but they remained insular in temperament.

Patricia Clare Ingham, in her *Sovereign Fantasies: Arthurian Romance and the Making of Britain*, uses psychoanalysis to query the notion of 'Englishness'. Focusing on the particular example of the 'diametrically opposed . . . political agendas' that informed medieval British responses to the Arthur legend, Ingham shows that 'the meaning of British sovereignty in Arthur's story . . . was contested throughout England, Wales and Scotland from Monmouth's time well into the late medieval period' (Ingham 2001: 23). The prophetic character of Arthur's projected return was employed as a symbol of British sovereignty by such diverse figures as Richard II, using his Welsh connections to defend his throne, Henry Tudor, exploiting Welsh ties as he raised the banner of Arthur against Richard III at Bosworth, and Owain Glyndwr, leading a messianic Welsh rebellion against Henry IV. In literature, Arthurian hopes and anxieties fed into the genre of romance as it developed in England and Wales in books as varied in their nationalist sensibilities as *The Red Book of Hergest*, the alliterative *Morte Arthure* and *Sir Gawain and the Green Knight.* Ingham's psychoanalytic approach reminds us of the inseparability of fear and desire and demonstrates how unfeasible it is to contemplate a uniform notion of 'Englishness'.

Yet as interpreters of an earlier culture we want spatial-temporal unities and historical categories we can grasp. The editors of *Essays on Ricardian Literature in Honour of J. A. Burrow* accept their honoree's notion of a distinct Ricardian literature even as they recognize the limitations of studying literature as a distinct discipline and urge us to expand our horizon. In the book's opening essay A. C. Spearing argues that Ricardian poetry displays no 'unifying vision' and that the works even of Chaucer, Langland and Gower 'record a struggle to find ways of saying things for which their culture provided no ready formulations or artistic forms' (in Minnis, Morse and Turville-Petre 1997: 22). The book's editors emphasize the incongruity of seeking unity in individual voices by juxtaposing more formalist examinations of prominent individual writers with more generalizing chapters that encourage us to think about the kinds of values and cultural conditions that define a common literary or historical moment. Charlotte Morse's closing essay explores the convoluted history of critical response to Burrow's positing a distinct Ricardian poetry comparable to Elizabethan or Romantic poetry, suggesting that medievalists now adopt the term *Ricardian studies*, which she sees as analogous to the popular locution *medieval studies* in that it rejects the ahistorical privileging of a single voice found in a phrase like *the age of Chaucer* in favour of the kind of current cross-disciplinary cultural exploration that acknowledges multiple and conflicting voices. Morse's conclusion crystallizes the stakes involved in medievalists' embracing inclusive theoretical constructs in our exploration of 'Englishness':

> Broadening Burrow's perspective to Ricardian studies, embracing the issues he addressed, and expanding beyond them gives us the flexibility to keep the aesthetic, rhetorical, political, ethical, spiritual and intellectual dimensions of Ricardian writing alive in and to the culture we inhabit. (In Minnis, Morse and Turville-Petre 1997: 344)

Reception, Patronage, Literary and Social Affinities

Who were the people who wrote literary texts in medieval England? What did they read? With whom did they associate? Who were their readers and how did their response differ from ours? Who were their patrons? For a few late medieval writers we can find substantive answers to these questions, but for many of their contemporaries the questions can be answered only in small part, and sometimes hardly at all. Literary historians therefore are devising new critical strategies to get at answers, so much so that the kind of localization of literary production imagined in these questions underlies much of the historicizing quest that marks current medieval literary study.

The publication in 1989 of Paul Strohm's *Social Chaucer* encouraged medievalists to return to thinking about literature in terms of an author's local associations. This idea is not new, but in drawing a picture of what he calls 'the king's affinity' Strohm advances the Marxist/historicist project of interrogating literary production and reception in the context not only of the vertical structures of patronage, but also the lateral structures uniting people in comparable social circumstances. More recently, Strohm has pursued a series of studies that use the symbolism of particular historical events as a springboard for exposing hidden structures and conflicts in the larger culture. In *Hochon's Arrow* he interrogates the unfulfilled threat made by a servant of the magnate Thomas Austin to shoot Mayor Nicholas Brembre's associate Hugh Fastolf, and unveils the factional politics that were lived daily by the London citizenry in the 1380s. In *England's Empty Throne* (1998) he examines official accounts of the unprecedented burning for heresy of William Sautre in 1401 and argues that the Lancastrians used such relatively insignificant threats as those posed by Lollardy to create a language that justified their usurpation and continuing occupation of the throne. As these examples suggest, Strohm is as much interested in how observers read the events as in the events themselves, and it is reflective of his evolving interest in historical contingency that in his recent books the writings of chroniclers have largely displaced literary texts.[8]

Strohm is more extreme in his theoretical commitment to history as the primary object of study than are most literary scholars, but even when answers to the questions of literary association appear in more familiar guises, a historicist bent is rarely absent. Thus when Christine Chism treats 'the revival of the dead and the past' in eight standard alliterative works, she predicates her analysis on the poets' common interest in the 'embodied and spectacular performance of history'. Chism acknowledges the importance of such literary qualities as metre, genre and voice, but her book's announced theoretical agenda is unabashedly cultural and historical: 'these poems (1) investigate the historical antecedents of medieval structures; (2) dramatize the questioning of cultural centers from outsider (or provincial) perspectives; and (3) centralize the historical contingencies of a world in flux rather than aiming primarily at more transcendent concerns with the afterlife' (Chism 2002: 1–2). Starting from a perspective that locates culture in historical event rather than in aesthetic accomplishment, she finds historical testimony even in works belonging to the *Pearl*-tradition of meditative devotion.

Locating culture in the literate audience of fifteenth-century writers who canonized Chaucer as the father of English poetry, Seth Lerer's *Chaucer and his Readers* embraces a historicism that proclaims that 'the aim of literary studies should be, not the interpretation of individual texts, but the study of the conventions of interpretation, and thus of the production and reception of texts' (Lerer 1993: 8, quoting Victoria Kahn). Dismissing the value of the singular literary endeavour as a cultural indicator, Lerer challenges modern readers to embrace textual variation and thereby to appreciate textual instability or *mouvance* as a distinguishing characteristic of literary production and reception in a manuscript culture. All Chaucer manuscripts presumably date to the fifteenth century or later. These manuscripts, which inscribe medieval response, show that Chaucer was read minutely, personally, and with a deep respect for what later writers saw as his definition of poetic practice. The fifteenth-century Chaucerians' imitation of and self-imposed subjection to the master's method, authority and immediate relevance thus illuminate the cultural significance of Chaucerian practice in ways that an untheorized devotion to a putatively recuperable fourteenth-century Chaucerian text makes obscure.

Religion

No community was more important to a writer in our period than that which nurtured one's belief. Three principal directions, based on the monumental work of scholars in the 1980s and early 1990s, have competed to redirect study of late medieval religion. Eamon Duffy, focusing on the institutionalized operation of faith, has assembled a compendium of information on traditional practices. His position is that we should seek to understand how most people thought and behaved. Anne Hudson and Margaret Aston, fastening upon oppositional beliefs, have amassed voluminous documentation of Lollard practices. Their position is that by focusing on dissident thought and behaviour, we can come to understand the tensions affecting both dominant and resistant belief. Carolyn Walker Bynum, directing attention to women religious, has documented the particularities of female spiritual practice. Her premise is that patriarchal documentation simultaneously appropriates and marginalizes the affective spirituality practised by large numbers of women and many men.[9] Taken together, the volumes produced by these archival scholars have offered medievalists much information upon and against which to construct theoretically informed analyses that spotlight the political character of late medieval spiritual practice. Curiously, it is Duffy's work that has generated the least direct interest, perhaps reflecting the scholarly tendency to be more interested in opposition than in dominant practice.

David Aers and Lynn Staley view spiritual discourse as inherently political. In their jointly authored *The Powers of the Holy* they postulate that in the closing years of the fourteenth century, before Bishop Arundel joined with the newly triumphant Lancastrian monarchs to enforce political and religious orthodoxy, writers who resisted a fairly mild communal pressure to conform 'were able to express divergent views and explore issues relating to both power and authority'. In particular, Langland, Julian of Norwich and Chaucer used the relative freedom afforded to literary discourse to challenge spiritual and political orthodoxy in ways that reflect, more or less cautiously, sympathy to Wycliffite concerns. Aers claims that Langland and Julian addressed the fractious issue of the 'humanity of Christ' by using images that privilege dissent, while Staley contends that Chaucer and Julian used the language of devotion to advance perspectives that covertly challenged the 'dominant ecclesiastical and political institutions' on whose good will and support they ostensibly depended. Through dextrous use of the language and imagery of gender, the three writers 'signal their awareness – inevitably political – that the call to Christ is a call to consciousness' (Aers and Staley 1996: 261–3). Aers and Staley's argument depends on a recognition of how politically charged are the intertwined languages of orthodoxy and dissent on the one hand, and the intertwined moods and subjects of female 'affective' piety and male 'analytic' piety on the other.

Sarah Beckwith's *Signifying God* similarly asserts the interconnectedness of the spiritual and the political as figured in the dissent-riddled symbolism of the York Corpus Christi plays. These popular spectacles incorporated performers and audience in an inherently politicized response to orthodox authority: performing the sacred in a public space necessarily obscured the boundaries between sanctified and profane spaces both symbolic and physical. As Beckwith puts it, 'When Corpus Christi, the little host under clerical jurisdiction and subject to strict ritual control and construction, is extended into the drama of the town, it risks its own meanings, finding them difficult to guarantee' (Beckwith 2001: 47). To dramatize the suffering of Christ was to appropriate a theological discourse that questioned the substantive nature of the sacrament. The fact that the corporate community of York manufacturers and labourers living in the very seat of English ecclesiastical authority involved itself in this vital debate as a municipally sanctioned spiritual practice requires us to read the York plays as political statement.

Violence and the Other

An idea shared by almost all the scholars I have mentioned is that history lies on the margins. It is in the victims, the resistant ones, and the individuals and groups subjected to authoritarian discipline, that a culture's desires are articulated, even though their voices are often muted or denied the attribution of eloquence afforded the sanctioned literati. The study of late medieval literature, so long focused on retrieving the polished diction of the canonical greats, has moved, in search of their history, to the edges, both geographically to Wales, Scotland, Ireland and the north of England, and textually to the manuscripts, chronicles and ecclesiastical and governmental documents that record less exquisite aesthetic moments. I will close this digest by addressing the theory governing approaches to two current issues at the edge of traditional literary work: violence (which is inextricably associated with power) and the Other, as psychoanalysts term the ego's apprehension of difference from itself.

The violence that maintained the social order is frequent in medieval texts, sometimes overt, sometimes simply threatened. Corinne Saunders's *Rape and Ravishment in the Literature of Medieval England* stands at what the author calls 'the convergence of two streams of scholarly discourse', the one situating itself at the critical distance of 'a historian of *mentalités*' seeking to inscribe acts of rape and abduction in the specific 'cultural, literary, and imaginative contexts' of medieval England; the other defining itself in the strict terms of current gender theory, responding to rape as the act that 'epitomizes all that is most fundamental and offensive in the power relationships of the sexes, in the social construction of gender differences, in the ferocious ideologies of hegemony and power' (Saunders 2001: 1–2). The former approach acknowledges culture difference; the latter insists on the primacy of essentialist values. As a literary historian focusing on the denotation of a word, *raptus*, Saunders places her study primarily in the *mentalités* camp, but as a modern feminist scholar, a woman reading and responding to a language enunciated almost entirely by men, she brings to the surface the horror embedded in unemotional male diction. Sexual violence is thus historicized as part of the cultural legacy of patriarchy.

Violence often becomes a response to what is perceived as Other, that is, what is peculiar, disturbing, resistant, transgressive, or foreign. Because these notions are personal, critical foci vary according to what it is about ourselves we wish to uncover in the past. Most recently, scholarly interest has fastened upon women and men who resisted the heterosexual norm: elective virgins and homosexuals.[10] For example, Sarah Salih offers an illuminating discussion of gender in regard to the distinctly medieval professions of virginity. Drawing upon Bynum's assertion that medieval religious women 'strove not to eradicate body but to merge their own humiliating and painful flesh with that flesh whose agony, espoused by choice, was salvation', Salih queries whether 'fleshly abjection is the only position medieval women can adopt'. Rather than assuming a gender-specific bodily sameness in all those genitally female, she insists on the distinctiveness of virginity from womanliness, contending that 'medieval virgins and medieval women . . . have different experiences of the body', that virginity may be considered 'a deployment, not a denial, of the body', and that 'virginity is not a denial or rejection of sexuality, but itself a sexuality . . . a culturally specific organization of desires' (Salih 2001: 5–10).

While notions of virginity underline the alterity of medieval experience, Robin Hood embodies the familiar stuff of legend, the classic insider turned outsider to turn hierarchy upside-down and serve the common good. In this he stands for much of what we know of the popular folk culture of late medieval England. But it is the subtitle of Thomas Hahn's collection, *Robin Hood in Popular Culture: Violence, Transgression, and Justice*, that indicates the direction taken by this look at popular culture.[11] A Bakhtinian delight in transgression explains the celebrity of the hero whose adventures have been reprised for upwards of eight centuries, and as we look with historicist eyes at the bloody justice meted out by and against Robin and his band we find a world that is both distinctly medieval and characteristically colonial. The outlaw inhabits the native forest, interacts with the foreign ruler and his surrogates in violent encounters, and asserts popular folk justice as being morally superior to the legal machinations of sheriff and court. Robin Hood himself exists powerfully in the oral consciousness (people and places are named after him), figures strongly in the literary tradition, and appears fleetingly in local records as a model of the renegade. His presence asserts popular English values in the face of externally imposed royal (hence French) and clerical (hence Latin) cultural hegemony.

The political response to resistance is to institutionalize behaviour. In a study of the evolution of medieval attitudes towards law, Richard Firth Green documents how the word *trouthe*, which once embodied the personal pledge, was transformed into an indicator of judicial practice, and how the violence that initially enforced the private agreement came to be reserved to the institutions of church and state. *Trouthe* appears frequently in both the public sphere, where it features in the development of contractual law, and the literary sphere, where notions of obligation, fidelity, honour, righteousness and factuality play a vital role. Green cites contemporary records in Latin and French that contextualize his reading of Middle English usage, examines a wealth of particular cases that make intelligible larger cultural norms, considers the developing relationship between folk law, the king's law and ecclesiastical law as they reflect the differing oral/popular and scribal/institutional understandings of *trouthe*, shows how similar to the medieval conflict is the clash between traditional law and colonial law depicted in late twentieth-century Nigerian literature, and, in all, demonstrates how much power – sometimes raw, sometimes more controlled – was invested in the definition and enactment of a word. Although its philological subject might seem conservative, this compendium offers a vivid demonstration of how the contributions of theorists have transformed the discipline of medieval studies.

Conclusion

Medievalists are a practical lot, and this has made some of us resistant to theory. Why get caught up in the latest fad or the newest jargon when there are so many facts out there to deal with? Interrogating what Strohm calls 'engaged theory' provides what I think is a practical answer to why theory must matter to us. Medieval literary studies have always been interdisciplinary. Even when formalist new criticism ruled the theoretical roost or structuralism ran wild, medievalists have treated texts as verbal artefacts to be considered in the context of other cultural survivals of their time and space. What distinguishes the past few years is that we bring to our texts increasingly sophisticated questions about the cultural circumstances of textual production. We see a poem in a manuscript and realize how much our understanding of that poem depends upon our understanding of the manuscript. We see a literary canon and realize how much our understanding depends upon our understanding of the cultures in which the constituent elements of that canon were produced, received, and identified as worth studying. We still occasionally gain new material knowledge: recovered documents, information about scribes, details about the conditions of medieval life. But much of what we have come to understand about our texts comes from the new questions that critical theorists have enabled us to ask. We understand more about medieval attitudes towards gender and sexuality, power and violence, materiality and spirituality because theorists have taught us that these are subjects worthy of inquiry.

See also: 2 English Society in the Later Middle Ages, 3 Religious Authority and Dissent, 4 City and Country, Wealth and Labour, 6 Manuscripts and Readers, 7 From Manuscript to Modern Text, 8 Translation and Society, 9 The Languages of Medieval Britain, 17 Literature and Law, 20 Middle English Romance, 21 Writing Nation, 23 Lyric, 24 Literature of Religious Instruction, 25 Mystical and Devotional Literature, 29 York Mystery Plays, 30 The *Book of Margery Kempe*, 31 Julian of Norwich, 32 *Piers Plowman*, 33 The *Canterbury Tales*, 34 John Gower and John Lydgate, 35 Thomas Hoccleve, 36 The Poetry of Robert Henryson, 37 *Sir Gawain and the Green Knight*, 38 Malory's *Morte Darthur*.

Notes

1 M. H. Abrams and Stephen Greenblatt (eds), *The Norton Anthology of English Literature*, 7th edn, 2 vols (New York: Norton, 2003).

2 David Damrosch (ed.), *The Longman Anthology of British Literature*, 2nd edn, 2 vols (New York: Longman, 2003).

3 *Pearl*, and of course the *Pearl*-poet more generally, remain vital to individual scholars; see Derek Brewer and Jonathan Gibson (eds), *A Companion to the Gawain-Poet* (Cambridge: Brewer, 1997), and John Bowers, *The Politics of Pearl: Court Poetry in the Age of Richard II* (Cambridge: Brewer, 2001).

4 A key resource for study of vernacularity is Jocelyn Wogan-Browne, Nicholas Watson, Andrew Taylor and Ruth Evans (eds), *The Idea of the Vernacular: An Anthology of Middle English Literary Theory, 1280–1520* (University Park: Pennsylvania State University Press, 1999).

5 An important book treating postcolonial theory is Cohen 2000.

6 Derek Pearsall, *Old English and Middle English Poetry* (London: Routledge and Kegan Paul, 1977), p. 120.

7 A key work on English identity, focusing on the period immediately before that considered in this volume, is Thorlac Turville-Petre, *England the Nation: Language, Literature, and National Identity, 1290–1340* (Oxford: Clarendon Press, 1996).

8 Paul Strohm, *Social Chaucer* (Cambridge, Mass.: Harvard University Press, 1989); *Hochon's Arrow: Usurpation and the Language of Legitimation 1399–1422* (Princeton: Princeton University Press, 1992); Strohm 1998. Strohm decries what he calls 'the preference for culture over history, akin to the current triumph of anthropology over history as the preferred disciplinary companion of literary studies' (Strohm 2000: 149), but his approach is none the less akin to that developed in Geertz's famous account of how the observation of a cockfight served to instruct him in Balinese culture; see Clifford Geertz, 'Deep play: notes on the Balinese cockfight', *Daedalus* 101 (1972), 1–37; rpt. in *The Interpretation of Cultures* (New York: Basic Books, 1973), pp. 412–53.

9 Eamon Duffy, *The Stripping of the Altars: Traditional Religion in England c.1400–c.1580* (New Haven, Yale University Press, 1992); Margaret Aston, *Lollards and Reformers: Images and Literacy in Late Medieval Religion* (London: Hambledon Press, 1984); Anne Hudson, *Lollards and Their Books* (London: Hambledon Press, 1985); and Carolyn Walker Bynum, *Jesus as Mother: Studies in the Spirituality of the High Middle Ages* (Berkeley: University of California Press, 1982) and her *Holy Feast and Holy Fast: The Ritual Significance of Food to Medieval Women* (Berkeley: University of California Press, 1987). See also Shannon McSheffrey, *Gender and Heresy: Women and Men in Lollard Communities 1420–1530* (Philadelphia: University of Pennsylvania Press, 1995).

10 Useful applications of queer theory to medieval studies appear in: Glenn Burger and Steven F. Kruger (eds), *Queering the Middle Ages* (Minneapolis: University of Minnesota Press, 2001); Carolyn Dinshaw, *Getting Medieval: Sexualities and Communities, Pre- and Postmodern* (Durham, N.C.: Duke University Press, 1999); Louise Fradenburg and Carla Freccero (eds), *Premodern Sexualities* (New York: Routledge, 1996); and Allen J. Frantzen, *Before the Closet: Same-Sex Love from Beowulf to Angels in America* (Chicago: University of Chicago Press, 1998). The seminal historical text is John Boswell, *Same-Sex Unions in Premodern Europe* (New York: Villard Books, 1994).

11 Due in large measure to the influence of Stephen Knight, Robin Hood studies are in vogue; see Stephen Knight, *Robin Hood: A Complete Study of the English Outlaw* (Oxford: Blackwell, 1994); Stephen Knight (ed.), *Robin Hood: Anthology of Scholarship and Criticism* (Cambridge: Brewer, 1999); Stephen Knight and Thomas Ohlgren (eds), *Robin Hood and Other Outlaw Tales* (Kalamazoo, Mich.: Medieval Institute Publications for TEAMS, 1997).

References and Further Reading

Aers, David and Staley, Lynn 1996. *The Powers of the Holy: Religion, Politics, and Gender in Late Medieval English Culture.* University Park: Pennsylvania State University Press. A reading of Chaucer, Julian of Norwich and Langland as participants in a debate over the representation of Christ's humanity.

Beckwith, Sarah 2001. *Signifying God: Social Relation and Symbolic Act in the York Corpus Christi Plays.* Chicago: University of Chicago Press. An exploration of the spiritual and the political as figured in eucharistic symbolism.

Cannon, Christopher 1998. *The Making of Chaucer's English: A Study of Words.* Cambridge: Cambridge University Press. A history of Chaucer's vocabulary, focusing on his adoption of new words and the provenance of those words.

Chism, Christine 2002. *Alliterative Revivals.* Philadelphia: University of Pennsylvania Press. A study of the representation of the past in eight Middle English alliterative poems.

Cohen, Jeffrey Jerome (ed.) 2000. *The Postcolonial Middle Ages.* New York: St Martin's Press. Fifteen essays that interrogate Western assumptions about the significance of time, race, religion, nationality and cultural dominance in medieval studies.

Cooney, Helen (ed.) 2001. *Nation, Court and Culture.* Dublin: Four Courts Press. Eleven essays that reassess fifteenth-century English poetry in relation to court and manuscript cultures.

Fein, Susanna (ed.) 2000. *Studies in the Harley Manuscript.* Kalamazoo, Mich.: Medieval Institute Publications for TEAMS. Sixteen essays that examine the scribes, contents, social contexts and languages of MS Harley 2253.

Green, Richard Firth 1999. *A Crisis of Truth: Literature and Law in Ricardian England.* Philadelphia: University of Pennsylvania Press. A history of the use of the word *trouthe* in literary and legal documents as it reflects the transition from oral to written culture.

Hahn, Thomas (ed.) 2000. *Robin Hood in Popular Culture.* Cambridge: Brewer. Twenty-three essays exploring the meaning of the Robin Hood legend in medieval and modern popular culture.

Hanawalt, Barbara A. and Wallace, David (eds) 1996. *Bodies and Disciplines: Intersections of Literature and History in Fifteenth-century England.* Minneapolis: University of Minnesota Press. Twelve essays treating the interplay between literature and history, with a focus on local, institutional and corporeal history.

Ingham, Patricia Clare 2001. *Sovereign Fantasies: Arthurian Romance and the Making of Britain.* Philadelphia: University of Pennsylvania Press. An exploration of the agendas that informed medieval response to the Arthur legend from Geoffrey of Monmouth onward.

Lerer, Seth 1993. *Chaucer and his Readers: Imagining the Author in Late Medieval England.* Princeton: Princeton University Press. An exploration of how fifteenth-century readers of Chaucer created his persona as father of English poetry.

Minnis, A. J., Morse, Charlotte C. and Turville-Petre, Thorlac (eds) 1997. *Essays on Ricardian Literature in Honour of J. A. Burrow.* Oxford: Clarendon Press. Fourteen essays on various topics in Ricardian literature, honouring the coiner of the term 'Ricardian Poetry'.

Pearsall, Derek (ed.) 1999. *Chaucer to Spenser: An Anthology of Writings in English, 1375–1575.* Oxford: Blackwell. A survey of writings that articulate the continuity of literary traditions over the period from Chaucer's *Parliament of Fowls* to Spenser's *Shepherd's Calendar.*

Salih, Sarah 2001. *Versions of Virginity in Late Medieval England.* Cambridge: Brewer. An examination of professions of female virginity as indicative of medieval attitudes towards gender, identity and the body.

Saunders, Corinne 2001. *Rape and Ravishment in the Literature of Medieval England.* Cambridge: D. S. Brewer. An exploration of attitudes about rape and abduction.

Strohm, Paul 1998. *England's Empty Throne: Usurpation and the Language of Legitimation, 1399–1422.* New Haven: Yale University Press. An exploration of the complex response of Lancastrian rulers and subjects to the deposition and murder of Richard II.

—— 2000. *Theory and the Premodern Text.* Minneapolis: University of Minnesota Press. An effort to expand our understanding of medieval thought by challenging the silences and evasions in medieval texts through a confrontation with theory.

Trotter, D. A. (ed.) 2000. *Multilingualism in Later Medieval Britain.* Cambridge: Brewer. Fourteen essays treating the multilingual character of writing in the British Isles in the fourteenth and fifteenth centuries.

Wallace, David (ed.) 1999. *The Cambridge History of Medieval English Literature.* Cambridge: Cambridge University Press. Thirty-two essays on writing in the British Isles from the Norman Conquest to 1550.

2

English Society in the Later Middle Ages: Deference, Ambition and Conflict[1]

S. H. Rigby

In trying to understand the meaning and significance of any literary text, particularly one from a culture as alien to modern readers as that of late medieval England, we necessarily have to put that text into some broader context. In recent years, an extremely popular context in which to understand medieval literature has been that of the social structure, social change and social conflict of the period. In this perspective, works of medieval literature come to be seen as social interventions in which the power relations of their time are reinforced or challenged. Literary critics thus ask whether any particular piece of imaginative literature buttresses the contemporary social hierarchy through its reproduction of the dominant ideology of the day, or whether it provides a dissident or questioning voice which challenges orthodox views about class, status and gender inequalities (Rigby 1996).

This approach to literature has much to recommend it but one problem is that medieval historians themselves are by no means agreed among themselves as to the nature of English society in the later Middle Ages. As a result, an appeal to historical context may provide a rather insecure foundation on which to build an edifice of literary interpretation. The reality of social inequality in late medieval England and its centrality for the social commentators of the time are points which hardly need labouring. Our main interest here lies rather in late medieval *responses* to such inequality and in how they are represented in both the literature of the time and modern historiography. Such responses can be divided into three main categories: deference, individual ambition and social conflict.

Social Inequality: Theory and Reality

The necessity for hierarchy and inequality within society were, of course, the commonplaces of the 'official' social theory of the late medieval period itself. In his *Pilgrimage of the Life of Man* (1426), John Lydgate took for granted the absurdity of the idea that all people should be of one social condition. Such equality between rich and poor would only produce 'confusioun' in the world and would cause all to suffer, including the poor themselves.[2] Medieval authors had long presented the social hierarchy in terms of the three estates of the *oratores*, *bellatores* and *laboratores* (those who pray, those who fight and those who work) and this familiar model of society continued to be reproduced in the later Middle Ages. Preachers such as Thomas of Wimbledon in his famous sermon of 1388, and poets such as John Gower in his *Vox clamantis*, were agreed that the social order consisted of three estates: the clergy, whose duty is to teach society the way to salvation; the knights, who bear arms to defend society; and the peasantry, who till the fields to feed society.[3]

Yet, in reality, the tripartite theory hardly provided an accurate picture of the contemporary social hierarchy. Rather, the prime purpose of the theory was to offer a moral justification of social inequality and, in particular, to urge the members of the third estate to accept the rule of their superiors. As Wimbledon put it, servants and bond men should be 'subject and low' and in dread of being 'displeasing' to their lords (102–3). Thus while, in the tripartite theory, it was the clergy in their entirety who constituted the first estate in order of pre-eminence, with the other estates ranked beneath them, in practice the inhabitants of late medieval England were perfectly capable of adopting an alternative vision of the social pyramid. Here the hierarchy of wealth, status and power cut across the division between clergy and laity so that the ranks within each could be horizontally equated. Society was then seen as being divided not into the three classic orders of the tripartite theory but rather between what Thomas Walsingham's *Historia Anglicana* called *proceres* (nobles), *mediocres* (the middling) and *pauperes* (the poor).[4] Bishop John Stafford, the chancellor, adopted this perspective in a sermon preached to the parliament of 1433 which divided society into three groups: first, its 'mountains', the *prelati, proceres et magnati* (prelates, nobles and magnates) whose duty was to promote social peace; second, its 'hills', the *milites, armigeri et mercatores* (the knights, esquires and merchants) whose duty was to provide justice; and, third, its *cultores, artifices et vulgares* (the peasants, craftsmen and common people), presumably the 'plain' of society, whose duty was to obey their betters.[5] Even finer social gradations were possible. In his mid-fifteenth century *Book of Nurture*, John Russell, marshal to Humphrey, Duke of Gloucester, had to deal with the thorny problems posed by the order of precedence in seating arrangements in a noble household. He divided potential guests into five groups, each of which in turn had its own internal gradations according to birth, income and dignity. Within each group there was a horizontal equation between the ranks of the clergy and the laity, from archbishops and dukes, through bishops and earls, mitred abbots and barons, unmitred abbots and knights, to parish priests and esquires.[6]

Social Deference

How did the inhabitants of late medieval England respond to these prevailing structures of social inequality? Were the social hierarchies of the day accepted by all or did they provoke resistance from those who found themselves excluded, in varying degrees, from access to wealth, status and power? Our first model of English society in the later Middle Ages is that presented to us by historians such as Maurice Keen who sees England before the eighteenth century as a 'deference society', i.e. one characterized by 'an ordered gradation' of social ranks which are hierarchically arranged 'by scales which regulate the respect and the kind of service which one man or woman may expect of another, or may expect to pay another'. 'In the minds of men of that age, the relations of deference and service that persisted between the grades (of society) were the basis of social order, of its essence: they had not yet come to regard social distinctions as divisive, as forces with the potential to tear society apart' (Keen 1990: 1; see also Bennett 1983: 67).

This emphasis on the need to see societies in terms of how contemporaries themselves perceived them, and the consequent belief that pre-industrial societies, including that of late medieval England, were neatly ordered and harmonious status-hierarchies is now an orthodoxy in many quarters of social history and of sociology. Again and again, pre-industrial society is presented to us as lacking social mobility and as being one in which social hierarchy depended upon some consensus about social evaluation. As a result of such consensus, social conflict is seen as being paralysed from within by the stranglehold of some 'common culture' or 'dominant ideology', a view actually anticipated in the fifteenth century by the preacher Robert Rypon in his sermon *Loquentes vobismetipsis*: 'the unity of the state exists in the agreement of its minds'.[7] In the field of urban history, for instance, a number of historians have argued that shared ideological norms, a belief that to disobey one's social superior was 'to commit a sin', and a general acceptance that 'the rich should lead and dominate', formed the basis of urban political life (Thrupp 1962: 14–27). It was this ideal of community and of amity between the social classes that was symbolized by urban dramas such as the York Corpus Christi cycle.[8]

The need for deference to one's superiors stressed by the orthodox social theory of the medieval period had two different aspects. First, it involved a general hostility to individual social mobility and a stress on the need to accept one's place on the social ladder. As Wimbledon said, repeating the words of St Paul (1 Corinthians 7: 20), each man should see what estate 'God hath clepid him and dwell he there in', accepting the need to work 'accordyng to his degree' (99–101). A hostility to individual social promotion can also be detected in the snobbery which, in 1448, led John Wyndham to denounce the *arriviste* Pastons as 'churls of Gimingham' or which made Margery Kempe tell her husband that he should never have married someone of her status, her father having been a mayor of Lynn and alderman of the Trinity guild there.[9] Within literature, this suspicion of social mobility can be seen in works such as Gower's *Vox clamantis* where he claims that 'When a poor man is elevated in the city through an unexpected fate, and the unworthy creature is allowed to reach the height of honour, then nature suddenly groans at the changed state of things and grieves at the unaccustomed rarity' (5.15, p. 215).

Second, the deferential outlook meant that medieval social theorists not only criticized individual social ambition but also attacked any broader attempts to change the social order or to alter the balance of privileges enjoyed by particular groups. Social inequality was thus presented as part of the hierarchical ordering of the universe as a whole, from God, down through angels, men, women, animals, plants and minerals – a hierarchy within which the lower should always serve the higher. To challenge this arrangement was to be guilty of the sin of pride by questioning the wisdom of God who had ordained everything in its rightful place. Thus even those clerical writers, such as William Langland, Thomas Brinton and John Bromyard, who attacked the abuses of those landlords who mercilessly tallaged (taxed) their tenants, could only recommend the virtues of patient poverty to those who suffered: just as wild beasts are afflicted in winter but are recompensed by God with the bliss of summer, so the poor who suffered in this world would be rewarded with joy in the next (Rigby 1995: 313–14).[10] As God asks in Julian of Norwich's *Revelations*, 'What shuld it agrevyn the to suffre awhile, seing it is my will and my worshippe?'[11] Those among the lower orders who refused to accept their traditional position within society were likely to be met with open hostility, as in Gower's *Vox clamantis* which depicts the Peasants' Revolt of 1381 in terms of a nightmare vision in which farmyard beasts turned into ravening monsters and refused to know their place, the asses demanding to be as horses and the domesticated fowl daring 'to assume the eagle's prerogatives for themselves' (1.7, p. 61).

However, deference was not simply an abstract theory which was set out in the teachings of a Wimbledon or the verses of a Gower. Nor was it merely an attitude evident in the snobbery of the aristocrat against the *parvenu*. Rather, deference was embodied in a variety of social institutions and in the concrete practices of everyday life. Russell's concern with the due hierarchy to be observed in the banqueting hall was typical of a broader concern that all should, literally, be put in their proper place. This concern with precedence can be seen in many areas of late medieval English society from the seating arrangements in parliament (which caused quarrels between Lords Grey and Beaumont in 1405, between the earl of Warwick and the earl Marshal in 1405 and 1425, and between Lords Hastings and Talbot in 1426) down to local parish churches, where parishioners occupied the benches or went up to make their offerings in order of their social standing. Indeed, despite the fine words of clerical moralists and of poems such as the mid-fifteenth-century *Farewell this World*, for whom Death was the great leveller,[12] even the ritual of death and burial tended to reflect the realities of secular social stratification, with those of wealth being able to acquire burial locations of particular spiritual potency. The need to reinforce the existing social hierarchy permeated even the institution of individual confession. Since, as religious manuals such as *Of Shrifte and Penance* (late fourteenth century) taught, to harm one's lord by working slowly was to break the commandment against theft,[13] priests were required to quiz their parishioners in confession on whether they had 'failed in reverence to their lords or . . . withheld their bounden services to their lords', whether they had worked 'feebly and remissly' and whether they had been guilty of murmuring and withdrawing from work when rebuked for their slackness.[14]

Social Ambition

Yet, despite the contemporary emphasis on the need for all to know their place in the social hierarchy, Keen's view that later medieval England was primarily a 'deference society' has not gone unchallenged. Indeed, Keen himself is far too perceptive a historian to fail to draw our attention to the reality of mobility and conflict within late medieval society (Keen 1990: 22–3, 40–1, 121). In this case, however, it may be useful to turn our attention to the accounts of late medieval society offered to us by historians such as F. R. H. du Boulay and Michael J. Bennett, accounts which, rather than stressing social deference, focus on the importance of personal ambition and of individual social mobility, both within and between the different classes and ranks of society (du Boulay 1970: 79; Bennett 1983: 247).

Underlying much of the social mobility of the late medieval period was the high mortality resulting from regular outbreaks of epidemic disease. England's population plummeted from perhaps five million or more before the Black Death of 1348–9 to around 2.75 million in 1377, and by 1524 it was perhaps still as low as 2.25 million or less. Negative replacement rates for the population as a whole meant that places on the higher rungs of the social ladder were now waiting to be filled. Within village society, declining population and the leasing of manorial demesnes meant that land was available and was relatively cheap. As a result, the numbers of cottagers and smallholders could decline, as at Halesowen where these groups fell from forty-three per cent of the village's population before the Black Death to only thirty-five per cent afterwards, whereas the proportion of wealthy peasants there rose from eighteen to twenty-six per cent (Razi 1980: 144–50). Middling peasants could now rise into the top rank of village society and their places be taken by those formerly below them. Rising wages and low grain prices meant that the incomes of labourers and cottagers were likely to improve, much to the dismay of moralists such as Langland whose *Piers Plowman* criticizes those labourers who would not deign to eat yesterday's vegetables, cured bacon and cheap ale but instead demanded high wages so that they could buy fresh meat and fish (B 6.307–19).[15]

However, the gains of this period were often greatest for the upper ranks of village society. The ability to pay the entry fines necessary to acquire vacant holdings, the need for money or credit to acquire property on the land market, and the ownership of the livestock required for a larger holding, all allowed the existing peasant elite to improve its position even further. In practice, of course, the degree to which the upper peasantry benefited varied from place to place and, in some villages, the middling peasants had a greater share in the post-plague advances than in those places where the gains of the rich meant that village society became more polarized. Moreover, even the richer peasants faced difficulties in transmitting their gains to future generations. A lack of heirs and the effects of agricultural depression, particularly in the mid-fifteenth century, meant that holdings were often soon dispersed rather than being passed on intact. As a result, while men could rise *within* village society, promotion to the gentry was rarely the result of landed accumulation alone.

Both medieval poets, such as Gower, and modern historians tend to see medieval urban society as particularly mobile (Bennett 1983: 109). The fifteenth-century *Discourse of Weights and Measures* certainly assumed that trade would function as a means of social advancement when it recommended the rates of mark-up on goods needed to help 'poor beginners' to 'prove thrifty men' in their peddling trade.[16] Higher up the urban social scale, the London trades tended to recruit from the ranks of those described as 'husbandmen' and 'yeomen' and £1 or £2 could suffice as a premium for a start in the metal- and leather-working trades (Thrupp 1962: 215–19). In the provinces, entry to the ranks of the artisans has been seen as even more open. Tradesmen in Chester and other north-west towns seem to have been drawn from families of 'low birth', including the peasantry (Bennett 1983: 120). Thrupp argued, from the London evidence, that, once on the ladder, lesser families could aspire to join the ranks of the higher wholesale traders – with the sons of workers in base metals rising to be goldsmiths and the families of the lesser victualling trades providing members of the vintners' and grocers' companies. More recently, on the basis of the York evidence, Heather Swanson has questioned how easy it was for artisans to rise into the ranks of the merchants. Nevertheless, the high mortality rates of the period and the tendency for merchants to divide estates and fortunes on their deaths did mean that towns were relatively open to those outsiders with sufficient wealth. In 1397, for instance, over two-thirds of the aldermen of Preston were first-generation members of the town's guild merchant (Bennett 1983: 132). If town government was becoming more formally oligarchic in this period, in the sense that popular influence was becoming more restricted, urban society was never dominated by hereditary patriciates of long-lasting mercantile dynasties. Those who were rich enough were guaranteed entry into the ruling plutocracy.

Traditionally, promotion of urban merchants, particularly those of London, to membership of the rural gentry has been seen as a common form of late medieval social mobility and this certainly was one of the routes to social respectability. Yet, while significant numbers of wealthy merchants did acquire land, they still made little overall impression on the character of the landed gentry in particular counties. Besides, many successful merchants showed little interest in using their wealth to gain access to the ranks of the gentry and for many townsmen the use of the title of 'merchant' may have been, in effect, a proclamation of their own gentility. Certainly, in York, it was the onset of economic recession in the late fifteenth century which encouraged merchants to invest in rural property on a permanent basis rather than any lack of respectability associated with commercial wealth *per se*.

Yet, despite the variety of routes to social advancement available in urban society, we should perhaps hesitate before accepting the view of the late medieval period still popular with literary critics in which it is seen as an era characterized by the rise of a commercial middle class, a class which embodied a 'new world' of money, trade and economic individualism which was to be satirized by Chaucer in works such as the Shipman's Tale and the Wife of Bath's Prologue. In fact, recent work by economic historians has tended to concentrate on the two centuries *before* the Black Death as the period which was vital in the commercialization and urbanization of medieval English society. Thus while specific towns did experience the growth of a wealthy merchant class in the late fourteenth century – particularly textile centres such as Colchester, benefiting from the switch from raw wool to manufactured cloth in England's export trade which began in this period – it is more difficult to see the post-plague period as one of a qualitative transformation in the commercialization of the national economy.

Indeed, at least as significant as the growth of trade and of a mercantile class for the emergence of a middle class in this period was the rise of lay lawyers, administrators, professionals and bureaucrats (see below).

The existence of endemic plague, with its high mortality rates and negative replacement rates, meant social mobility not only in the towns and within the village community but also within the upper ranks of landed society, among the gentry and the peerage. Men were now less likely to be succeeded by direct male heirs which, given the tendency for fathers to put the interests of their daughters before those of their brothers and collateral male relatives, meant that women were far more likely to inherit land. Given the sluggish land market of the period, marriage to an heiress was often the easiest way to acquire the land needed for power and status even if, because of the tendency of land to attract more land, such mobility was often within, rather than between, particular social groups. The rise of the Dallingridge family of Sussex from relative obscurity, a rise eventually symbolized by the construction of Bodiam Castle by Sir Edward Dallingridge in the late 1380s, was certainly facilitated by a series of advantageous marriages which brought the family property in Sussex, Lincolnshire, Northamptonshire and Kent (Saul 1998).

Along with marriage, service in office, particularly service to the Crown, provided the other main avenue of personal advancement within late medieval English society. Among the most dramatic examples of such promotion were those which occurred in time of war when military service offered lucrative prizes and the opportunity for men to move up through the ranks. Robert Knolles was probably a bowman when he began his military career in the 1340s but rose to being a company commander and, finally, to a knighthood, his profits from wartime plunder being reinvested in property in London, Kent, Norfolk, and Wiltshire (Bennett 1983: 182). However, despite the comments of contemporaries such as Gower, whose *Mirour de l'omme* attacked those covetous knights who fought for personal gain instead of for justice,[17] the rewards of military service, including wages, ransoms, plunder and office, should not be overemphasized. Although it is difficult to estimate the profits of warfare, it seems that dramatic windfalls of the kind enjoyed by Knolles were far from typical. For many, such as John Talbot (d.1453) whose gains from war only just covered his costs, war was a more hazardous investment. Given the dynastic instability of the period, hitching one's fortunes to a particular court or political faction was, potentially, also a source of spectacular rewards although such gambles entailed potentially fatal risks of their own (as shown by John Howard, a member of the East Anglian gentry promoted to the peerage by Edward IV who eventually died fighting in the Yorkist cause at Bosworth Field).

Less dramatically, service to the Crown in administrative office was another means of individual advancement. This was certainly the case in this period, as it had been before, for clerical high-flyers. Thomas Savage (d.1507), whose service as dean of the chapel of the royal household and president of the council led to his promotion to the sees of London and York, spoke for many such men when he told the king that 'he was of litil substaunce but a poer gentylman and a yongar brother and had no thing to take to but of the kinges grace as thawe his highnes had made hym out of claye and brought hym to the honor that he is cumed to'.[18] Of course, as shown by the poem of complaint *Male Regle* (1406), written by Thomas Hoccleve, clerk of the Privy Seal Office,[19] not all of those in royal service obtained the benefices, promotion, or rewards which they would have liked. Indeed, the costs of obtaining the university degrees which were increasingly necessary for promotion within the late medieval church may perhaps have reduced the chances of clerical preferment of those of humble birth in this period. Nevertheless, for the sons of urban artisans, the church may still have offered an easier route to social advancement in this period than entry into the merchant class (Swanson 1989: 165–8).

It was not only clerics who enjoyed the rewards of royal administrative service. From the late fourteenth century, the educational, literacy and administrative skills which had traditionally been the monopoly of clerics were increasingly being provided by lay administrators – even to monasteries and episcopal households. Families such as the Rempstons of Nottinghamshire, who came to local prominence on the basis of the profits arising from the lengthy service of Sir Thomas Rempston (d.1406) to the house of Lancaster both before and after 1399, show the rewards available from such administrative labours. The one-hundred-strong staff of the royal Chancery was overwhelmingly clerical in 1388 but by 1461 it was predominantly lay in composition, even though the Chancery had lagged behind the Exchequer in the process of laicization, with the decades around 1400 being crucial for the emancipation of many judicial, legal and administrative functions from clerical control (Bennett 1983: 194–8).

Those successful in administrative office had often been trained in law, a career which was an increasingly popular route to social advancement. This route is exemplified by the rise of Thomas Kebell, the younger son of a *parvenu* Leicestershire gentleman who, by the time of his death in 1500, had amassed an estate of over 3,000 acres and a fortune of over £800 worth of chattels from a career which had begun with entry to the Inner Temple and ended with his promotion to the offices of attorney-general of the duchy of Lancaster, sergeant-at-law and king's sergeant (Ives 1983). Poets such as Gower, whose *Mirour* called on the king to confiscate the ill-gotten gains of those who grew rich from the law (24313–816), may have disapproved of the law as a route to social promotion but, in practice, the profits of a legal career provided the means by which families such as the Willoughbys of Wollaton were able to acquire land and so join the upper gentry, their new position often being consolidated through marriage to an heiress. The legal profession may not have produced such a dramatic example of mobility as the de la Pole family, who began life as merchants of Hull and rose to being dukes of Suffolk but, in terms of its overall impact, the law probably had a greater effect on social mobility than did commerce or the church. Certainly, those yeomen who rose to gentility were far more likely to do so through manorial administration, law and the other professions than through agriculture alone.

Finally, promotion through royal service was only one instance, if the one which offered the greatest potential rewards, of social mobility through connection with, or service to, some great lord. Sir Edward Dallingridge, for instance, forged valuable links with the first and second earls of Arundel and with Sir Edward Despenser, with whom he served in France, as well as with John, Duke of Brittany – connections which may well have helped his acquisition of office in local government (Saul 1998). More specifically, paid service to some lord was a potential route to social promotion. Again, in this field a legal training was useful. Even Westminster lawyers could also serve as estate officials, while most of those called to the bar ended up in the provinces engaged in a wide range of legal-administrative posts, such as clerks of the court, stewards, accountants, rent-collectors, receivers, controllers of the household and general administrators. Indeed, all of the paths to individual advancement noted above tended to be smoothed by the vertical social ties of personal patronage whether in trade or a military career (Bennett 1983: 121, 175) or in law and estate administration where men such as Thomas Kebell made the most of their access to great magnates (Griffiths 1980: 121–3; Ives 1983: 29–30).

Patronage was just as important for a successful career in the Church, as shown by the sponsorship from his manorial lord which set William Wykeham on the road to the bishopric of Winchester. Once successful, clerics who had risen socially could themselves become the patrons of others. For instance, Thomas Rotherham, having climbed from obscurity to become archbishop of York, then helped sponsor the clerical career of two of his nephews, Geoffrey and John Blythe, by promoting them to wealthy canonries at York Minster; both men themselves eventually being promoted to the episcopal bench. As Rotherham's obituary notice admiringly put it: 'he was especially kind to his kinsmen, showering them with temporal possessions, others with marriages and yet others with benefices'.[20]

The later Middle Ages were thus a period when individuals were ready to take full advantage of the opportunities available to them. This does not mean that people's attitudes in this period had suddenly become markedly different from those of earlier centuries. On the contrary, the church, education, the law and Crown service had been a source of social advancement from at least the twelfth century, and the pace of such mobility had accelerated as early as the reign of Edward I (1272–1307). It was rather that the period from the mid-fourteenth century saw a further widening of the opportunities for people to put existing aspirations into practice as a result of high mortality, warfare, the growth of government and an expansion of lay literacy. As a result, English society became socially and geographically more mobile as those of lower social rank and from areas distant from the capital began to enjoy the benefits of careerism.

Of course, the extent and means of social mobility were relatively narrow when compared with those found in modern society. In the twenty-three years of Edward IV's reign, for instance, only eight barons were created by promotion into the peerage from the ranks of the gentry. Nor need we assume that there was a unilinear trend towards greater mobility in every social sphere. Indeed, the fifteenth century may have been a time of relative stability for the landed elite when compared with the century after the Conquest or with the failure of families in the thirteenth century through debt or political miscalculation. Yet, although real, hindrances to social mobility in the later Middle Ages tended to be a matter of practicality, such as the limited land market of the period or the costs of obtaining the university degrees increasingly needed for clerical promotion, rather than the result of any internalization of the ideology of deference or of any formal or legal barriers to movement between the orders.

The significance and extent of personal ambition in the later Middle Ages have important implications for how we make sense of English society in this period. First, people's willingness to seize the openings which were becoming available tends to cast doubt on the view of England as simply a deference society revealing, as it does, a discrepancy between, on the one hand, the deferential ideal of keeping to one's place in the social hierarchy which was so often extolled in our sources and, on the other, the attitudes and values which were implicit in people's actual behaviour. Second, these alternative, non-deferential values did not always remain implicit but could also receive explicit expression. For instance, the attempt by the authorities, through the Sumptuary Act of 1363, to keep everyone in their place by requiring all to dress in a manner appropriate for their 'estate and degree' is well known, but what is often forgotten is that there is no evidence that this law was ever enforced and that, in the very next parliament, the Commons successfully asked for the law to be repealed, the king affirming in reply that 'all people shall be as free as they were at all times before the said ordinance'. Similarly, while authors such as Gower and Chaucer could denounce those who saw the church in terms of personal advancement, the wills of clerical testators (like those of civil lawyers), such as William Wykeham and Thomas Rotherham, show an explicit awareness that educational provision was a means by which men like themselves from humble backgrounds could, as Rotherham put it, 'come to greater things'.[21]

Third, while individual social mobility is often seen as a conservative force, functioning as a safety valve for social tension and creating an obstacle to class consciousness, the tendency for individuals in late medieval England to take advantage of the openings available to them could lead to broader social change and result in a structural redistribution of wealth and opportunity. An obvious example is the way in which, to the dismay of both the landlords and the authors of literary works such as *Piers Plowman* (6.307–9) and Gower's *Mirour* (26437–520) and *Vox clamantis* (5.9–10), wage-labourers used the post-plague labour shortage to demand illegal levels of wages and to obtain short-term contracts which left them free to seek better terms elsewhere. Similarly, women in towns such as London and York also took advantage of the high mortality and labour shortage of this period to enter trades from which they had previously been excluded even if, in general, women tended to remain in low-status forms of employment which were less likely to require formal apprenticeships (Rigby 2001).

Social Conflict

Finally, social ambition has a broader historical significance in the sense that personal aspirations could also be expressed in the form of wider social struggles. This brings us to our third model of late medieval England, one which focuses on the conflicts which arose from contemporary social relations – the later Middle Ages as presented to us by historians such as Rodney Hilton and Robert Brenner. We often think of social conflict as mounted from below, in the form of popular struggles such as workers' strikes or peasant revolts. Yet, in fact, conflict can also be engendered from above by those seeking to defend their existing privileges from the ambitions of those beneath them in the social hierarchy and thus to maintain the latter's exclusion from wealth, status or power, as can be seen in the case of the labour laws of 1349 and 1351, which attempted to keep down wages in an age of post-plague labour shortage, or the sumptuary legislation of 1363. For many historians, the immediate post-plague period was one of rising social tensions as a seigneurial offensive from above in defence of the social status quo – an offensive aided and abetted by the state – clashed head-on with the awakening 'usurpatory' ambitions of peasants and labourers from below. It was these tensions which were to explode in the dramatic events of the Peasants' Revolt of 1381, a revolt which even witnessed revolutionary demands for the expropriation of the landlord class (Hilton 1977: 224–6; Rigby 1995: 110–24).

More typically, however, the peasant struggles of the later Middle Ages did not seek a revolutionary transformation of society but rather sought to effect a marginal social redistribution of resources through action at a local level. The non-deferential attitudes and values underlying such social resistance are rarely made explicit in our sources and have to be deduced instead from the willingness of peasants and labourers to assert their interests in their actual deeds. Rarely do we hear the voices of those such as the tenant of the prior of Worcester who persuaded his fellows not to answer in court for their refusal to render their customary hoeing services on the grounds that this arrangement was 'nothing but stupidity'. Certainly, literary works of the period, including poems such as Gower's *Vox clamantis*, or anonymous works such as *On the Rebellion of Jack Straw* (1381) and *On the Slaughter of Archbishop Sudbury* (c.1381),[22] tend to present popular protest from the viewpoint of its enemies rather than from that of those who actually participated in it. Even when a work such as *What Profits a Kingdom* (1401) presents popular revolt as a response to injustice, it is still more inclined to cite the 'gret harm' done in such risings as a warning to the lords about how they should behave than to sympathize with the actions of the rebels themselves.[23]

Yet, if we seldom hear the voices of the late medieval commons directly, the significance of the local, piecemeal social struggles undertaken by the peasants and labourers of late medieval England should not be underestimated. The withering away of serfdom, the assertion of personal and tenurial freedom, the decline of labour services, the end of manorial restrictions and impositions, a switch to low money rents, and the virtual disappearance of entry fines on many manors – these were no mean achievements. A classic instance of such successful peasant resistance to manorial impositions and restrictions is provided by the struggles of the tenants of the Bishop of Worcester in the fifteenth century where, although the peasants did not question their lord's right to claim rent *per se*, they did successfully challenge his claims for extra manorial dues, such as recognitions, tallages, heriots and court fines, with the bishop's court rolls being quite explicit that manorial levies went uncollected 'because the tenants refuse to pay' (Dyer 1981). Similarly, despite the state's efforts to limit wage increases and to restrict the movement of employees, wage-labourers in both town and country were able to obtain a marked increase in real wages and a *de facto* mobility of labour during this period, with workers frequently refusing to swear to obey the labour legislation, and even, on occasion, attacking the royal justices who attempted to enforce it (Rigby 1995: 115).

The difficulty facing the historian is how to weigh instances of conflict and resistance against those of deference and submission. In practice, it seems impossible to draw up a balance-sheet of social protest and acquiescence so as to conclude that one was more typical than the other. Certainly, not every tenant was involved in an endless struggle with his lord: even with the rising living standards of the later Middle Ages, most peasants and labourers were chiefly concerned with the immediate task of securing their daily maintenance. It was perhaps this dull economic compulsion, rather than any enthusiastic internalization of the ideology of deference, which explains the failure of society totally to break down, as it had threatened to do for a few weeks in 1381. None the less, it may still be useful for historians to foreground conflict rather than conciliation, not in the sense that it was numerically more typical but rather because such conflict was a crucial determinant of social change and of the paths of long-term economic development which such change opened up. Here we enter the later Middle Ages as interpreted for us by Brenner who claims that the successes of the English peasantry in their struggles against their lords in the later Middle Ages were not simply a product of population decline, which strengthened the bargaining position of tenants against their landlords. Rather, the ability of the peasants to organize to throw off manorial impositions and restraints was itself an independent variable in the equation: population decline could just as logically have led to the intensification of serfdom, as it did in seventeenth-century Bohemia, as to its demise (Aston and Philpin 1985: 34–46, 192–212). Certainly, even those who do not share Brenner's original denial of *any* causal role to population fluctuations in bringing about social change can still accept his eventual conclusion that such fluctuations acquired their significance 'only in connection with specific, historically-developed systems of social-property relations and given balances of class forces' (Aston and Philpin: 1985: 21, 213; Rigby 1995: 139–43).

Conclusion: Literary Ideals and Social Reality

A view of late medieval England as a 'deference society' may have provided the starting-point of our analysis but, as we have seen, an appreciation of the extent of contemporary social mobility and an awareness of the significance of social conflict are also crucial if we are to grasp the reality of the social changes which occurred in this period. It was in this rapidly changing society that poets such as Gower, Langland, Chaucer, Hoccleve and Lydgate were writing. When these writers came to discuss the nature of the good society, they did so by addressing the themes of deference, ambition and social conflict. Of these it was, inevitably, deference which they presented as vital for the creation of rightful social order. As Gower's *Confessio Amantis* put it, just as it was natural that the 'crop' should be above the 'root', so the temporal rulers should be respected in their estate while the people should remain 'in obeissance'.[24] Similarly, Langland's advice to the poor was to remember wise Cato's words: 'bear patiently the burden of poverty' (B 6.314). Both the orthodox Langland (C 5.65–7), and the Lollard author of *Pierce the Ploughman's Crede* (c.1393–1401),[25] were agreed that those of low birth were more suited to labouring and cleaning out ditches than to chasing after the wealth, status and power that promotion in the church could bring. Those individuals who sought to attain a higher rung on the social ladder for themselves were thus likely to be confronted with the moral indignation of a Gower or, as in the case of the Wife of Bath, the Franklin and the five Guildsmen, with the ironic satire of a Chaucer. Those whose collective struggles actively challenged the existing social hierarchy provoked an even more hostile response from works such as Gower's *Vox clamantis*, which presented the Peasants' Revolt of 1381 as diabolically inspired (1.10), or Chaucer's Knight's Tale, where the complaints and the rebellion of the 'cherles' (2459) are cited as prime instances of the malign influence of Saturn on human affairs. However, if deference was the ideal beloved by the chattering classes of late medieval England, it was those people who rejected such deference, in their actual, everyday practice, pursuing instead the paths of ambition and social resistance, who were to determine the future of England's social and economic development.

See also: 3 Religious Authority and Dissent, 4 City and Country, Wealth and Labour, 5 Women's Voices and Roles, 16 War and Chivalry, 17 Literature and Law, 18 Images, 21 Writing Nation, 23 Lyric, 29 York Mystery Plays, 30 The *Book of Margery Kempe*, 32 *Piers Plowman*, 33 The *Canterbury Tales*, 35 Thomas Hoccleve.

Notes

1 I should like to thank R. H. Britnell, P. Brown, R. Brown-Grant and R. G. Davies for their extremely helpful comments on earlier drafts of this paper. Thanks – and apologies – are also owed to the historians whose work I have drawn upon here but who, for reasons of space, could not be listed in the notes and bibliography below.

2 John Lydgate, *The Pilgrimage of the Life of Man*, ed. F. J. Furnivall, 3 vols, EETS es 77 (1899), 83 (1901), 92 (1904).

3 *Wimbledon's Sermon 'Redde Rationem Villicationis Tue': A Middle English Sermon of the Fourteenth Century*, ed. J. K. Knight (Pittsburgh, Pa.: Duquesne University Press 1967), lines 38–56; John Gower, *Vox clamantis*, in *The Major Latin Works of John Gower*, trans. E. W. Stockton (Seattle: University of Washington Press, 1962), 3.1.

4 Thomas Walsingham, *Chronica monasterii S. Albani Thomas Walsingham, quondam monachi S. Albani, historia Anglicana*, ed. H. T. Riley, 2 vols, Rolls ser. (1863, 1864), II 49.

5 *Rotuli Parliamentorum* (London: 1767–1832), IV, p. 419.

6 John Russell, *Book of Nurture*, in *The Babees Book*, ed. F. J. Furnivall, EETS os 32 (1868), pp. 115–239 (pp. 185–94).

7 *Preaching, Politics and Poetry in Late-Medieval England*, ed. A. J. Fletcher (Dublin: Four Courts, 1998), pp. 145–69.

8 J. Goldberg, 'Craft Guilds, the Corpus Christi Play and Civic Government', in *The Government of Medieval York: Essays in Commemoration of the 1396 Royal Charter*, ed. S. Rees Jones, Borthwick Studies in History, 3 (York: Borthwick Institute, 1977), p. 142.

9 *The Book of Margery Kempe*, ed. S. B. Meech and H. E. Allen, EETS os 212 (1940), p. 9, lines 18–25.

10 *The Sermons of Thomas Brinton, Bishop of Rochester (1373–1389)*, ed. M. A. Devlin, 2 vols (London: Camden Society, 3rd ser. 85, 86, 1954).

11 *Julian of Norwich: A Revelation of Love*, ed. M. Glasscoe (Exeter: University of Exeter Press, 1986), chs 64, 65.

12 *English Verse 1300–1500*, ed. J. Burrow (London: Longman, 1977), pp. 306–9.

13 *Of Shrifte and Penance*, ed. K. Bitterling, Middle English Texts, 29 (Heidelberg: Universitätsverlag C. Winter, 1998), p. 61.

14 G. R. Coulton, *Social Life in Britain from the Conquest to the Reformation* (Cambridge: Cambridge University Press, 1938), pp. 341–2.

15 William Langland, *The Vision of Piers Plowman: A Complete Edition of the B-Text*, ed. A. V. C. Schmidt (London: Dent, 1989).

16 A. Hanham, *The Celys and their World* (Cambridge: Cambridge University Press, 1985), p. 5.

17 John Gower, *Mirour de l'omme (The Mirror of Mankind)*, trans. W. B. Wilson (East Lansing, Mich.: Colleagues Press, 1962), lines 24049–156.

18 R. W. Hoyle, 'The Earl, the Archbishop and the Council: the Affray at Fulford, May 1504', in *Rulers and Ruled in Late Medieval England: Essays Presented to Gerald Harriss*, ed. R. E. Archer and S. Walker (London: Hambledon, 1995), pp. 242, 246.

19 *Hoccleve's Works Volume I: the Minor Poems*, ed. F. J. Furnivall, EETS es 71 (1892), pp. 25–39.

20 R. B. Dobson, 'The Educational Patronage of Archbishop Thomas Rotherham of York', *Northern History* 31 (1995), 68–9.

21 Dobson, 'Educational Patronage', p. 66.

22 *Political Poems and Songs*, ed. T. Wright, vol. 1, Rolls ser. (1859), pp. 223–6, 227–30.

23 *Historical Poems of the XIVth and XVth Centuries*, ed. R. H. Robbins (New York: Columbia University Press, 1959), pp. 39–44.

24 John Gower, *Confessio Amantis*, in *The English Works of John Gower*, 2 vols, ed. G. C. Macaulay, EETS es 81 (1900), 82 (1901), I, Prol., lines 104–18.

25 William Langland, *Piers Plowman: An Edition of the C-Text*, ed. D. Pearsall, York Medieval Texts, 2nd ser. (London: Arnold, 1978), 5.65–7. *Pierce the Ploughman's Crede*, in *The Piers Plowman Tradition*, ed. H. Barr (London: Dent, 1993), pp. 61–97, lines 744–59.

References and Further Reading

Aston, T. H. and Philpin, C. H. E. (eds) 1985. *The Brenner Debate*. Cambridge: Cambridge University Press. Reprints Brenner's controversial class-based account of late medieval social and economic change along with the views of his critics and Brenner's own reply to the debate.

Bennett, M. J. 1983. *Community, Class and Careerism: Cheshire and Lancashire Society in the Age of Sir Gawain and the Green Knight*. Cambridge: Cambridge University Press. An important regional study of social mobility.

du Boulay, F. R. H. 1970. *An Age of Ambition: English Society in the Later Middle Ages*. London: Nelson. A lively account of late medieval English society with an emphasis on social mobility.

Dunning, R. W. 1981. 'Patronage and Promotion in the Late Medieval Church.' In *Patronage, the Crown and the Provinces in Later Medieval England*, ed. R. A. Griffiths (Gloucester: Sutton), pp. 167–80. An illuminating examination of the church as a means of social mobility.

Dyer, C. 1981. 'A Redistribution of Incomes in Fifteenth-Century England?' In *Peasants, Knights and Heretics*, ed. R. H. Hilton (Cambridge: Cambridge University Press), pp. 192–215. An excellent case-study of class conflict in the countryside.

Given-Wilson, C. 1987. *The English Nobility in the Later Middle Ages*. London: Routledge and Kegan Paul. The most up-to-date survey of the late medieval English peerage and gentry.

Griffiths, R. A. 1980. 'Public and Private Bureaucracies in England and Wales in the Fifteenth Century'. *Transactions of the Royal Historical Society* 5th ser. 30, 109–30. A useful source on office as a means to social advancement.

Hatcher, J. 1977. *Plague, Population and the English Economy, 1348–1530.* London: Macmillan. Still the best introduction to the economic history of the period.

Hilton, R. H. 1977. *Bond Men Made Free: Medieval Peasant Movements and the English Rising of 1381.* London: Methuen. Looks at the rising of 1381 within the wider context of medieval social conflict.

Ives, E. W. 1983. *The Common Layers of Pre-Reformation England: Thomas Kebell – A Case Study.* Cambridge: Cambridge University Press. A classic case-study of mobility through the legal profession.

Keen, M. 1990. *English Society in the Later Middle Ages, 1358–1500.* London: Penguin. A useful introduction to late medieval English society with an emphasis on deference.

Platt, C. 1996. *King Death: The Black Death and its Aftermath in Late Medieval England.* London: UCL Press. Emphasizes the social impact of plague.

Razi, Z. 1980. *Life, Marriage and Death in a Medieval Parish: Economy, Society and Demography in Halesowen, 1270–1400.* Cambridge: Cambridge University Press. An important case-study of rural demography and social structure.

Rigby, S. H. 1995. *English Society in the Later Middle Ages: Class, Status and Gender.* Basingstoke: Macmillan. Surveys social structure, social change and social conflict.

—— 1996. *Chaucer in Context: Society, Allegory and Gender.* Manchester: Manchester University Press. Discusses modern attempts to contextualize late medieval literature.

—— 2001. 'Gendering the Black Death: Women in Later Medieval England.' In *Gendering the Middle Ages*, ed. P. Stafford and A. B. Mulder-Bakker (Oxford: Blackwell), pp. 215–54. Provides references to the debate about the social position of women.

—— (ed.) 2003. *A Companion to Britain in the Later Middle Ages.* Oxford: Blackwell. Includes chapters on late medieval English economy, society, politics, religion, education, art and literature, along with guidance on further reading.

Saul, N. 1998. 'The Rise of the Dallingridge Family.' *Sussex Archaeological Collections* 136, 123–32. A fascinating case-study of social mobility amongst the gentry.

Swanson, H. 1989. *Medieval Artisans: An Urban Class in Late Medieval England.* Oxford: Blackwell. A useful survey of this urban class.

Thrupp, S. L. 1962. *The Merchant Class of Medieval London.* Ann Arbor: University of Michigan Press. A classic study, first published in 1948.

3
Religious Authority and Dissent

Mishtooni Bose

In the 'prolog' to *The Reule of Crysten Religioun* (1443), Reginald Pecock identified his target audience as comprising two 'soortis of peple'. To the first group belonged those who insisted on reading the Bible in English ('her modiris langage'), and valued the New Testament over all other books written either in Latin or 'þe comoun peples langage'. The second group was drawn from a broader constituency: those who read not only the Bible in English, but also other 'unsauery bokis' in the vernacular, which they used clandestinely ('as fer as þei dare for drede of her prelatis') and which they considered 'noble and worþi and profitable bookis to alle cristen mennes leernyng and rewling' (18).[1] Pecock's motives were not solely polemical. He broadened his projected audience to include not only 'undisposid men' of the kinds described but also 'weel disposed cristen men of þe lay partie' (19), for whose intellectual acumen he had high regard. These people, he argued, required 'stable doctryne' in more durable forms than the sermons by which such doctrine was conventionally delivered. In *The Repressor of Over Much Blaming of the Clergy* (c.1449), he emphasizes that 'the wickidli enfectid scole of heresie among the lay peple in Ynglond . . . is not ȝit conquerid' because of the inadequate methods employed by a clergy over reliant on preaching as the principal or sole means of religious instruction (I, 89).[2]

Pecock could imagine how easily some of the 'weel disposid' laypeople might slip into the category of the 'undisposid' if their spiritual and intellectual hunger was not anticipated and satisfied by the clergy. He was able to draw important distinctions between potential and actual heretics, between 'þe lay peple' broadly conceived and the narrower subcategory of 'erring persoones . . . whiche ben clepid Lollardis' (I, 127–8). In making such distinctions, he not only offers an exposure of the social pathologies of heresy, but goes further, writing about both constituencies of the laity as if they were not merely firmly embedded but even closely juxtaposed in the London communities with which he was most familiar. This may have been an accurate account of encounters with religious attitudes that were less easily distinguished from 'orthodoxy' than might be supposed; and whether or not what he offers us here is documentary evidence, it remains significant that he is even capable of imagining such a juxtaposition. Produced as it was after sixty or seventy years of religious controversy in England, Pecock's vernacular programme is a wholesale attempt to think freshly about relations between clergy and laity and to construct them more hopefully. Notwithstanding his unequivocally harsh words about 'Lollardis' in the *Repressor*, his general reluctance to use this notoriously ambiguous term of abuse, and his ubiquitous attention to semantic nuance, no less than his interpellation of the reader of the *Repressor* as his 'brother', are all part of a strenuous attempt to defamiliarize a worn-out set of controversial positions and perceptions.

In order to understand more fully what was at stake in this vernacular experiment, it is necessary to obtain an overview of the controversial ideas to which Pecock's works were a belated response, and of the intellectual climate in which he was writing. Developments in scholarship over the last twenty years have made this an easier task than it once was, as we are now more familiar with the rich seam of writing, including sermons, dialogues and polemical treatises, that rehearses views derived directly or indirectly from the arguments of John Wyclif (Hudson 1985, 1988). The editing and revaluation of many of these writings has had the practical and invaluable consequence of considerably extending the canon of late medieval literature written in English (Hudson 1978, 2001; Hudson and Gradon 1983–96). Historians have, likewise, continued to be attentive to the confluence of political and ecclesiastical manoeuvres that tied the emergence and expression of dissent in this period ever more closely to the threat, whether real or imagined, of sedition (Aston 1984: 1–47; McNiven 1987). It has also become necessary to take into account the possible impact on vernacular literature of the anti-Wycliffite legislation that was intended to inhibit the range of scholarly and textual practices, from translation to dissemination, by which further controversy might be fostered (Watson 1995). I will begin by offering an overview of some of the topics of debate in the Wycliffite controversies, before discussing some of the characteristics of controversial writing, the necessity of distinguishing between reforming and dissenting discourses, the importance of literature in preserving arenas in which relationships between religious authority and dissent could continue to be negotiated, and the limitations of censorship legislation in helping us to imagine the intellectual and religious climate of late medieval England. As we shall see, Pecock's deliberate refusal to address either one of his projected lay audiences exclusively – to separate 'dissenters', that is, from those who acknowledge 'authority' – offers a salutary lesson for modern readers seeking to understand the relationships between them during this period.

The Wycliffite Controversies

The chronology and detail of the religious controversies that arose from the writing, activities and supporters of John Wyclif have been established and discussed lucidly elsewhere (Catto 1992: 186–261; McNiven 1987; Rex 2002: 25–87). The necessarily brief summary of controversial ideas offered here is intended, first, as a guide for readers encountering these issues for the first time and, second, to emphasize some of their more important implications for our reading of the literature of this period. It is helpful to think of the controversies as falling loosely into four phases. The first phase is given shape and focus by Wyclif's gradual progress 'from a schoolman to an evangelist' (Catto 1992: 218). The second phase lasted from Wyclif's death in 1384 to the passing of *De heretico comburendo*, the statute that enforced the burning of relapsed or impenitent heretics, in 1401. Despite intense hostility to Wyclif's ideas, from which ten heresies and fourteen errors were extracted and condemned at the Blackfriars Council in 1382, and an intellectual environment increasingly affected by repressive ecclesiastical and royal legislation, this phase witnessed a burgeoning of activity among Wyclif's clerical supporters. They produced their translations of the Bible during this period, together with other original writings in a variety of genres, and continued to enjoy some political support.

The third phase lasted from 1401 until the execution of Sir John Oldcastle in 1417, after an abortive rebellion that received some Wycliffite support. This period saw a dramatic narrowing of possibilities for ecclesiastical and social reform along Wycliffite lines, particularly where clerical endowment was concerned, and the culmination of the sequence of repressive legislation that had begun under Richard II (Richardson 1936; Simpson 2002: 333–43). This was a critical period given particular focus and intensity by the legislative zeal of Thomas Arundel, Archbishop of Canterbury. As well as being responsible for *De heretico comburendo*, Arundel instigated further anti-Wycliffite legislation during this period, including the *Provincial Constitutions* of 1407–9, which built on previous legislation and whose impact will be discussed later in the chapter. During this period, former followers of Wyclif who had recanted and established successful ecclesiastical careers (such as Philip Repingdon, Bishop of Lincoln), channelled their energies in conventionally sanctioned ways, notably by prosecuting the cause of ecclesiastical reform (Catto 1999: 154, 160). After the execution of Oldcastle, the cause lost political momentum, and the intellectual sustenance that it had initially received from Oxford gradually petered out. This inaugurates the fourth phase, which lasted from the aftermath of the Oldcastle execution until the first phase of the Reformation. To describe it as the 'underground' phase of Wycliffism is misleading, as it implies that expressions of dissent became less important or coherent once they had largely ceased to be nourished by the clerical activities of writing, translating and disseminating intellectual work. In fact, the literature generated by heresy trials of this period shows that a range of identifiably heretical beliefs continued to be firmly held, stealthily disseminated and passionately defended in different parts of the country throughout the remainder of the fifteenth and well into the sixteenth century. The phase of the charismatic Wycliffite preachers linking academic and extramural worlds gradually gave way to one in which dissent was largely fostered and nourished in increasingly well-documented communities, whose beliefs and activities can be glimpsed in legal transcriptions that also occasionally offer us vital insights into a broad spectrum of religious practices that cannot be accommodated by the narrow term 'heresy' (Catto 1999; McSheffrey 1995; Plumb 1995).

Crucial to Wyclif's emergence as a controversial figure was the fact that the subject-matter of his writings was immediately pertinent to the world beyond the schools. His theory of dominion, namely that men received the power of dominion from God through grace alone and that the unrighteous could not therefore exercise it, inevitably called into question the right of the church to hold property and to receive further endowments; and hostility to ecclesiastical temporalities was to prove one of the most politically durable legacies of the controversies to which his views gave rise. Among his many later controversial ideas was the view of a church composed solely of the predestinate, and in the last period of his life Wyclif's works attacked 'every form of idolatry: not only undue obedience to the carnal church, but the claims of the friars . . . the complaisance of secular lords, the cult of images and above all the idolatry of the eucharist' (Catto 1992: 212). It took Wyclif some time to arrive at that last, and arguably most notorious, tenet of his thought, namely the rejection of transubstantiation (which posited the conversion, upon consecration, of the whole substance of the bread into the whole substance of the Body of Christ) and the insistence that the substance of the bread remained after the words of consecration had been spoken. Yet it is equally important to bear in mind the context in which he arrived at this view. The process whereby the doctrine of transubstantiation was developed is itself a classic instance of the gradual construction and clarification of Christian 'orthodoxy' over centuries. As Ian Levy points out, '[B]y the time Wyclif arrived at Oxford in the middle of the fourteenth century the parameters of eucharistic theology had been narrowed to a degree unknown even a century before' (Levy 2003: 214–15). Wyclif's having moved to a dissenting position that was eventually hereticated may thus be seen as part of the much longer process described by Robert Swanson: 'because Western Christianity developed, indeed was transformed, between 1100 and 1500, heresy was almost a necessary concomitant' (Swanson 1994: 280).

It is possible to trace, both through the lists of official condemnations produced by the authorities and in recognizably Wycliffite writings, the spectrum of views that provoked such controversy. These views, derived from Wyclif's works but sometimes inflected differently, or de-emphasized in individual Wycliffite texts, have been conveniently grouped by Anne Hudson under three headings: theological, covering 'the eucharist, the sacraments, confession, images, pilgrimages, purgatory, and prayers to the saints'; ecclesiastical, that is 'the nature of the church, and papacy and church hierarchy, the temporal wealth and power of the church, "private religions", the duty of the clergy'; and political, covering 'the relation of the secular ruler to the church, the problem of dominion, the notion of common property, the questions of war and oaths, the sources of law' (Hudson 1988: 278–9). Despite only surviving in texts produced by opponents of the Wycliffites, the *Twelve Conclusions* of 1395, which cover criticisms of the church, the priesthood and the sacraments, as well as advancing arguments that would today be called pacifist, are a representative summary of some of the views that came to be associated with Wycliffism (Hudson 1978: 24–9, 150–5). The authors' description of themselves as 'pore men, tresoreris of Cryst and his apostlis' is typical of the self-deprecating rhetoric of normative Wycliffite discourse. Their appeal to 'þe lordys and þe comunys of þe parlement' is also characteristic, deriving from Wyclif's own appeals to such powers to bring alleged ecclesiastical abuses to an end. Most significant is the announcement that these conclusions are offered 'for þe reformaciun of holi chirche of Yngelond': this is not the separatist language of a disempowered group, but the idiom of would-be reformers who still felt themselves to be in possession of the political initiative. The state of the contemporary church is compared unfavourably with that of the apostolic church; clerical celibacy is attacked on the grounds that it 'inducith sodomie in al holy chirche'. The authors deny that God's body 'be uertu of þe prestis wordis schulde ben closed essenciali in a litil bred'. Exorcism, pilgrimages, the use of religious images in worship, confession and absolution are all attacked, as are 'special preyeris for dede men soulis' because these are procured through 'þe giftis of temperel godis to prestis and to almes housis', thus sustaining the corrupt practices associated with ecclesiastical endowment. In the language of the *Conclusions* and other dissenting literature of this period we can see emerging a core vocabulary and set of topics that together constitute an identifiable, coherent discourse.

Our concentration on the Wycliffite controversies should not, however, obscure what Pecock's careful distinctions between different constituencies of laypeople remind us, namely that categories of belief and behaviour that subsequently come to be defined as dissenting or even heretical often grow out of, and may even continue to flourish alongside, mainstream and officially sanctioned religious activities and impulses. The theological curiosity that could be nudged towards either compliance with authority or expressions of dissent can be seen fermenting in Langland's *Piers Plowman* vignette of the unlearned busying themselves with theological mysteries: they 'gnawen god with gorge' (C 11.42).[3] Some seventy years later, Pecock's fraternizing with a theologically curious 'lay partie' would produce a similar, though markedly more sympathetic, vignette: 'Certis ofte han men and wommen come to me and seid: "Thus hath a doctour sed in this mater . . . and thus hath this famose precher prechid"' (I, 91).[4] The most fruitful perspectives in recent research emphasize the strong elements of continuity between the particular reforming impulses, theological curiosity and spiritual hunger that crystallize in identifiably Wycliffite thought and those that flourish elsewhere in English religious and intellectual life. It is telling that the fact of this continuity has been drawn on both by scholars concerned to marginalize the emphasis on Wycliffism in modern historiography of the period and by others with different motivations (Rex 2002: 78–80). Some, for example, have sought to emphasize the extent to which the beliefs and religious practices that came to be identified as 'Wycliffite' or 'Lollard' grew up alongside, or out of, a common core of late medieval religious practices, and specifically emerged from a widely shared impulse to explore, deepen and refine the quality of religious faith as believed, professed and practised (Thomson 1989). Others have sought to stress the continuities between Wycliffite scholarly practices – principally the translation or dissemination of texts, or both – and those of other writers (Somerset 1998). The implications of one recent study are that Wycliffism both draws sustenance from, and reveals with a compelling degree of transparency, a broader cultural phenomenon: the trajectory whereby ideas fermented in the schools and were disseminated in the extramural world, eventually leaving their imprint on the thinking of later generations who may have been constrained by them, or at the least obliged to take them into account (Ghosh 2002). The claim that Wycliffism is one variation in the broader patterns of the intellectual and religious renaissance of the late fourteenth century does not, therefore, prevent our seeing the controversies as an invaluable trace element that renders the intellectual and textual processes of that renaissance more readily visible and intelligible to us.

Reform, Dissent and Theological Exploration

One recent observation neatly sums up the prevailing situation in current scholarship: 'Now that Lollard studies are on the map, everything else seems to have moved' (Somerset 2003a: 16). In focusing on the Wycliffite controversies, it is necessary to decide carefully how much gravitational force we should allow them to exert on our reading of other theologically adventurous literature written during this period. In the wake of this burgeoning of scholarship, therefore, our task must be to ensure that our reading of late medieval English literature is informed by our growing understanding of the Wycliffite controversies without its being unhelpfully overwhelmed by them. Late medieval English writing, whether in poetry or prose, and across a range of genres – satire, vision, hagiography and pseudo-hagiography, testimony, dialogue, quasi-scholastic treatise – created many different arenas in which it was possible to imagine alternative configurations of political, religious and social institutions (Simpson 2002). Critics have traced the range of theological energies at work in the literature of this period, and have shown how its topical and methodological diversity eludes explication solely in terms of a particular controversy (Aers 2002, 2003; Watson 1997a, 1997b). As Nicholas Watson points out in relation to prose works produced between 1370 and 1420: 'However violently some of these prose texts assert that there are only two such positions, orthodox and heretical . . . analysis of any single group of texts complicates this model' (Watson 2002: 95). Likewise, the urgent questions regarding salvation, the nature of the sacraments, ecclesiology, the value of penance and the role of learning that animate *Piers Plowman* have many points of origin, from the Great Schism and contemporary scholastic controversies to the devotional literature of earlier generations and Langland's individual agenda which, as his textual revisions reveal, evidently matured in dialogue with a range of controversial stances (Aers 2002). 'Thinking in poetry', a process memorably traced by J. A. Burrow, was hardly hospitable to an exclusively Wycliffite or even a proto-Wycliffite agenda (Burrow 1993).

In order to appreciate the distinctions between Langlandian and Wycliffite intellectual worlds, it is instructive to compare the ways in which Langland and an anonymous Wycliffite writer sought to represent the mind on its quest for an authentic understanding of faith beyond that provided by the church's authoritative modes of explanation. At the beginning of his quest 'for to seke Dowel', in *Piers Plowman* C.10, the first interpretation of 'Dowel' is offered to Will by two Franciscan friars. Will's response is inconclusive: 'Y have no kynde knowlechyng to conseyue al this speche / Ac yf y may lyue and loke y shal go lerne bettere' (56–7). Not for the first time, Will's appetite for a different mode of instruction, as much as for substantial knowledge, brings an encounter to an end. Will's dissatisfaction with the friars' teaching methods, his hunger for alternative modes of 'knowing', seems to make contact with Wycliffite concerns. In the course of criticizing the alleged evasiveness of friars, an anonymous Wycliffite author argues that logic cannot account for the manner in which transubstantiation is supposed to take place. His prose modulates from disputation with an imagined opponent to a direct plea: 'But, frere, tell me how Y schulde trowe':

> And ȝif thei seien this mater is sutil, and men mai not understonde it, wel we witen that God bindith not men to believe ony thing which thei mai not understonde – as we seien of the Trinite (III, 353).[5]

This is an explicit denunciation of the church's apparent unwillingness to explain what William of Auxerre, a schoolman of an earlier generation, had called the *quare* and *quomodo* – the 'whys and wherefores' – of the Christian faith. It is the 'how' in this indignant request that is most important for the present discussion, in that it expresses profound dissatisfaction with the church's preferred modes of explanation to the laity. Not only is the idiom of instruction found wanting; also in question is the friars' custodianship of that idiom. At first, therefore, there might seem to be some continuity between this and Will's outburst against the Franciscans' methods of teaching. From this point onwards, however, Langland and the Wycliffite writer travel in very different directions. *Piers Plowman* culminates in the imaginative appropriation and reliving of biblical events, facilitated by the progressive stripping away, indeed the reversal, of the cultural and institutional processes by which *boc* had been converted into *scriptura* (and the code-switching from prestige language to 'mother tongue' here is, as ever in Langland, fully significant). The Wycliffite writer, however, stays resolutely in the academic arena, and even extends its idioms into the extramural world: his is a far less open-ended quest for an account of the mysteries of faith that can satisfy 'resoun of kynde'. Although both use the model of the intellectual quest, and this Wycliffite writer, in common with many others, communicates a sense of intellectual excitement at the possibilities of cultural translation and intellectual transgression, we are bound to feel the distance and difference between the range of imaginative and intellectual possibilities opened up by *Piers Plowman* and the narrowing of argumentative focus achieved in Wycliffite polemic. It is therefore essential that our growing understanding of the Wycliffite controversies should not pre-empt the full realization, as we read Langland and other writers, of the different directions that theological exploration could take. As David Aers writes in relation to Langland's exploration of eucharistic theology, 'we must be careful not to read *Piers Plowman* with the prejudice that it must fit an "orthodoxy" shaped by the Church's war to eliminate Wycliffite inflections of Christianity' (Aers 2002: 65). It becomes necessary to attune ourselves to hearing a variety of voices across a wide discursive spectrum, and to note points of both contact and distance between 'Wycliffite' and 'non-Wycliffite' writings.

Moreover, when considering literary responses to the development of religious controversy, we are faced with a situation that is best described as a surplus of representation. When summarizing Pecock's descriptions of lay behaviour above, I treated his descriptions as if he could be entirely trusted to tell us the truth in this matter. In fact, for all his openness in so many respects, his accounts remain frustratingly one-sided and largely unverifiable. Pecock's works are not the only examples of the text constituting the events. The same could be said of the *Testimony of William Thorpe* (c.1407) and the *Book of Margery Kempe* (1430s), both of which overwhelm and displace the nuggets of factual information by which any of the events that they narrate might be independently verified. They thus pose their own interpretative enigmas, to which we will now turn.

William Thorpe and Margery Kempe: A Surplus of Representation

There are promising points of comparison between the *Testimony of William Thorpe* and the *Book of Margery Kempe*. Both are retrospective accounts that seek in some measure to demystify the Lancastrian clergy. Thomas Arundel, Archbishop of Canterbury, is the most obvious fulcrum between them, interrogating Thorpe at Saltwood Castle in 1407 and holding an even less formal 'dalyawns' with Kempe in Lambeth (c.1413). Kempe endures more formal interrogation in the presence of the Abbot of Leicester in 1417 and subsequently by Henry Bowet, Archbishop of York. Both texts evoke the atmosphere of heresy trials without ever quite taking their readers there (Jurkowski 2002: 294). Rather, it is the privilege of these representations to turn what might superficially be taken for scenes of formal interrogation into more complex arenas of negotiation, calling into question the distribution of religious authority between the ecclesiastical hierarchy and its humble interlocutors, and representing that authority as transactional and apparently still negotiable. They thus complicate the notion of a univocal 'religious authority', suggesting that the spiritual authority achievable by the minor cleric Thorpe or the vulnerable Kempe can be readily uncoupled from the debased currency of institutional authority, which remains the tarnished preserve of the Arundels and Bowets.

Closer inspection of these apparently shared elements, however, calls them into question in turn. Notwithstanding their obviously provocative qualities, these texts clearly emanate from radically different cultural standpoints, interpellating their readers in ways that are measurably distinct from one another. This can be seen in relation to their respective 'anatomies' of the Lancastrian clergy. The *Testimony* is a version of events that took place in 1407, but much of Thorpe's oral account invokes the 1380s and '90s as decades of relative intellectual freedom that he identifies with the flourishing of a dissenting community within clerical ranks, eulogizing his teachers in an autobiography of religious formation that stands in interesting counterpoint to the one offered by Will in *Piers Plowman* C.5.1–104 (Copeland 1996). The *Testimony* draws attention to the fact that the Lancastrian church retained in its ranks once prominent Wycliffites, such as Philip Repingdon, who had since recanted, and Thorpe calls into question the authenticity of their Christian conduct.[6] The text thus attempts to expose a lack of uniformity and degree of compromise and even dissimulation inherent in the fabrication and maintenance of univocal ecclesiastical 'authority'. For Thorpe, 'religious authority' is located elsewhere.

In the *Book*, by contrast, the focus remains on the necessity of validating Kempe as an individual. Like the *Testimony*, the *Book* is retrospective, re-creating for readers of the 1430s and afterwards a broader temporal trajectory that includes the distinctive religious and political atmosphere of the 1410s, the last decade on which Arundel stamped his decisive character. For all Kempe's criticisms of individual clerks, however, the *Book* leaves the wider ecclesiastical structures unchallenged. The recurring concerns for Kempe, as she negotiates different social encounters and seeks to satisfy her spiritual desires within the existing apparatus offered by the church, are pragmatic and individualistic, and are paralleled and amplified by one of her scribes, as his own quest to verify the authenticity of her testimony is written into the *Book*. The orientation of the *Testimony*, by contrast, is collective, insisting on the residual power of Thorpe's membership of a fully fledged counter-culture that is resolutely at odds with the prevailing ecclesiastical order.

These differences lead to further points of contrast. The *Book* may seem as assured in its pseudo-hagiographic purpose as the *Testimony* undoubtedly is, but crucially, in its diffusion of *auctoritas*, it is altogether less rigid in its dealings with its readers. Thorpe's conscience and testimony form the moral and rhetorical centre of the *Testimony*. Despite the force of Kempe's presence, it is far harder to locate an unequivocal centre in the *Book*. Its rhetorical position can be viewed as one 'whose relation to formal authority, if correct, is hardly one of childlike obedience' (Watson 1999a: 563–4). Alternatively, it can be read as a frank enunciation of clerical, and particularly episcopal, rather than lay priorities (Rees Jones 2000). It is not difficult to see whence the latter view draws its strength. The *Book* constructs a world in which the all-purpose term of abuse 'Lollard' and accusations of heresy are bandied about with relish not only by the monks at Canterbury (who cannot wait, it seems, to bypass the sequence of trial, recantation, relapse and condemnation in their haste to get to the spectacle of the 'tonne' and the 'cartful of thornys'), but also by laypeople. In marked contrast with representatives of the lay power, such as the memorably belligerent Steward and Mayor of Leicester, the church's representatives are usually accommodating, resilient and imaginative in their treatment of the challenging Kempe. 'The church' in this text is polyvocal, admitting dissent within and between its ranks, as we see in the markedly different ways in which Kempe is viewed by the supportive Carmelite, Alan of Lynn, and his censorious Prior Provincial, Thomas Netter. While the *Testimony* is uncompromisingly and proudly dissenting in its desire to represent the Lancastrian church as vulnerable in its orthodox self-image, the *Book* at least allows this lack of uniformity, which it does not seek to disguise, to be viewed as a potential source of strength. Thus, while both texts test the bounds of discursive and religious freedom, there are significant differences between the degrees to which they are prepared to grant freedom of interpretation to their readers.

By insisting on the power of texts to confer authoritative surpluses that may outlast anything achieved in fact, the *Testimony* and the *Book* insist on the charisma of texts as events. The *Testimony* systematically confers on Thorpe and his fellow dissenters the kind of lasting cultural authority that they could never achieve in their own lives (Copeland 2001: 191–219); and the same appears to have been true of Margery Kempe, for whom the *Book* achieves a similar kind of consummation. Notwithstanding the enactment of repressive legislation during this period, much of its surviving English literature, whether written by self-conscious dissenters, or by avowedly orthodox clergy, or from a range of positions in between, is capable of creating arenas in which religious authority remains negotiable and dissent refuses either to recognize itself as such or to confess its powerlessness. It is to the further survival of these arenas that our discussion now turns.

Censorship and Hermeneutics: Spectres of Orthodoxy?

Several broader themes can be pursued through the study of the Wycliffite controversies: the challenge to academic freedom; the attempts by legislators to align heresy with sedition; and the progress and possible effects of censorship. The sequence of legislation generated by the Wycliffite controversies culminated in Archbishop Arundel's *Provincial Constitutions* of 1407–9, legislation belatedly replicated in the archdiocese of York in 1462 (Spencer 1993: 164). I will concentrate here on the implications of this legislation.

It was when considering the difficulties of distinguishing 'radical orthodoxy' from expressions of dissent in the context of 'vernacular Wycliffism' that Anne Hudson opened up a promising and still fertile line of enquiry for research (Hudson 1988: 390–445). One of the most influential interventions in this enquiry has been the turning of attention to the ways in which Arundel's *Constitutions* sought to regulate the freedom of religious expression, principally by insisting on the licensing of preachers, forbidding translation of the scriptures, or any portion of them, into English, and circumscribing the pursuit of speculative theology (Spencer 1993: 163–88; Watson 1995). It has long been recognized that censorship enacted long before 1407 constrained the conditions under which Langland and other late medieval writers were working, culminating in the situation articulated by Anne Hudson in relation to *Piers Plowman*: 'unusually, perhaps uniquely, it is a poem whose impact became more unorthodox as time passed' (Hudson 1988: 408).

Although attempts to read 'down' from censorship legislation are often problematic and inconclusive, there is no doubt that the existence of such legislation necessarily modifies our perceptions of the hermeneutic environment of individual pieces of writing, and questions remain as to what extent we incorporate our knowledge of them into our reading of fifteenth-century texts. Recent research has recognized that the Constitutions were 'partly unenforceable' (Watson 1999b: 344). Social class acted as a crucial point of differentiation when it came to enforcing them (Aston and Richmond 1997: 19–21; Spencer 1993: 37–8; Watson 1995: 857). Second, the practical effect of this legislation is called into question by the existence of manuscript miscellanies in which unimpeachably orthodox and identifiably heterodox materials mingled (Hudson 1988: 423–7). Third, the evidence that survives from episcopal registers strongly suggests that Arundel's legislation was only patchily enforced by bishops, reminding us that then, as now, effectiveness and continuity in institutional administration depended strongly, if not wholly, on the temperaments and interests of particular individuals. Finally, close and contextual reading of the language of the *Constitutions* has demonstrated that they should be more properly viewed as legislation aimed principally at the 'radical Latin' used in the academic world, and at Oxford in particular, and only secondarily at the extramural generation and dissemination of vernacular literature (Somerset 2003b: 145–57; 2004: 73–92). The cumulative force of these studies has been to suggest that, rather than providing a reliable measure of the extent of religious and discursive freedom in fifteenth-century England, Arundel's *Constitutions* show that aspirations and fantasies are codified in legislation as surely as they are ever expressed in fiction.

It remains to be decided to what extent the *Constitutions* cast a shadow over literary bids for discursive freedom in the ensuing decades. To illustrate what is at stake here, we can consider three poems: the anonymous romance *The Anturs of Arther*; a poem attributed to John Audelay (*fl.*1426), *De tribus regibus mortuis*; and an untitled dialogue by him in which Marcol, a fool, instructs 'Salamon', a wise man, in criticisms that should be levied at clergy and laity respectively. The textual history of the *Anturs* is complex, but for the purposes of our discussion it is most useful to bear in mind that a version appears in the post-*Constitutions*, mid-fifteenth-century 'Thornton manuscript' (Lincoln Cathedral MS 91). Formal and thematic connections between *De tribus regibus mortuis* and the *Anturs* have already received critical attention.[7] In the former, three kings on a boar hunt are confronted by the ghosts of their fathers. In the *Anturs*, Guenevere, separated with Gawain from the rest of an Arthurian hunting party, sees the ghost of her mother rise shrieking from the Tarn, covered with toads and serpents. The ghosts have dire warnings for their children, urging them to offer masses for their parents and to abandon their materialism. The three kings build a 'mynster' expressly for this purpose, while Guenevere promises to offer 'a myllion of Masses' for her mother. These poems are unimpeachably orthodox in their insistence on the efficacy of the sacraments in ensuring the salvation of souls.

As has been noted elsewhere, Audelay's dialogue is a more complex case (Simpson 2002: 378–80). It is a particularly valuable witness for our purposes because Audelay was writing in the 1420s, far into the cultural watershed that may have been inaugurated by the *Constitutions*. This enables us to judge more precisely what risks he was taking by allowing the 'Salamon and Marcol' dialogue to channel a satirical and overtly Langlandian idiom, clearly identifiable through Audelay's references to 'Mede þe maydyn' and a sprinkling of other Langlandian locutions. Written in the same thirteen-line alliterative stanza form as *De tribus regibus mortuis* (though with a slightly differing rhyme scheme), this intriguing poem never overplays its hand by succumbing to polemical sclerosis (10–46).[8] It delicately and self-consciously balances its criticisms of different levels of the ecclesiastical hierarchy, including friars, secular priests and curates, but it never presents itself as univocally anticlerical, equally chastising the laity for neglecting their religious duties. While commending, as surely as the previous two poems, the church's ministering of the sacraments by which salvation is ensured, it also expresses profound impatience with an apparent loss of ecclesiastical leadership and consensus, a dangerous vacuum created by a widespread lack of learning (which Pecock's vernacular programme was also designed to address). Above all, its rapid shifts between arguments and addressees insist more broadly on the necessity of keeping different perspectives in play, and on the vitality of a particular post-Langlandian poetic tradition in facilitating this.

The formal and generic affiliations between this turbulent poetic arena and the other two poems oblige us to consider where we should draw our boundaries when defining the limits of controversial literature during this period. It is possible that the passionate endorsement of the offering of masses for the dead in both *Anturs* and *De tribus regibus* would have been read with a new self-consciousness on the part of avowedly orthodox fifteenth-century readers alert to Wycliffite assaults on the legitimacy of the established church to minister such rites (it will be remembered that the offering of prayers for the dead outraged the authors of the *Twelve Conclusions*). In the Audelay manuscript we have the further suggestive juxtaposition of *De tribus regibus* with a poem in a closely related alliterative form that openly aligns itself with a Langlandian, polyvocal position. It is at this point, however, that we inevitably recall the first two poems' membership of a broader genre of writing in which mortals are confronted by religiously informed supernatural beings, as in *Pearl* or *St Erkenwald* or, somewhat further afield, the *Gast of Gy* (the latter a particularly good example because of its source in a Latin prose treatise written in France, unconnected with the Wycliffite controversies). Consideration of these poems together reminds us that on their diachronic journeys, such texts may temporarily acquire further accretions of significance through new synchronic affiliations.

Conclusion

The historiography of the Wycliffite controversies exposes the extent to which pragmatic position-taking underpinned the sequence of legislation against heresy and the fragility and inconsistency of its subsequent enactment (McNiven 1987; Jurkowski 2002). As is shown through the development of eucharistic theologies, doctrines that were orthodox for one generation could be seen as dissenting by later ones. It is consequently more helpful to think of the English religious writings of this period in terms of their relative discursive openness and closure than to assign texts more straightforwardly to the ranks of the 'orthodox' and 'heterodox'. Such a perspective frees us from the risk of merely replicating the categories and classifications whereby writers sought to position themselves and others. In rejecting the false clarity that the documents generated by legislators such as Arundel sought to impose, we will remain responsive to the imaginative and intellectual explorations taking place in the literature.

See also: 24 Literature of Religious Instruction, 25 Mystical and Devotional Literature, 26 Accounts of Lives, 30 The *Book of Margery Kempe*, 32 *Piers Plowman*.

Notes

1 R. Pecock, *The Reule of Crysten Religioun*, ed. W. C. Greet, EETS os 171 (1927).
2 R. Pecock, *The Repressor of Over Much Blaming of the Clergy*, ed. Churchill Babington, 2 vols, Rolls ser. (1860).
3 William Langland, *Piers Plowman: An Edition of the C-Text*, ed. Derek Pearsall, York Medieval Texts, 2nd ser. (London: Arnold, 1978).
4 See note 2, above.
5 T. Arnold (ed.), *Select English Works of John Wyclif*, 3 vols (Oxford: Oxford University Press, 1968–71).
6 *Two Wycliffite Texts*, ed. Anne Hudson, EETS os 301 (1993).
7 Thorlac Turville-Petre, '"Summer Sunday", "De Tribus Regibus Mortuis", and "The Awntyrs off Arthure": Three Poems in the Thirteen-line Stanza', *RES* 25 (1974), 1–14.
8 *The Poems of John Audelay*, ed. Ella Keats Whiting, EETS os 184 (1931).

References and Further Reading

Aers, David 2002. 'The Sacrament of the Altar in *Piers Plowman* and the Late Medieval Church in England.' In *Images, Idolatry and Iconoclasm in Late Medieval England*, ed. Jeremy Dimmick, James Simpson and Nicolette Zeeman (Oxford: Oxford University Press), pp. 63–80. Discusses Langland's exploration of eucharistic theology and is particularly valuable for its emphasis on the independence of his imaginative exploration of this central Christian theme.

—— 2003. 'Walter Brut's Theology of the Sacrament of the Altar.' In *Lollards and their Influence in Late Medieval England*, ed. Fiona Somerset, Jill Havens and Derrick Pitard (Woodbridge: Boydell), pp. 115–26. Continues Aers's exploration of continuity and discontinuity between late medieval theologies by outlining in detail the professed beliefs of the Wycliffite Walter Brut.

Aston, Margaret 1984. *Lollards and Reformers: Images and Literacy in Late Medieval Religion*. London: Hambledon Press. Essential collection of articles with broader range of topics than the title implies.

—— and Richmond, Colin (eds) 1997. *Lollardy and the Gentry in the Later Middle Ages*. Stroud and New York: Sutton Publishing and St. Martin's Press. Innovative collection of articles that explore this question from the perspectives of textual, intellectual, political and social history.

Burrow, J. A. 1993. *Thinking in Poetry: Three Medieval Examples*. The William Matthews Lectures 1993. London: Birkbeck College. For all that has been written on 'vernacular theology' since this series of three short lectures was delivered, it remains invaluable for its elegant, intuitive anticipation of many of the insights subsequently developed at greater length by others.

Catto, Jeremy 1992. 'Wyclif and Wycliffism in Oxford 1356–1430.' In *The History of the University of Oxford. Vol. 2: Late Medieval Oxford*, ed. J. I. Catto and Ralph Evans (Oxford: Oxford University Press), pp. 175–261. An admirably lucid, subtle and detailed narrative of the nature and impact of the controversies surrounding Wyclif's career and writings as far as these affected Oxford; draws out the links between institutional and intellectual history.

—— 1999. 'Fellows and Helpers: The Religious Identity of the Followers of Wyclif.' In *The Medieval Church: Universities, Heresy, and the Religious Life*, ed. Peter Biller and Barry Dobson. Studies in Church History, Subsidia 11 (Woodbridge: Boydell and Brewer), pp. 141–62. An account that emphasizes fluctuations in commitment to a coherent 'Wycliffite' identity; particularly valuable for its treatment of members of the Oxford circle (including Nicholas Hereford and Philip Repingdon) who defected from Wycliffism early on.

Copeland, Rita 1996. 'William Thorpe and his Lollard Community: Intellectual Labor and the Representation of Dissent.' In *Bodies and Disciplines: Intersections of Literature and History in Fifteenth-Century England*, ed. Barbara A. Hanawalt and David Wallace (Minneapolis and London: University of Minnesota Press), pp. 199–221. Thorough examination of the representational ambitions and complexities of the *Testimony*.

—— 2001. *Pedagogy, Intellectuals, and Dissent in the Later Middle Ages: Lollardy and Ideas of Learning*. Cambridge: Cambridge University Press. Situates Lollard cultures within broader institutional and intellectual histories, with a particularly welcome focus on the diachronic development of pedagogic ideas and on contemporary academic discussions of controversial topics such as the 'literal sense' of scripture.

Ghosh, Kantik 2002. *The Wycliffite Heresy: Authority and the Interpretation of Texts*. Cambridge: Cambridge University Press. Detailed, lucid account of the place of hermeneutics in the Wycliffite controversies, examining works in Latin and English (including the Wycliffite sermons and Nicholas Love's *The Mirror of the Blessed Life of Jesus Christ*).

Hudson, Anne (ed.) 1978. *Selections from English Wycliffite Writings*. Cambridge: Cambridge University Press. The most useful and representative selection available, with comprehensive notes and helpful chronology.

—— 1985. *Lollards and their Books*. London and Ronceverte: Hambledon Press. Seminal articles on all aspects of Wycliffite textuality, book production and dissemination, the impact of legislation, and topics on which suspected heretics could be interrogated.

—— 1988. *The Premature Reformation: Wycliffite Texts and Lollard History*. Oxford: Clarendon Press. The most comprehensive study of Wycliffite literature and culture: essential reading.

—— (ed.) 2001. *The Works of a Lollard Preacher*. EETS os 317. Oxford: Oxford University Press. An edition of the sermon *Omnis plantacio*, and two tracts: *Fundamentum aliud memo potest ponere* and *De oblacione iugis sacrificii*.

—— and Gradon, Pamela (eds.) 1983–96. *English Wycliffite Sermons*, 5 vols. Oxford: Clarendon Press. Edition of the sermons with comprehensive introduction and commentary.

Jurkowski, Maureen 2002. 'The Arrest of William Thorpe in Shrewsbury and the Anti-Lollard Statute of 1406.' *Historical Research* 75, 273–95. Building on evidence from a recently discovered document in the Public Records Office that sheds light on the 'informal' nature of Thorpe's interrogation by Arundel, this article gives further insights into the precarious background to Lancastrian anti-Lollard legislation.

Levy, Ian 2003. *John Wyclif: Scriptural Logic, Real Presence and the Parameters of Orthodoxy*. Milwaukee, Wis.: Marquette University Press. A clear discussion of the evolution of medieval eucharistic theology and the development of Wyclif's thinking in this context.

McNiven, Peter 1987. *Heresy and Politics in the Reign of Henry IV: The Burning of John Badby*. Woodbridge: Boydell. Lucid and authoritative account of the political manoeuvring that accompanied, and in many respects propelled, the Wycliffite controversies; far wider-ranging than the subtitle suggests.

McSheffrey, Shannon 1995. *Gender and Heresy: Women and Men in Lollard Communities 1420–1530*. Philadelphia: University of Pennsylvania Press. Substantial contribution to our understanding of the social history of later Lollardy.

Plumb, Derek. 1995. 'The Social and Economic Status of Later Lollards' and 'A Gathered Church? Lollards and their Society.' In *The World of Rural Dissenters, 1520–1725*, ed. Margaret Spufford (New York: Cambridge University Press), pp. 103–31, 132–63. Detailed articles that pursue the identities of, and connections between, known Lollards and argue that they were thoroughly integrated in their local communities.

Rees Jones, Sarah 2000. ' "A Peler of Holy Church": Margery Kempe and the Bishops.' In *Medieval Women: Texts and Contexts in Late Medieval Britain – Essays for Felicity Riddy*, ed. Jocelyn Wogan-Browne, Rosalynn Voaden, Arlyn Diamond, Ann Hutchinson, Carol Meale and Lesley Johnson (Turnhout: Brepols), pp. 377–91. Usefully provocative essay that goes against the grain of Margery-centred readings by developing the argument that the *Book* was written 'by men, for men and about men'.

Rex, Richard 2002. *The Lollards*. London: Palgrave. Sceptical account that questions the prominence of Wycliffism in recent historiography and literary histories of this period and provides useful summaries of the main events.

Richardson, H. G. 1936. 'Heresy and the Lay Power under Richard II.' *English Historical Review* 51, 1–28. Still essential, clear summary of action taken against heresy in the late fourteenth century.

Simpson, James 2002. *The Oxford English Literary History. Vol. 2: 1350–1547 – Reform and Cultural Revolution*. Oxford: Oxford University Press. Literary history of the whole period that describes the transition from 'Medieval' to 'Renaissance' English literature in terms of the narrowing of discursive possibilities.

Somerset, Fiona 1998. *Clerical Discourse and Lay Audience in Late Medieval England*. Cambridge: Cambridge University Press. Stimulating study of the ideological implications of the use of academic discourse in vernacular controversy during this period; particularly useful for its consideration of Wycliffite and non-Wycliffite examples and for showing how vernacular experimentation grew out of academic textual and argumentative practices.

—— 2003a. 'Introduction.' In *Lollards and their Influence in Late Medieval England*, ed. Fiona Somerset, Jill Havens and Derrick Pitard (Woodbridge: Boydell), pp. 9–16. Introduction to an essential collection of new articles that includes a comprehensive bibliography of primary and secondary sources in this field.

—— 2003b. 'Expanding the Langlandian Canon: Radical Latin and the Stylistics of Reform.' *Yearbook of Langland Studies* 17, 73–92. Usefully directs attention away from binary oppositions between 'Wycliffite' and 'non-Wycliffite' thinking by concentrating on the spectrum of topics shared by *Piers Plowman* and identifiably Wycliffite texts.

—— 2004. 'Professionalizing Translation at the Turn of the Fifteenth Century: Ullerston's *Determinacio*, Arundel's *Constitutiones*.' In *The Vulgar Tongue: Medieval and Postmodern Vernacularity*, ed. Fiona Somerset and Nicholas Watson (University Park: Pennsylvania State University Press), pp. 145–57. Uses Ullerston's *Determinacio* as a means to establish the latitude of clerical attitudes towards translation at the turn of the century, and conducts some important revisionist reading of the *Constitutiones*, concluding that they were 'much less than a fully implemented system of draconian censorship'.

Spencer, Helen L. 1993. *English Preaching in the Late Middle Ages*. Oxford: Clarendon Press. Comprehensive study of the contents and contexts of sermons in this period, including the evidence of manuscript collections and the impact of legislation.

Swanson, Robert 1994. 'Literacy, Heresy, History and Orthodoxy: Perspectives and Permutations for the Later Middle Ages.' In *Heresy and Literacy, 1000–1530*, ed. Peter Biller and Anne Hudson (Cambridge: Cambridge University Press), pp. 279–93. Usefully sceptical article that calls into question possible assumptions about relationships between heresy and literacy and usefully complicates the notion of an absolute boundary between the literate practices associated with orthodoxy and heterodoxy respectively.

Thomson, J. A. F. 1989. 'Orthodox Religion and the Origins of Lollardy.' *History* 74, 39–55. Subtle account that emphasizes 'the narrowness of the margin between orthodoxy and dissent' in late medieval England.

Watson, Nicholas 1995. 'Censorship and Cultural Change in Late-Medieval England: Vernacular Theology, the Oxford Translation Debate, and Arundel's Constitutions of 1409.' *Speculum* 70, 822–64. A ground-breaking intervention in the critical study of this period; some of its conclusions have since been modified (not least by Watson himself), but it is stimulating and wide-ranging, and its implications still require further examination.

—— 1997a. 'Conceptions of the Word: The Mother Tongue and the Incarnation of God.' *New Medieval Literatures* 1, 85–124. Examines the exploration of incarnational theology by a variety of late medieval writers in English.

—— 1997b. 'Visions of Inclusion: Universal Salvation and Vernacular Theology in Pre-Reformation England.' *Journal of Medieval and Early Modern Studies* 27, 145–87. Examines the theme of salvation in late medieval English literature; particularly valuable for its awareness of the diversity of models and attitudes available to writers at this time.

—— 1999a. 'The Middle English Mystics.' In *The Cambridge Guide to Medieval English Literature*, ed. David Wallace (Cambridge: Cambridge University Press), pp. 539–65. A survey of the scholarly evolution of this field and a fresh, sceptical reconsideration of the usefulness of the terms 'mystic' and 'mysticism' in relation to late medieval English religious writing.

—— 1999b. 'The Politics of Middle English Writing.' In *The Idea of the Vernacular. An Anthology of Middle English Literary Theory 1280–1520*, ed. Jocelyn Wogan-Browne, Nicholas Watson, Andrew Taylor and Ruth Evans (Exeter: University of Exeter Press), pp. 331–52. Discussion of the political and cultural conditions in which writing in the vernacular took place, with slight but significant modification of Watson's earlier claims regarding the effect of Arundel's *Constitutions*.

—— 2002. '"Et que est huius ydoli materia? Tuipse": Idols and Images in Walter Hilton.' In *Images, Idolatry and Iconoclasm in Late Medieval England*, ed. Jeremy Dimmick, James Simpson and Nicolette Zeeman (Oxford: Oxford University Press), pp. 95–111. Dense and characteristically lucid study that includes an appendix summarizing Hilton's life and works; valuable for its awareness of the plurality of theological positions in vernacular writing during this period.

4

City and Country, Wealth and Labour

Sarah Rees Jones

Cities are dynamic places. They are full of people, noise and movement. They are often seen as dangerous, immoral and frightening places, but at the same time they are places of opportunity and creativity. These conflicting emotions that the experience of city life evokes in us today are also to be found in the conflicting reactions to the relationship between city and country and the problems of wealth and poverty, labour and leisure in later medieval English culture and literature.

In the travels of Margery Kempe, the provocative bourgeois wife, the English people are seen through the prism of their major cities and towns – of London, Canterbury, Norwich, Bristol and York, as well as Leicester and Lynn. In her *Book* these towns give shape to the nation, marking out its compass points and indicating the central points of both secular and ecclesiastical power, as well as the centres of prosperity and of exchange in both material goods and new ideas. Indeed the *Book of Margery Kempe* can be read as a debate about both the potentials and dangers of urbanization in early fifteenth-century England. Were towns and townspeople a source of prosperity and welcome innovation in the fifteenth century? Were they communities that should be cherished and promoted – as John Lydgate in his *Troy Book* had King Priam build and people New Troy (2.485–800).[1] Or were towns and their traders dangerous parasites that threatened to undermine the moral and spiritual strength of the established order? Like London and the various trades described in the opening passage of William Langland's *Vision of Piers Plowman*, were towns and markets simply potential sources of corruption tempting churchmen into all kinds of profiteering and sin (1–99)?[2]

Later Medieval England: A Rural Idyll?

This debate about the value of towns and trade looks in two directions. It looks backwards to the long tradition of writers describing regional geographies through an idealized eulogy of their cities and of the wealth of their hinterlands. Yet not all writers imagined England as the homeland of the new Troy. The influential encyclopedist Bartholomaeus Anglicus, writing from Paris in the early thirteenth century, and drawing on still earlier authors such as Bede, imagined England as a country without towns, but with an abundant and productive countryside which supplied the towns of Flanders with the essential raw materials from which their industries flourished and traded with the rest of Europe:

> [*De Anglia*] . . . þerinne ben many ryuer[s] and greete. And also þere ben margarites, preciouse stones. Þere ben beste glebe and londe and beren gode and divers fruyte. Þere ben namelyche many shepe with gode wolle. Þere ben many hertes and oþer wylde bestes. Þere ben fewe wolues or noone. Þerefore shepe þer ben ful many and þei may be sekerly left withoute warde in pasture and in feeldes . . .
>
> . . . Inglonde is a stronge londe and sterne and þe plenteuouseste corner of þe world, ful ryche a land that vnneþe it nedeþ helpe of any londe, and eueryche other lond nedeþ helpe of Inglonde. Inglonde is full of myrthe and to game and men ofte tymes able to myrthe and to game, free men of herte and with tonge, but þe honde is more bettir and more free þan þe tonge.
>
> [*De Flandria*] . . . þe men [are] . . . ryche of all manner merchandise and chaffare . . . Bi here crafty werke a grete dele of þe world is ysokerede and yhulpe in wollen cloþes. For of precious wolle that þei haue oute of Inglond, wiþ sotil crafte þei make noble cloþes and senden by see and eke bi londe into many londes. (bk. 15, ch. 13, p. 734, lines 10–16, 26–32; ch. 68, p. 760, lines 7–9, 12–16)[3]

Bartholomaeus thus anticipated, by several centuries, two key elements of the 'central-place theory' of modern economic historians: first, that England's medieval economy, whether urban or rural, developed as part of a larger transnational economic region centred on the great manufacturing and trading cities of the Low Countries, the Rhineland and northern France; second, that town and country were mutually interdependent in their economies, prosperity and general well-being. Rural producers did not simply feed the towns, and derive access to luxuries and manufactured goods in return. Rural production in itself shaped and determined the extent and prosperity of the urban network. Without the countryside towns could not exist, but equally the vitality of towns nourished their whole region – spiritually and intellectually – as well as in the promotion of material wealth. As Bartholomaeus claimed for his own adopted city:

> . . . Parys bereþ the prys. For as sometyme þe citee of Athene, modir of liberal artes and of lettres, norse of philosofres, and welle of alle sciences, [hiȝte Grece and] made [it] solempne in science and þewes among þe Grekes, so Parys in thise tymes [hyteþ and makeþ solempne in science and in þewes] not ooneliche Fraunce, but also al þe othere dele of Europa. (bk. 15, ch. 57, p. 759, lines 15–20)

One important aspect of Bartholomaeus' idyllic vision of England's place in Europe that would not, however, have been shared by many of his native countrymen, and is certainly no longer supported by economic historians, is that England was a predominantly rural country with no towns. England's later medieval urban network was centred on some twenty larger county towns, ports and cathedral cities. The largest provincial cities included York, Bristol, Norwich, Coventry and Lincoln which all had populations in the region of 10–20,000. These larger towns acted as centres of regional government as well as nodal points of both regional and international trade. London, with a population of perhaps as much as 80,000 by 1300, was England's dominant city. Over the next two centuries it emerged as the only metropolis in England, together with Southwark, Westminster and other suburban settlements. By 1300 the urban network already also encompassed a hierarchy of smaller towns and local markets extending across the countryside, much of which had developed in the twelfth and thirteenth centuries. In Essex, for example, the towns of Braintree, Chelmsford, Brentwood, Epping, Baldock, Chipping Barnet and Royston were all developed in the twelfth century. These smaller centres were a product of rural growth and reflected the interest of peasant farmers in marketing surplus produce as well as the engagement of larger-scale estates in commercial activity.

English writers were only too aware of the presence of markets and trade in the medieval countryside – and of the degree to which money circulated in the promotion of wealth. This social reality provided a fertile territory in which writers could, like Bartholomaeus, extol the virtues of prosperity. Equally it enabled them to explore the more negative values attributed to towns, trade and money in a different intellectual tradition, and particularly in religious didactic literature which found an extreme expression in the view that 'God made the clergy, knights and labourers, but the devil made the burghers and usurers'.[4] Indeed, these two perspectives provided the basis for a dynamic medieval tradition of debating the relative merits of the active and contemplative lives through the medium of town versus countryside, or immersion in the world versus retreat from it. Building on these literary traditions the ambiguous nature of the market became a central feature of much later medieval vernacular writing. In the works of Langland, Geoffrey Chaucer, Thomas Usk and Thomas Hoccleve discourses of money and of exchange run throughout, providing a universal and powerful metaphor for social relations on a par with (and often substituted for) the power of love. In the Shipman's Tale, Chaucer explicitly writes about the power of money in negotiating intimate sexual relationships where the reader might expect him to write about conjugal love or duty. Similarly, in *The Regiment of Princes*, Hoccleve plays upon the interchangeability of love and money in his story of John of Canace, the elderly father who tricked his children into caring for him by pretending that he had a chest full of money that they would inherit (4180–361).[5] Hoccleve concludes by claiming that lack of money (rather than love) is the ultimate cause of his own personal isolation, but it was no use hoarding either money or love at home. Usk concurs in his *Testament of Love*: like love, money needs to travel the world in order to work and in order to create real wealth (2.105–21).[6] Both money and love are ultimately social rather than personal assets.

By the end of the fifteenth century, two very different works illustrate the embeddedness of these ways of thinking. The rhymes of the London Lickpenny (also attributed to Lydgate) evoke the colour, sound, vivacity and exciting opportunity of the big city.

In verse after verse money (but only money) makes anything possible for the country visitor to London, from buying a legal judgement, to buying the finest produce and goods, to hiring a barge to escape the city, for 'Of all the lond it [London] bearethe the prise':

> Then I hied me into Estchepe.
> One cried, 'Ribes of befe, and many a pie!'
> Pewtar potts they clatteryd on a heape.
> Ther was harpe, pipe and sawtry.
> 'Ye by Cokke!' 'Nay by Cokke!' some began to cry;
> Some sange of Jenken and Julian, to get themselvs mede.
> Full fayne I wold hadd of that mynstralsie,
> But for lacke of money I cowld not spede.
>
> (89–96)[7]

In the end, as the narrator travels back to the country and his plough; the final verse reminds us of the greater calling of Christ Jesus:

> Then I conveyed me into Kent,
> For of the law would I medle no more;
> By-caus no man to me would take entent,
> I dight me to the plowe, even as I ded before.
> Jhesus save London, that in Bethelem was bore,
> And every trew man of law, God graunt hym souls med;
> And they that be othar, God theyr state restore: –
> For he that lackethe money, with them he shall not spede!
>
> (121–8)

It is difficult to be sure just which we should be more engaged by: the literally upbeat tempo of the city or the modest piety of the final verse. The audience must weigh the two in the balance, and then perhaps draw the obvious conclusion. The poem evokes something of the same internal reflection encouraged by the ambiguous discourse on wealth in the Londoner Thomas More's *Utopia*, published in 1516. In the city-state of Utopia there is no money and no private property, all property is owned in common and distributed according to need, and all citizens spend some time learning agriculture in the country. But is this a practical and realizable idyll in the modern world? Do money and private wealth have a role to play in creating civic order? *Utopia* demands that readers work out their own answer. These two very different late medieval works show how far writers' experience by 1500 had reshaped the old debates about the value of money, and the virtue of town versus country, into a new platform on which modern ideas could be built. Many modern writers who have imagined the relationship between town and country as a dialogue between progress and backwardness, between capitalism and feudalism, between enlightenment and superstition, or conversely between corruption and a state of natural grace, are foreshadowed in later medieval writing.

The Fourteenth-Century Crisis and its Impact

In the period 1350 to 1500 the role of towns in the life of the countryside, and in the production and consumption of wealth and culture, was thrown into relief as never before. In the early fourteenth century climate change, crop failures and famine weakened the population so that the Black Death in 1348–9 and subsequent epidemics of infectious diseases had a dramatic impact on English society. There was a fall in England's population from a maximum of about six million in c.1300 to as little as 2.5 million by the mid-fifteenth century. Such shifts in the population resulted in fundamental changes in the distribution of wealth, and the structure of all kinds of markets, and in the forging of new social relationships and ideas.

The impact was perhaps the most profound in rural communities. Between 1300 and 1500 there were radical changes in the ways in which many rural tenants were able to farm land and control their labour. Servile tenures, by which some peasant cultivators were tied to the manor of their lord and compelled to perform labour services, largely disappeared. Instead much farmland was leased on contractual tenancies in return for a cash rent. The abandonment of the principle of such personal dependence created a new social culture in which there was no longer a legal barrier between wealthy peasant cultivators and men of minor aristocratic or mercantile origin. Status was much more likely to be described in terms of occupation and wealth than of legal tenure, and these new distinctions were reinforced in social and cultural practice – for example, in the rise of occupational associations such as craft guilds. The new languages of status also fuelled the social satire of writers such as Chaucer and Langland whose works are filled with sketches of characters identified by and through their occupations.

In this new climate some peasant cultivators flourished and contributed to the formation of a new 'middling class' of small independent farmers. Families such as the fifteenth-century builders of Frogs Hall at Barrow in Suffolk marked their new status through slightly more conspicuous consumption or by their use of new social titles (such as husbandman and yeoman). They had a little more to spend on culture and leisure – on joining fraternities, getting involved in the running of the parish, owning a few books, and perhaps educating their children – and indeed, such farmers were often the effective leaders of their communities, in the absence of any resident gentry. Those who earned wages by working for others, such as carpenters and the many casual labourers, also experienced a real rise in their modest standard of living.

Yet it is important not to exaggerate the improvement in living standards. For many countrymen the loss of servile tenure also meant the loss of protected tenancies, and they joined the ranks of the rural working population who never rented land at all but remained an underclass surviving on wages or bed and board. These waged workers, of whose greed Langland complains in the ploughing of the half-acre episode in *Piers Plowman* because they only worked until their bellies were full (6.105–330), may have enjoyed a modest 'golden age' after 1350, but it did not last long. Although better paid than previously, such workers often had little security of employment, and the general economic contraction of the mid-fifteenth century made their position even more precarious. If in the shorter term higher wages brought benefits to some, in the longer term wages alone were not enough. The ownership of land and of farming rights remained the best guarantee of sustained prosperity and such ownership was far from equally available to all. Over the longer term, minor gentry and townsmen were often better placed than many peasantry to buy up land in the new post-plague economy. In the manors of west Suffolk it was the minor gentry, and only a very few wealthy peasants, who succeeded in buying up and monopolizing the grazing rights in the common fields. Their success as sheep farmers was at the expense of the poorer tenants in these villages and fuelled the anger that ultimately culminated in the popular uprising known as Kett's Rebellion in 1549.[8]

A second reason for caution in estimating the impact of the fourteenth-century crisis on England's economy was that there were very significant regional variations in the ways in which local economies were affected. Grains and pulses were the staple food crops for the production of the bread, pottage and ale of which the common medieval diet was largely composed. Such agriculture was particularly badly hit after 1350 as the number of mouths that needed feeding dramatically declined. Some corn-producing areas did continue to thrive throughout the period, particularly where there was good access to a large centre of population, and especially to London. Even places whose soils were not particularly well suited to agriculture, such as Stepney to the east of London, specialized in corn if they could sell it to the city.[9] Many other corn-producing communities declined. Some villages were gradually deserted altogether.

The largest concentration of evidence for such failed agricultural communities is clustered in a midland belt stretching from the south-west to the north-east. All of these communities lay just too far from the London grain market to make it worth growing grain for export to the metropolis. Instead, pastoral farming of all kinds of livestock became more important, reflecting the stronger demand for meat, wool and leather goods, their lower labour costs, and the ability to move such products over greater distances in search of a market. Cattle from Warwickshire, for example, could be walked to distant markets in London.

Other communities survived by developing industry. The timber, iron and glass industries flourished in woodland areas, such as the Forests of Arden and Dean, and the Surrey Downs.[10] The brewing of beer, which began to replace ale as the preferred drink in the south, was concentrated in port towns from Southampton to Lynn which could easily import hops from the continent. The flourishing woollen cloth industry of the fifteenth century developed in specific regions such as Suffolk and Essex, or Gloucestershire and Wiltshire, which benefited from access to overseas markets, good sources of capital investment and credit, and ready access to raw materials.[11] Extractive industries were also relatively prosperous. The mining of iron ore, lead, coal, tin and other minerals, in places such as Derbyshire, Durham, Northumberland and Cornwall, all became relatively more important sources of wealth in regions where agriculture was marginal and there was a good non-local demand for their products. Fishing was another industry that prospered in the fifteenth century as fishing grounds were extended out across the Atlantic.[12] Yet so successful were the fishermen of Somerset, Devon and Cornwall that they began to take over the traditional fish markets of south- and east-coast fishermen as far north as Great Yarmouth on the Norfolk coast. As was also the case with the new brewing and cloth industries, one community's relative prosperity was often the cause of another community's decline.

One overarching theme is clear: the growth of the London metropolitan market and its impact on the regions. The regions which weathered the fourteenth-century crisis most successfully lay to the south of a line drawn broadly between the Severn and the Wash, which all enjoyed relatively easy access to London and to the key markets of the Low Countries and the Rhineland. The north–south divide in England's economy was becoming firmly entrenched. One symptom was the decline of the great northern cities of Lincoln and York, which by 1500 had about halved in size and fallen out of the 'top ten' of England's towns, to be replaced by southern cities such as Exeter, Salisbury and Canterbury. Some isolated areas in the north did enjoy some economic buoyancy, such as the cloth towns of West Yorkshire, areas within the Pennine dales, the Humber estuary and Newcastle-upon-Tyne, but this was not enough to compensate for the general economic decline of the north in the fifteenth century.[13]

These shifts in the pattern of rural wealth had important social consequences. Where the new economy did flourish after 1400 it depended on an ability to specialize in niche products for markets both locally and further afield. This led to the development of a more extended urban hierarchy in which a commercial culture was more deeply ingrained than it had been before 1300, and a new wave of urbanization of the countryside as demand for small local markets increased. The new sources of employment were often in manufacturing of various kinds and this also promoted the growth of small and new towns, such as the new cloth towns of Suffolk and the Cotswolds. In the counties near London new market towns flourished, such as Maidstone or Saffron Walden, which supplied the metropolis with basic goods. Others, such as St Albans in Hertfordshire, developed specialist functions as innkeeping towns on the main roads into the capital. The spread of trade and industry in these parts of the countryside also relied upon the injection of capital and credit from the towns. In Essex and Suffolk, for example, cloth-making developed in a number of villages as well as in to the main centre at Colchester itself, but investment in the industry was increasingly concentrated in the hands of an elite of merchant clothiers based in the larger towns. Indeed, by the mid-fifteenth century the credit networks of London merchants extended over much of England, adding a new element to the bond between town and country, and between the metropolis and the regions.[14]

This urbanization of the countryside resulted in smaller towns replacing the larger cities in supplying basic manufactured goods to rural consumers. The growth of artisan occupations in small towns was reflected in the development of a more urban culture, such as the multiplication of guilds and guild halls, schools and hospitals, and in the spread of concern about the kinds of social nuisances associated with more urban places. Meanwhile the cities increasingly specialized in providing more expensive goods and professional services. Exeter, Bristol and London all made the transition successfully:

basic industries, such as tanning, relocated to suburban or even rural locations while financial, commercial and legal services, and the retail industry, engaged an increasingly large proportion of their residents.

Towns thus became the centres of a new consumerism. Prosperous town-dwellers revelled in new choices of clothing, furnishings and foods, lived in more elaborate houses, owned a greater variety of books, and enjoyed a wider range of cultural pursuits from religious fraternities and schools to taverns and gaming. By the later fifteenth century much of this urban culture was to be found even in quite small towns, such as Greenwich and Gravesend in Kent, whose residents were increasingly sophisticated in their tastes compared with their simpler country cousins.[15] Nowhere rivalled London, which was the preferred centre for fashionable shopping among the provincial gentry, and which also provided specialized educational centres to train the new professional elites, such as the Inns of Court or the many schools endowed by trading companies and wealthy merchants. London benefited from its proximity to the royal courts at Westminster and to important Continental markets, but the southern capital's success was at the expense of its northern counterpart. The city of York continued to provide high-class retail and professional services. It developed a distinctive cultural identity in its performance of religious drama and its adherence to particularly introspective and orthodox forms of piety. But ultimately the city went into decline as its merchants lost their premier position in overseas trade and as royal governments became firmly entrenched in the London region. The London base of so many fifteenth-century vernacular writers thus reflects the unrivalled dominance of the city – commercially, financially, politically and culturally – which gave it a particularly cosmopolitan character and which in turn no doubt influenced their view of English society.

Towns therefore attracted migrants from the countryside, from the gentleman entering the legal profession to the migrant labourer in search of casual work. This was another factor that contributed to the depopulation of the countryside in the years around 1400, and deepened the crisis in agriculture as some areas suffered shortages of labour. The issue of how to regulate the supply of labour between town and country became central to much post-plague debate: how the new industries were to be resourced (in terms of both manpower and money); how far these costs should be passed on to the consumer; how the agricultural economy might be protected; and how the new wealth of traders, craftsmen and labourers could be made to contribute to society. These were not new problems. London and other towns had legislated on prices and wages since at least the thirteenth century, while the local courts of rural communities were an equally well-established forum for the regulation of work in the countryside.[16] What was so different after 1349 was the national level of the response. Parliament responded with a range of national legislation reflecting the interests of the ruling elite as they sought to preserve pre-plague conditions and forms of production by curbing wage inflation, controlling the movement of workers between town and country, compelling workers to accept and fulfil contracts from employers, controlling the occupations of craftsmen, protecting landlords and regulating prices, consumption and trade.[17] All of this was to be enforced by justices chosen from gentry and mercantile elites who had the effective power to bypass traditional local communal courts. It was the new imposition of non-local law, coupled with the clumsy attempt to tax the perceived new sources of income through the imposition of three poll taxes in 1377–81, which in 1381 provoked widespread national popular unrest, now known as the Peasants' Revolt.

London was at the epicentre of the revolt in 1381, and Andrew Prescott has recently shown how it became an urgent matter for the urban elite to downplay Londoners' role in the revolt by blaming the uprising on an unruly mob of uncouth commoners from outside the city who took it by force.[18] For literate elites working and living in London these were frightening times, and their response to the rebellion, like much of their response to the social tensions of the time, was designed to preserve their own position and to leave posterity with an indelible impression of civic order imposed on rural incivility: 'And the commons of Southwark rose with [the commons of Kent] and cried to the keeper [of London Bridge] to let them enter [the city] or otherwise they would be undone. And for fear of their lives, the keepers let them enter, greatly against their will.'[19]

While there is broad agreement about the kinds of changes affecting town and country, historians do not agree at all about why or how these changes came about. One school has focused on demographic change as the major engine of social change in the later Middle Ages. They have debated the degree to which the countryside was already overpopulated, and the people undernourished, by 1300 – factors which deepened the impact of plague and other diseases that swept England in the 'age of bacteria' after 1350.[20] Others have switched their attention from mortality to fertility, arguing that increasing age at marriage, as the result of an increased availability of employment for women after the plague, may have reduced the birth rate and so further reduced the population after 1350.[21] This model has received the most attention from literary scholars, yet not all historians are convinced of its general applicability.[22]

The theories of monetarist historians have been less discussed by non-specialists.[23] Yet fluctuations in the circulation of bullion and the increasing use of money of account and credit were clearly fundamental to the development of medieval markets, which were both highly unstable and susceptible to political manipulation.[24] A 'shortage of money', much complained about by contemporaries, was a recurrent problem in the fourteenth century and particularly in the 'Great Slump' of the mid-fifteenth century. Indeed, a decline in the volume of currency in circulation may have had a more damaging impact on local economies than did the plague, inhibiting commercial development and restricting the rise in living standards, particularly since the severest shortages were in the 'everyday' currency of silver pennies.

A third area of debate has revolved around class relationships and the rise of the state. The fundamentally inequitable distribution of resources within both rural and urban societies both heightened the impact of natural disasters on an impoverished tenant population and ultimately restricted the degree to which working people could benefit from the freeing up of resources after the plague. The growing demands of the state, in terms of both an increased burden of royal taxation and an increasingly costly royal administration imposed at a local level, also worked to conserve power in the hands of traditional elites, to channel increasing resources into the processes of government, and to limit the growth of the market.[25]

While historians are proving adept at weaving these and other factors together, it remains the case that there are many different, and very often conflicting, explanations of the chronology, nature and causes of social change in town and country in later medieval England. This is a dynamic field in which much remains to be learnt and in which little real consensus has yet emerged.

Writing, Anxiety and Authority

At one time, literary scholars simply used such social history as the given context in which they could locate the social anxieties of literary works. The relationship between the 'real' world of records and the 'imagined' world of literary texts has since been considerably challenged by the rise of cultural history. Many scholars now recognize that the so-called 'pragmatic' sources on which social history is conventionally based, such as guild records, manorial estate accounts, and even buildings and archaeological finds, are essentially idealized texts that are shaped by the cultural heritage and aspirations of their makers and users. Estate accounts, for example, were designed to record services that the landlord believed were due to the estate, and were in that sense an idealized description of duties owed, rather than a straightforward financial record of the income and expenditure of the estate officials. Similarly, the medieval houses of cities such as London and York can be interpreted as incorporating idealized elements into their design which reflected conservative social aspirations (the hall), the imperatives of the market place (the shop), and new ways of idealizing gender roles in the bourgeois family (the parlour). Contemporary writers were familiar with such architectural 'rhetoric'. In *Troilus and Criseyde*, Chaucer plays upon Criseyde's dilemma as to whether she should acknowledge her feelings for Troilus, by using the intimate, private and public spaces in such a house (the closet, chamber, garden, hall and windows overlooking the street) as metaphors for the negotiations Criseyde must make between her personal desire and her public image (2.1114–239).

Pragmatic sources may thus be read as idealized texts alongside literary works.[26] One consequence of this intertextual approach is a reappraisal of the impact of the fourteenth-century crisis itself. There is a growing recognition that post-plague writing of all kinds drew upon literary and moral conventions established well before 1300, and that these conventions shaped the ways in which contemporaries recorded and interpreted events. An event such as the Black Death fitted well into a biblically informed understanding of social crisis heralding the apocalypse and could best be explained as a punishment for sin and the subversion of natural authority.[27] It has also been argued that the very use of writing contributed to the crisis itself.[28] The movement from oral custom to written record over the thirteenth and fourteenth centuries constituted a revolution in forms of understanding, which in turn contributed to a crisis of trust between the governors and the governed. The revolt in 1381 was in part a rejection of the increased use of records in local administration and against the new forms of truth and authority which the use of such writing implied.

In the use of administrative writing, however, it is necessary to distinguish between crown and local administrations, and between urban and rural contexts. While all administrations were using more written records in the century before 1350, the fourteenth-century crisis had different impacts on the use of writing in town and country. On rural manors, many landlords withdrew from direct farming of their estates and so stopped keeping a record of servile tenant obligations. The new farmers rarely kept written records and still less often preserved them in archives. Ironically, the tenants who made a bonfire out of the manorial accounts of the abbey of Bury St Edmunds in 1381 did so at just the time that the use of such records in recording servile obligations was already in decline.

In other contexts the impulse to keep records increased. Throughout society there was concern that a generation of opinion-formers had been destroyed by the plague and that collective memories of custom were in danger of being lost. This fear was perhaps most acute in self-governing towns where the practice of government was collective, and the memory of established custom rested in the minds of perpetually re-elected governing councils. In his preface to a new collection of London's civic customs in 1419, John Carpenter recorded his fears in a form which echoed that of many of his peers across Europe:

> Due to the fallibility of human memory . . . and as not infrequently all the aged, most experienced, and most discreet rulers of the royal City of London have been carried off at the same instance by pestilence, younger persons who have succeeded them in the government of the City, have on various occasions been often at a loss from the very want of written information.[29]

There was a considerable expansion in the number and range of urban custumals from the mid-fourteenth century onwards. The *Red Books* of Bristol and the *Memorandum Books* of York were started in the 1340s and 1370s, while the great custumals of Norwich, King's Lynn and Coventry date from the 1390s to 1420s. Even in cities with an established tradition of keeping custumals, the compilers of legal registers after the Black Death, such as the compilers of London's *Letter Book H* (1377–99), considerably extended the range of materials copied for posterity.[30]

The ostensible purpose of these collections of town laws was the preservation of the *status quo*, through the creation of a definitive archive of custom. The process of committing such customs to record, however, was also highly inventive and was often overtly political. In London the decade 1374–84 was one of civic turmoil and disputed elections, at the centre of which competing mayors Nicholas Brembre and John Northampton fought to impose their own political agenda on the city in the making of new laws. The final defeat of Northampton's party was celebrated in 1387 by the ceremonial burning of his new custumal, the Jubilee Book. In Norwich, also, in 1414 the traditional office-holders of the town complained that new upstarts, even people 'of the smallest reputation', were seeking to wrest control of the city from them by the use of novel and therefore suspicious charters, where traditionally their authority had been supported by custom alone.[31]

The imperative to keep better archives in towns was not a response just to plague, but also to the need to defend the autonomy of boroughs from the encroachment of new royal laws. Fundamental to the authority of self-governing boroughs was the regulation of trade and in particular the sale of foodstuffs. From the mid-fourteenth century new parliamentary laws concerning trade, enforced by new crown-appointed commissions, threatened this autonomy. Collections of borough customs concerning these trades thus occupied a central place in the new urban custumals. In the new *Memorandum Books* of the city of York many folios are dedicated to the copying of the parliamentary statutes that impinged on the corporation's established jurisdiction, and of related records that proved that such legislation was properly administered within the city.[32]

In fact many of the customs copied into such registers were already somewhat archaic. The thirteenth-century laws against forestalling and regrating, and the assize of ale, were no longer regarded as adequate by the fifteenth century, when local courts resorted to ever more innovative procedures in their attempts to regulate an increasingly wide range of trades, and used new agencies, such as guilds, for their enforcement. This did not prevent town clerks including ancient laws in their new collections, just as it did not prevent John Carpenter claiming that the origins of London's self-government did not lie with the kings of England but stretched back into antiquity well before the Norman Conquest.[33] These conservative legal collections were as much a means of asserting burgal independence by inheritance and history as an assertion of their current legal competence. When Langland described the sin of avarice in very similar terms to those of an urban custumal – as the draper who overstretches his cloth, his wife the Brewster who adulterates her ale and profiteers by selling it by the cupful, and Rose the Regrator who makes an unfair profit selling door to door (5.186–225) – he was citing laws that were familiar symbols of urban self-government but that had already been overtaken by newer forms of retail practice and regulation.

Where Langland was preoccupied by the rhetoric of archaic civic custom, by contrast Chaucer's appreciation of business in the Shipman's Tale was much more in keeping with contemporary practice. Chaucer recognized that the place of trade was as much in the home as in the shop or the market-place, that buying and selling went on all day and night regulated only by the personal timepiece and not by the quasi-ecclesiastical hours of the official borough market place, and that the relative moral standing of the merchant and the monk had become confused. He played upon these ambiguities in his tales, forcing readers to reassess their own moral priorities. Chaucer's writing therefore reflects not so much that of the rigid certainties of compilations of London law, but the records of the London mayor's court where witnesses were cross-examined to reveal the full messiness of real lives lived out of concord with written custom. Many such cases are thoroughly 'Chaucerian' in their ambiguous elision of references to money, sex and law. In 1395, for example, Thomas ate Hay, a brewer, who suspected a chaplain of having a relationship with his wife, accused the chaplain of breaking into his home and damaging and stealing various household goods. The chaplain, William Rothewell, claimed that he had every right to enter since the house was a common inn where he lodged and he denied the theft. The brewer's version of the tale was supported by his neighbours and the chaplain was thrown into prison until he could pay punitive damages for the alleged theft.[34] This was one of many cases where an association was suggested between infidelity and the theft of property.

This case shows one way in which customary law could be inventively manipulated by both parties to address a personal problem which lay beyond the rigid parameters of the law itself. The invention worked because of the elision between the brewer's work and his family life and the shared location of both within his household. Most work was indeed based in family enterprises attached to homes where it was regulated by the head of the household whose workers included a range of dependants from waged labourers to live-in servants and the householder's own children and spouse. The kind of work these dependants did for the householder included domestic tasks as well as 'productive' labour.

In the years following the plague such family enterprises were especially fragile. In the Suffolk village of Walsham le Willows in Suffolk in 1349 the Rampolye family lost at least seven members across three generations – and was thus unable to maintain its customary tenancies of farmland.[35] Such families suffered the double trauma of bereavement and the collapse of their traditional livelihood, as natural supplies of labour were disrupted and waged labour became more expensive. In an urban context the difficult conjunction of lack of family, lack of money and personal infirmity is eloquently expressed in the response made by the London Fusters (who made saddle trees) to complaints about their high prices in 1350. They complained that 'owing to a life of labour they were now feeble in strength, could find no apprentices or serving men to help them, and at a time when they needed more comfort in food and clothing than before, were forced to raise their prices in order to afford the necessities of life, such as a gallon of beer which had doubled in price'.[36] When debate raged about the proper distribution of wealth and the appropriate reward of labour, this discourse was inevitably linked to the values and comforts of domestic life. The home was where both love and money, but also love and work, were most easily elided, confused and contested.

The two figures on whom these anxieties most naturally fell were the wife and the apprentice. Both represented relationships where love and work were most difficult to separate. Working women had long been a fact of life, but their engagement in non-domestic occupations could be easily demonized by literate elites troubled by the dramatic dislocation of post-plague markets which was so easily explained by reference to sin. So the merchant's wife, Elizabeth Moring, who entered into trade independently of her husband, was portrayed as a vain woman tempted into prostitution in order to fund purely frivolous desires[37] – just as women trading illegally on the city staithes could be maligned by association with prostitutes in the court records, even though their immediate business was the sale of fish and other foodstuffs.[38] The regulation of the labour of women was thus a particular source of contention and attempts to impose the new labour laws could be interpreted as a threat to traditional family values. In 1360 Thomas Crake by 'force of arms' withdrew his wife Denise from the service of Sir Philip Nevyle for whom she had been compelled to work under the new Statute of Labourers.[39] The enforcement of the statute was clearly understood as compromising the husband's natural authority over his wife. Some of the greatest anxieties expressed in both the literature and the records of the period thus concerned the challenges to 'masterliness' at work and at home. Masters not only headed families and ran businesses, but were also the backbone of government, providing the minor officials upon which all systems of law and order depended. Such men bore the full brunt of the emotional, economic and political effects of the fourteenth-century crisis. The master was a uniquely anxious figure after the plague: bereaved and uncertain of his authority both inside and outside the home.

In the period after the plague new ways thus had to be found to nurture and retain a junior workforce. In both town and country employers preferred live-in service, where workers could be rewarded in bed and board, or in tied housing, rather than as waged labour which was both more expensive and tainted with subversion and disorder. Poignantly, this desire to reinforce the household grew at the very time that biological familial ties became more fragile due to the impact of epidemic disease. New forms of discourse were needed to reproduce traditional forms of authority in new ways in a situation where personal insecurity and personal loss, both emotional and material, were so closely intertwined. This is particularly apparent in the emergence of rules for the guidance of apprentices who lived with their masters and mistresses as members of their family but were also a critical element in the workforce. As a potential master householder himself, the apprentice was also a particularly vulnerable character who personified the regeneration of social power structures as well as family enterprises. Apprenticeship was thus much more closely defined and regulated as a stage of life and a category of service after 1350. Indentures spelt out in detail the expected moral, social and professional conduct of the apprentice, clearly separating productive work from all domestic activities including sexual activity.[40] The frisky apprentice in Chaucer's Cook's Tale, who transgresses these boundaries, is punished not just by failing his indentures but by losing all moral standing in the town as he descends into the life of a pimp.

Of course many apprentices and masters broke such hopelessly idealistic rules. Poorer craftsmen, in particular, found it hard to attract apprentices and to afford the rigid separation between domestic and productive employment that the rules imagined. Apprenticeship worked best as a privileged educational code for wealthier craftsmen in the elite mercantile trades that dominated civic positions of power. It was a way of setting such men apart from lesser craftsmen, and helped acculturate prosperous young migrants from the countryside into elite circles in the town. The closer circumscription and definition of masterliness which indentures of apprenticeship implied thus operated in towns, like the ownership of land in the country, to restrict the social groups that could aspire to the full benefits of occupying a position of mastership in society. In this context moral impropriety in Chaucer's failed apprentice once again becomes a method of contrasting the fecund abundance, and sheer fun, of life in the city with the dry constraints and formal social hierarchies of written civic law.

Conclusion

For better or worse, the city is often seen as a place ruled by money, with its heart in the market-place. English authors frequently lamented the way in which the countryside had been penetrated by the mercantile values of the city in a 'world turned upside-down'. Yet at the same time vernacular authors benefited from the new market for their services that the growing consumerism of an educated urban audience permitted, just as they grew intellectually and artistically from exploiting the paradoxes of city life. They also worked in a world where there was not always a clear distinction between 'literary' and 'pragmatic' texts, either in their production or in their imagination. 'Pragmatic' writing (from rent accounts to registers of law), far from being a simple record of what happened, provided a fertile environment for the construction of ideals and values. Such writing had its own literary ancestry and its composers struggled to find new languages appropriate to the politics of wealth and labour in their own time.

See also: 2 English Society in the Later Middle Ages, 5 Women's Voices and Roles, 6 Manuscripts and Readers, 7 From Manuscript to Modern Text, 16 War and Chivalry, 21 Writing Nation, 29 York Mystery Plays, 30 The *Book of Margery Kempe*, 32 *Piers Plowman*, 33 The *Canterbury Tales*, 35 Thomas Hoccleve.

Notes

1 John Lydgate, *Troy Book: Selections*, ed. Robert R. Edwards (Kalamazoo, Mich.: Medieval Institute Publications for TEAMS, 1998).

2 William Langland, *The Vision of Piers Plowman*, ed. A. V. C. Schmidt (London: Dent, 1978).

3 Bartholomaeus Anglicus, *De Proprietatibus Rerum, On the Properties of Things*, trans. John Trevisa [c. 1398], 2 vols, general editor M. C. Seymour (Book 15 ed. D. C. Greetham) (Oxford: Clarendon Press, 1975).

4 G. R. Owst, *Literature and Pulpit in Medieval England*, 2nd edn (Oxford: Basil Blackwell, 1961), pp. 553–4.

5 Thomas Hoccleve, *Regiment of Princes*, ed. C. R. Blyth (Kalamazoo, Mich.: Medieval Institute Publications for TEAMS, 1999).

6 Thomas Usk, *Testament of Love*, ed. R. A. Shoaf (Kalamazoo, Mich.: Medieval Institute Publications for TEAMS, 1998).

7 'The London Lickpenny', in *Medieval English Political Writings*, ed. James M. Dean (Kalamazoo, Mich.: Medieval Institute Publications for TEAMS, 1996).

8 Mark Bailey, 'Sand into Gold: the Evolution of the Fold-course System in West Suffolk, 1200–1600', *Agricultural History Review* 38 (1990), 40–57.

9 Patricia Croot, 'Settlement, Tenure and Land Use in Medieval Stepney: Evidence of a Field Survey c.1400', *London Journal* 22 (1997), 1–15.

10 Jean Birrell, 'Peasant Craftsmen in the Medieval Forest', *Agricultural History Review* 17 (1969), 91–107.

11 J. N. Hare, 'Growth and Recession in the Fifteenth-Century Economy: the Wiltshire Textile Industry and the Countryside', *Economic History Review* 2nd ser. 52 (1999), 1–26.

12 Maryanne Kowaleski, 'The Expansion of the South-Western Fisheries in Late Medieval England', *Economic History Review* 2nd ser. 53 (2000), 429–54.

13 A. J. Pollard, *North-Eastern England during the Wars of the Roses: Lay Society, War and Politics 1450–1500* (Oxford: Clarendon Press, 1990), pp. 30–80.

14 Derek Keene, 'Changes in London's Economic Hinterland as Indicated by Debt Cases in the Court of Common Pleas', in *Trade, Urban Hinterlands and Market Integration c.1300–1600*, ed. J. A. Galloway (London: Centre for Metropolitan History, 2000), pp. 59–82.

15 Catherine Richardson, 'Household Objects and Domestic Ties', in *The Christian Household in Medieval Europe c. 850–c. 1550*, ed. Cordelia Beattie, Anna Maslakovic and Sarah Rees Jones (Turnhout: Brepols, 2003), pp. 433–48.

16 Anthony Musson, 'New Labour Laws, New Remedies? Legal Reaction to the Black Death "Crisis"', in *Fourteenth Century England I*, ed. N. Saul (Woodbridge: Boydell Press, 2000), pp. 73–88.

17 Anthony Musson and W. Mark Ormrod, *The Evolution of English Justice: Law, Politics and Society in the Fourteenth Century* (Basingstoke: Macmillan, 1999), pp. 93–6; Christopher Given-Wilson, 'The Problem of Labour in the Context of English Government, c.1350–1450', in Bothwell and Goldberg 2000: 85–100.

18 Andrew Prescott, 'Theatre of Rebellion: Representations of the Peasants' Revolt in London's Civic Culture, 1381–1981', paper presented to the Harlaxton Medieval Symposium, *London and the Kingdom: A Conference in Honour of Caroline Barron*, July 2004, proceedings forthcoming.

19 *Anonimalle Chronicle*, cited in R. B. Dobson (ed.), *The Peasants' Revolt of 1381* (London: Macmillan, 1970), p. 156 and note.

20 Michael Moissey Postan, 'Some Economic Evidence of Declining Population in the Later Middle Ages', *Economic History Review* 2nd ser. 2.3 (1950), 221–46; Bruce M. S. Campbell, 'Agricultural Progress in Medieval England: Some Evidence from Eastern Norfolk', *Economic History Review* 2nd ser. 36 (1983), 26–46; John Hatcher, 'Mortality in the Fifteenth Century: Some New Evidence', *Economic History Review* 2nd ser. 39 (1986), 19–38.

21 Richard M. Smith, 'Geographical Diversity in the Resort to Marriage in Late Medieval Europe: Work, Reputation, and Unmarried Females in the Household Formation Systems of Northern and Southern Europe', in *'Woman is a Worthy Wight': Women in English Society, c.1200–1500*, ed. P. J. P. Goldberg (Stroud: Sutton, 1992), pp. 16–59.

22 Judith M. Bennett, 'Medieval Women, Modern Women: Across the Great Divide', in *Culture and History 1350–1600: Essays on English Communities, Identities and Writing*, ed. David Aers (Detroit, Mich.: Wayne State University Press, 1992), pp. 47–76; John Hatcher, 'Understanding the Population History of England 1450–1750', *Past and Present* 180 (2003), 83–130.

23 But see D. Vance Smith, *Arts of Possession: The Middle English Household Imaginary* (Minneapolis and London: University of Minnesota Press, 2003), pp. 108–53; Paul Strohm, *England's Empty Throne: Usurpation and the Language of Legitimation*, 1399–1422 (New Haven: Yale University Press, 1998).

24 N. I. Mayhew, 'Numismatic Evidence and Falling Prices in the Fourteenth Century', *Economic History Review* 2nd ser. 27 (1974), 1–15; J. H. A. Munro, *Wool, Cloth and Gold: The Struggle for Bullion in Anglo-Burgundian Trade, 1340–1478* (Brussels and Toronto: University of Toronto Press, 1978); John Day, *The Medieval Market Economy* (Oxford: Blackwell, 1987).

25 W. Mark Ormrod, 'The Crown and the English Economy', in *Before the Black Death*, ed. Bruce M. S. Campbell (Manchester: Manchester University Press, 1991), pp. 149–83.

26 Felicity Riddy, 'Mother Knows Best: Reading Social Change in a Courtesy Text', *Speculum* 71 (1996), 66–86.

27 Rosemary Horrox (trans. and ed.), *The Black Death* (Manchester: Manchester University Press, 1994), pp. 93–110.

28 Steven Justice, *Writing and Rebellion: England in 1381* (Berkeley, Los Angeles, and London: University of California Press, 1994); Richard H. Britnell, 'Pragmatic Literacy in Latin Christendom', in *Pragmatic Literacy, East and West, 1200–1330*, ed. R. H. Britnell (Woodbridge: Boydell and Brewer, 1997), pp. 3–24; Richard Firth Green, *A Crisis of Truth: Literature and Law in Ricardian England* (Philadelphia: University of Pennsylvania Press, 1999).

29 *Liber Albus: The White Book of the City of London*, ed. H. Riley (London, 1861), p. 2.

30 *Calendar to Letter-books Preserved among the Archives of the Corporation of the City of London at the Guildhall: Letter-Book H*, ed. R. R. Sharpe (London: City of London Corporation, 1907).

31 *Records of the City of Norwich*, ed. W. Hudson and J. C. Tingey, 2 vols (Norwich, 1906), I, 80–2, 88–9.

32 York City Archives A\Y, B\Y.

33 *Liber Albus*, ed. Riley, pp. 11–12, 29, 302–4, 311–13.

34 *Calendar of Select Pleas and Memoranda of the City of London*, ed. A. H. Thomas, Vol. 4: *1381–1412* (Cambridge: Cambridge University Press, 1932), pp. 218–19.

35 Horrox (ed.), *The Black Death*, pp. 256–62.

36 *London Plea and Memoranda Rolls*, ed. Thomas, Vol. 2: *1323–64* (1926), p. 239.

37 *Memorials of London and London Life*, ed. H. Riley (London: Longmans, 1868), pp. 484–6. Cf. the Shipman's Tale.

38 *London Plea and Memoranda Rolls*, ed. Thomas, Vol. 5: *1413–37* (1943), pp. 138–9, 151.

39 P. J. P. Goldberg (trans. and ed.), *Women in England, c.1275–1525: Documentary Sources* (Manchester and New York: Manchester University Press, 1995), p. 176.

40 *York Memorandum Book B/Y*, Vol. 3, ed. Joyce W. Percy, pp. 4–5.

References and Further Reading

Bailey, Mark 2002. *The English Manor c.1200–c.1500*. Manchester: Manchester University Press. Selection of manorial records in translation together with an introductory commentary.

Barron, Caroline 2004. *London in the Later Middle Ages: Government and People 1200–1500*. Oxford: Oxford University Press. Comprehensive account of the institutions of London government.

Bennett, Judith M. 1996. *Ale, Beer and Brewsters in England: Women's Work in a Changing World 1300–1600*. New York and Oxford: Oxford University Press. Draws on literary sources and historical records to analyse the changing perception of women's work in town and country.

Bothwell, James and Goldberg P. J. P. (eds) 2000. *The Problem of Labour in Fourteenth-Century England*. Woodbridge: Boydell and Brewer. Interdisciplinary essays on the perception and regulation of labour in town and country.

Britnell, Richard H. 1986. *Growth and Decline in Colchester, 1300–1525*. Cambridge: Cambridge University Press. Exemplary study of an urban economy and society based on one of England's best-preserved urban archives.

—— 1993. *The Commercialisation of English Society 1000–1500*. Cambridge: Cambridge University Press. 2nd edn 1996. A reassessment of the chronology and nature of commercial development in medieval England.

—— and Hatcher, John (eds) 1996. *Progress and Problems in Medieval England*. Cambridge: Cambridge University Press. Essays focusing on the nature of, and diverse reasons for, change in the medieval economy.

Dyer, Christopher C. 2002. *Making a Living in the Middle Ages: The People of Britain 850–1520*. New Haven and London: Yale University Press. A study of material conditions of daily life drawing on historical records and archaeology.

Goldberg P. J. P. 1992. *Women, Work, and Life Cycle in a Medieval Economy: Women in York and Yorkshire c. 1300–1520*. Oxford: Clarendon Press. Analysis of the changing patterns of women's work and marriage after the Black Death.

Grenville, Jane 1997. *Medieval Housing*. Leicester: Leicester University Press. The archaeology of housing in town and country.

Kowaleski, Maryanne 1995. *Local Markets and Regional Trade in Medieval Exeter*. Cambridge: Cambridge University Press. A prosopographical study of the integrated economies of town and country.

McIntosh, Marjorie 1998. *Controlling Misbehavior in England, 1370–1600*. Cambridge and New York: Cambridge University Press. Study of neighbourhood courts in rural and small urban communities.

Miller, Edward (ed.) 1991. *The Agrarian History of England and Wales. Vol. 3: 1348–1500*. Cambridge: Cambridge University Press, 1991. Major reference work containing essays organized thematically and by region.

Palliser, David M. (ed.) 2000. *The Cambridge Urban History of Britain. Vol. 1: 600–1540*. Cambridge: Cambridge University Press. Major reference work, organized chronologically and thematically by region.

Poos, Lawrence R. 1991. *A Rural Society after the Black Death: Essex, 1350–1525*. Cambridge and New York: Cambridge University Press. Combines landscape study with demographic, economic and cultural history.

Razi, Zvi and Smith, Richard (eds) 1996. *Medieval Society and the Manor Court*. Oxford and New York: Clarendon Press. Major reference work on England's surviving manorial records.

Roberts, Brian K. and Wrathmell, Stuart 2000. *An Atlas of Rural Settlement in England*. London: English Heritage. A survey of the regional character of rural settlement derived from landscape surveys and maps, combining geography and archaeology.

Schofield, Phillipp R. 2002. *Peasant and Community in Medieval England 1200–1500*. London: Palgrave Macmillan. A general introduction to rural life including some focus on political and cultural history.

Smith, Richard M. (ed.) 1984. *Land, Kinship and Life-cycle*. Cambridge: Cambridge University Press, 1984. Pioneering collection of essays on demographic history.

Williamson, Tom 2003. *Shaping Medieval Landscapes: Settlement, Society, Environment*. Macclesfield: Windgatherer Press. Reinterpretation of the archaeology and historical significance of different settlement landscapes.

5
Women's Voices and Roles

Carol M. Meale

In some quarters, during the medieval period, the senses were thought to open dangerous pathways to women, and hence to all of mankind.

> Eue bi heold. on þe forbodene Appel. & seiȝ him feir. and tok a delyt in þe biholdynge. And tok hire lust þerto & eet þerof: & ȝaf hire lord. Lo hou holy writ spekeþ. And hou inwardliche hit telleþ: how synne bi gon . . . Eue heold in paradys. long tale with þe Neddre. Tolde hym al þe lesson þat God heede I. tauȝt hire. And Adam of þe Appel. And so þe fend þoruȝ hire word. vnderstod anon riht. hire vnstablenesse: & fond wey touward hire. of hire forlorenesse.[1]

> (Eve looked at the forbidden apple and to her eyes it appeared delectable and she took delight in beholding it. And she took her pleasure there, and ate of it, and gave it to her lord and husband. See how Holy Writ speaks and how, through innermost meaning, it tells how sin began . . . Eve, in paradise, held a long conversation with the adder. She told him all the lesson about the apple which God had taught her and Adam. And so through her words, the fiend understood immediately her lack of stability and found a way to approach her, to her destruction.)

These quotations are taken from the late fourteenth-century copy of the text most properly known as the *Ancrene Wisse* in Oxford, Bodleian Library MS Eng. poet. A. 1. A work which circulated widely from the time of its composition in the early thirteenth century through to the sixteenth, it survives in seventeen manuscripts in English, French and Latin; although intended for women, its appeal was widespread between the sexes, and between lay and enclosed audiences.[2] The clerical cynosure which the text embodies was widespread; sermons, popular poetry and the visual arts abounded in similar misogynist sentiment, acting as a constant reminder to women that, like Eve's, their nature was such as to act as a gateway to evil and damnation, unless vigilance was unceasing. The question which has to be confronted when investigating women's history is therefore the complex one of how women contended with this ethos within their own lives: did they internalize this gendered construct, promulgated by a masculine elite; or did they negotiate with it, thus enabling mental and physical space through which to express themselves, their needs and their desires?

To look at the social, cultural and economic realities for women at this time suggests that negotiation was a primary strategy. Women owned and shared books; they composed texts, although their authority to do so was hedged around by prejudice; they communicated by letter; they commissioned works of art, from manuscripts to architecture; and they participated in administration and commerce. Even when they entered an enclosed life, whether as professed religious or anchorites, recent research demonstrates that a proportion of women, at least, exerted choice. This much must now be accepted as a given. At the same time, however, their legal position in regard to men remained one of subordination, while views of their biological (and, closely connected, their psychological) functioning also confined them to a position of inferiority. From birth to marriage, so received wisdom goes, they were effectively the property first of their fathers (or legal guardians) and then of their husbands, and it was only in widowhood they they could find a degree of autonomy. Again, though, ongoing research offers evidence that a more subtly nuanced argument is called for – one which allows for fluctuation within these prescribed stages of a woman's life-cycle, and one which is alert to differences of class and regional practice. Arguably, it is the tension generated by the oppositions within female experience which continues to dominate current academic assessments of their independence and achievements, and shapes the interpretative models and discourses which are themselves informed by specific historical and ideological climates. For these reasons, the study of the story of women must be incremental, layer upon layer of rediscovered fact and individual interpretation forming a complex, stratified landscape in which the observation of minutiae is all-important.

Women, Education and Writing

The terms 'women' and 'writing' still sit uneasily together, not least because the physical act of writing was not necessarily synonymous in the Middle Ages with composition. Of only two named women to whom authorship may be attributed, Julian of Norwich and Margery Kempe, we know that the latter – apparently completely illiterate – employed two amenuenses to copy her *Book*; and the verdict remains open as to whether Julian, during her time as an anchoress, received sufficient literacy training to have enabled her to write, as well as compose, her *Revelation of Love*. The issue is one which extends beyond the boundaries of 'literary' composition to encompass the ability to write of women from the gentry and mercantile classes whose voices are heard in the surviving collections of family letters – those of the Pastons, the Stonors, the Plumptons, the Armburghs and the Celys,[3] and also those of the numerous aristocratic and royal women who, for reasons similar to those of their male counterparts, had recourse to letter-writing for business and organizational, as well as personal, purposes (Crawford 2002).

While we know that many of these women were sufficiently skilled to add their own signatures to documents sent in their name, it is difficult to know whether they employed secretaries because of the freedom to do so conferred by their financial and social freedom – as was the case with many men – or through necessity. Many scholars have achieved a consensus on this point, following Norman Davis's magisterial assessment of Agnes and Margaret Paston's use of dictation,[4] but this seems too sweeping a judgement, given that: Margaret Plumpton, while still a child in her future father-in-law's household, could speak French and was learning her psalter; Elizabeth Stonor could both read and write (if somewhat shakily); and the one letter from Margaret Cely to her husband, George, is considered by the collection's editor to be holograph. It would seem a prerequisite to undertake a far more thorough investigation into the educational opportunities open to girls than has hitherto been carried out before generalizing from particular examples.

The promise which this field of research holds is indicated by David N. Bell's questioning of the level of literary attainment in nunneries in late medieval England, in which institutions, it is still widely believed, the majority of educated girls were trained. In an incisive analysis he draws distinctions between levels of literacy – in Latin, French and English – from 1066 onwards and concludes that among monks, not simply nuns, levels of acquaintance with anything but English declined steadily, as universities grew and took the power of education, and hence the highest form of literacy, the study of Latin, away from enclosed institutions. And universities, of course, were not open to women. He then points to a startling contrast in the sheer numbers of books produced in the fifteenth and early sixteenth centuries acquired by male and female institutions: fifty per cent of the books recorded from nunneries date from this period, whereas 'only around 13%' do so from monasteries (Bell 1995: 76). He further points out the considerably lower number of nunneries than monasteries, and their comparative poverty. It is important to see how his study is complemented by others which point to the prevailing conditions in specific regions and institutions.[5]

Nunneries, though, did not offer the only means by which girls and young women could acquire education and skills which may well have included literacy. Elementary schooling within individual households is one possibility, perhaps initially conducted under the auspices of the woman of the house and, in some cases, if the family were sufficiently wealthy, through the offices of a resident chaplain. It should be remembered, for example, that while John Paston II is renowned for his collection of books (of which he made an inventory) his sister Anne owned a copy of John Lydgate's *Siege of Thebes* which in July 1472 was on loan to the Earl of Arran, and Margaret herself left Anne her 'premer' and her daughter-in-law, Margery, her 'massebook' (I, 516–18, 575, 386–7).[6] Anne, like other young women of her class, had been placed in another gentry household, in her case that of Sir William and Dame Elizabeth Calthorpe of Burnham Thorpe in Norfolk, during 1469–70 (I, 42, 339, 348). Although this particular placement seems to have ended with some disagreement between the two families, it is revealing how efforts were made to 'finish' the training of young women in households of similar or higher status. It seems not unlikely that cultural attainments, in addition to those of household governance and the ever-important political ties, were promoted by such arrangements.

Another avenue for attainment, for girls of the urban middle classes, was that of apprenticeship, as Caroline Barron has stressed; and she also, perhaps most significantly, established the existence of some few schoolmistresses, the informality of their employment – lying outside the interests of ecclesiastical, civic and mercantile authorities – meaning that 'they have left only brief traces in the records' (Barron 1996: 147–8). It may be, as Barron notes, that London was atypical in this as in many other regards by comparison with the rest of the country, but her note referring to one Maria Mareflete, registered as 'magistra scolarum' in the Corpus Christi guild roll of Boston, serves as a reminder that it is by steadily working through local archives that we will accumulate evidence.

In terms of magnitude, it is in letter collections that the voices of medieval women are best represented. Whether dictated or not, it is here that we can understand that women kept their eyes and ears open to the local and national politics which impinged upon them and their families. Margaret Paston's contribution in particular, spanning the years 1441–78, provides an unparalleled source of information as to how the two interacted. Caught up in the battle between local East Anglian lords who were also major factional players nationally and internationally, Margaret's reportings of comings and goings, her fears for the maintenance of her family's dignity and lands, put flesh upon the bare bones of lists of dates, events and names (I, 215–382). In terms of how these experiences were described and reflected upon, the Paston women in general demonstrate what Roger Dalrymple called 'a marked fluidity in . . . stylistic approaches and practices' (Daybell 2001: 16), encompassing formal epistolary features and the natural rhythms of speech – the latter often incorporating aphorisms and echoes of popular lyricism. In contrast, the women of the Stonor family demonstrate less stylistic range, but for Alison Truelove this serves to confirm that women had 'appropriated' the masculine tradition of the ars dictaminis, 'the practice of of literary composition through dictation, letter-writing . . . as a verbal rather than manual skill' (Daybell 2001: 55).

It is, though, in a letter surviving within the Armburgh Papers, that perhaps the most striking example of a medieval woman's voice may still be heard. Within this collection, consisting essentially of documents relating to a long-drawn-out dispute over land inheritance stretching from c.1420–50, Joan Armburgh writes to John Horell of Essex in 1429/30 about what she sees as his act of treachery in relation to her and her maternal family, in whose care he had been brought up, in aiding the despoiling of lands in Radwinter by her legal opponents (13, 120–3).[7] In a lengthy, bitter, yet tightly controlled missive, she pours scorn upon him using all the verbal means at her disposal. Calling him 'an vnkynd bird that foulyth his owne nest', 'the develes child, fadre of falshode', she thanks God that she is 'strong y nogh to by tymbre for a peyre galwys to hange the vpon'. She laments the destruction of the woodland which she felt to be rightfully hers and, in particular, her garden, her 'peretrees', 'appiltrees', and all those 'that berith frut'. She goes on to visualize him sitting in a tavern with his drinking-partners, talking as 'a fals prophete', foretelling the day when a hare should sit upon the empty hearth of the ruined house. While this last metaphor for destruction has literary antecedents, as Christine Carpenter points out, it is essentially an ancient, popular and oral usage. Not so is her more erudite deployment of the image of the eagle, drawn from the medieval bestiary tradition. Describing Horell as the eaglet which against nature ('vnkynd') 'wol smyte the damme with the bylle', she invokes the allegorical tradition whereby the eagle represents Christ who, when confronted with recalcitrant offspring (mankind) 'drowe hem in to the pytte of helle'. Finally, she states her intention to go to law, to 'gete me a juge to syttyn vndyr commyssion'. Fuelled by emotional wrath as the letter is, it is considered in its balancing of various modes of discourse and through it Joan demonstrates her personality to be that of a woman of such determination as to give even the redoutable Margaret Paston a run for her money. Although we do not know whether Joan herself wrote the letter – the collection survives only in copies made, presumably, for the family's own record – there can be no doubt that the voice belongs to her.

The factor which unites all this female correspondence with the authored texts by Julian of Norwich and Margery Kempe, with which I began this section, is the mixture of the colloquial and the technical – legal and religious – which characterizes the language used. The 'homeliness' of the imagery of Margery's *Book* is often commented upon, but even Julian was not above likening the bleeding head of Christ, which she sees in her vision, to everyday experiences. In their plenitude, she likens the droplets of blood 'to the dropys of water that fallyn of the evys after a greate showre of reyne', and in their disposition on his forehead, to 'the scale of heryng'.[8] It is worth remarking at this point that while distinctions between Julian and Margery with reference to their ways of life are frequently made – the middle-class wife and failed business woman, who apparently never withdrew from the world, against the enclosed recluse – Julian's physical circumstances were not so withdrawn from worldly concerns as is assumed. She conversed, of course, with the many visitors, including Margery, who came to her for spiritual guidance, but also the position of her cell, attached to St Julian's church, was anything but peaceful. Although to the east it was bordered by open fields and woodland, to the west it was very different. The cell was reached by an alleyway from King Street which, in medieval Norwich, was one of the busiest commercial thoroughfares of the city. From here, narrow alleys led down to staithes on the river Wensum, at which ships docked and goods were loaded and unloaded, accompanied by all the noise and bustle which such activities entailed. King Street itself was built up with dwellings, and excavation and renovation are proving how notable some of them were. Enclosed Julian may have been, but cut off from the sounds and smells of the world she was not.

Julian is, however, an exception to all these writing women so far discussed in that we have little idea of her personal history – of whether or not, for example, she was a mother. Yet it is still possible to recreate a historical context for her. With regard to other female writers of texts in other literary genres, though, we enter an unknown territory. If the strong case for the authorship of a number of the lyrics in the Findern collection, Cambridge University Library MS Ff.1.6, is accepted,[9] it is possible to hazard a guess at the kind of gentry environment in the region of Derbyshire in which they lived. No such possibility exists in relation to those who wrote in other literary genres, the most important of which are the sub-Chaucerian *The Floure and the Leafe* (1460–80) and *The Assembly of Ladies* (c.1470–80).[10] The acceptance of both of these poems into the female canon has long been disputed. The former narrative has been most readily adopted into this canon largely, it would seem, because it is a more accomplished poem. But the *Assembly* is in many ways a more intriguing work, partly because of the problems it presents for literary critics and for the glimpses which it offers into the difficulties confronting women attempting to write in a masculine genre.

A dream allegory in which many women, within the vision, seek redress for wrongs done to them by men at the court of Lady Loyalty, the poem has been criticized for its seeming lack of motivation and direction, of clarity and resolution, and what has been seen as its superfluity of detail of clothing and court procedure. In short, it is a jumble of literary motifs and *topoi*. From a feminist viewpoint, though, the irresolution – the setting in a maze, with all the metaphorical weight which this lends to the directionless wanderings of the various women, with some (the pun is intentional) 'masyd in theyr mynd' (38) and others 'For verray wrath' overstepping the boundaries of the railings (41–2) – can be interpreted as the bewilderment felt by women in negotiating a path through the experience of love. And men, it comes as no surprise, do not fare well in this depiction. I should like to extend this argument by suggesting that the maze, additionally, represents a woman *author's* attempt to negotiate her way through the courtly discourse of love, a discourse established by men and which embodies masculine desire. It acts as a sustained commentary on the lack of availability of models of female secular writing in English. This reading leads to answers concerning the poem's vexations: the protagonist's tetchy response to being asked for her motto ('It is inough that my clothyng be blew', she remarks to the court porter, Countenaunce [313]) and her persistent questioning of everyone and everything she sees. Exposition is needed here because, unlike in *The Floure and the Leafe*, the rules are abstruse and essentially alien. The narrator herself does not know of what she should complain. She cannot even think of any good reason for writing her book except that by doing so 'it shuld nat out of remembraunce', and she relies upon the knight or squire (his status is unclear) who encourages her to recount her story in the first place to give it a title (742, 750–3). Well may the narrator wake 'Al amased' (739): she is both subject of her poem and, as author, subjected within it to the demands of a literary discourse within which she does not feel (or express herself) at ease.

There is another vital question to which the *Assembly* may hold the key to the answer, and that is whether or not women were able to compose within the genre of romance. Analysing stylistic and linguistic usage, Derek Pearsall concluded that the rhyme royal version of Generides, now Cambridge, Trinity College Library MS 0.5.2, was written by the author of the *Assembly* and, on the same grounds, that *The Floure and the Leafe* was not.[11] As a corollary, he concludes that a romance could not have been written by a woman and that, therefore, the dream vision was not. Yet there is nothing inherently improbable in a woman's choosing to write a romance, since they were readers of such texts. In France, Christine de Pizan was mistress of many different literary genres and there is an echo of Pearsall's conclusion in the suppression during the medieval period of Christine's authorship of the military treatise known in English as *The Fayttes of Armes and of Chyualrye* in one of the two manuscript traditions.[12] In England it is not necessary to look any further for evidence of a form of censorship than the recasting of the spiritual and biological complexities of Margery Kempe's *Book* into a brief and anodyne religious pamphlet published by Wynkyn de Worde c.1501.[13] It would seem that prejudice concerning female authority over the written word is an enduring phenomenon and one which must still be challenged. What cannot be denied, however, is women's undoubted command of differing verbal registers as genre, circumstances or occasion demanded.

Patronage, Books and Social Networks

Assessing women's roles in patronage of the arts is easier in some areas than in others. With architecture, for example, it is generally assumed that commissions originated with men. This is broadly true when looking at large institutional buildings, be they cathedrals or educational establishments. It is not coincidental that the curators of the Age of Chivalry exhibition of 1987 chose John de Grandisson, Bishop of Exeter (1327–69) and William of Wykeham, Bishop of Winchester (1367–1404) to exemplify patterns of commissioning, when it was men who had the power, wealth and influence to develop such outstanding buildings as Exeter Cathedral and the church of Ottery St Mary in Devon, Winchester College, and New College, Oxford.[14] In the Gothic exhibition of 2003 the balance was slightly redressed by including a section on Lady Margaret Beaufort, in the design and execution of whose foundations of the Cambridge colleges of Christ's and St John's the patroness's wishes are still in evidence.[15] Lady Margaret is also known to have taken a keen interest in domestic architecture, especially in the renovations and improvements to her principal residence during her latter years, at Collyweston, Northamptonshire (Jones and Underwood 1992). Although Henry VI's queen, Margaret of Anjou, was also an educational patron, being the foundress of Queens' College, Cambridge in 1447, there is no evidence that she took a similar interest in architecture, any more than did her successor as benefactress of Queens', Elizabeth Woodville. But Lady Margaret was not alone among aristocratic women in her interest in architecture. Alice Chaucer's last husband, William de la Pole, Earl of Suffolk, was probably instrumental in remodelling the Chaucer manor house of Ewelme, Oxfordshire, during the 1440s, but there is ample material evidence surviving to show her keen interest in design, embarking upon several such projects after William's death in 1450. John Goodall suggests that she may have been actively involved with the plans for the Divinity School at Oxford, of which she was a benefactress, in 1454 (Goodall 2001: 11–12); she certainly commissioned the tomb of her husband when he was reburied at the Hull Charterhouse in 1459; the chantry chapel and her own tomb at Ewelme church bear the stamp of her vigorous intervention, in its celebration of both her own lineage and her devotional preferences; and, most unusually, she seems to have directed the enlarging of her late husband's family chantry in Wingfield church, Suffolk in the 1460s (Goodall 2001: 269–72).

It is, of course, partly class and wealth which single out Margaret and Alice from others of their sex, both in the scale of their ambitions and their ability to achieve them. This is not to say that women drawn from lower ranks did not share their interest – especially in regard to places of devotion – but records are simply not extant to substantiate their involvement. In numerous gentry and urban widows' wills provision is made for improvements and additions to be made to their parish churches but, even if the buildings still stand, it is often impossible to know whether women played any decision-making role in their design.

With other artefacts, such as manuscripts, interpretation is not always so difficult. Books of hours and other illustrated texts often provide evidence as to women's patronage, sometimes in the form of heraldic decoration, paintings showing a woman at prayer or in the act of begging for intercession, or in the inclusion of a patron's name within particular prayers. The figures which Kathleen Scott gives for respective female-to-male patronage in these cases are, however, disturbing: eighteen to forty-six. This situation she attributes in part to 'the quick absorption of wealthy women in marriage, and to the general disposition of wealth', further remarking that 'ownership and use by a man and woman, and further actual ownership and use by women, is undoubtedly disguised under the ownership marks of coats of arms' (Scott 1996: I, 29). At the more sumptuous end of the market, an exceptionally fine non-liturgical book, London, British Library MS Cotton Julius E.IV, Article 6, containing the Pageants of Richard Beauchamp, earl of Warwick (figure 5.1), was almost certainly made for Anne (Neville), Countess of Warwick, Beauchamp's daughter, perhaps in an attempt to regain her possessions confiscated by the crown after her husband's death in 1473, or possibly to educate her grandson, Edward, heir to the throne, in the nobility of his ancestor. Containing fifty-five pen drawings of high calibre, accompanied on each page by brief explanatory captions, this is a unique survival from England (Scott 1996: II, 355–9).[16] It seems appropriate that it should have been commissioned by a woman who was one of the most avid book collectors of her time. Lower down the scale, socially and artistically, a manuscript in York Minster Library, MS Add. 2, known as the 'Bolton Hours' (Scott 1996: II, 119–21), has been attributed to the patronage of Margaret Blackburn/Bolton, daughter and subsequently wife of members of the York mercantile and civic elite.[17] Produced in all likelihood by a member of the Dominican order in York, it is a demonstration of the capacity of urban laypeople to acquire books outside the metropolis. London may have been the centre of the book trade, but it did not have a monopoly.

Illuminated manuscripts do not, though, constitute the primary means by which the reading habits of women may be recovered. For this, it is necessary to turn to other sources: chance survivals of book inventories; testamentary mentions of titles or codices (often brief), and undistinguished, sometimes second-hand, manuscripts which contain records of female ownership or reading interaction. There is often little distinction to be drawn between women of different classes in respect of the type of research which has to be undertaken. Alice Chaucer's eclectic tastes are demonstrated in an inventory

Figure 5.1 The earl and his wife and son in a storm at sea, from the Beauchamp Pageants: London. British Library, MS Cotton Julius E IV, art. 6, f. 28r. (By permission of the British Library.)

of the items she brought from Wingfield to Ewelme in 1466. Of the twenty-one volumes listed, fourteen were for chapel use. The contents of the remainder include romance, religious didacticism, educational instruction, and possibly more than one work by Christine de Pizan (Goodall 2001: 12, 207).[18] It is unlikely that this list forms the totality of Alice's library. Alice's will does not survive, but that of Cicely (Neville), Duchess of York (d.1495), does. Mother of kings and grandmother of Henry VII's queen, Elizabeth, Cicely's choice of reading material – lives of the saints and of Christ, and several mystical treatises by European women and by Walter Hilton – suggests the tastes of one who, long used to worldly vicissitude, turned to piety and contemplation. Her household ordinance from these years is also extant, revealing a rigorous round of private and communal prayer and edifying mealtime discussions, although both will and ordinance reveal that she never abandoned her duties as mistress of a noble household (Armstrong 1973). There are similarities between Cicely and her near-contemporary, Lady Margaret Beaufort (d.1509). Both continued to play an active role in the world as befitted their station; both were eulogized for the piety of their lives (although Lady Margaret could be a harsh and demanding mistress); both took care that their inner circles and households were governed with becoming propriety; and Lady Margaret, at least in the last years of her life, was patron, reader and – this marks her out as different from Cicely – translator of devotional works. What also distinguishes her is her role as a patroness of the printing trade: in her relations with Wynkyn de Worde and Richard Pynson she exemplifies a religious zeal verging on the evangelical (Jones and Underwood 1992; Powell 1998). Her life thus bridges traditional distinctions between medieval and early modern, patron and consumer as she was of books produced by means both ancient and new.

These three examples of women whose lives are so well documented are a rarity. With those of lesser social standing it is hard to reconstruct a cultural matrix into which they may be fitted. The range of women who owned books, and their multifarious tastes, can be documented (Meale 1996), but the next stage is to examine the provenance and ownership of manuscripts of particular texts. One reward of this approach is to establish reading, and hence social, networks. Copies of the Middle English translation from Latin of John of Hildesheim's *Three Kings of Cologne* (c.1400) have led to an examination of the women, both professed and lay residents, connected with the prestigious house of the Minoresses at Aldgate in London. Such detailed work has uncovered layers of interaction between the aristocracy, gentry and urban elite who had ties with this Franciscan order of St Clare (Boffey 1996). Other evidence may be more specifically regionally based, where there can often be a happy convergence of testamentary evidence and extant books sufficient to establish shared interests. Recent research into the life of Isabel Lyston, a gentry widow of Norwich – whose will lists the bequest of the romance of *Partonope of Blois* and *The Life of St Margaret* to one of her daughters – has revealed that the same daughter took as her second husband Andrew Sulyard of Wetherden in Suffolk, whose own mother, Anne Andrew, was herself a book-owner and relative of Thomasin Hopton, the possessor of a small but choice collection of books.[19]

It is of note that a great deal of the evidence of this aspect of women's culture comes from East Anglia – the area in which Julian and Margery lived. Whether this is directly related to East Anglia's position as a national and international trading centre in the fifteenth century is a moot point. But before leaving this discussion of women's self-expression through their choice of reading matter I should like to look at one more woman in relation to her milieu. In 1443, Thomas Drew, a chaplain of the parish of Salle in Norfolk, bequeathed to Lady Ela Brewes a book of devotions, with images, which had formerly belonged to her father, Sir Miles Stapleton (Norwich, NRO Norwich Consistory Court, 224 Doke). This book can in all probability be identified as Oxford, Bodleian Library MS Bodley 758, a copy of writings on the Passion by Michael de Massa. The manuscript, containing some of the best provincial work of the time, is notable for its grisaille illustration of the Crucifixion, in which the wounds of Christ are highlighted in red; and for its representations of the author of the piece, who was a fourteenth-century Augustinian monk, and of its scribe, Ralph de Medylton, who wrote the codex in 1405 under the commission of Ela's father (Scott 1996: II, 78–9). Medylton was a member of the house of Trinitarian canons founded at Ingham in

Norfolk by Ela's grandfather, another Sir Miles, in 1361. When Ela drew up her will on 16 October 1456 (Norwich, NRO, NCC Brosyard (8)) her principal concern, after the welfare of her soul, was for her family. To her surviving brother, Edmund Stapleton, she left her white psalter (there is no mention of the book with images). Although she wrote her will in Woodbridge, Suffolk, requesting burial in the chancel of the priory there, next to her late husband, Robert, her links with her family home at Ingham and the parish of Salle remained important. She left forty shillings towards the building of a tower at Ingham church, where members of her family were buried. Her connection with Salle came about through the manor of Stinton, which lay partially within the parish of Salle: the living was in the gift of the family and Ela, who retained Stinton as part of her jointure following her husband's death, presented a new rector in 1440. Thomas Drew, chaplain, would appear to have had a crucial part in this parish community in which Ela retained a leading role. He was evidently close enough to both Ela and her father to have shared an interest in religious texts. Since Bodley 758 is in Latin, it is tempting to speculate that he may have read this book with Ela. It could have been he who lent the Stapleton volume in 1430 to William Wode, rector of the parish, for in that year one Edmund Southwell made a copy of the text by Michael de Massa for Wode in the rectory at Salle. This is now London, Lambeth Palace MS 505. Ela's natal family, the Stapletons, had other religious and bookish concerns, but then so did her descendants. Through the marriages of her children and grandchildren she became connected with many of the most notable (and book-owning) East Anglian families, among them the Yelvertons, the Hoptons and the Pastons. It was her granddaughter, Margery Brews, who married John Paston III, and who sent to him her famous Valentine verses in 1477 (I, 662–3).

The acquisition of knowledge about the circumstances in which books were owned and used by women is ongoing, but it is a vital exercise. The quantity of detail which it is possible to recover about Ela Brewes and women like her, and about the circles into which they were born and moved, is key to understanding women's positions and how they functioned within late medieval society.

Women, Power and Status

Power and privilege did not come without their costs. Of the three noblewomen mentioned above, Alice Chaucer and Cicely Neville lived as widows for many years and so, de facto, had to involve themselves in the administration and management of their estates. Alice had the additional onus of ensuring all was in order for her husband's heir, John, until he became of age. She was also politically astute enough to arrange in 1458 for the marriage of John to Elizabeth Neville, daughter of Cicely and Richard Neville, the Duke and Duchess of York, thus cementing her reinstatement after the political execution of her husband in 1450, and the subsequent parliamentary attempt to remove her from the presence of the Lancastrian king, Henry VI. Margaret Beaufort, like Alice, fought tirelessly for her son, although they did not meet from 1470, when he went into exile in France, until after Bosworth, in the autumn of 1485. During this time she plotted on his behalf and, following his coronation as Henry VII, she continued to advise him (Jones and Underwood 1992: 60–92). Of these two women it was perhaps Lady Margaret who gained the most satisfaction from her offspring: Henry, after all, was founder of the Tudor dynasty, while the de la Pole fortunes, which had grown so spectacularly through William, began a steady decline with his son.

Widowhood was not the only reason why women had to bear administrative responsibilities. During the war with France men were frequently away from their lands for years at a time and, even when their menfolk were not abroad fighting but were busy seeing to affairs elsewhere, women from the nobility and gentry had to shoulder the burdens of management. Margaret Paston, once more, has left ample testimony to the trials which this entailed. Perhaps the best-known example of her fortitude and resourcefulness can be found in the description of the pillaging of the manor of Gresham in January 1449, given in a petition submitted to Henry VI in the summer of 1449, outlining the events of January of that year (I, 51–3). At the centre of a dispute concerning possession of this manor were the Pastons and Robert Hungerford, lord Moleyns. The latter finally took matters into his own hands and on 28 January sent to the 'mansion' where Margaret had taken up residence 'a riotous peple to the nombre of a thowsand persones . . . arrayd in maner of werre'. Moleyns's men drove out Margaret and the dozen people with her and proceeded to rifle and destroy the building. Margaret had been prepared: in 1448 she had written to her husband requesting crossbows and axes among other weapons. Meanwhile, her men had made 'barris to barre the dorys crosse-wyse', wickets throughout the house 'to schete owte atte, both wyth bowys and wyth hand gunnys', and holes through which handguns alone could be deployed. If sheer force of will could have combated strength of numbers, there is little doubt as to what the outcome of the attack at Gresham would have been.

Urban women were arguably more free to make choices about their lives than their gentry and noble contemporaries. As a result of her researches into the careers of London's women, Barron concluded that, in comparison with the sixteenth century, the fifteenth was a 'Golden Age' in terms of their ability to enter apprenticeships and trade as femes soles, that is as individuals with a legal identity separate from that of their husbands (Barron 1989). Judith Bennett disagreed with Barron in a paper in which she described the evidence to be adduced 'from miscellaneous contracts and cases' as 'examples and anecdotes' (Bennett 1992: 159). The debate continues. In a collection of essays on the widows of London from 1300 to 1500 it becomes clear that, while women had little, if any, access to the prestigious and wealthy great livery companies of the city, they were able to carry on in their late husbands' trades, as tanners, in one case as a skinner, as bell-founders, and as silkwomen (Barron and Sutton 1994). London, in the opportunities it offered women, may well have been different from other towns and cities, but only further specialized research into regional centres and practices will either confirm or deny this. London widows, for instance, were allowed the freedom of the city so long as they remained unmarried, but Exeter differed, while in Hull,

Nottingham, Shrewsbury and Canterbury, in order to trade, women had to buy a licence. Women of the peasant classes, too, were disadvantaged in relation to men. They could participate in small-scale retailing of any surplus of food, when they were employed in the same jobs as men on the land, but the period of their employment could be shorter than that of their male counterparts, and they were consistently paid less, even following the Black Death of 1349 (Mate 1999: 30–1). Neither were all widows in the countryside and in cities so fortunate under the law as those considered thus far. Social and economic pressures could be exercised to ensure that gentry heirs gained what they considered to be their due before their mother's or mother-in-law's death, leaving these older women with considerably reduced means, despite the legal access to dower (from the husband) and jointure (from the marriage settlement) to which they were theoretically entitled (Mate 1999: 92, 81–2).

Other investigations into the status of women are based on different theoretical models, such as demographical studies and diachronic analysis of women's participation in particular trades. For York, for example, ecclesiastical archives reveal a demographic pattern which is distinctive: young women, often migrants into the city, worked as servants and chose either to marry later than might be expected, in their early to mid-twenties, or not to marry at all (Goldberg 1992). Not all historians are in agreement with Goldberg's conclusions. As Mavis Mate has pointed out, poll-tax returns for the late fourteenth century show that there were more women in the city than men, that servants were often ill paid, as well as being dependent, and that their employment prospects were limited to poorly paid occupations (Mate 1999: 56–7). It may be possible to argue against Goldberg's thesis on these generalized grounds, but the detail and rigour of his documentary analysis are compelling. Again, it should be borne in mind that the gathering of evidence for any case should be incremental. So much is true of Bennett's investigations into women's involvement with the brewing trade, in which she has traced the gradual lessening of women's influence once beer production overtook that of ale in the 1430s (Bennett 1996). A number of factors could have accounted for this. Ale, brewed with malt, water and yeast, did not have a long shelf life so was not produced on a large scale. In consequence, production was usually local and could be carried out without large labour demands, sometimes as part of a household economy where the wife contributed income in this way. (Not that this was true of Margery Kempe: in her attempts at brewing 'sodenly þe berm wold fallyn down þat alle þe ale was lost euery brewyng aftyr oþer', 9–10). Once hops were introduced into the recipe, however, large-scale manufacture became possible, involving investment in machinery and labour. And once major capital was involved, in this, as in so many other trades and crafts, women were edged out.

Never were women so marginalized, though, as when they became prostitutes. In cities around the country such women were stigmatized by not being allowed to live within the enclosing walls. In York, for example, there was an unfortunate civic correlation drawn in 1301 between women and animals: 'No one shall keep pigs which go in the streets by day or night, nor shall any prostitute stay in the city' (Goldberg 1995: 210). A pig could be killed and its slayer choose to cut off its trotters, while a prostitute could be imprisoned 'for a day and a night', and have the roof timbers and door of her house confiscated by a bailiff. In Bristol, prostitutes, along with lepers, were banned from the city in 1344 and such prohibitions continued to be re-enacted in other English cities throughout the medieval period, from Bishop's Lynn to Leicester, Rochester to Exeter (Karras 1996: 18–20). The stews of Southwark, on the south side of the Thames, were especially notorious, and the moral hypocrisy inherent in the practice of prostitution here is overt: Southwark lay under the jurisdiction of the Bishop of Winchester, in whose ecclesiastical court these women could be tried and fined. In a London Borough ordinance of 1382, it was decreed that prostitutes should be marked out from other women through the wearing of a hood of 'ray', or striped cloth (Goldberg 1995: 211). As Karras points out, much of the medieval moral aversion to the trade in female flesh was precisely because of its commercial aspect. Women were viewed not only as morally debased by the sin of lust, but as guilty of venality and, in cases where they dressed extravagantly or wore make-up, pride (Karras 1996: 109–11). These women were indeed seen as the daughters of Eve.

The women whose marginalization is recorded here may have come from the lowest social strata but noble and regnal women were not immune to ostracism, albeit of a different nature. In 1441 Eleanor Cobham, second wife of the heir presumptive to the throne, Humphrey, Duke of Gloucester, was indicted for sorcery and witchcraft, on the basis that she had dabbled in necromancy, ostensibly in order to determine the date of Henry VI's death. Her marriage was annulled and she was imprisoned until her death at Beaumaris in Anglesey in 1452, five years after that of her former husband.[20] Henry IV's second wife and queen, Joan of Navarre, likewise was accused of witchcraft against her stepson, Henry V, in 1419 and held a prisoner (although under a more liberal regime than Eleanor's) until 1423.[21] In hindsight, political and financial expediency can be held to account for these charges, but such is their nature that they pose the question of the potency of masculine rebuke against perceived gender transgression. Imprisonment was also the fate of Margaret of Anjou (latterly in the charge of Alice Chaucer), until she was finally and ignominiously returned in 1476 to France, where she died as a pensioner of the French king in 1482. Two other English queens died in religious seclusion at the Cluniac house at Bermondsey: Katherine of Valois (d.1437), widow of Henry V who caused a scandal by marrying an obscure Welsh squire named Owen Tudor; and Elizabeth Woodville (d.1492), widow of Edward IV. The reasons underlying their retirement from the world remain obscure: perhaps disgrace, illness or, in Elizabeth's case, devotional inclination.[22] Examples such as these serve to reinforce the notion that rank did not necessarily protect women.

Two predominant themes emerge from this survey. First, that dynamic changes took place in English society from 1350 onwards and in the course of these changes, whether they concern the economy following the devastation of the plague, the status of the English language, or developments in education, women's roles were diverse and themselves in a state of flux. They could be beneficiaries of an expanding economy, as in fifteenth-century York or London; or they could be instrumental in furthering learning, as the evidence from nunneries increasingly suggests. Second, the varying fortunes of the women discussed here demonstrate clearly that all generalizations must be deconstructed. Each narrative of a woman's life, each example and anecdote, to adapt Bennett's phrase, goes towards recovering the history of women. The process of recovery entails a painstaking historical and geographical mapping of experience in relation to circumstance, and it is far from complete. If we really wish to understand the Middle Ages, we would do well to heed the words of a (male) adviser to Margery Paston, which she reported to her husband in 1481: 'on word of a woman shuld do more than the wordys of xx men' (I, 665).

See also: 2 English Society in the Later Middle Ages, 4 City and Country, Wealth and Labour, 6 Manuscripts and Readers, 7 From Manuscript to Modern Text, 9 The Languages of Medieval Britain, 19 Love, 20 Middle English Romance, 22 Dream Poems, 23 Lyric, 26 Accounts of Lives, 30 The *Book of Margery Kempe*, 31 Julian of Norwich.

Notes

1 A. Zettersen and B. Diensberg, *The English Text of the Ancrene Riwle: The 'Vernon' Text* (Oxford: Oxford University Press, 2000), pp. 21, 25.

2 Y. Wada (ed.), *A Companion to Ancrene Wisse* (Cambridge: Brewer, 2003), *passim*.

3 C. Carpenter (ed.), *Kingsford's Stonor Letters and Papers* (Cambridge: Cambridge University Press, 1996); J. Kirby (ed.), *The Plumpton Letters and Papers*, Camden Society 5th ser., 8 (1996); A. Hanham (ed.), *The Cely Letters and Papers* (London: Oxford University Press, 1975). For the Paston and Armburgh letters and papers, see below, notes 6 and 7.

4 N. Davis, 'The Language of the Pastons.' *Proceedings of the British Academy* 40 (1954), 119–39; cf. V. O'Mara, 'Female Scribal Ability and Scribal Activity in Late Medieval England', *Leeds Studies in English* 27 (1996), 87–130.

5 E.g., P. Lee, *Nunneries, Learning and Spirituality in Late Medieval English Society: The Dominican Priory of Dartford* (Woodbridge: York Medieval Press in association with the Boydell Press, 2000).

6 N. Davis (ed.), *Paston Letters and Papers of the Fifteenth Century*, 2 vols (Oxford: Clarendon Press, 1971–6).

7 C. Carpenter (ed.), *The Armburgh Papers: The Brokeholes Inheritance in Warwickshire, Hertfordshire and Essex c.1417–c.1453* (Woodbridge: Boydell Press, 1998).

8 M. Glasscoe (ed.), *Julian of Norwich: A Revelation of Love* (Exeter: University of Exeter, 1986), p. 8.

9 S. McNamer, 'Female Authors, Provincial Setting: The Re-Versing of Courtly Love in the Findern Manuscript', *Viator* 22 (1991), 279–310.

10 D. Pearsall (ed.), *'The Floure and the Leafe' and 'The Assembly of Ladies'* (Manchester: Manchester University Press, 1980).

11 D. A. Pearsall, '*The Assembly of Ladies* and *Generydes*', *Review of English Studies* ns 12 (1961), 229–37.

12 A. T. P. Byles (ed.), *The Book of Fayttes of Armes and of Chyualrye* (London: Oxford University Press, 1932), p. xv.

13 S. B. Meech and H. E. Allen (eds), *The Book of Margery Kempe* (Bungay: Oxford University Press, 1940), pp. 353–7.

14 J. Alexander and P. Binski (eds), *Age of Chivalry: Art in Plantagenet England* (London: Weidenfeld and Nicolson in association with the Royal Academy, 1987), pp. 463–75.

15 R. Marks and P. Williamson (eds), *Gothic: Art for England 1400–1547* (London: V&A Publications, 2003), pp. 246–53.

16 Cf. A. Sinclair (ed.), *The Beauchamp Pageant* (Donnington: Richard III and Yorkist History Trust in association with Paul Watkins, 2003), pp. 13–23.

17 P. Cullum and J. Goldberg, 'How Margaret Blackburn Taught her Daughters: Reading Devotional Instruction in a Book of Hours', in *Medieval Women: Texts and Contexts in Late Medieval Britain – Essays for Felicity Riddy*, ed. Jocelyn Wogan-Browne, Rosalynn Voaden, Arlyn Diamond, Ann Hutchinson, Carol Meale and Lesley Johnson (Turnhout: Brepols, 2000), pp. 217–36.

18 Goodall's transcription and identification of these books is in places faulty; cf. C. M. Meale, 'Reading Women's Culture in Fifteenth-century England: The Case of Alice Chaucer', in *Medievalitas: Reading the Middle Ages*, ed. P. Boitani and A. Torti (Cambridge: Brewer, 1996), pp. 81–101.

19 C. M. Meale, 'Wives, Mothers and Daughters: Lineage, Books and the Will of Isabel Lyston of Norwich (1490)', in *'Much Heaving and Shoving': Late Medieval Gentry and their Concerns – Essays for Colin Richmond*, ed. Margaret Aston and Rosemary Horrox (Lavenham: Aston and Horrox, 2005), pp. 95–108; C. M. Meale and J. Boffey, 'Gentlewomen's Reading', in *The Cambridge History of the Book in Britain. Vol. 3: 1400–1557*, ed. L. Hellinga and J. B. Trapp (Cambridge: Cambridge University Press, 1999), pp. 526–40.

20 R. A. Griffiths, 'The Trial of Eleanor Cobham: An Episode in the Fall of the Duke Humphrey of Gloucester', *Bulletin of the John Rylands Library* 51 (1968–9), 381–99.

21 A. R. Myers, 'The Captivity of a Royal Witch: The Household Accounts of Queen Joan of Navarre, 1419–21', *Bulletin of the John Rylands Library* 24 (1940), 263–84 and 26 (1941–2), 82–100.

22 R. A. Griffiths, *The Reign of Henry VI* (Berkeley and Los Angeles: University of California Press, 1961), pp. 60–1; A. F. Sutton and L. Visser-Fuchs, 'A "Most Benevolent Queen": Queen Elizabeth Woodville's Reputation, her Piety and her Books', *The Ricardian* 10 (1995), 214–35 (234–5).

References and Further Reading

Armstrong, C. A. J. 1973. 'The Piety of Cicely, Duchess of York: A Study in Late Mediaeval Culture.' In his *England, France and Burgundy in the Fifteenth Century* (London: Hambledon Press), pp. 135–56. Originally published in 1942; Armstrong discusses Cicely's will and household ordinance.

Barron, C. M. 1989. 'The "Golden Age" of Women in London.' *Reading Medieval Studies* 15, 35–58. Seminal account of the late medieval period.

—— 1996. 'The Education and Training of Girls in Fifteenth-century London.' In *Courts, Counties and the Capital*, ed. D. E. S. Dunn (Stroud: Sutton), pp. 139–53. Survey, followed by investigation of miscellaneous documentary sources revealing hitherto unknown material.

—— and Sutton, A. (eds) 1994. *Medieval London Widows 1300–1500*. London and Rio Grande: Hambledon Press. Valuable collection of essays on individual women (mercantile and noble) and on women who chose to live as vowesses.

Bell, D. N. 1995. *What Nuns Read: Books and Libraries in Medieval English Nunneries*. Kalamazoo, Mich. and Spencer, Mass.: Cistercian Publications. A ground-breaking catalogue and discussion.

Bennett, J. M. 1992. 'Medieval Women, Modern Women: Across the Great Divide.' In *Culture and History 1350–1600: Essays on English Communities and Writing*, ed. D. Aers (Hemel Hempstead: Harvester Wheatsheaf), pp. 147–85. Polemical essay which attempts to break down the boundary between the study of women in the medieval and in the modern periods, arguing for a diachronic approach to the history of women.

—— 1996. *Ale, Beer and Brewsters in England: Women's Work in a Changing World, 1300–1600*. Oxford: Oxford University Press. Detailed feminist analysis.

Boffey, J. 1996. 'Some London Women Readers and a Text of *The Three Kings of Cologne*.' *The Ricardian* 10, 387–96. Examination of women linked by shared reading of particular manuscripts and texts.

Crawford, A. (ed.) 2002. *Letters of Medieval Women.* Stroud: Sutton. Includes biographies and translations of letters from women from a cross-section of society.

Daybell, J. (ed.) 2001 *Early Modern Women's Letter Writing, 1450–1700.* Basingstoke: Palgrave. Essays by Roger Dalrymple on the Paston women, Jennifer C. Ward on noblewomen, and Alison Truelove on the Stonors.

Goldberg, P. J. P. 1992. *Women, Work, and Life Cycle in a Medieval Economy: Women in York and Yorkshire c.1300–1520.* Oxford: Clarendon Press. Detailed analysis of the demography of marriage in the area and a new and much needed study of women's role in the workforce.

—— (ed.) 1995. *Women in England c.1275–1525: Documentary Sources.* Manchester: Manchester University Press. Translations of archival sources relating to women in the lower echelons of society.

Goodall, J. A. A. 2001. *God's House at Ewelme: Life, Devotion and Architecture in a Fifteenth-Century Almshouse.* Aldershot: Ashgate. Architectural and historical study of Ewelme and its foundation by Alice and William de la Pole.

Jones, M. K. and Underwood, M. G. 1992. *The King's Mother: Lady Margaret Beaufort, Countess of Richmond and Derby.* Cambridge: Cambridge University Press. Impressive and objective biography of possibly the most influential woman of her time.

Karras, R. M. 1996. *Common Women: Prostitution and Sexuality in Medieval England.* Oxford: Oxford University Press. A history of one aspect of medieval society and culture which refuses any easy categorization of women as victims or as individuals in control of their destiny.

Mate, M. E. 1999. *Women in Medieval English Society.* Cambridge: Cambridge University Press. A useful survey, with excellent bibliography, of women's lives from c.600 to 1530; its chief strength lies in its exploration of economic and legal issues.

Meale, C. M. (1996) '". . . alle the bokes that I haue of latyn, englisch and frensch": Laywomen and their Books in Late Medieval England.' In *Women and Literature in Britain 1150–1500*, ed. C. M. Meale, 2nd edn (Cambridge: Cambridge University Press), pp. 128–58. Survey of women's book ownership from the middle classes to royalty; discusses the range of texts represented and the problems inherent in interpreting the evidence.

Powell, S. 1998. 'Lady Margaret Beaufort and her Books.' *The Library* 6th ser. 20, 197–240. The first study to deal exclusively with Margaret's learning and devotion as interpreted through her book ownership and patronage.

Scott, K. L. 1996. *Later Gothic Manuscripts, 1390–1490*, 2 vols. A Survey of Manuscripts Illuminated in the British Isles, vol. 6. London: Harvey Miller. Catalogue invaluable in its erudition and coverage.

Ward, J. (ed.) 1995. *Women of the English Gentry and Nobility 1066–1500.* Manchester: Manchester University Press. Companion volume to Goldberg 1995.

PART II
The Production and Reception of Texts

6
Manuscripts and Readers

A. S. G. Edwards

One of the distinctive dimensions of a manuscript culture is the possibility of more direct relationships between manuscripts and readers than can obtain in a developed print culture. Readers were necessarily in closer contact with those who supplied the works they read and hence had the opportunity to shape both the form and the content of those works. Moreover, the reader generally formed one component in a larger entrepreneurial nexus that included stationers, scribes and decorators who each had their own potential to affect the final form that constituted the manuscript book.

To say that every manuscript is by definition unique is to take refuge in the banal. But it is clear that medieval readers often saw the potential to individualize the manuscripts they owned. This individualization could take various forms. It might be restricted to the addition of a mark of ownership – for example, a name, or a shield bearing the owner's arms, usually added in the upper or lower margins of the first page. Those who prepared manuscripts speculatively, not at the behest of a specific commissioner, would sometimes leave blank shields in the design of the manuscript to be filled in later to accommodate this form of self-representation. For such gestures of visible identification were perhaps more than simple marks of ownership; they provided an explicit connection between the book and the social status of its possessor that correlates aspects of identity with forms of taste, literary or otherwise, depending on the kind of book with which the owner was identified.

Decoration and Illustration

More ambitious forms of decoration were possible if the commissioner and creators of the manuscript were in close consultation from its inception, and if the commissioner was sufficiently wealthy and the creators had sufficient artistic resources. Some owners sought to impose their own identities on books they owned by the inclusion of miniatures of themselves. This is quite common in a number of de luxe manuscripts (Scott 1989). Sometimes manuscripts contain miniatures showing the poet or author actually presenting his work to the dedicatee, as in various manuscripts of the poems of John Lydgate and Thomas Hoccleve. The fact that such miniatures also appear in manuscripts clearly commissioned by persons other than the original dedicatee suggests the evidential limitations of such visual data. In these instances, the image is a recollection of an original context, not a confirmation of the specific historical origins of the manuscript in which it appears. It testifies to the circulation of visual as well as textual models. Thus an image of Lydgate praying before the shrine of St Edmund, which appears in the actual copy presented to the king, now British Library MS Harley 2278, also appears in other de luxe copies, like British Library MS Yates Thompson 47 and the Arundel Castle manuscript, which draw on the same elaborate cycle of illustrations that appears in the presentation copy (Scott 1982).

This circulation of 'standardized' sequences of illustrations which affluent patrons could commission with their choice of work(s) is demonstrable in other instances. It can be seen in some manuscripts of Gower's *Confessio Amantis* (Griffiths 1983) or of Lydgate's *Troy Book* (Lawton 1983). That these groups of manuscripts seem to draw on such established sets of pictures, of course, lessens the possibility that readers or commissioners had any direct role in this aspect of manuscript preparation. But they must certainly have approved the fact of such illustration and its attendant additional time and expense. This in its turn allows us to infer something about the nature of the reader for this kind of de luxe production, if only in terms of his or her economic standing. On occasions, sudden loss of wealth or life may leave traces on surviving manuscripts, most obviously in a manuscript like Cambridge, Corpus Christi College MS 61 of Chaucer's *Troilus and Criseyde*, which contains a famous frontispiece miniature but no other pictures, even though spaces have been left for them throughout the manuscript.

The *Troilus* manuscript is not the only instance of illustration being left incomplete in a Middle English manuscript. In some instances, such incompleteness was seized on by a subsequent owner as an opportunity to enhance and enlarge the manuscript to create a new form for the book. A notable example is British Library MS Royal 18 D. II, another manuscript of Lydgate's *Troy Book* together with his *Siege of Thebes*. Only part of the ambitious programme of decoration was completed for its initial owner, Sir William Herbert, Lord Pembroke, at some point in the third quarter of the fifteenth century. By the early sixteenth century it had come into the possession of Henry Percy, fourth Earl of Northumberland, seemingly on the occasion of his marriage to Herbert's daughter, Maud, whose arms were added to it. It then came into the possession of the fifth earl, also Henry Percy, who arranged that the missing miniatures be added and also that the manuscript be enlarged to include a number of works directly associated with the Percys; for example, Skelton's poem on the death of the fourth earl, William Peeris's verse history of the Percy family, and several sets of verses painted on the walls of Wrexill and Leconfield, both Percy houses. Such 'personalizing' to reflect concerns of family history and status shows clearly how the concerns of readers could help to reshape the nature of the manuscript book in their own image.

Size and Audience

Not all readers, of course, came from the upper levels of society. And other forms of manuscript than the grand and expensively produced can sometimes offer a way of understanding audience. There is, for example, a copy of the Wycliffe translation of the Bible into Middle English, that now survives as two fragments thousands of miles apart, one in California as Huntington Library HM 501 and the other as Tokyo, Keio University Library MS [170X@9/6]. The most immediately striking feature of these fragments is their size. They are extremely small, approximately 145 × 85 mm, the size of book that is easily concealed. In view of the heretical status of the followers of John Wycliffe and of the writings associated with him in the later medieval period in England, it is understandable that the owner of such a work would wish to have it in a form that could be hidden from enquiring authorities who sought to suppress such unauthorized translations of the Bible. The form of these fragments provides a gloss on the social, political and religious conditions of one class of readers.

Size and form can be revealing in other ways. Not all small books were necessarily illicit. Some may have been designed in this way to meet the needs of readers who wished for portable books. A number of small books of hours survive to enable pious lay people to pursue their devotions where and when they wished. These books often seem to have been designed for women readers and may have provided a model for other, more literary, religious collections aimed at the same readership. For example, Cambridge University Library MS Additional 4122 is another very small book; it measures 85 × 123 mm. It contains verse lives of the female saints Margaret and Dorothy, and of the Virgin Mary. The conjunction of small size and female subject-matter makes it tempting to assume that the actual content was given a physical form specifically designed to meet the needs of a woman reader (Edwards 2003a).

At the opposite extreme are manuscripts of remarkable size, sometimes termed 'coucher books', books too large to be carried and which needed to be supported for reading with a lectern. The most weighty of these (in every sense) is the Vernon manuscript in Oxford, Bodleian Library MS Eng. poet. a. 1, which weighs about 22 kilos and measures 544 × 393 mm. It is an enormous assemblage (382 leaves survive) of religious and devotional works in Middle English, in both verse and prose. The preparation of such a book, not just in terms of its copying and decoration (which would literally have taken years), but also in terms of the actual assembling of such a wide range of texts, can only have been undertaken with a clear sense of its place within a particular religious institutional environment. It is a public book, one that could never have been envisaged as a means of private study but which would probably have to have remained set in a fixed position on a lectern, where it would be the focus of some form of collective contemplation through being read aloud.

Collections and Booklets

Between these extremes of size lies a vast range of manuscripts produced to meet the needs of different categories of readers – manuscripts created to furnish entertainment or to preserve information of various kinds, whether practical, devotional, religious or simply educational. Often manuscripts combine materials from some or all of these broad categories. One example which must stand for many is Oxford, Bodleian Library MS Ashmole 61. It is a manuscript of modest size and decoration, copied by a single scribe. It includes romances of various kinds (*Sir Isumbras*, *The Earl of Toulous*, *Lybeaus Desconus*, *Sir Orfeo*), saints' lives (St Eustace, St Margaret), verse prayers and other religious verse (including the *Northern Passion* and the *Short Charter of Christ*), Richard Maydestone's psalm translations, courtesy texts (*How the Wise Man Taught his Son*, *How the Good Wife Taught her Daughter*, *Stans Puer ad Mensam*), practical verse (Lydgate's *Dietary*), a comic tale (*King Edmund and the Hermit*) and a comic debate (*The Carpenter's Tools*) and such satiric verses as Lydgate's *Ram's Horn*. It is not easy to categorize the audience for such a heterogeneous collection. Its potential appeal is so wide-ranging as to constitute the appeal of a virtual library in itself.

Manuscripts containing such a range of materials are not uncommon and indicate processes of construction and accumulation to satisfy a wide range of readers' tastes. In some circumstances those responsible for the creation of manuscripts were able to anticipate such tastes and to create pre-packaged collections of texts to satisfy them. These collections are defined by modern scholarship as 'booklets' and provide the prospective purchaser with a means of assembling, either gradually or immediately, groups of texts on various subjects or in various literary modes. Such collections do not provide a secure guide to the interests of readers, but they do offer some insight into the sorts of works that were felt to be commercially viable in a particular place at a certain time. One group of poetry manuscripts demonstrates this with particular clarity. It is the so-called 'Oxford group', so named because the manuscripts are all in the Bodleian Library: MSS Fairfax 16, Tanner 346 and Bodley 638. These collections were assembled by different scribes at points between the 1440s and the end of the fifteenth century, yet they possess a considerable degree of uniformity in content, even though in some cases the manuscript is copied by more than one scribe. They all contain poems by Chaucer (his *Legend of Good Women*, *Book of the Duchess*, *Parliament of Fowls*, *Anelida and Arcite* and the lyric 'Pity'), Lydgate (*The Complaint of the Black Knight* and *Temple of Glas*), John Clanvowe (*The Cuckoo and the Nightingale*) and Hoccleve (*The Letter of Cupid*); in addition, there are other texts common to at least two of these manuscripts. These booklet collections seem to have been produced in London by professional scribes. But they offered models of assembling texts that were widely imitated (Boffey and Thompson 1989). For example, it seems that some of the poems in the Findern manuscript (Cambridge University Library Ff. 1. 6) very probably derived from booklet collections of the kind in the 'Oxford group'; this shows that by the mid-fifteenth century the influence of such collections had become sufficiently widely diffused to have reached Derbyshire, where the late medieval members of the Findern family lived.

Selection and Reading

Of course, not all audiences could be satisfied by such pre-packaged transmission of assemblages of texts. It was also possible for works to be drawn together in distinctive ways which reflect the preoccupations of their readers. We see this clearly with some of the forms in which individual tales from within the sequence of the *Canterbury Tales* were selected and realigned on distinctive generic grounds. For example, British Library MS Harley 1239 selects several of these tales – the Knight's, Clerk's, Man of Law's, Wife of Bath's and Franklin's, together with *Troilus and Criseyde* – to create a generically coherent anthology of Chaucerian romances. Manchester, Chetham's Library MS 6709 conjoins Chaucer's Second Nun's and Prioress's Tales with several of Lydgate's saints' lives to create a hagiographical collection. At times, the collocations reveal something of the diversity of generic responses that are possible. Although the Man of Law's Tale is excerpted in a context that suggests it is seen as a romance in Harley 1239, in the only other manuscript in which it occurs separately, Cambridge University Library Ee. 2. 15, it appears with Middle English saints' legends.

Some narratives from the *Canterbury Tales* achieved an extensive free-standing identity. Melibee and the Prioress's Tale both appear separately in five manuscripts each and the Clerk's Tale in four (Silvia 1974). A similar interest in isolating favourite stories from their larger structure occurs with John Gower's *Confessio Amantis*, another large collection of narratives. One episode, 'The Three Questions', appears extracted from the main sequence in five manuscripts, the Tale of Tereus in three, and a number of others in two (Edwards 1998). It is not easy for modern sensibilities to fully grasp the appeal of some of these narratives, but their popularity is doubtless related to their exemplary, didactic functions.

Such processes of selection could extend even further, to the isolation of smaller units from within works. Some passages or even individual stanzas from longer works came to achieve distinct, separate identities in their own right as free-standing poems. Lydgate's *Fall of Princes* (c.1432–8) became a notable repository of passages of moral generalization or gnomic aphorism; dozens of extracts from it survive. Virtually none of these draws on the narrative portions of Lydgate's texts, his accounts of famous men brought low by Fortune, portions which reflect his ultimate source, Boccaccio's *De casibus virorum illustrium*. Instead they draw on the moralizing envoys he invented which offer widely applicable generalizations about the human condition. One of the most popular of these extracts is a single stanza beginning 'Deceit deceiveth and shal be deceived'. It survives in more than a dozen copies, often copied in informal hands on to flyleaves of manuscripts, a testimony to its succinct and easily memorable distillation of commonplaces (Edwards 1971).

The appetite of readers for distilled proverbial verse formulations is also seen in the wide appeal of one stanza from John Walton's verse translation of Boethius' *Consolation of Philosophy* (c.1410). This stanza reads (I have modernized some spellings):

Right as poverty causes soberness,
And feebleness enforsis continence,
Right so prosperity and riches
The mother is of vice and negligence;
And power also causes insolence,
And honours oft times changes thewis, *personal qualities*
That is no more perilous pestilence
Than high estate given unto shrews.

This survives as an extract in nine manuscripts and some copyists thought sufficiently highly of it to ascribe it to Chaucer (Boffey 1996).

On occasions, readers were more creative, even merging passages from works by different authors to create a new poem. One example is a poem in the Findern manuscript (folio 150). Here passages from Lydgate's *Fall of Princes* are joined to stanzas from Chaucer's *Troilus and Criseyde* about the evils of false speaking. The poem is too long to quote here; but someone was sufficiently well versed in both these poems to perceive a congruence of tone and subject-matter that permits an act of creative misreading.

The appeal of such generally applicable moralized verses had a firm grip on medieval readers. Its appeal can still be seen, after the introduction of printing into England, in *The Prouerbes of Lydgate*, printed by Wynkyn de Worde c.1510. In spite of its title, the pamphlet includes extracts from Lydgate's *Fall of Princes*, with other of his lyrics and two of Chaucer's short poems, 'Fortune' and 'Truth'. It confirms the continued existence of an audience with an appetite for brief passages of generalized moral exhortation. The demand was sufficiently great for de Worde to reprint the *Prouerbes* about a decade later.

The processes of excerption we see with verse also occur with prose texts, although their identification is often harder to establish. But devotional and didactic works seem to have particularly lent themselves to forms of selection. *Pore Caitif* survives in more than fifty manuscripts; in its fullest form, it is a collection of fifteen separate tracts on various aspects of devotional life. A quite large number of manuscripts, at least fifteen, contain only selected parts of the text. And the compilation of the collection itself reflects antecedent processes of compilation: it incorporates borrowings from such materials as the religious writing of Richard Rolle and Walter Hilton as well as passages from the devotional treatise originally composed for anchoresses, the *Ancrene Wisse*. *Pore Caitif* hence demonstrates the processes of recycling and fragmentation that formed a part of readers' engagement with longer religious works.

Ancrene Wisse itself serves to remind us of the ways in which prose texts could become adapted to changing audiences over time. Originally conceived for a local, female readership in the early thirteenth century, it became a very different work in later manuscripts as it was adapted to different audiences, and it continued to be copied in various forms until the end of the fifteenth century. The earlier, implied audience of enclosed anchoresses ('ancren') becomes wider in later versions. One late fourteenth-century one, Cambridge, Magdalene College MS Pepys 2498, addresses itself specifically to 'men & wymmen', while others make no gender specification at all.

Ancrene Wisse also reveals the tendencies to excerption I have already noted. For example, two manuscripts, British Library Royal 8. C. i and Cambridge, Gonville and Caius College 234/120, contain only selected forms of the longer work. And certain sections seem to have achieved a separate identity. One, for example, appears both as part of the devotional treatise, *The Chastising of God's Children*, and in an early printed version of Richard Rolle's *Emendatio vitae* (Edwards 2003b). Few works can demonstrate such a sustained appeal and remarkable adaptability over time.

Religious prose works seem to have been particularly susceptible to processes of adaptation and selective redeployment. One need only think of the longer and shorter forms of Julian of Norwich's *Revelations* or the different forms of Margery Kempe's autobiography to see how these processes apply to important canonical works (Edwards 1981). Selection could also be the impulse to imitation in some contexts. I have already mentioned Cambridge University Library Ff. I. 6, the so-called 'Findern' manuscript. It includes works by Chaucer, Gower, Lydgate, Hoccleve and others – some, again, in selected forms. In addition, members of the family added a number of lyrics which, since they survive uniquely here, suggest that they were of their own or local composition. Such environments suggest forms of interplay between readers and the works they read that found expression in attempts at literary emulation.

It seems possible that some of the poems or extracts in the Findern manuscript were either composed or copied by women readers. Evidence of more precisely definable gendered or social preoccupations among manuscript readership is not always easy to find except in those instances where a female readership is specified, as in the early manuscripts of the prose devotional work *Ancrene Wisse*, and the related texts of the 'Katherine Group', works clearly conceived for a female anchoritic audience. Certain kinds of devotional collections, particularly of female saints' lives, also seem designed specifically for a female audience. Most of Osbern Bokenham's *Legendys of Hooly Wummen*, written in Suffolk in the early 1440s, specify the female patrons who commissioned them. Other collections of such lives, whether in verse or prose, vary in the degree of explicitness with which they identify their audiences, but can often be shown to have female associations.

Reader Response

Some readers occasionally left clear indications of their responses to what they were reading. A famous instance is one of the manuscripts of Chaucer's *Canterbury Tales*, now Paris, Bibliothèque Nationale fonds anglais 39. This was actually owned by a Frenchman, Jean, comte d'Angoulême, while hostage in England from 1412 to 1445. It contains a number of comments on the relative merits of particular tales in the hand of the scribe, John Duxworth. Either Duxworth or Jean himself seems to have been responsible for the value judgements on various tales that are incorporated into rubrics. The Knight's Tale is characterized as 'valde bona' (very good). Other tales, those of Sir Thopas and the Canon's Yeoman, are held to be 'valde absurda' (very silly). The Monk's Tale is 'valde dolorosa' (very sad). The judgements may be naive, but they provide testimony to some level of feeling about what has been read that seems direct and personal.

Such contemporary forays into forms of literary criticism are relatively rare. But scribes often felt inclined to engage with the texts they were copying in a more localized way. These engagements often took place quite literally in the margins and took the form of direct response to the works they were transcribing. For example, in British Library MS Harley 2251 there occurs a series of extracts from Lydgate's *Fall of Princes* that offer critical comments on women. They are seemingly derived from an exemplar prepared by another fifteenth-century scribe, John Shirley, and the comments attached to them in this manuscript may be copies of his own. The comments reflect quite violent disagreement with the sentiments expressed in his text: 'Pees or ye shall be shent [destroyed]', runs one. The tone is often hard to recover and complicated by the fact that Shirley seems to have known Lydgate himself. Are these perhaps the heavily jocular views of the scribe, addressed playfully to 'his' author? Or does the embodiment of the comments in the text reflect some personal intensity of disagreement? It is not possible to answer such questions with confidence, but the comments offer a rare insight into some kind of direct relationship between text and reader.[1]

Sometimes particular works seem to have generated a wider variety of responses from their readers. This appears to have been the case with Chaucer's *Troilus and Criseyde*. The margins of the manuscripts of it show concerns ranging from the local and explanatory to the significance of actual events in the poem. Sometimes readers sought to clarify hard readings, as in the line 'O soule, lurkynge in this wo, unneste' (4.305), where several manuscripts provide an explanatory gloss to the difficult *unneste*: 'go out of this neste'. On other occasions a reader can seem to respond directly to the emotional effect of the narrative. When Criseyde rebukes Troilus, 'Wol ye the childish jalous contrefete / Now were it worthi that ye were ybete' (3.1168–9), the scribe in one manuscript shows his understanding that her threat to beat Troilus is not to be taken seriously by adding the comment 'ye with a ffether' (Boffey 1995).

Adaptation and Transmission

There are odder responses of this kind. One rather comic example is British Library MS Harley 7333, which contains a copy of Chaucer's *Canterbury Tales*. The manuscript was prepared for, and possibly by, an Augustinian religious house in Leicestershire. Chaucer's religious readers do not seem to have objected very much to the ruder of Chaucer's fabliaux, at least at the level of plot. But particular details seem to have grated on their sensibilities. In the Reeve's Tale, where the narrator announces that Symkyn's

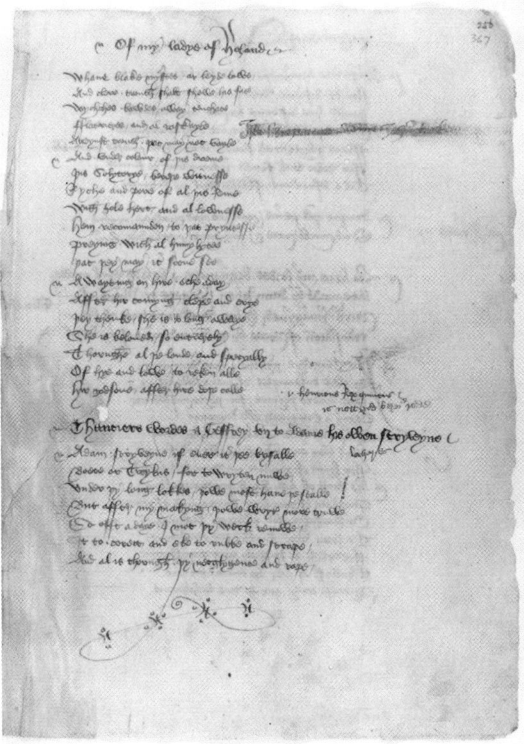

Figure 6.1 The unique text of Chaucer's 'Adam Scriveyn': Trinity College, Cambridge, MS R. 3. 20, p. 367. (By permission of Trinity College Library, Cambridge.)

wife was 'yfostered in a nunnerye' (3946), he has clearly gone too far. In this manuscript 'nunnerye' is changed to 'dairy'.

Such interventions by scribes in the texts they were copying – a process which is itself the subject of a lyric by Chaucer about his scribe, 'Adam Scriveyn' (figure 6.1) – took other forms as well. There is evidence that scribes were disposed to adapt their witnesses to their own preoccupations or those of their audience. For example, a number of the changes in manuscripts of Langland's *Piers Plowman* seem to be the result of the copyist's replacing names in his original with ones from his own experience; in one manuscript the place name 'Winchester' becomes 'Wynchelsey' (Winchelsea) while in another the proper name 'Watte' is replaced by 'bratram' (Bertram).[2] In larger contexts, we have the examples of the spurious ending of Chaucer's *Parliament of Fowls*, as it appears in Bodleian Library MS Arch. Selden. B. 24, seemingly constructed to meet the needs of a courtly Scottish audience; or the various recensions of Lydgate's *Temple of Glas*, in which the text is extensively reshaped, in forms not all certainly by Lydgate himself, to create what are, in effect, different poems to reflect its appropriateness to specific audiences.

In certain genres, notably romance and lyric, the boundary between reader and work is a more permeable one. It is clear that romances were particularly prone to extensive adaptation and expansion as they moved from audience to audience. This is an inevitable consequence of what was, at least in part, oral transmission. Verse romances seem largely to have been composed to be read aloud, or sung. As works transmitted in this way were intermittently written down they reflect the form of the text at its latest performance and therefore reveal local pressures of adaptation, with tendencies to considerable variation. The tendency can be seen in its most extreme form in a popular romance (it survives in six manuscripts) like *Lybeaus Desconus*, where the processes of addition and substitution are striking across the range of witnesses involving, in some manuscripts, the interpolation of lengthy passages.[3] It can be observed in a didactic romance like *Robert of Sicily*, which was also widely popular (there are ten manuscripts) and which produced versions ranging in length from nearly 500 lines to only seventy lines, yet each preserving a coherent version of the narrative (Powell 1998). It was clearly a romance that was seen as being particularly capable of radical reshaping according to the susceptibilities of different audiences. Other long romances, such as *Bevis of Hampton* and *Guy of Warwick*, survive in manuscript and early printed forms so distinctive that their shared identity exists at the level of plot rather than through any close shared verbal relationship. The transmission of verse romance, with its obvious performative constraints, under which texts could be compressed or expanded or otherwise readapted in response to a particular audience, suggests a particularly fluid relationship between manuscript, text and audience.

In other forms, like the lyric, this sense of audience can also become particularly problematic. An example is provided by a religious lyric, which is described, rather tendentiously, by its latest editor as 'An Anchoress's Hymn to the Virgin'.[4] The poem survives in two manuscripts, in one of which it is described as the work of 'an holy Ankeresse of Maunsffeld' (i.e., Mansfield). But in the other it is credited to the canon of John Lydgate, and its high aureate style certainly seems consistent with other of his lyrics (it begins 'Heile glorious Virgine grounde of al oure grace'). The problem admits of no clear-cut resolution; but it reminds us how, particularly for lyrics, we often lack any clear contexts for their composition.

In some instances lyrics can seem to represent in striking ways the 'do-it-yourself' propensity of medieval readers as they constituted new poems out of older materials. One particularly striking instance of this is Richard of Caistre's Hymn.[5] In its fullest form the hymn comprises twelve quatrains, divided into two equal sections; it survives this way in a large number of manuscripts. But it is in itself based on an earlier, shorter lyric, stanzas from which survive in different forms, some as brief as a single stanza, in various fifteenth-century manuscripts. Examples of such selection and adaptation by readers are seen in other forms, in which both class and gender may have had roles. A well-known sixteenth-century example of readerly recycling of earlier poems is the Devonshire manuscript (British Library Additional MS 17492), in the compilation of which a number of courtly ladies were involved, where passages from Chaucer's *Troilus and Criseyde*, from Hoccleve and Sir Richard Roos (copied from Thynne's 1532 edition of Chaucer), are reworked as lyrics to meet the social and amatory purposes of a courtly circle and joined with other lyrics by distinguished contemporary members of their circle, notably Thomas Wyatt and Henry Howard, Earl of Surrey (Seaton 1956). In these environments, a 'text' seems to have been seen as little more than a series of stanzaic blocks, to be excerpted, modified or rearranged according to the predilections of readers.

This difficulty is compounded by the lack of textual stability for the texts of some lyrics. A surprising number of different versions of the 'same' poem can survive, adding or excising stanzas, presumably in ways that reflect forms of occasional adaptability. For example, a recently discovered manuscript of Skelton's lyric 'Manerly Marjery Milk and Ale' includes one completely new stanza in a brief poem.[6] A number of Lydgate's shorter poems survive in extremely variant versions, in ways that suggest that readers saw the texts not as fixed forms but as assemblages of materials to be selected from for their own purposes and possibly expanded by them. Only rarely do authors seem to have been able to retain any firm control over their lyric corpus, as with Hoccleve who, near the end of his life, carefully prepared his own copies of many of his shorter poems. But this was not a foolproof way of proceeding; there is at least one instance where stanzas from his *Male Regle* are excerpted and rewritten to create an entirely different poem.[7] Hoccleve was a professional scribe, who understood better than most authors the practicalities of textual transmission in a manuscript culture. But his experience could not prevent his poem being appropriated in new ways by new readers.

The Middle English Reader

So far this chapter has focused on the relationship between manuscripts, texts and readers and the kinds of ways in which texts were reshaped by and for those who read them. One comes back to the question of readers, those who obtained, read and possibly collected books. The construction of their identity of the books they owned is difficult and uncertain work. Not all early owners signed their books; books that contain the same name turn out not to have the same signature; and where lists of books owned by an individual survive they cannot usually be connected to surviving books.

But occasionally it is possible to establish a little about the reading and collecting of an individual who had a pronounced interest in works relevant to medieval English literature. Such a collector was William Carent (1395–1476) of Ash, Dorset. Carent seems to have had a particular interest in works in English. The most notable among the manuscripts with which he has been associated is a sumptuously illustrated copy of Lydgate's history of the Troy legend, the *Troy Book*, now Manchester, Rylands Library MS Eng.1. He also seems to have had an interest in Chaucer. His will records his ownership of a manuscript of the *Canterbury Tales*, one that cannot now be identified. But he had other more pious interests. His interest in Lydgate extended to his verse life of the Virgin, the *Life of Our Lady*, produced in the south of England c.1470, now New Haven, Beinecke Library MS 281, which contains the family arms. He also owned

British Library MS Additional 11748, the principal content of which is the English version of Walter Hilton's *Scale of Perfection.* This manuscript also contains an inscription on its flyleaf (folio 1) bequeathing 'hunc librum et librum vocatum gratia dei' (this book and the book called the grace of God) to the abbess and convent of Shafton in Dorset. The 'librum vocatum gratia dei' is probably a version of Guillaume de Deguileville's *Pèlerinage de l'âme (The Pilgrimage of the Soul)*, either in French or English. The English version is not infrequently termed 'The Book of Grace Dieu', and the fact that all the other books owned by Carent noted above are in English suggests the likelihood that his copy was too.

All these works were ones with a wide circulation; there are over fifty surviving complete manuscripts of the *Canterbury Tales*, nearly as many of Lydgate's *Life of Our Lady* and Hilton's work, and more than twenty of Lydgate's *Troy Book*. Ten complete copies of *The Pilgrimage of the Soul* are known as well as other extracts from it. Clearly Carent had an interest in popular English works of various kinds, literary, historical and devotional. It is hard to know how representative his literary tastes may have been. But the surviving evidence suggests a degree of coherence in his focus on English works.

In this he provides clear evidence of a response to new literary market forces that had begun to emerge by the early fifteenth century. During the fifteenth century English established itself linguistically as the dominant literary language in England, in contrast to its earlier status as the poor relation of Anglo-Norman and Latin. These market forces were quite specifically concerned with the production of English works by contemporary writers – Chaucer, Gower, Langland and, a little later, Lydgate, Hoccleve and John Walton, among others – to satisfy the demands of new kinds of readers with a growing sense of the cultural value of the vernacular. Commercial structures were created to meet the demands of such readers and from 1476 they were complemented by the new potentiality of print, when the earliest small Caxton quarto volumes of English verse began to appear after he set up his printing-shop in Westminster.

For the next century manuscript and print were to provide parallel potentialities for satisfying the demands of readers. But there were forms of interpenetration between them: printed books were decorated by their owners to look like manuscripts; printed books were copied back into manuscripts; printed books and manuscripts were bound up together; and readers sought works for their libraries in both forms. Such activities blurred the distinction that history has created between the two modes of textual transmission and remind us of the permeability that late medieval culture saw between them. Print was initially simply another way of reading to add to the diversity of forms of manuscript reading we have seen.

See also 3 Religious Authority and Dissent, 5 Women's Voices and Roles, 7 From Manuscript to Modern Text, 9 The Languages of Medieval Britain, 18 Images, 20 Middle English Romance, 23 Lyric, 25 Mystical and Devotional Literature, 26 Accounts of Lives, 30 The *Book of Margery Kempe*, 31 Julian of Norwich, 34 John Gower and John Lydgate, 35 Thomas Hoccleve, 36 The Poetry of Robert Henryson.

Notes

1 For text and discussion see A. S. G. Edwards, 'John Lydgate, Medieval Antifeminism and Harley 2251', *Annuale Medievale* 13 (1973), 32–44.

2 See further, G. Kane (ed.), *The A Version: Will's Visions of Piers Plowman and Do-well* (London: Athlone Press, 1960), p. 137.

3 For details of this variation see Maldwyn Mills, ed., *Lybeaus Desconus*, EETS os 261 (1969).

4 Alexandra Barrett (ed.), *Women's Writing in Middle English* (Harlow: Longman, 1992), pp. 277–9.

5 Carleton Brown (ed.), *Religious Lyrics of the XVth Century* (Oxford: Clarendon Press, 1939), pp. 98–100.

6 A. S. G. Edwards and Linne R. Mooney, 'A New Version of a Skelton Lyric', *Transactions of the Cambridge Bibliographical Society* 10 (1994), 507–10.

7 M. Trudgill and J. A. Burrow, 'A Hocclevean Balade', *Notes and Queries* ns 45 (1998), 178–80.

References and Further Reading

Boffey, Julia 1995. 'Annotation in Some Manuscripts of Troilus and Criseyde.' *English Manuscript Studies 1100–1700* 5, 1–17. Catalogues the poem's range of headings and marginal glosses and discusses the process by which such material accumulated from the activities of scribes and readers.

—— 1996. 'Proverbial Chaucer.' *Huntington Library Quarterly* 58, 37–47. Examines processes of excerption and attribution in relation to a stanza from John Walton's Boethius translation.

—— and Edwards, A. S. G. 1999. 'Literary Texts.' In *The Cambridge History of the Book in Britain*, ed. J. B. Trapp and Lotte Hellinga (Cambridge: Cambridge University Press, 1999), vol. 3, pp. 555–75. A general survey of the circulation of literary texts during this period.

—— and Thompson, John J. 1989. 'Anthologies and Miscellanies.' In Griffiths and Pearsall, pp. 279–315. A study of the construction of collections of texts.

Edwards, A. S. G. 1971. 'Selections from Lydgate's *Fall of Princes*: A Checklist.' *The Library*, 5th ser. 26, 337–42. Identifies and discusses excerpts from Lydgate's poem.

—— 1981. 'Towards an Index of Middle English Prose.' In *Middle English Prose: Essays on Bibliographical Problems*, ed. A. S. G. Edwards and D. Pearsall (New York: Garland), pp. 23–41. Examines some of the ways in which prose texts were excerpted or otherwise reconstituted by readers.

—— 1998. 'Selection and Subversion in Gower's *Confessio Amantis*.' In *Revisioning John Gower: New Essays*, ed. R. F. Yeager (Kalamazoo, Mich.: Medieval Institute Publications, 1998), pp. 257–67. Examines various selections from Gower's poem.

—— 2003a. 'Fifteenth-Century English Collections of Female Saints' Lives.' *Yearbook of English Studies* 33 (2003), 131–41. Assesses evidence for the audiences of Middle English female saints' lives.

—— 2003b. 'The Manuscripts.' In *A Companion to the Ancrene Wisse*, ed. Yoko Wada (Cambridge: Boydell and Brewer), pp. 103–14. A consideration of the audiences for this widely circulating prose devotional work.

Griffiths, Jeremy 1983. '*Confessio Amantis*: The Poem and its Pictures.' In *Gower's Confessio Amantis: Responses and Reassessments*, ed. A. J. Minnis (Cambridge: Boydell and Brewer, 1983), pp. 163–77. An examination of the illustrations in Gower's poem.

—— and Derek Pearsall (eds) 1989. *Book Production and Publishing in Britain, 1375–1475*. Cambridge: Cambridge University Press. The most comprehensive account of manuscript culture in late medieval Britain.

Lawton, Lesley 1983. 'The Illustration of Late Medieval Secular Texts, with Special Reference to Lydgate's *Troy Book.*' In Pearsall 1983: 41–69. Considers the functions of illustration in some Middle English works.

Pearsall, Derek (ed.) 1983. *Manuscripts and Readers in Fifteenth-Century England.* Cambridge: Boydell and Brewer. An important series of studies of medieval readership in relation to literary texts.

Powell, Stephen D. 1998. 'Multiplying Textuality: Generic Migration in the Manuscripts of *Robert of Sicily.*' *Anglia* 116, 171–97. An analysis of the various manuscript forms of this pious romance.

Scott, Kathleen L. 1982. 'Lydgate's Lives of Saints Edmund and Fremund: A Newly Located Manuscript in Arundel Castle.' *Viator* 13, 335–66. An examination of an important series of illustrated saints' lives.

—— 1989. '*Caveat lector*: Ownership and Standardization in the Illustration of Fifteenth-Century English Manuscripts.' *English Manuscript Studies 1100–1700* 1, 19–63. A study of the ways in which owners of manuscripts imposed their identities on them.

Seaton, Ethel 1956. 'The Devonshire Manuscript and its Medieval Fragments.' *Review of English Studies* ns 7, 55–6. Identifies selections from various Middle English poems in this manuscript.

Silvia, D. S. 1974. 'Some Fifteenth-Century Manuscripts of the *Canterbury Tales.*' In *Chaucer and Middle English Studies*, ed. B. Rowland (London: Allen and Unwin, 1974), pp. 153–63. Considers the manuscript evidence for the popularity of particular Tales.

7
From Manuscript to Modern Text

Julia Boffey

Many changes have taken place since the Middle Ages in the forms in which texts were produced and the processes by which they were communicated to audiences. While much concerning these changes remains irrecoverable for modern readers and scholars, we can none the less attempt some understanding of their possible significance. This chapter will attempt to reconstruct what can be known about the circumstances of textual production and reception in England in the late Middle Ages in order to pinpoint some of these significant changes, and it will ask what implications such circumstances may have for the ways in which later Middle English texts were and are experienced and understood.[1]

Manuscript Culture

Until the mid-fifteenth century England, like the rest of the Western world, was a manuscript culture: one in which the written word was committed by hand onto a writing surface (the Latin *manuscriptum* derives from *manu*, by hand, and *scriptum*, written). The technology of printing with movable type was not introduced into Europe until the second half of the fifteenth century, and not established in England until 1476 (Hellinga 1982). Before then each book was a unique product, copied by one or more scribes, and unlikely to be replicated in significant numbers. Book production in these circumstances was labour-intensive and costly, even before processes of decoration and binding.[2] Parchment or paper had to be prepared, inks and pens made; copying probably took place on single sheets which would be folded into 'quires' (constituent gatherings of leaves for the book) only once the pages had been filled. Flourishing and rubrication might then be added, with further levels of decoration, illumination and illustration according to the quality of product desired (Alexander 1992; de Hamel 1992, Shailor 1989). Binding was generally left to the owner or purchaser of a manuscript, and was only rarely an integral part of a book's production.

The item generated by these processes could differ in a number of respects from modern conceptions of a 'book': it might never be bound, or it might be bound with several other manuscripts; it might grow, as other items were added in blank spaces or on extra leaves; it would probably lack a title of any recognizable sort; and it would be unlikely to possess any of the reader aids we now expect. Because the separate stages of production were rarely integrated, some might be omitted or unfinished: many medieval manuscripts have blank spaces for decoration or illumination that was never completed. The fifteenth-century book which is now London, British Library MS Royal 17. D. vi illustrates some of the means by which a volume could grow. It began life as a selection of the poems of Thomas Hoccleve (c.1366–1426), copied by a single scribe, and including a presentation miniature and a marginal drawing of Geoffrey Chaucer at the point in *The Regiment of Princes* where his name and image are invoked (figure 7.1).[3] At some point after its production, coats of arms were added to these illumina-

Figure 7.1 Presentation scene with Thomas Hoccleve (kneeling) in the act of offering his book to Henry V, from Hoccleve's *Regiment of Princes*: London, British Library, MS Royal 17 D. VI, folio 40. (By permission of the British Library.)

tions on behalf of the book's owners. Later still, a variety of shorter texts were appended by different hands on blank leaves at the start and end of the Hoccleve anthology. The many personal names copied informally onto the opening leaves of the manuscript suggest that it passed through the hands of several fifteenth- and early sixteenth-century readers before reaching the owner who donated it to the royal library.[4]

Authorship

Typically, medieval manuscripts contain very little information about authors. Sometimes a scribe may add a note commenting on a work's origins, or attributing it to a named figure, but very often this information is absent. Authors' identities, and the nature of their relationships to works which were copied, seem not always to have mattered, and the notion of compiling a book from an author's 'collected works' was not a familiar one in the Middle Ages (Root 1913). A small number of manuscripts contain an author's own copy of his work and are therefore what is known as autograph copies or holographs, but more often than not authors seem to have preferred to employ scribes. The works of the Augustinian canons Orrm (*fl.* c.1170) and John Capgrave (1393–1464), together with those of Hoccleve, are among the few substantial bodies of Middle English literary writing to survive in holograph.[5] While the involvement of scribes as intermediaries in the processes of transmission may have saved authors some time and labour, it could bring other problems. Chaucer famously castigated a scribe named Adam for his unreliable copying of authorial exemplars (figure 6.1), ruing the amount of time spent on correction: 'So ofte adaye I mot thy werk renewe, / It to correcte and eke to rubbe and scrape' ('Chaucers wordes unto Adam, his owne scriveyn', 5–6).

Scribal carelessness or interference, along with a general insouciance about textual authority, did little to promote authorial status in relation to medieval texts. The notion of the author as a construct would not have seemed in any way strange to the Middle Ages. The production of texts in a manuscript culture in fact accommodates a wide range of possible relationships between author and reader. The early audiences of Hoccleve's autograph collections, probably acquaintances to whom the copies were presented as gifts, would bring a very intimate knowledge of the 'author' and his circumstances to their responses to his writing, just as listening audiences who heard an author recite his own works (perhaps in contexts similar to that famously created by the artist of the frontispiece to one manuscript of Chaucer's *Troilus and Criseyde*)[6] would have a very special sense of authorial presence. But in other situations, authors may have seemed far more remote. When the anonymous author of *Sir Gawain and the Green Knight* refers to the romances he regards as analogues to his own poem, he writes not of authored works but of the material forms in which these have (presumably anonymously) been available to him, 'stori stif and stronge / With lel letters loken' ('powerful stories, [set down] in loyal, linked letters', 33–4), and Thomas Malory's many references to the French books from which he drew the matter of the *Morte Darthur* (completed c.1469) do not specify authors.[7]

If the senses of 'author' were variable, so too, of course, were the meanings of 'audiences'. An author writing for a particular dedicatee or patron, perhaps with an eye to some kind of reward, might have narrowly limited expectations about the critical reception of his work: the suppositions made by John Lydgate (c.1370–1449) about the reception of *The Fall of Princes*, an enormous compendium of exemplary stories written for Humphrey, Duke of Gloucester, are closely tied to his understanding of Humphrey's interests, and to the progress of his relationship with a figure from whom he hoped for benevolence and support.[8] Works like the *Confessio Amantis* of John Gower (1330?–1408), dedicated and rededicated to successive English kings and undertaken 'for Engelondes sake' (Prologue, 24), seem to anticipate an audience close to their author in time and preoccupation.[9] But occasionally it is possible to glimpse an authorial sense of a more distant posterity and of audiences whose understanding is not necessarily going to replicate that of the close-knit circle of actual or implied early readers. The narrator of Chaucer's *Troilus and Criseyde*, while careful to cultivate the 'yonge fresshe folkes' constructed as the poem's audience (5.1835 ff.), none the less considers the possibility that the work may be 'red . . . or elles songe (5.1797) in more distant future contexts, and worries about the uncomprehending nature of unknown audiences. For a later author like John Skelton (c.1460–1529), who could envisage publication in both manuscript and printed form, the possibilities of communicating beyond an immediate circle were obviously striking: his *Garland of Laurel* explores some of the implications of authorial fame and posterity.[10]

Because autograph manuscripts survive in such small numbers, and explicit comments on the physical processes involved in authorship hardly at all, it is difficult to reconstruct much about the ways in which medieval texts came into being. Some authors may have worked at rough drafts on wax tablets or scraps of parchment or paper, and there is a little surviving evidence of 'work in progress' of this kind.[11] Others may have dictated to scribes or indeed simply have carried their 'works' in their memories for oral recitation: this form of composition might have been especially common in relation to lyrics and other performable works, and in these cases such copies as survive may simply represent the accident of someone having decided to commit the 'text' to written form. For works like plays, the notion of single 'authorship' anyway needs redefinition. In these cases several 'authors' may have brought into being a 'text' whose essential life was realized in performance. The 'Book' of Margery Kempe (c.1343–after 1438) presents another conundrum about authorship, since Margery herself seems to have been largely illiterate, and to have 'composed' an account of her experiences only with the help of amanuenses who may also have acted as editors.[12]

Reading and Other Forms of Reception

Just as hard to define as the circumstances in which works were 'authored' are the ways in which they reached readers or 'audiences'. Plays are again an obvious example: few of the citizens of York or other major English cities which mounted civic cycles of religious (or mystery) plays can have had much sense of or even interest in the written forms in which the performances they saw were recorded.[13] Many romances also make reference to what seem to be conventions of oral performance. 'Herkneth to me, gode men, / Wives, maidens, and alle men, / Of a tale that ich you wile telle', and 'Litheth and lestneth and herkneth aright / And ye shull here a talking of a doughty knight' are typical of the way in which many begin.[14] Fictional episodes such as that in *Troilus and Criseyde* which depicts Criseyde with her ladies listening to a reading of the story of *The Siege of Thebes* (2.78–112) indicate that listening must have been a skill as much if not more practised than reading.

'Performability' may be suggested by matters such as the content and generic affiliations of a particular work. The anonymous early comic story *Dame Sirith*, for example, surviving in a single late thirteenth-century manuscript (Oxford, Bodleian Library MS Digby 86*),[15] involves dialogue and other features suggestive of dramatic performance.[16] In other cases, indications from the surviving written copies can offer some evidence. Chaucer's *Parliament of Fowls*, to take one example, a Valentine's Day dream poem which includes a debate in which many birds argue about a question of love, may well have been performed. The written copies (all of which are in manuscripts produced after Chaucer's death in 1400) do not introduce it as a performance of any kind, but they do in different ways all blur the nature of the song which finally establishes harmony between the birds and brings the dream to a close, as if the 'text' for this was never available in any clear form to a scribe.[17] In contrast, there are other instances in which the songs are the only fragments to survive in written form from longer performances which must have followed some notional script: 'ballades' from the 'sotelties' or pageants which served as entertainments at large-scale ceremonial banquets were sometimes copied into accounts which preserve otherwise only sketchy narratives of the contexts in which the poems played a role.[18]

Instances such as these remind us that surviving written copies of medieval texts may inscribe only a fraction of the meaning that certain works had for their earliest audiences. Responses like laughter, intakes of breath or knowing glances are unlikely to be recorded for posterity in written form. These are aspects of meaning which cannot possibly be concretized and at a chronological distance can only be matters of speculation (unless, as on rare occasions, they have been preserved in the form of personal accounts, such as Jean Froissart's record of his readings of *Meliador* to Gaston Phebus, Conte de Foix).[19] In contrast, the material aspects of medieval books are often revealing, suggestive of a number of kinds of 'value'. Some of these might be relatively straightforward to interpret: a book-owner of means would want an appropriately distinguished copy of an important work, such as a psalter or an apocalypse, and would be prepared to pay for the costly materials that would go into the making of a large, beautifully written, illuminated manuscript. Book producers might see the commercial attraction of promoting new works, and it has been suggested that an editorial team may have sponsored the production of copies of the *Canterbury Tales* after Chaucer's death in 1400 (Stevens and Woodward 1997). A book intended as a gift might be designed specifically for the tastes of the recipient, the costliness of its production reflecting the degree of respect or gratitude which its donor wished to express. Froissart's account of the preparation of a book of his own lyrics for presentation to Richard II in England in 1390 reports in telling detail the exquisite workmanship: 'it was illuminated, nicely written and illustrated, with a cover of crimson velvet with ten studs of silver gilt and golden roses in the middle and two large gilded clasps richly worked at their centres with golden rose-trees'. The king was impressed by the gift, and took it to his private chamber to scrutinize its delights.[20]

The labour-intensiveness of the processes of book production, along with the cost of the materials involved, inevitably meant that books were fairly precious objects: not only were they good gifts for the purposes of those bent on conspicuous generosity, but they also often figured in inventories of valuable possessions and as disposable property in wills (Rosenthal 1982). They could, in these contexts, signify meanings which had little necessary connection with the texts they contained. Leaving a book to a relative could be as much a statement about family piety as a commendation of the book's contents. And in some cases, books may have been desirable *objets de luxe*, fashionable accessories which signified the owner's prestige and up-to-the-minute tastes: the numbers of surviving illustrated apocalypse manuscripts, and of illustrated copies of the *Roman de la rose*, suggest that these may have among the favourite 'display' volumes. But appearance was not everything, or at least not in every context. The dreamer-narrator of Chaucer's *Parliament of Fowls* reads the highly influential and intellectually prestigious 'Dream of Scipio' in a battered and perhaps well-thumbed copy, an 'olde bok totorn' (110); Hoccleve and the friend who features in his 'Dialogue' borrow and lend books in order to discuss their contents rather than their material worth. The cultural value of books which preserve authoritative texts from former ages is stated powerfully in the Prologue to Chaucer's *Legend of Good Women* ('yf that olde bokes were aweye, / Yloren were of remembraunce the keye', F25–6), and the potential of books and written records in other, more politically charged, contexts is reviewed in the alliterative poem *Mum and the Sothsegger*.[21]

Modes of Manuscript Production

The variety of forms of author–audience relationship in the Middle Ages is matched by a similar range of methods of book production. The most straightforward model, that of the holograph manuscript, seems to have been less in evidence than its obvious advantages might suggest, presumably because most authors were not trained scribes. Hoccleve's expertise, gained from his training as a Privy Seal clerk, was unusual, and even he periodically complains about the physical discomforts of close work (see the Prologue to *The Regiment of Princes*, 967–1022). The next most straightforward model of production is that involving one scribe copying one or more texts from one or more exemplars or copy-texts, a process that could take place in both private and commercial contexts. The copy of the *Canterbury Tales* which is now Glasgow, Hunterian Library MS U. 1. 1. (197), seems to be an example of domestic production of this kind, largely copied by one Thomas Spirleng for his own and his father's use, and other survivals indicate that it became an increasingly popular mode of book production throughout the fifteenth century. A Yorkshire gentleman named Robert Thornton produced two books by this method, seemingly aiming at companion volumes of romances and pious materials (the manuscripts are now BL Additional 31042 and Lincoln Cathedral 91*; another individual named Rate copied a number of romances for a volume whose careful editing and bowdlerization suggest that it may have been for family use.[22] It is often difficult to identify the extent to which single-scribe productions of this kind were the fruit of private or of commercial impulses, particularly in contexts such as that of a large household, where a clerk might have copied a book to order without any record of payment. But in certain cases it is clear that individual scribes were employed for payment on specific projects: the accounts which the scribe William Ebesham submitted for copying undertaken on behalf of members of the Paston family are still in existence.[23]

The appearance of several different scribal hands in a manuscript does not automatically mean that a book must have been commercially produced, since a number of modes of informal production might have involved collaboration. Household contexts are again important here, since they provided environments in which exemplars could be sought and exchanged, and in which ready labour might be available from a multiplicity of scribes, both trained and amateur. The so-called 'Findern manuscript' (Cambridge University Library Ff. 1. 6*) has been described as the product of informal local collaboration of this kind, with different hands supplying romances, extracts from Gower's *Confessio Amantis* and Chaucer's works, and a number of lyrics on various subjects; and Aberystwyth, National Library of Wales MS Porkington 10, a collection with a homelier and more pious flavour, could have similar origins.[24] In an urban environment, neighbours with common interests could organize themselves into loose collaborations of the sort which produced what have been called 'common-profit books', selections of edifying texts copied in a number of different hands for local circulation.[25] The processes involved here replicate some features of what has been called the 'pecia system', a mode of production by which university students replicated copies of their set texts: like the men involved in making common-profit books, these students had shared interests and the proximity conferred by urban living.

Even in the context of the increasingly important and profitable metropolitan book-trade, the production of copies of literary texts appears to have remained a fluid business. Structures of commercial book production were not the highly organized *scriptoria* made up of copyists housed together in business premises which have sometimes been imagined, but instead much more loosely assorted collaborations between individuals who did piece-work in their own homes (Christianson 1999; Doyle and Parkes 1978). The role of a stationer who commissioned a volume (either because it had been requested from him by a client, or because he wished to put it on speculative sale) might have been to line up freelance contributors and supply them with materials and copy, rather than to house them directly and oversee their work. The suitability of the increasingly prevalent 'booklet' mode of manuscript production, by which individual scribes worked on groups of gatherings which would form self-contained booklets within a larger compilation, probably matched these patterns of labour organization quite effectively.

The physical processes of manuscript construction and some of these methods of scribal organization have interesting implications for the production of literary texts. Just as a number of books were 'compilations' which drew together various texts and bits of texts copied by various scribes (Parkes 1976), so too a number of Middle English works seem conceived as loose collections of smaller units: the *Canterbury Tales* (called, not insignificantly, 'The book of the tales of canterbury', in some of its early manuscripts) and the *Legend of Good Women*; Gower's *Confessio Amantis*; Hoccleve's 'Series'; Charles of Orleans's collection of love poems.[26] And, conversely, some short poems seem to have circulated in groups, of a standard size to fill a gathering or a booklet, where context might offer a prompt to interpretation. Some of Chaucer's lyrics and shorter poems were transmitted in this way, loosely associated with other texts of similar lengths and with preoccupations such as Sir John Clanvowe's *The Cuckoo and the Nightingale* and Hoccleve's translation of Christine de Pizan's *Epistre de Cupide*.[27] The notion that distinct scribal hands, or separate gatherings or booklets, might suggest a number of 'voices' in a book is not one to press too far, but it is perhaps worth acknowledging.

Print Culture

A printed book clearly offers its reader an experience very different from that held out by a manuscript. Printed letters are more uniform than those produced by hand, and a printed book generally gives a sense of having been produced as a whole, without the variation in scribal hand or hands usually detectable in a manuscript. One reader's copy of a certain book will look pretty much like another reader's copy of that same printed edition, without the variation that is inevitable in manuscript books, even those which result from some attempt at mass production. A printed book is more likely to be a defined entity, with a clear beginning and end, than a manuscript is (in this latter case many changes and adaptations may have been made after the initial stage of copying). And it retains fewer material signs of the individuals who have contributed to its production: here are no holograph copies, no scribal notes (unless in the form of marginal annotations by later readers), although there may be some kind of printer's mark, or a printed colophon which gives details of the printer's name and premises.

It is hard to imagine the responses of fifteenth-century readers encountering printed books for the first time. Much has been written about readers' feelings that printing somehow devalued or cheapened the written word, and about their lingering preferences for finely produced manuscript books (Bühler 1960; Hindman and Farquar 1977; Eisenstein 1979/1983). But as products of cutting-edge new technology, printed books must have had a certain cachet and desirability, and the evidence of importations and purchases suggests that discriminating book-buyers were certainly keen to acquire them in some numbers. The two processes of production were in fact to co-exist for some centuries. Manuscript circulation became more generally confined to certain categories of text, and to particular milieux, while printing established itself as the swiftest and most economically viable method of disseminating texts in large numbers: school books, law books, books associated with the processes of sixteenth-century religious reform, for example.

Much more obviously and usually than is the case with manuscripts, printing foregrounds individual texts as commodities and encourages elision of any distinction between 'book' and 'work': the availability from a printer of large numbers of copies of, for instance, Lydgate's *Temple of Glas* or Chaucer's *Troilus and Criseyde* endows each of those two texts with a distinct existence that is harder to apprehend when they circulate in manuscript copies with other texts or (as sometimes) in fragmentary form. Something of the form of the manuscript compilation may have been retained for those readers who bound numbers of printed texts together into single volumes, but in general it seems likely that printing promoted a keener understanding of textual integrity than would have existed in a purely manuscript culture. Such printed compilations as were made also enjoyed an existence different from one-off manuscript anthologies: Tottel's *Songes and Sonettes* or 'Miscellany' of 1557 (*STC* 13860–8) and the later *Paradise of Dainty Devises* (*STC* 7516–21) have a fixity which is not anticipated in any manuscript anthologies of Middle English verse.

The impulse to collect together and contain within a single volume the works of an individual author seems also to have developed as print culture established itself (Edwards 2000a). Few surviving Middle English manuscripts attempt this in any significant way: the early Chaucer collection which is now Cambridge University Library MS Gg. 4. 27* (containing the *Canterbury Tales*, *Troilus and Criseyde* and some of Chaucer's minor poems) seems to have been a one-off, and holograph manuscripts like Hoccleve's collections of his own works have a special status.[28] Not until 1526, and Richard Pynson's printing of three separate volumes containing Chaucerian and other verse (*STC* 5086, 5088, 5096), does any significant attempt seem to have been made to define Chaucer's *oeuvre*. But by the 1530s the large, printed single-author collection seems to have been a recognizable commodity: Godfray's printed edition of Chaucer's works (edited for him by William Thynne; *STC* 5068) was followed by later printings of the collected works of authors such as More (*STC* 18076) and Skelton (*STC* 22608).

Textual Transmission

The replication of texts in a manuscript culture depends on the successive copyings and recopyings of numbers of scribes whose efforts in the processes of transmission may be likened to the ripples spreading from a stone thrown into water – an analogy also used of the movement of sound by the eagle who instructs the dreamer-narrator of Chaucer's *House of Fame* (782–822). The processes by which a compositor or a team of compositors prepare pages of type for a printed book, 'setting' from copy-text which might take the form of a manuscript or another printed book, leave open similar possibilities for variation and change, although in this context the ripple effect will be a factor only if the text goes through a number of editions which necessitate new settings of type. But both compositors and scribes were likely to introduce variants of different kinds into their own versions of the texts they copied. Some of these are likely to be mechanical errors in writing or setting type: transposing letters or mistakenly writing or choosing one letter in place of another. Some might relate to omission or to the copyist losing his place: eyeskip. Still other variants stem from uncertainty – points, for example, where a scribe or compositor has had to guess a reading because his copy was illegible or damaged – and sometimes from ingenuity, where a scribe or compositor has introduced a new reading on the supposition that it improves on what is in his exemplar. In some cases the changes introduced can be of considerable scale and impact: a scribe who 'translates' a Middle English text into his own dialect as he copies it, for example, can change its flavour in a radical way; a copyist or a compositor who decides to edit his copy, perhaps by dividing it into headed sections or by glossing it, can make it into something significantly new.

Reconstructions of the processes by which Middle English texts were transmitted are taking increasing account of the range of possible kinds of scribal or other intervention. Recent work on the *Ancrene Wisse*, for instance – an early Middle English prose treatise for anchoresses which survives in a number of manuscripts in a number of different forms – points to some continuum of overlapping functions in which both author and successive different scribes were implicated in the forging of variants between the different copies, as revisions and adaptations of the text were made for new audiences and new purposes (Millett 1994). Similar processes of dynamic transmission are characteristic of forms like romance, where interventions such as those of the bowdlerizing scribe Rate (see above) have complicated the textual history of works like the *Erl of Tolous*.

Different degrees of scribal intervention can produce variant forms or sometimes what are more properly described as new versions or adaptations of the works from which they originated (the French term *remaniement* has proved useful to textual critics searching to define some of these rehandlings). The scribe of one manuscript of the prose text known as *The Three Kings of Cologne* (now in London, British Library MS Additional 36983) adapted a number of its concluding chapters so that their initial letters would, when read in sequence, produce the name 'THOMAS', so generating a variant form of the 'standard' text.[29] The comprehensive makeover which William Caxton gave Malory's *Morte Darthur* when he decided to print it in 1485 (*STC* 801) constitutes editorial intervention and generates a new version. Collation with the text in the single surviving manuscript, discovered in the library of Winchester School only in 1934 (and now London, British Library MS Additional 59678*), has demonstrated that the preparation of the printed edition involved substantial modernization and the division of the text into separately headed chapters.[30]

Instances such as these illustrate just a few of the many forms of variation which were made possible, even perhaps encouraged, by the circumstances of textual transmission in the medieval period. The fluid medieval conception of authorship, largely untrammelled by notions of plagiarism or copyright, allowed for forms of borrowing, adaptation and rewriting which often render superfluous the notion that a particular text may originate with one specific author. Other possibilities of reformulation were brought about by the scribal replication of texts and the multiple considerations which might influence a scribe to change the form of what he copied. The peculiarly unfixed nature of the texts generated and transmitted in this culture was explored by the French medievalist Paul Zumthor as *mouvance*, a quality of flexibility characteristic of the shifting forms of medieval texts (Zumthor 1972).

Reconstructing Texts for Modern Readers

Mouvance is relatively hard to accommodate in the production of usable scholarly editions of medieval texts, and it has not been widely acknowledged until comparatively recently in textual scholarship. This has tended to follow long-established procedures, assuming that the 'original' version of any text, that closest to the author if not his autograph, has some claim to special correctness and authority, even though, as we have seen, the existence of scribes like Chaucer's Adam meant that this was not necessarily always the case. Each subsequent act of copying, it is usually supposed, is likely to introduce errors of various kinds and gradually to 'corrupt' the author's words; and traditional textual criticism (following nineteenth-century precedents for the editing of classical texts) has seen its job as that of restoring the author's words as closely as possible to their original forms in order faithfully to reflect her or his 'intentions'. Much of the apparatus supplied to readers of nineteenth- and twentieth-century editions of Middle English texts has concerned itself primarily with textual matters: bodies of textual variants, analyses of the habits and preferences of particular scribes, and classification of the kinds of error they were likely to make; and diagrams of the relationships between different manuscripts and of the 'genealogy' of particular texts.

Modern editions of Middle English texts have for the most part (at least until recently) been produced within a traditional frame of reference (Edwards 2000b; Machan 1994). They might be 'critical' or 'best-text', establishing a text on the basis of recension, that is through critical assessment of the relationship between the different witnesses or surviving forms. Editions of this kind take account of variants, and of material evidence relating to the date of production of the different witnesses and the relationship of these to the presumed original, and use the evidence to deduce which witness is 'best', or closest to a putative original. The edition will reproduce largely what is in this witness except at points where there seem compelling grounds for emendation to forms from the corpus of variants preserved in the other witnesses. Single-text editions, in contrast, offer a text based on what has been preserved in only one of a range of available witnesses, and are likely to take little account of matters such as variants. N. F. Blake's edition of the *Canterbury Tales*, for example, reproduces only what is in the Hengwrt manuscript (Aberystwyth, National Library of Wales MS Peniarth 392), without reference to the so-called Ellesmere manuscript (San Marino, California, Huntington Library MS EL 26 C 9*) which has been the basis of other modern scholarly editions.[31] 'Eclectic' editions do not establish a base text or follow a single manuscript, but instead attempt a synthesis of material from all surviving witnesses, in the hope that the best sense can be generated from the widest possible number of sources.

Important criteria governing the decisions made by a would-be editor relate both to the nature of the work to be edited and to the readership for which the edition is to be prepared. An edition of a work surviving in multiple copies and in a number of different forms, such as Gower's *Confessio Amantis*, obviously involves more complex editorial work than an edition of a work which has been preserved in only one witness, like *Sir Gawain and the Green Knight* and its companion poems in London, British Library MS Cotton Nero A. x*. Matters like the modernization of orthography (relating especially to obsolete forms like thorn and yogh, or to –i- and –y-), punctuation, the provision of glosses and explanatory notes, and the presence of an editorial apparatus including variants and textual notes, will all be matters determined by the audience expected for the edition. The principles followed in J. A. Burrow's edition of *Sir Gawain and the Green Knight* for Penguin Books, aimed at a wide general readership, are clearly different from those in the same editor's *Book of Middle English*, prepared for undergraduate users, and different again from those followed in his experimental parallel text of the poems making up Hoccleve's *Series* for the scholarly purposes of the Early English Text Society.[32] And an edition like Peter Meredith's *Mary Play*, which aims both to justify extracting one sequence of plays from the N-Town cycle and to discuss possible features of its original performance, is in effect much more a contextualizing study than an edition.[33]

Both the theory and practices of textual criticism are continually evolving. In some instances, the discovery of new witnesses, or more exhaustive study of existing witnesses, can necessitate revision of what has been established by existing scholarship. This has been the case with the different versions of *Piers Plowman*, extended relatively recently from the sequence of A-, B- and C-texts to accommodate the complication of a further Z-text.[34] Other new initiatives have constructed texts on experimental editorial principles, such as for example the collaborative efforts to produce authorial versions of Hoccleve's poems by 'translating' those of his writings which have not been preserved in holograph into forms consistent with those he did employ.[35] Electronic editions can go still further, making available images of all the witnesses of any particular text, or exploiting hypertext links to make variant texts simultaneously visible and allow readers to edit for themselves. Recent developments in digital imaging are bringing ever closer the point where readers can go electronically straight to facsimiles of all the witnesses of any work in which they may be interested, thus in part recreating the reading experience of those who first consulted the manuscripts or early printed books in which the work was recorded.

Back to Manuscripts?

What special benefits are there in consulting manuscripts and early books directly, or in the form of the increasingly faithful reproductions made possible by advancing technology? At the most obvious level, the material forms in which early works have been preserved remind us of their alterity, and thus prompt the various processes of historicizing imagination and research which can enhance our understanding. These processes involve scrutiny of many different aspects of material presentation: studying the programmes of illustration in manuscripts of the *Roman de la rose*, or the arrangement of large capitals which seem to indicate significant divisions of the text of Malory's *Morte Darthur*, or the annotations noted by a scribe in the margins of a text he copied. But they are all aspects of meaning which are likely to be hidden from the reader who relies simply on a modern edition. To understand even a little of the gap between early witnesses and the modern forms in which we may know any work is also to begin to comprehend the crucial role that successive readers and editors may have played in directing its interpretation.

See also: 6 Manuscripts and Readers, 18 Images, 20 Middle English Romance, 27 Medieval English Theatre, 29 York Mystery Plays, 30 The *Book of Margery Kempe*, 32 *Piers Plowman*, 33 The *Canterbury Tales*, 34 John Gower and John Lydgate, 35 Thomas Hoccleve, 38 Malory's *Morte Darthur*.

Notes

1 These matters are explored in relation to French texts by such works as Febvre and Martin 1958, and Martin, Chartier and Vivet 1982, and discussed in relation to English books by McKenzie 1986, Griffiths and Pearsall 1989, and Hellinga and Trapp 1999.

2 The costs are not easy to compute. A scribe who worked for the Norfolk Paston family in the fifteenth century charged 1d. for each leaf he copied; a large, bound and splendidly illuminated mass book cost Abbot Litlington over £27 in 1384 (Bell 1937).

3 For Hoccleve's poems, see Charles Blyth (ed.), *Thomas Hoccleve: The Regiment of Princes* (Kalamazoo, Mich.: Medieval Institute Publications for TEAMS, 1999) and F. J. Furnivall and I. Gollancz (eds), *Hoccleve's Works*, 2 vols, EETS es 61 (1892) and 73 (1897), revised in one volume by A. I. Doyle and J. Mitchell (1970); J. A. Burrow and A. I Doyle (intro.), *Thomas Hoccleve: A Facsimile of the Autograph Verse Manuscripts*, EETS ss 19.

4 See M. C. Seymour, 'The Manuscripts of Hoccleve's *Regiment of Princes*', *Edinburgh Bibliographical Society Transactions* 4.7 (1974), 255–97.

5 Orrm's series of verse homilies synthesizing Gospel accounts of the life of Christ survives in Oxford, Bodleian Library MS Junius 1, and is discussed by M. B. Parkes, 'On the Presumed Date and Possible Origin of the Manuscript of the *Ormulum*', in *Five Hundred Years of Words and Sounds: A Festschrift for Eric Dobson*, ed. Eric G. Stanley and Douglas Gray (Cambridge: Brewer, 1983), pp. 115–27. Capgrave's manuscripts are reviewed by Peter J. Lucas, *From Author to Audience: John Capgrave and Medieval Publication* (Dublin: University College Dublin Press, 1997), and those of Hoccleve by Seymour, 'Manuscripts', and J. A. Burrow, *Thomas Hoccleve*, Authors of the Middle Ages, 4 (Aldershot: Variorum, 1994).

6 Reproduced in many contexts: see Elizabeth Salter and M. B. Parkes, introduction, *Troilus and Criseyde: A Facsimile of Corpus Christi College, Cambridge, MS 61* (Cambridge: Brewer, 1978) and Kathleen L. Scott, *Later Gothic Manuscripts, 1390–1490*, 2 vols (London: Harvey Miller Publishers, 1996), II, 182–5.

7 *Sir Gawain and the Green Knight*, ed. J. R. R. Tolkien and E. V. Gordon, 2nd edn ed. Norman Davies (Oxford: Clarendon Press,

1967); Terence McCarthy, 'Malory and his Sources', in *A Companion to Malory*, ed. Elizabeth Archibald and A. S. G. Edwards (Cambridge: Brewer, 1996), pp. 75–95.

8 *The Fall of Princes*, ed. H. Bergen, 4 vols, EETS es 121–4 (1924–7).

9 *The English Works of John Gower*, ed. G. C. Macaulay, 2 vols, EETS es 81 and 82 (1900–1).

10 *John Skelton: The Complete English Poems*, ed. J. Scattergood (Harmondsworth: Penguin, 1983), pp. 312–58.

11 Michelle Brown, 'The Role of Wax Tablets in Medieval Literacy: A Reconsideration in the Light of a Recent Find at York', *British Library Journal* 20 (1994), 1–16.

12 Barry Windeatt (ed.), *The Book of Margery Kempe* (Harlow: Longman, 2000).

13 Richard Beadle, 'The York Cycle: Texts, Performances, and the Bases for Critical Enquiry', in *Medieval Literature: Texts and Interpretation*, ed. Tim William Machan (Binghamton: State University of New York at Binghamton, 1991), pp. 105–19.

14 *Havelok the Dane* and *Gamelyn*, in *Middle English Verse Romances*, ed. Donald B. Sands (New York: Holt, Rinehart, and Winston, 1966), pp. 55–129, 154–81.

15 *All asterisked manuscripts can be consulted in facsimile reproductions, of which details are supplied by R. Beadle in McCarren and Moffat 1998: 319–81.

16 The text survives in Oxford, Bodleian Library MS Digby 86; see J. A. W. Bennett and G. V. Smithers (eds), *Early Middle English Verse and Prose*, 2nd edn (Oxford: Oxford University Press, 1968), pp. 77–95.

17 Ralph Hanna III, 'Presenting Chaucer as Author', in *Medieval Literature*, ed. Machan, pp. 17–39 (esp. 29–34).

18 See, for example, 'Sotelties for the Coronation Banquet, A. D. 1432', in *Secular Lyrics of the Fourteenth and Fifteenth Centuries*, ed. R. H. Robbins (Oxford: Clarendon Press, 1952), pp. 98–9.

19 Selections as Froissart, *Chronicles*, trans. and ed. Geoffrey Brereton (Harmondsworth: Penguin, 1968), p. 264.

20 *Chronicles*, ed. and trans. Brereton, pp. 403, 408.

21 See Helen Barr (ed.), *The Piers Plowman Tradition* (London: Dent, 1993), pp. 137–202 (esp. lines 1343ff.)

22 John J. Thompson, *Robert Thornton and the London Thornton Manuscript: British Library MS Additional 31042* (Cambridge: Brewer, 1987). On Rate see Lynne S. Blanchfield, 'The Romances in MS Ashmole 61: An Idiosyncratic Scribe', in *Romance in Medieval England*, ed. M. Mills, Jennifer Fellows and Carol Meale (Cambridge: Brewer, 1991), pp. 65–87, and her 'Rate Revisited: The Compilation of the Narrative Works in MS Ashmole 61', in *Romance Reading on the Book: Essays in Medieval Narrative Presented to Maldwyn Mills*, ed. Jennifer Fellows, Rosalind Field, Gillian Rogers and Judith Weiss (Cardiff: University of Wales Press, 1996), pp. 208–20.

23 A. I. Doyle, 'The Work of a Late Fifteenth-Century English Scribe, William Ebesham', *Bulletin of the John Rylands Library* 39 (1956–7), 298–325 and G. A. Lester, *Sir John Paston's 'Grete Boke': A Descriptive Catalogue, with an Introduction, of British Library MS Lansdowne 285* (Cambridge: Brewer, 1984).

24 Daniel Huws, 'MS Porkington 10 and its Scribes', in *Romance Reading on the Book*, ed. Fellows et al., pp. 188–207.

25 Wendy Scase, 'Reginald Pecock, John Carpenter and John Colop's 'Common Profit' Books: Aspects of Book Ownership and Circulation in Fifteenth-Century London', *Medium Ævum* 61 (1992), 261–74.

26 Mary-Jo Arn (ed.), *Fortunes Stabilnes: Charles of Orleans's English Book of Love* (Binghamton, N.Y.: Medieval and Renaissance Texts and Studies, 1994).

27 Thelma Fenster and Mary Carpenter Erler (eds), *Poems of Cupid, God of Love* (Leiden: Brill, 1990); John Scattergood (ed.), *The Works of Sir John Clanvowe* (Totowa, N.J.: Brewer, 1975).

28 J. A. Burrow and A. I. Doyle (intro.), *Thomas Hoccleve: A Facsimile of the Autograph Verse Manuscripts*, EETS ss 19 (2002).

29 C. Horstmann (ed.), *The Three Kings of Cologne*, EETS os 85 (1886).

30 See James W. Spisack, *Caxton's Malory*, 2 vols (Berkeley: University of California Press, 1983).

31 N. F. Blake (ed.), *The Canterbury Tales by Geoffrey Chaucer, Edited from the Hengwrt Manuscript* (London: Arnold, 1980).

32 J. A. Burrow (ed.), *Sir Gawain and the Green Knight* (Harmondsworth: Penguin, 1972); J. A. Burrow and Thorlac Turville-Petre (eds), *A Book of Middle English* (Oxford: Blackwell, 1992); J. A. Burrow (ed.), *Thomas Hoccleve's Complaint and Dialogue*, EETS os 313 (1999).

33 Peter Meredith (ed.), *The Mary Play from the N-Town Manuscript* (London: Longman, 1987).

34 A. G. Rigg and Charlotte Brewer (eds), *Piers Plowman: The Z Version* (Toronto: Pontifical Institute of Medieval Studies, 1983).

35 Burrow (ed.), *Thomas Hoccleve's Complaint.*

References and Further Reading

Alexander, Jonathan J. G. 1992. *Medieval Illuminators and their Methods of Work*. New Haven and London: Yale University Press. A general introduction.

Bell, H. E. 1937. 'The Price of Books in Medieval England.' *The Library*, 4th ser. 17, 312–32. Provides useful detail.

Bühler, Curt 1960. *The Fifteenth-Century Book: The Scribes, the Printers, the Decorators*. Philadelphia: University of Pennsylvania Press. A wide-ranging survey.

Christianson, C. Paul 1999. 'The Rise of London's Booktrade.' In Hellinga and Trapp 1999: 128–47. On London's communities of bookmakers.

de Hamel, Christopher 1992. *Medieval Craftsmen: Scribes and Illuminators*. London: British Museum Press. An introduction, attractively illustrated.

Doyle, A. I. and Parkes, M. B. 1978. 'The Production of Copies of the *Canterbury Tales* and the *Confessio Amantis* in the Early Fifteenth Century.' In *Medieval Scribes, Manuscripts, and Libraries: Essays Presented to N. R. Ker*, ed. M. B. Parkes and Andrew G. Watson (London: Scolar), pp. 163–210. Establishes the existence of loosely associated groups of metropolitan scribes whose activities could be flexibly coordinated.

Edwards, A. S. G. 2000a. 'Fifteenth-Century Middle English Verse Author Collections.' In *The English Medieval Book: Studies in Memory of Jeremy Griffiths*, ed. A. S. G. Edwards, Vincent Gillespie and Ralph Hanna (London: British Library), pp. 101–12. On attempts to bring together 'collected works' in manuscript.

—— 2000b. 'Representing the Middle English Manuscript.' In *New Directions in Later Medieval Manuscript Studies: Essays from the 1998 Harvard Conference*, ed. Derek Pearsall (Woodbridge: York Medieval Press in association with the Boydell Press), pp. 65–79. On post-medieval strategies for representing Middle English texts.

Eisenstein, Elizabeth 1979. *The Printing Press as an Agent of Change: Communications and Cultural Transformations in Early Modern Europe*, 2 vols. Cambridge: Cambridge University Press. Abridged as *The Printing Revolution in Early Modern Europe* (Cambridge: Cambridge University Press, 1983). Argues that the spread of printed books was responsible for reform of different kinds.

Febvre, L. and Martin, H.-J. 1958. *L'Apparition du livre*. Paris: Editions Albin Michel. Trans. David Gerard as *The Coming of the Book: The Impact of Printing, 1450–1800*. London: Verso, 1990. A Europe-wide overview.

Greetham, David 1992. *Textual Scholarship: An Introduction*. New York: Garland. A comprehensive textbook: see especially chapters 2 and 5.

Griffiths, Jeremy and Pearsall, Derek (eds) 1989. *Book Production and Publishing in Britain, 1375–1475*. Cambridge: Cambridge University Press. Articles on many aspects of the production and circulation of manuscripts.

Hellinga, Lotte 1982. *Caxton in Focus: The Beginning of Printing in England*. London: British Library. A concise introduction to Caxton's activities.

—— and Trapp, J. B. (eds) 1999. *The Cambridge History of the Book in Britain. Vol. 3: 1400–1557*. Cambridge: Cambridge University Press. A comprehensive collection of essays, covering both manuscript and printed books.

Hindman, S. and Farquar, J. D. 1977. *Pen to Press: Illustrated Manuscripts and Printed Books in the*

First Century of Printing. College Park: Art Dept, University of Maryland. Especially useful on matters such as illumination and the provision of woodcuts.

McCarren, Vincent and Moffat, Douglas (eds) 1998. *A Guide to Editing Middle English*. Ann Arbor: University of Michigan Press. On editing and editorial procedure, with much practical advice.

McKenzie, D. F. 1986. *Bibliography and the Sociology of Texts*. London: British Library. Short and stimulating.

Machan, Tim William 1994. *Textual Criticism and Middle English Texts*. Charlottesville: University Press of Virginia. Medieval and modern notions of what constitutes a 'text', an 'author', a 'work'.

Martin, H.-J., Chartier, R. and Vivet, J. P. (eds) 1982. *Histoire de l'édition française. Vol. 1: Le Livre conquérant: du Moyen Age au milieu du XVIIème siècle*. Paris: Promodis. A survey of French book production valuable for comparative purposes.

Millett, Bella 1994. '*Mouvance* and the Medieval Author.' In *Late-Medieval Religious Texts and their Transmission: Essays in Honour of A. I. Doyle*, ed. A. J. Minnis, York Manuscripts Conferences, Proceedings Series, 3 (Cambridge: Brewer), pp. 9–20. On the interventions of authors and scribes in processes of textual revision and variation.

Parkes, M. B. 1976. 'The Influence of the Concepts of *Ordinatio* and *Compilatio* on the Development of the Book.' In *Medieval Learning and Literature: Essays Presented to R. W. Hunt*, ed. J. J. G. Alexander and M. T. Gibson (Oxford: Oxford University Press), pp. 115–41. Analysis of matters such as layout, glosses, and collocation of texts.

Pearsall, Derek (1993–4). 'The Uses of Manuscripts: Late Medieval English.' *Harvard Library Bulletin* ns 4 (Winter), 30–6. Argues for the value of studying original manuscripts.

Root, Robert K. 1913. 'Publication before Printing.' *PMLA* 28, 261–74. A seminal early study.

Rosenthal, J. T. 1982. 'Aristocratic Cultural Patronage and Book Bequests, 1350–1500.' *Bulletin of the John Rylands Library* 64, 522–48. Considers evidence from wills and other sources.

Shailor, Barbara A. 1989. *The Medieval Book*. New Haven: Yale University Press. A clear and attractive introduction.

Stevens, Martin and Woodward, Daniel (eds) 1997. *The Ellesmere Chaucer: Essays in Interpretation*. San Marino, Calif.: Huntington Library, and Tokyo: Yushodo. Essays on one of the earliest and most important manuscripts of *The Canterbury Tales*.

Zumthor, Paul 1972. *Essai de poétique médiévale*. Paris: Seuil. Trans. Philip Bennett as *Towards a Medieval Poetics* (Minneapolis: University of Minnesota Press, 1992). Elaboration of the notion of *mouvance*, with reference mainly to French texts.

8
Translation and Society

Catherine Batt

(a) Yit last the venym of so longe ago,
That it enfecteth hym that wol beholde
The storye of Tereus, of which I tolde.
(Chaucer, 'Legend of Philomela')[1]

(b) A tale eek . . . in honur and plesance
Of yow, my ladyes, as I moot needis . . .
Wole I translate and þat shal pourge, I hope,
My gilt as cleene as keuerchiefs dooth sope.
(Hoccleve, *Series*)[2]

(c) holy wryt was translated out of Hebrew ynto Gru and out of Gru into Latyn and þanne out of Latyn ynto Frensch. Þanne what haþ Englysch trespased þat hyt myȝt noȝt be translated into Englysch? . . . Kyng Alured . . . translatede . . . þe Sauter out of Latyn into Englysch . . . Also þou wost where þe Apocalips ys ywryte in þe walles and roof of a chapel boþe in Latyn and yn Freynsch.
(Trevisa, 'Dialogue between the Lord and the Clerk')[3]

(d) '. . . y preye ȝow purcharite to techen us lewed men trewlyche þe soþe aftur oure axynge.'

'Broþer, y knowe wel þat y am holde by Christis lawe to parforme þyn axynge; bot naþeles we beþ now so fer y-fallen a-wey from Cristis lawe, þat ȝif y wolde answere to þyn axynges y moste in cas vnderfonge [*receive*] þe deþ . . . for now þe worlde is ful of wykkednesse . . .'
(*A Fourteenth Century English Biblical Version*)[4]

Translations in Contexts

Recent scholarship agrees that 'translation' is central to literary critical investigation and evaluation of later medieval British culture (Simpson 2002; Wallace 1999: 486) and, in its narrowest and broadest definitions, from linguistic 'transferral of meaning' to interpretative literary interplay between cultures and texts, a matter of pressing academic interest. As translation practice materially constitutes later medieval British literature, however, the question is less the status of a text's 'transfer' from one defined culture to another, than the scrutiny of translation itself as a site of later medieval Britain's cultural emergence (for theorization, see Bhabha 1994; Simon 1996). In the complex multilingual context of medieval Britain, translation constitutes the space of cultural creativity, and simultaneously defines it. While its individual expressions mandate strenuous investigation within socio-political and rhetorical contexts, those contexts are potentially difficult to recover. Furthermore, post-medieval critical treatments of translation, through their divergent ideologies, may make various demands of, and assumptions about, its nature and status, and so map out the very subject of their inquiry in radically different, even contingent, ways (Evans 1994). While any reconstruction of medieval translation's cultural spaces has to be alert to the complexities of medieval literature's 'situatedness' (Wogan-Browne, Watson, Taylor and Evans 1999: 316), modern readers' engagement with this literature itself forms a continuum of its 'frame of translation'. Translation's constitutive and conceptual functions define Middle English literature's particular multi-layeredness and hermeneutic open-endedness.

The late medieval examples cited above illuminate aspects of translation's culturally specific imbrication with literary, rhetorical, social, gender, moral and religious questions, as well as inviting readerly interventions. They also expose how, while Englishing a text is generally understood to facilitate greater dissemination, 'translation' does not reach a homogeneous 'society', but might serve, or indeed figure, specific groups and communities, united in particular ways. Chaucer's narrator, introducing the story of Philomela in the *Legend of Good Women* (late 1380s), alarmingly describes as chronic contagion the repetition of Ovid's gruesome tale of rape, child-murder and cannibalism, and gives an unexpected and frightening twist to the formulation of literary culture as continuity. Chaucer's route to Ovid is via the French *Ovide moralisé*, which reworks the classical tales according to religious allegory's exigencies, and plays on the relation between, and the authoritativeness of, Christian and classical, vernacular and Latin texts, especially where it incorporates a twelfth-century vernacular retelling (attributed to Chrétien de Troyes) of the legend of Philomela which, it declares, cannot be improved on. The French redactor, Rita Copeland argues, invokes classical rhetorical procedures to give the vernacular a status that antagonistically displaces Latin authority (Copeland 1991: 117–18). The Chaucerian notion of 'contagion' moves beyond a rhetorical frame for establishing authority and licenses the reader to construct for her- or himself a narrative of unsavoury continuities for a story transformed in the telling between Ovid's and Chaucer's versions. Chrétien's historicizing excuse for Tereus's violence against his sister-in-law, and the insistence on Tereus's helplessness in the face of 'love', exacerbate the human cruelty of Ovid's original. The *Ovide moralisé* provides the unsympathetic and disturbing gloss that the brutally raped Philomela represents the unstable vain pleasures of the world, to which Procne/the wayward soul urges Tereus/the body – a reading that might lead one to question the soundness of the writer's execution of

St Paul's dictum that everything is written to instruct us.[5] The Chaucerian version, given the *Legend* narrator's richly ambiguous self-presentation as far as concerns the text's sexual politics and, indeed, his failure to complete the story, leaves open the question of how the story 'infects' authorial intention and emphasis. With one brief remark, Chaucer invokes and troubles literary continuity, draws the reader into the text, and turns the spotlight on her or his own responsive 'situatedness'.

Thomas Hoccleve, meanwhile, in the course of his *Series* (c.1419–21), writes himself-as-author into a 'Dialogue' with a solicitous 'Friend' about his work's nature and reception. At this point (extract b), in evident homage to the interpretative frame of Chaucer's *Legend of Good Women* (which makes amends for previous 'heresy' against the God of Love), 'Hoccleve' declares one translation project – the Englishing of 'The story of a certain Roman Empress', from the popular Latin story-collection, the *Gesta Romanorum* – his penitential compensatory measure for the 'offence' which Friend claims that another, earlier translation (his 1402-dated *Letter of Cupid*, a reworking of Christine de Pizan's French poem) has given the 'ladies', whose good opinion he must now retrieve. Hoccleve's imagery (jocularly) suggests that his redemptive translation-work will 'cleanse' him, both spiritually and socially. It reworks his pious hope, from earlier in the 'Dialogue', that he might 'clense' his soul, 'foul and vnclene' through his body's 'gilte', by translating Henry Suso's work on the 'art of dying' (which translation ultimately forms the penultimate work in Hoccleve's *Series*).[6]

The *Series* playfully represents later medieval British translation practice and its role in the vagaries of literary production. An introspective 'Compleint' is followed by the 'Dialogue' with Friend, who takes on roles as editor, reader, commissioner and censor (virtually his first move is to object to Thomas's circulating the first poem), and effectively reshapes the *Series*. Although Duke Humphrey and the Countess of Westmoreland are named respectively as a patron and as a dedicatee, Friend, who suggests alternative plans for literary work, and even intervenes in textual production, provides a foil to the narrator's sense of literary autonomy. Translation, the substance of the work, is conceptually the space where the vernacular writer self-consciously theorizes and culturally locates his literary project. The poems evolve from concerns with canonicity, authorial intention and responsibility, the chances of medieval book circulation and production, and the consequences of reader reception. Once disseminated, a text is subject to vaguely defined and yet powerful lobbies (if one believes Friend's account of ill-willed ladies) that will have a material effect on future productions – even if the *Series* suggests, through Friend's machinations, that a putative audience's requirements may not ultimately be met. Dissemination seems 'circular' and literary, as Friend names the Wife of Bath as representative of female opinion,[7] articulating a relation between gender and interpretation, a familiar trope in and beyond medieval discussions of translation. The 'Chaucerian' subtext, however, demonstrates that translation does not take place in some hermetically sealed-off relationship between 'source' and 'target' language, but draws on the broader contexts of its own culture for expression and meaning. Translation makes for literature that is pragmatic, continually 'in process', collaborative and highly self-aware.

When Hoccleve self-consciously deploys a trope about the penitential and salvific effects of translation, he claims common moral ground with the work of (*inter alios*) writers of vernacular medical texts, for whom translation is an act of Christian charity that profits both soul and body. The Dominican Henry Daniel prefaces his (c.1379) Middle English Latin-derived uroscopy with modesty topoi familiar from other contemporary accounts of translation, and requests that others correct his work with good will, 'for charity' motivates him.[8] For Daniel, the vernacular helps disseminate his medical work, although Bible translators, who write under fear of suppression, also assert that they act out of charity, and a friar's apparently straightforward generous sharing of clerical knowledge carries a political charge in the heightened climate of the later fourteenth century that speaks to issues of authority and power more than to an uncomplicated mediation of knowledge made universally available.

John Trevisa, by comparison (extract c), outlines a seemingly straightforward role for the translator as mediator and disseminator of knowledge, in the *Dialogue between the Lord and the Clerk* that prefaces his own translation of Ranulf Higden's *Polychronicon* (1387). This robustly one-sided exchange offers a fictionalized relationship between the patron (in Trevisa's historical circumstance, Lord Thomas of Berkeley) and the scholar he wishes to translate this Latin history. The Lord, initially acknowledging Latin's use as a lingua franca, but proposing that English broadens lay, non-learned access to 'informacion and lore', impresses on the Clerk the need to translate the Bible into English for the good of all. In its claims for the vernacular's place in a chain of language-mediated learning, Trevisa's text aligns with the humanist argument of Nicole Oresme's prologue to his own translation of Aristotle's *Nicomachean Ethics*, part of the ambitious translation project Charles V of France (1364–80) oversees, and which included Augustine's *City of God* as well as the Bible – a programme for which later fourteenth-century England offers little parallel. Oresme claims that French, a 'noble' language, is a suitable medium for the dissemination of information for 'the common good', as Latin and French have the same practical function: historically, Latin, like French, was a people's 'mother language'.[9] Trevisa's Lord confirms the practical necessity of translation, and traces historical precedent for scripture in the vernacular in the work of Werferth, Alfred and Bede. The *Dialogue*, in arguing for English explication of the Gospel, refers also to the decoration of a chapel's walls with the Apocalypse 'in Latin and in French', which suggests that English takes its place in a culturally vibrant simultaneous deployment of insular languages as religious registers and devotional aids (a subject I return to below). This element of pragmatic multilingualism arguably informs the Lord's attitude to the translated text as a continuing, renewable process: 'no . . . man . . . makeþ so good a translacyon þat he ne myȝt make a betre . . . bote Ich wolde haue a skylfol translacion þat myȝt be knowe and vnderstonde'.[10] The Clerk concludes the *Dialogue* by invoking God's aid with a prayer celebrating God's act of creation, which affirms his orthodoxy as it confirms the validity of his own work, and intimates that the reiterative aspect of translation may share something with that of prayer.

As Fiona Somerset suggests, for all the 'openness' the Lord desires, the Dialogue partakes of other 'translations': the Lord appropriates the Clerk's language and reasoning, even his pastoral concerns, in arguing for the responsibility of giving the less learned access to texts; and other projects Trevisa engaged in reinforce the sense that translation into English intimated, 'for clerics, the threat of a kind of disendowment' (Somerset 1998: 93). Yet, while the *Dialogue* promotes a universally available knowledge, the book itself circulated primarily among clergy, gentry and nobility (Wogan-Browne et al. 1999: 324–5). Trevisa's *Dialogue* conveys important, late medieval reflections on translation, some of which the later General Prologue to the Wycliffite Bible also rehearses, especially the plea for the English to have a Bible 'in here modir langage'; the importance of making scripture 'open' to as many as possible; and the author's inviting correction: 'and I preie, for charite and for comoun profyt of cristene soulis, that if ony wiys man fynde ony defaute of the truthe of translacioun, let him sette in the trew sentence and opin of holi writ'.[11] But while the *Dialogue* has its own political contingencies, the producers of the Bible will not share Trevisa's privileged position, and their work will be received in a very different climate.

Only a few years later than Trevisa, the 'Brother', in another dialogue, prefacing a later fourteenth-century translation of the Epistles (d), tells his would-be students of 'Christ's law' (a 'Brother' and a 'Sister') that to teach them is potentially life-threatening. The instructor does not specify the danger, aside from the general remark on how a sinful and troubled humankind characterizes the times, but he compliments the less learned Brother on his arguments for seeking knowledge and asserts that love 'that is above reason' must have motivated this access of eloquence. The teacher justifies his translation of New Testament texts (which here follow on naturally from elementary instruction in the Ten Commandments) by saying that he too acts out of love which, if it goes against reason, is nevertheless consonant with the behaviour of Christ, who is love. This commentary, boldly appropriating and supplanting the terms of academic discourse, and with its audience of mixed religious, is clearly caught up in the political and ecclesiastical controversies surrounding Bible translations, which will culminate in the 1401 civil statute that establishes the death penalty for heresy, and in Arundel's 1409 *Constitutions* that forbid the unauthorized translation of biblical texts. The Wycliffite Bible Prologue shares the Brother's stance; there, clerical selfishness keeps the word of God from the less learned, and charity is the impulse to translation, which is also potentially dangerous: 'the lewid puple crieth aftir holi writ to kunne it and kepe it with greet cost and peril of here lif [and so] with comune charite to saue alle men in oure rewme whiche God wol haue sauid, a symple creature hath translatid the bible out of Latyn into English'.[12] For David Lawton (1999: 478), the Brother's fear of death is political; for James Morey, a doctrinal 'fear' of God is the issue (2000: 41–2). How one reconstructs and weights the political background clearly affects interpretation.

Perspectives on Middle English Translation

Writers' observations on translation practice are inevitably also political comments on their culture and the place of texts within it: the examples above convey something of the authors' awareness of issues beyond the immediate practical task of rendering the language of a source text into the English vernacular – and, of course, *how* one translates also has political ramifications. Translation focuses issues of literature's function and accessibility, and the authority of the writer; the relations between authors, patrons and audiences; how texts respond to (or even retrospectively construct) one another; and the status of the vernacular, its purposes and the possibility of its political control. These issues do not exert the same influences and pressures throughout the period, of course, or indiscriminately across the range of literatures within a particular periodization. (This essay began with 'examples' so as to emphasize translation's organic and dynamic nature, and its embeddedness in other cultural factors.) To determine translation's cultural spaces, and how it shapes the parameters of later medieval literary culture, one has to be aware of the complexity with which linguistic, rhetorical, institutional and historical factors interrelate.

Medieval thinking about translation is itself complex, and subtly deployed. Medieval Western culture in general predicates itself on the continuity of *translatio studii et imperii*, the idea that 'translation', in the sense of the carrying across of culture (both artistic and political) from the civilization of Greece to Rome, is the mainstay of authorization. Rita Copeland's magisterial and highly influential account of how classical rhetorical theory and practice relate to translation, *Rhetoric, Hermeneutics and Translation in the Middle Ages* (1991) identifies, within this cultural paradigm, conflicting but ultimately interacting scholastic models for the reception and continuity of past literatures that speak especially to anxieties about the 'authorization' of the vernacular in the face of learned languages. Copeland traces how 'translation' has roots in a grammar-based – or, more broadly speaking, 'hermeneutic' – tradition of exegesis, by which it has a subordinate role, supplementing and illuminating a source text. But the medieval understanding of translation also rediscovers, by way of hermeneutics, the rhetorically grounded translation method of Cicero, whose finely polished Latin performances supersede his Greek sources: 'translation . . . displaces the originary force of its models' (1991: 4). Copeland draws particular attention to medieval translation theory's use and reworking of St Jerome's careful negotiations of Cicero's classical rhetoric, and of 'sense-for-sense' or 'word-for-word' procedures in relation to biblical and non-biblical translations (1991: 42–62). For Copeland, the dominant later medieval model of translation, at the 'intersection' of rhetoric and hermeneutics, remains primarily one of 'textual appropriation' (1991: 55). As the vernacular secures, through translation, the means to usurp Latin academic discourse, Chaucer and Gower can be seen to 'displace' their antecedents and 'supplant' the 'originals' on which they depend.

The *translatio studii* model in general, with its sense of continuity and rupture, offers the opportunity for vernacular writers to register 'a sense of dependence on and difference from Latin thought and culture' (Wogan-Browne et al. 1999: 318). (That Chaucer's Philomela tale refines this formulation as a 'continuity of disruption' demonstrates sophisticated awareness.) Copeland elucidates translation's place in the context of 'competitive' literary inheritance, and the 'legitimizing' of vernacular writing, within particular scholastic terms. This central thesis is not presented as an all-inclusive model for translation (Copeland 1991: 5), for Copeland also touches on the Wycliffite Bible's promotion of translation as collaboratively arrived-at means of access rather than exclusivity (1991: 225–6), and discusses Chaucer's *Boece* as potentially in 'complementary relationship' with Jean de Meun's own French translation of Boethius (1991: 143).

That vernacular texts might speak 'across' to one another rather than simply 'hierarchically' reminds one that medieval literature engages on several levels. Roger Ellis, by analogy with the scholastic concept of 'authorial intention', lightheartedly notes the importance of the 'intencio lectoris' in constructing Chaucer's meaning (Ellis 2000: 446), drawing attention to translation's propensity to make space for readers – the writer of the English text, the addressed audience, the historical reader. Later Middle English literature's constitution through translation adumbrates issues that include, and go beyond, ideas of 'authorization', displacement and competitiveness, and directly solicit active response and dialogue. Readings of 'English literature' as either the product of French cultural dominance or the result of deliberate efforts to 'displace' Latin, French and Italian (Wogan-Browne et al. 1999: 333; 319–20; but see also 330) work from divergent assumptions of different relational status for the languages concerned. Literary histories in general tend to prioritize English language production in accounts of British literary 'tradition', 'against' other languages (even insular languages), but it is perhaps more fruitful to see (especially fourteenth-century) English literature's particular constitution of itself through translation less as Chaucer's initiative – the result of one court poet's interaction with European culture and a dedication to the mother tongue that is to have impressive political and cultural consequences – than as a continuing response to the insular historical linguistic situation in which some strata of society have access to Latin, English, Continental French and Anglo-Norman French, and for whom language may be as much 'interactive' as 'competitive'. This historical situation – in which, for example, legislation sits alongside divergent practice, so that while the 1362 Statute of Pleading confirms English as the language of law-courts, French continues in this capacity (Machan 2003: 163), and in which code-switching between languages is a feature of everyday professional life, from business and law to medicine – makes for a culture acutely aware of how language and register interconnect, and for which literature is a continuing exchange, dialogue and collaboration between texts, readers and writers.

Against this background, use of English may be as much a choice as a necessity. If in 1324 Hugh the Despenser can rally English troops in Gascony with an appeal to the preservation of England's 'language' ('de tout nostre lange' (Rothwell 1994: 57)), while Robert Mannyng's *Chronicle* (completed 1338) can invoke a 'symple' English (as distinguished from a more abstruse literary 'strange Inglis') as the means to communicate with a broad audience (Wogan-Browne et al. 1999: 21), then language is not uncomplicatedly allied to 'nationhood', and interpretation of its significance clearly needs careful contextualization (Ormrod 2003). It seems important to evaluate the fourteenth century in terms of a sense of insular identity of which vernaculars form a part, rather than to associate only the English vernacular with a sense of 'national' literature (and to assume that the 'national' is always at issue). When, in 1354, Henry, first Duke of Lancaster, asks for the poor French of his devotional treatise to be excused 'because I am English',[13] he is arguably as much owning to a distinct insular register as apologizing for provincialism and cultural marginality. Edmund of Abingdon's *Speculum ecclesiae* (c.1213–14) circulates in Anglo-Norman and English, as well as Latin, versions (a Latin fourteenth-century version retranslates the Anglo-Norman) for lay and religious audiences, suggesting Latin and vernacular might work within a model of reciprocity and not always hierarchically.[14] The mid-thirteenth-century Anglo-Norman version of this text, the *Mirour de sainte eglyse*, retains a Latin reference to the *Song of Songs*, and further supplies a Middle English lyric ('Nou goþ sunne under wode')[15] as a further meditational dimension to its description of the Passion. The translator's interpolation alerts us to an audience's capacity to process different languages, and also to the text as collaborative mediated enterprise. The *Ancrene Wisse*, originally in Early Middle English, but reworked in Anglo-Norman and Latin, shows how a text is adapted to the needs of specific communities.[16] The immensely popular *Brut* chronicle (of which some 250 manuscripts survive) has a history of composition in Anglo-Norman, translation and accretion in Middle English from the late fourteenth century onwards, and translation and recension into Latin; versions were produced and circulated in all these languages (and in Continental French) into the fifteenth century, and were popular with a range of social backgrounds including the aristocracy, religious houses, gentry and merchant classes. A 'decorum' of language register thus exists alongside the use of English as pragmatic necessity.

That English negotiates literary space for itself in a multilingual culture invites one to consider translation less a 'bridge between already given cultural entities' than a site of 'cultural creation' (Simon 1996: 152). English literature's productive self-consciousness over the fact and idea of translation grows out of the paradoxical nature of translation itself, which may assert power (St Jerome likens one translation method to 'marching' a 'captive' original text into the new language),[17] but may also reformulate the question of 'authority' with regard to the 'original' or to the translated text. Translation contributes to the plurality that characterizes the medieval generally: texts draw on many disparate 'voices', from sources to patrons, and so they are not 'beholden to imply a single authoritative voice' (Simpson 2002: 65). Translation may present itself as 'multivoiced', but may also be 'silent' – examples are Chaucer's *Boece*, or the fifteenth-century English prose *Merlin*. As a cultural space, imagined aside from specific linguistic relation to an 'original', 'translation' is ever open to reconstruction. Chaucer's fiction of Lollius in *Troilus and Criseyde* elides Boccaccio's source-poem, and draws the reader in to engage with the possibilities of and pressures on translation into English as a creative act, challenging ways of thinking about cultural placing. Later medieval translation may identify itself as the locus of heightened literary creativity and inventiveness and simultaneously provide metatextual comment that suggests particular artistic control. Malory's declared and actual translation practice in *Le Morte Darthur* poses hard questions about how one locates and uses cultural traditions, and Chaucer and Lydgate too use this space to comment on political and ideological constraints and problems. If translation is the locus of what Homi Bhabha calls a culture's 'presencing' (1994: 5), for the reader, recognizing how English text, metatext and source may overlap as much as be distinct makes for a rich critical space in which to consider medieval literature's specificity.

How does one reconcile this knowing cultural complexity with recent views on fifteenth-century literature as the product of proscription and the site of intense cultural policing? Earlier criticism may have misconstrued it in part on account of a post-Romantic equation of 'translation' with derivativeness and inferiority. Recent work situates translation in the context of power relations between lay and ecclesiastical, state and individual, in sharper, more clearly historicized perspectives that map literature within ecclesiastical and state legislation and engineering – specifically, Arundel's *Constitutions*, and claims such as John Fisher makes for English as part of a Lancastrian propagandist nationalist enterprise (Machan 2003: 162–3). This threatens to reproduce the earlier model of a vibrant and intellectually stimulating late fourteenth-century culture giving way to a less imaginatively engaged and culturally timid fifteenth century, in which translation is in the service of institutions. The rest of this essay considers the Bible translation debate as a particular political context for literature, touches on literature as subject to state legislation, and suggests that, rather than provide a key to 'how to read' fifteenth-century literature, such foci alert us to the careful interpretative negotiations that later medieval works demand.

Translation, the Bible and the Metatext of Translation

Translation has always been a source of concern and anxiety in relation to the Bible, as central events in the history of its dissemination, such as the reception of Jerome's translation, make evident, for it exemplifies tensions between preserving an originary 'Word' of God and the inevitably human mediation of that Word in its promulgation (Stanton 2002). Translation further raises problems about access and interpretation particularly worrying to arbiters of institutionalized religion, and recent studies of later medieval Bible translation emphasize the extent to which debates about the Bible's availability in English are ultimately less concerned with translation *per se* (which is not to deny the theorizing force of some of the arguments) than with fuelling broader contests about political and theological power and authority and who has access to them (Lawton 1999: 457). Translation becomes politically charged because John Wyclif mobilizes the vernacular in his challenge to ecclesiastical dominance, particularly in his determination to make accessible to the laity the arguments around transubstantiation, and to make the Bible serve as a means of access to the divine (Hudson 1988; Lawton 1999). The Wycliffite translation project, and reactions to it, illustrate the continuing need to consider evidence within its specific historical context, demonstrate continuities with past attitudes, crystallize some important thinking in the area, and precipitate political and cultural crisis.

Before the 'early version' of the Wycliffite Bible (*c* 1380–4) consolidates a movement for a complete prose translation of the text, knowledge of the scriptures, while apparently 'piecemeal' to those who are familiar with the concept and actuality of 'the Bible' as an integral text bound in one volume, was extensive. In the Anglo-Saxon period, Alfred's translation of the Psalter (which John Trevisa and the Wycliffite Prologue author take for precedent) is part of a self-conscious programme which simultaneously consolidates translation as a pedagogical necessity and the Anglo-Saxon king's own political position (Stanton 2002: 121–7). Robert Stanton has argued that in the ninth century Alfred's and in the eleventh century Aelfric's work, in the context of other biblical translation and glossing and Anglo-Saxon culture generally, valorizes the vernacular by carving out for it a space as the necessary mediator of the authoritative word, fulfilling a function that the Latin text could not itself supply (Stanton 2002: 101–43).

Continuity with post-Conquest practice lies in the Bible's contiguity with its interpretative apparatus, and its subjection to political and ecclesiastical mediation. The lay devout would know biblical quotation, paraphrase and narrative from the liturgy, sermons, glossed books of the Old and New Testaments, and other devotional literature, as well as encyclopedic works and universal histories (the *Polychronicon* is just such a text). The Bible is, then, 'translated' in complementary cultural and devotional contexts specific to certain individuals' and communities' spiritual and intellectual needs. Orrm's *Ormulum* (c.1170–80), for example, an ambitious and unfinished commentary project for the liturgical year's Gospel readings, offers homiletically contextualized close summaries of scripture (Morey 2000: 71–80, 320–30). The *Cursor mundi* (c.1300), drawing on Latin (both the Vulgate and Peter Comestor's immensely popular compendium of biblical synopsis, commentary and classical history, the *Historia scholastica* (c.1169–75)), and on French and Anglo-Norman sources, retells salvation and world history and constitutes for itself an eager community united by an understanding of the 'Englis lede [language]' (Wogan-Browne et al. 1999: 268–71). Among Middle English sermon and homily cycles are: the *Northern Homily Cycle* (c.1315) and the *Mirror*,[18] both of which originate in Robert of Gretham's Sunday Gospel collection; the *Miroir*, one of many surviving Anglo-Norman texts that testify to parallel and intersecting interests with Middle English productions in terms of glossed books of the Old Testament; verse biblical narratives; gospel harmonies; Apocalypses; Lives of Christ; and other devotional material.[19]

The 1215 Lateran Council promoted vernacular biblical texts in its injunction to provide for the 'various rites and languages' of those united in a common faith – although there is also a concomitant anxiety that only the licensed should preach (Morey 2000: 34) – and John Pecham's 1281 *Syllabus* and Archbishop Thoresby's mid-fourteenth-century provisions belong to this initiative (Wogan-Browne et al. 1999: 335–6). Lay access to biblical material facilitated individual engagement with scripture and its Church mediation. The resultant body of writings provides an illuminating context for what modern criticism too often isolates as 'canonical' literature – for *Piers Plowman*, and *Pearl*, invite analysis in terms of the importance they accord translation in an understanding of scripture, for example (Simpson 2002) – and also (arguably) for a collectively constituted 'vernacular theology', the continuing development of which legislation will frustrate (Watson 1995: 823).

The Wycliffite Bible departs from the norm in its project to supply a 'full' text of the scriptures 'free' of contextualization, and yet, belonging to a wide-ranging programme of educative reform that includes biblical commentary, works to some extent within established precedent in terms of both its production and its self-presentation (and it does not eradicate 'commentary'). The 250 manuscript witnesses have a complex history of translation and revision (Hudson 1988: 238–47), but they recognizably belong to two different trends. The process by which a Later Version (c.1395–7), with its greater concessions to English word order, replaces the 'word-for-word' method of the Early Version, difficult of access without the Latin text alongside, echoes in large the approach of Richard Rolle's *English Psalter* (c.1345), which gives the text verse by verse – first in Latin, with a word-for-word translation as a guide to the Latin and then in paraphrase, with a brief commentary (Lawton 1999: 470–1). The General Prologue itself assembles and repoliticizes important ideas about scripture, as well as supplying a commentary to the task in hand (although its survival in only eleven manuscripts suggest it was not considered integral to the translation). Some of the Prologue's arguments are familiar, but reworked to make particular demands of the reader. Where such as Trevisa recommend lay access, the Prologue, itself (daringly) a work of 'charity', like the translation, invites the Bible reader to work through the text's 'opyn and derk' parts in a spirit of 'mekenes and charite', one's guide in 'trewe vndirstondyng and perfectioun of al holi writ'. Drawing on Nicholas Lyra, the author emphasizes that allegorical meanings are underwritten by God: in a world in which human mediation can be an obstacle – the author has gone to some lengths to assemble the means to an authoritative source-text, 'to make oo Latyn bible sumdel trewe' – communal human endeavour, inspired by God, nevertheless effects the task. Thus, 'for charite and for comoun profyt of cristene soulis', the work is declared open to emendation and supplementation, and translation and spiritual understanding alike are seen as part of the same process: 'with good lyuyng and greet trauel [*effort*], men moun [*may*] come to trewe and cleer translating, and trewe undurstonding of holi writ'.[20]

Recent work powerfully and provocatively reads the attitudes to language and society here within fourteenth-century social and cultural preoccupations. Andrew Cole (2002), as one example, traces in Chaucer's prologue to his *Treatise on the Astrolabe* a shrewd assimilation of Wycliffite usage (in the distinction between the 'naked' as vacuous and the 'open' with what is accessible to understanding (1146–8)) that accords it particular status as vernacular translation theory. Nicholas Watson's observation that there is not necessarily a clear divide between what might be tolerated as 'orthodox' and what might be denounced as 'heretical' with regard to translation portrays a pre-Arundel world capable of accommodating a spectrum of views. In the dispute known as the 'Oxford Translation Debate' of 1401, the voices of the Dominican Thomas Palmer and the Franciscan William Butler range against that of Richard Ullerston, a version of whose text later surfaces as a Lollard tract on translation (Watson 1995: 841). The arguments bespeak ideology rather than linguistic historical actuality, which latter belies Palmer's claims that English is a crude language ill-equipped to convey scriptural meaning (Watson 1995: 842). There are concerns with the maintenance of hierarchy, and a fear that Bible translation will overturn class and decorum, leading to contempt for learning and an end to Latin. Ullerston's refutations acknowledge historical and linguistic precedent, and the value of translation, and express faith in the established Church's ability to keep order. That the Oxford debate arguments are not always internally consistent, elude brief summary and, the Lollard tract suggests, are susceptible to different political appropriations, gives the impression of a pragmatic attitude to vernacular translation, and reinforces the sense of political manipulation: above all, Bible translation emerges as the contested site of social and political control.

Simpson's 2002 tracing of 'orthodox' and 'evangelical' modes of thought on the Bible between 1350 and 1547 brilliantly revises a distinction between 'medieval' and 'Renaissance' attitudes. The 'orthodox' stance sees reader, text and institution in productive interaction, whereas the 'evangelical' position considers that the individual's 'direct' access to the integral, 'plain' Bible is enough. This distinction makes for a continuity, on the 'orthodox' side, from *Piers Plowman*'s endeavour to engage the spiritual self fully, with Scripture and within the bounds of the Church, to (c.1395–c.1460) Reginald Pecock's ill-fated expression of trust in reason, and Thomas More's faith in Church-sanctioned scriptural meaning (1529), while the 'evangelical' position links Wyclif's idealizing conceptualization of the Bible with Tyndale's translation strategies for his sixteenth-century New Testament – and yet, as Tyndale's history and that of his text show, one cannot escape the contingent and the political: there is no 'pure' text (Simpson 2002: 458–501). Simpson's attractive broader thesis sees the move from medieval to Renaissance as a 'narrowing' of cultural practice, whereby the early fifteenth-century assertion of Church control anticipates sixteenth-century centralizing initiatives. His formulation, however, stops short of addressing Arundel's place in a medieval pluralistic culture. Perhaps the 'liberties' some late fourteenth-century literary groups enjoyed could only ever be precariously maintained. If the history of English culture makes translation simultaneously a site for dynamic cultural revision and exploration and for the staking of cultural claims, it must also be the site where the political asserts claims to cultural space.

Fifteenth-Century Translation

Arundel's *Constitutions*, 'one of the most draconian pieces of censorship in English history' (Watson 1995: 826), in force into the sixteenth century, formalize the connection between heresy and vernacular (Watson 1995: 843). Directed against Wyclif and his followers, with their guarding of clerical privilege and their prescriptions and proscriptions of academic behaviour and thought, the *Constitutions* have, Watson argues, a devastating effect on the culture, most particularly in their forbidding of unauthorized translation of scripture into English, whether as 'book, libel [*short work*], or treatise' (Watson: 1995: 829). While Watson's Appendix of extant devotional works in Middle English (many of them translations) offers compelling evidence for a falling away of vernacular theological writings after 1410, enforcement of the legislation, and the effect on readers, appears uneven (and the Wycliffite Bible and other fourteenth-century texts continue to circulate). The fact of censorship clearly demands that we be alert to specificities of social context. The *Canterbury Tales*, along with biblical translation, notoriously constitute evidence in one John Baron's 1464 heresy trial,[21] yet Henry VI owns a copy of the Wycliffite Bible, as do other aristocrats (Hudson 1988: 233). In the case of Hoccleve's *Series* it is not clear what kinds of censorship are at issue when the narrator explicitly declines to translate a portion of Henry Suso's text (relating to the Eucharist), but translates without comment a lesson for All Souls' Day that uses John's Apocalypse.[22] A gentry-woman such as Eleanor Hull may still, in the 1440s, translate a *Commentary on the Penitential Psalms* for her own – and perhaps coterie – use (see Wogan-Browne et al. 1999: 291–2). The circulation of fourteenth-century literature, or fifteenth-century translations of Continental works of mystical devotion, such as Mechtild of Hackeborn's *Book of Ghostly Grace* (c.1400–40), is difficult to assess.

In a censorship culture, translation (as literature and as reader-reception) may operate as a site of resistance as well as of conformity. Nicholas Love famously presents his officially sanctioned *Mirror of the Blessed Life of Jesus Christ*, translated from pseudo-Bonaventure, as 'edifying' to the unlearned who, like children, need the 'mylk of lyght doctrine', not weightier spiritual food (Wogan-Browne et al. 1999: 253), but Margery Kempe, who also has Bonaventure on her reading-list, evidently does not receive her religious texts as 'lyght doctrine'. The effects of the *Constitutions* are clear in (for example) Caxton's not printing a Bible, yet, within these constraints, Osbern Bokenham's 1443–7 Englishing of Jacobus de Voragine's *Golden Legend* can self-consciously draw on scholastic (and less elevated) tropes to negotiate the status of his work as devotional literature (Johnson 1994).

Modern assessments of Chaucer's 'heirs', Hoccleve and Lydgate, often emphasize state control. While it is unlikely, linguistically speaking, that the Lancastrians could have had a monopoly on English language promulgation (Machan 2003), commentators differ on the effects of the political proscriptions under which 'Lancastrian' poets such as Hoccleve and Lydgate apparently labour.[23] For Simpson, the very condition of the medieval obviates the possibility of literary 'propaganda', as writers place themselves in complex, historically situated, relation to their material (2002: 64–5). Hoccleve's translations of advice literature in his *Regiment of Princes* may invite the reader/ruler to engage critically with the counsel promulgated. Lydgate's major works – *The Siege of Thebes* (1422–3), *The Troy Book* (1412–20), *Reason and Sensuality* (pre-1420) – arguably constitute an 'authoritative' cultural assimilation of Latin and French *roman antique* models that also acknowledge Chaucer's influence; but at every level, whether of relations to patrons or sources or textual fidelity, translation is the very ground of the relativization of concepts of authority and power.

Caxton's printing career, which is also a translation programme – he translated a quarter of the 108 books he published – is bounded by narratives of *translatio imperii*: the French *Recuyell of the Histories of Troy* (c.1473), and the *Eneydos* (c.1490), a French version of Virgil's *Aeneid*. In his printing choices and in his explanatory prologues, Caxton consolidates fifteenth-century tastes for translations of Continental vernacular literature of princely and self-governance, instruction, romance, history and hagiography, and revisits those concerns – the transferral of learning, the status of English (linked with 'nation'), the vagaries of book circulation and production, anxieties concerning readership and 'ownership' of particular texts (now in the setting of his own hopes and anxieties for printing) – that the extracts prefacing this essay illustrate. Caxton emerges as typically 'medieval' in the way Simpson defines how medieval translation situates itself in historical relation to its source (2002: 64–5), and often makes explicit the text's 'accretions' – previous readings and glossings, prologues, past patrons and conditions of production, as well as the 'present' reader/translator's response. Caxton's additions to the *Recuyell*[24] recognize the story's importance in terms of cultural capital, and exploit *translatio*'s continuities and ruptures. That narrative accounts agree only on the *destruction* of Troy has powerful resonance for Caxton, writing in a 'troublous' time: 'how dredefull and jeopardous it is to begynne a warre'. As for the translation, Caxton tells how his patron Margaret, Duchess of Burgundy, has to order a demoralized and self-declaredly inadequate translator to complete it. Across his output, Caxton confirms English vernacular authors in a literary canon, and here he celebrates (and is initially inhibited by) Lydgate's inimitable verse account of the destruction of Troy; and yet Caxton sees an opportunity for a prose translation. Translation constitutes and supplements canonicity. Caxton returns to similar themes with the *Eneydos*,[25] connecting past and present empire in its dedication to Prince Arthur, worrying over the diachronic and synchronic variance of English even as he negotiates a register 'not overrude ne curyous' by which to translate his source, and submitting the text to the correction of John Skelton as an accomplished translator of Latin classics. Gavin Douglas, an earnest translator, 'to Virgillis text ybund'[26] for his own *Eneados*, thinks Caxton misappropriates Virgil's authority. Simpson considers Douglas 'Renaissance' in his concern with textual fidelity (118–20), although Douglas is 'medieval' in his provision of commentary, prologues, expansions and explicit supplementing of Virgil with Mapheus Vegius' 1428 'Book XIII' and, of course, in using Troy narrative as a founding cultural text for Scottish literature (Wogan-Browne et al. 276).

Middle English literature, to a greater or lesser degree, recognizes translation as the ground of its 'presencing', and of provisionality as much as of affirmation. The particular appeal of a 'translation' culture is the space it makes for the reader in the play of textual transmission and creation at the same time as it demands awareness of historical specificity in the retrieval of meaning. As we reconstruct the contexts of medieval literature, translation offers a means to acknowledge, in the provisionality of our own responses, the possibility of continual rediscoveries, which makes critical engagement both humbling and intellectually exciting.

See also: 1 Critical Approaches, 3 Religious Authority and Dissent, 6 Manuscripts and Readers, 7 From Manuscript to Modern Text, 9 The Languages of Medieval Britain, 10 The Forms of Speech, 11 The Forms of Verse, 12 England and France, 13 Britain and Italy, 14 England's Antiquities, 15 Jews, Saracens, 'Black Men', Tartars, 18 Images,

21 Writing Nation, 23 Lyric, 24 Literature of Religious Instruction, 25 Mystical and Devotional Literature, 30 The *Book of Margery Kempe*, 32 *Piers Plowman*, 33 The *Canterbury Tales*, 34 John Gower and John Lydgate, 35 Thomas Hoccleve, 38 Malory's *Morte Darthur*.

Notes

1 Chaucer, *Legend of Good Women*, 2241–3.

2 Thomas Hoccleve, *Series 2: A Dialogue*, in *'My Compleinte' and Other Poems*, ed. Roger Ellis (Exeter: University of Exeter Press, 2001), pp. 154–5, lines 820–6.

3 Ronald Waldron, 'Trevisa's Original Prefaces on Translation: a Critical Edition', in *Medieval English Studies Presented to George Kane*, ed. Edward Donald Kennedy, Ronald Waldron and Joseph S. Wittig (Cambridge: Brewer, 1988), pp. 285–99 (p. 292, lines 132–46).

4 *A Fourteenth Century English Biblical Version*, ed. Anna C. Paues (Cambridge: Cambridge University Press, 1904), p. 4.

5 *Ovide Moralisé*, ed. C. de Boer, printed discontinuously in 5 vols of the *Verhandelingen der Koninklijke akademie van Wetemschappen*, 15–43 (Amsterdam: Johannes Mueller, 1915–36), 21 (1921), lines 2183–3684.

6 Ed. Ellis, p. 137, lines 205–17.

7 Ed. Ellis, p. 151, lines 694–700.

8 F. M. Getz, 'Charity, Translation, and the Language of Medical Learning in Medieval England', *Bulletin of the History of Medicine* 64 (1990), 1–17 (p. 13).

9 Nicole Oresme, *Le Livre de Ethiques d'Aristote*, ed. Albert Douglas Menut (New York: Stechert, 1940), pp. 97–101.

10 Ed. Waldron, p. 293, lines 158–64.

11 *The Holy Bible . . . in the earliest English versions made . . . by John Wycliffe and his followers*, ed. Josiah Forshall and Sir Frederic Madden, 4 vols (Oxford: Oxford University Press, 1851), I, 57.

12 Ibid., I, 57.

13 Henry, Duke of Lancaster, *Le Livre de Seyntz Medicines*, ed. E. J. Arnould, Anglo-Norman Texts, 2 (Oxford: Blackwell, 1940), p. 239.

14 Thomas Bestul, *Texts of the Passion: Latin Devotional Literature and Medieval Society* (Philadelphia: University of Pennsylvania Press, 1996), pp. 12, 42.

15 *Mirour de Seinte Eglyse*, ed. A. D. Wilshere, Anglo-Norman Text Society 40 (London: Anglo-Norman Text Society, 1982), pp. 67–9.

16 *Ancrene Wisse: Parts Six and Seven*, ed. Geoffrey Shepherd (Exeter: University of Exeter Press, 1985), pp. ix–xiii.

17 D. Robinson (ed.), *Western Translation Theory from Herodotus to Nietzsche* (Manchester: St Jerome Publishing, 2002), p. 26.

18 *The Middle English* Mirror*: Sermons from Advent to Sexagesima*, ed. Thomas G. Duncan and Margaret Connolly (Heidelberg: Winter, 2003).

19 Ruth J. Dean and Maureen B. M. Boulton, *Anglo-Norman Literature: A Guide to Texts and Manuscripts* (London: Anglo-Norman Text Society, 1999), 'Religious Literature', pp. 238–492.

20 Ed. Forshall and Madden, I, 2; 53; 57; 60.

21 Anne Hudson, *Lollards and their Books* (London: Hambledon, 1985), p. 142.

22 Ed. Ellis, pp. 222–5.

23 Cf. Paul Strohm, 'Hoccleve, Lydgate and the Lancastrian Court', in Wallace 1999: 640–61 with Simpson 2002.

24 N. F. Blake (ed.), *Caxton's Own Prose* (London: Deutsch, 1973), pp. 97–101.

25 Ed. Blake, pp. 78–81.

26 *Virgil's* Aeneid *Translated into Scottish Verse by Gavin Douglas*, ed. David F. C. Coldwell, 4 vols, Scottish Text Society, 3rd ser., 25, 27, 28, 30 (Edinburgh: Blackwood, 1957–64), II, 11, line 299.

References and Further Reading

Bhabha, H. K. 1994. *The Location of Culture.* London: Routledge. Theorizes postcolonial 'translation'; potentially highly productive for thinking about medieval cultural situations.

Cole, A. 2002. 'Chaucer's English Lesson', *Speculum* 77, 1128–66. Argues for Chaucer's indebtedness to Wycliffite theorizing, with special attention to the *Treatise on the Astrolabe.*

Copeland, R. 1991. *Rhetoric, Hermeneutics and Translation in the Middle Ages.* Cambridge: Cambridge University Press. An intellectually rigorous study of medieval translation, concentrating on its academic contexts.

Ellis, R. 2000. 'Translation.' In *A Companion to Chaucer*, ed. P. Brown (Oxford: Blackwell), pp. 443–58. Considers different approaches to Chaucer's work as translation; includes a useful annotated bibliography.

——, Price [Wogan-Browne], J., Medcalf, S. and Meredith, P. (eds) 1989. *The Medieval Translator.* Cambridge: Brewer. The first in the series of studies of medieval translation theory and practice (published since vol. 5, 1996, at Turnhout: Brepols), comprising papers from the Cardiff Conference on the Theory and Practice of Translation in the Middle Ages: wide-ranging material and theoretical/critical approaches.

Evans, R. 1994. 'Translating Past Cultures?' In *The Medieval Translator 4*, ed. R. Ellis and R. Evans (Exeter: University of Exeter Press), pp. 20–45. Examines the theorizing of medieval translation.

Hudson, A. 1988. *The Premature Reformation: Wycliffite Texts and Lollard History.* Oxford: Clarendon Press. The authoritative guide to the subject.

Johnson, I. 1994. 'Tales of a True Translator: Medieval Literary Theory, Anecdote and Autobiography in Osbern Bokenham's *Legendys of Hooly Wummen.*' In *The Medieval Translator 4*, ed. R. Ellis and R. Evans (Exeter: University of Exeter Press), pp. 104–24. Outlines the complexity of Bokenham's engagement with translation theories and with the reception of his work.

Lawton, D. 1999. 'Englishing the Bible, 1066–1549.' In Wallace 1999: 454–82. A lucid account of Bible translation, emphasizing social contexts and controls.

Machan, T. 2003. *English in the Middle Ages.* Oxford: Clarendon Press. A study of the use and status of English in medieval England, especially attentive to the linguistic aspects of interpreting the evidence.

Morey, J. 2000. *Book and Verse: A Guide to Middle English Biblical Literature.* Urbana and Chicago: University of Illinois Press. Brings together valuable documentation for twelfth- to thirteenth-century literature (excluding Wycliffite writings and drama).

Ormrod, W. M. 2003. 'The Use of English: Language, Law, and Political Culture in Fourteenth-Century England', *Speculum* 78, 750–87. A finely tuned historical contextualization of later medieval language usage.

Rothwell, W. 1994. 'The Trilingual England of Geoffrey Chaucer', *Studies in the Age of Chaucer* 16, 45–67. Stresses the complex interrelations of Latin, French and English.

Simon, S. 1996. *Gender in Translation: Cultural Identity and the Politics of Transmission.* London and New York: Routledge. Explores feminist issues in (post-medieval) translation theory and practice.

Simpson, J. 2002. *The Oxford English Literary History. Vol. 2: 1350–1547: Reform and Cultural Revolution.* Oxford: Oxford University Press. Locates translation as central to an understanding of medieval literary culture.

Somerset, F. 1998. *Clerical Discourse and Lay Audience in Late Medieval England.* Cambridge: Cambridge University Press. A nuanced account of the politics of translation of Latin material into English, 1370–1410.

Stanton, R. 2002. *The Culture of Translation in Anglo-Saxon England.* Cambridge: Brewer. Establishes an insular context for vernacular translation.

Wallace, D. (ed.) 1999. *The Cambridge History of Medieval English Literature.* Cambridge: Cambridge University Press. These informative essays continually address translation issues.

Watson, N. 1995. 'Censorship and Cultural Change in Late-Medieval England: Vernacular Theology, the Oxford Translation Debate, and Arundel's Constitutions of 1409', *Speculum* 70, 822–64. An influential and provocative argument, exploring the background to Arundel's legislation and assessing its impact on fifteenth-century culture.

Wogan-Browne, J., Watson, N., Taylor, A. and Evans, R. 1999. *The Idea of the Vernacular: An Anthology of Middle English Literary Theory, 1280–1520.* Exeter: University of Exeter Press. Theorizes and contextualizes translation and vernacularity in Middle English texts; includes a wide range of medieval accounts of writing and translation practice.

PART III
Language and Literature

9
The Languages of Medieval Britain

Laura Wright

This chapter is about the language resources that are currently available for readers of medieval British texts. It will concentrate on multilingualism and the presence of linguistic variation. It will also consider some recently developed methodologies, which depend upon a sensitivity to variation. Perhaps the most significant thing about this chapter is the plural noun in its title: medieval Britain was a multilingual society. Very few people outside the British Isles would have understood English, and many within the British Isles would not have understood it, and probably never even heard it spoken during their lifetime.

Multilingualism

Taking the year AD 400 as a rough starting-point, we assume that most of the speakers within the territory at that time would have been speakers of languages belonging to the Celtic family. The language of the speakers in the area later known as Wales developed into Welsh; speakers in the Cumbrian area spoke Cumbrian Celtic; speakers in Cornwall spoke an early form of Cornish Celtic; the language of the speakers in the area later known as Scotland later developed into Scottish Gaelic; the language of those on the Isle of Man developed into Manx; and speakers in Ireland spoke an early form of Irish Gaelic. There were probably speakers of another language family, known as Pictish, in the far north of Scotland.

Britain was visited by settlers from the nearby continent, who spoke languages belonging to an entirely different language family, known as the Germanic family. Parts of what we now call England, Scotland, Ireland, Wales and the Isle of Man were settled by these immigrants, who spoke two distinct branches of the Germanic family of languages. The first branch to reach Britain was West Germanic, a variety of which later developed into the language now known as Old English. The other branch was North Germanic, which developed into the language known as Old Norse, which then developed into the languages spoken in Scandinavia today. Speakers who left homelands in Scandinavia, collectively known as Vikings, settled around the coastline of the mainland, chiefly in the north and east, and also on the islands, including Ireland, the Isle of Man and the small islands in the Bristol Channel, bringing the Norse language with them. So from our starting-point in AD 400 until the eleventh century, Celtic Britain was visited by waves of settlers speaking both Old English and Old Norse – although they would not have used those labels as they are later, modern creations.

Early medieval Britain was broadly trilingual, with the three main languages being the Celtic family (Welsh, Cumbrian, Cornish, Scottish Gaelic, Irish Gaelic and Manx), the West Germanic family (Old English), and the North Germanic family (Old Norse, spoken by the Vikings). As the Germanic settlers came from the nearby Continent, lying to the east, they settled in the eastern parts of the territory, which became the stronghold of the English language. Today the last vestiges of the Celtic family – Welsh, Scottish Gaelic and Irish Gaelic – are spoken in the western area where the Continental settlers did not penetrate. Manx, Cornish and Cumbrian are no longer spoken as native languages, but revivalists keep their memory alive by means of reading and writing.

With the coming of Christian missionaries to Britain we can add another language, the language of the church, which is Latin. This might have been as early as the second century AD, via individual Roman converts. Thus, the authors and composers of medieval literature lived in a multilingual environment – but which language or languages they were exposed to depended very much on whereabouts in the territory they lived. In the early part of the period at least, a speaker would have had to be well born and educated in order to hear or use Latin.

In everyday use, these languages were not kept distinct from each other, but were mixed, to varying degrees. Perhaps the most mixed were English and Dano-Norwegian, in the territories where the Vikings settled. They settled in greatest numbers in the area known as the Danelaw, which is the part of England that was ruled from Denmark in the ninth century. It comprised four main regions: Northumbria; the areas around and including the towns of Lincoln, Nottingham, Derby, Leicester and Stamford; the region of East Anglia; and the south-east Midlands including parts of Bedfordshire. However, the Vikings were great seafarers and they also settled many other coastal parts of Britain, such as the small islands of Grassholm (Old Norse *holmr*, 'small island') off north Wales, and Lundy in the Bristol Channel (Old Norse *lundi*, 'puffin'). After the first generation of settlers had died out, it is not known for certain how long Dano-Norwegian continued to be spoken in Britain. Settlers continued to arrive from Scandinavia throughout the second half of the first millennium and into the second. The Scandinavian language had considerable influence on English as a whole, and the dialects spoken in the region of the Danelaw in particular. Many familiar present-day English words have a Norse etymology, such as *sky*, *anger*, *egg*, *skin*, *fellow*, *take*, *call*, *both*, *same*, as did the surnaming pattern of adding *-son* to a parent's name, such as *Anderson*. Grammatically, from contact with Old Norse-derived languages, Middle English gained such features as the *they/them/their* pronouns (which replaced the Old English *hie/hem/hiere* forms, although *hem* is still with us under low stress, written *'em*), the introduction of *are* to replace *been*, and the introduction of third person *-s* to replace *-th*. Parts of England under the Danelaw can be identified today by their Old Norse place-name suffixes (such as towns and villages ending in *-by*, 'town', *-dale*, 'valley', *-thwaite*, 'piece of land', *-toft*, 'piece of ground', *-thorp*, 'village'); and dialects within the area contain higher proportions of grammar derived from Old Norse. As the Vikings were not literate, we do not have texts written in Early or Middle Dano-Norwegian. Writers continued to write in Old English or Latin throughout the contact period.

Yet we do have another legacy from the centuries of contact between English and Dano-Norwegian, and that is the considerable structural change that took place in English. Twelfth-century English is very unlike ninth-century English. In twelfth-century written English we begin to see the loss of nominal case inflections and variable loss of verb inflections, an enormously simplified relativizer and article system, loss of grammatical gender in nouns and adjectives, and progress towards modern English word order. These changes are all typical of a creoloid situation, whereby speakers of languages which are structurally similar (Old English and Old Norse both being Germanic languages) compromise in order to understand each other by focusing on the stems of words and word order, rather than on morphology (that is, grammatical relationships indicated by small particles such as suffixes or stem-vowels).

Post-Conquest English is known as Middle English: the main developments of Middle English are its grammatical differences from pre-Conquest English as just mentioned, its huge absorption of words from other languages into English, and the vast amount of dialectal variation found around the country. There were two main feeder languages into the Middle English wordstock: Dano-Norwegian and Anglo-Norman.

As mentioned, Dano-Norwegian donated a very large number of words to the core English wordstock – and even more to the dialects within the Danelaw area – and had a profound effect on the grammar of English. But it also acted as a barrier to the spread of language developments south of the Danelaw. The southern boundary of the Danelaw is still marked in the speech of very young children in a rather recondite manner – recondite to adults, that is. During the eleventh century a sound-change emerged in the south known as Southern Voicing (the dating of this sound-change is contested; it may have begun considerably earlier). It spread northwards from the south coast until it reached the Norse contact zone of the Danelaw administrative boundary, and then began to recede southwards again in the fifteenth century. Southern Voicing refers to the voicing of the word-initial voiceless consonants [f, s, θ] to [v, z, ð], so that *frog* was pronounced *vrog*, *summer zummer*, and *thick* as though it began with the same phoneme as *there*, up to the southern limit of the Danelaw. In the London area, which is about twenty to thirty miles south of the southern Danelaw boundary, very young children have a truce-term, which is *fainites*. A truce-term is shouted whenever a child needs to obtain momentary respite from a chasing game. The temporarily powerful child, the one doing the chasing, always grants the respite to the potential victim while they tie their shoelace, fix their glasses, or whatever motivated the request for a truce. Truce-terms are only used within a specific age group, and have very little currency outside that group. They vary considerably around Britain. By and large they are abandoned and forgotten once a child grows to be ten or eleven. The London form *fainites* has a minority variant, *vainites*. The word *fainites* is probably of Anglo-Norman origin, from the Anglo-Norman French verb *feindre* meaning 'to pretend, feign, turn a blind eye to', which is what the temporarily powerful child does when he or she grants a brief moment of mercy to a potential victim. As with so many Anglo-Norman words, the original French sense altered in Britain, and the *fainite* group came to signify a momentary truce or cessation. In the southern region this word underwent Southern Voicing, and to this day adults in their forties remember saying *vainites* from such places near the southern Danelaw boundary as Southgate, Borehamwood, London Colney, St Albans and Chigwell. However, the Old Norse contact region to the north seems to have prevented the spread of this sound-change, and within the Danelaw other truce-terms prevail.

By 1400, the Middle English lexicon had been transformed by the flood of words – and prefixes and suffixes – entering from Anglo-Norman French. Anglo-Norman is a rather misleading name: it is not a half-English, half-French hybrid, but a French dialect. It is the dialect that came over from France with William the Conqueror and his followers, and it is predominantly that of Normandy, but it contains elements from Central French dialects as well. Originally, Anglo-Norman was spoken in Britain by a very limited set of speakers, that is, those of French origin. But as they settled around the country and had descendants, Anglo-Norman French began to be Anglified – and Middle English began to be Normanized. Many Anglo-Norman-derived words were actually coined by speakers who were born in Britain, just as there are numerous Anglo-Norman words found in British texts which are not recorded in France at all. Others, which had counterparts in France, often had semantic nuances that were very different from the British ones. Not only did Anglo-Norman have a huge influence on the Middle English lexicon, it also continued to be used as a written language into the 1700s in the field of law. The main written uses for Anglo-Norman in Britain, apart from in literature, were in the bureaucratic fields of administration and legal language. However, Anglo-Norman fused with Middle English for more everyday writing purposes (see the section on historical code-switching, below), and the register of some of the Anglo-Norman loanwords into Middle English tells us that usage could be very homely. Compare the affectionate term that adults use to children in the Danelaw area and points north (*my duck*), and the affectionate term that adults use to children south of the Danelaw (*my poppet*). *Duck* may be from an Old Norse term *duck*, meaning 'doll' (cf. Danish *dukke*, Old Swedish *dokka*, and Middle Low German *docke*, all meaning 'doll'), and *poppet* is from Anglo-Norman *poupet*, meaning 'doll'.

As well as donating much of the wordstock to Middle English, Anglo-Norman also donated many suffixes used in word-formation, such as *-acy*, *-age*, *-al*, *-acioun*, *-aunce*, *-erie*, *-esse*, *-ite*, *-ment*. These were not only available for coining new Anglo-Norman words, but soon became attached to words of Old English and Old Norse derivation as well, such as *bondage* (ON + AN), *husbondrie* (OE + ON + AN), *hunteresse* (OE + AN). A line (357) from Chaucer's Parson's Tale (c.1386) will show the intrinsically mixed nature of Middle English (ML = Medieval Latin):

OE	OE	OE	OE	AN + AN	OE	OE + OE	OE	OE
I	sey	nat	that	honestitee	in	clothynge	of	man

OE	OE + OE	OE	OE + AN + AN	OE	AN	OE	ML/AN + ML/AN + AN
or	womman	is	vncouenable,	but	certes	the	superfluitee

OE	ML + ML/AN + ML/AN	ON + AN	OE	OE + OE	OE	AN + AN + AN
or	disordinat	scantitee	of	clothynge	is	repreuable.

During the medieval period the Celtic group of languages spoken in Britain – Welsh, Cornish, Irish Gaelic, Scottish Gaelic, Manx, perhaps Cumbrian – were mainly restricted to their various regions. By and large, they did not donate many words to English, but it is possible that there was some grammatical influence. There was a grammatical constraint known (among many other names) as the Northern Personal Pronoun Rule, which may be a contact feature from Celtic. It seems to have started on the Scottish border and to have become quite widespread during the Middle English period. It is illustrated by the following example.

> wiche is giffen to al sentis or holy men, þat cleueþ togeder in charite, weyþer þei knowe þam bodily or noȝt
>
> (which is given to all saints or holy men, who cleave together in charity, whether they know them bodily or not)
>
> [*Rosarium theologie*, late 1300s][1]

At first sight it seems like quite a complicated rule (although in practice it is not): in the north, the third person plural present tense indicative marker was *-es*, unless the word *they* was adjacent, in which case the marker was *-e* or zero. In the south, the third person plural present tense indicative marker was *-eth*, even if the word *they* was adjacent. There was a small pocket in the eastern Midlands around the Wash where the third person plural present tense indicative marker was *-eth*, unless the word *they* was adjacent, in which case the marker was *-en*, *-e* or zero. The example above from the *Rosarium theologie*, written somewhere near Peterborough, comes from the eastern Midlands pocket. The form *cleueþ* takes the *-eth* suffix which marks the plural, but the form *knowe* has no suffix, because it is blocked by the adjacent *they*. The essence of the rule is that in the north and Midlands, the word *they* had the effect of blocking the suffix (whether *-s* or *-eth*) on the following verb. In the south, *they* had no effect.

So in late Middle English, the Northern Personal Pronoun Rule was operative in the northern part of the country, with the dividing line around the Wash. It seems to have been a fairly categorical rule in northern Middle English. By the end of the Middle English period, non-categorical use of the Northern Personal Pronoun Rule had reached London. It is present as a variable, not an absolute, rule in the Cely Letters (1472–88), which were written by a family of wool merchants based in London who also had northern connections. By the 1500s it is found in various London texts, albeit at a low frequency ratio, and so what might be visible in the Cely correspondence is the mechanism by which it reached London; that is, via the speech of northern traders.

Classical Latin was the language of the church, and so many medieval British texts were written in this language. Medieval Latin, a dialectal variant, was written in Britain too, particularly in the fields of civic administration and law. Although Latin has donated an enormous number of words and grammatical particles to English over the centuries, the main contribution from classical Latin was yet to come, in the early modern period.

As seafarers and traders crossed the English channel and arrived at the ports, they brought numerous Continental languages with them. I will single out for mention the languages of the Low Countries, that is Middle Low Dutch and Middle Low German. These two languages added many words within the fields of expertise of their speakers, which included seafaring, fishing and brewing beer. For example, to this source we probably owe such homely Middle English words as *cropling* (a type of small stockfish), *halfwoxfish* (a half-grown stockfish), *palingman* (a seller of eels), *pickle-herring* (herring in a spicy sauce), *raclefish* (a kind of stockfish, probably a strip of halibut, salted and dried), *shaft-eel* (a type of middle-sized eel) and *shotten-herring* (a herring that has spawned), as well as that staple of the medieval diet, the word *stockfish* itself (air-dried fish). All of these were everyday fare, easily available in the London markets.

Historical Code-switching

Speakers in medieval Britain did not share our concepts of discrete languages, and their notions of what was 'French' and what was 'English' were far more fluid than ours. Today we tend to think of languages as distinct entities: English is English and French is French, and the two are separate. Yet, one of the most widespread practices in the world today is that of code-switching; that is, veering from one language to another in the space of a few words. Many medieval texts switch from language to language, with the structure of the switches varying according to the function of the text, sometimes from word to word, sometimes from line to line, sometimes from paragraph to paragraph or rubric to rubric. Systematic code-switching between languages is found in such medieval texts as medical writings, other scientific texts, legal texts, administrative texts, sermons, other religious prose texts, literary prose, poems, drama, accounts, inventories, rule-books and letters. Some illustrations follow (these and other examples occur in Schendl 2000: 80–5):

1. Religious prose text in English and Latin: sermon (early fifteenth century)

Domini gouernouris most *eciam* be merciful in punchyng. *Oportet ipsos attendere quod* of stakis and stodis *qui deberent stare in ista vinea quedam sunt* smoþe and lightlich wul boo, *quedam sunt* so stif and so ful of warris *quod homo* schal to-cleue hom *cicius quam planare.*

(The lord's governors must also be merciful in punishing. They should take notice that of the stakes and supports that should stand in this vineyard, some are smooth and will easily bend, others are so stiff and so full of obstinacy that a man will split them sooner than straighten them out.)

2. Letter in English and Anglo-Norman: from R. Kingston to King Henry IV (1403)

Tresexcellent, trespuissant, et tresredoute Seignour, autrement say a present nieez. Jeo prie a la benoit trinite que vous ottroie bone vie ove tresentier sauntee a treslonge durre, and sende yowe sone to ows in helþ and prosperitee; for in god fey, I hope to almighty god that, yef ye come youre owne persone, ye schulle haue the victorie of alle youre enemyes.

(Most excellent, mighty and revered Sir, otherwise I know nothing at present. I pray to the blessed trinity to grant you a good life with the fullest health of the longest duration, and send you soon to us in health and prosperity; for in good faith, I hope to almighty God that, if you come yourself, you shall have a victory over all your enemies.)

It has often been assumed that texts which show code-switching are indicative of an ill-educated scribe, who did not know the other languages fully. However, studies on present-day code-switching show that, on the contrary, the speakers usually have a full grasp of both languages, but choose to switch for social and discourse-pragmatic reasons.[2] Similarly, it can frequently be demonstrated that the scribe of a code-switched text did in fact command the grammar and vocabulary of all the languages used, but that he chose to combine them. At present, we are not fully sensitive to the discourse-pragmatic reasons for medieval code-switching, and it is one of the things to which the present-day reader of a medieval text is deaf.

Middle English Dialectal Variation

One of the main characteristics of medieval texts written in English is their dialectal variation. Standard English was not to evolve until the early modern period, so whenever medieval writers applied ink to parchment, they would spell words according to how they sounded in their own accent, and they would use the wordstock and grammatical structure that pertained to their own dialect. The term *accent* refers to the sounds that come out of a speaker's mouth: it is possible to speak any language with any accent. You could speak Greenlandic with a German accent – although in practice you're only likely to do so if your native tongue is German. The term *dialect* refers to the words spoken in a given area, the order in which they are placed, and the grammatical particles which fuse them together.

Dialectal variation is a direct result of the passage of time. The reason there is so much dialectal variation in present-day Britain compared with, say, New Zealand, is because English has been spoken continuously in Britain for roughly one a half thousand years. That is to say, communities have lived, uninterruptedly, on the same plot of land since that land was settled, for all that time. As a result, dialects change almost imperceptibly from village to village, and a British village, unless it is in inhospitable terrain, is usually less than ten miles distant from the next village. This is known as a dialect continuum: if you were to start at a village on the south coast, and walk northwards until you met the old boundary of the Celtic language, Scottish Gaelic, in the highlands of Scotland, you would not notice the language change from village to village, but by the time you had walked through ten villages and were a hundred miles from your starting-point, the difference would be noticeable.

A dialect is made up of all the words that are used by the speakers in a given region, and all the grammatical rules that they use. However, an individual speaker would not have used all of those words, nor necessarily all of the grammatical variants. From studying medieval linguistic variation in a given region, the main picture that emerges is one of controlled variation. There was a tendency for scribes to have a major variant. For example, there were 144 instances of the third person plural form of *shall* written in Norfolk documents known as guild certificates between November 1388 and February 1389. Today, if we want to write the third person plural form of the word *shall* we have only two choices: we write either *shall* or *'ll*. In the Norfolk certificates the scribes spelled *shall* as follows:

> shul (20%), shal (11%), shullen (10%), schal (8%), schullen (6%), schul (6%), shuln (4%), scholen (3%), schully (3%), schuln (2%), sshullen (2%), schulen (2%), shule (2%), schun (1%), shulle (1%), sal (1%), shulle (0.7%), schullyn (0.7%), schulyn (0.7%), shullyn (0.7%), shulen (0.7%), sschullon (0.7%), schullo*n* (0.7%), scullen (0.7%), sullen (0.7%), schulne (0.7%), shun (0.7%), xuln (0.7%), sholen (0.7%), schole*n* (0.7%), sshollen (0.7%), schulle (0.7%), sshull (0.7%), sulle (0.7%), sul (0.7%), shole (0.7%), schalle (0.7%), scal (0.7%), shall (0.7%), scha (0.7%).

These can be separated out into *u*/*o* + *n* variants: 44%; *u*/*o* variants: 32%; and *a* variants: 23%. Hence there were forty ways of spelling plural *shall* in this one text type in Norfolk in the winter of 1388–9. There was nothing wrong or ill-educated about this. Medieval East Anglian clerks were particularly prone to spelling variation, perhaps more so than in any other part of the country: 'In East Anglia (especially Norfolk), and also in Lincolnshire, an individual writer's range of variant spellings for a single word is generally greater than in most other counties' (McIntosh, Samuels and Benskin 1986: II, x). In London, by contrast, in exactly the same text type, that is, in guild certificates written for the same purposes during the same four months, there were only five different ways of spelling third person plural *shall*: schul (80%), shul (9%), schulle (5%), schal (4%), schule (2%). This gives 96% *u* variants and just 4% *a* variants. One of the main processes of standardization was the elimination of variation. The London scribes had moved further towards this state in 1388–9 at ratios of 96% : 4% for plural *shall*, whereas the Norfolk scribes were still writing according to the normal medieval practice at this date, with three main variants at 44% : 32% : 23%.

Minority variants in medieval texts, be they spelling variants or grammatical variants, are not 'errors', or insignificant; they encode information about the variation in the speech of the writer. Each writer used a subset of the features available in his or her dialect, and accordingly had a stylistic 'fingerprint'. In published versions of medieval texts, minority variants are occasionally silently edited out, or a footnote appended as though they needed an explanation. In the Norfolk guild certificates of 1388–9, for example, the major variants for marking the third person singular present tense indicative (*-th, -s*) were also available as minority variants for marking the plural. The same is also true vice versa: the major Norfolk third person plural marker (*-n*) was also available as a minority singular marker. There was nothing erroneous about this: consistency was not considered to be a virtue in Middle English writing.

Historical Sociolinguistics

The discipline of sociolinguistics which developed in the second half of the twentieth century has led to the establishment of the field of historical sociolinguistics. Sociolinguistics looks at how social groupings manifest themselves in the human voice. When a native Briton hears another native Briton whom they have never met, on the radio or on the telephone, they are able to make informed guesses about certain personal attributes. This is because when a British person speaks English, regardless of what they actually say, they necessarily give away information about their age, their sex, the social class to which they belong, and perhaps the region in which they learnt to speak English. A listener might be able to infer information about their politics, or their schooling, and even deduce such lifestyle choices as what kind of music they prefer to listen to, and what style of dress they are likely to adopt. In north America, the listener would also be able to make an informed guess about the race of the speaker. On the island of Tristan da Cunha, the listener would also be able to make an informed guess about whether the speaker had spent a period time off the island or not (although the concept of the anonymous Tristanian speaker does not exist, as there are fewer than 300 people there). Sociolinguists who study present-day speech are interested in discovering which of these variables pertain to which speech communities – for example, the variable of ethnicity, which is so salient in North America, is unimportant on Tristan da Cunha, where practically everybody shares the same ethnicity. In Britain, people's skin colour is encoded less in their voice than it is in North America (for example, working-class teenagers born, raised and living in, say, Leeds are likely to have the same kind of Yorkshire dialect and accent, regardless of ethnicity). Sociolinguists then analyse the ways in which speakers and listeners can do all this, and ask: Is gender signalled by intonation in a given dialect? Is age signalled by vocabulary in a given speech community? What are the precise nuances of spoken difference between the middle-middle-class speakers in a city, and the upper-middle-class speakers of the same age, gender and political leanings in the same place? Sociolinguists who study present-day varieties of English have many ways of trying to discover, independently of speech, how members of communities signal their membership. Indices might include occupation, education, wealth, length of time the family has lived in that place, and many other social factors. They then work out how these correlate with the features of accent and dialect used by such speakers.

Historically, it is fascinating to try and reconstruct social relationships via the evidence that remains of how people spoke. In the medieval period, such evidence is necessarily textual – speakers cannot be interviewed as they would be today. The first step is to divide up the textual evidence into genres, which linguists refer to as text types. One of the most useful text types for the purposes of analysis and comparison is the personal letter. Personal letters usually have an addresser and an addressee, and if their letters have survived, it is often possible to find out something about their biographies. One of the best preserves of people's correspondence is the judiciary courts. If a family's correspondence was subpoenaed at some point then it may still exist in repositories such as the National Archives (formerly the Public Record Office), along with other details of the people involved in the court case. Terttu Nevalainen and Helena Raumolin-Brunberg have set up an electronic *Corpus of Early English Correspondence*, comprising letters from over 700 people writing in England between 1420 and 1680. An electronic corpus is a body of writing tagged for variables which, it is envisaged, might be linguistically salient in expressing some kind of social attribute. For example, in the *Corpus of Early English Correspondence* the fields tagged in the sender database include: name, title, year of birth, sex, rank, father's rank, social mobility, place of birth, domicile, education, religion, career and migration history.

During the late medieval period, the notion of rank was very different from that of today. People were divided into one of two social classes: either they belonged to the gentry, or they did not. The gentry was subdivided into the nobility, that is, royalty, dukes, marquesses, earls, viscounts and barons; and the gentry proper, that is, knights, esquires and gentlemen. The nobility were addressed as *my Lord* and *Lady*, the knights as *Sir* and *Dame*, and the esquires as *Mr* and *Mrs*. The gentry could hold certain professional occupations, such as those of army officer, government official, lawyer, doctor, merchant, clergyman or teacher. The non-gentry, grouped according to socio-economic status, comprised: the yeomen, merchants and husbandmen, who were addressed as *Goodman* and *Goodwife*; the craftsmen, tradesmen and artificers, who were addressed according to their occupation; the poorest social group, including the labourers, who were addressed as *Labourer*, and the cottagers and paupers who had no title at all.

Let us look at the variable *ye/you* in the *Corpus of Early English Correspondence*. In early Middle English, *ye* was used in subject position, and it marked plurality, whilst *you* was used in object position, also marking plurality.

> ȝef ȝe abideþ mine here,
> ȝe schule an oþer wise singe
>
> (if you (all) await my army
> you (all) shall sing another tune)
> [*The Owl and The Nightingale*, c.1260][3]

'Lordinges,' he said, 'bifor ȝou here
Ich ordainy min heiȝe steward'

('Lordings,' he said, 'before you [all] here
I ordain my high steward')
[*Sir Orfeo*, 1325–50][4]

Singularity was marked by *thee* and *thou*. In the fourteenth century, this system began to change, and *you* began to be used in subject position, as today. As *you* usage increased over the fifteenth century, *ye* and *you* began to lose their function of marking plurality, and by the end of the period they were used for both singular and plural referents, in both subject and object position:

Now telleth **ye**, sir monk, if that **ye** konne . . .
[MilP, before 1400]

No mor to **you** at thys tyme, Jhesu kepe **ȝe**
[Richard Cely the Younger, 1478][5]

As *thee* and *thou* lost their function of marking singularity they became marked for social function. By the beginning of the late medieval period, *thou/thee* came to be the form used from a social superior to a social inferior, so that lords would say *thou* to their servants, and servants would reply with *you* to their lords. Among social equals, *thou/thee* was the form used to an interlocutor with whom the speaker was intimate – including addresses to God. *Thou/thee* was also the form used when the speaker wished to give offence. *You*, by contrast, was the polite, unmarked form of address, and it is found regularly in courtly romances. This is the backdrop against which all late medieval texts were written: each and every instance of *ye/you* and *thee/thou* begs the question as to why another form was not used. However, the distribution sketched here is not yet fully understood. It is not uncommon to find the same speaker switching from *you* to *thou* or vice versa in the course of a single speech to the same interlocutor, often signalling a moment of high emotional tension.

When subject usages of *ye/you* are scrutinized in the *Corpus of Early English Correspondence*, it is found that the change was led by the upper gentry, closely followed by the lower gentry. However, the nobility lagged considerably behind, continuing to use *ye* and *you* in the traditional way – although as this group often employed professional secretaries, it is possible that we are seeing their very professionalism – that to be a secretary meant writing in a conservative way. Yet royal letters also show the move away from *ye* towards *you* at the same rate as the upper gentry, and they too employed secretaries. So it looks as though the change started in the more middle ranking social group, and then spread to the two extremes – although of course there is little direct data from the poorer groups because fewer of them could write. Taking the thirty years 1520–50, the distribution is as follows:

Rank	You (%)
Nobility	8
Upper gentry	48
Lower gentry	36
Merchants	25
Non-gentry	29

Thereafter *ye* drops out of usage altogether. Consequently, when coming across an instance of a second person subject pronoun in late medieval literature, the reader needs to remember that there were three choices in subject position over the period (*ye/you/thou*); that use of *you/thou* depended on the attitude of the addresser towards the addressee; and that *ye/you* usage was conditioned by rank as well as date of writing. All of this is easy to miss if the author has written *you*, the form which survives today.

Historical Pragmatics

One of the developments of recent decades is the field of historical pragmatics. This is to do with the language of immediacy as opposed to the language of distance. For example, it asks, in relation to written texts: Was the reader known to the author, as in a private letter, and hence writing intimately? Was there spontaneity, that is, free topic development, or was a model or template being followed, as in a religious or medical text? Is the language formal, as in a legal document, or is there high personal emotional content, as in drama? Historical pragmatics is concerned with the background culture of communication; that is, the kind of writing conventions that prevailed in a given society, conditioning not only the kind of thing an author would say in a given context, but also how they would say it. Unlike the field of historical sociolinguistics, the study of historical pragmatics does not lend itself to the searching of electronic corpora. If you are interested in a sociolinguistic question such as whether the women in Chaucer's tales use language differently from the men, then you can tag all the women's dialogue, and tag all the men's, and then search them according to each grammatical and lexical feature that you want to look at, until you arrive at a conclusion. If, however, your interest is in pragmatics, then you are likely to be searching across several text types. If a speaker insults another in a dialogue, how do we know the attitude of that speaker, whether playful, ironic or offensive, and how can we judge the force of the insult? What kind of person said, say, *Marry!* in 1350, and what kind of person avoided it at all costs? Had that distribution changed fifty years later? Was there likely to be a difference between the usage of, say, a middle-aged female in a country village and that of a middle-aged female London speaker? It can be notoriously difficult today to distinguish between sarcasm, irony, slander, defamation, insinuation and cynical observation. What may be said in public as an ironic comment may be heard, or repeated, as an offensive insult, with a resulting court case to clarify the matter. One person's swear word of strongest force, uttered only upon extreme provocation, can be another's intimacy marker, used to indicate that they are in friendly company and an informal setting. Religious people may avoid the utterance of *God!* as a discourse marker, while for other speakers it may be an indicator of topic change or attitudinal change, used to signal an answer to a question (*God no!*, *oh God yes!*), or perhaps the closure of a speech-turn (*God, I should hope not!*). It is easy to miss the force of obsolete expletives which pertain to the religious semantic field, as the religious culture of the late medieval period was so much stronger than ours is today.

Marry used to be a direct reference to the Virgin Mary, but by the end of the medieval period speakers would not necessarily have been aware of this. A search of usages as instanced by the *Oxford English Dictionary* shows that *marry* began to be used as a discourse marker in the late fourteenth century, particularly as a marker of address (*marry, sir*) and as an emphasis marker (*marry, yes*). The heyday of *marry* was around 1600, so from a medievalist's point of view this discourse marker is growing in usage over the period, and we would expect to see more and more kinds of character represented as using it as the period wears on. Its typical site is at the beginning of a second turn in conversation, often at the beginning of an answer to a question or a response to a statement, expressing a reaction to what went before. It usually signals some kind of emotional involvement or colouring, whether to a greater or lesser degree:

Sec. Pastor. Say what was his song? hard ye not how he crakyd it, Thre brefes to a long.
Tert. Pastor. Yee **mary** he hakt it, Was no crochett wrong, nor no thing that lakt it.
[c.1460][6]

(*Second shepherd.* Tell us: what was his song?
Did you not hear how he trilled it,
Three short notes to a long one?
Third shepherd. Yes, sure thing, he warbled it,
Not a crotchet was wrong,
Nor was anything missing.)[7]

We have already touched upon social rank in late medieval literature. In a hierarchical society, it is possible, indeed normal, for members of that society to live in close proximity – under the same roof – and yet not to have reciprocal speaking rights. Masters and mistresses could speak to servants whenever they chose. But servants could not utter whatever came to mind to their masters and mistresses with the same freedom. Although the employers could talk to their servants at will, the kind of speech acts they directed at them were not the same as those that they directed to other members of society. Orders and commands were predominant in the master-to-servant relationship, and also in the master-to-apprentice relationship. In other words, speakers self-edit. They decide which speech acts are appropriate under which circumstances and those circumstances are social ones. Just as the social situation has changed, so the propriety of uttering, say, a command, has changed over time. Nowadays, few English speakers are comfortable issuing a command, except from parent to child, and we have evolved an elaborate politeness code to circumnavigate the use of the imperative. This is a post-medieval creation. In present-day written texts, probably the only places that imperatives are routinely found are instruction manuals and recipes – where the reader is at liberty to ignore them.

Social rank also dictated the kinds of knowledge, experience and quotidian routine readers could assume when interpreting a text. This is known as exophoric reference, meaning reference to 'things in the real world', that is, knowledge shared by author and reader alike, as opposed to matter which pertains in a work of fiction but not outside that fiction. To illustrate this, let us consider Chaucer's Prioress in the *Canterbury Tales*. She is depicted in the General Prologue as speaking the French of 'Stratford atte Bowe' (125), referring to the Priory of Stratford at Bow in Essex. Nowadays, the general area of Stratford is 'a humdrum and not very prepossessing corner of the vast East London sprawl', but in the late 1300s it was frequented by royalty and other persons of fashion (Rothwell 2001: 187). It has sometimes been assumed that Chaucer's reference to the kind of French spoken by the Prioress at Stratford must imply incompetence on the Prioress's part; that the Prioress wasn't very sophisticated and had never been to Paris, and that this was evident in her use of French. However, a historical pragmatic approach does not make this assumption, because it is derived from the kind of value that today's society places on speaking Parisian French. Taking a historical pragmatic approach, the first task is to assemble as much evidence as we can about the kind of French that was used in Stratford in the late 1300s. This includes: (a) administrative London documents written in the business variety of the day, which was a rule-governed mixture of Anglo-Norman and Middle English, as used daily by Chaucer himself in his post as Controller of Customs a few miles upriver from Stratford; (b) other administrative texts written in the mixed language business variety, such as the accounts and registers of religious houses, as well as the output of the London civic bureaucracy in general; (c) translations of Latin religious works into Anglo-Norman, undertaken by nuns and monks in the various religious houses in the area, such as the work of a nun at Barking Abbey who translated the *Life of St Edward* and probably the *Life of St Catherine* into French verse; (d) other Anglo-Norman literary activity undertaken at religious houses, including the composition of grammatical texts and didactic material used in teaching; (e) Anglo-Norman legal texts, texts on conveyancing, deeds and procedural processes of the courts of law, including treatises on interpretation and practice, almost certainly in a spoken context; and (f) private letters, as Anglo-Norman was the language used by the gentry, both male and female, when writing letters.

The language of all of these documents demonstrates the close relationship between the religious houses, the universities, higher administration, royalty and the law, and Anglo-Norman French. Anglo-Norman was a working language of government, and its usage implied education and a seriousness of intent. It was indeed unlike the French of Paris, in both wordstock and grammar. But there was no standard variety of French in the late 1300s, any more than there was a standard variety of English, so to invoke a norm against which the Prioress can be judged is anachronistic. How then are we to interpret the reference to her use of Stratford French? It must imply that she was competent at the default working register of her day; that she led a working life. Does it also imply that she is insular, and ignorant of Continental customs?

This question has to be left hanging, because the multilingual situation of Britain is not fully understood. We know that the routine mixing of three or more languages was a norm among those who could write, and we know that they did not distinguish between those languages in the way that we do. Linguistic correctness and consistency were not recognized virtues, and hence could not be transgressed. Multiplicity of expression and semantically repetitious glossing were far more common then than now, as speakers from different dialect backgrounds optimized communication by any means they could. It cannot safely be assumed that Anglo-Norman and medieval Latin *of themselves* indicated a high register; rather, that the speech act dictated the form, and those languages were used for a wide range of speech acts.

See also: 2 English Society in the Later Middle Ages, 8 Translation and Society, 10 The Forms of Speech, 11 The Forms of Verse, 14 England's Antiquities.

Notes

1 Christina von Nolcken (ed.), *The Middle English Translation of the Rosarium Theologie* (Heidelberg: Winter, 1979), p. 58, lines 12–14.

2 See Schendl 2000 and references therein for a discussion of medieval code-switching.

3 *The Owl and the Nightingale*, ed. Eric Gerald Stanley (Manchester: Manchester University Press, 1960), lines 1702–3.

4 *Sir Orfeo*, ed. Kenneth Sisam, in his *Fourteenth Century Verse and Prose* (Oxford: Clarendon Press, 1921), lines 204 and 205.

5 *Cely Letters*, ed. Alison Hanham (London: Oxford University Press, 1975), p. 31, letter 34.

6 Martin Stevens and A. C. Cawley (eds), *The Towneley Plays*, EETS ss 14 (1994), lines 946–51.

7 Translation by Ruth Kennedy of Royal Holloway College.

References and Further Reading

Blake, N. (ed.) 1992. *The Cambridge History of the English Language. Vol. 2: 1066–1476*. Cambridge: Cambridge University Press. The standard work to consult about the Middle English language.

Fischer, A. 1998. 'Marry: From Religious Invocation to Discourse Marker.' In *Anglistentag 1997 Giessen: Proceedings*, ed. R. Borgmaier, H. Grabes and A. H. Jucker (Trier: WVT Wissenschaftlicher Verlag), pp. 35–46. Outlines the rise and fall of *marry* from the fourteenth to the nineteenth centuries, and considers the function of discourse markers.

Gregory, S. and Trotter, D. A. (eds) 1997. *De Mot en Mot: Aspects of Medieval Linguistics – Essays in Honour of William Rothwell*. Cardiff: University of Wales Press and the Modern Humanities Research Association. A collection of essays looking at French, English, Portuguese, Latin and Spanish.

Helsinki Corpus of English Texts: http://khnt.hit.uib.no/icame/manuals/HC/INDEX.HTM. A computerized collection of extracts of continuous text, containing a diachronic part covering the period from c.750 to c.1700.

Historical Thesaurus of English: http://www2.arts.gla.ac.uk/SESLL/EngLang/thesaur/homepage.htm. The *Historical Thesaurus of English* contains the vocabulary of English from the earliest written records to the present, taken from the *Oxford English Dictionary*.

Jucker, A. H. 2000. 'English Historical Pragmatics: Problems of Data and Methodology.' In *English Diachronic Pragmatics*, ed. G. di Martino and M. Lima (Naples: Cuen), pp. 17–56. Considers the historical pragmatic approach to English. See abstracts from the *Journal of Historical Pragmatics* at www.es.unizh.ch/ahjucker/JHP.htm.

Kastovsky, D. and Mettinger, A. (eds) 2001. *Language Contact in the History of English*. Frankfurt am Main: Lang. A collection of essays dealing with French, English, Latin, Irish and Scandinavian, among other languages.

Kurath, H. and Kuhn, S. M. (eds) 1952–2001. *Middle English Dictionary*. 12 vols. Ann Arbor: University of Michigan Press. Comprehensive analysis of lexicon and usage for the period 1100–1500.

Latham, R. E., Howlett, D. R., Powell, A. H. and Sharpe, R. (eds) 1986–. *Dictionary of Medieval Latin from British Sources*. London: British Academy and Oxford University Press. Indispensable guide to the study of the Latin Middle Ages in Britain from the sixth century to the sixteenth.

Linguistic Atlas of Early Middle English. http://wwwestrni.unibg.it/siti_esterni/anglistica/slin/IHD-atlases.html. Maps regional early Middle English spelling distribution, still under construction.

Machan, T. W. 2003. *English in the Middle Ages*. Oxford: Oxford University Press. Explores the social meanings, functions and status of English in the late medieval period.

McIntosh, A., Samuels, M. L. and Benskin, M. (eds) 1986. *A Linguistic Atlas of Late Medieval English*. 4 vols. Aberdeen: Aberdeen University Press. An atlas of regional later Middle English spelling distribution.

Nevalainen, T. and Raumolin-Brunberg, H. (eds) 1996. *Sociolinguistics and Language History: Studies Based on the Corpus of Early English Correspondence*. Amsterdam: Rodopi. A collection of essays demonstrating the historical sociolinguistic method.

Rothwell, W. 2001. 'Stratford atte Bowe Revisited.' *Chaucer Review*, 36, 184–207. Explains why the French of Stratford cannot be merely unlike the French of Paris.

——, Stone, L. W. and Reid, T. B. W. (eds) 1977–92. *Anglo-Norman Dictionary*. London: Modern Humanities Research Association. The Anglo-Norman hub is still under construction at http://anglo-norman.net/, but it is now searchable.

Schendl, H. 2000. 'Linguistic Aspects of Code-Switching in Medieval English Texts.' In Trotter 2000: 77–92. A catalogue of medieval text types which routinely code-switch between languages.

Simpson, J. A. and Weiner, E. S. C. (eds) 1989. *The Oxford English Dictionary* (2nd edn). 20 vols. Oxford: Clarendon Press. Now searchable at *Oxford English Dictionary*: http://www.oed.com. *OED* is the accepted authority on the evolution of the English language over the last millennium.

Trotter, D. A. (ed.) 2000. *Multilingualism in Later Medieval Britain*. Cambridge: Brewer. A collection of essays dealing with Welsh, English, Latin and French.

Wright, L. (ed.) 2000. *The Development of Standard English, 1300–1800: Theories, Descriptions, Conflicts*. Cambridge: Cambridge University Press. A collection of essays considering the processes of standardization.

10
The Forms of Speech

Donka Minkova

'The Forms of Speech' is an ambitious title: no single chapter can meet the expectation of complete coverage of the linguistic properties of Middle English. It is appropriate therefore to start with a disclaimer: this chapter will concentrate on the phonological features of fourteenth- and fifteenth-century English that are particularly relevant to the scansion of verse. This is not to say that grammar, word formation and semantics are of no interest. They certainly are. The remit of this chapter, however, is to provide information about the phonological setting in which verse was composed and copied.

Many of the foundational texts in English medieval literature are in verse; most of the authors included in Part VII 'Readings' are known primarily for their poetic works. This is not an accident of manuscript survival. Like painting, song and dance, the composition of verse is a basic form of creativity in human communication. In Old and Middle English culture poetry was a highly regarded vehicle of verbal expression, a natural choice for imparting knowledge, observing rituals, religious instruction, moral edification and amusement. In secular, courtly and devotional circles poets were held in high regard; they were often the arbiters of right and wrong, they were the esteemed story-tellers of the past, and their art had emotional appeal, vigour and prominence not matched by other forms of writing. John Trevisa (*fl.*1387), whose encyclopedic translations enjoyed great popularity in the fourteenth century, remarked that 'Writinge of poetes is more worthy to preisynge of emperoures þan al þe welþe of þis worlde'.[1] His contemporary William Langland paired for prestige and wisdom 'patriarkes and prophetes and poetes bothe' (10.336).[2] Geoffrey Chaucer referred admiringly to the poetry of Dante, Petrarch and John Gower; Gower, Robert Henryson and John Lydgate, in their turn, placed Chaucer on a par with the 'laurelled' poets of the classical past and tried to imitate him.

In a society where the pleasures of reading were not enjoyed by many, even among those who had some leisure on their hands, listening to verse must also have been a favourite form of entertainment. The mnemonic and aural aesthetic effects of medieval poetry acquire particular significance in the minimally literate context of verse delivery. The versification skills of a poet, gauged by the cohesion of the sounds and rhythms of a poetic piece, would be as central to its success and popularity as its subject-matter, its imaginative appeal, and the choice of diction and rhetorical devices.

The words *poet* and *poesy*, 'poetic composition', were not current in English until the beginning of the fourteenth century, yet neither the cultural esteem for poetry, nor the formal features of verse dating from the middle of the century onwards, were new in our period. Alliterative verse had been composed and admired by the Anglo-Saxons. The Continental model of syllable counting (isosyllabism) had been borrowed soon after the Norman Conquest; by the beginning of the thirteenth century important literary compositions such as *The Owl and the Nightingale* and *The Ormulum* attest to the understanding and approval of the innovative rhythmic patterns by speakers of English. Thus, although the poetry of the late Middle English period survives only in textualized form, its artistic effects rely on the same phonological components of verse that are found in earlier and later compositions. Such components are sound repetition (alliteration and rhyme), syllable counting and rhythmic organization, and the division of the speech continuum into half or full lines flanked by pauses.

Appreciation of the poetry of the period presupposes familiarity with the linguistic ingredients of verse. The following sections will survey the linguistic features relevant to the understanding of the cohesive elements and the metrical structure of Middle English verse.

The Middle English Linguistic Landscape

Our linguistic outline will start with a survey of the correspondences between spelling and the pronunciation of individual sounds during the century-and-a-half addressed by this volume. The focus will be on the pronunciation difficulties that a speaker of modern English is likely to run into when reading Middle English poetry.

Once again, a caveat is in order: no single list or chart can represent accurately the reconstructed pronunciation of Middle English, because 'Middle English' is an idealized picture of an aggregate of distinct dialects which were constantly evolving. One consequence of the political and cultural changes after the Norman Conquest of 1066 was the decentralization of literary activities in the vernacular and the displacement of English as the primary language in monastic culture. Theological and pedagogical writing was often in the hands of non-English speakers. For at least three hundred years after the Conquest English was competing with French and Latin in areas where some uniformity could be expected: in legal, administrative and scholastic discourse. Throughout the Middle Ages, of course, English was never displaced as the dominant vernacular language, but its various forms were not sanctioned by Church and state in a way comparable to the dialect of Wessex in the Anglo-Saxon period. It flourished locally, and during the fourteenth century it began to regain its position as the language of learning and official records. The 'recovery' of English was relatively swift; by the end of the fifteenth century only Latin persisted as an alternative learned language.

Although English was the leading language of choice in literary works in our period, its relegation to the periphery of officialdom meant also that it was a language without well-defined norms. Each geographical area had its own scribal and literary traditions. Dialects differed both in their phonological structure and in their morphology, syntax and vocabulary, and already in the fourteenth century these differences became the subject of contemporary commentaries. One of the more famous disparaging comments on the strangeness of dialects is Trevisa's elaboration of Ranulph Higden's reference to the speech of the northerners: 'Þe longage of þe Norþhumbres, and specialliche at ȝork, is so scharp, slitting, and frotynge and vnschape' (L *stridet incondita*). Chaucer's often cited and presumably comical imitation of the student's northern speech in the Reeve's Tale is the earliest example of dialect characterization in a literary work. Northerners, too, found the speech of outsiders objectionable: in the *Second Shepherd's Play*, a northern composition, one of the shepherds berates his fellow Mak for using southern forms with: 'Now take outt that sothren tothe / And sett in a torde!" (215–16).[3]

The main dialect divisions of Middle English are known as Northern, Midland and Southern. Within the south, a separate dialect, Kentish, developed in the counties of Kent and Sussex. The Midland dialect area splits further into two distinct varieties: East Midland and West Midland. These regional variants were constantly changing. Moreover, within that regionally and temporally dynamic linguistic landscape there must have existed social distinctions which are beyond recovery. Bundling together the fourteenth-century southern variety of Chaucer's English with Henryson's Scots English at the close of the medieval period is as gross a generalization as it would be to compare a late nineteenth-century speaker of Southern British English to a speaker of Scots English in the early twenty-first century. Nevertheless, there are some major phonological differences between Middle English and modern English that are valid for most of the readings in Part VII of this companion.

Consonants

By 1350 the inventory of consonants in English had reached its present-day state, except for the lack of the palatal fricative /ʒ/ as in *measure, vision*.[4] Simplifying somewhat, because the issue does not affect verse structure, double consonants in spelling, as in *bedd* 'bed', *sterre* 'star', were pronounced as single consonants, *pace* the widespread emphasis on the double consonants in some modern readings of Chaucerian rhymes like *cuppe : uppe, dette : sette, innę : synnę, stallę : allę.*

The full set of Middle English consonants is shown in the chart below:

	Labial	Dental	Alveolar	Palatal	Velar
Voiceless stops	p	t			k
Voiced stops	b	d			g
Voiceless fricatives	f	θ	s	š	h, x, ç
Voiced fricatives	v	ð	z		
Affricates			č, ǰ		
Nasals	m	n			
Liquids		l, r			
Approximants				j	w

Some differences between the Middle English pronunciation of individual consonants and consonant groups and their values in modern English which may affect their use in verse, and indeed the structure of the verse line, are as follows:

(1) In the early part of the period the pronunciation of the consonant written <h> (or <ch>, <qu>, <ȝ>) was regularly sounded as an aspirated velar initially before vowels in words of native origin: *hand*, *house*, *hard*, *hundred*, etc., although even in that subgroup /h/ dropping was common in weakly stressed words such as auxiliaries and pronouns: *(h)ave*, *(h)im*, *(h)em*. Words of Latin origin had lost /h/ initially and between vowels already in Vulgar Latin/Proto-Romance (c.200–600), but when later Old French borrowed Germanic words with the /h/ preserved, e.g. *haste*, *harbinge*, a great deal of vacillation occurred within Old French and Anglo-Norman: *(h)orrible*, *(h)omage*, *(h)erb*. In the fifteenth century even in native words the <h-> could be omitted, prompting spellings such as <ard> for *hard*, <undred> for *hundred*. Such spellings occur more often in southern texts. They indicate widespread instability of the pronunciation of initial /h/ in that area, most likely the consequence of the stronger hold of French there. The composers of alliterative verse familiar with that variation made use of it by allowing the matching of vowels and <h-> in the alliterative texts which have southern associations. Such /h/-less pronunciations are commonly attested by the alliteration in Langland, and even the considerably more northern *Gawain* poet occasionally pairs orthographic <h-> with a vowel:

For ye han **h**armed us two in that ye **e**ten the pudding — *PP* 13.106
THIS **h**anselle hatz **A**rthur of **a**uenturus on first — *SGGK* 491[5]

A related change is the simplification of /hw/ to /w/. Today it is a familiar feature of most varieties of British English, except for Scots, Northumberland, partly Welsh, Irish English and, marginally, in US and Canadian English. The loss of /h/ in the /hw/ cluster originated in the southern dialects of ME around the end of the twelfth century. Loss of /h/ was especially common in weakly stressed interrogative words *what*, *which*, *where*, but it affected also major class words with an etymological /hw/: *wheat*, *white*, *whale*, *wharf*, etc. In the north /hw/ was preserved, and strengthened to /xw/, often spelled

<qu->, bringing the pronunciation closer to /kw/. Again, the practice of the alliterative poets reflects the dialectal differences in the pronunciation of <wh->:

Now awaketh **W**rathe, with two **wh**ite eighen	*PP* 5.133
What! hit **wh**arred and **wh**ette, as **w**ater at a mulne	*SGGK* 2203
Quirland all on **qu**eles quen þe **qu**ene entres	*WA* 5420[6]

In word-medial position the spellings <-h->, <-gh->, <-ch->, <-ʒ-> stand for the velar and palatal fricatives [x], [ç], which are retained throughout the fourteenth century in pronunciation before /t/, so *laughter*, *taughte* with [xt], and *right*, *fighten* with [çt]. During the fifteenth century the medial fricative began to disappear, as indicated by the rhyming practice in *The Castle of Perseverance*: <*syth*> 'sight': <*lyth*> 'readily' (OE liðe), and in the later play *Mankind*: <*out*> 'aught': <*flewte*> 'flute'. In some words (*cough*, *rough*, *tough*, etc.) the velar and palatal fricatives [x], [ç] were gradually changing to /f/ in final position during the fourteenth century. The change spread to the northern areas in the fifteenth century. The vocalization of the final consonant in words like *bough*, *plough*, *thorough* also started in the fourteenth century. Chaucer rhymes <*ynow*> 'enough': <*now*>, and in *Mankind* we find the rhyme <*thorow*> 'through': <*avow*>.

(2) The initial letters in the clusters <kn-> and <gn-> were still pronounced in the fourteenth century. The test for this reconstruction comes from the use of such words in alliteration, stretching to the end of the fifteenth century in William Dunbar's northern dialect:

And his **c**loke of **C**alabre with alle the **k**nappes of golde	*PP* 6.270
And **g**nawen **G**od with the **g**orge whanne hir **g**uttes fullen	*PP* 10.057
He **k**ysses hir **c**omlyly, and **k**nyʒtly he melez	*SGGK* 974
To **k**nychtis, and to **c**leirkis, and **c**ortly personis	*TTMWW* 435[7]

(3) For the orthographic cluster <wr->, the default pronunciation throughout the period seems to have been with the /w/ in place, especially in Scotland where the cluster survives to this day. This is reflected in the alliterative practice:

Wylde **w**ordez hym **w**arp wyth a **wr**ast noyce	*SGGK* 1423
Than **wr**ing I it full **w**ylely and **w**etis my chekis	*TTMWW* 438

There is some evidence that simplified pronunciations were beginning to appear in the south in the fourteenth century. Langland occasionally, and the *Gawain* poet very rarely, resort to <wr-> : /r/ alliteration, but it is safe to assume that the cluster was mostly alive in the careful pronunciation of their contemporaries.

(4) The sequence [sj] in Middle English had not coalesced into a single /š/. In stressed position the preservation of [s] is suggested by alliterative pairings such as *suren*

'to assure' : *sithen* 'since' : *serven* 'to serve' (*PP* 5.540), and *asoyled* 'absolved' : *surely* : *sette* (*SGGK* 1883). In unstressed position the sequence occurs in the French suffix *-sio(u)n* / *-cio(u)n*; there the /sj/ had not developed into /š/ either: *condicion*, *devocion*, *nacion*, *proporcion* still have [-si-]/[-sj-]. In Chaucer and during the fifteenth century the suffix is disyllabic, rhyming on *-on*, e.g., *destruccion : person* (SumT 2007–8), *proporcion : upon* (CYT 754–5).

Vowels in Stressed Syllables

Middle English saw rapid change in the quality and the quantity of many vowels. In the beginning of our period the southern dialects of Middle English, which eventually became the basis of the emerging fifteenth-century southern standard, had five short vowels and seven long monophthongal vowels:

Short vowels			Long vowels		
ɪ		ʊ	iː		uː
			eː		oː
ɛ		ɔ	ɛː		ɔː
	a			ɑː	

The colon here is a typographical convenience to mark vowel length; it corresponds to the macron (¯) diacritic used in dictionaries, some edited manuscripts, and glossaries. The tables below illustrate the approximate reconstructed values of the Middle English vowels matched to the phonetic symbols above; to the left of the symbols are modern English words whose typical pronunciation in General American English corresponds to the International Phonetic Association symbol in the second column. The last column lists some of the most common Middle English spellings for the respective vowels.

Short vowels

Modern English	ME value	Middle English	ME Spelling
WITH	ɪ	*with, synn*	*i, y*
SET	ɛ	*set, went*	*e*
RAM	a	*ram, harm*	*a*
CAUGHT[8]	ɔ	*God, strong*	*o*
BUSH, HOOK	ʊ	*bush, some*	*u, v, o*[9]

The only vowel which requires a comment here is the vowel /ʊ/, because of its variant spelling with <o>, which can be confusing. A reference to the etymology of the word and its modern form helps. The pronunciation of Chaucer's rhyme in GP 7–8 *yronne* 'run, past part.' : *sonne* 'sun' or GP 265–6 *tonge* 'tongue' : *songe* 'sung' is with /ʊ/, exactly like *cuppe : uppe*, *curses : purses*, etc.

Long Vowels

Modern English	ME value	Middle English	ME Spelling
EAT, FIEND, BEE	iː	*finde, why, wyde*	*i, y, ij*
MAKE, MAID	eː	*see, here, feend*	*e, ee, eo, oe, ei*
SWEAR	ɛː	*sweren, eten, sea*	*e, ee, ea*
MASTER	ɑː	*made, tale*	*a, aa*
ROSE, COAT	oː	*boot, moon*	*o, oo, oe*
AWNING, PAW	ɔː	*bone, boot* 'boat'	*o, oo*
DO, SOUP	uː	*thou, now*	*ou, ov, ow*[10]

The chart above is 'conservative' and conceals an important development: during the period covered by this volume the long vowels were undergoing changes that brought them closer to their modern English values. By all accounts, the Great Vowel Shift, a series of changes which altered the shape of the long vowel system dramatically, and which made Chaucerian pronunciation so markedly different from ours, was already under way by about 1400–50. The Great Vowel Shift affected the high (/iː/, /uː/) and the high-mid vowels (/eː/, /oː/) first. The evidence for the early stages of the shift is mostly from occasional spellings, but also from rhymes, e.g. *dome* 'doom': *meúm* L. pron. (*Everyman*); *gees* 'geese' : *lys* 'lice' (*The Castle of Perseverance*). Although the raising and diphthongization of the long vowels does not affect the structure of verse *per se*, it is important to note that by c.1500 two vowels had already reached their modern values: Middle English /eː/ had become /iː/ (as in *see*, *feel*), and the Middle English /oː/ had become /uː/ (*boot*, *moon*). Also by c.1500 the Middle English high vowels /iː/ (*find*, *why*) and /uː/ (*thou*, *now*) were no longer monophthongs – they had started developing into the diphthongs /əj/, /əw/, although the modern values of /aj/ and /aw/ cannot be reconstructed until after c.1600.

The diphthongs that developed out of Middle English /iː/ and /uː/ during the fifteenth century joined a variety of diphthongal vowels that had been in the language from at least the early stages of Middle English. The diphthongs of late Middle English were: /ij/ as in *stil(e)* 'stile', /ej/, as in *weʒ* 'way', /ew/ as in *newe* 'new', /iw/ as in *stiward* 'steward', /uw/ as in *ful* 'fowl', /ow/ as in *bowe* 'bow', /aw/ as in *lawe* 'law', and /oj/ as in *joye* 'joy'.

Vowels in Unstressed Syllables

The most far-reaching single event in the phonology of Middle English, which affected profoundly the syllable composition of the lexicon and hence the way subsequent generations figure out the structure of medieval English verse, was the reduction and loss of final unstressed vowels. The levelling out of the different vowel qualities in unstressed syllables had been under way since at least the tenth century. The resulting vowel sound, if retained, was a mid-central, qualitatively 'neutral' vowel, some kind of schwa, [-ə]. Orthographically, it is usually represented by <-e>, but one also finds <-i> in northern texts and <-u> in texts from the West Midlands.

The behaviour of schwa differs depending on whether it is final in the word or followed by a consonant. Already before the middle of the fourteenth century final schwa had been largely abandoned in weakly stressed words such as pronouns, auxiliaries and some adverbs, and in any relatively unstressed words within a phrase, such as the French titles *sir*, *dam*, *frer*, which are commonly followed by a more strongly accented proper name. Final schwa had also been either lost or weakened at the end of trisyllabic words: *almes(s)* 'alms' (OE *ælmesse*), *orrest* 'battle' (AN *orrosta*), and when it was at the end of weak preterites: *cleped(e)* 'called', *loved(e)*, *maked(e)* 'made'.

Spelling and scansion indicate also that schwa must have been regularly elided in hiatus, i.e. before a vowel-initial word, or a word beginning with a 'weak' <h->, i.e. <h->-initial form words and Romance words: <madim> for *made him*, <mostic> for *moste ic*, *thilk(e) honour*, *other(e) herbes*, etc. The loss was more advanced in the northern dialectal areas. Although some grammatical categories, notably weak singular monosyllabic adjectives, plural adjectives, and possibly infinitives, appear to preserve the final *-e* in the south as the preferred option until the end of the fourteenth century, it is safe to assume that during the fifteenth century the loss was completed even in the southern dialects. It was during the fifteenth century that the use of the orthographic final <-e> as a marker of vowel quantity began to be introduced in words like *home*, *wife*, although Caxton's practice in this respect is still erratic.

The following lines from the Chaucer's General Prologue to the *Canterbury Tales* illustrate loss of <-e> in trisyllabic words (*whistlynge*), in the modal auxiliary (*myghte*, *koude*), in hiatus (*myghte his*, *laughe and*), and in weakly stressed titles (*Sire Knyght*):

And whan he rood, men myghte his brydel heere
Gynglen in a whistlynge wynd als cleere GP 169–70
In felaweshipe wel koude she laughe and carpe GP 474
Sire Knyght, quod he, my mayster and my lord GP 837

Loss of final <-e> was not confined to such instances, however. It would not be an exaggeration to say that *any* final <-e> in the fourteenth century, especially in the north, could be dropped in speech. The latitude that this allows poets in composing syllable-counting verse is much discussed; we will return to this question in the following chapter. When in need of an extra syllable, Chaucer apparently kept or elided final <-e> for purely metrical reasons:

Yit hadde he but litel gold in cofre GP 298
No lenger thanne after Deeth they soughte PardT 772
That hath doon synne horrible, that he PardP 379

The realization, or non-realization, of the unstressed final <-e> at line ends in Chaucer is a subject of long and heated debates, but of little linguistic or metrical interest. Linguistically, it is unrevealing. Metrically, the presence of a syllable after the last stressed syllable at the line end is a universally recognized variant in isosyllabic verse. Nevertheless, if we strive towards 'authenticity', some tendencies defined on the use of the words line-internally may be helpful. Thus, if a word like *vice* appears regularly as a monosyllable (as it does in Chaucer's WBT 955, SqT 101, PhyT 87, PardT 507, SNT 476), and only once (MkT 2502) as a disyllable, it is more likely that a rhyme like *vice : nyce* is masculine. Even so, it is a matter of statistical probability, not a mandate. Compiling statistics on the line-internal use of every relevant word would be hugely labour-intensive and potentially unrewarding. Lacking that, the choice of masculine vs. feminine rhymes in <-e> can be left to the modern reader.

Within about a century, between Chaucer's death in 1400 and the end of our period, the option of special metrical use of final <-e> which had been licensed by conservative pronunciations in the south became a recessive archaic feature, erratically used. The understanding of the syllabic structure and regularity of earlier verse was in jeopardy. A line such as *but ofte time hire colde mowth he kiste* (*TC* 4.1161) would have become a string of eight (and not ten or eleven) syllables. Conversely, the complete loss of <-e> from originally disyllabic nouns, adjectives, adverbs and many verb forms increased the proportion of monosyllables in the native component of the language. This is an important linguistic factor in the repeated triumphs of syllable-counting verse in Middle and early modern English.

When followed by a consonant, <-e-> was relatively stable. Even in this environment, however, it could be dropped, or syncopated, affecting the metrical organization of the verse line. Syncopation of the unstressed vowels in inflectional endings (*-eth*, *-es*, *-ed*) was common in the fourteenth century after another unstressed syllable: *pílgrim(e)s*, *mártir(e)s*, *pálmer(e)s*, *ánswer(e)d*, etc., and when the next word was vowel-initial:

> God loved he best with al his hoole herte
> At alle tymes, thogh him gamed or smerte, GP 533–4

In fifteenth-century verse, syncopation of the inflectional unstressed syllable progressed further towards its present-day status. Other syncopations which were optional in speech and in verse, but did not leave a permanent trace on the language, will be discussed in the following chapter. For further details on Middle English spelling and pronunciation, the reader should consult Jordan 1974 and McIntosh, Samuels and Benskin (eds) 1986.

The Prosodic Features of Middle English

A discussion of the ways in which the ingredients of verse are organized in the various metrical forms cannot proceed without clarifying the meaning and scope of two separate but related terms: *prosody* and *metre*. In literary scholarship, especially in works dating from before the middle of the twentieth century, *prosody*[11] can be used as a synonym for versification, or the study of the forms of metrical composition. This will not be the use of the term here. Instead, we will follow its use in linguistics, where *prosody* refers to speech-based phenomena whose domain may stretch over a string of sounds or syllables, such as stress and intonation. Thus *stress* (or *accent*, used as a synonym) is the prosodic prominence given to one syllable over an adjacent syllable in the same word or phrase. The terms *metre* and *metrical* will be used for the description of the structure of verse. A strong, or more prominent, slot in a verse template is a metrical *ictus*,[12] a word synonymous with *beat.*

The prosodic properties of the spoken language exist quite independently from any form of verse. The salient properties of verse in a particular language, on the other hand, draw directly on the prosody of speech. Within the history of English the relationship between prosodic and metrical patterns is of special interest because of the mixed linguistic situation in the country and the centrality of Latin and French in the cultural setting of verse composition.

While the individual sounds of Middle English have been studied and described in painstaking detail by generations of philologists, its prosodic properties have attracted less attention. There are good reasons for that. One can imagine that a scribe would be inclined to record vowel and consonant innovations by using non-traditional spellings and various diacritics, and by correcting an extant manuscript copy. The orthographic recording of prosodic features, however, is restricted to conjectures based on the confusion or omission of letters. We can *infer* that in Middle English the word *corune* 'crown' (OF *corone*, *corune*, L *corōna*) maintained stress on the penultimate syllable, as in Latin, because already Orrm (c.1200) wrote <cruness> 'crowns'; the initial (pre-tonic) syllable could be omitted only if it was unstressed. When the loanword *palace*, from OF *palais*, L. *palātium* appears spelled <pales> (c.1387), <palas> (c.1400), <palys> (c.1420), it is safe to assume that in the second half of the fourteenth century the second syllable of the word was no longer stressed. Similarly, we *know* that the Old English prefix *ge-* was unstressed because it was written *y-* or altogether omitted in Middle English. Because of the conventional nature of spelling, however, such clues are not readily forthcoming.

Typological considerations are also of importance in prosodic reconstruction. Across languages, and certainly in all forms of modern English, the propensity of a word to attract stress is determined by its function. Major class words – nouns, adjectives, verbs, many adverbs – have to be stressed in isolation or as heads of phrases. Function words – articles, prepositions, conjunctions, pronouns and auxiliaries – are commonly attached to a major class word; prosodically they function as *clitics* and are unstressed. This is a universal distinction and it is safe to project it back onto Old and Middle English.

Save for such orthographic and typological help, our knowledge of the history of English prosody is based on verse structure. The cohesive elements of verse – alliteration, rhyme and the positioning of a word in the verse line – are reliable guides to word and phrasal stress. As we will see, however, one should always be wary of circularity: it is often hard to decide whether a certain pattern in verse reflects a prosodic feature truly, or whether the exigencies of verse override the 'normal' accentuation of a word.

This issue will be addressed in the next chapter in the context of more general metrical constraints.

Word Stress in Middle English: The Basic Pattern

The prosodic contour of a major class word depends on its composition. Words can be simple, or *underived*, meaning that they have only one root, possibly an inflection, but no derivational affixes; thus *deck*, *friends*, *mountain*, *pleasures* are underived words. Derived words can have one root and one or more *derivational* affixes: *bedecked*, *unfriendly*, *mountainous*, *displeasure* are derived words. Words formed by combining two or more roots – *greenhorn*, *folklore*, *throughout*, *welcome* – are *compounds*. Compounds can be expanded further by derivational affixes: *greenhornish*, *folkloristic*, *unwelcome*, etc. are both compounds and derived words. The addition of inflexions does not affect stress placement, no matter whether the inflexion is added to a simple, a derived or a compound word.

Another very important factor in the determination of stress in Middle English is the etymological source of a word or an affix. During Middle English the language absorbed large numbers of words of Romance origin; approximately 10,000 words were borrowed between 1066 and about 1500.[13] In some instances, notably in the accentuation of underived disyllabic words, the principles of Germanic stress placement and the fundamentally different principles of stress in Latin and Old French serendipitously produced the same result. However, most polysyllabic borrowed words came into English with a very distinct prosodic contour, initiating the prosodic split of the vocabulary along etymological lines, a split which deepened during the Renaissance and is now part of the phonology of English.

The basic rule for stress placement in Middle English for all native words is a continuation of the Old English and Common Germanic pattern of stressing the first syllable of the root: *béren* 'to bear', *becúmen*, *búxom*, *fínger*, *blíþe* 'happy'. The same pattern of stress is observed in compounds: they behave like two simple words put together, with the left one having stronger prominence than the right one, resulting in a primary-secondary contour: *chíld-bèringe*, *níghtingàle*, *hándiwòrk*, *spérehèd* 'spearhead'. Prefixes, in particular the prefixes of verbs, were unstressed. Derivational suffixes with distinct semantic content: *-dom* 'state', *-had*/*-hod* 'status', *-er(e)* 'agent', *-lac* 'action', *-ful* 'quantity', could attract secondary stress, especially if they were attached to a disyllabic base, e.g. *mártyrdòm*, *máidenhòd*, *gódspellèr(e)*, *tónnefùl*. When attached to a disyllabic base, some suffixes whose form does not echo self-standing words, *-ing*, *-ly*/*-lich*, *-ness*, *-ish*, *-ship*, can also be realized with some degree of stress in verse – usually in rhyme position. Examples of this are Chaucerian (and later) rhymes such as *thing : wynnyng*, *dich : smoterlich*, *blesse : heuynesse*.

The accentuation of Romance borrowings is more complex. For disyllabic words borrowed early, stress on the initial syllable of the word was the default: *mammon*, *minus*, *moral*, *novel*, *pagan*, *palate*, *primer*, *sermon*, *solid*. Words which were borrowed as trisyllabic followed the Latin stress rule: if the penultimate syllable was light, the antepenultimate was stressed: *melody*, *mystery*, *regimen*, *patient*, *Samuel*, *violent*. Such words also fit the native model of word-initial main stress; a secondary prominence on the final syllable could be forced by the requirements of metre and rhyme, so Chaucer rhymes *pacient : sent*, *Samuel : wel*, *violent : yhent*. This is comparable to the metrical use of the native suffixes in the Chaucerian rhymes cited above. Of the words surveyed so far, then, stress in both native and borrowed words shared the function of marking the beginning of the most important part of the word, its root. In linguistic terms such type of accentuation can be described as *left-prominent* and *morphologically governed*. These are the characteristics of the Germanic Stress Rule.

When describing the native patterns of stress and their perseverance in Middle English, we must mention the 'invisibility' of prefixes to stress rules. Native prefixes (*a-*, *y-*, *be-*, *for-*, *to-*) were never stressed. Middle English borrowed many French prefixes: *con-*, *de-*, *dis-*, *en-*, *ex-*, *mal-*, *mis-*, *pre-*, *pro-*, *re-*, *sub-*, etc. The great majority of verbs with such prefixes still have stress on the etymological root – *confirm*, *deduct*, *displease*, *enlist*, *expose*, etc. – although the accent of many nouns and adjectives has been shifted on to the first syllable in later times: *comfort*, *convict*, *envy*, *exit*, *preface*, *present*, *record*, etc. This is predictable in view of the overwhelming pattern of initial stress in nouns and underived adjectives in the language in general. In Middle English, the default case is for the borrowed prefixes to remain unstressed, mirroring the behaviour of the native prefixes:

'Abyde', quoþ on on þe bonke abouen ouer his hede — *SGGK* 2217
Þat he beknew cortaysly of þe court þat he were — *SGGK* 903

Bot he defended hym so fayr þat no faut semed, — *SGGK* 1551
No more mate ne dismayd for hys mayn dintez — *SGGK* 336

The alliterative practice in late Middle English occasionally allowed the matching of the left edge of prefixes to the initial sounds of roots.[14] The interpretation of this evidence depends on the consistency of the alliterative usage of a prefix, its transparency as such, and on how systematic a particular poet is in his use of alliteration. In principle, however, it is safe to approach such evidence with the understanding that the need to satisfy alliteration or rhyme may override the pronunciation current in the contemporary language, especially if the word in question is a recent borrowing.

Prosodic Innovations in Middle English

All of the cases discussed so far represent a continuation of the familiar Anglo-Saxon stress patterns. We now turn to the introduction of a typologically different way of assigning stress. Stress in Latin was determined on the basis of the weight of the penultimate syllable, so it is assigned from *right to left*, and is *phonologically governed*. This type of accentuation is known as the Romance Stress Rule. These are taxonomies devised by modern linguists; for the medieval English speaker, the only relevant difference between the Germanic and the Romance patterns would be that in the latter case the left edge of a word's root could be an unstressed syllable. Such stress contours would have been perceived as somewhat odd by monolingual speakers of English; it is not surprising therefore that words which were borrowed early and used frequently changed their pronunciation so that it followed the Germanic Stress Rule.

The first foreign pattern of stress in Middle English appeared in trisyllabic Romance loanwords with a heavy middle syllable.[15] Words of the type *calendar, sinister, membrane* (L. membrāna), *memento, placebo* (L. placēbo), *smaragdus* must have been pronounced with the accent on the middle syllable, at least initially. This pronunciation could be retained even after the loss of the third/final syllable. A special, and much discussed case, is presented by originally trisyllabic words with a long middle syllable, which lost their final syllable either in Old French and Anglo-Norman or in the transition from Anglo-Norman to Middle English: *divers(e), legend(e), maner(e), honour(e), montayn(e)* 'mountain' (L. montāna), *natur(e), tempest(e), sentenc(e), solemn(e)*, etc. The position taken in many handbooks is that the accentuation of such words in Middle English vacillated between initial and final stress (not counting the <-e>). The line *In dívers art and in divérse figures* (FrT 1486) is often cited as an example of how Chaucer manipulated the available options so that the strong position in the verse would be filled by a stressed syllable. The generalization must be treated with extra caution, however. To illustrate how a blanket assumption about variable stress in French loanwords can be misleading, let us look at the following pair, cited by Halle and Keyser (1971: 103), whose book was a milestone in the study of English historical prosody:

To the clepe I, thow goddesse of *torment*	*TC* 1.8
That euere derk in *torment* nyght by nyght	*TC* 5.640

On the face of it, the positioning of the noun *torment* 'proves' that it had two variant pronunciations in Chaucer's language. However, if we survey all instances of the same word in the *Canterbury Tales* and *Troilus and Criseyde*, we find only two uses of end-stressed *tormént*, MLT 845 and *TC* 1.8, and in both cases the noun is in rhyme position. On the other hand, Chaucer uses that noun twenty-one times elsewhere in his verse, and every single time it must be accented on the first syllable; for example:

That doubleth al my *tórment* and my wo	KnT 1298
And al hir bisy *tórment*, and hir fir	KnT 1382
in langour and in *tórment* furyus	FrankT 1101

Such distribution presents compelling evidence that the noun *torment*, widely attested in Middle English since c.1300 (*MED*), must be reconstructed with initial stress in everyday speech. Putting the accent on the second syllable in rhyme position is as artificial as the promotion of *-ing* in the rhyme *thing : wynnyng*, or the promotion of the native suffix *-y* in *I : unworthy*. Such information regarding the distribution of French loanwords in Middle English verse is not readily available in the handbooks; it is of particular importance when we try to assess the regularity of the metrical form that a poet is using. It informs judgements which involve susceptibility to foreign influence and the poet's craft: sing-song, or even doggerel-like versification, versus 'artistic' violations of the norm to avoid monotony. The value of more detailed knowledge of how a poet uses a particular word is of course well known to textual editors. By way of illustration, the scansion of the following Chaucerian lines may be considered ambiguous:

Resoun wol nought that I speke of slepe	*TC* 3.1408
By which *resoun* men may wel y-se	*TC* 4.1048
And by the same *resoun*, thynketh me	SqT 406

If we assume that *resóun* is a widespread and accepted accentuation (it does rhyme with *adoun* 'down' at CYT 1198–9), the question that these lines raise is whether Chaucer allowed nine syllables in a line, composing what is known as a 'Lydgatean' line. Knowing that in *all* other appearances of the word *reason* in *Troilus* and the *Canterbury Tales*, a total of nineteen instances, Chaucer consistently places initial stress on the word suggests a different interpretation of the metrical structure in those lines. Those are 'headless' lines, a common variation on the metrical template, which allows the first weak syllable of the line to be omitted altogether.

Innovative prosodic contours in Middle English were found also in the Romance loanwords with derivational suffixes. As noted in the previous section, the derivational suffixes inherited from Old English could attract stress, but that stress was never stronger than the stress on the root of the word. There was no stress-shifting in derived words: the stress on the first syllable of the root was never affected by the addition of a suffix: *mártyr – mártyrdòm, máiden – máidenhòd*, etc. Middle English borrowed a large number of Romance suffixes such as *-ance/-ence, -esse, -(i)er, -io(u)n, -ité(e), -ment, -ous*. In the source language these suffixes carried the main stress of the word. In English, a stress-timed language in which the principle of rhythmic alternation has always favoured stresses occurring at regular intervals, a secondary stress was inserted two syllables to the left of the original primary stress: *èloquénce, gèntillésse, partìculér, humànitée, pàrlemént*, etc. In current linguistic terminology, this stress alternation is covered by a universal prosodic constraint called *LAPSE, which prevents the occurrence of stress lapses, or put differently, the occurrence of long strings of unstressed syllables.[16]

*LAPSE was observed in the native vocabulary (*mártyrdòm, máidenhòd, tónnefùl*), only the order of the prominences was main accent followed by a secondary one. During Middle English the combined influence of *LAPSE and the pre-existing model of main stress followed by a secondary stress in polysyllabic words triggered a reversal of the prominences in the borrowed vocabulary too: *éloquènce, partículèr, humánitèe, párlemènt*. As with the disyllabic words, e.g. *nature, reason, torment*, the accentual history of the polysyllabic words attests to the continuing vigour of the left-prominent Germanic pattern of word stress. This is not surprising: in spite of the influx of 10,000 Romance loanwords, words of Germanic origin continued to constitute the bulk of the core vocabulary of Middle English, accounting for seventy-five to ninety-five per cent of the wordstock, depending on register. It was only during the Renaissance that the balance began to shift in favour of non-Germanic patterns, bringing about the co-existence of two typologically different systems of stress in modern English.

For Middle English the switch of the main stress to the initial syllable, e.g. *èloquénce* to *éloquènce*, did not create a novel pattern because of the pre-existing native model of *máidenhòd.* Seen in the larger context of prosodic typology, however, the accentuation of derived Romance words introduced a major new paradigm of stress-shifting in English. For the first time in the history of the language words derived from the same root started to exhibit disparate prosodic contours: *móral–morálitèe, párish–paríshonèr, sólemn–solémpnitè, vólume–volúminòus.*

The details of the accentuation of polysyllabic words in Middle English are complicated further by the instability of the syllabic composition of the newly adopted words and because of the strong tendency of the main stress to dock on to the initial syllable irrespective of the etymologically 'proper' stress. In stress-alternating verse suffixed polysyllabic words, including proper names, were realized with their stressed syllables separated by a buffer unstressed syllable.

See also: 9 The Languages of Medieval Britain, 11 The Forms of Verse, 32 *Piers Plowman*, 33 The *Canterbury Tales*, 37 *Sir Gawain and the Green Knight.*

Notes

1 John Trevisa (trans.), *Polychronicon Ranulphi Higden monachi Cestrensis*, bk. 1; ed. Churchill Babington, Rolls ser., 41, (1865), I, 7.

2 *The Vision of Piers Plowman*, ed. A. V. C. Schmidt (London: Dent, and New York: Dutton, 1978). Online text distributed through the University of Michigan, Humanities Text Initiative (www.hti.umich.edu). Unless otherwise noted, all further references to *Piers Plowman* (*PP*) in this and the next chapter will also be to the B-Text.

3 Text cited from the online version available from the University of Michigan, Humanities Text Initiative, using *The Towneley Plays*, ed. George England and A. W. Pollard, EETS es 71 (1897).

4 Slashes include the symbols for classes of distinctive *sounds*, phonemes, following the transcription principles of the International Phonetic Association. Square brackets enclose a specific realization of a class of sounds, or an allophone. Letters will be enclosed in angled brackets.

The Middle English letter yogh <ʒ> does *not* represent /ʒ/, a sound which was not introduced until the seventeenth century. Instead, it stands for /g/, /h/, /j/, /s/, /z/.

5 This and all further citations of *Gawain* (*SGGK*) are from *Sir Gawain and the Green Knight*, ed. J. R. R. Tolkien and E. V. Gordon, rev. Norman Davis (Oxford: Clarendon Press, 1967). Text made available through the Electronic Text Center, University of Virginia Library (http://etext.lib.virginia.edu).

6 *WA: The Wars of Alexander*, ed. Hoyt Duggan and Thorlac Turville-Petre, EETS. ss 10 (1989).

7 *TTMWW*: William Dunbar, *The tretis of the twa mariit women and the wedo*, ed. James Kinsley (Oxford: Clarendon Press, 1958).

8 The pronunciation of the GOD-type vowel in many varieties of American English is a lower and unrounded sound /ɑ/

9 The spelling with <o> occurs when the etymological <u> (as OE *sume* 'some') is adjacent

to <m>, <n>, <u>, <v>, i.e., letters that are also written with down-strokes (minims).

10 The representation of /u:/ by <ou> and its word-final variant <ow> follows the practice in French.

11 Latin *prosōdia* 'the accent of a syllable' is from the same word in Greek where it also means 'a song sung to music, an accompaniment' (*OED*). Historically, the term was also used to mean 'the pronunciation of words'.

12 From Latin *ictus* 'blow, stroke, thrust'.

13 The estimate is from Baugh and Cable 1993: 174.

14 The issue of initially stressed prefixed words is treated most exhaustively in Duggan 1990. For further discussion, see Minkova 2003: 55–60.

15 A syllable is heavy if its vowel is long or if it ends in a consonant.

16 For Middle English the effect of the universal *Lapse constraint is equivalent to the so-called 'countertonic accentuation', a term coined specifically for the accentuation of classical and Romance loanwords in English. A full account of the origin and history of the term and the nature of countertonic accentuation is found in Danielsson 1948: 39–54.

References and Further Reading

Baugh, A. and Cable, T. 1993. *A History of the English Language*, 4th edn. Englewood Cliffs, N.J.: Prentice-Hall. A valuable introductory text, especially in the coverage of historical events influencing language change.

Blake, N. 1977. *The English Language in Medieval Literature*. London: Dent. The monograph makes a persuasive case for the importance of language study for the understanding of literature.

—— 1992 (ed.) *The Cambridge History of the English Language. Vol. 2: 1066–1476*. Cambridge: Cambridge University Press. The best in-depth and most comprehensive linguistic survey of Middle English.

Danielsson, B. 1948. *Studies on the Accentuation of Polysyllabic Latin, Greek, and Romance Loan-Words in English with Special Reference to those Ending in -able, -ate, -ator, -ible, -ic, -ical, and -ize*. Stockholm: Almqvist and Wiksell. An excellent collection of relevant linguistic material.

Duggan, H. N. 1990. 'Stress Assignment in Middle English Alliterative Poetry.' *Journal of English and Germanic Philology* 89, 309–29. Argues that alliteration on some prefixes reflects the actual pronunciation of these forms in the spoken language.

Fisiak, J. 1968. *A Short Grammar of Middle English: Orthography, Phonology and Morphology*. Warsaw: Wydawnictwo Naukowe, repr. 1996. A useful and straightforward structuralist account of the areas in the title.

Halle, M. and Keyser, S. J. 1971. *English Stress: Its Form, Its Growth, and Its Role in Verse*. New York: Harper and Row. A ground-breaking attempt at a generative account of the history of stress and verse, many aspects of which have been incorporated into later theories of prosody and metre.

Ikegami, M. T. 1984. *Rhyme and Pronunciation: Some Studies of English Rhymes from* Kyng Alisaunder *To Skelton*. Extra Series, 5. Tokyo: Hogaku-Kenkyu-Kai Keio University. As in the subtitle.

Jordan, Richard 1974. *Handbook of Middle English Grammar: Phonology*, trans. and rev. Eugene Crook. The Hague: Mouton. The most detailed single-volume description of Middle English sound changes (no prosody).

Lass, R. 1992. 'Phonology.' In Blake 1992, pp. 23–156. An excellent monograph-length linguistic exposition of the phonological and prosodic facts and theoretical issues.

McIntosh, A., Samuels, M. L. and Benskin, M. (eds) with the assistance of M. Laing and K. Williamson 1986. *A Linguistic Atlas of Late Mediaeval English*, 4 vols. Aberdeen: Aberdeen University Press. A reference source of permanent value.

Middle English Compendium 1998–. Ann Arbor: University of Michigan. Electronic access: www.hti.umich.edu/mec/. Includes, among others, Hyperbibliography, *MED*, Corpus of Middle English Verse and Prose.

MED 1954–2001. *Middle English Dictionary*, ed. H. Kurath, S. M. Kuhn and R. E. Lewis. 12 vols. Ann Arbor: University of Michigan Press. An indispensable research tool based on the analysis of a collection of over three million citation slips.

Minkova, D. 1991. *The History of Final Vowels in English.* Berlin and New York: Mouton de Gruyter. A study of the causes, spread and consequences of unstressed vowel loss in English.

—— 1997. 'Constraint Ranking in Middle English Stress-Shifting'. *Journal of English Language and Linguistics* 1, 135–75. Demonstrates that the widespread assumption of ubiquitous 'doublet' stress forms of French borrowings in Middle English is unwarranted and argues for the stability of the Germanic root-initial stress pattern.

—— 2000. 'Middle English Prosodic Innovations and their Testability in Verse.' In *Placing Middle English in Context*, ed. I. Taavitsainen, T. Nevalainen, P. Pahta and M. Rissanen (Berlin: Mouton de Gruyter), pp. 431–61. Argues against variable stress in all French words and offers details on the prosody-to-metre matching depending on position in the line.

—— 2003. *Alliteration and Sound Change in Early English.* Cambridge: Cambridge University Press. The study uses alliterative evidence in Old and Middle English to trace the development of major phonological changes in English phonology and prosody.

Mossé, F. 1952. *A Handbook of Middle English*, trans. James A. Walker. Baltimore: Johns Hopkins University Press, repr. 1968. A standard Middle English textbook for over half a century with excellent philological descriptions of the selected readings.

Schumacher, K. 1914. *Studien über den Stabreim mittelenglischen Alliterationsdichtung.* Bonner Studien zur englischen Philologie, Heft XI. Bonn: Peter Hanstein. The largest set of data on the patterns of Middle English alliteration; a reference source of lasting value.

Wright, J. and E. M. 1928. *An Elementary Middle English Grammar*, 2nd edn. London: Oxford University Press. The 'elementary' in the title is too modest for the detail and sophistication of this outstanding philological work.

11
The Forms of Verse

Donka Minkova

Verse composition depends on and mirrors the prosodic organization of speech. While the metrical forms favoured by poets at a particular time cannot be separated from the shape of the contemporary language, the selection of a particular form may also be motivated by considerations of tradition, innovation, and even fashion. In late Middle English the poets responded fully to these factors: the inherited tradition of alliterative writing blossomed in the West Midland and north-western regions, while the Continental model of syllable-counting was the dominant form of verse elsewhere.

Alliterative Verse in the Fourteenth Century

Alliterative verse is the oldest form of poetic composition in English. The classical corpus of Old English verse follows well-defined metrical standards. By the end of the tenth century, deviations from the strict norms of versification indicate that composers and scribes no longer fully understood the linguistic rationale of the earlier tradition. New Continental fashions, especially after the Norman Conquest, accelerated the demise of Old English metre. The last surviving pieces of alliterative poetry which can be scanned following the rules of Old English versification are two short poems, *Durham*, c.1100, and *The Grave*, c.1150, a total of forty-five lines. Early Middle English compositions such as *The Proverbs of Alfred*, *The Worcester Fragments of the Soul's Address to the Body*, *The Bestiary*, Laȝamon's *Brut*, are 'hybrids' mixing rhyme, alliteration and syllable-counting in often erratic patterns. For about a hundred years following Laȝamon's *Brut*, between 1250 and 1350, the only specimens of alliterative verse that have survived are 'debased and dubious remnants'.[1]

Whether the absence of strict alliterative verse in our records from that period reflects a complete cessation of such composition or not is beyond recovery. Arguably, the appeal of alliteration as an ornamental feature of rhymed verse and of prose continued unabated not just as an echo of the earlier tradition but as a predictable consequence of the universal human fascination with patterned sounds. Very importantly, alliteration as a creative device was grounded in the prosody of the language. Stress on the first syllable of the root was the dominant contour in English word accentuation during the fourteenth and fifteenth centuries. It is no surprise that a significant portion of the literary activity during that time is channelled into the composition of alliterative verse.

The aural, artistic and mnemonic effects of alliterative verse are achieved through a repetition of the initial *sounds* of stressed syllables across the verse line. Placing sound identity at the core of such verse has important implications for the interpretation of how poetry was created and transmitted in medieval times. If a poem shows consistent phonetic matching, irrespective of the orthography, that suggests that for all those involved in its composition, copying and delivery, it was the sound echo that mattered most in keeping the line together. This aural aspect of alliterative verse must have been valued very highly in Middle English; higher density and increased scope of the alliteration are consciously sought after and become measures of the artistry of a piece.

Renewed interest in the composition of alliterative verse around the middle of the fourteenth century, especially in the West Midlands and the north-west, produced a body of alliterative verse of lasting value. The 'fashion' for composing alliterative verse was apparently localized and relatively short-lived, although London associations and a diffusion of the tradition northward in the fifteenth century complicate the picture. As in every other verse tradition, the pieces we have inherited bear the individual marks of their authors and scribes. Nevertheless, many of the alliterative patterns and rhythmic regularities cut across the entire tradition. The description below will refer to the general characteristics of Middle English alliterative verse in terms of (a) metrical features – the number and distribution of ictic and non-ictic positions, and (b) parametrical features – the specifically Middle English patterns of alliteration. The examples will be drawn from *Sir Gawain and the Green Knight* (*SGGK*)[2] and William Langland's *Piers Plowman* (*PP*)[3] – the masterpieces that are also the subject of other chapters.[4]

Metrical Constituents of Middle English Alliterative Verse

In its most abstract and idealized form, the constituent structure of Middle English alliterative verse can be represented by the following scheme:

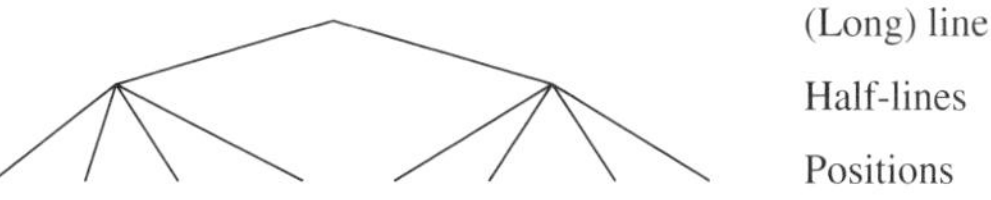

The basic unit of Middle English alliterative verse is what is known as 'the alliterative long line'. The long line is a syntactically complete entity: line-ends coincide with clause or phrase boundaries. The long line is further divided into two half-lines, also referred to as the A-verse and the B-verse. Each half-line also tends to be a self-contained phrase, which implies at least a minimal pause between the two parts. The pauses are rarely marked by the scribes or typographically set off in the editions of the 'revival' verse, but the mid-line pause is easy to locate from the rhythm of the line and/or from the alliteration, since the identity of sound straddles the two half-lines, as in the frequent patterns *aa(a): ax*.[5] Here are some examples of the division of long lines into half-lines:

A-Verse	*B-Verse*	
Dere dyn vpon day,	daunsyng on nyȝtes,	
Al watz hap vpon heȝe	in hallez and chambrez	*SGGK* 47–8
How bisie they ben	aboute the maze?	
The mooste partie of this peple	that passeth on this erthe	*PP* 1.6–7

Although we call the two parts 'half-lines', the division of the long line is syntactically, and also metrically, uneven. The B-verse tends to be subordinated to the A-verse; the A-verse is longer, it has more stressed syllables, it can have three alliterating positions, and is usually syntactically indispensable and more important semantically.

The principle on which alliterative metre rests, shared by all types of metre in English, is the recurrence of prominences in a particular order across the verse line. A prominence in the abstract metrical scheme is also known as the strong (S) position, *ictus*, or *lift*. The regular overlap of linguistic stress and metrical ictus is what justifies the designation of alliterative verse as 'strong stress metre'.[6] An ictus is normally filled by a syllable bearing linguistic stress as described in the previous chapter. An ictus can accommodate only one syllable.

The default number of lifts across the long line is four, the first three of which must alliterate. The desire for additional ornamentation often led Middle English poets and scribes to add extra alliterating words in the first half-line, or to position an alliterating syllable in the rightmost ictus. Thus, in the A-verse we sometimes find three alliterating words, although the third alliteration is structurally redundant, as in *SGGK* 47 above.

In the B-verse alliteration on the first lift is obligatory but, unlike in Old English, where this would be completely irregular, the second ictus can also be filled by an alliterating syllable:

His lif liked hym lyȝt, he louied þe *lasse*	*SGGK* 87
May no sugre ne swete thyng aswage my *swelling*	*PP* 5.121

The one-to-one correspondence between metrical position and linguistic material (one position = one syllable) does not apply to the weak (W), or *non-ictic* positions, also known as *dips*. Dips are filled by unstressed syllables and they vary in size: they can host a single unstressed syllable (weak dips), or they can enclose a string of two or more unstressed syllables (strong/heavy dips). Alliteration on a syllable which is unambiguously in a dip, as on the prepositions *with* in *Gawain* 384 and *for* in *Piers* Prologue, 42, is accidental.

Wyth what weppen so þou wylt, and *wyth* no wyȝ ellez	*SGGK* 384
Faiteden *for* hire foode, foughten at the ale.	*PP* Prol.42

The Distribution of Constituents in the Half-line

Plotting the distribution of lifts and dips in Middle English alliterative verse is one of the great challenges in the study of its metre. J. P. Oakden's comprehensive statistical report (Oakden 1930–5: I, 181–200), the first attempt to survey the entire set of relevant texts, failed to identify the regularity with which certain combinations of stressed and unstressed material was avoided by the poets. In the mid-1980s two scholars, Thomas Cable and Hoyt Duggan, working independently and using different methodologies, discovered patterns of great stability, especially in the B-verse. They disagree on many points, yet jointly their studies have enriched greatly our knowledge of the medieval poets' versecraft.[7]

We will start with a description of the characteristics of the A-verse. As noted in the previous section, the A-verse is commonly heavier than the B-verse. The 'weight' of the half-line in this context is measured in one of two ways: A-verse can be heavier because it has three ictuses which may, but do not have to, alliterate:

And meled þus much with his muthe . . .	*SGGK* 447
Gauan gripped to his *ax* . . .	*SGGK* 421
Sleep and sory sleuthe . . .	*PP* Prol.45
Lowed to *speke* in Latyn . . .	*PP* Prol.129

Since the norm is for each half-line to have two ictuses, three-ictus verses are also known as 'extended'. This type of extension is not allowed in the B-verse.

Another way of calibrating the weight of the A-verse relative to the B-verse is by counting the co-occurrence of 'strong' dips. The following A-verses are examples of that pattern:

And he þat wan *watz not* wrothe . . .	*SGGK* 70
Bothe in wareyne *and in* waast . . .	*PP* Prol.163

The pattern of two ictuses and two strong dips is so common that it can be regarded as the 'unmarked' type of A-verse.[8] Other patterns are possible, notably two-ictus A-verses with only one strong dip. What does *not* occur with any degree of commonness, except in Langland, is the combination of three lifts and two strong dips. Another non-occurring combination in the A-verse is that of two ictic positions and no strong dips. Although a formula for what constitutes an ideal A-verse cannot be given, the identification of non-occurring patterns helps: the minimum number of lifts is two, as is the maximum number of strong dips. It is also clear that the preferred distribution of lifts and dips tended to be a trade-off in favour of a relatively stable verse length: the more ictuses, the fewer strong dips; the fewer ictuses, the greater the likelihood of two strong dips.

One feature of metre, observed in many verse forms, including Old English verse and rhymed isosyllabic verse, is that the abstract scheme is adhered to much more strictly at the right edges of the various domains, the verse or the line, than at the left edges. Put differently, the beginnings of lines tend to be free, the endings tend to be strict. For Middle English alliterative verse, this translates into limitations on the structure of the B-verse that are not imposed on the A-verse. The structure of the B-verse requires that it should have exactly two ictuses, and that the first of these lifts should alliterate.

. . . watz sesed at Troye	*SGGK* 1
. . . unholy of werkes	*PP* Prol.3

Recall, however, that unlike in Old English, where the second ictus in the B-verse could never alliterate, in Middle English alliteration on the second ictus is allowed:

. . . no wont þat þer were . . .	*SGGK* 131
. . . whan softe was the sonne . . .	*PP* Prol.1

A further condition on the metricality of the B-verse is that one and only one of the dips must be strong, as in *-sed at* in *SGGK* 1 or *-ly of* in *PP* Prol.3. Except for Langland, this feature is observed fairly consistently in the corpus. For Langland, whose long line is commonly observed to be longer than that of the other poets, the first constraint, the occurrence of one strong dip, is always obeyed. The second part of the constraint, the proscription against more than one strong dip, is violated, though not very frequently:[9]

. . . *at ful* tyme *of the* day	*PP* 5.489
. . . *that he ne* hath *it at* even	*PP* 5.552

Another property shared with Old English verse and, as we will see, with rhymed verse is that no more than a single weak syllable should be allowed at the right edge of the B-verse. Whether or not the presence of at least one weak syllable at the right edge of the long line was considered mandatory is not a settled issue, although the scholarly consensus is that the feminine (S W) ending is the preferred pattern.[10] In a theory of gradient metricality, in which the basic matrix allows some well-defined violations, a masculine verse-ending (S) would be an acceptable variant, while a dactylic ending (S W W) would not.

I have described Middle English alliterative verse in terms of its basic metrical constituents and their distribution. As in every other type of verse, there are some absolute constraints, which have to be obeyed, or the result is an unmetrical line. There are further, weaker tendencies, which create variability of the template, increase the 'interest' of the verse, and avoid monotony, but do not constitute unmetricality. The inviolable constraints on the structure of Middle English alliterative verse are:

- In either verse at least one of the dips must be strong.
- The A-verse requires a minimum of two lifts and allows a maximum of three.
- The B-verse requires two and only two lifts.
- The B-verse cannot end on more than a single weak syllable.

Additional features, or variations on the basic template, are:

- The long line is divided into two uneven half-lines.
- The A-verse tends towards an inverse correlation between lifts and strong dips.
- The B-verse (in Langland) can have two strong dips.
- The B-verse can end on a strong syllable.

Alliterative Patterns in Middle English Unrhymed Verse

Structurally, the default distribution of alliterating ictuses in the long alliterative line follows the pattern *a a* / *a x*. Additional ornamental alliteration is found on the third ictus of the A-verse (*a a a* /), or on the second ictus of the B-verse (/ *a a*), and in rare instances up to five stressed syllables in the long line can alliterate. When the A-verse has three ictuses, the position of the non-alliterating one is free, i.e., the A-verse can be (*x a a* /), (*a x a* /), (*a a x* /). All of the examples cited in the previous section conform to one of these structural patterns. Other patterns, such as cross-alliteration (*a b* / *a b*), verse-internal alliteration (*a a* / *b b*), and a variety of 'defective' alliterations, occur occasionally; they are referenced in the specialized literature.

A frequently noted distributional peculiarity of Middle English alliterative verse is that sometimes the alliteration binds not just a single long line, but runs through two and even more consecutive lines:

Þe tulk þat þe **tr**ammes of **tr**esoun þer wroȝt
Watz **tr**ied for his **tr**icherie, þe **tr**ewest on erþe *SGGK* 3–4

This overzealousness in alliteration is found rarely in Langland.[11] It was a device liked by the *Gawain* poet and the other poets in the 'classical' part of the corpus.

A final point regarding the alliterative patterning in Middle English has to do with the selection of alliterating sounds. The tradition was not only structurally distinct, it was also distinct in terms of how it absorbed and reflected the phonological attributes of fourteenth- and fifteenth-century English. The main technical points specific to Middle English alliterative versification are illustrated and discussed briefly below:

1. Strong tendency to alliterate on identical vowels.

And his arsounz al after and his aþel skyrtes,	*SGGK* 171
For if hevene be on this erthe, and ese to any soule	*PP* 10.297[12]

2. Cluster onsets alliterate as groups.

And al bigrauen with grene in gracios werkes	*SGGK* 216
Til Sleuthe and sleep sliken hise sides	*PP* 2.99

These two peculiarities of Middle English alliterative versification point to the poets' keen ear and delight in the aesthetic and mnemonic powers of sound identity. In both cases their preferences are linguistically motivated. The density of vowel alliteration in Old English is higher than that found in the Middle English corpus at a ratio of 5 : 1, but then all vowels alliterated freely with each other because of the insertion of a glottal stop at the left edge of vowel-initial stressed syllables, a characteristically Germanic phenomenon. It is likely that the influx of Romance vocabulary in Middle English obscured the glottal stop and changed the perception of what constitutes 'identity' for the vowels. The poets therefore avoided vowel alliteration, and when they resorted to it they tended to choose identical vowels. Cluster alliteration, another distinctively Middle English feature, is also based on the properties of the sounds in the cluster: <s->-initial clusters are most cohesive. The patterns in (1) and (2) are congruent with a view that the composition of Middle English alliterative verse was primarily sound-based. The next characteristic feature, *Liaison* alliteration, also supports such a position:

3. *Liaison* alliteration (in the 'classical' corpus).

An oþer noyse ful newe / neȝed biliue	*SGGK* 132
Þe tweyne yȝen and þe nase, / þe naked lyppez,	*SGGK* 962

In these lines the poet based the alliteration on the pronunciation of two words within a larger phonological unit, where the word boundaries are blurred and the final consonant of the word to the left is assigned to the beginning of the following stressed syllable: ***an** oþer* becomes *a **-n**other.* The fact that such alliterations exist at all is a very strong argument in favour of the speech-based character of the composition. Another diagnostic for the aural nature of a particular composition is offered by the practice of alliterating on sounds that have different realizations in the dialects.[13]

4. Dialectal borrowing in alliteration: /f-/ : /v-/ (in Langland).

Than for any vertue or fairnesse or any free kynde	*PP* 2.77
The viker hadde fer hoom, and faire took his leeve	*PP* 19.484

The next two characteristics are more likely prompted by the visual shape of letters. The separation of /sp-/, /st-/, /sk-/ is disallowed in the Germanic and Old English alliterative verse. Note that both practices illustrated below, the splitting of the traditionally cohesive clusters, and the alliteration on similar but not identical sounds, are associated with Langland. Although they are found occasionally in the other poems of the corpus, there are no examples of them in the Gawain poems.

5. The clusters /sp-/, /st-/, /sk-/ alliterate on /s-/ (in Langland).

And sette **s**colers to **s**cole or to som othere craftes	*PP* 7.31
Thanne **S**ymonye and **C**yvylle **s**tonden forth bothe	*PP* 2.72

6. /s-/ : /š-/ alliteration (in Langland).

And sette Mede upon a **sh**errеve **sh**oed al newe	*PP* 2.164
And seide ful **s**oftely, in **sh**rift as it were	*PP* 3.372

The Constituents of Syllable-counting Verse

For all its technical virtuosity and literary appeal, Middle English alliterative verse was the 'other' form of verse in the period covered by this volume, regionally restricted and unpopular with poets and audiences closer to the Continental verse models. Though probably not a direct descendant of the Anglo-Saxon tradition, alliterative verse was analogous to it in two of its most fundamental properties: alliteration as the structural 'glue' of the line, and an uneven number of syllables per verse. Both features were easy to implement in Middle English: alliteration and root-initial stress go together, and the variability of the syllable count echoes the flexibility of the unstressed 'buffers' between the natural lexical prominences in speech.

Early on in Middle English, a new type of versification based on the *rhymed isosyllabic iambic line* spread across the country. The model was made known in England through contacts with the Anglo-Normans. *Rhyming* appears occasionally as an embellishment in Old English verse, but it often relies on inflections, and it is not structurally indispensable. *Isosyllabism* is a genuinely innovative component of Middle English verse. It is based on the iteration of equal measures, or feet, across the verse line; lines have the same number of feet. Until Chaucer started using five feet, or ten syllables, per line, Middle English isosyllabic poetry was written in eight-syllable, or tetrameter lines.[14] The lines were linked in couplets or larger groups by end-rhymes.

The *iamb*, a binary sequence of a weak and a strong position (W S), was the dominant type of metrical foot in Middle English verse. There were good linguistic grounds for the robustness of the iamb in metre. The gradual loss of inflexions in Middle English went hand in hand with an increased use of prepositions, and prepositions attach prosodically to the next word, creating W S strings: *to God*, *by word*, *in hand*, *with cheer*. Prefixes, frequently used to derive verbs and adverbs, are unstressed, so that their natural contour was W S: *behold*, *forgive*, *perform*, *asleep*, *today*. Phrase-level and sentence-level contours in English have always been right-strong: *five books*, *my lord*, *full well*, *he spoke*,

I laugh. Finally, the poets had a considerable inventory of handy 'fillers': semantically dispensable monosyllabic words: *and*, *full*, *now*, *for*, *some,* the grammatically redundant 'pleonastic' *this*, *that.* Put differently, although individual major class words retained their trochaic shape, in connected speech iambic cadences were sufficiently frequent and easy to construct; this permits an effortless 'fit' between the prosody of the language and the metre of verse.

Exact syllable-counting cannot be claimed for all of the verse written in non-alliterative mode in Middle English. The difficulties are both linguistic and textual. Linguistically, a decision on what constitutes a syllable is hard because it depends on the grammatical type of the word and its syllabic composition, on the placement of the word within a phrase, and on the presumed dialect and chronology of the poem. The problem with the extant texts is that the poems derive most often not from an original, but from randomly surviving copies, some of them possibly influenced by intermediate transmission from memory and by word of mouth. The metrist's goal is to combine the linguistic and textual information and to reconstruct the abstract model that the poets and scribes must have had in mind. The next section will summarize the rules of syllabification and metre-to-prosody matching that can be used as criteria for assessing the metrical skills and efficacy of Middle English isosyllabic poetry.

Counting Syllables in Isosyllabic Verse

Isosyllabism, stress alternation in the form of iambs and rhyme are the three properties that jointly define the tetrameter and the pentameter composed in Middle English. Of these, only the presence and the importance of rhyme have been universally acknowledged. Isosyllabism and stress alternation are issues that continue to be debated. The position taken here is that Chaucer and the best practitioners of the tradition intended to write verse with an equal number of syllables per line.

Counting syllables in verse requires reference to phonetic processes that occur in speech, but are not necessarily reflected in the orthography. The historical processes that led to the loss of final <-e> were described in the previous chapter. Here the scope of *elision* and *syncopation* of unstressed vowels is expanded to include speech forms which do not result in permanent language change. Although the examples will be drawn from the pentameter portions of the *Canterbury Tales*, it should be understood that they are instantiations of familiar linguistic principles characterizing the behaviour of unstressed vowels in speech and applicable to all forms of verse.

1. ELISION. The final vowel of an unstressed syllable can be elided when adjacent to another vowel, both across a word-boundary and within a word. The most common realization of elision is associated with the final <-e>, but unstressed [i] can also be elided. In the latter case the vowel [i] changes to a palatal approximant [j] in the onset of the following syllable: an originally trisyllabic sequence becomes disyllabic, as in *many a*, *bisy a*, *bisier*, *myrie I*:

And many a breem and many a luce in stuwe	GP 350
Nowher so bisy a man as he ther nas	
And yet he semed bisier than he was	GP 321–2
But ye be myrie, I wol yeve yow myn heed!	GP 782

Here belong also cases of contraction of the negative particle *ne* and the definite article *the* with a following vowel-initial word. Although occasionally marked by the scribes, the contraction does not have to be orthographic:

That ye n' arette it nat my vileynye	GP 726
Th' estaat, th' array, the nombre, and eek the cause	GP 716
In the ende of which an ounce, and namoore	CYT 1266
And to the ymage of juppiter hem sente	SNT 364

2. Syncopation. The medial vowel of an unstressed syllable is skipped. Syncopation can occur within the boundaries of a single word, or across word boundaries. Syncopation occurs commonly in inflectional endings after another unstressed syllable: *yéddingg(e)s* 'recitations', *pílgrim(e)s*, *mártir(e)s*, *pálmer(e)s*, *ánswer(e)d*, etc., and when the next word is vowel-initial or *h*-initial:

Of yeddynges he baar outrely the pris	GP 237
God loved he best with al his hoole herte	GP 533

The inflexion can be syncopated also in front of a consonant-initial unstressed syllable:

It is ful fair to been ycleped madame	GP 376
Cometh neer, quod he, my lady prioresse	GP 839

Throughout the history of English, unstressed syllables ending in /r/, /l/, /m/, /n/ have had pronunciation variants in which the schwa is syncopated: *never*, *water*, *eagle*, *bosom*, *heaven*. When a vowel-initial unstressed syllable follows, the sonorant is reassigned to the onset of the following syllable, and a trisyllabic sequence becomes disyllabic:

And herde oon crien water as he were wood	MilT 3817
The feeld of snow, with th' egle of blak therinne	MkT 2383
Of his bosom, and shewed it to the preest.	CYT 1118
Youre vertu is so greet in hevene above	KnT 2249

It should be emphasized again that the elisions and syncopations described here are not *ad hoc* adjustments devised in order to make Chaucer's verse, or any other Middle English verse, regular from the modern reader's point of view. These processes are well motivated phonologically and are not confined to Middle English, or even to English.

Elisions and syncopations in the spoken language create variability of form, and it is this variability that must be taken into account before a line is declared 'irregular' and before a poet's versecraft is considered deficient.

In addition to the linguistically based accommodations, two verse-specific conventions influence the interpretation of syllabic regularity. First, an extra *unstressed* syllable at the end of the line is optional – this carries over from the Continental models. Whether the rhyme is masculine or feminine in iambic metre is entirely optional; the final unstressed syllable is outside the metrical frame, it is *extrametrical.*

The other apparent deviation from the exact syllable count is a familiar and well-recognized metrical variant: the *unstressed* syllable at the left edge of the line may be missing, so that the total number of syllables in a pentameter is nine, not counting the optional feminine rhyme:

Twenty bookes, clad in blak or reed	GP 294
Swere and lyen, as a womman kan	WBP 228

Such lines are known as 'headless' or 'acephalous'. They are particularly common in Chaucer's tetrameter verse. In the metrical literature on Chaucer the appearance of a curtailed first foot has raised doubts about the wisdom of positing an eight- or ten-syllable norm for verse which may have seven or nine syllables (or nine and eleven, counting the feminine rhyme). This phenomenon, however, is not just a random omission of *any* syllable in the line; it is constrained by position and by type: it occurs only at the left edge of the line where metrical freedoms are tolerated, and the syllable omitted is always unstressed. The strong position is always and obligatorily filled.

The combination of the described phonetic rules and the metrical conventions of ignoring the weak syllables at the line-edges produces a high level of metrical conformity. In Chaucer's pentameter verse syllabic regularity can be argued for ninety-nine per cent of the lines. No one can claim, of course, that either Chaucer or the fifteenth-century scribes *never* allowed a line with a syllable count that defies the eight- or ten-syllable matrix. The set of exceptions most frequently evoked in this context are the so-called 'Lydgatean lines'. They may have only nine syllables, but they start with an unarguably weak syllable. In addition, they have a stress clash usually across the caesura. Lydgate definitely composed such lines. Whether Chaucer did or not is still debated, but editors usually emend them, tacitly discounting them from the set of norms in Chaucer's metrical system.[15]

The Iambic Tetrameter

The Middle English iambic *tetrameter*, or the four-beat/octosyllabic line, as it is alternatively known, is a blend of two principles: the strict syllable counting of the Old French and Anglo-Norman *vers octosyllabe* and the stress alternation that characterized English speech. The term 'four-beat' emphasizes the similarity to the four-beat norm of Old

English verse and the dominance of the four-beat model in Middle English alliterative verse. The term 'octosyllabic' emphasizes the uniformity in the length of each line. *Tetrameter* is preferred here because it combines the information about the number of beats with the notion of measure: a tetrameter line consists of four units, each of which has a single strong and a single weak position:

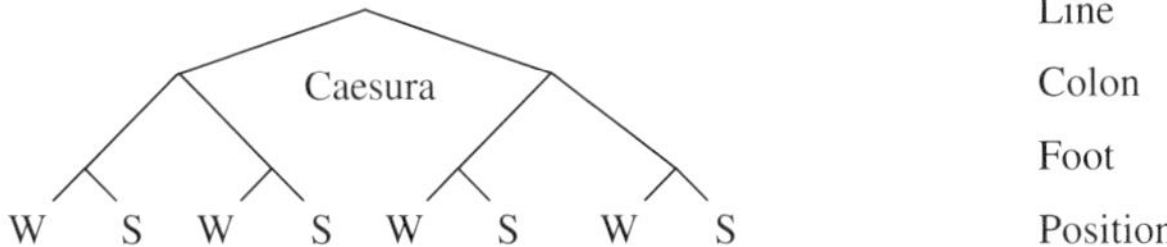

The balanced binary division of the line into two parts (cola), and the further division of each colon into two feet, each foot consisting of two syllables, was the most common and straightforward type of metre in English until Chaucer introduced the metrically much more complex pentameter. Each of the four components corresponds to constraints on the organization of the linguistic material: weak positions (Ws) are filled by unstressed syllables, strong positions (Ss) are filled by stressed syllables. The division into feet is needed because feet at the left edge of the line and feet at the right edge have different properties: the first foot can be 'defective', i.e., it may lack a filled W position, in which case the line is *headless*. Inversion of the first foot, i.e., S W instead of W S can occur, while it is prohibited in the last foot of the verse. The division into cola is justified by the frequent syntactic break after the first two feet, known as a metrical *caesura*. The existence of the line is validated by rhyme and syntax. Until Chaucer experimented with the tetrameter, Middle English verse was end-stopped, meaning that each line-ending coincided with a major syntactic break – the end of a clause or phrase.

Verse in regular iambic tetrameter in English began to appear by c.1200, *The Owl and the Nightingale* being the earliest specimen of almost perfect syllabic regularity. Among the full-scale tetrameter compositions in rhyming couplets before Chaucer are *Genesis and Exodus*, Robert Mannyng's *Handling Synne*, *Sir Orfeo*, *Havelok the Dane*, *Cursor mundi*, and, in Chaucer's lifetime, John Barbour's *The Bruce* and John Gower's impeccably crafted *Confessio Amantis*. We will focus on Chaucer, but the principles of analysis apply to all verse written in the same form.

When Chaucer came on the scene, the iambic tetrameter was well established. It is no surprise that in addition to his early translation of the *Roman de la rose*, where the tetrameter would have been a natural choice of form following the octosyllabic original, two of his early poems, the *Book of the Duchess* and the *House of Fame*, are also in this form. Unlike his predecessors, however, Chaucer must have found the form insufficiently challenging. At the beginning of Book Three of the unfinished *House of Fame*, he refers disparagingly to his own effort in versification:

> Here art poetical be shewed,
> But for the rym is lyght and lewed
> Yit make hyt sumwhat agreeable,

Though som vers fayle in a sillable;
And that I do no diligence
To shewe craft, but o sentence
HF 1095–1100

He did follow the model diligently enough. The metre of the poem is smooth and regular, the syllable count is also entirely within the limits of the model. What is new and unexpected, however, are run-on lines, or lines with enjambment, in which a syntactic and prosodic unit straddles two lines:

O wikke Fame! – for ther *nys*
Nothing so swift, lo, as she is! *HF* 349–50

'I am thy frend.' And therewith *I*
Gan for to wondren in my mynde *HF* 582–3

Making his tetrameter verse more interesting by creating metrical tension at line-ends was not enough for Chaucer; the *House of Fame* was his last tetrameter piece. The major innovation for which he is recognized in the history of English metre is the introduction of the iambic pentameter, the most significant event in the history of English versification in the period covered by this volume.

Chaucer's Metrical Innovation: The Iambic Pentameter in English

There are only a few anonymous poems before Chaucer that can be described as pentameter verse; it was Chaucer who developed and perfected the form in the *Parliament of Fowls*, *Troilus and Criseyde*, the *Legend of Good Women* and most of the *Canterbury Tales*. Isosyllabism was not new in England in the fourteenth century. Verse in 'long' isosyllabic lines of ten syllables plus an optional eleventh unstressed syllable was composed in France, Italy, Portugal and Spain. The first component of the pentameter, the string of ten syllables per line, then, was a borrowed element. As in any other kind of 'borrowing' in English, however, the original was anglicized: the 'foreign' ten-syllable line was restructured rhythmically. The *English* decasyllabic line is not a simple string of ten syllables with one peak usually on the fourth syllable and another one on the tenth, as had been the case in French. Chaucer's pentameter combines the ten-syllable count with stress alternation: the ten syllables are further structured into five iambs. The abstract pattern is illustrated below:

/\		/\		/\		/\		/\		Foot
W	S	W	S	W	S	W	S	W	S	Position
His	top	was	dok	ked	lyk	a	preest	bi	forn	GP 590

Ideally, weak positions are filled by unstressed syllables, and strong positions, or ictuses, are filled by stressed syllables, as in the line above. However, the abstract pattern and its realization as the poet matches syllables to positions may diverge. A relatively simple case of divergence is illustrated in the following line where prepositions, which are linguistically weakly stressed, are placed in ictic positions:

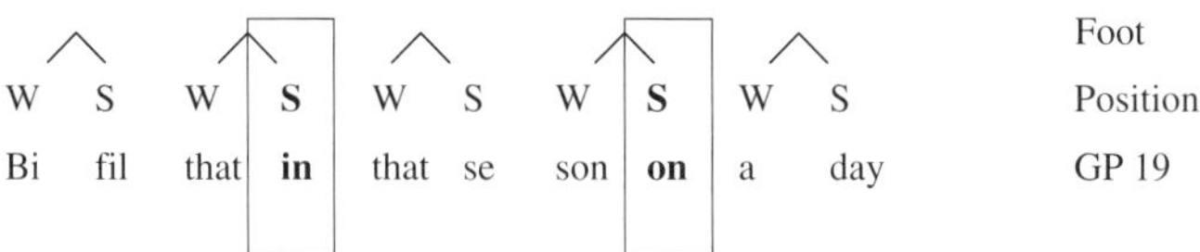

This, and other types of mismatching of prosody to metre have led to heated scholarly debates concerning the nature of Chaucer's verse. It has been argued that Chaucer's pentameter line is a four-stress line. The position taken here, which unifies Chaucer's metre with the pentameter verse written subsequently, is that the abstract pattern has exactly five ictuses. In matching prosody to metre, two issues are especially relevant: the flexibility of monosyllables, and the fixedness of polysyllables.

Monosyllabic words are free to appear in either foot position. Naturally, of course, one would expect lexical monosyllables – nouns, adjectives, verbs, adverbs – to be placed in the ictic or the even positions in the line, and the function words to be placed in the non-ictic or odd positions. Since prominence is only a relative property of adjacent syllables, however, adjustments are readily available: the boxed prepositions in GP 19 above are *promoted* metrically because they are flanked by even weaker syllables. Such promotions are very common in Chaucer. If the lines below are read without some prominence on the boldfaced words, one may get the impression that there are only four stresses per line – this is partly what has prompted the labelling of Chaucer's pentameter 'four-stress metre'.

And **at** a knyght than wol I first bigynne	GP 42
And born hym weel, as **of** so litel space	GP 87
In hope to stonden **in** his lady grace	GP 88

The inverse adjustment, *demotion* of lexical monosyllables, is rare but also possible:

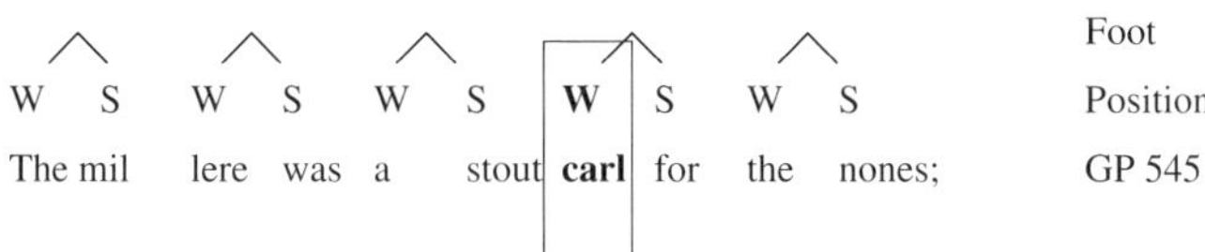

The matching of polysyllabic words to the abstract metrical frame is constrained by their prosodic contour: S W words (*hundred*, *perced*, *huntying*, *mighty*, *sondry*, *shortly*, etc.) are aligned so that their first syllable falls on the strong branch of the iamb. Prefixed words (*assent*, *entune*, *foryeve*, *discreet*, *bihinde*, *agayn*, *bitwix*, etc.) fill the whole foot. The positioning of trisyllabic words is in accord with their stress pattern, as described in the previous chapter. The following lines illustrate unproblematic matching of polysyllabic words to the metrical positions in the pentameter:

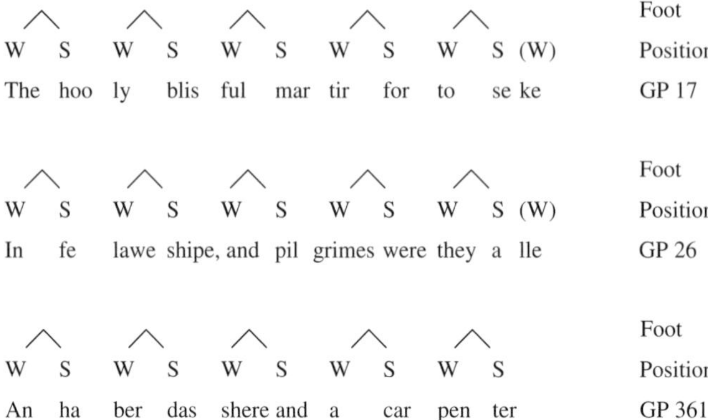

Except for the minor rhythmic adjustments, promotion of *for* in GP 17 and *and* in GP 361, such scansions are completely routine. Absolute regularity in verse, however, may be too much of a good thing, and all good poets find ways of avoiding monotony by introducing variations on the rhythm of the line. Such variations create 'tension', a metrical term referring to the divergence between the abstract scheme and its realization. By the very nature of metre-to-prosody matching, tension can be recognized and interpreted only in the context of overall regularity, such as we find in Chaucer. For him, the most frequent and, indeed, defining mode of tension is the rhythmic inversion of the prominences within the foot, commonly known as 'trochaic substitution', the positioning of a linguistic S W entity into a metrical W S slot. This is illustrated below: the bottom row represents the linguistic stresses of the words in the line:

^		^		^		^		^			Foot
W	**S**	W	S	W	S	W	S	W	S	(W)	Position
Un	der	his	belt	he	bar	ful	thrif	ti	ly		GP 105
S	**W**	W	S	W	S	W	S	W	S	W	Stress

The window of tension here is the first foot: there can be no doubt that the word *under* was stressed on the first syllable. Unlike the monosyllabic mismatches, where a minor rhythmic promotion or demotion satisfies the metre, here the rhythmic essence of the metre is violated. Placing *under* against the expectations of the iambic pentameter of the surrounding lines breaks the strict rhythmic alternation and introduces a different rhythm: *Under his belt* is rhythmically S W W S, a 'triple', distinct from the routine 'duple' contours of S W S W S strings. The source of this rhythmic modulation in Chaucer is twofold: triple rhythms were common in speech and carried over to iambic verse in English from its very inception; they occur already in the twelfth-century *Ormulum*. The second source is the Continental, and especially the Italian, decasyllabic model, where duples and triples alternate across the line.

Trochaic substitutions are distributed unevenly across the line. The strict iambic alternation is most easily broken at the left edge of the line; this is in accord with the general observation about the metrical looseness at the beginning of the line – recall the parallel phenomenon of headlessness. About 6.2% of Chaucer's tetrameter and pentameter lines (outside the *Canterbury Tales*) have an inverted first foot.[16] For the *Canterbury Tales* the figure is 9.4%, no doubt reflecting the conversational immediacy of some of the tales. Substitution at the right edge of the line is vanishingly rare: at the end of the line the metrical constraints are always obeyed. The following graph shows the distribution of inverted feet across the verse line in the entire corpus of Chaucer's verse, following the counts in Li (1995).

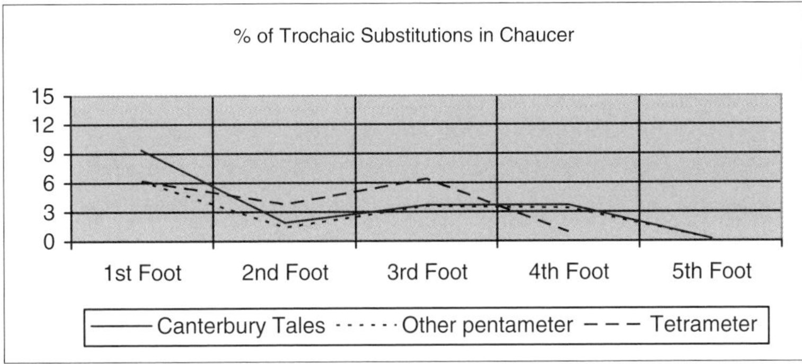

Here are some *CT* examples of trochaic inversions in the first four feet:

Redy to wenden on my pilgrimage — GP 21
Of his **offryng** and eek of his substaunce. — GP 489
Ful semely **after** hir mete she raughte. — GP 136
The smylere with the knyf **under** the cloke — KnT 1999

The rhythm of the last foot is inviolable. It hosts the rhyme, which means that the strong position of the last foot *must* be realized as stressed. This is the position in which a compound has to shift the main stress onto the second root rather than the first, as in the following lines where the rhyming words are given in parentheses:

Ther nas quyk-silver, lytarge, ne brym**stoon** (*noon*) — GP 629
Men myghte hir rowtyng heere two fur**long** (*strong*) — RvT 4166
Right so a wyf destroyeth hire hous**bonde** (*bonde*) — WBP 377

The strictness at the right edge means that native words with derivational suffixes will have to be realized with artificial prominence on the suffix. In Chaucer this option is most often exercised with *-yng(e)* and *-ness(e)*. In rare instances even an unsuffixed SW word placed in the last word is apparently meant to be pronounced with stress on the second syllable, as in the rhyme *felawe : awe* in GP 653:

Wo occupieth the fyn of oure glad**nesse** (*dresse*)	MLT 424
And he al redy was at his bid**dyng** (*thing*)	CYT 1109
Hym terve, I pray to god, for his fals**hede** (*rede*)	CYT 1274
And if he foond owher a good fel**awe** (*awe*)	GP 653

In these examples the structural requirement of the metre overrides the natural prosodic contour. In that sense such rhymes are odd and would have attracted the listeners' attention. Such conventional rhyming is sometimes interpreted as representing possible fourteenth-century pronunciation. This is misguided. As discussed in the previous chapter, neither native words nor automatically *all* Romance words had doublet forms in Chaucer's time. Understanding that the matching of stress to ictus is flexible at the beginning of the line and completely inviolable at the end of the line gives us a more discriminating view of contemporary pronunciation and also provides a metric of the care with which a poet chose his rhymes. Mismatches at the left edge violate the metre, but they also create a desirable artistic effect by introducing rhythmic variation. Mismatches at the right edge are forced by the metre; it is the prosody of the form that can be violated; the violation is conventional and does not have to reflect the prosody of speech.

Like elision and syncopation in phonology, the metrical regularities defined here have validity outside the concrete Chaucerian material; the same or very similar patterns are found in all syllable-counting verse in English, from Gower, Barbour, Lydgate, Hoccleve, Henryson to Milton and Shakespeare. Chaucer's poetic works are at the core of the history of English metre and provide a standard against which the technical proficiency of his contemporaries and followers can be measured. In this context the modern reader can share Lydgate's ardent appreciation of Chaucer:

Til that he cam and thorugh his poetrie
Gan oure tonge firste to magnifie
And adourne it with his elloquence . . .
(*Troy Book* 3.4240–2)[17]

What Chaucer rendered magnificent was not only the language itself; he also left a lasting imprint on our literary and cultural heritage by transforming the structure of English art verse.

A final note concerns the organization of the individual lines into larger verse units: couplets and stanzas. Since the entire tradition of syllable-counting verse in the fourteenth and the fifteenth century is also a tradition of rhyming, the lines have to be paired in a particular sequence. The oldest and most common type of rhyming in English is the couplet, which was also one of Chaucer's favourite forms. His masterpiece *Troilus and Criseyde* and the *Parliament of Fowls* are written in stanzas of seven lines each, known as *rhyme royal*. This is also the way some of the *Tales* are organized: the Man of Law's Tale, the Clerk's Tale, the Prioress's Tale and the Second Nun's Tale. It was also a form favoured by Hoccleve and Lydgate. The French model of eight-line stanzas was used by Chaucer in his early composition, *ABC*, and again in the Monk's Tale. Other stanza-types are also found, but they are not frequent. The rhyme arrangements in the various forms are easy to identify and their description is not controversial.

See also: 9 The Languages of Medieval Britain, 10 The Forms of Speech, 32 *Piers Plowman*, 33 The *Canterbury Tales*, 37 *Sir Gawain and the Green Knight*.

Notes

1 Pearsall 1977: 152.

2 *Sir Gawain and the Green Knight*, ed. J. R. R. Tolkien and E. V. Gordon, rev. Norman Davis (Oxford: Clarendon Press, 1967). Text made available through the Electronic Text Center, University of Virginia Library (http://etext.lib.virginia.edu).

3 *The Vision of Piers Plowman*, ed. A. V. C. Schmidt (London: Dent; New York: Dutton, 1978). Online text distributed through the University of Michigan, Humanities Text Initiative (www.hti.umich.edu).

4 This should not be taken to imply that the poets followed the same rhythmical constraints. Langland's metrical laxness compared to the 'classical' corpus of the *Gawain* MS and the alliterative histories is widely discussed in the relevant scholarship. Especially useful in tracking the specifics of Langland's metrical practice are the studies by Duggan (1986, 1987).

5 In this notation, *a* = alliterating stressed syllable, *x* = non-alliterating stressed syllable. Parentheses enclose optional syllables. In much of the literature on Middle English metre *x* is also used as the equivalent to an unstressed syllable, in the notation which uses the slash (/) for a stressed syllable, so *SGGK* 3: *Þe tulk þat þe trammes* is represented as x/xx/x

6 For the rationale and history of this term see Cable 1991.

7 The reader interested in the history of the scholarship and the arguments used should consult the works by Cable and Duggan in the references section, below. I am much indebted to their provocative and insightful treatments of the controversial metrical issues.

8 Duggan 2001: 488 found that 'most Middle English alliterative poets wrote two-stressed a-verses without two strong dips in fewer than fifteen percent of their lines'.

9 The placement of two strong dips in the B-verse in Langland occurs in 4% to 8.4% of cases depending on the manuscript (Duggan 1986: 577).

10 Cable (1991: 92) is a proponent of a rule requiring 'exactly' one unstressed syllable at the end of the B-verse. Duggan (1988) found that the rule was violated in approximately 15% of the cases in his corpus of fifteen poems.

11 For statistics on the frequency of this special cohesive device in Middle English see Oakden 1930–5: I, 156.

12 For the linguistic rationale of vowels alliterating with <h->-initial words see the previous chapter.

13 Recall the discussion of <wh-> : <w-> alliteration, which is also sound-based, in the previous chapter.

14 The Latin *septenary* model, used most famously by Orrm and the poet of *Poema morale*, is a

sequence of seven iambic feet plus an extra weak syllable. The first four feet form a complete iambic tetrameter half, followed by a *catalectic* half, i.e. the strong part of the final foot is missing.

15 Syllabic regularity in Chaucer's pentameter in relation to editing is discussed in Minkova and Stockwell 2003.

16 The figures are based on a count by Li 1995: 234.

17 From John Lydgate, *Troy Book: Selections*, ed. R. R. Edwards (Kalamazoo: Medieval Institute Publications for TEAMS, 1998).

References and Further Reading

Baum, Paull F. 1961. *Chaucer's Verse.* Durham, N.C.: Duke University Press. Though much in this book has been criticized, it remains a useful starting-point for the study of Chaucerian metre.

Borroff, M. 1962. *Sir Gawain and the Green Knight: A Stylistic and Metrical Study.* New Haven: Yale University Press. Though superseded in many of the details, the 'Metre' part of the book is foundational in the study of classic Middle English alliterative metre.

Cable, Thomas 1991. *The English Alliterative Tradition.* Philadelphia: University of Pennsylvania Press. The coverage and theoretical claims in this important study by one of the foremost scholars of English alliterative verse go beyond what the title suggests.

Duggan, Hoyt 1986. 'The Shape of the B-Verse in Middle English Alliterative Poetry.' *Speculum* 61, 564–92. Discusses constraints on the distribution of stressed and unstressed syllables in the B-verse.

—— 1987. 'Notes Toward a Theory of Langland's Metre.' *Yearbook of Langland Studies* 1, 41–70. A discussion of the metrical constraints specific to Langland's alliterative practice.

—— 1988. 'Final -e and the Rhythmic Structure of the B-verse in Middle English Alliterative Poetry.' *Modern Philology* 86, 119–45. Discusses the interplay between metre and the realization of final -e.

—— 1990. 'Stress Assignment in Middle English Alliterative Poetry.' *Journal of English and Germanic Philology* 89, 309–29. Argues that alliteration on some prefixes reflects the actual pronunciation of these forms in the spoken language.

—— 1997. 'Metre, Stanza, Vocabulary, Dialect.' In *A Companion to the Gawain-Poet*, ed. D. Brewer and J. Gibson (Cambridge: Brewer), pp. 221–42. A concise survey of metrical issues in the four poems in MS British Library Cotton Nero A.x.

—— 2001. 'Some Aspects of A-Verse Rhythms in Middle English Alliterative Poetry.' In *Speaking Images: Essays in Honor of V. A. Kolve*, ed. C. Brewer and R. Yeager (Asheville, N.C.: Pegasus Press), pp. 479–503. An innovative study which evaluates the metrical norms for the A-verse.

Gaylord, A. T. (ed.) 2001. *Essays on the Art of Chaucer's Verse.* New York: Routledge. A very important collection of classic and more recent essays; a must for the serious student of Chaucer's metre.

Halle, M. and Keyser, S. J. 1971. *English Stress: Its Form, Its Growth, and Its Role in Verse.* New York: Harper and Row. A ground-breaking attempt at a generative account of the history of stress and verse, many aspects of which have been incorporated into later theories of prosody and metre.

Kaluza, M. 1911. *A Short History of English Versification*, trans. A. C. Dunstan. New York: Macmillan. A very useful reference book covering verse forms 'from the earliest times to the present day'.

Kane, G. 1981. 'Music "neither Unpleasant nor Monotonous".' In *Medieval Studies for J. A. W. Bennett*, ed. P. L. Heyworth (Oxford: Clarendon Press), pp. 43–63. An influential piece on the Middle English verse structure.

Li, Xingzhong 1995. 'Chaucer's Metres.' Ph.D. thesis, University of Missouri, Columbia. A statistically based investigation of the metrical principles underlying Chaucer's verse.

McCully, C. B. and Anderson, J. J. 1996. *English Historical Metrics.* Cambridge: Cambridge University Press. The most comprehensive recent collection of linguistic and philological research work on English historical metrics with two-thirds of the essays covering various aspects of Middle English verse.

Minkova, D. and Stockwell, R. 2003. 'Emendation and the Chaucerian Metrical Template.' In *Chaucer and the Challenges of Medievalism: Studies in Honor of H. A. Kelly*, ed. D. Minkova and T. Tinkle (Bern: Lang), pp. 129–41. Argues in favour of defining Chaucer's iambic pentameter in terms of syllable count.

Mustanoja, T. F. 1979. 'Chaucer's Prosody.' In *Companion to Chaucer Studies*, ed. B. Rowland, rev. edn (Oxford: Oxford University Press), pp. 65–95. A helpful survey of Chaucerian metrical studies.

Oakden, J. P. 1930–5. *Alliterative Poetry in Middle English*, 2 vols. Repr. in 1 vol. Hamden, Conn.: Archon Books, 1968. A very influential classic study, dated, but still valuable for its organization, data and comprehensiveness.

Pearsall, D. 1977. *Old English and Middle English Poetry.* London: Routledge and Kegan Paul. An admirably clear and informative full-scale discussion of the entire body of early English verse.

Stockwell, R. and Minkova, D. 2001. 'The Partial-Contact Origins of English Pentameter Verse: The Anglicization of an Italian Model.' In *Language Contact in the History of English*, ed. D. Kastovsky and A. Mettinger (Bern: Lang), pp. 337–63. Explores the relationship between Continental metrical models and the native prosody in Chaucer.

PART IV
Encounters with Other Cultures

12

England and France

Ardis Butterfield

Until the fall of Calais in early 1558, England was a European country. Indeed, as late as the 1530s, Henry VIII was styling himself 'King of France'. To speak of 'England and France' in this period is thus to imply a distinction that simplifies the intricately interwoven relationship between their peoples. This chapter takes as its theme the variety of images of France that were formed and projected within late medieval England. It explores the ways in which French culture and French writing permeated 'English' culture and 'English' writing, both as an image of cultural aspiration to the English and as a source of cultural resistance. It investigates some of the ways in which English writers seemed to perceive French culture as well as how they absorbed it and responded to it.

Early Affiliations

The deep-rooted relationship between England and the French extends even further back than the eleventh century. If the Norman Conquest in 1066 stands out in this story it is worth remembering that Anglo-Saxon kings had many close dealings with the Continent from the mid-ninth to the mid-eleventh centuries, particularly through marriage alliances with the aristocratic rulers of East and West Francia, Flanders and Normandy. None the less, through the rather haphazard circumstances of the Norman invasion, it was the relationship with the Normans that turned out to be crucial in the literary history of the English. Norman French, along with Latin, became the main language of administration and the Church and of educated lay culture.

It was not until a second invasion, that of the Angevin Henry II in 1153, that the literary implications of this relationship fully emerged. Before then, histories dominated: first Eadmer's *Historia novorum in Anglia* (c.1095), then a spate of further chronicles in both Latin and French, in which the Norman, and later the Plantagenet, place in the history of the English was given due weight. The implicit insecurity of rulers in wanting to shore up their political authority by such means corresponded to problems of succession and family faction. Henry II had an interestingly mixed ancestry: grandson on his mother Matilda's side to Henry I, his father was Geoffrey of Anjou, Matilda's second husband, drafted in to prevent other claimants to Henry's throne from gaining ground. It was ironic that the first post-Conquest king to have both an insular and a Continental parent should be the king under whom literary culture in England exploded into life.

The existing interconnectedness of English and Continental intellectual society was reinforced through the vast extent of Henry II's territorial possessions. As an Angevin ruler, Henry controlled most of what is now north-west France: Anjou itself, Maine, Normandy and Brittany. After marrying Eleanor of Aquitaine in 1152 he gained great areas of south-west France: Aquitaine and Poitou. Including England, Henry's Angevin empire far outweighed the possessions of the Capetian kingdom of France. From this perspective we can see that England was but one element in a large-scale linking of separate feudal regions.

It would be misleading to describe the literature produced in England in the twelfth century in narrowly insular terms. The geographical range of Henry's control meant that the ruling French elite in England had a broader outlook than Normandy alone. Henry's marriage was a significant factor. Eleanor's court in Aquitaine and that of her daughter, Marie de Champagne, were famous for their patronage of poetry, learning and music. This period of Angevin supremacy across Europe coincided with a remarkable sequence of writings in French. The greatest romance writer of the Middle Ages, Chrétien de Troyes, and the greatest lyric authors – the second-generation troubadours (from the south) and first-generation trouvères (from the north) – flourished under Eleanor's and Marie's encouragement. It is in their writings, and those of a chaplain, Andreas, who produced an odd, ironic treatise on love, that modern scholars discovered 'courtly love'.[1] Although there has been much (modern) debate about courtly love, there is no disputing the overwhelming influence of these early Occitan and French writers of song and of romance on the Western culture of love through to our own times.

Their influence has been misunderstood. One problem with the term 'courtly love' as C. S. Lewis, for example, defined it, is that it conjures up an impression of pretty, silent women adored by dominating yet emotionally humbled men. Although women are indeed largely silent and idealized in medieval song, the picture of complacent stasis in the male–female relationship is false. Irony, black humour and obscenity in many troubadour love songs point to a world where this relationship is seen as troublingly asymmetrical. The woman (*domna* in Occitan, *dame* in French) is a contradictory symbol of power and inarticulacy: she is at once acutely vulnerable and emotionally overwhelming, irrelevant and central. Inherently unstable, this female image feeds a culture of love that constantly finds new ways of generating fractured, rhetorically ingenious writing.

Conventionally, the beginnings of French literature in the Middle Ages are told as a separate story from the beginnings of English. English, in turn, is seen as highly dependent on French at the beginning, but then able to achieve independence and, finally, triumphant success in its own right. Yet the actual state of their affair cannot be summarized so simply. Most of the earliest surviving writing in French was produced for the Plantagenets, either in England itself or in areas (such as Aquitaine) of what is now France but was then under English/Angevin rule. The very work that in the late nineteenth and early twentieth centuries was taken by French literary historians most to define France and the French, the *Chanson de Roland*, was probably composed in the late eleventh century, but its first surviving version occurs in an Anglo-Norman manuscript c.1140–70. The first written versions of the celebrated story of Tristan and his love for Isolde were by authors living and working in England: Béroul and Thomas (known as Thomas of England). The collection of jewel-like but often bizarre short stories or *lais* by a woman styling herself Marie de France offers another example of poetry that is part of the modern canon of medieval French literature yet was written in England.

But this is not to claim some kind of jingoistic priority for England in the history of French literature. It is rather to show that the very terms of the distinction are inadequate. The circumstances of Angevin domination meant that Aquitaine was no more or less English than England was French. Of course, the different regions within the empire were hardly homogeneous or indistinguishable; none the less, from the point of view of literary production, the use of French to exert a cohesive cross-continental cultural language was powerful and paramount.

Prologue: Marie de France

The Prologue written by Marie de France to a collection of twelve of her *lais* encapsulates the relations between England and the French at this earlier stage. Marie herself is a shadowy figure: little is known about her beyond what can be deduced from her name, her dedication of her writings to a noble king (generally agreed to be Henry II) and the surviving manuscripts. With such a precarious sense of who she is and why she writes verse, the Prologue makes all the more intriguing reading. While she pays homage to the ancient, revered texts of the classical poets, she insists on doing something different in her own work. Rather than present a Latin text, she chooses short, popular oral and sung tales from the Breton vernacular, and treats them as if they were worthy of the same respect as the ancients. Her rare status as a woman writer makes this decision even more striking though not necessarily any clearer. Is this a woman's decision? What would that mean? The *lais* themselves do not offer transparent answers. Most of them tell strange, often surreal stories of love and magic in which the lovers' passion is hard to interpret within the frame of the narrative. For example, there is a knight who can transform himself into a bird, a king who is scalded to death, and a wronged werewolf who, biting off the nose of his ex-wife, creates a line of female descendants without noses. What is clear, however, is that Marie is fascinated by the socially and critically destabilizing power of these stories. At the heart of our earliest surviving love narratives from the English-Angevin Middle Ages is a mysterious but clever version of love, written by a woman, in which fantasy, morality and the art of writing provide a potent and unsettling mix. This female perspective, moreover, is presented as an act of cultural translation of the highest ambition.

The rest of this essay will be concerned with both these things: the destabilizing role of women in medieval love narratives, and the issue of cultural translation: how can one literary culture express its relation to another, more powerful and prestigious, one? Marie raises these questions particularly sharply, as we have seen. For not only are they pressing questions for her as a writer; she asks them as a female writer 'from France' writing in England. For each of the following four writers of the later English medieval period their relationship with French writing turns crucially on the problematic place held by women in their French sources.

I will argue, further, that each work – *Sir Gawain and the Green Knight*, Malory's *Morte Darthur*, Gower's *Confessio Amantis* and Chaucer's *Legend of Good Women* – raises distinctive questions about how medieval authors treated sources. In particular, they prompt us to rethink some of the ways modern readers of English medieval authors have tended to approach the French material. The assumptions of traditional source study die hard, even when a term such as intertextuality is preferred. Yet neither approach necessarily does justice to the challenges of reading one culture through another.

These works have been selected because between them they draw on two of the most deeply influential elements of French inspiration for writers in all the main vernaculars across Europe – including Italian, German, Spanish and Galician-Portuguese. I am referring to two strands of romance: the huge Arthurian tradition that spread from the twelfth century onwards and a newer kind of love narrative from the thirteenth century embodied in the two-authored *Le Roman de la rose* by Guillaume de Lorris and Jean de Meun.[2] There were many other genres of French writing, not least the lyric, but these two types of romance can be taken as representative of what France meant to later medieval English writers. *Sir Gawain and the Green Knight* and Malory's *Morte Darthur* make the first pairing, showing aspects of English response to Arthurian material over a century (from the last quarter of the fourteenth century to c.1470). The second pair, Gower's *Confessio Amantis* and Chaucer's *Legend of Good Women*, draw deeply from the *Rose* and its fourteenth-century French successors, the *dits* of Guillaume de Machaut and Jean Froissart.

The Arthurian Tradition I: *Sir Gawain and the Green Knight*

Sir Gawain has survived with hardly any of the signals that we now expect of poems: an author, a date, a social context, an audience. Scholars have agreed from studying the dialect of the unique manuscript only that it was written down, and perhaps also composed, in the north-west Midlands. Partly because of this northerly, non-metropolitan linguistic location, and partly because of its distinctive style supported by its unique survival, *Gawain* has tended to strike most modern readers as a rather English work.

Under the influence of a persuasive reading by John Burrow, it is widely regarded as being centrally about *trouthe*, a virtue understood in medieval culture as comprising loyalty, integrity, honour and consistency. Burrow sees the two contracts in the story as the measure of and guide towards the poet's determination to put *trouthe* foremost. What is clever, structurally, about the poem is that this first contract (the beheading game) turns out to depend, or rather to have depended, on the second (an exchange of winnings).

The lucidity of this view is beguiling. I think for many readers the moral argument of the poem is not clear, but baffling. A major symptom of bafflement occurs in the comic eruptions that puncture the poem. In the first contract, for example, there is so much ludicrous exaggeration in the description of the Green Knight that our reaction is at least partly composed of amusement and incredulity:

> For the hede in his honde he haldes up even,
> Toward the derrest on the dece he dresses the face;
> And hit lyfte up the yye-lyddes, and loked ful brode,
> And meled thus much with his muthe, as ye may now here.
> (444–7)

(For he holds up the head plainly in his hand, and turns the face towards the highest-ranking [of the company] on the dais, and it lifted up its eyelids and stared very boldly, and spoke the following with his mouth, as you may now hear.)[3]

The moving eyelids on the severed head both add to and detract from the terror of public decapitation: they add to it because they make us flash forward imaginatively to what Gawain's head will do in similar circumstances, but they also detract from it because they comically and conclusively shift the mode of the narrative from realism to romance. The workings of this contract, I suggest, include a repressed, at least partially comic, allusion to its outcome which is not primarily moral but more like a curious blend of horror tempered by fantasy. The second contract, the exchange of sexual favours with the lady of the house, redoubles the effect of comic dislocation. Not only are the very terms of the bargain full of suggestion, but we also wonder how Gawain is going to be able to exchange *this* sort of gain with the host. The double-edged anticipation reaches its first climax at the end of the first day. How closely is he going to stick to his part of the bargain? Is he going to kiss the host in *precisely* the same way as he was kissed by the lady? The sexual frisson in the air is hammed up by the poet's description of the kiss:

> He hasppez his fayre hals his armez wythinne,
> And kysses hym as comlyly as he couthe awyse.
> (1388–9)

(He clasps his fair neck within his arms, and kisses him as beautifully as he possibly could.)

The effect is again a comically disruptive antidote to the moral version of the situation: if this is only the first day of exchanges, what will be performed on the last? In short, seriousness is often deflated in the poem through implied comic predictions which distract us from having too firm a hold on the moral imperatives of any particular situation. My argument here is not that the poem is *not* serious, but that it has a problem with the serious.

The question of how seriously we take Gawain's fault is linked to how seriously we take Gawain himself. One of the subtlest sources of comedy in the bedroom scenes and one of the lady's most potent weapons against Gawain is her constant appeal to his reputation. What does she mean? Here, even more puzzlingly, the poem offers nothing but contradiction and insinuation. Her obvious innuendo is that he is a good lover, but this conflicts with Gawain's reputation in the poem for superlative virtue and, in particular, for *clannesse* or chastity. Not only is chastity one of his five pentangle virtues, but he is also dedicated to the Virgin Mary.

At this point of apparent hiatus, French romance provides, after all, a context. Gawain is not isolated; this is one of the fissures in the poem that reveals a vast Continental hinterland. Gawain has a reputation because he happens to be the most frequently cited character in medieval French romance. It is perhaps surprising to discover that more is written about him than about any other Arthurian knight, including Lancelot and Tristan. Unlike them, though, he is not always the hero: more often he has important subsidiary adventures in romances where other knights are the centre of attention – and this again is unique to him. His romance career stretches over a long period: from the earliest French romances by Chrétien de Troyes in the late twelfth century, to fifteenth- and sixteenth-century prose and ballad versions in French and English. And despite the seriousness of some of the English versions such as the alliterative *Morte Arthur* his standing in French is always more ambiguous.

Gawain never gains a reputation in French romance, he has it already: it belongs with his stock character. Moreover, especially in the later romances, this characteristic of Gawain becomes self-knowing. Gawain knows that he has a reputation, and frequently refers to it. The result is that the sense of his reputation becomes curiously abstracted: the sense of who Gawain is does not depend particularly on what Gawain does. This perhaps explains the existence of another, seemingly disparate element in Gawain's reputation – his reputation with women. Unlike Lancelot, or Arthur, or Tristan, Gawain does not form half of a romantic pairing. There is no single lady, like Isolde or Guinevere, with whom he is associated. The reason is that he has affairs with any number of ladies, and cannot be made to settle down with any of them. He will swear undying loyalty to the first pretty young maiden he comes across in an adventure. They usually consummate their love with remarkable promptness (at least in the later romances), only for Gawain then to find an unavoidable reason for leaving.

Altogether, though, Gawain's luck with women is very variable. Some girls, such as Tanree in one of the Continuations of Chrétien's *Le Conte du graal*, spend half their lives simply waiting for Gawain to ride by. Tanree, when Gawain finally appears as she is idly combing her hair by a fountain, is so excited that she immediately suggests that they go to her manor for him to do what he likes with her. She is infatuated with him because of his name and renown. He duly deflowers her, but then leaves again. Her lament on his departure is revealing. How stupid she was, she says, to think that he would stay. All women who have heard of him fall in love with him. Someone with his reputation cannot be expected to be faithful.

Other girls treat him less generously. The Male Pucelle in *Le Conte du graal* causes him nothing but trouble and humiliation. Another girl in a Continuation sets him a trap. She offers herself to him, but refuses to sleep with him until the early morning. Gawain just manages to contain his impatience, but while he is waiting he discovers a knife that she was about to use to kill him. When she joins him in bed she tries but fails to find the knife, and at this point the ever gentle, ever courteous Gawain turns nasty and rapes her. Somewhat inexplicably the experience causes her to fall in love with him after all, and she goes to much trouble to ward off the vengeance of her brothers against Gawain for his act.[4]

At first sight, it is odd that Gawain should be regarded both as a paragon and as a smooth-talking heart-breaker. On reflection, though, it is of course a version of the celebrity phenomenon very familiar in our own culture. The two kinds of reputation are not mutually exclusive but connected. The girls after all desire him precisely because of his reputation. In this sense, female admiration of Gawain enhances rather than detracts from his general standing among the Arthurian knights. On the other hand, we can also see how readily the combination of virtue and sexual appeal lends itself to comedy. One of the best exploitations of this is the late twelfth- or early thirteenth-century romance *Le Chevalier à l'épée*. The plot is strikingly close to the temptation episode in the English *Sir Gawain and the Green Knight*. Gawain, having lost his way in the forest, is offered hospitality in a castle. The host urges him to sleep with his daughter. Scarcely able to conceal his relish, but dubious of the host's intentions, Gawain does as he is told. Just as he is about to 'accomplish his desire' the girl warns him that he is in a trap. If he goes any further, a sword hanging above him is going to jump out and strike him. Gawain is very taken aback:

> Never before in the whole of his life had he ever heard tell of such a dire threat, and so he suspected that she had told him all this to protect herself, so that he could not satisfy his desire. On the other hand, he reflected, it could not be concealed – indeed would be generally known – that he had lain with her all alone, both of them naked, in her bed, and that he had, on account of a single word, desisted from making love to her. It is more becoming to die in honour than to live long in shame.[5]

The joke here is a clever twist on the usual Gawain predicament. His reputation is hanging, quite literally, over him, but here it is phrased entirely in terms of sexual prowess: his honour will be lost not if he does deflower the girl, but if he does not. The story goes on to conflate the two kinds of reputation (Gawain as paragon and Gawain as lady-killer) even more mischievously. Gawain saves his honour to the extent of getting two wounds from the sword, but not of losing his life. In the morning the host proclaims him the best knight of all: the sword has chosen him to pass the test, and he can now marry the daughter.

Gawain is treading close to ridicule in *Le Chevalier à l'épée*. The test of his worth demands not courage, or courtesy, or martial skill, or even strength, but an acute awareness of the embarrassment of sexual failure. This propensity for comic humiliation sets Gawain apart from most other Round Table knights. Nearly all the Arthurian plots represent some kind of testing process for each knight. The better the knight, the more significant the test of his virtue, so that failure gains often tragic proportions. The problem for Gawain is that his virtue is always being set up for a fall. Most of Gawain's failures never rise to tragedy; they only succeed in being embarrassing, or funny, or both. For this reason, Gawain – in Old French romance – makes an unusual kind of hero. In many ways, in fact, he cannot be called a hero: he never quite manages to live up to it, despite his reputation. He may be described as the best knight, but in practice he always falls short of Lancelot or Perceval, and he also fails to achieve the Grail – the most important symbol of perfection in Arthurian romance.

As a hero, then, we could say that Gawain, instead of having a tragic flaw, has a comic flaw. It would be misleading, however, to think that his penchant for embarrassing situations overturns his serious qualities, although the case has been argued. There is no comedy without the prior assumption of his high reputation: the two characteristics feed off each other; one does not cancel the other out. It is important to recognize this central tension in the Gawain character-model when we reread the English romance; our 'background' for the English Gawain is full of shifts and strains.

Let me return to the fourteenth-century English version of Gawain. I have been discussing four main strands in the French Gawain's generic character: his status as a paragon of courtly and chivalric virtue; his reputation as a ladies' man; his tendency, while being tested, towards ritual comic humiliation; and his inability quite to reach the stature of hero. All these elements figure in the English poem. The pivotal relationship between Gawain as paragon and as ladies' man is one of the poem's central structural devices, in the way that the clever interlacing of the Beheading Game plot and the Castle Temptations adventure counterpoises Gawain's high virtue and his susceptibility to women. The English Gawain also risks comic humiliation. Note, for example, how many times people respond to him by bursting into loud laughter: Bertilak laughs at him, the court laughs at him, Morgan le Fay must be laughing behind his back. In addition, there is the more subtle, implicit comedy of the two contracts: the farcical black humour of the Beheading Agreement and the powerful sexual embarrassments of the Exchange of Winnings.

His equivocal status as a hero in French romance similarly finds a match in the English poem. In particular, the strains in his generic make-up help to explain why we have such a problem in the poem: first, how seriously to take Gawain; and second, how seriously to view his fault. For Gawain, as we have seen, always falls short of expectation. We are never sure that the heroic is really *his* mode. From this point of view the poet takes a certain risk in setting Gawain up so high at the start of the poem, because the expectation in his generic model is that he will fall. Moreover, I would argue that this sense of awkwardness of fit between Gawain as paragon and Gawain as excessively contrite sinner is part of the comedy.

Another element we recognize in the English version is the mischievous association of women with Gawain's fall. Gawain *would* have to be brought down by a love token (a 'luf lace' as the girdle is immediately called by the poet as soon as Gawain tries to hide it). It is beautifully funny to see Gawain riding off at dawn to meet the Green Knight so wonderfully (and unwittingly) compromised by his clothes: his helmet covered in embroidered figures of love and the green girdle – this damaging symbol of generic discomfiture – wrapped round his waist. No wonder he erupts in embarrassed fury against womankind. It always comes down to women with Gawain: he has never been very good at dealing with their tricks without losing his dignity.

Finally, there is comic irony in the English poem's presentation of Gawain's virtue. It seems a little cruel to make Gawain of all people, with *his* reputation, have to lie in a bed and refuse a lady's advances. The sharp reversal of the comedy of *Le Chevalier à l'épée* reminds us that chastity, of all virtues, is the one most ambiguously associated with Gawain. That Gawain is virtuous by accident is made to seem less than purely noble: it is undignified in its very contingency, and undone by his deliberate attempt to save his life.

The traditional language of source study does not fit the case of *Sir Gawain and the Green Knight* and French Arthurian romance very easily. The correspondences are not specific verbal borrowings but a result of something more like a long cultural memory. It is possible to trace plot patterns, such as the Beheading Game and the Temptation scene, but we cannot be sure that the English author knew particular romances such as *Le Chevalier à l'épée* or *La Mule sans frein*. Yet even if we were, his approach clearly involves more than borrowing a plot. Throughout the English poem, the figure of Gawain keeps developing moments of extra dimensionality: the author is drawing on a wider knowledge of his stock character and alluding to his audience's memory of that character's literary life. By this relatively late stage in the Arthurian tradition, individual Arthurian characters have developed complex layers of literary existence, and possess fluctuating and hence not readily confinable meanings. I have been arguing that the stress points arise precisely out of the uncontrollable associations of Gawain and women.

The Arthurian Tradition II: Malory's *Morte Darthur*

Malory's *Morte Darthur* is more directly saturated with French textual references. It may be useful first to give a brief outline of the material he uses. After the twelfth-century verse narratives by Chrétien, Arthurian romance developed huge, expanded cycles in prose throughout the thirteenth century and the early fourteenth. There were two main types: the Lancelot–Graal material, also known as the Vulgate cycle, and the Tristan branch, known as the *Prose Tristan*. The Lancelot–Graal cycle itself had five distinct branches, all with their own complex history of expansion and adaptation. Malory seems to have known four of them: the *Suite du Merlin*, the *Lancelot 'proper'*, *La Queste del saint graal* and *La Mort le roi Artu*. Malory's opening section on Arthur comes from the *Suite du Merlin* (probably in a late version). The next section on Arthur, called by the pioneering French editor of Malory, Eugène Vinaver, 'The Tale of Arthur and Lucius', comes largely from an English alliterative poem known as the *Alliterative Morte Arthure*. Lancelot's book is drawn from the *Lancelot 'proper'* (the third branch of the Lancelot–Graal cycle); this is followed by the only section in the work for which there is no agreed source: 'The Tale of Sir Gareth'. Malory takes 'The Book of Sir Tristram' from the first two books of the *Prose Tristan*. However, although the third book of the *Prose Tristan* tells the story of the Grail, Malory chooses instead to base his 'Tale of the Sankgreal' on the version that comes in the fourth branch of the Lancelot–Graal cycle: *La Queste del saint graal*. Finally, the last two parts of Malory, on 'Lancelot and Guinevere' and the 'Morte Arthur' itself, come from two sources: *La Mort le roi Artu* (the fifth branch of the Lancelot–Graal cycle) and a fifteenth-century English stanzaic version of the same French story, known now as the stanzaic *Morte Arthur*.

The very obviousness of the *Morte* as a work of translation creates its own problems. The scale and complexity of the range of material, and the fact that Malory draws on English as well as French versions, means that modern readers have come to very different conclusions about the methods and results of Malory's reading. A surprising number of Anglo-American readers have seen Malory's work as coming through this labour with 'a distinctly English spirit';[6] conversely, for Vinaver, Malory was less an adapter of English traditions of writing romance than a translator of the great French cycles. Even when the full range of sources is surveyed, few modern readers of Malory (since Vinaver) have been sufficiently in command of the French writings to comment either in detail or in general on Malory's reactions to them. And those who have made detailed studies of Malory in relation to the English sources have inevitably left these issues to do with French sources to one side.

In this sense, the question about cultural translation posed by Marie surfaces in Malory in a particularly interesting form. Not only does Malory read French Arthurian romance, but he also reads it through English versions, which in turn are readings and renderings of French. We have a seemingly impossible task of observing a myriad instances of distancing and realignment, of an adjustment of perspectives that are themselves in the process of being adjusted. The French material, in turn, is not static but a vastly complex process of rereading and reinterpreting within a moving current of expanding narratives that do not just precede Malory, but continue in parallel with his work in the fifteenth century and beyond. Both *Sir Gawain* and Malory are part of this wider current: whatever the precise angle of their displacement from it, they cannot escape also being positioned within it.

One of the best, but also most difficult, examples of Malory's position within the French Arthurian tradition concerns his treatment of Guinevere. Modern English readers of Malory have debated Guinevere's role at length; many find her oddly situated in the homosocial tensions of the last part of the *Morte*. Arthur states baldly:

> wyte you well, my harte was never so hevy as hit ys now. And much more I am soryar for my good knyghtes losse than for the losse of my fayre quene; for quenys I might have inow, but such a felyship of good knyghtes shall never be togydirs in no company. (685)[7]

and he goes on to lament bitterly the breakdown of relations between him and Lancelot: 'alas, that ever sir Launcelot and I shulde be at debate!' (685). Arthur seems to regard Guinevere as a necessary but replaceable commodity; Lancelot, by contrast, stirs his deepest emotional responses. Tension is created by the strength of the bond between Guinevere and Lancelot: ironically, Arthur needs Guinevere less because she is his own queen, than because she is Lancelot's mistress. Guinevere and Lancelot help create and maintain the bond between Arthur and Lancelot. Thus Arthur is wrong: Guinevere is the crucial factor in creating stability out of instability. Adultery, paradoxically, is vital to the honour of the king.

What is difficult to gauge is how much of this is Malory. Again, the approach of most modern readings of Malory depends on extracting this judgement: Malory's view is deemed to have been found if a line or passage can be shown *not* to have a source. Yet while this may have value in the case of specific moments of comment, it cannot help much with the larger perspectives on character and narrative perspective. Like Gawain, Guinevere is the product of multiple prior narrative reshapings: she does not come to Malory unformed, but rather with a certain degree of stubborn autonomy. The triangular relationship between her, Lancelot and Arthur develops from Chrétien, but not necessarily in a straight line. Not only do we need to take account of how Chrétien's imperious, extreme and famously uncompromising Guinevere is read and re-presented in the thirteenth-century French prose version; we also need to allow for the possibility that Malory read Chrétien direct, as well as the stanzaic English interpretation of *La Mort le roi Artu*. There is not space to do this here; my point is rather that since Guinevere is crucial to our larger understanding of the destruction of the Arthurian court, we need to see her in as large a perspective as we can, which means going behind and back through her many biographies. But the longest perspective is clear: Guinevere is the most visible instance in Malory's *Morte Darthur* of the *domna*. She is the modern fifteenth-century embodiment of the contradictory asymmetries of love articulated in the eleventh century through the passionate analyses of the troubadours.

The *Rose* Tradition

In some ways the Arthurian tradition seems a special case of literary relationship because it has a recognizable narrative identity. Despite their bewildering variety the narratives are all working to elucidate a single story. I have been arguing that the still widely used model of source study cannot account adequately for traditions of such long historical coherence. What, then, of the *Roman de la rose*? On the face of it the *Rose* does not produce a comparable tradition since the narratives that follow it are more disparate.

The *Rose* itself is one of the best examples in that its second part, by Jean de Meun, so radically differs from the first. Perhaps coherence can be found, none the less, not in narrative so much as in method: the art of the *Rose* presupposes that the writer will be interested above all in the means and literary process of expressing love.

Briefly, outside the Arthurian tradition, thirteenth-century narrative is dominated by not one but two *Roses*: the double work by Guillaume de Lorris and Jean de Meun, and another, roughly contemporary with Guillaume's, by the sharper-tongued Jean Renart. Both *Roses* were highly influential, and both in terms of their treatment of lyric. Guillaume (and later Jean) made lyric the subject of narrative, in every sense; Jean Renart cut lyrics into his narrative, a practice which was imitated closely by Guillaume de Machaut and Jean Froissart, amongst others, in the fourteenth century.[8]

Gower: *Confessio Amantis*

In the last part of this essay I want to consider the response of two more English authors to French writing: John Gower and Geoffrey Chaucer. In both cases, this response has created difficulty for modern readers. With respect to Gower, first of all, it remains a central question about the *Confessio Amantis* as to why Gower chose to base so huge a moral edifice on love. The *Confessio* is a substantial work in eight books, structured around the device of confession. Each book cumulatively works through the Seven Deadly Sins, but these are expounded by a priest of Venus rather than of the Church, and applied specifically to love. The lover confesses his sins of bad behaviour as a lover, and Genius the priest illustrates his answers by means of a collection of over a hundred narratives from a wide range of sources, including Ovid. Although Gower has received much praise for his narrative skill, not every reader has been convinced by his choice of frame. The topic of love and the device of confession seem to pull in different directions. Considering that in his other two large-scale works, the Latin *Vox clamantis* and the French *Mirour de l'omme*, Gower presents himself as a fairly strident moralist, it seems odd that in the third he should adopt the secular language of love so thoroughly.

An important reason can be found in the double structure of Guillaume and Jean's *Rose*: Gower, like many other fourteenth-century vernacular writers, saw Jean's appropriation of Guillaume's mantle of authorship as a model for his own self-presentation as author. Love was *the* subject of French writing, and hence became the subject of various constructions of vernacular authorship across Europe. Like the continuators of the *Rose* such as Gui de Mori, the author(s) of *Le Roman de Fauvel*, and then Machaut and Froissart, Gower was drawn into its powerful orbit. The view of Gower as someone who fundamentally disapproved of the *Rose* is misplaced. He is best seen as another continuator, an inveterate glossator and interpreter, participating in rather than rejecting the tradition of commentary that built up around the *Rose*. At the same time, the *Confessio* also shows how the activity of continuation was not straightforward. The contortions of structure, especially evident in the complexly layered ending of the work, speak of the clever yet also obscure sleights of hand in the structure of the *Rose*. One author hands over to another in the *Rose*, but only retrospectively and through a trick; Gower likewise plays tricks with authorship, pushes himself forward as a narrator and a generalized young lover, and then as an old, disillusioned author. In short, we should not be surprised by our puzzlement over the *Confessio*: it continues processes of dislocation that not only started much earlier in French writing but also became a key topos for vernacular authorial self-presentation.

Chaucer: the *Legend of Good Women*

My chosen Chaucerian text, the *Legend of Good Women*, has often been linked with the *Confessio* on the grounds of comparing its structure as a tale collection and of closeness of date. Once more, it functions both as a work in which the response to French models is overt and profound, and also as one that has struck modern readers as particularly hard to interpret in its entirety. One of the main questions concerns the relation of the Prologue (which survives in two distinct forms) to the collection of nine (actually eight-and-a-bit) legends; another concerns its state of completion – just how unfinished is it? The two questions are related in the sense that readers have often wondered whether Chaucer could not be bothered to finish it, since the legends, apparently written as a penance under instruction from Alceste, the God of Love's consort, are short and slight. The Prologue, by contrast, has some of the most mature reflection in all Chaucer's writings on the relation of a modern author to past literary masterpieces.

If Gower's most direct mentor is Jean de Meun in his role as reader of Guillaume's *Rose*, then Chaucer's Prologue, at least at first, is more immediately recognizable as a version of Jean Renart's *Rose*. Renart sets forty-eight songs or extracts into his romance, including stanzas from thirteen high-art love songs from the trouvères and three from the troubadours. The fashion for doing this spread quickly and widely during the thirteenth century, and by the fourteenth was the defining mode of writing love narrative for the great master of love poetry and music, Guillaume de Machaut, and his younger contemporary (who was the same age as Chaucer), Jean Froissart. Chaucer's decision to place a *ballade*, the formal epitome of French fourteenth-century lyric art, into his Prologue, places him squarely in that mode. The use of song, for Renart and his later followers, was a sophisticated means of cutting in glancing perspectives on authorship, whether the songs were by somebody else (as they were in Renart's romance) or by the author of the narrative (as they were in Machaut and Froissart). We can see, then, that the conjunction of the formal disruption of the ballade within the narrative couplets of Chaucer's Prologue and comment on the role of the author is entirely to be expected from a French point of view.

A little later we learn that Chaucer has committed a crime, and the crime was to be a translator:

> Thow art my mortal fo and me werreyest,
> And of myne olde servauntes thow mysseyest,

And hynderest hem with thy translacyoun . . .
. . . Thow mayst it nat denye,
For in pleyn text, it nedeth nat to glose,
Thow hast translated the Romauns of the Rose.
(G Text, 248–50, 253–5)

He is also blamed for describing Criseyde as false in *Troilus and Criseyde*. Both these acts are crimes of heresy against the God of Love. In isolation, the logic of these lines is hard to understand. Is this a genuine repudiation of the *Rose* on Chaucer's part? Among many conflicting modern interpretations, some have assumed that Chaucer is trying to move on from the French courtly tradition and is therefore parodying this kind of criticism of Chaucer's alleged antifeminism, while others have held back from the thought that Chaucer could have been so crudely flippant about the topic of representing women.

Here again, reading the French context more closely can be of some help. Exactly the same kind of repudiation occurs in a pair of poems by Machaut: the *Jugement du roy de Behaingne*, and the *Jugement du roy de Navarre*.[9] In the second, Machaut as narrator is criticized for not having supported the cause of women in the first: he is hauled up before a law court, denounced at length and ordered to write a *lai* as penance. Clearly, lumping 'the French courtly tradition' together as a single target for Chaucer is misguided: Machaut can hardly be accused of betraying the *Rose*. More complexly, the *Rose* tradition is itself, as I have suggested earlier, centrally concerned with the dislocation provided by Jean de Meun's reading of Guillaume's *Rose*. Reaction and controversy are courted by the double *Rose*; they are not separable from its intricate, and in some ways inconsistent, agenda. Chaucer, like Gower and Froissart, and like Machaut before them, is continuing the process of glossing the *Rose* through the form of Renart's *Rose*. Glossing and commenting, an originally academic activity, can be contentious: in all these authors, there is a deep recognition of the contortions of a 'courtly' position, and of the difficulties of articulating it for a new generation.

I want to relate this, finally, back to the woman with whom we began, Marie de France. Her bold expression of the complex project of cultural translation resonates through Chaucer's Prologue more audibly than we might expect, given the passage of time. Yet his own cultural position – also a writer in England – is remarkably close to hers. She is burdened with the task of translating into French, he with translating into English; for both the solution is not to smooth over the difficulties but to embrace them. As both of them saw, the role of woman in the courtly culture of love is not just fundamentally awkward, but fundamental to a writer trying to convey in other words, in another language, the essence of that culture's aspirations. Women do not just surface troublingly from the deep structure of a text, as they do in *Gawain*; the trouble they cause constitutes the writer's topic. This became the subject of much debate in the fifteenth century through another woman writer, Christine de Pizan, and her extended 'querelle' with the *Rose*.

In reading and interpreting the literary relationship between England and France in the later Middle Ages we find that it is expressed as much as a subtext as an overt exchange. Traditional source study cannot detect the large part of that more subterranean dialogue. The greater part of this dialogue is a form as much of implicit argument as of respectful reference. In that sense, the term intertextuality, at least in its modern sense, also has its drawbacks, since the relationships involve something more than physical texts: sudden vistas of memory, indirect recall and even purposeful oblivion. They are also, in the special case of England and France, based on several centuries of social, political, familial and linguistic common ground, shared on the island and on the Continent. We need an approach to this long cross-cultural history that sees books as shared commodities, but also as keys to the less tangible social experience of memory. Chaucer, after Marie de France, puts it like this:

> And yf that olde bokes were aweye,
> Yloren were of remembraunce the keye.
> (F, G Texts, 25–6)

See also: 5 Women's Voices and Roles, 8 Translation and Society, 9 The Languages of Medieval Britain, 13 Britain and Italy, 14 England's Antiquities, 16 War and Chivalry, 18 Images, 19 Love, 20 Middle English Romance, 23 Lyric, 33 The *Canterbury Tales*, 34 John Gower and John Lydgate, 37 *Sir Gawain and the Green Knight*, 38 Malory's *Morte Darthur*.

Notes

1 See, most famously, C. S. Lewis, *The Allegory of Love* (Oxford: Oxford University Press, 1936), p. 4.

2 Guillaume de Lorris and Jean de Meun, *Le Roman de la rose*, ed. F. Lecoy, 3 vols. Les Classiques Français du Moyen Age 92, 95, 98 (Paris: Champion, 1965–70); trans. F. Horgan (Oxford and New York: Oxford University Press, 1994).

3 *Sir Gawain and the Green Knight, Pearl, Cleanness, Patience*, ed. J. J. Anderson (London: Dent, 1996), lines 444–7; translation mine.

4 Busby 1980: 200–2.

5 Trans. Elizabeth Brewer, *Sir Gawain and the Green Knight: Sources and Analogues*, 2nd edn (Woodbridge: Brewer, 1992), p. 117. For the French text, see *Two Old French Gauvain Romances*, ed. R. C. Johnston and D. D. R. Owen (Edinburgh and London: Scottish Academic Press, 1972), p. 44, lines 576–89.

6 Terence McCarthy, 'Malory and His Sources', in Archibald and Edwards 1996: 75–95 (95).

7 *Malory: Works*, ed. E. Vinaver, 2nd edn (Oxford: Oxford University Press, 1971), 20.2, 28–32, p. 685.

8 Ardis Butterfield, *Poetry and Music in Medieval France from Jean Renart to Guillaume de Machaut* (Cambridge: Cambridge University Press, 2002), pp. 217–23.

9 Guillaume de Machaut, *Le Jugement du Roy de Behaigne and Remede de Fortune*, ed. and trans. J. I. Wimsatt and W. W. Kibler (Athens: University of Georgia Press, 1988); B. A. Windeatt (trans.), *Chaucer's Dream Poetry: Sources and Analogues* (Cambridge: Brewer, 1982).

References and Further Reading

Archibald, Elizabeth and Edwards, A. S. G. (eds) 1996. *A Companion to Malory*. Cambridge: Brewer. Very helpful synthesis of recent research.

Busby, Keith 1980. *Gauvain in Old French Literature*. Amsterdam: Rodopi. A detailed exploration of the figure of Gauvain in Arthurian romance.

Butterfield, Ardis 1997. 'French Culture and the Ricardian Court.' In *Essays on Ricardian Literature in Honour of J. A. Burrow*, ed. Alistair Minnis, Charlotte C. Morse and Thorlac Turville-Petre (Oxford: Clarendon Press), pp. 82–121. An account of the role of French culture in the Ricardian period, including Chaucer and Gower.

—— 2003. 'Chaucer's French Inheritance.' In *The Cambridge Chaucer Companion*, 2nd edn, ed. Jill Mann and Piero Boitani (Cambridge: Cambridge University Press), pp. 20–35. A broad-based discussion of the significance of French literary and cultural assumptions within Chaucer's writing.

Calin, William 1994. *The French Tradition and the Literature of Medieval England*. Toronto: University of Toronto Press. A conspectus of Anglo-Norman and Middle French literature and its relations to English writing throughout the medieval period.

Echard, Siân (ed.) 2004. *Companion to Gower*. Cambridge: Brewer. Collection of the most recent work on Gower's life and writings.

Crane, Susan 1999. 'Anglo-Norman Cultures in England, 1066–1460.' In *The Cambridge History of Medieval English Literature*, ed. David Wallace (Cambridge: Cambridge University Press), pp. 35–60. Surveys Anglo-Norman writing and its cultural significance.

Gaunt, Simon and Kay, Sarah (eds) 1999. *The Troubadours: An Introduction*. Cambridge: Cambridge University Press. Lucidly introduces the work of the troubadours.

Gilbert, Jane 2004. 'Becoming Woman in Chaucer: "On ne naît pas femme, on le meurt".' In *Rites of Passage: Cultures of Transition in the Fourteenth Century*, ed. Nicola F. McDonald and W. M. Ormrod (York: York Medieval Press), pp. 109–29. An illuminating reading of Chaucer's *Legend of Good Women* and *Book of the Duchess*.

Hult, David F. 1986. *Self-Fulfilling Prophecies: Readership and Authority in the First 'Roman de la Rose'*. Cambridge: Cambridge University Press. An influential discussion of Guillaume de Lorris's *Roman de la rose*.

Muscatine, Charles 1957. *Chaucer and the French Tradition*. Berkeley: University of California Press. Classic account of 'courtly' and 'bourgeois' style in French writing and Chaucer.

Putter, Ad 1995. *'Sir Gawain and the Green Knight' and French Arthurian Romance*. Oxford: Oxford University Press. A study of French Arthurian romance in relation to the English poem.

Saul, Nigel (ed.) 1994. *England in Europe 1066–1453*. London: Collins and Brown. Informative historical essays ranging from the Norman Conquest to the end of the Hundred Years War.

13
Britain and Italy: Trade, Travel, Translation

Nick Havely

Italian and English were both during this period still in the process of forming and establishing themselves as literary languages. In Italy the prominence of the Tuscan vernacular and of the 'three crowns of Florence' (Dante, Boccaccio and Petrarch) was clearly evident in the later fourteenth century; yet the 'Tuscanization' of Italian literary culture was by no means complete, and there were other vernacular traditions, both north and south of Florence, that continued to attract patronage and readers. Moreover, these literary forms of Italian *volgare*, whose varieties and potentialities Dante had surveyed in his Latin treatise *De vulgari eloquentia* (c.1302–5), continued to co-exist – sometimes uneasily – with Latin. Some of the major Italian humanists, such as Leon Battista Alberti (1404–72), were committed to both media; while others, like Lorenzo Valla (1407–57) considered the vernacular to be unfit for public use.

'Out of Latyn'

Geoffrey Chaucer's East Midlands dialect was also one of a number of literary vernaculars that major English writers continued to use. In his 'tri-lingual England', too, Latin, like French, was a major medium (Rothwell 1994); and Latin in various ways, as we shall see, provided linkage between British and Italian culture over these centuries. Even in 'that most remote little corner of the world, England' (as Boccaccio described it in his *Genealogia* 15. 6), it was clearly recognized that Latin was not only the international language of the elite and the clergy but also a vigorous living presence in its homeland of Italy. Around 1407, for instance, a Lollard polemicist, discussing the languages in which the Bible existed, notes that 'Italie hath it in Latyn, for that is ther moder tonge'.[1] And it may be that Chaucer is indirectly (and more playfully) acknowledging the Latin/Italian lineage when he conceals the Tuscan origin of his source for the *Troilus* (namely, Boccaccio's *Filostrato*), claiming instead: 'That of no sentement I this endite, / But *out of Latyn* in my tonge it write' (*TC* 2.13–14).

In several English fifteenth-century texts, such as the pseudo-Chaucerian *Tale of Beryn*, *Lumbard* is also used to describe a form of Italian.[2] It is not (at least according to present evidence) until 1485 and Caxton's Preface to his edition of Malory that *Ytalyen* is spoken of as a literary medium; but the commercial importance of Venice and Genoa and the political power of Milan during the fifteenth century are reflected in references to the practical usefulness of *Lumbard* as a language for travellers and traders around the Mediterranean.

Trade, Travel and Translation: Four Languages

Trade is one of the major activities that helped to shape medieval English perceptions of Italy and to develop cultural contacts. Genoese, Florentine and Venetian merchants in London and Southampton came to play important parts in the commercial and cultural scene from Chaucer's time onwards. Moving within the circles frequented by Chaucer there were, for instance: Gualtero dei Bardi, who was resident in London from about 1351 to 1391 and King's Moneyer from 1361; Niccolò da Lucca who was, over the last quarter of the century, representative for Florentine and Lucchese firms – combining this varied career with a role as valued agent on the Continent for John of Gaunt; and two members of the Alberti company, who performed a literary task for Richard II, transporting a book of the miracles of Edward II to Rome and presenting it to the Pope.[3]

We do not know what specific books were brought back from Italy by this senior managerial class, nor precisely how they communicated with the likes of Chaucer and John of Gaunt. Tuscan merchants at this level, however, are known to have been among the early readers of Boccaccio; and conversations between them and their foreign hosts and clients could have made use of a variety of languages, from English and French through 'corrupt Latin' (Rothwell 1994: 53–4) to the *Lumbard* that was reckoned to be of use to fifteenth-century traders. The subsequent consolidation of the Italian communities, especially in London, was also likely to make cultural, as well as commercial, exchange easier. Groups or 'nations' of Italian residents were subject to consular control in the early fifteenth century and by 1409 there was a Venetian vice-consul in London (Ruddock 1951: 134–6). In Southampton a Venetian became Sheriff in 1453 and a Florentine, Cristoforo Ambruogi, held the office of mayor twice, in 1486 and 1497 (Ruddock 1951: 171, 184).

It was not all plain sailing. The conspicuous presence of prosperous Italian merchants in England also generated rivalry, resentment and, at times, outright hostility. Already in the mid-thirteenth century the chronicler Matthew Paris was commenting on the size of houses bought up by the Lombards in London.[4] Towards the end of the century John Gower is expressing a commonly held attitude about 'Lombard foreigners' when he complains that 'in order to deceive they put on an appearance of being our friends, yet beneath that they have set their hearts on plundering us of our silver and gold'.[5] In the 1430s the *Libelle of Englyshe Polycye* voices a sturdy insular disdain for the luxury goods imported by the Florentines and Venetians – as 'nifles, trifles . . . thynges not enduryng' – while also deploring the arrogance of these alien traders, who can 'ryde aboute' and buy up more Cotswold wool than 'we Englisshe may getyn in any wyse'.[6] Other kinds of transaction are reflected in references to Italian physicians and women servants, and to the presence of Italian churchmen from papal nuncios through learned friars to ordinary priests, while intellectual traffic and careerism in the fifteenth century – as we shall see – bring several humanists from Italy to live and work in England.

Travel, like trade, was a two-way traffic, however. For travellers from England, taking the usual route through France and across the Alps, the journey to Italy would have taken five or six weeks. Couriers could cut this down to twenty or thirty days, but it was not until the introduction of riding posts in the early sixteenth century that the journey time was further reduced (Parks 1954: 511–13). Despite such length, however, it was a well-trodden route, frequented by churchmen with business at the papal Curia, by pilgrims bound for Jerusalem via Venice, or visiting the holy city for the jubilees of 1300, 1350, 1390, 1423, 1450 (and then every twenty-five years), by scholars attracted to the major Italian universities, and by diplomats like Chaucer on missions to city-states such as Genoa, Florence or Milan in order to deal with matters of trade, or military alliances or other royal business.

Among this last group, we know that Chaucer travelled the route at least twice: first in 1372–73, to arrange a designated port for Genoese shipping and, possibly, to deal with Florentine bankers; and second in 1378, to negotiate with the Visconti of Milan and the English mercenary Sir John Hawkwood about 'matters concerning the conduct of our war' (i.e., England's war with France). How much he saw, heard or gathered of Italian culture on either of these journeys remains conjectural. There is no evidence that he met any particular Italian writers (such as Boccaccio) in Florence on the first journey or that he was able to obtain texts of their vernacular works (like *Filostrato* or *Decameron*) from a Visconti scriptorium on the second. It is quite possible, though, that he would have heard more about Boccaccio as the grand old man of Tuscan letters, who was to begin delivering his lectures on Dante in Florence later in 1373; and he could well have gained some informed impressions about the works of the 'three crowns' of Florence cheaply by word of mouth, rather than more expensively on the page. What he saw of Italian art, architecture or political life in the two cities likewise remains uncertain; but over the 1370s he could have become aware of the contrasts between the declining 'associative polity' of Florence and the ascendant signorial despotism represented by Milan (Wallace 1997: 13–54).

Perceptions and impressions formed during these years eventually contributed in various ways to poems of the next two decades. The *House of Fame*, the *Parliament of Fowls* and the *Troilus* all address the precedence of Dante as vernacular author, while (in the latter two cases) appropriating narrative from Boccaccio. The later images of Italian absolutism and the politics of Lombardy in the Clerk's and Monk's Tales (MkT 2399–406) and in the *Legend of Good Women* (G Prologue, 353–88) owe a good deal to Chaucer's encounter with the Visconti court in 1378 and to his awareness of Petrarch's earlier association with the 'tyrauntis of Lumbardye' (Wallace 1997: 261–331). For

Chaucer, therefore, as for a number of later writers – John Tiptoft, Earl of Worcester (1427–70), and Thomas Wyatt and others from the sixteenth century onwards – travel was followed by what can broadly be termed 'translation': the carrying over and appropriation of lyric, narrative and discursive materials and traditions.

In Chaucer's case, however, the relationship between the two processes – the missions to Florence and Milan and the reinventing of Italian narratives – was not a straightforward matter of cause and effect. Unlike more leisured English gentleman scholars (such as Tiptoft) or later expatriates and dilettanti, Chaucer did not go to Italy for lengthy periods to read and write. For him, a number of other concerns and cultural contacts contributed to the project of translation. Among these was his continuing involvement with the politics and the literature of France.

French literary culture had, over the course of the fourteenth century, become preeminent in its own right and was also a significant intermediary for the transmission of Italian texts and influences. Since early in the century the papacy's residence in Avignon had drawn Italian financiers, merchants, craftsmen and artists (including Simone Martini) to the southern French city.[7] With the expansion of its university and the papal library under the pontificate of John XXII (1316–34), the city was also a growth point for learning in the pre-humanist period; and Petrarch, whose later childhood had been spent in Avignon, returned there in 1326–7 and again at intervals during 1337–53 (Simone 1969: 43–8).

Jean Daudin's French translation of Petrarch's moralistic encyclopedia, *De remediis utriusque Fortunae*, brings us close both in place and time to Chaucer. It is important to remember that Chaucer's contacts with France and Italy are interwoven during the late 1370s and that one well-documented visit to France (as a member of the English mission to the peace negotiations at Montreuil-sur-Mer) took place in between his two Italian journeys, during 1377. Daudin's vernacular version of Petrarch – then hot off the scriptorium – could well have provided a talking-point during breaks in the meetings; and it has been suggested that around this time Chaucer could have made contact with another French friend of Petrarch, Philippe de Mézières (Hanly 2000: 157–9).

Transformations of the story of Griselda from Boccaccio's Italian (*Decameron*, Day 10) to Petrarch's Latin and on to Philippe's French and Chaucer's English (Clerk's Tale) – are symptomatic of the busy interaction between the four languages in the late fourteenth century. Translation of both Petrarch's and Boccaccio's work, especially their Latin works, would continue through the fifteenth century and provide a basis for the renewed interest in their vernacular writing in the sixteenth. Dante's *Commedia* would by that time be eclipsed by the cult of Petrarch and the popularity of Boccaccio; and in Britain it would have to wait until the beginning of the nineteenth century for its first complete published translation (Henry Boyd's in 1802). At the end of the fourteenth and the beginning of the fifteenth centuries, however, copies, commentaries and indeed translations were still testifying prolifically to the *Commedia*'s status in Italy and abroad.

The 'Grete Poete of Ytaille'

For most people in the fourteenth century, as now, Dante was the authority on Hell. There was even a popular belief – recorded by Boccaccio in his short biography, the *Trattatello in laude di Dante* – that he had gone there. In consequence, the story goes, one of the poet's more credulous admirers remarks on seeing him in a Verona street that 'his beard looks all frizzy and his face all scorched with the heat and smoke down below'.[8] Boccaccio's 'Dante' is said to have been amused by this literal-mindedness, but the poet of the *Inferno* had in some way invited such a response through the narrative's constant assertions about the vision's authenticity.

It is no coincidence, then, that the very first known reference to Dante in English presents him as a source for the torments of Hell. In Book 1 of Chaucer's dream poem, the *House of Fame* (written in the late 1370s or early 1380s), the narrator has been following the story of Virgil's *Aeneid* as depicted on the walls of a temple of Venus, and has reached the point in Book 6 where the hero makes a journey through the underworld. At this point Dante is named as an *auctor* on Hell, alongside Virgil and the late-Roman poet Claudian (*HF* 439–50).

Dante's *Commedia* also develops a positive concept of afterlife in its other two worlds (Purgatory and Paradise), by imagining the soul's capacity to change to a higher state of being: the potential of the human 'worm' to become the 'angelic butterfly which ascends unhindered to God' (*Purgatorio* 10.124–6).[9] This process is reflected in the ascent of 'Dante' as lover and with the development of the *Commedia* as a love poem dominated by the figures of the Virgin Mary, St Lucy and Beatrice. Beatrice is encountered by 'Dante' at the end of the ascent that has led him, under the guidance of Virgil, down through the circles of hell and up through the terraces of Purgatory to the summit of the earthly paradise, where he sees her for the first time since her death across a stream as part of a solemn pageant in an Edenic setting. It is not – at least initially – a joyful reunion of lovers, but rather a quasi-confessional encounter in which 'Dante' is forced, under severe examination by Beatrice, to reassess his former life and his present spiritual state (*Purgatorio* 30.55–31.90). Such a scenario, in which a visionary meets a familiar female figure across a stream in a paradisal setting and is subsequently directed by her to scrutinize his own spiritual state, is one that will also be familiar to readers of a late fourteenth-century English poem in the *Gawain* manuscript: *Pearl*. Some of the parallels could be attributable to the common and long-established tradition of representing authoritative ladies (like Reason and Nature in the *Romance of the Rose*) in an idealized setting; but, as several critics have argued, the scene in *Pearl* may be influenced in part by the prominent encounter at the end of the *Purgatorio* (Putter 1996). It is quite possible that this anonymous but learned English poet (who in *Cleanness* cites the *Romance of the Rose* and its author by name) had some direct knowledge of the *Commedia* and some awareness of its crucial role in the transformation of medieval love lyric.

Chaucer, too, recognized the potential of the *Commedia* as a poem about love. His highly ambiguous garden of love in the *Parliament of Fowls* presents outcrops of allusion to Dante's earthly paradise alongside the more substantial strata laid down by his reading of Boccaccio's temple of Venus in Book 7 of the *Teseida*. A yet more sophisticated and more extensive appropriation of Dante's erotic language takes place at a climactic point in Chaucer's *Troilus* (3.1261–7) when the poet audaciously puts in the mouth of a pagan lover the words that Dante's St Bernard addresses to the Virgin Mary at the start of the final canto of the *Paradiso* (33.13–21). Such an exalted allusion requires us – as does Troilus's devotional discourse elsewhere in the poem – to consider what this lover's experience amounts to when viewed in the cosmic perspective that his own words open up (Wetherbee 1984: 109–10).

There are differing views about the degree of reverence accorded to Dante as *auctour* by Chaucer, from the initial references in the *House of Fame* onwards. Yet his prominence as a precedent is evident from the fact that he and Petrarch are the only two vernacular writers to whom Chaucer gives the title of *poete* (for example in the Wife of Bath's Tale, 1125–6 and the Clerk's Tale, 31). This is a title that Chaucer never claims for himself, although it was conferred upon him by several of his French and English contemporaries and followers (Gower, Deschamps, Lydgate). Instead, he describes himself less ambitiously as *makere* – for instance, at the end of the *Troilus*, where he presents himself as the author of a 'litel . . . tragedye' rather than a more ambitious kind of *comedye* (*TC* 5. 1786–8). By the time he had completed the *Troilus* Chaucer had made this imposing precedent a significant part of his poetic agenda by naming Dante or alluding transparently to the *Commedia* at a number of points of departure in his main works: at the end of Book 1 and the beginnings of Books 2 and 3 of the *House of Fame*; at the entry into the garden of love in the *Parliament of Fowls* (120–47); and, perhaps most strikingly, in the reworking of Dante's exordium to the *Purgatorio* (1.1–12) in the 'proem' to Book 2 of the *Troilus* (1–11).

Recognition of the *Commedia*'s precedent as ambitious vernacular project is not otherwise registered in surviving English texts of Chaucer's time, and references to Dante (at least those known to us at present) are quite sparse during this whole period in Britain. There is, for example, an anecdote about Dante in Gower and four references of rather more interest in Lydgate's translation of Boccaccio's *De casibus*, *The Fall of Princes* (1431–8), in the translator's prologue (303), Book 3 (3858), the Prologue to Book 4 (136) and in Book 9 (2511–52). Indeed, it could be argued that the proliferation of manuscripts and printed editions of Chaucer's own work did as much as anything to keep Dante on the horizon for the English reading public during the fifteenth century. From this point of view, it looks as if we have the Wife of Bath to thank for the first printed reference to Dante in English. Her description of 'the wyse Poet of Florence / That hight daunte' appears on folio 148v of Caxton's 1477 edition of the *Canterbury Tales*, as in the subsequent editions of 1483, 1492 and 1498. Caxton's printer, however, must have found the name of the Italian poet somewhat unfamiliar, since shortly after this the devil's reference to learning about hell in the Friar's Tale (as mentioned above) cites not Dante but *dauid* ('David', folio 155v).

The name was given its correct form in Caxton's next edition of the *Tales* (1483), and there is some evidence that Dante was more than a mere name to some English clerics and scholars earlier in the fifteenth century – especially to those with experience of international travel and an interest in literary culture. Despite unease on the part of some early humanists about its use of the vulgar tongue, the *Commedia* at the end of the fourteenth century retained its status as a text worthy of commentary, copying, illustration, and even its first translation into Latin.[10] A couple of internationally minded English readers also seem to have taken a share in this process of presenting Dante to a wider audience. At the Council of Constance (1414–18) two English bishops, Robert Hallam (of Salisbury) and Nicholas Bubwith (of Bath and Wells), encouraged work on a further Latin translation of and commentary upon the *Commedia* by the Franciscan Bishop of Rimini, Giovanni da Serravalle; and it is known that there were copies of this text in the Wells cathedral library and at Oxford still in the early sixteenth century.[11] Neither of these English copies survives, but Serravalle's translation was widely disseminated and was probably used by Reformation writers from the early sixteenth century onwards, in their attempts to conscript Dante as a witness against Rome.

The Oxford copy of Serravalle's Dante is said to have been presented to the University by Humphrey, Duke of Gloucester (1390–1447), and we shall return to the wider implications of his Italian contacts in the last section of this chapter (Petrina 2004: 199–204). Interest in Dante specifically is shown by at least two scholars associated with him. The Italian Tito Livio Frulovisi was in England as the Duke's 'poet and orator' in 1337 (Weiss 1967: 41–5; Saygin 2002: 254–9) and alludes to Dante in one of the Latin comedies he wrote while a member of the ducal household (Petrina 2004: 326–7).[12] And John Whethamstede (d.1465) – Abbot of St Albans, friend of Duke Humphrey and author of a number of encyclopedic works during the first half of the fifteenth century – cites the *Commedia* (twice) and the *Monarchia* (on the subject of papal power, as the Reformation polemicists were later to do) and shows knowledge of Serravalle's commentary, which was probably the source he was using.[13] Whethamstede was an omnivorous bibliophile who had visited Italy for the Councils of Pavia and Siena in 1423 and who, like the two English bishops at Constance a few years before, had taken advantage of a conference trip to catch up with new developments and resources in literature (Weiss 1967: 32). Among the contemporary Italian authors he refers to are the humanists Coluccio Salutati and Leonardo Bruni; but, as his references to Dante indicate, he was also interested in the older generation of Italian writers; and his work shows knowledge of the Latin writings of both Petrarch and Boccaccio.

The 'Lauriat Poete' and 'Lollius'

Whethamstede's emphasis on the Latin works of Boccaccio and Petrarch, and on access even to Dante's *Commedia* through Latin, is perfectly understandable according to the standards and priorities of his time and of the later fourteenth century too. Indeed, it is quite possible that in Chaucer's time, English encounters with the work of both Boccaccio and Petrarch were mostly through their moralistic and encyclopedic Latin works rather than through their vernacular writing, towards which Petrarch especially showed an ambivalent attitude. In the 1370s the papal library at Avignon (according to its inventory) was a centre for the diffusion of both authors' major Latin writings; and by the end of the century several of these would be produced in French by the translation industry centred upon the royal court in Paris (Petrarch's *De remediis* in 1376–7 and the first version of Bocaccio's *De casibus* in 1400). These French connections might have provided the channels through which learned English churchmen (of the generation before Hallam and Bubwith, the patrons of Serravalle) and elite lay readers encountered or heard of Boccaccio and Petrarch.

Boccaccio, like Petrarch, also seems to have cultivated a reputation as a Latin author, especially during the last quarter-century of his life. His monumental *De casibus virorum illustrium* ('Of the Fall of Famous Men') appeared in two versions (1355–60 and 1373–4); his *De mulieribus claris* ('On Famous Women') was written in 1361–75; and his encyclopedic project on pagan myth, *De genealogia deorum*, occupied him intermittently from the middle of the century until the 1370s when copies begin to circulate. The influence of *De casibus*, with its sequence of falls from Adam to contemporary figures, is evident in both the plan and the subtitle of Chaucer's Monk's Tale, which – with its account of the recent fall of Bernabo Visconti (2399–406) and its version of Dante's Ugolino (2407–62) – is in other ways too an Italianate narrative.[14] Despite the Knight's interruption of the Monk's Tale, it was still felt that the fall of famous men (and Boccaccio's *De casibus* in particular) could, like other kinds of 'mirrors for princes', provide suitably edifying material for aristocratic and royal readers. Laurent de Premierfait, secretary to the Duc de Berry, produced two versions for his employer, in 1400 and 1409 (Simone 1969: 64). John Lydgate's *Fall of Princes* (which is based on Premierfait's translation) was commissioned by Humphrey, Duke of Gloucester in 1431 and its 36,000 lines were completed in 1438 (Wright 1957: 5–21); and the seven surviving illustrated manuscripts of the work reflect patronage and reception at a high social level.[15]

Royal patronage was also received during the fifteenth century for French and German versions of Boccaccio's hundred or so stories of famous women, *De mulieribus claris*; and the anonymous author of a partial translation into English (c.1440–50) seems also to have hoped in vain for such support (Wright 1957: 28–32). This collection was certainly known in earlier fifteenth-century England, to John Whethamstede (Weiss 1967: 36 n. 8) as well as to Lydgate, who refers to it in lines 3201–4 of his *Siege of Thebes* (completed in 1422), and to Humphrey of Gloucester, who is known to have owned copies of it and of *De casibus* (Weiss 1967: 64 with n. 13). It has also been argued that Chaucer's version of the story of Cleopatra in his *Legend of Good Women* may have been influenced by it and *De casibus* (Godman in Boitani 1983: 285–91); and he could well have recognized Boccaccio's *De mulieribus* as one important precedent (among others) for a programme of narratives about women.

Chaucer may also have known something of or about one of Boccaccio's other major Latin projects: the encyclopedic *De genealogia deorum*. Its authority as a 'handbook of mythology' was explicitly recognized in England by Abbot John Whethamstede, by Lydgate from the 1420s, by Humphrey of Gloucester and by Caxton; and it continued to be drawn upon as a compendium of pagan myth during the sixteenth and seventeenth centuries – for example, by Hoby, Spenser, Jonson and Heywood (Weiss 1967: 36 with n. 8 and 64 with n. 13; Wright 1957: 36–7).

Less authoritative, yet more obviously important for Chaucer at least, were Boccaccio's early vernacular poems, especially the *Filostrato* (c.1335), which is the main narrative source for the *Troilus*, and the epic twelve-book *Teseida delle nozze d'Emilia* (c.1339–41) which Chaucer condensed into the two thousand lines of the Knight's Tale. When compared to his recurrent and reverential references to Dante as the 'grete poete of Ytaille' and to the 'lauriat poete' Petrarch, Chaucer's silence with regard to Boccaccio is striking. Not much later (in the 1420s) Lydgate would be quite specific in naming the author and his place of origin as 'Bochas de certaldo', along with a major work ('the Genologye'), and in assigning him status in the Italian pantheon of writers 'next Fraunceys Petrak' (*Siege of Thebes*, 3538, 3541, 3543).[16] Various reasons have been advanced or suggested for Chaucer's refusal or inability to cite the author who was his most substantial source for two of his major works, as well as for a number of important passages elsewhere. By comparison with the daunting precedents of Dante and Petrarch, the early work of Boccaccio might have seemed less imposing for an ambitious later writer; and perhaps Chaucer might even have wished to avoid comparisons between what he was doing with the vernacular in *Troilus* and what Boccaccio had done in *Filostrato* (see Havely 1980: 12; Taylor in Koff and Schildgen 2000: 54–5 with n. 22, and 70 with n. 63).

Boccaccio was also the author of an incontestable vernacular classic of the mid-fourteenth century: the *Decameron*. His hundred tales circulated among the Italian mercantile class with whom Chaucer is known to have had dealings.[17] A readership for the work in France around this time is also indicated by the fact that Laurent de Premierfait, the translator of *De casibus*, followed that project quickly with a version of the *Decameron* in 1414 (Wright 1957: 113). Chaucer's response to the *Decameron* in the *Canterbury Tales* is not so precisely demonstrable as is his use of *Filostrato* or *Teseida*; but there are striking affinities in the narrative procedures of the two collections and clear parallels between the Reeve's, Shipman's, Clerk's and Franklin's Tales and stories in Boccaccio (Cooper 1997). Again – as with *De casibus* and *De mulieribus claris* – Chaucer is very likely to have been aware of the narrative programme of the *Decameron* as an important vernacular project and precedent. Recent discussion of the relationship between Chaucer's and Boccaccio's framed collections has focused not so much upon demonstrations of specific influence as upon shared themes and concerns, such as debate, voice, fiction, confession, anticlericalism and modernity (Edwards 2002; Koff and Schildgen 2000).

By contrast, on the sole occasion when, in the *Troilus*, Chaucer turns to Petrarch's best-known vernacular work, the *Canzoniere*, he does so in a very specific and innovative way. His main narrative source, the *Filostrato*, showed indebtedness throughout to the lyric traditions of the *dolce stil nuovo* (including Dante), and there had been a tendency for Boccaccio's hero Troiolo to modulate into that sweet old style at moments of stress or excitement. As early as Book 1 of the *Troilus*, when his lover-hero is under similar pressure, Chaucer proceeds to outdo or update Boccaccio by giving his Troilus a more modern lyric voice – translating the fourteen lines of Petrarch's sonnet 88 into the three seven-line stanzas of the 'Canticus Troili' (*TC* 1.400–20). This is the first English translation of a Petrarch sonnet before the sixteenth century but, just as importantly, it forms part of Chaucer's process of developing his own lyric perspective in the *Troilus* (Wallace 2000: 228–9). Here, as elsewhere in his greatest complete poem, Chaucer uses one 'auctor' as a means of departing from and gaining perspective upon another. He uses the opening of Dante's *Purgatorio* for this purpose at the start of the second book of *Troilus*, while here, in the middle of the first, he turns momentarily but significantly from 'Lollius' to 'the lauriat poete'.

Into and Out of Latin: Italian Humanism in Fifteenth-Century Britain

Petrarch's sonnets were to return to English with Thomas Wyatt (c.1503–42) and Henry Howard, Earl of Surrey (c.1517–47), as part of a Europe-wide 'Petrarchism' which in the sixteenth century also included French poets such as Ronsard and du Bellay. This reappearance of the vernacular Petrarch followed the renewal of the *Canzoniere*'s poetic presence in later fifteenth-century Italy, through Poliziano's *Stanze per la giostra di Giuliano*.[18] Through much of the fifteenth century, however, Petrarch was the 'clerk' rather than the 'poet', and was influential in England and elsewhere through his Latin moral treatises rather than his Italian love poetry. It is primarily his Latin work that continues to be diffused through Avignon in the early fifteenth century (Simone 1969: 61–3); and in particular it is his series of dialogues on prosperity and adversity (*De remediis utriusque Fortunae* of the mid-1350s) that not only, as we have seen, was the first of his works to be translated into a European vernacular (Daudin 1376–77), but also recurs in lists of English collections during the period, including those of Duke Humphrey of Gloucester and libraries at Cambridge and Oxford (Weiss 1967: 64, with n. 12; 161, with nn. 1 and 4; and 177, with n.2).

If Petrarch is to be regarded as 'the father of humanism', then we shall have to define the term more flexibly within a fifteenth-century context. Humanism in this period had more to do with precision in Latin style and scholarship than with secular values or the notion of the autonomous 'dignity of man' (Burke 1990: 1–2). Petrarch's *De remediis*, for instance, is ambitious and precise in its classicism, but it is also deeply rooted in medieval encyclopedic and contemplative traditions – and that may account for its appeal (along with works like *De viris illustribus* and Boccaccio's *De casibus*) to higher-class French and English readers. Patrons of humanistic learning in fifteenth-century England included some of the elite laity, such as Humphrey of Gloucester and John Tiptoft, Earl of Worcester; but learned abbots and bishops – such as John Whethamstede of St Albans, William Grey of Ely and James Goldwell of Norwich – are at least equal in importance, as keen gatherers of Italian humanistic texts (Burke 1990: 9–10; Weiss 1967: 176–8).

Both clerics and illustrious lay patrons of this sort were aware of the wider range of contemporary Italian learning and what it could offer them. Early in the fifteenth century, John Whethamstede's encyclopedic writing draws, as we have seen, upon Petrarch and (particularly) Boccaccio; but he also shows knowledge of the Florentine political and educational writer, Coluccio Salutati (1331–1406) and especially the great promoter of 'civic humanism', Leonardo Bruni (1370–1444) (Weiss 1967: 36, with nn. 9–10 and 13). Bruni is also known to have been in contact with Whethamstede's friend Humphrey of Gloucester during the 1430s and was (unsuccessfully) wooed by the Duke to come to England. He had produced a highly successful new translation of Aristotle's *Ethics* in 1416–17; he was also (to judge from the number of his works available) the Italian humanist best known to English readers, to whom he directed a project for a version of the *Politics* – completed and sent to Humphrey in 1438 (Saygin 2002: 66; Weiss 1967: 41, 47–9).

Humphrey of Gloucester was more successful in drawing into his service two less well-known Italian humanist scholars. Tito Livio Frulovisi was in England during 1437 and around that time wrote a life of Henry V, a poem in praise of Humphrey himself and two plays which are 'the first Renaissance comedies composed in this country' (Saygin 2002: 254–9; Weiss 1967: 41–5). His successor, Antonio Beccaria, was in Humphrey's household for rather longer (1438/9–45/6). Beccaria was employed as secretary and translator – producing (among other items) a Latin version of Boccaccio's misogynistic prose fantasy, the *Corbaccio* – and he seems to have been particularly important to Humphrey as a speechwriter (Weiss 1967: 45–6; Saygin 2002: 118, 259–62). The precise benefits that the Duke derived (or hoped to derive) from his association with and employment of such scholars remains uncertain, and we cannot be sure how much of their work he actually read. Yet for ambitious magnates like him, the humanists' cultivation of classical antiquity and their practised rhetorical skills would have been seen as a highly negotiable currency in the world of politics and diplomacy. For the Duke's purposes, it would probably have been more important to receive the plaudits of Frulovisi's *Humfroidos* and to retain the oratorical services of Beccaria than to have to wade through Bruni's translations of Aristotle.

Of the fifteenth-century Italian humanists to have visited Britain, the two most eminent had close associations not with the Court but with the Church. Poggio Bracciolini, the assiduous hunter of manuscripts and promoter of the idea of a 'Renaissance', was, at an early stage (1418–23) of his long career, in the service of Duke Humphrey's political rival, Cardinal Beaufort (Saygin 2002: 237–54), while the Sienese nobleman, Aeneas Sylvius Piccolomini – proponent of Roman eloquence, writer of comedy and the future Pope Pius II (1458–64) – is known to have visited Scotland on a short diplomatic visit in 1435 (Jack 1972: 3, with n. 4). We should not see such visitors as intellectual 'missionaries' (Burke 1990: 4) seeking to make a benighted northern Europe free for humanism; but, on the other hand, by no means all were reluctant exiles, here to complain about the weather and the food. Indeed, it seems that for a significant number of them (such as Poggio), employment abroad worked very well to further their career development back in Italy (Saygin 2002: 240).

Reciprocal benefits were also beginning to be derived by British travellers to Italy during the fifteenth century. We have already seen how the learned clergy took advantage of their travel opportunities; and there is probably scope for more study of the fifteenth-century Councils of the Church (such as Constance in 1414–18 and Basel in 1431–9) as contexts for cultural exchange. In conclusion, we can turn to two very different British visitors as examples of the relationship between travel and translation around the end of our period: the English earl, John Tiptoft (1427–70) and the Scots bishop, Gavin Douglas (1474/5–1522).

Of the two it is Tiptoft who is the better-documented as visitor to Italy. Like a number of his contemporary countrymen, he seems to have taken advantage of the educational opportunities provided by humanist teachers such as Guarino Veronese (1374–1460) at Ferrara and Pier Paolo Vergerio (1370–1444) (Kirkpatrick 1995: 89–91). During a lengthy period in Italy, from 1458 to 1461, he is known to have studied (possibly law) at the University of Padua, to have attended the school at Ferrara, to have become acquainted with Guarino during the last year of the master's life, and to have reduced the humanist pope Pius II to tears by demonstrating an Englishman's eloquence in Latin oratory (Kirkpatrick 1995: 91–3; Weiss 1967: 113–22). Books he collected in Italy formed the basis of one of the major individual libraries in England at that time; following his execution in 1470, the collection was bequeathed to Oxford and Cambridge (Weiss 1967: 115–18). He was an early example of the kind of Italophile English gentleman who was to become ever more common during subsequent centuries, when the *giro d'Italia* and the Grand Tour provided a kind of gap year for the ruling classes.[19] The results of his travels were not, however, to be measured solely by the length of his library catalogue. He also ventured, among other less successful translations, a version of a humanist text: Buonaccorso da Montemagno's dialogue on nobility, *Controversia de nobilitate* (Kirkpatrick 1995: 93; Weiss 1967: 118–19). Here the English aristocrat articulately transmits the theme of personal versus inherited worth that had exercised so many of the non-noble Italian humanists, and in so doing provided an important source for the debate about nobility in one of the major early Tudor interludes, Henry Medwall's *Fulgens and Lucrece*, which was probably first performed for Cardinal Morton's household in the 1490s.

Gavin Douglas, on the other hand, did not directly translate any of the Italian humanist or vernacular texts, and (as far as we know) did not spend so long in Italy as Tiptoft had. Yet his response to Italian writers is considerably more wide-ranging, complex and questioning; and it carries significant implications for the relationship between Britain and Italy in the early sixteenth century. Scotland in the late fifteenth century had strong trading links with much of northern Europe, including France; and its cultural contacts extended more widely, including well-documented visits by Scottish clerics to Rome (Bawcutt 1976: 23–4; Jack 1972: 2). Italian clerics were visitors or residents during the period; Italian minstrels are known to have been present at the court of James IV (1473–1513), and the dependence of an educated class on the University of Paris provided (as it did in England) an important intermediary link with Italian humanist culture (Bawcutt 1976: 24–7). By his own account, in 1515, Douglas had at some point 'passit his tyme in . . . France and Rome'; and his clerical career (leading to the bishopric of Dunkeld in 1515) involved contacts with the papal Curia and the Lateran Council of 1512–17 (Bawcutt 1976: 24). According to one of his editors, he 'may have studied abroad from 1505 to 1509', although there is no evidence of his attending Italian universities or of contacts with humanists while in Italy.[20] It is known, however, that a study-guide by one of Tiptoft's masters, Guarino of Ferrara, was in use at Douglas's home university (St Andrews) shortly before his time (Burke 1990: 12, with n. 37); and the works of other humanists, such as Lorenzo Valla and Poggio Bracciolini, were available in Scotland (Jack 1972: 22). Above all, references in Douglas's own works show familiarity with Italian writing from Petrarch and Boccaccio to Valla, Poggio and Landino (Bawcutt 1976: 32–3, 164–7). His *Palice of Honour* (1501) explicitly pays tribute to (or records quarrelling between) the first four of these writers (lines 903, 910, 915, 1232–3), and it is possible that this vision poem may have been influenced to some degree not only by Chaucer's *House of Fame* but also by Petrarch's *Trionfi* (Jack 1972: 23–7). His major work, the translation of the *Aeneid* (completed in 1513), continues demonstrably to draw upon the resources of Italian humanism. In the extended Prologue to Book 1, for example, 'Jhone Bocas (Boccaccio) in the Genealogie' is cited as an authority for myths about journeys to the underworld (204), while several lines (127–30) are given to summarizing Lorenzo Valla's insistence upon the need for lengthy study of Virgil's meaning.

Douglas's *Aeneid* is of course (to revert to Chaucer's phrase) 'out of Latyn', but it has a partially Italian perspective that sharpens its awareness of linguistic issues and differences: the resources of 'our awyn langage' (111); the limits and imperfections of Scots/English 'besyde Latyn' (359, 380); and the status of the writer's own 'stile vulgar' (492). The Scottish poet's 'vernacular humanism' (to use Bawcutt's apt phrase) can thus be seen as addressing crucial linguistic and stylistic questions that would also preoccupy those writers in English who, in increasing numbers over the following century, were to translate out of Latin or out of Italian.

See also: 4 City and Country, Wealth and Labour, 8 Translation and Society, 9 The Languages of Medieval Britain, 12 England and France, 14 England's Antiquities, 15 Jews, Saracens, 'Black Men', Tartars, 19 Love, 23 Lyric, 33 The *Canterbury Tales*, 34 John Gower and John Lydgate, 37 *Sir Gawain and the Green Knight*.

Notes

1 C. Bühler, 'A Lollard Tract on Translating the Bible into English', *Medium Ævum* 7 (1938), 173.

2 *The Tale of Beryn*, ed. F. J. Furnivall and W. G. Stone, EETS es 105 (1909), line 2662.

3 G. Holmes, 'Florentine Merchants in England, 1346–1436', *The Economic History Review* ser. 2, 13 (1960–1), 193–4, with n. 7, and 197.

4 Matthew Paris, ed. H. R. Luard, *Chronica majora. Vol. 5: 1248–1259.* Rolls ser. 57 (1880), p. 246.

5 Gower, *Mirour de l'omme*, lines 25437–40 (my translation), ed. G. C. Macaulay in *The Complete Works of John Gower*, vol. 1 (Oxford: Clarendon Press, 1899).

6 See *The Libelle of Englyshe Polycye: A Poem on the Use of Sea-Power 1436*, ed. Sir George Warner (Oxford: Clarendon Press, 1926), lines 344–51 and 456–9.

7 B. Guillemain, 'Les Italiens à Avignon au xive siècle', in *Rapporti culturali ed economici fra Italia e Francia nei secoli dal XIV al XVI: Atti del colloquio italo-francese, Roma 18–20 febbraio 1978* (Rome: Giunta centrale per gli studi storici, 1979), esp. pp. 67–9.

8 Boccaccio, *Trattatello*, in *Giovanni Boccaccio: opere minori in volgare*, ed. M. Marti (Milan: Rizzoli, 1969–72) 4. 349 (my translation). There is a new English version: *The Life of Dante*, trans. J. G. Nichols (London: Hesperus, 2002).

9 *Dante: Commedia*, ed. A. M. Chiavacci Leonardi, 2nd edn, 3 vols (Milan: Mondadori, 1997).

10 On the Latin translation by Matteo Ronto (probably in the 1390s) see W. P. Friederich, *Dante's Fame Abroad 1350–1850* (Chapel Hill, N.C.: University of North Carolina Press, 1950), p. 78.

11 For an account of Serravalle's English connections, see D. Wallace, 'Dante in Somerset: Ghosts, Historiography, Periodization', *New Medieval Literatures* 3 (1999), 9–38.

12 R. Weiss, 'Per la conoscenza di Dante in Inghilterra nel quattrocento', *Giornale storico della letteratura italiana* 108 (1936), 357 and n. 8.

13 See Weiss 1936 (n. 11 above): 358 and 359, n. 6; and Petrina 2004: 351–2.

14 See P. Boitani, 'The *Monk's Tale*: Dante and Boccaccio', *Medium Ævum* 45 (1976), 50–69.

15 On Duke Humphrey's active role in Lydgate's composition of the *Fall of Princes*, see Wallace 1997: 332–3. For discussion of some of the illustrated copies, see V. Kirkham, 'Decoration and Iconography of Lydgate's *Fall of Princes* (*De casibus*) at the Philadelphia Rosenbach', *Studi sul Boccaccio* 25 (1997), esp. p. 297 with n. 1 and 300. D. A. Pearsall, in *John Lydgate* (London: Routledge, 1970), argues that such de luxe manuscripts 'would have been admired rather than read' (p. 250).

16 John Lydgate, *Siege of Thebes*, ed. A. Erdmann and E. Ekwall, EETS es 108 (1911) and 125 (1930).

17 For evidence, see V. Branca, *Boccaccio: The Man and his Works*, trans. R. Monges (New York: Harvester, 1976), pp. 197–200.

18 On the importance of Poliziano's 'narrative recasting' of Petrarch, see Gordon Braden, *Petrarchan Love and the Continental Renaissance* (New Haven, Conn., and London: Yale University Press, 1999), pp. 75–8.

19 The best introduction to subsequent travel by the English gentry in Italy remains John Stoye's *English Travellers Abroad, 1604–1667: Their Influence on English Society and Politics*, rev. edn (New Haven, Conn., and London: Yale University Press, 1989).

20 D. F. C. Coldwell (ed.), *Selections from Gavin Douglas* (Oxford: Clarendon Press, 1964), p. xx.

References and Further Reading

Bawcutt, Priscilla 1976. *Gavin Douglas: A Critical Study.* Edinburgh: Edinburgh University Press. Essential study of Douglas's 'vernacular humanism'; see especially ch. 2 ('The Cultural Background').

Boitani, Piero 1983. *Chaucer and the Italian Trecento.* Cambridge: Cambridge University Press. Wide-ranging collection of essays, moving from the historical and cultural contexts to Chaucer's dealings with particular Italian authors and texts.

Burke, Peter 1990. 'The Spread of Italian Humanism.' In *The Impact of Humanism in Western Europe*, ed. Anthony Goodman and Angus McKay (London and New York: Longman), pp. 1–22.

Explores the various kinds of 'reception' of Italian humanism.

Cooper, Helen 1997. 'Sources and Analogues of Chaucer's *Canterbury Tales*: Reviewing the Work.' *Studies in the Age of Chaucer* 19, 183–210. Asserts the primacy of the *Decameron* as model for the *Tales*, and reviews the parallels; see especially pp. 192–9.

Edwards, Robert R. 2002. *Chaucer and Boccaccio: Antiquity and Modernity*. Basingstoke and New York: Palgrave. Argues that 'Boccaccio's representations of antiquity and modernity furnish powerful models for Chaucer to extend, resist and reconceive'.

Hanly, Michael 2000. 'France.' In *A Companion to Chaucer*, ed. P. Brown (Oxford: Blackwell), pp. 149–66. Concise account of contacts and influences, with attention to French 'carriers' of Italian culture.

Havely, N. R. 1980. *Chaucer's Boccaccio*. Cambridge: Brewer, repr. 1992. Prose translations of *Filostrato* and parts of *Teseida* and *Filocolo*, with introduction, notes and appendices.

Jack, R. D. S. 1972. *The Italian Influence on Scottish Literature*. Edinburgh: Edinburgh University Press. See especially ch. 1 on 'The Mediaeval Period.'

Kirkpatrick, Robin 1995. *English and Italian Literature from Dante to Shakespeare: A Study of Source, Analogue and Divergence*. London and New York: Longman. Particularly knowledgeable about the Italian contexts; chs 1 ('Chaucer and the Italians') and 2 ('Education and Politics, 1350–1550') are especially relevant.

Koff, Leonard M. and Schildgen, Brenda D. (eds) 2000. *The 'Decameron' and the 'Canterbury Tales': New Essays on an Old Question*. Madison, Wis. and London: Fairleigh Dickinson University Press and Associated University Presses. Discussions of reception, influence and broader themes (locality, consolation, confession, anti-clericalism) and five essays on specific tales.

Parks, George B. 1954. *The English Traveller to Italy, I: The Middle Ages*. Rome: Edizioni di storia e letteratura. Well-documented survey of the range of travellers: clerical, diplomatic, mercenary and scholarly. Part 3 deals with the period from 1300 to 1500.

Petrina, Alessandria 2004. *Cultural Politics in Fifteenth Century England: The Case of Humphrey, Duke of Gloucester*. Leiden: Brill. Stimulating reassessment of Humphrey's politics and links with Italian humanists.

Putter, Ad 1996. *An Introduction to the 'Gawain'-Poet*. London and New York: Longman. Considers the case for the poet's knowledge of Dante (pp. 4–6 and 188–9).

Rothwell, W. 1994. 'The Trilingual England of Geoffrey Chaucer.' *Studies in the Age of Chaucer*. On the interactions of English, French and Latin as used by the literate classes.

Ruddock, Alwyn A. 1951. *Italian Merchants and Shipping in Southampton 1270–1600*. Southampton: University College. Traces the role of the Genoese, Venetians and Florentines in London as well as Southampton.

Saygin, S. 2002. *Humphrey, Duke of Gloucester (1390–1447) and the Italian Humanists*. Leiden: Brill. Stresses the importance of Humphrey's patronage for his public and political image, and reviews the evidence about Italian humanists employed in England from 1418 to 1445 (ch. 19).

Simone, Franco 1969. *The French Renaissance: Medieval Tradition and the Italian Influence in Shaping the Renaissance in France*. London: Macmillan. Pioneering work on the relationships between fourteenth- and fifteenth-century French and Italian culture. Chs 1 (on Avignon) and 5 (on the reception of Petrarch in France) are especially relevant here.

Wallace, David 1997. *Chaucerian Polity: Absolutist Lineages and Associational Forms in England and Italy*. Stanford, Calif.: Stanford University Press. Extensive essay in comparative historicism, with a particularly valuable account of 'Chaucer in Florence and Lombardy' (pp. 9–64) and close attention to the Italian sources and contexts for the Knight's, Clerk's and Monk's Tales.

—— 2000. 'Italy.' In *A Companion to Chaucer*, ed. P. Brown (Oxford: Blackwell), pp. 218–34. Concise thematic approach to Chaucer's dealings with Italy and Italian writers – addressing the political contexts, the influence of the *Decameron*, the Monk's Tale and *De casibus*, and the Italian presences in the *Troilus*.

Weiss, Roberto 1967. *Humanism in England during the Fifteenth Century*, 3rd edn. Oxford: Blackwell. Despite much subsequent scholarship, this remains a work to reckon with. It contains especially useful accounts of (for example) Abbot

Whethamstede (pp. 30–8), Humphrey of Gloucester (chs 3 and 4) and John Tiptoft (pp. 112–22).

Wetherbee, W. P. 1984. *Chaucer and the Poets: An Essay on 'Troilus and Criseyde.'* Ithaca, N.Y., and London. Perceptive treatment of classical and vernacular intertextualities, with an especially illuminating chapter on 'Dante and the *Troilus*' (ch. 5).

Wright, H. G. 1957. *Boccaccio in England, from Chaucer to Tennyson*. London: Athlone Press. A diligent survey, although now outdated in its critical approach. Chs 1–3 include relevant material.

14

England's Antiquities: Middle English Literature and the Classical Past

Christopher Baswell

At the height of his fortunes in the great alliterative *Morte Arthure*, King Arthur has enjoyed a series of triumphant encounters with the Roman Empire. He has met the emperor Lucius's demand for England's delinquent tribute as a Roman colony with his own genealogical claims to 'mine heritage, the empire of Rome' (643).[1] He has enforced this claim on the battlefield, moved his army down into central Italy, and received the submission of Rome: 'Now we may revel and rest, for Rome is our owen!' (3207). Arthur has almost inverted the geographical trajectory of Roman empire. At this moment of glory, however, Arthur has a terrifying dream of kings, himself among them, ascending and falling from Fortune's wheel.

A 'philosopher', summoned to interpret the dream, tells Arthur that indeed 'thy fortune is passed' because he has shed blood in 'surquidrie', excessive pride (3394–9). And that very day, Arthur hears that his nephew Mordred, whom he left as warden of England, has usurped his throne, married his wife Waynor, and incestuously sired a child with which she is pregnant. Arthur's vengeance on Mordred will lead to both their deaths. In the same dream exegesis, though, the philosopher also associates the men Arthur saw around Fortune's wheel with the 'Nine Worthies', a canonical group of great heroes of pagan antiquity (Alexander, Hector and Julius Caesar), the Old Testament (Judas Maccabeus, Joshua and King David), and the Christian era. These last three lie in the future: Charlemagne, Godfrey of Bouillon and Arthur himself (3408–39). Arthur will be the next to join this cultural lineage of classical heroism, yet heroic glory and death here are profoundly intertwined.

Arthur's encounters with the ancient past in the *Morte Arthure* – his insistent genealogical derivation from it, his ambition to rival it, his fate tragically to join it – provide a key instance of Middle English poetry's engagement with classical story, especially the narratives of Troy and Rome. In the pages that follow, I want to suggest the verbal inheritance of the Latin classical past in learned poets like Geoffrey Chaucer and John Gower, poets who enrich their work by extensive borrowings and echoes, and thereby come to rival those sources as figures of linguistic prestige and cultural authority. But at the same time, I explore the less overtly learned but ultimately more powerful roles of classical story in the cultural and historical imagination of later medieval England.

Classical antecedents were sources of delight and aspiration, including the persistent English ambition to an imperial expansion that would replicate yet invert Rome's, as Arthur so briefly did. The ancient past was also threatening, a model as much of potential downfall as of heroic or imperial ambition. Does the encounter with antiquity provoke rebirth (as Arthur hoped), or lead inevitably to another imperial 'sepulture' (4340) with which the poem ends? Are ancient characters models for political and moral behaviour, or is the encounter with such fathers and mothers strangely tainted by their own deaths and by hints of incestuous or patricidal desire? Further, I extend the arena of the 'classical' past beyond its traditionally western boundaries, and suggest briefly how stories at the borderland of the Greco-Roman Near East (and beyond) offered even more fascinating and frightening arenas of alternative imagination: other kinds of history and origin, other models of social order, other genders of power.

The Trojan Origins of Britain

Especially in England, Troy and Rome were at once points of genealogical origin and models of pride and downfall. In one of the early encounters of the British and Roman armies in the *Morte Arthure*, Arthur's knight Sir Clegis explicates his coat of arms to a haughty opponent, the King of Syria:

> Mine armes are of auncestry envered with lordes, *acknowledged*
> And has in banner been borne senn Sir Brut time;
> At the citee of Troy that time was enseged,
> Oft seen in assaut with certain knightes;
> Forthy Brut brought us and all oure bold elders
> To Bretain the brodder within ship-bordes. *Great Britain*
> (1694–9)

Sir Clegis summarizes a mythical history of the Trojan origins of Britain. Indeed, another great Arthurian poem of slightly earlier origin, *Sir Gawain and the Green Knight*, opens and closes with similarly dense summaries of Trojan fall and British foundation. There, Trojan origins bracket a defining challenge to the young Arthurian court and its emblematic hero Gawain. Will their reaction contribute to foundational glory or prefigure a fall repeating Trojan sensuality, faithlessness and vanity?

Geoffrey of Monmouth had given the story of Britain's Trojan origin canonical form in his Latin *History of the Kings of Britain* (c.1138).[2] Geoffrey narrates how survivors of Troy, led by Aeneas, arrived in Latium where they would ultimately found Rome. Aeneas's great-grandson Brutus commits accidental patricide. Exiled, Brutus finally arrives at a western island that he names for himself – Britain – and where he founds a city he calls New Troy; it is later called London. To the extent, then, that *Morte*

Arthure depicts a battle for dominance between family lines, the background of Geoffrey's *History* raises a spectre of civil war. This would echo fearfully in a nation that had experienced kings dethroned by collateral family across the fourteenth century, from Edward II to Richard II. Moreover, even if Lucius represents a Trojan descent collateral with Arthur's, Rome itself is an older, patriarchal source for Brutus and British royalty. In this context, Lucius's death is not without echoes of patricide.

Geoffrey also connects later British kings, Arthur's ancestors, to the Roman imperial line through marriages during the era of Roman colonization. He thus extends a widely held notion of the westward movement of world power – *translatio imperii* – from Troy to Greece to Rome, and now to Britain. The book itself performs a related idea of *translatio studii*, the westward transmission of learning. Like Troy or Rome, though, Geoffrey's Britain is susceptible of decline, especially as a punishment for pride.

Geoffrey's Latin *History* was an amalgam of legend, fiction and more solid documentary sources. It had its detractors, but quickly took on the status of fact in some settings, while in others it trod a permeable line – always unstable in medieval writing – between history and romance. It was adapted to French verse by the poet Wace as the *Roman de Brut* (presented to Eleanor of Aquitaine in 1155). This in turn was adapted into English verse at the very beginning of the Middle English period in a magnificent *Brut* poem by Laȝamon, c.1190–1205, which emphasizes battle and militant heroism (Laȝamon 1995: vii–xii).[3] Laȝamon's self-conscious use of archaic diction may suggest a quest for an early Middle English 'classical' style to suit his material. The Brutus narrative reached yet wider audiences in the thirteenth to the fifteenth centuries, with the production of French and then English prose chronicles, all usually called *Brut* and enormously widespread in manuscript copies (Matheson 1998: 1–49).[4]

The many languages of the *Brut* tradition – Latin, French, English, and the Welsh source that Geoffrey claims – should remind us of the continuously multilingual quality of medieval English classicism. Latin and French collections of ancient story were widely available, and Latin verse versions of classical stories (especially Troy) were a popular form of school exercise. A Latin manuscript like London, British Library Stowe 56, for instance, from around 1200, contains the First Crusade chronicle of Baudri of Bourgeuil, a summary of Norman history, Dares Phrygius's *Historia de excidio Troiae*, the Latin Apollonius of Tyre story, several texts about Alexander the Great, and Geoffrey of Monmouth's *History*; it is a manuscript then of classical history relevant to the Normans and the Angevins, with territorial interests extending to the site of another antiquity already mentioned, the eastern Mediterranean and the Holy Land.

Both Virgil's *Aeneid* and Statius's *Thebaid* had also been redacted and creatively reworked in French in the *Roman d'Eneas* (c.1155) and the *Roman de Thèbes* (1152 or slightly earlier); and the late antique (and fictive) 'eyewitness' accounts of Dares and Dictys (*Ephemeris belli Troiani*) had been elaborately reimagined in Benoît de Sainte-Maure's *Roman de Troie* around 1160 or soon after (Baswell 2000: 31–41). Several of these texts – a French verse version of Baudri's crusade chronicle, the *Eneas* and the *Thèbes* – appear in the late fourteenth-century manuscript London, British Library Additional 34114, offering a French language analogy to the interests of Stowe 56;

Additional 34114 is a grand, beautifully decorated manuscript of aristocratic preoccupation reflecting the imperious if not imperial ambitions of its owner, Henry Despenser, Bishop of Norwich, and his aristocratic family (Baswell 2002: 40–58).

Middle English Troys

Even the alliterative *Morte Arthure* and *Sir Gawain*, though they engage the spectre and promise of Troy and Rome, keep that classical past somewhat at bay by strategies of marginalization, restricting it to fairly brief references. At the same time, Middle English literary culture produced a number of texts in which the fall of Troy and its imperial aftermath in Rome and Europe are absolutely central. Even while they provide a genealogical past of heroic glory and imperial foundation, the legends of Troy and Brutus also tie their European heirs to stories of arrogance, national disaster and versions of fatality lacking either the causality or comfort of Christian belief. The Trojan past in Middle English literature is the realm of the undead: it promises imperial (or urban) rebirth, but it also figures inescapable loss, and features the building of both cities and of tombs.

As with the *Brut* tradition, the fuller story of Troy also found its way into Middle English from both its Latin and French sources, and appealed to an ever-wider range of readerships: aristocratic, gentry and urban bourgeois. An apt instance is the fourteenth-century *Seege or Batayle of Troye*. A fairly short version of about 2,000 lines, the *Seege* combines apparently learned sources and oral poetic conventions. It casts the ancient uncanny in a more local, perhaps Celtic, mode: Paris judges among 'ffoure ladies of eluene land' (508), for instance, not three classical goddesses.[5] This poem also suggests the range of uses a single text could serve. Of its four surviving manuscripts, one (London, Lincoln's Inn 150) is largely popular in its content and shows links to oral performance; in another (London, College of Arms Arundel XXII) the *Seege* introduces a more learned and historical interest, followed by a Middle English Troy history translated from Geoffrey of Monmouth and from Wace (Guddat-Figge 1976: 228–31, 214–15).

By far the most influential narrative of the Trojan War and its aftermath was the *Historia destructionis Troiae*, loosely drawn from the *Roman de Troie*.[6] It was completed in 1287 by the Sicilian jurist Guido delle Colonne, and survives in about one hundred and fifty manuscripts. It was translated into Middle English verse, more or less completely, three times in the later fourteenth and early fifteenth centuries, including a version by John Lydgate that itself survives in nineteen manuscripts (Benson 1980: 35–129). The following discussion will concentrate on the vigorous and fluent alliterative version, the most faithful to Guido, known as the *'Gest Hystoriale' of the Destruction of Troy* (hereafter, *Gest*).[7]

Guido, and the *Gest* after him, write a genuine history, often of heroic proportions. Yet that heroism occurs within a sequence of events paradoxically trivial in their origins: vanity, jealousy, lust, social competition, transgressions of diplomatic protocol. 'What mighty were marrit [*ruined*], & martrid to dethe; – / Of kynges, & knightes, & other kyde [*famed*] Dukes, / That thaire lyves here lost for a lighte cause!' (5552–4). The closest Guido comes to a positive notion of history is an early passage (now missing from the *Gest*) that notes the many great nations founded as a result of Troy's fall (*Historia*: 9–10). There are no grand imperial or divine perspectives here; rather, men and women are trapped in disasters whose inevitability is pressed upon the audience by prophecy and the narrator's persistent digressions about future consequences.

The working of councils 'for the comyn proffet' (9320), intriguingly relevant to parliamentary developments in later medieval England, increasingly degenerates into private treachery and false representations in the *Gest*. The identities of city or nation are progressively atomized into the preservation of clans (especially those of Eneas and Antenor) or the pursuit of private love (especially Achilles' for the Trojan princess Polexena). The *Gest*'s grandeur is that of private heroism, most often resulting in tragic death and an accelerating series of tombs, as Priam's sons and allies are killed off. The most elaborate is Hector's tomb, which becomes a narrative magnet for later events like Achilles' first sight of Polexena. Hector's is 'a marvelous toumbe', 'a prise werke' of dazzling artisanal skill (8733–66). His corpse receives equally skilled attention, scientifically preserved 'as a lede [*man*] upon lyve' (8789), seated visibly beneath a lifelike martial sculpture. Hector's corpse is an emblem, I think, of Troy's own textual survival as a simultaneous model of disaster and empire, preserved somewhere between certain death and the artisanal (or poetic) representation of life.

Translatio Studii: Chaucer, Gower, Lydgate

The ancient narratives mentioned so far come into Middle English texts at several removes from any antique source, although this did not diminish their authenticity for medieval audiences. The early Latin sources of the Troy story – Virgil's *Aeneid* and the late-antique accounts of Dares and Dictys – were continuously available in Latin and much studied in medieval England, as were other major classical poems like Statius's *Thebaid* and the works of Ovid. All three poets were respected and imitated for their stylistic refinement, and both influenced popular histories. Horace, less a narrative poet than Virgil or Ovid, was none the less widely read and mined for moral tags as well as stylistic imitation; in prose Seneca (the younger) was used similarly (Baswell 1995: 15–40).

All these texts are almost inevitably read through the optic of the learned commentaries by which they were surrounded in most manuscripts. These could be quite literal and historical, as in the annotations of the influential late-antique Virgil commentator Servius. A smaller but important commentary tradition approached some ancient poetry as allegory. The twelfth-century commentary on the *Aeneid* attributed to Bernard Silvestris links the epic to stages of spiritual growth in the hero Aeneas (Baswell 1995: 41–135). The episodic quality of Ovid's poetry made it even more attractive to allegorists and moralists. As classical story became attractive material for sermon exempla in the earlier fourteenth century, stories from the *Metamorphoses* were widely quoted and retold for these ends, especially by learned friars (Minnis 1982: 16–19, 109–18).

Chaucer's classicism has received a great deal of study (Fyler 1979; McCall 1979; Minnis 1982) and will not occupy much space here. Chaucer was as energetic a reader of ancient Latin as he was of later French and Italian literatures, and the work of his entire career is dense with echoes and references to the Latin classics, and to antique story from Thebes to Christian Rome. Probably his earliest long poem, the *Book of the Duchess*, opens with the story of Ceyx and Alcione from the *Metamorphoses* (11.410–740); and its dream sequence begins in a chamber painted with scenes from the *Romance of the Rose*, lit by stained glass in which is depicted 'hooly al the storye of Troye' (325). This scene – Troy casting light on erotic allegory – emblematizes Chaucer's engagement with the motives and erotic tragedy of ancient story. The poem also typifies his linguistic syncretism, for the Ceyx and Alcione episode, certainly deriving from Ovid, is also strikingly similar to the story as told in the fourteenth-century French *Ovide moralisé* (McCall 1979: 14–22).

This very variety of sources, and their frequent contradictions, become the thematic crisis of the *House of Fame*, whose dream episode features clashing versions of the love affair of Dido and Aeneas. Here, self-conscious echoes of the opening of the *Aeneid* ('I wol now synge, yif I kan, / The armes and also the man', 143–4) begin a story that is indebted equally to Ovid: 'Rede Virgile in Eneydos / Or the Epistle of Ovyde, / What that she wrot or that she dyde' (378–80). Later scenes in the poem feature classical and post-classical writers literally fighting over their versions of the past; the dream poem becomes almost a nightmare of classical authority and its contradictions (Baswell 1995: 239–48). Ovidian and other versions of ancient heroines also occupy the *Legend of Good Women*.

Troilus and Criseyde – a classical tale whose most immediate source is Boccaccio's *Filostrato*, yet occasionally emended directly from Virgil – is set with great care in the declining days of Trojan power. Its narrator none the less constantly tries to push Trojan history aside and focus on the doomed affair of Troilus and Criseyde; Book 3 practically burrows into their private, almost ecstatic experience. This summons again the sense of old Troy as a troubling precedent for New Troy. *Troilus*, further, is full of references to the even more disastrous story of Statius's *Thebaid*, with its history of civil war, incest and fratricide (Wetherbee 1984: 111–44). The Theban legend reappears in the first of the *Canterbury Tales*, the Knight's Tale, another instance of a classical story borrowed from Boccaccio but reflecting Chaucer's deep knowledge of Statius. Indeed in most manuscripts the tale is headed with Latin lines from the last book of the *Thebaid*; Chaucer himself, or an early copyist, draws the reader's attention to his Latin models. Other *Canterbury Tales* reflect contact with Ovid of course, and with Horace, Seneca and (perhaps indirectly) the historian Livy.

This Latinate side of Chaucer's work, and his multilingualism, link him closely with his friend and fellow poet, Gower (c.1330–1408), who wrote lengthy works in Latin, French and English. Gower displays his Latin erudition much more overtly than does

Chaucer, especially in his decision to compose his *Vox clamantis* in Latin verse that is sometimes virtually a mosaic of lines from Ovid. Gower displays intimate knowledge of Latin poets like Virgil and Statius as well (Yeager 1990: 12–14, 52–60). Part of the poem's dream story involves a journey away from a 'New Troy' destroyed by beasts who suggest the rebels of 1381, and later a return to an island of 'Brute'. Gower thus sets his Latin poem in the world of imperial Trojan foundation, with symbolic analogies between London and Troy that are left implicit in Chaucer. Equally classicizing is Gower's Middle English *Confessio Amantis*, the confession of a lover to 'Genius', the priest of Venus who guides him through the deadly sins as they relate to worldly love, as well as the remedies of each sin. These are illustrated by narrative examples drawn in great part from Ovid, often viewed through the allegorizing of earlier commentators (Harbert 1988: 86–97). Yet Gower's stories often burst past their local exemplary intention, as in his Ovidian tales of Pygmalion (4.371–445) or Jason and Medea (5.3247–4229). Ovidian story can be as disruptive to the poem, at times, as it is morally controlled at others.

By rendering classical story in the vernacular, both Chaucer and Gower were aware of opening new, unstable arenas of emotional and moral complexity – part of the claim both are laying to Middle English as an emerging classical language. This complexity is especially apparent in Gower's persistent concern about love engendering war and social upheaval. Troy is the predominant instance, especially the life of Paris. In the face of such upheaval, Gower's narrator yearns in the prologue for renewed harmony from a new Arion, the mythological harper who 'broghte hem alle in good accord' (Prol. 1065). Indeed, the poem ends with the Lover revealed to himself as an old man, beyond worldly love; he returns instead to hopes for harmony and love in the social order.

Ambitions to a stylistic lineage that might parallel Trojan genealogy are especially overt in John Lydgate's *Troy Book*. This is the most ambitious of the three Middle English Troy narratives based on Guido delle Colonne; it explicitly links Trojan empire with English royal lineage and imperial ambitions. Lydgate (c.1370–1449) produced his version between 1412 and 1420, during which years his patron Henry V assumed the throne (1413) and pursued his claim to the French crown by both battle and diplomacy. The closing sections of *Troy Book* celebrate the Treaty of Troyes and Henry's marriage with Catherine Valois. Lydgate spent his life as a monk of Bury St Edmunds, though he studied at Oxford and travelled widely. His interests in antique story and literature profited from a renewed interest in classical texts and myth at the beginning of the fifteenth century (Pearsall 1970: 22–82). The renewed interest in classical learning provides context for many of Lydgate's additions to Guido, such as the expanded (and Virgilian) version of Aeneas's fate, and lengthy mythological explanations around the Judgement of Paris.

In writing an authoritative Troy story enmeshed with Henry's imperial ambitions Lydgate was also consolidating English poetry – itself still a usurper of Latin's prestige – as a worthy medium of classical gravity. And the armature for Lydgate's purposes was his laureate predecessor 'My maister Chaucer' (5.3521), especially the Chaucer of classical story and classical echoes discussed above:

> The noble Rethor that alle dide excelle;
> For in makyng he drank of the welle
> Undir Pernaso, that the Musis kepe,
> On whiche hil I myghte neuer slepe.
> (3.553–6)

Lydgate folds a Chaucerian presence into *Troy Book*, first by insisting on his own inadequacy compared to his predecessor. Yet he lays claim to being Chaucer's only genuine poetic heir. Further, especially as the story approaches the affair of Troilus and Criseyde, Lydgate increasingly puts aside his Latin source in favour of Chaucer's version, even Chaucer's language. Chaucer becomes the 'classical' model for narrating England's imperial ancestry, in a style further classicized by Lydgate's characteristic rhetorical amplification and his use of Latin-derived 'aureate' diction.

The more literal usurpation that lurks behind *Troy Book* is that of Richard II by Henry IV in 1399. Lydgate's introductory and closing verses carefully align Henry V with legitimate Trojan descent (he will rule 'by successioun' over 'Brutys Albyoun', Prol. 103–4). Far more daring, in this historical setting, is Lydgate's decision, apparently without explicit commission, to narrate the far more overtly disturbing Theban legend, in his *Siege of Thebes* (1421–2). This story concentrates at its surface a number of threats more implicit in the stories discussed above: incest, usurpation, civil war, fratricide and urban disaster. The Theban legend hovers at the edges of Chaucer's and Gower's classicism, but had never been retold in its entirety in Middle English before Lydgate. Lydgate's capacity to register unresolved tensions, without letting them quite interrupt his poetic voice, serves him well in the *Siege*. The poetic mantle of Chaucer is assumed in this poem by the fiction that it is the first story in the return journey of the *Canterbury Tales*. It thus echoes both the General Prologue and the Knight's Tale, to which the *Siege* is a pendant and a prehistory.

In the *Siege*, ideals of love and loyalty are constantly undermined by pride, hasty anger and unmotivated aggression. Lineages are ended or interrupted. Even an admirable king like Adrastus ends the poem in despair over the death of his allies and heirs. Even true loyalty, such as that of Tideus to Polyneices ('Polymyte'), begins with a pointless fight and ends in disaster. Yet Lydgate presents his story as both an exemplary and a cautionary mirror for princes, of an intriguingly and unnervingly modern sort, full of unresolved conflict. Adrastus is the poem's 'merour . . . / Of kyngly fredam' (2723–4); he practises exogamous marriage, plans military strategy, listens to his counsellors, and pays his armies fast and fairly. Parliaments and councils are emphasized, often conflicting with outbreaks of aristocratic violence. There are related incompatibilities between urban and royal social orders, and between the more contemporary powers of written documents and archaic models of chivalric procedure. Antique civil strife becomes, in the *Siege*, the site of dark confrontation between current civil orders.

Classical Story in the Auchinleck and Thornton Manuscripts

As the historical and legendary preoccupations of the *Brut* tradition and its related classical stories such as Thebes, Troy and Rome were moving into French and then English from the twelfth to the fifteenth centuries, other and more imaginatively adventurous classical narratives, less connected to British history and newer English territorial ambitions, were also beginning to appear in Middle English. Several such works appear in the 'Auchinleck Manuscript' (Edinburgh, National Library Advocates 19.2.1), an enormous collection of primarily secular romances, and a great deal else, produced with considerable care and expense around 1330–40, in a quite professional London workshop.[8] Among the manuscript's texts are a number of 'English' romances such as *Guy of Warwick*, *Bevis of Hampton*, *Of Arthour and of Merlin* and *King Richard*. The manuscript also suggests a user interested in the historical framework of these romances, through the *Liber regum Anglie*; despite its title, this is an English metrical chronicle in the *Brut* tradition, but very much shorter.

Auchinleck is not exclusively a manuscript of English stories, however. It also contains a version of the 'Breton lay' *Sir Orfeo*, and the earliest English Alexander romance, *Kyng Alisaunder* (originally complete, now a fragment in this manuscript). Both these poems recount stories of the classical past well outside the Trojan tradition and its complex genealogical links to England. *Sir Orfeo* and *Kyng Alisaunder* both experience the past as a site of terrors encountered, but conquered and assimilated; and equally they experience the past as a source for certain, if limited, forms of wonder and delight. *Sir Orfeo* in particular adapts its antique stories to a theme of literal renaissance.

Sir Orfeo appears to reflect knowledge of several early Latin versions of the Orpheus myth, as well as the mediation of the medieval commentary traditions. And while the poem uses these sources with great liberty, its very boldness and creativity place *Sir Orfeo* among the most authentically classical poems in Middle English. The Middle English takes this famous story of the underworld and its eruption into mundane life, and reimagines it through the optic of a specifically English uncanny.

The myth of Orpheus and Eurydice was widely known across the Middle Ages, through versions by Virgil (*Georgics* 4.453–527), Ovid (*Metamorphoses* bks 10–11) and even more often through Boethius's *Consolation of Philosophy* (3.metrum 12). By the fourteenth century, this famous episode had also been retold many times in mythological handbooks. It was interpreted allegorically, moreover, in texts like Pierre Bersuire's *Ovidius moralizatus* and the French *Ovide moralisé*, both of which made classical stories available as examples for preaching. These treatments were sometimes simplistic (approaching Orpheus as a Christ figure who tries to save the errant soul Eurydice, for instance) but rarely dogmatic; they often suggested multiple and mutually inconsistent allegories. While *Sir Orfeo* may develop allegorical notions of the protagonist as leader and even saviour, it profits more from the precedents of free and innovative interpretation (Friedman 1970: 104–36).

Sir Orfeo responds brilliantly to this famous myth and its ambient traditions. Orfeo is both a harpist and a king (specifically of Winchester in the Auchinleck manuscript's version) who loses his wife when she is mysteriously carried off by the king of Fairy in an act of tyrannical will enacted under a threat of violence. The poem reimagines the ancient underworld in terms of the Celtic fairy kingdom – a kingdom, moreover, that functions as a sort of dream version and dark alternative to that of Orfeo himself. The Fairy king's is a static realm of tyranny, death and emptily repetitive ritual such as the hunt Orfeo will later witness.

As the tale is told by Ovid, Orpheus retreats to the wilderness after losing Eurydice a second and final time. In this setting of narcissistic solitude, he harps to the trees and animals, and turns to homosexual desire, for which he is ultimately dismembered by enraged Maenads. The poet of *Sir Orfeo* folds some of this into his version: his Fairy king threatens dame Heurodis with dismemberment if she refuses to go with him, and after losing his wife Sir Orfeo spends a period of woodland reversion almost into a wild man. In the Middle English, this leads to Orfeo's sighting the Fairy king's hunt and entering his realm. There, in a daring reversal of the classical story, Orfeo does succeed in restoring the life of dame Heurodis, not through the Fairy king's mode of threatened violence, but by music, words and diplomatic cunning. Classical episodes of alienation, violence and death are thus refigured as verbal negotiation leading to rebirth and restoration.

An added closing episode of recognition and reconciliation with the steward to whom Orfeo had entrusted his kingdom tips thematic attention away from conjugal desire and towards good rule and faithful stewardship, although music and Orfeo's harp itself link together all the poem's episodes and issues. In a poem that largely observes the simple paratactic style of Breton lays and their heritage of oral performance, the recognition scene – sparked by the harp – occurs in a long and mannered sentence of conditional clauses ('Yif ich were Orfeo the king . . .', 558–74) that climax in Orfeo's promise to leave his kingdom to the steward. Both the syntax and the plot turn enact an ordered transmission of knowledge and rule. The passage offers classically derived rhetoric as an alternative to the occluded declamatory style and wilful mystery of the Breton lay. Rhetorical classicism, loyal stewardship and kingship linked to musical art all converge, then, at the close of *Sir Orfeo.* In this poem, we can speak of a genuinely renaissance reaction to the antique past, reconfiguring its stories to explore renewal of both an individual life and the state.

The Auchinleck manuscript also contains, as noted above, the antique narrative *Kyng Alisaunder*, a long poem (over 8,000 lines) mostly in octosyllabic couplets, which explores some of the same issues of kingship and wonder found in *Sir Orfeo.* Historical accounts of the empire of Alexander the Great, versions of his education by Aristotle and fantastic accounts of his travels were all enormously widespread across medieval Europe. Greek and Latin historians, as well as biblical references, record his conquests. Alexander's story was cut loose from later imperial claims upon Trojan or Roman descent, since his empire famously crumbled upon his premature death. This mixture of legend and history made for an imaginative space in which extreme and sometimes deeply anxious versions of human identity (religious, political, genealogical) might play out, along with critiques of imperial ambition and cupidity. Such themes inform the two major Old French Alexander romances (one in Anglo-Norman) as well as the many redactions of his story (at least six) in Middle English and Middle Scots, and extensive summaries in poems like Gower's *Confessio Amantis*. *Kyng Alisaunder* announces itself as a learned 'storye ymade of maistres wyse' (669), explicitly drawing on the Anglo-Norman *Roman de toute chevalerie* and 'the latyn' (3511), probably Walter of Chatillon's *Alexandreis* (Bunt 1994).[9]

Sir Orfeo's verbal ploys and diplomatic cunning become more daring and playful in *Kyng Alisaunder*'s many episodes of disguise, by which Alexander slips in and out of hostile courts. Even his counsellors think this can be 'woodhede and foly' (4274). A great conqueror, this Alexander is also a great lover and a great trickster. The climactic instance of both falls near the end: already aware of his fated death, Alexander poses as his own ambassador to visit Queen Candace and consummate a long courtly flirtation. Like many women in *Kyng Alisaunder*, Candace never gives up her power in the face of love, a contrast with other classical stories that is emphasized as she sings, when Alexander first meets her, 'of Dido and Eneas, / Hou love hem ladde by strange bride [*bridle*]' (7619–20).

Disguise and subversion also play in Alexander's conception: the mage and exiled king Neptenabus takes on the guise of Jupiter Ammon and sleeps with Olympias, the wife of his conqueror Philip of Macedon. Troubled paternity and chaotic lineage haunt the rest of the poem, in taunts about Alexander's illegitimacy ('hores son', 2687), but especially in his travels among geographical wonders in the poem's second half. Incestuous mixing among the Ethiopians means that 'Noman ne knowes there other [*relative*], / Fader the son, ne suster the brothere' (6296–7); such extreme models threaten genealogy and the fundamental order of the state. Alexander kills Neptenabus, and will be poisoned by a judge he had dismissed, tellingly named Antipater. The poem also encounters, often respectfully, other versions of identity in alternate faiths such as Judaism and Brahmanism.

A related, more domestic arena of social anxieties opens up in romances in the 'Thornton Manuscript' copied for his own use by Robert Thornton, a member of the Yorkshire gentry, about a century after the Auchinleck manuscript. Thornton's book provides an important index of educated provincial taste in the later Middle Ages (Guddat-Figge 1976: 134–42). Along with a prose Alexander story and our unique copy of the alliterative *Morte Arthure*, it also contains the romance *Octavian*, about a Christian Roman emperor, and crises of lineage and class. Like *Kyng Alisaunder*, *Octavian* makes paternity and adultery central issues, and features repeated scenes of disguise. The emperor's marriage is barren for seven years. When his wife does conceive twin boys, she is accused of adultery by the emperor's wicked mother; she and her twins are exiled, leaving the empire again without an heir. The romance equally involves a series of virtuous and strong mothers: the wronged empress herself (who finds her way safely to Jerusalem), a lioness who suckles one of the twin sons, and even the wife of a Paris burgess who raises the other. A series of militant adventures climaxes in a war against a Saracen sultan and the seduction of his daughter by the son raised in Paris, 'Florent', who plays with disguise much as Alexander does. This same twin, earlier purchased (after some haggling) by the merchant Clement, reveals himself as a natural aristocrat and is identified as the emperor's lost son. The splintered family finally reunites and the imperial line is restored at Rome. Like many late Middle English romances, *Octavian* at once parodies and honours some bourgeois values, and yet criticizes archaic and wasteful aspects of chivalric ideology.

Classical narratives like *Orfeo*, *Alisaunder* and *Octavian* thus explore issues at once unnerving and decidedly contemporary, in the imaginative freedom of antique settings largely unloosed from the restrictions both of genealogical connections and Christian ideology. To different extents, each of them pulls back from its darkest imaginings, amending the past (*Sir Orfeo*), inventing reconciliation and lineal continuity (*Octavian*), or leaving its terrors in a past kept separate by the very absence of lineage (*Alisaunder*); and each imagines a deep connection between good rule and artifice, be it music, language or disguise.

Geography and Social Orders at the Edge

The return to a centre and the re-establishment of male power or lineage, however, are not the only trajectories available to these unsettling antique stories. The conquests of Alexander push medieval readers' attention persistently eastward, far beyond the Mediterranean boundaries of the other major antique story traditions. It is no accident that such geographical exoticism accompanies other sorts of extremity: non-Christian religions, anti-imperial ethics, unnerving kinship systems, politically and militarily powerful women like Candace and the Amazons. *Octavian* presses modestly at some of the same edges. From its epicentre at Rome it reaches Paris to the west and Jerusalem to the east; it features women, especially mothers, both good and bad, but persistently strong.

A small but influential group of antique stories goes even further in featuring these motifs of exotic geography and of women whose powers pose unnerving alternatives to ideologies of empire and patrilineage. Probably the most widespread instance is the story of Albina, a nightmare of patrilineage that appears as the prologue of almost all manuscripts of the English *Brut* chronicle. The king of Syria, with the Roman-sounding name Dioclician, is an imperial conqueror of all the nations around him. He marries his own cousin and hence his thirty-three offspring verge towards the incestuous; more problematic yet, all are female. This situation only worsens when Dioclician marries them to his subject kings. As his eldest daughter Albina says, 'I am come of a more hyere kynges blod than my housband is' (p. 3), and all the daughters insist that the prestige of their lineage trumps the obligations of their gender. They refuse obedience to their husbands, bringing two models of social order into dangerous conflict. The daughters adopt that key medium of male power, the sword, and slay all their husbands in their beds. Dioclician, enraged, exiles his daughters on a boat; it ultimately arrives at a fertile island which Albina names for herself: Albion. She and her sisters later have sex with incubi (thus achieving genealogy without the help of human males) and produce the race of giants that Brutus must conquer upon his own arrival before he renames the island for himself.

Such anxiety-laden versions of antiquity attract attention from the two chief classically oriented poets of Middle English, Gower and Chaucer, especially through some of the classical women who appear in both *Confessio Amantis* and the *Legend of Good Women*: Procne and Philomela, Medea, Ariadne and Cleopatra. The geography of the Albina story and many of its narrative motifs are replicated in Chaucer's Man of Law's Tale (a version of which had already appeared in Gower's *Confessio*): a classical setting, an imperial father, a Syrian marriage unwanted by the daughter, movement by rudderless ship from there to England, and the production of offspring once in England. The roles of murderous women are indeed distributed elsewhere in this tale, to the two mothers-in-law, who also usurp such forms of usually male power as the sword and royal letters sent under seal. The Syrian mother gets called a 'virago' (358) – a woman who acts like a man – and the Northumbrian mother is 'mannysh' (782). The Man of Law's heroine, Custance, may seem a remarkably passive double for the redoubtable Albina. Yet Custance converts the Northumbrians to Christianity, apparently before the mission of Augustine of York; like Albina, she leaves a crucial mark on the island before the usual male 'founder' of Roman Christianity reaches there. Further, Custance is in one way more effective than Albina, in that her son will ultimately install the genealogy of exoticized antique Northumbria permanently on the Roman imperial throne. And at one point, moreover, that son appears as fatherless as Albina's offspring: 'A mooder he hath, but fader hath he noon' (1020).

Incest, mentioned in several contexts above, is perhaps the deepest threat to social identities formed through patrilineage and the orderly transmission of dominion. Custance's story is nowhere about incest, but a number of its scenes closely repeat scenes from famous incest narratives; and any such echoes are accentuated by the Man of Law's protest, in his Prologue, that he will not speak 'Of swiche unkynde abhomynacions' (88). The antique Near East is the site for the most elaborate meditation on this theme in Middle English, Gower's version of the widely known 'Greek Romance' of Apollonius of Tyre (Yeager 1990: 216–29). Seeking to wed the daughter of King Antiochus, Apollonius uncovers that king's sexual violence against his daughter, then flees Antioch and even his own city to avoid the king's murderous schemes. There follows a convoluted plot in which Apollonius acquires then loses a beloved (and exogamous) wife and daughter, usually at sea, and ultimately regains both. Repeatedly, the plot threatens to move again into sexual violence, even incest, or death itself. In each case, however, these dangers are avoided by emotional decency, and even more by the civilizing arts of music, medicine, education and story-telling, exercised as much by women as by men. If King Antiochus's desire for his unspeaking daughter made him 'wylde' and 'unkinde' (8.309–12), the music and learned speech of Apollonius's daughter Thais draw her own father out of a speechless lethargy and briefly 'salvage' behaviour and teach him to love her 'kindly' (8.1699, 1707). Gower's tale looks hard at the horrors of sexual disorder but uses mirror settings to imagine socialized alternatives; yet his antique time and edgy antique geography also allow him to propose a world where powerful women and the arts are the sources of social restoration.

Troy and the Ends of Medieval Classicism

We may turn, briefly, to classicism at the close of the Middle Ages by returning yet again to Troy, the narrative that had supported both the central imperial imagination and much of the erotic imagination of all medieval England. Three late medieval Troy narratives characterize broader developments in classicism in the period (Baswell 1995: 270–84). In 1490, William Caxton printed his *Eneydos*, almost a translation of the French *Livre des Eneydes* (1483), which Caxton (in a self-authorizing gesture) claims is translated from Virgil's *Aeneid.* The book focuses largely on Dido, and several versions of her story that had come into prominence in vernacular and Latin Troy texts. The narrative voice scarcely registers the contradictions among these stories. However little he may be aware of it, Caxton registers the crisis of multiple versions and interpretations that had troubled Chaucer's *House of Fame* more than a century earlier. This multiplicity extends to the expanding and ever less convergent audiences – townsmen, clerks and nobles – to whom Caxton addresses his book.

Two reactions emerge to these increasingly ramified and unresolved versions of classical story; both point towards important developments among early modern writers in England. At roughly the same time as Caxton, the Scottish poet Robert Henryson produced his superb *Testament of Cresseid*, which he presents as a sixth book of Chaucer's *Troilus and Criseyde.* Here, Henryson imagines Cresseid's decline after her abandonment by her Greek lover Diomede; he includes a moving episode of the leprous Cresseid seeing Troilus in triumphant procession just before she dies. This is Henryson's own imaginative intervention in classical story, a gesture that points towards the careers of Philip Sidney and Edmund Spenser. Further, by attaching his work to Chaucer's, Henryson extends gestures noted in Lydgate, by which Chaucer is registered as the heir to Latinity in an emergent English classical canon.

Gavin Douglas's 1513 translation of the entire *Aeneid* into late Middle Scots in some ways complements Henryson. It is a remarkable accomplishment that helps draw humanist classicism into a broader English-reading literary world. Douglas explicitly sneers at Caxton's 'buke of Inglys gross', and addresses himself to a newly restricted audience of 'worthy noblys' for whom he will write in 'knychtlyke stile' (Prol. 1.139, 237, 9.31). Yet, like the humanists he emulates, Douglas uses the inherited commentary tradition, and registers many medieval reactions to his story by inserting them into his often brilliant prologues to each book; these, along with other introductory materials and his own prose glosses, neatly imitate the structure of early printed copies of the *Aeneid* and their manuscript sources. Together, these three works, around the turn of the sixteenth century, suggest the continuing power of Troy to engage the imagination of empire, love and death.

See also: 5 Women's Voices and Roles, 6 Manuscripts and Readers, 7 From Manuscript to Modern Text, 8 Translation and Society, 9 The Languages of Medieval Britain, 12 England and France, 13 Britain and Italy, 15 Jews, Saracens, 'Black Men', Tartars, 18 Images, 19 Love, 20 Middle English Romance, 21 Writing Nation, 33 The *Canterbury Tales*, 34 John Gower and John Lydgate, 36 The Poetry of Robert Henryson.

Notes

1 www.lib.rochester.edu/camelot/teams/tmsmenu.htm is the main page for the on-line version of TEAMS Middle English Texts, also available in print: affordable student editions, with solid introductions and bibliography, of the alliterative *Morte Arthure*, John Gower, *Confessio Amantis* (extensive selections), Robert Henryson, *The Testament of Cresseid*, John Lydgate, *Siege of Thebes* and *Troy Book: Selections*, *Octavian*, *Sir Orfeo*.

2 Geoffrey of Monmouth, *The History of the Kings of Britain*, trans. Lewis Thorpe (Harmondsworth: Penguin, 1966).

3 Laȝamon (Laȝamon), *Brut or hystoria Brutonum*, ed. and trans. W. R. J. Barron and S. C. Weinberg (Harlow: Longman, 1995). An edition with facing-page translation eases access to Laȝamon's difficult early Middle English.

4 *The Brut or the Chronicles of England*, ed. F. W. D. Brie, EETS os 131 (1906), 136 (1908).

5 *The Seege or Batayle of Troye*, ed. Mary Barnicle, EETS os 172 (1927).

6 Guido delle Colonne, *Historia destructionis Troiae*, trans. Mary E. Meek (Bloomington: Indiana University Press, 1974). With a solid and accessible introduction.

7 *The 'Gest hystoriale' of the Destruction of Troy*, ed. George A. Panton and David Donaldson, EETS os 39 (1869), 56 (1874).

8 www.nls.uk/auchinleck/. A complete digitalized facsimile of the Auchinleck manuscript, with introduction, transcriptions and full bibliography organized by topic or text.

9 *Kyng Alisaunder*, ed. G. V. Smithers, EETS os 227 (1952), 237 (1957).

References and Further Reading

Baswell, Christopher 1995. *Virgil in Medieval England: Figuring the* Aeneid *from the Twelfth Century to Chaucer*. Cambridge: Cambridge University Press. Surveys the multiple commentary traditions (rhetorical, historical, allegorical) around the *Aeneid*, and their impact on medieval vernacular literature in England.

—— 2000. 'Marvels of Translation and Crises of Transition in the Romances of Antiquity.' In *The Cambridge Companion to Medieval Romance*, ed. Roberta L. Krueger (Cambridge: Cambridge University Press), pp. 29–44. Old French versions of classical story and their later development in Middle English.

—— 2002. 'Aeneas in 1381.' *New Medieval Literatures* 5, 7–58. Explores reactions to the Troy story in the aftermath of the Peasants' Revolt of 1381.

Benson, C. David 1980. *The History of Troy in Middle English Literature*. Woodbridge: Brewer. Fullest survey of versions of Guido delle Colonne in Middle English.

Bunt, Gerrit H. V. 1994. *Alexander the Great in the Literature of Medieval Britain*. Mediaevalia Groningana, 14. (Groningen: Forsten). A brief survey of Alexander traditions in England and their connections with earlier Latin versions.

Federico, Sylvia 2003. *New Troy: Fantasies of Empire in the Late Middle Ages*. Minneapolis: University of Minnesota Press. Politics, literature and the Troy tradition in later fourteenth-century England.

Friedman, John Block 1970. *Orpheus in the Middle Ages*. Cambridge, Mass.: Harvard University Press. Strong on developments in the mythographical tradition.

Fyler, John M. 1979. *Chaucer and Ovid*. New Haven, Conn.: Yale University Press. Affinities between the styles and poetic self-conceptions of Chaucer and Ovid.

Guddat-Figge, Gisela 1976. *Catalogue of Manuscripts Containing Middle English Romances*. Munich: Finke. A technical catalogue, useful for exploring the companion texts found with classical story in medieval England.

Harbert, Bruce 1988. 'Lessons from the Great Clerk: Ovid and John Gower.' In *Ovid Renewed: Ovidian Influences on Literature and Art from the Middle Ages to the Twentieth Century*, ed. Charles Martindale (Cambridge: Cambridge University Press), pp. 83–97. An accessible survey; the collection also has a fine essay on Chaucer and Ovid by Helen Cooper.

Kiser, Lisa 1983. *Telling Classical Tales: Chaucer and the Legend of Good Women*. Ithaca, N.Y.: Cornell University Press. Chaucer's 'legends' of ancient women in the context of classical reading.

Matheson, Lister M. 1998. *The Prose Brut: The Development of a Middle English Chronicle*. Tempe, Ariz.: Medieval and Renaissance Texts and Studies. The fullest account of the many versions of the *Brut*; especially strong on the class and geography of its readers.

McCall, John P. 1979. *Chaucer among the Gods: The Poetics of Classical Myth*. College Park: Pennsylvania State. Classical mythography in the Middle Ages, and Chaucer's selective and creative response to it.

Minnis, A. J. 1982. *Chaucer and Pagan Antiquity*. Cambridge: Brewer. The best survey of Chaucer's engagement with classical learning and his historical sense of the antique past.

Nolan, Barbara 1992. *Chaucer and the Tradition of the Roman Antique*. Cambridge: Cambridge University Press. Chaucer's *Troilus and Criseyde* and the *Knight's Tale*, within the broad tradition of earlier medieval vernacular classicism.

Pearsall, Derek 1970. *John Lydgate*. London: Routledge and Kegan Paul, and Charlottesville, Va.: University Press of Virginia. Useful chapters on Lydgate's intellectual milieu, and discussion of *Siege of Thebes* and *Troy Book*.

Severs, J. Burke and Hartung, Albert E. (eds) 1967–98. *A Manual of the Writings in Middle English: 1050–1500*. New Haven: Connecticut Academy of Arts and Sciences. Fascicles 1 (Romances), 12 (Chronicles and other historical writing) and 24 (Tales) survey further texts containing classical story.

Tinkle, Teresa 1996. *Medieval Venuses and Cupids: Sexuality, Hermeneutics, and English Poetry*. Stanford, Calif.: Stanford University Press. Medieval developments of the classical gods of love, with strong surveys of medieval mythography.

Wetherbee, Winthrop 1984. *Chaucer and the Poets: An Essay on* Troilus and Criseyde. Ithaca, N.Y.: Cornell University Press. The finest study of classical echoes in *Troilus*, especially as mediated by Chaucer's reading of Dante.

Yeager, Robert F. 1990. *John Gower's Poetic: The Search for a New Arion*. Cambridge: Brewer. Ovid's impact on Gower's poetry, both Latin and English.

15

Jews, Saracens, 'Black Men', Tartars: England in a World of Racial Difference

Geraldine Heng

> Britain's liminality, its otherness, its being on the edge of the world . . . make it in some sense strange and unpredictable.[1]

Medieval England, in its dramatically contrasting responses to the non-European, non-Christian nations, races and communities it encountered and found to be irreducibly alien can at first glance appear – like Britain – to be a collective entity altogether strange and unpredictable. For instance, in a European century in which canon law inveighed against heresy, and heretics were persecuted in inquisition and crusade, the English monarch Edward I and his courtiers, in an extraordinary gesture of benevolence, attended a Mass of East Syrian liturgy in 1288 celebrated by Rabban Sauma, a Nestorian monk born in China, of Ongut or Uighur extract, who had been sent with companions on a mission to the West by Arghun Khan, the Il-Khan of the Persian Khanate of the Mongol empire. The Mongols represented by Sauma – a nomadic militant people usually called 'Tartars' in English records – had been horrifically evoked earlier in the century by the chronicler of St Albans, Matthew Paris (recording events in narrative and letter under the years 1238, 1241, 1242 and 1243) as a population of *cannibals*: a monstrous, inhuman race of men with abnormally large heads, who fed on raw flesh and human beings ('carnibus crudis et etiam humanis vescuntur'), and who were bent on devastating the Western world after having successfully conquered the East.[2]

Not only did these inhuman, animalistic men drink blood (IV, 76), but chiefs and followers alike in war fed on the cadavers of the slain, with the mutilated paps of virgins savagely killed by repeated rape saved up as delicacies for the chiefs (IV, 273). Naming the Great Khan, Genghis, by name ('rex eorum, Zingiton vocatus'), the chronicler of St Albans focuses on the rapacious hands, bloody teeth and eager jaws of the Mongols, emphasizing their readiness at all times to eat the flesh of men and drink human blood (vi, 77). The English chronicler's understanding that Tartars were cannibals was not unique: Latin Christian authors, and even the Franciscan and Dominican emissaries to Mongol Eurasia – who compiled eyewitness ethnographies – attested in letter and travel account, chronicle and commentary, annals and encyclopedias, to a mindset in the thirteenth-century Latin West that the Asiatic steppe peoples of the north were anthropophagi.[3]

If, to Latin Christians, Sauma's masters comprised a race of rabid aggressors of repellent aspect and subhuman practices, the Asiatic monk himself belonged to a heretical sect of 'wicked Christians' – in the words of Roger Bacon, thirteenth-century scientist–encyclopedist – whose founder, Nestorius, Patriarch of Constantinople, had been condemned for heresy in 431 by the Council of Ephesus, with his followers subsequently exiled and dispersed across the Eastern world. Indeed, Sauma had earlier been intensely and closely probed, in lengthy disputations with the cardinals of Rome, on key Nestorian deviations from the Latin Christian faith and professions, and had had to assure the cardinals that he journeyed to the West neither to dispute with Latin Christianity nor to proselytize. Performed expressly at Edward's behest, Sauma's oriental Mass with its heretical liturgy culminated in the English king's receiving the Eucharist from the Nestorian emissary of the unclean Tartar empire. After the Mass Edward seized the opportunity, in an extraordinary pronouncement, to declare the unity and undivided oneness of the Christian faith in the countries of the Franks.[4]

Were we to desire an example of unequal English response to alien communities and nations, we need hardly look any further than here, in the English king's benign participation in a heretical sacramental rite – whether as a public act of international diplomacy, or in genuine piety, or both – and his gracious magnanimity to the Nestorian emissary of an empire-mongering race feared and detested in the Latin West. For Edward I of course is historically remembered for legislative and governmental virulence toward another community of aliens with which England transacted – English Jews – and infamous, in particular, for his mass expulsion of the Jews in 1290, scarcely two years after his equable generosity towards the Nestorian representative of the Tartars.

The English king is also memorialized as an energetic crusader against yet another community of the foreign, Muslim infidels; he had refused, as Prince Edward, to be deflected from his crusading mission by his father Henry III, Pope Clement IV, the overwhelming cost of the enterprise, or domestic unrest (Tyerman 1988: 131). On crusade in the Holy Land in 1271, he successfully recaptured Acre, Nazareth and Haifa with little over a thousand men, courageously surviving an Islamic assassin's assault with a poisoned blade the year after; at his death in 1307, the pious king desired that his heart be taken on crusade by English crusaders asked to serve in the Holy Land for a year. If the public actions, legislative policies and official pronouncements of an English monarch may be taken as an index of the temper of the times, what might we then understand of medieval England's widely divergent responses and attitudes to the radically other races and nations it encountered?

In the Jaws of the Nation: Jews, English Identity and the Production of Historical Race

From the late thirteenth century to the fifteenth, the range of English responses to cultural encounters with a variety of racial and religious others becomes historically intelligible when we grasp that the kind of difference represented by each community encountered is subjected to a mechanism of selection that is tacitly in place during the period. This mechanism of selection, which operates on a principle of usefulness to the consolidation of English collective identity, implicitly orders alien nations into a hierarchy of intelligibility that prioritizes among the various forms of difference they represent. A prioritized hierarchy means that some forms of encountered difference are tacitly deemed worthy of engagement for the yields they seem to promise, while other forms of difference are refused, and become useful and of value only by virtue of the process of their exclusion.

In the late thirteenth and fourteenth centuries, a dream of conversion and empire in the Latin West, and the prospective vision of an expansive, universal, Latin Christendom reaching across the globe, made gestures of rapprochement towards the Mongol empire – including unlikely sacramental gestures like the English Edward's – a worthwhile undertaking for pope and monarch alike, and indeed of particular interest to monarchs of outward-looking countries like England that were in the process of calibrating the character, and the range of meanings, of their collective identity and place in the world.

As a race of aliens outside Europe and England – and a global race palpably successful in the creation of a worldwide empire – Mongols were courted, despite their uncanny otherness, not only for their military value as allies against other cultural enemies (in particular, Muslims occupying the Holy Land) but also as a potential threshold in the expansion of Latin Christianity through the conversion of their populations, and for the lure and power of their example as successful globalists and empire-makers. Pope after pope wrote to Mongol khans urging conversion and instruction in the faith, and requested critical support for Catholic missions in Eurasia, West Asia and the Far East; English and French kings exchanged envoys and letters with Mongol khans, with Edward also engaging contingently in military alliances with Abaga Khan from as early as 1271.[5]

But the mechanism of selection that deemed one foreign nation worthy of engagement also operated to exclude other communities of aliens. Most notably, Jews – a community of internal aliens of ambiguous and contradictory status in England – troubled England's aggressively Christian culture of the late thirteenth century, by virtue of both their presence in the English homeland and the intimate interdependence of Christian majority and Jewish minority populations within England's borders. After their fiscal profitability to England's economy had been exhausted through centuries of imposed legislative and governmental exactions, the Jewish minority population of unassimilated internal aliens became of greatest value to the English collectivity, as matters developed, through their forcible expulsion and excision from English life.[6]

English collective identity from the thirteenth to the fifteenth centuries incrementally underwent key transitions. A body of recent historical, sociological and cultural scholarship has concurred in seeing the most important of these transitions as shaped by historical circumstances and cultural forces functioning in tandem to facilitate the emergence of a medieval form of the nation in England (Forde, Johnson and Murray 1995; Heng 2003; Menache 1985; Turville-Petre 1996).[7] The outcome was not an English nation-*state*, in the eighteenth- and post-eighteenth-century sense of that corporate entity, but a medieval configuration of an imagined political community – a community desired and projected by the polity through a range of popular articulations – and that is seen as arching over and across the many internal divides of class, region, status, occupation, language and local interests in the country, so that it is the unity and oneness (rather than the internal fragmentation of the collective community of the English) that is especially emphasized.

Key to the cohesion of an overarching English community otherwise riven by internal conflicts of interest is the outlining of the limits of membership in the privileged community through the specification of those who are outside it, by being demonstrably *not* English: those who are set apart, by virtue of religion, origin, phenotype, language, cultural practices and race, from any prospect of inclusion or belonging. Jews, 'aliens in medieval England to a more profound degree than perhaps anywhere else in western Europe' (Stacey 2000: 166), admirably served the centuries-long consolidation of English identity through the long haul: while they were resident in England; through their very removal from the homeland; and in the centuries afterwards, when the only figures of Jews to be found were those that existed exclusively in the English communal imagination and its wilful cultural creations of murderous, profaning Jewish ideotypes.

That England was obsessively focused on the alien minority in its midst is attested by the overwhelming attention and surveillance accorded to English Jews, so that modern scholars are driven to remark on the 'really exceptional feature of the history of the Jews in England', the oddity of 'how intensely they were recorded by the state: in no other country was a separate government department set up to control specifically Jewish affairs in the way the Jewish Exchequer did in England' (Skinner 2003: 2). English exceptionalism in over-documenting, regulating and controlling Jews concedes, of course, the importance of Jews as economic agents in English life – to crown, monastic houses and populace alike – and an economic dependence on Jewish financial activity that partially accounts for the periodic mob massacres of Jews by the Christian English populace and opportunistic seizure and destruction of records of debt to Jewish financiers.[8] Beyond the economic imperative, however, England's exceptionalism among the countries of Europe also ramified in a variety of ways that were in excess of economic rationality. For England

> is . . . where the new anti-Semitic myths of Jewish greed, filth and diabolism found some of their earliest and most elaborate iconographic representations, on the west front of

> Lincoln Cathedral, for example, and in the famous Cloisters Cross. England was also the first European country to stigmatize its entire Jewish population as coin-clippers and hence criminals . . . England saw the earliest royally sponsored efforts to convert Jews in numbers to Christianity; and in 1290, it witnessed the first permanent expulsion of an entire Jewish community from any European kingdom. (Stacey 2000: 165)

England was the first European nation to require, in 1218, the wearing of the Jewish badge a scant three years after the Fourth Lateran Council's Canon 68 required by fiat that Jews be identified from Christians by a difference of dress. The *tabula* to be worn, a visible marker of Jewish apartness and non-belonging, eloquently testified to the historical project of publicly identifying and naming a minority population that was not to be perceived as part of the national community of the Christian English (Despres 2002: 148; Roth 1964: 95–6). The rapidity with which England moved to administer this instrumental device for specifying difference was not, moreover, an isolated instance.

More durable than the badge was England's early, and thereafter repeated, elaboration of a cultural mechanism that scholars today refer to as the ritual murder libel against the Jews: 'it is notable . . . that the earliest and most frequent accusations of ritual child murder occurred in English settings' (Skinner 2003: 9):

> from the 1140s onwards, hardly a decade passed in which Jews were not accused of ritually murdering a Christian child . . . [Except for] two allegations in northern France . . . the child murder charge does not appear at all before the mid-thirteenth century and remains uncommon even then. It was . . . almost an entirely English enthusiasm. (Stacey 2000: 169)

The expulsion of 1290, it has been said (Menache 1985), was the visible culmination of a process in which medieval nations-in-the-making like England and France rid themselves of an 'Israel of the flesh' – troublingly represented by a living Jewish minority in residence – to facilitate the substitution of an 'Israel of the spirit' represented by the Christian English (or the Christian French) themselves as the new chosen people of God: an imaginative reconfiguration that forms a crucial step in the momentum of medieval nation-making and identity-consolidation. This insight is supported by institutional and cultural manifestations of various kinds. Historically, the creation by Henry III in 1232 of a *domus conversorum* (a hostel for the accommodation of Jewish converts to Christianity) did indeed result in the disappearance of Jews-in-the-flesh, more than half a century before Henry's son's mass expulsion of the community. Conversion, of course, is a form of identity death that ensures the vanishing of Jews – through the transformation of former Jews into new Christians. The conversionist sermons required by Edward I in 1280, which were preached by Dominicans and aimed at turning Jews from Judaism, were further attempts at reducing the presence of Israel-in-the-flesh.[9]

Cultural artefacts also bear witness to other strategic reconfigurations. It has been argued that the Hereford *mappamundi*, created either around the time of the expulsion, c.1290, or slightly later, c.1300,[10] is part of a range of documents that makes an important distinction between the Israelites of the Old Testament, 'who prefigured Christians, yet because of historical necessity could not be Christians' and medieval Jews, 'born after Christ'.[11] The map carefully names and distinguishes by legend the race of biblical Israelites ('populus israel'; 'filiorum Israel') whose most important stories are narrated and linked through textual and pictorial traditions. Post-biblical Jews, by contrast, are not referred to as the people of Israel but as 'Iudei' and are depicted as idolaters, so that the biblical group of Israelites on the Hereford map can be embraced as the predecessors of Christians, even as the group of post-biblical Jews is condemned in the very moment of their naming.[12] Like the Hereford world map, *Mandeville's Travels*, another cultural text that renders an expansive account of global geography, history, cosmology and ethnography, makes a similar distinction between biblical Israelites and post-biblical – medieval – Jews within its own context of the mid- to late fourteenth century, both artefacts in their own ways serving 'medieval nationalism' in the 'construction of [English] identity'.[13]

If 'England was severe in implementing the Fourth Lateran Council's anti-Jewish legislation' (Despres 1994: 415–6) and brutal in the expurgation of an entire community by executive order, the stigmatization of Jews as a vile and malignant race occurred most effectively and durably in the informal realm of culture, rather than in the formal realm of state and canon law. Among the array of cultural instruments advanced against English Jews, the accusation of Jewish ritual murder of innocent Christian boy children of tender years – who were putatively seized, tortured and crucified by Jews in symbolic, purposeful re-enactments of the killing of Christ – has a special status. The accusation of ritual murder accrued ever-greater force through its repeated recitation over generations, involving different children in different cities, and coalesced as a formidable technology of power wielded against English Jews – a technology of power with the ability over time to bring about the legal state execution of English Jews on the basis of a cultural fiction.

Installed in England before anywhere else in Europe, the accusation of ritual murder began in Norwich in 1144 and was repeated at Gloucester in 1168, Bury St Edmunds in 1181, Bristol in 1183 or 1260, Winchester in 1192, 1225 and 1232, London in 1244, the 1260s and 1276, Lincoln in 1255 and Northampton in 1279.[14] Ritual murder stories had a way of transforming the child victims at the centre of the anti-Jewish accusations into child martyrs whose veneration then often produced monastic shrines with ecclesiastical support – devotional sites around which feelings of Christian community could gather, pool and intensify. Seven such shrines were established in England, of which three (at Norwich, Bury and Lincoln) survived till the Reformation (Stacey 2000: 170).[15] Shrines of child martyrs and accusations of ritual murder were thus mutually interactive cultural partners in invented testimony against the Jews, and served in multilayered ways to buttress local, regional and national identities and group purposes.[16] Together they bear witness, in fact, to the power and volitional force of informal mechanisms that narrate communal belief; for they show how, in different ways from formal mechanisms like law, informal cultural instruments marshal group consensus and advance the ends of majority-group power by telling key stories that manipulate affect and emotion.

In August 1255, when the putrefied body of an eight-year-old boy named Hugh, the son of a widow, Beatrice, was discovered in the city of Lincoln, and the Jews of Lincoln were accused of slaughtering the child, the anti-Jewish discourse of ritual murder had been well sedimented in English culture for more than a century. A predictable series of events followed, and on 4 October 1255, by order of Henry III, ninety-one Jews were imprisoned and one person executed for the martyrdom of Hugh; on 22 November, eighteen more Jews were executed, 'drawn through the streets of London before day-break and hung on specially constructed gallows'.[17] Nineteen Jews were thus officially executed – legally murdered – by the state through acts of juridical rationality wielding a discourse of power and affect compiled by communal consent over the generations against a minority target.

When state executions of targeted group victims – victims condemned by community fictions allowed to exercise juridical force through the violence of law – occurred in the *twentieth* century, such official practices have often been understood by historical scholarship to constitute *de facto acts of race* – institutionalized crimes of a sanctioned, legal kind committed by the state against members of a targeted internal population. In the twentieth century, the phenomenon of legalized state violence against target groups within national borders regularly occurred. In the United States, an example might be Franklin Roosevelt's Executive Order 9066, an order that created ten internment camps across seven states for the incarceration of 111,000 Japanese Americans during World War II, on the presumption that Japanese Americans constituted a community of internal aliens who would betray their country, the United States of America, to the enemy nation of Japan in wartime, simply by virtue of their race.

Were we to hold thirteenth-century applications of state power to parallel standards of ethical measurement as twentieth-century applications of state power, we would have to understand that the historical execution – the legal murder – of nineteen Jews in 1255 in England, on the basis of a community belief in Jewish guilt and malignity, constituted an act of *medieval* racism committed by the state against an internal minority population. That scholarship has yet to come to this fundamental acknowledgement attests to the dominance of canonical race studies in the twenty-first century by definitions of race and racisms compiled from historical examples across an overly limited range of historical time (generally, the eighteenth to the twentieth centuries, when questions of skin colour, biology and pseudo-scientific racisms dominated definitions of race and racisms) in the countries of the West. Were we to apply a fundamental working hypothesis of race as *differences that are conceptualized in a strategically invoked essentialism as absolute and fundamental*, and that are *used to distribute powers and positions differentially to human groups* in an historical period, we see that in medieval England the institution of the Jewish badge, the expulsion order and the legal execution of nineteen Jews all bear witness to the consolidation of a community of Christian English – otherwise internally fragmented and ranged along numerous divides – through the exercise of legislative and juridical violence against *a human group that has, on these historical occasions, spectacularly entered into race.*

The example of medieval Jews also helps us to understand the forms of racial law that were in place in the medieval West. Fourth Lateran's Canon 68, mandating that Jews be publicly set apart from the Christian populace by a difference in dress (and facilitating the legal manipulation of Jewish populations in England and Europe) can be seen as a species of racial law that authorizes racial government. Canon 68 arises out of, witnesses and contributes to the rise of a political Christianity in the West that installs an 'internal frontier' within national borders, reinforced by discourses of affect – like ritual murder libel in the story of young Hugh of Lincoln – which mobilize communal fear and hate through stories of race.[18] The gradual coalescence of England's collective character, as a national community united across disparate (but always Christian, and European) peoples, thus pivoted on the political-legal emergence of an abjected Jewish minority *into race*, under forms of racial government supported by political Christianity.[19]

The resilience of ritual murder as a story to be told and retold about English Jews – a story of quintessential Jewish malevolence directed at the vulnerable core of the Christian English *domus* represented by its family life – testifies to the efficacy of cultural mechanisms in harnessing group sentiment satisfactorily. To underscore the story's tenacity, Langmuir tracks the spectacle of Jewish guilt through three thirteenth-century chronicles (Matthew Paris's *Chronica majora* and the Burton and Waverley annals) and an Anglo-Norman ballad, to Chaucer's Prioress's Tale, Marlowe's *Jew of Malta*, the Bollandists in the *Acta sanctorum* of the eighteenth century, and Francis Child's collection of twenty-one divergent versions of the ballad of 'Sir Hugh' or 'The Jew's Daughter' in the nineteenth century. Langmuir notes wryly that, even in 1911, a brochure published in Lincoln still directed people to 'the very well in the Jew's house in which Hugh's body had been thrown'.[20]

In fourteenth- and fifteenth-century England other anti-Jewish fictions also gained in prominence and popularity, and occasionally dovetailed into the story of ritual murder to create finely complex aesthetic hybrids like Chaucer's rendition of Jewish homicide in the Prioress's Tale of the *Canterbury Tales.* Popular anti-Jewish fictions of late medieval England include the Host desecration libel that narrates how Jews covertly acquire and torture the consecrated Host (which bleeds yet remains whole, thus proving the authenticity of eucharistic transubstantiation while foiling attempted deicide) and the story of the 'Jew of Bourges', a Marian miracle tale in which the Virgin poignantly saves a Jewish boy cast into an oven by his own father for having received the Host. Thematically, these fictions efficiently work in late medieval England to buttress faith in eucharistic Real Presence, intensify popular devotion and reinforce the cult of the Virgin. They may feature plot trajectories that end in the pivotal selective conversion of Jews to the Christian faith, the superiority of which is then affirmed as the Christian community itself is enlarged and strengthened, in fiction, by the new recruits.

Whether the plot of Jewish guilt was acted out in public spectacles of community drama (at Corpus Christi, in the *Croxton Play of the Sacrament* and the N-Town *Assumption of the Virgin*) and preached publicly in sermons, or depicted in recreational and devotional materials intended for individual and family use in private reading, meditation and prayer (psalters and books of hours, compendia such as the Vernon manuscript),[21] Jews were thus forced, post-expulsion, to enact and re-enact a set of ritualized gestures in which they were once again identified, marked, punished and relocated outside the English Christian community – or, alternatively and with equal vengefulness, converted and conscripted into that community – but this time in the medium of *culture.*

Thus lodged and ritualized in culture, the gestures of diabolical Jewish guilt, post-expulsion, could be usefully renewed and elaborated, proliferating through a variety of cultural forms, and plotted with local variations, to affirm and witness the legitimacy, authenticity and ultimate solidity of Christian identity, subjectivity and corporate life in England. Whether they are stories of bleeding, suffering Hosts that retain their integrity and wholeness under sacrilegious Jewish torture, dramatic performances of Jews assaulting Mary's bier with the intention of desecrating her body, or miracle tales in which little boy children are hurt by murderous Jews, these rituals of Jewish culpability specialize in eliciting a spectrum of passionate emotional response. Drawing on the dependability of human passions, they tapped an amassed archive of affect in the medieval cultural imagination – pathos, rage, indignant laughter – to unite and pull together the English Christian community, whose collective identity, and devotional and corporate life, were thus sustained by the repeated renaming and re-expulsion of the alien in pious and recreational acts of solidarity.

From *Outremer* to Home: Saracens, Islam, a History of Crusades, and Medieval English Literature

Medieval habits of thinking and understanding by means of analogy, coupled with an historical tendency in the Latin West to perceive conspiracies among infidel nations when Christian territory was invaded, contributed to a mindset, in England as in Europe, that Jews and Muslims in their difference from Christian folk were proximately alike: two alien communities linked by points of resemblance and historical ventures, it was thought, against the West. Examples of endeavours in which Jews were reportedly collaborating with Muslims included the Arab–Berber invasion of Visigothic Spain in 711, Abd-al Rahman's encounter with Charles Martel at Poitiers in 732, the Fatimid Caliph al-Hakim's destruction of the Holy Sepulchre in 1009, and Saladin's resettlement of Jerusalem after its Islamic reconquest in 1187 (Heng 2003: 78–82).[22]

Indeed, the royal physician to Henry I, the Spanish scholar and Jewish convert to Christianity, Petrus Alphonsi, had insinuated in his twelfth-century *Dialogue of Peter and Moses* that Jews had been complicitous in the very creation of Islam, when he suggested that the prophet Muhammad, founder of Islam, had been influenced by a heretical Jew earlier in life. Revealingly, the strictures on dress in Fourth Lateran's Canon 68 were addressed not only to Jews, but to *both* Jews *and* Saracens, as if the two infidel races were halves of a single body of semitic aliens.[23] The association of the infidel *within*

Europe (Jews) and the infidel *without* (Muslims) is manifested in medieval literature with particular vivacity. The thirteenth-century Middle High German *Parzival* sees no contradiction in designating the Sultan of Babylon 'the Baruch', while the late Middle English *Richard Coer de Lyon* accuses Saladin's Muslims of well-poisoning, a favourite anti-Jewish calumny of the fourteenth century, especially during the plague years. Examples of such twinning of Muslims and Jews abound, and Islam has even on occasion been depicted as if it were a species of Judaism, as Paul Olson notes, in pointing out how Islamic law, in Chaucer's Man of Law's Tale, is defined as 'sacrifice', like 'Old Testament Judaism'.[24] Conversely, Judaism is conflated with Islam (often thought to be a pagan religion organized around idolatry) on the Hereford world map:[25] the demon-headed idol in the Near East defecating a string of coins is worshipped by 'Iudei' (dedicated devotees of money), and the idol's name is 'Mahum' (i.e., 'Mahound,' a form of 'Mahomet' which appears to contract the prophet's name and 'hound').

The ability to understand one alien people and their religion as proximately substitutable for another meant that historically, when crusades against Muslims were called out, the projective massacre of the Islamic infidel in the East was preceded by massacres performed on the Jewish infidel in Europe, prior to any arrival in the Holy Land – a phenomenon on display from the First Crusade on.[26] In England, even the coronation of a crusader king, Richard Lionheart, in 1189, occasioned the massacre of Jews at Westminster and London, with the violence spreading to Lynn in Norfolk, Norwich, Stamford and York. The events were celebrated by English chroniclers like Richard of Devizes and William of Newburgh with as much relish as the slaughter of Muslims in Richard's campaigns in the Holy Land.[27]

In the crusades against the Saracens, England's signal role has long been underemphasized, despite the fine scholarly efforts of Tyerman (1988), Lloyd, Luttrell, Keen and others, because it has been overshadowed by the massive documentation on French crusading history in the East.[28] Yet from the inception of the crusading movement, the royal family and ruling caste of England were in the forefront of crusade leaders, with prominent responsibility for the only two crusades that can be considered successful in the interminable history of European hostilities in the Holy Land: the First and the Third. Robert Curthose, eldest son of the Conqueror and heir to the throne of England, was the highest-ranking military leader in the First Crusade, an eleventh-century venture dominated not by royals (although the English contingent included members and relatives of the royal family, including Odo, Bishop of Bayeux, half-brother of the Conqueror, Stephen of Blois, husband to Adèle, daughter of the Conqueror, and Robert and Adèle's cousin, Robert of Flanders), but by baronial Normans from England, France and southern Italy.

The Third Crusade, the other crusading enterprise historically considered effective, at least in ideological and strategic terms, was led by a twelfth-century English king, Richard Lionheart, and Philip Augustus of France (Philip being outperformed militarily, diplomatically and ideologically by the larger-than-life Richard). Despite repeated failures in European crusading in the East thereafter, the deep investment of English royalty and nobility in crusading and the Holy Land endured through the next centuries, rooted in part by historical blood ties between the ruling dynasties of England and Jerusalem. Edward I, a committed thirteenth-century crusader, was genealogically linked, like his forebears and descendants, to the Latin kingdom of Jerusalem through his great-great-grandfather Geoffrey Plantagenet, son of Fulk of Anjou, Jerusalem's third king. In the fourteenth century, chivalric nobles continued to be held up for admiration and emulation because they were crusaders: Henry Grosmont, first Duke of Lancaster and Earl of Derby (and great-grandfather of Henry IV) is praised by John Capgrave as 'the father of knights' by virtue of his extensive crusading missions in the Near East, Prussia, the Mediterranean and Spain.[29] The urgencies and unresolved fate of the Holy Land meant that the crusade, as Maurice Keen puts it, continued to be 'very much in men's minds in England . . . among the highest and most influential in the realm, in the late 1380s and 1390s', and late medieval English knights continued to risk 'body and fortune' in what was 'still widely regarded as the highest expression of chivalrous dedication'.[30] Tyerman, with others, emphasizes the special allure of the Levant through the centuries: 'as a focus of idealism and a goal of ambition, the Holy Land was unrivalled' (1988: 280).

Medieval England's absorption with crusading, Saracens and the Holy Land is of critical importance because, as I show in *Empire of Magic* (Heng 2003), the long history of crusading in the East has been intimately intertwined with the emergence and development of medieval romance – a genre that witnesses some of the finest extant examples of Middle English poetry and prose, including the extraordinary *Sir Gawain and the Green Knight*, the alliterative *Morte Arthure*, *Mandeville's Travels* and Malory's (and Caxton's) *Morte Darthur*. Indeed, Arthurian romance and the King Arthur legend itself, I have argued, first coalesced in literary form in Geoffrey of Monmouth's *History of the Kings of Britain* in 1130–9 as a form of cultural rescue in response to trauma in the First Crusade – the trauma of crusader cannibalism committed on the bodies of Saracens in Syria – which called forth a reconstituted species of cultural fantasy when historical narration, as a genre, faltered in the negotiation of traumatic crisis.[31]

Medieval romance in general, and Arthurian romance in particular, I suggested, developed as a narrative system in which history and fantasy collided and merged, each into the other, without apology, at the precise junctures where both history and fantasy could be mined to best advantage – producing a genre in which historical traumas, crises and pressures could safely be brought into discussion and explored in a medium in which pleasure, not anxiety, was paramount. Out of crusading encounters with the East, Geoffrey's chronicle–romance developed exemplary models, a characteristic vocabulary and a structure of desire that would shape and serve elaborations of medieval romance thereafter. With literature primarily from England in Latin, French and English from the twelfth to the fifteenth centuries as examples, I described how key historical developments in England – the idea of a medieval English nation, crises in knighthood and the encroachment of forms of modernity threatening chivalric feudalism, the rise of conversion and missionizing as alternative forms of conquest to military adventurism, and the expanding sense of an infinitely enlarging world in which England was located – found expressive voice by retelling the history and meaning of the crusades against the Saracens and Islam.

'The Middle Ages', as R. W. Southern observes, 'were the Golden Age of the Islamic problem' (1962: 13), and it should not surprise that Saracens and their religion pervasively inhabit the documents of medieval English culture, both within and outside contexts of crusading. Muslims and Islam are ruminated upon in philosophical and quasi-scientific treatises, encyclopedias, sermons, chronicles, travel literature, allegorical and didactic texts, maps, manuscript illuminations, carvings, collections of tales, drama, poetry and, of course, romances. Saracens appear as warriors and knights, princesses and queens, hybrid monstrosities, giants, idols and false gods, the prophet Muhammad in his various incarnations, priests, magicians, Sultans, nurses, merchants and traders, converts, advisers, mothers-in-law, husbands, travellers, Moors, Turks, black men, legendary pairs of lovers, and even babies. Late medieval English culture also exhibits the full range of descriptions of Islam proffered throughout the Latin Middle Ages as explanatory accounts of the religion, with descriptive traits derived from alternative, even competing, accounts sometimes overlapping. Islam is variously portrayed as a Christian heresy, as a species of paganism, as in some ways resembling Judaism, or as a monotheism in its own right with self-distinguishing features and traditions.

The elaboration of Islam as a Christian heresy is exemplarily represented by Langland's *Piers Plowman* and Higden's *Polychronicon*, where Muhammad is depicted as an ambitious Christian clerk who would be pope (*PP* B 15.390–415, C 18.165–7),[32] and is taken by Muslims for their Messiah (*PP* C 18.159) despite being in reality a false prophet practising witchcraft and necromancy (*Polychronicon* VI, 18–23).[33] Muslims are none the less often seen, in variants of this representation, to share critical common ground with Christians in their love for, and belief in, one God (*PP* B 15.392–4, C 18.132–5), and the view of Islam as a monotheistic offshoot of Christianity acknowledges, in its fashion, commonalities in the heritage of both religions.

By contrast, the depiction of Islam as a polytheistic pagan apparatus turning on idol worship and false gods – a depiction ubiquitous in the popular Middle English 'crusading' or 'Saracen' romances influenced by Old French *chansons de geste* – is an aggressive polemical stance of denigration and dismissal. Romances in the English Charlemagne/Roland cycle, like the *Sultan of Babylon* and *Otuel and Roland*, or hybrid popular fictions like *Bevis of Hampton* and the *King of Tars*, exuberantly feature a multiplicity of Saracen gods and idols (of which four favourites in the pantheon – 'Mahoun', 'Tervagant', 'Appollo/Appolyn' and 'Jove/Jovin' – are commonly invoked by name) and represent a contact zone in culture where the enemy contestant for the Holy Land and their false gods can be defeated in fictional contests functioning as an imaginative correlative to historical crusades. Polytheistic Saracen idols are also visually evoked in manuscript illustrations and carvings,[34] and by the sixteenth century, one scholar remarks, Islam had been furnished with about a dozen deities in this tradition.[35]

Intriguing glimpses also sporadically exist of an Islam accurately represented in its key features beyond any particular resemblance to Christian equivalents or referential relation to Christianity. A remarkable example can be seen in *Mandeville's Travels*, when an accurate transcription of the central Islamic profession of faith ('there is no God but God, and Muhammad is His prophet') is offered by the narrator: 'there is no God but one, and Muhammad [is] his messenger'.[36] Also remarkable in this instance is the direct quotation of the avowal, in which the Arabic designation for God, 'Allah', appears, when the *Travels* attempts the transliterated Arabic, garbling the alien polysyllables only moderately: 'La ellec olla syla Machomet rores alla'.[37] The Arabic designation for God rarely appears, as such, in medieval English literature, even when Muhammad ('Makomete'), the Koran ('Alkaron'), and a monotheistic supreme deity ('grete God') with Muhammad as his prophet ('Goddes message[r]') are accurately invoked (e.g., in Chaucer's Man of Law's Tale, 332–4, 336, 340).

How Islam and Saracens are depicted depends substantially, of course, on the context and purpose of discussion in which the religious foe appears. The daunting magnitude of the international endeavour of crusade and/or conversion of the infidel was analysed in theological, military and political terms in sober treatises, as well as handled with larky insouciance in imaginative literature. Peter the Venerable, who commissioned the first translation of the Koran by the English scholar Robert of Ketton in 1143, and who well understood Islam's global reach, soberly estimated that 'Islam contained a third, or possibly even a half, of the people of the world' (Southern 1962: 43). Roger Bacon, whose knowledge of the strength of the Islamic religion was derived from Islamic intellectual traditions of rational philosophy represented by distinguished intellectuals like Avicenna/Ibn Sina (whose authority Bacon cites as readily as Augustine's and Aristotle's), gloomily lamented in his *Opus maius* of the thirteenth century that there were in reality few Christians, and the world was occupied by infidels.[38]

In medieval English romance, however, a different attitude prevailed, and emirs and sultans, along with their military hordes, were shown to be eminently vanquishable, and their royal heirs (warriors of note) only too ready to consort with the Christian enemy, turn renegade and convert to Christianity. In romance, the younger generation of Islamic nobles, like the redoubtable Ferumbras and Otuel, may possess prowess, dignity and courage – rendering them worthy opponents and highly desirable as recruits – but they are also ever ready to undermine the Islamic patrilineage from which they spring, and their conscription into the ranks of Christianity neatly robs Muslim dynasties of a royal line of succession, at least in literature. Royal daughters and other Saracen princesses, who are invariably beautiful and, as Jacqueline de Weever shows, often *whitened* in the narrative to seem more aesthetically desirable, more potentially, *intrinsically*, European, turn out to be aggressive seductresses who long for the love and bodies of Christian knights, and are unabashedly vocal in articulating their desire.[39] Saracen princesses, too, turn traitor to the Islamic cause, marry the Christian men they single-mindedly court, and cheerfully convert to Christianity. Islamic families, it would seem, can willy-nilly be trusted to disintegrate from within, by themselves, once they encounter Christians, such is the strength of one religion and the weakness of the other. After all, as the *Chanson de Roland* has it, 'pagans are wrong and Christians are right' (1015).

If romance themes of sex and seduction, family betrayal, religious apostasy and Christian military triumph blithely reassure, entertain and speculate, they are also often rounded off with the exhibition of spectacular Saracen monstrosity in the form of Saracen giants: giants who may be depicted as dramatically black, with the head or face of an animal, sexed as female, or possessing giant babies. Like the apostate Saracen warriors and princesses, Saracen giants are invested figures and, accordingly, are awarded individual exotic names (Alagolafre, Estragot and Barrok in the *Sultan of Babylon*, Gulfagor in *Sir Ferumbras*, Ascopart in *Bevis of Hampton*, Amiraunt in *Guy of Warwick*, Baliagog in *Sir Tristrem*, Vernagu in *Roland and Vernagu*) and put on display as exotic exhibits for gawking consumption.[40] Just as the royal apostates who are paraded in their beauty, bloodlines and prowess represent the martial-erotic sublime in the Saracen universe, the monstrous giants in their spectacular extremity anchor the demonic pole of the exotic Saracen panorama (Heng 2003: 284, 448 n. 46, 426 n. 9).

A single Saracen monster is a unique freak of nature, but the repeated materialization of hybrid bestial-human Saracen giants in romance after romance, along with the depiction of she-giants, and giant children – monstrous *families* – is an imaginative argument for the viability of the existence of monstrous races. These giants and their right-sized Saracen human counterparts, moreover, come from everywhere within a heterogeneous, expansive East that spans, but extends beyond, the geopolitical Islamic empire: Alexandria, 'Babylon', Egypt and Ethiopia, in Africa; Ascalon in the Levant; Baghdad in West Asia; Andalusia in the Iberian peninsula; and even India. Converging upon Christian centres from an Islamic 'Orient' that stretches from the West, to the South, to the East, in an encompassing sweep of cardinal points that designate the horizons of the world, Saracens in romance are none the less neatly managed and contained by the military and conversionist strengths of triumphal Christianity.[41]

Global and Cartographic Race: Blackness, Monsters, Tartars and Others in the Mapping of the World

In cultural depictions of Saracens as black (not only giants, but sultans, warriors and other Saracens are singled out for identification in various contexts of medieval English culture as black, or bluish-black, in skin colour) we see how an important discourse on colour, at work in the description of the races of the world, is in the process of stabilizing in England and Europe in the thirteenth to the fifteenth centuries. Saracens are designated as black, of course, because of their infernal religion (the association of blackness with the devil has a cultural history that long antedates this period); and in one fourteenth-century romance, *The King of Tars*, a literal bleaching of skin colour is dramatically depicted when the Saracen Sultan of Damascus converts to Christianity and is baptized. At baptism, the Sultan transforms from being 'black and loathly' and black and 'foul' (*King of Tars*, 928, 799, 393) to 'all white' without any taint (929–30), like his Christian wife the princess of Tars, a fair beauty whose whiteness of skin has been trumpeted early and repeatedly.[42]

Yet another Middle English text of the fourteenth century, the *Cursor mundi*, features a Saracen bleaching that does not even require the sacrament of baptism or the narrative logic of romance. When four Saracens, who are 'black and blue(-black) as lead' (8072) meet King David, and the king holds forth three rods blessed by Moses to kiss, the Saracens transform from black to white on kissing the rods, taking on, we are told, '*the hue of noble blood*' (8119–22, emphasis mine)[43] (Edwards 1992; Kelly 1993). In illuminations, a thirteenth-century Canterbury psalter not only visually represents devils and those possessed by devils as black, but also depicts the vicious-looking executioner of John the Baptist as a black African phenotype – following in this a perceptible artistic development in Europe, from the thirteenth century, of depicting 'executioners and torturers' who harass biblical luminaries, including Christ, as black men with negroid features and hair.[44] With a range of cultural artefacts exhibiting a colour dualism in which white is valued positively, as the colour of the noble-born and Christians, and black is valued negatively, as loathly and foul, and the colour of infernal heathens and killers, the activity of a colour line in medieval culture can be seen to exist – a colour line in which the desirability of whiteness as a central, defining category of group identity is in the ascendant.

Because religion is the dominant discourse, the master-discourse, of the medieval period, the assigning of a hierarchical difference of colour (white over black) to human beings is often decided upon by a hierarchy of religious difference (Christianity over Islam). But nature, operating in the form of environment, climate and the influences of geographical location, can also assign and predispose colour, and Ranulph Higden's *Polychronicon*, Bartholomeus Anglicus's *De proprietatibus rerum* and John Metham's *Physiognomy* are among a number of texts which, following classical tradition, explain that Ethiopians, Moors, Africans, Indians and others are black because of the heat of the sun. However, although natural causes, in medieval theories of climate, physiognomy and environment, may proffer explanations for the blackness of some human races, the *negative value* of blackness is not thereby assuaged, nullified or dissolved by virtue of natural origin and natural explanation so that black and white then become neutral descriptors of human difference and connotatively equal terms. Indeed, Higden's *Polychronicon* insists that the African sun, in making the men of Africa short of body, black of skin and crisp of hair, also makes them cowards at heart, while Europe brings forth men who are fairer of shape, greater of body, mightier of strength, hardier and bolder of heart, since all that lives and grows does better with cold than with heat.[45] *De proprietatibus rerum*, which also observes that cold lands produce white folk and hot lands produce black, similarly insists that white is a visual marker of inner courage, while the men of Africa, possessing black faces, short bodies and crisp hair, are cowards of heart and guileful.[46]

In this anthropological mapping of the world wherein races and populations are geographically identified by location, physically described and then ascribed moral attributes according to their somatic features and geographical habitats, we see the incipience, if not the maturation, of a system of value and meaning in which to be European, Christian, of elite status, and imbued with courage, strength and moral virtue, *is to be white*. The project of European identity-making that is in process from the thirteenth to the fifteenth centuries is vested in a description of the world that anatomizes alien nations, populations and races in ways that would secure and stabilize the moorings of what it means to be Christian and European.

One genre that therefore answers very satisfactorily to the needs of the historical moment is the *mappamundi*, or world map, a genre that spectacularly lends itself in multiple ways to the dissection of the world and its constituent populations. A thirteenth-century English *mappamundi* such as the richly detailed Hereford, with its more than 500 pictures, 420 towns, fifteen biblical events, five scenes from classical mythology, thirty-three plants and animals, and thirty-two peoples of the earth,[47] puts on display the 'cosmological, ethnographic, geographical, historical, theological and zoological state of the world',[48] in significant part by the insertion of distinctive objects, legends and peoples that it locates into place as stakeholders for the meaning of a site. Europe is ubiquitously visualized on the Hereford in this way by architectural features such as fortifications and cathedrals – the built environment that symbolizes advanced civilization – and bordered by natural features such as rivers (figure 15.1).

Outside Europe, however, place is often represented as ethnography and zoology, with regions being identified as the habitat of peoples and animals that are distinctive by virtue of their difference. Each vector of the world is thus made visible and projected on the map through a landscape identified by its relative distance from Europe in *human and cultural*, as well as spatial, terms. In its most grotesque and spectacular forms, cartographic race on *mappaemundi* is equated with the monstrous races of malformed, bestial or hybrid populations located by the Hereford and other English *mappaemundi*, like the Duchy of Cornwall and Psalter maps, in Asia and Africa,[49] lands which teem with human monsters of many kinds (figure 15.2). Very palpably on these maps, the depiction of pygmies, giants, hermaphrodites, cynocephali, sciapods, troglodytes, panotii, blemmyae and other malformations of the human inherited from classical tradition harnesses the inheritance of the ancient past to a late medieval survey and dissection of the world that reflects on the meaning and borders of European self-identity and civilization. Race appears on the map, outside Europe, and pressing on the edges of the Latin West.

Though much has been written on a uniquely medieval sense of the marvellous that celebrated 'wondrous diversity' through prolific depictions of freaks and monsters in literature, art and cartography, the insistence that medieval absorption with freakery and monstrosity differs from modern absorption should not suggest to us that medieval pleasure would therefore be of a simply and wholly innocent kind. We see that Gerald of Wales's depiction of Ireland as the habitat of monstrosities and barbarities of diverse, wondrous kinds, in his *Topography of Ireland*, compiles a highly interested anatomy of Ireland that serves the purposes of twelfth-century Anglo-Norman elites embarked on the colonial project of subjugating an Ireland conveniently represented as in need of England's civilizing influence and normality.

Scott Westrem and others have also underscored how one particular monstrous race singled out in late medieval descriptions of the world like *Mandeville's Travels* – the

Figure 15.1 Western Europe, from the Hereford *mappamundi*: Hereford Cathedral Library, MS. (By permission of the Dean and Chapter of Hereford Cathedral and the Hereford Mappa Mundi Trust.)

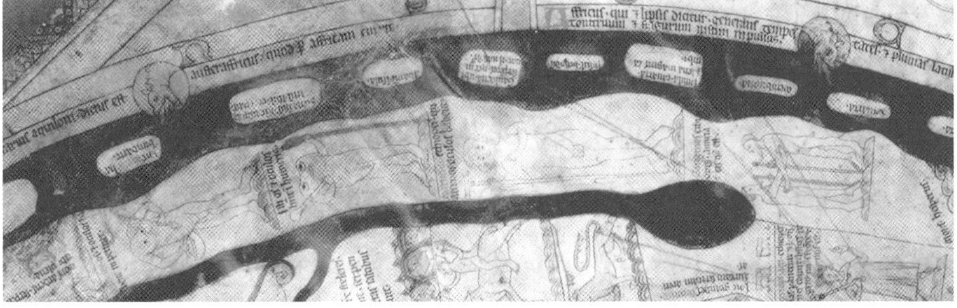

Figure 15.2 The monstrous races, from the Hereford *mappamundi*: Hereford Cathedral Library, MS. (By permission of the Dean and Chapter of Hereford Cathedral and the Hereford Mappa Mundi Trust.)

unclean monstrous race of cannibals traditionally supposed to have been enclosed by Alexander the Great behind a barrier of mountains in north-west Asia, bordering Europe – are identified with medieval *Jews*, also defined as unclean and monstrous by virtue of the blood libel against them.[50] The eschatological tradition that these enclosed unclean descendants of Cain would break forth in the last days of the world to war on Christendom, often supported by the very tangibility of the creatures visibly marked out on *mappaemundi*, is thus a racial script whose sub-theme, in marking Jews as one of the monstrous races, presents them as a perennial, looming threat to Christian Europe, and whose ultimate malignity would only be hideously realized at the end of time. Finally, if there is a symbolic evocation, on the Hereford *mappamundi*, of the relationship between race and chaos, it would be located in the largest single edifice on the map: an imposing Tower of Babel, key image in the biblical narrative of the fabulous origin of proliferating human diversity, and a resonant figure of incommensurate and unassimilable differences among human populations. Babel is a looming architectural presence that towers above the castles and cathedrals, the built environment, of civilized Europe.

Cartographic and imaginary race ultimately issues a grid through which the European cultural imagination perceives and understands global races and the alien nations of the world. Gregory Guzman (1991) details how a race of Tartars, disseminating from Central Asia, was understood by authors in the Latin West, including Matthew Paris, through a conceptual grid, supplied by classical authors, of the monstrous cannibal races of the world and their geographic locations. Equated, then, with the imaginary race of cannibalistic monsters cartographically located in north-west Asia, are historical races: Jews (in *Mandeville's Travels*), Tartars (in the *Chronica majora* of Matthew Paris) and Turks (in the Hereford *mappamundi*).[51] The 'Monstrous Races tradition', as Debra Strickland's recent art-historical study puts it, 'provided the ideological infrastructure' for ruminating on and understanding 'other types of "monsters", namely Ethiopians, Jews, Muslims, and Mongols' (2003: 42). Even our four marvellously black Saracens who meet with King David and undergo a wondrous cutaneous transformation, in the encyclopedic Middle English *Cursor mundi*, are pointedly not only Saracens bearing great riches, but also ambassadors from a monstrous race: with their mouths located in their chests (8078), they are a subpopulation of the blemmyae, a favourite race of freaks described in English literature as early as the tenth-century Old English *Wonders of the East* (section 15), whose early medieval survey of the world also located and described Ethiopians (section 32).[52]

Race – whether imaginary, or historically grounded, determined by religion, nature or geographical-environmental conditions – is what the rest of the world has. The utility of race in the late medieval period, made visible and projected through a variety of cultural forms, answers well in this time to the specification of an authorized range of meanings for Christian, European identity, the disarticulation of that identity from its founding genealogies like Judaism, and the securing of new moorings (including imperial moorings, launched by missionizing and conversion efforts across the globe) apposite to the historical moment. The field of forces within which *homo europaeus* appears in the late Middle Ages overlaps, thus, with the grid in which racial thinking is made. The consequences, in the final analysis, can be political: as the Bishop of Winchester says on the subject of Tartars and Saracens, and as Matthew Paris reports, England (and by extension, Europe) should leave the dogs to devour one another, so that they may all be consumed and perish; and when Latin Christians proceed against those who remain, they will slay the enemies of Christ and cleanse the face of the earth, so that the entire world will be subject to one catholic church (III, 489).

Yet, extrapolating from the Bishop of Winchester's darkly savage military humour, the conversionist dreams and projects of popes in the fourteenth and fifteenth centuries, and the avid interest of cultural texts in the skin colour of Christian Europeans and an elite membership of noble blood, it would also be true to say that race makes an appearance in the late Middle Ages not only through fantasmatic blacks, historical Jews and the collections of hybrid humans pressing upon the edges of civilization, but can also be found at the centre of things, in the creation of that strange creature who is nowhere, yet everywhere, in cultural discourse: the white Christian European in medieval time.

See also: 2 English Society in the Later Middle Ages, 16 War and Chivalry, 20 Middle English Romance, 21 Writing Nation, 37 *Sir Gawain and the Green Knight*, 38 Malory's *Morte Darthur*.

Notes

1 Peter Brown, 'Higden's Britain', in *Medieval Europeans: Studies in Ethnic Identity and National Perspectives in Medieval Europe*, ed. Alfred P. Smyth (Basingstoke: Macmillan, 1998), pp. 103–18, (p. 110).

2 Henry Richards Luard (ed.), *Matthæi Parisiensis monachi sancti Albani, chronica majora*, 7 vols, Rolls ser. 57 (1872–84), III, 488–9.

3 Guzman 1991 lists six Latin writers who expound on the cannibalism in thirteenth-century documents.

4 James A. Montgomery (trans.), *The History of Yaballaha III* (New York: Columbia University Press, 1927), pp. 59, 65–6; Sir E. A. Wallis Budge (trans.), *The Monks of Kublai Khan Emperor of China* (London: Religious Tract Society, 1928), pp. 177, 186–7.

5 See Simon Lloyd, *English Society and the Crusade 1216–1307* (Oxford: Clarendon Press, 1988), pp. 240–50; James Muldoon, *Popes, Lawyers, and Infidels: The Church and the Non-Christian World 1250–1550* (Philadelphia: University of Pennsylvania Press, 1979), pp. 78–85, 92–6; Christopher Dawson (ed.), *Mission to Asia*, Medieval Academy Reprints for Teaching, 8 (Toronto: University of Toronto Press, 1980); Heng 2003: 269, 272–4.

6 James Shapiro, *Shakespeare and the Jews* (New York: Columbia University Press, 1996), p. 42.

7 See Claus Bjørn, Alexander Grant and Keith Stringer (eds), *Nations, Nationalism, and Patriotism in the European* Past (Copenhagen: Academic Press, 1994); and also David B. Leshock, 'Religious Geography: Designating Jews and Muslims as Foreigners in Medieval England', in *Meeting the Foreign in the Middle Ages*, ed. Albrecht Classen (New York: Routledge, 2002), pp. 202–25; Geraldine Heng, 'The Romance of England: *Richard Coer de Lyon*, Saracens, Jews, and the Politics of Race and Nation', in *The Postcolonial Middle Ages*, ed. Jeffrey Jerome Cohen (New York: St Martins Press, 2000), pp. 135–71; Diane Speed, 'The

Construction of the Nation in Middle English Romance', in *Readings in Medieval English Romance*, ed. Carole M. Meale (Cambridge: Brewer, 1994), pp. 135–57.

8 Roger of Howden and Roger of Wendover, for instance, document the burning of debt papers in the anti-Jewish attacks following Richard I's ascension to the English throne: William Stubbs (ed.), *Chronica magistri Rogeri de Houedene*, 4 vols, Rolls ser. 51 (1868–71), III, 33–4; Henry G. Hewlett (ed.), *Rogeri de Wendover liber qui dicitur Flores historiarum ab anno domini MCLIV annoque Henrici Anglorum regis secundi primo*, 3 vols, Rolls ser., 84 (1886–9), I, 176–7.

9 Cf. John Edwards, 'The Church and the Jews in Medieval England', in Skinner 2003: 85–95; and Anthony Bale, 'Fictions of Judaism in England before 1290', in Skinner 2003: 129–44 (143–4).

10 Scott Westrem, *The Hereford Map: A Transcription and Translation of the Legends with Commentary* (Turnhout: Brepols, 2001), p. xv.

11 Leshock, 'Religious Geography', pp. 205, 212.

12 Ibid., pp. 211–12.

13 Ibid., pp. 219, 205, 202.

14 See Robert C. Stacey, 'From Ritual Crucifixion to Host Desecration: Jews and the Body of Christ', *Jewish History* 12.1 (1998), 11–27 (23); Gavin Langmuir, 'The Knight's Tale of Young Hugh of Lincoln', *Speculum* 47 (1972), 459–82 (462–3); *Encyclopedia Judaica*, 17 vols (Jerusalem: Keter, 1972–82), IV, 1122 and VI, 748.

15 Cf. Stacey 2000: 168–9; Gavin Langmuir, 'Thomas of Monmouth: Detector of Ritual Murder', *Speculum* 59 (1984), 820–45; Anthony P. Bale, '"House Devil, Town Saint": Anti-Semitism and Hagiography in Medieval Suffolk', in Delany 2002: 185–210 (186); Bale, 'Fictions of Judaism' pp. 133, 136.

16 Cf. Stacey, 'From Ritual Crucifixion', pp. 21–4 for a nuanced reading of the tale of the boy martyr, Adam of Bristol (c.1260).

17 Langmuir, 'Knight's Tale', pp. 477–9.

18 Etienne Balibar and Immanuel Wallerstein, *Race, Nation, Class: Ambiguous Identities* (London: Verso, 1991).

19 Cf. Langmuir, 'Knight's Tale', p. 479; Colin Richmond, 'Englishness and Medieval Anglo-Jewry', in Delany 2002: 213–27 (224–5).

20 Langmuir, 'Knight's Tale', p. 460.

21 Cf. Despres 1996, 2002; her 'Immaculate Flesh and the Social Body: Mary and the Jews', *Jewish History* 12 (1998), 46–69.

22 See also W. Montgomery Watt and Pierre Cachia, *A History of Islamic Spain* (Edinburgh: Edinburgh University Press, 1965), pp. 12, 14, 32; Allen Harris Cutler and Helen Elmquist Cutler, *The Jew as Ally of the Muslim: Medieval Roots of Anti-Semitism* (Notre Dame: Indiana University Press, 1986), pp. 87, 93; Heng, 'Romance of England', pp. 142–5; Steven Runciman, *A History of the Crusades*, 3 vols (Cambridge: Cambridge University Press, 1951), II, 467.

23 On the etymology of 'Saracen' see, e.g., Norman Daniel, *The Arabs and Medieval Europe* (London: Longman, 1975), p. 53.

24 Paul A. Olson, *The Canterbury Tales and the Good Society* (Princeton, N.J.: Princeton University Press, 1986), p. 94.

25 Westrem, *Hereford Map*, pp. 121, 123, maps 3, 7, 8.

26 Shlomo Eidelberg (ed. and trans.), *The Jews and the Crusaders: The Hebrew Chronicles of the First and Second Crusades* (Madison: University of Wisconsin Press, 1977).

27 John T. Appleby (ed.), *Cronicon Richardi Divisensis de tempore regis Richardi primi* (Toronto: Nelson, 1963), pp. 3–4; William of Newburgh, *Historia rerum Anglicarum*, ed. Richard Howlett, Rolls ser., 82, 4 vols (1884–9), I, 294–9, 308–22.

28 Lloyd, *English Society*; Anthony Luttrell, 'English Levantine Crusaders, 1363–1367', *Renaissance Studies* 2:2 (1988), 143–53; Maurice Keen, 'Chaucer's Knight, the English Aristocracy, and the Crusade', in *English Court Culture in the Later Middle Ages*, ed. V. J. Scattergood and J. W. Sherborne (London: Duckworth, 1983), pp. 45–62.

29 F. C. Hingeston (ed.), *Liber de illustribus Henricis*, Rolls ser. 7 (1858), p. 161.

30 Keen, 'Chaucer's Knight', pp. 57, 60.

31 Geraldine Heng, 'Cannibalism, the First Crusade, and the Genesis of Medieval Romance', *differences* 10:1 (1998), 98–174.

32 William Langland, *The Vision of Piers Plowman: A Critical Edition of the B-Text*, ed. A. V. C. Schmidt, 2nd edn (London: Dent, 1995); *Piers Plowman by William Langland: An Edition of the C-text*, ed. Derek Pearsall (London: Arnold, 1978).

33 *Polychronicon Ranulphi Higden monachi Cestrensis*, ed. Churchill Babington and Joseph Rawson Lumby, 9 vols, Rolls ser. 41 (1865–86).

34 Michael Camille, *The Gothic Idol: Ideology and Image-making in Medieval Art* (Cambridge: Cambridge University Press, 1989).

35 James A. Bellamy, 'Arabic Names in the *Chanson de Roland*: Saracen Gods, Frankish Swords, Roland's Horse, and the Olifant', *Journal of the American Oriental Society* 107 (1987), 267–77 (268–9). Cf. Melitzki 1977.

36 George F. Warner (ed.), *The Buke of John Maundeuill* (London: Roxburghe Club, 1889), p. 71; P. Hamelius (ed.), *Mandeville's Travels*, vol. 1, EETS os 153 (1919), p. 92.

37 Ibid. In the Egerton manuscript, the avowal quoted is slightly more latinate: 'La elles ella sila Machomet rores alla hec' (ed. Warner, p. 71). Both Cotton and Egerton are missing one reference to Allah in the original Arabic, and resemble imperfectly heard and mimicked quotations. In Arabic, the profession of faith is: 'La illaha illa Allah wa Muhammad rasul [*messenger*] Allah' (Arabic transliteration by courtesy of my Islamicist colleague Denise Spellberg).

38 John Henry Bridges (ed.), *The Opus majus of Roger Bacon*, 3 vols. (Oxford: Clarendon Press, 1897–1900), III, 122.

39 Jacqueline de Weever, *Sheba's Daughters: Whitening and Demonizing the Saracen Woman in Medieval French Epic* (New York: Garland, 1998).

40 See Melitzki 1977; but also Alice Lasater, *Spain to England: A Comparative Study of Arabic, European, and English Literature of the Middle Ages* (Jackson: University of Mississippi Press, 1974); and Maria Rosa Menocal, *The Arabic Role in Medieval Literary History* (Philadelphia: University of Pennsylvania Press, 1987) on the transmission of Arabic culture from Spain.

41 David Lawton, 'History and Legend: The Exile and the Turk', in *Postcolonial Moves: Medieval through Modern*, ed. Patricia Clare Ingham and Michelle R. Warren (New York: Palgrave, 2003), 173–94 (p. 192).

42 Judith Perryman (ed.), *The King of Tars* (Heidelberg: Winter, 1980).

43 *Cursor mundi*, ed. Richard Morris, 7 vols, EETS as 57, 59, 62, 66, 68, 99, 101 (1879–93).

44 Jean Devisse, *The Image of the Black in Western Art*, vol. 2 (New York: Morrow, 1979), pp. 70–5 and figs. 24, 25.

45 Ed. Babington and Lumby, I, 50–3.

46 *On the Properties of Things: John's Trevisa's Translation of* Bartholomaeus Anglicus De Proprietatibus Rerum, ed. M. C. Seymour et al., 3 vols (Oxford: Clarendon Press, 1975–88), II, 752–3, 763. Cf. Strickland 2003: 38–9.

47 Evelyn Edson, *Mapping Time and Space: How Medieval Mapmakers Viewed their World* (London: British Library, 1997), p. 142.

48 Westrem, *Hereford Map*, p. xv.

49 Catherine Delano-Smith and Roger J. P. Kain, *English Maps: A History* (Toronto: University of Toronto Press, 1999), p. 39.

50 Scott Westrem, 'Against Gog and Magog', in *Text and Territory: Geographical Imagination in the European Middle Ages*, ed. Sylvia Tomasch and Sealy Gilles (Philadelphia: University of Pennsylvania Press, 1998), pp. 54–75.

51 Westrem, *Hereford Map*, p. 137, map 4.

52 *Three Old English Prose Texts*, ed. Stanley Rypins, EETS os 161 (1924).

References and Further Reading

Daniel, Norman 1993. *Islam and the West: The Making of an Image*, rev. edn. Edinburgh: Edinburgh University Press. Classic, foundational study on Western understanding of Islam; highly influential and much cited in scholarship.

Delany, Sheila (ed.) 2002. *Chaucer and the Jews: Sources, Contexts, Meanings*. New York: Routledge. Useful new resource on the subject of Chaucer and Jews; includes a chapter on the emergence of a 'virtual' Jew in post-expulsion English culture.

Despres, Denise 1994. 'Cultic Anti-Judaism and Chaucer's Litel Clergeon.' *Modern Philology* 91, 413–27. Key article on late medieval eucharistic culture and the Jews.

—— 1996. 'Mary of the Eucharist: Cultic Anti-Judaism in Some Fourteenth-Century English Devotional Manuscripts.' In *From Witness to Witchcraft: Jews and Judaism in Medieval Christian Thought*, ed. Jeremy Cohen (Wiesbaden: Harrassowitz), pp. 375–401. An important essay on Marian miracle tales and anti-Jewish sentiment.

—— 2002. 'The Protean Jew in the Vernon Manuscript.' In Delany 2002: 145–64. A crucial essay on how devotional manuscripts and books of private reading create intentional communities bound by anti-Jewish sentiment.

Edwards, Paul 1992. 'The Early African Presence in the British Isles.' In *Essays on the History of Blacks in Britain: From Roman Times to the Mid-Twentieth Century*, ed. Jagdish S. Gundara and Ian Duffield (Aldershot: Avebury), pp. 9–29. On the historical presence of black Africans in the British Isles in Roman Britain and in the fourteenth to the sixteenth centuries.

Forde, Simon, Johnson, Lesley and Murray, Alan V. (eds.) 1995. *Concepts of National Identity in the Middle Ages*. Leeds Texts and Monographs, ns 4. Leeds: University of Leeds, School of English. Wide-ranging anthology, including a state-of-the-art discussion of the subject of medieval nations and nationalisms.

Giffney, Noreen 2003. 'Que(e)rying Mongols.' *Medieval Feminist Forum* 36, 15–21. An essential bibliographical resource on Mongols.

Guzman, Gregory G. 1991. 'Reports of Mongol Cannibalism in the Thirteenth-Century Latin Sources: Oriental Fact or Western Fiction?' In *Discovering New Worlds: Essays on Medieval Exploration and Imagination*, ed. Scott Westrem (New York: Garland), pp. 31–68. Pivotal essay on how inherited traditions from antiquity formed an interpretative grid through which Mongols were rendered intelligible to medieval Europe.

Heng, Geraldine 2003. *Empire of Magic: Medieval Romance and the Politics of Cultural Fantasy*. New York: Columbia University Press. Study on the interrelationship of the crusades and medieval romance, with chapters on race, medieval nation-making and Europe's relationship to the Near East, Eurasia, India and China.

Kelly, Kathleen Ann 1993. '"Blue" Indians, Ethiopians, and Saracens in Middle English Narrative Texts.' *Parergon* ns 11.1, 35–52. Important article discussing varieties of skin colour as indicators of race in Middle English narratives.

McCulloh, John 1997. 'Jewish Ritual Murder: William of Norwich, Thomas of Monmouth, and the Early Dissemination of the Myth.' *Speculum* 72, 698–740. Comprehensive discussion of the ritual murder accusation in England, with a judicious reconsideration of hypotheses of the myth's provenance.

Melitzki, Dorothee 1977. *The Matter of Araby in Medieval England*. New Haven, Conn.: Yale University Press. Still the best book-length resource on matters 'Arabian' and Islamic in medieval English culture, literature and intellectual life, with almost two-thirds of the volume devoted to literature and literary analysis.

Menache, Sophia 1985. 'Faith, Myth, and Politics: The Stereotype of the Jews and their Expulsion from England and France.' *Jewish Quarterly Review* 75, 351–74. An indispensable article on how the English and French conceptualized themselves as national peoples through the expulsion of Jews.

Roth, Cecil 1964. *A History of the Jews in England*, 3rd edn. Oxford: Clarendon Press. Still the standard essential study on the history of Jews in England from the Conquest to the nineteenth century.

Skinner, Patricia (ed.) 2003. *The Jews in Medieval Britain: Historical, Literary and Archaeological Perspectives*. Woodbridge: Boydell Press. Excellent new resource on Jews in Medieval England; extends across a variety of topics.

Southern, R. W. 1962. *Western Views of Islam in the Middle Ages*. Cambridge, Mass.: Harvard University Press. Short, useful study (originally a series of lectures) on formative stages in medieval European understanding of Islam; accessible and engaging.

Stacey, Robert C. 2000. 'Anti Semitism and the Medieval English State.' In *The Medieval State:*

Essays Presented to James Campbell, ed. J. R. Maddicott and D. M. Palliser (London: Hambledon), pp. 163–77. Trenchant, pivotal study of the role played by Jews in medieval nation (and state) formation: an indispensable essay.

Strickland, Debra Higgs 2003. *Saracens, Demons, and Jews: Making Monsters in Medieval Art*. Princeton, N.J.: Princeton University Press. Important new art-historical study on 'monstrous races' and historical Jews, Saracens and Mongols; surveys a broad spectrum of art.

Tolan, John 2002. *Saracens: Islam in the Medieval European Imagination*. New York: Columbia University Press. Excellent new study, with chapters on Spain, the Crusades, the friars and Eastern Christian reactions to Islam.

Turville-Petre, Thorlac 1996. *England the Nation: Language, Literature, and National Identity 1290–1340*. Oxford: Clarendon Press. Indispensable study on medieval English nationalism and the critical role of language and literature.

Tyerman, Christopher 1988. *England and the Crusades, 1095–1588*. Chicago: University of Chicago Press. Superbly comprehensive historical survey on medieval England and the crusades.

PART V
Special Themes

16
War and Chivalry

Richard W. Kaeuper and Montgomery Bohna

Chivalry and war strongly marked the literature and culture of medieval England as of north-west Europe generally. Lay folk of privileged status shaped their sense of their rights and their social and cultural role through chivalric ideas. In a complex, hierarchical, religious and turbulent society, knights negotiated their connections with violence, piety, honour, status, love and gender relationships through chivalry. Warfare, the *raison d'être* of both the lay elite and chivalry itself, was also endemic to Europe throughout the later Middle Ages; however, one conflict in particular characterized the era for contemporaries and historians: the prolonged wars between France and England collectively called the Hundred Years War (1337–1453). Seeking to understand these powerful forces this chapter moves gradually from the world of ideology out to the countryside and the battlefield, exploring the chivalric framework, literary comments on war, the technical medieval literature of war in both France and England, and finally the modern debate about the conduct and consequences of war.

Chivalric Ideology[1]

The great danger in the study of chivalry as a force in society and a theme in literature is the all but irresistible tendency to read history backwards. The problem, of course, arises from the refusal of chivalry to die out decently with the close of the Middle Ages. It lived on stubbornly in survivals and revivals well into the Victorian era and beyond. Thus we may erroneously come to view medieval chivalry through Victorian lenses, imagining it to be the sort of social force Victorians wanted it to be, a pure force for good in the world, a force that civilized and socialized the rougher side of men, subordinating violence to order, increasing piety, and enforcing what the Victorians would have termed a proper respect for women. Chivalry can even be mistakenly reduced to little more than an idealized code of courtly love. If any of these ideals seem lacking when we dip into medieval texts, we deplore the 'decline of chivalry' in the very age in which it flourished.

If we actually study the literature that conveys chivalric ideals before we decide what chivalry was, a more complex and interesting picture emerges. The chivalry of the Middle Ages may not even consist entirely of qualities we can admire. It was the tough warrior code of the lay aristocracy. Tensions, complications and even contradictions are only to be expected and should make us cautious about asserting what 'ideal chivalry' inevitably had to say about warfare, women, piety, or a host of other topics. Textbook lists of ideal qualities – largess, courtliness, prowess, service to ladies and the like – are not so much wrong as inadequate. They fail to reveal the stresses within knights or the uneasiness over their role in a rapidly developing society. We can gain a better sense of the complexities by examining the centrality of prowess and then turning to love and piety, evaluating the common conception that these gentler qualities counterbalanced the unruly vigour of prowess.

The Centrality of Prowess

The one quality we can be sure to find near the centre of any discussion of chivalry in later medieval English literature and culture is prowess, or rather prowess double-bonded with honour, usually termed *worship*. Prowess was the glorious means to win honour, the glorious good. Any scholarly list of half a dozen chivalric components without emphasis on the centrality of this linked pair cuts the pounding heart out of chivalry.

Repeatedly, prowess is virtually equated with chivalry. Even if other traits are admired, a man must have prowess to count. Havelok's regality shows in his birthmark and mysterious light; his prowess shows his knighthood (2042–3, 2187–8, 2314).[2] *Lancelot of the Laik* announces that largess must be given first to those who show prowess and just such men are considered the most qualified to be king's counsellors (1705–8, 1718–20).[3] As soon as a character appears in a text the readers or hearers are assured that he does, in fact, possess the requisite prowess. We meet the father of the eponymous hero in *Perceval of Galles*, for example, and are at once given nearly 150 lines assuring us of his prowess (15–152).[4] Isumbras, Eglamour, and Robert of Cisyle must be satisfied by more concise credentials in their romances, but the same valorization appears (*Isumbras* 8–12; *Eglamour* 4–12; *Robert of Cisyle* 9–15).[5] Malory has Merlin tell Arthur of his relatives beyond the sea, Ban and Bors, noting that they are both kings but quickly also assuring him that they are 'marveillous good men of her handes' (13).[6] Not long thereafter, Arthur assures Ban he has witnessed his 'dedys full actuall' (23). Bevis of Hampton, leaving his young son to the care of a forester, gives only this advice for his education (1743–4): 'Right sone as he is of eld, / Tech him bere spere and schelde!' The dying Duke of Normandy in *The Siege of Milan* wants his son to 'hawkes and houndes forgo / And to dedis of armes hym doo' (307–8) so that he can avenge his father on the Saracens.[7] Charlemagne in *The Sultan of Babylon* urges young knights to learn the essentials from the experienced:

For worthynesse wol not be hadde,
But it be ofte soughte,
Nor knighthode wole not ben hadde,
Tille it be dere boughte.
Therefore ye knightes yonge of age,
Of oolde ye may now lere,
How ye shalle hurle and rage
In felde with sheelde and spere . . .
To wynnen honourys in righte
(923–30, 934).[8]

Chivalric praise won at spearpoint (*Ywain and Gawain* 45),[9] as authors of romance insist, is innate in knights and proves their nobility.[10] The lady being rescued by Ywain's prowess in *Ywain and Gawain* notes that he kills at every stroke and exclaims, 'yon es a nobil knyght' (1884, 1892–3). Sir Eglamour's squire, responding to his lord's question whether he has suffered any dishonour, links nobility with prowess in his response:

Ye ar on of the noblest knyghth
That ys knowen in Cristyanté.
In dede of armes, be God on lyve,
Ye are counted worth othur fyve.
(92–5)

In other words, chivalry is in an important sense physical – it can be *done* by hands-on prowess. The young Horn insists that he will 'do pruesse' in the field before he can woo Rymenhild (*King Horn* 560).[11] William of Palerne, thrusting himself into the thick of the fight, 'blessed' many of his foe 'with his ownne hond' (1192, 1195).[12] John Lydgate regularly pictures what he terms the manly quality of prowess in just such terms. He praises Troilus for his ferocity that none could withstand 'Whan that he hilde his bloodly swerde on hond' (*Troy Book* 4886).[13] 'And his knyghthod schortly to acounte,' Lydgate continues, 'Ther myght in manhod no man him surmounte' (4889–90). In the grand tournament at Logres, in the *Prose Merlin*, 'men myght se many feire chevalries don on bothe parties' and Merlin declares that Arthur has given proof he 'is right a worthi man, and a gode knyght shall he be of his honde' (pp. 94–5, 101).[14] Of the young squires (just becoming Arthurian heroes) Merlin proclaims, 'And thei have doon many feire chivalries and yoven many grete strokes that thei ought to be commended and preised of all the worlde' (168). Even when magic has temporarily reduced him to a dwarf later in this romance, Gawain 'dide many prowesses, for though he were a duerf and mysshappen, he hadde not loste his strengthe nether his hardinesse, and many a knyght he conquered' (325).

Our image of this prowess done cannot be accurate if it is sanitized or bowdlerized into moral courage alone or pictured as pre-Raphaelite images of romantic strife. Courage indeed was required, but the blood-spilling carnage of fighting with edged weapons must be kept in mind for it is portrayed and even celebrated in chivalric literature. Havelok, defending a house against robbers, has twenty wounds head to toe and bleeds like water from a well, but mows down his enemies (1776–1920). The newly knighted Horn slays more Saracens than can be counted and returns with their chief's head on the point of his sword (609–48). In *Isumbras* the hero hits one opponent so hard his eyes 'styrten out' (608). The final fight of this text slaughters precisely 20,003 Saracens and 'Gret joye it was to see' (737–41). Guy of Warwick not only regularly kills with the standard lance and sword, he can also employ his fist alone, a staff grabbed from a passing stranger, his hunting horn, or an axe that comes to hand (A 5325–6, A 5744, A 6807–8, A 6893–6, A 5789–90).[15] With knightly weapons he and other manly heroes not only sever heads from trunks horizontally at the neck, they cleave even armoured enemy heads vertically to the eyes or the chin; with better effort they cut the body to the belt or right through entirely (e.g., *Guy of Warwick* 1394, 1398, 2957; *Sir Tryamour* 308–9;[16] *Prose Merlin* pp. 89, 106, 128–9, 133, 146). Trophy heads of enemies are often presented to superiors. Lancelot, in *Lancelot of the Laik*, shows good form: 'Fro sum the arm, fro sum the nek in two; / Sum in the feild lying in swoun, / And sum his suerd goith to the belt al dounne' (1098–100). Such blows (which increase Arthur's love, according to the *Stanzaic Morte Arthure* (500–3)[17] are termed in this text a 'marvell' and 'wonderis' (3175, 3180), and such language is often found. It is used by Lydgate for whom manliness is proved by actions such as those of the embattled Hector who 'began / Armys, leggis, shuldres, by the boon, / To hewen of amyd his mortal foon' (884–6).

Such chopping seems to be valued as a good in itself. It is also efficacious; after all, it achieves closure in any dispute. Reasoning unsentimentally with her lady, the widow of the Storm Knight who has been killed by Ywain in *Ywain and Gawain*, Lunette makes a strongly pragmatic case: if two knights fight and one kills the other, is he not the better man (999–1002)? Most issues in the romances of this period are settled by the fighting of knights. Greater prowess even resolves the case on behalf of the god of the victorious warrior, as in *The Sultan of Babylon* (1308–26) or *The Siege of Milan* (where God blows the fire applied by the Sultan to a crucifix into the offender's eyes and then Roland splits him to the waist with a great falchion: 406–86).[18] At the end of *Lybeaus Desconus*, the hero seems threatened by a different kind of fight altogether. Two 'clerks' have imprisoned the lady he must rescue and have already used their sorcery to build a fantastic apparition of a palace, to cause an earthquake, and to turn the lady into a 'worm'.[19] Yet in the end the issue must be settled by the standard knightly fight in which they can manage nothing more spectacular than a poisoned sword. The hero, significantly, is relieved when he hears their horses neighing as the clerks approach through the devastation of the earthquake to do battle – it will be his kind of fight after all, conducted with swords, shields and spears from horseback.

We need to recognize also that the capacity to fight in this manner is based more on professionalism than on a deep moral code. A good fighter in search of honour is recognized as a man of chivalry, whether or not he is a good man. King Rion in the *Prose Merlin* is animated by the ambition to rip beards from thirty kings and form them into a mantle to wear 'in dispite' of the defeated. This text clearly views his ambition with disapproval and characterizes Rion as 'a right . . . crewell man'. Yet it also recognizes him as 'right myghty of londe and of peple, and full of high prowesse' (85). Similarly, the steward in *Amis and Amiloun* is recognized as 'A douhti knight at crie' although his bad character is immediately made evident by the statement that he seeks with envy and indignation to bring both heroes of the romance to shame through guile and treachery (205–10).[20] Havelok thinks of forgiving the evil Godrich, telling him, 'For I see thu art so wight / And of thy body so good knight' (2720–2). Lady Lyonet in the *Morte Darthur* refers to two good knights who are 'murtherers' shortly before Sir Gareth characterizes another as a good knight who follows shameful customs – hanging defeated knights from trees, shields about their necks, gilt spurs at their heels (pp. 194, 196). Arthur admits him later to the Round Table as a reformed man and no man-murtherer (208). Nor is even the right religion necessary. In texts such as *The Sultan of Babylon* (979–90), *The Siege of Milan* (226–8) and *Guy of Warwick* (2923) even Saracens are termed chivalrous and perform wonders of arms with their hands in the best knightly manner. *The Siege of Milan* calls the Saracen fighter Sir Darnadowse, for example, 'A nobill knyghte and a chevallrouse' (995). Bevis of Hampton is even dubbed by a Saracen (969–70). There seems in this romance some possibility that good heathen warriors go to heaven (4014–16, but see 4224–39). Professional prowess, in short, is recognized.

Inclusive professionalism scarcely prevents the highly competitive dimension of chivalry. Knightly honour is won through prowess done on other knights' bodies. A practising knight himself, Sir Thomas Malory regularly shows in his *Morte Darthur* how much he cares about the competitive ranking of knights winning worship upon the bodies of worthy opponents.[21] A classic statement, early in his great book, has Balayne tell his brother Balan that knowing the location of King Ryons, Arthur's enemy, they must go 'in all goodly haste to preve oure worship uppon hym' (p. 44). When Lancelot is caught in the queen's chamber in the great crisis near the end of the *Morte Darthur*, he calls out that he will disprove Agravain's accusation 'as a knyght shuld . . . uppon you wyth my hondys' (p. 677). Similarly, Perceval wants to win his symbolic knightly spurs 'Appone the Sowdane' (*Perceval of Galles* 1596). Revenge, of course, drives much of the competition of body against body. Examples defy citation, but we should note how Bevis of Hampton gets an early and much admired start. Pledging revenge on his father's killer at age seven, he gains entrance to the hall by cleaving the head of the resisting porter; he denounces the killer seated on the dais, and even gives him three youthful blows to the head, toppling him though failing to kill him (313–18, 415–50).

Tournament, of course, is the most frequent outlet for competition. In romances if actual warfare is not available a tournament is arranged to enable the competition to continue. Sometimes a tournament even occurs during warfare, creating a second layer of competition within the plot. In the *Prose Merlin* the knights want to hold a tournament even during the succession of desperate engagements of the Saxon war, a desire that Queen Guinevere counters with sensible advice (p. 211). Romance, of course, always imagines tournaments as fought fiercely with edged weapons as a simulacrum of war, not as merely colourful, if rough, sport. Thus, even in tournament, knightly competition often leads to serious trouble as mock war turns real, revenge is taken, fighters turn 'wrothe oute of mesure' (*Morte Darthur* 647), or reasons for later revenge accumulate. The tournament held to celebrate the wedding of Arthur and Guinevere in the *Prose Merlin* (455–61) quickly gets out of hand in classic fashion. A death in a tournament, casually mentioned in Guy of Warwick (1824–34) leads to a war in which Guy, of course, shines. Bevis of Hampton cannot resist a tournament even when it will mean a delay and diversion from rescuing his wife (and seems tempted by the prize offered – another lady!). Tirri, Bevis's companion in arms, responds vigorously to the news of this tournament given by Bevis:

> 'Ye, sire,' a sede, 'by Sein Thomas of Ynde!
> Whan were we wonded be byhind?
> We scholle lete for non nede,
> That we ne scholle manliche forth uns bede!'
> (3775–8)

Such a drive for manly competitiveness and the rewards it brings raises large questions about chivalry and an ordered society. In romance this competitiveness is at least one powerful force in the slowly building tidal wave that destroys the fellowship of the best body of knights in the world, as the collapse of the Round Table demonstrates.

Warrior Courtesy, Love and Piety

Writers of chivalric literature were not heedless of the problems inherent in prowess or the need for guidelines and limitations, even as they praised prowess to the skies. Prowess is assumed to entail courtesy, but this acts as a channel to violence, rather than a block. Repeatedly, statements and incidents in romance from our period show a set of ideals about how warriors should fight. The role of horses and the advantage of a mounted man appear often. An honourable man will dismount to fight on equal terms with his dismounted foe (*Lybeaus Desconus* C 333, L 356; *Perceval of Galles* 1685–9). Amis, who unhorses the wicked steward in *Amis and Amiloun*, dismounts to fight and announces the principle: 'it were gret vilani, bi Seyn Jon, / A lieggand man for to slon, / That were yfallen in nede' (1336–80). When Tryamour thrusts his spear accidentally into his opponent's mount, he even offers the man his own horse (1219–27). Several honourable men will not come all together against a single enemy (*Perceval of Galles* 1421–4). An opponent who loses or breaks his sword should be shown mercy; or at least both fighters should turn to equal weaponry (knives in a case from the *Siege of Milan*, a Saracen showing this courtesy to Arthur, 1058–68). No 'wepenless' man should be killed, as Lybeaus Desconus intones (L 386). In fact, any defeated knight must be shown mercy: as one of Malory's knights proclaims, 'a knyght withoute mercy ys withoute worship' (p. 66). Such maxims obviously form an important link between medieval chivalry and later ideas of 'gentlemanliness'. Yet we need to realize that all such medieval ideals are cordoned off by the bounds of status; they apply among the knightly, not between the knightly and all those they consider sub-knightly. We cannot transform the knight into Everyman. We must remember that chivalric ideology set them apart as proud warriors in a distinctly hierarchical society.

Even limited protocols for ideal combat can point us towards what are usually considered by modern scholarship the kinder and gentler components of chivalry – love and piety. Such qualities raise again the important question of the role chivalry played not only in individuals, but in a medieval society developing multiple forms of order, and particularly in the public peace championed by resurgent royal power. Examining those issues, we must always remember the centrality of prowess in chivalry that we have already discussed.

Love comes to mind at once as an inseparable aspect of romance genre. Is not romance basically about knights and ladies? Lancelot, Guinevere (and Arthur), Tristan and Isolde (and Mark) play crucial roles in the *Morte Darthur*; the first three also dominate the *Stanzaic Morte Arthur*. In these works and others drawing heavily on French originals love language appears – in *Ywain and Gawain*, for example. And love generates action in less famous works. Eglamour, ill for love, does all to win his lady; Guy of Warwick fills thousands of lines with action designed to win the love of Felice.

An insistence on analytical caution will win no popularity, but is necessary. Even in such unsurpassed tellings as Malory's the love themes show the general unease of Middle English literary works over highly formal courtly love ideas originating in France. And in English romance, as in French, misogynistic sentiments are spoken (e.g. *Troy Book* 129, *Prose Merlin* 59). Moreover, love seems linked to prowess rather than acting as a restraining force on its vigour. We need to look more closely at knights and ladies.

A first step is simple. As a knight was not Everyman, he did not rescue Everywoman. The concern is almost exclusively for socially elite women, for damsels and ladies. The *Prose Merlin* announces the ideal standard: no damsels may be sexually forced in Arthur's realm (p. 328). The famous chivalric oath in the *Morte Darthur* likewise intones this standard: no rape of 'ladyes, damesels and jantilwomen and wydowes' (p. 75). They are rather to be helped to maintain their rights. Sadly, as with most rules, this one is necessary because of contrary behaviour, as the pages of Malory's book and many others reveal. In the *Prose Merlin*, three sons of King Lot debate gender relations among the elite with a focus on the lovely daughter of their most recent host. Agravain frankly proposes rape, justifying himself by saying it is expected that a knight will take what he can, that only scorn from other knights would greet any reluctance. The other two responses please us more – Gaheries proposes taking the maiden to a place of safety, and Geheret proposes mutuality as the key to love. Yet the later record of all three with women is stained and the sour voice of Agravain lingers.[22] Elite women suffer rape in chivalric literature – it is how Arthur is engendered and that is far from the only case – and peasant girls, shepherdesses and the like should always beware.

Any sample of chivalric literature shows, moreover, how regularly even elite women appear as prizes to be won (with praise for their beauty and a keen eye for the acreage they inherit). In *Perceval of Galles* the hero's father has been given Arthur's sister in marriage because of his prowess and Perceval himself weds the splendidly named Lufamour after he kills the Sultan who besieged her (18–24, 1733–6). The prize awarded Guy of Warwick for his service against the Saracens is the hand of the Byzantine princess; he walks to the very altar before thinking of his beloved Felice, at home in misty England, whose love he has long been fighting to win. One of the innumerable ladies to be won by the victor in a tournament appears in *Amadace*, promised to 'he that first is inne the fild, / And best thenne justus thare' (479–80). Lydgate thinks it right that the first Greek knight into Troy took the king's daughter, though he wishes he had properly married her (*Troy Book* 84).

The women are not always helpless victims. Josian, saving herself for Bevis from the man who married her by force, hangs the offender from the marriage bed with a slipknot in a 'towaile' (3219–24). She makes other would-be lovers recoil by taking herbs that give her the appearance of a leper (297). She and Rymenhild in *King Horn* are even more romantically forward than their chosen knights. Ladies may, however, be abandoned after the fighting and winning. The *Jeaste of Sir Gawain* focuses on Gawain's fighting with the woman's father and brothers whose honour has been besmirched by Gawain's union with their daughter and sister. If Gawain proves he is 'of hys hondes a man' (409), the unfortunate woman is beaten as a harlot and left to wander, separated from her family.[23]

Chivalric romance usually, however, pictures the lady wanting the winner and accepted by him. The link with prowess becomes clear. If love inspires knightly prowess, prowess inspires love from the lady. In a tournament Sir Tryamour encounters the king of 'Naverne':

> Soche a strokk he gaf hym tho,
> That all men hyt syen,
> The blode braste owt at hys eerys
> And hys stede to grownde he berys
> (787–91)

The effect on the watching lady is decisive: 'Then that lady of grete honowre, / Whyte os lylly flower, – / Hur love was on hym lente' (793–5). The reciprocal role of love in inspiring prowess is never doubted. *The Sultan of Babylon* states it almost as a maxim:

> For he was nevere gode werryour
> That cowde not love aryght:
> For love hath made many a conqueroure
> And many a worthy knighte
> (975–8)

If loving a woman is a part of knighthood, it remains closely linked to prowess. Fighting to prove the superior beauty of his lady, Lybeaus Desconus unhorses a doubter with such vigour that the man breaks his backbone with a 'crake' heard by the crowd

(L 1009–20). Guinevere in the *Stanzaic Morte Arthure* needlessly worries that Lancelot, besotted by the Maid of Astolot, will give up prowess. 'May she never be so dear to you / That you give up performing deeds of arms; / Since I must remain alone in sorrow, / I would at least like to hear of your deeds of prowess' (Benson and Foster's helpful translation of 756–9).[24] The importance of Lancelot's prowess to her is as strikingly real as her utterly groundless fears: Lancelot goes on smiting opponents, moved by love for the queen. In the *Prose Merlin* Guinevere symbolically girds on the young Arthur's sword. During the ensuing bloody battle against the Saxons, Merlin admonishes Arthur for not earning through prowess the kiss she also gave him (193–4). Horn looks at the ring given him by his love (bearing her engraved name) and kills a hundred Saracens – only a warm-up exercise for the slaughter to follow (1615–22). He looks at his ring later, in Ireland, and puts his sword through the heart of the Saracen champion, a giant (880–5). The link between sexuality and violence is further underscored by Malory's using the phrase 'have adoo' both in the sense of knightly combat with men and knightly copulation with women.

Any lines separating prowess, prize-winning, sexuality and love seem blurred. Guy of Warwick is rejected by Felice, his lord's daughter, first because he has not been knighted, then because, though knighted, he has not done marvels of prowess, then because he is not the best knight of them all. These spur pricks set him galloping across Europe and Asia Minor, fighting, winning, dismembering opponents by the score. As already noted, he nearly takes the Byzantine princess offered as a prize. Guy seems at times more bonded with Tirri, his companion at arms, than with any woman. The two become sworn brothers and pledge mutual troth (4905–28). When they are separated, Tirri wishes to die (A 5890–1). When Guy finally returns to marry a willing Felice, he and she enjoy just fifteen days and nights together before his 'conversion' and a new life of prowess, now in the service of God.

Although love is linked to prowess, it seems to take a distinctly second place in importance. As one scholar sagely observed, 'what Tristram values above all is not the presence of his beloved, nor the joy of sharing every moment of his life with her, but the high privilege of fighting in her name'.[25] Could not the same be said even of Lancelot's relationship to the queen?

Finally, we need to consider piety in relation to chivalry. No reader of romance can miss the presentation of knights as pious. It may be announced almost randomly, as when we learn in the midst of a great fight in *Gologras and Gawain* that Arthur and his knights love God and Saint Ann (580–1),[26] or it may be the very framework of the tale. Some romances, such as *Isumbras* and *Guy of Warwick*, focus on great sins or a lifetime of sin and end with heroic penances. Robert of Cisyle, full of pride, cannot believe God could put down one so mighty as he, the 'flour of chivalrye', who lays all his enemies low. Flattened by divine might, he can only, near the end of his romance, repeatedly intone a personal litany of repentance, 'Lord, on Thi fool Thou have pité' (348, 356, 360, 364).

Yet analytical caution is again advisable. An almost irreducible self-confidence usually animated chivalry, leading to a virtual appropriation of religion within chivalric ideology, a selecting and transforming of religious ideas that would valorize knighthood.

This ideology regularly claims that God blesses knightly fighting, a claim that best resonated in crusade-like encounters (even though set historically well before crusade existed). Sir Tryamour journeys to the Holy Land to 'were in Goddys grace' (132) hoping to beget an heir by the grace of a grateful God. Eglamour wields a sword found by St Paul in the Greek Sea (256–61). Charlemagne in *The Siege of Milan* dreams that an angel gives him a perfect sword and awakes to find a very physical sword in his hand to be used against Christ's enemies (109–44). The dying Duke of Normandy in this text sees heaven open for warriors in reward for fighting Saracens (313–24). Heroes regularly call upon God or the blessed Virgin in their fighting and cut down their enemies with this heavenly aid.

Chivalric texts, however, also like to picture knights meriting and receiving such aid and valorization in quotidian, secular conflicts. God's aid directs the sword hand of Bevis (meeting tests of prowess to win Josian's hand) as he kills a boar, a dragon and a lion; it also guides the sword that cuts through the shoulder of a very human opponent and another human's hand. Faithful old Sir Roger may be finally overwhelmed by his lady's abductors in *Sir Tryamour*, but his body remains uncorrupted in its grave, as if God recognized him as a lay saint. Guy of Warwick's 'conversion' seems initially to change his armour for pilgrim garb. Yet he is quickly drawn back into solving the same sorts of problems – restorations, rescues – by the same method of knightly combat that filled the romance before his conversion, except that now he accepts no reward and reveals his identity only reluctantly and selectively. At the end of his life he actually becomes a hermit and dies in the odour of sanctity, as does Lancelot in the *Morte Darthur*. Yet neither would be a romance hero had he not first lived a long life of heroic prowess. Malory famously manages to transmute even the grail quest – in the French original a searing critique of worldly knighthood – into the greatest adventure God has given Arthurian chivalry. *Amis and Amiloun* makes the general point nicely. It values loyal friendship over any formally religious virtue and shows divine approval in the final miracle. Disloyalty, a stain on the honour of chivalry, is treated as sin (301–6) and the great evil in this text as in others is shame. Little wonder that Richard of Normandy in *The Sultan of Babylon* tellingly calls Jesus the 'King of honoure' (2841).

Views of War in Medieval Literature

Medieval England in the era of the Hundred Years War was no spawning ground for pacifism of a modern sort; most people probably considered war necessary and noble, even an antidote to sloth or lechery. Some ardently hoped it would prove profitable. Yet thoughtful writers expressed fears about the costs and benefits of particular phases of the almost continuous warfare and sometimes worried over wars among Christians in general.

Leading intellectuals show the tension. John Lydgate's books are replete with praise for Henry V as conqueror and glow with admiration for victorious manliness; yet fears and cautions surface. In the *Siege of Thebes* Lydgate worries about knightly force prevailing over right (1774–87) and insists that victory must be rooted in right and 'trouthes excellence' rather than 'falssenesse' (2236–9, 2248–53; 2495–505).[27] In *Troy Book* he hopes for an ideal knighthood, worries again over trouth and treson, and proscribes sternly any coveting or robbing:

> No swiche pelfre, spoillynge, nor robberie
> Apartene not to worthi chivalrye:
> For covetyse and knyghthod, as I lere,
> In a cheyne may nat be knet yfere
> (5363–6).

John Gower accepted the invasion of the French kingdom claimed for the English crown and wanted English knights to join enthusiastically in the effort, prowess serving as an antidote to sloth (e.g. *Troy Book* 69–82). Yet he castigates harmful knightly practices at home and abroad. The knight somehow 'through pure honour . . . must seek prowess of arms' (Ançois par fine honesteté / Droit la pruesce d'armes quere' 23663–4).[28] Prowess of the sort featured in romance, based on pride or amour, must give way to fighting for God. Repeatedly in the *Mirour de l'omme*, he denounces covetousness as the cause of unjust war and the spur for detestable looting and pillaging of the poor. A late Gower poem, *In Praise of Peace*, denounces war – except for crusade – as 'modir of the wronges alle' (106) and blesses peace as 'beste above alle ertheley thinges' (63).[29]

Geoffrey Chaucer may show greater prudence and reserve, but he raises questions of much relevance to war even in such conventional works as the Tale of Melibee, and the lyrics 'The Former Age' and 'Lack of Stedfastnesse'. His tales and translations have a timeless quality; yet the contemporary relevance of the questions is apparent. Is war caused by deplorable covetousness? Do men start wars without knowing how they may end?

Even greater tensions agitate the alliterative *Morte Arthure*, an anonymous and almost schizophrenic work.[30] Early in this text lords in Arthur's court intone heroic platitudes about glorious war and even praise Christ for its return after a period of dulling peace. Arthur crosses the Channel as a liberator, dispatching the oppressive giant on Mount Saint Michael, and as rightful lord reclaims his inheritance from the hard and illicit grasp of Rome. Fighting is presented in the valorizing epic tradition. Yet the campaign steadily goes off the rails. Arthur defeats Lucius, who had tormented his people, but becomes himself a tormentor. His downfall seems no surprise after we have witnessed his overweening ambition for conquest. Some scholarship also connects *Wynnere and Wastoure* with a vigorous debate over war policy at the court of Edward III, often seen as the model for Arthur in the alliterative *Morte Arthure*.[31]

Possibly borrowing from the late twelfth-century work of Chrétien de Troyes, the anonymous Middle English *Perceval of Galles* shows Perceval's mother wanting to escape a chivalric world where deeds of arms are done. After the death of her husband at the hands of the Red Knight, she has fled into the woods so her son must only deal with the beasts rather than engage in jousts and tournaments (163–76). His innate knightly vocation will out, of course; and when he learns of knighthood by seeing three splendid knights in the woods – he thinks one of them must be God – and announces his desire to be made a knight, his mother grieves so she thinks she will die (385–8). The theme is echoed in the *Lybeaus Desconus* in which the hero's mother again tries to keep him safe by keeping him away from knights. Yet her fear is for what he might do no less than what he might see, for her 'dughty childe' was 'full savage / And gladly wold do oute-rage / To his ffellawes in fere' (12–24).

Unjust warfare plays a role in the symbolic fall of Arthur in some works. Fissures in the Round Table broaden ominously in Malory's *Morte Darthur*, of course, although Malory seems not to blame war *per se*. A perspective closer to that of the alliterative Morte *Arthure* reappears in *The Awntyrs of Arthur.* Gawain puts a significant and fearful question to the terrifying apparition that admonishes both the queen and him:

> How shal we fare . . . that fonden to fight,
> And thus defoulen the folke on fele kinges londes,
> And riches over reynes withouten eny right,
> Wynnen worshipp in were thorgh wightnesse of hondes?
> (262–5)

In answer the ghostly figure (Guenevere's mother come from torment) tells him Arthur is too covetous and foretells the fall of the Round Table fellowship (266–312).

Thus the perils of war did not go unquestioned in a highly warlike era. The chivalric literature we have already examined, however, shows attitudes unlikely to nourish lasting concerns for peace. A very human aggressiveness worked against it, no less than a desire for profit. The centrality of prowess in chivalric ideology (subordinating even love and piety) meant that idealizing calls for only defensive war, or war for God, or war free of pride and greed, were likely to be honoured more in the breach than the observance.

Military Literature in England

A perceived need thus generated a vernacular military literature of the later Middle Ages. It can be divided into two categories: texts drawn from classic works, especially Vegetius's *De re militari*, and texts which are based to a greater or lesser degree on the personal experience of late medieval soldiers themselves.

The first English version of *De re militari* was translated by an anonymous clerk in 1408 for the use of Thomas, Lord Berkeley. While for the most part following Vegetius faithfully, the translator 'modernized' his text by adding references to the use of gunpowder artillery in siege warfare. Although the general tone of this work endorses the conventional contemporary sense of the higher moral calling of knighthood, it also reflects the tension between the knightly ideal and the destructive dimension of the pursuit of prowess in its condemnation of 'oure crystene knyghts that werreth noght fore none of the skylles but for cruelte of wrechyng or elles for couetise'.[32]

Knyghthood and Bataile, a verse paraphrase of Vegetius composed anonymously between 1457 and 1460 by a supporter of the Lancastrian cause in the Wars of the Roses, while alluding to the turbulent political context, follows a tradition of medieval writing on chivalry in seeing a reform of knighthood as the solution to England's contemporary troubles; implicitly then, the author acknowledges the tension between knighthood's potential as a source of strength –

> If chiualer, a land that shal defende
> Be noble born and have lond & fee
> With thewys good, as can noman amende *morals*
> Thei will remembir ay their honeste

– and the dangers of chivalry's failure: 'What helpeth it, if ignobilittee / Have exercise in werre and wagys large' (p. 11).[33]

Finally, the influence of Vegetius is traceable beyond specifically military literature: 'the ideal of knighthood that appears in medieval military manuals . . . based on Vegetius, informs the very spirit of Malory's [*Morte Darthur*] . . . [whose] use of Vegetius also reflects his philosophy of knighthood, one that was strongly influenced by the tradition of the military manuals'.[34]

Although belonging to the category of personal military experience only at second hand, the *Boke of Noblesse* of William Worcester owes more to this tradition of military writing than to the classical tradition of *De re militari*.[35] As private secretary from 1438 to 1459 to Sir John Fastolf, one of the leading English captains in the last stages of the Hundred Years War, Worcester must have been privy to a store of personal experience which few contemporary Englishmen can have matched. Worcester's explicit purpose, like that of the author of *Knyghthode and Bataile*, is the reform of knighthood as a means to recover England's domestic stability and international reputation; for Worcester, the solution to the political turbulence of the Wars of the Roses is renewed war with France, and the prerequisite to this is the rediscovery by English gentlemen of their true calling, the vocation of arms.

Costs and Consequences

Two broad historiographical debates have arisen about the Hundred Years War. The first has concerned the social and economic consequences of the war, originally defined in largely economic terms of gain and loss but increasingly in a broader context of state-formation, public order and social security. The second debate relates to the military dimensions of war-making, and turns on the question of strategic or technological innovation. Neither debate can be said to have concluded, and important contributions to both are certain to appear, while to some extent the obviously interrelated nature of the two questions is increasingly the subject of investigation.

The question of the social consequences of the Hundred Years War was first raised in an article published in 1942 by the Marxist economic historian M. M. Postan.[36] Confining his observations largely to England, Postan argued that the war 'was not so much the mainspring as a make-weight' which had significant influence only on aspects of England's economy where 'changes were taking place anyhow'.[37] Postan saw the war as having a significant impact, however, in redistributing wealth from the traditional aristocracy and great magnates such as the Duke of Lancaster to lesser men, 'the "kulaks" of the English countryside', and therefore accelerating the rise of *nouveaux riches* such as the de la Poles who, Postan asserted, represented 'a new and rising class'.[38]

Twenty years later K. B. McFarlane replied to Postan's essay with a call for greater precision in evaluating the war's socio-economic consequences. McFarlane attempted, despite the gaps in late medieval financial sources, to draw up a 'balance-sheet, however rough' of the war's costs, taking into account various forms of taxation, changes in the wool trade, and the profits or costs of the war itself in the form of plunder, ransoms, forced contributions, occupation of enemy territory and the like.[39] He concluded that, far from 'a circular tour of English rural wealth' which tended to impoverish the English economy, the war in fact produced a balance-sheet profit when the spoils of war were taken into account. Furthermore, far from redistributing wealth to a new class of capitalist *nouveaux riches*, the profits of war remained largely in the hands of 'the class traditionally associated with martial prowess', the chivalric landowning aristocracy: 'the de la Poles . . . were the exceptions'.[40]

With an article published in 1964, Postan replied to McFarlane's view by insisting on a distinction between the costs of war in terms of 'material resources and economic activities diverted to war' and McFarlane's 'financial or bullionist' reckoning.[41] But Postan briefly moved beyond a purely economic analysis by broaching the question of the wider social cost of the war and asking what effect the diversion of England's landowning aristocracy might have had on the administration of justice and public order: 'have not constitutional historians been telling us how indispensable knights had become in the conduct of local government and how great was the burden of administration and service they bore in the shires?'[42] Despite this digression, however, the greater part of Postan's argument accepted McFarlane's terms of reference and turned on the 'bullionist' issue of the war's balance-sheet: 'however generous we may be in our estimates of net gain from offices, booty, estates and even ransoms, we should still find it very difficult to make them equal the five millions plus spent on national and private accounts'.[43]

With the question of the Hundred Years War's consequences framed largely in terms of economic or even purely monetary terms, the broader question of the war's socio-political consequences has begun to receive attention only relatively recently. Revisiting the issue of 'costs and profits', A. R. Bridbury criticized the appeal to the 'arbitrament of the balance sheet' as anachronistic:

> the implication . . . is that war, far from being a normal feature of social life in the Middle Ages, was an aberration of conduct which diverted people from nobler, or simply more practical and useful purposes . . . But neither cost nor the frustration of hope is commonly taken to be conclusive as a condemnation of any particular social activity.[44]

He concluded that the question of economic cost was moot: 'in such a society making war did not waste resources: it employed them'.[45]

Since the mid-1970s, the issue of the impact of the Hundred Years War on French and English society has tended to be viewed in broader social and political rather than solely economic terms. It has been suggested that one of the most important consequences was the diversion of resources, not economic but governmental, away from the further elaboration of the peace-keeping and administrative aspects of the emerging state in both France and England. If it cannot be established with any reliability who the winners were in financial or economic terms, there is abundant evidence to conclude that public order in both kingdoms was a loser.[46] Moreover, if the war harmed public order and the process of state-building on both sides of the Channel, it has been argued that throughout much of France the effect of the war was the virtual collapse of civil society itself in the face of 'warlordism': the domination of swathes of countryside by freebooting garrisons, *routier* captains and mercenary companies amounted in contemporary eyes to nothing less than 'a disastrous reversion to an age of barbarism and anarchy, of arbitrary lordship and abject serfdom'.[47]

Conduct of War: Military Revolution?

While the debate over economic and social consequences has spanned almost sixty years, the military dimensions of the war have received relatively little attention. In those same sixty years, excepting the occasional professional soldier,[48] very few scholars showed much interest in the central business of warfare, even while taking considerable interest in closely related topics such as organization and finance.[49] While it was argued that the strategic, tactical, technological and organizational innovations of the two centuries after the Hundred Years War constituted a 'military revolution' for early modern Europe,[50] military developments during the Hundred Years War itself were largely ignored. Recently, however, the case for the importance of the Hundred Years War has been made by Clifford Rogers. In an article originally published in 1993, Rogers adopted the concept of 'military revolution' in order to describe the conjunction of tactical and technological change which characterized the Hundred Years War.[51]

In Rogers's view, during the Hundred Years War two developments 'revolutionized the conduct of war'.[52] The first was a tactical shift from heavily armed cavalry relying on the psychological impact of their massed charge to carry the day, to lightly armed infantry reliant primarily on missile weapons (at first the longbow and later the arquebus or musket) for victory. The second was a shift, thanks to the introduction of gunpowder artillery, in the balance between military fortification and the means available to overcome it: the evolution of effective siege artillery ended the centuries-long supremacy of defensive fortifications.

The consequences of these two revolutions in warfare, Rogers argues, can be detected at many different levels. For the Hundred Years War itself, the result of the infantry revolution was that 'major cavalry actions on the field of battle became rare', while English armies consisting of longbow-armed infantry won a series of spectacular victories at Crécy, Poitiers and Agincourt and in smaller engagements. Over the longer term the use of effective missile weapons, first bows and later handguns in combination with long thrusting weapons such as the pike, resulted in European warfare becoming more lethal; this greater lethality in turn changed the nature of European warfare so that, in the era of European expansion and conquest immediately following the end of the Hundred Years War, the conquistadors and empire-builders of the sixteenth and seventeenth centuries engaged the natives of the Americas, Africa and Asia with a style of warfare at once unfamiliar, shocking, brutal and devastating.[53] More broadly Rogers ties the infantry revolution to the rising 'political influence of the commons', ascribing both the Great Revolt of 1381 and the steady development of the House of Commons to the 'increased ability of the people to resist oppression by military means'.[54] Meanwhile, the consequence of the artillery revolution, by placing the means to reduce castle and town walls in the hands of only those rulers able to afford the expensive new technology, was to accelerate the transformation of medieval monarchies into centralized 'nation-states': 'regional interests lost their ability to defy central authorities, small states and semi-independent regions were gobbled up by their larger neighbors'.[55]

While Rogers's thesis on the military importance of the Hundred Years War has largely framed the issues, many other studies on military aspects of the war have appeared in the last decade. Rogers himself has complemented his initial work with a lengthy study of Edward III's strategy, while others have fleshed out the idea of an 'infantry revolution' through detailed case-studies of battlefield tactics and technology.[56] Military leadership, naval warfare, the structure and organization of armies and the use and evolution of artillery have all received renewed attention in the last decade.[57]

See also: 2 English Society in the Later Middle Ages, 5 Women's Voices and Roles, 19 Love, 20 Middle English Romance, 21 Writing Nation, 37 *Sir Gawain and the Green Knight*, 38 Malory's *Morte Darthur*.

Notes

1 Unless noted otherwise, all Middle English texts are TEAMS series (Kalamazoo, Mich.: Medieval Institute *Publications*).

2 *Havelok the Dane* in Donald B. Sands (ed.), *Middle English Verse Romances* (New York: Holt, Rinehart and Winston, 1966), pp. 55–130.

3 *Lancelot of the Laik and Sir Tristrem*, ed. Alan Lupack (1994).

4 *Sir Perceval of Galles and Ywain and Gawain*, ed. Mary Flowers Braswell (1995).

5 *Sir Isumbras* and *Sir Eglamour of Artois* in *Four Middle English Romances*, ed. Harriet Hudson (1996); *Robert of Cisyle* in *Amis and Amiloun,*

Robert of Cisyle, and Sir Amadace, ed. Edward Foster (1997); *Bevis of Hampton* in *Four Romances of England*, ed. Ronald B. Herzmann, Graham Drake and Eve Salisbury (1999).

6 Malory, *Works*, ed. Eugène Vinaver, 2nd edn (Oxford: Oxford University Press, 1977).

7 *The Siege of Milan* in *Three Middle English Charlemagne Romances*, ed. Alan Lupack (1990).

8 *The Sultan of Babylon* in *Three Middle English Charlemagne Romances*, ed. Lupack.

9 *Sir Perceval of Galles and Ywain and Gawain*, ed. Braswell.

10 Specific comment: *Perceval of Galles*, ed. Braswell, 354–7; general cases: Torre and Gareth in Malory, *Works*, ed. Vinaver, pp. 61, 179; *Havelok*, ed. Sands in his *Middle English Verse Romances*, pp. 79–105.

11 *King Horn* in *Four Romances of* England, ed. Herzmann et al.

12 *William of Palerne*, ed. G. H. V. Bunt (Groningen: Bouma's Boekhuis 1985).

13 John Lydgate, *Troy Book Selections*, ed. Robert R. Edwards (1998).

14 *Prose Merlin*, ed. John Conlee (1998).

15 *The Romance of Guy of Warwick*, ed. Julius Zupitza, EETS es 42, 49, 59 (1883–91), repr. 1966 (as single volume).

16 *Sir Tryamour* in *Four Middle English Romances*, ed. Harriet Hudson (1996).

17 *King Arthur's Death: The Middle English Stanzaic Morte Arthur and Alliterative Morte Arthure*, ed. Larry D. Benson, rev. Edward E. Foster (1994).

18 *The Siege of Milan* in *Three Middle English Charlemagne Romances*, ed. Lupack.

19 *Lybeaus Desconus*, ed. M. Mills, EETS os 261 (1969).

20 *Amis and Amiloun, Robert of Cisyle, and Sir Amadace*, ed. Foster.

21 See his careful list of those who even 'overmacched' Gawain, for example, p. 97.

22 *Merlin, or The Early History of King Arthur: A Prose Romance*, ed. Henry B. Wheatley, vol. 2, EETS os 36 (1867), pp. 525–7.

23 In *Sir Gawain: Eleven Romances and Tales*, ed Thomas Hahn (1995).

24 In *King Arthur's Death*, ed. Benson, rev. Foster.

25 Malory, *Works*, ed. Vinaver, p. 750.

26 In *Sir Gawain: Eleven Romances and Tales*, ed. Hahn.

27 John Lydgate, *The Siege of Thebes*, ed. Robert R. Edwards (2001).

28 John Gower, *Mirour de l'omme (The Mirror of Mankind)*, trans. William Burton Wilson, rev. Nancy Wilson van Bosch (East Lansing, Mich., 1992).

29 'In Praise of Peace', in *The English Works of John Gower*, ed. G. C. Macaulay, EETS es 81, 82 (1900–1).

30 *Alliterative Morte Arthure* in *King Arthur's Death*, ed. Benson, rev. Foster.

31 Juliet Vale, *Edward III and Chivalry: Chivalric Society and its Context 1270–1350* (Woodbridge: Boydell Press, 1982), pp. 73–5.

32 New York, Pierpont Morgan Library MS M. 775, folio 110, quoted in Diane Bornstein, 'Military Manuals in Fifteenth-Century England', *Medieval Studies* 37 (1975), 470–1. Cf. G. Lester (ed.), *The Earliest English Translation of Vegetius' De Re Militari* (Heidelberg: Winter, 1988).

33 *Knyghthode and Bataile*, ed. R. Dyboski, EETS os 201 (1935).

34 Diane D. Bornstein, 'Military Strategy in Malory and Vegetius' *De Re Militari*', *Comparative Literature Studies* 9 (1972), 128.

35 William Worcester, *The Boke of Noblesse*, ed. J. G. Nichols (London: Roxburghe Club, 1860; repr. New York: Franklin, 1972).

36 M. M. Postan, 'Some Social Consequences of the Hundred Years War', *Economic History Review* 12 (1942), 1–12.

37 Ibid., p. 12.

38 Ibid., pp. 11–12.

39 K. B. McFarlane, 'England and the Hundred Years War', *Past and Present* 22 (1962), 3–18.

40 Ibid., p. 11.

41 M. M. Postan, 'The Costs of the Hundred Years War', *Past and Present* 27 (1964), 34–53.

42 Ibid., p. 38.

43 Ibid., p. 50.

44 A. R. Bridbury, 'The Hundred Years War: Costs and Profits', in *Trade, Government and Economy*, ed. D. C. Coleman (London: Weidenfeld and Nicolson, 1976), pp. 81–2.

45 Ibid., p. 94.

46 Kaeuper 1988: 132–3.

47 Nicholas Wright, *Knights and Peasants: The Hundred Years War in the French Countryside* (Woodbridge: Boydell, 1998), p. 61. Cf. Guy Bois, *The Crisis of Feudalism* (Cambridge: Cambridge University Press, 1984), p. 335, for a description of the local effects of the later stages of the war as 'Hiroshima in Normandy'. For a useful synthesis of the war's local impact, see Michael C. Jones, 'War and Fourteenth-Century France', in *Arms, Armies and Fortification in the Hundred Years War*, ed. Anne Curry and Michael Hughes (Woodbridge: Boydell Press, 1994), pp. 103–20; repr. in Rogers 1999, pp. 343–64.

48 A. H. Burne, *The Crécy War* (London: Eyre and Spottiswoode, 1955) and his *The Agincourt War* (London: Eyre and Spottiswoode, 1956).

49 Cf. G. L. Harriss, *King, Parliament, and Public Finance in Medieval England to 1369* (Oxford: Clarendon Press, 1975); J. B. Henneman, *Royal Taxation in Fourteenth Century France*, vol. 2 (Philadelphia: American Philosophical Society 1976); H. J. Hewitt, *The Organization of War under Edward III, 1388–62* (Manchester: Manchester University Press, 1966).

50 Michael Roberts, 'The "Military Revolution", 1560–1660' in his *Essays in Swedish History* (Minneapolis: University of Minnesota Press, 1967), pp. 195–225, repr. in *The Military Revolution Debate*, ed. Clifford Rogers (Boulder, Colo.: Westview Press, 1995), pp. 13–35; Geoffrey Parker, 'The 'Military Revolution', 1560–1660 – a Myth?', *Journal of Modern History* 48 (1976), 195–214; and his *The Military Revolution: Military Innovation and the Rise of the West 1500–1800* (Cambridge: Cambridge University Press, 1988).

51 Clifford Rogers, 'The Military Revolutions of the Hundred Years War', *Journal of Military History* 57 (1993), 241–78, repr. in *The Military Revolution Debate*, ed. Rogers, pp. 55–93.

52 Ibid., p. 56.

53 Ibid., p. 63. On this point Rogers acknowledges his debt to Parker, *Military Revolution*.

54 Ibid., pp. 61–2.

55 Ibid., p. 74.

56 Clifford Rogers, *War Cruel and Sharp: English Strategy under Edward III, 1327–1360* (Woodbridge: Boydell Press, 2000); Kelly DeVries, *Infantry Warfare in the Early Fourteenth Century: Discipline, Tactics, and Technology* (Woodbridge: Boydell Press, 1996); Mathew Bennet, 'The Development of Battle Tactics in the Hundred Years War' and Robert Hardy, 'The Longbow', both in Anne Curry and Michael Hughes (eds), *Arms, Armies and Fortifications in the Hundred Years War* (Woodbridge: Boydell Press, 1994), pp. 1–20, 161–81.

57 Andrew Ayton, 'Sir Thomas Ughtred and the Edwardian Military Revolution', in *The Age of Edward III*, ed. J. S. Bothwell (Woodbridge: York Medieval Press, 2001), pp. 107–32; Ian Friel, 'Winds of Change? Ships and the Hundred Years War', pp. 183–93; Andrew Ayton, 'English Armies in the Fourteenth Century', pp. 21–38; Anne Curry, 'English Armies in the Fifteenth Century', pp. 39–68; John Kenyon, 'Coastal Artillery Fortification in England in the Late Fourteenth and Early Fifteenth Centuries', pp. 145–9; Robert D. Smith, 'Artillery and the Hundred Years War: Myth and Interpretation', pp. 151–60; all in Curry and Hughes, *Arms, Armies and Fortifications*.

References and Further Reading

Allmand, Christopher T. 1988. *The Hundred Years War: England and France at War, c.1300–c.1450.* Cambridge: Cambridge University Press. Ably supplements Perroy.

—— (ed.) 1976. *War, Literature and Politics in the Late Middle Ages.* Liverpool: Liverpool University Press. Wide-ranging and still valuable.

Bradbury, Jim 1985. *The Medieval Archer.* Woodbridge: Boydell. Standard reference.

—— 1992. *The Medieval Siege.* Woodbridge: Boydell. Useful introduction.

Contamine, Philippe 1972. *Guerre, état et société à la fin du moyen âge: études sur les armées des rois de France 1337–1494.* Paris: Mouton. Invaluable despite its age.

Curry, Anne 1993. *The Hundred Years War.* Basingstoke: Macmillan. Useful overview.

DeVries, Kelly 1996. *Infantry Warfare in the Early Fourteenth Century.* Woodbridge: Boydell. Interesting assessment of an important topic.

Kaeuper, Richard W. 1988. *War, Justice and Public Order: England and France in the Later Middle Ages.* Oxford: Clarendon Press. Assesses the conflicting roles of the late medieval state as warmaker and law-giver.

—— 1999. *Chivalry and Violence in Medieval Europe.* Oxford: Oxford University Press. The most recent substantial treatment, based largely on literary sources.

Keen, Maurice H. 1984. *Chivalry.* New Haven, Conn.: Yale University Press. Comprehensive if somewhat dated.

Nicholson, Helen 2004. *Medieval Warfare: The Theory and Practice of War in Europe 300–1500.* Useful brief survey.

Painter, Sidney 1940. *French Chivalry: Chivalric Ideas and Practices in Mediaeval France.* Baltimore: Johns Hopkins University Press. Classic.

Perroy, Edouard 1965. *The Hundred Years War,* trans. W. B. Wells. New York: Capricorn Books; first published in French in 1945. Remains the best single-volume narrative.

Prestwich, Michael 1996. *Armies and Warfare in the Middle Ages: The English Experience.* New Haven, Conn.: Yale University Press. Accessible and broad survey.

Rogers, C. 1999. *The Wars of Edward III: Sources and Interpretations.* Woodbridge: Boydell Press. Useful excerpts from sources plus eight important essays.

—— 2000. *War Cruel and Sharp: English Strategy under Edward III, 1327–1360.* Woodbridge: Boydell. Argues that military strategy in France evolved from earlier fighting against the Scots.

Rose, Susan 2002. *Medieval Naval Warfare, 1000–1500.* London: Routledge. The most recent survey.

Strickland, Matthew (ed.) 1992. *Anglo-Norman Warfare.* Woodbridge: Boydell. Collection of reprinted essays of seminal importance.

Sumption, Jonathan 1991–9. *The Hundred Years War,* 2 vols. Philadelphia: University of Pennsylvania Press. Magisterial narrative.

Wright, Nicholas 1998. *Knights and Peasants: The Hundred Years War in the French Countryside.* Woodbridge: Boydell. Impact of war on the French rural population.

17
Literature and Law

Richard Firth Green

> Just as it is important to mix truth with falsity, if falsity is to be accepted, so it is important to mix falsity with truth, if truth is to be accepted. All lawyers know this. Indeed, it may be called one of our Rules of Law.
>
> Hilaire Belloc, *The Cruise of the Nona*

The emerging field of law and literature is really an amalgam of two conceptually distinct areas of study. The older (and the one more likely to appeal to the general reader) seeks to make jurisprudential sense of literary works in which lawyers and trials figure prominently – works such as Shakespeare's *Merchant of Venice*, Melville's *Billy Budd*, Kafka's *Der Prozess*, or Camus's *L'Etranger.* Although professional lawyers may undertake such studies – as Judge Richard Posner's fine book *Law and Literature* (1998) – Theodore Ziolkowski's *The Mirror of Justice* (1997) proves that this is an area where the informed lay person still has much to contribute. The more recent branch of the discipline concentrates on the application of literary analysis, primarily rhetorical or narratological analysis, to actual legal texts: litigants' claims and denials, witnesses' statements, judges' findings and so on. This has been largely the preserve of legal specialists and, encouraging as it may be for literary scholars to discover that their subject has attracted the notice of hard-headed professionals, most of the prominent figures in this field (Peter Goodrich, Richard H. Weisberg and James Boyd White, for example) are themselves lawyers, and where outsiders like Peter Brooks or Jerome Bruner have ventured into this territory, they have often done so in collaboration with a legal colleague. There is an obvious reason: legal discourse presents formidable obstacles to the non-specialist and few literary critics will be willing to follow Stanley Fish's example of taking a law degree in order to prepare themselves for it.

For those drawn to the study of law *in* literature there is no lack of medieval material for them to work on: a list of all those Middle English works which incorporate trials, portray legal dilemmas or invite legal commentary would be a considerable one. Archaic procedures like ordeal or trial by battle appear frequently in romance (*Amis and Amiloun*,

Ywain and Gawain, *Athelston*, Chaucer's *Man of Law's Tale*, or Malory's story of Lancelot and Meliagaunt are obvious examples), although (as in *Sir Launfal*) we sometimes encounter less theatrical forms of trial. Debate poems, like *The Owl and the Nightingale* or Chaucer's *Parlement of Fowles*, often employ legal terminology, as do morality plays like *The Castle of Perseverance* or *Everyman*. For those who share Justice Oliver Wendell Holmes's view that the Bad Man will generally possess a privileged insight into the workings of the law, there are a number of medieval outlaw tales to provide us with such a perspective: they range from the Anglo-Norman *Foulk le Fitz Waryn* and the Chaucerian *Tale of Gamelyn* at one end of the social scale to the *Gest of Robyn Hode* and *Adam Bell, William of Cloudesly and Clym of the Clough* at the other. Many shorter poems, like the early fourteenth-century *Simonie* or the fifteenth-century *London Lickpenny*, satirize legal abuses, and numerous pulpit exempla in collections like the *Gesta Romanorum* or the *Alphabet of Tales* are directed against lawyers and their clients. Of all the writers to show familiarity with legal procedure and terminology, William Langland is the most prolific, not only in episodes like the marriage of Lady Mede or the jousting for Jerusalem but in countless allusions and analogies (as John Alford's *Piers Plowman: A Glossary of Legal Diction* amply demonstrates). Occasionally we even find Langland expressing a legal principle that is nowhere explicitly articulated in the legal literature. There are, for example, several recorded instances of medieval criminals who managed to survive a hanging being granted an automatic pardon (incidentally, this was no longer the case in Blackstone's England), but only in *Piers Plowman* do we find it expressed as an actual point of law: 'It is noght used on erthe to hangen a feloun / Ofter than ones' (B 18:380–1).[1]

When John Alford and Dennis Seniff compiled their bibliography of *Literature and Law in the Middle Ages* in 1984, there were already a substantial number of scholarly studies of Middle English literary works in which the law plays an important part, and over the last twenty years their number has increased considerably; what I wish to concentrate on here, however, is the rather more problematic approach of reading medieval law *as* literature. If this is a daunting task for modernists who have not been trained in the law, the obstacles faced by medieval literary critics are doubly formidable: not only must they come to terms with arcane and archaic legal discourses – and there were three principal ones (those of canon, civil and common law) operating simultaneously in medieval England – but they must also wrestle with foreign tongues (Latin and law French), since only the fledgeling Court of Chancery recognized English records in medieval England. On the positive side, readers interested in the common law (and it is the home-grown common law, not canon or civil law, that brings us closest to the *mentalité* of the period) can enlist the aid of Frederick Pollock and Frederic Maitland's wonderfully lucid *History of English Law*, but apart from its age (it was first published in 1895), this work suffers from the obvious disadvantage that it breaks off at the beginning of Edward II's reign, well before the first great flowering of English literature at the end of the fourteenth century. Unfortunately, Maitland's most brilliant successor, F. C. Milsom, writes the kind of dense legalese that will discourage all but the most persistent researcher, and those seeking an accessible introduction to medieval English law will probably do better to turn to historians like Theodore Plucknett or, more recently, Anthony Musson and W. M. Ormrod, than to the lawyers themselves.

Categorizing, Story-telling and Persuasion

In a book on legal story-telling called *Minding the Law* (2000), Anthony G. Amsterdam and Jerome Bruner distinguish 'three commonplace processes of legal thought and practice' (a literary theorist might call them discursive fields): categorizing, story-telling and persuasion.

> What distinguishes a contract from something 'not worth the paper it's printed on'? That's legal categorizing. How do you describe to the court the circumstances surrounding the contract's alleged breach? That's legal storytelling. You tell the story differently – in a quite different tongue – depending upon whether you represent the plaintiff or the defendant in a breach of contract case. That's legal rhetorics. *Categorization*, *narrative*, and *rhetorics* – the stuff of everyday life in the law. (2)

This insight clearly has implications for the literary critic, even though writers really share only two of these fields (narrative and rhetoric) with lawyers. The third (categorization) is more likely to be shared with philosophers, social scientists or literary theorists than with poets or novelists. This distinction is a significant one.

Very few lawyers, I suspect, would accept a symmetry among Amsterdam and Bruner's three fields. For many, the law's primary business is categorization and its application is simply a matter of deciding on appropriate categories. In McQuaker v. Goddard, for example, the plaintiff was bitten by a camel in a zoo and his claim to damages turned on whether camels are to be categorized as wild animals or tame ones (obviously, in England, camels do not belong in the same category as dogs and cats, yet in their countries of origin it is doubtful whether they can ever be categorized as wild). In deciding the category (camels are *not* wild animals) the court effectively decided the case. Of course, the legal issue in McQuaker v. Goddard is particularly clear-cut; had the defence argued that McQuaker was bitten not by their client's camel but by his neighbour's labrador, there would have been a factual question to put to a jury and the arts of story-telling and persuasion might have become more important. For those legal theorists, such as H. L. A. Hart and Ronald Dworkin, who view the law as primarily a matter of applying rules, narrative and rhetoric must always play subsidiary roles, at best greasing the wheels of the law, at worst liable to throw it off its tracks. The United States, with its long tradition of jurisprudential iconoclasm (embodied earlier in the school known as Legal Realism and currently in the Critical Legal Studies movement), has shown itself relatively hospitable to a wider view of legal process, but even there voices have been raised against allowing story-telling equal time with categorization. For instance, Martha Minow, a sympathetic commentator, has written:

> On reflection, I think good judgments *could* emerge when people turn over in their minds competing narratives about both a particular claimant and a larger social struggle, but there is no guarantee. Being able to appeal to some overarching principles and even some mid-level concepts lends at least the sense of some consistency in judgments across contexts and over time, which matters to the rule of law.[2]

If the boundary between these fields appears negotiable in the twenty-first century, it seems at least possible that earlier centuries too were aware of its permeability.

Rhetorics, the third in Amsterdam and Bruner's trinity, can claim a venerable legal ancestry. Indeed, the modern study of rhetoric, as it has come down to us via the trivium of the medieval universities, originated in the forensic instruction of Roman lawyers like Cicero and Quintilian. At this distance of time, however, it is very difficult to catch much of its flavour in the medieval English courtroom. The Year Books (the 'termes' that Chaucer says his Man of Law had by heart) report thousands of cases from the late thirteenth century down to the beginning of the seventeenth, but although they ostensibly record verbatim exchanges between opposing attorneys, with occasional remarks, questions and opinions from the bench, their style is generally anything but expansive. For the most part their subjects are concerned with arguing technical niceties, and although something might be said of their broader strategies (a heavy reliance on analogies and hypothetical cases, for example), there is little sign of their use of the more topical arts of persuasion. Perhaps this is inevitable, given that they are pleading their cases before a panel of judges, not a jury of laymen, but there are reasons for supposing that the dry shorthand of the reporters misses some of the verbal subtlety of the actual exchanges. Pleaders, after all, were employed to *counter*, 'tell a tale', and the plea they entered for their clients was known as a *counte*, 'a story'; attorneys, like poets, might even *doner colour*, 'give colour', to these stories, although colour clearly has a narrower sense in law French than it does in the *artes rhetoricae*. Even through the dry reportage, however, individual voices can sometimes be heard, particularly from the bench: 'My client is a poor man and knows no law', says a pleader early in Edward II's reign; 'It is because he knows no law that he has retained you', snaps back one of the judges. And in the next reign we again catch the unmistakable note of judicial sarcasm: 'I am amazed that *Grene* makes himself out to know everything in the world – and he is only a young man' (Holdsworth 1936: 551). If, like their Parisian counterparts, medieval English law students had indulged a taste for theatre, we might now have in English a courtroom drama as brilliant as the French farce of *Maître Pierre Pathelin*, but not until Elizabethan times do the English Inns of Court emulate the Basoche of Paris, and by then we have other sources from which to reconstruct the rhetorical texture of the law in action.[3]

When we turn to the question of legal narrative, however, we are on surer ground. All lawsuits, of course, tell a story of some kind and those recorded in the Year Books are no different:

> As the Serjeants state their different cases you will hear . . . stories of all manner and degrees of people from Kings and Archbishops and Earls to farm labourers and vileins;

> stories of the relations and dealing of these people with each other, illustrating the social conditions of the time; stories illustrating what people ate and drank and how much, and what were the current prices of all sorts of things, from cattle-sheds to apple-trees, from wine to herrings and eggs. You will hear much of ecclesiastics . . . of their quarrels amongst themselves and with their neighbours, of their disputes about patronage and tithes and debts and the like, and sometimes of their extremely overbearing treatment of their lowly dependents. (Bolland 1925: 13)

The author of this passage is a man who spent much of his life editing the Year Books of Edward II's reign, so perhaps it is not surprising that he detected more narrative energy in his sources than a less partial reader might have done. Most, in fact, would probably find the stories preserved in the Year Books unusually dry and unrewarding. There are two main reasons for this. In the first place the story the plaintiff's lawyer tells the court (his *counte* – or what modern lawyers sometimes refer to facetiously as the 'name, blame, claim' stage of the trial) was entirely oral. We often learn about it in the Year Books only indirectly, through the points of law that it raised – points the judges had to settle before it was fit to be told to a jury. The second reason is that this story would have been subject to extremely narrow formal constraints; in Amsterdam and Bruner's terms the subjugation of *narrative* to *categorization* in the medieval English courtroom would have been particularly harsh.

Forms of Action

Personal and real cases at common law from the Middle Ages down to the era of Victorian legal reform could be litigated only under one of a number of 'forms of action'; what this meant in practice is explained, with his usual cogency, by F. W. Maitland:

> Let it be granted that one man has been wronged by another; the first thing that he or his advisers have to consider is what form of action he shall bring. It is not enough that in some way or another he should compel his adversary to appear in court and should then state in the words that naturally occur to him, the facts on which he relies, and the remedy to which he thinks himself entitled. No, English law knows a certain number of forms of action, each with its uncouth name, a writ of right, an assize of novel disseisin or of *mort d'ancestor*, a writ of entry *sur disseisin* in the *per* and *cui*, a writ of *besaiel*, of *quare impedit*, an action of covenant, debt, detinue, replevin, trespass, assumpsit, ejectment, case. This choice is not merely a choice between a number of queer technical terms, it is a choice between methods of procedure adapted to cases of different kinds.[4]

Maitland famously claimed that the medieval forms of action 'rule us from the grave', but in the twenty-first century this rule has become fairly light. It will, of course, make a difference to the way the modern lawyer tells her client's story in court whether she conceives of the wrong he has suffered as being a breach of contract or a tort, but it is fair to say that her narrative freedom will be nowhere nearly as restricted by her choice as that of her medieval predecessor.

The medieval lawyer believes a tort has been committed against his client (this is called a *trespass* in Maitland's list), but unless he can make it seem as if this wrong was committed 'with force and arms' and 'against the king's peace' the court (at least until the middle of the fourteenth century) will not listen to his story. In fact, he must carefully frame his whole narrative in such a way as to accommodate this procedural requirement. Of course it may well be that force really was used, that the king's peace really was disturbed, and that his client's front door actually was broken down by an angry neighbour with an axe; but if not, his only recourse is to make it sound *as if* it happened that way. He is compelled to modify or adapt the facts of the case in order to make them fit a predetermined pattern. In other words, where categorization and narrative are forced into such stark competition the inevitable result will be legal fiction. Many years ago Owen Barfield argued that we can observe in the practice of legal fiction some of the most fundamental processes of the poetic imagination (and indeed, of linguistic consciousness itself) at work. Without going quite that far, I would like to spend the remainder of this paper examining the workings of legal fiction in late medieval England in order to discover what they may be able to tell us about the narrative sensibilities of the period.

Legal Fictions

The distinguished legal historian J. H. Baker has warned us against failing to discriminate among a wide variety of practices that are commonly called legal fictions. At one end of the scale he finds those things that 'cannot be called true or false in a factual sense' (2001: 44) and might better be regarded as *rules of law* than legal fictions; an 'implied' contract is litigated *as if* an express contract had been made and 'promissory estoppel' allows a plaintiff redress *as if* he had been expressly promised something; but in neither case is anything more than a terminological distinction being made. Closer to a true legal fiction is what might be called a *statutory fiction* where a court 'deems' something to have been intended by a lawmaker that is not expressly stated; if a tripe stall in Bolton is deemed to be a refreshment house 'within the meaning of the act' lay people are likely to feel that a liberty has been taken with the language, and although lawyers (like poets) will claim that they have a right to take such liberties they risk provoking resentment by doing so. Most people may not know what promissory estoppel is but they do know a house when they see one. Some statutory fictions verge on the metaphysical – like the one that deemed all British naval vessels to reside within the parish of Stepney – but (from a legal point of view) to take such fictions literally would be like arguing that John Donne was mistaken when he claimed that 'both th'Indias of spice and mine' were in bed with him. Not for nothing does Daniel Quilp refer to 'the beautiful fictions of the law' and 'those charming creations of the poet, John Doe and Richard Roe' (*The Old Curiosity Shop*, ch. 33).

At the other end of the scale are those legal fictions in which, for procedural purposes, factual claims are made in court that are patently untrue. They are of two basic types: *evidence fictions*, in which the court chooses to accept formal proof of something that did not happen (or fictitious proof of something that did happen); and *litigation fictions* in which some fact or event that was at one time required for the prosecution of a case has become merely a formal precondition of its coming before the court. In the 1930s film *The Gay Divorcee*, Ginger Rogers spends a platonic night in a hotel room with a total stranger (the improbable Rodolfo Tonetti) in order to supply formal proof of adultery for a collusive divorce suit – a clear example of a comparatively recent evidence fiction. Good modern instances of litigation fiction, on the other hand, are fairly hard to come by, although Eben Moglen has argued that commercial suits against perfectly respectable companies brought under the civil provisions of the US *Racketeer Influenced and Corrupt Organizations Act* offer one example.[5] For Baker, what distinguishes rules of law and statutory fictions from evidence fictions or litigation fictions is that the former are purely verbal while the latter are in some sense factual. There is, however, another way to look at this: the first two are deliberately anti-formalistic (they assume terminology to be flexible and capable of redefinition); the second two, on the other hand, are deeply formalistic (they attempt to adapt life to terminology rather than the other way around). Significantly, while the second category is comparatively uncommon in modern law, it was the first that was the rarer in the late Middle Ages. Statutory fiction, narrowly defined, was treated with grave suspicion in medieval England; statutes came to be construed with such *rigor iuris* that one early Tudor act against stealing horses, mares and geldings (in the plural) had to be redrafted because it was felt to condone the theft of single animals (Bellamy 1984: 149).

In what follows, then, I shall be concentrating on typical medieval forms of litigation fiction and evidence fiction, but I should also like to consider a further category (one that on the surface barely appears to be a fiction at all), that of equivocation. Equivocation may be distinguished from the usual form of evidence-fiction, however, in that it involves a truth intended to mislead rather than a fiction that deceives no one. I will discuss each of these types in turn.

Litigation Fictions

Around the beginning of July 1316, Simon de Rattlesdene bought a barrel of wine from Richard and Mary de Grunestone in the Suffolk port of Orford. The wine had apparently suffered on the voyage for when he got it home he found that it tasted of seawater. Richard and Mary evidently refused to refund him his money (over £4), and he sued them in the Court of Common Pleas. His counsel must have informed him that, since he could not produce a written contract, there was no form of action available; there was no writ to recover damages for having been sold defective wine. Accordingly, Simon decided to sue them, as the lawyers would say, *in trespass*. This, then, according to his attorney, is what really happened:

> Simon by his attorney complains that whereas the same Simon had bought from the aforesaid Richard at Orford the aforesaid tun, and had left it in the same place until, &c., the aforesaid Richard and Mary on the Thursday in the Octave of St John the Baptist in the ninth year of the present king's reign [1 July 1316] with force and arms, namely with swords and bows and arrows, drew off a part of the wine from the aforesaid tun and instead of the wine so drawn off they filled the tun with salt water so that all the aforesaid wine was destroyed &c. to the grave damage &c. and against [the king's] peace &c. whereby he says that he is worse off and has suffered damage to the value of £10. (300–1)[6]

It is characteristic of such litigation fiction that it generally 'works off the record', as Baker puts it (2001: 55). Only the sheer improbability of anyone's acting as Richard and Mary are said to have done here (that, and the fact that other defendants around the same time are complaining about false allegations of force being made against them) suggests that my introductory narrative is the more likely account of what really happened.[7]

The empty *vi et armis* provision in trespass is only one of a number of such formal litigation fictions to arise in the late Middle Ages, but it might well be argued that fiction was built into the very fabric of late medieval pleading itself. Since only the final issue between the parties was sworn to by them and then put to a jury, there were few constraints on the truth of minor allegations that might be made in the process of arriving at this issue. Thus, in a 1330 case concerning the right to present to a church living we find the Year Book reporters shaking their heads over a blunder committed by the defendant's lawyer in conceding that the current parson had been presented by the plaintiff's father (Baker 2001: 113). By telling this quite unnecessary truth the pleader had forfeited his client's case even though 'he could safely have alleged that the church was filled by a stranger as parson, by the presentment of a stranger (who never had any right), for this is not traversable' (not, in other words, subject to formal proof). By the late fourteenth century such fictitious allegations in pleading (known as *giving colour*) had become a standard weapon in the lawyer's armoury. The irony that 'statements that were wholly false and known to be so should operate to turn the course of proceedings whose intent was to find facts and do justice' has been noted by D. W. Sutherland (1981: 184).

Evidence Fictions

If litigation fictions work off the record, evidence fictions are even more opaque. It is quite clear, however, that medieval witnesses were no less ready than their descendants to construct fictional testimonies where necessary, and we may occasionally encounter external confirmation that this is what is going on. One of the richest sources of personal narratives among English legal archives are proof-of-age inquests in which witnesses attesting to the majority of a feudal heir are asked to state how they can be sure of his or her age; their standard response is to recall something important that had happened to them in the same year as the birth. Thus on 7 June 1423 John Borham of Sandon in Essex testified that Walter Fitz Wauter was baptized in the church of Wodeham Wauter on 22 June 1400, a date he particularly remembered because on that very day 'he was playing with other fellows of his at Chelmesford at football and broke his left leg'.[8] This vivid detail might be easier to credit if another witness had not broken his left leg playing football at Little Laver the day Thomas Enfield was baptized (8 October 1401), a third suffered the same misfortune at Thorpe on the day of Walter Howse's baptism (16 May 1402), and a fourth at Layer Marney when John Marny was baptized (15 August 1402). Rather that assuming that early fifteenth-century Essex was a hotbed of soccer hooliganism, we might better suppose that witnesses had learned that such stock stories would save them having to hang around in court.[9] In fact, so common were such evidence fictions that preachers used to inveigh against them from the pulpit: more than one told his parishioners about a group of witnesses who had invented accidents to themselves and their families to support their memory of a day on which a contract was supposed to have been drawn up, and were then punished for their perjury by having those very accidents befall them.[10]

A similar kind of fiction crept into the findings of local juries where there was a popular sentiment against the punishment of what was felt to have been an excusable homicide. The law treated killing in self-defence with grave suspicion and juries quickly learned that if they were to save a good neighbour from the gallows they must enter a special verdict that included a number of vital circumstantial details: the killer must always have been cornered while fleeing for his life, for example, and the weapon used must always have been a relatively harmless household implement found to hand, not some lethal weapon brought for the purpose. Sometimes we are lucky enough to be able to check these special verdicts against an earlier coroner's inquest. In 1341, for instance, such an inquest had reported that Robert Bousserman had returned home at midday to find John Doughty having sexual intercourse with his wife and had promptly dispatched him with a blow of his hatchet. English law did not tolerate such *crimes passionelles* (although French custom seems to have been more lenient), but the local jury evidently felt that this killing was excusable; this is what it reported at Bousserman's subsequent trial:

> John Doughty came at night to the house of Robert in the village of Laghscale as Robert and his wife lay asleep in bed in the peace of the King, and he entered Robert's house; seeing this Robert's wife secretly arose from her husband and went to John, and John went to bed with Robert's wife; in the meantime Robert awakened and hearing noise in his house and seeing his wife had left his bed rose and sought her in his house and found her with John; immediately John attacked Robert with an [*illegible*] knife and wounded him and stood between him and the door of Robert's house continually stabbing and wounding him and Robert seeing that his life was in danger and that he could in no way flee further, in order to save his life he took up a hatchet and gave John one blow in the head. (Greene 1985: 42–3)

Some such verdicts sound inherently implausible – like the tale of the man who stood with a loaded bow in his hand while his assailant 'having no respect for the arrow in the bow', rushed upon it and disembowelled himself[11] – but in this case, without the corresponding coroner's report, we would have little reason to suspect that the jury's account of Robert Bousserman's homicide was a pack of lies.

Lawyers tend to hold a rather benevolent view of legal fiction: if it speeds up business and enables justice to be done what harm can there be in it? Like Mr Pickwick's attorney, Perker, they are apt to forget that even the most benign legal fiction will look suspiciously like falsehood to the lay person: 'I don't exactly know about perjury, my dear sir . . . Harsh word, my dear sir, very harsh word indeed. It's a legal fiction, my dear sir, nothing more' (*The Pickwick Papers*, ch. 40). With John Doughty's fictional manslaughter, however, we are moving into a territory where we can no longer regard legal fiction as entirely victimless or innocent. There is a tendency to use the pejorative term *equivocation* for legal fictions that patently pervert the course of justice, but we should still recognize that there is an essential kinship between the two activities.

Equivocation Fictions

In 1220 Hamo Moor accused a man called Philip King of having stolen his mare. Philip said that he got it from his father-in-law, Edward, and Edward said that he bought it from a man called Elias Piggun.

> And Elias Piggun being asked where he got that mare, says that before the war she was given to him at Cardiff in Wales together with some pigs, by a certain man in consideration of lessons in sword-play, and that he possessed her for six weeks, and brought her from Wales into these parts, and sold her to Edward for three shillings and a penny, outside Waltham at the cross. But as to the sale he produces no suit [supporters], but confesses that he and Edward were alone together. And Edward says the same. (125)[12]

Again, this convincing little account (none of whose details Piggun would have had to swear to) turns out to be a pack of lies; what gives it away, finally, are those 'lessons in sword-play' [*de skermia*]. There are two points of law we need to know in order to understand what is really going on here: the first is that at this date Hamo's accusation (technically, it is called an *appeal*), unless settled more amicably, could ultimately end in a trial by combat; the second is that anyone who mistakenly bought stolen goods had the option of transferring the formal accusation of theft onto the person from whom they were purchased (the technical term for this is *vouching to warranty*). Now Philip does seem to have got the mare from his father-in-law Edward, but Edward's title to her was evidently far from secure. At any rate he clearly did not fancy his chances of defending it on the field of combat so he vouched to warranty a professional: Elias Piggun may have *said* that he was a man who made his living giving lessons in sword play, but from where Hamo stood he looked remarkably like a hired champion (a *campio locatus*).

The facts, insofar as they can be known in the case of Hamo v. Piggun, emerge because the justices became suspicious and empanelled an inquest of no less than twenty-four men from four different villages to look into the matter. There is a certain amount of partiality from the representatives of the different villages, but all agree that Piggun had never legally owned the mare; whether he had taken on the warranty for money or because he had been promised the hand of Edward's daughter (presumably Philip's sister-in-law), however, is left unsettled. One particularly interesting detail is volunteered by the men of Waltham: they say 'that after this action had begun in the court of Cheshunt, Philip handed over the mare to Elias Piggun, the would-be warrantor, in order to enable him to swear safely' (126). The whole rigmarole about receiving the mare in exchange for lessons in sword play is simply false (though, it should be noted, unsworn) testimony; this little charade about having nominal ownership of her, however, is a legal fiction or, if you prefer, an equivocation. It anticipated the moment when Piggun might have to swear on the field of combat.

My final example is also from the thirteenth century and it too involves trial by combat. It comes from a revealing little 'handbook for felons' called the *Placita corone* (c.1250). One of the dilemmas the author sets out to solve is how to get someone off an accusation of homicide brought not by the sheriff but by relatives of the dead man. Like Hamo's action against Piggun, this was technically an *appeal* and could potentially end in trial by battle. Normally, the author suggests, the best way of getting out of an indictment for homicide was to purchase a royal pardon, but these private appeals posed a bit of a problem because they were not covered by such pardons. However, there was still a way, he tells us, and this was a trick he had got from no less an authority than a royal judge called Roger de Thurkelby. The accused (the *appellee*) must turn up on the field of combat on the appointed day and swear to his innocence as required by law:

> And as soon as the appellor takes the field against him to defeat him, as the necessity of the occasion demands, the appellee, if he is sensible, and always provided he is not strong enough to defeat his adversary at the first blow, will raise neither shield nor club but will say the word now; and this means that he confesses the deed for which he is appealed and for which he was liable to be hanged in such a case. And therefore let him take care that he have the king's charter on him and that he show it to the judge or to those who are there in his name. (7)[13]

Normally someone who cries recreant on the field of combat is dragged straight off to the gallows, but (and here's the beauty of the thing) the hangman cannot touch anyone who has the king's pardon on him. Not only do you get off scot-free, but you even have an action against your appellor for disturbing the king's peace.

The contrasts between this situation and the case of Hamo v. Piggun are striking. In both, the crude resolution of trial by combat (already obsolescent in the thirteenth century) is employed in defence of an unjust claim, but the methods used are altogether different. Piggun, we might guess, is not a wealthy man, nor did he personally steal

Hamo's mare; he is a principal in the case only by virtue of a legal fiction built upon the voucher to warranty. The hypothetical homicide in the *Placita corone*, on the other hand, has enough wealth and influence to procure a royal pardon for himself; he is a genuine principal and as likely as not guilty of murder. Even more marked, however, are their respective attitudes towards perjury. Piggun, we will recall, had had technical possession of the mare, 'in order to enable him to swear safely'. Should he have had to fight Hamo to prove whose oath was sound, he wanted to be sure he was covered; a man would lose his eternal soul for swearing a false oath. The Cheshunt villagers who served on the inquest reported that Piggun had declared before the whole parish that he took up the warranty 'for God's sake, and asked all men to pray for him so truly as true it was that he did this for God's sake and not for lucre' (*pro Deo et non pro denariis*). Calculated perjury, however, is an essential element in the strategy of the *Placita corone*: if guilty, the appellee automatically perjures himself when he swears before entering the field of combat (as the procedure requires) that he is innocent. If he really is innocent, of course, his crying recreant will expose him to the public shame of being reputed a perjurer, though perhaps he might still hope for a more lenient verdict on Judgement Day. Either way he seems far less concerned about the fate of his soul than Elias Piggun. And what is still more shocking is that he is counselled to this course of action by one of the king's judges. The ultimate fate of the two men is equally striking: Elias Piggun, at worst an accessory after the fact, is sentenced to mutilation by the loss of a foot (a mutilation calculated to put him out of business), while the *Placita corone*'s appellee, with the judge's connivance, gets off scot-free.

Of the many 'pleasant fictions of the law,' wrote Dickens in *Nicholas Nickleby*, 'there is not one so pleasant or practically humorous as that which supposes . . . the benefits of all laws to be equally attainable by all men, without the smallest reference to the furniture of their pockets' (ch. 46). No doubt Dickens would have felt that the respective fates of these two appellees amply justified his cynicism, but a reading of their legal narratives teaches us more than this. It might appear that the interplay of truth and falsehood, legal fact and legal fiction, formalist and relativist attitudes to the relationship between language and the actual world, was so convoluted in the medieval courtroom that normal social assumptions about honesty and veracity must have been regularly abused there, particularly by those with power and influence. This alone might seem to explain the remarkable interest in the law that we have noted in the literary works of the period, and to corroborate Ziolkowski's contention that great literature will often respond to those moments in history 'when the tension between law and morality is increased to the breaking point' (1997: 16). Closer inspection, however, suggests that the situation is more complex.

Legal attitudes to truth, though clearly in a state of flux, were not entirely unprincipled in the later Middle Ages. All our cases make it plain that where no oath was involved, most people felt perfectly free to embroider the truth in court, or (if they experienced any reluctance) that their attorneys were quite happy to do it for them. On the other hand, few medieval people would have taken the swearing of an oath as lightly as the *Placita corone*'s appellee (or his adviser Judge Roger Thurkelby) and we are left with the dominant impression that most were deeply affected by its sacral nature. Moreover, where an oath was involved, it mattered greatly whether they were being asked to swear that something had happened (a judicial oath) or to the truth of a statement (an evidentiary oath); to swear that you had not stolen Roger's horse was one thing, to swear to a true saying (a *voir dite* or *verdict*) that Simon had not stolen Roger's horse was quite another. Both might lead to legal fictions, but fictions of rather different kinds: in the first instance truth might be as narrow, as legalistic, as equivocal as one could make it; in the second, as circumstantial, as generous, as partial as it needed to be. That people came to identify the commodification of the first kind of truth with the very institution of the law itself helps explain much of the cynicism expressed in literary works like *The Simonie* or *London Lickpenny* (not to mention *Piers Plowman*), but it does more. It furnishes the masterplot of a great many medieval romances in which generosity of spirit is brought into conflict with narrow literalism, and where the fictions of the poet do battle with the fictions of the law.

See also: 20 Middle English Romance, 28 Morality and Interlude Drama, 32 *Piers Plowman*, 33 The *Canterbury Tales*, 38 Malory's *Morte Darthur*.

Notes

1 William Langland, *The Vision of Piers Plowman: A Critical Edition of the B-Text*, ed. A. V. C. Schmidt, 2nd edn (London: Dent, 1995).

2 Martha Minow, 'Stories in Law', in *Law's Stories: Narrative and Rhetoric in the Law*, ed. Peter Brooks and Paul Gewirtz (New Haven, Conn.: Yale University Press, 1996), pp. 24–36 (p. 30).

3 Howard Graham Harvey, *Theatre of the Basoche: The Contribution of the Law Societies to French Mediaeval Comedy* (Cambridge, Mass.: Harvard University Press, 1941).

4 Frederic William Maitland, *The Forms of Action at Common Law: A Course of Lectures* [1909], ed. A. H. Chaytor and W. J. Whittaker (Cambridge: Cambridge University Press, 1976), pp. 1–2.

5 Eben Moglen, 'Legal Fictions and Common Law Legal Theory: Some Historical Reflections', *Tel-Aviv University Studies in Law* 10 (1991), 33–52. Baker, however, would probably regard this as a simple statutory fiction; in other words, large companies (and even government agencies) are *deemed* to be racketeers for the purposes of the lawsuit.

6 J. H. Baker and S. F. C. Milsom (eds), *Sources of English Legal History: Private Law to 1750* (London: Butterworths, 1986).

7 There are always two sides to any lawsuit, and it is always possible that Simon left his wine standing on the quay for a while, enabling Richard and Mary to claim that the contamination had occurred after the sale.

8 R. C. Fowler, 'Legal Proofs of Age', *English Historical Review* 22 (1907), 101–5 (102).

9 It is perhaps even more likely that the court reporter (for an appropriate fee) undertook to supply suitable stories for the record.

10 J. A. Herbert, *Catalogue of Romances in the Department of Manuscripts in the British Museum*, vol. 3 (London: Trustees of the British Museum, 1919), p. 633.

11 Naomi D. Hurnard, *The King's Pardon for Homicide before A.D. 1307* (Oxford: Clarendon Press, 1969), p. 302.

12 Frederic William Maitland (ed.), *Select Pleas of the Crown*, vol. 1 (London: Selden Society, 1888).

13 J. M. Kay (ed. and trans.), *Placita corone: or La corone pledée devant justices* (London: Selden Society, 1966).

References and Further Reading

Alford, John A. 1988. *Piers Plowman: A Glossary of Legal Diction.* Cambridge: Brewer. A valuable guide to vernacular legal terminology, not only in Langland.

—— and Seniff, Dennis P. 1984. *Literature and Law in the Middle Ages: A Bibliography of Scholarship.* New York: Garland. A useful bibliography covering the whole of the European Middle Ages; in need of updating.

Amsterdam, Anthony G. and Bruner, Jerome 2000. *Minding the Law.* Cambridge, Mass.: Harvard University Press. A lawyer and a psychologist offer valuable insights into the uses and effects of legal story-telling.

Baker, J. H. 2001. *The Law's Two Bodies: Some Evidential Problems in English Legal History.* Oxford and New York: Oxford University Press. A leading historian of the Common Law discusses the nature and meaning of legal fiction.

Barfield, Owen 1947. 'Poetic Diction and Legal Fiction.' In *Essays Presented to Charles Williams* (London: Oxford University Press), pp. 106–27. Explores connections between legal and literary language; Barfield was a member of the Inklings and a trained lawyer.

Bellamy, John G. 1984. *Criminal Law and Society in Late Medieval and Tudor England.* Gloucester: Sutton, and New York: St Martin's Press. Surveys criminal legislation from Richard II to Elizabeth I, concentrating on summary process, witnesses, riot, penal laws and benefit of clergy.

Bolland, William Craddock 1925. *A Manual of Year Book Studies.* Cambridge: Cambridge University Press. A dated, but still useful, introduction to the Year Books.

Brooks, Peter 2000. *Troubling Confessions: Speaking Guilt in Law and Literature.* Chicago: University of Chicago Press. Applies insights drawn from the analysis of fictional confession scenes to legal cases.

Green, Richard Firth (1998). *A Crisis of Truth: Literature and Law in Ricardian England.* Philadelphia: University of Pennsylvania Press. Uses developments in fourteenth-century Common Law to throw light on the concept of 'truth' in Ricardian authors such as Chaucer and Langland.

Greene, Thomas Andrew 1985. *Verdict According to Conscience: Perspectives on the English Criminal Trial Jury, 1200–1800.* Chicago: University of Chicago Press. Studies the English jury from its medieval origins to the eighteenth century; views institutional history in its social and cultural contexts.

Goodrich, Peter 1996. *Law in the Courts of Love: Literature and Other Minor Jurisprudences.* New York: Routledge. A lawyer discusses alternative dispute resolution in terms of medieval Courts of Love.

Holdsworth, William S. 1936. *A History of English Law*, 4th edn, vol. 2. London: Methuen, and Sweet and Maxwell. The standard institutional history of English law; only the first three volumes deal with the Middle Ages.

Musson, Anthony and Ormrod, W. M. 1999. *The Evolution of English Justice: Law, Politics, and Society in the Fourteenth Century.* Basingstoke: Macmillan, and New York: St Martin's Press. Takes the development of the Common Law from where Pollock and Maitland leave off; discusses the cultural and social context of the law drawing on literary materials.

Plucknett, Theodore F. T. 1956. *A Concise History of the Common Law*, 5th edn. Boston: Little, Brown. A useful history of the Common Law, written by a historian rather than a lawyer.

Pollock, Frederick and Maitland, Frederic William 1898. *The History of English Law before the Time of Edward I*, 2nd edn rev. by S. F. C. Milsom. London: Cambridge University Press, 1968. Largely the work of Maitland, it remains fresh and perceptive after more than a hundred years.

Posner, Richard A. 1998. *Law and Literature*, 2nd edn. Cambridge, Mass.: Harvard University Press. A pre-eminent American jurist distinguishes between literary and legal approaches to ethical problems.

Rosenthal, Joel T. 2003. *Telling Tales: Sources and Narration in Late Medieval England.* University Park: Pennsylvania State University Press. Studies late medieval narrative construction in witness statements (including proof-of-age testimony) and private letters.

Steiner, Emily and Candace Barrington (eds) 2002. *The Letter of the Law: Legal Practice and Literary Production in Medieval England.* Ithaca, N.Y., and London: Cornell University Press. A valuable collection of essays on the connections between literature and law in medieval England.

Sutherland, D. W. 1981. 'Legal Reasoning in the Fourteenth Century: The Invention of "Color" in Pleading.' In *On the Laws and Customs of England: Essays in Honor of Samuel E. Thorne*, ed. Morris S. Arnold, Thomas A. Green, Sally A. Scully and Stephen D. White (Chapel Hill: University of North Carolina Press), pp. 182–94.

Symposium: Law and Literature 1982. *Texas Law Review* 60, 373–586. A ground-breaking collection, including the opening shots in the debate between Stanley Fish and Ronald Dworkin on whether what is interpreted (i.e., a work of literature or a legal text) already has meaning, or whether the act of interpretation itself determines the meaning.

Ziolkowski, Theodore 1997. *The Mirror of Justice: Literary Reflections of Legal Crises.* Princeton, N.J.: Princeton University Press. Studies literary responses to the failure of legal systems to adjust to changing social circumstances; includes discussions of *Njal's Saga* and *Renard the Fox*.

18
Images

Peter Brown

The plural in the title of this essay indicates a twofold application of the word. In the first place, 'image' denotes the familiar literary device whereby writers fashion a visual impression of a place, person or thing, whether for literal or figurative use. However, in the period covered by this book, 'image' also applied to the representation of religious objects, people and scenes (whether carved, sculpted or painted) in churches and elsewhere.[1] The use of such images was a source of much debate. My topic is the way in which the use of literary images in secular writing becomes embroiled in the controversy over religious images.

Secular and religious images, whether verbal, graphic or plastic, belong in the same frame of reference because medieval writers showed no compunction about transferring the terms of religious image-making to secular contexts, and because the interpretation of all images belongs to the same economy of mind: they function as sense signs producing mental simulacra in the imagination, which are in turn processed by the faculties of reason and understanding.[2]

The emphasis of the present essay is on two secular writers, John Gower (c.1340–1408) and Thomas Hoccleve (1367?–1426), who were active when the debate on images had taken a particular turn, in response to radical ideas promoted by the Lollard followers of the Oxford reformer, John Wyclif. Although both Gower and Hoccleve are clear-cut in their stated attitudes towards Lollard issues, their literary practice reveals a much more ambiguous and conflicted set of ideas (Strohm 1999: 660).

John Gower's *Vox clamantis*

For Gower in *Vox clamantis* 2.10, the word *imago* or 'image' means a religious object such as the statue of a saint.[3] He is particularly exercised by its capacity to distract believers from focusing attention on the essence of the faith, to the extent that the image, rather than what it signifies, becomes the object of veneration. Gower condemns such image-worship in forthright terms: Christians thereby become traitors to God and void of reason. For in praying to statues carved in wood and stone they are worshipping the mute products of their own creation, not their Creator. It effects an inversion, since the natural world was made to be servant, not master. Simple logic reveals the insanity of subjection to carved images, for the same tree that provides wood for a statue is also used to make a plough, or light a fire (Isaiah 44: 13–20). Graven images may, however, be used in positive and constructive ways, as a means to strengthen devotion to God and the saints. But they are rendered worthless if the intention behind their manufacture is to elicit offerings from the devout, or to display the wealth of the donor. Furthermore, God explicitly prohibited to Moses any attempt to create a sculptured likeness (Exodus 33). The true image of God is the human body united with the faculty of reason, and it is by virtue of this creation by God that he merits worship.

The one image that should be worshipped is the sign of the Cross, in honour of the crucified Christ. It is an image accessible not only in material form as 'wood worthy of reverence' but also as an interior image (*signa*, line 553) 'stamped on our minds'.[4] The Cross is emblematic of power (the conquering of hell, overthrow of the devil, redemption of mankind), of salvation (the defeat of death) and of personal purgation (it purifies feelings, cleanses the mind, brightens the heart). The Cross therefore expresses the distilled essence of the Christian faith: all sacred things, says Gower, 'pleasantly combine . . . together in the Cross'.[5]

Gower's argument – which is part of a more general attack on clerical vices, as found in Books 3 and 4 – has a topical application. For Gower's is one among many clamorous voices, growing in number and intensity from the late 1370s, urging a reconsideration of the nature, purpose and function of representations in paint and wood of persons and scenes from biblical and devotional sources. The hostility to religious images became so intense in some quarters that they were deliberately destroyed. Henry Knighton's *Chronicle* records a case in Leicester (before 1389) involving Richard Weytestathe, a chaplain, and the vegetarian William Smith, who used a painted wooden statue of St Katherine as fuel to cook cabbage, thus inflicting a new martyrdom (Aston 1988: 133–4; Hudson 1988: 76).[6] At roughly the same time, according to the *Chronicon Anglie*, Sir John Montague removed images from the chapel of the manor at Shenley and hid them but for an image of St Katherine, which he placed in a bakehouse.[7] Such episodes were not the sudden flaring of spontaneous iconoclasm in an atmosphere of revolutionary fervour, but one outcome of a controversy that had been simmering for some time. The debate pre-dates Wyclif, who – whatever the excesses of his followers – had relatively mainstream views on the uses and abuses of images (Aston 1988: 98–104; Jones 1973: 29–31).[8]

It would be a mistake to regard the debate as one that soon polarized, or remained stable. On both radical and conservative wings there were many shades of opinion and numerous intermediate positions, as the case of Walter Hilton demonstrates.[9] So, while hostility to religious imagery came to be readily associated with the Lollard position, and an occasion for persecution and death (Aston 1988: 122),[10] in details that position could overlap with the views of others who would not otherwise be regarded as remotely heterodox (Hudson 1988: 301–9; Stanbury 2000: 464–5). This was especially true of the debate in its formative stages, and it was towards the end of the formative stage that Gower made his intervention, subsequently endorsing it when he revised the work c.1386 and again c.1399 (Fisher 1965: 102).

In order to position Gower's views in relation to the wider debate we might compare them with those expressed in a treatise setting out Lollard attitudes to images (Jones 1973: 31–7). The surviving manuscript, in London, British Library MS Additional 24202, is from the early fifteenth century and occurs in a collection of religious tracts which are 'critical of the contemporary church though not all overtly heretical'.[11] Like Gower, the author of 'a tretyse of ymagis' condemns images as no more than inert objects, emphasizes the moral and spiritual waywardness of image-worship, criticizes the motives behind their making, calls on biblical authority to support his argument, reminds his readers that the living human being (especially Christ), made in God's image, is the authentic object of worship, and identifies the Cross as exempt from his strictures. At the same time, he introduces different slants, is more specific in targeting abuses and their practitioners, and extends the agenda of items linked to image-worship. All in all it is a much more pointed and polemical piece of writing than Gower's, and reads as an intervention in a continuing and fierce controversy.

For the Lollard writer, religious images entail a heresy of representation, showing Christ and the saints in a splendour far removed from the biblical record. Underneath, the images are, as for Gower, dead – no more than brightly painted stones. Their effect on the gullible and unwary is spiritually devastating. Elaborate images cause forgetfulness of their originals, contradicting what those persons stood for (simplicity, poverty, humility) and bringing their admirers into error concerning Christ, the apostles and saints, and indeed the nature of Christian belief itself. Worse, 'rude' worshippers waste their temporal goods in making offerings to images while ignoring deeds of charity to poor, needy and ill neighbours, falsely believing that the most impressive images merit the most generous gifts. But in all this they are deceived, mistaking the material image for the spiritual reality it should represent, blinded to the worthlessness of the object they adore. Instead, they attribute to it semi-magical powers, even miracles, and so become little better than heathens at the mercy of the devil. Such idols are perversions of what, ideally, they might be, as Gower also recognized: the stimulus to a devout mental image, 'bokis of lewid men to sture them on the mynde of Cristis passion'.

The kind of image the Lollard writer attacks has not arisen by chance. He is as suspicious as Gower about the intentions and ulterior motives behind their manufacture. For the manipulation of images to represent more than their unadorned scriptural source is an exercise in vainglory, reflecting the sinful state of the perpetrators. They are responsible for leading the simple people into error in order to derive material gain – 'wynnyngis', or donations. They thus promote heresy by diverting to their own use the energy and money that should be targeted at charitable work. 'They' in this instance are 'rich endowid clerks' who by virtue of this practice are blatant hypocrites, preaching charity to the poor while at the same time encouraging gifts to dead images, so depriving the poor, the bedridden and the afflicted of alms, and neglecting the hungry and cold – the very people they are bound to succour as a means of attaining heavenly bliss (Aston 1988: 124–9). Images are thus a means whereby proud and covetous clerks exploit and control the unwary, devices designed by the agents of Antichrist to rob the poor of faith, hope, charity and worldly goods, and to maintain themselves in pride, greed and lust. Nor is offering to images justified on biblical grounds. It is a newfangled thing with no scriptural basis. The incontrovertible anchor-point of the biblical argument is the same for the Lollard writer as it was for Gower: the first two commandments against strange gods and graven images (Exodus 20: 3–4).

Again like Gower, he directs attention away from dead, false, painted representations towards true, living counterparts. Neighbours are *quick* images, so serving the poor with charity is a better way of worshipping their maker – that is, by attention to those human forms, made in the likeness of God, that replicate Christ's poverty and suffering. And since Christ took human form, the Crucifixion is for the Lollard writer, as it was for Gower, permissible as a reminder of what Christ endured – though even here the *kind* of image is important: it should be simple, uncomplicated, unadorned.

The author of 'A tretyse of ymagis', writing when the debate had become more polarized, ventures into territory that Gower does not countenance. But the underlying attitudes towards images, as expressed by Gower and the Lollard writer, are remarkably similar. And this is surprising. For if we are used to thinking of the Lollards as developing a fundamental critique of the church, one that came to be associated with political radicalism, we are no less used to regarding Gower as conservative, if not downright reactionary, with the first book of *Vox clamantis* serving as one of the chief sources of evidence.[12] The work is prefaced by a flattering dedication to Archbishop Thomas Arundel, the persecutor of the Lollards.[13] On the other hand, the later books of *Vox clamantis* mount a sustained attack on the abuses of authority, and claim to be expressing the voice of the people (Ferster 1996: 129–32).[14]

Why then this sharp disparity between the sympathies implicit in Gower's attitude to images, and the vitriol he directs at the rebels of 1381 (Federico 2003: 3–18)? The customary explanation adduces evidence from the textual history of *Vox clamantis*: Book 2 onwards was written before the events of 1381; Book 1 was written in direct response to them, and appears to indicate a fundamental rethinking by Gower of his political stance. It may be that Gower was alarmed by the tendency of the rebels to target literate figures like him, a private gentleman and landowner.[15] But it is also worth considering the claims he makes for his work as a 'mirror', producing by means of memory and association what is denied to actual sight, namely a sharper and fuller perceptiveness. In this respect, Gower's choice of genre is significant because of the dream vision's particular virtues. It allows him access to truth, the significance of which 'disturbs the depths of my heart', and enables him to create a kind of distance from the turmoil of rebellion, to achieve as need demands a sense of heightened reality, to imply that what he writes is divinely inspired, and above all to represent the uprising in striking, surreal images.

There can be little doubt that Gower recognized the power of such images to alter consciousness. He claims that dream images can provide a *better* understanding of the conditions of the time than other modes of analysis by revealing deeper structures of meaning than those apparent on the surface of events. Moreover, dreams provide what he calls 'memorable tokens' of certain important occurrences. The term he uses is *signa* (line 16), the same word as the one he used in 2.10 to describe mental images formed by meditating upon the Cross as object. However, they are not a means merely of chronicling notable events in visual terms, but of rhetorical representation – that is of depicting key aspects of the revolt in ways designed to persuade the reader of their negative or positive qualities within a moral and political scheme that categorizes the uprising as deplorable.

There is no avoiding the striking contradiction between Gower's attitude to images in 2.10, where he counsels restraint, and in Book 1, where images of his own sprout and flourish in abundance as if from some *Vox clematis*. But the contradiction may be more apparent than real. It could be that he, 'moral' Gower, was acutely aware that, as a writer, he was himself by analogy a creator, manipulator and controller of images and hence responsible for ensuring that the effects they achieved were consonant with the intentions behind them. For both sections are about the tendency of the ignorant to go astray and lose reason when confronted by a powerful, influential and attractive force – be it that of a visually impressive religious icon, or of Fortune, herself a kind of political idol (Olsson 1987: 147), or that of a demagogue offering the enticing prospect of redress for wrongs suffered to 'stupid minds' prone to imagine more than they should (2). Second, *Vox* 2.10 is concerned with images that are books for the unlettered and which must therefore be tightly controlled, whereas the book as a whole is written in Latin for the intelligentsia, whom Gower presumably trusts to take from images the meanings they are intended to convey (Fisher 1965: 105–6). Finally, as order is re-established in the aftermath of revolt, man resumes his proper place, made in the image of God, and with reason his paramount faculty once the delusory images produced in the ferment of revolt have evaporated (1.18). Man as the image of God and Reason (p. 88), we know from 2.10, is worthy of worship. The correct hierarchy is restored, subservience and subjection reinstated (1.21) after being turned upside-down by wild, animalesque forces. It is the surrendering of reason to religious enthusiasm, of the 'rational' to the 'brutish', and the subservience of the worshipper-cum-idolator before a thing that should be servant, not master, that the abuse of religious images entails. It is perhaps no coincidence that at this particular place in Book 1 of *Vox clamantis* Gower should address the Cross as a token of salvation – that one image exempted from his strictures, and which acts here as a constant reminder of integrity, stability and dependable truth.

For the most part the images Gower creates in Book 1, his 'memorable tokens', are the very antithesis of what he associates with the Cross, for they express again and again the inversion of hierarchical order, and contempt for its gradations. The longest lasting inversion is that of the dream itself, not merely as a mirror image of the peasants' uprising, but in enabling Gower to show how the revolt gave reality itself a different hue, a dream-like quality, it having been for him a living nightmare of transgression, of space invaded, of boundaries broken and privacy violated. Even the sanctioned, festive, socially rehabilitating inversions associated with the June feast of Corpus Christi – the day on which the rebels entered London – suddenly become serious and menacing, the invasion a parodic Corpus Christi procession bent on desecration.[16]

Among the topsy-turvy images Gower describes paradise becomes hell, reasonable people become madmen, peasants become animals, domestic beasts revert to a wild state, arable land lies fallow, country invades city, citizens are rusticated, the subservient become masters, freemen become constrained, the weak defeat the strong, the sheep assault their shepherd, new Troy (London), undergoing its own fall, becomes an anti-Troy with no heroes (though plenty of traitors). Gower himself feels dehumanized, dislocated, bewildered (Olsson 1987: 145). The outcome of this relentless dynamic is the production of images memorable precisely because they capture the process of inversion, the metamorphosis of one thing into another to produce hybrids, grotesques: pigs that are wolves, asses that become lions, farmhands who are frogs. In all this, Gower draws on a library of imagined forms familiar to his readers from the Bible and Ovid and elsewhere.[17]

If it is difficult to detect in the proliferation of images in Book 1 of *Vox clamantis* any of the reticence and resistance to images Gower evinced in 2.10, it is the case that in Book 1 he deploys images in response to a particular occasion and need, in order to achieve certain effects and purposes, not in order to have them admired for their own sake. Again, there is a sense of relief when the chimeras of the revolt fade, the invented images become redundant, and he turns to the one true image of the Cross. And we should also note the relative lack of rhetorical colour in the following books. If Gower was not a crypto-Lollard, he certainly shared some of the Wycliffites' misgivings about images. At the same time he abrogated to himself the creation and control of elaborate, awe-inspiring, vivid representations of a world turned upside-down. While he remained true to his Lollard-leaning views on the function of images, that did not prevent him from dedicating his work to a persecutor of heretics, or from condemning popular demand for the kinds of social and religious reform for which he had earlier seen a need (Echard 2003). Hoccleve, the subject of the next section, is no less contradictory in his attitude to images, but his starting-point is very different.

Hoccleve's *Regiment of Princes*

It is not unusual to find in the margin of a late medieval manuscript a drawing of a hand with an extended index finger. A two-dimensional outline in ink, often hastily sketched, and inserted by a scribe or reader, it indicates a noteworthy section of the text.[18] However, on folio 88 of London, British Library, MS Harley 4866 (after 1411) the convention is transformed almost beyond recognition.[19] The pointed hand depicted there is not schematic, but lifelike, executed in skin-coloured tints, and shaded to suggest depth and modelling (figure 35.1). It is a right hand, attached to an arm, and the arm to the body of a man who is familiar from the polychrome covers of modern books: Geoffrey Chaucer (Perkins 2001: 119–21). It accompanies the text of

The Regiment of Princes by Hoccleve, a work that is part autobiography, part mirror for princes, part petition (Scanlon 1990),[20] and addressed to Henry of Monmouth, Prince of Wales (the future Henry V).

The familiarity of the portrait should not obscure its extraordinary impact within its original context. Here is Thomas Hoccleve's Chaucer in a manuscript which may have been executed under the author's direct supervision[21] – Chaucer as Hoccleve remembered him and wished him to be remembered in a portrait dating from the time of the poem's completion in 1411.[22] According to his own testimony, among the qualities valued by this clerk of the privy seal were Chaucer's skills as a writer, his piety and his dependability as a source of wisdom and authority. So the picture shows him holding a rosary in his other hand, wearing a *penner* or inkhorn around his neck, dressed in gown and headgear of a sober grey colour, and with a carefully composed facial expression, created in three-quarter profile, suggesting that its owner is serious, of an age that commands respect, and focused (he looks and points steadily in one and the same direction). Furthermore, the image 'leaps out of the page': it is the only image embedded in the text of the *Regiment of Princes*; it appears, unexpectedly, towards the end of the poem; its lush colours contrast with the monochrome of the script; its size (approximately 7 cm × 4 cm) is relatively large in relation to the whole page; and by being placed against a flat, lozenge-pattern background, and overlapping the frame with his hand, Chaucer seems – in contrast to the linearity of the text – three-dimensional, as if leaning out of a window in a wall to call attention to some significant event .

The significant event is the production of this extraordinary image. Chaucer points to lines in the text where their author explains:

> . . . I have heere his liknesse
> Do make, to this ende, in sothfastnesse,
> That they that han of him lost thoght and mynde
> By this peynture may ageyn him fynde.
> (4995–8)

Viewed as an event in the history of art, the image is indeed significant,[23] but its more immediate function is different: while the portrait draws attention to the text, the text also directs attention to the portrait, informing the reader's response to it. For Hoccleve, the image of Chaucer is intended not merely as an icon of literary greatness, but also as a means to an end – as a way in which those who have forgotten Chaucer's significance ('lost thoght and mynde') can recapture it. That process might well be stimulated through Chaucer's outward appearance, as shown in the portrait, but the true ends in view are the inner qualities of Chaucer's writing – qualities that might then be further internalized in the life or poetry of the admiring reader. It is an image designed to stir reading (or listening) memories, to encourage a return to Chaucer's writings, to aid thoughtfulness, to incorporate Chaucer posthumously, as an icon of national identity, in Prince Henry's political agenda (Pearsall 1994: 398), and to reinforce the authority of Hoccleve's role as an adviser to princes by linking his poem vividly with a revered writer who wrote poems of advice to the Prince's father, Henry IV (Perkins 2001: 118–19; Scanlon 1990: 240–2).

The lines quoted above are embedded in two stanzas, headed by the image, which describe in greater detail the process Hoccleve has in mind, which is analogous to the use of images in religious meditation:

> Althogh his lyf be qweynt, the resemblance *extinguished*
> Of him hath in me so fressh lyflynesse
> That to putte othir men in remembrance
> Of his persone, I have heere his liknesse
> Do make . . .
>
> The ymages that in the chirches been
> Maken folk thynke on God and on his seintes
> Whan the ymages they beholde and seen,
> Where ofte unsighte of hem causith restreyntes *hindrance*
> Of thoghtes goode. Whan a thyng depeynt is
> Or entaillid, if men take of it heede, *carved*
> Thoght of the liknesse it wole in hem breede.
> (4992–5005)

Not to have imaginative access to Chaucer is a grievous error, comparable to the neglect of religious images (Knapp 2001: 119–24). If the images found in churches are left unseen the result is moral torpor and the inhibition of virtue: 'restreyntes / Of thoghtes goode'. Actually looking at them, on the other hand, makes people think about god and the saints. But they are a stimulus to devotion, not objects of worship or admiration in themselves. Hoccleve's interest is not in the sign, useful and functional though it may be, but in what it signifies. Furthermore, paintings and carvings, once viewed with attention, or 'heede', are possessed internally, imaginatively, and can be summoned up as it were by remote access. That in turn provokes meditation: 'Thoght of the liknesse it wole in hem breede'. Thus the production of an image (Chaucer) commissioned by Hoccleve enables others to possess him in their internal lives, much as Hoccleve does.

At least, that is his pious wish, founded upon what might be seen as a naive understanding of the identity between outer show and inner nature. Such naivety might well be strategic in a poem designed to promote the integrity of a prince whose father usurped the legitimacy of Richard II's reign.[24] Other problems hedge his endeavours. The *Regiment*, of which there are forty-three complete or substantial copies, is 'far and away Hoccleve's most successful poem in its day' (Burrow 1990: 56; Perkins 2001: 151–4; Simpson 2002: 204). The manuscripts of the poem circulated not only in court circles, but also among religious, gentry and professional owners; its readers included priests, physicians, lawyers, administrators and writers (Perkins 2001: 171–7).[25] But the portrait survives only in two manuscripts: Harley 4866 and British Library MS Royal 17.D.vi (an inferior version). It has been removed from a third (British Library MS

Arundel 38), while a seventeenth-century copy has been inserted in a fourth (Philadelphia, Rosenbach Museum and Library, MS 1083/10).[26] Was the cult of Chaucer too esoteric to have produced the kind of general and widespread effect Hoccleve wanted? Worse, the very basis on which the mechanism of devotion rests is itself contested. Hoccleve acknowledges as much only to dismiss it, as if a more elaborate rehearsal of the counter-arguments to his project might result in its being fatally undermined. In the third stanza on folio 88 he writes:

> Yit sum men holde oppinioun and seye
> That noon ymages sholde ymakid be.
> They erren foule and goon out of the wey;
> Of trouthe have they scant sensibilitee.
> Passe over that! Now, blessed Trinitee,
> Upon my maistres soule mercy have;
> For him, Lady, thy mercy eek I crave.
> (5006–12)

The allusion is to the contemporary attacks on religious images such as had surfaced in Lollard circles. As we have seen, such attacks argued that, far from providing a means to spiritual improvement, religious images are an impediment and a distraction – objects of admiration in their own right, and thus the focus of idolatry (Pearsall 1994: 405–6). That Hoccleve was ideologically opposed to reformist thought we know from an earlier section of the poem (211–399) in which John Badby, burnt for heresy at Smithfield in 1410, is given short shrift for denying transubstantiation (another Lollard issue).[27] But the very act of appropriating religious ideology to serve secular ends itself undermines the orthodox position that Hoccleve ostensibly adopts. The controversy over the right use of religious images is sidestepped and put to questionable use as a means of giving iconic status to a literary saint – itself a manoeuvre designed to curry favour with the regime-in-waiting. What also undermines Hoccleve's stated political position on images is his literary practice. The internalizing of Chaucer's image, far from leading to some higher, unassailable truth, as was the intention of such practice in a pious context, instead drives the poet ever more inward, to an examination of his own subjectivity. It is, indeed, a process that validates inwardness as an end in itself, rather than as a means to transcendence of self.

I will take as my example the topic of old age. In his portrait, Chaucer is relatively venerable, depicted as he might have looked towards the end of his life, with grey hair and beard. (He died at the age of sixty, or thereabouts.) Now the key authority figure in the *Regiment of Princes* is 'A poore old hoore [*grey-haired*] man' who happens to walk by when Hoccleve's persona is in a state of abject anxiety, aggravated by insomnia (120–6). The old man greets him courteously, but Hoccleve is too immersed in his 'seekly distresse' to reply. Yet the old man is concerned about Hoccleve's melancholic state of 'drery cheere, / And . . . deedly colour pale and wan' (127–8) in which, as he later says, his wits have become 'disparpled' [*scattered*] (209). Having recognized that his true nature has become distorted ('Al wrong is wrestid'), the old man attempts to shock him out of introversion and into normality by asking 'Sleepstow, man? / Awake!' and shaking him 'wondir faste'. Hoccleve answers at last with a sigh and a 'who is there?' and 'this olde greye' replies 'I . . . / Am here' (130–4).

Who this 'I' is becomes an intriguing question as the rest of the prologue develops. At first Hoccleve is rude and arrogant and tries to send him away, saying that the old man's words are annoying and only make a bad situation worse. But the old man, now calling Hoccleve 'My sone' (143) in a paternal or pastoral, and certainly a caring, mode, won't go. Instead he offers relief from sorrow through conversation, therapy through dialogue or confession: 'If that thee lyke to ben esid wel, / As suffre me with thee to talke a whyle' (148–9). He identifies Hoccleve's problem as stemming in part from his relative youthfulness and lack of experience but, discovering that Hoccleve is literate, the old man looks forward to a complete cure, for 'Lettred folk han gretter discrecion' (155). Still Hoccleve rejects his overtures, scorning the old man's self-appointed role as a doctor, and disparaging his appearance outright: 'Cure thyself that tremblest as thow goost, / . . . thou art as seek almooste / As I' (163–7). In spite of his advice on the use of images, Hoccleve has not, at this stage of his story, learnt how to penetrate outward appearances. Nor does he believe that the old man can possibly understand his condition: 'thou woost but litil what thow meenest' (173).

But the old man persists, gradually teasing a confession out of his new-found son, and pointing out that to be isolated and alienated may lead to madness, 'a dotid heede' (200). So he offers his services as a guide, and the conversation now turns to a wide range of topics, including poverty, extravagance, the temptations of youth, money, reputation, marriage, sexuality and patronage. Hoccleve is much encouraged by his exchanges with the old man, who swears loyalty, old and poor as he may be: 'swich as that I am, sone, I am thyn' (1992). Hoccleve, for his part, has formed an equally close bond and does not wish to be parted:

> 'What, fadir, wolden yee thus sodeynly
> Departe fro me? Petir, Cryst forbeede!
> Yee shall go dyne with me, treewely.'
> 'Sone, at o word, I moot go fro thee neede.'
> 'Nay, fadir, nay!' 'Yis, sone, as God me spede.'
> 'Now, fadir, syn it may noon othir tyde, *happen*
> Almighty God yow save and be youre gyde.'
> (1996–2002)

Hoccleve is sufficiently recovered and energized to begin the *Regiment* proper, in which he offers counsel to the Prince of Wales on the management of 'images' more generally, while at the same time petitioning him for the payment of his overdue annuity. Before he begins, he invokes Chaucer, calling him 'maister deere and fadir reverent' (1961).

The old man has been variously identified as almsman, go-between, surrogate for Hoccleve, alter ego, truth-teller, Carmelite friar and academic doctor. But such is the consanguinity of the Chaucer in Hoccleve's portrait and the old man in the prologue to the *Regiment of Princes* that the latter might be thought of, if not as an animated version of the former, at least as a figure with strong affinities. Here is the elderly guide taking an active role in the life and imagination of Hoccleve, much as Chaucer's works did (Patterson 2001: 465–6). As the old man says to the narrator of the *Regiment*: 'swich as that I am, sone, I am thyn' (1992). However, the Chaucerian ambience is not focused only on the old man. For the debate on youth and age, and the contempt of the young for the old and its dire consequences, see the Pardoner's Tale. For the comic exchange between the old man and Hoccleve ('Awake!' 'It's me!') see Mercury's exchange with Morpheus in the *Book of the Duchess* (178–86). See the same poem for an account of melancholy and the effects of insomnia, and for a therapeutic dialogue between a reluctant, introverted, sorrowing man and a persistent interlocutor – a dialogue that includes the repeated line borrowed by Hoccleve: 'Thow wot full litel wot thou wenest' (*BD* 743, 1137, 1305).

While it is important to be aware of allusions, and to recognize the affinities between Chaucer and the old man, there is nothing resolved or mechanistic about the processes at work here. On the contrary, the image and influence of Chaucer in Hoccleve's prologue are dynamic, shifting, heartfelt, subject to constant renegotiation. For Hoccleve, 'Chaucer' (the man and his works as indivisible entity) is not a mine to be quarried but a father-figure with whom to engage in an act of filial piety designed at once to understand and possess for himself the source of his own existence as a writer.[28] Thus 'Chaucer' – the man and his narratives – becomes a structure of thought and feeling, a way of thinking through independently, and articulating, Hoccleve's own preoccupations, and of writing about them in ways that are at once original and recognizable by a particular reading community.

What all of this points to is something of the complexity of the relationship between text and image. In decrying the Lollard position on religious images, as it applies by extrapolation to his own case, Hoccleve was right but for the wrong reasons (Knapp 2001: 129–34; Tolmie 2000: 285). Certainly the image of Chaucer works by association, and the topic of age is one which becomes a source of meditation and debate with the prologue to the *Regiment*. But in so doing the image changes its nature, moving from a visual to an imaginative status, and undergoing refraction through the regular literary devices of characterization, dialogue and dramatic situation. It might be that the literary image is so complex and different that the Lollard case ceases to apply. All of which opens up a discursive space quite at odds with the poem's larger project, which is to reinforce political and religious orthodoxy as a way of enhancing what might be called the image of Prince Henry. Insofar as legitimacy and succession were issues that needed to be addressed under the general rubric of the Prince's image, the integrity of Hoccleve's literary descent from Chaucer might be seen as a way of expressing a literary analogy that reinforces the legitimacy of the future Henry V – except that, as we have seen, the literary expression of a father and son relationship is full of fissures, discontinuities, ruptures and anxiety (Strohm 1999: 645).

The late medieval debate on images, whether one examines it within contexts that are religious or secular, material or literary, is one that admits of no easy resolution. For it is founded upon a series of linguistic and religious paradoxes that cannot be neatly divided into discrete positions. Two of the basic tenets of the Christian faith – that Christ was God made flesh, and that each person was an image of God – conferred on human existence and the material world an inherent sanctity, however much they were despoiled by sin. Furthermore, the narratives of Christ's life, and the legends of the saints who modelled themselves on his example, were constructed in terms of episodes that led naturally to the repetition and memorializing of key persons and events, and so to the veneration of symbolic representations. Those representations had their ultimate sanction in the canonical texts of a Bible brim-full of images subtly deployed across the whole gamut of literary artifice – texts that were themselves subject to a huge accretion of commentaries that expounded the hidden significance, the underlying patterns, of holy writ.

Once the whole notion of image-making – whether verbal or material – became politicized, as it did in the 1380s, then it became incumbent upon individuals to take positions on a divisive issue could not be easily resolved. It is not surprising, therefore, that practitioners of literary images, such as writers of the calibre of Gower and Hoccleve, find themselves impaled on the horns of a dilemma. While they ostensibly adopt and articulate one position (different in each case), their literary practice points in another direction. To this extent their work witnesses to their struggle to reconcile the imperatives of their social existence (as producers of literature within a network of patron, audience and political faction) with the often contradictory and uncomfortable priorities that develop as a consequence of reflective writing.

See also: 2 English Society in the Later Middle Ages, 3 Religious Authority and Dissent, 22 Dream Poems, 25 Mystical and Devotional Literature, 33 The *Canterbury Tales*, 34 John Gower and John Lydgate, 35 Thomas Hoccleve.

Notes

1 *MED* 1a, 1b, 2a.

2 Simpson 2002: 389, 436–7; Douglas Kelly, *Medieval Imagination: Rhetoric and the Poetry of Courtly Love* (Madison: University of Wisconsin Press, 1978), pp. 26–9; Nicolette Zeeman, 'The Idol of the Text', in *Images, Idolatry, and Iconoclasm in Late Medieval England: Textuality and the Visual Image*, ed. Jeremy Dimmick, James Simpson and Nicolette Zeeman (Oxford: Oxford University Press, 2002), pp. 43–62 (pp. 43–4); V. A. Kolve, *Chaucer and The Imagery of Narrative: The First Five Canterbury Tales* (London: Arnold, 1984), pp. 20–32.

3 Latin text in *The Complete Works of John Gower*, ed. George Campbell Macaulay (Oxford: Clarendon Press, 1899–1902), vol. 4 (1902); trans. Eric W. Stockton, *The Major Latin Works of John Gower: The Voice of One Crying, and The Tripartite Chronicle* (Seattle: University of Washington Press, 1962), pp. 109–11.

4 *Signa* is the plural of *signum*, in general 'a mark, token, sign, indication', meanings 'very frequent in all styles and periods' (Lewis and Short I); it also designates an image in the sense of a work of art (figure, statue, picture) and is synonymous with *imago* (II.C).

5 See Margaret Aston, 'Lollards and the Cross', in *Lollards and their Influence in Late Medieval England*, ed. Fiona Somerset, Jill C. Havens and Derrick G. Pitard (Woodbridge: Boydell Press, 2003), pp. 99–113; Hudson 1988: 307.

6 *Knighton's Chronicle 1337–1396*, ed. and trans. G. H. Martin, Oxford Medieval Texts (Oxford: Clarendon Press, 1995), pp. 292–9; cf. Sarah Stanbury, 'The Vivacity of Images: St Katharine, Knighton's Lollards, and the Breaking of Idols', in *Images, Idolatry, and Iconoclasm*, ed. Dimmick et al., pp. 131–50; Kamerick 2002: 64–7.

7 Joy H. Russell-Smith, 'Walter Hilton and a Tract in Defence of the Veneration of Images', *Dominican Studies* 7 (1954), 180–214 (201).

8 Anne Hudson (ed.), *Selections from English Wycliffite Writings* (Cambridge: Cambridge University Press, 1978), p. 180.

9 Nicholas Watson, '"Et que est huius ydoli materia? Tuipse": Idols and Images in Walter Hilton', in *Images, Idolatry, and Iconoclasm*, ed. Dimmick et al., pp. 95–111; Kamerick 2002: 34–7.

10 See *Two Wycliffite Texts: The Sermon of William Taylor 1406; The Testimony of William Thorpe 1407*, ed. Anne Hudson, EETS os 31 (1993), esp. pp. 56–61.

11 Hudson (ed.), *Selections*, p. 179, which see for an edition of the text.

12 David Aers, '*Vox Populi* and the Literature of 1381', in *The Cambridge History of Medieval English Literature*, ed. David Wallace (Cambridge: Cambridge University Press), pp. 432–53 (pp. 439–44).

13 Cf. *Confessio Amantis*, Prologue 346–51, 5.1803–24, in *The English Works of John Gower*, ed. G. C. Macaulay, vol. 1, EETS es 81 (1900).

14 *Vox clamantis* 3.15, lines 1267–70; 7.25, lines 1447–70. See Paul Miller, 'John Gower, Satiric Poet', in *Gower's 'Confessio Amantis': Responses and Reassessments*, ed. A. J. Minnis (Cambridge: Brewer, 1983), pp. 79–105 (pp. 102–5); Steven Justice, *Writing and Rebellion: England in 1381*, New Historicism, 27 (Berkeley, Los Angeles and London: University of California Press, 1994), pp. 207–13.

15 Andrew Galloway, 'Gower in his Most Learned Role and the Peasants' Revolt of 1381', *Mediaevalia* 16 (1993), 329–47.

16 Paul Strohm, *Hochon's Arrow: The Social Imagination of Fourteeth-Century Texts* (Princeton, N.J.: Princeton University Press, 1992), pp. 45–56.

17 Bruce Harbert, 'Lessons from the Great Clerk: Ovid and John Gower', in *Ovid Renewed: Ovidian Influences on Literature and Art from the Middle Ages to the Twentieth Century*, ed. Charles Martindale (Cambridge: Cambridge University Press, 1988), pp. 83–97 (pp. 83–7).

18 For examples, see the index entry for '*Note bene*/index signs . . . hands' in Ann Eljenholm Nichols, Michael T. Orr, Kathleen L. Scott and Lynda Denison, *An Index of Images in English Manuscripts from the Time of Chaucer to Henry VIII, c.1380–c.1509: The Bodleian Library, Oxford. Vol. 1: MSS Additional–Digby* (Turnhout: Harvey Miller Publishers, 2000).

19 Kathleen L. Scott, *Later Gothic Manuscripts, 1390–1490*, 2 vols, A Survey of Manuscripts Illuminated in the British Isles, 6 (London: Harvey Miller, 1996), II, 160–2.

20 Anna Torti, The Glass of Form: Mirroring Structures from Chaucer to Skelton (Cambridge: Brewer, 1991), pp. 87–106.

21 Thomas Hoccleve, *The Regiment of Princes*, ed. Charles R. Blyth, (Kalamazoo, Mich.: Medieval Institute, Publications for TEAMS 1999), pp. 16–17. All quotations are from this edition.

22 For Hoccleve's life see John Burrow, *Thomas Hoccleve*, Authors of the Middle Ages, 4 (Aldershot: Variorum, 1994).

23 James H. McGregor, 'The Iconography of Chaucer in Hoccleve's *De Regimine Principum* and in the *Troilus* Frontispiece', *Chaucer Review* 11 (1976–7), 338–50; Jeanne E. Krochalis, 'Hoccleve's Chaucer Portrait', *Chaucer Review* 21 (1986–7), 234–45; David R. Carlson, 'Thomas Hoccleve and the Chaucer Portrait', *Huntington Library Quarterly* 54 (1991), pp. 283–300; Alan T. Gaylord, 'Portrait of a Poet', in *The Ellesmere Chaucer: Essays in Interpretation*, ed. Martin Stevens and Daniel Woodward (San Marino, Calif.: Huntington Library; Tokyo: Yushodo, 1995), pp. 121–42.

24 Paul Strohm, *England's Empty Throne: Usurpation and the Language of Legitimation 1399–1422* (New Haven, Conn., and London: Yale University Press, 1998), pp. 180–6.

25 See also M. C. Seymour, 'The Manuscripts of Hoccleve's *Regiment of Princes*', *Transactions of the Edinburgh Bibliographical Society* 4 (1974), 253–97 (255–8).

26 Derek Pearsall, *The Life of Geoffrey Chaucer: A Critical Biography*, Blackwell Critical Biographies, 1 (Oxford, and Cambridge, Mass.: Blackwell, 1992), pp. 285–91; Pearsall 1994: 395–6; Perkins 2001: 155–9.

27 Peter McNiven, *Heresy and Politics in the Reign of Henry IV: The Burning of John Badby* (Woodbridge and Wolfeboro, N.H.: Boydell Press, 1987), pp. 199–219; and cf. Hoccleve's diatribe against the Lollard rebel Oldcastle in *Hoccleve's Works: The Minor Poems*, ed. Frederick J. Furnivall and I. Gollancz, EETS es 61 (1892) and 73 (1897), rev. edn Jerome Mitchell and A. I. Doyle repr. in one vol. (1970), pp. 8–24, esp. lines 409–24.

28 A. C. Spearing, *Medieval to Renaissance in English Poetry* (Cambridge: Cambridge University Press, 1985), pp. 103–10; Ethan Knapp, 'Eulogies and Usurpations: Hoccleve and Chaucer Revisited', *Studies in the Age of Chaucer* 21 (1999), 247–73; Ruth Nissé, '"Oure Fadres Olde and Modres": Gender, Heresy, and Hoccleve's Literary Politics', *Studies in the Age of Chaucer* 21 (1999), 275–99 (278–91); Patterson 2001: 461–3.

References and Further Reading

Aston, Margaret 1988. *England's Iconoclasts. Vol. 1: Laws against Images.* Oxford: Clarendon Press. Compendious and indispensable account of all aspects of the image controversy.

Burrow, J. A. 1990. 'Hoccleve and Chaucer.' In *Chaucer Traditions: Studies in Honour of Derek Brewer*, ed. Ruth Morse and Barry Windeatt (Cambridge: Cambridge University Press, 1990), pp. 54–61. Although Hoccleve is seen as 'Chaucerian,' his lack of imagination and evocation of public and private life, make his poetry distinctive.

Echard, Siân 2003. 'Gower's "bokes of Latin": Language, Politics, and Poetry.' *Studies in the Age of Chaucer* 25, 123–56. Gower speaks for the people against social and clerical abuses even as he condemns the rebellion of 1381.

Federico, Sylvia 2003. *New Troy: Fantasies of Empire in the Late Middle Ages.* Medieval Cultures, 36. Minneapolis and London: University of Minnesota Press. A psychoanalytical and historicist approach to the myth of Troy as found in late fourteenth-century English literature.

Ferster, Judith 1996. *Fictions of Advice: The Literature and Politics of Counsel in Late Medieval England.* Philadelphia: University of Pennsylvania Press. Ch. 8 is on political aspects of Gower's work, and ch. 9 on Hoccleve's *Regiment* as a mirror for Prince Henry that counsels, pressures and criticizes.

Fisher, J. H. 1965. *John Gower: Moral Philosopher and Friend of Chaucer.* London: Methuen. The standard biography, now somewhat dated.

Hudson, Anne 1988. *The Premature Reformation: Wycliffite Texts and Lollard History.* Oxford: Clarendon Press. A foundational work for the study of Lollard controversies, including those concerned with images.

Jones, W. R. 1973. 'Lollards and Images: The Defense of Religious Art in Later Medieval England.' *Journal of the History of Ideas* 34, 27–50. A ground-breaking and still influential study.

Kamerick, Kathleen 2002. *Popular Piety and Art in the Later Middle Ages: Image Worship and Idolatry in England, 1350–1500.* The New Middle Ages. New York: Palgrave. Ch. 1 for Lollard attitudes and the orthodox rejoinders; ch. 2 for attitudes to idolatry in a range of devotional vernacular literature.

Knapp, Ethan 2001. *The Bureaucratic Muse: Thomas Hoccleve and the Literature of Late Medieval England.* University Park: Pennsylvania State University Press. Pages 107–27 for an account of Chaucer as Hoccleve's literary father in the *Regement.*

Olsson, Kurt 1987. 'John Gower's *Vox Clamantis* and the Medieval Idea of Place.' *Studies in Philology* 84, 134–58. Gower explores the individual in relation to different contexts (political, social, legal) represented as distinct places (e.g. England in 1381).

Patterson, Lee 2001. '"What is me?": Self and Society in the Poetry of Thomas Hoccleve.' *Studies in the Age of Chaucer* 23 (2001), 437–70. Reads the *Regiment* as a wide-ranging critique of the *modus operandi* of Lancastrian rule.

Pearsall, Derek 1994. 'Hoccleve's *Regement of Princes*: The Poetics of Royal Self-Representation.' *Speculum* 69, 386–410. Hoccleve colludes with his patron in promoting a favourable image of the ruler.

Perkins, Nicholas 2001. *Hoccleve's 'Regiment of Princes': Counsel and Constraint.* Cambridge: Brewer. Essential reading: a comprehensive account of all aspects of Hoccleve's poem.

Scanlon, Larry 1990. 'The King's Two Voices: Narrative and Power in Hoccleve's *Regement of Princes.*' In *Literary Practice and Social Change in Britain, 1380–1530*, ed. Lee Patterson, The New Historicism: Studies in Cultural Poetics, 8 (Berkeley, Los Angeles and London: University of California Press), pp. 216–47. The *Regiment*'s structure reflects Henry's simultaneous need for advice and for independence from it.

Simpson, James 2002. *Reform and Cultural Revolution.* Oxford English Literary History, vol. 2: *1350–1547.* Oxford: Oxford University Press. The *Regement* reveals the interdependence of king and subjects (pp. 204–14).

Stanbury, Sarah 2000. 'Visualizing.' In *A Companion to Chaucer*, ed. Peter Brown (Oxford: Blackwell), pp. 459–79. The image controversy as a context for Chaucer's practices.

Strohm, Paul 1999. 'Hoccleve, Lydgate and the Lancastrian Court.' In *The Cambridge History of Medieval English Literature*, ed. David Wallace (Cambridge: Cambridge University Press, 1999), pp. 640–61. The *Regiment* displays anxiety and reassurance about Henry's legitimacy.

Tolmie, Sarah 2000. 'The *Prive Scilence* of Thomas Hoccleve.' *Studies in the Age of Chaucer* 22, 281–309. Hoccleve writes a coercive poem, threatening the revelation of secret material, unless his annuity is paid.

Wetherbee, Winthrop 1999. 'John Gower.' In *The Cambridge History of Medieval English Literature*, ed. David Wallace (Cambridge: Cambridge University Press), pp. 589–609. A recent and succinct introduction to Gower's works more generally.

19
Love

Barry Windeatt

Off love were lykynge of to lere,
And Ioye tille all that wol here,
That wote what love may meane;
But who so have grette haste to love,
And may not com to his above,
That poynte dothe louers tene.
Fayre speche brekyth never bone;
That makythe these lovers ilkone
Ay hope of better wene,
And put themselffe to grete travayle
Wheddyr it helpe or not avayle:
Ofte sythes this hathe be sene
(*Ipomadon*, Prologue, 1–12)[1]

(Of love it would be a pleasure to learn and a joy to all that will hear, who know the meaning of love; but whoever is overhasty in love and cannot attain his goal, *that* gives lovers grief. Fair words break no bones – they make each of these lovers always entertain higher hopes and put themselves to great effort, whether or not it is of any avail: very often has this been observed.)

In its novelistically detailed narrative, *Ipomadon* is one of rather few romances in English to develop any extended fiction of idealizing love and courtship that Chaucer calls 'fyn lovynge' (*LGW* F 544), and nineteenth-century scholarship formulated as 'courtly love': a ritualized devotion to an unattainable lady.[2] Like Chaucer in *Troilus and Criseyde*, the *Ipomadon* poet constructs an implied audience for his poem, an elite who know what love means, and a brief summary of his romance confirms his prologue's point that eloquence and patient endeavour play a special role in such love:

The beautiful, young, orphaned Queen of Calabria, named only as 'the Fere' ('the Proud One'), vows to marry none but the best knight in the world. Without having met or seen her, Ipomadon, the king of Apulia's son, falls in love with the Fere by report. He goes

> to her court incognito and serves as her cupbearer for three years. Known only as the 'straunge valett', he courts ridicule by devoting himself to hunting and feigning cowardice concerning deeds of arms. The Fere, who has secretly fallen in love with him, is tormented that his handsomeness is not matched by knightly prowess.
>
> Ashamed by the Fere's reproaches, Ipomadon leaves her court to travel far and wide, winning renown by tourneying. Urged by her barons to marry, and hoping to entice back her 'straunge valett', the Fere announces a three-day tournament and consents to marry its winner. En route to this event, Ipomadon goes incognito to the court of his uncle, King Mellyagere of Sicily, where he plays the fool as 'Drew-le-reine', the devoted servant of the Sicilian queen, who falls in love with him. Again, he pretends to care only for hunting. Each day he sets off as if to go hunting, but then proceeds incognito to the Fere's tournament and wins all three days in successive disguises of white, red and black armour. Instead of claiming the Fere, however, Ipomadon disappears again, although it is by now clear that the 'straunge valett', 'Drew-le-reine', and the white, red and black knights are all the same person.
>
> When Ipomadon (having by now succeeded his father as king) hears that the Fere is besieged by the grotesquely ugly Sir Lyoline of Inde, he returns to Mellyagere's court disguised as a fool, and is the only volunteer when the Fere's confidante Imayne arrives to seek a champion for her lady. On the way Ipomadon rescues Imayne in various exploits; she falls in love and vainly attempts to seduce him. Ipomadon duly defeats the black-armoured Lyoline, but as Ipomadon has deliberately worn black armour, the outcome is unclear to onlookers. Ipomadon pretends to be Lyoline and is set to disappear once more when the Fere's cousin Cabanus challenges him. During their combat Cabanus notices Ipomadon's ring, which identifies him to Cabanus as his long-lost half-brother. They are joyfully reconciled; the Fere and Ipomadon are married at last.

Not unlike Chaucer's *Troilus*, this narrative foregrounds a lover hero whose qualities take him to the brink of absurdity or beyond it, but are thereby all the more admirable (or question-provoking) as an expression of love's idealism. *Ipomadon* acknowledges that its hero is 'a straunge lover' in his eccentric reluctance to shed his disguises and claim the lady his service has won many times over. As with much medieval romance, pursuit of love is aligned with those chivalric accomplishments that allow the lover to deserve his lady's favour. Experience seemingly subverts the Fere's plan, by having her fall in love with a comically cowardly anti-hero. Yet, contrary to appearances, love and her subconscious have indeed discerned her best partner. Embarrassed by his unworthy failings, the haughty lady longs for her love to turn into the best knight but will only marry a man she can rule: 'I shall take non . . . But I may weld hym þat me wanne!' (5255–9). Having fallen in love with an idea of this heroine, the hero spends most of a fantastically protracted narrative devoted to his lady's service while disguising and absenting himself from her, perhaps symbolizing a deeper male fear ('In her presoune shall he nat be', 4343). So mysterious are his constant disappearances that he is thought to derive from the fairy world (3991–2). Yet insofar as the hero or narrative ever explains Ipomadon's eccentric avoidances, it is that he never feels he succeeds in living up to the Fere's vow to marry the best knight ('And euer more in my hert I thought, / To hyr vowe I corded nowghte', 8565–6). It is as if he cannot match her idea of him and needs her to remain unattainable (but he is quickly on the scene if a rival suitor appears). Only chance rediscovery of a half-brother draws the hero away from indefinite avoidance of his lady, marriage, sexual fulfilment and closure. Such a pattern of postponed fulfilment strikingly develops the prologue's recommended avoidance of undue haste into a celebration of the preserved chastity not only of the lady but also of the hero.

In his singularity, Ipomadon can only represent a typical courtly lover in the sense that the exception gloriously proves the rule. Here is love as teasingly problematic, as a cue for debate and puzzling over after the romance has been read, as a prompt for such *demaundes d'amour* as Chaucer's texts pose ('Yow loveres axe I now this questioun: / Who hath the worse, Arcite or Palamoun?' KnT 1347–8). This is love that is 'courtly' in its personal courtliness of refined feeling and bravura behaviour as much as in its connection with courts and the exalted rank of its protagonists. It is a cult and sect loyally defended by members, as in Clanvowe's *Boke of Cupide*, where the dreamer indignantly overhears a cuckoo ridiculing love as defended by a nightingale.[3] From such courtliness stems much 'fayre speche' propounding questions of love, but only infrequently uttered directly between lovers. Lovers remain mysterious, imaginary constructions to each other, because mostly separated. Absence, secrecy and disguise, conventional in love narratives, highlight the lovers' sense of an inner private self, prompting those subject to love to extended soliloquizing and introversion on the paradoxes of their helpless fixation and its folly, which none the less is an undying commitment.

Impossible to resist and beyond reason, love is a source of good and the reformation of the heart: sensitive, compassionate, constant. Such love can be played as a form of game, pursued through its rules and role-play, in which the overwhelming power of love implies the abjection of the lover, who is fictionalized as the servant, feudal vassal and knight of his lady, whom he reverences and who holds the power to heal the sickness that he suffers. Since love in its disturbance of behaviour and well-being was commonly diagnosed in medieval medical writings as a form of illness, the lover's classic symptoms – moping, pallor, loss of appetite, insomnia – imply the beloved's role as the physician, who with her favour may cure in her lover a sickness believed to be potentially fatal.[4] In such service-unto-death the lover's obeisance to his lady is also often represented as a quasi-religious devotion and observance towards one fictionalized as all-powerful, perhaps 'La Belle Dame Sans Merci', the title of a French poem translated into English.[5] Yet serving implies deserving, and the 'penance' of the lover's suffering looks forward to the lady's favour and even her sexual concession of herself, viewed as her mercy and her 'grace', through which the lover enters the heavenly bliss of fulfilment.

Love Celestial

> For this have I herd seyd of wyse lered,
> Was nevere man or womman yet bigete
> That was unapt to suffren loves hete,
> Celestial, or elles love of kynde.
> (*TC* 1.976–9)

With a love affair in prospect, the pagan Pandarus presents to Troilus as traditional lore what Chaucer's medieval Christian audience would find familiar: that while all humankind have the potential for love, there are two ways – 'celestial' (heavenly, of God) and 'of kynde' (of our human nature and directed at our fellows). Christian expositions of love attended more to virtuous love properly directed, whether to God or in an accord of wills between fellow Christians, based on reason in disinterested mutual amity and charity. To such loves passionate love offered only disruption and distraction, but early readers of Chaucer's *Troilus* could have known no comparably sustained exploration of love in English – other than the love of God. Nor was there one so avant-garde in bringing 'love of kynde' into debate with 'love celestial' in the context of a culture founded on a theology of redemption through love ('the Fader that formed us alle / Loked on us with love and leet his sone dye / Mekely for oure mysdedes, to amenden us alle', *PP* 1.166–8).[6] That 'love celestial' had expressed itself through the mystery of God's Incarnation at the Annunciation to the Virgin Mary. The N-Town Play of the Parliament of Heaven dramatizes how the Trinity debate the Incarnation as a 'loveday' or reconciliation, with the Holy Ghost like a suitor ('I, Love to ȝoure lover xal ȝow lede', 118),[7] an intervention that *Piers Plowman* catches with kinetic intensity of poetic language: 'For the heighe Holy Goost hevene shal tocleve, / And love shal lepe out after into this lowe erthe, / And clennesse shal cacchen it' (12.140–2).

It is more than coincidence that this same period in later medieval England, which sees the flowering of devotional literature fostering an inner life moved by loving longing for God, should also see explorations of 'love of kynde' as never before in English. Texts concerned to realize the fullness and probe the limits of 'love of kynde' might notice the model of love's power in devotional texts. Here was analysis of the exercise of self-sacrificing service in contemplative texts that seek to instil a love reciprocating something of God's limitless love for us. Julian of Norwich's textured vision of the Lord and his servant, who is at once Adam, Christ and all humankind ('The servant . . . rynnith in grete haste for love to don his Lord's will . . . And ryth thus continualy his lovand Lord ful tenderly beholdyth him, ch. 51)[8] is a major analytical step on the way to the realization of the rootedness of all in love that ringingly concludes her account of her revelations: 'And in this love he hath don all his werke; and in this love he hath made all things profitable to us; and in this love our life is everlestand' (ch. 86).

It is from mystical and devotional texts on 'love celestial' that secular writers might derive a sense of individual potential for growth through love, of love as dynamically transformative, and of loving as the measure of the self. According to the anonymous *The Cloud of Unknowing* 'al þe liif of a good Cristen man is not elles bot holy desire' (133),[9] and in *The Scale of Perfection*, Book I, which he wrote for an anchoress, Walter Hilton asks, 'For what is a man but hise thoughtes and his loves?', and continues, 'As moche as thou lovest thi God and thyn even Cristene and knowest Hym, so moche is thi soule; and if thou litil love Hym, litil is thi soule' (ch. 87).[10] It is by such capacity for love that the soul grows and is ultimately measured and valued, as Richard Rolle makes clear in his *Incendium amoris*: 'He who loves much is great, he who loves less is less; because according to the greatness of the love that we have in us, we are valued by God' (ch. 7),[11] and hence love is 'the sweetest and most useful thing a rational soul can ever acquire' (ch. 41).

From mystical texts might also derive a sense of how delay and frustration can be managed and structured as aspects of a life of loving, longing and quest, within a context of separation and distance from the beloved. Frustrating delays actually serve to prove the truth and strength of love, as the *Cloud*-author makes clear ('alle holy desires growen bi delaies; & ȝif þei wanyn bi delaies, þen were þei neuer holy desires', 132), for a longing love directed towards God – unlike some worldly object – can never fail to find its mark, as is underlined by the *Cloud*-author's *Epistle of Discretion of Stirrings*, citing the 'Book of Loue', the biblical Song of Songs, whose sensual imagery was interpreted as Christ's love song to the soul: 'soche a blinde schote wiþ þe scharp darte of longyng loue may neuer faile of þe prik [target], þe whiche is God' (72).[12] It is through progressively more demanding understandings of love in *Piers Plowman* that the dreamer's unending search for how to do well, do better and do best can be successively redefined as the poem unfolds through a structure of quest and yearning (10.189; 9.200–11; 13.138–40). Few texts convey more vividly than *Piers Plowman* how instrumental love is – 'Love is leche [*physician*] of lif and next oure Lord selve, / And also the graithe gate that goth into hevene' (1.204–5) – and how imperative: '"Lerne to love," quod Kynde, "and leef alle othere"' (20.208).

If courtly love-longing implied courtly protagonists and a refined readership (with story outcomes that tend to confirm the status quo), it was an imperative of 'love celestial' that the humblest folk, unencumbered by learning, could gain the most immediate loving access to God; Langland's Conscience tells Clergy: 'For oon Piers the Plowman hath impugned us alle, / And set alle sciences at a sop save love one' (13.124–5). Apprehension of the divine depends much less on intellect, knowledge or learning than on a capacity for loving, and Rolle prefaces his *Incendium* by declaring roundly that he writes not for theologians bogged down in interminable academic questionings but for the 'simple and unlearned, who are seeking to love God rather than amass knowledge'. For Rolle, God 'is not known by argument, but by what we do and how we love'; the *Cloud*-author with his customary forthrightness argues, 'For whi loue may reche to God in þis liif bot not knowing' (33), and declares, 'þerfore I wole leue al þat þing þat I can þink, & chese to my loue þat þing þat I cannot þink. For whi he may wel be loued bot not þouȝt. By loue may he be getyn & holden; bot bi þouȝt neiþer' (26). For mystical writers, love's radical bypassing of conventional bookish hierarchies of literate authority is yet another paradox of its dynamically enabling and renewing power. Contemplation of 'love celestial' held out nothing less than the prospect that 'oure soule, bi vertewe of þis reformyng grace, is mad sufficient at þe fulle to comprehende al him by loue', for as the *Cloud*-author went on to explain:

> o louyng soule only in it-self, by vertewe of loue, schuld comprehende in it hym þat is sufficient at þe fulle – & mochel more, wiþ-oute comparison – to fille alle þe soules & aungelles þat euer may be. & þis is þe eendles merueilous miracle of loue, þe whiche schal neuer take eende. (18–19)

Mixed Loves

It sit hire naught to ben celestial
As yet, though that hire liste bothe and kowthe;
But trewely, it sate hire wel right nowthe
A worthi knyght to loven and cherice,
And but she do, I holde it for a vice.
(*TC* 1.983–7)

Pandarus's debatable strategy to see love 'Celestial, or elles love of kynde' as alternative choices for Criseyde – by implication never coterminous and mutually exclusive – foregrounds the relation between such loves as a theme in the poem. Yet even if 'love celestial' – in the end, and at our end – would always be privileged in medieval culture, and other loves recanted, the use of erotic language in texts addressing divine love, and of religious language in texts on 'love of kynde', points to constant negotiation in interpretation and understanding of loves.[13]

To inscribe something of what the *Cloud* terms the 'eendles merueilous miracle of love' – whether 'celestial' or 'of kynde' – medieval writers tend to draw on the same lexicon of metaphorical language for the progressive stages of love. The beginnings of love in looking can be represented as a wounding, as being struck, pierced and transfixed. Troilus feels himself 'Right with hire look thorugh-shoten and thorugh-darted' (1.325), and no very different idiom is employed to express the mystical love of *The Mirror of Simple Souls*: 'And in þis beholdinge, ful often loue comeþ to hir wiþ his rauysshinge dartes, and woundeþ hir so sweteli þat sche forȝetiþ al þat sche afore sawe and wiste' (260).[14] This sense of love as a wound inflicted conveys love's pain, heightened consciousness and need for relief, as when Margery Kempe describes herself as 'a creatur al wowndyd wyth lofe and as reson had fayled' (ch. 41),[15] or when Troilus repents of his former life, reflecting 'so soore hath she me wounded . . . with lokyng of hire eyen' (2.533–4). More audaciously, *The Orcherd of Syon* understands God's own love-wound as his need for us ('O eendelees & infinyte good, O al woundid in loue, me semeþ þat þou hast nede of us wrecchide creaturis', 376).[16]

Whether in celestial love or love 'of kynde', the lover's symptoms draw on the same conventional idioms. There is 'the fir of love' that burns Troilus (1.490), just as there is Kempe's 'unqwenchabyl fyer of lofe whech brent ful sor in hir sowle' (ch. 41). Ipomadon 'wax wan and pale off hewe' (196), and in a love lyric in his *Ego dormio* Rolle declares of Christ 'Now wax I pale and wan for loue of my leman [*lover*]' (33).[17] The sigh-filled sleeplessness that afflicts a courtly lover like Ipomadon ('Off all the nyght he slepyd no þinge / But lay wyth many a sore sykynge', 1058–9) also marks Rolle's 'A Songe of the Love of Jesus': 'Lufe us reves þe nyght rest' (47).[18] Each lover's sense of removedness from the beloved finds some outlet in the lyric impulse, whether the beloved is the lady or the divine. Troilus repeatedly puts his feelings into lyric form, as does Ipomadon ('A songe of love he gan to syng / "For her ay mys I fare" ', 2454–5), but for Rolle too in his *Ego dormio*: 'My songe is in seghynge, my lif is in langynge, /

Til I þe se' (32),[19] and in a love lyric to Jesus: 'I sit and synge of loue-langynge þat in my brest is bredde' (45). It is through love lyric and love letters that in *Troilus* the lover's longing attempts to bridge the distance of separation, but Christ too can be a lover-knight to the soul, and Hilton's *Scale of Perfection* sees the scriptures as: 'not ellis but swete lettres, sendynges maad atwixe a lovend soule and Jesu loved' (2.43). In absence and separation Troilus daydreams so fixedly about Criseyde 'That, as he sat and wook, his spirit mette [*dreamed*] / That he hire saugh [*saw*]' (1.362–3), while in *Ego dormio* Rolle is 'euer his loue þynkynge, and oft sithe þerof dremynge' (26), yet his love is celestial. Criseyde's body sits amongst her prattling women friends but 'For Troilus ful faste hire soule soughte' (4.699), just as in Rolle's chapter on love in his *Emendatio vitae*: 'Loue suffreth not a lovinge soule for to dwelle in hire self but it rauischeth hire out of hire self vnto hir louede, so þat sche is more verryly wher she loueth þan þer þe bodi is þat liueth & feeleth bi hire' (Cambridge University Library MS Ff.5.30, folio 158).

To all such contexts, the sense of suffering in languishing for love gives a potent charge. Pandarus recalls Troilus 'so langwisshyng to-yere / For love, of which thi wo wax alwey moore' (3.241–2), and Margery Kempe is deeply moved by words repeated in a sermon, 'Owr Lord Jhesu langurith for lofe' (ch. 78), perhaps because they declare a love that it was impossible fully to reciprocate. The *Cloud*-author lays it down as a rule that 'it is þe condicion of a trewe louer þat euer þe more he loueþ, þe more him longeþ for to loue' (45). What he has in mind is Mary's contemplative love for Christ in the gospel story of Mary and Martha (Luke 10: 38–42), and he alludes to the courtly convention of lovesickness to convey Mary's sense of sinful separation from Christ as 'langwisching sekenes for lackyng of loue' (46). In the context of both celestial and courtly love, the craving that is in love-longing can be symbolized by thirsting. In his first 'Canticus Troili' Troilus sings, 'For ay thurst I, the more that ich it drynke' (1.406), and in his late letter to the departed Criseyde his longing is a despairing thirst ('So thursteth ay myn herte to byholde / Youre beute, that my lif unnethe I holde', 5.1406–7). For Julian of Norwich, the same idiom can reinterpret Christ's thirst on the cross: 'this is the gostly thrist of Criste, the luf longyng that lestith and ever shall' (ch. 31).

Whether celestial or courtly, a love-longing likened to consuming thirst may be followed by a fulfilment compared with intoxication. In his *Incendium Amoris*, Rolle remarks that 'Love is a spiritual wine, intoxicating the minds of the elect' (ch. 41), and in *The Prickynge of Love* the fluctuations of love-longing and love-drunkenness are part of the game of love that sports with lovers' feelings: 'This is the game on love: his absence schal make thee for to morene aftir him and lyve in longyng, and his presence schal fille thee with pyment of his swetnesse and make thee liik drunken' (ch. 26).[20] The lovers in *Ipomadon* are said to know little of the art of love but share an equal passion 'For bothe one draught they drowe' (1255). Criseyde may even be alluding to the mistakenly drunk love-potion of Tristan and Iseult when she asks herself, after seeing Troilus ride past, 'Who yaf me drynke?' (2.651). Criseyde may reason to herself about love that one need not be 'drynkeles for alwey' (2.718) to avoid drunkenness, but the discourse of some mystical texts implies an irresistibly intoxicating love-drunkenness of the spirit, as when *The Mirror of Simple Souls* describes how 'sche drinkeþ, soule nouȝted-drunken, soule fre-drunken, soule forȝeten-drunken, but riȝt drunken and more þan drunke of þat sche neuer dranke ne neuer schal drinke' (276). A kind of alcoholism of mystical love features in *The Ladder of Four Rungs*, where 'So doth God Almyghty to his loveris in contemplacion as a taverner [*tavern-keeper*]' who like some latterday drug-dealer trades on the addictions of his regulars 'there he seeth hem in the strete' until they have beggared themselves for love (113–14).[21]

For writers about both secular and celestial love, the sheer intoxication of love can express itself partly in dance. In the analysis of love-drunkenness in his encyclopedic *Confessio Amantis*, Gower mentions dance as a consequence: 'Bot am so drunken of that sihte . . . / And thanne I mai wel, if I schal, / Bothe singe and daunce and lepe aboute, / And holde forth the lusti route' (6.183, 186–8).[22] More startling is how *The Chastising of God's Children* (a compilation for a female religious) remarks on 'a gostli drunkennesse' that 'sum men in that tyme bien stired wiþ al þe membris of her bodi, so þat þei muste skippe, ren or daunce' (103).[23] In the *Roman de la rose* love is represented as a courtly 'carole' or dance-song – and the 'olde daunce' of love is known to the Wife of Bath and Pandarus – but there is also a dance of 'love celestial' in which Christ leads the dancers. In *Incendium amoris* Rolle declares: 'For Christ himself yearned, so to speak, for our love, when he hastened with such fervour to his cross to redeem us – but it is truly said that "Love precedes the dance and gives the lead"' (ch. 42), and the same idea recurs in *Ego dormio* ('How God of mageste was deynge on þe roode: / Bot soth þan is hit said þat loue ledeth þe rynge', 30). Addressed to a nun, *A Deuout Treatyse called the Tree & XII. Frutes of the Holy Goost* discusses 'desire of Ihesu . . . whan such swete teeris gon afore and ledyn þe daunce of loue' (101),[24] while Troilus is said to bear himself in secret love 'As though he sholde have led the newe daunce' (2.553).

In the long tradition of wooing and nuptial imagery for 'love celestial' between the soul and the divine are models of much greater daring than anything found in texts devoted to 'love of kynde'. In the Chester Play of the Resurrection Christ talks as a lover-knight who has rescued man's soul, 'my deare lemmon [sweetheart]', from 'a dungeon deepe' (345),[25] but *A Talkyng of þe Loue of God* can eroticize the Harrowing of Hell as how Christ 'led out your dear love, man's soul, to your bright bower, full of bliss, to live in your embrace always without end' (34–5).[26] Yet if Pandarus expresses unease that his go-between role has made him 'swich a meene / As maken wommen unto men to comen; / Al sey I nought, thow wost wel what I meene' (3.254–6), no such unease prevents Rolle from opening his *Ego dormio* by casting himself in his writing as the surrogate wooer, who will metaphorically bring to Christ's bed the nun to whom the treatise is addressed:

> Forþi þat I loue þe, I wowe þe, þat I myght haue þe as I wold, nat to me, bot to my Lord. I wil becum a messager to brynge þe to his bed þat hath mad þe and boght þe, Crist, þe kynges son of heuyn, for he wil wed þe if þou wil loue hym. (26)

Just as Criseyde complies with her uncle's wishes (3.580–1), so the nun in *Ego dormio* will please the go-between, Rolle, by returning the love proffered her by his royal master ('He asketh þe no more bot þi loue, and my wil þou dost, if þou loue hym', 26). And although romance tradition provides for attempted seductions of the hero by forward hostesses and assorted temptresses (which lies behind the lady's embarrassing visits to the guest bedroom in *Sir Gawain and the Green Knight*), little in romance is as direct as the account, in Rolle's chapter on love in *Emendatio vitae*, of how the soul is to ravish Christ:

> þou boldely entrest into þe privee bedstede of þe endeles king of hevene. þou alloone dredest not for to ravische Jhesu Crist. He it is whom þou hast souht and whom oonly þou hast loued. Cryst is þin owen: hold him faste! (CUL MS Ff.5.30, f.159)

An urgent, earnest tone here compares markedly with the comedy that is rarely far from women's unwanted seduction attempts on heroes of romance, as with the besotted Imayne's efforts to get into bed with Ipomadon who, like Gawain, has an idea of what is coming, and takes unromantic evasive action:

> Grewosly vp starte hee
> And sayd, 'What devill art þou?'
> In his mowthe her hande he gate,
> Right as he wolde haue eyton þat; *eaten*
> 'Mercy!' she cryde nowe.
> (7189–93)

The account of how Troilus, in bed at last with his own lady, joyfully explores Criseyde's naked body before he makes love to her –

> Hire armes smale, hire streghte bak and softe,
> Hire sydes longe, flesshly, smothe and white
> He gan to stroke, and good thrift bad ful ofte
> Hire snowisshe throte, hire brestes rounde and lite
> (3.1247–50)

– is remarkable not only for what it so frankly describes but also for its unapologetic and unembarrassed celebration of sensual pleasure in physical love, quite without prurience and titillation (unlike its Italian source here). Chaucer's boldness in what *Troilus* enacts as sexual experience contrasts with how much remains confined to the lover's erotic fantasies in *Confessio Amantis*:

> Somdiel I mai the betre fare,
> Whan I, that mai noght fiele hir bare,
> Mai lede hire clothed in myn arm:
> Bot afterward it doth me harm
> Of pure ymaginacioun;
> For thanne this collacioun

I make unto miselven ofte,
And seie, 'Ha, lord, hou sche is softe,
How sche is round, hou sche is smal!
Now wolde God I hadde hire al
Withoute danger at mi wille!'
And thanne I sike and sitte stille,
Of that I se mi besi thoght
Is torned ydel into noght.
(4.1139–52)

Troilus's loving exploration of Criseyde's body has been preceded by unusual comic indignities when the unconscious male lover's body is chafed by his lady and his friend and then stripped, but it is a commonplace of contemporary devotional literature to make Christ's body the focus of exploration. In addressing Jesus, *A Talkyng of þe Loue of God* undresses him in imagination: 'For within you are gathered all things that may ever make anyone worthy of another's love: fairness, beautiful face, white flesh under clothes make many a man beloved and more dear' (27). When Margery Kempe reports Christ speaking of getting into bed with her, after her marriage to the Godhead in Rome ('For it is convenyent the wyf to be homly wyth hir husbond . . . Therfore most I nedys be homly wyth the and lyn in thi bed wyth the', ch. 36), it is noticeable that, since Christ gives the instructions, it is Kempe's spiritual foreplay with his body that is anticipated rather than the other way round: 'And therfor thu mayst boldly take me in the armys of thi sowle and kyssen my mowth, myn hed and my fete as swetly as thow wylt' (ch. 36). Christ's feet are also the focus for the speaker of *A Talkyng*, who is imagined at the foot of the cross in a fusion of spiritual ecstasy and physical intimacy of devotion:

> I suck the blood from his feet; that sucking is extremely sweet. I kiss and embrace and occasionally stop, as one who is love-mad and sick with love-pain. I look at [Mary], who brings him, and she begins to smile, as if it pleased her and she wanted me to go on. I leap back to where I was and venture myself there; I embrace and I kiss, as if I was mad. I roll and I suck, I do not know how long. And when I am sated, I want yet more. (61)

No carnal love is represented with such urgent physicality in medieval English writing. As to kissing, perhaps the fullest sense of its ardent mutual sensation conveyed by any medieval English author is written by a monk – in the Latin meditations of the Monk of Farne, which look back to older meditative traditions:

> The more dearly a bridegroom loves his bride, the longer he is wont to linger over the kisses which he imprints on her lips, and the more ardently he knows his love to be returned, the more closely does he press his lips to hers. Consider, then, the kiss of God, which has remained one unceasing kiss ever since he touched the lips of flesh with the lips of his Godhead, for having once assumed flesh he has never laid it aside. Has he not pressed his mouth close to our mouths in kissing us? So closely in very truth has he

> pressed it in this kiss, that the one who kisses and the one kissed have thereby become one, since the Word was made flesh that one who was man might also be God, and one who was God also man. (67)[27]

This is also one of many devotional texts where entry into Christ's wounded side through contemplation brings with it a language redolent of erotic union ('I open my side to draw thee into my heart after this kiss, that we may be two in one flesh', 64). Addressing the soul in the lyric 'In a valley of this restless mind', Christ remarks of his wounded side: 'This is hyr chambre, here shall she rest, / That she and I may slepe in fere' (42).[28] Yearningly inviting Christ into their souls, the language used by speakers of mystical texts often carries an erotic charge, as in Rolle's *Emendatio vitae* ('With your sweet heat penetrate a soul languishing for you and to you. Kindle with your heat the inner recess of my heart and illuminate with your shining light my inmost chamber', 57).[29] *A Talkyng of þe Loue of God* concludes and climaxes with a kind of love-death that draws together these various motifs:

> There I shall suck of your side, which opens towards me so wide, without moving at all, and there I will stay . . . There I will live and die, locked in your two arms . . . love of my life, my death, my bliss, because you made me your dear lover, I put me between your arms, I embrace you between my arms. Now give me consciousness of you forever . . . (69)

Imploring Jesus 'let me now die in your blissful arms from all the love of this world into the love of you' (53), this text comes near to conflating death with love's climax, and in a unique passage, extant in one copy of *Ego dormio*, Rolle anticipates a form of mystical *Liebestod* or love-death:

> In þis degre of loue þou wil couait þe deth, and be ioyful when þou hirest men name deth, for þat loue maketh þe as siker of heuyn when þou deyest as þou now art of deile [*grief*], for þe fyre of loue hath brent away al þe roust of syn. And I wene, fro þou or I or anoþer be broght in to þis ioy of loue, we mow nat lyue longe after as oþer men doth, bot as we lyue in loue, also we shal dey in ioy, and passe to hym þat we haue loued. (32)

The fervour of such contexts only contrasts with the often serio-comic theme of the lover's threatened death in secular texts – a health problem usually cured promptly by physical consummation. In Malory's 'Book of Sir Tristram' Sir Kehydius falls in love at first sight with La Beall Isode and dies for love of her (493),[30] but dying for love was more often stratagem than event. Thomas Hoccleve's *Letter of Cupid* complains of lovers: 'They seyn so importable is hir penance, / That, but hir lady list to shewe hem grace, / They right anoon moot steruen in the place' (26–8),[31] and a poem of Charles d'Orléans wryly suggests that dying for love is all talk: 'But many suche as ye in wordis dy / That passyng hard ther graffis [*graves*] ar to spy' (5294–5).[32]

Love of 'Kynde'

Luf makys me, as ye may se,	
Strenkyllid with blood so red;	*besprinkled*
Luf gars me haue hart so fre,	*makes*
It opyns euery sted;	*place*
Luf so fre so dampnyd me,	
It drofe me to the ded;	
Luf rasid me thrug his pauste,	*power*
It is swetter then med.	*mead*
Thomas of India (372)[33]	

Appearing to the disciples in this Wakefield mystery play as the love that conquers death, the resurrected Christ casts himself as a lover-knight impelled by love for his beloved ('For oon so swete a thyng . . . / Man sawll, my dere derlyng, / To batell was I broght . . . / Yit lufe forgate I noght' (372). Countless lyrics also give voice to the familiar image of the Man of Sorrows, in which Christ like a wounded lover reproaches onlookers with how much he suffers for his love of man's soul. How could such claims for 'love celestial' be resisted? The interfusion of medieval idioms of 'love celestial' and 'love of kynde' in both secular and religious texts sets the goals and demands of those loves in telling juxtapositions that promote love of God: *The Prickyng of Love* recommends 'ȝif þou wolt al-gatis [*anyhow*] loue fleshli loue, I praie þe loue þou none þan þe flesh of Ihesu Criste' (5).

One of the psychologically shrewdest readings in Middle English of how a shared sexual attraction develops is found not in romance but as the concluding chapter on 'hou goostli love is turned into fleschli love' in Hilton's *Eight Chapters on Perfection.* Hilton acutely analyses how mutual influence, reluctance to differ and growing self-delusion license progressively permissive behaviour, and so:

> thei coveiten eche of hem to handle and feele othir, and kisse othir, as semeth to hem as it were devocioun and good love . . . And sumtyme thei seien that thei mai doon thus, and 'though it be a synne, yit it is no gret synne'. And thus, ai bi litil and litil, goostli love falleth and dieth, and flesschli love wexeth and quekeneth. And aftir this, bi processe of tyme, the fervour of love wexeth so moche . . . that neither of hem wole ayenseyn othir for displesynge of either othir in ony thinge that either of hem wil doon, though it were deedli synne. (147)[34]

After this stage, no talking, touching or kissing can satisfy and they 'consenten to the deede of leccherie, and fulli to performe it, yif that thei myght have leiser' (148). Since in Hilton's analysis all this may follow from 'mysrulynge of love', it is as well to be suspicious of any love that is secretly and singly directed to any other person: an apt conclusion to his little treatise's larger counsel of perfection.

Yet where one spiritual director analyses how 'love of kynde' may subvert 'love celestial', another is unafraid, addressing an audience of nuns, of drawing on the familiar symptoms of lovesickness in order to promote a lesson in celestial love. In *The Doctrine of the Hert*, a 'tretice made to religious wommen', the final chapter analyses seven tokens of 'extatik love' (253–64),[35] which recall the signs of 'the loveris maladye / Of Hereos' suffered by Palamon and Arcite in the Knight's Tale (1373–4), as also by Troilus and Ipomadon:

1. Lovers say little and are hard to understand (as with Arcite: 'no man koude knowe / His speche nor his voys', 1370–1); just as spiritual lovers understand only each other;
2. Lovers have dry limbs (Arcite 'lene he wex and drye as is a shaft', 1362); just so, spiritual love dries up all fleshly lust;
3. Lovers' eyes are sunken (like Arcite's 'eyen holwe', 1363); just as spiritual lovers' eyes are sunk deep into inward love;
4. Lovers weep only for the beloved, impatient with music in her absence (cf. KnT, 1367–8; *TC* 5.459–62); just as spiritual lovers weep and sing in their soul;
5. Irregular pulse (cf. *TC* 3.1114–15); just as the spiritual lover's pulse 'skipped out gostly from itself into God';
6. Deafness of lovers to all but mention of the beloved (cf. *TC* 1.730–1); such is spiritual deafness to all worldly tidings;
7. Lovers' pleasure in reminders of their beloved (cf. *TC* 5.561–81); transports over intimations of God.

Here a text directed at nuns, which declares fleshly love a form of madness, deploys what it evidently assumes its readership will recognize as conventional symptoms of courtly lovesickness, before reinterpreting them spiritually to analyse the transformative effect of 'love celestial'.

Hilton's *Eight Chapters* and *The Doctrine of the Hert* bespeak the poise with which medieval English writing moves discriminatingly between love's idioms and priorities. 'But firste reserve the honoure to God, and secundely thy quarell muste com of thy lady,' declares Malory, 'And such love I calle vertuouse love' (1119). Least theoretical of writers, in his great English Arthuriad Malory works out an accommodation between his ideals of virtue, honour and constancy (in love as in all things) and the open adultery of his Continental sources. In contrast with modern manners ('But nowadayes men can nat love sevennyght but they muste have all their desyres'), the love he depicts is for Malory something extraordinary:

> But the olde love was nat so. For men and women coude love togydirs seven yerys, and no lycoures lustis was betwyxte them, and than was love trouthe and faythefulnes. And so in lyke wyse was used such love in kynge Arthurs dayes. (1120)

By emphasizing its pastness and its cultural difference, Malory implicitly affirms that love is socially constructed, and that its value may be defined by circumstance and opportunity. This enables the *Morte* to value Lancelot's love more by what its loyalty achieves than by moral absolutes, and even to advance a link between Guinevere's consistency in her adulterous passion and her pious end ('whyle she lyved she was a trew lover, and therefor she had a good ende'). In its constancy such love seems relatively unabashed by 'love celestial' and negotiates its own terms with it, as in the Maid of Astolat's resolute refusal on her deathbed to repent of the unreciprocated love for Lancelot that is killing her:

> And othir than good love loved I never Sir Launcelot du Lake . . . And sitthyn hit ys the sufferaunce of God that I shall dye for so noble a knyght, I beseche The, Hyghe Fadir of Hevyn, have mercy uppon me and my soule, and uppon myne unnumerable paynys that I suffir may be alygeaunce of parte of my synnes . . . I take God to recorde I was never to The grete offenser nother ayenste Thy lawis, but that I loved thys noble knyght, sir Launcelot, oute of mesure. And of myselff, Good Lorde, I had no myght to withstonde the fervent love, wherefore I have my deth! (1093–4)

If Chaucer's *Troilus* narrative – of a young man's extramarital affair with a beautiful widow – is the frankest and fullest exploration in Middle English of sexual love enjoyed, the religious idiom in which pagan Troilus perceives a metaphysical dimension to his fulfilment boldly sets 'love of kynde' in debate with 'love celestial'. When Troilus, in bed with Criseyde, exclaims: 'O Love, O Charite! / . . . Benigne Love, thow holy bond of thynges' (3.1254, 1261) he draws on a nexus of terms found in contemporary texts addressing 'love celestial'. *The Chastising of God's Children* declares: 'For charite is a bond of loue, whiche drawiþ us to God, in whiche loue we forsaken ouresilf, and þerwiþ we bien ooned to God' (136), and Rolle prays 'Swet Jhesu, bynd me to þe in charite' in one of his *Meditations on the Passion* (71). When Troilus addresses his lady's eyes that have ensnared him –

> Ye humble nettes of my lady deere!
> Though ther be mercy writen in youre cheere,
> God woot, the text ful hard is, soth, to fynde!
> How koude ye withouten bond me bynde?
> (3.1355–8)

– he also echoes some of the idiom of 'love celestial' in Rolle's *Meditations*: 'Cache me, lord, in to þe nette of þy mercy þat is holy chirche, and kep me þat I neuyr brek out of þe bondis of charite' (74). But whereas *The Chastising* distinguishes 'charite' from 'loue of kynde' in spite of their outward resemblance – 'Neþeles þe loue of kynde is as liche to charite as to þe worchyng outward as two heeris of oon hed; but þe willis and þe menynges bien myche discordynge and ful vnliche' (136) – in *Emendatio vitae* Rolle expounds the role of charity so as to include both love between lovers and 'love celestial': 'Charity is the noblest, most excellent and sweetest of virtues, which we know to join lover with lover and to couple Christ with the elected soul for ever' (60), and both such current views form part of the contemporary climate in which Chaucer's first audiences interpreted Troilus's association of love and 'charite' in his experience.

In its remarkably monolithic reading of *Troilus*, twentieth-century criticism explained the poem's idiom of 'love celestial' by its own favoured critical perspective of irony, which allows the poem's narrative to be seen as a whole with the devoutly Christian sentiments at its ending. In this now standard reading, the pagan Troilus confuses 'love of kynde' with 'love celestial' until the poem's conclusion. Here, the language of prayerful entreaty compellingly echoes contemporary espousals of 'love celestial', so that Chaucer's invitation 'O yonge, fresshe folkes, he or she, / In which that love up groweth with youre age, / Repeyreth hom fro worldly vanite' (5.1835–7) might recall for early readers of *Troilus* the argument of such a treatise as Rolle's *Contra amatores mundi*:

> O young men who until now have been deceived, now at least learn to love; but instead love him whom you have not loved before. Come with me; hear of love; desire to love – but taste eternal love which gives life, not temporal love which kills. For I too am a young lover, though a wonderful one, since I think continually of my love, and do not withdraw from her embraces. (ch. 3)[36]

For 'love of kynde' is usually to be recanted or transcended. In Thomas Usk's *The Testament of Love*, in which Lady Philosophy's visit to Boethius is rewritten into Lady Love's visit to the imprisoned Usk, the prisoner's 'Margaret' is both loved woman and symbol of grace: his love moves towards the 'celestial'.[37] Inside Gower's allegorical frame to *Confessio Amantis* – the confessor's exposition of the deadly sins, as exemplified in tales of diverse kinds of love – is the biographical thread of the poet-lover's confession of his devotion to his lady, which ends with his recantation of a love for which he is grown too old. Yet however eloquently the ending of *Troilus* privileges 'love celestial', the revocation of *Troilus* among 'my translacions and enditynges of worldly vanitees' in the Retractions to the *Canterbury Tales* indicates that its ending does not preclude the poem's being recanted. A debate between 'love of kynde' and 'love celestial' produces a shifting negotiation and mutual commentary in different contexts over the course of Chaucer's poem: 'love celestial' offers a concluding yet not conclusive perspective on *Troilus.* As with Malory's Maid of Astolat, 'love of kynde' may be gravely 'oute of mesure', it may squander life and it may kill. Yet if it be true, it may represent some atonement for one's larger imperfection and a way to God:

> 'Why sholde I leve such thoughtes? Am I nat an erthely woman? And all the whyle the brethe ys in my body I may complayne me, for my belyve ys that I do none offence, though I love an erthely man, unto God, for He fourmed me thereto, and all maner of good love comyth of God'. (1093)

See also: 5 Women's Voices and Roles, 16 War and Chivalry, 20 Middle English Romance, 23 Lyric, 25 Mystical and Devotional Literature, 29 York Mystery Plays, 30 The *Book of Margery Kempe*, 31 Julian of Norwich, 32 *Piers Plowman*, 33 The *Canterbury Tales*, 35 Thomas Hoccleve, 36 The Poetry of Robert Henryson, 38 Malory's *Morte Darthur.*

Notes

1 Rhiannon Purdie (ed.), *Ipomadon*, EETS os 316 (2001).

2 On interpretations of courtly love see Boase 1977 and O'Donoghue 1982; for the classic exposition, Lewis 1936. On Chaucer, see Kelly 1975 and Windeatt 1992; on courtliness, Burnley 1998; on the visual arts, Camille 1998.

3 V. J. Scattergood (ed.), *The Works of Sir John Clanvowe* (Cambridge: Brewer, 1975).

4 On lovesickness, see Beecher and Ciavolella 1990 and Wack 1990.

5 Walter W. Skeat (ed.), *Chaucerian and Other Pieces* (Oxford: Clarendon Press, 1897).

6 A. V. C. Schmidt (ed.), *William Langland: The Vision of Piers Plowman*, 2nd edn. (London: Dent, 1995).

7 Steven Spector (ed.), *The N-Town Play*, EETS ss 11–12 (1991).

8 Marion Glasscoe (ed.), *Julian of Norwich: A Revelation of Love*, 3rd edn (Exeter: University of Exeter Press, 1993).

9 Phyllis Hodgson (ed.), *'The Cloud of Unknowing' and 'The Book of Privy Counselling'*, EETS os 218 (1944).

10 Thomas Bestul (ed.), *Walter Hilton: The Scale of Perfection* (Kalamazoo, Mich.: Medieval Institute Publications for TEAMS, 2000).

11 Margaret Deanesly (ed.), *The 'Incendium Amoris' of Richard Rolle of Hampole* (Manchester: University of Manchester Press, 1915); trans. Clifton Wolters as *The Fire of Love* (Harmondsworth: Penguin, 1972).

12 Phyllis Hodgson (ed.), *Deonise Hid Diuinite*, EETS os 231 (1958).

13 Links between love and religious idiom seem to occur universally: see Dronke 1965.

14 M. Doiron (ed.) 'Margaret Porete: *The Mirror of Simple Souls* – A Middle English Translation', *Archivio Italiano per la Storia della Pietà* 5 (1968), 241–355.

15 Barry Windeatt (ed.), *The Book of Margery Kempe* (Harlow: Pearson, 2000; repr. Woodbridge: Boydell and Brewer, 2004).

16 Phyllis Hodgson and Gabriel M. Liegey (eds), *The Orcherd of Syon*, EETS os 258 (1966).

17 S. J. Ogilvie-Thomson (ed.), *Richard Rolle: Prose and Verse from Longleat MS 29 and Related Manuscripts*, EETS os 293 (1988).

18 Hope Emily Allen (ed.), *English Writings of Richard Rolle* (Oxford: Clarendon Press, 1931).

19 Ed. Ogilvie-Thomson.

20 H. Kane (ed.), *The Prickynge of Love*, 2 vols (Salzburg: Institut für Anglistik und Amerikanistik, 1983).

21 Ed. Hodgson.

22 G. C. Macaulay (ed.), *The English Works of John Gower*, EETS es 81–2 (1900–1).

23 Joyce Bazire and Eric Colledge (eds), *The Chastising of God's Children and the Treatise of Perfection of the Sons of God* (Oxford: Basil Blackwell, 1957).

24 J. J. Vaissier (ed.), *A Deuout Treatyse called The Tree & XII. Frutes of the Holy Goost* (Groningen: Wolters, 1960).

25 R. M. Lumiansky and D. Mills (eds), *The Chester Mystery Cycle*, EETS ss 3 (1974).

26 M. Salvina Westra (ed.), *A Talkyng of þe Loue of God* (The Hague: Nijhoff, 1950). Only the translation is cited in this chapter.

27 Hugh Farmer (ed.), *The Monk of Farne: The Meditations of a Fourteenth-Century Monk* (London: Darton, Longman and Todd, 1961). For the Latin text, see Hugh Farmer, 'The Meditations of the Monk of Farne', *Analecta Monastica* 4 (1957), 141–245.

28 Douglas Gray (ed.), *A Selection of Religious Lyrics* (Oxford: Clarendon Press, 1975).

29 Nicholas Watson (ed.), *Richard Rolle: 'Emendatio vitae', 'Orationes ad honorem nominis Ihesu'* (Toronto: Pontifical Institute of Mediaeval Studies, 1995). Citations from Latin in this chapter are translated.

30 E. Vinaver (ed.), *The Works of Sir Thomas Malory*, 3 vols, 3rd edn, rev. P. J. C. Field (Oxford: Clarendon Press, 1990).

31 Roger Ellis (ed.), *Thomas Hoccleve: 'My Compleinte' and Other Poems* (Exeter: University of Exeter Press, 2001), p. 94.

32 Mary-Jo Arn (ed.), *Fortunes Stabilnes: Charles of Orleans's English Book of Love* (Binghamton: Center for Medieval and Early Renaissance Studies, 1994), p. 336.

33 Martin Stevens and A. C. Cawley (eds), *The Towneley Plays*, EETS ss 13–14 (1994).

34 B. Windeatt (ed.), *English Mystics of the Middle Ages* (Cambridge: Cambridge University Press, 1994).

35 Ed. Windeatt.

36 Paul F. Theiner (ed.), *Contra Amatores Mundi* (Berkeley: University of California Press, 1968).

37 Gary W. Shawver (ed.), *Thomas Usk: Testament of Love* (Toronto: University of Toronto Press, 2002).

References and Further Reading

Beecher, Donald A. and Ciavolella, Massimo (eds) 1990. *A Treatise on Lovesickness*. Syracuse, N.Y.: Syracuse University Press. Comprehensive study of the sixteenth-century treatise by Jacques Ferrand in its tradition.

Boase, Roger 1977. *The Origin and Meaning of Courtly Love*. Manchester: Manchester University Press. Accurately subtitled 'A critical study of European scholarship'; on the notion of courtly love since the term 'amour courtois' was used by a nineteenth-century medievalist, Gaston Paris.

Burnley, David 1998. *Courtliness and Literature in Medieval England*. Harlow: Longman. Includes ch. 9 on 'Courtly Love'.

Camille, Michael 1998. *The Medieval Art of Love: Objects and Subjects of Desire*. London: Laurence King. Study of courtly visual culture and artefacts associated with love.

Dronke, Peter 1965. *Medieval Latin and the Rise of European Love-Lyric*, 2 vols. Oxford: Oxford University Press. Wide-ranging study of patterns, motifs and traditions.

Kelly, H. A. 1975. *Love and Marriage in the Age of Chaucer*. Ithaca, N.Y.: Cornell University Press. Studies literary representation of love in fourteenth-century historical contexts.

Lewis, C. S. 1936. *The Allegory of Love*. Oxford: Oxford University Press. Enduring critical intelligence and panache; more reservations about the historical style: 'Every one has heard of courtly love, and every one knows that it appears quite suddenly at the end of the eleventh century in Languedoc . . . love of a highly specialized sort, whose characteristics may be enumerated as Humility, Courtesy, Adultery and the Religion of Love' (p. 2).

O'Donoghue, Bernard 1982. *The Courtly Love Tradition*. Manchester: Manchester University Press. Anthology of Continental texts, with introduction.

Wack, Mary Frances 1990. *Lovesickness in the Middle Ages: The 'Viaticum' and Its Commentaries*. Philadelphia: Penn University Press. Comprehensive commentary on Constantine's influential text.

Windeatt, Barry 1992. *The Oxford Guides to Chaucer: 'Troilus and Criseyde'*. Oxford: Clarendon Press. Discusses aspects of 'A Debate about Love' in the poem (pp. 215–50).

PART VI
Genres

20
Middle English Romance

Thomas Hahn and Dana M. Symons

Sir Thomas Malory's *Morte Darthur* occupies a pivotal position in English literary history, as the latest and greatest of medieval romances.[1] Its massive, comprehensive character gives it the appearance of incorporating every Arthurian story Malory could lay hands on. It is fundamentally coherent and continuous, telling the entire story of Arthur and his knights, from Uther Pendragon's begetting of Arthur to the death of the king and the dissolution of the Round Table. It tells its stories in prose, anticipating the premier medium for English fiction through to the present day. Its language and idiom bridge the gap of medieval and modern, making it accessible to the common reader, and so it has been continuously in print from its first edition (1485) to the present time. Finally, it neatly marks the final moment of medieval romance, surviving both in a single medieval manuscript and in a near-contemporary mass-produced print. In all these ways, then, the *Morte Darthur* would seem to give us a snapshot – perhaps, given its bulk, better to say a feature film – of the nature of English romance at the end of the Middle Ages.

In fact, the overall picture of medieval romance formed through a reading of the *Morte Darthur* seriously distorts several centuries of writing, reading and performance. Among the most striking features of the *Morte* is Malory's systematic refusal to have anything to do with widely read and performed native materials. Although Malory must have heard many an English verse romance, and in his reading must surely have encountered dozens of English texts in prose and verse, the thousand or so pages to which modern editions of the *Morte* extend contain only the faintest traces of earlier English romances. In his attachment to 'the French boke', as he calls his written sources, Malory showed himself nostalgically old-fashioned, and brilliantly clairvoyant, anticipating precisely what post-medieval readers would find most engaging about chivalric adventure and love. His investment in these older, high literate narratives, and his evasion or exclusion of vernacular romances, also anticipate the conventional judgement of literary histories, namely that this genre – arguably the most popular form of non-religious writing in medieval English – hardly deserves notice. Most anthologies – the path by which readers ordinarily come to the writings of the Middle Ages – include short excerpts from Malory, all or part of the utterly exceptional and atypical romance *Sir Gawain and the Green Knight*, and no substantive or representative examples of verse romance. Such restricted access precludes any attempt to make sense of the popularity these stories enjoyed in their own time.

Audience and Performance

The familiarity and attachment of diverse audiences to romance emerges conspicuously in the numbers and variety of surviving examples. More than 150 of these narratives have come down to us from the English Middle Ages, and we know there were many more than that through allusions by other writers to stories that no longer exist.[2] Moreover, audiences of all kinds encountered these romances not just in writing, but through recitations, songs and performances, individual and collective, private and public, amateur and professional. Like Criseyde and the women of her household in Chaucer's *Troilus*, groups might read such stories to one another, or a court might appropriate a romance as the 'libretto' for a masque, as Edward I did with the story of *Sir Gawain and Dame Ragnelle*. The relatively low quality of some manuscripts and the layout of texts suggests that these were sometimes used as performance scripts, whether by professional performers, travelling minstrels or *gisours*, or by talented locals. An unusually detailed account of a presentation, though it occurred in the sixteenth century, can perhaps offer a richer picture of the nature and appeal of these stories.

In 1575 the London courtier Robert Laneham wrote a letter, smacking of the distance of the cosmopolitan intellectual and antiquarian, in which he offers an eyewitness account of the festivities put on for Queen Elizabeth's visit to Kenilworth. He pays special attention to one Captain Cox, a Coventry mason by trade, but also a performance artist 'hardy as Gawin': Cox acts, sings, recites, professes 'Philosophy, both morall and naturall' and carries a sheaf of papers he might use as scripts, bound with a whipcord. He also possesses 'at his fingers ends' – that is, available for immediate recall and command performance – a vast repertoire of stories, including ballads, songs, perhaps plays, and certainly romances; he knows 'king Arthurs book', a huge mix of other chivalric narratives, and 'Syr Gawyn'.[3] Far from being a bardic rhapsode, the Captain draws on an urban and artisan environment; moreover, although he seems never to have quit his day job, like many medieval performers before him he enjoyed a lively local reputation, and his performances brought the entire social scale together, old and young, from field and town, London and the countryside, from Queen to commoner.

Laneham also describes another performer who, 'after a littl warbling on his harp for a prelude, came foorth with a sollem song, warraunted for story oout of King Arthurs acts, the first booke and 26 chapter, whearof I gate a copy'.[4] Laneham quotes just enough of the Arthurian material to confirm that it derived from a printed copy of Malory's *Morte*. Indeed, the anonymous minstrel's performance seems to have entailed turning Malory's prose version of Arthur's Roman war back into alliterative verse, reversing the very process that Malory had used when he appropriated the one English romance he relied on as a major source. His presentation strikingly demonstrates the pleasure 'live' audiences must have taken in rhythm and poetry, and the capacity of even a post-medieval amateur to extract verse romance from beneath layers of prose and print. Presumably when back in the city Laneham may have preferred literary romances of the sort Philip Sidney and Edmund Spenser were beginning to imagine, but he and his fellow listeners seem fully prepared to take pleasure in the old, popular narratives as the occasion allowed. Laneham's inventory underscores the heterogeneity of Captain Cox's repertoire, reflecting both the variety and dynamism of vernacular romance and the widely differing tastes of audiences. The two episodes also make clear how readily performance traditions swallowed up texts, and made them – whether elite, literate, modern, mechanically reproduced, it did not seem to matter – grist for their presentations.

Turning once again to Malory, and especially to the single English romance he uses as a major source, the alliterative *Morte Arthure* (about 1375),[5] may help clarify further the dialectic of competing cultural registers. Although critics have suggested that the *Morte* more resembles a chronicle, epic or tragedy than it does a romance, its very tendency to push against these generic boundaries sets it apart as one of the greatest literary writings in Middle English. The author took pains to transform his Latin source, Geoffrey of Monmouth, into alliterative long lines that, despite their connection to native oral traditions, would have challenged even the earliest readers through their density and artfulness. Moreover, he has saturated the poem with structural, thematic and linguistic repetitions and contrasts, all of which complicate the narrative, demanding high levels of readerly engagement. The poem is filled with spectacular scenes of mayhem and violence that, just because they are so minutely choreographed, tend to bring readers up short, rather than allowing them to dash blithely through the bloodshed. The action oscillates between gallant, admirable chivalric exploits and power-mad, catastrophic destruction of life; aria-like speeches, delivered in stylized modes that vividly recall oral traditions, punctuate the narrative as stop-action commentary. Ultimately these features coalesce, in the manner of high-art writing, and press the reader with political and moral ambiguities; indeed, modern critics continue to debate whether the *Morte* exalts medieval kingship or offers a searing indictment of imperial ambitions, either in the mythical Arthur or in the policies of a living king like Edward III.

For Malory, whose ambition was to write the whole book of Arthur, such heightened literary effects would have thwarted his narrative's momentum, and dark ambiguities had no place in an episode near the outset of the king's reign. He therefore simply stripped away what from an aesthetic perspective might seem the high points, and reshaped the *Morte* as a vigorous account of Arthur's crushing victories. What is more, when Malory's *Morte Darthur* moved from manuscript to print, either Malory himself, William Caxton, his printer, or some other knowledgeable reviser extended this stripping down process, systematically regularizing language, idiom and syntax in this section of the book, excising poetic formulas and obscure diction, thereby making it more accessible for ordinary readers. Through this process of streamlining its narrative, highlighting the spectacular aspects of its action, and eschewing poetic diction, the printed edition of the *Morte Darthur* ironically draws upon those signature features that endowed popular vernacular romance with its appeal. When, a century after its appearance, the anonymous Elizabethan minstrel took the printed edition of Malory as a script for his own verse performance, he was surely not restoring the rugged density and elegance that marked the fourteenth-century poem, but pushing Malory's narrative still further towards the widely relished models provided by medieval English romance.

Stories of Sir Gawain

Laneham's mention of 'Syr Gawyn' as part of Captain Cox's repertoire immediately invokes an association with *Sir Gawain and the Green Knight*, the most celebrated, best known of all English romances, at least for readers schooled in the modern canon. In medieval England, however, *Gawain* seems to have found only a tiny readership. Moreover, despite conventional gestures towards popular oral traditions (requests for attention, the contention that the story has circulated widely), neither the Captain nor his audience would have enjoyed listening to *Gawain*, for no live audience has the wherewithal to answer the demands of this supremely literary poem. The romance proclaims its uniqueness by choosing to tell an extravagant story, extra-canonical to the Arthurian tradition, but completely self-contained. It unfolds its plot in language that far outruns the alliterative *Morte Arthure* in difficulty, combining dialectal enigmas, archaic forms, specialized vocabularies and extreme literary compression; its plot is unparalleled in English for its dazzling, spiralling structures that seem to repeat endlessly and to reward repeated attention. Although in its ambition and achievement it resembles other experiments in romance, like Chaucer's *Troilus* or his Knight's Tale, finally it stands apart from all other examples of the genre, a conclusion brought home even more forcefully when *Sir Gawain* is placed alongside the dozen or more broadly popular Gawain romances that circulated in Middle English – a juxtaposition that would have conditioned all medieval readers' first responses to the poem. The relative obscurity of *Gawain* meant that even an insatiable reader like Malory would not have encountered it; at the same time, had he come across it, it seems quite unlikely that he would have incorporated it into the *Morte Darthur*. The suffusing, self-conscious artistry that mark it as an elite work would have clotted the narrative directness and momentum Malory sought so strenuously to convey.

A much more likely candidate for Captain Cox's 'Syr Gawyn', and a much more representative example of medieval romance in England, is the sole medieval progeny produced by *Gawain*, *The Greene Knight* (c.1500). The composer's decision to create this poem advertises his attachment to the narrative enchantment of *Gawain*, and he holds fast to the earlier work's storyline. At the same time, however, *The Greene Knight* literally digests the longer romance, streamlining the narrative through its determined spelling out of motives and events, its domestication of the challenging and mysterious, and its explanation of marvels and ambiguities. If we as modern readers take *Gawain* as an aesthetic touchstone, it becomes difficult not to read the transformed text as '*Gawain* for dummies'. Yet the composer's design cannot have been to produce a bad high-art romance; he aimed instead for a poem that would offer audiences genuine pleasures, though determinedly different from those of *Gawain*. Reducing the story in length to only one-fifth of the earlier poem, *The Greene Knight* promises – and delivers – non-stop, spectacular action. It scraps the atmospherics and set pieces, the connoisseur descriptions and subtle dialogue that give every reader pause in *Gawain*. The transformed figure of Sir Bredbeddle (aka the Green Knight) seems scarcely a vegetation god, an ogre or a moral inquisitor, but simply a 'jolly sight to seene' (79) and a 'venterous knight' (94), whose direct challenge to Arthurian chivalric values gives every indication of easy resolution.[6] In place of the awed silence that in *Gawain* overtakes the court when the Green Knight appears, here the entire fellowship leaps forward; stock scenes like the exchange with the porter and the irascibility of Sir Kay likewise cue listeners and readers to enjoy patterned confrontation for its own sake, rather than to contemplate motives or search out ambiguities. The multiple temptations, hunts, exchanges and blows that organize *Gawain* all become single events in *The Greene Knight*, and the relations between them, so richly unspecifiable in the earlier poem, are here made unmistakably plain for the audience. All of this makes the poem coalesce and speed towards its conclusion, and the sense of things coming together finds support in narrative motifs of convergence and communion: the Green Knight actually sits down and shares a meal with the Round Table after making his challenge, and Sir Bredbeddle is ultimately brought back to Arthur's court and joins its fellowship. The repetitions, the rapid pace and clear trajectory of the plot, and the insistent disclosures all combine to encourage the audience to find immediate pleasure in the exaggerations and sensationalism of the action, to enjoy each episode as it hurtles past, rather than to suspend judgement or worry at interpretation.

The Interplay of Elite and Popular Elements

Captain Cox's appearance before the broadest possible audiences, performing both tales with ancient oral pedigrees and modern appropriations, casts some of the strongest light we have on the constant scuffling of high and low cultures. Our capacity to recognize their separability tempts us to look past the dynamism of the form and the cultural process that it gives voice to. Attempts, like the present essay, to specify the nature and appeal of romance run the risk of muting the edgy dialogue of popular and elite that fuelled the genre for medieval audiences. Alliterative romances, for example, frequently exploit this dialectic, flaunting idioms, techniques and themes explicitly linked to native oral traditions, yet drawing on literate, often Latinate, sources, and in this way at once bridging and deepening the gap between high and low. Moreover, as exceptional poetic efforts like *Gawain* and the alliterative *Morte Arthure* strikingly illustrate, elite writers were not only aware of the omnipresence of such stories, they sometimes tried to appropriate or reshape them for their own purposes and audiences. The self-conscious artistic aspirations of writers like the *Gawain* poet, Geoffrey Chaucer and John Gower, and the emergence of a palpable canon of English Literature, no doubt intensified the negative valence associated with popular and performance texts. At the same time, however, many authors continued to regard verse romance as the default genre for long narrative: alongside the enduringly popular English tales of *Guy of Warwick* and *Bevis of Hampton*, bookish writers produced lengthy accounts of the fall of Thebes, the war at Troy and the adventures of Alexander the Great. These expansive accounts of foundational myths and martial exploits may well have appealed to wide readerships, though they seem to have targeted niche audiences as well: John Lydgate's *Siege of Thebes* – a conspicuous example of a literary writer producing a non-popular romance – was recast in prose by a reviser who inserted materials drawn from expert writing on military strategy, presumably for readers especially attached to such matters.

We may perhaps gauge the hopes that high culture entertained for romance as a distinctly literary genre by glancing at represented scenes of reading from Chaucer's *Troilus and Criseyde.* This 8,000-line poem – with its intense demands on readerly attention, its self-reflexivity and endless allusions to other writing, its verbal pyrotechnics and troublingly self-absorbed narrator – stands as a paragon of what romance might be as a form of elite writing. In addition, within the *Troilus* Chaucer stages two moments that idealize the forms of engagement he hoped readers would feel with his own poem. Near the beginning of the poem, Pandarus visits Criseyde, and finds her and the ladies of her household sitting in her 'paved parlour', listening intently to a 'mayden reden hem the geste / Of the siege of Thebes' (2.82–4). The narrative, presumably a vernacular story analogous to the English *Troilus* (and perhaps the inspiration for Lydgate's *Siege of Thebes*), is twice described as a book and once as a 'romaunce' (2.85, 95, 100). This 'parlour' book therefore seems to be a large, de luxe volume meant for household use rather than for private reading – a 'coffee-table' romance. Pandarus's apology for interrupting the session makes clear that elite and sophisticated readers paid close attention to such texts, and his avowal, 'Al this [story] knowe I myselve' (2.106), affirms that such canonical Greats are just the sort of cultural capital on which keen and cultivated readers should spend disposable time. Pandarus reinforces the value of the private reading through which he must have learned 'Al this' when, having bedded Criseyde and Troilus in the more intimate space of his *litel closet*, 'he drow hym to the feere, / And took a light, and fond his contenaunce / As for to looke upon an old romaunce' (3.979–80). Presumably both these scenes rehearse the kinds of reading Chaucer hoped his own 'litel bok' would attract: whether communal or individual, reading the romance of *Troilus and Criseyde* presents itself as a serious pastime, clearly soliciting lively, continuous, rapt attention from its ideal audiences, and promising them a form of shared, enduring knowledge, newly canonical but of permanent worth. Romance at this elite level refuses immediate, shared gratification in familiar, preordained plots; instead, it models refined social behaviours and achieved cultural capital, even as it enables readers, through the exacting practice of enjoying the poem, to integrate these qualities to their developing vernacular identities. Such knowledge could only be found in written texts, not in ephemeral performances or fragile scripts meant for recitals.

As the ultimate successors to a half-millennium-long tradition that has associated narratives with the printed word, solitude and analysis, twenty-first-century readers come well prepared to appreciate the peculiar pleasures of a romance like *Gawain* or Chaucer's *Troilus*. At the same time, the increasing absorption of stories in broadcast, electronic and filmic forms has heightened our awareness of how immediacy and participation (virtual or physical) shape or enhance narrative meaning. The reciprocity of high and low that marks romance in medieval England arose from and depended upon an analogous range of shifting experiences and expectations. Although the pleasures live medieval audiences may have shared inevitably elude us just because of their remote and ephemeral character, it none the less makes sense to try and work out the differing responses romance in its various forms may have generated for listeners and readers. One source of evidence for the distinctive features of popular romance comes from the reactions to such tales by 'official culture'. These responses give an idea not only of the characteristics of the vernacular romance in England, but also of its power as entertainment in its own right. The entertainment value of these performative pieces for audiences from a variety of social registers emerges clearly in attempts to silence the genre, which range from outright condemnation of street performances to a more subtle censure illustrated through the attempts to appropriate and rework popular romances in ways that undermined the very traits that gave them their broad appeal. Such responses signal an anxiety on the part of elite culture about the status of writing in English, and a perception that these popular entertainments were the rivals of serious literary efforts. In part these interventions intended to undo the exclusive association of the mother tongue with oral, public performances and with 'frivolous' amusements, thereby opening a space for literary production in the vernacular whose composition and consumption required leisure, money and education.

Condemnations of popular versions of a story set the concerns of more literary writers against those of their more performative counterparts, suggesting in turn something about the pleasures of popular narratives for their audiences. For example, Robert Mannyng of Brunne complained in his *Chronicle* that the oral performances he encountered were flawed because they did not match the written versions he favoured:

I see in song, in sedgeyng tale *recited*
Of Erceldoun and of Kendale:
Non tham says as thai tham wroght, *composed*
And in ther sayng it semes noght. *worthless*
(93–6)[7]

Here Mannyng attacks the recited songs and tales on the grounds that they do not accurately or fully reproduce written versions. For *literati* like this chronicler, the value of a text resided in its fixed enclosure in written words, where meaning is gleaned by a solitary reader who has the leisure to spend time uncovering various possible interpretations of the text. The ability to please an audience whose taste is geared towards immediate reception in fact eradicates the pleasures a literate audience prefers. Mannyng's insistence on the rigidity of a 'good' version points conversely to the importance of flexibility in a popular narrative: it suggests that one benefit of transmission by mouth in a public context is the possibility that the story can be tailored to (or even by) a particular audience on the spot.

The grounds on which popular versions of a story were excoriated reveal the qualities that distinguished them from literary writing. Mannyng, for example, complains about street performances of Tristan and Iseult, one of the most widely known tales of the Middle Ages; he dismisses these renditions as inaccurate or inauthentic because they leave out important details:

That may thou here in *Sir Tristrem*,	
Over gestes it has the steem,	*takes the prize*
Over alle that is or was,	
If men it sayd as made Thomas.	*recited; composed*
But I here it no man so say	*hear no one recite it*
That of som copple, som is away.	*Save in various couplets, something is missing*
(97–102)	

As in his more general complaint, Mannyng considers that the omission of any part of the 'original' written text – where 'of som copple, som is away' – renders the public recital deficient. The inscribed copy of Thomas's story safely preserves the meaning of *Tristan and Iseult*, and the quality or authenticity of any subsequent version will depend on just how fully it reproduces its source. The omissions and improvizations characteristic of performance produce the 'crippled' versions that so irritate Mannyng. A look at Thomas of Britain's highly literary Anglo-Norman version of the Tristan story suggests that what Mannyng missed was the emphasis on the characters' thoughts and inner turmoil. The pointedness of Mannyng's complaints insistently deflects us from the realization that in order to accommodate the psychological detail he considers intrinsic to the story, literary narratives on their side exclude the qualities that made the popular stories pleasurable for their audiences.

In contrast to Mannyng's worry that something may be left out, Thomas of Britain's French version of the Tristan story explicitly inveighs against the diversity of the material, the presence of digressions and the inclusion of too many episodes in a single narrative. Thomas instead endows his poem with authority through a process of exclusion, explaining that, although the tale has many variants, he will unify it by reciting only what is necessary (2104–7).[8] In reviewing multiple retellings of the story (perhaps written as well as oral), Thomas recognizes that some versions disagree about certain events (2108–9); as author, he sorts through this 'surplus' material, jettisoning episodes that do not conform to the whole, in this way creating an organic narrative. Thomas's view is that the additional material somehow mars the tale and compromises 'the truth' (2149) of the single, coherent narrative he intends to pass on. Thomas's conviction that the 'true' story of Tristan will demand stripping away excess meaning points to how a popular version might look, suggesting it is episodic and full of digression, incorporating a diversity of material rather than abiding by a tightly knit storyline.

The Appeal of Popular Romance

In this view, popular narratives were at once deficient (leaving out authentic bits) and excessive (including all sorts of material extraneous to the organic narrative). What kinds of pleasure might medieval audiences have found in romances that seemed so skewed from an elite, literate perspective, and just who made up the audiences that found those pleasures? *Sir Tristrem*, an English romance of the early fourteenth century, illustrates the investment such tales had in episodic narrative comprised of 'highlights' interspersed with more detailed moments of spectacular, quick-paced action. The emphasis here is on the pacing of the narrative. There is no room for meditative speeches ventriloquizing the internal wrangling of characters with their consciences, or for long exegetical passages on the part of the narrator. The action is quick and dirty. Relatively early in the tale, King Mark is forced to pay a tribute to Ireland: three hundred pounds each of gold, silver, coin and latten (a brass-like alloy) each year, and, most terrible, in the fourth year, 'Thre hundred barnes fre' (Three hundred noble children, 946).[9] As Mark prepares to hand over the children to Moraunt, Tristrem argues that Mark should refuse to pay and offers to fight Moraunt instead. After a quick exchange of words in which Tristrem's challenge is reciprocated by Moraunt, the two men sail away to an isolated place where they can fight undisturbed.

The description of the battle occupies a full sixty lines (1030–89). The combat begins with clouts to one another's helms and continues with a joust where Tristrem and Moraunt exchange blows with their lances. Reading over the two stanzas that encompass the fight on horseback, it is impossible to tell whether the two men joust several times, with the action foreshortened to quick flashes of multiple tilts, or whether the same hits are simply being described repeatedly as a way of emphasizing the action. But whether the action is reiterated or contracted, it operates on an almost cinematic level, representing the action in much the same way that a film repeats a spectacular event several times from different angles, or compresses a series of similar events by quickly flashing from a moment in one scene to a similar action in another. In the visual medium, both dilation and compression operate to heighten the impact on the viewer, and the action of the joust seems to work similarly in the text. After each man has hit the other's shield, the narrator adds a second hit by Moraunt, even though it is not clear that the two have started another tilt:

Moraunt with his might	
Rode with gret raundoun	*violence*
Ogain Tristrem the knight,	*Against*
And thought to bere him doun.	*overthrow him*
With a launce unlight	*stout lance*

He smot him in the lyoun,	*on his shield*
And Tristrem that was wight	*valiant*
Bar him thurch the dragoun	*Pierced*
In the scheld.	
That Moraunt, bold and boun,	*stout*
Smot him in the scheld.	*Hit*
(1035–45)	

Similarly, in the next stanza, Tristrem suddenly leaps on his horse, even though he does not seem to have been unseated, suggesting that this is either a reprise of the action that has just taken place in the previous stanza or a compressed view of new events. *Sir Tristrem*'s repetitious lingering over the details of battle offers an episodic narrative that thrives on lively dialogue, quick-paced action, bloody battles or other spectacular scenes, while avoiding any kind of inner turmoil or tension about meaning. The colloquial, formulaic tone of the poem invites audiences to join enthusiastically in its performative aspects, and enjoyment of popular romances like *Sir Tristrem* would in part derive from an intense familiarity with other works of the same sort – pieces that catered to the same taste.

Although the guardians of high culture frequently condemned popular narratives outright, such censure itself confirms their familiarity within all ranks of society. Even writers invested in producing an elite literary culture in English – and who were perforce hostile to mere 'rhyming' or entertainment – might 'stoop' to appropriate or refurbish characteristic features of the genre. The features that mark *Sir Tristrem* as typically 'low' are precisely what Chaucer consistently reproduces within inverted commas, as it were, in his send-up of popular romance in the *Canterbury Tales*, the Tale of Sir Thopas. For example, Chaucer regularly undermines the spectacular effects that give Middle English romance special appeal, so that the absent presence of these elements becomes a central source of the high literary enjoyment that Chaucer's tale provides. When the narrator describes Sir Thopas as 'a knyght [that] was fair and gent / In bataille and in tourneyment' (715–16), he makes claims about Thopas's prowess, yet no battle ever takes place to exemplify the knight's supposed valour. Promising a struggle, the tale lingers instead over the boasting that usually precedes a fight. The humour here resides in the knowledge that Thopas's behaviour stands in stark contrast to that of the heroes of popular romance, who can certainly boast with the best of them, but whose boasting leads to exciting, action-packed combat.

Exoticism and Magic

Popular romances habitually intensify the element of spectacle through recourse to the exotic. Such details may colour the nature or the context of the hero's encounters, or the behaviour and appearance of his enemies. This is a particular staple of the Charlemagne romances, because the enemies are 'Saracens', opponents who are religiously, culturally, linguistically and racially distinct from their European rivals. For example, in the early fifteenth-century *Sultan of Babylon*, the narrator explains that the Sultan 'and his sone Sir Ferumbras' propitiated 'Here [Their] goddis of golde' with 'frankensense / That smoked up so stronge' before blowing 'hornes of bras' and drinking 'beestes bloode' (677–84).[10] This ceremony is accompanied by a strange combination of foods:

> Milke and hony ther was,
> That was roial and goode.
> Serpentes in oyle were fryed
> To serve the Sowdon with-alle. *as well*
> (685–8)

The offerings to golden idols and the peculiar meal take place with ritualized chanting that the narrator first reports and then translates, underscoring not simply the linguistic but the cultural unintelligibility of the Sultan's court to outsiders: '"Antrarian, antrarian," thai lowde cryed / That signyfied "Joye generalle"' (689–90). The fundamental nature of the differences that separate 'ordinary' Christians from these outlandish aliens surfaces still more vividly on the eve of battle, when the narrator describes the army the Sultan has gathered against the French from countries all over the world:

> Thre hundred thousand of Sarsyns felle, *fierce*
> Some bloo, some yolowe, some blake as More, *blue; yellow; Moor*
> Some horible and stronge as devel of helle.
> He made hem drinke wilde beestes bloode,
> Of tigre, antilope and of camalyon, *giraffe*
> As is her use to egre her mode, *excite their courage*
> When thai in were to battayle goon.
> (1004–10)

The fiendish qualities of this enemy army, their exaggerated dissimilarities in skin colour, and the recital of their practice of drinking tiger, antelope and giraffe blood to excite their courage in battle all point to the irreducible barbarity of the enemies Charlemagne and his knights must defeat, at the same time that such 'barbarity' eddies through the poem as entertainment for the romance audience.

Where some romances exaggerate the alien details of people or landscapes, in ways that parallel the fixation in saints' lives with 'heathens' and 'barbaric' lands, the Breton lays as a group emphasize the magical aspects of romance narratives. In recycling motifs of folk and fairy tales, these stories deploy fairies, magic, alchemy or demonic characters to fashion an exoticism that distinctively enhances the narrative's spectacle. The lays focus with some frequency on familial relationships and the problems that arise when bonds of kinship and love fall out of balance, and in this way stake out a space for thrilling and sensationalistic scenes. In *Sir Orfeo*, for example, a romance based on the classical tale of Orpheus and Euridice, the hero is a ruler whose wife Heurodis is abducted by the fairy king. Orfeo must give up his own kingdom and travel to the Celtic Otherworld to rescue Heurodis before he can reclaim his royal status and regain his kingdom. His journey offers many opportunities for spectacular visions of the fairy realm, including the fairy king's castle, with its hundred towers, red-gold buttresses, richly enamelled vaulting, gold pillars, and dwellings made of precious stones, as well as a wall that puts on display people who were thought to be dead but were instead brought to the fairy realm and left sleeping:

Sum stode withouten hade,	*stood; head*
And sum non armes nade,	*no arms had*
And sum thurth the bodi hadde wounde,	*through; body*
And sum lay wode, y-bounde,	*crazy, bound*
And sum armed on hors sete,	*horse sat*
And sum astrangled as thai ete;	*choked; ate*
And sum were in water adreynt,	*drowned*
And sum with fire al forschreynt.	*shrivelled*
Wives ther lay on childe bedde,	
Sum ded and sum awedde,	*driven mad*
And wonder fele ther lay besides	*wondrous many*
Right as thai slepe her undertides;	*Just; their*
Eche was thus in this warld y-nome,	*taken*
With fairi thider y-come.	*enchantment brought here*

(391–404)[11]

In the midst of this multitude of the mortally wounded, with their bodies now headless, armless or otherwise fatally maimed, asphyxiated, drowned, burned, or dead in childbirth, Orfeo sees his own wife whom he has come to rescue. Like the descriptions of battle in *Sir Tristrem*, Ragnelle's appearance in *The Wedding of Sir Gawain and Dame Ragnelle*[12] or the appearance, customs and behaviour of the Sultan and his people in *The Sultan of Babylon*, the spectacular details of fairyland offer exotic or uncouth details to delight audiences.

Sir Orfeo stands out as a striking and relatively early experiment in grafting literary sources and art traditions onto popular models of narrative. Modern critics have found much to say about this romance, highlighting the treatment of classical myth, the function of music, the allegorical play of kingship and personal sovereignty, or the nature of refined love – in short, teasing out rudiments of truth and beauty, the cherished concerns of high art. Such modern readings of *Sir Orfeo* unquestionably arise from the inherent interest of these matters, but they originate as well in the patterns of interpretation inculcated by elite literacy, which values above all dense, figurative language, coherent, sustained narratives and the contemplation of abstract, often psychological complexities. Textual and formal analysis has much less to say about those elements that bind *Sir Orfeo* to the popular romances that saturated the consciousness of most medieval listeners and readers, and that would have constituted the primary filter for making sense of this unusual poem. The great majority of romances that circulated in medieval England resembled *The Greene Knight* and *Sir Tristrem* much more than they did *Gawain*. The fleeting yet compulsive and recurrent pleasures such stories held for long-dead audiences, elusive though these may be, deserve our assessment just because this promises to deliver a fuller, richer, more just sense of medieval people's lives and experiences than that provided by professedly exceptional works of art. At the same time, however, understanding why, how and how much popular romances mattered in medieval England constitutes a crucial, even necessary preliminary to recovering the meaning of elite works like *Gawain* and Chaucer's *Troilus*, since these stories form the ever-present ground against which high art defines itself.

Generic Definitions

Paradoxically, one obstacle to our grasping the nature and appeal of popular romance is that, in isolating discrete features or formulating rigid definitions, we run the danger of disguising the dynamism and fluidity that mark the genre in the English Middle Ages. The fixation with settling on a stable generic definition originates in the needs of modern scholarship: medieval scribes, authors and reciters casually used *romance* as the default category for sustained narratives of different kinds. *The Romance of the Childhode of Jhesu Christe*, for example, occurs in an anthology that includes *The Siege of Jerusalem* and *The Siege of Milan* ('romances' of battle and action), *Duke Roland and Sir Otuel* (a Charlemagne romance with affinities to *The Sultan of Babylon*) and *The Romance of King Richard the Lion Heart*, a wildly popular account of Christian-Islamic hatred and hostility that survives in six other manuscripts and ten early printed editions. One can only marvel at the capaciousness of a genre that as easily accommodates the adventures of the baby Jesus as military and crusading exploits. Even a distinct subcategory like the alliterative romances illustrates the variegated character of the genre: although the dense and playfully self-conscious language of *Gawain* virtually compels absorbed reading, many other poems like *The Wars of Alexander* and the *Morte Arthure* frequently render the sounds and formulas of their long lines as surface ornament, a form of 'linguistic spectacle' whose pleasure lies in immediate apprehension, which may or may not accompany applied criticism. 'Bookish' romances with direct literary sources, like the *Morte Arthure*, the *Awntyrs of Arthure*, or *Gologras and Gawain*, often display the highest concentration of alliterative poetry; writers and reciters alike seem not, however, to have revered such studied artifice, but to have felt it a spur to revise and improvise, as the four differing texts of the *Awntyrs* makes clear. Alliterative romances might even directly challenge the 'French books' associated with the most elite literate culture: in the midst of the French prose romance of Alexander, recorded in a manuscript routinely described as among the most beautiful books produced in the Middle Ages (Oxford, Bodleian Library MS Bodley 264), an English scribe noted that 'Here fayleth a processe [episode] of this rommance'. Readers are directed to turn to the end of the manuscript, where they may enjoy the alliterative *Alexander and Dindimus*,[13] and then to resume with the French. The scribe plainly considered the English romance an indispensable supplement to the immense French book, and in this way an equal or rival for cultural prestige. Finally, verse romances not only retained their popularity until the end of the Middle Ages, but occasionally (like Malory's *Morte*) became mass-produced artefacts: *Golagras and Gawain*, for example, exists only as a printed book, published in Edinburgh in the early sixteenth century.

Conditions of Production

The material conditions and the media – manuscript, print, oral traditions – in which romances circulated provide some further contexts for appreciating their appeal. Approximately thirty English literary manuscripts survive from before 1400, while some 600 manuscripts – twenty times as many – date from the fifteenth century (Edwards and Pearsall 1989: 257). Such numbers no doubt reflect the depredations wrought by engaged use and remoteness of time, but reflect even more dramatically a prodigious increase in literary activity and the emergence of an acknowledged canon of literary writing by 1400. These developments acutely diminished the stature of popular narrative traditions, branding them as subliterate. In convincing readers that their *poesie* was worth much more than the parchment it was written on, elite writers invested *belles lettres* – English *writing* – with cultural capital; this cachet inevitably exacerbated the gap between the technologies of preservation associated with literacy and with the performance environment of popular narrative. The image of Captain Cox, as late as the sixteenth century, scurrying about with scraps and scripts and loose printed sheets all bound with a whipcord, readying himself for a recital, stands in stark contrast to the man of letters whose 'litel bok' of romance might run to eight thousand lines, and might be reproduced as a de luxe manuscript with authorial frontispiece, as in the Cambridge *Troilus* (Corpus Christi College Cambridge MS 61, c.1399–1413).

The earliest manuscript collections of romances attest both the movement of the genre from oral to literate forms, and its stature as the default category of vernacular narrative. Compendia begin to appear around 1300, with *King Horn* and *Floris and Blanchfleur* as two of the three items in one anthology (Cambridge University Library MS Gg.4.27 [2]), and *King Horn* and *Havelok the Dane* making up two of the thirteen items in another (Oxford, Bodleian Library MS Laud Misc. 108). The Auchinleck Manuscript (Edinburgh, National Library of Scotland Advocates' MS 19.2.1, c.1330–40) is the most impressive anthology of romances left from the English Middle Ages; its portfolio of seventeen narratives (out of a total of forty-four items) documents a massive appetite not only to hear but also to own popular vernacular fictions, and it evinces a willingness to spend disposable income on English romance. These manuscripts participate in a wider phenomenon, in which English audiences beginning around 1300 took their reading matter more determinedly into their own hands, with individuals or households (rather than ecclesiastical authorities or institutions) sponsoring the production or seeking the ownership of vernacular texts. The Yorkshireman Robert Thornton, for example, copied the romances of *Percival of Galles*, *Sir Isumbras*, *Sir Eglamour of Artois* and *Sir Degravant*, as well as the alliterative *Morte Arthure*, for his library (in Lincoln Cathedral Library MS 91). Although 'serious' writing warranted systematic reproduction (by the early 1400s multiple copies of Gower, Chaucer, and perhaps *Piers Plowman*, were being turned out by professional scribes and illuminators in London), romances held their appeal. Fully two-thirds of the romances survive in codices dated to 1440 or later (Meale 1989: 217) and many traditional stories, like *Guy of Warwick*, continued to be printed throughout the sixteenth century, and then enjoyed an afterlife as ballads, 'gestes' or recitals, or printed chapbooks. Literary romances that incorporate elite literary values, like *Gawain* and the alliterative *Morte Arthure*, often survive in single copies reflecting the taste or initiative of a private reader.

Faced with such elusiveness and seeming obsolescence, what is a literary historian to do? Might the best course be to leave the great bulk of romances alone, and use an essay like this to produce a few more ingenious readings of narratives like *Gawain*? Such a course entails not only neglecting massive evidence about what mattered to medieval writers and audiences but also corroborating the commonplace assumption that stories which lack 'literary artistry' – realistic detail, dense verbal texture or psychological development – are self-evidently deficient. The process of assessment embedded in such history (implicitly conceding that medieval romances are 'bad' because they do not correspond to our expectations at the beginning of the twenty-first century) stands in contrast to a more positivist approach where one simply inventories what survives, perhaps appending brief summaries that confirm a modern reader's sense of the remoteness and feebleness of medieval romance. The present essay has tried to steer a third course, offering some sense not only of what was read, or of what one should read now, but also of how reading (and listening) *otherwise* might bring meaning and pleasure to audiences, then and now. Such arguments allow us to expand the literary canon in terms of form, content and new media (where attempts to appreciate medieval performance art in themselves make it 'new'). They also provide an intellectual platform from which to grasp the role narrative plays in shaping the ordinary experience of people, or in giving voice to particular interests or groups outside elite culture. Finally, as a pedagogy within literary studies, this broadly cultural understanding of old texts may increase our capacity to make sense not simply of highly complex or artful narratives but also of stories that through their seeming artlessness inform our deepest identities and social connections. Medieval romances surely played such a part in the lives of their earliest audiences; recapturing any genuine sense of their impact and pleasure will require informed and inventive reading on the part of twenty-first-century students and scholars.

See also: 6 Manuscripts and Readers, 7 From Manuscript to Modern Text, 14 England's Antiquities, 15 Jews, Saracens, 'Black Men', Tartars, 16 War and Chivalry, 19 Love, 37 *Sir Gawain and the Green Knight*, 33 The *Canterbury Tales*, 38 Malory's *Morte Darthur*.

Notes

1 Sir Thomas Malory, *Works*, ed. Eugène Vinaver, 2nd edn, Oxford Standard Authors (London: Oxford University Press, 1971). Based on the revised text of Vinaver's 3–volume Oxford English Text's edition of 1967.

2 Severs 1967 gives a list of Middle English romance titles with approximate dates of composition.

3 *Robert Laneham's Letter*, ed. Frederick J. Furnivall. New Shakespeare Society, ser. 4, vol. 14. (London: Kegan Paul, Trench, Trübner, 1890), pp. 29–30. The letter describes the twelve days of elaborate festivities the earl of Leicester held for Queen Elizabeth at Kenilworth in 1575. (In all quotations from Middle English texts, we have used modernized letter forms in place of thorn and yogh, and have silently expanded ampersand to *and*.)

4 *Ibid.*, p. 41.

5 In *King Arthur's Death: The Middle English Stanzaic Morte Arthur and Alliterative Morte Arthure*, ed. Larry D. Benson, rev. Edward E. Foster (Kalamazoo, Mich.: Medieval Institute Publications for TEAMS, 1994), pp. 129–284. This volume is published in the TEAMS Middle English Texts Series, which produces inexpensive student editions that are also made available on-line at www.library.rochester.edu/camelot/teams/catalog.htm.

6 In *Sir Gawain: Eleven Romances and Tales*, ed. Thomas Hahn (Kalamazoo, Mich.: Medieval Institute Publications for TEAMS, 1995), pp. 309–35. Also includes editions of *The Wedding of Sir Gawain and Dame Ragnelle*, *Sir Gawain and the Carle of Carlisle*, *The Avowyng of Arthur*, *The Awntyrs off Arthur*, *The Knightly Tale of Gologras and Gawain*, *The Turke and Sir Gawain*, *The Marriage of Sir Gawain*, *The Carle of Carlisle*, *The Jeaste of Sir Gawain*, and *King Arthur and King Cornwall*; published in the Middle English Texts Series: see n. 5, above.

7 Robert Mannyng, *The Chronicle*, ed. Idelle Sullens, Medieval and Renaissance Texts and Studies, 153 (Binghamton, N.Y.: Medieval and Renaissance Texts and Studies, 1996).

8 Thomas of Britain, *Tristran*, ed. and trans. Stewart Gregory, Garland Library of Medieval Literature, 78 (New York: Garland, 1991). Includes Old French text and facing-page modern English translation.

9 In Alan Lupack (ed.), *Lancelot of the Laik and Sir Tristrem* (Kalamazoo, Mich.: Medieval Institute Publications for TEAMS, 1997), pp. 143–277. Published in the Middle English Texts Series and available online: see n. 5, above.

10 In Alan Lupack (ed.), *Three Middle English Charlemagne Romances: The Sultan of Babylon, The Siege of Milan, and The Tale of Ralph the Collier* (Kalamazoo, Mich.: Medieval Institute Publications for TEAMS, 1990), pp. 1–103. Published in the Middle English Texts Series and available on-line: see n. 5, above.

11 In *The Middle English Breton Lais*, ed. Anne Laskaya and Eve Salisbury (Kalamazoo, Mich.: Medieval Institute Publications for TEAMS, 1995), pp. 15–59. This volume also contains editions of *Lai le Freine*, *Sir Degaré*, *Emaré*, *Sir Launfal*, *Sir Gowther*, *Erle of Tolous* and *Sir Cleges*, published in the Middle English Texts Series and available on-line: see n. 5, above.

12 In *Sir Gawain*, ed. Hahn, pp. 41–80. See n. 6, above.

13 *Alexander and Dindimus*, ed. Walter W. Skeat, EETS es 31 (1878, repr. 1930).

References and Further Reading

Aertsen, Henk and MacDonald, Alasdair A. (eds) 1990. *Companion to Middle English Romance.* Amsterdam: VU University Press. Nine essays addressing a variety of themes in both popular and literary romances.

Amodio, Mark C. (ed.), with the assistance of Sarah Gray Miller 1994. *Oral Poetics in Middle English Poetry.* New York: Garland. Contains several essays on the relationship between oral and literary works.

Barron, W. R. J. 1987. *English Medieval Romance.* London and New York: Longman. A comprehensive inventory of romance writing in medieval England.

Boffey, Julia and Thompson, John J. 1989. 'Anthologies and Miscellanies: Production and Choice of Texts.' In *Book Production and Publishing in Britain, 1375–1475*, ed. Jeremy Griffiths and Derek Pearsall (Cambridge: Cambridge University Press), pp. 279–315. A thorough examination of contents and circulation of manuscript collections, including those preserving romances.

Crane, Susan 1986. *Insular Romance: Politics, Faith, and Culture in Anglo-Norman and Middle English Literature.* Berkeley: University of California Press. A comparative and contrastive study of narratives in the bilingual and multicultural contexts of post-Conquest England.

Edwards, A. S. G. and Pearsall, Derek 1989. 'The Manuscripts of the Major English Poetic Texts.' In *Book Production and Publishing in Britain, 1375–1475*, ed. Jeremy Griffiths and Derek Pearsall (Cambridge: Cambridge University Press), pp. 257–78. A survey of manuscript production, and of patterns of use and survival, for major writers like Chaucer, Gower and Langland, with some notice of romance collections.

Hardman, Phillipa (ed.) 2002. *The Matter of Identity in Medieval Romance.* Cambridge: Brewer. Essays addressing a range of popular but less studied Middle English romances.

Hebron, Michael 1997. *The Medieval Siege: Theme and Image in Middle English Romance.* Oxford: Clarendon Press. Concentrated study of a topos that finds a variety of representations in medieval romances.

Knight, Stephen 1986. 'The Social Function of the Middle English Romances.' In *Medieval Literature: Criticism, Ideology and History*, ed. David Aers (Brighton: Harvester Press), pp. 99–122. A materialist critique of representations among the traditional orders of society in English romances.

Krueger, Roberta L. 2000. *The Cambridge Companion to Medieval Romance.* Cambridge: Cambridge University Press. Broad collection of essays on both continental and English romance.

Matthews, William 1964. 'Alliterative Song of an Elizabethan Minstrel.' *Research Studies* 32, 134–46. Discusses the anonymous minstrel's song based on Malory from Robert Laneham's letter.

Meale, Carol M. 1989. 'Patrons, Buyers and Owners: Book Production and Social Status.' In *Book Production and Publishing in Britain, 1375–1475*, ed. Jeremy Griffiths and Derek Pearsall (Cambridge: Cambridge University Press), pp. 201–38. An account of the peculiarities of foreign and domestic book-making and ownership in later medieval England.

Putter, Ad 2004. 'Story Line and Story Shape in *Sir Percyvell of Gales* and Chrétien de Troyes's *Conte du Graal*.' In *Pulp Fictions of Medieval England: Essays in Popular Romance*, ed. Nicola McDonald (Manchester: Manchester University Press), pp. 171–96. A consideration of the relation of popular romance in late medieval England and earlier, high literate narrative.

Saunders, Corinne (ed.) 2004. *A Companion to Romance.* Oxford: Blackwell. A survey from ancient times to the present, with five essays dedicated to medieval romance in England.

Severs, J. Burke (ed.) 1967. *A Manual of the Writings in Middle English, 1050–1500. Vol. 1: Romances.* New Haven: Connecticut Academy of Arts and Sciences. A useful compendium of information on the romances, including summaries and information on manuscripts, editions and early scholarship.

21
Writing Nation: Shaping Identity in Medieval Historical Narratives[1]

Raluca L. Radulescu

A mixture of epic, myth, romance, historical detail, prophecy, and later of political propaganda, late medieval historical writing engages with issues of great importance in the process of shaping national identity. Kingship, the governance of the realm, and domination in the British Isles, over Scotland, and outside, over France, attracted a wide readership. The higher echelons of aristocratic society, the royal household, as well as the increasingly politically aware town and country gentry circles, showed an interest in chronicles about the history of the nation. Consequently, alongside prophecies and incipient propaganda, historical writing helped to crystallize a sense of collective identity and the image of the past. The development of the *Brut* chronicles (the starting-point of the present survey), which survive in a significant number of manuscripts and printed editions, is representative of the evolution of the genre in the vernacular.

Writing history in the later medieval period was a preoccupation spreading outside the monastic environment, its initial setting, into the spheres of the town and the country house. As the 'full-scale monastic chronicle' entered a period of decline in the fourteenth and the fifteenth centuries (Gransden 1982: xii), the new chroniclers, mostly town clerks, manifested an increased interest in the writing of history, which found a reading public outside the royal court.

Surveys of historical writing in the later medieval period are available in C. L. Kingsford's *English Historical Literature in the Fifteenth Century* (1913), updated in L. M. Matheson (1984) and A. Galloway (1999). The two-volume work by A. Gransden (1982) remains the most comprehensive guide to medieval historical writing to date, while E. D. Kennedy's volume (1989) lists the main tracts, the surviving manuscripts and the secondary sources for the study of historical pieces. All of these surveys need updating; recent theses and scholarly work on the various aspects of historical writing have brought to light new areas of interest as well as new sources to be taken into account in the assessment of the bias, function and use of such texts. For this reason, in the present chapter, late medieval historical texts will be classified into three categories:

chronicles, whether of local or national importance; genealogical tracts written with the purpose of instruction or propaganda; and historical poetry, which celebrated events or political figures of the day.

The *Brut* Chronicles

The *Brut* chronicles, surviving in over 240 manuscripts written in Latin, Anglo-Norman and Middle English, have recently received increased scholarly attention, rightly being acknowledged as the equivalent of a medieval bestseller. Surpassed in number only by Wycliffite translations of the Bible, the *Brut* chronicles are a rich source for the study of medieval readers' interest in national history (Matheson 1984: 210).[2] There are considerable differences between the variants of these chronicles and, as a result, their classification has been and remains problematic. The extant manuscripts are heavily annotated and the relationships among the various continuations are complex. Their widespread ownership (geographically and across social classes) gives evidence of the popularity of this account of British history in a period dominated by increased anxiety over the political future of the nation.

Also known as *The Chronicles of England* (the title given by William Caxton to his first edition of the text in 1480), the *Brut* chronicles contain a prose history of the English nation from its first settlements, combining historical, mythical and chivalric elements, and also accommodating into its narrative political verses and prophecies in prose. They were composed first in Anglo-Norman, then in Latin in the fourteenth and fifteenth centuries (Kingsford 1913; Matheson 1999: 5–6); afterwards, translations from Anglo-Norman into English were undertaken in the late fourteenth and early fifteenth centuries. In addition, at least one of the Latin *Bruts* appears to have been translated into Latin from English. This complex process of translation and adaptation stands as evidence of the representative status of these chronicles for the development of historical writing in England. Linguistic change was accompanied by changes in style and bias, which reflect the movement from a narrative written for a courtly audience, designed to suit its tastes and interests, to vernacular adaptations and continuations. The additions incorporate debates over kingship and governance during the Wars of the Roses, and Lancastrian and Yorkist views of contemporary events (Gransden 1982: 73–4; Kingsford 1913: 114). Initially composed for a relatively small audience, restricted both socially (to the aristocracy) and linguistically (to the use of Anglo-Norman), the *Brut* found a wider audience for its translation in the vernacular among country gentry and urban circles (Matheson 1999; Radulescu 2003a). The upper-class style of the narrative was not altered, yet the fifteenth-century additions display partisan views of contemporary events.

The courtly aspect of the chronicle was preserved in the Middle English *Brut*, where the accounts of political events during the fourteenth century contain references to the coats of arms of the barons present at the parliament of Westminster in 1321, which was called 'the parlment with the whit bende', where they were wearing 'cote-armur of grene clothe' (213).[3] There are other references to chivalry. For example, the author deplores the battle of 'Burbridge' (Boroughbridge), when the prisoners were 'robbed, and bonde as theues', that brought shame unto them all: 'Allas the shame & despite, that the gentil ordre of Knyghthode there hade at that bataile!' The destruction of the chivalric spirit is shown to have been caused by internecine strife, as 'in that bataile was the fader ayeins the sone, and the vncle ayeins his nevew' (220). The cause of the disaster is justified, in a patriotic tone, through an attack on the mixing of English blood with the blood of other nations, which brought 'so miche vnkyndenesse' that had never been seen before 'in Engeland amonges folc of on nacioun'.

The patriotic tone of the narrative is derived from the various sources of the *Brut*. One of them, Geoffrey of Monmouth's *Historia regum Britanniae*, also provided the first author(s) of the *Brut* with the story about the discovery and settlement of Britain. Brutus, the great-grandson of the Trojan hero Æneas, comes to Albion and fights the giants living there; after his killing of the giants the new country is given his name. The story is complemented by the anonymous founding myth of Albina, the daughter of the King of Syria, Dioclitian, and her thirty-two sisters who, feeling superior to their husbands, kill them and are banished by their father; they leave their homeland, sail until they find an isle and settle there. The island is called Albion, after the name of the eldest sister, and the sons of these sisters with the devil are the giants defeated by Brutus and his kinsmen.

The *Brut* continues with British history including that of King Arthur, the only king to whom several chapters are dedicated, and then of the Anglo-Saxon kingdoms, followed by an account of the English kings up to Henry III in 1272. The narrative was initially added to in order to bring the narrative to the death of Edward I in 1307, then to 1333, and finally to 1461. These continuations as well as other factors have been used as criteria of classification for the existing manuscripts by Matheson (1998). In his classification there are several groups: the Common Version, which originally covered the period until 1333, with many additions up to 1461; the Extended Version, which incorporates an exordium and details from the *Short English Metrical Chronicle*; the Abbreviated Version, which is a short version combining elements from the first two; and another group called by Matheson 'Peculiar Texts and Versions', which contains all the remaining texts incorporating original developments as well as peculiar texts that draw on the *Brut* as a source (Matheson 1984, 1999). The last version to 1461 was chosen by Caxton as the base text for his edition of the *Chronicles of England* in 1480, which subsequently went through thirteen editions until 1527, proving an 'enormous' influence on 'how Englishmen in the fifteenth and sixteenth centuries viewed their native history' (Matheson 1984: 210). The impact of the historical narrative of the *Brut* did not stop at the advent of the printing era; material already contained in the printed edition continued to be copied into manuscripts, such as Glasgow University manuscripts Hunterian 74 and Hunterian 228 (Matheson 1985: 596; 1999: 129, 162). It is these fifteenth-century continuations that have attracted increased scholarly attention in recent years, thanks to the discovery of new manuscripts and versions which require a reassessment of their provenance, authorship and bias.[4]

In 1482, Caxton printed his second edition of the *Chronicles of England*; in the same year he also published an edition of John Trevisa's translation of Ranulph Higden's *Polychronicon*. In doing so he promoted Higden's universal history, which, although written over a century beforehand, had acquired a readership almost as impressive as that of the *Brut* (Matheson 1985). Higden's *Polychronicon* is an encyclopedia in seven books covering the universal history from the Creation to Higden's own time (1327–60s), subsequently translated into English by Trevisa in 1387 at the request of his patron, Thomas Lord Berkeley. Higden drew upon numerous authorities, from Pliny and Suetonius to St Augustine and Isidore of Seville. His erudition and interest in historical detail place Higden in the great tradition of early medieval historical writing in England represented by Bede, Florence of Worcester, William of Malmesbury, Geoffrey of Monmouth, Henry of Huntington, John of Salisbury and Gerald of Wales. Higden's work is indicative of his literary tastes and political views, especially with reference to Edward III's reign, 'an age when patriotism was in the ascendant' (Gransden 1982: 51). Inasmuch as it reflected the level of national consciousness, it was, in a sense, a 'patriotic work', and ultimately, through its translation into English, a universal history that reached a large audience and became a landmark in the tradition of late medieval writing in the vernacular (Gransden 1982: 52).

The Appeal of Genealogy

It is not surprising that fifteenth-century readers became interested in history written in the vernacular; learning from the history of the nation was a way of claiming a share in the national past at a time when national sentiments were running high. Some readers highlighted their family's involvement in particular events by writing their names in the margin of the *Brut* at points which mark battles of national importance; this gesture has been identified by a critic as the reflection of an 'urge towards self-definition through the reading of history' (Meale 2000: 215–16). Similarly, the identification of the political actors of contemporary history in the prophecies incorporated in the narrative also points to these readers' growing interest in interpreting contemporary events. Political prophecy, an 'important and integral part of the narrative' of the *Brut*, was a 'living language' in which 'people communicated their feelings about people, king and nation', and represented a discourse with a particularly important role to play in the interpretation of the historical text (Coote 2000: 26, 14). To the same extent, the genealogical trees, accompanied by roundels, whether of the kings of England or of aristocratic families, which appear in the margins of *Brut* manuscripts, have a twofold purpose: on the one hand they helped readers to memorize dates and reigns; on the other, they showed an alignment of personal history with the national one (figure 21.1). In this respect the *Brut* chronicle represents the central focus of any study of historical writing in the later medieval period, since it brings together all the different strands in this genre and forms the basis for history-writing in the sixteenth century and beyond.[5]

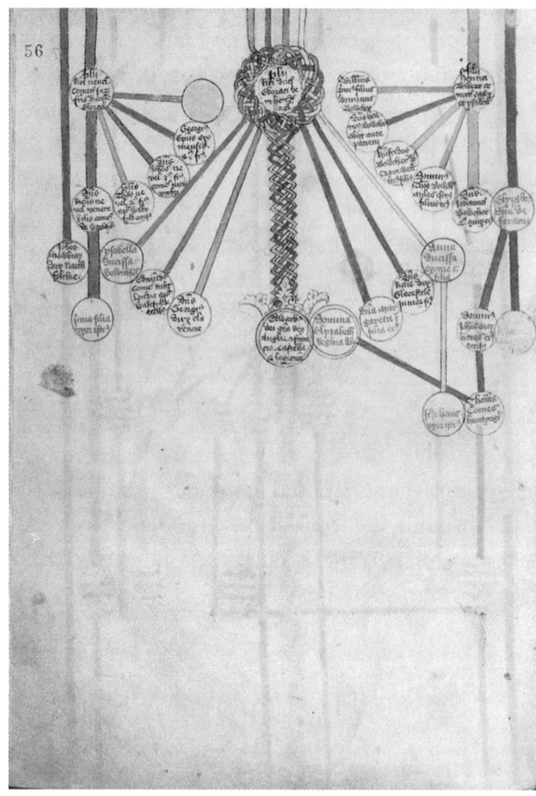

Figure 21.1 Last page of a genealogy of the Kings of Britain, from Brutus to Edward IV, preceding a copy of the Middle English *Brut*: Dublin, Trinity College, MS 505, p. 56. (By kind permission of the Board of Trinity College Dublin.)

The development of prophecy and genealogy alongside chronicles in the vernacular points to an awareness among readers and writers of the necessity to define, discuss and interpret historical events and the problem of royal succession. An early aid for the teaching of history (especially biblical history), genealogy had already developed in Europe before it reached England in the thirteenth century. The ease of use (genealogical rolls could be read from top to bottom and opened one section at a time) and the scarcity of text were determining factors in the growth of popularity of this genre with the royal court, where the visual impact of the genealogy of kings was used as a tool for political propaganda. In England genealogical material in either roll or codex format accompanied the development of the traditional narrative of the *Brut*; its primary function was to emphasize the unbroken line of kings descended from Brutus, the great-grandson of Æneas. Fifteenth-century productions of royal genealogies reflected the factional strife between the two houses of Lancaster and York and the continuing English claim to the crowns of France and Spain. The genealogies are now classified as the Long and Short English and Latin pedigrees and survive in the form of a significant number of copies dating from the second half of the fifteenth century, mainly from the reign of the Yorkist Edward IV (Kennedy 1989). The interest in genealogical charts had started with the reign of Henry VI, when the English claim to France was depicted both visually and textually as a means of rallying support for the campaigns in France from the country and town gentry. The debate over the rightful heir to the English throne later fuelled the production of more royal pedigrees which justified the Lancastrian or Yorkist descent from the line of English kings described in the *Brut* chronicle. Over thirty pedigrees were produced for Edward IV after 1461, and fifteen of them included his British descent from Cadwallader and Arthur; indeed it is likely that many more were in circulation at the time (Kennedy 1989: 2676–7, 2889–90).

The imagery in these manuscripts helped their readers to reflect upon their sense of belonging to the nation and to memorize the most important events in their history. Prophecy and genealogical material formed a recurrent topic in miscellanies owned in aristocratic and gentry circles to the extent that they provided the means to express allegiance to one or the other of the royal houses and an active involvement in the 'making' of history. The mere possession of a politically biased genealogical chronicle was in itself potentially dangerous, as is proved by the case of Thomas Dervent, gentleman, who was arrested in the early years of Edward IV's reign because he owned a Lancastrian pedigree of the 'true and verray lynyall descent from noble progeniteurs to your highnesse as rightfull and verrey enheritour to the crownes of Englond and Fraunce'.[6] Examples of books functioning as incriminating evidence for their owners' political convictions abound in the history of all periods; however, particular instances like the one just mentioned point to the increase in the consumption of historical texts in the vernacular in the later part of the fifteenth century.

What is more, a number of genealogies even incorporated family history alongside the main royal line, as does New York Public Library MS Spenser 193, which contains the genealogy of the Boteler-Sudeley family side by side with the English kings. This genealogical roll also includes the anonymous version of Lydgate's historical poem now known as the 'Kings of England'. According to Linne Mooney, the versified chronicles of the English kings, like Lydgate's, enjoyed an 'enormous popularity' – a claim justified by the number of manuscripts which contain them (over thirty-six) – and were used to 'bolster aristocratic or popular support' for the king (Mooney 1989: 256). Referring to a *Brut* manuscript which contains the coats of arms of the Hopton family in Yorkshire, Meale considers that annotated chronicles which display their owners' personal investment in historical events denote a 'broader movement within England to consolidate a sense of national identity through historical writing' (Gransden 1982: 253; Meale 2000: 215). Similarly, other noble families chose to represent their family line next to the royal descent; such examples are: the Percys' and the Talbots' rolls, the Beauchamp Pageant, to which the Neville connection was added (now London, British Library MS Cotton Julius B iv: see figure 5.1); the Salisbury roll, which is a history of the Neville family, now London, British Library MS Loan 90; the Rous roll, which deals with the history of the Warwick family (now extant in two versions, Latin and English, which are London, College of Arms, Warwick Roll, and London, British Library, MS

Additional 48976, respectively); and the Clare roll, now London, College of Arms 3/16, which is a pedigree of the lords of Clare. It therefore becomes clear that late medieval English rolls and genealogical chronicles were produced not only as royal propaganda, as Alison Allan has argued (Allan 1979), or merely as objects of pride for their owners, but also as manifestos of their personal investment in the political struggle and a reflection of their desire to establish their family's ancestry at a time of social and political instability.

Royal genealogical chronicles did continue to function as political propaganda throughout the fifteenth century. Although not common in English, propaganda in history appeared a few times before that (Gransden 1975). However, it was not until Henry V that an English king's achievements were celebrated in both Latin and English in no less than three biographies: the anonymous *Gesta Henrici quinti* (written c.1416–17 and covering events to 1416), Thomas Elmham's *Liber metricus de Henrico quinto* (covering Henry's reign to 1418), and the most popular of them, Titus Livius Frulovisi's *Vita Henrici quinti* (written in 1437), which was translated into English. Built around the most significant historical events of Henry's reign, yet 'all written to promote the policy of the central government' (Gransden 1982: 197), these tracts led to the development of historical writing in the vernacular and influenced English chroniclers like John Hardyng, as will be shown below.

The London Chronicles

Portraits of rulers are also present in other chronicles dating from the last decades of the fifteenth century. These are the London chronicles, which are closely related to the *Brut*, and to several other chronicles written during Edward IV's reign, which display a strong Yorkist bias and were written in order to promote the interests of this royal house. The London chronicles developed out of the annals kept by successive aldermen and mayors of the city and reflect, to a large extent, the economic interests and political allegiances of the merchant class and their biased views of contemporary events. Originating long before the Wars of the Roses, these texts described the settlement of the city, and landmarks in its activity through the centuries. The fifteenth century saw an exceptional growth in the number of vernacular versions which were later printed in city chronicle form. The authors of these chronicles were in favour of the French war, as it could bring them significant profits, and supported the Yorkist Edward IV, whose ascent to the throne they presented in positive terms. Among the most well-known is 'Gregory's Chronicle', named after its author, William Gregory, skinner, Sheriff of London in 1436–7 and Mayor of the city in 1451–2 (Kingsford 1913: 97). His chronicle was continued anonymously up to 1470, three years after his death. Gransden emphasizes the 'evident' Yorkist sympathies of this and other London chronicles, especially in their praise of Edward IV and attacks on Henry VI's counsellor, the Duke of Suffolk, who was blamed for the loss of the French territories (Gransden 1982: 243). Through their interest in issues of national importance and the emphasis they placed on kingship and the governance of the realm, these chronicles shaped English national consciousness in subsequent centuries (Gransden 1982: 220–48; Matheson 1984: 214). A recent reassessment of the London chronicles disagrees, however, with earlier critical opinion (McLaren 2002); to this extent, it can safely be said that a lot more research is needed into the use, sources and relationships of these chronicles.

Equally important for the understanding of the London chronicles is their context in commonplace books compiled in the city, like Richard Hill's anthology (now Oxford, Balliol College MS 354), which contains a chronicle up to 1536 alongside English folk songs, carols, lyrics and religious poems, Robert Arnold's manuscript, in which the chronicle finishes in 1502, and Robert Bale's manuscript, in which the chronicle covers the years 1437–61 (although his authorship of the chronicle is not certain). Another important chronicler is Robert Fabyan, alderman and member of the drapers' company and from 1493 Sheriff of London, who in 1504 completed the *New Chronicles of England and France*, a text which had a great influence on early modern historiography.

The audience for all of these chronicles (the merchants and the London oligarchy) and the ever-broadening audience of the *Brut* (initially courtly but later including the gentry) overlapped. Both audiences influenced in turn the writing of other, shorter chronicles and historical notes in the vernacular, like those contained in London, British Library MS Additional 48031A, a fifteenth-century miscellany known after the scribe who compiled the collection as *John Vale's Book*. Vale was a member of the household of Sir Thomas Cook, an alderman and later the Mayor of London in the 1460s. The documents included in the book, including deeds, bills, political pamphlets and newsletters, a short chronicle, and two unique variants of Sir John Fortescue's *Governance of England* and John Lydgate's *Serpent of Division*, were collected by Thomas Cook senior and his more famous son, Sir Thomas, and by their family and servants.[7] By the 1460s Sir Thomas Cook had made enemies, and was imprisoned on the grounds of helping the Lancastrians; it was his Lancastrian reputation that brought him freedom at the Readeption of Henry VI in 1470; interestingly, he had helped Edward IV financially, only to become prominent in the parliament of the Readeption of Henry VI.

Vale's short chronicle of the events from 1431 to 1471 displays similar vocabulary to that contained in the contemporary political documents he copied into his collection, and summarizes the main upheavals of the rules of both Henry VI and Edward IV while deploring both reigns. Vale suggests that the strife in the realm during the Wars of the Roses was the result of subjects' disobedience to the anointed king, Henry VI, and that Humphrey Duke of Gloucester's murder in the early years of Henry's reign marked the beginning of the general decline in the country. The chronicler blames the king's 'insaciable, coveitous personnes and diabolic counseillours' for their disastrous advice regarding the French territories. He suggests that the failure of their counsel was due to their social inadequacy for the political role of royal counsellor, as they were not 'comen of the blood roiall, but they that were broughte up of noughte'. By contrast, the first thirty-nine years of Henry VI's reign are described as a period when he 'reigned in grete nobley, worship, welthe and prosperite', which ended because of circumstances outside his control, which led to his 'falle mooste dolorous' as well as 'many and divers grete mischefes, lossis, insurreccions and civile bataylis to thextreme pointe of the utmoste destruccion and depopulacion of subgiettes and people' (178).[8] Vale's use of political concepts like governance and counselling resembles both the mirrors for princes tradition and contemporary political documents, copies of which he included in his collection (187–8). Vale's text is also representative of biased views of history and the development of historical pieces for personal (or very restricted) use. Thus it belongs to a group of historical texts written during the Wars of the Roses which were influenced by the propaganda material put forth by the opposing royal houses which was intended to function as a means of rallying 'popular support, particularly that of the expanding middle classes' (Gransden 1982: 251).

Similarly, a strong political bias is found in another contemporary Lancastrian chronicle, once attributed to John Warkworth, in which the king's counsellors are attacked because of their disregard for the king's peace and the common weal of the realm. 'Warkworth's' *Chronicle* was written, according to internal evidence, at some time between the fall of the Duke of Clarence, brother to Edward IV (1478) and the presentation of the *Brut* to Peterhouse College in 1481 (Matheson 1999: 89).[9] In *Warkworth's Chronicle* Henry VI's Readeption is presented as an occasion 'whereof all his goode lovers were fulle gladde, and the more parte of peple' (*Warkworth's Chronicle*: 11). Like Vale, the chronicler blames Henry's counsellors, 'myscheves peple that were aboute the Kynge', who were 'covetouse towarde them selff' and did not defend 'the comone wele of the londe', and thus the French territories were lost (*Warkworth's Chronicle*: 11–12). The chronicler excuses Henry's political mistakes, as 'alle [was] bycause of his fals lordes, and nevere of hym', and blames Edward IV's failure to bring peace in the realm and resolve the conflicts inherited from the previous reign; although he had good counsellors, his governance was not strong enough, with the result of 'one batayle aftere another, and moche troble and grett losse of goodes amonge the comone peple' (*Warkworth's Chronicle*: 12). An increasing interest in interpreting contemporary events is evident in these comments which voice popular discontent with the Yorkist policies.

Yorkist Chronicles

Complaints of the same nature, though from a Yorkist perspective, appear in a fifteenth-century continuation to the *Brut* chronicle, in which Suffolk, counsellor to Henry VI, was made a scapegoat for the disaster of the French war (Marx 2003: 66) as well as other abuses and even the heavy taxation:

> the realme of Englonde was oute of all good governaunce . . . for the king [Henry VI] was simple and lad by covetous counseyll . . . And suche ymposicions as were put to the peple, as taxes, tallages, and quynzymes . . . For these mysgouernaunces, and for many other, the hertes of the peple were turned awey from thaym that had the londe in gouernaunce, and theyre blessyng ws turnyd into cursyng. (78)

The similarity in sentiment in this version of the *Brut*, in the London chronicles, and in other Yorkist chronicles, is striking. Good kingship and a concern for the common weal of the realm are increasingly addressed. Anxieties over the future of the nation led fifteenth-century chroniclers to comment on political themes and to ponder internecine strife and political discord. The successes of Henry V's rule were the standard against which both his son, the Lancastrian Henry VI, and the Yorkist opponent, Edward IV, were measured. The partisan bias of these chronicles of the Wars of the Roses is evident; yet, while defending one or the other of the factions, the historical discourse was being shaped in the vernacular and a political vocabulary created.

The Yorkists' declared aim was to redress the political situation and in their attempt to persuade the population about their intentions they appealed to what the author of the *Brut* seems to imply was a shared understanding of the common weal of the realm (520).[10] The 'bad' counsellors were 'sett Aparte, & might nat reul as thei did Afore' (522), and peace was established once again: 'ther was A concorde & pees made Among those lordes, & thei wer sett in pees' (525), but for a short time. This passage refers to the events in 1458, when Richard Duke of York and Henry VI's lords reached an agreement. During Edward IV's reign, however, similar discontent with the king's policies led to more internal conflicts and civil war.

If these chronicle accounts take the form of propaganda, they also incorporate traditional elements found in medieval historiography, like prophecy and hagiographical elements. In the debate over a good king's qualities, his moral standards become essential: in the Lancastrian chronicles Henry is portrayed as a saint – for example, in the description of the miracles performed at the exposition of his corpse in St Paul's – while Edward's greed is particularly deplored: 'And anone after the Kynge brake the seyd Archebysschoppes mytere, in the whiche were fulle many ryche stones and preciouse, and made therof a croune for hyme self' (*Warkworth's Chronicle*: 25).

By contrast, in two Yorkist chronicles, the *Historie of the Arrivall of King Edward IV*, and the *Chronicle of the Rebellion in Lincolnshire*, Edward IV is the beneficiary of a personal miracle upon his return to the throne in 1471, on Palm Sunday: the statue of St Anne, covered and boarded up as the tradition prescribed from Ash Wednesday to Easter Day, suddenly reveals itself at the moment when Edward is kneeling in prayer before it (*Arrivall*: 14). The chronicle continues in a similar style, placing emphasis on Edward's exceptional qualities, especially his concern for peace in the realm. For example, at the point where the dispute between Edward and Richard Neville, Earl of Warwick (the 'Kingmaker') is described, the King's image is that of a tolerant, magnanimous, peace-loving ruler, who is happy to forgive and forget the disobedience of his subject.

In the *Chronicle of the Rebellion in Lincolnshire* Edward is similarly presented as a good king, whose qualities become apparent in his treatment of two rebels, this time his brother George Duke of Clarence and the Earl of Warwick; Edward is 'a prince enclined to shew his mercy and pite to his subgettes', some of whom 'unnaturally and unkyndly, withoute cause or occacion yeven to theym by our saide soveraigne lorde, falsly compassed, conspired, and ymagened the final destruccion of his most roiall personne, and of his true subgettes' (*Chronicle of the Rebellion*: 5). Any action against such a king has a direct effect on his subjects, and on the commonwealth, because whoever goes against the king goes against all the people in the realm. The end of the chronicle presents precisely this feeling, as the Duke of Clarence and the Earl of Warwick are shown to have plotted 'to the likly uttur and finalle distruccion of his rialle person, and the subversion of alle the land, and the common wele of the same' (*Chronicle of the Rebellion*: 18). This passage strongly resembles the end of the *Arrivall*, where Edward's achievements are praised by comparison to the 'crwell, and mortall battayles' he had to fight during the early years of his reign, and the effort he put into the 'discomfeture [of] dyvars great assembles of his rebells, and riotows persons, in many partyes of his land' (*Arrivall*: 39).

In another Yorkist chronicle, now contained in London, British Library MSS Harley 116 and 326, the anonymous author similarly tackles the issues of kingship and governance of the realm (Radulescu 2003b). Henry of Derby, later Henry IV, is described as the usurper of the crown of England, and his heirs Henry V and Henry VI, of the line of Lancaster, as equally unrightful kings of England: 'Thies thre harryes hath kepte the crowne and occupied the crowne of England fro the rightfull heires this xx yeres and thre' (folio 145r). Kennedy categorizes this chronicle, now known as *The Chronicle from Rollo to Edward IV*, along with other chronicles with a Yorkist bias (Kennedy 1989: 2702). The chronicler emphasizes the image of Henry of Derby as a disloyal subject at the time of his return from his exile in France with armed forces: he swore an oath that he would not pursue violence against his king Richard II and his countrymen (folio 144v), and yet he later imprisoned and deposed the king. On the other hand the qualities that are essential for a king and the governance of the realm, loyalty and keeping one's word, are present in the portrayal of Richard Duke of York, whose claim to the throne of England is said to be rightful, as the commons recognized him as true heir to the crown (folio 145r). However, York made the same allegations of loyalty as Henry upon his return from Ireland, when he swore an oath of obedience, undertaking to support his king and respect his royal person, only to claim the crown for himself later. The same techniques are used by both sides: incipient forms of propaganda in the fifteenth century meant manipulation of the accepted core of ideals of a period, to serve one's political purposes.

These issues created a climate of uncertainty in fifteenth-century England, and a strong king was expected to rule the realm. Edward IV's second reign was the result of a similar breach of loyalty, which the Yorkists portrayed as cunning use of a situation: Edward sailed to England and, upon landing, he was not welcomed by his people. In *The Historie of the Arrivall* the author describes how Edward swore an oath that he had only come to claim his inheritance as the son of the Duke of York; yet later he fought the Lancastrians and regained his throne. In this light, Edward IV's 'arrival' and tactics ironically appear to us, despite the author's eulogy to Edward, as a copy of Henry IV's tactics: the Yorkists had learnt something from the lesson of history, while the chronicle in Harley 116 and 326 represents one more example of the influence of propaganda on historical writing.

Chronicles in Verse

Representative of a change in style and bias, the chronicle written by John Hardyng puts forth a verse history of the kings of England up to the fifteenth century at a time when most historical writing was in prose. Hardyng based his work mainly on Geoffrey's *Historia* and the *Brut*, yet also used a variety of sources, from Apuleius, Bartholomaeus Anglicus, Nennius, Bede, Florence of Worcester and even the *vita* already mentioned, the *Gesta Henrici quinti*. His chronicle is an example of historiography combined with romance elements, as he chose to incorporate not only Arthur's reign, but also the Grail quest (including the presence of the character of Lancelot and other details from the Vulgate *Mort Artu*) into his narrative (Gransden 1982: 250).[11] Hardyng's life is described at the beginning of his chronicle, where he explains his early involvement in the political events of the northern families of the Percies and the Umfravilles, in whose households he lived, and his service to Henry V, to whom he presented a number of documents – some of them forged – relating to the English claim to Scotland (Kennedy 1989: 2646). In 1457 Hardyng presented the first version of his chronicle (and some more documents) to Henry V's successor, in the hope of securing protection and financial support. This is now known as the Long Version, surviving in only one manuscript, London, British Library MS Lansdowne 204, probably the presentation copy made for Henry VI. Later Hardyng sought the help of Henry's rival to the throne, Richard Duke of York, for whom he wrote the second version of the chronicle. After Richard's death, he revised this version further and dedicated the final version in 1464 to Richard's son, Edward IV. Hardyng's *Chronicle* now survives in twelve complete manuscripts and four fragments and was printed twice by Grafton in 1543 (Kennedy 1989: 2836); its popularity in the later medieval and early modern period made it a staple of Tudor historiography.

Hardyng's shifting allegiances were reflected in his changing dedications and the different political bias of the two versions. He adapted the sections which contain descriptions of contemporary events in ways which would please his new patron, Edward IV; his way of switching political views thus mirrors similar tendencies in contemporary prose chronicles written and commissioned by the two factions, the Lancastrian and the Yorkist. Hardyng's *Chronicle* also displays the main interests of fifteenth-century historians: England's claim to Scotland; the issues of rightful inheritance and good governance raised by the two rival dynasties; and their attempts to justify them using the Arthurian tradition. Each side tried to argue, in propagandistic fashion, through commissioned materials, that it had a better title to the throne of England than the other; as shown above, genealogical rolls had already been produced for a few decades when Hardyng started his chronicle. Hardyng's achievement was to put together a chronicle incorporating the earlier traditions, like the narrative of the *Brut*, and romance elements such as the Grail quest, with contemporaneous accounts of political events he had witnessed.

Hardyng's verse chronicle is unusual in a century dominated by vernacular prose as a medium for historiography; his intention seemed to be to insert his work both into the romance tradition and into that of the earlier verse chronicles, like Wace's twelfth-century chronicle (who translated into French Geoffrey's *Historia*) and the fourteenth-century chronicle of Robert of Gloucester. Hardyng also represents the aspirations of a sector in English society which became more involved in both politics and literary enterprise – the fifteenth-century English gentry. He manifests similar anxieties over justified kingship and good governance as contemporary chroniclers, and voices his anxieties over the future of the nation. When Hardyng narrates the conflict between King Richard II and Duke Henry, later King Henry IV, he stresses the political qualities of the policies displayed by Henry, in opposition to Richard's. When Henry returns to England to claim his father's inheritance, he swears allegiance to Richard and pledges his intention to contribute to the good governance of the realm by helping the king to 'voyde out of [the royal] house' the 'eiuill condicion' (350–1).[12] However, Henry continued his political action by deposing Richard; Hardyng explains that 'duke Henry of Lancaster was made Kyng by resignacion, renunciation, and deposayle, and election of the parliamente, and crowned at Westmynster on saynte Edwardes daye in Octobre'. Furthermore, he describes how the parliament deposed him because of his 'misgouernaunce', while 'no man then repugned' Henry, who was justified in taking on kingship, as a result of a 'free election' (350). The 'election' of the new king is also presented as a popular decision, and the reasons for deposing the former king are his 'mysrule and wrong gouernyng' (354).

Hardyng's allegiance first to the Lancastrians (his first dedication was to Henry VI) and then to the Yorkists (the new dedication was to Richard Duke of York, King Edward IV's father) may be one of the reasons for his apologetic attitude towards both Lancastrian kings, whose natural qualities put them on the throne of England. Hardyng excuses the Lancastrian kings for Henry of Derby's disloyalty to Richard II, whom he deposed, while he also states that neither Henry V nor Henry VI was aware of the injustice. When describing the circumstances of Henry V's death, Hardyng points out that 'for all his rightwisnes and iustice that he did he [Henry V] had no conscience of vsurpement of the croune', for which reason the author of the chronicle petitions God to take pity on such a great king. Henry's qualities as a good king not only ensured the peace and stability inside his country, but also 'through the lawe and peace conserued was the encrease of his conquest, and els had he been of no power to haue conquered in out landes' (388).

In the same way Hardyng praises the qualities of King Henry VI's reign and both prays for and advises Edward IV to show the same qualities of a good king (by treating Henry with generosity), in order to avoid further strife in the country. He reminds Edward of the reasons for the dethronement of his ancestor, Richard II, namely that the commons disliked his governance, being 'full glad . . . of his deposicion' and cherished the new King Henry IV for his 'full good policie', which ensured 'peace [*without stryfe*] in his daye' (409–10). Once more Edward is urged not to follow his ancestor's example, but rather the example of good Lancastrian governance. In Hardyng's line of argument the ideal qualities of the king are emphasized, rather than the political rivalry of the houses of Lancaster and York, an attitude that reflects gentry concerns with ideal kingship and governance of the realm.

Hardyng finishes his chronicle with Edward's claim to the crowns of England, France and Spain, an important issue at the end of the fifteenth century, which emphasized the renewed ambition of the English to regain the glory of the mythical British past. Hardyng's *Chronicle* thus displays a concern with creating a narrative of dynastic descent and national pride, similar to the *Brut* tradition, and discusses kingship and governance in the context of contemporary political events. Hardyng's *Chronicle* is important for its bringing together of traditional elements from the *Brut* and other chronicles, and for its bridging of the gap between biased Lancastrian and Yorkist political material (for example, in the genealogical rolls), thereby producing a more coherent view of history which reflected contemporary interests in kingship and governance.

Last but not least the historical poems written in the later medieval period reflect popular discontent with the government or the king. The allegory of the king seen as a wise gardener, commonly found in most complaint or debate literature, was appropriated into the popular political poetry of the fifteenth century, a topic amply discussed by Scattergood (1971). Such poems, sometimes written in remote corners of England, incorporate political prophecies (Beadle 2002); they represent an area of vernacular literature which enjoyed widespread circulation because of its topical relevance.

In conclusion, as the present survey has demonstrated, historical writing in late medieval England developed to an unprecedented extent, reflecting an increased interest in national history and the image of the past. The popularity enjoyed by the *Brut*, and by genealogical and political chronicles, contributed to the process of shaping both a political vocabulary understood at all levels in society and a discourse which influenced historical writing in subsequent centuries.

See also: 2 English Society in the Later Middle Ages, 4 City and Country, Wealth and Labour, 5 Women's Voices and Roles, 8 Translation and Society, 16 War and Chivalry, 20 Middle English Romance, 33 The *Canterbury Tales*, 34 John Gower and John Lydgate, 35 Thomas Hoccleve, 38 Malory's *Morte Darthur*.

Notes

1 I would like to thank Professor E. D. Kennedy for his useful suggestions, which have helped to improve the argument in this article and saved me from some pitfalls.

2 Some ideas and quotations from original material in this survey are developed out of my analysis of vernacular historical and political writing (Radulescu 2003a, ch. 2).

3 *The Brut or The Chronicles of England*, ed. Friedrich W. D. Brie, 2 vols, EETS os 131 (1906) and 136 (1908). Page references are to the latter volume.

4 See the new editions by Matheson 1999 (*Warkworth's Chronicle*) and Marx 2003 (*An English Chronicle*).

5 For a detailed analysis of the impact of the *Brut* in the sixteenth century see Marx and Radulescu 2006.

6 The document that attests to Dervent's arrest is Public Records Office, Ancient Petitions,

SC8/107/5322, cited in Sutton and Visser-Fuchs 1998: 140.

7 The details of Vale's life, the career of his master, Sir Thomas Cook, and the manuscript production, are discussed by Sutton and Visser-Fuchs in the editors' introduction 1998: 73–123.

8 *The Politics of Fifteenth-Century England: John Vale's Book*, ed. M. L. Kekewich, C. Richmond, A. F. Sutton, L. Visser-Fuchs and J. L. Watts (Stroud: Alan Sutton for Richard III and Yorkist History Trust, 1995). A complete edition of the manuscript, except Fortescue's *Governance of England*, containing an extensive introduction that is particularly useful for an understanding of fifteenth-century history and politics.

9 For reasons of consistency and to avoid confusion, references to the printed texts of the following three fifteenth-century chronicles are taken from K. Dockray (ed.), *Three Chronicles of the Reign of Edward IV: John Warkworth's Chronicle, Chronicle of the Rebellion in Lincolnshire, History of the Arrival of King Edward IV* (Gloucester: Sutton, 1988) and are mentioned by their title rather than the editor's name.

10 See n. 3, above.

11 For Hardyng's sources, see Kennedy 1989: 2836–45.

12 *The Chronicle of Iohn Hardyng*, ed. Henry Ellis (London: Rivington, 1812).

References and Further Reading

Allan, A. 1979. 'Yorkist Propaganda: Pedigree, Prophecy and the "British History".' In *Patronage, Pedigree and Power in Later Medieval England*, ed. C. Ross (Gloucester: Alan Sutton), pp. 171–92. A landmark study of genealogical rolls and codexes used for propaganda purposes during the Wars of the Roses.

Beadle, R. 2002. 'Fifteenth-century Political Verses from the Holkham Archives.' *Medium Ævum* 71, 101–21. Contains an analysis of a recently discovered, and previously unpublished, fragment of political verses which combine the political opinions of a remote community with contemporary interpretations of prophetical material.

Coote, L. 2000. *Prophecy and Public Affairs in Later Medieval England.* York: York Medieval Press, and Woodbridge: Boydell. Provides a timely reassessment of medieval prophecy seen as an essential component of historical discourse.

Galloway, A. 1999. 'Writing History in England.' In *The Cambridge History of Medieval English Literature*, ed. D. Wallace (Cambridge: Cambridge University Press), pp. 255–83. The latest (brief) survey of historiography in England from Bede to the end of the medieval period.

Gransden, A. 1975. 'Propaganda in English Medieval Historiography.' *Journal of Medieval History* 1, 363–82. A study of some aspects of early propaganda in medieval historiography in the vernacular.

—— 1982. *Historical Writing in England. Vol. 2: c.1307 to the Early Sixteenth Century.* London and Henley: Routledge and Kegan Paul. The most comprehensive survey of late medieval historical writing in England to date; although it focuses only on the main writers and works, and requires updating, it remains the staple work in historiography and an indispensable guide for research.

Kennedy, E. D. 1989. *Chronicles and Other Historical Writing.* Vol. 8 of *A Manual of the Writings in Middle English* (New Haven, Conn.: Connecticut Academy of Arts and Sciences). The most comprehensive (commented) survey of manuscripts and secondary sources for late medieval English historiography.

Kingsford, C. L. 1913. *English Historical Literature in the Fifteenth Century.* Oxford: Clarendon Press. A very useful survey of the main authors and genres, although now superseded by Gransden's and Kennedy's studies.

Marx, W. 2003 (ed.) *An English Chronicle 1377–1461.* Medieval Chronicles, 3. Woodbridge: Boydell Press. A new, complete edition of a continuation to the *Brut* chronicle previously known as 'Davies' chronicle' (after its nineteenth-century editor). It contains an excellent, comprehensive introduction dealing with *Brut* variants, sources and the development of the *Brut* narrative.

—— and Radulescu, R. (eds) 2006. *Readers and Writers of the* Brut *Chronicle.* Special issue of *Trivium* 36. Brings together the latest research into the sources, transmission and circulation of different variants of the *Brut.*

Matheson, L. M. 1984. 'Historical Prose.' In *Middle English Prose: A Critical Guide to Major Authors and Genres*, ed. A. S. G. Edwards (New Brunswick, N.J.: Rutgers University Press), pp. 209–48. A very useful though brief guide to the main chronicles and related material (in prose) in the period.

—— 1985. 'Printer and Scribe: Caxton, the *Polychronicon*, and the *Brut*.' *Speculum* 60, 593–614. Advances the idea that Caxton was the author of the continuation of the *Brut* up to 1461.

—— 1998. *The Prose Brut*: *The Development of a Middle English Chronicle.* Medieval and Renaissance Texts and Studies, 180. Tempe: Ariz.. The most comprehensive classification to date of all the surviving *Brut* manuscripts and variants, with discussions of their ownership, provenance and circulation.

—— 1999. *Death and Dissent: Two Fifteenth-century Chronicles: The Dethe of the Kynge of Scotis, Translated by John Shirley, and 'Warkworth's' Chronicle, the Chronicle Attributed to John Warkworth, Master of Peterhouse, Cambridge.* Medieval Chronicles, 2. Woodbridge: Boydell Press. A comprehensive new edition of these two texts; the second is a Lancastrian continuation to the *Brut.* Matheson here discusses, in great depth, the relationships between some late versions of the *Brut* and their ownership, provenance and circulation.

McLaren, M. R. 2002. *The London Chronicles of the Fifteenth Century: A Revolution in English Writing.* Cambridge: Boydell and Brewer. This is the latest reassessment of London chronicles.

Meale, C. M. 2000. 'The Politics of Book Ownership: The Hopton Family and Bodleian Library, Digby MS 185.' In *Prestige, Authority and Power in Late Medieval Manuscripts and Texts*, ed. F. Riddy, York Manuscripts Conferences, 4 (Woodbridge: Boydell for York Medieval Press), pp. 103–31. Discusses the appropriation of history by its gentry readers, taking as an example a miscellany containing a copy of the *Brut.*

Mooney, L. 1989. 'Lydgate's "Kings of England" and Another Verse Chronicle of the Kings.' *Viator* 20, 255–89. Discusses the importance of Lydgate's widely circulated poem and its continuous use almost a hundred years after its composition.

Radulescu, R. 2003a. *The Gentry Context for Malory's Morte Darthur.* Arthurian Studies, 55. Cambridge: Brewer. Ch. 2 tackles all the major late fifteenth-century historical and political texts and discusses their gentry ownership as well as their impact on gentry political attitudes.

—— 2003b. 'Yorkist Propaganda and the *Chronicle from Rollo to Edward IV*.' *Studies in Philology* 100, 401–24. An edition and analysis of a previously unpublished short Yorkist chronicle, highlighting the importance of considering the manuscript context of historical pieces.

Scattergood, V. J. 1971. *Politics and Poetry in the Fifteenth Century.* London: Blandford. The most comprehensive study of late medieval political poetry to date.

Sutton, A. F. and Visser-Fuchs, L. 1998. *Richard III's Books*: *Ideals and Reality in the Life and Library of a Medieval Prince.* Stroud: Sutton. Gives extensive discussions of the various tracts, including historical ones, that were in circulation in late medieval England.

22
Dream Poems

Helen Phillips

As a genre medieval dream poetry has an importance – numerically and in the range, and frequently the serious nature, of its subject-matter – that may surprise the modern reader. This is partly because, although dreams have always fascinated humans, cultural, scientific and poetic approaches to dreams have changed over the centuries. In the medieval period narratives framed by the device of a dream are not airy, fantastical or highly personal extravaganzas, as they can be at times in the cultural worlds of the Romantics, the Victorians, or the post-Freud era. Medieval dream poetry is rooted in classical and biblical concepts of dream and vision that imbued dreaming with the potential for august, profound, even divine meaning. The fact that in the thirteenth century a revolution happened, with the *Roman de la rose*, whereby this visionary and learned genre also became used for exploring the subject of human sexual passion, taking the experience of desire as a subject for serious literature in a serious genre, not only widened the subject-matter of dream poetry thereafter but raised questions about the place and value of passion, in Western society and Christian ideology, together with related questions about gender, interiority, emotionality, sexuality and the social mythologies of *cortoisie*. While the troubadour lyric and the birth of romance are rightly considered vanguards of the Western development of the idea of romantic love, it is within the dream genre that medieval writers were able to treat the subject discursively as well as experientially, and to sift, debate and contemplate the complexities and contradictions of passion and the states of consciousness it creates. By the late medieval period the dream poem and other types of courtly *dits amoureux* were also arenas for the exploration of further subjects such as masculine identity, unhappy marriage, misogyny and feminism. Dream poetry seems also to have stimulated self-conscious and often metafictional experimentation in the treatment of issues like the relationship of reader and writer to text, time in narrative, the fictional self, textuality and fiction. In the hands of Guillaume de Machaut, Jean Froissart, Geoffrey Chaucer and some of their fifteenth-century successors, it often seems the most sophisticated of all medieval literary genres, posing questions about the mysteries of writing and reading, and interior consciousness and the external world.

Among secular genres only romance rivals the dream narrative for the attention of writers, and the dream poem commanded a wider spectrum of subjects and styles. The genre's dominance is all the greater if we consider as one genre (as we should) dream poems together with other texts, related types of *dits amoureux,* where the narrator enters the core material through similar framing devices: through entry into a garden or temple, through overhearing events, or waking out of sleep and wandering forth into a landscape. There need not be literally a dream for a text to make clear that its narrator has been granted entrée into an especially significant, magic or revelatory realm. Some of the most profound narratives of this genre are not explicitly dreams, including Dante's *Divine Comedy* and Boethius's *Consolation of Philosophy*, as well as many charming or poignant shorter poems where a narrator may frame lovers' plaints or debates, or receive instruction, by saying that he suddenly came upon, saw or heard a scene and its actors. 'Dream poem', although established in modern critical parlance, is a misleading critical term if applied too rigidly to this wide genre of framed narratives.

The form was used for topics as diverse as political theory (e.g., *Songe du vergier*, 1376–8), elegy (*Pearl*, c.1400), royal celebration (*The Kingis Quair*, 1424), heraldic and political topical allegory (Rothelay's late fourteenth-century 'Half in a dreme'), a Latin treatise on the function of music (*Gregory's Garden*, c.1280–1300), and antifeminism (Mathéolus's *Liber lamentationum*, widely known through Le Fèvre's French translation, c.1372). Like other areas of medieval literary culture, dream poetry as composed and read in Britain between 1350 and 1500 was supranational and multilingual. Among dream texts composed in Britain we find French (for example, *Le Songe vert*, c.1349 or 1390s) and Latin (John Gower's *Vox clamantis*, c.1382), as well as Middle English. British poets' classical and European reading was often wide: Chaucer's compositions indicate inspiration from, among other dream and vision texts, Dante's *Divine Comedy* (influential on his *Legend of Good Women* and *House of Fame*), Boethius, Alain de Lille's *De planctu Naturae*, and three French writers who were among the greatest innovators in fourteenth-century dream poetry, Machaut, Froissart and Oton de Graunson (the two last working for part of their lives at the English court). Dream poems with wide readership include Middle English translations – for example, those of the *Roman de la rose* and Guillaume de Deguileville's *Pèlerinage de la vie humaine* and *Pèlerinage de l'âme.*

Social and Political Dream Poems

The serious and moral, indeed divinely sent, teaching that characterized early dream narratives made the genre an obvious one for political comment, giving powerful authority to what was presented, while distancing the speaker from personal responsibility for the message. Sometimes the content is fairly trivial and propagandist, as in Rothelay's praise of the de Vere family ('Half in a dreme') mentioned above. Dream poetry also includes some of the most interesting medieval writing on social and political issues. It often illustrates the fact that there is not really a separate concept of the political in the period. *Piers Plowman* combines spiritual and political reform as the twin subjects of its visions. Topical observations may be obscured in dream poetry by allegorical and generalized treatment and merged with timeless motifs of moralization or regret, such as Reason, Fortune or worldly mutability. The two personified protagonists of *Winner and Waster* might be supposed to represent, as in modern translation of their names, 'producer and consumer', but this debate on the relative value to society of opposed economic forces concentrates on two groups of rich men: those who accumulate money and hoard it (the Pope, lawyers, friars, merchants) and those who spend it (knights).[1] Workers and producers of the wealth are virtually ignored. The two sides rule armies whose fighting is halted by the king. Winner's boast of his own frugality and well-stocked house is countered by Waster's derision: he should use his wealth to help the poor. 'Winner' here is being conceived more in terms of the moral topos of the sin of avarice than in any political or economic conceptual structure of the creation and distribution of wealth. Both claim morality on their side. Winner paints a sordid picture of Waster's profligate habits; Waster ripostes that his spending helps society. Both claim concern for the poor. Both invoke the characteristically medieval apprehension of the threats to social stability and happiness as coming from mutability, social disruption and God's wrath against sinners. Their largely timeless debate perhaps, however, obliquely reflects the economic crisis in the post-Black Death years, with Edward III's expensive French campaigns of 1352–3. The king sends Winner to Rome and Waster to London, suggesting a clergy/knight division. The implication may be that Waster will stimulate wealth creation, and a surplus will be sent to keep Winner, who will furnish money for royal wars if required. As so often in medieval poetry, the audience of the debate is presented with complex, even contradictory, arguments: matter for continuing debate perhaps in the audience's sociable circle after the poem, rather than the delivery by the author of a simple and single message. This manuscript text is unfinished but it is hard to see how any decisive, single resolution of the arguments could have emerged.

John Gower began Book 1 of *Vox clamantis* by describing wandering out on a sunny June day, then lying in bed visited by strange terrors.[2] He finally falls asleep and dreams towards dawn – a time marked in classical dream theory as likely to bring significant dreams. His Prologue alludes to the apocalyptic visions of the Bible, referring to St John, author of the book of Revelation, and Daniel, whose dream of Nebuchadnezzar's statue being toppled was often taken by fourteenth-century writers as a warning of the fall of governments and decline of society. Their dreams, he says, were significant dreams, not idle ones. Often a troubled, melancholy dream narrator of this kind is suffering lovesickness but here, as in some other dream poems, his anxiety is moral and social. Gower's first subject is the 1381 Rising. He presents the rebels as animals, maddened with rage, irrationally destroying civil order. Gower's perspective is strongly pro-government, like that of many chroniclers, with fervent praise for those who crushed the rebellion. He ends Book 1 saying that his 'vigiles sompnii', wakeful dream, is no ordinary dream brought by sleep but 'sompnia vera', true dreams.

These dream narratives with social themes illustrate the ease with which, in medieval thinking and the dream genre, different aspects of life – religious, moral and political – interpenetrate. Texts presented as love visions may also include political motifs or topical implications: Chaucer's *Parliament of Fowls*, with its quarrelsome classes in parliament, raises questions about the chivalric social myth of *gentilesse* and social hierarchical order, as well as the cosmic order symbolized by Nature; the G prologue of his *Legend of Good Women* offers sharper warnings about tyranny (perhaps relevant to Richard II in the 1390s) than might be suspected initially from its elegant dream of the God of Love.

Framing Devices and Fictions of Beginning

Medieval dream poetry is often marked more by didacticism than dreaminess – and, of course, ancient dream theories saw didacticism and opportunity of access to truths usually veiled from humans as characterizing those real-life dreams worthy of serious interpretation.[3] Dream poems have first-person narrators and they make obvious recipients for instruction from an authority figure, who may be a deity, human or a personification. These authoritative dream guides go back to classical dream narratives such as Cicero's *Somnium Scipionis* (c.55 BC). Dreams often enclose debates and allegorical figures and action. The framing device of the dream can be a comparatively straightforward device to package didactic or entertaining material: examples include the encyclopedic moral lessons presented in Stephen Hawes's *Example of Virtue* (before 1503) or Alain Chartier's *Quadrilogue invective* (1422), concerned with France's military defeat and political demoralization, and translated about fifty years later into Middle English ('for profite by good exhortacion', its last sentence says), doubtless because its lament for national decline and its moral analysis equally fitted late fifteenth-century England.[4]

A framing device closely related to the dream – that of the narrator waking up rather than sleeping, and setting about his task – is a favourite preliminary stratagem, often used for subject-matter that can be regarded as a devout or dutiful exercise. Translators are particularly given to this variant on the dream frame. Thomas Brampton's translation of the *Penitential Psalms* (c.1420), Richard Roos's translation of Chartier's *La Belle Dame sans merci* (c.1450), and Henry Bradshaw's *Life of St Werburge* (c.1513), compiled from several sources, enclose their translations within this particular 'fiction of beginning', with its air of energetic duty. While medieval authors choose and deploy frames with evident finesse, there may also be in the history of the book another reason for the popularity of this type of structure during the medieval period, a reason unconnected with ancient dream theories or religious visionary tradition. Before the era of the modern book, framing devices had some of the functions of the modern peritextual features of binding, cover design and illustration, title-page, introduction and so on, which present the book as a discrete object and one whose character and subject can be predicted from these 'wrap-round' features. Different types of framing device can appropriately add gravitas or suggest a mood; to take just two obvious cases, a debate between body and soul is introduced as a vision that came to the author while drowsing in bed on a winter's night in the darkness before dawn ('Als I Lay in a Winteris Nyt'), whereas many a love debate or lament begins with the author sleeping, waking, or wandering out at dawn in spring, as in 'The Clerk and the Nightingale', a late fifteenth-century debate about women.

Analysis of dream poems reveals that their use of frames and the first-person narrator are rarely merely conventional or perfunctory. The *Roman de la rose* had firmly established the seasonal opening as virtually a standard part of the dream poem but later poets seem to calculate carefully the different effects of a winter, spring or harvest reference. While sunny spring mornings tend to be the default settings, associated with love and the start of the medieval year or a new day, thus providing parallels to the start of the narrative itself, other seasons, weather, or time of day may be used to foreground and foreshadow darker or complex themes. The *House of Fame*, contemplating the reputation of poets after death, the tragedy of Dido and a period of creative barrenness suffered by the poet, begins in December. The *Temple of Glas*, a profoundly complex literary structure, centred on the theme of thwarted loves, begins gloomily and uneasily with winter, a darkened moon (symbolizing women's oppression?) shrouded in misty cloud. Its dream then starts ambiguously, with both dazzling sun and windswept clouds, and then the poem's first subject, a crowd of unhappy lovers, appears. The device that closes this text, the dreamer waking at hearing melody, aptly fits the hope offered to unhappy lovers by the end of the long dream.[5]

Chaucer's *Book of the Duchess* delays its spring seasonal opening until unconventionally late, within the fictional dream: its unhappy narrator falls asleep only to dream of waking up amid May sunshine, a paradox that suits the complex mixture of lament and celebration around the Black Knight's love and memories that forms the dream's main subject. A spring opening can have particular aptness. The cheerful dream of male desire in the fifteenth-century *Isle of Ladies* is prefaced by a description of a young man on a May night in bed, thinking about his lady, and Clanvowe's *The Cuckoo and the Nightingale* (1392?), where the dreamer overhears the birds disputing about love, begins with springtime and the narrator's own desire, and ends tying the poem specifically to royal Valentine's Day celebrations. The birds are going to hold a St Valentine's Day parliament outside the Queen's bedroom window at Woodstock.

In *Vox clamantis* the frame's June setting matches the month when the 1381 Rising took place. *Parliament of the Three Ages* begins with a Maytime poaching expedition and ends with sunset and the sound of a bugle. This frame delicately underlines for the reader the lesson of life's transience, with implications about the heedless pursuit of gain and pleasure in this world: very appropriate for a poem depicting the successive ages of man, where Youth's joy in tournaments, like Middle Age's preoccupation with his estate, falls into triviality against the coming of death which Old Age confronts.

Fictions of Closure

The dream's ending, the transitional event that brings the narrator back from dream to waking, seems often as carefully contrived as the initial framing device. It is often a sound or jolt (and in this detail the literary dream recalls real-life dreaming experience). In Mathéolus's misogynist dream (where he sees married men, as the greatest of all martyrs, given the highest place in heaven) he wakes to hear his wife nagging. Skelton's *Bowge of Court* (1498) ends with the dreamer thinking he is falling out of a ship and fear awakens him. In Froissart's *Paradis d'Amours* (composed probably in England while Froissart was secretary to Queen Philippa of Hainault, 1361–9), when the narrator dreams that he is finally with his lady and she is welcoming his love and proposes they walk together, he is touched by Pleasure and trembles. That frisson of joy wakes him. The dream in *The Assembly of Ladies* ends when water splashes on the dreamer's face. In *Le Songe vert* the dreamer sees a new flower, the *fleur de lis* (his future lady), while he is sitting in a tree and is enraptured. When he leaps from the tree to protect the flower from thistles, the fall awakes him. Several texts end with a bell. Critics differ over the meaning of the bell striking twelve at the close of the elegy-like *Book of the Duchess*, but it certainly suggests some kind of completion or acceptance of the ending of a period of time. Deguileville's dreamer wakes just as his dream self is dying and going to heaven: a real-life bell summons him to Matins and he finds he is awake and back in his bed in his own monastery. Here the dream's end and the text's end are a new day's start – in the real world of continuing Christian endeavour.

This is not the only dream in which the whole of a man's life passes: Hawes's *Pastime of Pleasure* and *Example of Virtue* do the same. This illustrates one aspect of dream poets' propensity for playing with different types of time, as well as the spiritual message offered by the ending of many religious revelations: that the truths glimpsed in dream must be applied to the daily life of the Christian that continues after the dream and after the end of the fiction. *Pearl* sees its dreamer wake up just as he fails to cross over into heaven but then concludes with his setting out again on his own real-life journey with renewed purpose to make himself a pearl fit for the Lord's use, at the real future closure of his own life. The dream genre, from Boethius onwards, could be combined with the *consolatio* genre, the didactic instruction offered by a vision leading not just to mental enlightenment but to emotional consolation, for a narrator who at the poem's start, as in *Pearl*, was plunged in despair or anger against divine dispensation.

Dream endings can, like seasonal openings, be cleverly startling or ambiguous in their atmosphere. *The Castell of Pleasure* delays its seasonal passage to its close: the dreamer wakes to a thunderstorm. He had thought the sound that woke him was the melody within the dream; however, real life with its mutability, in human experience as well as weather, proves more changeable than this happy fancy. The first dream of the two that comprise the *Isle of Ladies* ends with the dreamer waking in a bedroom full of smoke (symbolizing mystification?). His second dream ends with his marrying his lady but, just as his dream self is enjoying the music and dancing at his own wedding feast, he is so eager to join in he jumps up and finds he has fallen out of bed. Far from having won his lady he sees around him no lady or wedding but just a bedroom with old tapestries of hunting, showing hurt deer dying of their wounds. His longing is so great he decides to send the completed book, the dream narrative, as a plea to his lady, asking her to marry him. Otherwise he will have to return to his dream.[6]

Narratological Themes

There are other cases where, in metafictional fashion, the dream changes into the very book the reader is perusing (in the previous example, its first peruser would be the lady). Chaucer at the close of the *Book of the Duchess* announces he will now write the book of the dream. *The Assembly of Ladies* ends with the author's discussing with a knight, immediately after waking, the name of the book. Yet the text begins with her saying that she will *tell* the story of her dream to the knight. Such phenomena reflect the late medieval fluidity between oral and written texts and are also instances of a widespread interest in experimenting with metafictional devices in dream poetry. The imitations of Chaucer's 'Go Little Book' envoy (from *Troilus*) in the fifteenth century and the Tudor period illustrate the same fascination with the relationship between the fictional dream experience and the completed, physical volume. Some poems end with self-conscious allusion to the difference between fiction and reality in the matter of time. In *Le Chevalier des dames*, a mid-fifteenth-century French feminist text, the dreamer discovers on waking that he has been away twenty-two days and the book of the dream is now complete and lying on his pillow. The twenty-two days tease the reader: are they the time spent in a dream or the time spent writing a book? This foregrounds how far the interest in dreaming evinced by many medieval authors was frequently also an interest in the nature of writing and fiction.

This foregrounding of relationships between the fictional experience, dreaming and the actual book which the reader now holds and the author wrote, produces at times dramatizations of the first-person narrator as a scribe or secretary. The narrator of *La Belle Dame sans merci* says he is but a scribe, for example. This persona, a denial of simple and direct authorial identification with the core experience, may reflect the patron's importance in medieval literary production. Machaut's narrator in the *Dit de la fontainne amoreuse* (c.1360) hears a lover's lament through a bedroom wall and writes it all down, later presenting it to the lover, who represents Machaut's patron, the Duc de Berry. The oblique relationship of the narrator (as scribe or mere observer) to the experience at the poem's centre in some of Machaut's *dits amoureux* must be one of the inspirations for the passive narrators Chaucer creates, both in dream poems and elsewhere: men who cannot be held responsible for the interpretations that may be drawn from what they present to their readers. His devices include characterization of the narrator as old, naive, ignorant of love, or a mere translator of other men's ideas and sentiments.

Medieval dream poems are rooted, then, as much, if not more, in literary traditions and meditation on the nature of books as in the real-life experience of dreaming. The core experience, the dream, is often framed by bookishness in two ways: it emerges from the narrator's prelude, which may describe the reading of a book or invoke great poets of the past (for the fifteenth century this might mean a reference to Chaucer); and, as we have seen, the concluding frame may bring to the reader's attention the fact that the dream turns into a book, or send the 'little book' forth to its reader. That indecisiveness in Chaucer's conclusions that witnesses to the complexity of ideas in his dream poems produces at the close of the *Parliament of Fowls* talk not of a book, a decisive finished text emerging out of his vision, but of returning in puzzlement to the world of the reader, back to yet more books. The *Parliament* has its dreamer end as inveterate reader not authoritative *auctor*. Although the 'secretary' role may reflect traditional economic ownership of the text by a patron, dream poets (with Chaucer and Machaut as early examples) may also promote and advertise their own presence, their roles as authors and their careers as poets through anagrams of their names, lists of their works or a focus on fame. This trend heralds the increasing confidence and prominence of the individual secular author, a development intensifying with the advent of printing, when authors become more assertive about ownership of their writing in the face of printer-publishers. Yet, while issues of authorship and ownership, and the prestige of the creative artist, hover controversially round these ways of presenting the first person narrator, and the relation of dreamer to narrator/recorder, it is also true that the figure of the narrator as a dreamer, advancing through a strange landscape which unfolds before his eyes, as an *ingénu* in a world he does not understand, strongly resembles the experience of a reader, advancing watchfully through a narrative.

Books and the Dream

The device of referring to a book before a dream derives from Chaucer's dream poems, perhaps inspired by French precedents, including Deguileville's *Pèlerinage de la vie humaine* which cites the *Roman de la rose* and then presents a dream quest which subverts the erotic quest of the *Rose* into a journey towards understanding God's design for salvation. Sometimes the book, juxtaposed with the ensuing dream, suggests a way of interpreting the dream's material. William Nevill's *The Castell of Pleasure* (printed c.1515–18) begins with Ovid's tale of Phoebus and Daphne, foreshadowing its subject of a lover's desire thwarted by a disdainful woman but finally triumphant, and also introducing a theme of pride before a fall, just as Nevill will return to the theme of the transience of earthly pride and prosperity at the dream's close.[7] Mutability is also suggested by the time-setting picture he paints, just before sleeping, of the shadows falling on the hills from the setting sun, chimney smoke going up from households, curfew rung, and people needing lodging knocking urgently to find somewhere for the night. The relationship of book to dream in Chaucer's dream poems is elusive and suggestive, never directive. The message voiced in Chaucer's retelling of Ovid's *Metamorphoses* tale of Ceyx and Alcyone, before the dream in the *Book of the Duchess*, about accepting transience, perhaps suggests a stoical consolation which the reader can apply to the Man in Black's sorrows later, within the dream. It is, however, instructive that critics have differed in what message they believe this Ovidian section provides. The juxtaposition of Dido's story and the dream in the *House of Fame* similarly challenges the reader to create interpretation, rather than providing a guide to the poet's meaning. The device of the book read before the dream is one of the 'layering' structures beloved of dream poets (the concept is Jacqueline Cerquiglini's) and such layering and the juxtaposition of often puzzling elements can make the characteristic structures of this genre inherently dialectic as well as didactic. Authors may cite a famous book and set up a creative conflict between that written existing text and the data in their own new vision. Chaucer questions the place of sexual desire in an ordered cosmos in the *Parliament of Fowls* after introducing the world-denying, transcendental vision of Cicero's *Somnium Scipionis*. *The Kingis Quair* invokes Boethius's *Consolation of Philosophy* yet draws from it (lines 33–40) a new, very un-Boethian, message that a virtuous young man will win worldly success.[8] The two late medieval secular poets seem to be challenging the other-worldly ideologies of the classical texts they cite. The literary precursors against which a new dream is constructed in Chaucer's *House of Fame* and *Legend of Good Women* are particularly intriguing, the first introducing the tale of Dido, the second citing Chaucer's own previous writings (*Troilus* and the *Romaunt of the Rose*) deemed to be misogynist. In both cases the topics dominating the ensuing dream include literary tradition and the afterlife of writers and writings, together with the theme of women and their reputation in literary, masculinist tradition. 'Fame', the central subject of the *House of Fame*, has done harm, or at least delivered a mixed fate, to Dido and to the other heroines of old who are celebrated in the *Legend*. Henryson's *Testament of Cresseid* begins with a 'dooly sessoun' prefiguring a 'cairful dyte', a 'tragedie' (lines 1–4): this is Spring (or, with appropriately penitential wording, Lent) but with hail showers.[9] The season's gloom and turmoil are matched by a literary allusion which introduces ideas of tragedy and also of ambiguous interpretations. The poet tells of going to bed and reading one book: Chaucer's *Troilus and Criseyde*, sympathetic to Criseyde. His own revelation follows but in the form of another book, as well as a kind of vision from the past, in a brilliant twist on the expectations likely to be held by readers of dream poetry: first, that a dream will follow the reading of a book and, second, that the ending of a dream poem may depict a book emerging from the dream experience. The second book appears to be the poem of the dream itself. This is another case where the poem's core narrative is in creative conflict with the book read when the narrator retired to bed.

Dreaming and Dream Narratives

Occasionally dream poems do provide moments of striking similarity to real dreams. William Dunbar's *Golden Targe* (c.1503), for example, has a sudden shift where a crowd of allegorical personages vanishes only to reappear on a boat. Guns and other noises around the boats cause a rainbow bridge to shatter. The commotion wakes the dreamer.[10] The surface of Langland's fictional narrative in *Piers Plowman* is frequently chaotically varied, with phantasmagorical diversity of subject, shifting abruptly between large and small perspectives, theological ideas, figures from human history, textual quotations, comic or political vignettes, disparate voices and sudden movements. In moving so giddily from rats and mice to biblical statements, or contemporary London scenes, or personifications of cosmic power such as Truth and Reason, and crossing readily between different kinds of time (historical, liturgical, apocalyptic and autobiographical), the narrative resembles real-life dreaming more than most medieval literary dreams. The effect is not merely of verisimilitude but of a startlingly illuminating revelation of how all human life in its diversity – history, texts, contemporary social life and personal spiritual endeavour – relates to the great patterns of God's creation, God's plan in history and the practices of the Church. There are a series of dreams, many dream-guides and no simple didactic lessons. The surface chaos of Langland's dreams creates a revelation of a deeper unifying order, as the reader begins to perceive how the same patterns are repeated. We are not surprised when, at the spiritual climax of the dreamer's journey of discovery, the Easter dream is a coalescence of motifs from different parts of the narrative and different areas of Christian experience: Jesus, dressed as a medieval knight going to joust, is also historically entering Jerusalem on Palm Sunday, and is both Piers the Plowman and the Good Samaritan.[11]

Dream Traditions in the Later Middle Ages

Piers Plowman is only one dream poem that created a school of further poems in its wake. Although not specifically presented as dreams, a number of alliterative poems on contemporary political crises and abuses, the 'Piers Plowman Tradition', testify to its wide influence. These include *Piers the Plowman's Crede* and *Mum and the Soothsayer.* The tendency of powerful and innovative dream poems to generate successors is, like the fact that virtually all the major poets of the late medieval period composed dream poems, an indication of the genre's importance. Two French poems, both influential in England, initiated the fashion for palindrome compositions reversing the message of a previous text. Jean le Fèvre, having translated the *Liber lamentationum* of Mathéolus with its misogynist dream, composed his own *Livre de Leesce*, where Lady Leesce ('Delight') contradicts his aspersions and defends women. Machaut's *Dit dou roy de Behaigne* was followed by the *Dit dou roy de Navarre* which reversed its conclusion. Le Fèvre's and Machaut's palindromes seem to have been known to Chaucer, whose *Legend of Good Women* similarly uses the dream genre not only to survey his own position as writer but to reverse the alleged misogyny of his previous writings. Chartier's *Belle Dame*, known in both France and England, similarly generated successors (including an apology of his own) with diverse attitudes to its attack on the merciless – and robustly independent-minded – woman of its central debate.

Fifteenth-century 'Chaucerian' poetry, many of the writings of Lydgate and Hoccleve, and the anonymous *Assembly of Ladies* and *Isle of Ladies*, illustrate how much Chaucer's legacy to England's national literature was felt to lie in the courtly dream poem. The genre continued, as it had always done, to change and innovate. The late medieval and Tudor periods see a new interest in using the dream frame as a showcase for lyrics. That had already happened in fourteenth-century French literature: Machaut and Oton de Graunson are the masters at combining narrative, dream and inset lyric in complex layered structures. Chaucer makes sparing use of inset lyrics. John Skelton places a sequence of exquisite lyrics and delicate and amusing compliments to a group of women in the circle of the Countess of Surrey, within a dream frame in his *Garland of Laurel* (begun before 1495).[12] It opens with his saying that, in a gloomy meditation, he fell asleep. He dreams of the Queen of Fame and Dame Pallas (Athene), who complain of his dullness. This leads to the series of lyrics and his own crowning as laureate. Like Chaucer in the *Legend of Good Women*, he lists his poems, like a curriculum vitae. He wakes with the sound of triumphant shouts and trumpets. It is finely balanced between self-promotion and self-deprecation, between the poet's sense of aristocratic patronage and the judgement of history, Fame, on his own creative oeuvre. It illustrates, like Machaut's *Voir Dit* and Chaucer's *Legend*, a concern on the part of poets for the preservation of their fame within a European vernacular tradition that by now rivalled the classical heritage. Skelton's recital of his own oeuvre in the dream goes hand in hand with the appearance of former English poets Chaucer, Gower and Lydgate: he is taking his own place in a national literary tradition. Like Chaucer in the *Legend*, his literary fame is linked to his respect for women: he is crowned because he has never defamed women.

The framed *dit amoureux*, this large genre which includes dream poetry, has been called by Sylvia Huot a 'lyrico-narrative' hybrid genre, for the affinities its approach to passion owes to lyrics, as well as the complex relationships between narrative frames and lyric sequences in the structure of some dream texts.[13] The genre is one of the ancestors of the Elizabethan poetic miscellany and the sonnet sequence. Chaucer in the *Legend of Good Women* experiments with using the dream as a frame for introducing a story collection of tales, perhaps abandoning this because he hit upon the alternative device of the pilgrimage as a frame for a new collection, the *Canterbury Tales*.

Another development in fifteenth-century French and English framed narratives is an interest in the defence of women against misogyny and in the problems of unhappy or abusive marriage. Again, the *Legend of Good Women* seems in the forefront of developments. It harnesses the cause of the virtuous woman to the glamour of the courtly love literary tradition: its Alceste is the model of perfect womanhood as perfect wifehood. In its own way it opposes the masculinist ethos of the *Roman de la rose*, as Deguileville had done from a specifically Christian outlook. Framed narratives that continue this feminist interest include several by Christine de Pizan, including the *Epitre du dieu d'Amours* and *Cité des dames*, and the female-authored *Assembly of Ladies* and *Flower and the Leaf*, the latter of which presents a vision of the virtuous knight, a 'new man' of virtue, continence and constancy as well as prowess. Chaucer's *Legend* condemns the faithless Jason and Theseus and praises the constant Piramus. The 'new man', as a glamorous knight from chivalric literature who is also dedicated to defending women from misogynists (including Jean de Meun, author of the *Roman de la rose*), also appears in the French *Chevalier des dames* and *Champion des dames*.

Dream poems show surprisingly little interest in dream theory. They may occasionally, as Chaucer does in the *Book of the Duchess*, mention famous dreams and the great treatise on dreams composed by Macrobius, his *Commentary on Somnium Scipionis*, c.390, but this seems often little more than literary decoration. There certainly was medieval curiosity about dreams and their interpretation, as the popularity of dream-interpretation books like the *Somniale Danielis* indicates, but medieval dream poetry, which can tell us much about the history of human thinking on the mysterious structures of writing and reading (much that was forgotten by the intellectual world until the advent of recent literary theory), is of little interest in the history of ideas about dreaming. Authors of romances often use dreams within their narratives with interesting prophetic, symbolic or psychological import. Yet the massive tradition of medieval dream poetry, as a genre, seems to stand apart both from medieval speculations about dreaming and from dreams within romances. The extraordinary formal potential and virtuosity we see in dream poetry seems to have created a genre with its own absorbing dynamics, preoccupations, intellectual achievements and formation of traditions.

See also: 18 Images, 20 Middle English Romance, 23 Lyric, 32 *Piers Plowman*, 34 John Gower and John Lydgate, 35 Thomas Hoccleve, 36 The Poetry of Robert Henryson.

Notes

1 *Winner and Waster* in *Alliterative Poetry of the Later Middle Ages*, ed. Thorlac Turville-Petre, London: Routledge, 1989, pp. 38–66.

2 *Vox clamantis* in *The Latin Works of John Gower*, ed. G. C. Macaulay, 4 vols, Oxford: Clarendon Press, 1902, pp. 3–313.

3 Macrobius, *Commentary on the Dream of Scipio*, trans. William H. Stahl, New York and London: Columbia University Press, 1952, ch. 3.

4 In *The Works of Alain Chartier*, ed. James C. Laidlaw (Cambridge: Cambridge University Press, 1974).

5 *Lydgate's Temple of Glas*, ed. J. Schick, EETS es 60 (1891).

6 *The Isle of Ladies*, in *The Floure and the Leafe, The Assembly of Ladies, The Isle of Ladies*, ed. Derek Pearsall, (Kalamazoo, Mich.: Medieval Institute Publications for TEAMS, 1990), pp. 63–140.

7 William Nevill, *The Castell of Pleasure*, ed. Roberta D. Cornelius, EETS os 179 (London: Oxford University Press, 1930).

8 James I of Scotland, *The Kingis Quair*, ed. John Norton-Smith, Medieval and Tudor Series (Oxford: Clarendon Press, 1971).

9 Robert Henryson, *The Testament of Cresseid*, in *The Poems of Robert Henryson*, ed. Denton Fox (Oxford: Clarendon Press, 1981), pp. 111–31.

10 William Dunbar, *The Golden Targe*, in *The Poems of William Dunbar*, ed. James Kinsley (Oxford: Clarendon Press), 1979 pp. 29–38.

11 William Langland, *Piers Plowman: A Parallel-Text Edition of the A, B, C, and Z Versions*, ed. A. V. C. Schmidt (London: Longman, 1995).

12 John Skelton, *The Garland of Laurel*, in *The Complete Poems of John Skelton*, ed. John Scattergood (Harmondsworth: Penguin, 1983) pp. 312–57.

13 See Sylvia Huot, *From Song to Book: The Poetics of Writing in Old French Lyric and Lyrical Narrative Poetry* (Ithaca, N.Y.: Cornell University Press, 1987), pp. 1–2, 83–90, 219–41, 302–37.

References and Further Reading

Barr, Helen (ed.) 1993. *The Piers Plowman Tradition: A Critical Edition of Pierce the Ploughman's Crede, Richard the Redeless, Mum and the Sothsegger, and The Crowned King*. London: Dent. An accessible edition with excellent introductory essays.

—— 1994. *Signes and Sothe: Language in the Piers Plowman Tradition*. Cambridge: Boydell and Brewer. An important critical analysis of the poetics of late medieval political dream poetry.

Boffey, Julia 2003. *Fifteenth-Century Dream Visions.* Oxford: Oxford University Press. An excellent anthology of texts with critical introductions.

Brown, Peter (ed.) 1999. *Reading Dreams: The Interpretation of Dreams from Chaucer to Shakespeare.* Oxford: Oxford University Press. Original essays examining a wide range of approaches to theories of dream interpretation, from medieval culture through Milton to modern literature.

Brownlee, Kevin 1984. *Poetic Identity in Guillaume de Machaut.* Madison: Unversity of Wisconsin Press. A demonstration of the complexity with which author, narrator, text and patron are handled in Machaut's dream poetry: an illuminating critical analysis for the late medieval genre generally, in English as well as French.

Davidoff, Judith M. 1988. *Beginning Well: Framing Fictions in Late Middle English Poetry.* London: Associated Universities Presses. A very helpful guide to the way medieval authors frame dream poems and similar courtly narratives.

Edwards, R. R. 1989. *The Dream of Chaucer.* Durham, N.C., and London: University of North Carolina Press. An interesting critical approach to Chaucer's use of the dream genre.

Huot, Sylvia 1987. *From Song to Book: The Poetics of Writing in Old French Lyric and Lyrical Narrative Poetry.* Ithaca, N.Y. and London: Cornell University Press. Combines a scholarly examination of the compilation of courtly manuscripts of lyrics and *dits amoureux* with a critical analysis of the ways in which lyrics and narratives are creatively merged by many late medieval writers.

Kruger, Steven F. 1992. *Dreaming in the Middle Ages.* Cambridge: Cambridge University Press. An interesting examination of the literature and theory of dreaming in medieval literature.

Langland, William 1995. *Piers Plowman: A Parallel-Text Edition of the A, B, C and Z Versions*, ed. A. V. C. Schmidt. London and New York: Longman. An invaluable new edition, replacing Skeat's century-old parallel-text edition.

Lynch, Kathryn 1988. *The High Medieval Dream Vision.* Stanford, Calif.: Stanford University Press. A useful survey of major dream visions.

Macrobius 1952. *Commentary on the 'Dream of Scipio'*, trans. William H. Stahl. New York and London: Columbia University Press. Stahl provides a useful introduction to this seminal classical text for the medieval authors of dream visions.

Minnis, Alaistair J., with Scattergood, V. J. and Smith, J. J. 1995. *Chaucer's Shorter Poems.* Oxford Guides to Chaucer. Oxford: Oxford University Press. An original and stimulating exploration of Chaucer's dream poetry.

Phillips, Helen 1997. 'Frames and Narrators in Chaucerian Poetry.' In *The Long Fifteenth Century: Essays for Douglas Gray* (Oxford: Clarendon Press), pp. 71–99. Examines the construction of narrators and a variety of framing devices in French and English courtly narratives of the fifteenth and early sixteenth centuries.

—— and Havely, Nick (eds) 1997. *Chaucer's Dream Poetry.* Harlow: Longman. Offers new editions of all Chaucer's dream poems with critical essays on the genre and the individual texts.

Russell, J. S. 1988. *The English Dream Vision: Anatomy of a Form.* Columbus: Ohio University Press. Explores the idea that late medieval English dream narratives represent a distinct tradition.

Spearing, A. C. 1976. *Medieval Dream-Poetry.* Cambridge: Cambridge University Press. This remains the best introductory survey of ancient and medieval dream literature.

23
Lyric[1]

Rosemary Greentree

'Oh, to vex me, contraries meet in one'

Anyone who seeks the essence and boundaries of the medieval English lyric may find John Donne's line an apt expression of the task's pleasures and exasperations. The Middle English lyric attracts contraries of matter and manner, metre, diction and form. The slightest of structures may bear the weight of serious content with a paradox or exploration of holy mysteries in a form equally suited to celebration. Apparently artless forms may prove sophisticated and lavishly allusive. The disparate members of this genre vary from the glorious to the mundane; the range can only be sketched here. Vexation comes from attempts to define the genre, to confine its members within a few descriptive sentences. Every statement can be questioned, every adjective is ambiguous, every category has exceptions.

Expectations of the Middle English Lyric

Some qualities are called 'lyrical' when they are found in poetry of any era: a hint of music, even without accompaniment; evocation of the poet's mood; emphasis on sensations rather than narrative; allusive depiction of material. The reader expects any or all of these in poems called lyrics. Middle English short poems called 'lyrics' may then seem far from lyrical. The genre's distinguishing marks are not well defined, and lyrics may differ almost as much from one another as from members of other genres. The term is a driftnet that has caught almost any short poem of the period.

Many Middle English lyrics conform to all present-day expectations. Some appear with music and others suggest singing and dancing in their words and metre; many express love's emotions. But there are prayers, meditations and sermon verses; some imply a narrative, and others transmit knowledge. There are political verses, prophecies, theological paradoxes and mnemonic advice. General anthologies of medieval English literature usually include only lyrics that answer modern expectations, including love songs to the Virgin and earthly beloveds, carols and poems of life and death. Anthologies devoted solely to lyrics present a wider range.

Characteristics of Lyrics

There are some constants in the genre. Ann S. Haskell notes a 'cluster of characteristics', including brevity, metrical pattern, rhyme scheme, theme and occasional hints of a plot.[2] To John Burrow, the term 'usually means no more than a short poem', but he emphasizes 'the most characteristic *axis* of lyric poetry: the "I" addressing the "you" ', and distinguishes that 'I' from any other personal utterance, since the lyric 'I' 'speaks not for an individual but for a type' (Burrow 1982: 61). The voice of the lyric 'I' is always present, sounding many notes: laughing, weeping, expressing countless human feelings, praying, teaching or passing on scraps of knowledge.

Modern editions seldom reflect the medieval manuscript context of the poems. Modern editors group lyrics according to time of composition and common themes, but their original compilation was generally less systematic, often related to the availability of space or the scribes' sources. British Library MS Harley 2253, for example, contains the celebrated 'Harley lyrics', generally classified in printed editions as religious, secular and political. One may now read the religious and secular works in Brook's and Brown's editions, and the political poems in Robbins's, but in the manuscript the lyrics mingle with works in other genres and languages.[3]

Lyrics may be additions to longer compositions. Brief, mnemonic lyrics were included in sermons, as tags to reinforce the preacher's messages. Carols and hymns in dramatic works set the scene or advance the plot. Commonplace books reveal their compilers' interests, tastes and values. John Grimestone's is a Franciscan's handbook, with religious parodies of secular songs; Richard Hill's preserves the 'Corpus Christi Carol' (see below) and other lyrics, with puzzles, recipes and the birth dates of his children; the Findern manuscript begins as a formal anthology but ends in household accounts.[4] The love-song 'Bryd one brere' is written on the back of a Papal Bull of 1199.[5] Some sections of larger works could function as formed poems. The song of Troilus, 'Canticus Troili', from *Troilus and Criseyde* (1.400–20), is Chaucer's rendering of a sonnet by Petrarch. Such appropriation and extraction exemplify the free use of isolable lines, in an age when reference to 'myne auctor' might seem more respectable than originality, and copyright was unknown. The context of lyrics inevitably influences their interpretation, as in the case of '*De amico ad amicam*' and '*Responcio*', described later.

Knowledge of the Poet

The 'lyric I' who addresses the 'you' implied in Middle English lyrics is a general, typical figure, an 'I' without ego, who may make the reader a participant in the poem. Anonymity helps efface the poets of many medieval lyrics, removing distractions to focus attention on the poem itself.[6] Aspects of style may suggest a particular poet, place or time of composition. Some political verses recount historical events, and some poets describe their situations, but a manuscript's time of compilation does not necessarily reveal the dates when its contents were written, and biographical details may be fictions. These factors can enhance or diminish the reader's appreciation of a work. Acrostics and other devices sometimes reveal a poet's name or the place of composition. However, the lack of details of a poet's life and state of mind spares the reader fruitless speculation, since it is both easier and more profitable to concentrate on the lyric 'I'.

The Art of the Middle English Lyric

Medieval English lyrics seem often to communicate more directly than more recent poems, with fewer poetic devices. The works are by no means artless, and frequently their art conceals itself. Many are complex and refined, and some conform to intricate constraints of metre and composition. The exquisite 'I syng of a myden' (Brown 1939: 119) combines delicacy and poise in a simple structure, filled with implication and allusion:

I syng of a myden that is makeles, *maiden; matchless*
kyng of alle kynges to here sone che ches. *her; she chose*

he cam also stylle ther his moder was *quietly; where*
as dew in aprylle, that fallyt on the gras.

he cam also stylle to his moderes bowr
as dew in aprille, that fallyt on the flour.

he cam also stylle ther his moder lay
as dew in aprille, that fallyt on the spray. *shoots*

moder & mayden was neuer non but che –
wel may swych a lady godes moder be![7] *such*

This fifteenth-century poem takes and transforms a few lines from the six quatrains of a thirteenth-century lyric of the Annunciation, 'Nu this fules singet hand maket hure blis' (Brown 1932: 55). The later poem gracefully recalls the story of the Annunciation, emphasizing the role of the Virgin Mary as mother and maiden; the adjective 'makeles' distinguishes her as without either mate or peer. In the alliance of spare structure and abundant imagery the art of the later lyric is sure and unobtrusive; its elegant economy makes the earlier poem seem cumbersome. The stress on Mary's choice and active office as God's mother rather than on her as the passive bearer of God's son reverses the message of the thirteenth-century lyric and enhances the significance of her participation in the event.[8]

A fifteenth-century poet could afford to be this brief, because it was possible to rely on an audience's familiarity with the material in this time of affective piety. The poem's five couplets suggest the Virgin's mystical number, five, and thus her Joys, of which the first, the Annunciation, celebrated on 25 March, marked the first day of the medieval year. The falling of dew recalls Gideon's fleece (Judges 6: 36–40), a metaphor for Mary's chaste conception of Christ. April, the first month of her pregnancy, is often associated with the coming of spring and love, and floral images frequently signify the Virgin. The imagery's rich implications and the elegant juxtaposition of courtly references and allusions to nature, within an austere structure, reveal the sure touch of a sophisticated poet. Succinct references to familiar figures for familiar material create a fresh, refined work of art.

Although many Middle English lyrics seem direct in expression and without poetic artifice, others are more complex, like this fifteenth-century work of theological paradoxes (Brown 1939: 187) which eventually leaves the answers to faith:

A God and yet a man?
    A mayde and yet a mother?
Witt wonders what witt Can   *can know*
    Conceave this or the other.

A god, and Can he die?
    A dead man, can he live?
What witt can well replie?
    What reason reason give?

God, truth itselfe, doth teach it;
    Mans witt senckis too farr vnder   *sinks*
By reasons power to reach it.
    Beleeve and leave to wonder!

The poet archly entertains profound questions within a simple form as easily suited to a frivolous song, in lines marked by alliterative repetitive staccato which restrict a facile flow and compel the reader to consider the contradictory implications of the words. In style and content these lines resemble a quatrain ascribed to Bishop Reginald Pecock, 'Witte hath wondir that resoun ne telle kan' (Brown 1939: 186). The similarities suggest that Pecock is a source of inspiration for if not the author of the more polished poem quoted above.

Religious and Secular Lyrics

Criticism may classify Middle English lyrics as 'secular' or 'religious', poems of flesh or spirit, of this world or the next, but 'secular' does not exclude spiritual references, as it may in current usage. The world of the lyrics is Christendom, where Christian and pre-Christian teachings mingle, and pagan customs may gain new purposes.[9] Lyrics of love illustrate this blurring of boundaries. Most lyrics called religious tell of love – divine love for mankind or humanity's for God, Christ, the saints, and especially for Mary. Some courtly lyrics resemble praise of the Virgin: the gulf between the courtly lover and his distant mistress resembles that implied in lyrics celebrating Mary as Queen of Heaven and Empress of Hell, and her beauty is often described in the terms used for worldly mistresses. Other poems stress the intimate relationship with Mary as mother. Many secular love lyrics include prayers for the lady or thanks for her presence; mnemonics use saints' days to mark the seasons, and few poems lack any reference we would now call religious.

Similar forms can shape poems of sharply different meaning, as two lyrics from the Harley collection demonstrate. Their first stanzas show a close resemblance. (I use Brook's titles for these and other Harley lyrics.) 'The Way of Woman's Love' (Brook 1968: 71–2) describes the pains of courtly love:

Lutel wot hit anymon	*knows; any man*
hou derne loue may stonde,	*secret love*
bote hit were a fre wymmon	*immodest*
that muche of loue had fonde.	*experienced*
The loue of hire ne lesteth no wyht longe,	*her; not at all*
heo haueth me plyht & wyteth me wyth wronge.	*she; promised; blames*
Euer ant oo, for my leof icham in grete thohte,	*always; beloved*
y thenche on hire that y ne seo nout ofte.	*do not see often*

'The Way of Christ's Love' (Brook 1968: 70–1), however, proclaims Christ's generous love:

Lutel wot hit anymon	
hou loue hym haueth ybounde,	*has bound*
that for vs o the rode ron	*on the Cross; bled*
ant bohte vs with is wounde.	*redeemed; his*
The loue of him vs haueth ymaked sounde,	*us; healed*
ant ycast the grimly gost to grounde.	*cast; terrible ghost*
Euer ant oo, nyht ant day, he haueth vs in is thohte;	*thought*
he nul nout leose that he so deore bohte.	*will not lose; dearly bought*

The former poem pleads 'Ledy, thyn ore!' [mercy] (17), and the latter 'Crist, thyn ore!' (14); all stanzas in both poems conclude with a refrain of the 'O and I' form.[10]

There are many religious parodies of worldly songs, generally composed by the clergy, particularly by the Franciscans – their title, *joculatores dei*, freely rendered by Robbins as 'the singing fools of Our Lord'.[11] Richard de Ledrede, the Franciscan Bishop of Ossory, wrote pious Latin verses for the tunes of vernacular works, and his Red Book preserves some secular originals. One concerns 'The Maid of the Moor' (Robbins 1955: 12–13), whose identity is a source of continuing speculation. The first two stanzas read:

Maiden in the mor lay –	
in the mor lay –	
seuenyst fulle, seuenist fulle.	*a week*
Maiden in the mor lay –	

in the mor lay –
seuenistes fulle ant a day.
Well was hire mete. *good; food*
wat was hire mete?
the primerole ant the *primrose*
the primerole ant the –
Welle was hire mete.
Wat was hire mete?
the primerole ant the violet.

The repetition of questions and answers creates the effect of a children's rhyme, and the poem has been read as a gentle account of a maiden's death and burial. Other proposals offer religious explanations, and identify the maid as the Virgin Mary, or Mary Magdalene, or an allegorical figure for the soul.[12] The poem's contemporary references and context show that the more seemly Latin lyric 'Peperit virgo' (The Virgin gave birth) was to replace these English stanzas in the Red Book.[13]

Political Lyrics

The range of political lyrics is considerable. The poems maintain old national prejudices, tell of battles lost or won, describe policies and offer advice to the powerful, deplore evils of the times and show their consequences. Poets express their beliefs either directly or through allusion. They may disclose historical events at length, as in Lydgate's account of 'The Kings of England' (3–6), or briefly, as in the grim couplet of the year 1391: 'The ax was sharpe, the stokke was harde, / In the xiiii year of Kyng Richarde'.[14]

Another terse poem summarizes 'Abuses of the Age' (144) in general terms:

Bissop lorles *uneducated*
King redeles *unadvised*
Yung man rechles *heedless*
Old man witles *witless*
Woman ssamles *shameless*
I swer bi heuen kyng, *heaven's*
Thos beth fiue lither thing *are; evil*

This list is elaborated in many other works. These wrongs lead to other abuses ('The Bisson Leads the Blind', 127–30) and to the instability and injustices of a topsy-turvy world in such poems as 'This World Is Variable' (148–9), 'London Lickpenny' (130–4) and 'The World Upside Down' (150–2). There are poems about lax clergy ('The Land of Cockaygne', 121–7) and friars' evil deeds ('The Orders of Cain', 157–62). Bad counsel given to kings may explain disastrous policies ('Advice to the Court, II (1450)', 203–5); deceptions may be practised on unwise old men ('Old Hogyn's Adventure', Robbins

1955: 33–4). Poems of 'galaunts' deride foolish young men in rich foppish attire ('Huff! A Galaunt', 138–9), and others condemn the scandalous dress of women ('The Pride of Women's Horns', 139). More optimistically, Lydgate presents a Latin list of evils with English solutions ('Advice to the Several Estates, I', 232–3).

Three poems of the Battle of Agincourt (1415) illustrate variation in the treatment of an event. A stirring alliterative ballad, 'The Battle of Agincourt' (74–7), vividly conveys the gruesome scene and names heroes of the field. 'The Agincourt Carol' offers thanks for victory (91–2; Greene 1977: 257–8), merely saying that 'dukys and erlys, lorde & barone, / were take & slayne, & that wel sone' (17–18). Another carol, 'The Rose on Branch' (92–3; Greene 1977: 258) alludes more distantly to the rose and the fleur-de-lis, symbols of England and France.

Heraldic symbols signify political figures and parties in many poems of the Wars of the Roses. 'The Rote is ded the Swanne is goon' ('Prelude to the Wars (1449)', 201–3), refers to Yorkist figures through their badges. Symbols become metaphors in the triumphant account of the 1450 'Arrest of the Duke of Suffolk' (186–7): 'Now is the Fox drevin to hole hoo to him hoo hoo'. Suffolk's badge of the clog and chain, used to tether tame apes, inspires the epithet 'Iack napys, with his clogge' (19). The poem prays that God will save the king and feed no more such apes, and warns other powerful men, 'dukes, erles, and barons alle' (29), echoing the Agincourt carol. Falls from grace may inspire strongly didactic works, as in 'The Lament of the Duchess of Gloucester (1441)' (176–80), where each stanza ends, 'All women may be ware by me'.

Middle English Lyrics and Lyrics in Other Languages

Many lyrics in Middle English show debts to other languages, particularly French and Latin. Although they have the forms and moods of French and Latin poems, and some are translations, they have a distinctively English accent.

Some works in other languages provide inspiration rather than passages for translation. The solemn Latin hymn 'Stabat iuxta Christi crucem' prompts poems that may follow its metrical pattern, but explore rather different paths. English versions imply an observer of the Crucifixion, and often concentrate on the Virgin's sufferings. In 'stod ho there neh / that leueli leor wid spald ischent' ('she stood there nigh / that dear face put to shame with spittle', Brown 1932: 8–9) the poet first considers the humiliations and agony of Jesus but concludes with a prayer to Mary. The Latin work inspires 'Iesu cristes milde moder / stud biheld hire sone o rode' (Brown 1932: 83), in which the poet describes and addresses the Virgin, concluding 'Bring hus, moder, to thi sone' (64). The Latin also inspires a dialogue between Mary and Jesus on the Cross, 'Stond wel moder ounder rode / Bihold thi child with glade mode [*heart*]' (Brown 1932: 87–91). In each case the English poet presents Mary as both suffering human mother and divine mediatrix, creating a more intimate impression than the more detached Latin hymn.

In the *chanson d'aventure*, a French form, the poet describes wandering in the countryside, with a light-hearted encounter or an overheard conversation. Two English poems in similar style show how the form can be exploited for different purposes. 'Als i me rode this endre dai / O mi pleyinge' (Brown 1932: 119–20), better known by its burden 'Nou springes the sprai', tells of a maiden who cries vengefully of her betrayer:

als i me rode this endre dai	*as, a day or two ago*
o mi pleyinge,	*to amuse myself*
seih i hwar a litel mai	*saw; where; maiden*
bigan to singge:	
'the clot him clingge!'	*clod*
wai es him i louue-longinge	*woe; in*
sal libben ai,	*live ever*
Nou sprinkes the sprai,	*tender shoots*
al for loue icche am so seeke	*sick*
that slepen i ne mai.	

So begins a Harley lyric, 'The Five Joys of the Virgin' (Brook 1968: 65), of different mood. Although this could suggest an earthly beloved, the 'suetest of alle thinge' is the Virgin:

Ase y me rod this ender day	
By grene wode to seche play,	*seek entertainment*
mid herte y thohte al on a may,	*with heart I thought; maiden*
suetest of alle thinge	*sweetest*
Lythe, ant iche ou telle may	*listen; I you*
al of that suete thinge	*sweet*

The poet of 'Nou springes the sprai' seeks to comfort the maiden he meets; that of the Harley lyric seeks comfort as he recounts Mary's joys. Descriptions such as 'mi solas nyht ant day, / my ioie ant eke [*also*] my beste play, / ant eke my louelongynge' (14–16), equally fitting in a poem of worldly love, were used without incongruity in lyrics of love of the Virgin.

The young knight or clerk of a *pastourelle* meets a shepherdess, in a tale told from his point of view, and generally intends to seduce the girl. The economy of the English poems and their differences from the French works imply an audience already familiar with the form. The Harley lyric, 'De Clerico et Puella', 'My deth y loue, my lyf ich hate, for a leuedy shene [*bright*]' (Brook 1968: 62–3) is told entirely in dialogue, with no need for description, concluding with the sharp-tongued girl's sudden change in disposition. 'The Meeting in the Wood', 'In a fryht as y con fare fremede' (Brook 1968: 39–40), sets the conventional scene briefly before presenting the dialogue. The maiden at first rebuffs her suitor, fearing disgrace and her family's rejection, but she too has an abrupt change of heart. Allusions to clothes, offered and declined, recall the *pastourelle* 'L'autrier jost'una sebissa' (The other day beside a hedge) of the French troubadour Marcabru. As Rosemary Woolf remarks, these variations in the English *pastourelles*, and resemblances in mood and motif, suggest a poet familiar with French and Latin poems and audiences at ease in these languages.[15]

Macaronic Lyrics

Macaronic lyrics are products of an era of mingled languages, when Latin was used by the clergy, and French by the court, while Middle English was becoming an acceptable literary language. These lyrics combine languages in various ways. One might expect awkward effects, yet the contrary is the case. Thoughts are elegantly expressed, their meanings enhanced by the rhythms and timbres of the languages chosen. This stanza of a hymn to the Virgin (Brown 1932: 26–7) demonstrates the counterpoise of mood and language:

Of on that is so fayr and bright	*one*
velud maris stella	*like the star of the sea*
Brighter than the day-is light	*day's*
parens & puella	*mother and maiden*
Ic crie to the, thou se to me,	*look upon*
Leuedy, preye thi sone for me	*Lady*
tam pia,	*so holy*
that ic mote come to the	*might*
maria	

The movement of the English lines perfectly expresses the tender informality of an approach to Mary as mother and mediatrix, aptly balanced by the decorous Latin. The Latin phrases, in their conventional descriptions and titles for the Virgin, offer a doctrinal foundation to the spontaneity of the poet's pleas. The interplay of the liturgical and familiar languages is itself a metaphor for a progression from formal distance to the intimate affection typical of thirteenth-century Marian devotion.

Two poems that gracefully demonstrate particular characteristics of the three languages, in isolation and interaction, form the love letters known as '*De amico ad amicam*' (From the lover to his mistress) and '*Responcio*' (Reply). The first begins:

A celuy que pluys eyme en mounde	*To the one I love most in the world*
Of alle tho that I have found	
Carissima	*dearest one*
Saluz ottreye amour,	*may love grant greetings*
With grace and joye alle honoure	
Dulcissima	*sweetest one*

'*Responcio*' reads:

A soun treschere et special	*To her dear and special friend*
Fer and ner and overal	*far; near*

In mundo,	*in the world*
Que soy ou saltz et gré	*may he be in health*
With mouth, word and herte free	
Jocundo	*cheerful*

These stanzas and glosses come from texts emended by Leo Spitzer, who comments on the 'specific climate' of each of the languages and its contribution to their effects: 'The English – that of genuine feeling, the French – of conventional courtesy, the Latin – of epigrammatic terseness'.[16] Julia Boffey observes the 'chameleon-like nature' of these poems and the effects of their manuscript contexts. In the courtly MS Cambridge University Library Gg.4.27 they seem 'exquisitely courtly', but in the more clerical British Library MS Harley 3362 they appear 'exquisitely clerkly, and essentially comic; the gracefully turned sentiments here become exuberant learned play'.[17] Fluent harmony is an enjoyable and consistent characteristic of the macaronic lyrics. They seem paradoxically unforced, moving easily between languages in common use, to exploit particular characteristics for effect.

Lyrics of Earthly Love

Earthly love is both celebrated and deplored in lyrics of the castle and village, in voices that speak of distant courtly love the boisterous wooing of young country folk. The terms may be extravagant, and tell more often of sorrow than of joy.

Courtly love lyrics depict wretched lovers and the unattainable objects of their yearnings, but the lovers' sufferings often seem to be conventional rather than deeply felt. Their sentiments may be gracefully composed, as in this poem of love's wounds (Robbins 1955: 150):

Go hert, hurt with aduersite,	
And let my lady thi woundis see	*wounds*
And sey hir this, as y say the:	*tell*
far-wel my Ioy, and wel-com peyne,	*pain*
Til y se my lady Agayne.	

The complexities of this lyric's setting, for performance by three singers, argue for a polished performance rather than expression of the lover's pain, but the stanza elegantly displays his lavish despair in the conceit of the messenger, his wounded heart. A quatrain (Robbins 1955: 144) found among the traditional contents of a preaching book (MS Harley 7322) is affecting in its directness:

Me thingkit thou art so loueli	*I think*
So fair & so swete,	
That sikerli it were mi det	*surely; death*
Thi companie to lete.	*give up*

Many conventional figures recur in the lyrics of love. The lover's feelings of simultaneous love and hatred, and his wish to woo the lady in the form of a bird, have been inherited from Latin lyrics. Frequently he threatens to live in tormented sorrow in the woods, with play on the word *wode* meaning 'forest' and 'mad'.

Among the conventions is the detailed description of the beloved, beautifully exemplified in the Harley lyric 'Blow, Northerne Wynd' (Brook 1968: 48–50). The poem tells of a 'burde of blod ant of bon' (10), beginning with her 'lokkes lefliche [*beautiful*] ant longe' (13), selecting details of her face and figure, 'al / ywraht [*made*] . . . of the beste' (31–2). Her beauty extends to her disposition, famous as 'graciouse, stout [*stately*], ant gay' (38), and the poet compares her virtues to jewels and flowers.

Heo is coral of godnesse	*she*
heo is rubie of ryhtfulnesse,	*virtue*
heo is cristal of clannesse	*purity*
ant baner of bealte;	*banner; beauty*
heo is lilie of largesse,	*generosity*
heo is paruenke of prouesse	*periwinkle; prowess*
heo is solsecle of suetnesse	*marigold; sweetness*
ant ledy of lealte	*loyalty*
(45–52)	

The lover, by convention, must love from a distance, and he recounts his torments at Love's court. Love urges him to tell the lady and beg a remedy, 'er then thou falle ase fen of fote' (before you fall like mud from a foot) (74). The final stanza also conforms to custom in its account of the poet's sufferings:

For hire loue y carke ant care	*grieve*
for hire loue y droupne ant dare,	*languish; lie motionless*
for hire loue my blisse is bare	
ant al ich waxe won;	*become pale*
for hire loue in slepe y slake,	*become weak*
for hire loue al nycht ich wake,	
for hire loue mournyng y make	
mor then eny mon	*any*
(77–84)	

Happiness in love seems rare, welcome and refreshing. The Harley lyric 'Alysoun' (Brook 1968: 33; Brown 1932: 138–9) merely hints at the lover's sufferings, as in the first stanza:

Bytwene Mersh ant Aueril	
when spray biginneth to springe,	*leaves begin to grow*
the lutel foul hath hire wyl	*little bird has her will*
on hyre lud to synge.	*language*

Ich libbe in loue-longinge	*live*
for semlokest of alle thynge;	*fairest*
he may me blisse bringe;	*she*
icham in hire baundoun.	*I am; power*

Glimpses of spring and of Alysoun's beauty and the refrain's joyous rhythm counter these thoughts:

An hendy hap ichabbe yhent	*fair fortune I have received*
ichot from heuene it is me sent	*I know*
from alle wymmen mi loue is lent,	*taken away*
ant lyht on Alysoun	*settled*

Details of Alysoun's appearance glance at the traditional picture of medieval beauty, but without conspicuous exaggeration. The poet simply calls her 'feyrest may [*maiden*] in toune' (29), and notes 'hire browe broune, hire eye blake' (15), rather than the conventional grey of most ladies' eyes.

A Harley lyric of surprises is 'The Fair Maid of Ribblesdale' (Brook 1968: 37), which demonstrates absurdity by stretching conventions of description to their logical extremes. Formal style depicts a lady from head to toe, with radiant complexion, pink cheeks, grey eyes, white teeth and graceful figure, before listing details of her impeccably virtuous disposition. The Fair Maid, however, is introduced as one among 'wilde wymmen' (1). She shines brightly, 'Ase sonnebem [*sunbeam*] hire bleo [*face*] ys briht' (7), with her head like 'the sonnebeem aboute noon' (14). Incongruous details disturb the decorum of her description. Her eyes are 'gray ynoh' (16), and her eyebrows, 'bend [*arched*] and heh [*high*], / whyt bytuene ant nout to neh [*not too near*]' (25–6). The reader must decide how grey are her eyes and how far apart her eyebrows. Evenly arranged teeth within her conventionally smiling red mouth are 'white ase bon of whal [*whale bone*]' (40), which is also the material of the buckle on her indelicately enticing jewelled girdle (67). Strangest of all, her neck, resembling a swan's, is 'a sponne [*span*] lengore then y mette [*found*]' (44) and both of her arms 'an elne [*ell*] long' (52). The poet would rather be with the Maid 'then beon [*be*] pope' (46), and concludes that 'He myhte sayen that Crist hyme seye/that myhte nyhtes neh hyre leye / heuene he heuede here' [He might say that Christ looked on him who might lie near her at night – he would have heaven here] (82–4). The dazzling, wanton Fair Maid, of symmetrical but singular proportions, provokes laughter before love, and an irreverent approach to accustomed patterns of *descriptio*. The poem suggests irony and parody to several critics.[18] Unlike its subject, the lyric is elegantly formed, and reveals a clerical sense of humour, which may imply an origin at the Cistercian abbey near Ribblesdale.[19]

Another clerkly song seems to praise women (Robbins 1955: 35) in nine stanzas that offer generous compliments, beginning.

In euery place ye may well see,	
that women be trewe as tirtyll on tree,	*turtle dove*

Not lyberall in langage, but euer in secreet	*licentious; discreet*
& gret Ioye a-monge them ys for to be.	*joy*

Each is undercut by the burden 'of all Creatures women be best: / Cuius contrarium verus est' [*of which the truth is the contrary*]. The joke is best made and enjoyed by the clerks, whose facility with Latin allows the easy contradiction of the English lines. Many popular lyrics of clerks and love tell of betrayed maidens, as does that of the clerk Jankin and another Alison (Greene 1977: 278; Robbins 1955: 21–2), artfully interwoven with the mass she attends on Christmas Day.

Kyrie,' so 'kyrie,'
Jankyn syngyt merie.
With 'aleyson.'

As I went on Yol Day in owre prosessyon	*Yule*
Knew I joly Jankyn be his mery ton.	*by; note*
Kyrieleyson.	*Lord have mercy*

Jankin reads the epistle, and sings the Sanctus in polyphonic style, with notes – in Alison's homely metaphor of chopping vegetables – 'smallere than wortes to the pot'. He winks as he brings the 'pax brede' and affectionately treads on her foot. The last stanza tells her fate:

Benedicamus Domino, Cryst fro schame me schylde;	*Let us bless the Lord; shield*
Deo gracias therto: alas, I go with chylde!	*Thanks be to God*
Kyrieleyson.	

This is Alison's story, but the poet is clearly a clerk. Other lyrics of girls and clerks (usually a John, Jak, or Jankin) have similar endings, seen in 'This endyr day I mete a clerke, / And he was wylly [*crafty*] in his werke' (Robbins 1955: 18–19), 'Ladd Y the daunce a Myssomur Day' (Robbins 1955: 22–4), and 'The last tyme I the wel woke' (Robbins 1955: 19–20).[20]

Few lyrics of love are in a woman's voice, and fewer express the pleasures conveyed in 'Off seruyng men I wyll begyne, / Troly, loley' (Greene 1977: 272; Robbins 1955: 32–3). Among entries in a manuscript owned by the Findern family are some short poems now thought to be the work of women. The titles given by Robbins (1954), Beadle and Owen (1977), and McNamer (1991) reflect changes in criticism of these poems, and in critics' ideas of the poets, first as men employing the conventions of courtly poetry and later as women speaking without artifice.[21] 'Where y haue chosyn stedefast woll y be' (McNamer 1991: 303; Robbins 1954: 632) is called 'To his Mistress' by Robbins, 'Without Variance' by Beadle and Owen (1977), and 'A Woman Affirms her Marriage Vow' by McNamer. 'This is no lyf alas that y do lede' (McNamer 1991: 308; Robbins 1955: 156) has the titles 'The Cruelties of his Mistress' (Robbins 1954), 'Love's Sorrow' (Robbins 1955, Beadle and Owen) and 'A Woman's Lament' (McNamer). Of course, women's writing is not artless: McNamer acknowledges the playful nature of 'Whatso men seyn / Love is no peyn' (McNamer 1991: 304; Robbins 1954: 632), called 'Feigned Love' by Robbins and by Beadle and Owen, but 'Men "Make but Game"' by McNamer.

Carols

Carols make up one of the largest and most varied groups among the Middle English lyrics, but all share the common characteristic of the burden, and owe their origin to the round dance or *carole* and sometimes to pre-Christian customs. They were not confined to any religious season or usage, and Greene's collections show the range of their subjects and forms. They tell of the Nativity and the Passion, of Christ, the Trinity, the Virgin and saints, of love and mortality, of women and marriage. Some are satirical, and others convivial or political. Several have already been noted, and two others will illustrate some of the moods.

There are several carols to accompany the Boar's Head and to tell how to serve it (with mustard, bay leaves and rosemary). A macaronic carol (Greene 1977: 80) captures the grand and joyful atmosphere of the Christmas feast.

Caput apri refero	*I bring the boar's head*
Resonens laudes Domino	*Singing praises to the Lord*
The bores hed in hondes I brynge,	
With garlondes gay and brydes syngynge;	*birds*
I pray you all, helpe me to synge,	
Qui estis in conviuio	*Who are at the banquet*

An entirely different work is the 'Corpus Christi Carol' (Greene 1977: 195–6):

Lulley, lulley; lully, lulley;	
The fawcon hath born my mak away.	*falcon; mate*
He bare hym vp, he bare hym down;	
He bare hym into an orchard brown.	
In that orchard there was an hall,	
That was hangid with purpill and pall.	
And in that hall ther was a bede,	
Hit was hangid with gold so rede.	
And yn that bed ther lythe a knyght	*lies*
His wowndes bledyng day and nyght.	
By that bedes side ther kneleth a may,	*maid*
And she wepeth both nyght and day.	
And by that beddes side ther stondith a ston,	*stands*
'Corpus Christi' wretyn theron.	*'Body of Christ'*

Versions from the nineteenth and twentieth centuries maintain aspects of the bleeding knight and his virgin attendant (Greene 1977: 196–7). Greene's notes summarize many of the comments on this 'hauntingly beautiful carol', and he remarks that it 'has been subjected to more praise and more critical discussion than any other in this collection' (Greene 1977: 423). Critics have discerned Arthurian and eucharistic imagery, but Greene sees it as a political allegory in which the falcon represents Anne Boleyn (through her heraldic badge) winning Henry VIII from Catherine of Aragon and precipitating separation from the Roman Catholic church.

Mundane Lyrics

The idea of lyrics that are mundane seems a contradiction in terms, yet some poems in lyric collections deal only with aspects of everyday life, far from spiritual considerations or the emotional extravagances of courtly love. Some seem intended for oral transmission, whereas others reveal the influence of reading. They reveal the culture of their time, with its values and attitudes, and assist in the transmission of knowledge.

A charm to be said before a journey (Robbins 1955: 60) illustrates the intermingling of influences we might now call religious and secular, which to a medieval traveller were simply aspects of everyday life:

Here I ame and fourthe I mouste,	*am; forth I must {go}*
& in Iesus Criste is all my trust.	
no wicked thing do me no dare,	*injury*
nother here nor Elles whare.	*neither; elsewhere*
the father with me; the sonne with me;	
the holly gosste, & the trienete,	*Holy Ghost; Trinity*
be by-twyxte my gostely Enime & me	*between; spiritual enemy*
In the name of the father, & the sonne,	
And the holly goste, Amen.	
Amen.	

There are charms to protect against theft and fever. 'Seynt Iorge our Lady knygth / he walked day he walked noygth' (Robbins 1955: 61) invokes St George to protect a vulnerable horse from the Night Goblin. Medieval science is preserved in rhymes about teeth, bones, complexions, diet, bloodletting and even secrets of the philosopher's stone (Robbins 1955: 58–84).

Some poems about money attest to different levels of literacy in the audience. The following pithy verse (Robbins 1955: 81) could be heard and retained by any listener:

He that spendes myche & getes nothing,	*much*
And owthe myche & hathe nothing,	*owes*
And lokes in his porse & fyndes nothing	*purse*
He may be sorye and saie nothing.	
Quothe K. L.	

All may know that harsh truth, but a rhyme of the perils of lending (Robbins 1955: 81) is for a reader who enjoys the elegant arrangement of words on a page:

<table>
<tr><td>I had my
I lent my
I askyd my
I lost my</td><td>}</td><td>good</td><td>{</td><td>and my
To my
Of my
and my</td><td>}</td><td>ffrend</td></tr>
</table>

I made of my ffrend my ffoo:
I will be war I do no more soo.

The terse warning of the association of riches and litigation (Robbins 1955: 81) is still apt:

Pees maketh plente.	*peace; plenty*
Plente maketh pryde.	
Pryde maketh plee.	*{legal} plea*
Plee maketh pouert.	*poverty*
Pouert makethe pees.	

These verses are generally without imagery; one depicting the calendar as a tree is unusual (Robbins 1955: 62):

I wot a tree XII bowys betake,	*know; boughs; has*
LII nestys bethe vp ymad;	*nests; made up of*
In euery nest beth bryddys VII.	*are birds*
I-thankyd be the God of heuene	*wonderful*
And euery bryd with selcouth name.	

The best known of all Middle English lyrics is a mundane one, another rhyme of the calendar (Robbins 1955: 62):

Thirti dayes hath nouembir,
April, iune, and septembir;
Of xxviij^{ti} is bot oon,
And all the remenaunt xxx^{ti} and j.

This poem embodies the contraries of the genre. Although undistinguished artistically, it is the most enduring, known to countless speakers of English. It demonstrates the worth of the short poem as a means of recording and transmitting knowledge, preserved because it is useful. It also illustrates a kind of Middle English lyric that has nothing to do with music or emotion.

Resolution?

Is it possible to resolve all the contradictions of the poems classified as 'Middle English lyrics'? Some undoubtedly suggest music; some express emotion; some imply narratives; some inspire silent thoughts, or offer instructions, arguments or warnings. When such poems have only their brevity in common, it is hard to place all of them into one family, and short poems of other eras and cultures are not normally squeezed into one category in this way. Those not readily accommodated in a group such as carol or hymn can of course be simply called 'Middle English short poems', with descriptive additions to indicate their subject matter or style. Some are lyrical and memorable by any estimation, and most of them afford valuable glimpses of medieval English life.

See also 5 Women's Voices and Roles, 7 From Manuscript to Modern Text, 8 Translation and Society, 9 The Languages of Medieval Britain, 11 The Forms of Verse, 12 England and France, 19 Love, 24 Literature of Religious Instruction, 29 York Mystery Plays.

Notes

1 My thanks are due to Tom Burton, Dallas Simpson and Philip Waldron for their helpful comments on an earlier version of this chapter.

2 Anne S. Haskell, 'Lyric and Lyrical in the Works of Chaucer: The Poet in his Literary Context', in *English Symposium Papers, 3*, ed. Douglas Shephard (Fredonia, N.Y.: SUNY College at Fredonia), pp. 1–45 (2–5).

3 From the Harley lyrics Brown 1932: 131–63 offers religious and secular lyrics and a political piece ('A Song of Lewes'); Brook 1968 presents religious and secular lyrics; Robbins 1959: 7–29 prints political poems.

4 Facsimile as Richard Beadle and A. E. B. Owen (eds), *The Findern Manuscript: Cambridge University Library MS. Ff.1.6* (London: Scolar, 1977).

5 John Saltmarsh, 'Two Medieval Love-Songs Set to Music', *Antiquaries Journal* 15 (1935), 1–21.

6 See Woolf 1968: 4–5; and John Burrow, 'Poems without Contexts', *Essays in Criticism* 29 (1979), 6–32.

7 I generally use the lyric transcriptions of Carleton Brown, Rossell Hope Robbins, Richard Leighton Greene and G. L. Brook, but change thorn and yogh to their modern equivalents, remove brackets and italics, and add marginal glosses.

8 Thomas Jemielty, '"I Sing of a Maiden": God's courting of Mary', *Concerning Poetry* 2 (1969), 53–9, and Michael Steffes, '"As Dewe in Aprylle": "I Syng of a Mayden" and the Liturgy', *Medium Ævum* 71 (2002), 66–73, expand these points.

9 Greene 1977 describes such customs, in particular in 'The Carol as Popular Song' (pp. cxviii–cxxxviii) and 'The Carol and Popular Religion' (pp. cxxix–clix).

10 Summarized by Richard Osberg, 'A Note on the Middle English "O&I" Refrain', *Modern Philology* 77 (1979–80), 392–6.

11 R. H. Robbins, 'The Authors of the Middle English Religious Lyrics', *JEGP* 39 (1940), 230–8 (231). Among the Franciscans are some of the few lyric poets whose names are known, including William Herebert, John Grimestone, James Ryman and Thomas de Hales.

12 D. W. Robertson, Jr., 'Historical Criticism', in *English Institute Essays 1950*, ed. Alan S. Downer (New York: Columbia University Press, 1951) sees the Maid as the Virgin.

Joseph Harris, '"Maiden in the Mor Lay" and the Medieval Magdalene Tradition', *Journal of Medieval and Renaissance Studies* 1 (1971), 59–87 considers her identification with Mary Magdalene. Mahmoud Manzalaoui, '"Maiden in the Mor Lay" and the Apocrypha', *Notes and Queries* 210 (1965), 91–2, discerns the soul.

13 Richard L. Greene, 'The Maid of the Moor in the *Red Book of Ossory*', *Speculum* 27 (1952), 504–6 examines the lyric's context. Siegfried Wenzel, in 'The Moor Maiden – a Contemporary View', *Speculum* 49 (1974), 69–74, and 'A New Occurrence of an English Poem from the Red Book of Ossory', *Notes and Queries* 228 (1983), 105–8, discusses contemporary references.

14 References are to Robbins 1959 unless otherwise noted.

15 Rosemary Woolf, 'The Construction of *In a Fryht as Y Con Fare Fremede*', *Medium Ævum* 38 (1969), 55–9; repr. in *Art and Doctrine: Essays on Medieval Literature: Rosemary Woolf*, ed. Heather O'Donoghue (London: Hambledon, 1986), pp. 125–30.

16 Leo Spitzer, 'Emendations Proposed to *De amico ad amicam* and *Responcio*', *Modern Language Notes* 67 (1952), 150–5 (152).

17 Julia Boffey, 'The Manuscripts of English Courtly Love Lyrics', in *Manuscripts and Readers in Fifteenth-Century England: The Literary Implications of Manuscript Study*, ed. Derek Pearsall (Cambridge: Boydell and Brewer, 1983), pp. 3–14 (p. 14).

18 Arguments for parody are presented by: T. L. Burton, '"The Fair Maid of Ribblesdale" and the Problem of Parody', *Essays in Criticism* 31 (1981), 282–98; David Jauss, 'The Ironic Use of Medieval Poetic Conventions in "The Fair Maid of Ribblesdale"', *Neophilologus* 67 (1983), 293–304; and Daniel J. Ransom, *Poets at Play: Irony and Parody in the Harley Lyrics* (Norman, Okla.: Pilgrim, 1985). Theo Stemmler presents a contrary view in 'My Fair Lady: Parody in Fifteenth-Century Lyrics', in *Medieval Studies Conference Aachen 1983: Language and Literature*, ed. Wolf-Dietrich Bald and Horst Weinstock; Bamberger Beiträge zur Englischen Sprachwissenschaft, 15 (Frankfurt: Lang, 1984), 205–13.

19 Marion Glasscoe, 'The Fair Maid of Ribblesdale: Content and Context', *Neuphilologische Mitteilungen* 87 (1986), 555–7.

20 Neil Cartlidge, '"Alas, I go with chylde": Representations of Extra-Marital Pregnancy in the Middle English Lyric', *English Studies* 79 (1998), 395–414, offers further interpretation of these poems.

21 Because the edition by Beadle and Owen (see note 4) is a facsimile I have noted the more accessible sources in Robbins's and McNamer's articles.

References and Further Reading

Boffey, Julia 1985. *Manuscripts of English Courtly Love Lyrics in the Later Middle Ages*. Manuscript Studies, 1. Woodbridge: Brewer. Examines all aspects of the manuscripts, including their authors and the circulation of the poems.

Brook, G. L. (ed.) 1968. *The Harley Lyrics: The Middle English Lyrics of MS Harley 2253*, 4th edn. Manchester: Manchester University Press. Offers full texts and commentary on the Middle English religious and secular lyrics of this manuscript in their original form.

Brown, Carleton (ed.) 1932. *English Lyrics of the XIIIth Century*. Oxford: Clarendon Press.

—— 1939. *Religious Lyrics of the XVth Century*. Oxford: Clarendon Press.

—— 1952. *Religious Lyrics of the XIVth Century*, 2nd edn, rev. G. V. Smithers. Oxford: Clarendon Press. Brown's and Robbins's editions are generally considered the most accurate transcriptions of the Middle English lyrics. Each volume has a full introduction and presents each lyric in its original dialect.

Burrow, John 1982. *Medieval Writers and their Work: Middle English Literature and its Background 1100–1500*. Oxford: Oxford University Press. The chapter on lyric is particularly helpful for its discussion of the lyric voice.

Davies, R. T. (ed.) 1963. *Medieval English Lyrics: A Critical Anthology*. London: Faber, and Evanston, Ill.: Northwestern University Press, 1964. Supplies texts in a standardized dialect, with comprehensive glosses and notes and a full introduction.

Dronke, Peter 1996. *The Medieval Lyric*, 3rd edn. Cambridge: Brewer. Considers the relations and themes of lyrics in the Romance and Germanic languages.

Fein, Susanna (ed.) 2000. *Studies in the Harley Manuscript: The Scribes, Contents and Social Contexts of British Library MS Harley 2253*. Kalamazoo, Mich.: Medieval Institute Publications for TEAMS. Examines many aspects of the manuscript, and the works of all genres and languages.

Gray, Douglas 1972. *Themes and Images in the Medieval English Religious Lyric*. London: Routledge. Examines the development of the lyric tradition and its effects on the conduct of life, in a full, perceptive account of the religious lyric.

Greene, Richard Leighton (ed.) 1977. *The Early English Carols*, 2nd edn. Oxford: Clarendon Press. The most comprehensive of Greene's examinations of this genre, with introduction, texts, and detailed notes on the individual works.

Greentree, Rosemary 2001. *The Middle English Lyric and Short Poem*. Annotated Bibliographies of Old and Middle English Literature, 7. Cambridge: Brewer. Annotations of editions and critical works from 1839 to 1997.

McNamer, Sarah 1991. 'Female Authors, Provincial Setting: The Re-Versing of Courtly Love in the Findern Manuscript.' *Viator* 22, 279–309. Reads the lyrics from a feminist perspective, and finds fresh interpretations.

Robbins, Rossell Hope 1954. 'The Findern Anthology.' *PMLA* 69, 610–42. Offers traditional views on the lyrics, considered to be the work of male poets.

—— 1955. *Secular Lyrics of the XIVth and XVth Centuries*. 2nd edn. Oxford: Clarendon Press.

—— 1959. *Historical Poems of the XIVth and XVth Centuries*. New York: Columbia University Press. The *Secular Lyrics* and *Historical Poems* complete the collections begun by Brown. Robbins has also contributed many other editions and works of criticism, particularly in journal articles.

Spitzer, Leo 1951. '*Explication de Texte* Applied to Three Great Middle English Poems.' *Archivum Linguisticum* 3, 1–22, 137–65. Considers 'Blowe, northerne wynde', 'Lestenyt lordynges boþe elde and ȝyng' and 'I syng of a myden'.

Stevens, John 1961. *Music and Poetry in the Early Tudor Court*. London: Methuen; Lincoln: University of Nebraska Press. Relates the poems to the music and customs of the court, and provides texts and music from Tudor song-books.

Wenzel, Siegfried 1986. *Preachers, Poets, and the Early English Lyric*. Princeton, N.J.: Princeton University Press. One of Wenzel's many contributions to the examination of the lyrics found in sermons.

Woolf, Rosemary 1968. *The English Religious Lyric in the Middle Ages*. Oxford: Clarendon Press. Comprehensively considers the historical development of lyric themes in the thirteenth, fourteenth and fifteenth centuries.

24
Literature of Religious Instruction

E. A. Jones

Most readers, when they think of the 'literature of religious instruction', will think of Geoffrey Chaucer's Parson's Tale, and, having once thought of it, will turn over the leaf and choose another chapter of this Companion. Religious instruction does not have the appeal for the modern reader that it evidently had for the Middle Ages. Indeed, my title could be considered controversial: some readers will find 'literature of religious instruction' a contradiction in terms. The alternative descriptor 'works of religious instruction' may seem to capture better the utilitarian, penitential, drudging nature of religious didacticism. While I hope to show that this is not (always) a just description, it is worth pausing for a moment to note that the descriptor is also valuable in that, in a way which the Middle Ages seems likely to have recognized, it does not privilege textual over other forms of work, and also for its reminder that the work of religious instruction was accomplished through a range of means and media in addition to the literary.

The term 'literature of religious instruction' may be used in both general and specialized senses. There is little in the Middle English corpus which could not be described, at some level, as literature of religious instruction. Many of our key texts have been given, at one time or another, the label 'sermons in verse', with the reader left to supply the adverb 'merely'. Specialists in this field, however, reserve the term for a distinct class of texts whose genesis, content and form may all be accounted for with reference to the didactic or catechetic programmes of the late medieval church.

The Pecham Syllabus

Accounts of such programmes necessarily begin well before the period covered by this Companion, with the Fourth Lateran Council (or Lateran IV), called by the great reforming pope Innocent III in 1215. Among the most consequential of the Council's conclusions was the new emphasis it placed on the sacrament of Penance. Canon Twenty-one of the Council, known from its opening phrase as *Omnis utriusque sexus*, required everyone (male and female) over the age of discretion to make individual confession to his or her parish priest at least once a year, usually preparatory to receiving the Eucharist at Easter. But a meaningful confession requires a skilled confessor:

> The priest shall be discerning and prudent, so that like a skilled doctor he may pour wine and oil over the wounds of the injured one. Let him carefully inquire about the circumstances of both the sinner and the sin, so that he may prudently discern what sort of advice he ought to give and what remedy to apply, using various means to heal the sick person. (Shinners and Dohar 1998: 170)

The decree was thus part of a move, which had begun with the Gregorian reforms over a century earlier, towards the more complete professionalization of the clergy. It would henceforth not be sufficient for a priest simply to locate a sin in his penitential book and to read off mechanically the penance he was expected to impose. Now he was presented not with a sin, but with a sinner – an individual in need of an individual remedy – and in order to determine the most effective treatment he needed to consider a whole range of 'circumstances' contributing to (or mitigating) the sin:

> Quis, quid, ubi, per quos, quoties, cur, quomodo, quando,
> Quilibet observet animae medicamina dando.[1]

> [Who, what, where, by what means, how often, why, how, when, These things must be considered by anyone who is to give medicines for the soul.]

For these new challenges, the Council recognized, a well trained clergy was a pre-requisite.

The task of ensuring the sufficient education of parish priests was placed squarely with the bishops who ordained them. In England, a series of bishops, beginning with Richard Poore, Bishop of Salisbury, in statutes dating from between 1217 and 1219, put legislation into place to ensure that the clergy of their diocese was adequately educated to meet its pastoral responsibilities. As part of this process, several bishops specified the basic knowledge which priests might be expected to know, and to transmit to their parishioners.

The specification of such requirements was not new. Abbot Ælfric (?950–?1016) had declared that masspriests should preach to their parishioners on the subject of the *Pater noster* ('Our Father') and Creed (the Church's profession of faith, from *Credo* – I believe) and, at the beginning of the millennium, the 'Canons of Edgar' and the laws of King Cnut (1016–35) obligated every Christian to teach his children both prayers (Spencer 1993: 199, 206). With the *Ave Maria* ('Hail Mary'), these made up the three basic prayers of the Church which every Christian should know from childhood. In the post-conciliar period, however, this minimum syllabus was rapidly augmented: Richard Poore required his parish priests frequently to instruct their flock in the articles of the faith; the seven deadly sins were included by William of Blois, Bishop of Worcester, in 1229, and probably in 1239 Robert Grosseteste, Bishop of Lincoln, added to these requirements the Ten Commandments and the seven sacraments.

The culmination of this process, and the summation of thirteenth-century statute-making, was the set of Constitutions issued by Archbishop John Pecham of Canterbury at the Council of Lambeth in 1281. The ninth canon of Pecham's Constitutions was headed *De informatione simplicium sacerdotum* (Information for priests of simple learning), but is better known by its dramatic opening phrase as *Ignorantia sacerdotum*. 'The ignorance of priests', declared Pecham, 'casts the people down into the ditch of error, and the foolishness and lack of learning of clerics, whom the decrees of canon law order to teach the sons of the faithful, is all the worse when it leads to error instead of knowledge.' His remedy for such ignorance was to require every parish priest to expound four times a year to his parishioners, in English, 'without any fancifully woven subtleties', the basic tenets of the Christian faith (Shinners and Dohar 1998: 127, 128; Latin in Simmons and Nolloth 1901: 5–7).

Pecham's syllabus, with a fondness for sevens which we will encounter again, consists of seven elements (Shinners and Dohar 1998: 127–32):

I. The fourteen articles of the faith. These are the essential statements of Christian belief which are enshrined in the Creed. In fact, Pecham is unusual in specifying fourteen articles (of which, he says, seven pertain to the mystery of the Trinity, and seven to the humanity of Christ). Most other schemes have twelve articles, which equate with the twelve clauses of the Apostles' Creed, each of which, according to an early tradition, was uttered by a different apostle at Pentecost.
   (i) I believe in God the Father Almighty Creator of Heaven and earth
   (ii) And in Jesus Christ, His only Son, our Lord;
   (iii) Who was conceived by the Holy Ghost, born of the Virgin Mary,
   (iv) Suffered under Pontius Pilate, was crucified, dead, and buried;
   (v) He descended into hell; the third day He rose again from the dead;
   (vi) He ascended into Heaven, sitteth at the right hand of God the Father Almighty;
   (vii) From thence He shall come to judge the living and the dead.
   (viii) I believe in the Holy Ghost,
   (ix) The Holy Catholic Church, the communion of saints,
   (x) The forgiveness of sins,
   (xi) The resurrection of the body, and
   (xii) life everlasting.

II. The Ten Commandments (or Decalogue). The most important of the many injunctions issued by God to Moses on Mount Sinai in Exodus 20 (and reiterated in Deuteronomy 5), the Ten Commandments were recorded on two tablets of stone (the first three, relating to love of God, written on one tablet; the other seven, relating to love of neighbour, on the other) which were preserved in the Ark of the Covenant. There are slight differences in the order of the commandments between Exodus and Deuteronomy, and in how they are divided up between Roman Catholic and Protestant traditions. The Catholic arrangement is also the medieval arrangement:

(i) I am the Lord your God: you shall not have strange Gods before me.
(ii) You shall not take the name of the Lord your God in vain.
(iii) Remember to keep holy the Lord's Day.
(iv) Honour your father and your mother.
(v) You shall not kill.
(vi) You shall not commit adultery.
(vii) You shall not steal.
(viii) You shall not bear false witness against your neighbour.
(ix) You shall not covet your neighbour's wife.
(x) You shall not covet your neighbour's goods.

III. The two evangelical precepts. When asked by one of the Pharisees which was the greatest of the commandments, Jesus responded with two precepts: 'Thou shalt love the Lord thy God with thy whole heart and with thy soul, and with thy whole mind' and 'Thou shalt love thy neighbour as thyself' (Matthew 22: 35–40).

IV. The seven works of mercy. Six of these are taken from Jesus's account of the Last Judgement, when 'the Son of man shall come in his majesty' and separate the saved from the damned, 'as the shepherd separateth the sheep from the goats', according to whether they have fed the hungry, given drink to the thirsty, given shelter to strangers, clothed the naked, visited the sick, or comforted those in prison (cf. Matthew 25: 31–46). These good works are made up to seven by the addition of the burial of the dead from the list of Tobit's acts of charity: Tobit 1: 17–19 (not in the Authorized Version). In some schemes these become the seven works of bodily mercy, and are then complemented by the works of spiritual mercy: converting the sinner, instructing the ignorant, counselling the doubtful, comforting the sorrowful, bearing wrongs patiently, forgiving injury, and praying for the living and the dead.

V. The seven deadly sins 'and their fruits'. The seven are pride, envy, wrath, sloth, avarice, gluttony and lechery. The fruits of pride are 'boasting, ostentation, hypocrisy, schism, and other such things'; sloth includes spiritual sloth, 'from which a man takes delight neither in God nor in divine praises for him', and can lead to despair. One can commit the sin of gluttony by eating too often, or too finely, or too much, or in 'the overeager or voracious quality of one's eating', or 'in the over-meticulous and exquisite preparation of food meant to arouse the savory pleasures of taste'. (We may remember that St Augustine took his food only as a medicine.) 'It is not fitting', says Pecham, 'to say much about lust whose infamy infects every breath we take.'

VI. The seven principal virtues. These fall into two groups: the three theological virtues ('which were ordained by God') of faith, hope and charity (see 1 Corinthians 13: 13), and the four cardinal or principal virtues ('which were ordained by man for himself and his neighbours') of prudence, justice, temperance and fortitude. (Another tradition has a further set of seven 'remedial virtues' against the seven deadly sins: humility against pride, and so on.)

VII. The seven sacraments. Five ought to be received by all Christians: baptism, confirmation, penance (i.e. confession), the Eucharist (communion), and extreme unction (the anointing of the sick). The remaining two are received only by some, and are (generally speaking) mutually exclusive: holy orders and marriage – 'the first of which is appropriate for those seeking perfection, while the second is appropriate only for the imperfect'.

There was little here that had not previously appeared in the work of other thirteenth-century bishops, but Pecham's syllabus gained added force and influence by virtue of being the first statement of the elements of the faith to have been issued by an Archbishop of Canterbury for the whole of the southern province of the English church. This influence may be seen in its numerous derivatives and reissues during the remainder of the Middle Ages.

In 1357 the Archbishop of York, John Thoresby, issued a complementary syllabus for the northern province, which seems to have been based closely on Pecham. At the same time, 'forthi that nane sal excuse tham / Thurgh unknalechyng for to kun tham', Thoresby commissioned a certain John Gaytryge to translate his rudiments of the faith into English (Simmons and Nolloth 1901: 22). A rather different use of the syllabus was seen in 1409 when, as part of the repressive backlash against the Wycliffite heresy, Archbishop Arundel issued a set of constitutions which Nicholas Watson has called 'one of the most draconian pieces of censorship in English history' (Watson 1995: 826). Among other measures, Arundel demanded that all potential preachers should submit themselves to their bishop for examination and licensing, and that any (including parish priests) who had not been thus licensed 'shall simply preach in the churches where they have charge, *only* those things which are expressly contained in the provincial constitution set forth by John, our predecessor, of good memory, to help the ignorance of the priests, which he beginneth, "Ignorantia Sacerdotum"' (Watson 1995: 827, n. 14; my italics). Copies of Pecham's decree were to be available in every church in the province within three months. From Pecham's original intention, to specify the minimum knowledge that priests should impart to their parishioners, the syllabus had come to represent the maximum range of subjects that they might safely discuss with them (Watson 1995: 828).

There are documented reissues of *Ignorantia sacerdotum* in the fifteenth century by Bishop Stafford of Bath and Wells (1424–43) and Archbishop Neville of York (1465–76). It is the first item in William Lyndwood's analytical collection of English canon law, the *Provinciale* (1433), and also (in the form of Neville's reissue) in Thomas Wolsey's equivalent compilation of ecclesiastical legislation from the northern province made in 1518. The Pecham syllabus has been labelled 'the high point of pastoral legislation in medieval England' (Boyle 1955: 81), and this does not seem an exaggeration.

Teaching the Syllabus

It is one thing to specify a syllabus of the rudiments of the faith. To ensure its universal dissemination among both clergy and laity, as envisaged by Lateran IV, is quite another. In the event, the work of religious instruction was carried out through a wide range of means, some public and some private, both within the church and without.

For Pecham, as we have already seen, instruction in the syllabus was to come from the pulpit, although he gave few clues as to how such instruction might best be delivered. We should not automatically assume that it was expected always to come in sermon form. An earlier thirteenth-century legislator, Bishop Alexander Stavensby of Coventry (1224–38), for example, accompanied his stipulations on clerical education with a ready-made treatise on the deadly sins which was to be read 'by the priests to all their parishioners on every Sunday or other festivals' (Spencer 1993: 202). Pecham's more extensive syllabus was to be expounded once every quarter, although canonists left it to individual priests' discretion as to whether to attempt a full treatment in one sitting, or to spread the syllabus over several Sundays. In either case, preachers were presented with considerable difficulties in attempting to fulfil their dual responsibilities to the work of expounding the syllabus and to the exegesis of the gospel reading of the day. Some free-standing expositions of the syllabus (on the lines of Stavensby's earlier treatise) survive in books which we can place in the ownership of parish priests. These might have been read on any opportune Sunday or feast day. Some of the extant sermon-cycles incorporate treatments of one or more elements of the syllabus into their annual round of Sunday sermons, particularly in Lent and Advent. Others again take their cue from particular Sunday readings to expand upon one or more of the elements of the syllabus, although in these cases systematic coverage was difficult to achieve (Spencer 1993).

Priests were also encouraged to make use of the opportunity both to assess their parishioners' knowledge of the faith, and to offer some one-to-one tuition, which was offered by the confessional. Pecham did not refer to instruction during confession, though it had been a feature of earlier statutes (notably Grosseteste's of 1239). But his northern counterpart Thoresby is much more explicit about how, when and where his syllabus of 'sex thinges' is to be delivered, enjoining, in addition to regular preaching,

> . . . that parsons and vikers and all paroche prestes
> Enquere diligently of thair sugettes, in the lentyn tyme,
> When thai come to shrift, whethir thai kun this sex thinges,
> And if it be funden that thai kun thaim noght,
> That thai enȝoygne tham opon his behalue,
> And of payne of penaunce for to kun tham.
>
> (Simmons and Nolloth 1901: 22)

A particularly dramatic confessional encounter is recorded in the early sixteenth-century *A Lytell Geste How the Plowman Lerned his Pater Noster*. The rich and successful plowman begins well enough:

In lenten tyme þe parsone dyde hym shryue.
He sayd, 'Syr canst thou thy beleue?'
The plowman sayd vnto the preste:
'Syr, I beleue in Ihesu Cryste,
Whiche suffred deth and harowed Hell,
As I haue herde myne olders tell.'
The parsone sayd, 'Man, late me here
The saye deuotely thy Pater Noster,
That thou in it no worde do lacke.'
Than sayd the plowman, 'What thynge is that
Whyche ye desyre to here so sore?
I herde neuer therof before.'
The preest sayd, 'To lerne it thou arte bounde,
Or elles thou lyuest as an hounde.
Without it saued canst thou not be,
Nor neuer haue syght of the deyte.'[2]

The plowman would do anything rather than have to learn the prayer, and so the canny parson makes a deal with him. If he will give some of his wheat to forty poor men of the parish, the parson will pay him double its value, on condition that he can correctly report all forty men's names, in the correct order. The plowman agrees, and so the parson sends them – first *Pater*, 'feble, lene & olde', followed by *noster* and *qui es in celis*, right down to *Sed libera nos a malo* and, the last of them, *Amen*.

Few priests will have been as inventive as this. But if they wanted to enliven their instruction, or otherwise render it more memorable, in many cases they would have had to do little more than to gesture at the interior of the church in which they stood. The whitewashed austerity of our present-day churches gives little notion of the busy, colourful interior of the medieval church. And where the Elizabethan church had its Decalogue boards, with their sober listing of the Ten Commandments, the Apostles' Creed and the Our Father, the medieval priest had available to him the full array of the 'visual catechism'[3] afforded by medieval church decoration and furniture.

The articles of the faith appear, each one with the apostle responsible for its composition, in many surviving stained glass windows (one of the finest examples being the sixteenth-century series of windows in the south aisle of Fairford, Gloucestershire); the twelve apostles, each accompanied by his article of the Creed, were also a popular subject for the painted panels of the lower half of the roodscreen – the partition between the chancel and nave of a medieval church. The seven works of mercy feature in many surviving wall paintings, often arranged around a figure of Christ, or a man or a woman. A window at All Saints North Street in York depicts the donor, a former mayor of the city, performing each of six of the works of mercy (burial of the dead being omitted). The seven deadly sins also occur in many of the extant murals, often schematized in the form of a tree. A well-preserved example at Hessett (Norfolk) has a tree growing out of a dragon's mouth (figure 24.1). The tree divides into seven branches, each terminating in a smaller dragon's head. In the dragons' jaws stand figures personifying

Figure 24.1 The Seven Deadly Sins: wall painting at the church of St Ethelbert, Hesset, Suffolk. (Courtesy of *Medieval Wall Painting in the English Parish Church*, www.paintedchurch.org, and with thanks to Anne Marshall.).

the sins: at the top, Pride, a young dandy; below him, Lust, a couple in passionate embrace; Wrath, with dagger and whip and so on. Representations of the seven virtues are found less frequently, although in a wall painting at Cranborne (Dorset) a tree of vices is complemented by a tree of virtues. The commandments also seem to have been depicted rather rarely (though there is an extant window at Ludlow). The seven sacraments are a popular subject for windows: at Doddiscombsleigh (Devon), the sacraments are depicted on panels surrounding a central figure of Christ; red lines radiate outwards from Christ to the hands of the priests, showing them mediating the divine power. In the last century of the Middle Ages, the continuing vigour of catechetic art is manifested in some forty-seven sacrament fonts, almost all in East Anglia. The usual design of the font was an octagonal bowl, and this provided eight panels, on seven of which the sacraments were carved in relief, while the eighth usually showed Christ (often the

Crucifixion). These visual representations of individual elements of the catechetic syllabus were also combined into overall iconographic schemes, as for instance the series of windows at Fairford or Doddiscombsleigh, or the painted west wall of Trotton (Sussex), which has at its apex a scene of the Last Judgement while, flanking the west door and window, on the left side the seven deadly sins issue from seven dragons' mouths each of which emerge from an appropriate part of a man's body, and on the right a man is surrounded by seven medallions each portraying one of the works of mercy.[4]

Instruction was not, however, confined within the churches, even if, as we move outside them, it becomes harder to identify its forms and to trace the lines of its communication. We would like, for instance, to have more details of the York Creed and *Pater noster* plays that complemented the city's famous Corpus Christi plays, but whose texts have not survived. Although our knowledge of either play is sketchy, it seems likely that both were, like the Corpus Christi play, substantial processional performances which were put on by civic guilds rather than the ecclesiastical hierarchy. The Creed play is first heard of in the mid-fifteenth century, and was staged once every ten years, generally in late summer, until its final performance in 1535. The play may have taken the form of a series of pageants in which each article of the Creed would be associated with an apostle, a typologically related Old Testament prophet and a dramatic scene (as, for example, the fourth article – 'He suffered under Pontius Pilate' – might be illustrated with a tableau or play of the Crucifixion). *Pater noster* plays are recorded at York, Beverley and Lincoln, and seem similarly to have linked dramatic scenes to an exposition of the prayer. In York, the *Pater noster* play is mentioned first in 1389, and (like the Corpus Christi play) managed to continue in performance well beyond the Reformation; in fact, its final performance, in 1572 (three years after the last staging of the Corpus Christi cycle), proved to be the last instance of the medieval civic drama in the city.[5]

From public spaces to private instruction, the route from bishop's palace, to parish church, to parishioners' homes is mapped out clearly by Thoresby, who commands:

> That all that haues kepyng or cure undir him
> Enioygne thair parochiens and thaire sugettes,
> That thai here and lere this ilk sex thinges,
> And oft sithes reherce tham til that thai kun thaime,
> And sithen teche tham thair childir, if thai any haue,
> What tyme so thai er of eld to lere tham.
> (Simmons and Nolloth 1901: 20–2)

We have already seen that pre-Conquest legislation required parents to teach their children the basic prayers of the church. At baptism in the later Middle Ages, godparents swore to see to it that their godchildren were taught *Pater, Ave* and Creed (Duffy 1992: 53). In the mid-fifteenth century, Peter Idley's book of *Instructions to his Son*, incorporating material on the syllabus reworked from *Handlyng Synne* (see below), gives an indication of the range of information that the most diligent parents might aim to impart; it enjoyed some popularity, surviving in ten manuscripts. For the fortunate and male, parental or godparental instruction might be supplemented by education in the rudiments of the faith as part of the programme offered by cathedral song schools and other providers of primary education. Among the contents of the standard school reader of the period was a verse treatise on confession and the examination of penitents, the *Peniteas cito*, and surviving schoolmasters' books offer further evidence of the centrality of catechesis in elementary education (Gillespie 1979; Woods and Copeland 1999).

As we move into the private sphere, books increasingly play a leading role in the work of religious instruction. Before turning to a consideration of the texts involved in this process, we should briefly recall that the medieval book was a vehicle for visual as well as verbal communication. There is considerable correspondence between the iconography of church decoration and that of the manuscript page. The catechetic syllabus in particular lent itself readily to schematic or diagrammatic representation. One of the earliest post-Lateran aids for priests is Grosseteste's *Templum domini* ('The Lord's Temple'), which briefly summarizes the elements of the faith in tabular form. A popular device was the Wheel of Sevens or Seven Septenaries, which linked, within seven segments of seven concentric circles, the seven petitions of the *Pater noster*, the sacraments, the seven gifts of the Holy Spirit (wisdom, understanding, knowledge, counsel, fortitude, piety, fear of the Lord), the seven virtues, works of mercy, deadly sins and either the remedial virtues or sometimes the beatitudes (from the 'Sermon on the Mount' in Matthew 5: 3–11).[6]

The Literature of Religious Instruction

The earliest books complemented the efforts of Lateran IV to raise standards among the parish clergy by improving their knowledge of the faith they were supposed to teach, their understanding of the sacraments they performed and their skill as confessors. Some of the early confessors' manuals in fact pre-date the Council, and are indicative of the intellectual climate out of which *Omnis utriusque sexus* emerged. These manuals, and those produced in the aftermath of Lateran IV, are designed expressly to educate the priest in his new role as 'doctor of souls'.

In England, one of the most influential examples of the manual for parish priests is the *Oculus sacerdotis* ('The Priest's Eye'), written in Latin in the 1320s by William of Pagula, himself a parish priest in the diocese of Salisbury (Boyle 1955). The first of its three parts offers detailed guidance for confessors; the second part is an expansion and exposition of the Pecham syllabus, and the third is a more detailed treatment of the seven sacraments. It was a long-lived and popular work (over fifty manuscripts survive, and a more focused digest of it, the *Pupilla oculi*, was printed in 1510), but its Latin put it out of the intellectual reach of those priests whose ignorance legislators like Pecham were most concerned to remedy. For these, John Myrc, a regular canon of Lilleshall (Shropshire), wrote his *Instructions for Parish Priests* in the late fourteenth century. As he says,

ȝef thow be not grete clerk,
Loke thow moste on thys werk;
For here thow myȝte fynde & rede
That þe be-houeth to conne nede:
How thow schalt thy paresche preche,
And what þe nedeth hem to teche,
And whyche þou moste þy self be
(lines 13–19; Bryant and Hunter 1999: 52).

Myrc's short work is based on the *Oculus sacerdotis*, and is dominated by a series of detailed instructions on how to hear confession, which include advice as to the deportment of the confessor (pull your hood down over your eyes; remain impassive throughout the penitent's confession; don't spit) as well as a virtual script for him to read from as he examines the penitent on his knowledge of *Pater*, *Ave* and Creed, and enquires into his sins using as prompts the articles of faith, the Ten Commandments, the seven deadly sins, and venial sins associated with the five wits or senses, and offering the seven virtues as remedies against the sins.

Alongside, and gradually supplanting, these elementary guides to the priest's duties, was the group of texts usually labelled 'manuals of religious instruction'. These were often longer, more leisurely, compositions, less specifically directed towards the remedy of an immediate deficiency than something like Myrc's *Instructions*, more compendia of everything necessary for one to live well in the faith. As such, they contain much that will have been of use to the parish priest in carrying out his duties of preaching and instruction. But at the same time, they were not so specialized as to alienate the layperson. The period covered by this Companion is characterized by a rapid expansion of lay literacy, and accompanying this we find both a tendency for works originally intended for the clergy to reach lay readers (sometimes through translation and/or adaptation, sometimes simply through manuscript copying and changes in ownership), and also the growth of what we might think of as a self-help literature for the pious laity. This process culminates in the era of printing, which saw not only the wider dissemination of pre-existing texts of this sort, but also the emergence of designedly lay books like *The Kalender of Shepherdes*, with its mixture of almanac lore and the elements of the catechetic syllabus, all illustrated in pithy text and vivid woodcuts (Duffy 1992: 82–4).

This literature is of undoubted interest to the religious historian, but what is there here for the student of literature? First of all, there is a great deal of attractive writing, in a range of styles. The author of the immensely popular fourteenth-century *Speculum vitae* begins his (still unedited) poem in uncompromising fashion:

I warne yow first at the begynnyng
I wil make no vayn spekyng
Of dedis of armes ne of amours
As done mynstrels and gestours

> that makyn spekyng in many place
> Of Octavyan and Isambrace
> and of many other gestis.
> (quoted Duffy 1992: 69)

Or, as he might have put it, 'Thou getest fable noon ytoold for me' (ParsP, 31). Nevertheless, illustrative stories, or exempla, are one of the most characteristic and immediately appealing features of many of these texts. Some of the earliest and most celebrated appear in the expanded translation of the Anglo-Norman *Manuel des pechiez* composed by Robert Mannyng of Brunne in 1303, *Handlyng Synne*. Here biblical and hagiographical stories are found alongside tales like that of Florentius and his Bear and the Witch and the Cow-milking Bag, all told with a fine balance of economy and relish, and a talent for vivid narrative in octosyllabic couplets that we do not find again in English until Chaucer.

As well as stories, there is, as we might expect, much sombre impressiveness in this literature (the magnificent peroration to the Parson's Tale springs to mind); but there is also humour. This is from the account of gluttony in the fourteenth-century *Book of Vices and Virtues*:

> Þe tauerne is þe deueles scole hous, for þere studieþ his disciples, and þere lerneþ his scolers, and þere is his owne chapel, þere men and wommen redeþ and syngeþ and serueþ hym, and þere he doþ his myracles as longeþ þe deuel to do. In holy chirche is God ywoned to do myracles and schewe his vertues: þe blynde to seen, þe croked to gon riȝt, brynge wode men in-to here riȝt wytte, doumbe men to speke, deue men here herynge. But þe deuel doþ þe contrarie of al þis in þe tauerne. For whan a glotoun goþ to þe tauerne he goþ riȝt ynow, and whan he comeþ out he ne haþ no fot þat may bere hym; and whan he goþ þidre he hereþ and seeþ and spekeþ and vnderstondeþ, and whan he comeþ þannes-ward all þes ben y-lost, as he þat haþ no witt ne resoun ne vnderstondynge. (Francis 1942: 53–4)

But the literature of religious instruction is notable less for the originality of its content, than for the variety of ways in which that content is marshalled, organized and made available to the user. As Michael Sargent has pointed out, it was 'primarily in devotional literature that writers of English first faced the technical problems of the composition of book-length prose treatises'.[7] The solutions found by the authors of this literature range from the neat, to the elegant, to the baroque. Some we have encountered already, in other contexts. The linked groups of sevens which lent themselves to diagrammatic presentation also provide the structure for a number of works, including the *Speculum vitae*, which takes as its starting-point the seven petitions of the *Pater noster*, and relates these to the other sevens of the usual syllabus. The trees of vices and/or virtues that we have seen employed in church decoration also provide a structuring principle for several texts, the most important of them being the late thirteenth-century French *Miroir du monde*. With the contemporary and closely related *Somme le roi*, this was one of the most influential of all works of religious instruction; there are extant translations into most of the important European languages, and ten independent renderings into English (Francis 1942). The image of a tree and its branches allows the indulgence of the Middle Ages' passion for the division and subdivision of topics: the seven branches of the tree of death represent the seven deadly sins, while the many subsidiary sins are the branches and twigs that derive from each of the boughs. A complementary tree of life structures the discussion of the virtues. In versions of the *Somme*, like the *Book of Vices and Virtues*, the tree device is used alongside the memorable image of the seven-headed beast of the Apocalypse. The seven heads are the seven deadly (or capital) sins:

> Of þese seuene heuedes comen alle manere of synnes, and þerfore þei ben y-cleped heued vices, for þei ben heuedes of alle eueles and of alle synnes. (Francis 1942: 11)[8]

The late fourteenth-century *Desert of Religion* has (despite its name) a veritable allegorical forest, comprising trees not only of the seven sins and seven virtues, but also of the commandments, sacraments, works of mercy and much else besides, to a total of no fewer than twenty trees.

One of the most extravagant of allegorical schemes is that of the fifteenth-century *Jacob's Well*, a long and still only partially edited text which describes itself as a sequence of ninety-five sermons, though whether these 'sermons' were really designed for public preaching must be open to some doubt. It describes the making of a 'depe well' out of a 'schelde', or shallow, pit.

> Þis pytt is þi body, þat is clepyd be doctourys þe pytt of lust. Þis pytt is so schelde of kynde þat it hath no kyndely spryng to receyve þe water of grace. But þis pytt, þi body, hath v. entrees, þat arn þi v. bodyly wyttes: þi syȝt, þin heryng, þi smellyng, þi mowth, þi towchyng.

Through these 'entrees' comes in the water of sin. This water must first be removed using the scoop of penance.

> But ȝit, vnder þis watyr in ȝoure pytt, whan þe watyr is scopyd out, is deep wose [*ooze*] be-nethe, þat is, þe vij. dedly synnes, in whiche þe soule styketh sumtyme so faste þat he may noȝt out, but schulde peryssche . . . My werk & labour schal be to tellyn what is þis wose of þe vij. dedly synnes, & how ȝe schal caste out þis wose, ffirst wyth a skeet [*scoop*] of contricyoun, and after wyth a skauell [*spade*] of confessioun, and þanne schouelyn out clene þe crummys, wyth þe schouele of satisfaccyoun. (Brandeis 1900: 1–2)

After this, the water-gates of the five senses must be stopped, before digging deeper to expose the circumstances of sin. This done, 'þi welle is depe ynow in perfeccyoun for to springe watyr of grace', and it is time to begin building. Once the ground has been levelled with equity, and the foundations of the articles of the faith have been laid, building can commence, using a mortar made from a mixture of sand (consideration of sins), water (tears of compunction) and lime (Christ, 'why3t as chalk'). The plumb-line of truth keeps the walls straight. A ladder (charity) is next required, having as its rungs the ten commandments, the seven bodily and seven spiritual works of mercy, 'praysinges & thankynges to god and prayerys', the *Ave Maria*, and the seven petitions of the *Pater noster*. Finally, '3e muste haue a wyndas, & a roop, & a bokett, to drawyn vp watyr to drynke, be-cause 3oure welle is so deep' – the windlass being one's mind, the rope faith, and the bucket 'gostly desyre to all goodnes'. The well is now complete, whereupon

> drawe vp þis bokett of desyre fro all euyll to all goodnes, wyth þe roop of trewe beleue, and loke þi roop be threfold to-gedere in on, in feyth, hope, & charyte. And, be þe wyndas of þi mynde, wyth þis roop made my3ty in thre lynkes, schal be turnyd vp þe bokett of þi desyre in goodnes, fylled wyth watyr of grace, to contemplacyoun in heuenly thinges, in whiche contemplacyoun þou schalt, in þe bokett of desyre, drinke þi fylle of þe sweet watyr of grace. (Brandeis 1900: 3–4)

Although generally anonymous, these are all self-contained texts, evidently conceived as a whole. Such texts have tended to attract the majority of critical attention, at least until recently. They are, however, outnumbered by the large number of compilations which were put together to satisfy the increasing (and increasingly diverse) demand for literature of religious instruction. Some of these, like the compilation of fifteen short tracts known as *Pore Caitif*, were immensely popular, and serve to question the easy distinction between 'text' and 'compilation'; others are much more clearly *ad hoc* assemblages, designed for, and increasingly compiled by, individuals for guidance in their particular form of living, whether active or contemplative, priest, vowess, or proponent of the 'mixed life'. The latter conception of a life which, while lived in the world, could still allow access to the mysteries of contemplation, probably lies behind works like *Pore Caitif*, in which basic catechetic material on the Creed, commandments and *Pater noster* gives way, as the compilation proceeds, to more 'mystical' material from Richard Rolle and other authors.

Literature and Religious Instruction

With *Pore Caitif* we can start to see links between the literature of religious instruction and other categories of Middle English writing. I shall conclude by considering a few ways in which the project of religious instruction intersects with the more obviously literary elements of the Middle English canon.

There are, first of all, some texts which make sense only in the context of the catechetic syllabus, such as Dunbar's 'The Tabill of Confession', or the apparently cryptic lyric 'Kepe well X. & flee from sevyn; / Spende well V. & cum to hevyn'.[9] More commonly, however, the stuff of religious instruction is present incidentally in texts whose primary interest lies (more or less distantly) elsewhere. In addition to the many exempla which they provide (from Lucifer's deadly sin of pride onwards), the Mystery Plays offer several moments that rely on, even as they reinforce, their audience's knowledge of the elements of the faith: the ten commandments in the Moses plays, and again in Christ's encounter with the Doctors; the composition of the Creed in some Pentecost plays, and the works of mercy in the Last Judgement. At (arguably) the other extreme of the canon of Middle English religious literature, the arcane and intensely specialized writings of the 'mystics' reveal their foundations in the more mundane matter of religious instruction. Rolle's early *Judica me Deus* is in part a reworking of the *Oculus sacerdotis*, and even a work more central to his reputation as a mystical author, such as the *Form of Living*, contains a long chapter on the sins of thought, deed and omission. Much of the first book of Walter Hilton's *Scale of Perfection* is taken up with an analysis of the 'image of sin' in the soul, which is identified as the seven deadly sins and their circumstances.

The debt of the Ricardian poets to the catechetic tradition is also apparent. A searching (and probably professional) interest in the sacraments runs throughout the works of the *Pearl*-poet. Gower's *Confessio Amantis* is, of course, structured around a confessional inquisition in which Genius interrogates Amans on the sins he has committed through his five wits, and warns against the seven deadly sins and their subsidiaries. *Piers Plowman*'s confession of the seven deadly sins (B-text 5, expanded version in C-text 6) animates the personifications found in representations like that at Hessett,[10] to extraordinarily vivid effect (as, later, does Spenser in his procession of the sins: *Faerie Queene* 1.4); here the circumstantial analysis of sin is employed in the generation of narrative of striking particularity, as the sin of gluttony (for example) becomes Gluttony's sins (Woods and Copeland 1999: 395).

And so to the Parson's Tale, which emerges as a fine yet atypical example of the Middle English literature of religious instruction, sharing with the rest of that literature its situatedness in response to the confessional and catechetic demands of the post-Lateran Church, but differentiated by its single-minded narrowness of focus and almost total eschewing of the imagery and exempla which in other texts enliven the austere subject-matter. The least literary of the literature of religious instruction, it is 'the tale to end all tales' (Patterson 1978: 380).

See also: 3 Religious Authority and Dissent, 6 Manuscripts and Readers, 7 From Manuscript to Modern Text, 23 Lyric, 25 Mystical and Devotional Literature, 29 York Mystery Plays, 32 *Piers Plowman*, 33 The *Canterbury Tales*, 34 John Gower and John Lydgate.

Notes

1 Quoted by D. W. Robertson, 'A Note on the Classical Origin of "Circumstances" in the Medieval Confessional', *Studies in Philology* 43 (1946), 6–14 (p. 7). Cf. Woods and Copeland 1999: 393.

2 *IMEV* 8182; *STC* 20034. Printed London: Wynkyn de Worde, 1510. I have added modern capitalization and punctuation. See also Duffy 1992: 84–5.

3 See A. E. Nichols, *Seeable Signs: The Iconography of the Seven Sacraments 1350–1544* (Woodbridge: Boydell Press, 1994), p. 158. Nichols is referring specifically to seven-sacrament fonts, but the term seems equally applicable to a wider range of church furniture and decoration. I am very grateful to David Griffith for his help with the following paragraph.

4 See also the on-line database of British wall paintings of the sins and works of mercy maintained by the University of Leicester History of Art Department at www.le.ac.uk/arthistory/seedcorn/contents.html.

5 A. F. Johnston, 'The Plays of the Religious Guilds of York: The Creed Play and the Pater Noster Play', *Speculum* 50 (1975), 55–90; S. K. Wright, 'The York Creed Play in Light of the Innsbruck Playbook of 1391', *Medieval and Renaissance Drama in England* 5 (1991), 27–53.

6 For an illustration, see L. F. Sandler, *The Psalter of Robert De Lisle* (London: Harvey Miller, 1983), 52.

7 'Minor Devotional Writings', in *Middle English Prose*, ed. A. S. G. Edwards, (New Brunswick, N.J.: Rutgers University Press, 1984), pp. 147–75 (p. 163).

8 'Capital' is from Latin *caput*, head.

9 Spencer 1993: 196. The verse is *IMEV* 1817.

10 C. David Benson, '*Piers Plowman* and Parish Wall Paintings', *Yearbook of Langland Studies* 11 (1997), 1–38.

References and Further Reading

Anderson, M. D. 1995. *History and Imagery in British Churches*. London: Murray. A classic survey, first published in 1971, that is still a good introduction to its subject.

Barratt, A. 1984. 'Works of Religious Instruction.' In *Middle English Prose*, ed. A. S. G. Edwards (New Brunswick, N.J.: Rutgers University Press), pp. 413–32. A survey, primarily bibliographical, with an emphasis on identifying opportunities for editorial and other forms of research in this area.

Boyle, L. E. 1955. 'The *Oculus Sacerdotis* and Some Other Works of William of Pagula.' *Transactions of the Royal Historical Society* 5th ser., 5, 81–110. A foundational study on Latin pastoral manuals.

—— 1985. 'The Fourth Lateran Council and Manuals of Popular Theology.' In *The Popular Literature of Medieval England*, ed. T. J. Heffernan, Tennessee Studies in Literature, 28 (Knoxville: University of Tennessee Press), pp. 30–43. A concise and informative survey from one of the principal authorities in the field. The essay by Judith Shaw in the same volume is also useful.

Brandeis, A. (ed.) 1900. *Jacob's Well*, Part 1 (all published). EETS os 115. Inventive allegorical coverage of the Pecham syllabus in prose. Only the first half of the text is included in the edition, but valuable nevertheless.

Bryant, G. F. and Hunter, V. M. (eds) 1999. *'How thow schalt thy paresche preche': John Myrc's* Instructions for Parish Priests, Part 1 (all published). Barton-on-Humber: Workers' Educational Association. Text and parallel translation with introductory material on the clergy in late medieval England, suitable for the beginning student.

Duffy, E. 1992. *The Stripping of the Altars: Traditional Religion in England 1400–1580*. New Haven, Conn.: Yale University Press. Important and controversial assertion of the vigour of pre-Reformation Catholicism.

Francis, W. N. (ed.) 1942. *The Book of Vices and Virtues*. EETS os 217. Middle English prose translation of the hugely influential French *Somme le roi*.

Gillespie, V. (1979). '*Doctrina* and *predicacio*: The Design and Function of Some Pastoral Manuals.' *Leeds Studies in English* ns 11, 36–50. Stresses the variety of functions and audiences served by Middle English catechetic texts, with particular discussion of *Speculum Christiani* and Gaytryge.

Pantin, W. A. 1963. *The English Church in the Fourteenth Century*. Notre Dame, Ind.: University of Notre Dame Press (first published 1955). Chs. 9 and 10 in particular are still a useful survey of manuals of religious instruction in Latin and English.

Patterson, L. W. 1978. 'The "Parson's Tale" and the Quitting of the "Canterbury Tales".' *Traditio* 34, 331–80. Identifies the Parson's Tale as a manual for penitents, and argues that it provides an ending to the *Canterbury Tales* of appropriate, if negative, finality.

Raymo, R. R. 1986. 'Works of Religious and Philosophical Instruction.' In *A Manual of the Writings in Middle English 1050–1500*, vol. 7, ed. A. E. Hartung (New Haven: Connecticut Academy of Arts and Sciences), pp. 2255–378 and notes. Exhaustive bibliographical survey.

Shinners, J. and Dohar, W. J. (eds) 1998. *Pastors and the Care of Souls in Medieval England.* Notre Dame Texts in Medieval Culture, vol. 4. Notre Dame, Ind.: University of Notre Dame Press. An anthology of primary texts in translation illustrating all aspects of its topic, including (in ch. 5) the priest's responsibility for instruction.

Simmons, T. F. and Nolloth, H. E. (eds) 1901. *The Lay Folks' Catechism.* EETS os 118. Usefully brings together texts of Pecham and Thoresby's Latin decrees, Gaytryge's 'catechism', and an adaptation of it, formerly thought to be Wycliffite.

Spencer, H. L. 1993. *English Preaching in the Late Middle Ages.* Oxford: Clarendon Press. Ch. 5, 'The Preaching of *pastoralia*', is particularly valuable in this context.

Watson, N. 1995. 'Censorship and Cultural Change in Late-Medieval England: Vernacular Theology, the Oxford Translation Debate, and Arundel's Constitutions of 1409.' *Speculum* 70, 822–64. One of a series of essays defining Watson's notion of 'vernacular theology', and arguing for Arundel's Constitutions as a watershed in the production of Middle English religious texts.

Woods, M. C. and Copeland, R. 1999. 'Classroom and Confession.' In *The Cambridge History of Medieval English Literature*, ed. D. Wallace (Cambridge: Cambridge University Press), pp. 376–406. A suggestive linking of pedagogical and penitential discourses, with a Foucauldian slant.

25
Mystical and Devotional Literature

Denise N. Baker

Writing more than a century ago, Dean Inge observed that no English word 'has been employed more loosely than "Mysticism"'. This statement is as true today as it was in 1899 when he published *Christian Mysticism*. *Mystical* continues to be employed even when words like *mysterious, vague, spiritual, occult*, or *weird* are more appropriate to the context. The second term in the title of this chapter, *devotional*, is less often misused only because it is seldom used by non-specialists. A discussion of mystical and devotional literature should obviously begin with an attempt to identify the kinds of texts under consideration.

Such an explanation is not easy, though, because during the late medieval period neither word had the specific meaning it does in this chapter. During the fourteenth and fifteenth centuries, *mystical* referred to the symbolic or figurative meaning of the Bible. The texts identified as mystical in this chapter would have been referred to as contemplative and placed in the Christian tradition of spiritual practices reserved for those in contemplative rather than active life, that is, professed religious. The goal of this spiritual programme is to achieve a heightened consciousness of God described by such terms as union, presence, ecstasy or deification. Rather than focusing on philosophical questions about the nature of mysticism or theological debates about the orthodoxy of particular mystics, this chapter will concentrate on five authors known as the Middle English mystics: Richard Rolle, Walter Hilton, the anonymous author of the *Cloud of Unknowing* and related texts, Julian of Norwich and Margery Kempe.

The term *devotional* refers to an object or practice that stirs a religious emotion of awe, reverence or piety. As Richard Kieckhefer explains, devotional Christianity was so diffuse in the late Middle Ages that is it difficult to define precisely. He places it midway on the conceptual map between the liturgical and the contemplative. Performed by either individuals or groups with variations in structure and differing degrees of official sanction, devotions are defined by their objects rather than by their forms (Kieckhefer 1987: 76). In addition to practices like pilgrimage or objects like relics, devotionalism also manifests itself in art and literature; some examples of the latter will be discussed in the second part of this chapter.

The study of mystical and devotional literature has flourished in the last two decades for several reasons. The initial impetus to examine this literature more carefully came from feminist scholars, because the earliest texts attributed to women in medieval England were by the visionaries Julian of Norwich and Margery Kempe. Likewise, guides for women in religious life, either nuns or anchorites, were written by Richard Rolle and Walter Hilton. At the same time, other scholars were revising their approach to mystical and devotional texts. Rather than debating whether a text describes an authentic mystical experience or dismissing devotional texts as evidence of the overwrought sentimentality of late medieval religion, they focused on the language and circulation of these texts.

Analyses of the language of mystical and devotional texts have been both aesthetic and cultural. As Bernard McGinn astutely observes, these works are as metaphorically complex as those traditionally regarded as literary:

> Mystical masterpieces . . . are often close to poetry in the ways in which they concentrate and alter language to achieve their ends . . . [and employ] verbal strategies in which language is used not so much informationally as transformationally, that is, not to convey a content but to assist the hearer or reader to hope for or to achieve the same consciousness. (McGinn 1991: xiv, xvii)

The figurative language and rhetorical strategies of mystical and devotional texts thus merit careful study. The works of the *Cloud* author and Julian of Norwich, in particular, explore theological issues with a poetic resonance that continues to entrance readers today. The *Cloud* author, in fact, explicitly discusses the challenge of expressing an experience of transcendence that is beyond words and warns his disciple,

> & þerfore beware þat þou conceyue not bodely þat þat is mente goostly, þof al it be spokyn in bodely wordes, as ben þees: UP or DOUN, IN or OUTE, BEHINDE or BEFORE, or ON O SIDE or ON OÞER.[1]

Much devotional literature also exhibits remarkable linguistic complexity. The artistry of mystical and devotional literature undoubtedly belongs within the purview of literary and rhetorical analysis.

Moreover, as critical attention has turned from a concentration on the aesthetic qualities of literature to a broader focus on culture, the importance of mystical and devotional texts to our understanding of late medieval England has become apparent. Pointing out the anachronism of the exclusionary category 'Middle English mystics', Nicholas Watson argues,

> the fourteenth-century 'mystics' are part of a huge cultural experiment involving the translation of Latin and Anglo-Norman texts, images, conceptual structures – the appa-

> ratus of *textual authority* – into what contemporary commentators termed the 'barbarous' mother tongue, English: a language whose suitability as the vehicle for complex thought of all kinds was a matter for serious doubt. As such, Rolle, the *Cloud* author and the rest are involved in the same socio-political discussion as Chaucer, Langland and the Lollards. (Watson 1999: 544)

Mystical and devotional works must thus be studied in conjunction with other contemporary texts to provide an accurate panorama of the development of the language and the culture of medieval England. Both the texts originally written in Middle English and those translated from Latin or Continental sources contributed to the development of a vernacular theology which enabled new authors and audiences to participate in the expression of religious ideology.

Mystical and devotional literature in the vernacular also provides significant evidence about the emergence of a literate laity whose interest in these texts is preserved in records of ownership and patronage. Although few individuals owned books in late medieval England, Margaret Deanesly's analysis of 7,600 medieval wills reveals that those vernacular books bequeathed were more often works of piety or devotion than romances or chronicles. According to these records, Nicholas Love's *Mirror of the Blessed Life of Jesus Christ* was probably the most popular book of the fifteenth century; and Rolle and Hilton the most popular authors (Deanesly 1920: 349, 352–6). Studies of manuscript production and ownership have revealed that contemplative and devotional texts originally composed for spiritual elites, such as monastics or recluses, circulated widely in the vernacular among the fifteenth-century laity.

Late medieval women, either in convents or households, were often the readers or, occasionally, the writers of such mystical and devotional literature. The fifteenth-century libraries of female religious communities, especially the Bridgettines of Syon, the Benedictines of Barking and the Dominicans of Dartford, included a more impressive collection of such vernacular literature than those of their male counterparts, most likely because few women could read Latin (Bell 1995: 76). Laywomen were also familiar with many of these same texts. Cicely, Duchess of York and mother of Edward IV and Richard III, would listen during dinner to readings from Hilton's *Mixed Life*, or a translation of Pseudo-Bonaventure's *Meditationes vitae Christi*, or the lives of saints recorded in the *Golden Legend*, or the accounts of continental visionaries like Mechtild of Hackeborn, Catherine of Siena and Bridget of Sweden (Hutchison 1989: 225). Even the illiterate Margery Kempe reports that her spiritual adviser read such books to her.

Many mystical texts were, in fact, composed by women. On the Continent, influential visionaries range from Hildegard of Bingen in the twelfth century through a multitude of women writing in the vernacular in the subsequent three centuries, including Bridget of Sweden and Catherine of Siena, whose works were translated into Middle English in the fifteenth century. Unlike their Continental counterparts, the English writers Julian of Norwich and Margery Kempe, whose books each survive in only one medieval manuscript, were not widely recognized as authors during their lifetimes. None the less, they were able to compose their books because of the unique nature of mystical and visionary experience as a direct manifestation of divine authorization.

Mystical Literature

The earliest member of the group known as the Middle English mystics, Richard Rolle, died in 1349, probably a victim of the bubonic plague or Black Death. Although his life falls outside the period 1350–1500, Rolle must be included in this study because he was not only the first but also the most prolific and popular of the so-called Middle English mystics. His works survive in nearly 500 manuscripts dating from 1390 to 1500 and excerpts from his writings are included in such compilations as the *Pore Caitif* and the *Disce mori*. Writing in both Latin and English, Rolle produced texts in many of the genres of religious literature: translations of and commentaries on various books of the Bible, expositions of prayers, a pastoral manual, autobiographical treatises, epistolary guides for contemplatives, meditations on the Passion of Christ, lyric poems and miscellaneous short prose pieces. Rolle's English works fall into the last four categories and two of his Latin texts, the *Incendium amoris* and the widely circulating *Emendatio vitae*, were translated into English in the fifteenth century.

In the autobiographical passages of the *Incendium amoris*, Rolle recounts his reception of the three unique attributes of his mysticism: *fervor* (fire), *canor* (song) and *dulcor* (sweetness). The prologue begins with a report of his initial experience of the fire of love:

> I cannot tell you how surprised I was the first time I felt my heart begin to warm. It was real warmth too, not imaginary, and it felt as if it were actually on fire. I was astonished at the way the heat surged up, and how this new sensation brought great and unexpected comfort. I had to keep feeling my breast to make sure there was no physical reason for it! But once I realized that it came entirely from within, that this fire of love had no cause, material or sinful, but was the gift of my Maker, I was absolutely delighted, and wanted my love to be even greater.[2]

In chapters fifteen and thirty-one Rolle offers similarly dramatic reports of his personal reception of *canor* and *dulcor*. As we shall see, his emphasis on these sensations and his conflation of literal and figurative language influence later readers like Margery Kempe but prove controversial for Walter Hilton and the *Cloud* author.

Near the end of his life Rolle turns from Latin to English to compose three epistles for female disciples: *Ego dormio* for a nun at Yedingham; the *Commandment* for a nun from Hampole; and the *Form of Living* for Margaret Kirby, who was enclosed as an anchorite in December 1348. Since the early thirteenth century, vernacular works of spiritual guidance, like the *Ancrene Riwle* and the *Wooing of our Lord*, were written for female religious who could not read Latin. Rolle follows in this tradition, but rather than concentrating exclusively on ascetic and affective spirituality, as these earlier works do, he acknowledges that women in the contemplative life could achieve mystical union with God. His first two epistles, addressed to nuns at early stages in their spiritual development, are very brief and emphasize a turning away from the world in order to pursue the love of God. *The Form of Living*, composed about a year before his death, presents a more systematic treatment of the stages leading to the perfection of contemplation and provides much of the same advice as Rolle's most popular text, the Latin *Emendatio vitae*, probably addressed to the secular clergy.

Consisting of twelve chapters in most manuscripts, *A Form of Living* divides into two parts: the warnings against sin in the first six chapters and the explanations of love and contemplation in the last six. The first part does not provide a thorough analysis of the seven deadly sins as the *Ancrene Riwle* and the first book of Hilton's *Scale of Perfection* do, but rather catalogues various temptations and advises moderation in ascetic discipline. The second part focuses on love, identifying three degrees of love and associating the highest, singular love with the experience of fire and song, echoing passages in the *Incendium amoris*. In the final chapter Rolle repeats the typical medieval distinction between those in active and contemplative lives. Lay people and secular clergy in the first category are bound to obey the commandments and perform works of mercy. Those in religious life, either monastic or reclusive, devote themselves to contemplation, itself divided into a lower and a higher grade. The lower grade involves an affective piety, developed through meditation and prayer, that leads to purgation of sin; the higher grade involves a more intense concentration on God, culminating in the experience of the fire of love and a contemplative vision of heaven. By concluding with this discussion of the highest grade of contemplation, Rolle's *Form of Living*, unlike earlier anchoritic guides, boldly asserts that women in religious life can proceed beyond the ascetic and affective stages to experience the highest degree of perfection, contemplative union with God.

Despite the wide circulation of Rolle's works in late medieval England, his sensational mysticism remains outside the mainstream. The three authors who wrote in the last quarter of the fourteenth century – Walter Hilton, the author of the *Cloud of Unknowing* and related texts and Julian of Norwich – are today considered the pre-eminent Middle English mystics. Although each expresses a unique perspective in a distinctive style, all three situate their texts within a Christian tradition influenced by neoplatonism. The two branches of this tradition are represented by Augustine and Pseudo-Dionysius, the name scholars give to a fifth- or sixth-century Syrian wrongly identified in the Middle Ages as the Athenian whose conversion in response to Paul's preaching on the Areopagus is reported in Acts 17: 34. Although they often use the same metaphors of ascent, light and darkness, the Augustinian and Pseudo-Dionysian paradigms of contemplation involve contrasting assumptions about the nature of the relationship between the human and the divine.

Hilton is a traditional Augustinian who practises a cataphatic or affirmative process of contemplation; he presents a programme of penance and meditation to prepare for the spiritual movement inward to discover the *imago dei* residing in the higher reason. The *Cloud* author, in contrast to Hilton, exemplifies an apophatic or negative process because he insists on an ontological divide, a darkness or cloud of unknowing, between God and the created order. Therefore, rather than seeking the image of God immanent in the human soul, as Hilton does, the *Cloud* author concentrates on ridding the mind of all thought of created things in hopes of glimpsing the absolutely transcendent God. During the last quarter of the fourteenth century, both these authors composed works of guidance in the genre of the *Ancrene Riwle* and Rolle's *Form of Living* that present their contrasting programmes for achieving contemplative union with God. Hilton writes ostensibly for a nun and the *Cloud* author for a male religious, but both disciples are about to embark upon the solitary life.

Despite the contrasts between their two different traditions of Christian mysticism, the Augustinian and the Pseudo-Dionysian, Hilton and the *Cloud* author address many of the same issues in the *Scale of Perfection* and the *Cloud of Unknowing*. These similarities bring John P. H. Clark to conclude 'that there was some degree of interchange, and of mutual criticism and enlightenment, between Hilton and the author of the *Cloud*' (Clark 1991: 25). Clark indicates that the *Cloud* author's three allusions to another man's work refer to the first book of the *Scale*, which was finished by the mid-1380s; and Hilton's second book, finished just before his death in 1396, responds to some of the *Cloud* author's positions. Moreover, Hilton and the *Cloud* author may have lived in close proximity to each other. After being educated at Cambridge, with some training in the law, Hilton entered Thurgarton Priory of the Augustinian Canons in Nottinghamshire in the mid-1380s. Although we have no biographical information about the *Cloud* author, the earliest extant manuscripts of his works are in a north-east Midlands dialect, indicating that he may have resided in the same area of England as Hilton.

Hilton and the *Cloud* author both subscribe to some fundamental tenets of the medieval contemplative tradition. Like Rolle, both distinguish two states of life, that of the active laity and clergy who minister to them and that of the contemplatives, cenobites or solitaries who have withdrawn from the world to devote themselves to the act of contemplation. Hilton and the *Cloud* author also agree with Rolle that there are different levels of contemplation, but they identify three rather than two stages. Although they disagree about the first phase, with Hilton regarding it as knowledge of God acquired by reason without the special affection of devotion and the *Cloud* author identifying it as works of charity, they concur that those in active and contemplative lives can both participate in the second or devotional stage. The latter, like Rolle's lower grade of contemplation, involves contrition stirred by meditation on one's sins and compassion evoked by meditation on the manhood of Christ; Hilton regards this second level as affection without understanding. Both also insist, with Rolle, that the highest phase is reserved for those in contemplative life except in very rare cases. Despite these similarities with Rolle, both Hilton and the *Cloud* author are suspicious of his rather sensational accounts of *fervor, canor* and *dulcor.* Although these second generation authors use the metaphor of the fire of love, they warn their disciples not to mistake figurative for literal language and they criticize various types of false spirituality, some of which seems reminiscent of Rolle. The *Cloud* author's descriptions of the pretensions of immature contemplatives are especially amusing and his analysis of the deficiencies of language for discussing ineffable spiritual experiences is remarkably profound.

Hilton and the *Cloud* author, however, write for disciples at different stages of spiritual development. In Book 1 of the *Scale of Perfection* Hilton addresses beginners in the second stage of contemplation, including those in active life, the audience for whom he also writes the *Mixed Life*. He indicates three means for advancement: reading, meditation and prayer. These devotional practices, which the *Cloud* author also associates with the second stage of contemplation, are the focus of *Scale I*. Like the *Ancrene Riwle*, Hilton concentrates on analysing the seven deadly sins in order to destroy the image of sin obscuring the image of God within the soul; such purgation is the first rung on the *scala* or ladder to perfection. In Book 2 of the *Scale*, completed almost a decade later, Hilton changes the organizational schema from the three levels of contemplation to two stages of reform, in faith and in feeling. The former, corresponding to the first two levels practised by beginners and those proficient in contemplation, is sufficient for salvation; the latter is the highest state of perfection usually achieved only by those in contemplative life. After reiterating material from the first book, Hilton focuses on the higher rungs of the spiritual ladder leading from reform in faith to reform in feeling: entry into a luminous darkness by abandoning the world and turning to God, and meditation on the humanity of Jesus. The ultimate goal, however, is an affectionate understanding of divinity which occurs when the soul is conformed to and united with the image of the Trinity in a state of intellectual illumination and affective rapture.

Rather than concentrating on the earlier stages of contemplation, the *Cloud* author focuses primarily on the last step before union. As he warns in the prologue, his book is only for a contemplative who wishes to reach the state of perfection. He acknowledges the importance of the process Hilton sets forth, beginning with purgation of sin and employing reading, meditation and prayer as the means to contemplation. However, he refers his reader to another man's book, probably Hilton's, for an explanation of these initial steps. The *Cloud* author instead describes the twofold process of apophatic or negative contemplation involving the cloud of forgetting and the cloud of unknowing. Despite the similarities of terminology, this first cloud is very different from Hilton's luminous darkness because it is a metaphor for the process of emptying the mind of all thoughts of the created order, not just withdrawal from the world. Rather than bringing about illumination or opening of the inner eyes of the soul to God, as Hilton's luminous darkness does, the cloud of forgetting allows the contemplative to perceive

> a derknes, & as it were a cloude of vnknowyng, þou wost neuer what, sauyng þat þou felist in þi wille a nakid entent vnto God. Þis derknes & þis cloude is, howsoeuer þou dost, bitwix þee & þi God, & letteþ [*hinders*] þee þat þou maist not see him cleerly by liȝt of vnderstonding in þi reson, ne fele him in swetnes of loue in þin affeccion. & þerfore schap þee to bide in þis derknes as longe as þou maist, euermore criing after him þat þou louest; for ȝif euer schalt þou fele him or see him, as it may be here, it behoueþ alweis be in þis cloude & in þis derknes.[3]

The *Cloud* author asserts that this cloud of unknowing between the transcendent deity and the soul can be pierced only by love. The contemplative must therefore direct all his attention towards God by concentrating upon a single word, like *love* or *sin*, in the hope that he will experience stirrings or blind impulses 'speedly springing unto God as spacle fro þe cole'.[4] Rather than seeking God through introspection, the contemplative must remain in the cloud of unknowing while he waits for the transcendent deity beyond human conception to 'seend oute a beme of goostly liȝt, peersyng þis cloude of vnknowing þat is bitwix þee & hym, & schewe þee sum of his priuete, þe whiche man may not, ne kan not, speke'.[5] Depite his acute analysis and arresting metaphors, the *Cloud* author, influenced by Thomas Gallus's interpretation of Pseudo-Dionysius, believes that intellect and imagination only impede the contemplative's efforts. Even though he and Hilton both use the traditional figurative language of ascent, light and darkness, their apophatic and cataphatic methods are very different.

Julian of Norwich and Margery Kempe, the first English women identified as authors, like the female mystics on the continent, write about their own divinely inspired experiences, albeit in very different genres and styles, rather than producing works of spiritual guidance for others, as their male counterparts do. Both defend themselves from criticism for violating St Paul's prohibition against women speaking in public about spiritual issues by claiming divine authorization. Although Julian revises her short text extensively over twenty or more years to produce a long text that is six times the length of the original version, both women only compose one book which survives in a single medieval manuscript. Since Julian of Norwich and Margery Kempe are discussed in separate chapters, I only wish to address their relation to the male writers on contemplation who were their contemporaries.

Julian of Norwich writes in the same Augustinian tradition as Walter Hilton. It is sometimes assumed that she knew the *Scale of Perfection*. However, she was probably working on the two versions of her *Book of Showings* at the same time he was composing the two books of the *Scale*. None the less, Julian is conversant with the contemplative tradition that Hilton presents. Prior to the visionary experience in 1373, she had prayed for three gifts: a vision of Christ's Passion, a physical illness that would bring her to the brink of death, and the metaphoric wounds of contrition, compassion and wilful longing for God. The first two items in the final triad obviously result from the meditation on one's sins and on the Passion of Christ that Hilton identifies as the second level of contemplation; the third wound, longing for God, is the great desire and good will that, according to Hilton, knits Jesus to the human soul. Julian's revelations can be loosely grouped into three categories corresponding to these three metaphoric wounds. The visions of Christ's suffering during the Passion which predominate in the first twelve revelations incite her compassion and can be related to the visualization that occurs during meditation on the humanity of Jesus. The auditory showings about the nature of sin prevalent in Revelation Thirteen correspond to the contrition that results from meditation on one's sins. The ghostly or spiritual showings of the last three revelations are concerned with humankind's essential relationships with the persons of the Trinity. These last two topics are the focus of the substantial additions that Julian makes to the long text. Her development of an original theodicy or solution to the problem of evil in Revelation Thirteen and her creative exploration of the concept of Jesus as a mother in Revelation Fourteen attest to Julian of Norwich's maturation, over the course of twenty or more years during which she revised her *Book of Showings*, from a devout visionary to a sophisticated theologian who counteracts the emphasis on sin and a patriarchal deity in the Augustinian tradition.

About thirty years younger than Julian of Norwich, Margery Kempe had access to both devotional and contemplative literature even though she was an illiterate lay-woman. By the time she visited Julian in Norwich around 1413, she was familiar with books by Hilton and Bridget of Sweden, as well as Rolle's *Incendium amoris* and the Pseudo-Bonaventure's *Stimulus amoris*, possibly translated by Hilton as the *Prickynge of Love*. That her spiritual director read or paraphrased these books to Margery reveals how widely disseminated the text originally addressed to professed religious had become by the fifteenth century. As well as by Continental holy women, particularly Bridget who was also married, Margery was strongly influenced by Richard Rolle. In the early sixteenth century, while the unique manuscript copy of her *Book* was in the possession of Mount Grace Charterhouse, a reader, most likely a Carthusian, first called attention to the similarities between Rolle and Kempe in his annotations (Lochrie 1991: 120). For example, next to her admission that, 'Whan sche felt fyrst þe fyer of loue brennyng in her brest, sche was a-ferd þerof', the annotator writes in the margin, 'so s. R. hampall'.[6] This commentator clearly recognizes that Kempe is alluding to Rolle's own account of his reception of the gift of fire in his prologue to the *Incendium amoris*. Later scholars have noticed that Kempe uses the Middle English equivalents of Rolle's *fervor*, *dulcor* and *canor* to prove the validity of her way of life. Although Rolle's sensational mysticism was questioned by Hilton and the *Cloud* author, in Kempe's own day Rolle's texts circulated more widely than those of the second-generation Middle English mystics. As Mount Grace's possession of her manuscript and the annotator's comparison of her to Rolle suggests, Margery Kempe's *Book* was less controversial in her own time than it became in later periods.

Given the extraordinary flourishing of mystical literature in the last quarter of the fourteenth century, it is remarkable that Margery Kempe's *Book* is the only such text composed in England during the following century. Rather, copies of works of Rolle, Hilton and, to a lesser extent, the *Cloud* author, as well as translations from Latin and Continental vernaculars, predominate. Watson attributes the paucity of original English works on contemplation during the fifteenth century to ecclesiastical efforts to eradicate Lollardy, regarded as a dangerous heresy by the Church (Watson 1995: 825–35). Archbishop Thomas Arundel's Constitutions of 1409 resulted, Watson argues, in a decrease in the number and complexity of works of vernacular theology. Although translations of mystical literature from Latin and Continental vernaculars continued, the circulation of these works was for the most part limited to professional religious and high-ranking laity after 1410. Many of these translations were commissioned or copied by two religious orders which gained strong aristocratic support under the Lancastrians, the Bridgettine nuns of Syon and the Carthusians, a hermetic order whose English foundations increased from two to seven in the period between 1343 and 1415.

Among the most important translations from the Continental vernaculars are texts by the female mystics Bridget of Sweden, Catherine of Siena, Mechtild of Hackeborn and Marguerite Porete. Bridget and Catherine had gained fame in the second half of the fourteenth century as outspoken critics of the papal court at Avignon. Both women had dictated their revelations to amanuenses in the vernacular before they were translated into Latin. Seven Middle English translations of Bridget's *Liber celestis* are extant, probably based on a Latin manuscript in the Syon library, but their quality and degree of completeness vary considerably. Although known by Margery Kempe, Bridget's *Liber celestis* is different from her *Book* because it focuses on revelations related to specific occasions and provides little autohagiography. Catherine of Siena's *Dialogue*, translated into Middle English early in the fifteenth century and extant in three manuscripts and a 1519 edition by Wynkyn de Worde, is also associated with Syon. The Middle English title *Orcherd of Syon* indicates not only the connection with the foundation, but also the allegorical framework added to divide the text into seven parts, each consisting of five chapters, analogous to an orchard with thirty-five rows or alleys of trees. Mechtild of Hackeborn's *Liber spiritualis gratiae*, a record of the ecstatic visions of a thirteenth-century nun at the famous convent of Hefta, is abridged in the Middle English translation probably made for the Syon nuns and titled *The Booke of Gostlye Grace*. Perhaps the most remarkable of these translations of visionary text by continental women is the Middle English version of Marguerite Porete's *Mirror of Simple Souls*. Marguerite's book was condemned as heretical and she was burnt in Paris on 31 May 1310. The *Mirror* is in a different genre from the revelations of the other Continental women visionaries; it is an allegorical dialogue between the Soul, Lady Love and Reason describing the contemplative's spiritual ascent. A Middle English translation from the original French by M. N. survives in three manuscripts, including London, British Museum, MS Additional 37790, the Amherst manuscript, which also contains the short text of Julian of Norwich's *Book of Showings*. M. N. does not attribute the *Mirror* to Marguerite Porete and his glosses and explanations attempt to correct the passages for which she was condemned. This Middle English version gained special attention from three later Carthusians. Richard Methley of Mount Grace Charterhouse translated the *Mirror* into Latin and William Darker, a scribe at the Sheen Charterhouse, included it with the *Cloud of Unknowing* in Oxford, Pembroke College MS 221, which was annotated by James Grenehalgh.

Devotional Literature

Devotional literature is much more difficult to define and classify than mystical literature because these texts express or incite emotions of awe, reverence or piety in regard to a diversity of religious topics, ranging from sins to saints, in a variety of genres, from short prayers to long narratives. Not only are devotional texts much more numerous than mystical ones, but they were composed by a much broader range of authors, many of whom remain anonymous. Furthermore, most devotional literature is extant only in manuscript, not printed editions. Just as devotionalism itself is an intermediate phenomenon between the liturgy and contemplation, so devotional texts stand midway between the didactic literature promulgating the Church's catechetical programme to the laity and the contemplative literature originally written for professed religious. As we have already seen, devotions such as prayer and meditation constituted an important level in the spiritual progress towards perfection in the contemplative life and mystical texts recommend or report such practices. Likewise, sermons, treatises on sin, saints' lives and other primarily didactic genres may evoke the same emotions of awe, reverence or piety as devotional literature even though their primary purpose is to teach. The distinction among contemplative, didactic and devotional literature is sometimes difficult to make and involves judgements about the text's purpose and emphasis rather than clear generic affiliations.

Like mystical literature, Middle English devotional texts can also be traced to the Latin Christian tradition. Around the twelfth century an unprecedented interest in individual experience and introspective analysis developed. This self-reflection manifested itself in an affective spirituality expressed in religious practices, images and texts designed to elicit an emotional response from the faithful. Cistercians in the twelfth century and Franciscans in the thirteenth promoted affective spirituality in a variety of ways, the most pervasive and distinctive of which is meditation on the humanity of Christ, particularly his Passion and the suffering of his mother Mary. Prayers and hymns, lyric poems and prose narratives encouraged the faithful to respond to Jesus's expression of love for them with compassion, to engage emotionally and even physically with the suffering of their Saviour and his mother.

The most influential text in this Latin tradition is the *Meditationes vitae Christi* erroneously attributed to Bonaventure, who succeeded Francis of Assisi as minister general of the Friars Minor in 1257. Probably composed around 1300 by a Tuscan Franciscan, the *Meditationes* surveys the life of Christ from the Incarnation to Pentecost. As the author acknowledges in the prologue, he not only includes events recorded in the Gospels, but also amplifies them as 'they might have occurred according to the devout belief of the imagination and the varying interpretations of the mind',[7] in order to evoke an emotional response from the reader. The popularity and influence of *Meditationes vitae Christi* in late medieval England is demonstrated by the fact that more than a third of the 113 surviving manuscripts of the Latin text were held by English libraries and seven different Middle English adaptations of it were made, six of which focus on the Passion narrative that comprises the last quarter of the original (Sargent 1992: xix–xx).

The only Middle English adaptation of the full *Meditationes vitae Christi* is the *Mirror of the Blessed Life of Jesus Christ* made by Nicholas Love, a Carthusian of Mount Grace, in the first decade of the fifteenth century. Love's *Mirror* is extant in fifty-one manuscripts and, as Deanesly's survey of late medieval wills demonstrates, it was the most popular book of the fifteenth century. Although the addressee of the Latin *Meditationes* is a woman professed in religious life, Love's intended audience is lay men and women, simple souls for whose benefit he says he excises the more complex material in the Latin original. In the century since the Latin text was composed, meditation on the life of Christ, a devotional practice first recommended for those in monastic or reclusive life, had spread to the laity, both male and female. In the first decade of the fifteenth century, however, the availability of devotional and mystical literature for the laity was restricted by Arundel's Constitutions of 1409. Love's *Mirror* was approved by the Archbishop himself even before the legislation was published, so its wide circulation is due not only to the broad audience it addresses but also to the official sanction it received.

Conclusion

The study of mystical and devotional literature has been invigorated over the last two decades by new approaches. Previously dismissed for their overtly religious content, these texts attracted the interest of feminist scholars because so many were addressed to or written by women. At the same time, other scholars recognized the linguistic and rhetorical richness of these texts as well as their cultural and social significance as expressions of vernacular theology circulating widely among the laity in the fifteenth century. Many studies trace the affiliations among the Middle English texts and their Latin or continental predecessors. Such research illuminates works that employ unfamiliar and often perplexing vocabularies and conceptual paradigms. Some recent studies, though, have focused on contestations about gender or socio-political issues and others have begun to place these texts in conversation with those traditionally considered to be more literary. Much archival and editorial work remains to be done on devotional literature. The next decade thus promises exciting advances in the study of mystical and devotional literature.

See also: 3 Religious Authority and Dissent, 5 Women's Voices and Roles, 7 From Manuscript to Modern Text, 8 Translation and Society, 9 The Languages of Medieval Britain, 23 Lyric, 24 Literature of Religious Instruction, 26 Accounts of Lives, 30 The *Book of Margery Kempe*, 31 Julian of Norwich.

Notes

1 *The Cloud of Unknowing and Related Treaties on Contemplative Prayer*, ed. Phyllis Hodgson, Analecta Cartusiana, 3 (Salzburg: Institut für Anglistik und Amerikanistik, Universität Salzburg, 1982), p. 62.

2 Richard Rolle, *The Fire of Love*, trans. Clifton Wolters (London: Penguin Books, 1972), p. 45.

3 *Cloud of Unknowing*, ed. Hodgson, p. 9.

4 Ibid., p. 12.

5 Ibid., p. 34.

6 *The Book of Margery Kempe*, ed. Sanford Brown Meech, EETS os 212 (1940) p. 88, nn 2 and 3.

7 *Meditations on the Life of Christ: An Illustrated Manuscript of the Fourteenth Century*, trans. Isa Ragusa, ed. Isa Ragusa and Rosalie B. Green (Princeton, N.J.: Princeton University Press, 1961), p. 5.

References and Further Reading

Aers, D. and Staley, L. 1996. *The Powers of the Holy: Religion, Politics, and Gender in Late Medieval English Culture.* University Park: Pennsylvania State University Press. Placing Julian of Norwich's *Showings* in the context of contemporary culture, Aers contrasts her presentation of the Passion of Christ with orthodox and Wycliffite texts; and Staley considers the political implications of her *Book* in the context of the late fourteenth-century crisis of authority.

Baker, D. N. 1994. *Julian of Norwich's Showings: From Vision to Book.* Princeton, N.J.: Princeton University Press. Baker analyses Julian of Norwich's development from a visionary in the contemplative tradition to a theologian who challenges Augustinian ideology.

Bell, D. 1995. *What Nuns Read: Book and Libraries in Medieval English Nunneries.* Kalamazoo, Mich.: Cistercian Publications. Basing his studies on his comprehensive list of manuscripts and printed books once owned by medieval English nunneries, Bell analyses the literacy and learning of the nuns.

Clark, J. P. H. 1991. 'Introduction.' In *Walter Hilton: The Scale of Perfection*, ed. J. P. H. Clark and R. Dorward (New York: Paulist Press), pp. 13–68. Clark places the *Scale of Perfection* in the context of medieval Christian spirituality.

Deanesly, M. 1920. 'Vernacular Books in England in the Fourteenth and Fifteenth Centuries.' *Modern Language Review* 15, 349–58. Deanesly's classic article, based on a survey of some 7,600 English medieval wills, provides evidence of the circulation of late medieval mystical and devotional literature.

Edwards, A. S. G. 1984. *Middle English Prose: A Critical Guide to Major Authors and Genres.* New Brunswick, N.J.: Rutgers University Press. This volume includes several essays which offer informative introductions to mystical and devotional texts: J. A. Alford on Rolle, A. Minnis on *The Cloud of Unknowing* and Walter Hilton's *Scale of Perfection*, C. von Nolcken on Julian of Norwich, J. C. Hirsch on Margery Kempe, B. Nolan on Nicholas Love and M. G. Sargent on minor devotional writings.

Hutchison, A. M. 1989. 'Devotional Reading in the Monastery and in the Late Medieval Household.' In *De Cella in Seculum: Religious and Secular Life and Devotion in Late Medieval England*, ed. M. G. Sargent (Cambridge: Brewer), pp. 215–27. One of several essays in this collection tracing the dissemination of texts originally composed for professed religious to the laity; Hutchison focuses on the reading practices recommended to the Syon nuns in *The Myroure of Oure Ladye.*

Kieckhefer, R. 1987. 'Major Currents in Late Medieval Devotion.' In *Christian Spirituality: High Middle Ages and Reformation*, ed. J. Raitt with B. McGinn and and J. Meyendorff (New York: Crossroad), pp. 75–108. Kieckhefer provides an overview of the devotional themes of the late Middle Ages.

Lagorio, V. M. and Sargent, M. G. 1993. 'English Mystical Writings.' In *A Manual of the Writings in Middle English, 1050–1500*, ed. A. Hartung (New Haven: Connecticut Academy of Arts and Sciences), IX 3049–137, 3405–71. An indispensable summary of mystical and devotional texts composed in or translated into Middle English and a bibliography of primary and secondary materials.

Lochrie, K. 1991. *Margery Kempe and Translations of the Flesh.* Philadelphia: University of Pennsylvania Press. Lochrie's feminist interpretation approaches the *Book of Margery Kempe* from the perspective of cultural criticism.

McGinn, B. 1991. *The Presence of God: A History of Western Christian Mysticism. Vol. 1: The Foundations of Mysticism.* New York: Crossroad. With three of its four projected volumes already published, McGinn's survey of Western Christian mysticism is the definitive study.

Milosh, J. E. 1966. *The Scale of Perfection and the English Mystical Tradition.* Madison: University of Wisconsin Press. The only full-length scholarly analysis of the *Scale*, this book explicates Hilton's teachings in the context of the various religious traditions.

Minnis, A. 1983. 'Affection and Imagination in *The Cloud of Unknowing* and Hilton's *Scale*.' *Traditio* 39, 323–66. Minnis's article documents the influence of Thomas Gallus on the *Cloud* author's understanding of Pseudo-Dionysius and contrasts the attitudes towards imagination held by these Middle English mystics.

Riehle, W. 1981. *The Middle English Mystics*, trans. B. Standring. London: Routledge and Kegan Paul. (Originally published in German, 1977). In this comparative study of the language of medieval English and German mystics, Riehle concentrates on the imagery and metaphors they share.

Salter, E. 1974. *Nicholas Love's 'Myrrour of the Blessed Lyf of Jesu Christ'*. Salzburg: Institut für Englische Sprache und Literatur, Universität Salzburg. This is the definitive study of Middle English devotional texts on the life of Christ culminating in Nicholas Love's *Mirror*.

Sargent, M. G. 1992. 'Introduction.' In *Nicholas Love's Mirror of the Blessed Life of Jesus Christ*, ed. M. G. Sargent (New York: Garland), pp. ix–cxxxv. Sargent's introduction provides a thorough analysis of Love's revisions of the *Meditationes vitae Christi* and the circulation and influence of this Middle English adaptation.

Turner, D. 1995. *The Darkness of God: Negativity in Christian Mysticism*. Cambridge: Cambridge University Press. Turner analyses the central metaphors of the Augustinian and Pseudo-Dionysian traditions and the apopathic dialectics of the *Cloud of Unknowing*.

Watson, N. 1991. *Richard Rolle and the Invention of Authority*. Cambridge: Cambridge University Press. Watson provides the definitive study of both the Latin and English texts that constitute Rolle's canon.

—— 1995. 'Censorship and Cultural Change in Late-Medieval England: Vernacular Theology, the Oxford Translation Debate, and Arundel's Constitutions of 1409'. *Speculum* 70, 822–64. Watson argues that the Church's efforts to combat Lollardy, especially Arundel's Constitutions, led to a decline in the composition of texts of vernacular theology in the fifteenth century.

—— 1999. 'The Middle English Mystics'. In *The Cambridge History of Medieval English Literature*, ed. D. Wallace (Cambridge: Cambridge University Press), pp. 539–65. Watson argues that the texts of the Middle English mystics should be studied in the context of late medieval English culture rather than as part of the special category of mystical literature.

26
Accounts of Lives

Kathleen Ashley

The search for information about medieval lives can take us into many kinds of writing produced during the Middle Ages, whether or not formally categorized as 'life writing'. Chronicles, histories and court records incorporate portraits of prominent (or notorious) people, while letters give access to the everyday existence of more ordinary writers; even wills can be read as autobiographical documents. Beyond historical records, medieval poets and writers are often deliberately reflexive, employing autobiographical discourse in a rhetorically tantalizing way (de Looze 1997; Zink 1999). Although it is certainly possible to 'read autobiographically or biographically' – using the act of reading to construct a coherent account even if the writer did not intend to produce one – it might be more interesting to explore the medieval understanding of writing or reading a 'life'.

Such an exploration reveals immediately that medieval texts we label as 'biography' and 'autobiography' both resemble and differ from contemporary versions of these genres. Perhaps the most striking similarity is their popularity. Accounts of lives now routinely top best seller lists in America and elsewhere, while the exemplary life story was also ubiquitous in medieval culture – whether read aloud in church, represented visually in art and performance or owned for private reading. However, when we ask who wrote and read lives, under what conditions, or for what purposes, we begin to see the differences between the two eras and to understand that the generic concepts we now use do not identify the same object.

Political biographies of rulers had existed since classical times, and the Middle Ages added the spiritual autobiography or conversion narrative, as exemplified by Augustine's *Confessions* or Abelard's *History of My Calamities*. However, full-length examples of lives were rare in the medieval period and overlapped with other kinds of religiously focused biography, memoir, mystical writing and treatises.[1] Far more common are the collections of shorter lives, called 'legendaries' when they contained stories about saints, and 'catalogues' or 'mirrors' when covering historical figures. The majority of these texts were written in Latin with later medieval translations into the vernaculars. The immensely influential Latin compendium of biblical figures and saints, the *Legenda aurea* (1261–6) of Jacobus de Voragine, for example, was translated into French as the *Légende dorée* (1333–40), which was then translated into English and circulated in many manuscripts as the *Gilte Legende* (1438).[2] Later, William Caxton published a separate translation, and Voragine's text also inspired the Middle English *Stanzaic Life of Christ.* Whether in Latin, French or English, works structured by stories of lives circulated widely and appealed across class lines to religious and lay people alike.

The modern genre concepts of autobiography and biography were defined in the nineteenth century on the assumption that any narrative of a life should consist of a long chronological trajectory from birth to old age. The study of both genres has become a literary field in the past thirty years and has given rise to conferences and scholarly journals (*a/b: Auto/biography Studies*, *biography*). In a further development, biography and autobiography were subsumed under the broader rubric of 'life writing', now offered as a university degree programme. The focus of most recent academic study has been the 'literariness' of the genres, despite their seeming factuality and historical referentiality.

For the Middle Ages, the recognized genre of 'lives' referred primarily to saints' lives, or hagiography. 'Hagiography' is a word of Greek etymology (writings, *graphia*, about holy people, *hagios*) for the many kinds of literature produced for the cult of saints. Saints' lives constituted the most popular form of biographical narrative throughout the Middle Ages and the genre provided a paradigm for writing all lives. When, in the *Canterbury Tales*, Geoffrey Chaucer's tipsy Miller says he will tell 'a legende and a lyf' (MilP 3141) he employs the familiar code terms for a saint's life, which he then parodies by telling instead a comic 'cherles tale' about a hapless carpenter and his lusty young wife. Chaucer is the playful exception to the general rule that medieval accounts of lives are produced within a clerical milieu for straightforwardly pious and instructive purposes, but we may see in his clever appropriation of hagiographic terminology one of the clues to the genre's popularity. As Michel de Certeau suggests, hagiography has a kind of 'vacation' function in the religious life:

> In the fifth-century *Life of Melanie*, we are told that once she was 'sated' with canonical books and collections of homilies, 'she went through the lives of the Fathers as though she were eating desserts'. Tales of the saints' lives bring a festive element to the community. They are situated on the side of relaxation and leisure. They correspond to a free time, a place set aside, a spiritual and contemplative respite; they do not belong in the realm of instruction, pedagogical norms, or dogma. They 'divert' . . . The Saints' Lives are read during meals, or during monks' times of recreation. In the course of the year the readings intervene on holy days; they are recounted at places of pilgrimage and are heard during free hours. (de Certeau 1988: 273–4)

Perhaps these imaginative and recreative possibilities that de Certeau identifies in hagiography account for the ubiquity of saints' lives as well as the innumerable ways they could be appropriated.

Not all theorists of hagiography have taken such an open or liminal approach to the genre. An early medieval writer, Gregory of Tours, introducing his book on the lives of church fathers (*Liber vitae patrum*), asked the question, 'should we say the life or the lives of the saints?' For Gregory, this was a rhetorical question to be answered with the assertion that the lives and deaths of holy people all conformed fundamentally to the pattern of a single life, that of Christ.[3] Many scholars of medieval hagiography, biography and autobiography[4] have taken up Gregory's position that all accounts of lives written during the Middle Ages are primarily shaped by powerful models – whether Christ, the Roman ruler or another ideal type. As a result of the idealizing conventions dominating life-writing, they argue, we should not seek individual, personal or social identity in such accounts. They also follow Gregory in promoting a rather simple notion of what it means for a text or a life to be 'exemplary'.

Is there a way out of the confrontation between historicity and literariness implied by the concept of writing a life? Or a more complicated notion of identity and identification that may be at work in the texts? The current efflorescence of scholarship in both contemporary auto/biography studies and medieval hagiography studies would suggest the existence of productive critical tools that I will use in analysing the significance and appeal of accounts of lives for medieval culture.

The *Book of Margery Kempe* as Critical Test Case

To introduce some of the issues arising from the constructedness of life-writing, the representation of medieval identities and the reception of such texts, we might use the well-known fifteenth-century autobiographical narrative, the *Book of Margery Kempe*.[5] Historians have tended to articulate a binary of the individual versus the collectivity, arguing that valuing individuality is a feature of modern cultures. Some admit a limited 'discovery' of the individual in the 'twelfth-century Renaissance', but the consensus had been that medieval narrative offered 'types' rather than individuals – that personal histories not only reveal their exemplarity in following sacred patterns but are designed to function as exempla for readers.[6] Margery does model her self-representation in part upon Christ's Passion, which provides the example of an innocent victim suffering the persecutions of ignorant and evil people. The account of Margery's life, however, also illustrates her assertive individuality, one that escapes complete containment by any conventional typology. Scholars had difficulty placing Margery's *Book* within the genre of mystical literature after the sole manuscript was rediscovered in 1934 precisely because she did not follow the spiritualized model of the mystic's life offered by Richard Rolle or Julian of Norwich, but seemed altogether too concretely rooted in fifteenth-century society.

Another traditional crux in discussions of personal identity has to do with 'interiority' versus 'exteriority' the assumption being that selfhood is best defined by an inner-directed self-consciousness. As David Wallace notes of Julia Boffey's work (Boffey 1999), such forms of interiority as we find in fourteenth-century texts 'owe much . . . to penitential literature' (487),[7] so that even narratives of personal confession may be more conventional than authentically revelatory. However, Margery's description of her post-partum depression and her episodes of lustful imagining reveal the inadequacy of such binary categories, since the experiences simultaneously reveal her deepest, most personal emotions and function as negative exempla in her narrative of conversion.

Poststructuralist theories offer other ways of understanding the relationship between the personal and social. They challenge the idea of a unified 'self' able to act autonomously from society and use instead the concept of a 'subject', whose subjectivity is constituted by multiple ideological discourses and subject positions inflected by class, gender, age and so on. The individual and the social are mutually constituted in this view, while subjectivity has both inner and outer referents. Criticism of Margery's *Book* over the past twenty years has largely drawn on these theories to analyse her occupation of multiple subject positions within late medieval society: bourgeois wife, member of the civic elite as daughter of the Mayor of Lynn, businesswoman, mother of fourteen children, an author despite her illiteracy, a pilgrim, a practitioner of affective piety, a contemplative. It was Margery's loudly transgressive combination of her various social roles that provoked charges that she was a heretic and investigations into her orthodoxy.

Moreover, the subject's complex identity is, according to poststructural thought, shifting and even self-contradictory. The very multiplicity and volatility inherent in representing personal identity therefore provide the potential for negotiation – for deliberate play with dominant ideologies, typologies and discourses. It is possible, in other words, for a subject to have *agency* in manipulating conventions. Through her awareness of the dominant discourses of her society, Margery negotiates the hostile challenges to her orthodoxy by church and civil authorities, and she successfully manoeuvres her reluctant husband to take a vow of celibacy and release her from marital vows, which will in turn free her to pursue her religious goals. Towards the end of her narrative, Margery is clearly redefining the concept of being a virgin who can count on dancing in heaven with Mary and her virginal entourage. Although such a possibility was theoretically open only to women who had taken vows of chastity, Margery's conversation with Christ allows her to claim a place in that celestial dance by transforming virginity into a spiritual rather than a physical state. Her redefinition of virginity illustrates the strategies historically used by the bourgeoisie to create a validating ideology for lay piety, previously subordinated to ecclesiastical ideologies.[8]

Just as it has redefined issues of identity, poststructuralism has destabilized traditional notions of genre. It asks us to see fiction and rhetoric in presumably factual writing and it conversely emphasizes the historicity of all texts. Its interest in the hybridity or blurring of generic forms is particularly useful for understanding medieval genres. As we have seen, forms of medieval life-writing – including autobiography and biography – do not constitute defined literary genres that can be clearly differentiated from the spiritual confession or hagiography. Margery's *Book* is considered the first autobiography, but it is written as a biography in that she refers to herself in the third person as 'this creature'. It also positions itself to be a hagiographic text, since it attributes to Margery's life most of the medieval markers of sanctity: miracle-working, acts of charity, ability to mediate for others through prayer, divine visions and conversations, suffering and adversity. Margery intends to write a sacred biography, a 'treatise' about herself as an exemplary person who may be a candidate for canonization. Her book did not achieve its religious purpose in the fifteenth century, but it has brought her literary canonization in the late twentieth century.

Clearly, Margery's *Book*, as a generically and representationally complex text, has proved responsive to contemporary critical methodologies – but it is somewhat exceptional. In its tantalizing display of personal identity and ideological multiplicity, her *Book* invites interpretation. The more challenging task would be to pursue some of the same issues of identity and identification with apparently conventional, officially produced accounts of lives, to which we now turn.

Mirrors of Sacred Lives

Despite their manifest significance for medieval culture as judged by numbers of manuscripts or intertextual influence – and despite the impressive scholarship focused on their manuscripts, sources, language and provenance – mirrors of sacred lives are only just beginning to receive the interpretative attention they deserve. In reconsidering the significance of writing about lives, we might remind ourselves of the fundamental semiotic role played by the sacred life as the template for medieval interpretations of history. From the Gospels that are the originating and sustaining texts of Christianity to the liturgy of the Catholic church year, the narrative of Christ's life provided both frame and substance through which a medieval person came to understand his or her own reality. For medieval culture, the life of Christ was, in the words of semiotician Claude Lévi-Strauss, 'good to think with'. As a result, the exemplarity of that sacred life operated at a very profound level.

Some of the best-known, most widely circulated texts of the thirteenth, fourteenth and fifteenth centuries are structured around episodes in the life of Christ or the Virgin Mary. The Latin pseudo-Bonaventuran *Meditationes vitae Christi*, written at the end of the thirteenth century by a Franciscan from Italy, uses the Gospel accounts of Christ's life as the frame not just for doctrinal instruction but also as an imaginative catalyst for the reader's devotions. In this meditational text the explicit aim is to enable a reader, by attending to the minute details of Christ's earthly life, to learn how to live virtuously. But this exemplarity is not just externalized mimicry. The meditator observes the meaning of Christ's behaviour through a process of empathy – an affectionate comprehension – that generates the desired spiritual orientation:

> The Lord Jesus remained enclosed in the womb for nine months according to the human manner, benignly and patiently enduring and waiting for the proper time. Feel compassion for Him who reached these depths of humility! We must greatly desire this virtue and should never rise to pride, since the Lord of majesty has stooped so low that we can

> never sufficiently thank Him for this one benefit attained by such long imprisonment for us. But at the least we are aware of this benefit in our hearts, and in great affection render thanks to Him that He has elected us above the others.[9]

One can consider this 'imitation', but the term seems a crude one for the psychologically nuanced processes of identification explicitly called for in the passage, a process designed to generate both the inward predisposition to virtue and its outward behaviour.

The Latin text was translated into many European vernaculars, including at least ten separate Middle English translations. According to Michael Sargent, one of these translations, Nicholas Love's *Mirror of the Blessed Life of Jesus Christ*, 'was the most important literary version of the life of Christ in English before modern times . . . one of the most well-read books in late-medieval England' (ix).[10] Love's *Mirror* follows the long version of the Latin work and, like the *Meditationes*, embellishes the biblical narrative with human details and commentary that would assist the reader in identifying with the sacred events. For example, after his Resurrection from the grave, Jesus appears first to his mother, who is understandably overjoyed to see him alive. The scene shows Mary kissing and hugging her son, then she sits leaning against him while she 'bisily & curiously' examines all the parts of his body where he had been wounded, wanting reassurance he is not in pain (195). He then says he will go and find Mary Magdalene, which his mother thinks is a good idea given the Magdalene's emotional state; however, she makes him promise he will come again to comfort her '& so she lovely clippyng him & kissinge, lete him go' (197).

The scene with Mary Magdalene, too, amplifies the emotional response beyond the scriptural account and invites the reader to understand Christ's behaviour in human terms, not just allegorically. That amplification introduces a tension into the description. Ostensibly, the *noli me tangere* episode – Christ's asking Magdelene not to touch him when she tries to kiss his feet (John 20: 17) – is motivated by the desire to deter her 'unperfite affeccion to his manhode' now that he is a resurrected being. However, she defends her actions based on her overwhelming grief at his death, and the 'tweyn trewe lovers standen & speken to geder with grete likyng & ioy, & she curiously beholdeth his gloriouse body & asketh what hir liketh, & he in alle thinge answerede plesynglye to hir pay' (198).[11] As in the scene with his mother, Jesus ends up allowing the beloved woman to cuddle him, touch him, and ask anything she wants about him – playing up the human intimacy of the moment at the expense of the doctrinal point of Christ's untouchability.

The narrator then undercuts the doctrinal frame even further by reinterpreting Jesus' initial guarded response as something to be rationalized, speculating that Jesus must have decided to behave more lovingly so as to comfort her:

> And forthermore though oure lorde so straungely as it semeth answerede hir at the byginnyng biddyng hir that she sulde not touch him *nevereles I may not trowe, bot that afterwarde he suffrede hir to touch him, & to kysse both handes & feete,* or thei departeden. *For* we *mowe suppose & godely trowe that sithen he wolde so affectuously & specialy after his owne modere first*

> *before all othere visete & apere to that he wolde not thereby in any maner disturble hir or hevye hir, bot rather in alle poyntes confort hir.* And therfore the goode lorde that is so benynge & ful of swetnes, namely to all thoo, that trewly lovene him spake not to hir the forseide wordes in straunge manere & bostesly bot in misterye, shewyng hir in perfite affeccion as it is seide, & willing lift up hir herte holly to god & to hevenly thinges, as seith seynt Bernarde. (198–9; my italics)

At the end of the passage, the narrator returns with some difficulty to the spiritual mission of Christ (to lift Mary's heart wholly to heavenly things) by citing Saint Bernard's interpretation, but only after assuring the reader of Jesus's human concern to comfort those who love him. Although the theology of the Resurrection demands that Christ's godhead be emphasized, the narrative keeps subverting its mandate in order to show Jesus as an exemplary person whose words and actions provide a caring model to other sons and lovers. As we see, therefore, in attempting to demonstrate the paradoxical identity of an incarnated being who is both earthly and spiritual, the life of Christ could be representationally unstable. Likewise, the goal of reaching the laity by developing the human dimension of their subject occasionally conflicts in these texts with the clerical task of doctrinal exegesis.

The medieval narrative of a life is a complex construction, capable of doing various kinds of cultural work, sometimes simultaneously. In particular, when a work circulates widely and undergoes translation at a later time or in another place, it is usually revised to meet the needs of the new historical context. Love's early fifteenth-century *Mirror*, for example, goes beyond its Franciscan source as a manual of meditation and lay instruction to develop passages of anti-Lollard polemic. As Sargent points out, it 'played a major role in Archbishop Arundel's campaign against the Wycliffite heresy' (xv).[12]

Other translations in Middle English reshape their sources even more dramatically.[13] The clerical author of the *Stanzaic Life of Christ* says in opening that he had been asked by a worthy man to do a translation from Latin of stories about Christ's life, 'Of Jhesu Cristes Nativite / And his werkus on a rowe' (1).[14] Drawing from two widespread Latin texts – Ranulph Higden's *Polychronicon* and Voragine's *Legenda aurea* – the writer put together a rhymed version of the most important episodes in Christ's life: the Incarnation, Visitation, Nativity, Circumcision, Epiphany, Purification, Massacre of the Innocents, Boyhood, Passion, Resurrection, Ascension and Pentecost, as well as events commemorated during the liturgical seasons of Septuagesima, Quadragesima and Ember days. Whereas his two sources are compendia with diverse subjects and histories, for his adaptation the writer made a careful and focused selection of material, which was then organized by the framework of Christ's life.

While it may have been produced for a layman, the *Stanzaic Life* retains the exegetical tone of the *Legenda aurea*, with its lengthy interpretations of the spiritual significance of events. The narrative of Christ's Ascension, for example, is presented within the doctrinal structure of seven points and multiple sub-points (291–321). This poem sets up a different kind of relationship between Christ's life story and readers than did Love's *Mirror*, which offered Jesus's experience as an empathetic trigger for the individual reader's response and eventual moral transformation. The *Stanzaic Life* seems designed to develop a more cognitive imagination, using each episode of the sacred life to develop a spiritual understanding of history. Christ's life in the poem mirrors not exemplary human behaviour but the divine rationale behind historical events.

The Virgin Mary was the focus of many texts, and often her life story was incorporated into the overarching narrative of the Incarnation and the Passion (as we saw with Love's *Mirror*). Since the theological structure of Christianity was built upon the history of Christ's life, even texts that resemble treatises more than narratives (like the *Stanzaic Life*) have a structural relationship to the chronology of the sacred life. The liturgy that ritualized worship throughout the church year also takes its shape and significance from the narrative of the Incarnation and the Passion – featuring the lives of Christ and his mother.

The fifteenth-century monk and poet John Lydgate wrote a verse *Life of Our Lady* that was structured around the liturgical year, while the *Myroure of Oure Ladye*, written for the sisters at Brigittine Sion monastery (c.1450), provides an explanation in English of every element of their liturgical services. The nuns call themselves the 'daughters of Syon' (an identity taken from the biblical Song of Songs), and announce the purpose of their lives as being to praise Mary through the liturgy. The translation into their vernacular will help them achieve an 'inwarde understandinge' of what they 'synge and rede' (2).[15]

The three parts of the treatise – general principles, explanation of the seven days of services and explanation of feast days and masses – proceed primarily through analysis of liturgical references to Mary's life and her epithets (such as star of the morning, Queen of Heaven, rod of Jesse) to understand her role in Christian history. Although embedded within an exegetical framework, episodes in the life of Mary and her identity as redemptress become the 'myroure' to enable their devotion: 'Lyfte up the eyen of youre soulles towarde youre soverayne lady, and often & bysely loke and study in this her myrroure' (4). The concept of using a holy person's life as a mirror permeates hagiographic literature, and here the text itself is also a mirror – a vehicle for achieving understanding by the reader.

We see these images visualized in some Books of Hours, illuminated texts containing the Office of the Virgin that were designed for private lay devotion and became 'late medieval best sellers'.[16] Typically, a patron figure is portrayed in the margin, either kneeling in prayer or reading a book, with Mary or a saint in the central scene (figures 26.1, 26.2). In some illuminations, the person is represented inside the frame that marks the sacred space. The image tells us that by reading about the holy life or praying to the holy figure the owner of the Book of Hours establishes a meaningful reciprocal relationship to the sacred. The most famous illustration of this theme is found in the *Hours of Mary of Burgundy*, where Mary sits reading her prayerbook outside an open window. Through it is revealed a gothic chapel with the Virgin Mary, holding an infant Christ, being worshipped by several angels and aristocratic women – including a figure thought to be a representation of Mary of Burgundy herself. As Laurel Amtower points out, the 'adoration of the Virgin is not just image, not just imagination, but its own reality. It plays out as a part of the reader herself'. Amtower notes the 'mirroring of the

Figure 26.1 Hours of the Virgin, from a Book of Hours in Latin and Flemish, use of Rome, Flanders c.1480: Claremont Colleges, MS Kirby 1, folio 7v. (By permission of the Libraries of the Claremont Colleges, California.)

sacramental image above the contemplative reader' and the prayer on the facing page promising that the 'presence of the Virgin will be the reward for whoever contemplates and repeats her joys as specified in the Books of Hours' (Amtower 2000: 74, 75). Sponsler adds that there are two kinds of identification in play – with the divine figure and with the exemplary self represented in the illumination as engaged in spiritual experience (Sponsler 1997: 124). Thus, dramatized in 'the sacred space of the holy image', the devotional self steps importantly to centre stage (126).

Part one of the *Myroure of Oure Ladye* ends with an explicit discussion of why 'devoute redyng of holy Bokes' (65)[17] is recommended. The author distinguishes between different reading goals: 'dyverse bokes speke in dyverse wyses' (68). Some are designed to inform the spiritual understanding, to be used in self-scrutiny that will guide one toward better moral choices. Others 'sturre up the affeccyons of the soule', either by fostering feelings of love, joy, and hope of heavenly reward, or by recounting the 'foulnes & wretchednesse of syn to sturre up the affeccyons of hate and lothynge ther agenst'.

Figure 26.2 Saints Philip and James with patron and wife kneeling before open prayer books, from a Book of Hours in Latin and Flemish, use of Rome, Flanders c.1480: Claremont Colleges, MS Kirby 1, f. 155. (By permission of the Libraries of the Claremont Colleges, California.)

Yet other books, including the second part of the *Myroure*, the author says, combine the two methods; they both provide spiritual understanding and appeal to the emotions. He points out that it is description of the experiences of Christ and his mother, above all, that will trigger the positive inclination to praise and emulate, as well as feelings of dread and compassion that are deterrents (70). For the *Myroure*, as for Books of Hours, the representation of holy lives – which establishes an emotional relationship between the sacred and the worshipper – is considered an essential stimulus to the process of spiritual actualization in its reader.

Anthologies of Saints' Legends

In late medieval England, life stories from the Bible or hagiographic tradition were most commonly available in collections of lives. Their inspiration was Voragine's *Legenda aurea* whose original purpose, like that of other early collections of lives, was for clerical reading at the liturgically appropriate feasts in the church year.[18] By at least the thirteenth century, however, manuscripts containing saints' lives were being produced for the laity and circulated outside church-controlled liturgical contexts. The immensely popular *South English Legendary*, which survives in at least sixty complete copies, looks like a compendium of lives for feasts in the church calendar, but its use was probably not restricted to clerical contexts (Jankovsky 1977; Samson 1985). Such complex constructions could be appropriated for various kinds of cultural work, as we have pointed out. The *Legendary*, for example, might be used in a liturgical service and for lay instruction by the clergy, or it might provide readings for private devotions. It includes lives from universal Christian history, while some manuscripts include large numbers of local English saints, suggesting a nationalist agenda. Beyond pious and edifying purposes, saints' lives held high entertainment value for their audiences, which may explain the inclusion of the *Legendary* in many manuscripts containing romances and other non-religious literature (Gorlach 1974).

As a result of their open and attractive form, collections of lives became one of the most popular genres in the later Middle Ages, capable of revealing much about the culture that produced and consumed them. In what follows I focus on the ways in which writers and readers appropriated such accounts of saints' lives and thereby continue to explore the dynamics of identification and the resulting constructions of identity.

Lay Piety and the Formation of Social and Gender Identities

Throughout the late medieval period, hagiography continued to be produced and used within ecclesiastical settings or by churchmen for the education of the laity. From the thirteenth century on, however, the boundaries between the church and lay society became increasingly permeable, and hagiographic texts circulated across that boundary in new ways. Felicity Riddy has argued that 'the literary culture of nuns in the late fourteenth and fifteenth centuries and that of devout gentlewomen not only overlapped but were more or less indistinguishable' (Riddy 1996: 110).[19] The same devotional texts were read in both nunneries and gentry households, around which, Riddy suggests, pious women of all estates created a strong feminine subculture. That culture was primarily based on texts in the vernacular, while a similar male culture, cutting across religious–lay boundaries, included Latin texts.

In the wealth of scholarship on saints' lives that has been produced in the past two decades, one issue has dominated: the importance of gender. The question of identification has been particularly troublesome to many modern scholars when the saint is a female and the hagiographer male. One school of criticism simply believes that the point of view expressed in a male-authored saint's life inevitably censors any views challenging male and clerical power structures.[20] Although most collections of saints' lives contain stories of both male and female saints, the fifteenth century brought a resurgence of interest in the female saints, especially virgin martyrs whose life and death stories have also fascinated contemporary critics. The first critics tended to read the female martyrdom stories as emblematic of the containment if not the denigration of women; the sensational and violent tortures inflicted upon the female body in such lives seemed voyeuristic and misogynist.

A revisionist trend has now begun to offer other interpretations. Sheila Delany argues that 'the sadistic sexual politics of hagiography' is met by the 'affirmative sexual politics of women's moral strength and spiritual victory' (Delany 1992: xxxiii), while Karen Winstead carefully differentiates the treatment of the female martyrs in different eras and different authors. For Winstead, late thirteenth- and fourteenth-century virgin martyr legends offer a new paradigm of sainthood (Winstead 1997). Like the 'unruly woman' of parody and fabliau, the virgin martyr uses invective and even physical abuse to challenge the social norms and expectations. She functions as a semiotic construct which allows late medieval culture to explore its gender and power arrangements, rather than being an imitable example of conduct.

The assumption that lives of female saints inevitably focus on gender issues and appeal mainly to women has thus been challenged recently on various grounds, both semiotic and historical. As a sign, 'the feminine' might signify more than sexual identity, especially as a sacred category which transcends the limits of binary human identities by virtue of what Theresa Coletti calls the 'complicated incarnational relation of spirit and flesh' (Coletti 2004: 154). Where masculinity is associated with abusive earthly power, as it is in many saints' lives featuring tyrannical rulers, the female saint can represent positive alternatives and, especially where the female saint is identified with the Virgin Mary, femininity can play a central redemptive role in a narrative.

The saint's life could function as a cultural semiotic, but it could in some cases be more explicitly didactic and exemplary, providing models for social behaviour to its readers. Winstead argues that in fifteenth-century vernacular hagiography saints are likely to be represented as 'refined gentlewomen rather than triumphant viragos' (Winstead 1997: 113). The saints' lives written by John Lydgate (prolific writer and monk at Bury St Edmunds), Osbern Bokenham (Augustinian friar from Stoke Clare) and John Capgrave (another prolific author and Augustinian friar of Lynn), although written in religious houses, circulated among the literate laity to whom they explicitly modelled genteel and pious conduct.[21] These fifteenth-century writers, especially Bokenham, reveal the social context of hagiographic production, recounting conversations with bourgeois and upper-class patrons for whom they agreed to write the life of a saint. No longer under the exclusive control of the clergy, the literature of sanctity could now be commissioned by lay men and women, and the inherited narratives were reshaped accordingly to meet their needs. The result was in many ways the most straightforwardly exemplary form of saints' lives available in the Middle Ages, narratives that have useful lessons in appropriate behaviours for a culture bent on self-improvement of every kind.

Patron Saints as Personal Intercessors

As we have seen, there is evidence in records of readership and patronage that both men and women could identify with saints on grounds other than gender. The selection of a specific saint as personal patron often depended less on gender than on the particular powers or attributes associated with that saint. The benefits requested of a saint were not always spiritual – physical welfare and material prosperity were often reasons for petitioning a saint or reading her legend. Saint Margaret, for example, was 'the patroness of parturient women in the later middle Ages', as Wendy Larson points out (Larson 2003: 94). The text of the legend might be read or placed on the woman's belly. Although Margaret is a virgin martyr, it is neither her gender nor her martyrdom that has shaped the ritual use of her legend but her escape from the dragon's belly, which promises a power capable of ensuring a healthy human delivery. In this and many other cases, the petitioner hopes to access the power of a saint who has particular efficacy in dealing with his or her need.

Another connection between an individual and a saint might be based on identity of names. This possible relationship is more easily seen in manuscript illuminations, where a patron has commissioned an image of a saint or the text of the saint's life because they share the same name. It is likely that Mary of Burgundy had a special devotion to the Virgin Mary in part because of name identity. Foundations of chapels dedicated to one's name saint are also visible indications of that relationship.[22] Hagiographers, too, reflect the identity between saint and hagiography patron based on names. Bokenham begins and ends his life of St Elizabeth by reminding the saint of the special grace she owes to Dame Elizabeth Vere, presumably because she is the lady's name saint. Dame Elizabeth, he says, had 'particularly commanded me to compose your legend' and 'loves you affectionately in her heart' (Delany 1998: 195). Likewise, he concludes his life of St Katherine with the plea that she will be an intermediary for him with heaven and for his two patrons called Katherine. St Anne is petitioned on behalf of John Denston and his wife for a son, with the note that 'they already have a beautiful small daughter called Anne in honor of you' (41). Hagiographer, saint and patron thus participate in an intersubjective identification and set of spiritual obligations based on sharing a name.

Important (but relatively unexplored) relations between hagiographer and saint may arise when the birth-date of a medieval person and a saint's feast day coincide.

Hagiographers Simon of Walsingham and Osbern Bokenham both claim a special relationship to Sainte Foy/St Faith based on the coincidence of their birth and her feast on 6 October. Bokenham ends his translation of St Faith's life in his *Legends of Holy Women* with the statement: 'And especially, lady, because of your passion, show the grace of special favor to him who, from pure devotion, was translator of your legend into English. Grant him, lady, in his last hour of living to be cleansed from sin, for he on your day to live did first begin' (Delany 1992: 79). His life history is linked to the saint's passion history, motivating the writing of the life, and authorizing him to ask for special favours from the saint.

The early thirteenth-century Anglo-Norman monk Simon lived at the Benedictine monastery of Bury St Edmunds (Suffolk), site of a chapel dedicated to St Faith, and he was from Walsingham, near Horsham which had a priory also dedicated to St Faith. However, the major factor in his writing the life of 'Seinte Fey' seems to be the special bond based on his birth the very night of her passion. Ironically, he says, as her travail ceased, his began.[23] In writing her life he hopes to gain her favour, so she will intercede for him to reach 'la joie plenere' (70). She is, he reiterates throughout the poem in a kind of refrain, not just his special friend but 'la Deu amye' – the friend of God. This motif of friendship between the hagiographer and the saintly patron is extended to a third party, another friend who had asked him to write the life of Foy. This was a 'prudhome, men cumpaignun' who is great in science and reason but short in stature. The production of this saint's life is thus embedded in a triangular nexus of friendship between the human patron who has commissioned the work, the hagiographer, and the saintly subject who is the poet's holy patron.

Whether experienced as ecclesiastical ritual or personal identification, as metaphor or as literal model, saints' lives permeated the fabric of medieval culture, providing narratives, images and concepts through which the people of the time understood the meaning of their existence.

See also: 3 Religious Authority and Dissent, 5 Women's Voices and Roles, 8 Translation and Society, 9 The Languages of Medieval Britain, 18 Images, 21 Writing Nation, 24 Literature of Religious Instruction, 25 Mystical and Devotional Literature, 30 The *Book of Margery Kempe*, 31 Julian of Norwich.

Notes

1 There is a vividly detailed and lengthy life of Christina, a twelfth-century recluse who became prioress of Markyate, written in Latin by an unknown cleric; see the edition and translation by C. H. Talbot, *The Life of Christina of Markyate: A Twelfth-Century Recluse* (Oxford: Clarendon Press, 1959; repr. Toronto: University of Toronto Press, 1997), and the analysis of the meaning of her anchoritic life by Christopher Cannon, 'Enclosure', in *Medieval Women's Writing*, ed. C. Dinshaw and D. Wallace (Cambridge: Cambridge University Press, 2003), pp. 109–23. The categories of sacred biography and auto-

biography are difficult to distinguish in the later Middle Ages from mystical writings. For example, Julian of Norwich's *Revelation of Love*, a visionary text based on her spiritual experiences in late fourteenth-century Norwich, uses the first person.

2 On the legendaries, see Manfred Gorlach, *The South English Legendary, Gilte Legende, and Golden Legend* (Braunschweig: Technische Universität Carolo-Wilhelmina, 1972).

3 Gregory of Tours, *The Life of the Fathers*, trans. E. James, 2nd edn (Liverpool: Liverpool University Press, 1991), p. 2.

4 Heffernan 1988: 16 prefers the term 'sacred biography' to refer to a narrative of the life of a saint since he thinks 'hagiography' now connotes an 'exercise in panegyric'.

5 *The Book of Margery Kempe*, ed. L. Staley (New York: Norton, 2001).

6 See the discussion by Colin Morris, *The Discovery of the Individual 1050–1200* (Toronto: University of Toronto Press, 1987); also Caroline Walker Bynum, 'Did the Twelfth Century Discover the Individual?', in her *Jesus as Mother: Studies in the Spirituality of the High Middle Ages* (Berkeley: University of California Press, 1982), pp. 82–109.

7 *The Cambridge History of Medieval English Literature*, ed. D. Wallace (Cambridge: Cambridge University Press), p. 487.

8 On the appropriation and transformation of clerical ideologies and practices by the pious bourgeois laity, symbolized by Margery, see my essay, 'Historicizing Margery: The *Book* of Margery Kempe as Social Text', *Journal of Medieval and Early Modern Studies* 28, 375–92.

9 I. Ragusa and R. B. Green (eds), *Meditations on the Life of Christ: An Illustrated Manuscript of the Fourteenth Century* (Princeton, N.J.: Princeton University Press, 1961), p. 30.

10 M. G. Sargent (ed.), *Nicholas Love: The Mirror of the Blessed Life of Jesus Christ – A Reading Text* (Exeter: University of Exeter Press, 2004).

11 I have silently converted the Middle English thorn in Sargent's edition to 'th' in my quotations.

12 See also Nicolas Watson, 'Censorship and Cultural Change in Late-Medieval England: Vernacular Theology, the Oxford Translation Debate, and Arundel's Constitutions of 1409', *Speculum* 70, 822–64, on the politics of translation.

13 For illuminating discussions of many topics touched on in this essay, including addressing the audience, the reading process, translation, theories of the vernacular, and the politics of Middle English writing, see Jocelyn Wogan-Browne, Nicholas Watson, Andrew Taylor and Ruth Evans (eds), *The Idea of the Vernacular: An Anthology of Middle English Literary Theory 1280–1520* (University Park: Pennsylvania State University Press, 1999).

14 F. A. Foster (ed.), *A Stanzaic Life of Christ*, EETS os 166 (1926, repr. 1971).

15 J. H. Blunt (ed.), *The Myroure of Oure Ladye*, EETS es 19 (1873, repr. 1981).

16 See Amtower 2000: 46–77; also Lawrence R. Poos, 'Social History and the Book of Hours', in *Time Sanctified: The Book of Hours in Medieval Art and Life*, ed. R.S. Wieck (New York: Braziller, 1988), pp. 33–8.

17 See note 16, above.

18 Thomas J. Heffernan analyses the places in the liturgy where saints' lives would be read, in his 'The Liturgy and the Literature of Saints' Lives', in *The Liturgy of the Medieval Church*, ed. T. J. Heffernan and E. A. Matter (Kalamazoo, Mich.: Medieval Institute Publications, 2001), pp. 73–105.

19 Jocelyn Wogan-Browne makes the same argument about Anglo-Norman religious culture between the late twelfth and the early fourteenth centuries, that we cannot make sharp distinctions between secular and religious patrons and audiences. See her '"Clerc u lai, muïne u dame": Women and Anglo-Norman Hagiography in the Twelfth and Thirteenth Centuries', in *Women and Literature in Britain 1150–1500*, ed. C. M. Meale, 2nd edn (Cambridge: Cambridge University Press, 1996), pp. 61–85 (p. 62).

20 See, for example, Gail Ashton, *The Generation of Identity in Late Medieval Hagiography* (London: Routledge, 1999), p. 161.

21 On the use of lives of the virgin martyr Katherine in household manuscripts as a tool for socialization, see Katherine J. Lewis, 'Model Girls? Virgin-Martyr and the Training of Young Women in Late Medieval England', in

Young Medieval Women, ed. K. J. Lewis, N. J. Menuge and K. M. Phillips (New York: St Martin's Press, 1999), pp. 25–46.

22 Gail Gibson, *The Theater of Devotion: East Anglian Drama and Society in the Late Middle Ages* (Chicago: University of Chicago Press, 1989), pp. 96–106.

23 See the introduction with edition of the poem by A. T. Baker, 'Vie Anglo-Normande de Sainte Foy par Simon de Walsingham', *Romania* 66 (1940), 49–84. Walsingham's life of Foy is found in a diverse collection of saints' lives from several centuries in a manuscript owned by the Augustinian canonesses at Campsey (Suffolk); on this interesting manuscript and its rich implications for literary and women's history and hagiography study, see Jocelyn Wogan-Browne, 'Powers of Record, Powers of Example: Hagiography and Women's History', in *Gendering the Master Narrative: Women and Power in the Middle Ages*, ed. M. C. Erler and M. Kowaleski (Ithaca, N.Y.: Cornell University Press, 2003), pp. 71–93.

References and Further Reading

Amtower, L. 2000. *Engaging Words: The Culture of Reading in the Late Middle Ages*. New York: Palgrave. An exploration of medieval lay reading habits and the shaping of identity in the late Middle Ages.

Ashley, K. 1998. 'Historicizing Margery: The Book of Margery Kempe as Social Text'. *Journal of Medieval and Early Modern Studies* 28, 375–97. Argues that although the main intertext is the hagiographic life, both Margery's *Book* and her life may also be read as cultural documents of the late medieval transition to lay bourgeois piety.

—— and Sheingorn, P. 1999. *Writing Faith: Text, Sign, and History in the Miracle of Sainte Foy*. Chicago: University of Chicago Press. A study of hagiographic narrative as rhetorical construction and systems of representation.

Boffey, J. 1999. 'Middle English Lives.' In *The Cambridge History of Medieval English Literature*, ed. D. Wallace (Cambridge: Cambridge University Press), pp. 610–34. A discussion of how lives were represented to readers through records, letters, travelogues, biographies, saints' lives and Margery Kempe's *Book*.

Coletti, T. 2004. *Mary Magdalene and the Drama of Saints: Theater, Gender, and Religion in Late Medieval England*. Philadelphia: University of Pennsylvania Press. Argues that for medieval England the figure of Mary Magdalene poses issues of female religious authority and institutional life as well as the relationship of sexuality to spirituality.

de Certeau, M. 1988. *The Writing of History*, trans. T. Conley. New York: Columbia University Press. Essays on the theory of historiography, including a chapter on 'Hagio-Graphical Edification.'

Delany, S. 1992. *A Legend of Holy Women*. Notre Dame, Ind.: University of Notre Dame Press. Translations of Osbern Bokenham's fifteenth-century lives of virgin martyrs and other women saints.

—— 1998. *Impolitic Bodies: Poetry, Saints, and Society in Fifteenth-Century England – The Work of Osbern Bokenham*. New York: Oxford University Press. A political reading of Bokenham's legendary of women saints, emphasizing its 'corporeal semiotics' in the representation of textual, biological and institutional bodies.

de Looze, L. 1997. *Pseudo-Autobiography in the Fourteenth Century: Juan Ruiz, Guillaume de Machaut, Jean Froissart, and Geoffrey Chauc*er. Gainesville: University of Florida Press. An analysis, both historically and theoretically informed, of the pleasure medieval readers took in texts that challenged the fiction/fact boundary.

Gorlach, M. (1974). *The Textual Tradition of the South English Legendary*. Leeds Texts and Monographs, ns 6. Leeds: University of Leeds, School of English. Detailed analysis of the many manuscripts of this popular collection of saints' lives.

Heffernan, T.J. 1988. *Sacred Biography: Saints and Their Biographers in the Middle Ages*. New York: Oxford University Press. A survey of the hagiographic tradition from Gregory of Tours in the sixth century to fifteenth-century English lives.

Jankofsky, K. 1977. 'Entertainment, Edification, and Popular Education in *The South English Legendary*.' *Journal of Popular Culture* 11, 706–17. Argues that the *Legendary* was 'Englished' by inclusion of national history and local traditions along with moral edification.

Larson, W. 2003. 'Who is the Master of this Narrative? Maternal Patronage of the Cult of St Margaret.' In *Gendering the Master Narrative: Women and Power in the Middle Ages*, ed. M.C. Erler and M. Kowalski (Ithaca, N.Y.: Cornell University Press), pp. 94–104. Analysis of the gendered appropriations of the life and cult of St Margaret in the later Middle Ages.

Riddy, F. 1996. '"Women Talking About the Things of God": A Late Medieval Sub-culture.' In *Women and Literature in Britain, 1150–1500*, ed. C.M. Meale, 2nd edn (Cambridge: Cambridge University Press), pp. 104–27. Posits a female textual community, both lay and monastic, for devotional reading in later medieval England.

Samson, A. 1985. 'The *South English Legendary*: Constructing a Context.' In *Thirteenth-Century England*, ed. P.R. Coss and S. D. Lloyd (Woodbridge: Boydell), pp. 185–95. Places the *Legendary*, a popular work, in relation to patterns of pragmatic literacy in English.

Sponsler, C. 1997. *Drama and Resistance: Bodies, Goods, and Theatricality in Late Medieval England.* Minneapolis: University of Minnesota Press. An interdisciplinary examination of late medieval cultural texts, using cultural studies methodologies.

Staley, L. 1994. *Margery Kempe's Dissenting Fictions.* University Park: Pennsylvania University Press. A study of the fictional strategies of Kempe as author vs. Kempe as subject of the autobiography, emphasizing the *Book* as social critique.

Winstead, K. 1997. *Virgin Martyrs: Legends of Sainthood in Late Medieval England.* Ithaca, N.Y.: Cornell University Press. A study of the lives of virgin saints as complex cultural texts whose reception by diverse reading communities varies widely.

Wogan-Browne, J. 2003. 'Powers of Record, Powers of Example: Hagiography and Women's History.' In *Gendering the Master Narrative: Women and Power in the Middle Ages*, ed. M. C. Erler and M. Kowaleski (Ithaca, N.Y.: Cornell University Press), pp. 71–93. Study of hagiographic narratives in a collection of Anglo-Norman lives (the Campsey manuscript) demonstrates the activity of female religious communities in fourteenth- and fifteenth-century England.

Zink, M. 1999. *The Invention of Literary Subjectivity*, trans. D. Sices. Baltimore: Johns Hopkins University Press. Argues that a new awareness of subjectivity may be found in the thirteenth century and that French literature was 'invented' as a result.

27
Medieval English Theatre: Codes and Genres

Meg Twycross

Ask anyone who has a nodding acquaintance with late medieval theatre, and they will tell you that there are three major genres: mysteries (biblical plays tracing the history of the Fall and Redemption of Man); moralities (allegorical psychodramas); and interludes (cheerful, largely secular plays of no particular length, which comprise The Rest). In one way they would be right – and in another they would be very wrong. For one thing, this range is far too restricted, although it reflects the percentage of written texts that survive. For another, can we be certain that their medieval participants would have recognized them as genres?

Modern versus Medieval Terminology

If we mean by that, did they have a distinctive word for each of these groups of plays, which corresponded roughly to ours, the answer is, 'No'. They certainly did not use our terms.[1] Of these three labels, only one, *interlude*, would have been familiar to the original audiences. *Mystery* and *morality* were first applied to medieval theatre in the eighteenth century, when English antiquarians with a renewed interest in 'old plays' picked up the terms from scholars in France. They were not contemporary theatrical terms, and we are on shaky ground if we attempt to argue from them.

The words themselves were of course current in late medieval English. *Mystery* had much the same range of meanings as it has nowadays, and a few extra, because it is a blend of two words, *mysterium*, 'hidden thing', and *ministerium*, 'service'. The latter not only gave *mystery*, 'craft guild', in the sense of 'skilled service', but the temptingly ambiguous *mystery* 'a rite/service of the church', as in 'the mystery of the Blessed Sacrament'. This was also one of its meanings in French, which suggests that the biblical and saints' plays they called *misteres* were perceived as being of the same kind as, or even descended from, liturgical drama.[2] But it was never used this way in English. When Greg Walker states that they

> are often called Mystery Plays, partly because they deal with religious mysteries (making known the ways of God – and the central principles of the Christian faith – to their audiences), and also because . . . they were put on by the craft guilds: the organizations (part trade-regulating body, part religious confraternity) responsible for administering the crafts or 'mysteries' that dominated the urban economy (Walker 2000: 3)

he is recording our perception of the meaning, not the contemporary one. Historically speaking, both these explanations are complete moonshine.

Morality at the same period meant either 'virtuous theory or practice', or 'the interpretation of a story to bring out the hidden meanings', as in Henryson's *moralitas* of the story of *Orpheus and Eurydice*. Thomas Hawkins, in his 1773 *Origin of the English Drama*, was the first to adapt it as a theatrical term from French *moralité*. The word must have seemed appropriate because *Everyman*, one of his anthologized examples, is described in its prologue as 'By fygure a morall playe'. This sounds convincingly technical – *figure* suggests allegory, though in this context it actually meant nothing more than 'in the format of'[3] – and his new genre the *morality* presents models of virtuous behaviour. In fact the term *moral play* was a one-off, created on the pattern of 'moral fable', as in Lydgate's versions of Aesop.[4] It did not catch on; all other plays of the same kind published around the same time introduce themselves on the title pages as an *interlude*. Even today, there is no consensus about which plays are to be described as 'moralities' and which as '(moral) interludes'.

The term *interlude* is late medieval, but extremely slippery. It seems to refer to a shortish theatrical entertainment, on apparently any subject, sacred or secular, performed solo or by a number of players, which happens as an independent part of something else (Davis 1984). The 'something else', however, can be anything from the celebration of Christmas Day to a larger theatrical piece. The *Satire of the Three Estates* was described as an *interlude* when it was done at Linlithgow before James V of Scotland as a Twelfth Night entertainment in 1540 (Walker 2000: 538–9); by the time it had become a full-scale outdoor play in 1554, it had acquired its own Interlude, the comic entertainment played in the interval after (or during) the time when the audience 'mak collatioun'.

We have adopted the term for a particular type of short(ish) play written in the early Tudor period, partly because publishers started to use it that way in their blurbs:

> Magnificence: A goodly interlude and a merry made by Master Skelton, poet laureate, late deceased;
>
> A godely interlude of Fulgens cenatoure of Rome, Lucres his doughter, Gayus Flaminius, and Publius Cornelius, of the Disputacyon of Noblenes;
>
> A newe and a very mery enterlude of a Palmer, a Pardoner, a Potycary, a Pedler;
>
> A Brefe Comedy or Enterlude concernynge the Temptacyon of Oure Lord and Saver Jesus Christ by Sathan in the Desart.

Some are allegorical, some are not. Some are religious, some are secular. Some are biblical, some are classical. The one thing they have in common is that they are being marketed as scripts of a manageable length and fairly small cast-lists which you might like to buy for your household players to perform, probably on Twelfth Night. Nowadays their target would be the amateur dramatic company looking for a suitable one-acter.

One word they did use is *miracle*. Again, the range of meaning was very similar to ours, though it could mean 'marvel in general', rather than solely 'marvel executed though divine power'. There was a French literary collection of *Miracles of Our Lady*, many of which were dramatized. The only surviving English 'miracle play' in this sense of the word is the *Croxton Play of the Sacrament*, which relates a sensational and to us distasteful tale of how four Jews tried to destroy the Host and how it struck back.[5] Durham perhaps had a play of Theophilus, a version of the Faust legend, one of the most famous *Miracles of Our Lady*.[6] However, it was not restricted to the miraculous in the modern sense. The *Tretise of Miraclis Pleyinge*, an apparently unique attack on late fourteenth-century religious drama by a non-standard Wycliffite, by implication extends the word to mean all the marvellous and effective works of Christ.

As a theatrical term *miracle* dies out soon after 1400. Modern scholars have restricted it to a vanished genre about which we know very little, except that it appears to have been religious in subject-matter, about 'the Passioun of Crist and Hise seyntis',[7] performed out of doors and, at least in its earlier stages, by the minor clergy (King 2001) – hence the alternative name 'clerks' play' (Twycross and Carpenter 2002: 191–3). It was clearly immensely popular: the Wife of Bath goes gadding off 'to pleyes of myracles' while her husband is away (WBP 558). An ambitious late version was the open-air biblical play at Skinners' Well outside London, performed by the guild of parish clerks apparently annually from at least 1384 to 1410 (King 2001; Lancashire 1984: 543–9), which sounds like a prototypical mystery cycle. *Of Miraclis Pleyinge* however suggests that the *miracle* has become the province of (city?) businessmen, who are pouring money into productions which they should rather be spending on the needs of their poorer neighbours (Walker 2000: 200). Does this record the beginning of the great civic cycles of the next century?[8]

They also used the word *pageant*. The Latin equivalent and source is *pagina*, which just means 'page'. The base meaning is probably something like 'section'. We are most familiar with it in the context of processional wagon-drama, where it can mean 'an individual episode' (also used of free-standing plays like *The Conversion of St Paul*), or 'the script of the same', or 'the vehicle on which it is performed'. In descriptions of non-dramatic Corpus Christi processions, it also means 'a group of costumed characters' and even 'an emblem of the guild carried in the procession'. In Ipswich the dolphin carried by the Fishmongers and the bull carried by the Butchers are called *lez pagent*.[9] This has bedevilled investigation into the history of the York Corpus Christi Play: were its early *pageants* anything other than processional floats? In accounts of court entertainments, it refers to a vehicle, the 'device or pageant' which, as The Arbour of Gold in the Garden of Pleasure, or *le Fortresse dangerus*, often formed the focal point of an elaborate costumed disguising. 'To play his pageant' also entered popular slang meaning 'to play a role'. The most famous example of this is from the Paston Letters, where it is said of the Earl of Suffolk, 'ther was neuer no man þat playd Herrod in Corpus Crysty play better and more agreable to hys pageaunt then he dud';[10] but a poignant version comes from a poem on the death of Edward IV, 'I have pleyd my pagent & now am I past, / I wyll þat ye wytt I was off no grett elde'.[11] All the world's a stage, and every pageant is transient.

We find theatrical terminology in various places: in banns advertising forthcoming productions; prologues and epilogues; account books; and the very occasional description in a chronicle or didactic work. It is useless looking for critical treatments of contemporary theatrical genres. Medieval literary theorists did not discuss and had no developed critical vocabulary for them. Literary criticism, usually in Latin, dealt almost exclusively with the theatrical genres of the Roman Empire, up to 1500 years back. They knew about comedy and tragedy both in theory and from the works of Terence and Seneca, but what they extrapolated from these was a generalization about the overall shape of a narrative. *Comedy* is a 'Play þat begynnyþ with mornynge and sorow and endyth with merth',[12] and *tragedy* 'a dite of a prosperite for a tyme, that endeth in wrecchidnesse'.[13] The terms are not restricted to plays: Chaucer's Monk's Tale is a collection of very untheatrical tragedies.

So what did they call them? The answer seems at first to be impossibly general. They were called *ludus* in Latin – *play* or *game* in English.[14] The people who performed them were *players* (the word *actor* was not used in this context until 1581). This leads us to several intriguing conclusions about what theatre, as a genre, meant to them; and makes it clear that they did not consider that the possession of a script was essential.

We are so used to *play* as a theatrical term that we automatically assume that whenever it turns up in a theatrical context it will carry our sense. But it may not have had the same connotations for a fifteenth-century speaker. To begin with, *play* and *game* in general seem to have been interchangeable, as in *The Game and Play of the Chess*. This also obtains in purely theatrical contexts. After four-and-three-quarter hours of strenuous moral allegory, God in *The Castle of Perseverance* declares, 'þus endyth oure gamys' (3645).[15] The Banns to N-Town conclude:

> Now haue we told yow all bedene
> The hool mater þat we thynke to play.
> Whan þat ye come þer xal ye sene
> This game wel pleyd in good aray . . .
> (516–19)[16]

Conversely, when we hear that the citizens of Athens 'went to the theatre . . . to see plays', it transpires that they were watching athletics.[17] It would probably take us nearer to the medieval way of looking at it if we were to substitute the word *game* for *play* throughout.

Theatre as 'Game'

So what do these names imply about their perception of theatre? There seem to be several strands. First, it is festive: entertainment as opposed to hard work. The Banns to N-Town proclaim that the intention is 'þe pepyl to plese with pleys ful glad' (6). Religious plays take place on holidays: 'in grete festis & in Sondayys', when, according to *Dives and Pauper*, 'men mon lefully makyn merthe'. If to a modern audience the combination of entertainment and religion may seem strange, *Dives and Pauper* has the answer: 'þe reste & þe merthe & þe ese & þe welfare þat God hat ordeynyd in þe halyday is tokene of endeles reste, ioye & merthe & welfare in heuen blisse þat we hopyn to han withoutyn ende'.[18] Because they are festive and celebratory, they are all ultimately upbeat. The Corpus Christi Play is a divine comedy. The moral plays show the hero Mankind ultimately being saved, even though *The Castle of Perseverance* gives us an eleventh-hour cliff-hanger. The archetypal hero is Theophilus, not Faustus.

Next, it is not 'serious': compare the axiomatic distinction between *ernest* and *game*. This is a more difficult one. In one sense it merely points to the fact that plays are not, and are not meant to be, real life. They are make-believe. This must have been reinforced by the circumstances of playing. The plays took over and transformed everyday space: in processional religious drama, the city streets; in liturgical drama, the churches; in the moral and other interludes, the great halls of households, educational establishments or civic guilds; in other drama, churchyards, inn-yards, market-places. The audience shares this space: close enough for direct eye-contact, to be harangued and solicited. There was no point in creating an illusion of naturalism. Everything we know about the staging, particularly of the religious plays – the masks, the gold face of God; symbolic costumes like the 'sark wounded' of Christ, the crowns for the Maries, black and white costumes for the Damned and Saved Souls; the metaphors turned props; the male actors playing women – suggest that a degree of stylization was the norm (Twycross 1988; Twycross and Carpenter 2002: 198–200).[19] So do the use of allegory as a major mode, the demonstrative style, direct address, the way the actors at the end slip out of character to close the play with a blessing. All theatre is illusion, but this draws attention to the fact. It is unselfconsciously metatheatrical.

The *ernest/game* dichotomy could, however, be used as ammunition for an attack on the very existence of religious theatre. An extension and distortion of it, proffered in *Of Miraclis Pleyinge*, was that *play* = *bourde*, 'jest', and that those who played the miracles of God were, to reverse the Nun's Priest's dictum, making game of earnest. Such 'japing' is, says the author, tantamount to blasphemy.[20] But no one else seems to have worried about this, and the few existing statements of intent emphasize the plays' usefulness as a vehicle for the Christian message.[21] There is however some anxiety to demonstrate that although these games themselves are make-believe, they present true material. 'Of Holy Wrytte þis game xal bene / And of no fablys be no way' (520–1), declare the N-Town Banns.

Play, especially the verb, also implies the deployment of performance skills and invention. Absolon in Chaucer's Miller's Tale 'pleyeth Herodes upon a scaffold hye' in order 'to shewe his lightnesse and maistrye' (3383–4). It also suggests feats of physical dexterity and strength, as in 'sword-play'. The 'wake pleyes' in the Knight's Tale turn out to be Virgilian funeral games, including 'Who wrastleth best naked with oille enoynt' (2960). Robert Mannyng of Brunne bundles together under the heading of *pleyes* that the Christian should refuse to be involved in, 'myracles and bourdys / Or tournamentys of grete prys'.[22]

For there is no strong sense of demarcation between theatrical and other kinds of play. Alexander Carpenter, in his *Destructorium viciorum* (c.1425),[23] lists various kinds of *ludus* under different headings, according to their degree of moral danger. He classifies the *ludi* of jongleurs and minstrels (as conjurers?), of dice and knuckle-bones, under 'games of deception'; ring-dances (*chorea*, 'caroles'), other kinds of dance (*tripudia*), interludes, and other types of theatrical play (including the Roman amphitheatre) as 'games of lascivious emptiness and pleasure'; football, casting the stone, tournaments and jousts, as 'games of incautious action', because they can lead to gratuitous physical damage; and chess and music, especially to the glory of God, as 'honest social games'. We would distinguish games of skill or chance from performance-based plays, but there remains a grey area: where would you put *caroles* (often accompanied by song, and sometimes in dialogue form), jongleurs and minstrels, tournaments? What of mummings, disguisings, Royal Entries?

The mumming is a case in point (Twycross and Carpenter 2002: 83–100, 151–68). Originally a Christmas folk-custom involving a house-visit by roughly disguised persons who challenged the householder to play at dice, its distinguishing feature was that the visitors kept 'mum'. But when it was appropriated by City and Court as a suitable vehicle for ceremonial gift-giving, it began to acquire a story-line (mysterious visitors from foreign parts come to compliment local potentate) and elaborate costumes. It then acquired an interpreter figure who expatiated on the significance and the origins of the characters and the compliments they wished to pay. At what point does this become theatre? For theatrical it certainly is. The same goes for the disguising, whose name merely means 'dressing up', an interactive dance-form where the participants were costumed thematically. It was the ancestor of the Stuart masque and our modern ballet – save that the audience at Covent Garden are not invited to partner the dancers. It acquired elaborate mobile scenery and a brief romantic or political story-line. The dancers did not speak: but do we therefore say that ballet is not a theatrical genre?

We see tournaments as purely martial exercises, though elaborately costumed. It comes as a surprise to find that the participants and onlookers seem sometimes to have difficulty in distinguishing it from the disguising (Twycross and Carpenter 2002: 128). The same costumiers serviced both, combatants took on the personae of Arthurian knights, the Pope and Cardinals, the Seven Deadly Sins. Entries into the lists were cast in the form of romance challenges. There were the same opportunities for political or romantic subtexts. The only difference was that the physical skill exhibited was fighting, not dancing. The scenario, opposition as combat, was fixed, though the outcome necessarily remained open-ended. It was a game: was it theatre?

We have to remember that they did not have distinct buildings called *theatres* dedicated solely to the performance of drama. The nearest to these were the 'playing places' of East Anglia and elsewhere, where the major place-and-scaffold plays were enacted: but even they, once the theatrical game was over, could revert to venues for football or wrestling. Similarly, learned perception of the Roman *theatrum* was of the amphitheatre where *ludi* included chariot races, wild beast shows and gladiatorial combat, and they understood classical drama to be a public recitation by the poet accompanied by music and mime.

Their *ludus*, then, seems to have been something much more comprehensive and fluid than our *play*. The stress is on performativity. This might explain why *plays* in our sense happily accommodate other types of game. The modern critical search for thematic appropriateness may often be completely pointless. Cornelius asks Lucres 'what maner of passe tyme' she would like while they are waiting for Gaius to turn up: 'Wyll ye see a bace-daunce after the gyse / Of Spayne, whyle ye have no thynge to do?' (1809–11). Here it seems to be regarded as an addition to the main action, delightful but dispensable. The famous suggestion from the title page of *The Four Elements* (printed 1520), 'Also, yf ye lyst ye may brynge in a dysgysynge' (there are no hints about theme or characters), follows detailed instructions on what, alternatively, you can cut – 'muche of the sad (*serious*) mater' – if you wish to reduce the running time from one-and-a-half hours to forty-five minutes, a delightfully pragmatic approach to theatrical integrity.[24]

Sometimes these theatrical 'turns' are verbal; the *sermon joyeux* of Folly in *Satire*, on the traditional text *stultorum infinitus est numerus* (Ecclesiastes 1: 15); the quacksalver and his boy (a much-appreciated feature, with his patter and sleight of hand, of village fairs) in *Croxton*. Others show 'lightness and maistrie'. The Chester Herod juggles with his staff and sword; the Chester Shepherds wrestle with each other. You can make a thematic point of the second ('He hath put down the mighty from their seat and exalted the humble and meek'); it is difficult to see what Herod's dexterity does apart from add to his already flamboyant persona. The tossing in canvas of Mak the sheep-stealer is a carnival game, involving a straw-stuffed dummy, familiar from the Continent though not otherwise evidenced in England (though later, according to *Tom Brown's Schooldays*, it was a well-known schoolboy torture). Nowadays it is considered to be the punishment of Lent or Winter for outstaying his welcome. It is hard to see how this, or any other of the ingenious 'thematic' explanations which have been proffered, could be relevant here. It seems to be there purely to release the Shepherds' pent-up frustration, and the actors' energy.

Sometimes, however, an embedded disguising makes an essential contribution to the play's theme. In *Wisdom*, when Mind, Will and Understanding, the three faculties of the Soul, are corrupted, they signal their new worldliness by calling up

. . . a dance
Off thow þat longe to owr retenance, *those who belong to our retinue*
Cummynge in by contenance *miming*
þis were a dysporte.
(685–8)

The disguisings of their new retainers, representing Maintenance, Perjury and Lechery, provide a vivid visual illustration of the nature of their corruption. They are also used to make a political point, satirizing the Duke and Duchess of Suffolk: not verbally, but through coded signals in their costumes (Marshall 1992).

The dynamic of the theatrical event seems to dictate what goes where: often what seems bewildering on the page works perfectly in performance. There is no sense that it is tasteless or aesthetically improper to mix comedy and high seriousness, the kind of thing that drove neoclassical critics to hysteria over Shakespeare and led to the wholesale condemnation of tragicomedy as a bastard English invention.[25] Furnivall observed in 1896: 'Now, did the mixture of comic bits with most serious subjects take off the effect of the mysteries of Christianity performed before the common folk? I doubt it.' He recalls an account of a Passion play in Spain in which 'at one point a bell tinkled and in came a troupe of ballet girls in short frocks and flesh-tights, and danced a ballet. All the onlookers evidently took it as a natural and proper occurrence'.[26] Bogatyrev points out that this 'simultaneous use of the most diverse styles' is typical of folk theatre.[27]

Often one tone is deliberately played off against the other in the same plot. In *Mankind*, the serious discourse of Mercy is mocked and parodied by Mischief and the vices. It is meant to be subversive, but the target of the subversion is really the audience. They are seduced into playing along with the energetic villains, to be brought up with a jerk when disaster follows and the serious genre reasserts itself. This battle of two voices in which one is temporarily suppressed is particularly suited to the plot-line of the moral plays, but it also works most effectively in, for example, the Towneley *Cain*, and the York *Crucifixion*. The audience is side-tracked into sympathy with tithe-dodging, thus lawlessness, and eventually murder; and into willing the successful crucifixion of Christ.

Theatre and Literature

So did they, as their terminology suggests, see theatre as a game with a story-line, or conversely as the game version of a story, the difference between literature and theatre merely the method of delivery? The famous description of plays as 'quick [*living*] books' seems to support this (Walker 2000: 198; see Twycross 1988). Certainly they seem to have had few problems adapting literary narratives to plays: nothing is so wide-ranging or far-fetched that it cannot be staged. Forget about the unities of time and place. The Corpus Christi Play covers the entire chronology of the human race. The Digby *Mary Magdalene* ranges over the Mediterranean from Palestine to Marseilles. Miracles are merely a challenge to the director's ingenuity. Cosmic events like the Flood are managed by a mixture of description, make-believe and scenic audacity, anchored by recognizable human interaction.

It was perhaps easier to make the transition because much of medieval literature is so performative – to such an extent it is sometimes difficult to tell what was meant to be performed and what was not. Romances, and even biblical paraphrases, have 'minstrel' introductions. Some 'poems' are clearly performance texts. The early *De clerico et puella* ('Damishel, reste wel!') is even labelled as an *interludium*; it could have been done by one man with many voices, or a group of players. The thirteenth-century *Dame Sirith* is described as a *fablel* (fabliau), and has a narrator, but its dialogue has marginal character-headings for three voices; the fourth, non-speaking, character is a performing dog.[28] But is the later *De clerico et puella* ('My deþ I loue, my lif I hate') a literary 'dialogue at a window', or a performance text? Is Henryson's *Robene and Makyn* a dialogue poem or a *pastourelle* play?

Dialogue is obviously transferable to theatre. It also came naturally to medieval writers. Dialectic and disputation, theological, philosophical and forensic, were built into their educational system. Dynamically, not only do dialogues lay out both sides of an argument; by employing different voices they give a sense of interaction, engagement – and competition. St Bernard's analysis of the implications of the Redemption, the debate of the Four Daughters of God,[29] was adapted by three very different major plays: the N-Town *Parliament of Heaven*, *The Castle of Perseverance* and Thomas Chaundler's Latin academic drama *Liber apologeticus de omni statu humanae naturae*.[30] Even today, courtroom drama can be gripping, especially if we identify with the plaintiff or the accused – here the entire human race. In another forum, Buonaccorsa de Montemagno's *De vera nobilitate,* recycled as the main plot of *Fulgens and Lucres,* not only deals with a burning social issue (birth or merit?) but involves the audience in the outcome of a love affair – will Lucres, in the face of social pressures, choose the man who will suit her the best?

Another 'performative' feature was the use of direct address. The first-person authorial voice turns up embodied in a metatheatrical character called the Expositor, or Doctor (Twycross 1983: 82–8). At the other end of the spectrum, the literature of popular religious meditation invited the reader to imagine the figure of Christ or the Blessed Virgin speaking directly to him or her (Twycross 1983: 76–7). As an aid, some manuscripts supply both text and image. It is not surprising to find these adopted into plays, sometimes verbatim. On folio 67v of London, British Library Additional MS 37049, a figure of Christ crucified addresses the reader, 'Þou synful man þat by me gase, / A while to me turne þu þi face / Behold & se in ilk a place / How I am dyght / Al to rent & al to shent / Man for þi plyght'. The poem is lifted wholesale into the Towneley *Resurrection* (26.248–350, slightly rearranged): reader becomes audience.[31]

We could call this intertextuality, but it is pragmatic, rather than self-consciously allusive in a literary way, like Chaucer's writing. The plays share codes and genres with literature because they have the same aims. The Corpus Christi plays, for example, have three main functions: to show and tell; to explicate; and to move their audience emotionally. This affects the style they use, and the literature they draw on.

They show and tell the Christian narrative. Scholars have become so frustrated at the popular view that these plays are merely staged 'Bible stories' that we have perhaps gone too far the other way and emphasized everything but the story. But one of the few descriptions of the York Corpus Christi play, in 1426, calls it *quemdam ludum sumptuosum in diuersis paginis compilatum veteris & noui testamenti* (a certain lavish play put together in various pageants of the Old and New Testament). Banns, prologues and epilogues stress what the narrative is going to be or has been about: 'Now haue we told yow all bedene / The hool *mater* þat we thynke to play' (N-Town *Banns* 516–17); or, as the Chester Banns say simply, 'Be here on Whitson-Monday / Then beginneth the storie!' (213–14). The plays are part of the contemporary initiative of Englishing the Bible 'for lewed men', that is, for people who cannot read Latin fluently. They belong with the monumental verse retellings like the *Cursor mundi*, the *Northern Passion* (used by the York playwrights), the *Stanzaic Life of Christ* (used by Chester) and especially Nicholas Love's Englishing of Pseudo-Bonaventure's *Speculum vite Christi*, the *Mirror of the Blessed Life of Jesus Christ* (used by N-Town).

'Show and tell' also describes their theatrical style, which often sounds uncannily Brechtian. It is also extremely economical. Instead of the characters going through contortions of verisimilitude to convey information 'naturalistically', they merely tell the audience directly what they need to know (Twycross 1983). Characters introduce themselves: 'Saule ys my name – I wyll þat ye notify – / Whych conspyreth the dyscy-pylys wyth thretys and menacys' (*Conversion of St Paul* 21–2);[32] say how they feel– 'A, lorde, I trymble þer I stande, / So am I arow [*afraid*] to do þat dede' (York 21.141–2);[33] and what they are doing – 'ȝis, here is a stubbe will stiffely stande, / Thurgh bones and senous it schall be soght' (York 35.102–3). This demonstrative mode, which has been christened 'Behold and see' (Mills 1985), may have evolved by necessity in performance circumstances where the audience could not always be certain of seeing exactly what was going on, but it has the effect of underlining and presenting significant action: 'Jesu, my sone þat is so dere, / Now borne is he' (York 14.55–6).

The story-telling often includes a story-teller: plays are introduced or punctuated by the Presenter figure. Sometimes he acts as a purely narrative link (e.g. Chester 4.3–6).[34] At other times he has a much more interventionist role:

> To þe pepyl not lernyd I stonde as a techer,
> Of þis processyon to ȝeve informacyon;
> And to them þat be lernyd as a gostly precher,
> That in my rehersayl they may haue delectacyon.
> (N-Town *Procession of Saints* 9–12)

The plays belong to that branch of devotional literature which has a very strong guiding authorial voice. It was not enough just to tell the story. Since it was accepted that Scripture had many levels of meaning – literal, moral, allegorical, anagogical – it was the duty of the learned to explicate them (Twycross 1983).

Playwrights also took this mission seriously. Sometimes they did it by direct explication through the Presenter or some other authoritative character. The Chester Doctor (of Divinity) explains the typology of Abraham and Isaac:

> By Abraham I may understand
> the Father of heaven that cann fond *brought it about*
> with his Sonnes blood to breake that bond
> that the dyvell had brought us to.

By Isaack understande I maye
Jesus that was obedyent aye,
his Fathers will to worke alwaye
and death for to confounde.
(4.469–76)

The N-Town Moses expounds the Ten Commandments like a good parish priest: 'Desyre not þi neyborys wyff, / Þow she be fayr and whyte as swan / And þi wyff brown' (6.165–7).

Sometimes the characters themselves are their own commentators. They point out the exemplary nature of their own and other's actions: 'Euery childe xulde with good dyligens / His modyr to plese, his owyn wyl forsake' (N-Town 21.279–80), sometimes cynically: 'mede [*bribery*] doth most in every qwest, / And mede is maystyr bothe est and west . . . / With mede men may bynde berys [*bears*]' (N-Town 35.261–4). They also offer gems from the treasury of biblical exegesis. The Chester Three Kings, following the *Golden Legend*, explain the meaning of their gifts: gold signifies 'a kinges powere', frankincense the Godhead, 'and bodely death alsoe in good faye / by myrre I understande' (Chester 9.89–91). The Towneley Christ explains to John the Baptist that his Father has sent, to assist at the Baptism, 'his angels two / In tokyn I am both God and man' (19.145–6); the York Joseph assuages Mary's worry that they have no lamb for the Purification sacrifice because 'Oure babb Jesus . . . / He is the lame of God I say, / that all our syns shall take away' (17.257, 263–4). This fascination with signs, symbols and tokens is a continuous thread, though it appears differently in different cycles.

Theatre was ideally suited to stir up an emotional relationship with the figure of Christ the Man, to arouse compassion and thus love and emulation. Medieval piety familiarly focuses on the suffering of Christ and his saints, hoping to provoke tears. But besides the enumeration of broken sinews and bleeding flesh, it sets out to shock and destabilize by extravagant metaphorical flights of fancy. In the Bodley *Burial of Christ*, Mary Magdalene says to Joseph of Arimathæa: 'Cum hithere, Ioseph, beholde & looke / How many bludy letters beyn writen in þis buke, / Small margente [*margin*] her is', and he replies, 'Ye, this parchement is stritchit owt of syse' (271–4).[35] Metaphysical poetry before the event, it aims to enforce not only the horror of Christ's suffering but also its ultimate efficacy and meaning: here the 'parchment', Christ's skin, is the instrument on which the charter of the redemption of mankind is written. The metaphors lead away from the physical to the metaphysical, causing the audience to perceive the action in another dimension.

Allegorical theatre, too, has a solid grounding in literature. *The Castle of Perseverance* ultimately goes back to Hugh of St Victor's inventive allegory in *De anima*, many times translated and adapted (*Sawles Warde*, Robert Grosseteste's *Chasteau d'amour*), crossed with the rich quasi-scientific literature on the Ages of Man. We even find poems which seem like a sketch for a play, complete with marginal character designations and costume illustrations, like the engaging 'Seven Ages of Man' in London, British Library Additional MS 37049, where the Good and Bad Angels tussle over the Everyman figure from the cradle to the grave. Even the new-born baby speaks: which is precisely what he does in both *The Castle of Perseverance* and *The World and the Child.*

Theatre as Image

We have seen theatre as action and theatre as text: this last reminds us about theatre as picture. In fact, the description of theatre as a 'quick book' was contrasting it with the 'dead book' not of literature, but of image: 'betere they ben holden in mennus minde and oftere rehersid by the pleyinge of hem than by the peintinge, for this is a deed bok, the tother a quick'.[36] There is no room here to go into this topic in depth (see Twycross 1983), but anyone wanting to understand the Corpus Christi plays, for example, should immerse themselves not only in the individual iconographies of the biblical scenes, but also in the way in which these 'books' were to be read. Iconography is a literature in itself, with a whole language of narration, characterization, metaphor, metonymy and symbol.

Figure 27.1 The Nativity; the Virgin Mary, dressed as befits her spiritual status, is attended by the apocryphal midwives: stained glass at East Harling church, Norfolk. (By permission of Meg Twycross.)

A Taxonomy of Medieval Theatre

Medieval theatre thus belongs to several genres. Playwrights drew on familiar modes as they felt them to be appropriate and effective. The result is much more stylistically varied than we might at first expect. It might seem sensible to classify the different kinds by subject-matter. But since this is theatre, there are other considerations which can cut across a tidy content-based patterning. Audience is one; venue, another; occasion, a third. The three are often interconnected, but sometimes they can pull a genre apart.

For example, *Wisdom* can be classed as a moral allegory, but allegory on an intellectual level for a theologically as well as a theatrically sophisticated audience. Its approach is detectably different from that of the mass-audience *Castle of Perseverance* (though not crudely so: the *Castle* is by no means simplistic). Besides, it is designed for household performance indoors, probably in a Great Hall, while the *Castle* is written for outdoor place-and-scaffold staging on a grand scale. The difference between indoor and outdoor staging usually reflects the difference between implied audiences: indoor, essentially private, for a closed community (household, Inn of Court, school, university, guild), full of in-jokes, ellipses and allusions; outdoor, public, for a wider community, declarative, appealing to a universalized, shared knowledge. Linguists might like to try out the concepts of private and public discourse, though not in the modern idiom. Both deploy elaborate language, as they do extravagant production values: fine rhetoric, like fine costumes, was a necessary and expected pleasure.

Besides this, indoor and outdoor venues themselves vary. There is no room here to go into the details of staging (Beadle 1994: 37–84), but obviously it determines the way the material is presented. An outdoor biblical play performed on wagons, pageant by pageant, will be structured differently from one intended for place-and-scaffold staging. Individual episodes, playing to smaller audiences, will often have a more concentrated and intimate emotional focus, and will be able to switch between modes and scales (emotional, lyrical, mythical, forensic) more easily, but will miss out on the panoramic sweep of the wider arena. We think of indoor theatre as being largely Great Hall staging, but churches are also indoor venues, with a different atmosphere and acoustic. They can specialize in striking scenic effects, especially vertical ones, since there is a solid building to which to attach the ropes for flying machines and directional fireworks.

Occasion, too, is very important in determining mode, style and audience. All medieval theatre was to a certain extent occasional. Even if performances were not annual seasonal events, like the Corpus Christi play, the Christmas mummings or the Plough Monday plays, they were self-referential special occasions, bringing a community, large or small, together in a celebratory mood.

This tentative set of categories attempts to give some sense of the range of theatrical events in our period, and to redress the balance of the purely literary view of 'medieval drama'. Some of these survive as scripts; some (especially the less verbal ones) are described by chroniclers or ambassadors; some are known only by passing references in account books. In the luckiest cases, we have a combination of at least two of these.

Plays Whose Content Comes from the Christian Religion

First in time are **liturgical plays**, starting with the many versions of the *Quem quaeritis* (the words of the angel at the Sepulchre to the three Maries) first recorded in the *Regularis concordia* of Winchester c.975. Usually in Latin (though English creeps in later),[37] usually sung, they are embedded in a church service. This controlled their style and mode: formal, hieratic, and not unlike opera. The casts were of course all male clergy, except in nunneries, which may have affected the later English convention that women did not perform in public. Their avowed aim was to strengthen the faith of the laity: they related the liturgy to the stories behind the ritual, while drawing on all the familiar adjuncts of music, ceremony, incense and a powerfully theatrical use of light and dark to stir up religious responsiveness. Costumes were often vestments only slightly adapted, liturgical objects were used metonymically as props or even characters: so the Maries carried thuribles for spice-jars, and the processional Cross represented the risen Christ.

Some biblical narratives (the Purification of the Virgin Mary, the Entry into Jerusalem) were commemorated on the appropriate festivals by **liturgical processions**. Processions have their own theatrical dynamic (Twycross 1996: 1–33) and in some cases they featured costumed characters and some mimesis, like the Beverley guilds' *St Helena* and *Presentation,* and the Palm Sunday *processus prophetarum* of, for example, the London churches. There is cross-fertilization: a *Prophets* pageant often links the Old and New Testaments in the Corpus Christi Play, and the *Purification* and *Entry into Jerusalem* plays have strong formal processional elements.

The **biblical play**, our ***mystery***, is most familiar as an individual pageant in the major cycles (also not a medieval term: it does not even turn up in this meaning in the *OED*), such as the York Corpus Christi Play, and the Chester Whitsun Plays. They also however appear as singletons, presumably as parish and/or guild drama. The Northampton *Abraham* may be an example, and there are records of many *Resurrection* plays at Easter. The 'clerk's play'/*miracle* may also have featured individual episodes: for example, the play of the *Resurrection* in the churchyard at Beverley c.1220.

Plays about the Articles of the Faith, as in the (lost) *Creed* and *Paternoster* plays. We have no scripts, and know little about them from other sources, except that they were outdoors, episodic and probably processional. In stained glass, the Apostles' Creed is represented by a sequence of the Twelve, each carrying a banderole with his particular verse; the York *Creed Play* may have been a run of saints' plays. The *Paternoster* plays of York and Beverley were probably about the Seven Petitions of the Paternoster as a corrective to the Seven Deadly Sins: Beverley lists seven Sin plays, and an eighth called 'Viciouse'.

The **saint's play** was a prolific genre: surviving scripts, like *The Conversion of St Paul*, and the Digby *Mary Magdalene*, are merely the tip of an iceberg. They are evidenced very early: we know of a play of St Katherine at Dunstable c.1100. Known saints' plays emphasize the miraculous, expressed by grand special effects. The *Conversion of St Paul* is effected when *a feruent* (firework emulating a thunderbolt) *with gret tempest* strikes him from his horse. The Digby *Mary Magdalene* is a true spectacular with fiery devils, burning buildings, more *fervents*, the ground opening and swallowing up a temple and its occupants, a ship (on wheels?) which travels around the Mediterranean, and angels descending from heaven in a cloud.

Close to these are the plays about **miracles**, such as the *Croxton Play of the Sacrament* and the *Theophilus* play from Durham. The sensationalism of the former includes a bleeding Host, a detachable arm, and an exploding oven, out of which bursts *an image . . . wyth woundys bledyng* which reprimands the blasphemers and then turns again into the Host.

Moral Plays

This picks up *Everyman*'s term: they are plays which deal, prescriptively, with human behaviour.

Allegorical plays on the Life of Man shade from the epic, as in the *Castle of Perseverance*, through plays for a more limited cast, such as *Nature*, *Mankind* and *Everyman* itself, down to *The World and the Child*, ingeniously arranged as a two-hander. They can plot the whole life of Man from the cradle to the grave and beyond, or concentrate on a particular crisis point, such as the coming of death. They are particularly good on the mid-life crisis. Allegory is used as a tool for psychological analysis. This mode makes clever use of theatricality to present the nature of temptation: how, partly depends on the scale and venue of the production. A grand place-and-scaffold play like *The Castle of Perseverance* can present the assault of evil as a full-blown psychomachia, with a pitched battle centred on the siege of the castle. In an interlude like *The World and the Child*, this is translated to a fencing match with Folly, backed up with a lot of clever word-play and the seductions of low-life comedy. Since temptation comes largely from materialism and frivolity, the smaller-scale moral interludes can easily become comedies of manners.

The **political allegory**, such as *Magnificence* or *A Satire of the Three Estates*, uses the format of the moral play to present the fall and redemption of a ruler. Its manipulative tempters, insinuating themselves into the courtly arena, specialize in quick-witted repartee, sleight of hand, disguise, false names and veiled and not-so-veiled satirical references to contemporary politics. The plot works up to a dramatic peripeteia, out of which the ruler emerges chastened and reformed.

The **exemplum**. I adopt this term from sermon literature, to describe a play that is not exactly a saint's life, and not exactly a romance, but has a moral lesson. Not a very well-evidenced genre, but the story of the so-called *Dux Moraud*, an acting script for the lead character alone, an incestuous duke, is known from elsewhere, as is the plot of *Robert of Sicily*, familiar from the *Gesta Romanorum*. Unfortunately we have no script for this, only records of performance in 1452/3 at Lincoln and at Chester in 1529.[38]

Disputations and **debates**. Arguably a mode rather than a genre, they are included here because some plays are essentially dramatized debates. The characters may be generic with allegorical names (*Occupation and Idleness*), or typical (the main characters in *Fulgens and Lucres* – landed aristocracy versus new meritocracy). Sometimes they represent the viewpoints of different classes of society on a particular topic (*Gentleness and Nobility*, Heywood's *Weather*). Although they can be used to discuss theological matters, they tend to be vehicles for social or political discussion. They expect their audience to be excited by sheer intellectual fireworks, sometimes interspersed with bouts of fisticuffs. The format is also employed to discuss *questions d'amour*, as in *A Play of Love*: is it better to be loving-not-loved, loved-not-loving, a lover-loved, or neither-loving-nor-loved? These had been a parlour game in polite society ever since the twelfth century, and many of Henry VIII's court disguisings seem to have incorporated love-debates.

Plays on Secular Themes

Romances. A fifteenth-century chronicler records that in 1444 St Albans saw a performance of *Eglemour and Degrebelle*, apparently a version of *Sir Eglamour of Artois*, while in Bermondsey Abbey there was 'a play . . . of a knight cleped Florence'[39] which sounds suspiciously like Gower's *Tale of Florent* and the Loathly Lady. Are these the only surviving clues to a secular romance genre like the Dutch *abele spelen*?[40] Court pageant disguisings often had a romance theme, if not plot.

The classical genres of **comedy** and **tragedy** were at first played in Latin, then in English. *Terence in English* (the *Andria*, translated c.1500) looks impenetrable, but acts like a dream, and gives some idea of the attractions of the genre. Terentian comedy specializes in quick-fire twists and turns of plot, with stock (Athenian) bourgeois characters and eleventh-hour happy endings. Normally academic drama, played in schools and colleges, it also enjoyed a vogue in the courts of Henry VIII and Cardinal Wolsey.

Fabliaux/farces: early texts like *De clerico et puella* and *Dame Sirith* suggest that this genre, more familiar from literature, may have enjoyed an almost completely unevidenced popular life, emerging later in the Tudor interlude.

Robin Hood games seem to have turned into plays in our sense. As in the ballads, the proto-Marxist romantic hero provides a delightfully subversive break from real life. Henry VIII enthusiastically played at Robin Hood and Maid Marian.

Ceremonial Shows

In the **Royal Entry**, a sequence of scenarios, tailored to the person celebrated, builds up an implicit narrative such as the celestial journey of the soul, or the Entry into the Heavenly Jerusalem (Kipling 1998). Extravagant and expensive, with breath-taking scenic effects, they were often called *shows* or *sights*. Formal lengthy speeches full of biblical and classical allusion delivered by heroes of religion, mythology and history situated the royal person in a continuum of authority, by blood and by divine concession. They were designed simultaneously to exalt and to admonish: with supreme power goes commensurately great responsibility.

Theatrical Games with Implicit or Largely Non-verbal Scenarios

These include tournaments, mummings and disguisings. Some folk-games could be included here purely because we do not know if they had words or not: for example, is the 'summer game' the name of a genre or of an occasion? What happened at a 'king-game', and what was its relationship to a Robin Hood play? The St George Ridings (Lancashire 1984: nos 959, 1494) had a cast of characters; did they speak? Versions of some of these were taken up by the Court: in 1494 a *St George* play appeared as a disguising in Westminster Hall (Lancashire 1984: no. 959).

A collection of essays like this, which divides literature into a multiplicity of genres but treats theatre as only one, on a par with romance or lyric, is clearly missing the point in a very modern way. Medieval theatre is not one genre, but many, a multi-dimensional web of intersecting modes.

See also: 3 Religious Authority and Dissent, 7 From Manuscript to Modern Text, 8 Translation and Society, 18 Images, 20 Middle English Romance, 23 Lyric, 24 Literature of Religious Instruction, 25 Mystical and Devotional Literature, 26 Accounts of Lives, 28 Morality and Interlude Drama, 29 York Mystery Plays, 33 The *Canterbury Tales.*

Notes

1 Mills 1998 discusses this independently.

2 Graham Runnalls, 'Mystère "représentation théâtrale": histoire d'un mot', *Revue de Linguistique Romane* 64 (2000), 321–45.

3 The Dutch original says *een schoon boecxken ghemaeckt in den maniere van eenen speele ofte esbatemente*, 'a handsome booklet made in the fashion of a play or entertainment'.

4 *The Minor Poems of John Lydgate. Part 2: Secular Poems*, ed. Henry Noble MacCracken, EETS os 192 (1934), p. 598, line 936.

5 It uses the word *miracle* about the transformation of the Host into a living figure of Christ: 'Thus endyth the Play of the Blyssyd Sacrament, whyche myracle was done in the forest of Aragon, in the famous cité Eraclea, the yere of owr Lord God M[l] cccc. lxi' (Walker 2000: 233). Wherever possible, as here, references are to the texts in Walker 2000. Otherwise they are to the standard editions, as cited in these notes.

6 In *Non-cycle Plays and Fragments* ed. Norman Davis, EETS ss 1 (1970) 118–19.

7 *Tretise of Miraclis Pleyinge* in Walker 2000: 198.

8 However, the water is muddied by disapproving references elsewhere to the *Lud{us} qui vulgariter dicitur miraculos* ('play which is called *miracles* in the vernacular') as an undignified masked romp which suggests the Feast of Fools rather than a serious religious play.

9 *Records of Plays and Players in Norfolk and Suffolk, 1300–1642*, ed. David Galloway and John Wasson, Malone Society Collections, 11 (Oxford: Oxford University Press for the Malone Society, 1980), pp. 170, 173, 177, etc.

10 *Paston Letters and Papers of the Fifteenth Century*, ed. Norman Davis, 2 vols (Oxford: Clarendon Press, 1971–6), II, 426.

11 *Religious Lyrics of the XVth Century*, ed. Carleton Brown (Oxford: Clarendon Press, 1939), no. 159, 'The Lament of the Soul of Edward IV', lines 85–6.

12 *Promptorium parvulorum*, ed. A. L. Mayhew, EETS es 102 (1908), col. 351.

13 Chaucer, *Boece*, book 2, prosa 2, lines 71–2.

14 V. A. Kolve, in *The Play called Corpus Christi* (London: Arnold, 1966), developed this into an argument based on game theory: interesting and provocative, but outdated.

15 Line references are to *The Castle of Perseverance*, in *The Macro Plays*, ed. Mark Eccles, EETS os 262 (1969).

16 Line references are to *The N-Town Play*, ed. Stephen Spector, 2 vols, EETS ss 11 and 12 (1991).

17 *The Middle English Translation of Christine de Pisan's 'Livre du corps de policie'*, ed. Diane Bornstein, Middle English Texts, 7 (Heidelberg: Winter, 1977) p. 90; original reference from *MED*.

18 *Dives and Pauper*, ed. Priscilla Heath Barnum, vol. 1, pt. 1, EETS os 275 (1976), pp. 293, 295.

19 Articles on female roles in all-male casts in *Medieval English Theatre* 5:2 (1983) 110–80, 6:2 (1984) 96–100, 7:1 (1985) 25–51.

20 See Nicholas Davis, 'The *Tretise of Myraclis Pleyinge*: On Milieu and Authorship', *Medieval English Theatre* 12 (1990), 124–51.

21 E.g., the 1388/9 Guild Return for the Paternoster Guild of York, *REED: York* 6–7.

22 Robert of Brunne's *Handlyng Synne*, ed. F. J. Furnivall, EETS os 119 (1901) and 123 (1903), lines 4659–60.

23 Alexander Carpenter, *Destructorium viciorum* (Paris: Egidius de Gourmont, 1516).

24 *Three Rastell Plays*, ed. Richard Axton (Cambridge: Brewer, 1979), p. 30.

25 John Dryden, *Essay of Dramatic Poesy* in *The Major Works*, ed. Keith Walker (Oxford: Oxford University Press, 1987), p. 94.

26 *The Digby Plays*, ed. F. J. Furnivall, EETS es 70 (1896), p. xii.

27 Petr Bogatyrev, 'Semiotics in the Folk Theater', in *Semiotics of Art: Prague School Contributions*, ed. Ladislav Matejka and Irwin R. Titunik (Cambridge, Mass.: MIT Press, 1976), pp. 33–50.

28 Both texts in *Early Middle English Verse and Prose*, ed. J. A. W. Bennett and G. V. Smithers (Oxford: Clarendon Press, 1966), nos 6 and 15.

29 St Bernard, *Sermon on the Annunciation 1* (PL 183, cols 383–90); familiarized to English readers by Nicholas Love's *Mirror of the Blessed Life of Jesus Christ*, ed. Michael G. Sargent (Exeter: Exeter University Press, 2005) pp. 15–19.

30 Ed. Doris Enright-Clark Shoukri (London and New York: MHRA, 1974).

31 *The Towneley Plays*, ed. Martin Stevens and A. C. Cawley, EETS ss 13 and 14 (1994).

32 *The Late Medieval Religious Plays of Bodleian MSS Digby 133 and e Museo 160*, ed. Donald C. Baker, John L. Murphy and Louis B. Hall, Jr, EETS os 283 (1982).

33 *The York Plays*, ed. Richard Beadle (London: Arnold, 1982).

34 *The Chester Mystery Cycle*, ed. R. M. Lumiansky and David Mills, 2 vols, EETS ss 3 (1974) and ss 9 (1986).

35 In *Late Medieval Religious Plays*, ed. Baker et al.

36 *Tretise of Miraclis Pleyinge* in Walker 2000: 198.

37 The 'Shrewsbury Fragments', a liturgical play with dialogue in English apparently from the diocese of Lichfield, is the script of one singer who enacted Third Shepherd, Third Mary and Cleophas, the second pilgrim to Emmaus: *Non-Cycle Plays and Fragments*, pp. 1–7.

38 *Records of Plays and Players in Lincolnshire 1300–1585*, ed. Stanley J. Kahrl, Malone Society Collections, 8 (Oxford: Oxford University Press for the Malone Society, 1974), p. 32; *REED: Chester* 26.

39 Robert Bale's *Chronicle*, in *Six Town Chronicles of England*, ed. Ralph Flenley (Oxford: Clarendon Press, 1911), p. 117. References from Lancashire 1984: nos 373, 1353.

40 Hans van Dijk, 'The Drama Texts in the Van Hulthem-Manuscript', in *Medieval Dutch Literature in its European Context*, ed. Erik Kooper (Cambridge: Cambridge University Press, 1994), pp. 283–96.

References and Further Reading

Beadle, Richard (ed.) 1994. *The Cambridge Companion to Medieval English Theatre*. Cambridge: Cambridge University Press. The standard work.

Carpenter, Sarah 1983. 'Morality-play Characters.' *Medieval English Theatre* 5, 18–28. Self-presentation and characterization of allegorical characters and the Mankind figure.

Davis, Nicholas 1984. 'The Meaning of the Word *Interlude*.' *Medieval English Theatre* 1, 5–15. History and semantics of the term.

Gibson, Gail McMurray 1989. *The Theater of Devotion: East Anglian Drama and Society in the Late Middle Ages*. Chicago: University of Chicago Press. Sources and milieu, largely of the N-Town Plays.

King, Pamela M. 1987. 'Spatial Semantics and the Medieval Theatre.' In *Themes in Drama 9: The Theatrical Space*, ed. James Redmond. Cambridge: Cambridge University Press. Position and movement as a source of theatrical meaning.

—— 2001. '"He pleyeth Herodes upon a scaffold hye"?' In *Porci ante Margaritam: Essays in Honour of Meg Twycross*, ed. Sarah Carpenter, Pamela M. King and Peter Meredith, *Leeds Studies in English* ns 32, 211–28. Parish clerks and biblical drama, with particular reference to Absolon in Chaucer's *Miller's Tale*.

Kipling, Gordon 1998. *Enter the King*. Oxford: Clarendon Press. Royal entries.

Lancashire, Ian 1984. *Dramatic Texts and Records of Britain: A Chronological Topography to 1558*. Toronto: University of Toronto Press. Still a very useful gazetteer; to be updated by *Records of Early English Drama* (see below): NB: references to this work are to item numbers, not page numbers.

Marshall, John 1992. 'The Satirising of the Suffolks in *Wisdom*.' *Medieval English Theatre* 14, 37–66. Political satire in the allegorical play *Wisdom*.

—— 1994. '"Her Virgynes, as Many as a Man Wylle": Dance and Provenance in Three Late Medieval Plays.' *Leeds Studies in English* ns 25, 111–48. The use and connotations of dance.

McGavin, John J. 1990. 'Chester's Linguistic Signs.' *Leeds Studies in English* ns 21, 105–18. Signs and symbols in the Chester Plays.

Mills, David 1985. 'The "Behold and See" Convention in Medieval Drama.' *Medieval English Theatre* 7, 4–12. The demonstrative mode and self-description in medieval theatre.

—— 1998. *Recycling the Cycle: The City of Chester and its Whitsun Plays*. Toronto: University of Toronto Press. History, performance, milieu and the survival of the text.

Pettitt, Tom 1996. 'Mankind: An English *Fastnachtspiel*?' In *Festive Drama*, ed. Meg Twycross (Cambridge: Brewer), pp. 190–202. *Mankind* as a play for the winter revels, incorporating traditional sports and folk-play routines.

Records of Early English Drama 1979–. Toronto: University of Toronto Press. Ongoing series including *REED: York*, ed. Alexandra F. Johnston and Margaret Rogerson (1979); *REED: Chester*, ed. Lawrence M. Clopper (1979). Collected records from the earliest evidence to 1642.

Twycross, Meg 1983. 'Books for the Unlearned.' In *Themes in Drama 5: Drama and Religion*, ed. James Redmond (Cambridge: Cambridge University Press), pp. 65–110. Relates biblical plays, especially N-Town, to popular devotional literature.

—— 1988. 'Beyond the Picture Theory: Image and Activity in Medieval Drama.' *Word and Image* 4, 589–617. Medieval religious iconography as translated to theatre; theatrical images in action.

—— 1996. 'Some Approaches to Dramatic Festivity, Especially Processions.' In *Festive Drama*, ed. Meg Twycross (Cambridge: Brewer), pp. 1–33. Surveys current critical approaches and suggests some new ones.

—— and Carpenter, Sarah 2002. *Masks and Masking in Medieval and Early Tudor England*. Aldershot: Ashgate. Masking from late antiquity to the mid-sixteenth century; useful update to E. K. Chambers, *Medieval Stage*.

Walker, Greg (ed.) 2000. *Medieval Drama: An Anthology*. Oxford: Blackwell. Comprehensive selection with notes and introductions.

28
Morality and Interlude Drama

Darryll Grantley

In early English drama, the most clear-cut basis for generic categorization is between the Corpus Christi plays – the large scriptural cycles usually with urban auspices of production – and the unitary interludes destined for initial performance primarily in noble households. Other divisions of genre, most notably that between 'morality' or 'moral' plays and 'interludes', are much harder to sustain. When used, the term 'morality' is normally applied to earlier allegorical plays containing only a single universalized humanity figure alongside other characters who are personified abstractions or agents of heaven and hell. If any distinction is to be made between the morality plays and interludes, the latter can be regarded as having narratives that feature a fuller mixture of allegorical and 'historical' figures: a variety of individualized human types. Moralities could also be defined as dramatizing the Fall and redemption of man in microcosmic scale.[1] However, even here the narrative patterns vary between this classic scheme, found in *The Castle of Perseverance*, and the coming-of-death theme in *Everyman* – plays which additionally have very different modes of staging. Perhaps one further loose criterion of categorization might be between morality plays concerned either entirely or overwhelmingly with straightforward moral exhortation, and interlude plays that incorporate social issues and polemical argument into their focus. In the end, though, it can be questioned whether this particular distinction is worth making at all since the boundary between these two subgenres remains very unclear. In the sixteenth century and earlier the term 'interlude' could be applied to any type of play, so the modern critical distinction does not even have the force of early precedent.

This essay attempts to give an account of the moral and interlude drama from its beginnings up to (though not including) the London commercial drama housed in dedicated theatres in the last quarter of the sixteenth century. While it will take some note of chronology it also seeks to look at the various generic and staging categories, some of which are either confined to certain periods or somewhat period inflected. The complication in attempting a discussion of the early non-cycle drama is that there are various ways in which it can be categorized, such as in terms of auspices (the earliest known production contexts), method or thematic preoccupation. Research over the last decade or so has begun to yield information about the places of performance of interludes, and as further volumes of the geographically specific *Records of Early English Drama* project are published, understanding of performance places is likely to be enhanced. Nevertheless, the auspices of particular plays are often difficult to establish and necessarily remain a matter of speculation, so it is staging method that provides the most useful means of broad classification and also at times gives a clue to auspices. The main distinctions are between 'place-and-scaffold' and processional staging, represented by a minority of extant plays, on the one hand and the simpler, relatively non-scenic style on the other, suitable for hall or booth stages and clearly more appropriate for itinerant production. As the latter style is the one employed in most plays, continuing into the late sixteenth century and providing the model for the later commercial drama, the interludes using this method will be further categorized in terms of their preoccupations. Since the focus of the following discussion is on moral and interlude drama, certain types of play contemporaneous or overlapping in time with the interlude – such as the folk plays, secular farce, or neoclassical plays – are necessarily excluded.

'Place-and-Scaffold' Plays

'Place-and-scaffold' production involved an elaborate form of staging, requiring the erection of several scaffolds in a large playing space. This sort of staging is highly appropriate for the allegorical moral drama, since it entails strong visual associations and schematic arrangements. Characters routinely introduce themselves on their scaffolds – usually through self-descriptive boasts rather than dialogue – establishing both their identity and their conceptual role in the allegorical scheme of argument, while the appearance of the scaffolds associated with them can contribute an important iconographic dimension. The schematic placing of these structures visually underlines oppositions and moral associations, while the *platea* or unlocalized playing space either remains thus or becomes provisionally localized through dialogue and action. Scaffolds could be arranged linearly, as an illustration of the French Valenciennes Passion Play suggests, or in a circular scheme as indicated by the staging plans of some English and Cornish plays.[2] In the case of the latter arrangement, it is likely that the audience moved about the playing area to follow the action. The earliest extant play using this mode of staging is also the best example of it: *The Castle of Perseverance*, dating from the last quarter of the fourteenth or the first quarter of the fifteenth century. The play exemplifies several narrative motifs of the allegorical moral drama such as the *psychomachia* or struggle for man's soul between divine and infernal forces, and the coming of death, while something of the 'ages of man' topos is also present. It contains the fullest extant example in English drama of the debate between mercy and justice of the 'Daughters of God', a motif found in other literary genres as well. The frontispiece to the manuscript of the play has a staging plan showing the scaffolds for Flesh, the World, Belial, Avarice and God arranged in a circular pattern respectively to the south, west, north,

north-east and east with the Castle in the middle and provision for a ditch or barrier to be made around the *platea*. Despite the elaborateness of the staging requirements, a blank for the place name left in the Banns suggests the likelihood of this being a travelling play.

Another early moral play using 'place and scaffold' staging is *The Pride of Life* dating from the first half of the fifteenth century or possibly as early as the middle of the fourteenth century. Its auspices are unknown but it is possibly an Anglo-Irish or Kentish play. Extensive use is made of a messenger who moves about the *platea* between scaffolds such as that of the King and the booth of the Queen. Like *The Castle of Perseverance* this partially extant play has a strong *memento mori* function. A later interlude using place and scaffold staging is Sir David Lindsay's *Satire of the Three Estates*, a play dating originally from 1540 but in extant versions from 1552 and 1554. It is an elaborate piece, rambling and episodic in structure, with a very large cast of characters. Notable are the large number of stage directions, several quite complex, and some substantial structures including a body of water. Despite its challenging staging requirements, the play enjoyed three contemporary performances – two before the Scottish court, one of which is likely to have been indoors. It contains strongly anti-Catholic polemic but the tone is leavened by comic episodes, including folk-play elements and the banns for the play (for the production in Cupar, Fife) include a self-contained bawdy farce containing social satire. Although the main play's narrative scheme involves the classic pattern of corruption and redemption, the moral allegory is tempered by a substantial element of social comment; and, possibly as a consequence, the mode of staging contributes to the iconography of the play less here than in the earlier two plays.

Although place-and-scaffold staging is used for a small minority of plays, it does occur in a variety of genres. Among the extant examples are two saint plays, the Digby *Mary Magdalen* (c.1500) and the Cornish *Beunans Meriasek* (late 1400s). Both are very elaborate and present considerable technical challenges, especially the Digby play, since they seek to stage miracle and thus require magical effects. Both mix allegorical and non-allegorical modes of representation in their staging of legendary biography as religious example. Remaining examples of plays clearly or probably using this mode of staging are *Dux moraud* (now surviving only in fragmentary form), the Cornish mystery cycle, the *Origo mundi* (both mid-fifteenth-century) and the Digby Herod play *The Killing of the Children* (late 1400s). The only extant interlude likely to have had a processional staging (on pageant wagons) is another Digby play, *The Conversion of St Paul* (early 1500s).

Hall and Booth Plays

The considerable demands made by place-and-scaffold staging can generally be supposed to require substantial courtly or institutional resources, and while the auspices of most plays of this type are not known, it is probable that in most cases they involved state, civic or monastic bodies. The less elaborate form of staging, suitable for mounting performances in domestic halls, in educational institutions or on booth stages, is to be found in the rest of the early morality plays and interludes, although the variety and sophistication of staging arrangements in these plays, discussed below, should not be underestimated.

The early moralities are few in number yet vary remarkably in form and approach, though they are all characterized by the anatomized presence of a central humanity figure, surrounded by moral and other concepts or qualities allegorically presented as a range of abstractly named characters. The best-known of these is *Everyman* (c.1519), probably a translation of the late fifteenth-century Dutch play, *Elckerlijc*. This is the only fully fledged 'coming of death' play in the English repertoire, although several have elements of the *ars moriendi* motif. One of the striking features of the way the narrative is structured in the plays is the progressive shift of focus from exterior to interior dimensions of the central figure's life: from his wealth, through various levels of social relationship and kinship, to his physical and finally his spiritual qualities – a stripping away of the paraphernalia of human existence to reveal its essence.

The remaining early moral plays are all constructed around the *psychomachia* principle, most clearly evident in *Mankind*, an East Anglian play dating from between 1465 and 1470. The distinctiveness of this play lies in its interest in the corruption of language, and in language as a measure of moral corruption. It is replete with various forms of comic linguistic subversion, and the central figure also observably changes linguistic register according to the moral influences under which he falls. In fact, the use of both language and verse – now becoming a focus of scholarly interest – is rather more sophisticated in many interludes than has generally been considered.

Another occurrence of a generalized central figure is found in *Wisdom, Who is Christ* (1460–70) in the form of the Soul or 'Anima' composed of the elements of Mind, Will and Understanding whose fall into error leads to a graphic representation of the corrupt soul, disfigured and foully dressed. The play does not have a great deal of narrative action, but there is much ceremony and dance. Although its didactic focus is firmly on the religious question of salvation, *Wisdom* does make some reference to the sort of social issue and problem that preoccupies later interludes, such as social aspiration and judicial corruption. Two further plays that might be regarded as both having a generalized central figure and maintaining a 'morality' focus on personal fall and redemption are Henry Medwall's *Nature* (c.1496) and the anonymous *World and the Child*, or *Mundus et infans* (1500–22). *Nature* is a two-part play with a double fall and redemption scheme; it has a well-integrated role for the seven deadly sins and contains an example of the *remedia* trope as each of the allegorical virtue figures counsels Man on how to counteract an opposing vice. The two plays have some interesting similarities in that each has a prominent role for the figure of the World, and each is an 'ages of man' play. While Man in *Nature* embraces pride and lust in youth, later falling prey to covetousness (typically a sin of old age) in *The World and the Child*, the central figure changes identity several times to signal the stages of his progress through life. The play contains the best example of this topos among the surviving English interludes.

The rest of the plays in the interlude genre shift away from an exclusive engagement with the theological questions of fall and redemption, although this pattern continues to prevail in many as a narrative paradigm. What becomes more apparent is the interest in a range of secular topics of a social or political nature. Research in recent years has started to give some attention to the ways in which this drama – generally aimed at the politically and socially powerful – articulates many recurrent concerns of a changing society, relating to both state politics and social issues. As the interlude drama turns towards addressing these matters, its narratives move from being defined by the clear didactic purpose of the homiletic exemplum towards a broader enmeshment in the world of its audience. In the process its characters are relatively (though almost never entirely) detached from allegorical function and many are determined by theatrical exigencies or are modelled on recognizable social types. Ironically, this is often most true of the Vice, whose identity frequently owes as much to the role of theatrical engine or 'device' as it does to any moral notion.

Debates

One type of dramatic structure which persistently foregrounded the didactic is the debate. Debates are frequently contained within interludes, but some plays are either built around or entirely composed of them. An early example of a socially focused interlude is Henry Medwall's *Fulgens and Lucres* (c.1497), which might be described as a form of secular *psychomachia*. Medwall was chaplain to John Morton, one of the 'new men' to rise to prominence from relatively humble roots through his own abilities and education to become Archbishop of Canterbury. The play ranges two suitors in contention for the hand of Lucres, one born into nobility and the other risen by his own efforts. The climax is a debate, the outcome of which predictably favours the 'self-made' suitor who thus gains Lucres's hand. The play reflects the burgeoning aspiration and anxiety promoted by the social impact of the sixteenth-century educational revolution.

The contention between estates is also dramatized in a dialogue entitled *Gentleness and Nobility* (1527–30), generally attributed to John Heywood. This debate play 'in the manner of an interlude' involves a merchant, a knight and a ploughman, each advocating the value of his own estate, and ends with broad concurrence between the two more elite discutants about the nature of nobility. Although the ploughman is rejected, he does manage to deliver some satirical comments on the abuses of power in the realm. In both these plays, the only dramatic action comes from the lower-ranked figures – servants and the ploughman respectively – whose coarse behaviour justifies their demeaned status.

Whether or not Heywood wrote *Gentleness and Nobility*, he certainly reveals a fondness for the debate form in the plays more certainly attributed to him. *Pardoner and the Friar* (1513–21), *The Four PP* (1520–2),[3] *The Play of Love* (1520s or early 1530s), *Witty and Witless* (1520–33) and *The Play of the Weather* (1527–33) are all dramatic debates with little or no action. They vary in respect of how far they touch on social or religious issues and how far they simply seek to entertain, but although almost all the characters in them have a discursive function, it is clear that entertainment is in several of these plays a feature in its own right rather than principally a means to more effective instruction.

Topical Content

Although the list of extant examples is not very large, the general run of interlude drama shows a wide range of dramatic strategies, narrative patterns and thematic preoccupations. Many have a mixture of 'historical' characters with conventional names, and allegorical figures. The fact that this drama is primarily addressed to a target audience of the politically and financially empowered elite is reflected in the topics that they recurrently address. Although certain of them have principal issues on which they focus, each usually encompasses a variety of areas of concern. Some articulate sources of anxiety related to the self-interest of the elite in the changing society of the sixteenth century, such as the nature of nobility, the management of wealth, and problems of financial irresponsibility, usury and debt, bad serving-men and companions, foreigners in the realm, and court life and preferment. Other recurrent topics involve a more morally hortatory address to this sector of the population, including the oppression of the poor and bad landlordism, judicial corruption, excess in apparel, and drunkenness and related personal vices. The fall-and-redemption scheme so prominent in the moral drama is found in a minority of the generalized moralities, mostly from or before the middle of the century: *Hick Scorner* (1513–1616), *Impatient Poverty* (1547–8), *Wealth and Health* (1553–5); of these, only *Impatient Poverty* has anything like an everyman figure at the centre of the narrative.

The economic preoccupations of the play just cited are evident from some of the other titles, and continue to be present in later interludes. In these, the principle of illustrative narrative is still evident, if considerably varied from the fall-and-redemption scheme. *All for Money* (1559–77) has an episodic structure with a variety of narrative strands, not hanging together particularly well, although the corrupting power of money is the dominant idea. The play has some interesting dramatic devices, both verbal and visual. A strong visual presentation also characterizes *The Trial of Treasure* (1567), a play with little narrative development but made up rather of a series of demonstrative scenes. A similar approach is taken in another episodic play on an essentially economic theme, *The Contention between Liberality and Prodigality* (1567–8). Dramatic narrative is somewhat more fleshed out in *Apius and Virginia* (1559–67) which, although still developed in allegorical terms, offers a representation of family relationships rather than being made up of characters not embedded in identifiable social structures.

A small number of interludes have 'proverb' titles, a further indication of the move away from theological preoccupations in this drama towards a more secular perspective on human life and behaviour. However, in *Enough is as Good as a Feast* (1559–70) by William Wager the central figure becomes ensnared by worldliness and on his sudden death is carried off to hell. Although this is a Calvinist play with a clear predestinarian slant, the playwright also uses the moral framework to deal with a number of social and economic ills in the realm. *Like Will to Like* (1562–8), by Ulpian Fulwell, has no single central figure but two pairs of roistering companions. Their corruption is inspired by the Devil, but their transgressions and punishments are entirely conceived in secular terms – one of the pairs being led off at the end to execution and the other ending up in a paupers' hospital with gout. George Wapull's *The Tide Tarrieth No Man* (printed 1576) has an even larger number of errant figures and the play's preoccupations are overwhelmingly with economic problems: the play's prologue points to corrupt people detrimental to the well-being of the commonwealth and more specifically to the greedy who oppress the poor. The wide range of characters includes a covetous neighbour, a greedy landlord, an aspirant courtier, and an irresponsible young couple who marry illicitly, all of whom are involved in either perpetrating or falling victim to monetary corruption. The Christian perspective is restated iconographically at the end of the play with a visual display of theological slogans, but it is somewhat detached from the multi-faceted and secularly focused narrative that has gone before. Another proverb play, *The Longer Thou Livest the More Fool Thou Art*, is discussed below in another category.

Humanist 'Wit' Plays

Certain other interludes can similarly be grouped in terms of being cast in a specific mould, or having a similarity of topic, provenance of narratives, or discursive function. The most obvious of such groupings comprises the humanist 'wit' plays, which advocate the improvement of the self through education. Since they are connected to each other these have very similar plots in which, as in Medwall's *Fulgens and Lucres*, an advantageous marriage is set up as a reward for successful attainment of the educational goal. The earliest of these plays is John Redford's *Play of Wit and Science* (1539), written for performance by boys, probably at court. Based on Redford's piece is the anonymous *The Marriage of Wit and Science* (c.1569), also performed by boys at court, and modelled on this in turn is Francis Merbury's *The Marriage of Wit and Wisdom* (1571–9), possibly a university play (Cambridge) but offered for acting. All three show the standard fall-and-redemption scheme as the central figure of Wit is led astray from his studies by allegorized figures of boredom and physical pleasure, threatening the success of his marriage quest until his reformation at the end. The contest between the figures urging study and those providing sensual temptations constitutes a form of *psychomachia* with moral terms and a religious frame of reference, but the humanist connection between self-enhancement through education and social aspiration is clearly paramount. In all three plays it becomes evident that the potential bride is more socially elevated than the aspiring groom and in the middle play, *The Marriage of Wit and Science*, the bride's father actually speaks in justification of his decision to entertain the match in the face of this inequality. The Merbury play adds some fairly gratuitous dramatic action in the form of a subplot involving low-life non-allegorical characters, an indication perhaps of the changing priorities of the drama.

Another play that might be considered with this group, although it is not a 'wit' play as such, is John Rastell's *The Nature of the Four Elements* (1517–18). Its auspices are unknown, but it was probably intended for performance on Rastell's stage. This strongly humanist piece also reveals an interest in self-improvement through education, and dramatizes similar challenges to the attainment of it, but it goes further in that it attempts to provide the audience directly with substantive instruction, largely of a cosmographical and geographical nature, aside from its hortatory project.

'Upbringing of Youth' Plays

Thematically related to this group are several 'upbringing of youth' plays. Although the advent of humanist ideas had something to do with the preoccupations of these interludes, they might equally be seen to be addressing anxieties stoked by the gathering educational revolution of the sixteenth century and the increased social mobility to which it gave rise. Many contemporary social commentators such as Edmund Dudley, Thomas Elyot, Roger Ascham, William Harrison and Richard Mulcaster were writing about the phenomenon and urging the elite not to allow their children to become spoiled or neglect their education, lest they lose out in competition for state promotion to the children of 'meaner' men.[4] The consequences of the neglect of education are the subject of *Nice Wanton* (1547–53), probably a school play written in Edward VI's reign although the extant form is a revision for performance by boys before Queen Elizabeth. It features a sister and brother who are seduced from their studies, throw away their school books and end up dying of the pox and on the gibbet respectively. Poverty and a bad marriage are the punishment for the abandonment of education in *The Disobedient Child* (1559–70) by Thomas Inglelend and in an early sixteenth-century anonymous fragment, *The Prodigal Son*, printed by Rastell. *The Longer Thou Livest the More Fool Thou Art* (1559–68) by William Wager presents an adulthood of foolishness leading ultimately to damnation as the result of a lack of proper early rearing.

In contrast to the young subjects of these plays, who fail to recover from the consequences of their error, the other extant youth plays present a fall-and-redemption scheme. The anonymous *Misogonus* (1564–77) depicts a profligate young heir finally being brought to repentance by the appearance of a long-lost and virtuous brother in whose favour the father threatens to disinherit him. In *Lusty Juventus* (1547–53) by Richard Wever and *Youth* (1513–14), youthful arrogance and disposition to carnality are what lead their young protagonists astray, but in both cases there is redemption in the end. In all the plays of this group where parents are present, save the fragment, there is only a single parent, the most likely explanation for which is that it is the idea of parenthood which is being represented in plays that still adhere to an allegorical impulse. *The Life and Repentance of Marie Magdelene* (1550–66) by Lewis Wager describes the deceased parents of the errant female subject as moral and loving, but overindulgent and failing to provide sufficiently strict control. In most of these plays there is the clear supposition that the problems discussed pertain to the children of the elite, *The Longer Thou Livest the More Fool Thou Art* actually addressing itself to those who are 'like to have governation'. The plays are also Protestant in orientation, promoting the idea of individual responsibility for both economic and spiritual salvation.

Religious Polemic

Another thematically linked range of interludes is made up of those that engage in religious polemic, Protestant plays constituting the overwhelming majority. *New Custom* (1550–73) presents a variety of allegorical characters who contrast the simplicity and soundness of Protestant doctrine with the bullying corruption of Catholicism and, unusually, represents the principal Vice figure as being converted in the end. *The Conflict of Conscience* (1570–81) by Nathaniel Woodes is based on a received narrative, being the story of Francis Spera, a convert to Protestantism who subsequently lapsed back into Catholicism and thereafter fell into despair, believing himself damned. The play is in two versions with different endings, one concluding with the protagonist's suicide while the other has him achieving salvation through reconversion. The considerable output of the Protestant polemicist, John Bale, accounts for most of the other extant dedicatedly anti-Catholic plays. *God's Promises* and *Three Laws* (both 1538) view the history of the world in terms of a providential process with Protestantism as its final outcome, the latter play having the distinction of containing the first known discussion of homosexuality in English drama. *John Baptist's Preaching* (1538) makes an implicit analogy between John the Baptist striking against the old order of the Pharisees and Sadducees and the advent of the new order of Protestantism. Bale's religious polemic also includes *The Temptation of Our Lord* and *King John* (discussed below). Several other general-interest interludes also participate in the Reformation debate, including *Enough is as Good as a Feast*, *The Longer Thou Livest the More Fool Thou Art*, *Lusty Juventus* and *A Satire of the Three Estates*. The sole extant interlude to represent the Catholic perspective is *Respublica*, a Christmas play for boys written in the time of Queen Mary and perhaps performed at court. It does not deal with doctrinal issues but concentrates on the economic disruption and social hardships brought about by religious change.

Plays Based on Received Narratives

Other groupings of interludes can be made on the basis of the received narratives that form their basis, which may be of biblical, hagiographical, or historical and legendary provenance. Several plays based on these are still squarely in the spirit and form of interlude drama and contain Vice figures, a mixture of 'historical' and allegorical characters, a schematic arrangement and definition of characters, and plots that are constructed according to the recognized formulas of the genre. Like the urban Corpus

Christi cycles, a number of interludes employ biblical narrative, here usually treated very freely and expansively. The only non-saint play drawing on the New Testament is John Bale's *Temptation of Our Lord* (1538) dramatizing, as its title suggests, Christ's temptation in the desert, with a predictably anti-Catholic slant. The fact that the interludes based on the Old Testament choose episodes not selected for dramatization in the Corpus Christ cycles is worth noting, but given the small number of extant plays it is difficult to speculate on the reasons for this, except to reflect that the scriptural episodes in the cycles have a defined part to play in the Corpus Christi providential schemes, while the interludes are free of this imperative. While *Godly Queen Hester* (1525–9) reworks the book of Esther to create one of the few actively positive representations of Jews in early English drama, *Jacob and Esau* (1550–7) uses the story of Jacob's tricking his brother out of his birthright to articulate anxieties about errant heirs in the ranks of the elite; and *Virtuous and Godly Susanna* (1563–9) by Thomas Garter presents an allegorized version of the account of Susanna and the elders in the Book of Daniel. Loosely based on the third and fourth chapters of the Vulgate first Book of Esdras is *King Darius* (published 1565), which puts together a first part containing allegorical figures who fail to convert a Vice with, in the second part, a debate in the form of a wit-contest. In a not dissimilar vein to these plays are the few extant saint plays, two of which – the Digby plays *Mary Magdalen* and *The Conversion of St Paul* – draw partly or wholly on New Testament material. All these plays expand on the scriptural sources and manifest a strong interest in the theatrical possibilities of the narratives, a number even including a degree of gratuitous comic action. The only other surviving saint plays are Lewis Wager's *Life and Repentance of Marie Magdalene* and the anonymous Cornish *St Meriasek*, an elaborate dramatization of the life of a non-biblical saint which, in its demanding staging requirements and expansive, episodic narrative, bears some resemblance to the Digby *Mary Magdalen*. Wager's work, which might be termed a Protestant saint play, recasts the biblical story of the meeting of Mary Magdalene and Christ at the house of Simon the Leper into a strongly allegorical framework.

Several secular interludes take their narratives from history and legend, including the early proto-history play of *King John* (1538) by John Bale. As might be expected from this writer, the play uses historical reference very freely in the interests of anti-Catholic polemic, but is noteworthy for its attempt to foster patriotic sentiment through English history in the service of a political objective. It also makes liberal use of the traditional allegorical basis of the interlude, including Vice figures. A play that draws on legendary English history, also to make a political point, is *Gorboduc* (1562), written for performance in the Inner Temple by Thomas Norton and Thomas Sackville. It seeks to promote the case for a secure succession to the throne by portraying the disastrous consequences of divisions in the realm. It is on the borderline of what constitutes 'interlude' drama, and is in many ways more neoclassical in impulse: the actions are all off-stage and reported, there is a chorus, and the rhetoric and characters are generally those from a classical frame of reference. However, the allegorical thrust of the play is present not only in the names of some of the characters, but also in their schematic arrangement including a type of *psychomachia* that puts the king at its centre. Also in the allegorical spirit of interlude drama are the dumbshows that precede each act, although these may possibly be derived from a Continental dramatic tradition.

Classical tragedy is reworked as a form of tragicomedy by John Pickering in *Horestes* (printed 1567), the Oresteian legend being represented in the theatrical idiom of the interlude, with a Vice at the centre of the action, and the outcome being shaped according to the demands of moral illustration rather than fate. A different sort of mythic narrative is found in *Patient and Meek Grissell* (1558–61) by John Phillip, which dramatizes a version of the patient Griselda story drawn from Boccaccio's *Decameron*, but makes a Vice responsible for the trials of the heroine. Thomas Preston's *Cambises* (1558–69) tells, in an elaborate way, a story of royal corruption first found in Herodotus. Similar sources of literary legend provide the plots of *Fulgens and Lucres* and *Apius and Virginia*, both discussed above.

The Distinctiveness of the Interludes

An interest in the dramatization of received narratives, especially of a legendary or literary nature, is one of several ways in which the late medieval interlude tradition shades off at its edges into academically influenced, Continental and neoclassical forms which constitute a shift to early modern forms and sensibilities in the drama. However, despite being fairly diverse in nature, interludes can clearly be seen to constitute a distinct tradition, in the allegorical principles that underlie their construction, in the clear schematic frameworks in which their characters operate, and in the recurrence of certain dramatic strategies and devices found in them, such as changes of dress or name by the Vices and other figures. Although allegory was something that emerged from homiletic example, where secularization takes place in the interludes allegory is not abandoned but adapted. Notions of damnation or salvation in a theological sense give way to more immediately material (such as economic or legal) consequences of actions, while Vice figures come to be conceived in terms less of sin than of deviant social behaviour. Social, economic and political changes were to have their impact on the nature of drama of various sorts produced in the course of the sixteenth century. It was not only religious but economic factors that led to the decline in the production of drama by those urban communities in which it had been part of the civic culture, and turned towns instead into merely purchasers of the products of itinerant companies. Agricultural enclosure and other economic as well as ideological transformations in rural communities tended equally to undermine their festive culture and its theatrical dimensions. Monastic auspices for drama were also put paid to in the course of the century. On the other hand educational institutions such as universities and schools and the Inns of Court became more active in theatrical production and consequently more important as influences on the nature of drama. Finally, the emergence of a capitalist economy in the early modern period was to promote entrepreneurship with regard to the production and marketing of drama, particularly with the advent of the dedicated commercial theatres in the late 1560s and mid-1570s. The result of these various determining forces was, briefly, secularization and an increasing engagement of drama with social and political issues, the incorporation of foreign and classical formal models and narratives, and the enhancement of the saleability of drama through a shift in the balance between didacticism and entertainment value. Although it is true that the allegorically based interlude could and did incorporate all of these, they were ultimately to lead to its elision into and replacement by the modes of theatrical writing now identified with Christopher Marlowe, William Shakespeare, Ben Jonson and their contemporaries.

Staging the Interludes

An important dimension of these plays that emerges from their allegorical approach, minimalism and formal variety is their staging. The place-and-scaffold plays clearly have the greatest potential for complex staging, but some remarkable attempt at visual contrivance is present in many others too. Pyrotechnics are used in a number, most notably *The Castle of Perseverance*, the Digby *Mary Magdalen*, *King Darius* and *The Play of Love*. In several plays there are actions which require some ingenuity to perform but whose presence on stage testifies to an awareness of and interest in visual effect. These include the appearances of certain characters by being given birth to on stage in *All for Money*, a beheading in *Apius and Virginia*, a flaying in *Cambises*, hangings in *Horestes* and *A Satire of the Three Estates* and a near hanging in *The Contention between Liberality and Prodigality* (avoided by the breaking of the rope). Although the interludes do not generally make extensive use of sets, there are suggestions of elements of set in several, such as the 'Wit' plays, where there is some requirement for visual signification of location. Location might equally be signalled by the use of stage properties, such as a tombstone in *Apius and Virginia*, or a bed in *Magnificence*. Stage properties, in fact, play a significant role in many plays and perform a variety of signifying functions. Some of the more interesting examples include an orrery (for purposes of instruction) in *The Nature of the Four Elements*, a 'similitude of dust and rust' in The *Trial of Treasure*, and a two-sided shield with slogans in *The Tide Tarrieth No Man*, although the signifying function of properties is perhaps most clearly evident in the dumbshows in *Gorboduc*. Otherwise, visual features are provided by the most portable elements of the drama, the performers themselves. This often involves dress, either by characters drawing attention to their own attire or by their changing attire. One of the most remarkable examples is Anima's change of appearance to signal her fall into sin in *Wisdom*, when small boys dressed as devils run in and out from under her foul mantle. In the interludes, pride in attire is a recurrent way of dramatizing moral failings, but it also provides opportunities for satire on sartorial fashions and the articulation of anxieties about wastrel youth. Other ways in which performers create visual effect are in formal configurations, examples of which are found in the banquets of *King Darius* or *The Life and Repentance of Mary Magdalene*, or in (judicial) court scenes in several plays including *Mankind*, *Nice Wanton* and *Virtuous and Godly Susanna*. A recurrent feature of the performance arrangements of this drama is the doubling of parts, made explicit in the case of many interludes by the doubling schemes provided at the beginnings or ends of the texts. Doubling was necessitated by the small size of itinerant companies, but is sometimes used creatively to suggest connections between characters, most notably in Bale's *King John*. Another recurring element in performance is the entry of characters through the audience and interaction with the audience, especially on the part of Vice figures – something that proceeds naturally from the somewhat intimate staging circumstances usual in this drama. Finally, mention should be made of the performance of music and song in numerous interludes, sometimes fairly incidental to the action but at other times very integral to it.

The Study of Interlude Drama

In terms of modern research on early drama, aside from a recurrent focus on certain important moralities, the interlude tradition has tended to be something of a poor relation to the great urban cycles of Corpus Christi plays. The cycle plays have a format that is their own and they are clearly identifiable both as 'medieval' forms of drama and as being produced in specific contexts in the urban societies which produced them. The early moralities also have something of a particularity which sets them aside as a genre worthy of scholarly attention. Since the main body of sixteenth-century interludes, however, tends to run into and be regarded as constituting the earlier stages of a continuum with the late sixteenth-century and seventeenth-century products for the commercial stage, it suffers from relative obscurity on account of the huge cultural explosion of Renaissance drama. It is thus tempting for those who do not proceed from a particular basis of interest in medieval drama to see the interest of these plays simply as lying in their being imperfect precursors of the plays of the early modern London stage. However, apart from the fact that the interludes are invaluable as documents of social history, since their didactic and polemical elements clearly responded to the issues that concerned their audiences, they also have considerable intrinsic interest as theatre pieces. Their allegorical approach makes available enquiry into such matters as representation and character identity, the role of the visual in drama, expectations placed on audiences, the interaction of performers and audiences, and a whole host of other questions relevant to dramatic theory. Also of considerable potential theoretical interest is the fact that, as itinerant drama generally produced with highly limited resources and necessarily adaptable to a variety of spaces, interludes are early examples of minimalist theatre. Furthermore, they are able to yield perspectives on medieval and early modern performance since their relative flexibility in terms of form involves the development of a language of performance, in terms of both speech and action. Indeed, the thrust of much recent work on this drama focuses on the ways in which they function theatrically.

Their 'poor relation' status has resulted in less critical interest in interludes than in the Corpus Christi cycles, but the imbalance has begun to be rectified in the last two or three decades. As has been suggested at various points in this discussion, current scholarly interest appears to be going in a number of directions, including work on auspices and patronage, the engagement of the drama with both political and social issues of the period, and the language of the plays. There is also increasing interest in the visual aspects of the staging, including iconography – a dimension of the drama that has gained prominence through work produced under the aegis of the Early Drama, Art and Music project (studies on aspects of early staging published by the Medieval Institute of Western Michigan University) – and also in pyrotechnics, masks, music, the staging of effects and other technical aspects of staging. These are all areas of study promoted by the annual conferences of, and work published in, the journal *Medieval English Theatre*. Finally, there has also been considerable interest in the insights produced by modern performance. One area where there is immense potential for particularly useful work is in the production of good, easily accessible editions, since there is still too much concentration on the currently best-known examples of the genre.

See also: 27 Medieval English Theatre, 29 York Mystery Plays.

Notes

1 Cf. Potter 1975: 8: 'it is . . . possible to see the medieval religious drama as a totality, in which the morality play performs the same ceremony in the microcosm of the individual human life as that of the Corpus Christi cycle in the macrocosm of historical time'.

2 An illustration of the staging of the Valenciennes Passion Play occurs in Paris, Bibliothèque Nationale MS Français 12, 536 and is reproduced in Wickham 1974: 90–1. Staging plans for *The Castle of Perseverance* (Washington, Folger Shakespeare Library MS V.a.354, folio 191v), *Beunans Meriasek* (Aberystwyth, National Library of Wales MS Peniarth 105, folio 92v) and the Cornish Origo Mundi cycle (Oxford, Bodleian Library MS 791, folios 27, 56v and 85) are reprinted in Davidson 1991: 48, 45, 46, 43 and 44 respectively.

3 Alternatively *The Four Ps*, referring to the characters in the play: the Pardoner, 'Pothecary, Pedlar and Palmer.

4 Dudley, *The Tree of Commonwealth* (1509), ed. D. M. Brodie (Cambridge: Cambridge University Press, 1948); Elyot, *The Book Named the Governor* (1531), ed. S. E. Lehmberg (London: Dent, 1962); *Education or Bringing Up of Children* (1535), in *Four Tudor Books on Education*, ed. R. D. Pepper (Gainesville, Fla.: Scholars' Facsimiles and Reprints, 1966); Ascham, *The Schoolmaster* (1570), ed. L. V. Ryan (Ithaca, N. Y.: Cornell University Press); Harrison, *Description of England* (1577), ed. G. Edelen (Washington, D.C.: Cornell University Press, 1994); facsimile of Mulcaster, *Elementary* (1581): Menston: Scolar Press, 1970.

References and Further Reading

Bevington, D. 1962. *From Mankind to Marlowe: Growth of Structure in the Popular Drama of Tudor England.* Cambridge, Mass.: Harvard University Press. Looks at the early plays in respect of the practicality of staging them with limited casts, and their evolving theatrical strategies.

—— 1968. *Tudor Drama and Politics.* Cambridge, Mass.: Harvard University Press. A study of the political dimensions of the interlude drama.

Brown, D. H. 1999. *Christian Humanism in the Late English Morality Plays.* Gainesville: University Press of Florida. Explores humanist values and teaching in a range of sixteenth-century interludes.

Butterworth, P. 1998. *Theatre of Fire: Special Effects in Early English and Scottish Theatre.* London: Society for Theatre Research. Studies special effects, especially pyrotechnic, in early drama with reference to Continental practice.

Cartwright, K. 1999. *Theatre and Humanism: English Drama in the Sixteenth Century.* Cambridge: Cambridge University Press. Argues for a much stronger presence of humanist impulses in the interlude drama, especially in the ways the plays are made to appeal to their audiences.

Craik, T. W. 1962. *The Tudor Interlude: Stage, Costume, and Acting*, Leicester: Leicester University Press. Examines a wide variety of aspects of the plays as performed, with reference to a large number of interludes.

Davenport, W. A. 1982. *Fifteenth Century English Drama: The Early Moral Plays and their Literary Relations.* Cambridge: Brewer. General and wide-ranging study of the earlier morality drama in the broader contexts of contemporary writing.

Davidson, C. 1991. *Illustrations of the Stage and Acting in England to 1580.* EDAM Monographs Series, 16. Kalamazoo, Mich.: Medieval Institute Publications. Prints contemporary illustrations pertinent to early drama, as potential source material.

Forest-Hill, L. 2000. *Transgressive Language in Medieval English Drama.* Aldershot: Ashgate. A study of the aggressive aspects of the language of early drama, including the interludes, in the context of contemporary debate and law.

Grantley, D. 2003. *English Dramatic Interludes 1300–1580: A Reference Guide.* Cambridge: Cambridge University Press. A guide to a wide variety of aspects of the drama, by individual play, with plot summaries and bibliographies for each.

Happé, P. 1991. *Song in Morality Plays and Interludes.* Lancaster: Medieval English Theatre Monographs. Provides an index of songs and song cues in interludes, and editions of extant songs.

Norland, H. B. 1995. *Drama in Early Tudor Britain 1485–1558.* Lincoln: University of Nebraska Press. Deals with changing contexts of early drama, the move towards secularism and the emergence of new genres.

Potter, R. 1975. *The English Morality Play: Origins, History and Influence of a Dramatic Tradition.* London: Routledge and Kegan Paul. Views morality plays as acts of ritual and draws perspectives from modern performance.

Southern, R. 1973. *The Staging of Plays before Shakespeare.* London: Faber and Faber. Reconstructs probable staging of a large number of interludes, also detailing developments and modifications in staging techniques.

Twycross, M. and Carpenter, S. 2002. *Masks and Masking in Medieval and Early Tudor England.* Aldershot: Ashgate. Provides a comprehensive study of masks in early drama, including a section on morality plays and interludes.

Walker, G. 1991. *Plays of Persuasion: Drama and Politics at the Court of Henry VIII.* Cambridge: Cambridge University Press. Discusses in detail selected interludes in relation to contemporary Tudor politics.

—— 1998. *The Politics of Performance in Early Renaissance Drama.* Cambridge: Cambridge University Press. Studies the effects of audiences and circumstances of performance on Henrician plays, seen in terms of individual performances.

Westfall, S. 1990. *Early Tudor Household Revels: Patrons and Performance.* Oxford: Clarendon Press. Argues for the centrality of patrons in determining the political arguments in the drama and examines the role of interlude drama in the noble household.

White, P. W. 1993. *Theatre and Reformation: Protestantism, Patronage, and Playing in Tudor England.* Cambridge: Cambridge University Press. Argues for the patronage of early drama by Protestant authorities in the sixteenth century and examines the plays for reflections of this.

Wickham, G. 1974. *The Medieval Theatre.* Cambridge: Cambridge University Press. A look at early drama in general, including the morality plays, with a particular emphasis on contexts of production.

PART VII
Readings

29
York Mystery Plays

Pamela King

York's late medieval mystery play marked the climax of the festive year. It was performed on the great summer feast of Corpus Christi, the first Thursday after Trinity Sunday and the day on which the real presence of Christ in the host at Mass is celebrated (Duffy 1992: 91–130). York's is the only extant mystery cycle securely linked to the feast; the Chester cycle, the only other true cycle, was performed at Whitsun then at midsummer (Stevens 1987). The organization of the York cycle was delegated to the trade and craft guilds of the city, who together presented their audiences with a dramatized summary of the highlights of the Christian story. The Old Testament is represented by the Creation, Fall and Expulsion, Cain and Abel, Noah, Abraham and Isaac, and the Exodus. The focus in the New Testament is on a sequence of pageants from Annunciation to Epiphany, then, after a brief series drawn from the life of Christ, a detailed Passion sequence. The cycle ends with a Harrowing of Hell, Resurrection, Ascension, Assumption of the Virgin, and finally a spectacular Doomsday.

Staging the Pageants

The York Cycle was performed processionally on wagons. This performance is not to be confused with the Corpus Christi procession itself, in which guilds marched in their regalia with their banners, following the host in its monstrance. Corpus Christi processions still take place in a number of European cities, the one in Valencia being particularly elaborate and spectacular (figure 29.1). There, as in medieval York, there is a tradition of biblical plays, separate from the procession itself. York's play ousted the city's Corpus Christi procession from the feast-day to the following day some time before 1476.[1]

Each wagon was an elaborate vehicle, less a stage on wheels than the theatrical set for the pageant which was played on its deck or multi-storey decks, as well as on the street around. The records of York's guild of Mercers, who performed Doomsday, have

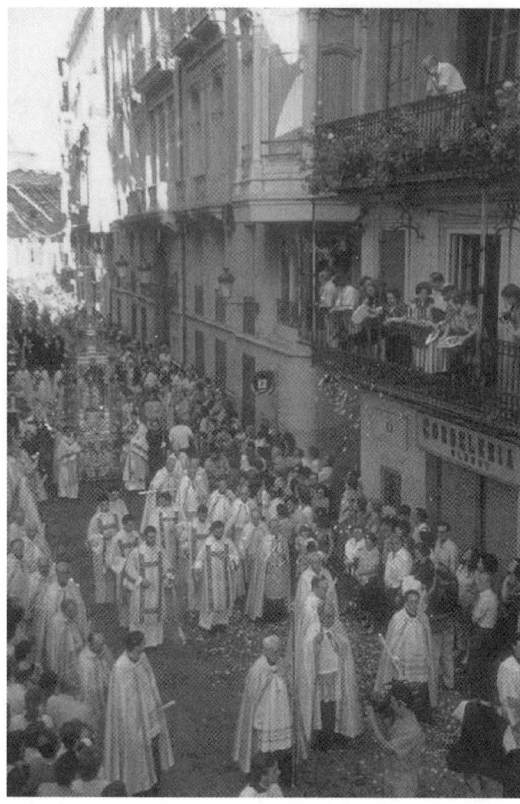

Figure 29.1 A modern Corpus Christi procession in Valencia, Spain. (By permission of Pamela King.)

yielded the single most illuminating piece of evidence of the physical aspects of performance in mid-fifteenth-century York. An indenture records the formal legal transfer of the properties of the guild to their appointed 'pageant masters' on 11 June 1433, including first, 'a Pageant with iv wheels, hell mouth', and later, 'a brandreth of iron that God shall sit upon when he shall sty up to heaven' and 'a heaven of iron with a nave of tree' (Johnston and Rogerson 1979: I, 55–6). The list also includes pieces of scenery including a wooden rainbow, costumes, wigs and masks and nine mechanical angels.

Despite its level of detail, the Mercers' indenture has raised almost as many questions as it has answered. Clearly, the wagon is designed especially for the play in which God, or more exactly Christ as judge and second person of the Trinity, returns to earth to divide the saved from the damned, before returning whence he came, winched up on his 'brandreth', a northern dialect word still current describing the iron basket on legs in which a log fire is lit within an open grate. Critical debate since the publication of the indenture has considered, for example: whether the wagon was oriented for playing side-on, like a proscenium stage, or end-on, like illustrations of sixteenth-century pageant floats; whether heaven was a revolving wheel – one etymological possibility offered by 'naffe' is the hub of a wheel – as it is illustrated in contemporary examples in painting; and whether information about one vehicle owned by one guild in one city, and known to have been replaced in 1501 by the accomplished carver of church furniture, Thomas Drawsword (Johnston and Rogerson 1979: I, 188–9) is a reliable source of information about pageant wagons in general.[2]

As modern reconstructions extrapolated from the Mercers' indenture and other more fragmented pieces of evidence about playing on wagons have shown, the short individual pageants of the York cycle are far from small-scale in the experience of an audience. A wagon constructed on two or even three storeys, as those plays set in heaven and hell as well as on earth demand, made of the likeliest fabrication materials of the time, oak and iron, would have been an imposing spectacle in the narrow streets of the medieval city. It had to be manoeuvred by hand round tight corners and between buildings with jettied first floors. Moreover, at the time when the scripts of the York pageants were written down, there were forty-eight or forty-nine pageants all proceeding in sequence along the route which began just after dawn at Holy Trinity Priory inside Mickelgate Bar and circumnavigated the city, finishing at Pavement. The pageants were performed in sequence at between twelve and sixteen identifiable 'stations' along the way (Twycross 1994: 38–42).[3]

There is a presumption that the constraints of space caused the pageants to be tightly choreographed. Physical organization on the pageant itself had to be instantly intelligible to audience members standing well back from the action. Contemporary visual arts, such as the stained glass windows of York's churches, offer standard iconographical arrangements for the moments of stillness which the texts suggest. In a play where several performers take the role of, for example, Christ, in a number of succeeding pageants, there can be no continuity of characterization, and there is evidence that many characters wore half- or full-face masks. Acting styles, gesture and movement, like visual placing, would have been stylized (Carpenter and Twycross 2002: 191–232).[4] It is unclear exactly who the actors were; fragmentary evidence suggests that some of the players were guild members, but others were bought or brought in for the occasion depending on the affluence and other circumstances of the guild. An early proclamation from York demands that all performers be 'good players, well arrayed and openly speaking' (Johnston and Rogerson 1979: I, 25). The names of no women players survive, although whether or not women ever did perform in York's mystery plays remains a matter of debate (Goldberg 1997: 145–7).[5] Certain things are, however, clear: the terms 'amateur' and 'professional' have little relevance in this context; the productions were not crude and neither staging nor acting was in any sense improvised; and the relationship between play and audience was complex (Twycross 1994: 43–55).

The Text of the Play and the Guilds of York

The text of the play survives in a single copy, the York Register, now in the British Library (Beadle and Meredith 1983). The Register was commissioned by the city government. Its paucity of stage directions illustrates that it was intended as a record of the established spoken text, rather than as a script for informing individual performers or what would in modern parlance be 'directors'. It is assumed that the guilds worked from separate 'originals' of their individual plays, none of which survives. Richard Beadle concluded from the evidence of how the main scribe was working in the York Register, commonly attributed to the late 1460s, that 'the undertaking was to him new and unusual, and that he had no model from which to proceed' (Beadle 1982: 10–11). One of the mid-sixteenth-century servants of the then Common Clerk, John Clerke, has been identified as 'Scribe C' – the third of four hands recognized as working on the compilation later in its life (Beadle 1982: 16–17; Johnston and Rogerson 1979: I, 324, 330, 351). When the material contained within the Cycle came to be viewed as theologically contentious in the mid-sixteenth-century, the Register, which had never been completed, was called in by the city council to be 'amended' (Johnston and Rogerson 1979: I, 354).

The performing of a Corpus Christi play in York considerably pre-dates the sequence of pageants which has come to be accepted as the canonical cycle, although dating and describing the genesis of the cycle and identifying the authors of the individual pageants remains a matter of informed speculation. Although there are references to guild merchants in York as early as the twelfth century, the term is ambiguous; the emergence in the city records, at the end of the fourteenth century, of guilds as highly organized occupational associations running apprenticeship schemes coincides with the earliest references to the Corpus Christi play. The reign of Richard II is also, however, the period at which systematic civic record-keeping began, so neither guilds nor play demonstrably burst upon a previously well-charted scene (Dobson 1997: 97–8). The national regulations on guild membership belong to the rash of mid-fourteenth-century labour legislation which attempted to exert central control over the opportunist and exploitative practices arising with labour shortages in the aftermath of the Black Death. In late fourteenth-century York a number of guilds registered their ordinances, and the earliest reference (1376) to a rental of a pageant house, the building used for garaging pageant wagons, is very close to the date of the earliest guild ordinances for the city. It now seems probable to the historians of late medieval York that the evolution of the Corpus Christi play, probably inspired by the city governors, was a catalyst in the development of a fully evolved guild structure rather than a product of it (Dobson 1997: 101–5). Although in the chillier economic climate of the late fifteenth century the city governors were themselves drawn from the evolved guild structure, a century earlier they were a class apart, a group of international merchants who had yet to feel the need to combine into a protectionist organization. None of the mayors of York from the late fourteenth or early fifteenth century appears as a member of any guild, each having moved by wealth and influence straight from the freedom of the city into the aldermanic elite. The willingness of the guilds to accept what the elite group sought to impose probably also lies in the social rather than the economic realm if pageantry was understood as a profile-raising activity – the opportunity to create 'a mirror of self-identity' as much as a demonstration of significant expenditure (Goldberg 1997: 148–60). Critical in this understanding of the successful co-evolution of the guilds and the play is the significance of the individual episode to its owning guild.

Individual pageants provided individual craft or trade guilds with the opportunity to display their skills and their wares and to sanctify their commercial activities. The first listing of the guilds against named episodes is the much altered *Ordo paginarum*, literally 'order of pageants' in the York A/Y Memorandum Book for 1415 (Johnston and Rogerson 1979: I, 16–26). Many of the attributions vary significantly from the position when the play was recorded in the Register. There is in short a picture of constant change and adaptation to fluctuating economic, social and religious circumstances which affected either an individual guild or the whole city. The connection between the subjects of individual pageants and the occupations of their owning guilds is apparent, although sometimes, as with the Shipwrights' *Building of the Ark*, more obvious than others. Contemporary illustrations of the nine orders of angels in their leather-and-feather suits may explain the affinity of the guild of Barkers and Tanners with *The Fall of the Angels* (I), whereas the bed from which Pilate reluctantly rises in *Christ before Pilate I: The Dream of Pilate's Wife* (XXX), demands a sumptuous display of the Tapiters' and Couchers' – tapestry-makers' and upholsterers' – craft (Goldberg 1997: 141–4). Prosperity and status also had a bearing on the episode which each guild held. The last pageant of the cycle, Doomsday, requires heaven, earth and hell, special effects and a large cast, and carried prestige for the very wealthy guild of Mercers. In matters of civic office, and consequently civic ceremony, the distinction between types of occupation is apparent. Tradesmen, whose wealth was tied up in capital, controlled the cycle as a whole, so the artisanal focus of individual pageants is symptomatic of interesting social and economic tensions (Beckwith 2001: 42–55). There are finer distinctions among different crafts, but over time all guilds would have experienced some fluctuation in their fortunes, as is reflected in the records of the cycle.[6]

The scripts gathered in the Register in the 1460s were probably written and modified across the whole of the Register's prehistory. The York play includes examples of almost every recognizable late medieval metrical form, from the rightly celebrated and immensely complicated alliterative stanza of the trial plays in the Passion sequence, to the seven-line so-called 'Burns stanza' – hallmark of the eponymous Scot who deployed it with sustained enthusiasm – of the *Baptism* (XXI). Claims have been made for common authorship of various groups of pageants, most notably those attributed to the 'York Realist', a rather unhelpful coinage depending on a very loose understanding of what constitutes realism. Other pageants have been linked together by stylistic features or by a shared common source: *Abraham and Isaac* (X) and *Moses and Pharaoh* (XI) were both influenced by the *Metrical Middle English Paraphrase of the Old Testament.* Equally, it is evident that much of what appears in the Register is the work of 'editors' intervening between the original author of a pageant and its changed circumstances of production, such as when *Christ before Pilate 2: The Judgement* (XXXIII) was forged out of more than one pre-existent script, or completely reworked, as the Tilemakers took over the whole episode (Beadle 1994: 100–8). In this context the designation of authorship for the play as a whole is relatively meaningless.

None the less, considerable interest has developed in identifying and describing the culture which generated the play and of approaching some understanding of what resources were available to the civic authorities in York were they to commission pageant texts *ab initio*. That question is best approached through an understanding of the content of the play, its treatment and emphases, its available explicit and latent social, political and religious agenda, and the specific political and ecclesiastical climate in York at the turn of the fifteenth century.

Content and Milieu

The York Cycle presents itself to the modern reader as a sequence of short episodes telling the story of the world from an orthodox Christian perspective, beginning with the Creation and ending with the Last Judgement – a biblical narrative sequence. This understanding of the cycle presents a number of problems. To begin with it is a perversely Protestant reading. The Bible was not available to the mass of the English laity until its translation into English ceased to be controversial, and the invention of the printing-press made whole bibles portable and affordable. One argument goes that the York Cycle was an ingenious alternative to Bible reading for a mass, lay and probably illiterate audience, but if that is its purpose, and we accept the questionable proposition that Bible knowledge was on the agenda of the medieval Church for the laity, there are some oddities, imbalances and lacunae in the story as told. A secondary issue arises when one begins to consider why this enterprise in prodigious story-telling should be chosen to celebrate Corpus Christi day. Here it may be argued that Corpus Christi day was a holiday for all, and the feast in the Church calendar closest to midsummer's day, so, if one were planning to tell the whole of the history of the world as a series of pageants performed on cumbersome wagons, in rhymed verse, twelve times over, it made sense to select a day when the weather was likely to be kind and the hours of daylight long. These are all issues which have borne re-examination.

The selection of episodes in the York play is remarkably similar to that in the surviving and other known English cycles. All the events commonly included are taken from the first two of the thirty-nine books of the Old Testament, the four Gospels of the New Testament, and a variety of apocryphal texts embellishing the Gospels. The arrangement is eccentric only if one comes to the cycle expecting a smooth biblical narrative; in fact something else altogether is going on.

Fundamental to Christianity is the relationship between the deity and the individual. For the Protestant this is a personal relationship, informed by the teaching and preaching of the Church. Communal prayer and worship create a focus and support the regulation of Christian behaviour, and ritual actions reinforce the understanding of the specifics of the relationship, but the relationship remains fundamentally a matter for the individual, with the Bible as his or her manual on how to fulfil the human side of the contract. For the pre-Reformation Roman Catholic, the relationship with the deity could not be achieved without the mediation of the Church. The priest's role was sacramental as well as pastoral. That is to say, without the intervention of an anointed priest, the seven sacraments of the Church – Baptism, Marriage, Confirmation, Ordination, Penance, the Mass and Extreme Unction – could not work. The priest's role was mystical and transformational: he alone could sanctify the water to wash away the inherited sin of Adam when the infant was baptized, and the oil with which the dying was anointed; he alone could change the wine of the Eucharist into the blood of Christ. And the sinner was impotent to seek forgiveness without the procedures of confession, contrition and satisfaction, administered by an anointed priest, which made up the sacrament of Penance.

How the Western medieval Church had evolved as an institution of this power cannot be explored here, but it is important to understand its nature and its procedures in order to understand the shape and emphases of the York Cycle. The Church interpreted Holy Writ as its pastoral agenda for the populace, and it did this through a predetermined calendar of worship codified in the liturgy. For the regular religious, the monk or nun, the liturgy dictated a whole programme of daily worship. For laymen and women, worshipping in their parish churches with the other members of their occupation or guild who would be their near neighbours, it was not so much the daily round of liturgical worship which governed their lives, but the annual calendar of feasts and fasts. Every week the liturgy at mass followed a fixed pattern allied to the appropriate point in the Church calendar. The major fixed feast of the Church was Christmas, prepared for by the long Advent fast. After Epiphany, the traditional time of gift-giving in emulation of the Magi, there was a variable period before the long fast of Lent which preceded Easter, the major moveable feast of the year, commenced. Thereafter the summer season was punctuated by further celebrations – for example, the feast of Pentecost (Whitsun), then at midsummer, Corpus Christi, and in mid-August the celebration of the Assumption of the Virgin Mary. The whole year, including the less eventful autumn season, was also marked by the regular observation of saints' days, both universal ones like that of St Michael the archangel whose feast in September, Michaelmas, was the traditional day for the settlement of debts, and local ones like St William of York and St John of Beverley. For the lay person the Church enforced its major fast during Lent as the time at which everyone made at least one annual confession; and feast days were, of course, periods of rest and respite from the monotonies of work.

Every week in the calendar has a programme of biblical reading attached to it, and it is from that pattern, rather than from the Bible itself, that the Corpus Christi play derives its overall balance and emphases. The majority of episodes in the Cycle cluster around the two major feasts of the year, Christmas and Easter. The events which take up the story following the Resurrection draw on further feasts from the summer season. Less obviously, the few episodes from Christ's adult life are all drawn from the Gospel readings in the liturgy between Christmas and Easter, rather than those read at other times of year (King 1998). All the Old Testament episodes in the York Cycle are also concentrated in the liturgy for worship between Christmas and Easter, forming the sequence of readings for matins in the Breviary for Septuagesima, the extended Lenten period. The Breviary was not a liturgical book used much for lay worship, but the presumably clerical authors of the cycle would have been familiar with this cluster of Old Testament episodes. For the laity, the significance of Old Testament events would be familiar from preaching based on the tradition of Bible commentary drawn from the writings of the Church Fathers, beginning with those of St Augustine. Medieval Christianity read the Old Testament through the New, that is symbolically, according to the principles of typology. Much of the Old Testament consists of prophecy, either direct or requiring interpretation. Typology allowed that certain events of the Old Testament were also prophetic. Accordingly, Noah's ark was the wood on which the man faithful to God was saved, prefiguring the way in which the wood of the Cross would offer salvation for all; Abraham's willingness to sacrifice his only son Isaac to fulfil God's will made possible God's own sacrifice of his Son; and Moses's leading the Israelites out of bondage in Egypt into the promised land prefigured Christ's rescue of the Old Testament prophets and patriarchs when he harrowed hell. The commonplace nature of these connections between certain Old Testament events and the events of the life of Christ is demonstrated by sequences of Old and New Testament scenes in the visual arts, such as those in the windows of the corona of Canterbury cathedral (Kolve 1966: 57–100).

Why did this particular sequence, however explicable, become attached to the feast of Corpus Christi? Devotion to Corpus Christi, to the Mass, was fashionable in late medieval York, as membership of the late-formed Corpus Christi guild demonstrates. The guild was a religious confraternity in which the well-to-do civic laity, male and female, rubbed shoulders with the secular clergy in order to undertake conspicuous acts of charity and also to ensure support for themselves should they become elderly, infirm or impoverished. These devotional tastes have their place in the ecclesiastical politics of the early fifteenth century where the then Archbishop of Canterbury, Thomas Arundel, was actively engaged in reasserting orthodoxy as a counter to the spread of the radical Wycliffite ideas of the preceding quarter-century. In 1410, the year following the publication of Arundel's Constitutions, regulating preaching, Nicholas Love presented his *Mirror of the Blessed Life of Jesus Christ* to the Archbishop. Love may have been the Augustinian prior of York in 1400 who then transferred to become prior of the North Yorkshire Carthusian house at Mount Grace in 1410. His reworking of the pseudo-Bonaventuran *Meditaciones vitae Christi* emphatically affirms orthodox doctrine and fast became the most prominent contemporary text of northern provenance. Its one significant area of addition to the *Meditaciones* is a section on the sacrament of the Eucharist, influenced by Henry Suso's *The Seven Poyntes of Trewe Love and Everlastynge Wisdome*. The contemplation of the events of Christ's life had become intimately bound up with the celebration of transubstantiation, through which the Incarnation was perpetually and mystically reprised.

Direct connections can be made between the devotional climate of the first decade of the fifteenth century in which sacramental orthodoxy was being revived, Love's chapter on the Eucharist, and the formation of the York Corpus Christi guild. Direct connections between Love's writing and the pageants, however, need to be viewed with circumspection, since at this period social patterns and economic differences had created fissures between the Minster, the regular religious in York's many religious houses, and the city's laity (worshipping for the most part in the city's numerous parish churches).

Church and city had also come through the particular trauma of the execution of its own Archbishop, Richard Scrope, for his part in the unsuccessful rebellion of 1405 which attempted the deposition of Henry IV. Factions in York apparently united throughout the fifteenth century in tenacious attempts to have Scrope canonized.

At the beginning of the fifteenth century, York was already a centre for the development of lay catechesis, largely due to the policies and writings of John Thoresby, Archbishop of York from 1352 to 1373. Thoresby instigated a campaign against the ignorance of the clergy, first by reissuing the late thirteenth-century Latin tract by John Pecham bluntly entitled *Ignorancia sacerdotum*, then by commissioning John Gaytrick, a Benedictine monk at St Mary's abbey in York, to translate it into English verse as the book known as *The Lay Folks' Catechism* (Hughes 1988: 149–73; Johnston 2002: 356–7). The *Catechism* offers guidance to the clergy on instructing their parishioners in the sacraments of the Church (particularly penance), and on preaching.

A project such as the composition, however fragmentary and protracted, of a cycle of pageants such as York's, presupposes not only the existence of an ecclesiastical intellectual milieu but access to works of reference beyond the liturgical and catechetical works accessible to the secular clergy. Roughly contemporary with Thoresby is the Augustinian friar, John Waldeby, whose celebrated sermons were retained in the extensive library of the friary of his order in York (Johnston 2002: 362–6). The order, known colloquially as the 'Friars Preachers', was celebrated everywhere as one of specialist sermon-writers and bibliophiles. Their house in York was situated on the route of the Corpus Christi procession and at one stage in the early fifteenth century it shared rental of the ninth station at which the plays called with the adjacent hospital of St Leonard's. Brothers also appear frequently among the membership of the Corpus Christi guild.

The Audience of the Play

Almost as inscrutable as the authors of the play is the original audience, their expectations, responses, and motives for attending the performance. It can probably be assumed that few watched the play through from start to finish. Processional production offers audiences a wide variety of possible viewing choices. It is possible to remain at one station throughout, seeing pageants in sequence; to take a break, then to move to a later station to catch up with missed plays; to follow a particular pageant round the route because of personal allegiance; to wander sociably round the route in one direction or another, watching pageants or parts of pageants as and when they are encountered; or to organize a party for the holiday in a house along the route and look out occasionally at the play as it winds past. The play has an overarching coherence arising from the patterns of worship it reflects and the significance of the occasion for which it was devised; equally its contributory pageants relate to that pattern but have their own internal cohesiveness. As with viewing, so with reading, where a knowledge of the whole can enrich understanding of a part, but the audience member can also construct a meaningful understanding from sampling individual episodes.

The play begins with the Barkers' (tanners) *The Fall of the Angels* (I) (Beadle 1982: 49–53; Beadle and King 1995: 2–7),[7] a text of deceptive simplicity. God the Creator opens with a stanza which defines the nature of deity. The first four lines all begin 'I am', translating the Hebrew name for God, 'Yahweh'. The first line ends 'without beginning' and the last line 'without any ending'. What follows in this long speech is an enactment of the doctrine of creation by word, as the Creator names things – heaven, earth, hell, angels – and, if the pageant is to make any sense, they appear. God is here both Creator and theatrical director. His nine orders of angels are created singing in heavenly harmony, a harmony mirrored by their orderly one-stanza-each speeches of praise, and broken when Lucifer as he falls also 'steals' an extra six lines. In accord with the theological explanation of the Fall offered by Thomas Aquinas, Lucifer is created spontaneously worshipping himself instead of his maker: 'All the mirthe that is made is marked in me!', a shocking usurpation of the first-person pronoun.

No records of the staging of the Barkers' pageant survive, but the text suggests that a spectacular set opened out in imitation of the process of creation. The pageant's entire cast are supernatural beings. The angels were in all probability dressed in suits and wings made of leather, as depicted in the stained glass windows of more than one of York's parish churches. All characters would have worn full- or half-face masks, such as those listed in the Mercers' indenture for their Doomsday. Like Doomsday, this first play names heaven, earth and hell, all of which would have been represented on the set. The opening and closing pageants have much in common in their probable visual arrangement, both featuring magisterial speech and action from the second person of the Trinity, who is both Creator and Redeemer. The action of both is also formal and symbolic: in the Barkers' pageant the angels appear and are swiftly identified as good and bad, destined for heaven and hell respectively, whereas in the Mercers' pageant it is humankind who rise up from their graves as black and white souls to be similarly divided.[8] In the first pageant, all of this, accompanied by music, was the opening spectacle which greeted the citizenry of York as dawn broke on Corpus Christi day, whereas Doomsday completed the cycle, again with heavenly harmony, at dusk.

The theological significance of Corpus Christi to the laity is threaded through the intervening pageants. In the late medieval Church the laity's opportunities to participate fully in the sacrament of the altar were very occasional; their regular experience of the mystical transformation of the Mass was as spectators. All manner of benefits were claimed for those who looked at the consecrated host, the body of Christ (Duffy 1992: 91–130).[9] The liturgical climax of the Mass for the laity was the moment at which the wafer became flesh, when Christ descended to be among the community of believers, and the miracle occurred at the moment when the priest, turning his back on the communicants, faced east and elevated the host. At this moment, bells pealed, incense was burnt, and the spectators were encouraged to murmur prayers of welcome.

In terms of biblical history, as opposed to liturgical ritual, God is scheduled to make three significant appearances, in turn to make, to be and to judge humankind. The first appearance is enacted in the Barkers' pageant, the last in the Mercers' Doomsday, whereas the second, Christ's sojourn on earth between Annunciation and Passion, occupies most of the intervening action. Unsurprisingly he is greeted, in liturgically approved manner, wherever he appears. These lyrics of greeting provide one of the poetic modes by which pageants on different subjects, in different metrical forms, and probably written by different authors, contribute to a unified whole, and an understanding of the pageants as telling the story of the Fall and the Redemption specifically as a celebration of those moments when the quotidian and the divine touch explains why a number of individual episodes are treated in the way they are.

The Tilethatchers' pageant of *The Nativity* (XIV) is an apparently modest little episode, probably played on the deck of a wagon representing the Bethlehem stable with the traditional thatched roof, familiar from the kind of late medieval French or Flemish manuscript illumination popularly reproduced on Christmas cards. In the York pageant there are two speaking parts only, Mary and Joseph; there is none of the clutter of attendant handmaids, midwives, innkeepers and their potboys which are optional inclusions in the scene. Yet the pageant is as theatrically audacious as it is simple, for it involves unavoidably the enactment of the birth of the Christ-child in full view of the audience. The birth takes place during the second stanza of a four-stanza speech, while Joseph is traditionally absent seeking fuel. The third stanza of Mary's speech welcomes her baby, God incarnate, and lyrically expresses all the paradoxes surrounding the helpless homeless infant who is simultaneously the all-power-wielding Father-Creator of all. It is written according to the common formula for the elevation lyric, each line beginning with an exclamatory 'Hail', the 'Salve' of the liturgy. It seems at least likely that the man playing the Virgin Mary knelt and turned his back on the audience, elevating the infant or doll which represented the Christ-child over his head, in the manner of the celebrant at Mass, at the moment of its birth. Accordingly the audience, accustomed to going to look upon Christ in the form of the host through the eyes of faith and devout imagination, either at the Mass or in the Corpus Christi procession, were treated to more directly available visual representations of him in the plays, as he was represented literally in the flesh, either as a new-born infant or as the man of sorrows displaying the wounds of the Passion.

It is the latter depiction of Christ that dominates the York play. As the Passion sequence progresses, Judas is to use the greeting formula to identify and betray Christ in the Cordwainers' *The Agony in the Garden and the Betrayal* (XXVIII), lines 248–51. The same formula is used with deep irony by Pilate's soldiers as they identify their victim with Corpus Christi in the Tilemakers' *Christ before Pilate 2: The Judgement* (XXXIII): '*Ave*, royal roy and *rex judeorum*, / Hail, comely king that no kingdom has kenned', lines 408–16. The Pinners' pageant of *The Crucifixion* (XXXV) is well known for its black humour, as four 'soldiers' ineptly attempt to pin the silent Christ to the cross on the ground. When the cross rises, the tone of the pageant changes abruptly as the audience is confronted by the most famous contemplative image in medieval Christendom. Christ speaks from the cross, addressing the on-stage and off-stage audience indiscriminately as, 'All men that walk by way or street'. The following speech, lines 253–64, in which all are enjoined to attend in turn to Christ's wounds, invokes the standard penitential practice of meditating on the five wounds, but it borrows its rhetorical structure from the Lamentations of Jeremiah (1: 12), a text from the Old Testament which is incorporated into the Good Friday liturgy.

A pattern of action, followed by freeze-frame for contemplation, characterizes the Butchers' *Death of Christ* (XXXVI). All the opening action of this pageant takes place in the shadow of the Cross, so that the dialogue between Pilate, Annas and Caiaphas competes for the audience's attention with the still and silent figure who looms over them. Pilate finally addresses the crucified Christ who again speaks, drawing attention directly to his wounds, enjoining the viewer to 'mend his mood' (118–30), that is, to improve his or her behaviour. As the play progresses, the Virgin Mary again is given dialogue deriving directly from the lyrical tropes of the liturgy, but this time her exclamations are all 'Alas' (131–43): this is the *planctus*, the lament, with which the passing of the living Christ from earth is marked in a broadly antiphonal opposition to the speeches of greeting with which his Incarnation is greeted. The iconic lament has already been anticipated in the plaints of the mothers of the innocents murdered by Herod's soldiers in the Girdlers' and Nailers' *The Slaughter of the Innocents* (XIX), lines 199–233. As the pageant proceeds, the instruments of the Passion are produced and other subsidiary characters' speeches bring them sequentially to the attention of the audience before they are integrated into the scene.

Other pageants have a more complex relationship with the feast day that the play celebrates. In particular, there are those whose subjects, although part of the overarching narrative of Fall, Redemption and Judgement, have their own sacramental or festive focus. For example the Bakers' pageant of *The Last Supper* draws on the biblical account of the event for its narrative sequence, but bases elements of the dialogue on the liturgy of the Mass. Its account of how Christ washed his disciples' feet is also heavily dependent on the liturgical ritual for Maundy Thursday. The opening of the pageant explains the origin of the sacrament of the altar, how the Eucharist supplanted the Jewish Passover feast as a type of sacrifice, and how that in turn relates in Christian doctrine to the shift from the Old Law of justice to the New Law of forgiveness and grace based on Christ's sacrifice. In the play's narrative sequence that sacrifice has yet to take place, but the pageant breaks historical verisimilitude because of the doctrinal burden which it bears. The institution of the Eucharist itself is missing from the pageant as the relevant leaf has been torn out, and there is no way of knowing how it was enacted.

The Barbers' *Baptism* is another pageant in which the historical account, in this instance drawn from two Gospel narratives, Matthew 3: 13–17 and John 1: 29–34, intersects with instruction on and enactment of a perennial ritual of the Church. Just as the play as a whole offers the opportunity to revivify the meaning of the ritual transubstantiation of the Mass by overtly connecting it with the historical Incarnation of Christ, so too the opportunity to have the audience instructed on the meaning of Baptism, the sacrament by which the laity is admitted to the body of the Church, by John the Baptist himself, compromises strict historical mimesis in this pageant.

Movement and Procession

The situation becomes more complicated still when a pageant represents an event which has its own annual processional festive celebration. The problematic pageant of the *Purification of the Virgin* (XVII) is a late addition to the Register. The feast of the Purification is celebrated as Candlemas, and in the Middle Ages was a significant winter festival of light, involving processions with numerous candles (Duffy 1992: 459, 589). Just as Corpus Christi coincides with midsummer, Candlemas is the feast of deepest winter. Records of English dramatizations of the Purification incorporating processions with candles and designed for performance at or around Candlemas do survive, including one from nearby Beverley, but the *Purification* pageant in the York cycle does not exploit the popular candle imagery at all. In the pageant, the focus is all on the meeting between Simeon and the infant Jesus, with Simeon offering long speeches of welcome and a commentary on the beneficial effects he feels of coming into contact with the Godhead. Corpus Christi has not entirely eclipsed the traditional festive meaning of the Purification, but the dramatist has selected a different emphasis appropriate to context. The affective and transformational meeting between Simeon and the Christ-child, humanity and divinity, was an alternative traditional focus for the event, known as *hypopanti*. Encounter and recognition form in general a commonplace organizational structure in liturgical ceremony: the movement of the *quem quaeritis*, in which the mourning Mary Magdalene seeks the body from the empty tomb and meets the risen Christ, is a movement from absence and loss to reunion. The meeting on the road to Emmaus works in a similar manner, and Epiphany celebrations too are organized around a pattern whereby the burden of meaning is conveyed by self-conscious patterns of convergence, greeting and divergence, of seeking and fulfilment. This underlying pattern is central to the meaning of Corpus Christi, which celebrates the arrival of the real presence of Christ at the moment of the elevation of the host at Mass. But a reading of the Purification as *hypopanti* varies the emphasis of Corpus Christi, with its focus on the assimilation of the substance of Christ into the individual, presenting instead the incorporation of Christ as a member of the civic community.

A comparable instance was recognized by Martin Stevens in the Skinners' *Entry into Jerusalem* (XXV) (Stevens 1987: 50–62). Here the elision of Corpus Christi with the festive procession traditional to Palm Sunday has a reflexive effect, as the Palm Sunday procession within the pageant enacts and mimics the Corpus Christi procession from which the plays emanate. Accordingly the play, by eliding one festive procession with the other, both dramatizes the full meaning of Corpus Christi and suggests a comparison between York and Jerusalem. The formulaic speeches of welcome which the eight burgesses of Jerusalem/York address to Christ are again based on the prayers muttered by the laity as the host passes them in its monstrance in the Corpus Christi procession. Stevens goes on to suggest that the royal entry, the ritual celebratory welcome of a visiting monarch to the city, of which York staged a number, is the mediating genre which suggests the form taken by the Skinners' pageant. It could equally be argued that the royal entry derives its meaning for the city from the pageants. For example, in York's welcome for Henry VII (an attempt to repair relations with the Crown, uneasy since the city's treasonable support for Scrope), the Virgin Mary – as Virgin Mary – warns Henry of York's privileged spiritual status, while as actor and citizen of York the speaker is also asking that Henry – as Christ's chosen knight – looks favourably upon the city. The reciprocities claimed in the Virgin's speech depend upon the city's understanding of its relationship with God, a relationship annually asserted and affirmed through the celebration of Corpus Christi (Johnston and Rogerson 1979: 49).

The York Cycle is far more than a devotional narrative presented by amateur actors on carts; the modes by which it expresses itself draw selectively upon the liturgy and devotional glosses for the laity, and offer a politicized commentary on the city's perception of itself and its relationship with God. In the latter half of the sixteenth century the Cycle went into slow decline, eventually falling prey to the doctrinal changes which were thoroughly embedded in English religious culture by the end of Elizabeth I's reign. Thereafter there followed centuries of neglect. Contrary to popular belief, this was not because imitating the deity was outlawed; no such law ever entered the statute books.[10] However, the succession of Lords Chamberlain saw to it that religious drama was not performed to public paying audiences for over three hundred years. In 1951 the York Cycle was revived as part of the Festival of Britain, and since then there have been a number of notable modern productions.[11]

See also: 3 Religious Authority and Dissent, 4 City and Country, Wealth and Labour, 23 Lyric, 24 Literature of Religious Instruction, 25 Mystical and Devotional Literature, 26 Accounts of Lives, 27 Medieval English Theatre, 28 Morality and Interlude Drama.

Notes

1 Pamela M. King, 'The York Plays and the Feast of Corpus Christi: A Reconsideration', *Medieval English Theatre* 22 (2000), 13–32 (p. 14, n. 4).

2 Peter Meredith, 'Development of the York Mercers' Pageant Wagon', *Medieval English Theatre* 1 (1979), 5–18; Meg Twycross, 'The Left-hand-side Theory: A Retraction', *Medieval English Theatre* 14 (1992), 77–94.

3 Philip Butterworth, 'The York Mercers' Pageant Vehicle, 1433–67: Wheels, Steering, and Control', *Medieval English Theatre* 1 (1979), 72–81; Eileen White, 'Places for Hearing the Corpus Christi Play in York', *Medieval English Theatre* 9 (1987), 64–76; David Crouch, 'Paying to See the Play: The Stationholders on the Route of the York Corpus Christi Play in the Fifteenth Century', *Medieval English Theatre* 13 (1991), 64–111.

4 On characterization see *Medieval English Theatre* 5 (1983), *passim*.

5 Meg Twycross, '"Transvestism"' in the Mystery Plays', *Medieval English Theatre* 5 (1983), 123–80.

6 E.g., Johnston and Rogerson 1979: I, 62–3 (Armourers), 47–8, 112–13 (Masons).

7 All quotations from individual pageants are taken from Beadle and King (eds) 1992.

8 Meg Twycross, 'More Black and White Souls', *Medieval English Theatre* 13 (1991), 52–63.

9 King, 'York Plays and the Feast of Corpus Christi'.

10 Olga Horner, 'The Law that Never Was: A Review of Theatrical Censorship in Britain', *Medieval English Theatre* 23 (2001), 34–96.

11 Reviews of modern productions, and critical reflections by directors and producers, are regularly published in *Medieval English Theatre.*

References and Further Reading

Beadle, R. (ed.) 1982. *The York Plays.* London: Edward Arnold. Full critical edition of the York Cycle.

—— 1994. 'The York Cycle.' In *The Cambridge Companion to Medieval English Theatre*, ed. R. Beadle (Cambridge: Cambridge University Press), pp. 85–108. Useful introduction to the manuscript sources.

—— and King, P. M. (eds) 1995. *York Mystery Plays: A Selection in Modern Spelling.* Oxford World's Classics. Oxford: Oxford University Press. Twenty-two pageants in modern spelling with brief critical introductions.

—— and Meredith, P. 1983. *The York Play: A Facsimile of British Library MS Additional 35290.* Leeds: University of Leeds, School of English. Photo-facsimile of the York Register with bibliographical introduction and notes.

Beckwith, S. 2001. *Signifying God: Social Relation and Symbolic Act in the York Corpus Christi Plays.* Chicago and London: University of Chicago Press. Monograph exploring the relationship between civic community and sacramental drama.

Carpenter, S. and Twycross, M. 2002. *Masks and Masking in Medieval and Early Tudor England.* Aldershot and Burlington, Va.: Ashgate. Detailed study and analysis of one aspect of theatrical practice including a section on mystery plays.

Dobson, R. B. 1997. 'Craft Guilds and City: The Historical Origins of the York Mystery Plays Reassessed.' In *The Stage as Mirror: Civic Theatre in Late Medieval Europe*, ed. A. E. Knight (Cambridge: Brewer), pp. 91–106. A York historian's review of theories of the origins of the York Cycle.

Duffy, E. 1992. *The Stripping of the Altars: Traditional Religion in England c.1400–c.1580.* New Haven, Conn., and London: Yale University Press. Comprehensive description of pre Reformation ecclesiastical practices in England.

Goldberg, J. 1997. 'Craft Guilds, the Corpus Christi Play and Civic Government.' In *The Government of Medieval York: Essays in Commemoration of the 1396 Royal Charter*, ed. Sarah Rees Jones (York: Borthwick Institute of Historical Research), pp. 141–63. Review of the relationship between guilds and the play, and of the role of women in the production of the cycle.

Hughes, J. 1988. *Pastors and Visionaries: Religion and Secular Life in Late Medieval Yorkshire.* Woodbridge: Boydell Press. Monograph on late medieval northern English devotional literature in its social and political contexts.

Johnston, A. F. 2002. 'The York Cycle and the Libraries of York.' In *The Church and Learning in Later Medieval Society: Essays in Honour of R. B. Dobson*, ed. C. M. Barron and J. Stratford, Harlaxton Medieval Studies, 11 (Donington, Lincs.: Shaun Tyas), pp. 355–70. A study of the library resources available in York when the pageants were written.

—— and Rogerson, M. 1979. *Records of Early English Drama: York.* 2 vols. Toronto and Buffalo, N.Y.: Toronto University Press. Reference work reproducing all civic records from York which refer to dramatic activity.

King, P. M. 1998. 'Calendar and Text: Christ's Ministry in the York Plays and the Liturgy.' *Medium Ævum* 67, 30–59. A study of the relationship between the selection of episodes in the York Cycle and the organization of biblical texts in the Missal.

—— 1999. 'Contemporary Cultural Models for the Trial Plays in the York Cycle.' In *Drama and Community: People and Plays in Medieval Europe*, ed. A. Hindley (Turnhout: Brepols), pp. 200–16. A study of practices and procedures drawn from the law and of the subversive potential of York pageants in performance.

Kolve, V. A. 1966. *The Play Called Corpus Christi.* Stanford, Calif.: Stanford University

Press. Provided the foundation for much late twentieth-century critical work on cycle drama.

Medieval English Theatre, 1– (University of Lancaster, 1979–). Themed journal with many articles on cycle drama and related topics.

Stevens, M. 1987. *Four Middle English Mystery Cycles: Textual, Contextual, and Critical Interpretations*. Princeton, N.J.: Princeton University Press. Monograph arguing for the distinctiveness of the York Cycle as city drama.

Swanson, H. 1989. *Medieval Artisans: An Urban Class in Late Medieval England*. Oxford: Blackwell. Useful historical discussion of the guild system.

Twycross, M. 1994. 'The Theatricality of Medieval English Plays.' In *The Cambridge Companion to Medieval English Theatre*, ed. R. Beadle (Cambridge: Cambridge University Press), pp. 37–84. Comprehensive study of the performative aspects and characteristics of medieval drama.

Woolf, R. 1972. *The English Mystery Plays*. London: Routledge and Kegan Paul. Detailed study of the subject-matter and sources of individual pageants in the extant mystery cycles.

30
The *Book of Margery Kempe*[1]

Ruth Evans

> To create was a fundament . . . Once created, the creature was separate from the creator, and needed no seconding to fully exist.[2]

One day, when the creature that is now generally known as Margery Kempe is praying before an altar of the Cross, she dozes off and has a vision of an angel, 'al clothyd in white as mech as it had been a litel childe beryng an howge boke be-forn hym'.[3] 'A,' she says to the child/angel, 'þis is þe Boke of Lyfe.' Seeing a picture of the Trinity painted in gold in the book, she asks, 'Wher is my name?' The child replies, 'Her is þi name at the Trinyte foot wretyn', and vanishes. Then Christ addresses her: 'Dowtyr, loke þat þu be now trewe & stedfast & haue a good feith, for þi name is wretyn in Heuyn in þe Boke of Lyfe' (206–7). This strangely haunting vision raises a number of issues about how to read the *Book of Margery Kempe*. I will argue that we must respect the *Book*'s singularity, and not reduce either text or protagonist to what is immediately familiar and comprehensible: a knowable human subject, a transparent account of historical reality.

Reading the Book

In far too many critical studies the object of analysis is displaced from the text to a person: either the author or the protagonist – usually both, since they are routinely conflated, even in the most savvy critical readings (Beckwith 1986; Dinshaw 1999; Lochrie 1991; Margherita 1995). One important exception to this tendency is Lynn Staley who separates author – 'Kempe' – and subject – 'Margery' (1994: 3) in a radical attempt not to circumscribe Kempe's authorial achievement. But Staley's (very influential) argument is still mortgaged to the belief that a book is the product of a single sovereign author who controls its meaning. One of the aims of the present essay is to trouble some of the liberal humanist assumptions that are still rife in scholarship on the *Book*, and to allow the text to proliferate meanings that are not limited by the figure of the author.

There is the question, first, of *which* name is inscribed at the Trinity's foot and in the celestial book. The *Book*'s protagonist is most frequently named 'þis/þe (for) (sayd) creatur'; she is called 'Margery' only sixteen times, always in direct speech, and 'Mar. Kempe of Lynne' (243) just once (Cowen 2000: 165, 171). 'Creatur' – someone created by God, or just a 'person' – is one of the *Book*'s key terms: a deliberately self-depreciatory self-naming, like its use of 'synful caytyf' (1), as in the titles of works like *Pore Caitif.* I will refer to the *Book*'s third-person narrator as 'the creature', 'she' or 'the protagonist', or use the formula 'the *Book* says'. This strategy is to separate the textual voice from the putative author, but my aim is very different from Staley's.

'Creatur' is a key term in the *Book* in more ways than that of self-naming. In the above passage, we might assume a massive hubris on the creature's part: so holy has she become that her name is second only to the Trinity. But the 'Boke of Lyfe' in which she cannot read her name is an allusion to the common late medieval topos of the book of Nature, specifically to the first of the four metaphorical 'Books of Life' classified by the twelfth-century theologian Hugh of Folieto: 'The first was written in Paradise, the second in the desert, the third in the Temple, the fourth has been written from all eternity.'[4] Further details in the passage confirm this. In religious uses of the book as metaphor, as E. R. Curtius notes, '[o]ften an angel writes down a man's good deeds' (318). Moreover, in the book of Nature topos 'every creature is a book' (319), and in homilists especially, '"scientia creaturarum" and "liber naturae" appear as synonyms': the '"book of the creature" remained a favourite concept of orthodox asceticism and mysticism' (320). The *Imitatio Christi* (c.1418), attributed to Thomas à Kempis, claims: 'Si rectum cor tuum esset, tunc omnis creatura speculum vitae et liber sanctae doctrinae esset' (If your heart were righteous, then every creature would be a mirror of life and a book of sacred doctrine).[5] This is how the *Book*'s protagonist figures her life and body in the *Book*'s closing prayers – as cosmic, containing the teeming multitudes of creation: 'gresys growing in al erthe, kyrnellys of corn, fischys, fowelys, bestys & leevys up-on treys whan most plente ben' (252). So the name that the child points out to her might simply be her preferred appellation, 'the creature'. Not hubris at all, but a sign of her inscription in the created world.

Not only is her name written in the book of Nature but she herself, as a 'creatur', constitutes that very book. I stress the creature-as-book metaphor because readers persistently represent the relationship between the lay author and her male clergial scribes in terms of the binary opposition orality/literacy, in which the female author/protagonist can never figure in terms of writing, only of speech. But the *Book* constantly resists such polarization. Like so many of the authoritative cultural models that the narrator uses to create her precarious subjectivity (saint's life, confession, Augustinian willed virginity, *imitatio Christi*, prophecy), the various models of 'writing' – which are central to the *Book* – are reworked to such an extent that they are simply resistant to being read in modern terms. If the *Book*'s female author claims agency and selfhood, she also sees herself as a book authored by God.

What then of her failure to recognize or read her own name? This scene first stages, and then assuages, the creature's anxiety about her special status. But it also suggests that her own identity is sometimes unrecognizable and that God's writing can be bafflingly unreadable. And although the 'creatur' comes to recognize her name as divinely written (that is, effortlessly), the first proem's elaboration of what Sarah Beckwith aptly calls the *Book*'s 'difficult genesis' (1986: 37) insists that writing the historically contingent *female* self is an extremely arduous business.

Yet there is a sense in which the creature-as-book is not 'written' at all. God's book is a metaphoric writing: natural, eternal, unfallen. The creature's desire throughout the text is to inscribe herself in this prelapsarian writing. Her yearning for virginity is one powerful manifestation of that desire. Another is the text's drive to efface itself as writing (which is why it is imperative to insist on its status as writing). In some ways, the *Book* is analogous to *Piers Plowman* in what I will call its rhetoric of transparency.[6] In the *Book*'s first proem, the narrator roundly declares that 'sche ded no þing wryten but þat sche knew rygth wel for very trewth' (5), as if meaning were always firmly under strict editorial control and as if 'trewth' (which can mean 'loyalty to God' as well as 'veracity', with its implication of artlessness) were the only criterion by which the work and its unity might be judged. This rhetoric of transparency is typical of one of the *Book*'s chief models: Nicholas Love's populist and officially blessed *Mirror of the Blessed Life of Jesus Christ* (1410). Love's translation seeks to efface itself as text in order to forge for its audience a sense of immediate, interiorized connection with the body of Christ. The *Book*'s rhetoric of transparency has led many readers to assume a unity of voice and writing: in reading the *Book*, they 'hear' the authentic voice of 'Mar. Kempe of Lynne', romantically 'struggling out of repression and inarticulation'.[7] But that voice is textual: it does not give us direct access to its author. The fact that the modern edition has a female signature has led to a reading practice in which, to cite Diane Purkiss's argument about early modern women writers, 'the textual voice is prized less for itself than as a sign pointing towards . . . an authorial presence'.[8] But there is no external evidence that connects 'Mar. Kempe of Lynne' (243) with the Margery Kempe of Lynn who was admitted to the Trinity Guild of Lynn in 1438 (358–9), and even less evidence that connects either of these figures with the supposed author 'Margery Kempe' (Salih 2001: 173). So we cannot even claim with any confidence that 'Margery's voice rings clearly from the text' (Fanous 2000: 171). In the dream-like Book of Life vision, as in the *Book* as a whole, that 'voice' does *not* speak to us 'clearly' but emerges indirectly, through a mixture of third-person past tense narration and direct speech. The reader must actively construct a meaning for this voice rather than passively hear it: the contrast between the 'lityl' child and the 'howge' book suggests a fantasy of the insignificant self confronted by the vastness of creation; the question 'Wher is my name?' reveals an insecurity about where her identity is located.

Yet modern readers are not entirely wrong to think of the *Book*'s protagonist in the anachronistic terms of post-Lockean possessive individualism. The drive to assert the self's singularity through what it can appropriate to itself (or through how it can harness a higher power to justify its will), is present throughout the *Book,* most strikingly in the episode where the creature sees the sacrament fluttering above the priest's head and Christ assures her that she is more privileged than St Bridget, her most envied hagiographic role model: 'My dowtyr, Bryde, say me neuyr in þis wyse' (47). And it is also evident in her out-sobbing of the saints (people complain that 'þer was neuyr saynt in Heuyn þat cryed so as sche dede', 105), in Christ's famous reassurance to her about her lack of virgin status ('trow þow rygth wel þat I lofe wyfes also', 48), in her on-off fasting, her wearing of white clothes, her frequent communion, and her anxious witnessing of Christ's refusal of Mary Magdalene's touch (238) – an episode in which she both identifies with the Magdalene and distances herself from her, knowing she would not be happy if Christ were to say to her 'Touch me not' (Dinshaw 1999: 161).

What is so compelling about the *Book* is its constant negotiation between the will to individualism and the sense of participating in a vast cosmic drama in which the self is always subject to a higher authority. The complex construction of the textual voice is crucial here. But first I need a detour through the issue of the *Book*'s authorship. While I resist the conflation of author and protagonist, I cannot (as Staley does) entirely sever extra-textual writer from intra-textual voice (Salih 2001: 171–3). But the connection is far from straightforward.

Language and Authorship

In the introduction to their 1940 edition, Sanford Meech and Hope Emily Allen ask a question that has left an indelible stamp on critical studies of the *Book*: 'Whose language is it?' (vii). There are four suspects: the historical author 'Margery Kempe'; the first and second amanuenses (the Englishman who had lived a long time in 'Dewchland' and the priest); and lastly 'Salthows', the scribe who copied out the only surviving manuscript of the *Book* c.1450. By 'language' Meech and Allen mean 'habits of speech and orthography'. But their question is not entirely innocent. In 1975, at a time when feminist criticism was recovering a 'lost tradition' of female authors, J. Hirsh argued that 'the second scribe, no less than Margery, should be regarded as the author of *The Book of Margery Kempe*' (1975: 150). Hirsh's (much-contested) presumption is that an illiterate Englishwoman living in the early fifteenth century could not have 'written' a book in her own right and that it was a male cleric who shaped and wrote it.

But the scene of writing in the *Book* is complex. In the first proem, we learn that certain 'worthy & worshepful clerkes' asked the creature to 'makyn a booke of hyr felyngys & hir reuelacyons' (3), some even offering to write them down 'wyth her owen handys'. Insofar as a 'hand' is handwriting, the implication is that the 'clerkes' offer to write down mechanically what is dictated to them. But insofar as the phrase asserts agency (doing it with their *own* hands) it may imply a more active intervention on their part – writing in Hirsh's sense of 'composition'. But the creature would not agree to its 'writing' because she had been 'comawndyd in hir sowle' that it was too soon. Some twenty years later, and since she is unable to write herself, she asks an Englishman living in Germany (probably her own son) to write the work, and he then writes 'as mech as sche wold tellyn hym for þe tym þat þei wer to-gydder' (4). Then he dies. She next asks a priest, but he is unable to read what has been written and backs off because of the narrator's bad reputation. In a scene reminiscent of literary myths of divine inspiration, such as Bede's account of the poet Cædmon, the priest is then miraculously able to read the mangled script of the first scribe and copies it out again in English, with the creature at his elbow intervening in the writing process: 'sche sum-tym helping where ony difficulte was' (5).

The act of writing here does not conform to our modern models of either literacy or dictation (Lochrie 1991: 103). Writing is presented as a collaborative exercise. Apart from the difficulties of determining the exact amount of scribal participation from the evidence of the two proems – and at least one further layer of scribal transmission exists between the second scribe's work and this, the Salthows copy (Cowen 2000: 159–60) – the mythical elements in the scene resist its reduction to a transcript of empirical reality. Undeniably, the *Book* is a crucible of different texts and voices: priests, friars, archbishops and bishops, laymen and laywomen, anchors and anchoresses, female saints' lives, popular lives of Christ, the second scribe. But is it really possible to identify with legal precision the various 'voices' within it?

Chapter 62 is often taken to be one of the places where we hear the authentic voice of the second scribe. It describes his change of heart towards the creature after Friar William Melton's attacks on her ostentatious sobbing in church, a reversal due to his reading a life of Marie of Oignies:

> Than þe preste whech wrot þis tretys thorw steryng of a worshepful clerk, a bacheler of diuinite, had seyn & red þe mater beforn-wretyn meche mor seryowslech & expressiowslech þan it is wretyn in þis tretys (for her is but a lityl of þe effect þerof, for he had not ryth cler mende of þe sayd mater whan he wrot þis tretys, & þerfor he wrot þe lesse þerof) þan he drow a-geyn & inclined mor sadly to þe sayd creatur, whom he had fled & enchewyd thorw þe frerys prechyng, as is be-forn wretyn. (153)

One of the difficulties of reading this passage is that the precise referents (is 'þe sayd mater' the sobbing of Marie of Oignies, saintly sobbing in general, or the creature's sobbing in particular?) depend on the position of the speaking voice, just as 'her' and 'þis' are designated in relation to the temporality of that voice. Yet whose voice do we hear? The various attributions of wrong reading and the apology for the scribe's faulty memory are neither uncomplicatedly the judgements of an author called Kempe (Lochrie 1991: 119) nor those of the priest.

One of the principal objectives of this passage is to present the saint's life as a legitimating model for the creature's inordinate weeping. So it is written from the creature's subject-position. But who is apologizing for the fact that in this 'tretys' the priest had only conveyed 'a lityl of the effect' (intention) because he did not have a clear 'mende' (memory) of the subject? Either party might lay claim to the apology. The critical word here is 'expressiowslech'. It is unique: the *MED* cites only this example, relating it to *expresseli*, and giving its meaning as 'clearly, fully, in detail'. But it is also related to *expressen* (*MED*: 'To put (something) into words', 'To give a name to (something)', 'To denote or mean') – in other words, 'meaningfully' or 'intelligibly'. At stake then is what is considered culturally meaningful or 'legible'. It is difficult to separate out here the various written texts (saint's life, 'tretys') from their various subject(-matter)s. The creature's legibility, and that of her written text, reside not in her intrinsic behaviour but in the cultural models that readers bring to bear on that behaviour. Nothing could pose more acutely how the business of understanding both written texts and other people depends on a series of intricate and gendered relations between 'mater', books and readers.

Hirsh inaugurated a line of criticism that seeks to establish authorship of the *Book* through analysis of stylistic data, but authorship is also constructed through the textual codes of the page itself. The title by which the text is now known, *The Book of Margery Kempe*, is that of the early sixteenth-century printed editions. But the preposition 'of' does not only mean 'by' (indicating authorship) but also 'about' (signalling subject-matter) or even 'belonging to', as in its medieval rubric, the 'boke . . . of Mountegrace': the book belonging to the Carthusian Priory of Mount Grace in North Yorkshire, where the manuscript was kept during the fifteenth century. Is *Book* its proper description anyway? It describes itself as a 'schort tretys' (1, 5) as well as 'a booke' (3) in the first and second proems. But is it a 'treatyse of contemplacyon', as de Worde describes it? Or even a 'Journal', as in Meech and Allen's curious label to the frontispiece of their edition? (Women's life-writings often take the form of daily journals but the *Book* is written at a temporal remove from the events it narrates.)

What constitutes this author's 'work' anyway? Is it only the medieval manuscript text? Or Wynkyn de Worde's gutted and sanitized 1501 version? Or Henry Pepwell's 1521 reprint, a text that repositions the author as 'a deuout ancres' (in its colophon) and places the devotional text attached to her name in the company of a number of other pre-Reformation devotional works? The bibliographic codes of Pepwell's edition include a woodcut Image of Pity which immediately precedes the extract from the *Book* and which is designed to function, like the reading of the text, as a pardon that offers a generous indulgence (Summit 2000: 126–38). This is the material book as efficacious object, not the work as a product of authorial genius or even less as expressive (to use medieval terms) of the *intentio* of its *auctor*. Nevertheless, the *female* 'signature' does have a historical function in the sixteenth-century printed versions: Pepwell and de Worde impose a female authorial imprimatur as a tool for resisting the forces of modernity ushered in by the Reformation (Summit 2000: 17).

The female author of the *Book* that looms so large in current criticism is a construct: an effect of the text's sixteenth-century rubrics, of a twentieth-century desire to find lost medieval female authors, and of assumptions about the *Book*'s generic status. In 1941, the *Book* was hailed as the first autobiography in English (Watt 1997: 27). According to Philippe Lejeune, the fundamental condition for autobiography is that there must be 'identity between the *author*, the *narrator* and the *protagonist*' (a view he has since modified).[9] Assumptions about the *Book*'s genre and its authorship have therefore been mutually informing in Kempe studies. Alternative generic categories have been proposed – 'autohagiography' (Salih 2001: 174), 'female sacred biography' (Staley 1994: 42) – but these have not always redirected attention towards the textual strategies through which identity is produced in the *Book*. This does not mean throwing out the idea of the female author altogether. But it does mean acknowledging that authorship is constructed culturally: we define as the writings of Margery Kempe those that circulated as hers – with the caveat that we know virtually nothing about the historical author.

Textual Subjectivity

The figure that emerges so powerfully from the text is a narrative self, created out of historical, institutional discourses. Chief among these are confession (Salih 2001: 176) and *imitatio Christi*, an almost literal identification with the body of Christ and with his suffering (Beckwith 1986, 1993). But the text offers more than a series of discursive subject-positions. It vividly evokes the multiple experiences of subjectivity: of being *myself* (alienated, troubled, cosmic), of appearing as an other to others (difficult, respected, whole), of being produced and circumscribed by social institutions (affective piety, heresy, the family), and of inhabiting a gendered body. For many readers what is so singular about the *Book* is that its protagonist experiences herself on so many levels (though not always with equal degrees of conscious reflection), often openly traversing the very stuff out of which the ego is made.

In understanding how this is achieved, the question of grammatical person is fundamental. Emile Benveniste argues that it is 'in and through language that man [*sic*] constitutes himself as a *subject*, because language alone establishes the concept of "ego" in reality, in its reality which is that of the being'.[10] For Benveniste, this subjectivity depends on the first person: 'Language is possible only because each speaker sets himself up as a *subject* by referring to himself as *I* in his discourse.'[11] But if subjectivity is an effect of language that depends on the capacity of the speaker to posit herself as 'I', then how can we read the subjectivity of the *Book*'s third-person protagonist: 'þis creatur'? Yet most readers feel strongly that she hangs together as a 'psychic unity that transcends the totality of the actual experiences it assembles'.[12] This subjectivity must be historicized: where post-Enlightenment autobiography offers an experience of the self on a Romantic voyage of self-discovery, the creature is pulled between subjection to the will of God and the desire to be a subject in her own right. In this tension we find continuities with modern and post-modern subjectivities. I will consider a passage that deals with the theme of dying for the love of God, since the model of sacrificial desire in late medieval literature plays constantly with subject–object relations in language.[13]

After an early episode where the monks of Canterbury threaten to burn her as a Lollard, the creature reflects on what it would be like to die for Christ:

> Sche ymagyned in hir-self what deth sche mygth deyn for Crystys sake. Hyr þowt sche wold a be slayn for Goddys lofe, but dred for þe point of deth, & þerfor sche ymagyned hyr-self þe most soft deth, as hir thowt, for dred of inpacyens, þat was to be bowndyn hyr hed & hir fet to a stokke & hir hed to be smet of wyth a scharp ex for Goddys lofe. Þan seyd owyr Lord in hir mende, 'I thank þe, dowtyr, þat þow woldyst suffer deth for my lofe, for, as oftyn as þow thynkyst so, þow schalt haue þe same mede in Heuyn as þow þu suffredyst þe same deth. & ȝet schal no man sle the, ne fyer bren þe, ne watyr drynch þe, ne wynd deryn þe, for I may not for-ȝetyn þe how þow art wretyn in myn handys & my fete; it lykyn me wel þe peynes þat I haue sufferyd for þe.' (29–30)

This is an extraordinary rewriting of the ethics of Christian self-sacrifice. The creature actively yearns to identify with the passionate suffering of her ascetic models: the virgin-martyr and Christ – and (perhaps covertly) the heretic. But she also seeks a way of evading the law that exacts dying as the ultimate act of Christian love. At first the creature is willing to contemplate dying for the love of God. But she fears her inability to endure the actual moment of death ('for dred of inpacyens'). So she imagines for herself an easy death: to be bound head and foot to a piece of timber and to be beheaded with a sharp axe. To see this as 'þe *most* soft deth' it is only necessary to recall the typically protracted *passio* of the female virgin: Chaucer's St Cecilia suffers for an agonizing three days, because Almachius's servant botches the beheading (the narrative of pious female survival requires that he does). 'Stokke' evokes the contemptuous Lollard word for an idol (whether consciously or unconsciously is impossible to know): the creature imagines herself, paradoxically, both burnt at the stake as a heretic and heroically bound to the very symbol of orthodoxy. The ambiguity of 'stokke' suggests her sense of being torn between contrary identifications. But the beheading also represents a fantasy of castration: for women, the imagined relation to the phallus, which is also the recognition of difference, and a move *away* from identification.

Christ's reassuring words praise her for imagining the possibility of sacrifice, but release her from any obligation to undergo it. It is enough for her to *imagine* that possibility to receive the same reward in heaven as if she had in fact died for his sake. This looks like casuistry (or cowardice), but here I think the *Book* asserts the power of willful thinking: as with its version of willed virginity (modelled, it must be said, on the standard Augustinian view), this thinking projects the self past its physical limits.

Her selfhood is also enacted through the permutations of grammatical person. Benveniste argues that language (and hence subjectivity) is made possible not only through taking up the 'I' but through the difference that arises through pronominal *contrast*: '*I* posits another person, the one who, being, as he [*sic*] is, completely exterior to "me," becomes my echo to whom I say *you* and who says *you* to me.'[14] This reciprocal 'echoing' allows the individual to emerge as a subject and produces the experience of consciousness of self. (In Benveniste's use of 'echo' I hear a reference to the Other's function as a narcissistic foil.) But this is inverted in the *Book*. The creature does not say 'I' (with some important exceptions): Christ does. In addressing her as *you*, Christ sets her up as a subject, but one that is seen from the place of the Other that Christ occupies. What the creature seeks is recognition from the Other. Christ's words produce for her this fantasy of recognition: in his gaze/speech she appears as object, rather than subject. Paradoxically, this produces for 'þe creatur' a sense of herself as gratifyingly 'whole'. Sacrifice covers over lack because it assumes that the Other does exist. By positing Christ as another person who is present (as I) and who engages in dialogue (I/you), the *Book* brilliantly explores over and over again how it might be to imagine oneself as the object of the Other's desire. Sacrifice is here structurally equivalent to Benveniste's reciprocal 'echo': the creature is willing to sacrifice her subject-position as 'I' in order to be recognized as an object in the eyes of Christ. Her strategies recuperate any sense of her inadequacy in falling short of the full sacrifice that the Other desires by rewriting the Other's desire so that it conforms to what she wants: 'I thank þe, dowtyr, þat þow woldyst suffer deth for my lofe, for, as oftyn as þow thynkyst so, þow schalt haue þe same mede in Heuyn as þow þu suffredyst þe same deth' (30).

If Christ's words speak her into being, then his wounds also write her into subjectivity. Christ assures her that he will not forget that she is 'written' on his body: the wounds on his hands and feet are a reminder both of her sinfulness and of his redemption of her sins, an allusion to the 'Charters of Christ' tradition, in which Christ's body is figured as a legal document on parchment, inscribed by the figurative pens of his tormentors. Writing is the traumatic memory of sacrifice, bodily sentience, sin and the promise of redemption. Christ has sacrificed himself in order that Christians might be redeemed: his painfully inscribed body bears witness to that sacrifice, just as in being written on that body the creature assures herself of her figurative participation in his sacrifice. In this writing, she is made (a) subject.

Jacques Derrida argues that sacrifice is the ultimate act both of subjectivity and of responsibility: my death is the only thing that is truly mine to give, and 'the gift of death' means 'assuming responsibility for one's own death'.[15] But the creature's ultimate refusal of the gift of death does not constitute an evasion of responsibility and of subjectivity. Rather, in religious sacrifice, as in the sacrificial postures of courtly love (indeed, the *Book* often imagines a passionate erotic connection with Christ), the subject imagines itself as seen from the place of the Other. This is difficult for those readers who see female agency as all-important. But the creature has no trouble recognizing her own subjection and even embracing it. Simone de Beauvoir argues that woman 'stands before man not as a subject but as an object paradoxically endued with subjectivity; she takes herself simultaneously as *self* and as *other*, a contradiction that entails baffling consequences'.[16] But Beauvoir describes the condition of post-Enlightenment, Western woman: a free citizen and yet subordinate. In early fifteenth-century England the discourse of liberation is simply not available.

Yet there is a tension between subjection and an emergent will-to-power within the *Book*'s dominant hagiographic model. The *Book*'s narrative strategies – especially its oscillations between third, first and second person – are an attempt to explore the various, shifting and contradictory meanings of subjectivity: as *subject to* as well as *subject of*. The text's understanding of its status as *writing* (it does not represent itself as an *oral* mode that simply happens to be written down) is crucial to this exploration. In the passage the constant qualifications ('Hyr þowt', 'as hir thowt', 'in hir mende') reinforce a sense of writing as reflection and hence produce the creature's sense of self, by creating a gap between the event of imagining and its memorial inscription. Jack Goody's observation about a thirteenth-century *trobaritz* poem illuminates my point: 'the written poem separates condition and reflection . . . [this feature] is promoted by writing, which creates an object outside oneself in a way that speech cannot do, at least in the same clear-cut fashion'.[17]

This pronominal strategy extends outwards into a nexus of shifting subject positions: Christ tells her, 'þerfor I preue þat þow art a very dowtyr to me & a modyr also, a syster, a wife, and a spowse' (31). These multiple identifications are the products of institutionalized discourse, represented by the standard Gospel injunctions to be an obedient Christian: 'He þat doth þe wyl of my Fadyr in Heuyn he is bothyn modyr, broþyr, & syster vn-to me' (31). Such shifts explain the moments when third-person narration suddenly slips into first-person narration. There are four instances of this 'I' in direct narration (there are of course hundreds in direct speech): when the first scribe comes to England, 'meued I trost thorw þe Holy Gost' (4); when Christ sends her great temptations for three years, 'of þe which on of the hardest I purpos to wrytyn for exampyl of hem þat com aftyr þat þei schuld not trostyn on her owyn self ne haue no joy in hem-self as þis creatur had' (14); when the anchorite in Lynn prophesies that she will be helped on her pilgrimage to Jerusalem, and the text comments: 'so it be-fel as þe ankyr had prophecyed in euery point, and, as I trust, xal be wretyn more pleynly aftyrward' (44); and finally when the text comments on the creature's enthusiastic praise of God: 'Wyth swech maner of thowtys & many mo þan I cowde euyr writyn sche worschepyd & magnified owr Lord Ihesu Crist' (214). I read these apparent intrusions as extensions of the practice of first-person reporting that is otherwise found only in direct speech, and which could belong as much to the creature as to her scribe(s). Or to no one in particular. Despite Benveniste's claims that subjectivity is an effect of referring to oneself as 'I', the opposite does not hold true. 'I' in a medieval text may be a grammatical placeholder, not an expression of personal experience. In any case, the editorial practice of inserting speech marks obscures for modern readers one of the characteristics of medieval manuscript textuality: a permeability between direct and reported speech. There is, however, another important consequence that arises out of the linguistic construction of subjectivity: the question of temporality.

The Subject of Time

Readers often remark upon the loose structural organization of the *Book*. One critic has even claimed that 'much Margery criticism can be seen, in one sense, as an indirect attempt to order this desultory text' (Fanous 2000: 157). Its 'desultory' nature has sometimes been attributed to the illiteracy and intensely visual piety of its female author, given to thinking in terms of spatial images, not in the linear chronology of written narrative. More recently, this supposed desultoriness has been explained in terms of the *Book*'s genre: that it does not claim to be historical fact but rather reconstructs a version of historical memory. This gets away from the routine assumption that the loose narrative sequence is a *hindrance* to our reading of the text. As Benveniste observes, 'Linguistic time is *self-referential*': it is 'internal to the discourse'.[18] The 'time' of the *Book* is the time of its narrator's memory of events. It is difficult to appreciate this, so much are Western cultures still gripped by Locke's idea of what Charles Taylor calls the 'punctual self': that through 'disengagement and rational control' the self is fully within our power to perfect.[19] The characteristic narrative temporality of the *Book* is not linear – it does not arrive punctually – but is organized in terms of 'episodic' or 'autobiographical memory' (remembering what, as distinguished from 'semantic memory', remembering how):

> Thys boke is not wretyn in ordyr, euery thyng aftyr oþer as it were don, but lych as þe mater cam to þe creatur in mend whan it schuld be wretyn, for it was so long er it was wretyn þat sche had for-getyn þe tyme & þe ordyr whan thyngys befellyn. (5)

Events are displaced because they are narrated from the protagonist's standpoint in the present of writing, 'lych as þe mater cam to þe creatur in mend'. So the *Book* prefers metaphorical links to metonymic ones, representing the creature's experience in terms of large symbolic patterns: weeping and roaring, contemplations of Christ's suffering, prophecy, misunderstanding.

What is also overlooked in considerations of the *Book*'s structure is the material form of the medieval codex. A typical instruction to the reader like that at the end of Chapter 16 – 'Rede fyrst þe xxi chapetre & þan þis chapetre aftyr þat' (38) – exploits the fact that the *Book* is what we would now call searchable. Marginal annotations, rubrication and chapter numbers in the *Book* allowed contemporary readers to navigate their way around it and to make their own meanings, not as readers of a disembodied *text* but of a material, spatially organized *book*. Just as the protagonist's subjectivity is an effect of language, so the *Book*'s temporality is an effect of both its subject's relation to the time of writing and the material dimension of the medieval book.

Dismemberment

A final aspect of the creature's subjectivity is her sense of being subject to forces from *inside* herself. The famous hallucination of 'mennys membrys' is an account of how the (illusory) wholeness of the ego is always under threat from forces within:

> And, as sche beforn had many gloryows visyonys & hy contemplacyon in þe manhood of owr Lord, in owr Lady, & in many oþer holy seyntys, ryth euyn so had sche now horybyl syghtys & abhominabyl, for anything þat sche cowde do, of beheldyng of mennys membrys & swech oþer abhominacyons. Sche sey as hir thowt veryly dyuers men of religion, prestys, & many oþer, bothyn hethyn & Cristen comyn be-for hir syght þat sche myth not

> enchewyn hem ne puttyn hem owt of hir syght, schewyng her bar membrys vn-to hir. & þerwyth þe Deuyl bad hir in her mende chesyn whom sche wolde han first of hem alle & sche must be comown to hem alle. & he seyd sche lykyd bettyr summe on of hem þan alle þe oþer. Hir thowt þat he seyd trewth; sche cowde not sey nay; & sche must nedys don hys byddyng, & ȝet wolde sche not a don it for alle þis worlde. But ȝet hir thowt þat it xulde be don, & hir thowt þat þes horrybyl syghtys & cursyd mendys wer delectable to hir a-geyn hir wille. (145)

What is striking about this passage is not so much that it scandalizes by its mention of priests' (and other men's) 'membrys' but that it stages an apparently unresolvable internal conflict. The sights are simultaneously 'horybyl' and 'delectable'. The careful parallelism and chiasmus of the repeated 'ȝet' clauses enacts contradictory surges, the first clause reversing her previous desire ('& ȝet wolde sche not a don it for alle þis worlde'), the second one then reversing that willed decision ('But ȝet hir thowt þat it xulde be don'), and ending with an expression of desire that once again reverses the previous decision: 'þes horrybyl syghtys & cursyd mendys wer delectable to hir a-geyn hir wille'. The passage offers imagos of the fragmented body, staging the always threatening return of corporeal disintegration: 'castration, mutilation, dismemberment, dislocation, evisceration, devouring, bursting open of the body'.[20] For Lacan, these images, usually appearing in dreams, are the subject's way of representing to itself 'a certain level of aggressive disintegration in the individual'.[21] The images haunt her: 'Wher sche went er what so sche dede, þes cursyd mendys abedyn with hir' (145). The fear of fragmentation is what drives her all-too-human attempts to secure a unified identity by identifying with something external to herself (mostly Christ).

It is not clear why the Devil instructs her to prostitute herself to various men of religion and other men, nor who is the mysterious 'summe on of hem' that the Devil claims she prefers over all others, nor what is especially sinful about the creature's desiring just one rather than all of them. Perhaps the fact that she feels she can choose, rather than allowing herself to be 'comown to hem alle'? That there is room, even in this guilty scene, for her autonomous desires? As Sarah Salih observes, the passage deals with masculine desires, but these are finally 'less frightening than her own; she fears not rape but pleasure' (2001: 225–6). This is a version of Jesus' temptation in the wilderness, but for the creature it is also a struggle between what she feels to be her true (sexual) desires (the Devil knows her own mind) and a rational knowledge of what is right, which she associates with her 'wille' (which is God-given). At the same time, the text also produces a withering critique of the phallus as the crucial signifier of clerical authority (Beckwith 1986: 53), both exposing and refusing the cultural imperative that it is by means of the phallus that the subject comes to occupy the position of the 'I' in discourse.

The presentation of indecent thoughts as temptations recalls an earlier episode where the creature's sexual desire for another man 'whech sche louyd wel', and with whom she arranges a churchyard tryst, is described as happening in 'þe secunde ȝer of hir temptacyons' (14). After consenting to the meeting, she lies by her husband but finds the thought of having sex with him 'abhomynabyl' (15). This episode too is haunted by images of dismemberment. Spurning her offer of sex, the man declares 'he had leuar ben hewyn as small as flesch to þe pott' (15). The same phrase is echoed later, when the creature asks Christ to do what he will with her: 'ȝyf it wer thy wille, Lord, I wolde for þi lofe & for magnifying of þi name ben hewyn as small as flesch to þe potte' (142). The recurrent image reminds us of the intertwining of late medieval erotic and religious discourses. The phrase calls to mind the *passio* of the female virgin martyr, her flesh lacerated and chopped into pieces, her body immersed in a cauldron. What the good Christian fears, from without and within, is disaggregation. The creature uses Christ to construct a protective carapace through which she can produce a fantasy of the self as a coherent whole.

Conclusion

The readings I propose here are an attempt to wrestle with the text's strange idiom and to find ways of talking about the subjectivity of the protagonist without essentializing her. We need to stop bickering over Meech and Allen's question 'Whose language is it?' Critical theory and book history converge in a shared understanding of writing as collaborative and of authorship as historically constructed. The task is not that of rescuing Margery/Kempe as an author. It is rather to propose a different set of materialist reading practices for the *Book*: readings that acknowledge its complexity of pronoun use, engage with the texture of its writing, and challenge any notion at all of 'self'.

See also: 3 Religious Authority and Dissent, 4 City and Country, Wealth and Labour, 5 Women's Voices and Roles, 6 Manuscripts and Readers, 7 From Manuscript to Modern Text, 18 Images, 19 Love, 24 Literature of Religious Instruction, 25 Mystical and Devotional Literature, 26 Accounts of Lives, 31 Julian of Norwich, 32 *Piers Plowman*, 33 The *Canterbury Tales*.

Notes

1 I am indebted to Nicholas Watson and Felicity Riddy for allowing me to read their unpublished work on the *Book*.

2 Jeanette Winterson, *Oranges Are Not the Only Fruit* (London: Pandora, 1985), p. 46.

3 *The Book of Margery Kempe*, ed. Sanford Brown Meech and Hope Emily Allen, EETS os 212 (1940): p. 206. Page numbers are given in the text.

4 E. R. Curtius, *European Literature and the Latin Middle Ages*, trans. Willard R. Trask (London and Henley: Routledge and Kegan Paul, 1953), p. 320.

5 2.4, cited in Curtius, *European Literature*, p. 320: my translation.

6 'The literary fiction is that there is no fiction, no design or "foreconceit"': Anne Middleton, 'The Audience and Public of *Piers Plowman*', in *Middle English Alliterative Poetry*, ed. David Lawton (Cambridge: Brewer, 1982), pp. 103–23 (p. 113).

7 Sue Ellen Holbrook, 'Margery Kempe and Wynkyn de Worde', in *The Medieval Mystical*

Tradition in England, ed. M. Glasscoe, Exeter Symposium, 4 (Brewer: Cambridge, 1987), pp. 27–46 (p. 27).

8 Diane Purkiss, 'Material Girls: The Seventeenth-Century Woman Debate', in *Women, Texts and Histories, 1575–1760*, ed. Clare Brant and Diane Purkiss (London: Routledge, 1992), pp. 69–101 (p. 71).

9 Philippe Lejeune, 'The Autobiographical Contract', in *French Literary Theory Today*, ed. Tzvetan Todorov (Cambridge: Cambridge University Press, 1982), p. 193.

10 Emile Benveniste, 'Subjectivity in Language' (1958), in *Problems in General Linguistics*, trans. Mary Elizabeth Meek (Coral Gables, Fla.: University of Miami Press, 1971), pp. 223–30 (p. 224).

11 Ibid., p. 225.

12 Ibid., p. 224.

13 See Simon Gaunt, 'A Martyr to Love: Sacrificial Desire in the Poetry of Bernart de Ventadorn', *Journal of Medieval and Early Modern Studies* 31 (2001), 477–506 (p. 494).

14 Benveniste, 'Subjectivity', p. 225.

15 Jacques Derrrida, *The Gift of Death*, trans. David Wills (Chicago and London: University of Chicago Press, 1995), p. 10.

16 Simone de Beauvoir, *The Second Sex* (1949), trans. H. M. Parshley (Harmondsworth: Penguin, 1972), p. 799.

17 Jack Goody, *Food and Love: A Cultural History of East and West* (London: Verso, 1999), pp. 110–11.

18 Benveniste, 'Subjectivity', p. 227.

19 Charles Taylor, *Sources of the Self: The Making of Modern Identity* (Cambridge: Cambridge University Press, 1992), p. 160.

20 Jacques Lacan, *Ecrits: A Selection*, trans. Alan Sheridan (London: Tavistock, 1977), p. 11.

21 Ibid., p. 4.

References and Further Reading

Aers, David 1988. *Community, Gender and Individual Identity: English Writing 1360–1430.* London and New York: Routledge. Ch. 2, 'The Making of Margery Kempe: Individual and Community', shows how Kempe and her book were shaped by the economic, class and social forces of medieval Lynn. (Extract reprinted in Staley 2001.)

Atkinson, Clarissa W. 1983. *Mystic and Pilgrim: The Book and the World of Margery Kempe.* Ithaca, N.Y.: Cornell University Press. Important woman-centred historical study that places Kempe within English and Continental mystical traditions.

Beckwith, Sarah 1986. 'A Very Material Mysticism: The Medieval Mysticism of Margery Kempe.' In *Medieval Literature: Criticism, Ideology and History*, ed. David Aers (Brighton: Harvester), pp. 34–57. Materialist-feminist demystification of Luce Irigaray's claim that the female mystic is a site of resistance to patriarchal culture.

—— 1993. *Christ's Body: Identity, Culture and Society in Late Medieval Writings.* London and New York: Routledge. Ch. 4, 'The Uses of Corpus Christi and *The Book of Margery Kempe*', discusses Kempe's identifications with Christ.

Cowen, Janet 2000. 'Naming and Shaming in *The Book of Margery Kempe*.' In *Essays on Anglo-Saxon and Related Themes in Memory of Lynne Grundy*, ed. Jane Roberts and Jinty Nelson (London: King's College Centre for Late Antique and Medieval Studies), pp. 157–79. On names and naming conventions in the *Book*.

Dillon, Janette 1996. 'Holy Women and their Confessors or Confessors and their Holy Women?' In *Prophets Abroad: The Reception of Continental Holy Women in Late-Medieval England*, ed. Rosalind Voaden (Cambridge: Brewer), pp. 115–40. On the negotiation of authority between Kempe and her confessors.

Dinshaw, Carolyn 1999. *Getting Medieval: Sexualities and Communities, Pre- and Postmodern.* Durham, N.C., and London: Duke University Press. Ch. 3, 'Margery Kempe Answers Back', offers a queer reading, and reads the *Book* alongside Robert Glück's 1994 novel, *Margery Kempe.*

Fanous, Samuel 2000. 'Measuring the Pilgrim's Progress: Internal Emphases in *The Book of Margery Kempe*.' In *Writing Religious Women:*

Female Spiritual and Textual Practices in Late Medieval England, ed. Denis Renevey and Christiania Whitehead (Toronto: University of Toronto Press), pp. 157–76. Compares the *Book's* treatment of time with hagiographic models.

Gibson, Gail McMurray 1989. *Theater of Devotion: East Anglian Drama and Society in the Late Middle Ages.* Chicago: University of Chicago Press. Ch. 3, 'St Margery: *The Book of Margery Kempe*', situates the *Book* in relation to regional devotional practices. (Extract reprinted in Staley 2001.)

Hirsh, John C. 1975. 'Author and Scribe in the *Book of Margery Kempe.*' *Medium Ævum* 44, 245–50. Influential article that argues that the second scribe, 'no less than Margery', should be regarded as the author of the *Book.*

Lochrie, Karma 1991. *Margery Kempe and Translations of the Flesh.* Philadelphia: University of Pennsylvania Press. First full-length feminist theoretical study.

Margherita, Gayle 1995. *The Romance of Origins: Language and Sexual Difference in Middle English Literature.* Philadelphia: University of Pennsylvania Press. Ch. 1, 'Margery Kempe and the pathology of writing', is a feminist psychoanalytic reading of the *Book.*

McEntire, Sandra J. (ed.) 1992. *Margery Kempe: A Book of Essays.* New York and London: Garland. Essential collection of essays, grouped in three sections: the woman, her work and her world.

Meale, Carol 2000. 'This is a deed bok, the tother a quick': Theatre and the Drama of Salvation in *The Book* of Margery Kempe.' In *Medieval Women: Texts and Contexts in Late Medieval Britain – Essays for Felicity Riddy*, ed. Jocelyn Wogan-Browne, Rosalynn Voaden, Arlyn Diamond, Ann Hutchinson, Carol Meale and Lesley Johnson (Turnhout: Brepols), pp. 49–68. On the influence of early English drama on Kempe's visions.

Salih, Sarah 2001. *Versions of Virginity in Late Medieval England.* Cambridge: Brewer. Ch. 5, 'Like a Virgin? The *Book of Margery Kempe*', is an important study of Kempe's 'performative' virginity.

Shklar, Ruth Nissé 1995. 'Cobham's Daughter: *The Book of Margery Kempe* and the Power of Heterodox Thinking.' *Modern Language Quarterly* 56, 277–304. Argues that Kempe consciously manipulates Lollardy to create her own model of dissent and to question her opponents' authority.

Staley, Lynn 1994. *Margery Kempe's Dissenting Fictions.* University Park: Pennsylvania State University Press. Influential study that distinguishes between Kempe the author and 'Margery' the protagonist, and considers Kempe's English national identity

—— (ed.) 2001. *The Book of Margery Kempe: A New Translation, Contexts, Criticism.* New York: Norton. Close translation of the *Book*, with supporting contextual material and nine critical essays, representing largely socio-historical approaches.

Summit, Jennifer 2000. *Lost Property: The Woman Writer and English Literary History, 1380–1589.* Chicago and London: University of Chicago Press. The section in Ch. 3, 'Margery Kempe as "devout anchoress": Henry Pepwell's Edition of 1521', discusses the *Book*'s early sixteenth-century reception.

Watt, Diane 1997. *Secretaries of God: Women Prophets in Late Medieval and Early Modern England.* Cambridge: Brewer. Fine study of Kempe as a prophet.

31
Julian of Norwich

Santha Bhattacharji

Julian of Norwich (1342–c.1416) is the foremost representative of the female visionary tradition in England. She is also one of the few medieval writers to have a large modern readership outside the academic community. Consequently, some of the reasons for her current fame are based on misunderstandings of her medieval context. She is sometimes thought ground-breaking where she is conventional (as in her discussion of the motherhood of Christ), and extreme where she is in some ways restrained (as in her depiction of Christ's crucified body). Conversely, some of her true originality has been overlooked, as this chapter will argue.

Julian's text, variously titled *Showings* (Colledge and Walsh 1978), *A Revelation of Love* (Glasscoe 1993) or, more commonly, *Revelations of Divine Love*,[1] has come down to us in two versions, the Short Text (Beer 1978; Windeatt 1994) and the Long Text. We have no concrete evidence as to when the texts were written, or in what order. Within the field of Middle English studies, as distinct from that of theology (where Julian's writings also currently attract much attention), the task of establishing a critical text and situating it accurately in its cultural and historical context is obviously of paramount importance. Most recent scholarship has therefore focused on these issues, producing, for instance, widely different theories as to dating. Furthermore, we have almost no biographical information concerning Julian herself, and have to deduce some kind of life story for her on the basis of the extremely guarded comments in her text. This too has produced widely different theories. Some scholars have argued that, before she became an anchoress, she was already a nun (Colledge and Walsh 1978: 43), others that she was a wife and mother (Ward 1988: 17–25). Some have seen her as highly educated (Baker 1994: 8–11; Colledge and Walsh 1978: 43–51), others as near illiterate (Pelphrey 1982: 18–28). These discussions will take on point and relevance as we explore Julian's actual text. In this chapter, therefore, we will first set Julian within the medieval tradition of 'mystical' writing, then examine some of the most salient aspects of the Long and Short Texts, and only afterwards proceed to issues surrounding the dating of the two texts.

Julian as a Mystical Writer

Julian can be set within the movement of medieval women visionaries, which was at its height on the Continent at this time. She can also be set more specifically within the group of fourteenth- and fifteenth-century medieval writers generally referred to as the English Mystics, primarily Richard Rolle, Walter Hilton and the anonymous author of *The Cloud of Unknowing*. In particular, she can be usefully compared and contrasted with the fifteenth-century Margery Kempe, our other major representative of the female visionary tradition in England. The current trend for redating Julian's texts to the early fifteenth century, when Margery was also being exhorted to write down her experiences, as she tells us,[2] makes this comparison between the two women particularly fruitful.

In an English context, Julian immediately stands out. Her distinctiveness is pinpointed by the colophon at the end of the Long Text (in London, British Library MS Sloane 1), which cautions the reader against taking bits of her text in isolation, on the grounds that it is 'hey divinitye and hey wisdam' (Glasscoe 1993: 135). What is meant by this phrase? When we look at Julian's three male predecessors, we can describe their work by the modern term 'ascetic theology', meaning that they outline a path or method – an *ascesis* – whereby one can draw closer to God. As for Margery, her narrative describes her personal conversion and development as a mystic, and her *Book* has been called 'the first autobiography in English'.[3]

In Julian we find none of this. While there is the vivid and compelling account of the near-fatal illness during which she received her sequence of sixteen 'shewynges' (Colledge and Walsh 1978: 281) on 8 May 1373, she does not outline either her personal spiritual journey or a method to be applied by others. Instead, she has an urgent, dense, tightly argued package of insights to share with us concerning the nature of God in Himself: theology in the strictest sense of the word. Indeed, this can be called in modern terminology 'mystical theology', in the sense that it involves knowledge of God that can only be known by faith, and is not immediately obvious to the fallen, limited human mind. Julian herself keeps using phrases such as 'full mystely', 'mysty example', 'hyd', 'an high mervelous prevyte hyd in god' (513, 519, 407). It is perhaps in this sense that she is writing 'hey divinitye'.

Indeed, her phrases recall the 'hid divinity' of the apophatic tradition exemplified in *The Cloud of Unknowing*, which has a very similar colophon warning the reader not to read the text selectively.[4] In the apophatic tradition, the inability of the human mind to conceptualize God with any adequacy is constantly reiterated, and the mind enters instead into a realm of imageless silence. Julian's complex style perhaps embodies a similar struggle to go beyond our normal concepts and patterns of thought, as we see in one of her most baffling statements: 'I saw god in a poynte . . . by which sight I saw that he is in althyng' (336). In this statement, 'poynte' is manifestly 'non-figural and non-referential' (Gillespie and Ross 1992: 72). Her efforts to explicate the 'mysty' dimension build up into a 'meta-narrative' (Baker 1994: 140) which both accompanies and interrupts the actual physical visions.

When we set Julian within the Continental visionary tradition, this explicatory dimension is not, at first glance, quite so unique. When we look at her great contemporary, Catherine of Siena (1347–80), we find a woman speaking with similar complexity about God's view of mankind. As in Julian, a lot of the complexity arises from a strong emphasis on God as the Trinity.[5] We have evidence that Catherine's text was known in England from the 1390s, as was the *Liber Celestis*[6] of Bridget of Sweden (Watson 1993: 653–5). In this latter work, both Jesus and Mary grant visions to Bridget about events that had no other witness, such as the conception of Christ in Mary's womb. The authority granted to these visions, at least by the laity, is suggested by Margery Kempe, to whom Christ asserts that 'it is trewe euery word that is wretyn in Brides [Bridget's] boke'.[7] Here, then, are two Continental women confidently asserting that they are giving us knowledge directly received from God.

Julian puts herself in a more subtle and difficult position. In both Catherine's and Bridget's writings, it is Christ himself or God the Father who speaks at length, offering interpretations of the visions, and these words are received in the same ecstatic trance in which the visual dimension of the revelation is received. Julian, however, distinguishes scrupulously throughout her work between the actual 'bodily' (physical) vision and what she understood by it: 'by this I saw', 'I vnderstood', 'as to my sight' (Watson 1992: 87). The careful separating out of her own voice from that of Christ, and her presentation of her insights not as direct revelation but as the fruit of years of personal reflection – 'the inward lernyng that I have vnderstodyn therein sithen' (519–20) – perhaps also support the impression that she is producing 'hey divinitye'.

More specifically, her reflection centres on the life of God, that is, on the internal love and working of the three persons of the Trinity. Julian's constant and distinctive emphasis on the Trinity lends enormous complexity to her work. Although the information that she has to share with her 'even-Christians' concerns God's attitudes towards human beings, these attitudes always originate in the relationships between the three persons of the Godhead. In contrast, Margery Kempe emphasizes her passionate engagement with the humanity of Christ, from which she much later passes on to the Godhead.[8]

The popular response to Julian has tended to overlook her Trinitarian emphasis. This is because Julian strives to find human, earthy, domestic images for the insights she has to communicate, so successfully that it is the images that command attention at first reading: Christ's body is so drained of blood that it is like a sagging cloth; God's love enwraps us as closely as our clothing; God the Father, in his azure robe, would rather sit down on the barren earth than anywhere else, if he cannot be enthroned in the city of our hearts (362, 299, 523–6). However, as we now proceed to examine Julian's own engagement with the humanity of Christ, we will keep her Trinitarian emphasis in mind: 'for wher Jhesu appireth the blessed trinitie is vnderstand, as to my sight' (297), an assertion she makes at the very moment the visions start, launching both narrative and meta-narrative simultaneously (Watson 1992: 87–8).

Julian's Visions of the Crucified Christ

As the Long Text is the more elaborate recension of Julian's work, being roughly six times as long as the Short Text, it is the version on which the following discussion will concentrate. Julian's text opens with a brief but absorbing personal narrative in which she tells us that she requested of God a near-fatal illness, which would befall her at the age of thirty, and which would enable her to lead the rest of her life more closely focused on God – what we might now call a 'disclosure' experience, in which an extreme situation awakens us to a perspective on life that we might not otherwise have.

Having made the request, Julian forgot about it, which might simply be realistically human, or could imply that she was being careful not to seek out extraordinary experiences in the apparently rather cautious and conservative religious climate in England (Watson 1993: 645–57). At thirty-and-a-half, she duly fell ill. Her parish priest, summoned to her deathbed, holds up a crucifix before her face; as she watches it, blood begins to pour down from under the crown of thorns. The intensity of the vision emerges in the similes with which she struggles to convey the cascading blood: it is as plentiful as raindrops falling off the eaves of a house; each drop spreads out like the scales of a herring; if it had been real it would have soaked the bed (311–12, 343). Julian's visions of the crucified Christ unfold from this point. She sees his body, already flayed by the scourging, slowly dry out from loss of blood and moisture as it hangs on the cross, turning blue, and then brown. Eventually she beholds the actual moment of death. Paradoxically, it turns out to be a moment of utter joy for Christ and complete well-being for Julian.

Up to this point, Julian's visions look as if they can be set within a fairly conventional tradition. Late medieval devotion strongly emphasized the use of the visual imagination (Baker 1994: 40–62) and provided handbooks, such as the *Meditationes vitae Christi*,[9] translated into English early in the fifteenth century by the Carthusian Nicholas Love,[10] to help the individual meditator picture the scenes of Christ's life in detail. Such handbooks encouraged the visualizing of each scene in chronological order, with particularly detailed attention being paid to the successive scenes of Christ's Passion. The effect of this pattern of devotion can be seen, for example, in the *Book of Margery Kempe*: Margery's first 'contemplation' focuses on the childhood of the Virgin Mary, then progresses to the birth of Christ, while the bulk of her *Book* shows us her repeated visualizing of the various stages of Christ's Passion. Margery's model, Bridget of Sweden, also beholds many different scenes of Christ's life. Thus, these texts present themselves as a sequence of discrete visions or topics.

Julian, in carefully dividing and numbering her material into sixteen visions, as she does in Chapter 1 of the Long Text, seems to be following the same pattern. However, we already see her unusualness emerging: her 'sequence' of visions actually consists of one prolonged beholding of Christ on the cross. The narrative element, to the extent that it can be isolated at all, ends with the moment of Christ's death in the eighth revelation, at the end of Chapter 21 – about a quarter of the way through the whole work;

a second brief narrative section introduces the last vision, in Chapters 66 to 70 (632–53). Throughout, Julian struggles to show us how everything she understood from the visions was part of one comprehensive whole, a point she emphasizes in her summary of the first revelation:

> The first is of his precious crowning of thornes; and ther in was conteined and specified the blessed trinitie with the incarnation and vnithing betweene god and man's sowle, with manie fayer schewynges and techynges of endelesse wisdom and loue, in which all the shewynges that foloweth be grvndide and ioyned. (281)

In contrast, the list of chapters which precedes Chapter 1, and which appears to be the work of a later scribe, omits this assertion of unity, perhaps implying a more traditionally sequential approach to the text.[11]

The second aspect of Julian's unusualness which emerges at this point lies in her particular description of the Crucified. Most visions of the time describe Christ's heavy shedding of blood. Julian seems initially to be following the same tradition, as her similes above show. However, other emphases creep in. She stresses the acute dehydration of the body, dried out not only by loss of blood and moisture but also by a cold sharp wind, culminating in Christ's words, 'I thirst' (358–60). Christ looks as though he is taking a week to die, resulting in Julian's striking description of his body slowly changing colour, from blue, to brown, to black, sagging downwards from the nails. Julian seems to be aware that her depiction is unusual: she defends the colour brown by referring to the 'Vernicle', the handkerchief of St Veronica who, according to legend, had wiped the sweat from Christ's face as he carried his cross. On this cloth, Julian reminds her audience, Christ's face is brown, black and downcast (328).

It is possible that Julian is here drawing on an older but parallel verbal tradition in the Middle Ages, in which the pallor, rigidity and dryness of the dying Christ are emphasized. This older tradition is embodied in the vernacular medieval Passion lyrics, many of which derive from some lines in the early medieval *Liber meditationum*, attributed in the later Middle Ages to St Augustine. These lines, beginning 'Candet nudatum pectus' (His bare breast glistens), emphasize the pallor of the dying Christ, and in particular use words like *arent*, 'dry out', and *rigent*, 'grow rigid', to describe what is happening to his limbs and sinews. Such details are echoed in Middle English lyrics in lines such as 'His leichende lyppes bycomen pale and hys bodi al dreie' and 'Mi blod is sched, my fles is falle, / Me thristet sore, for drink I calle'.[12] We see here not only the dryness, as the blood leaches from the body, but also the sagging ('falle') and the thirst. Julian might thus be drawing on materials which come from popular culture, like the tradition of the Vernicle and the imagery of the lyrics – an important consideration in evaluating her degree of literacy or otherwise. If so, she nevertheless reuses them in a way that gives us a strong impression of her independence and originality.

Her real independence emerges at the point of Christ's death, where the movement of her contemplation of his crucified body does not at all issue in the message that we might expect. In the religious lyrics, a dialogue between Christ and the meditator often accompanies the visual description, and culminates in a somewhat bargaining plea from Christ: 'ȝef thei weren kende to loven me outh, / Of al my peine me ne routh' (If men were disposed to love me at all, I would take no account of all my pain).[13] For Julian, in contrast, the culminating point of the Crucifixion, the moment of death, issues in the following exchange:

> Arte thou well apayd that I sufferyd for thee? I seyde: ȝe, good lord, gramercy; ye, good lorde, blessyd moet þow be. Then seyde Jhesu our good lord: If thou arte apayde, I am apayde. It is a joy, a blysse, an endlesse lykyng to me that evyr I sufferd passion for the; and yf I might suffer more, I wolde suffer more. (382)

Julian returns repeatedly to the core statement here: if I could suffer more, I would suffer more (385, 387), and clarifies this further: 'He seyde nott: yf it were nedfulle to suffer more, but if I might [could] suffer more' (387–8). She even repeats this phrase in her much later section on the motherhood of Christ (596). Thus one could argue that this perception of the free, willing outpouring of Christ's love to its limit, expecting no return other than the satisfaction of the recipient (392), is fundamental to Julian's whole thought.

In contrast, the dominant imagery for Christ's love at this time depicted Christ as lover-knight, wooing his lady, of which we can find a particularly sustained and well-worked-out example in the *Ancrene Wisse*.[14] While the imagery served to stress the desirability and beauty of each human soul in the eyes of God, it also made the response of the soul, its movement godward, of central importance. In the *Ancrene Wisse*, indeed, the lady is threatened with hell if she does not respond to her divine wooer. In contrast, Julian is emphasizing the movement of God towards man, purely for the sake of man's own well-being.

'All shall be well' and the Parable of the Lord and the Servant

Julian's 'narrative' of the visual dimension of her visions constantly gives way to the 'meta-narrative' of her spiritual understanding of the visions, and this more spiritual discussion eventually takes over the text altogether. The strictly visual episodes in the narrative of Christ's dying actually occupy only a few paragraphs, at the beginning of Chapters 4 (294–8), 10 (324–35), 12 (342–5), 16 (357–9) and 17 (360–5). Their vividness perhaps obscures how abstract are the vast majority of the things that Julian has to say, as her mind wrestled intensely with what she was seeing over the thirty hours or so in which she received the visions. The most striking insight afforded us into her intense mental wrestling occurs in her 'parable of the Lord and the Servant', which came to Julian in response to her anguished questioning on sin and judgement.

In fact, Julian's text has been termed 'a theological enquiry'[15] because in some ways her text is structured by her questions: 'What may this be?' 'What is synne?' 'How may this be?' (300, 336, 511). The initial response she receives, in the passage best known among Julian's popular readership, comes in Chapter 27: 'Synne is behouely, but alle shalle be wele, and alle shalle be wele, and alle maner of thynge shalle be wele' (405). The Middle English of this sentence does not yield its subtleties easily to modern attempts to translate it. 'Behouely', or 'behovabil' in MS Sloane 1 (Glasscoe 1993: 28), seems to have overtones of 'essential, deeply in-built part of the whole process', as we find in the related verb used in the later Wycliffite version of the Bible: 'Whethir it bihofte not Crist to suffer these thingis, and so to entre into his glorie?' (Luke 24: 26). In this case it is the Crucifixion which is essential and unavoidable, a concept which the Authorized Version renders as 'ought': 'Ought not Christ to have suffered . . . ?'

Similarly, the modal verbs have subtly shifted in meaning down the centuries, so that 'shalle' is also problematic, containing strong residual overtones of its Old English meaning of 'must' or 'is to'. The latter again suggests an ordained process – everything is to turn out well – a concept reinforced by Julian's enigmatic and distinctive teaching on a future 'great deed' that is to be done by Christ, and which will bring all things to resolution. When this deed is done, and we understand this 'hygh mervelous prevyte hyd in god', we shall 'verely se the cause why he suffered synne to come, in whych sight we shalle endlessely haue joye' (407). Understanding how sin fits into the whole picture will thus satisfy our questioning at a very deep level. The 'grett deed' by which 'he shalle make alle thing wele' (424) is amplified in Chapter 32 (422–6), and then rendered more complex in Chapter 36, where we discover that the deed is twofold: on one level it takes place at the end of time, but on another level it begins in this life (436–41). Thus Julian indicates that God's revelation of himself, and all his deeds, are not single, historical events, but processes stretching into the future: 'As I haue done I do now continually, and shall in coming of tyme', Christ says to her (440). We are now ready for Julian's twofold exegesis of her Parable of the Lord and the Servant. The parable was, apparently, given to her at the time of the original revelation, when she was struggling to understand everything that was being shown to her. The parable has attracted much comment because it shows Julian's method at its most developed.

First of all, in Chapter 50, Julian prepares the ground by expanding more than usual on the depth and perplexity of her questioning. She believes that our sinfulness makes us perpetually blameworthy in God's eyes, and she believes this both through the Church's teaching and 'by my owne felyng', through her own lived experience. (Intellectual reflection and personal 'felyng' continually act together in the Long Text.) In the visions, however, Julian sees no blame at all in God's attitude towards us. 'Betwene theyse two contraryes my reson was grettly traveyled', she tells us, and she fears that 'his blessed presens shulde passe fro my sight, and I to be lefte in vnknowing'. Here we are afforded a glimpse into the tension that Julian seems to have experienced at the time of the visions between her deeply absorbed gazing on Christ, and the furious activity of her own mind: 'my longing [for an answer] endured, hym continually beholding' (511). The tension erupts in a question: 'how shall I be esyde?' (512).

In the exceptionally long Chapter 51, Julian receives an answer, in the form of a visual parable. A servant stands ready before his seated lord, who gazes on him with great affection and sends him off on an errand. In his eagerness, the servant sets off at a run and falls into a pit. He is injured and helpless, and can neither get out of the pit nor turn round to see that his master is looking at him tenderly and without blame, for 'oonly hys good wyll and his grett desyer was cause of his falling' (516). The first level of the parable is shown 'gostly in bodily lycknes' (514). Then she is shown a second level, 'more gostly withoute bodily lycknes'. On the more purely spiritual level, Julian beholds the lord's intention not only to restore the servant to full well-being, but to 'reward' him (517) for all his pain, asking: 'fallyth it nott to me to geve hym a ȝyfte that be better to hym and more wurschypfull than his owne hele [health] shuld haue bene?' (518). At this point, says Julian, the showing of the parable vanished. She never ceased 'marveylyng' over it, but at that time 'culde I nott take there in fvll understanding to my ees' (519).

The two points that Julian is making here are highly unusual and daring: Adam fell purely through good will and eagerness; and in heaven mankind will be rewarded for all the suffering involved in the Fall, to such an extent that the 'gift' will be better than if Adam had never been injured in the first place. The second point, however, is not unorthodox, reflecting the teaching of the 'Exultet', a key text of the Easter Vigil service, which was the most elaborate church service of the whole year. The Exultet celebrates the 'happy fault', the 'necessary sin of Adam', which brought about the far greater gift of the redemption.[16] As Julian would probably have listened to the Exultet every year of her life, perhaps its ideas had sunk deeply into her mind. On the first point, that Adam sinned not through disobedience but through over-eagerness, she remains unusual within the Western Christian tradition. Julian is herself so startled at her perception that human beings are not blameworthy in God's eyes that she worries about straying into heresy: 'it semyth as I shulde erre' (512).

Denise Baker sees Julian's argument here as being typical of the general movement of her thought: 'Instead of the Augustinian emphasis on causes and consequences, her writing reflects a concentration on purpose and ends' (Baker 1994: 68). Baker's view is supported by the tendency towards final resolution we have already seen in Julian's concept of the 'great deed' to be done at the end of time, so that 'alle shall be wele'. In contrast, the dominant place accorded to the writings of St Augustine, in the Western tradition, tended to look back to the Fall in order to emphasize the doctrine of original sin. Julian, however, seems not so much interested in how sin starts, as in how it is that we are nevertheless not blamed for sin. Thus her parable is probably not meant to be read 'historically', as a rewriting of Genesis, but rather metaphorically, as we shall now see in her revisiting of the parable, which she undertakes in much greater detail.

She is eventually 'som dele esyd' (519) by three aspects of her ongoing reflection. Here we see her scrupulous distinction between the different layers of her experience: her reflection is made up of the original teaching received at the time of the visions; the 'inwarde lernyng' that she has gone through since; and the complete revelation as a whole 'whych oure lorde god of his goodness bryngyth oftymes freely to the sight of my vnderstondyng' (519–20). The fruit of her reflection emerges twenty years, save three months, later, when we get a second double-layered exegesis of the parable.

This time, the first level of interpretation reiterates that the servant is Adam, particularly in the sense of Everyman; the second level sees God the Son represented in the servant, who serves the Father by voluntarily descending into the pit to rescue Adam (533–4). The second exegesis, although presented after twenty years, is far more visually detailed than the first one, and specifies, for instance, that the lord is sitting at ease in an ample blue robe, while the servant is in a stained, worn, knee-length tunic, symbolizing the heavy work that he is to undertake (526–8). Since the servant is both Adam and the Son, and God cannot look on the Son with any blame at all, it follows that he looks on Adam in the same way (535). Through the co-inherence of the two levels of the servant image, Julian is at last able to answer her question: mankind is not blamed because it is subsumed into Christ. She expresses the idea in some typically bold language: 'When Adam felle godes sone fell; for the right onyng [*union*] which was made in hevyn, goddys sone might not be seperath from Adam, for by Adam I vnderstand alle men' (533).

Julian had been instructed to meditate carefully on every detail of the parable in order to find the solution to her questioning, which bears out her assertion that the whole sequence of visions is brought frequently to her mind's eye. Her dependency on the visual, and her lack of references in this difficult section of her work to any theologians who could have supported her points,[17] perhaps reinforce Julian's assertion that she is 'unlettered'; it also shows us what sophisticated thought could be produced by careful and repeated reflection on a visual image, where the image becomes as multilayered as any text.

The Motherhood of Christ

The lack of condemnation in God's attitude to man brings Julian on to an extended consideration (Chapters 58–63), of Christ as our mother, motherhood being the most appropriate image, she suggests, for the kind of love he shows us. As usual, Julian begins with a consideration of the Trinity: there are many strands to God's love for his creatures, and 'by the forseeng endlesse councell of all the blessyd trynyte' (591) he has chosen that the Second Person should become our mother through his wisdom (585) and his mercy, whereby we are remade (586). This motherhood expresses itself on earth in several key ways: through Christ all things were made, and thus through him we have our physical substance in the first place; Christ on the Cross is like a woman dying in labour, in order to bring forth her child; he feeds us in the Eucharist with his own substance, in the same way that a mother feeds the baby at her breast with milk made from her own body; he cleans us up as a mother does, for 'the moders service is nerest, reediest and suerest' (595).

Julian is not particularly original in this depiction of Christ. Anselm of Canterbury is one of the first medieval writers to develop the idea, in his 'Prayer to St Paul', where he addresses first Paul, and then Christ, as his spiritual mother.[18] Anselm draws on the scriptural image of Christ as a hen gathering her chicks under her wings (Matthew 23:

37) but subsequent writers, such as Hildegard of Bingen and St Bernard of Clairvaux, considerably extend the imagery (Bynum 1982). In England, a male contemporary of Julian, the Monk of Farne (d.1371), also uses the imagery in a striking way. For him, Christ on the Cross is like a mother with her arms open and her head lowered to kiss her children; he even speaks of entering Christ's womb in order to be born again.[19] Julian, however, gives us one of the most sustained considerations of Christ our Mother. She does not seem to be drawing directly on scriptural images, but on the sacramental idea of Christ feeding us on his substance, an emphasis that once again could have come from popular religious lyrics.[20] He needs ('hym behovyth', 596) to feed us, she says, perhaps remembering the physical experience of feeding a child at the breast. Distinctive to Julian is her focus on Christ as the mother who cleans us up, wanting us to run confidently to her/him when we fall, a focus that links in with her equally distinctive view of the body. Like many spiritual writers of the time, Julian accepts that physical life is full of pain and corruption (622–4), but that does not prevent her from instancing even the most basic physical processes as demonstrating God's creativity and love for his creatures:

> A man goyth vppe right, and the soule [*food*] of his body is sparyde [*closed up*] as [*in*] a purse fulle feyer. And whan it is tyme of his nescessery, it is openyde and sparyde [*closed up*] ayen fulle honestly. And that it is he [*God*] that doyth this, it is schewed ther wher he seyth he comyth downe to vs to the lowest parte of oure nede. (306–7)

Julian proceeds to emphasize our human frailty, not only within her section on the motherhood of Christ (Chapters 60–2), but thereafter to the end of the book. It is perhaps surprising, in view of the label 'optimistic' that is often attached to Julian's thought, that the Long Text culminates in a run of about fifteen chapters on the inevitability of human sin, but these follow on naturally from her discourse on frailty. They get overlooked, perhaps, in the light of the peroration that concludes the Long Text. Julian brings her searching 'theological enquiry' to an end by telling us that from the time of the visions, she desired often to know 'oure lords menyng': his meaning, his intention. After fifteen years, she tells us, she receives a revelation that 'loue was his menyng', and she expands these words into a beautifully crafted concluding paragraph to her whole work (732–4).

The Dating of the Short and Long Texts

The usual view of the Short Text is that it represents a first draft of Julian's book, which she would have written down fairly soon after receiving her visions in 1373 (Colledge and Walsh 1978: 19), maybe as a way of keeping them fresh in her mind. However, our modern, highly literate print culture perhaps makes us assume that we remember things by writing them down, whereas Julian emphasizes, as mentioned above, that God constantly brought the whole sequence of visions before the 'sight of [her] vnderstanding'.

In a ground-breaking and persuasive article, Nicholas Watson argues for dating the composition of the Short Text to the 1380s. In this version of her work, Julian mentions neither the breakthrough in her understanding of the parable of the Lord and the Servant which took place 'twenty years save three months' after the visions, nor the insight that 'love was his meaning', which occurred fifteen years after the visions, in 1388. It seems likely therefore that the Short Text was written before that year.

On the other hand, the Short Text includes some paragraphs and phrases which seem to be responding to controversies which became particularly acute in the 1380s. These controversies arose from the challenge to many traditional aspects of the medieval church raised by John Wyclif and the Lollards. One of their challenges was to the use of devotional images, which they argued could not be true representations either of spiritual realities or of historical events (Watson 1993: 659–64). Julian not only scrupulously records her belief in 'the payntyngys of crucyfexes that er made be the grace of god aftere the techynge of haly kyrke to the lyknes of Crystes passyonn, als farfurthe as man ys witte may reche' (202) but, as the quotation shows, does so in words that show an awareness of the Lollard criticisms. In addition, the Short Text shows a sensitivity about Julian's female gender which does not appear in the Long Text. This again suggests that Julian is responding to a particular controversy, that concerning the right of women to 'teach', since Lollard women were allowed to preach and comment on Scripture. 'Botte god for bede that ȝe schulde saye or take it so that I am a techere, for I meene nouȝt soo; for I am a woman, leued [*ignorant*], febille and freylle', she declares. But, like Margery Kempe a few years later, who came 'in no pulpit', she insists on her right to 'telle ȝowe the goodenes of god' (222).[21]

Watson goes on to argue that the Short Text is a carefully thought-out and polished work in its own right (Watson 1993: 667–72), and this would suggest that Julian took many years over its composition. In addition, he points out the 'dark' side of the Short Text – its ongoing preoccupation with doubt and sin, culminating in the four 'dreads' of the last chapter – and argues that Julian's maturation as a writer might have been a longer and more tentative process than the confident tone of the Long Text suggests.

A slow method of composition also has implications for the Long Text. It is possible that the insight of 1388 caused Julian to start reconsidering her whole understanding of the visions, and thus to begin the process that would issue in her enormously expanded longer version. The scribal heading to the last chapter of the Long Text states, 'The good lord shewid this booke shuld be other wise performid than at the first writing' (731, n.1), and the whole book now ends with the 'Love was his meaning' passage. The Long Text cannot have been written before 1393, because of the twenty-year gap before understanding the Lord and the Servant parable, mentioned above. As with the Short Text, we need not assume that the Long Text was written immediately after the insight of 1393; indeed, Watson argues that the parable of the Lord and the Servant is so significant to its entire line of thought that Julian might have needed many years to absorb it (Watson 1993: 678). The scribe's colophon at the beginning of the Short Text gives the date 1413, and if we assume that he was copying the Short Text because the Long Text was not yet completed, this would push the composition of the Long Text into the second decade of the fifteenth century.

We must also consider whether the Short Text might have been a later, abbreviated version of the Long Text, made, perhaps, under mounting fear of being thought heretical. In 1401 an Act allowing the burning of heretics was promulgated, and the first priest to be burned was William Sawtre in nearby King's Lynn. Furthermore, Archbishop Thomas Arundel brought in a set of Constitutions in 1409 severely limiting the writing of theology in the vernacular.[22] However, to fulfil the needs of the laity, writings were permitted which foregrounded an emotional response to Christ, rather than theological thought about him. Thus Nicholas Love's *Mirror of the Blessed Life of Jesus Christ* was approved by Arundel. More strikingly, *The Orchard of Syon*, a fifteenth-century translation of the *Dialogue* of Catherine of Siena, rewrites Catherine's highly abstract Trinitarian thought as a pious meditation, encouraging its readers 'to feel, not think, their way through the text' (Watson 1995: 836). The Short Text's colophon suggests that it is presenting us with this kind of work: in it 'er fulle many comfortabylle wordes and gretly styrrande to alle thaye that desires to be Crystes looverse' (201). Moreover, Julian's female gender, accentuated in the Short Text, perhaps reinforces this expectation; as Lynn Staley Johnson has pointed out, the removal of gender in the Long Text changes its genre, away from emotionally 'affective' writing (Johnson 1991: 831).

On the other hand, the Short Text does not read like an abbreviation of a longer work. The Long Text has expansions in almost every sentence – a technique that would arise naturally if the Long Text represents the rewriting of an already existing, more embryonic work. But it is difficult to conceive of cutting the Long Text to one-sixth of its length, by an inverse method, to create the Short Text. In fact we do have a compendium of extracts from the Long Text, dating from c.1500, the 'Westminster Manuscript', which shows us what an 'abbreviated' text might look like.[23] Consequently, most scholars adhere to the view that the Short Text was written first.

What all the evidence suggests is that, for various reasons, the Short Text was seen to be very acceptable in the climate of 1413, and thus is the version that gets copied in that year. It is possible that the Long Text was already in existence but, as an exceptionally sophisticated piece of vernacular theology, could not circulate freely after Arundel's Constitutions of 1409. We know from other texts, most notably Rolle's *Incendium amoris*, that a text could circulate simultaneously in versions of different lengths,[24] and the existence of the Short Text in 1413 does not therefore rule out the existence of the Long Text at that date. The extant full-length manuscripts of the Long Text are all post-medieval copies, and do not give us any clues as to the date of composition.

In Julian, then, we have a writer whose thought is being examined more and more seriously, with ever-increasing appreciation for its unusualness and profundity. The depth and originality of her thought are reflected in her bold and complex language: in Julian's hands, Middle English prose becomes a medium of great subtlety and originality.

See also: 3 Religious Authority and Dissent, 18 Images, 23 Lyric, 24 Literature of Religious Instruction, 25 Mystical and Devotional Literature, 26 Accounts of Lives, 30 The *Book of Margery Kempe.*

Notes

1 *Revelations of Divine Love*, trans. E. Spearing, Penguin Classics (London: Penguin, 1998); *Revelations of Divine Love*, trans. Clifton Wolters, Penguin Classics (Harmondsworth: Penguin, 1966). This is also the title of the *editio princeps* by Serenus Cressy (London, 1670).

2 S. B. Meech and H. E. Allen (eds), *The Book of Margery Kempe*, EETS os 212 (1940), p. 3. Margery was being urged to write down her experiences c.1418, twenty years before she finally dictated her book c.1438.

3 Barry Windeatt (trans.), *The Book of Margery Kempe*, Penguin Classics (Harmondsworth: Penguin, 1985), p. 9. Unless otherwise indicated, all subsequent references are to this edition.

4 Phyllis Hodgson (ed.), *The Cloud of Unknowing and the Book of Privy Counselling*, EETS os 218 (1944), p. 2.

5 E.g., Catherine of Siena, *The Dialogue*, trans. Suzanne Noffke, Classics of Western Spirituality (New York: Paulist Press, 1980), pp. 116–17.

6 Roger Ellis (ed.), *The Liber Celestis of St Bridget of Sweden*, vol. 1, EETS os 291 (1987).

7 Meech and Allen (eds), *Margery Kempe*, p. 47.

8 Ibid., p. 86.

9 Sr M. Jordan Stallings (ed.), *Meditationes Vitae Christi* (Washington, D.C.: Catholic University of America Press, 1965).

10 Nicholas Love, *The Mirrour of the Blessed Lyf of Jesu Christ*, ed. James Hogg and Lawrence Powell, Analecta Cartusiana, 91 (Salzburg: Institut für Anglistik und Amerikanistik Universität Salzburg, 1989).

11 Wolters, *Revelations*, pp. 49–59. For a discussion of these chapter lists, see Elisabeth Dutton, 'Compiling Julian: *The Revelation of Love* and Late-Medieval Devotional Literature', D.Phil. diss., University of Oxford, 2002, pp. 29–50.

12 Carleton Brown (ed.), *Religious Lyrics of the Fourteenth Century*, 2nd edn, rev. G. V. Smithers (Oxford: Clarendon Press, 1952), pp. 241, 85.

13 Ibid., p. 85.

14 G. Shepherd (ed.), *Ancrene Wisse, Parts Six and Seven*, rev. edn (Exeter: University of Exeter Press, 1991), pp. 21–6.

15 Brant Pelphrey, *Christ Our Mother* (London: Darton, Longman and Todd, 1989), p. 103.

16 J. Wickham Legg (ed.), *The Sarum Missal Edited from Three Early Manuscripts* (Oxford: Clarendon Press, 1916), p. 118: 'O certe necessarium ade peccatum et nostrum . . . O felix culpa'.

17 E.g., Irenaeus of Lyons, *Against Heresies*, which may have influenced Walter Hilton.

18 Benedicta Ward (trans.), *Prayers and Meditations of St Anselm*, Penguin Classics (Harmondsworth: Penguin, 1973), pp. 152–4.

19 A Benedictine of Stanbrook (trans.), *The Monk of Farne* (London: Darton, Longman and Todd, 1961), pp. 64–5, 73. Latin text: Hugh Farmer (ed.), 'The Meditations of the Monk of Farne', *Studia Anselmia 41: Analecta Monastica, series 4* (Rome, 1957), pp. 141–245, at pp. 182, 190.

20 E.g., Brown (ed.), *Religious Lyrics*, no. 48.

21 Cf. Meech and Allen (eds), *Book of Margery Kempe*, p. 126.

22 For the full Latin text of the Constitutions, see: www.umilta.net/arundel.html.

23 For the Westminster text, see: www.umilta.net/westmins.html.

24 See the list of 'long' and 'short' manuscripts of the *Incendium Amoris* in Margaret Deanesly (ed.), *The Incendium Amoris of Richard Rolle of Hampole*, University of Manchester Publications, History Series, 26 (Manchester: Manchester University Press, 1915), pp. 1–37.

References and Further Reading

Baker, Denise N. 1994. *Julian of Norwich's Showings: From Vision to Book*. Princeton, N.J.: Princeton University Press. Clear and insightful; probably the best introduction to Julian.

Beer, Francis (ed.) 1978. *Julian of Norwich's 'Revelations of Divine Love': The Shorter Version Edited from B.L. Add. M.S. 37790*. Middle English Texts, 8. Heidelberg: Winter. Very helpful introduction on the manuscript tradition, with a clear analysis of the subject-matter.

Bynum, Caroline Walker 1982. *Jesus as Mother: Studies in the Spirituality of the High Middle Ages*. Berkeley: University of California Press. The standard work on this important theme.

Clark, John P. H. 1981. 'Fiducia in Julian of Norwich.' *Downside Review* 99, 97–108, 214–29.

—— 1982a. 'Nature, Grace and the Trinity in Julian of Norwich.' *Downside Review* 100, 203–20.

—— 1982b. 'Predestination in Christ According to Julian of Norwich.' *Downside Review* 100, 79–91. A sequence of articles discussing Julian in the context of late medieval theology.

Colledge, Edmund and Walsh, James (eds) 1978. *A Book of Showings to the Anchoress Julian of Norwich*, 2 vols. Toronto: Pontifical Institute of Mediaeval Studies. Base text: MS Paris, Bibliothèque Nationale, fonds anglais 40. Puts Julian forward as a woman of exceptional learning, probably a nun of Carrow.

Gillespie, Vincent and Ross, Maggie 1992. 'The Apophatic Image: The Poetics of Effacement in Julian of Norwich's *Revelation of Love*.' In *The Medieval Mystical Tradition in England*, ed. Marion Glasscoe, Exeter Symposium, 5 (Cambridge: Brewer), pp. 53–77. A penetrating study of Julian's syntax and vocabulary, and her awareness of the limitations of language.

Glasscoe, Marion 1989. 'Visions and Revisions: A Further Look at the Manuscripts of Julian of Norwich.' *Studies in Bibliography* 42, 103–20. Discusses the different merits of the Paris and Sloane manuscripts.

—— (ed.) 1993. *Julian of Norwich: A Revelation of Love*, rev. edn. Exeter: University of Exeter. Based on London, British Library MS Sloane 2499. Minimal editorial interference, particularly in the punctuation, as Glasscoe wishes Julian's flowing sentence structure to show through; a compact and student-friendly edition.

Jantzen, Grace M. 1987. *Julian of Norwich: Mystic and Theologian*. London: SPCK. Julian's thought from the standpoint of modern theology.

Johnson, Lynn Staley 1991. 'The Trope of the Scribe and the Question of Literary Authority in the Works of Julian of Norwich and Margery Kempe.' *Speculum* 66, 820–38. Looks at female authors such as Hildegard of Bingen and Christine de Pizan, and considers issues such as the emotionalism expected in the work of a female author.

Nuth, Joan 1991. *Wisdom's Daughter: The Theology of Julian of Norwich*. New York: Crossroad. Modern feminist perspective on Julian's thought, emphasizing that Julian is producing a fully systematic and coherent theology.

Pelphrey, Brant 1982. *Love Was his Meaning: The Theology and Mysticism of Julian of Norwich*. Salzburg Studies in English Literature: Elizabethan and Renaissance Studies, 92.4. Salzburg: Institut für Anglistik und Amerikanistik, Universität Salzburg. Argues that Julian's theology is reminiscent of an older and wider Christian tradition, with parallels to Eastern Orthodox thought.

Riehle, Wolfgang 1981. *The Middle English Mystics*. London: Routledge and Kegan Paul. Particularly good on the Continental mystics and devout lay communities.

Staley, Lynn 1996. 'Julian of Norwich and the Late Fourteenth-Century Crisis of Authority.' In *The Powers of the Holy: Religion, Politics, and Gender in Late Medieval English Culture*, ed. D. Aers and L. Staley (University Park: Pennsylvania State University Press), pp. 107–78. Argues for Julian as politically aware, and looks at the effects of her excising her gender from the Long Text, thus producing an unsentimental, intellective discourse.

Tanner, Norman P. 1984. *The Church in Late Medieval Norwich, 1370–1532*. Studies and Texts, 66. Toronto: Pontifical Institute of Mediaeval

Studies. Important historical background, particularly on libraries, beguines and other anchorites.

Ward, Sr Benedicta 1988. 'Julian the Solitary.' In *Julian Reconsidered*, ed. Kenneth Leech and Sr Benedicta Ward (Oxford: SLG Press), pp. 10–31. A seminal article postulating that Julian had been a wife and mother before becoming an anchoress, not a nun.

Watson, Nicholas 1992. 'The Trinitarian Hermeneutic in Julian of Norwich's *Revelation of Love.*' In *The Medieval Mystical Tradition in England*, ed. Marion Glasscoe, Exeter Symposium, 5 (Cambridge: Brewer), pp. 79–100. Explores the complexity of Julian's language.

—— 1993. 'The Composition of Julian of Norwich's *Revelation of Love.*' *Speculum* 68, 637–83. A seminal article on the dating of the Short and Long Texts, which also provides a sensitive exploration of the Short Text in itself, restoring it to a place of interest in its own right.

—— 1995. 'Censorship and Cultural Change in Late Medieval England: Vernacular Theology, the Oxford Translation Debate and Arundel's Constitutions.' *Speculum* 70, 822–65. Historical considerations affecting the dating of the Long Text.

Windeatt, Barry (ed.) 1994. *English Mystics of the Middle Ages.* Cambridge: Cambridge University Press. Pages 181–213 for the Short Text from London, British Library MS Additional 37790. Very brief introduction and notes nevertheless give a clear general impression of the Short Text.

32
Piers Plowman

Stephen Kelly

Somewhere in London in the 1360s, an emaciated clerk falls asleep and dreams of home. Home is Cleobury or Shipton-under-Wychwood or Burford or Tewkesbury (Hanna 1993), but in our dream the clerk wanders the hills and crosses the brooks of his childhood and sees, as he could see only in a dream, polluted, riotous London arrayed before him. The innocence of his wanderings across childhood hills is darkened by his waking experience of London's corruption and injustice and its ignorance of God. When he wakes, the poem he will work on for the rest of his life, writing and rewriting, constantly revising, has been seeded. It provides a conflicted political conscience and extraordinary moral sense with devastating focus. And so the most shattering vernacular critique of medieval English society and its spiritual life is begun.

Or so the story goes in a convenient, if crude, précis of the dominant critical narrative of twentieth-century *Piers Plowman* studies. It has come to define what C. David Benson has recently termed the 'Langland myth': the critically convenient fiction of a righteous poet and his insistent, visionary and revisionary poetics (Benson 2004). But as in all myths there is some value in the story it purports to tell. It describes William Langland, the poet of three, or perhaps four, versions of *Piers Plowman* and his quest, in Anne Middleton's provocative terms, 'to revise the world' (Middleton 1997: 210). A project arguably unparalleled in English literature of the Middle Ages – for its audacious deployment of the vernacular, political courage and theological daring – it gained immediate favour among diverse 'estates' of readers, reaching aristocrats, women and the religious in around fifty-five complete manuscript copies within a short time after its initial dissemination.[1]

The story remains a critical fabrication: speculative, presentist (in its reflection of contemporary critical mores as opposed to historical 'realities') and undergirded by scholarly politics concerned to assert the cultural prestige of the poem and, by association, its scholars. While it admits the provisionality of literary histories, it also betrays their dependence upon the disciplinary circumstances within which they are conceived. As this essay will illustrate, *Piers Plowman* has been the subject of critical and political appropriation since its first appearance. Indeed, I will argue that Langland designed his poem to be appropriated as a form of 'heuristic fiction' in which the dominant cultural forms of his society could be critically reimagined by its readers. And as another exercise in appropriation, this essay will generate its own readings – and therefore its own histories – of *Piers Plowman*. However, in attending where it can both to the milieu of the poem and to the investments of literary history in the notion of *Piers Plowman* and its poet, it is hoped that this essay will signal, albeit briefly, how literary history has impoverished our understanding of the poem even as it has brought its existence into view. The essay is concerned with the historicity of *Piers Plowman*: its character as a text intervening in fourteenth-century documentary culture but subsequently remade in a series of historical appropriations. It will finally argue that the poem might be better understood – that it might divulge its historicity in a richer, more textured sense – by being assessed outside the purview of traditional literary studies.

Imagining the Author

That 'William Langland' is the author of *Piers Plowman* is evidenced by an inscription in Dublin, Trinity College Dublin MS 212, folio 89v, recording 'Willielmi de Langlond', son of 'Stacy de Rokayle', as author of 'Perys Ploughman'. Later, the Tudor playwright and anti-Catholic propagandist John Bale ascribed the poem to 'Robertus Langlande' born 'in comitatu Salopie in villa Mortymers Clyberi in the cleyelande within viij. myles of Malborne Hylles scripsit Peers Ploughman, li. i. "In a somer sonday [*seson*] whan sote [*warme*] was ye sunne"' (Hanna 1993: 158–9). The poem has been thought to support either name, with early critics feeling that the suggestions of the opening of Cambridge, Corpus Christi College MS 201 added weight to six separate ascriptions of the poem to a 'Robert' Langland: 'y Robt [Robert] in rosset gan rome abowhte', a notion which the poem's great Victorian editor, W. W. Skeat, dismissed and which was finally refuted in characteristically adroit fashion by George Kane (Kane 1965: 26–51). The suggestions of the text predominantly favour William: 'Will' is the narrator of the poem and although he functions as a personification of the faculty of *voluntas*, Langland probably follows the popular late medieval trope of self-naming in constructing his narrator. Anagrammatic signatures also support the view that the author of *Piers Plowman* was William Langland.[2] But now that authorship has been established, might we justifiably ask why we need to know?

It is a commonplace of essays such as this one to open with an account of the authorship of a text precisely because its sponsoring discipline – literary studies – has invested the idea of the author with critical significance. However, the 'author function', to draw on Michel Foucault's useful term, is not a recent phenomenon; it is not even as recent as Foucault himself presumed (Foucault 1984). The quest to identify the author of *Piers Plowman* arguably becomes an issue only when the milieu of his poem has passed. It is when the poem moves from being seen as a hortatory, politically and spiritually expedient critique of circumstances – either with a direct purchase upon, or in the memory of, its readers – to becoming 'antique' writing of an earlier age that Langland's name becomes a noun naming a body of writing. The marginal inscriptions in the Trinity College manuscript aside, for sixteenth-century antiquarians and printers the author's name has significance not necessarily because it provides the poem with a bio-bibliographical myth of origin but because it serves an ideological function in the present. For John Bale, Langland prophesied 'many things, which we have seen come to pass in our own days'. For the poem's first printer, Robert Crowley, Langland is significant because he answers a divine injunction: 'it pleased God to open the eyes of many to se hys truth, gevyng them boldenes of herte, to open their mouthes and crye oute agaynste the worckes of darcknes, as dyd John Wicklefe . . . and this writer' (quoted in Simpson 2002: 332). Both writers appropriate the deployment of prophetic discourses in *Piers Plowman* in order to advertise the importance of the poem and its poet for legitimating Protestant ideology – still open to accusations of historical novelty when they were writing. The figure of the Author is therefore important because he functions as a locus for a form of secular prophecy, heralding the end of the tyranny of the Roman Church. As Simpson says, 'Langland became, for a brief period from the death of Henry VIII until the Marian reaction in 1533, a critical representative of the enlightened few from "dercke and unlearned times", who had seen through to the evangelical future' (Simpson 2002: 333).

The quest for the Author is not limited to the sixteenth century. It achieves its fullest expression in the twentieth century, when it becomes a central concern of the burgeoning academic discipline of literary studies. The twentieth century consolidates and secures the notion that William Langland is the author of *Piers Plowman*. The poet is said to suffer from an obsession with textual revision, as if committed to 'perfecting' his poem. Conscious (or perhaps, more worryingly, unconscious) of the view that critical esteem depends upon the figure of the genius, early advocates of *Piers Plowman* sought to construct an image of the author as a troubled political or spiritual savant: the name 'Langland' could take its place beside other culturally and historically significant names like 'Chaucer' or 'Shakespeare' or 'Wordsworth' as the signifier of a particular kind of literature: *sui generis*, highly idiosyncratic, fused with the, albeit unknown, personal experience of the writer.

The 'author function' of William Langland thus becomes in the twentieth century the means by which a community of scholars identifies itself: we now have a *Yearbook of Langland Studies*; the internet, until recently, hosted a 'William Langland homepage'; we have a '*Piers Plowman* Tradition' – a prerequisite of canonicity, mimicking the immediate dissemination of Chaucerian apocrypha and the elaboration of a paternal 'author function' for Geoffrey Chaucer by Thomas Hoccleve, Robert Henryson and others in the fifteenth century. We are thus legitimated in our own interests in this next to unknown poet and his strange and difficult poem – or at least, we are according to the conditions of our discipline: were the readers of this volume hard-nosed historians, they might find such interest in the author a distraction from what the poem itself has to say (an enviable view, but generally not without its own presuppositions). And, as I shall argue later, we do this sprawlingly complex and contradictory poem an intellectual and historical disservice by shoehorning it into a particular literary 'canon'.

Interestingly, it is only when he needs to legitimate himself – when he needs to define a socially prescribed role for himself as an *auctor* – that Langland makes any sustained 'autobiographical' statement. In the C version of the poem the poet describes his life with his wife and child in Cornhill:

> Thus I awakede, woet God, whan I wonede in Cornehull,
> Kytte and I in a cote, ylothed as a lollare,
> And lytel ylet by, leveth me for soothe,
> Amonges lollares of Londone and lewede ermytes
> (C. 5.1–4)[3]

Lawrence Clopper and Middleton have both convincingly argued that it is only in the light of the second Statute of Labourers of 1388 that Langland feels compelled to identify himself with his poem (Clopper 1992; Middleton 1997). It is suggestive both of how he may have been perceived outside any immediate circle which sponsored his writing and of his need to wrest back his poem from misappropriation in the Peasants' Revolt, during which 'Piers Plowman' was recorded by chroniclers as one of the Revolt's leaders (Hudson 1988; Justice 1994). That being said, nowhere does Langland explicitly name himself; as Simpson argues, 'even if "William Langland" really was the name of the poet of *Piers Plowman*, he never anywhere says so in the poem, and instead schematizes the name so as to imply a dispersed or common authorship' (Simpson 2002: 341). We will return to this notion later in the essay.

'Inventing' *Piers Plowman*: Medieval Poem and Modern Text

And what of the poem itself? As already stated, it exists in three, or perhaps four, identifiable versions: an A-text of some 2,500 lines, whose eleven passus narrate three dreams; a B-text of around 7,200 lines, with twenty passus narrating eight dreams; and a C-text of eight dreams in twenty-two passus. Another version, the Z-text, is a redaction of A and may or may not be authorially sanctioned (Brewer and Rigg 1983; Hanna 1996).

Dating the poem, as with most Middle English writing, is dependent upon an unhappy mixture of 'internal' and 'external' evidence. On the basis of historical allusion the A-text is generally dated to the 1360s, and perhaps the close of the decade; the B-text, with its references to the Good Parliament and other contemporary events, is likely to have been copied around the late 1370s. It has been thought that the C-text must have been available in London in some form before 1388, the date of the execution of Thomas Usk, but this has been questioned.[4] Work by Simon Horobin and Linne Mooney on the Hengwrt–Ellesmere scribe, whom Mooney has come to identify as Adam Pinkhurst (Chaucer's 'Adam Scriveyn'), further consolidates the view that *Piers Plowman* is, definitively, a London text.[5]

The existence of the poem in three discrete versions is complicated by its dissemination in fifty-odd manuscripts. There are seventeen copies of the A-text and one fragment, and sixteen copies of B; the C-text boasts eighteen copies, and there are, fascinatingly, more than ten conjoined versions (Hanna 1993). *Piers Plowman* exists, then, not as a single text but as a series of texts, none of which is an authorial, or autograph, manuscript. The realization that the poem exists *as poems* is crucial to any attempt to understand the historicity of *Piers Plowman*. Furthermore, recent scholarship has challenged the notion that the versions of *Piers Plowman* were produced in a progressive sequence from A to C. Instead, it has been suggested that there was probably only one authorial version of the poem – B – and that the A version was an early release of a B draft designed to satisfy audience interest. Alterations executed in the C-text were made to compensate for the changing political and cultural circumstances in which Langland might have found himself. That he may not have been committed to writing *Piers* in a continual process of revision is suggested by the theory that the B manuscript from which he made revisions for C wasn't even a good copy of the text (Hanna 1996).[6]

The implications of the manuscript contexts of *Piers Plowman* and its multiple versions problematize scholarly discussion of the poem's authorship, which might be characterized as a quest for a stable and fixed origin. Textual production in medieval culture is a collective activity: the author rarely has control over the dissemination of his or her work (see, for example, Chaucer's 'Complaint to Adam Scriveyn' and the closing lines of *Troilus and Criseyde*). Hankering after the author is therefore, arguably, an anachronistic impulse: most literary texts, even after print, exist in multiple versions. Intriguingly, students of literature find this realization either deeply troubling or enormously liberating. Their reasons for doing so indicate a great deal about their vision of the historical and social utility of literary texts, a vision often subliminal and rarely articulated. Among students alarmed by this realization, the complexities of textual production in historically distant cultures are most unsettling, precisely because the figure of the author is compromised in favour of a more social notion of literary production.

However, for most readers of this book, *Piers Plowman* comes to them bound within the secure confines of a modern critical edition. The editorial culture of the poem in the twentieth century runs along parallel lines: on the one hand, we have the austere, intimidating and audacious Athlone editions, edited by George Kane, E. Talbot Donaldson and George Russell; on the other, we have two 'popular' and accessible editions, the B-text edited by A. V. C. Schmidt and the C-text edited by Derek Pearsall, as well as a parallel-text edition of all three versions of the poem by Schmidt, updating the 1857 edition of the poem's first major editor, W. W. Skeat.

While the Athlone, Schmidt and Pearsall editions all admit the inevitable choices they have made in presenting the text(s) of *Piers Plowman* – by prioritizing one manuscript over another – nowhere in their apparatus do they self-consciously examine the arguably anti-historical character of editorial practice. The *re-presentation* of historically distant texts for contemporary readers in the form of scholarly or critical editions belies the fact that the historical existence of the text edited for a contemporary readership may, as we saw above, be diffused, contradictory and multiple. The enabling premise and promise of any critical edition of a medieval text is the rescue of writing from a historically distant culture and its subsequent presentation as a modern printed text. While it is an enterprise guided by the admirable humanist endeavour of safeguarding the past achievements of human culture, it is one that, nevertheless, often risks eliding the historical complexity of the cultures within which, and for which, medieval texts were made.

It may seem paradoxical to suggest that the historical recuperation of a text actually denies its historicity. Editing, after all, is surely concerned with preservation. But editing is guaranteed by a set of value-judgements about what should be preserved. As Charlotte Brewer puts it, 'The job of the editor is a tricky one. He or she must scrutinize and analyse the scribally preserved evidence of Langland's words and produce for the modern reader something that approximates to a satisfactory reproduction of them' (Brewer 1996: 1). As Brewer indicates, 'Langland's words', the words of the Author, are prioritized in the editorial act. But the idea of the author in the Middle Ages was the site of a range of complex and politically contested assumptions. If vernacular authorship is beginning to garner cultural currency and therefore political significance in the fourteenth century, it is unlikely that medieval writers produced texts with the notion of themselves as authors in the sense espoused by contemporary editorial practice. Rather, it is often by appropriating the *auctoritas* of the clerical writer or by deferring to the powers of the reader that vernacular authorship is defended. The idea that Langland and Chaucer are somehow protean, that they break ground for later, more recognizably modern, notions of authorial creativity, is simplistic but also ignorant of the cultural specificity of later medieval textual practices. Hence, editing in the interests of an authorial voice is arguably a thoroughly unhistorical act because it misrepresents the culture in which texts were produced and disseminated. The origins of this misrepresentative impulse are fascinating in themselves, perhaps appearing in England with the early transmission of a Chaucerian canon in the fifteenth century. It is, as I suggested earlier, at the moment when the author's name becomes synonymous with a text or texts that the politics of editing become visible, as the presentation of the Author's Words, in parody of sacramental discourse, provides an editorial elect with a sacred duty. Other words – words which indicate the historicity of the text, its traffic from production through series of reading communities, such as those of scribes, copyists, redactors and indeed 'common' readers where they are to be found – are at most of secondary concern.

Nowhere is this distaste for the readers of *Piers Plowman* better signalled than in the Athlone B-text, edited by Kane and Donaldson. They take issue with the methods traditionally used by textual scholars to establish an authorial text. Since there is insufficient space fully to explore their presuppositions and procedures here, I will focus instead on their suspicion of the means by which editors establish the hierarchy of texts using what is known as 'stemmatic' evidence.[7] Stemmatic accounts of manuscript provenance trace the descent and dissemination of manuscripts by positing the notion that there is an authorial text which seeds the subsequent tree of variant manuscripts. Variance – 'error' or peculiarities specific to a given manuscript – is used to trace back to a base or urtext, which is assumed to be authorial in origin. Kane and Donaldson take issue, reasonably, with the assumptions of stemmatic research. There is too much subjectivity involved on the part of the textual scholar; too much reliance upon the action, or inaction, of copyists and scribes. For Kane and Donaldson, there had to be better procedures for establishing the authorial text. In a gesture which seems initially unproblematic but subsequently extraordinarily audacious, Kane and Donaldson declared that they could identify an authentically 'Langlandian line', based on repeated principles of alliteration and metre.[8] The editorial task in the Kane–Donaldson B-text is therefore a process of disinfection: clean away the interference and error and contamination of scribes in the various manuscripts of the B version; seek an identifiably Langlandian poetic register; reconstruct – and, most controversially, 'repair' where necessary – the author's words; finally, present the poem as it flowed from its poet's pen.

The poet's pen; Kane and Donaldson, and literary historians since, generally assume that the only way to establish *Piers Plowman* as historically significant is to reconstruct its author's agenda, motivation and poetics. The *materiality* of *Piers Plowman* – its existence in multiple manuscript copies beyond the editorial control of its author – has been ignored as an *integumentum*, a veil, behind which the true value of the poem lies. Hoyt Duggan, director of the *Piers Plowman* Electronic Archive, usefully characterizes the problems faced by the editor of *Piers Plowman* as follows:

> the recovery of an authorial text of *Piers Plowman* poses editorial problems only slightly less complex than the problems of editing the Greek Bible . . . Of the 54 surviving manuscripts, none is an autograph, none can be dated certainly as of the poet's lifetime. *The poem's very popularity poses a grave difficulty for modern editors: all of the surviving medieval copies are full of errors*, both subtle and blatant, serious and trivial. Like most other medieval poets, *Langland lacked control over the reproduction of his work*. Enthusiastic early readers often produced *inexpert* copies for their own use. These copies became in turn the bases for yet other copies, *with each copying accumulating fresh errors, conjectures, 'corrections,' and contamination* within and between versions. Authentic lines were garbled or omitted. Inauthentic lines were introduced *when scribes acted as amateur, self-taught editors*, sometimes mixing lines from the poem's three authorial versions and occasionally adding words or lines of their own.[9] (my emphases)

Duggan's language, albeit representative of the editor's dilemma, is riddled with problematic assumptions: the text's historical readers are ignored, even blamed, for 'error' or 'contamination'. The activities of readers are to be erased, as is suggested in a sentence of exquisite irony: 'The poem's *very popularity* poses a grave difficulty for modern editors: all of the surviving medieval copies are full of errors' (my emphasis). The modern editor, then, is to ignore the cultural situatedness of manuscripts of *Piers* – a situatedness indicated by those very 'errors' or by 'popularity' – in favour of a text rendered historically mute but at the same time ventriloquially expressive of a socially detached Author. That detachment, and the editor's recuperative agenda, is further suggested by Duggan's next sentence: 'Like most other medieval poets, Langland lacked control over the reproduction of his work.' The editor's perspective here misses a crucial point: it bears being repeated that medieval texts were produced under collective or corporate circumstances, with the author as a single, albeit central, figure among many. But it has come to be the task of the editor, as Kane and Donaldson famously declared in their Athlone B-text, to rescue the author from his contemporary readers or scribes.

Central to the view of modern editors, from Skeat, through the Athlone project, to Schmidt and Pearsall and the Electronic Archive, is the belief that *Piers Plowman* is the work of a culturally central and historically significant poet and that the poem should be recognized as such. Indeed, in a stroke of genuine scholarly brilliance, Kane and Donaldson fuse their editorial practice with a complex defence of Langland's poetic artistry. Similar in its commitment to defending *Piers Plowman*, but less fussy than the Athlone enterprise, is A. V. C. Schmidt's edition, which shares the view that Langland is a major medieval literary artist. In setting out this view, Schmidt has sought to make *Piers Plowman* not only inexpensive – the Everyman edition appears as an affordable paperback – but also immediately readable. But, as Andrew Galloway has recently pointed out, popular editions of *Piers Plowman*

> may easily distort the fluid, inchoate nature of late-medieval vernacular literary authority, hiding the possibilities that on occasion no manuscript reading may present what the author wrote and that no one version exists as a finished, literary object. (Galloway 1999: 62)

The reader of *Piers Plowman* must therefore be conscious that the poem they read is a historical and scholarly construction; understanding the historicity of *Piers Plowman* requires an understanding of its existence as *texts*.

The Necessity of Difficulty in *Piers Plowman*

If the impetus for the Athlone editions was to defend *Piers Plowman* and its author as culturally significant and worthy of sustained critical engagement, Schmidt's project has been even more ambitious as it seeks to establish *Piers Plowman* on the undergraduate curriculum, alongside the more accessible works of Chaucer and Thomas Malory. But the editorial defence of *Piers Plowman* is easily lost on precisely this readership as it struggles to come to terms with what is, by any measure, an extraordinarily difficult poem. For all the efforts of textual scholarship to present us with a coherent text – whether because it is the 'author's words' or because it has been cleanly, efficiently presented in a cribbed form – *Piers Plowman* will remain a supremely challenging poem.

Indeed, the editorial projects whose histories I have been assessing have struggled against the view that *Piers Plowman* was the work of a muddled, mediocre literary talent. But it is precisely the *difficulty* of *Piers Plowman* which has often led critics to make all sorts of dismissive or partial claims about the text. Famously C. S. Lewis dismissed most of *Piers Plowman*, complaining that Langland 'hardly makes his poetry into a poem'. Even champions of the poem have had to admit the text's often obfuscatory nature. In their selections from the C-text Elizabeth Salter and Pearsall suggested, for example, that 'the poem has no proper narrative structure . . . Langland is not committed to a narrative structure in any continuous way'. For Priscilla Martin, Langland 'is prepared to thwart our narrative expectations if inconclusiveness or re-statement best serve the cause of precision'.[10] How inconclusiveness serves precision is questionable, but Martin's paradox is illustrative of the narrative and conceptual complexity of the poem. For Middleton, by far the best critic of *Piers Plowman* in recent years, Langland's narrative practice can best be characterized in terms of the '"discontinuous" and disrupted episode' (Middleton 1982b).

Inconclusiveness, discontinuity, frustration, difficulty – these and other terms characterize contemporary critical discussion of *Piers Plowman*. The student bewildered by the poem itself can at least take some comfort from the fact that its professional readers are similarly unsettled. But what is the cause of the poem's difficulty? Is it indeed, as Lewis supposed, an issue of talent; was the poet of *Piers Plowman* an enthusiastic but ill-disciplined amateur?

That the poem's historical readers found *Piers Plowman* a difficult text is indicated by a range of rubrications and divisions added to the poem in its manuscript forms. Whether these are authorial we cannot know, but they certainly help the reader. The division of each section of the poem into *passus*, Latin for 'step(s)', is indicative of the exploratory and contemplative character of the reading experience. Many manuscripts, in this case of the B version, divide the poem into two large sections: a *Visio*, or 'vision', ending at the close of Passus Twelve; and a *Vita*, or 'life', lasting until the end of the poem.

These simple demarcations help orient the reader as a trade-off against the thoroughly disorientating narrative surface of the poem. Predominately allegorical – in the mode of the popular medieval species of allegory, dream-vision – *Piers Plowman* incorporates a bewildering range of late medieval discourses and genres in the interest of mounting as thorough a social critique as possible. Will, the poem's narrator, stumbles from one dream to the next in which the inequities of late medieval society are systemically exposed. He interrogates personifications of the institutions, virtues, vices and mental faculties which determine the character of individual life in late medieval England. His quest for 'kynde knowyng' – the capacity to understand and activate the mystery of the Incarnation and Resurrection within his own life, which he admits to Holi Chirche he does not yet possess – leads him away from the organized Church towards the figure of Piers the Ploughman, an agrarian Christ-figure who functions as a moral and ethical template for the poem. On the way, Langland deconstructs the institutional, political and epistemological underpinnings of his culture, thus razing his society to the ground so that it can be reconstructed on the rock of his Petrine ploughman. In doing so, he declares encyclopedic knowledge of late medieval political, legal and documentary discourses, including the registers of legal, scriptural, scholastic, satirical, allegorical, ecclesiastical, sermonic, psalmic, dramatic and clerical discourse.

For Steven Justice, *Piers Plowman* 'progresses by literary ascesis' (Justice 1993: 100), by the accrual of discourse upon discourse, genre upon genre. Confusion on the reader's part is inevitable, a fact recognized by Langland given that no one is as confused as his hapless narrator, Will. And yet with the reader's confusion comes a commitment to achieving understanding: we are trapped in the experience of interpretative suspense and so submit the poem to ever more concentrated forms of hermeneutic analysis. Reading allegory, reading *Piers Plowman*, is thus hard work. The bewildering character of Langland's narrative can be signalled by a very brief synopsis of the opening few passus. While the poem remains disorientating in its movement from one episode to another, by focusing on a single term and concept, work, we can see how narrative discontinuity in *Piers Plowman* serves a larger political and epistemological interest.

Revising the World: Reading (as) Work in *Piers Plowman*

Wandering on the Malvern hills, dressed as a hermit, Will falls asleep and dreams, famously, of a 'fair field full of folk' (Prologue); on the pattern of a typical estates satire they are arranged according to their 'estate' and their fidelity to 'proper' moral conduct: 'somme putte hem to the plough, pleiden full selde . . . / And some putten hem to pride, apparailed hem therafter' (B-text, Prol.20, 23).[11] It is significant that here Will celebrates those who work – who contribute to the maintenance of society – over those who do not; while a commonplace of estates satire, Langland's deployment of work as a trope of virtue will resonate throughout his poem. Indeed, the first seven passus of *Piers Plowman* are animated by a series of reflections upon his society's multiple conceptions of work. Work is introduced in the Prologue of the poem as the ideal means of maintaining the spiritual health and continuity of medieval society (Aers 1992: 35). Those who 'putten hem to the plough' (Prol.20) are contrasted with those who 'putten hem to pride' (Prol.23); this opposition reverberates throughout the Prologue and Passus One (Prol.138–9; 1.79–89, 128–30, 145–7) and the poem as a whole. That it will be a problematic opposition is evidenced by the fact of Will's marginal social status, his lack of a socially cohesive role. The ideal of work is thus problematized almost as soon as it is introduced.

However, Will's marginal status in the Prologue undermines his right to moralize on medieval society, 'the fair field ful of folk', or on the 'wastours' who have lost sight of the 'tour on the tofte'. Will's lack of hermeneutic authority, an authority he aped in the Prologue but which disappears with the appearance of 'a lovely lady of leere in lynnen yclothed' (1.3) in Passus 1, will culminate in a crisis of satire in Passus Eleven, which will in turn precipitate Will's defence of poetry as work in Passus Twelve. But in the intervening passus, work, as cohesive and morally informed activity, animates a meditation upon: the growing expectation of payment across all the strata of medieval society (Passus 1 and 2); the moral, ethical and spiritual implications of mercantile economics for a hierarchical society (Passus 3); and the dangers of bribery and social mobility for a judicial system sanctioned by a king whose identity is contrary to any sort of social movement or temporal change (Passus 4). Langland's satire of the detachment of Holi Chirche and of the corruption of the King's Council is radical but, with the close of Passus 4 and the beginning of Passus 5 we come to realize – retro-interpretatively – that it is at the same time politically normative. It seeks the defence and elevation of a model of social mutuality based upon work and directed away from a contingent 'dale' and towards eternity. The character of Reason may successfully reform the King's Council in Passus 4, but the full implementation of reform can only be achieved by deference to a spiritual economy. For this reason, the characters of Reason and Repentance attempt in Passus 5 to have the Seven Deadly Sins confess to their sinfulness.

The movement to penitential issues is thus signalled by the partial victory of justice in Passus 4, but the failure of any of the sins, all of whom recall the 'wastours' bemoaned in the Prologue, actually to repent, retrospectively subjects the discourse and institutions of justice and penitence to critique. Langland infers in his satire of political and ecclesiastical justice that fine words are simply not enough to secure salvation: deeds, works, must matter. But when the sinners set off on pilgrimage – a form of active, participatory penance that, on a superficial level at least, Langland should approve of – the actual practice of pilgrimage is attacked when the seasoned pilgrim does not know his way to Truth. Enter Piers the Plowman, whose moral credibility hangs on the popular trope of the ploughman as a socially cohesive figure. With the beginning of Passus 6, Piers's offer to lead the pilgrimage promises to renew the moral and social fabric of his culture by convening the folk in socially beneficial activity. Pilgrimage is equated with the ploughing of the half-acre, which Piers says he must complete before he can set off to Truth:

> Quod Perkyn the Plowman, 'By Seint Peter of Rome!
> I have an half acre to erie by the heighe weye;
> Hadde I eryed this half acre and sowen it after,
> I would wende with yow, and the way teche.'
> (6.3–6).

Such a sentiment returns the theme of work, with its multiple repercussions, to the foreground of the poem. And this is accentuated even further since the ploughing of the half-acre itself constitutes the pilgrimage. But Langland's sense of his society's spiritual crisis means that the ploughing fails, because the pilgrims-cum-labourers become uninterested and lazy. The Passus ends with the failure of the ploughing, and a prophecy of imminent famine.

None the less, the penitential significance of the ploughing of the half-acre informs the next passus, 7, with Piers receiving a pardon for his efforts. But in the B-text's most controversial moment (removed from the C version), Piers tears the pardon and rejects, in turn, its harsh morality, which seems to favour predestination, the authority of the priest who tries to decode it, and, subtextually, the very practice of the issuing of pardons at all. The morality of the pardon – the good shall be saved, the evil damned

– is problematic for Piers because it forecloses the need for morally informed, socially advantageous work. In fact, the rest of the poem reverberates with these implications. The next twelve passus describe Will's inner quest for Dowel, Dobet and Dobest, a quest never completed because in the strict terms of Truth's pardon, work seems ultimately to have little spiritual coherence. Grace *seems* already to have been determined and Conscience's quitting of the failed Barn of Unity in Passus 20 to look for Piers signals that only he can resolve the politico-theological dilemma with which the poem closes.

As the preceding critical synopsis should indicate, *Piers Plowman* is both thoroughly discontinuous but also tightly patterned thematically. Negotiating the difficulty of *Piers Plowman* requires the reader to enact a kind of 'double reading': she must read *with the narrative*, moving 'forward' to one epistemological or spiritual crisis or aporia after another; but she must also read 'retro-interpretatively', subjecting each latest crisis to retrospective analysis, and thus making sense, *post factum*, of earlier episodes. The double movement of understanding backwards and forwards is a difficult task (hard work!) for the reader. It requires, drawing on terms from Matei Calinescu's study of rereading, that the reader abandon the basic 'ludic involvement' necessary for engagement in ordinary narrative – precisely the kind of involvement demanded by the 'jangeleres' condemned in the Prologue – in favour of 'absolute absorption' in Langland's poem (Calinescu 1993: 138–56, 164–72).

Hence, the extent to which *Piers Plowman* is dependent for its success upon the hermeneutic competence of its readers amplifies my earlier point about the importance of material evidence of reception in the light of the poem's immediate dissemination, and once again brands as anachronistic a commitment to an authorial text or, indeed, cult of personality. As Simpson suggested earlier, Langland prefers to disperse authorship into a collective practice of textual interpretation. For Mary Clemente Davlin:

> The reader must participate in *Piers*, play with it, so that its purpose – a particular kind of experience at once aesthetic and religious – can be achieved . . . It is not unusual for medieval poems to have as their purpose some religious or moral change in their readers or audience . . . such change was a conventional expectation, and . . . readers were expected to read actively to the point that 'reading [could] be a kind of rewriting'. (Davlin 1989: 5)

Reading as rewriting: such a notion of reception places responsibility for the creation of meaning and the activation of its affects with an audience. While this is not an uncommon aspect of late medieval poetics it manifests in the context of *Piers Plowman* what I would like to term a 'social poetics'. *Piers Plowman* is a *social text*, a *corporate poem*; its strategies for negotiating the spiritual, epistemological and political dilemmas it narrates can only be activated by its readers, who move from reflecting upon the issues explored by the poem to assessing their impact on their daily lives.

Langland's achievement in making such a daring intervention in the documentary culture of late medieval English society is to foresee the capacity of poetry, and in particular fiction, to undertake this task. *Piers Plowman* grasps the opportunity of the imaginative and ambiguously referential character of fictive discourse in order to effectively ventriloquize the constituent voices of its culture. The poem seeks truth in untruth: acting as a 'heuristic fiction', it functions as both a critique of the cultural imagination of late fourteenth-century England and as a template for the imaginative revision and renewal of narratives of individual and communal identity by its readers. The poem is designed to be *instrumentalized* by its readers; it is to be used by individual readers as a tool with which to interrogate culture and their roles within it. The movement in Langland's text, from cultural critique (Prologue to Passus 7), to meditation on the self and its social existence (Passus 7–12), to the possibility (and value) of just action within a discordant society (Passus 13–20), is part of Langland's philosophical enquiry into the significance of the individual life within the transcendent framework of Christian history. The poem impels its readers, through the example of its narrator and surrogate reader, Will, to begin for themselves the imaginative process by which society can be re-envisioned, retold in terms more faithful to its source and justification in Christian ethics. To this end, Langland's poem elaborates a 'convocative' or 'apostolic' politics whose aim is the constitution of a 'narrative identity' for its audience. His 'heuristic fiction' allows society to be remodelled imaginatively; its aim is to put at issue and in question the reader's sense of identity and to invoke reflective, meditative reading as the primary means of (re)constituting a moral self.

Conclusion: Reading, Reception and the Future of *Piers Plowman*

For these reasons, the image of Langland with which we opened, of a lonely literary maverick, is no longer tenable. The poet of *Piers Plowman* could never have begun an experimental literary project which placed so great a demand upon his readers unless his readers were known – unless he was always already aware of an immediate audience or 'coterie' to whom, and for whom, he could write his poem. In recent years, the issue of a Langlandian coterie has become a 'hot' scholarly topic, with a number of essays proposing a range of London communities to which Langland might have belonged (Middleton 1982a).[12] It has been suggested, unconvincingly to my mind, that Chaucer and Langland might have shared an audience with an increasingly sophisticated taste for vernacular fictions (it is more likely that they shared scribes). Whether they shared an audience or not, their work does signal an appetite among readers for intellectually complex fictions; indeed, the ambition of *Piers Plowman*, and its immediate dissemination in the counties around London, suggests that its particular brand of 'social poetics' was extremely attractive to a diverse audience and that its capacity to intersect with other forms of political and religious discourse augmented its efficacy as reformist literature. Indeed, in their famous appropriation of the poem, the rebels of 1381 record the utility of *Piers Plowman*, and of the figure of Piers in particular, for providing popular dissent with the force of discourse (Justice 1994). However, the means by which they invoke *Piers Plowman* indicates their own distaste for the existential radicalism of Langland's reformism. We will remember that in Passus 7 of the B version, Piers abandons work and exits the half-acre in disgust, having destroyed the pardon from Truth. In encouraging Piers to return to work, John Ball, author of the insurgent letters in which reference to the poem is made, signals his awareness that Piers's radical suspension of work is cataclysmic for society and that, with the rebels about to set the world to rights, Piers can indeed return to ploughing. But in domesticating Piers, the rebels misunderstand his challenge – a challenge dependent first upon spiritual reform rather than social emancipation. Langland does indeed want to change society, but that change must come from within, issuing in communality, as a convocative stance informed by scripture – and his poem – rather than as activism contingent upon political opportunity.

Langland's revisions in the C version of *Piers Plowman* articulate his own awareness of the success of his poem's incursion into the documentary culture of later medieval England. But they also signal the capitulation of an extraordinary poetic enterprise. 'It is,' says Middleton, 'in essence, the situation of all literature distinct from instrumental discourse: the poem must be open to misprision if it is also to be open to its intended affective use. Its heteroclitic nature, its capacity to become a property of public discourse in several incommensurable ways at once, defines its social power and its wholly *ad hoc* authority' (Middleton 1982a: 123). The C version, for all its tidying of earlier unruly passages, articulates the failure of *Piers Plowman*, as Langland recognizes the dangers of misappropriation and regresses into a model of authorship which claims precarious ownership of a poetic discourse now made all too public.

As the arch traced by this essay indicates, *Piers Plowman* cannot be contained within the standard generic or epistemological categories of contemporary literary history. It is effusive, contradictory, and of course multiple in its versions and renditions. No edition, no matter how complex its apparatus, could hope to do justice either to the poem's dissemination or to its invitation to readers and scribes to amend, revise or enact its social poetics. *Piers Plowman* will for that reason remain elusive, beyond the reach of critical canons. However, the poem continues to invite us to recognize its interlocutionary power. That is, it invites us to reactivate its ethical and moral challenges in the context of our own lives; for example, the poem's potent identification of the politics of injustice remains as pertinent as ever. And if the poem continues to ask questions of readers about the ethical and political role of fiction and the social and moral agency of the individual, it poses particular questions for literary scholarship in the twenty-first century.

I should like to conclude by outlining some of these. To my mind, the contemporary scholar of *Piers Plowman* must make a decision about the character of her attention in the poem: either she is interested in the poem as the work of an author and therefore with base texts and definitive versions, as traditional literary studies has been, or she must define herself as a historian of textual culture, a 'textual anthropologist'. The latter choice invalidates the former, inasmuch as it incorporates the former's interests and surpasses them. The quest for an authorial text of *Piers Plowman* is a partial aspect of the complex cultural existence of the poem. From the perspective of a textual anthropology, each manuscript may manifest an appropriation of an earlier version, but is in no way deficient by comparison. Rather, each is an act of writing with as much cultural and historical interest as the next. The personalities pertaining to all, and the operations enacted in their production and dissemination, are now worthy of detailed comparative and non-judgemental investigation. The themes of the history and anthropology of textual cultures might therefore include, among others: the development of technologies of inscription and transmission; the origin, form and variety of discourses which textual practices come to employ (and their relation to one another); the development of tropes of authorship and readership and their attendant notions of agency and subjectivity. If this sounds considerably like the preoccupations of contemporary literary scholarship it is because literary scholarship is in the midst of just such a process of reorientation. However, the implications of such critical praxes for current disciplines are likely to be catastrophic. Their implications for medievalists, and for scholars of *Piers Plowman* in particular, could nevertheless be enormously energizing and liberating. Indeed, an appropriate response to the complexities of *Piers Plowman* demands that we take issue with disciplinary complacencies. In thinking through the viability of such critical transformations, we take the challenge of Langland's social poetics into new situations of historical and cultural pertinence.

See also: 2 English Society in the Later Middle Ages, 3 Religious Authority and Dissent, 4 City and Country, Wealth and Labour, 7 From Manuscript to Modern Text, 11 The Forms of Verse, 22 Dream Poems, 33 The *Canterbury Tales*.

Notes

1 I do not count here the Wycliffite or Lollard 'corpus' of writings, which mounts a similarly devastating critique of late medieval English society.

2 In addition to Kane 1965, see Anne Middleton, 'William Langland's "Kynde Name": Authorial Signature and Social Identity in Late Fourteenth-Century England', in *Literary Practice and Social Change in Britain, 1380–1530*, ed. Lee Patterson (Berkeley: University of California Press, 1990), pp. 15–81; and James Simpson, 'The Power of Impropriety: Authorial Naming in *Piers Plowman*', in *William Langland's Piers Plowman: A Book of Essays*, ed. Kathleen Hewett-Smith (New York: Garland, 2001), pp. 145–66.

3 William Langland, *Piers Plowman: An Edition of the C-Text*, ed. Derek Pearsall, York Medieval Texts, 2nd ser. (London: Arnold, 1978).

4 John M. Bowers, 'Dating *Piers Plowman*: Testing the Testimony of Usk's *Testament*', *Yearbook of Langland Studies* 13 (1999), 65–100.

5 Simon Horobin and Linne R. Mooney, 'A *Piers Plowman* Manuscript by the Hengwrt/Ellesmere Scribe and its Implications for London Standard English', *Studies in the Age of Chaucer* 26 (2004), 65–112. This is exciting new work which promises to revolutionize understanding of the contexts of production for *Piers Plowman*, and its intersections with London literary culture. Mooney's discovery of Adam Pinkhurst's work is published as 'Adam's Scribe' in *Speculum* 81 (2006), 97–138.

6 See also Wendy Scase, 'Two *Piers Plowman* C-Text Interpolations: Evidence for a Second

Textual Tradition', *Notes and Queries* 34 (1987), 456–63; and Jill Mann, 'The Power of the Alphabet: A Reassessment of the Relation between the A and the B Versions of *Piers Plowman*', *Yearbook of Langland Studies* 8 (1995), 21–50.

7 For sustained discussion of the brilliance and audacity of Kane–Donaldson see Ralph Hanna, 'Producing Manuscripts and Editions', in *Crux and Controversy in Middle English Textual Criticism*, ed. A. J. Minnis and Charlotte Brewer (Cambridge: Brewer, 1992), pp. 109–30; and Galloway 1999.

8 *Piers Plowman: The B Version – Will's Visions of Piers Plowman, Do-Well, Do-Better and Do-Best*, ed. George Kane and E. Talbot Donaldson (London: Athlone Press, 1975), pp. 128–220.

9 The *Piers Plowman* Electronic Archive: http://jefferson.village.virginia.edu/piers/report94.html A. Text by Hoyt N. Duggan.

10 Lewis, Salter and Pearsall, and Martin are quoted in C. David Benson, 'The Frustration of the Reader and Narrative in *Piers Plowman*', in *Art and Context in Later Medieval English Narrative: Essays in Honour of Robert Worth Frank, Jr.*, ed. Robert R. Edwards (Cambridge: Cambridge University Press, 1994), pp. 1–15. This is an excellent essay on why *Piers Plowman* is so hard to read.

11 William Langland, *The Vision of Piers Plowman: A Critical Edition of the B-Text*, ed. A. V. C. Schmidt, 2nd edn (London: Dent, 1995). All further references are to this edition.

12 Kathryn Kerby-Fulton, 'Langlandian Reading Circles and the Civil Service in London and Dublin, 1380–1427', *New Medieval Literatures* 1 (1997), 59–83; Kathryn Kerby-Fulton and Steven Justice, 'Reformist Intellectual Culture in the English and Irish Civil Service: The *Modus tenendi parliamentum* and its Literary Relations', *Traditio* 53 (1998), 149–203; and James Simpson, ' "After craftes conseil clotheth yow and fede": Langland and London City Politics', in *England in the Fourteenth Century: Proceedings of the 1991 Harlaxton Symposium*, ed. Nicholas Rogers (Stamford: Paul Watkins, 1993), pp. 109–27.

References and Further Reading

Aers, David (ed.) 1992. *Culture and History, 1350–1600: Essays on English Communities, Identities and Writing* (London: Harvester Wheatsheaf). A key collection of essays on late medieval literature and culture from a cultural materialist perspective.

Benson, C. David 2004. *Public Piers Plowman: Modern Scholarship and Late Medieval English Culture.* University Park: Pennyslvania State University Press. Usefully deconstructs some of the critical myths underpinning Langland scholarship.

Brewer, Charlotte 1996. *Editing Piers Plowman: The Evolution of the Text.* Cambridge: Cambridge University Press. A critical history of the editing of the poem, from Crowley to the electronic *Piers Plowman.*

—— and Rigg, A. G. 1983. *Piers Plowman: The Z Version.* Toronto: Pontifical Institute of Mediaeval Studies. An argument for a fourth version of *Piers.*

Calinescu, Matei 1993. *Rereading.* New Haven, Conn.: Yale University Press. A study of the interpretative conditions for the rereading of texts.

Clopper, Lawrence M. 1992. 'Need Men and Women Labor? Langland's Wanderer and the Labor Ordinances.' In *Chaucer's England: Literature in Historical Context* (Minneapolis: University of Minnesota Press). A consideration of Langland's perspectives on work in the light of labour legislation.

Davlin, Mary Clemente 1989. *A Game of Heuene: Word Play and the Meaning of* Piers Plowman. Woodbridge: Brewer. A study of the varieties of word-play and other rhetorical experimentation in *Piers Plowman.*

Foucault, Michel 1984. 'What is an Author?' In *The Foucault Reader*, ed. Paul Rabinow (Harmondsworth: Penguin), pp. 101–20. A classic study in the archaeology of the concept of authorship.

Galloway, Andrew 1999. 'Uncharacterizable Entities: The Poetics of Middle English Scribal

Culture and the Definitive *Piers Plowman.' Studies in Bibliography* 52, 59–87. A thoughtful guide to the presuppositions and pitfalls of modern editions of *Piers Plowman.*

Hanna, Ralph 1993. *William Langland.* Aldershot: Ashgate. A first port of call for readers interested in bio-bibliographical matters relating to William Langland.

—— 1996. *Pursuing History: Middle English Manuscripts and their Texts.* Stanford, Calif.: Stanford University Press. A characteristically combative discussion of contemporary textual studies with excellent essays on the versions of *Piers Plowman* and on editorial accounts of late medieval texts.

Hudson, Anne (1988) 'The Legacy of *Piers Plowman.*' In *A Companion to Piers Plowman*, ed. John Alford (Berkeley: University of California Press), pp. 251–66. A survey of the reception of Piers Plowman from the fifteenth century.

Justice, Steven 1993. 'The Genres of *Piers Plowman.*' In *Medieval English Poetry*, ed. Stephanie Trigg (London: Longman), pp. 99–118. A brilliant essay assessing the shifting generic allegiances of *Piers Plowman.*

—— 1994. *Writing and Rebellion: England in 1381.* Berkeley: University of California Press. For a controversial account of the role of documentary culture in the Peasants' Revolt.

Kane, George 1965. *Piers Plowman: The Evidence for Authorship.* London: Athlone Press. Finally put the 'authorship question' to bed, but led to the ossification of discussion of William Langland, at least until the 1980s.

Middleton, Anne 1982a. 'The Audience and Public of *Piers Plowman.*' In *Middle English Alliterative Poetry and its Literary Background*, ed. David Lawton (Woodbridge: Brewer), pp. 101–23. Sophisticated account of textual transmission, distinguishing between a 'coterie' Langland might have known and the wider public among whom his texts quickly circulated.

—— 1982b. 'Narration and the Invention of Experience: Episodic Form in *Piers Plowman.*' In *The Wisdom of Poetry: Essays in Honor of Morton W. Bloomfield*, ed. Larry D. Benson and Siegfried Wenzel (Kalamazoo, Mich.: Medieval Institute Publications), pp. 91–122. Key essay in understanding Langland's poetics and compositional methods.

—— 1997. 'Acts of Vagrancy: The C Version "Autobiography" and the Statute of 1388.' In *Written Work: Langland, Labor, and Authorship*, ed. Steven Justice and Kathryn Kerby-Fulton (Philadelphia: University of Pennsylvania Press), pp. 208–318. An invaluable essay delineating the relations between Langland's poetics and political legislation.

Simpson, James 1990. *Piers Plowman: An Introduction to the B-text.* London: Longman. A student-friendly and systematic study of the B version.

—— 2002. *Reform and Cultural Revolution.* Oxford English Literary History, vol. 2: *1350–1547.* Oxford: Oxford University Press. An exciting comparative account of late medieval literary history, with a compelling account of the Reformation construction and appropriation of medieval literature; excellent on the early modern reception of *Piers.*

33
Subjectivity and Ideology in the *Canterbury Tales*

Mark Miller

Chaucer's *Canterbury Tales* is a baggy monster of a poem, a sprawling collection of shorter works encompassing a variety of literary forms. The individual pieces are held together by the device of pilgrims telling tales on the way to Canterbury, but the purpose of that format is less to provide a tight formal architecture for the whole than to give Chaucer the freedom to explore whatever forms of cultural expression he found interesting. Besides such freedom, the device of pilgrim narrators allowed Chaucer to expand the scope of his long-standing interest in the relations between subjectivity and ideology. While his earlier work was aimed at a courtly audience and engaged the courtly literary forms of dream vision and historical romance, the different cultural locations of the *Canterbury* genres provided him with a wider range of subject-positions and ideological formations to investigate. In what follows I will focus on four *Canterbury Tales*, those of the Knight, the Wife of Bath, the Pardoner and the Parson. These texts engage some of the social and ideological formations of most interest to Chaucer, and provide some of his richest portraits of the psychologies those formations make possible. Focusing on these texts will suggest not only what an extraordinary project the *Canterbury Tales* is, but how valuable it can be as a window onto the psychic life of late medieval English culture.

Aristocratic Formalism in the Knight's Tale

Since Johan Huizinga, many historians and critics have characterized late medieval aristocratic culture as formalistic and theatrical.[1] That characterization has meant different things to different people, but what is shared by all concerned is an interest in a pattern of attitudes that shaped the chivalric way of life, including: a taste for the production and celebration of noble identity in tournaments, pageantry, processions and other performances; an appetite for displays of leisured refinement that functioned as class markers and sites of class solidarity, for instance through the ritualized enactments of hunting and dance and the connoisseurship involved in heraldry and the blazon; and an aestheticized concern with courtly manners, the formal structures of comportment that also both marked and made class identity, not least in the arena of erotic life, where the finesse of *fin'amors* gave expression to a heart that was 'noble' in a sense that united social class, aesthetic refinement and ethical sensibility. English literature of the late fourteenth century produced three great poetic investigations of this obsession with political, ethical, aesthetic and erotic formalism: *Sir Gawain and the Green Knight*, and Chaucer's *Troilus and Criseyde* and Knight's Tale. In what follows I will focus on the Knight's Tale, to suggest what drives this formalist imaginary and what connects its aesthetic, political, ethical and erotic dimensions.

Perhaps the most immediate way the Knight's Tale engages aristocratic formalism can be found in its literary structure. While the poem has an overarching plot, very little of it is devoted to narrative, and what narrative there is often serves merely to stitch together the real organizing structure of the poem, a series of quasi-theatrical displays, aesthetic set-pieces and tableaux.[2] From the opening of the poem, in which Theseus, in the midst of a homecoming procession after conquering the realm of 'Femenye' (866), encounters grieving Theban widows, dressed in black and kneeling two by two at the wayside, to the poem's conclusion, in which Theseus stands before a parliament he has called, delivering a politico-philosophical speech to move Athens past tragedy to a new alliance with Thebes, these set-pieces articulate the tale's governing ethos. One way they do so is by exhibiting Theseus's ethical exemplarity and fitness for rule. In his encounters with the Theban widows, and later with Palamon and Arcite battling over their love for Emily, Theseus finds himself initially moved to anger by what he perceives as intrusions on the celebratory performance of his nobility, but quickly corrects himself and responds to the plights of both mourners and lovers. As the Knight says, the noble heart is marked by its quick accessibility to pity, 'for pitee renneth soone in gentil herte' (1761). Even more important, Theseus shows in these scenes a capacity for rational self-governance that makes him a microcosmic model of the ideal *polis*. When feeling pity at the battling lovers, a still angry Theseus remains in a sense at war with himself, moved by incompatible passions just as Palamon and Arcite are driven to battle by the irreconcilable passions that control them. What ultimately distinguishes Theseus is the way he submits his warring passions to deliberation to arrive at the just and merciful solution of a tournament to manage Theban rivalry. That tournament, which Theseus oversees 'arrayed right as he were a god in trone' (2529), in turn becomes the site for adjudicating warring passions under the highly rule-bound conditions he sets. Submission to Theseus's will thus emerges as the political form that collectively enacts the noble self-mastery he exhibits in his own person.

This is of course a highly idealized picture of noble self-fashioning and of a political form modelled on it and, as a number of critics have argued, it has some unsavoury and disturbing aspects, even for the Knight (Leicester 1990: 221–382; Patterson 1991: 165–230; Wallace 1997: 104–24). The tensions and incoherencies in the Knight's ethos appear in a number of places, including the terrifying depiction of the temple of Mars, a deity whose random violence undoes the Knight's confidence in the civilizing power of military authority. Another locus of ethical and ideological tension appears in the Tale's highly aestheticized eroticism. Central to the Knight's ethos is an analogy he draws between Thesean self-rule and the Knight's own formalist literary sensibility. The Knight imagines Theseus's noble identity as a kind of beautiful form, an ordering of the elements of his psyche to accord with the governing principles of his will; and in similar fashion the Knight imagines his poem, and a number of aesthetic objects within it, as beautiful forms whose elements, disparate and even conflicting as they may be, are given order by the governing principles of his imagination. One of those objects is the enormous amphitheatre Theseus has built for the tournament, the symmetry and beauty of whose construction the Knight describes in loving detail, even as he gets drawn aside from his celebratory tone by the sometimes fearful representations that decorate the amphitheatre. Another such object is Emily. The Knight begins the scene of Palamon and Arcite's enamoration by describing Emily's beauty as the formal counterpart to the beauty of the garden that surrounds her: 'Emelye . . . fairer was to seene / Than is the lilye upon his stalke grene, / And fressher than the May with floures newe – / For with the rose colour stroof hir hewe' (1035–8). The Knight's narrative perspective here, like his perspective on the amphitheatre and Theseus's on the tournament, is that of a distanced, supervisory appreciation. Unlike, say, the portrait of Alisoun in the Miller's Tale, which appeals to the pleasures of taste and touch, this portrait of feminine beauty appeals only to sight, and later sound, both of which are senses that operate at a distance from their objects. The visuality of Emily's portrait focuses on a series of nested formal structures, including the highly cultivated and enclosed garden, its floral patterns of rose red and lily white, and the mirroring of those patterns in Emily's appearance. While Emily is literally contained within this structure, she is also figuratively constituted by it, so that her beauty seems inseparable from the idea of an aesthetic self-enclosure. Given the constitutive nature of this self-enclosure, the one element of strife in her portrait – the sense of competition between Emily's beauty and that of the flowers – only adds to the formal stasis of the scene. In these antagonistic elements whose reflection of each other provides for their common participation in a beautiful aesthetic structure, we have the picture of woman as perfect formal object nearly at its purest.

While such an aestheticized, objectifying portrait looks problematic to modern readers educated by feminism, and while it emerges as an object of critique in other Chaucerian works, its expression of a cultivated sensibility displayed in the appreciation of beauty might seem to fit in perfectly with the Knight's aristocratic ethos. But the function of Emily's beauty in the narrative, and the political and ethical ramifications of that function, complicate matters. It is precisely the combination of alluring beauty and self-enclosure we see in the portrait that so captivates Palamon and Arcite, leaving them in awe before a figure whose perfection and inaccessibility seem to Palamon in particular to make of her something divine; and that erotic captivation marks the Theban cousins as both ethically and politically suspect, lacking in Thesean self-command and in need of ordering by outside rule. Theseus, meanwhile, achieves his self-mastery partly by renouncing erotic passion, mocking the young lovers for their folly in being ruled by love, and declaring himself a follower of Diana, goddess of chastity. For the Knight, then, Emily's beauty has two quite different functions which tug his aristocratic ideal in incompatible directions. On the one hand, Emily's beautiful, divine perfection makes her such a ravishing object of desire that love for her becomes the engine of fratricidal conflict, a source of social and psychic disorder so powerful that it apparently cannot be allowed a place in the life of the ideal noble man. On the other hand, Emily's status as an aesthetic object makes her beauty something the Knight both admires and sees as a site for the display of a connoisseurship coextensive with chivalric refinement. Even Palamon and Arcite's abject and violent love for her, while represented at times as imprudent and silly, both provides the Knight's plot with its driving engine and final destination and retains a strong touch of glamour, a sense that erotic passion can more powerfully shape a world worth staking one's life on than Thesean deliberation ever could.

One way of putting the Knight's problem here is to say that what I have been calling aristocratic formalism actually means two distinct things, however important each may be to a sense of chivalric identity. One thing it means is a belief in the ethical and political efficacy of proper form, a belief exhibited in the tale by the formal hierarchies of value that allow Theseus to order his own will and by the political hierarchy that allows him to order the collective will of the *polis*. The other thing it means is the love of a formalized beauty that reflects the beauty of the divine and calls the subject ecstatically out of itself, remaking one's sense of oneself and the terrain of one's desire and action. These two aspects of aristocratic formalism can function in tandem with each other, as when a beautiful aesthetic object serves to link a particular ethical and political order with the ideal of a divinely ordered cosmos. That at least is what Theseus's amphitheatre is *supposed* to do, even if its success at pulling off the trick remains highly questionable. But the two aspects of aristocratic formalism can also tug against each other, as they do in the tale's representation of erotic desire. When that happens, the conflicts internal to aristocratic ideology become more visible, and the pressure to declare a solution, however illusory, becomes more powerful.

The Knight's most comprehensive attempt at such a solution comes in Theseus' long speech on the divine Prime Mover of the cosmos, which effectively ends the tale. The goal of the speech is pragmatic. Theseus wants to offer consolation for the death of Arcite that continues to haunt Athens, and he wants to do that partly because, with Arcite's death out of mind, he could marry Emily to Palamon and thus cement an alliance with Thebes. The principal conceptual support for both goals comes from a cosmic formalism that is the metaphysical counterpart to the aesthetic, ethico-political and erotic formalisms we have already discussed:

> The Firste Moevere of the cause above,
> Whan he first made the faire cheyne of love,
> Greet was th'effect, and heigh was his entente.
> Wel wiste he why, and what thereof he mente,
> For with that faire cheyne of love he bond

> The fyr, the eyr, the water, and the lond
> In certeyn boundes, that they may nat flee. . . .
> Thanne may men by this ordre wel discerne
> That thilke Moevere stable is and eterne.
> Wel may men knowe, but it be a fool,
> That every part dirryveth from his hool,
> For nature hath nat taken his bigynnyng
> Of no partie or cantel of a thyng,
> But of a thyng that parfit is and stable,
> Descendynge so til it be corrumpable.
> (2987–3010)

The universe, like the ideal polity Athens represents, is a harmonious whole, unified in its purposes by the will of a Prime Mover whose ruling power is shown to be rightful by the wisdom and beauty of his designs. The analogy between the divine Prime Mover and Theseus, 'arrayed right as he were a god in trone' before his amphitheatre, is supposed to provide Thesean polity with its ultimate guarantee. Further, the idea that the nature of every created thing lies in the divine whole from which it came is supposed to make mourning for the dead seem foolish: all that has happened to Arcite is that he has returned from the lower state of corruptible materiality to the higher one of participation in divine stability and eternity. In these two arguments the two aspects of aristocratic formalism are supposed to merge seamlessly. For here we have both a formal hierarchy that governs all value and provides order to the collectivity of the cosmos and a beautiful perfection that calls to us as the truth of our desire.

But even Theseus cannot maintain this vision for long. As he casts about for examples of finite material substances being ecstatically called back to the divine source of their being, what he sees is less a beautifully ordered cosmos than a world haunted by death and dissolution. The oak that lives so long is finally wasted, the stone under our feet is worn away, the broad river goes dry, great towns wane and men and women must die, the king as well as the page. Such reflections can have a consolatory effect of their own, but it is the consolation found in the thought that we might as well accept our fate since the world will go this way whether we like it or not: 'heer-agayns no creature on lyve, / Of no degree, availleth for to stryve' (3039–40). The idea that death is a horrible fate we cannot control is quite another thing from the idea that death offers reunion with the source of our true being and the principle and guarantor of cosmic order. When this further notion of consolation is translated onto the political sphere for which the cosmic one is supposed to provide an analogy, the justification of Thesean polity suffers a similar embarrassment. It is one thing to say that Athens, unlike Thebes, is a rationally ordered polity governed by a ruler whose wisdom, justice and mercy justify his absolute power, and quite another to say that the reason to obey him is that resistance to his will, however terrible and destructive, is futile. The speech thus remains suspended between a sense that the cosmic and political orders ought to mirror each other in a way that would reveal their rightness, and a sense that those orders are supported merely by the brute power of those they serve. The Knight may want Theseus's

Prime Mover speech to resolve the contradictions in the chivalric ethos, but the ultimate effect of the speech is to make those contradictions all the more evident.

Gender and Exchange in the Wife of Bath's Prologue

Let us turn now from the aristocracy to that enormous range of English society classed as the third estate, but comprised of so much more both demographically and ideologically than can be captured by the image of the feudal agricultural labourer. One reason for the expansion of the kinds of people and social relations included in the third estate was the spread of commodity exchange and a money economy throughout late medieval English society, beyond mercantile centres such as London into the farthest reaches of the English countryside (Keen 1990: 27–128). As a cloth-maker, the Wife of Bath is a rural small commodity producer, and as such a member of what some critics and historians have seen as the most dynamic segment of the English economy (Patterson 1991: 247–54, 324–33). One impact of this social position on the Wife lies in the way the trope of economic exchange governs much of her thinking about marriage, sexuality, friendship, gossip and social relations more broadly. Her husband, she tells us, 'shal be bothe my dettour and my thral' (155), making 'his paiement / . . . [with] his sely instrument' (131–2). The notion of debt here is partly that of the Pauline 'marital debt', the obligation spouses have to each other to make themselves sexually available, in order to preserve their partner from the burning of an unfulfilled desire that might drive them to the sin of extramarital sex. I will return to this notion later. For now I want to focus on the economic aspect of debt, in which sexual 'payment' is an attempt to balance the books of marital exchange. The Wife's claim here is that such exchange always redounds to her profit. Her husband 'shal it have both eve and morwe' (152), and however much 'payment' he may make in return, he remains perpetually her debtor, reduced to little more than sexual servitude. At other points in the text, however, the Wife gives voice to a more defensive sense of the politics of sexual economy. She angrily reports, for instance, her husbands' complaints that, while they can assess the value of almost any commodity they plan to purchase, they are not allowed to do so with their wives until it is too late (cf. 285–92). Whether or not the Wife can claim the advantage in her marital exchanges, then, she knows that such acts participate in a broader cultural imaginary in which the equation of women with commodities to be evaluated and exchanged by men is at least the object of male fantasy, if not quite – at least as she describes it here – a positively achieved social reality.

The idea that a commodified feminine body bears the burden of sexual exchange in the Wife's experience is borne out by a particularly moving passage in which she describes the strategy by which she seeks power over and profit from her husbands:

> Namely abedde hadden they meschaunce:
> Ther wolde I chide and do hem no plesaunce;
> I wolde no lenger in the bed abyde,

If that I felte his arm over my syde,
Til he had maad his raunson unto me;
Thanne wolde I suffre hym do his nycetee.
And therefore every man this tale I telle,
Wynne whoso may, for al is for to selle;
With empty hand men may none haukes lure.
For wynnyng wolde I al his lust endure,
And make me a feyned appetit;
And yet in bacon hadde I nevere delit.
That made me that evere I wolde hem chide.
(407–19)

By chiding and withholding herself sexually until her husband 'maad his raunson' to her, the Wife drives up her value from that of an already paid-for commodity to a partner in exchange, and moreover the partner on the 'wynnyng' or profitable side of the exchange. But while her proto-capitalist sense of the economics of scarcity and of the principle that 'al is for to selle' allows her to tip the balance of marital power in her favour, it also has its price. Although the passage begins with her chiding her husbands as part of her marital strategy, it ends with her chiding because she is disgusted at 'bacon', the shrivelled old husbandly meat that never gave her pleasure, and angry that her path to profit requires her to endure his desire and perform a sexual appetite she doesn't have. This disgust and anger suggest that the very means by which she hopes to claim back what the commodification of women has taken from her leaves her feeling polluted, frustrated and compromised. Profit of a kind there may be for her here – this is, after all, the way she gets power, money and land from her husbands – but she seems less than sure that such gains outweigh what she has traded away.

To understand just how much she has traded away, and in what terms, we need to expand our scope beyond questions of commodification and exchange, to include a broader look at the ideology of gender difference that finds expression throughout the Prologue, and indeed throughout much of the *Canterbury Tales*. This ideology, which has roots in clerical, philosophical, political, medical and literary discourses, organizes masculinity and femininity around an almost indefinitely large group of parallel oppositions, among them those between form or idea and materiality, soul and body, activity and passivity, rationality and desire, duty and pleasure, textual and cultural authority and personal experience, interpretation and text, and public and private.[3] The masculine is identified with the first term in each opposition, which is figured as morally or politically or even metaphysically superior to the second, which is identified with the feminine. As with the commodification of sexuality, while this antifeminist imaginary powerfully shapes the Wife's self-understanding, she does not merely allow it to dominate her, but rather seeks to turn it to her advantage. In the present case, that means systematically and often quite brilliantly reversing the poles of value in the structuring oppositions. Her own experience, she declares, authorizes her speaking voice in a way that transcends the claims of textual and cultural authority: 'Experience, though noon auctoritee / Were in this world, is right ynogh for me / To speke of wo that is in mariage'

(1–3). Further, she links her self-authorizing experience to a pleasurable body that becomes the source of narrative: 'My joly body schal a tale telle' (1185). Compared to the authenticity of the Wife's experience, clerical authority becomes little more than a deceptive and somewhat comical 'glossing', a thin patina of self-deception and outright lies that can never really efface the bodiliness and sexual pleasure it treats with such suspicion:

> Glose whoso wole, and seye bothe up and doun
> That they were maked for purgacioun *i.e., human genitals*
> Of uryne, and oure bothe thynges smale
> Were eek to knowe a femele from a male,
> And for noon oother cause – say ye no?
> The experience woot wel it is noght so.
> (119–24)

While keeping the terms of the masculinist gendered imaginary more or less intact, then, the Wife reclaims the pleasures of sexuality and the body as legitimate ends of married life rather than impediments to ideality, reason and duty, and in so doing she seeks to redeem the femininity she continues to associate with those ideologically denigrated terms.

The Wife's reclaiming of feminine experience, the body and sexual pleasure, like her pursuit of marital power through a commodified sexuality, involves one of the fundamental strategies of the oppressed: in each case, she takes the tools and terms of an oppressive patriarchy and turns them around on the oppressors. If the Wife's ability to do so suggests that patriarchal ideology is not a single and stable package of ideas, values and social relations, the instability of that ideology, and its consequences for the subjectivities of those who inhabit it, become even more palpable when we bring the two aspects of the Wife's strategy to bear on each other, and particularly when we attend to the place of the body in each. As we have seen, the Wife understands the body to be the ground of her identity and voice, the source of a self-authenticating experience that can counter the claims of masculine authority. At the same time, however, she understands the body, particularly in its sexual functions, to be a commodity, something whose use can be bought and sold, and therefore something essentially alienable, and even alienated, from her. This second aspect of her conception of the body, in which it is anything but a ground of identity and authenticity, comes across in a cluster of equally alienated terms she uses to represent her and her husbands' genitals: 'instrument' (149), 'harneys' (136), 'thing' (121), 'quoniam' (608). The body and sexuality, then, are sites of a more complicated and ambivalent set of attitudes for the Wife than may at first appear. While she clearly wishes to reclaim sex from the clerical horror of it, the necessity she faces of making use of a commodified sexuality, and of feigning a sexual appetite in doing so, distances her from what she otherwise sees as the principal site of her pleasures, and places her uncomfortably on the side of the falsifying 'glossing' of sexuality that opposes the frankness she so greatly values.

The price of the Wife's strategy for marital profit and power, then, is that she must trade away the very thing she takes to be the ground of her autonomy from the 'auctoritee' of her culture's antifeminism. In making this deal she finds herself in a commodified and instrumentalized body rather than a self-authenticating one. Even here, however, the Wife does not become a pure victim of patriarchy, for her alienation from the body brings with it another kind of defence from objectification. If her body is merely a commodity or instrument rather than something essential to her identity, then, when her husbands wish to assay her like an ox or wash-basin, perhaps their objectification of her reaches no further into her than the 'thing' with which they equate her. The same holds for her disgusting contact with husbandly 'bacon': perhaps all that happens there is that she allows her husbands the use of a thing that remains external to her, and *she* never really has to endure their desire. Perhaps, that is, she remains *inside* her body, wielding it like an instrument and selling its sexual use like a commodity, but all the while remaining in an interior privacy that her husbands can never touch. This, too, would have its costs, since insofar as she is detached in this way from the body's sufferings, she is detached as well from the pleasures she so wants to embrace. But at least she would be intact and unpolluted, and could in that sense claim victory over a patriarchy that demands her for its own uses.

The Wife's imagination of an instrumentalized and commodified body, then, however much it participates in her objectification, is also the locus of a desire for autonomy, for freedom from what an antifeminist culture and the men who make it want from her and take her to be. Yet even here we see signs of how flexible ideology is, how it manifests itself in contradictory ways that render it no less powerful for its incoherence. For in the Wife's desire for an autonomy that finds expression in tropes of intactness and freedom from violation, and that entails a withdrawal from and even disgust at sexuality, we can perceive another aspect of medieval antifeminism: the theological ideal of an autonomy that demands sexual renunciation and locates as one of its dominant emblems the intact virginal body, an ideal for which Paul is one of the major voices, and which informs the ideological compromise enacted by the notion of the marital debt we encountered earlier in this discussion. Of course the Wife is hardly an active proponent of such an ideal, and in fact she makes it one of her principal targets throughout her Prologue. But ideology does not reduce to a set of explicitly held positions, and the subject-positions of those who inhabit any given ideology are always rife with tension and contradiction. Far from being a sign of ideology's weakness, this is what makes it so flexible and persistent, capable of manifesting itself in so many different common-sense worlds, social formations and political agendas.

Perfection and Pollution in the Pardoner's and Parson's Tales

While my discussions of the Knight's Tale and the Wife of Bath's Prologue have focused on ideological issues concerning class, economy and gender, in each text those topics have opened into a further Chaucerian interest in ideals of ethical perfection and moral purity, and adjacent anxieties about ethical failure and moral pollution. These concerns have a long history in Judeo-Christian culture, and Chaucer took a particularly keen interest in them. I will conclude by turning more directly to this concern in two of the *Tales*, those of the Pardoner and the Parson. Since both tales are told by members of the clerical estate, this focus will also allow us to touch on the question of Chaucer's relation to ecclesiastical structures and religious authority.

By the late Middle Ages, the Church had for some time been plagued by widespread incompetence and corruption, and a constant sense that it was in need of some sort of radical reform if it was to live up to its appointed mission. Medieval culture produced many expressions of this sense of crisis and call to reform, including in England the radical critiques of Wyclif and the Lollards, the more ambiguous charges levelled in Langland's *Piers Plowman*, and the continual self-criticism and efforts at reform of the Church itself.[4] One of the hotspots for a sense of pervasive corruption was the practice of selling pardons and indulgences. In its ideal form, this practice was not really a case of 'selling' something at all. Rather, someone would make a charitable contribution to the Church, and the moral rectitude and religious concern shown in doing so would have the fitting consequence of lessening the period of the afterlife spent in Purgatory for the sins that even the most dedicated souls commit. Almost inevitably, however, the practice became a system for buying off sinful behaviour, and even for purchasing in advance the freedom to commit sinful acts. The gesture of religious and moral commitment thus became hard to distinguish from a *mere* gesture whose real motivation lay in sinful desire. Under such circumstances it is not surprising if those who found themselves called to the vocation of pardoner were often somewhat less than paragons of just conduct and religious devotion.

Chaucer's Pardoner exemplifies the corrupt excesses to which this practice could lead. A self-described con artist, he plays to his audience's vices and superstitions, offering them, in addition to pardons, bogus relics for which he claims magical powers, such as the shoulder bone of a holy Jew's sheep whose water will bring a man prosperity and allow a woman to sleep with all the priests she wants without her husband mistrusting her (350–71). The Pardoner is also a talented preacher, skilled at inducing his audience to weep for their sins – and line up to purchase the pardons he sells. All the while, as he repeats again and again in a gleeful display of his own corruption, he only pretends to care for the souls of those to whom he ministers; his holiness is pure hypocrisy, for 'myn entente is nat but for to wynne, / And nothing for correccioun of synne' (403–4). Yet, as a number of critics have argued, the eagerness and theatricality of the Pardoner's self-accusations suggest that his claim of being a hypocrite is something other than the sincere revelation of an inner truth. The Pardoner has some serious moral and religious concerns, which the loud profession that he cares about nothing but money dissimulates but cannot finally silence (Dinshaw 1989: 156–84; Patterson 1991: 367–421).

Among the places those concerns appear is an apparent digression on gluttony near the beginning of his tale (498–549). The passage revolves around a citation from Paul's first letter to the Corinthians: 'Mete unto wombe, and wombe eek unto mete, / Shal God destroyen bothe' (522–3). The context in Paul is a concern with autonomy, given particular force by the thought of an impending judgement: 'I will not be brought under the power of any. Meat for the belly and the belly for the meats, but God shall destroy it and them' (1 Corinthians 6: 12–13). The immediate purpose of the citation seems to be a cautionary one, alerting us to the moral danger inherent in being a creature that has to eat to survive, and that can, as a result, become a slave to natural necessity in a way that shows an improper appreciation of our ultimate destiny. The problem, for both Paul and the Pardoner, concerns the morally fastidious attitude towards the life of nutrition, and towards the human body more generally, encouraged by the intimation of a divine destruction of food and the stomach – a destruction of the body, as Paul has it later, that is sown in corruption, and its replacement by a nearly unimaginable body raised in incorruption, freed from, among other things, the process of digestion and the production of waste. This intimation all but implies that the very thing that keeps the human creature alive in its current condition, the assimilation of food, binds it to corruption, that is to a decay and death that can be traced to a state of collective moral deprivation and guilt by which we are enslaved.

The Pardoner responds to these Pauline intimations and the imperative of ethical perfection they express by calcifying them into a bewildered disgust aimed much more squarely at the sheer need for food than Paul would ever condone. In the lines preceding his citation from Paul, the Pardoner's ostensible target is gluttony, albeit a gluttony which he somewhat unconventionally elevates to the status of the primal sin: 'O glotonye, ful of cursednesse! / O cause first of oure confusioun! / O original of oure dampnacioun / . . . Corrupt was al this world for glotonye' (498–504). In the lines that follow the turn to Paul, however, what began as a critique of a particular, identifiable sin opens into a wild bodily imaginary fixated on disgust. When the Pardoner says of the drunkard that 'of his throte he maketh his pryvee' (527), he imagines the mouth, the opening through which drink pours into the throat, as an opening into a receptacle for waste, perhaps like the opening of the 'pryvee' itself, or perhaps like the bodily orifices through which urine and excrement pass. This collapse of upper and lower orifices and of food and waste continues as the Pardoner moves to the stomach: 'O wombe! O bely! O stynkyng cod, / Fulfilled of dong and of corrupcioun! / At either end of thee foul is the soun' (534–6). Here, the sounds that emanate from mouth and anus are conflated into a general foulness, and the stomach, the site for the digestion of food and the production of vital energy, becomes a sack of dung and corruption, as though the maintenance of life were not merely inseparable from but *indistinguishable* from the production of waste and death. The association of food with waste and death gets articulated further as the Pardoner comments on the efforts of cooks to make food pleasing to the palate: 'Thise cookes, how they stampe, and streyne, and grynde, / And turnen substaunce into accident / To fulfille al thy likerous talent!' (538–40). Substance and accident are technical terms from classical and medieval metaphysics: a substantial quality of a thing is a feature of a thing that helps make it essentially what it is, while an accidental quality of a thing is a feature of it that could change without changing what that thing essentially is. In making food tasty, cooks are destroying its essential nature, putting it through a process of metaphysical degeneration. In becoming pleasurable to eat, it has lost its nature as food. Pleasure and the taking of nutrition have now begun to seem irreconcilable. The consequences of this thought get expressed in the Pardoner's final comment in the passage, that 'he that haunteth swich delices / Is deed' (547–8). To live in such a way – and it ought to be unclear what 'in such a way' means, that is, whether this passage is directed towards gluttony considered as a particular sinful condition of some people, or towards the condition we are all in as human animals who naturally enjoy fulfilling our animal needs in pleasurable ways – to live 'in such a way' is to be spiritually dead, a kind of walking corpse deprived of contact with the divine source of life. Ultimately, such a picture of the human creature as deprived of its divine essence by its own natural needs lies behind the text's conflations of mouth and anus and food and waste. Taken to its logical extreme, the Pardoner's thought here is that there is no possibility for the taking of sustenance that is not simultaneously the assimilation of waste, the propagation of a living death.

I claimed earlier that the Pardoner's hypocrisy is a theatrical posture rather than the sincere revelation of an inner truth. The literalizing hyperbole of the Pardoner's disgust and the Pauline drive to moral purity that informs it can help us see why he would want to adopt this posture, why the thought of his hypocrisy is, perhaps surprisingly, a comforting one for him to have. The idea of hypocrisy tries to make sense of moral failure by relying on a clean split between a person's interior motives and their outward expressions: a hypocrite is someone who acts in one way while thinking and feeling something else. What is so powerful and disturbing about the Pardoner's disgust, however, is the way it violates boundaries between inside and outside, both literally, in its relocation of privy and excrement inside the body, and metaphorically, in the way the Pardoner's talk of gluttony expresses his sense of humans as infatuated with our own moral excrement, that is as attached to what should be driven outside the self by our love of God. The Pardoner's idea of himself as a hypocrite functions as a way of denying this frightening collapse of inner and outer, and of denying that the ultimate concerns behind that collapse matter to him. If he is a hypocrite, he only pretends to share Paul's moral and religious motivation. More importantly, the idea of hypocrisy reclaims for the Pardoner an unproblematic relationship to his own interiority, re-establishing the transparency of a singular intention and a will under his own control. The Pardoner's hypocrisy is thus not merely a show he puts on for the other Canterbury pilgrims. His is an inner theatricality as well, an attempt to stage for himself an identity not riven by the claim on it of an unrealizable perfection.

I have been discussing the Pardoner's Prologue and Tale as giving disoriented and anxious expression to the impossible demands of a perfectionist ideology that has had powerfully normative force in Christianity from its beginnings. One way to see how close to the norm the Pardoner actually is here is to note some similarities between his moral imagination and that of the Parson, perhaps the most idealized clerical figure on the Canterbury pilgrimage. This will enable us to close this essay by saying something as well about the question of Chaucer's religiosity and the ending of the *Canterbury Tales*. The Parson's Tale, as the last of the *Tales*, is often thought of as standing outside the Canterbury tale-telling game. The Parson explicitly rejects rhyme and the telling of fables, offering instead a moral and religious lesson, and his tale is followed immediately by Chaucer's retraction of his fictions, or at least of those that are 'enditynges of worldly vanitees' (1084). Does the Parson's Tale thereby encapsulate Chaucer's own judgement on the Canterbury pilgrimage, and even on his own poetic project?

The Parson's Tale is by genre a penitential manual, a handbook for layfolk designed to aid them in the reflection necessary for effective confession and penance (Patterson 1976: 331–80). Among the many late medieval examples of the genre, the Parson's Tale shows a marked impatience with the narrative exempla and poetic forms that often mediate such texts' moral and religious lessons. As the Parson says in taking up Harry Bailey's invitation to contribute to the Canterbury pilgrims' tale-telling,

> Thou gettest fable noon ytoold for me,
> For Paul, that writeth unto Thymothee,
> Repreveth hem that weyven soothfastnesse
> And tellen fables and swich wrecchednesse.
> Why sholde I sowen draf out of my fest,
> Whan I may sowen whete, if that me lest?
> (31–6)

This note of impatience with anything that might distract from 'soothfastnesse' accords with Chaucer's metaphorical use of the Parson's position as the *Tales*' final narrator. The day is late, the pilgrimage almost at an end, the destination draws near; and the Parson wants himself and everyone else to concentrate all of their attention on the goal of 'thilke parfit glorious pilgrimage / That highte Jerusalem celestial' (50–1). But if the Parson is a no-nonsense man motivated by a genuine concern with the care of souls, the pressure of that impending end and the judgement that attends it produces a moral hyperbole in the Parson's rhetoric that at times approaches that of the Pardoner. In his initial discussion of 'the causes that oghte moeve a man to Contricioun' (132), for instance, the Parson cautions that sinners, in reflecting on their misdeeds, should be careful to avoid doing so with delight. To drive home the point, he adds that sinners are 'foul and abhomynable, for ye trespassen so ofte tyme as dooth the hound that retorneth to eten his spewyng' (137). This is especially so for those who continue long in sinful habits, 'for which ye be roten in your synne, as a beest in his dong' (138). The association of sin with vomit and waste continues as the Parson warns beautiful women not to be 'a fool of hire body' (155): 'for right as a soughe wroteth in everich ordure, so wroteth she hire beautee in the stynkynge ordure of synne' (156). This is not the only kind of rhetoric the Parson uses, but he does return to it time and again throughout the tale, as though he thought that rubbing his audience's faces in their excremental sinfulness was necessary to keeping them trained on the beauty of the divine and the glory of the celestial pilgrimage. The issue for the Parson is not just the shortness of time. A citation from Bernard concerning the Last Judgement seems equally important: 'Ther ne shal no pledynge availle, ne no sleighte; we shullen yeven rekenynge of everich ydel word' (165). There are fewer clearer statements of the perfectionism of medieval

Christianity: we will be judged, that judgement will be for eternity, and every idle word will have to be accounted for. Under such circumstances, relying for motivation on the love of God and the natural desire in humans for participation in the joyous community of the blessed would seem to be too risky a proposition. At least for the Parson – and he is hardly alone in this – the consequences of failure weigh so heavily on moral life that he feels he must mobilize his audience, and by all rights himself as well, as much by fear and disgust as by the love that is supposed to be at the heart of the Christian message.

My point is not that the Parson is especially harsh or tortured, nor that Chaucer intends his tale as a critique of Christian ideology or the late medieval clergy. The Parson is not the Pardoner, the doctrine expressed in the Parson's Tale is fairly orthodox, and it may well approximate to what Chaucer, who never shows any particular attraction to Lollardy or other radical movements, himself believed. My point here is that religious and moral commitment no more reduce to a set of beliefs to which its subjects subscribe than do other forms of ideology. Even if Chaucer was a conventional late medieval Christian, he was capable of thinking critically and imaginatively about the difficulty of inhabiting Christian belief, and the ease with which its demands could tip over into moral fastidiousness and self-loathing. If the Pardoner exemplifies the full flowering of that tendency, the Parson exhibits its proximity to even the most idealized versions of vocational commitment.

See also: 2 English Society in the Later Middle Ages, 3 Religious Authority and Dissent, 4 City and Country, Wealth and Labour, 5 Women's Voices and Roles, 12 England and France, 16 War and Chivalry, 19 Love, 24 Literature of Religious Instruction, 32 *Piers Plowman*, 37 *Sir Gawain and the Green Knight*.

Notes

1 Johan Huizinga, *The Waning of the Middle Ages* (1924; repr. New York: Doubleday, 1954). See also Muscatine 1957: 175–90, Middleton 1984: 119–33 and Patterson 1991: 165–230.

2 Besides the discussions cited above, see Kolve 1984: 85–157.

3 Cadden 1993; Dinshaw 1989: 113–31; Patterson 1991: 280–321.

4 Keen 1990: 240–97; Aers and Staley 1996.

References and Further Reading

Aers, David and Staley, Lynn 1996. *The Powers of the Holy: Religion, Politics, and Gender in Late Medieval English Culture.* University Park: Pennsylvania State University Press. Attends to the ideological struggles within late medieval English religion.

Brown, Peter 1988. *The Body and Society: Men, Women, and Sexual Renunciation in Early Christianity.* New York: Columbia University Press. Account of how sexuality functioned as a cultural and metaphorical site for Christian thinking about autonomy, moral perfection and a redeemed sociality.

Burger, Glenn 2003. *Chaucer's Queer Nation.* Minneapolis: University of Minnesota Press. Relates Chaucer's interest in subject-positions that disturb conventional ideologies of gender and sexuality to the constitution of national and class identities in late medieval England.

Bynum, Caroline Walker 1991. *Fragmentation and Redemption: Essays on Gender and the Human Body in Medieval Religion.* New York: Zone Books. Topics include the sexualization and feminization of Christ, the somatic spirituality of women mystics, and scholastic theories of the relation between the body and personal identity.

Cadden, Joan 1993. *Meanings of Sex Difference in the Middle Ages: Medicine, Science, and Culture.* Cambridge: Cambridge University Press. Analyses the classical and medieval construction of 'masculine' and 'feminine', with special attention to medical and scientific discussions of reproduction, sexual pleasure, abstinence and gynaecology.

Dinshaw, Carolyn 1989. *Chaucer's Sexual Poetics.* Madison: University of Wisconsin Press. Analysis of the construction of gender and sexuality through tropes of reading and interpretation.

Fradenburg, L. O. Aranye 2002. *Sacrifice Your Love: Psychoanalysis, Historicism, Chaucer.* Minneapolis: University of Minnesota Press. Engages with Lacanian psychoanalysis to explore chivalric culture's constructions of love, sacrificial masculinity and the hyperbolized feminine love-object.

Howard, Donald R. 1987. *Chaucer: His Life, His Works, His World.* New York: Dutton. A critical biography of Chaucer that includes an evocative portrait of the social world in which he lived.

Keen, Maurice 1990. *English Society in the Later Middle Ages, 1348–1500.* Harmondsworth: Penguin. A wide-ranging and accessible social history of late medieval England.

Kolve, V. A. 1984. *Chaucer and the Imagery of Narrative: The First Five Canterbury Tales.* Stanford, Calif.: Stanford University Press. Close readings explore the ethos of each tale in relation to medieval visual culture.

Leicester, H. Marshall, Jr. 1990. *The Disenchanted Self: Representing the Subject in the* Canterbury Tales. Berkeley: University of California Press. Close readings of the Pardoner, the Wife of Bath and the Knight, informed by poststructuralism and psychoanalysis.

Middleton, Anne 1984. 'War by Other Means: Marriage and Chivalry in Chaucer.' *Studies in the Age of Chaucer: Proceedings* 1, 119–33. Discussion of aristocratic formalism and theatricality as essential to the ideal of a beautiful noble life.

Muscatine, Charles 1957. *Chaucer and the French Tradition.* Berkeley: University of California Press. Muscatine's formalist account of Chaucer's work in relation to French models continues to inform much critical work.

Patterson, Lee 1976. 'The Parson's Tale and the Quitting of the *Canterbury Tales*.' *Traditio* 34, 331–80. Examines the Parson's Tale in relation to the genre of penitential manuals and Chaucer's project in the *Canterbury Tales* as a whole.

—— 1991. *Chaucer and the Subject of History.* Madison: University of Wisconsin Press. Locates Chaucer's interest in subjectivity in the social history of late medieval England, with attention both to the historical construction of the subject and to medieval understandings of history as an analytical category.

Robertson, D. W., Jr. 1962. *A Preface to Chaucer: Studies in Medieval Perspectives.* Princeton, N.J.: Princeton University Press. This account of Chaucer as a didactic, moralizing poet stands in marked contrast to Muscatine's humanism, and for many years defined the terms for those who read Chaucer as a Christian poet.

Wallace, David 1997. *Chaucerian Polity: Absolutist Lineages and Associational Forms in England and Italy.* Stanford, Calif.: Stanford University Press. Analysis of Chaucer's engagements with the democratizing possibilities of associational politics, and his critique of political absolutism and philosophical and poetic idealism.

34

John Gower and John Lydgate: Forms and Norms of Rhetorical Culture

J. Allan Mitchell

John Gower (c.1330–1408) and John Lydgate (c.1370–1450) had very different careers – the one a wealthy landowner, the other a monk – and yet they shared a strong and self-conscious sense of vocation as public poets. Indeed, they often cast themselves as adamant truth-tellers and social reformers; each engaging energetically in the public sphere by pursuing topical issues and protesting current events such as church schism, revolt, heresy and war. Lydgate may be seen as heir to the 'Gowerian' *vox clamantis* – if not exactly as another lone voice crying out in the wilderness, then at least as an extremely concerned citizen.[1] Both attempt to speak truth to power, if sometimes at the behest of the powerful.[2] As a result, Gower and Lydgate may seem poles apart from Chaucer, who can hardly muster a comparable sense of mission. To be sure, such distinctions tend to overestimate the differences between the three poets, and it is not the purpose of this chapter to rehearse invidious comparisons. It is indeed worth recalling that in the fifteenth century Chaucer, Gower and Lydgate – identified as 'the fyrst rethoryens' by Osborn Bokenham[3] – were regularly praised for their eloquence. An expansive term covering not just formal elegance but also ethical and political sapience, eloquence provides an entryway into the difficulty and historical difference of Gower and Lydgate.

The aim of this chapter is to consider the theory and practice of eloquence in Gower and Lydgate. What I have called their shared vocation as poets derives from their assuming a sense of obligation and even entitlement as practitioners of secular rhetoric, participating as they do in forms of rhetorical culture that gave occasion to invent, improve, provoke, enable and judge the social order. In theory they join a tradition of public oratory deriving from Aristotle and Cicero, expressing venerable notions of rhetoric and *res publica* familiar to medieval writers. Rhetoric here has first of all to be understood as a pragmatic activity and attitude, a disposition towards words as much as a manner of disposing words. Gower and Lydgate both begin with the assumption that rhetoric is improving, humanizing, civilizing – not (or not *just*) artful embellishment. Such ideas survived in the handbooks of the ancients, but were also transmitted in thirteenth-century works of rhetorical and regiminal instruction such as Giles of Rome's *De regimine principum* and Brunetto Latini's *Livres dou trésor*. Here is how rhetoric, as a species of practical politics, is described in Brunetto's *Trésor*:

> that noble science which teaches us to compose and organize and say good and beautiful words, full of meaning, in keeping with the nature of the utterance . . . Without doubt we need it every day, and many things we can achieve merely by saying well the proper words, things we could not do through force of arms or any other means.[4]

The same complex of ideas can be found throughout the vernacular works of Gower and Lydgate. The *Trésor* is a source of the seventh book of the *Confessio Amantis* and probably informs the sixth book of Lydgate's *Fall of Princes*, to which I will return.

And yet in practice such exalted notions about the 'noble science' of rhetoric and the high calling of the rhetorician do not exhaust their meaning for either Gower or Lydgate. In their practical engagements with forms of rhetorical culture, more complex views of the craft emerge. I will examine exemplary instances where optimistic claims on behalf of eloquence are put under pressure by human ineptitude or powerlessness, or narrative complexity, and the contingencies of audience response. What is still not widely recognized is that alongside their clear moral stridency the poets express considerable ambivalence towards their rhetorical practice; they are mindful of its risks and rewards. At their best Gower and Lydgate are conscious of the available means of persuasion, but also of their liabilities; responsive to different audiences and communicative situations, but also vulnerable to their unpredictability; and sensitive to the pleasures of verbal artifice and the pressures they release, while also anxious about the duplicity it may foster. There are differences between Gower and Lydgate when it comes to rhetorical theory and practice, and I will note them in what follows; but both poets see rhetoric as holding promise for coping with vicissitudes and common vices, while unable to guarantee results. Coincidentally, Gower and Lydgate set forth their ideals by using the analogy of skilful and measured harping. Because they do not always find Gower's and Lydgate's didactic rhetoric congenial, modern readers may think of *harping* in its modern pejorative sense, but it is no small part of our critical labour to recover the rationale of this form of rhetorical culture. To begin with it may be useful to think of Gower's and Lydgate's rhetorical art as a means of communication rather than just description or self-expression. Rhetoric is an activity that seeks to engage audiences as potential respondents rather than (as is usual in modern fiction) voyeurs upon whom no clear responsibility is placed.

Gower's Problems of Persuasion

In *Confessio Amantis* (c.1390–3) Gower expresses optimism about rhetoric as a form of political discourse, and he does so by employing a favourite figure of rhetoric, the exemplum. Gower exemplifies his civic ideology with reference to two legendary harpists, the first Arion (in the prologue) and the second Apollonius of Tyre (appearing in the last book). Arion is invoked at the end of the polemical prologue, after the three estates have been harangued for sowing social division. The Latin annotation introduces Arion: *Hic narrat exemplum de concordia et vnitate inter homines prouocanda* (Here he narrates an exemplum about the stimulating of concord and unity among human beings).[5] The English verses express much nostalgia for Arion's music:

Bot wolde God that now were on — *would; one*
An other such as Arion,
Which hadde an harpe of such temprure, — *tunefulness (moderation)*
And therto of so good mesure
He song, that he the bestes wilde — *wild animals*
Made of his note tame and milde . . .
And every man upon this ground
Which Arion that time herde, — *heard*
Als wel the lord as the schepherde,
He broghte hem alle in good accord.
(1053–65)

The language of moderation and pacification signals the poet's characteristic concern with finding an antidote for the 'division' that plagues society. Gower is longing for a new Arion – perhaps a poet like himself (Yeager 1990: 237–44) – to cure the social ills of England. Harping is here bound up with assumptions about the capacity of eloquence to tame our refractory animal nature, produce social harmony and 'make pes wher now is hate' (1075). Related notions about the humanizing properties of rhetoric are elaborated later in the figure of another exemplary harpist, Prince Apollonius of Tyre, who plays his instrument with 'measure' and demonstrates his 'gentilesse' (8.767–89). He has been taken as an example of the good ruler (Peck 1978: 170), with his rhetorical competence ('Of wordes he was eloquent', 8.393) epitomizing all the most important princely qualities. The two harpists frame the *Confessio* and embody a rhetorical ideal.

But such idealism represents only part of Gower's thinking about rhetoric. Taken on their own, the examples might lead us to suspect the poet of wishful thinking insofar as he wagers social reform (*concordia et vnitate*) on the powers of rhetoric alone, and perhaps that is the point of these examples. His exemplary harpists exist in an idealized past, the new Arion precisely as a wish and Apollonius as a romance fantasy. There are grounds for thinking that Gower has a more nuanced view than we might at first suspect.

Gower speaks in his own strident voice in the prologue of the *Confessio*, while subsequent books are mediated though the equivocal impersonations of the fictional confessor Genius. A running question throughout is whether and how far to identify the poet with the priest, although when it comes to rhetoric the poet's views tend to become transparent. Genius identifies himself as a Ciceronian when he credits the great orator with teaching the original 'forme of eloquence, / Which is, men sein, a gret prudence'

(4.2651–2), and the identification of eloquence and prudence – made emphatic in the rhyming couplet – is recognizably Gower's own. Genius goes on to spell out the connections between rhetoric and right rule directly, in the seventh book of the *Confessio*, where the confessor becomes a surrogate for 'Aristotle' (and probably Gower). The book contains the earliest discussion of rhetoric surviving in English, covering some of the same ground as Brunetto (compare *Confessio* 7.1507–1640 and *Trésor* 3.1–78), Gower's main source for this part of the *Confessio*. But there are important differences. For one thing, Gower does not take up Brunetto's extended exposition of the parts of rhetoric. The truncated discussion in the *Confessio* ends with the example of the part Cicero played in the foiled Catiline plot against Rome. The example comes from Brunetto, and the Roman chronicle of which it is a part also frames Lydgate's rhetorical theory, as we shall soon see. In the *Confessio* Cicero and others are cited approvingly for speaking 'plein after the lawe' against Catiline, in contrast to Julius Caesar who attempted to arouse sympathy for the conspirator by using adorned 'eloquence' (7.1595–1628). Whereas in Brunetto Caesar's speech is parsed to illustrate a skilful use of rhetoric, Gower takes his 'eloquence' to demonstrate the duplicity of decorative speech. So rather than detail rhetorical forms and stratagems, Gower expresses disapproval of them.

But there is a more profound discrepancy between Brunetto's and Gower's discussions of rhetoric, and it has to do with their separate treatments of the divisions of the sciences (the *trivium*). The *Trésor* disposes the branches of human knowledge into the theoretical, practical and logical sciences, making rhetoric subsidiary to practical science. By contrast, Gower divides the parts of the human sciences into *theorique*, *rhetorique* and *practique* (7.30–53). Gower does a rare and astonishing thing by promoting rhetoric to a scientific category in its own right, seeing that previously it had only existed as a species of another science. The change represents the poet's view of the primacy of rhetoric as an elevated form of knowledge (Copeland 1992: 68–9). But Gower proceeds to make another change that is less auspicious for the status of rhetoric: the *Confessio* subordinates grammar and logic (i.e., dialectic) to rhetoric, three terms that had been on an equal footing in Brunetto's *Trésor*. With some patience we should be able to unpack the significance of this curricular adjustment within Gower's *trivium*.

Grammar and logic maintain their original, subsidiary position in the hierarchy of the sciences, but thanks to the promotion of rhetoric they stand in a new relation: they are placed under, instead of alongside, rhetoric. What are these subordinate sciences? According to the *Confessio* the discipline of 'Gramaire ferste hath forto teche / To speke upon congruite' (7.1530–1), while 'Logique hath eke [*also*] in his degre / Betwen the trouthe and the falshode / The pleine wordes forto schode [*declare*]' (7.1532–4). These are elliptical definitions, but one way to interpret them is to say that grammar provides for consistency of terms (resulting in *congruite*), while logic maintains integrity of thought (distinguishing *the trouthe and the falshode*). In making these related disciplines serve rhetoric, Gower's *Confessio* introduces a significant complication into the theory with consequences for the rest of what is said about rhetoric here and elsewhere. Rhetoric is no longer on a par with grammar and dialectic; they are instead instrumental to rhetoric. Gower is categorical: rhetoric is a verbal science that employs but is not bound to possess congruity or integrity. The issue is taken up in what remains of Book 7's discussion of rhetoric, and it points to difficulties scholars have often recognized in the construction of *Confessio Amantis* – the poem's apparent moral ambiguity or inconsistency.

Gower identifies the source of the problem himself. After putting grammar and logic in their place, Genius observes that rhetoric 'above alle erthli thinges / Is vertuous in his doinges, / Wher so it be to evele or goode' (7.1547–9). The sentence indulges in some momentary equivocation: 'virtue' here may be said to hover temporarily between its moral sense and some neutral sense (signifying mere power), only resolving into the latter meaning by the last line. If one experiences any such ambiguity here, then it is instructive. Just as the word *virtue* can be employed in two senses, so the *virtue* of words can be deployed for good or ill. Ulysses is then adduced as an example of rhetorical mendacity, for through his seductive eloquence he once persuaded Antenor to betray Troy (7.1558–64). Curiously enough, in the previous book of the *Confessio* Ulysses was cited as an exemplary practitioner: 'He was a worthi knyht and king / And clerk knowende of [*informed about*] every thing; / He was a gret rethorien' (6.1397–9). What are we to make of the discrepancy between these two examples? Looked at from the perspective of the seventh book, the favourable reference to Ulysses only serves to drive home the point that as a verbal skill rhetoric is morally neutral. Its *virtue* is its perlocutionary force, and it is a force that remains fundamentally independent of ethics. That has always been the charge brought against rhetoric: it is a sheer power of expediency.

Already we have seen Gower grappling with certain conceptual difficulties relating to his craft, and it does not take much searching to find examples of fraudulent or corrupting rhetoric in the *Confessio*. And yet it is also easy to find counter-examples. Indeed, one of the methods of the *Confessio Amantis* is to proceed by way of contraries or contraposition, as is evident in Gower's treatment of speech (Mitchell 2004: 74–6). Examples and counter-examples tend to multiply and are set in juxtaposition with each other in this poem, inviting and indeed compelling the reader to interpret. A string of examples in the third book is worth pausing over at this point, especially as they are limit cases about the efficacy of rhetoric. Here the practice of truth-telling raises difficulties for Gower's theory.

Genius introduces the discussion with the following prudent advice:

Sone, it is evere good to lere, *Son; learn*
Wherof thou miht thi word restreigne,
Er that thou falle in eny peine. *Before*
For who that can no conseil hyde, *counsel conceal*
He mai noght faile of wo beside, *fail {to obtain}*
Which schal befalle er he it wite, *before he knows it*
As I finde in the bokes write.

(3.724–30)

In support of the view that it is good to restrain the tongue there follow three exempla, the first being the Tale of Jupiter, Juno and Tiresias. Tiresias is called upon to judge between the god and the goddess whether men or women are 'more amorous' (3.745), and he decides 'withoute advisement [*consideration*]' (3.751) against Juno. For his verdict Tiresias is blinded by Juno, and in compensation Jupiter grants him the gift of prophecy. Truth-telling is both the cause and the effect of cruelty and suffering in this example, and a moralization follows concerning the necessity of 'hold[ing] thi tunge stille clos [*i.e., remain silent*]' (3.769). Next comes the Tale of Phebus and Cornide, an analogue of Chaucer's Manciple's Tale, in which a truth-telling crow – here called a 'fals bridd' (3.792) – informs Phebus about his wife's adultery. In revenge Phebus kills the bird and blackens its feathers, transforming the crow into a raven. The exemplum is directed against tale-bearing: 'Be war [*mindful*] therfore and sei [*say*] the beste, / If thou wolt be thiself in reste' (3.815–16). The third and last casualty of truth-telling is the nymph Laar, who tells Juno that Jupiter is having an adulterous affair, for which Laar loses her tongue and is consigned to hell. The moral: 'be thou non of tho [*those*], / To jangle and telle tales so, / And namely that thou ne chyde' (3.831–3).

Such monitory exempla exhibit typical habits of thought and potential ironies in Gower's (or Genius's) rhetorical practice, for besides the obvious fact that the voluminous *Confessio* hardly practises what it preaches in these instances, there are profound incongruities to reckon with. First, exemplary rhetoric is sometimes put to expedient rather than strictly moral ends: here discipline of the tongue eclipses moral considerations such as truthfulness or honesty, the assumption being that truth-tellers should weigh their own self-interest before saying anything at all. For indeed, in the first exemplum Genius says nothing against the treachery of Juno, and the moral so emphatically warns against unadvised speech that her brutality seems excusable. In the other two tales the real vice consists not in adultery, but in exposing adulterers.

A second set of issues relates to the fact that in the *Confessio* stated meanings regularly do not bring out everything that is significant in a given case. The focal interest of the previous examples is not hypocrisy, adultery or brutality but the question of when and how to give counsel. The monitory rhetoric is selective in its application, with the result that sometimes there seems to be a misalignment between the morals and the stories to which they are attached. Tiresias is an example of injudicious speech, but such a judgement seems beside the point if he is telling the truth; and anyway he does not seem to have had a choice whether to speak in the case. Where such incongruities are perceived, exempla can come across as crudely reductive. The labelling of the 'false bird' in the Tale of Phebus is perhaps a brazen example of the single-minded way the facts of the case are invented to suit the moral rather than the other way around.

To this point can be added the observation that the English moralizations are sometimes at odds with Gower's Latin annotations in the margins. For instance, in reference to Jupiter, Juno and Tiresias he writes: *Hic ponit Confessor exemplum, quod de alterius lite intromittere cauendum est* (Here the Confessor presents an instructive example how one must take care not to interfere in another's quarrel). The English generalizes the lesson of the exemplum so that it applies to incautious and contentious speech; the Latin specifies the danger of interfering in quarrels. Much attention has recently been paid to how (clerical) Latin and (lay) English compete with one another in the bilingual *Confessio*, resulting in either exegetical control over the lay vernacular (Copeland 1991: 202–5) or the vernacularization of clerical culture (Scanlon 1994: 247–9). However that may be, the present example seems designed to confuse those who would apply it one way or another – and so *ipso facto* misapply its good counsel.

Finally, exempla are sometimes in conflict with others in the *Confessio*, as observed earlier in reference to speech. The same vices that are tolerated in the foregoing tales about truth-telling are the ones cautioned against in other tales told, for example, against hypocrisy (the story of the Trojan Horse, 1.1077–225) and love-brokerage (the story of Echo, 5.4573–661).

For these and other reasons Gower has been suspected of undermining exemplary rhetoric in the *Confessio Amantis*. Are readers not invited to be suspicious of exempla for their literary and logical imperfections? Does the poet not simply expose the rhetoric as so much vain adhocery? Academic critics have for a long time faulted the rhetoric of exemplarity for its lack of congruity and integrity (which is to say, grammar and logic); because exemplification is such a common practice probably they are demanding more than is required of the phenomenon for it to be effective. Indeed, the main problems cited – expediency, incongruity and inconsistency – are not necessarily inimical to ethical deliberation. Recall that rhetoric is a practical art: it has a functionalist rather than normative orientation. John of Salisbury describes the exemplum as a rough-hewn and pragmatic device, serving 'more to persuade than to convince'. Even if exemplary rhetoric is reductive and even irrational, sometimes 'unsophisticated and straightforward ways of putting things are very useful'.[6] What it may lack in consistency or integrity the exemplum can make up in utility. This is not to say that all examples are created equal (that is, function equally). In the three cases about truth-telling from the *Confessio*, Gower is clearly provoking his audience to think *about* rather than simply *along with* the rhetoric. But insofar as the exempla provoke thought about truth-telling, they have already fulfilled their chief criterion of stimulating an ethical practice. Surely one indispensable lesson of prudent speech concerns its limits and effects, as is illustrated in the three exempla about the vulnerability of those who tell the truth. The tales convey their lesson by means of direct assertion but also indirectly in their equivocal rhetorical construction, for like the misunderstood prophet, the crow and the nymph, the exempla challenge us not to misconstrue their good counsel – if they possess any.

The *Confessio* exhibits a marked degree of internal tension and incongruity, but the heterogeneity of the work is unexceptional for a medieval poem. A recognizable ethical eclecticism informs this work so as to accommodate different audiences and circumstances. What the work ultimately depends upon is the prudence of its audiences as co-practitioners in the construction of meaning. Genius instructs his audience in the practice when he directs the lover to 'take that him thenketh good, / And leve that which is noght so' (8.260–1). But how does one know what it is good to 'take' or 'leve'? Gower is alive to the difficulty throughout the poem, and as we have just seen the poet expresses some strong reservations about audience reception. Think on the crow! But

Gower does not on that account throw his hands in the air, but rather offers those who seek virtue a practical solution in the Aristotelian doctrine of the mean (5.7641–3). Prudence consists in adjudicating and moderating extreme cases, discovering a middle way. With so many extreme cases in the *Confessio*, the doctrine has an obvious pertinence. Gower says that the *Confessio* itself goes the 'middle weie' (Prol. 13), taking on a mediating role, anticipating and entrusting to its audience the further ethical work of discovering the virtue of words. The main assumption of the doctrine is that the middle way is not some abstract and universal measure, but a relative mean (or meaning) that varies 'by comparison to us' (*Trésor* 153).

Lydgate's Theory of Practice

Like Gower, Lydgate starts from the assumption that rhetoric and right rule are intimately connected practices. And rhetoric is again likened to the music of the harp. Near the beginning of Lydgate's *Siege of Thebes* (c.1420–2) reference is made to the harpist King Amphioun who raised the walls of Thebes with the 'armonye [*harmony*] of his swete song' (203).[7] Amphioun appears in the discussion of rhetoric in Brunetto's *Trésor*, perhaps Lydgate's source for the reference. The effect of such enchanting harping is the building of a city, indeed a heroic civilization: the 'crafty speche' (226) of Amphioun stirs the first citizens 'Be on [*By one*] assent to make this cyté / Royal and riche that lich nowher noon [*i.e., having no rival*]' (238–9). Lydate's preoccupation with good governance and peacemaking – virtues associated with rhetoric – achieves its clearest expression in the concluding lines: 'I take record of kyng Amphyoun / That bylte Thebes be his elloquence / Mor than of pride or of violence' (286–8). According to Lydgate such eloquent harping signifies an allegiance to the order of words (associated with Mercury) rather than the sword (associated with Mars). Eloquent speech is here presented as a conciliatory and civilizing force. To be sure, the idealized vision of secular rhetoric must be set alongside historical examples given in the *Siege of Thebes* in which social harmony is not long sustained. One is invited to ask how Lydgate can persist in his belief when the sword repeatedly triumphs over the word (Simpson 1997). Problems of persuasion, to which we will return, are clearly on Lydgate's mind.

Lydgate's theory is elaborated in several places in his *Fall of Princes* (1431–8), a translation and amplification of a French version of Boccaccio's *De casibus virorum illustrium*.[8] The *Fall*, commissioned by Henry, Duke of Gloucester, recounts the lives of princes and their subjection to the vicissitudes of Fortune. In passages that are original to Lydgate in the first book (where he pays his respects to Chaucer), he waxes nostalgic about how poets once enjoyed the esteem of kings. He cites Julius Caesar who was enrolled in 'the scoole [*school*] off Tullius [*Cicero*]' (1.367), an example that leads to a flattering description of Gloucester and his charging Lydgate with the translation of Boccaccio. The juxtaposition suggests that Lydgate is himself nothing less than a new Cicero to a Caesar, not an utterly fanciful idea given statements elsewhere in the poem about the importance of his vocation and present commission. In the third book, for example, Lydgate has some verses commending poets for their industry and high office. He argues that poets should enjoy the patronage of kings, rather than having to beg for money and wine: 'Thei shold be quieet fro worldli mocioun [i.e., *relieved of worldly cares*]' (3.3839). In theory as in practice, Lydgate associates good writing with state power. That does not mean poetry and rhetoric are mere instruments of the powerful. Leading up to the discussion of patronage he speaks of the way poets convey their criticisms by means of indirection:

> Ther cheeff labour is vices to repreve — *chief; reprove*
> With a maner couert symylitude, — *certain covert*
> And non estat with ther langage greeve — *class (person of rank); grieve*
> Bi no rebukyng of termys dul and rude.
> (3.3830–3)

While it may at first appear that Lydgate is rehearsing a 'simple moralistic view of poetry' (Pearsall 1970: 233), or advocating a mollifying 'don't-rock-the-boat attitude' (Strohm 1998: 180), the poet is not yielding ground to the status quo. Like others, Lydgate recognizes the prudence of employing the 'couert symylitude'. Brunetto taught that when the subject-matter is unpleasant or the audience is 'predisposed against you . . . then you would have to have recourse to concealment' (*Trésor* 298). Lydgate expresses other notions beside these subversive ones, including the idea that rhetoric exists to uphold tradition and conserve institutions and disciplines. The fourth book has an original prologue in which writing is described a form of 'remembraunce' without which law, religion, philosophy and so on would cease to exist (4.1–154). To memorialize and monumentalize the past is one of the main functions of Lydgate's *Fall of Princes*.

But it is in the sixth book that Lydgate has the most to say about rhetoric. Here he rehearses familiar ideas, referring throughout to Cicero as the 'prince of elloquence' (e.g., 6.327) and twice invoking Amphioun (6.339, 3491). Some optimistic passages near the beginning of the book speak of rhetoric's civilizing and reformist function, as in the phrase 'eloquence rud peeplis to reffoorme' (6.385). But the book also shows Lydgate owning up to certain limitations and liabilities. The reference to Cicero as a 'prince of eloquence' is ominous in the context of the *Fall of Princes*, a portent that is borne out in an ensuing narrative chronicling the tragic downfall of the great Roman orator. Cicero is held in high esteem for his prudent and eloquent service to the republic (6.3130–50). His particular virtues are demonstrated in the judgement of Catiline (referred to above in the discussion of Gower's rhetorical theory), and also in the way he reconciles rulers and appeases enemies of the state. However, Cicero proves powerless before his own enemies: he was exiled twice and finally killed for exposing Antony's relationship with Cleopatra. Put alongside other references to the perils and persecutions of several great writers and orators (such as Seneca, Ovid, Dante, Boethius) found elsewhere in the *Fall*, Lydgate's remarks about patronage in the third book take on a different tenor. Clearly the republican poet will sometimes find himself more vulnerable because of his intimacy with power, as any rhetorician must recognize. This is not a special expression of Lydgate's private anxiety, of course, since here he is translating from the French. But in the first book the poet had drawn an original parallel between his own vocation and Cicero's, not a wholly propitious analogy after all.

The fate of Cicero leads logically to a defence of Ciceronian rhetoric, for the looming question becomes whether rhetoric fulfils its civic function. Lydgate, following his source again, turns to the hierarchy of the sciences in the latter half of the book, dividing human knowledge into the moral, the natural and the rational. The 'noble science' of rhetoric (6.3285), situated under the rational, aids ethical deliberation. Rhetoric 'weel shewes / What men shal uoide [*avoid*] & what thing vndirfonge [*undertake*], / And to that parti rethorik doth longe [*belong*]' (6.3295–7). Instructive differences now emerge between Gower's and Lydgate's treatments of rhetoric, for the science enjoyed a higher priority at the head of the *trivium* in the *Confessio Amantis*. Yet both poets agree on the practical benefits of rhetoric. What marks them out more sharply is the relative weight each gives to technical and stylistic matters, for unlike his predecessor Lydgate does not omit from his discussion the five parts of rhetoric. Gower, we recall, ignored that part of the *Trésor*. The difference is more conspicuous when we consider Lydgate's habitual description of rhetoric as 'sugared', 'aureate', 'coloured' or 'fragrant' (Ebin 1988: 19–48). He has in mind aesthetic and methodological considerations that were of less interest to Gower, who (as we have seen) takes Cicero's judgement of Catiline to illustrate the virtues of the plain-spoken orator against Caesar's embellished eloquence. Lydgate's 'poetical' impulses may now seem to stand out against the old 'rhetorical' ideology, reflecting a broader transition away from rhetorical science towards stylistics in late medieval culture (Copeland 1992: 73). However, it would be a mistake to polarize the two, since for Lydgate stylistic refinement and ostentation serve a basic civilizing purpose. He speaks of the great rhetors and writers Seneca, Cicero, Petrarch and Boccaccio as having acquired glory for their nations by refining and beautifying their respective languages. Chaucer is another vernacular poet who did his part to 'refourme [the English language] with colours of suetnesse' (1.278–9). Lydgate regularly protests that he is too dull to follow such august examples, but he is posturing (Pearsall 1970: 144–6). In fact he strives hard to 'sweeten' his rhetoric with aureate and archaic diction, florid digressions and catalogues, and a generally ornate and elevated style.

Lydgate is the more deliberately extravagant and dazzling poet by far, yet he nevertheless remains highly conscious of the problems and possibilities of verbal artifice. Several short didactic poems reflect on rhetorical situations and skills: some restate practical precepts of rhetorical theory, and in general they reflect a pragmatist's acknowledgement of the occupational hazards of rhetoric.[9] The *Debate of the Horse, Goose, and Sheep* reiterates the idea that fables employ similitudes and other forms of concealment to reprove tyrants (580–7). The opening of *Isopes Fabules* suggests fables may also have diverse applications depending on the disposition or 'lust' of the individual recipient (13). Lydgate's *Dietary* includes maxims such as, 'To every tale soone yif not credence' (105), sensibly imparted along with other rules of consumption and bodily nourishment. Several charming poems with epigrammatic refrains also reflect a rhetorician's pragmatism. *See Myche, Say Lytell, and Lerne to Soffar in Tyme* proffers worldly wisdom about restraining speech. *Consulo quisquis eris* is an adept if playfully exaggerated statement of one of the expedient first principles of rhetoric:

With hooly men speke of hoolynesse,	
And with a glotoun be delicat of thy ffare,	
With dronke men do surfetys by excesse,	*(i.e., speak excessively)*
And among wastours no spending that thou spare;	*wasters (spendthrifts)*
With woodecokkys lerne for to dare,	*woodcocks (game birds); hide*
And sharpe thy knyff with pilours for pilage;	*pillagers*
Lyke the market so preyse thy chaffare,	*price your wares*
And lyke the audience so vttre thy language.	*And according to; utter*
(17–24)	

Suiting the message to its audience has always been a requirement of rhetoric, an *ad status* principle set forth in the recurring last line. Some of the comparisons are more successful than others, and a few are pleasantly absurd such as the advice to be sleepy among the slothful and mad with madmen. The poet eventually interrupts himself and, retreating from the conclusions, urges that words should conform themselves to virtue. As an exercise in amplification by extended synonymy the poem works to drive home the point about being flexible and responsive, while also exploring the limits of such expediency. Elsewhere Lydgate is still more distrustful of the amphibious nature of rhetorical artifice. In *Say the Best, and Never Repent* the same rhetorical embellishments we have come to associate so closely with Lydgate are considered suspect: sweet rhetoric becomes a form of duplicity, as in the line about 'Sugurat gall [*poison*] with aureate eloquens' (11). Lydgate invented the term 'aureate' to describe what he values most in poetry (Ebin 1988: 25–8). One last instance to consider in this context is the self-referential *Ryme Without Accord*, in which the tensions between rhetoric and reason are embodied ironically in the poetry. The poem sets to rhyme and pentameter verse such discordant concepts as a cowardly knight, a false friend, a fighting priest and so on. Each stanza ends with a rhyming refrain, 'It may wele ryme, but it accordith nought', giving way in the last stanza to a desperate prayer – as if in flight from the inescapable paradox.

Like Gower, Lydgate can be circumspect about the intrinsic merits of rhetoric. His most compressed and witty exploration of the problem is the *Churl and the Bird.* The short fable, which bears close comparison with Gower's Tale of Phebus and Cornide and Chaucer's Manciple's Tale, is sceptical and self-referential about the prudence of proverbial moral rhetoric as such. The *Churl and the Bird* is said to have been translated out of the French from a 'paunflet [*pamphlet*] I radde & sauh but late' (35), though its exact source remains uncertain. It begins with hearty praise of moral rhetoric:

Problemys, liknessis & ffigures	*Riddles (Allegories), similitudes and figures of speech*

Which previd been fructuous of sentence,	*edifying*
And han auctoritees grounded on scriptures	*(i.e., possess authoritative doctrine)*
Bi resemblaunces of notable apparence,	
With moralites concludying in prudence.	
(1–5)	

There follows further description of the way poets use 'dirk parables' (16) and other figurative devices to convey their meanings stealthily: 'Poetes write wonderful liknessis, / And vndir covert kepte hem silf ful cloos [*themselves concealed*]' (29–30). Lydgate is describing common rhetorical techniques of indirection, concealment and similitude. At the same time he is announcing an interest in rhetorical theories that posit a *covert* sense veiled under *liknessis*, something that develops into a main theme of the fable. To understand the way this fable works it is necessary to proceed slowly, noting subtle shifts in meaning as the narrative progresses.

In the fable a churl traps a bird that regularly sings with 'soote [sweet] sewgred armonye' (73) from a laurel tree in his garden. Once captured she will not be constrained to sing, and demands to be set free with the promise that she will return every day to the tree. The bird argues that it is in her nature to be at liberty, adducing a theory of natural inclination also found in the Manciple's Tale. The churl threatens to roast the bird instead, in response to which she offers him three 'greete wisdames' (159) in exchange for freedom. The churl agrees and the bird flies to the laurel. But before proffering her 'wisdoms' she reflects on what she has just learned about traps and birdlime:

Eche man bewar, of wisdam & resoun,	
Of sugre strowid, that hidith fals poisoun;	*strewn*
Ther is no venym so perlious of sharppnesse,	*dangerous*
As whan it hath of triacle a liknesse.	*medicine*
(179–82)	

That sweet semblance (*liknesse*) may be treacherous becomes a major preoccupation of the fable, and it refers as much to the bird as to sugared birdlime, as we will see. The churl receives three proverbs from the bird: do not give credence to every tale you are told, do not desire the impossible, and do not grieve for lost treasure. The bird goes on to mock the churl for allowing her to escape, for she announces that concealed within the entrails of her body is a precious stone weighing one ounce: it is a golden jacinth that would have conferred upon the churl strength, riches, renown, beauty and peace. But the attempt to teach a churl the price of such a rare stone would amount to throwing 'perlis [*pearls*] whihte / To fore rude swyne' (256). For indeed, as she says, a sow will delight more in feeding her piglets chaff than precious fruit (257–9). Here another sense of 'likeness' and 'semblance' emerges, having to do with the way animal nature tends towards what is familiar and similar. There is another resonance here given the mention of pearls and fruit – both of them conventional symbols of eloquent and edifying speech. The citation from the Sermon on the Mount ('Neither cast ye your pearls before swine; lest perhaps they trample them under their feet; and turning upon you, they tear you', Matthew 7: 6) in which Jesus teaches his disciples not to squander their preaching on an unreceptive audience indicates that the bird is talking about sententious rhetoric. Is the stone in her body itself not an emblem of moral rhetoric? The bird has already implied the analogy. Looking back at the description of the jacinth one notices that its magical powers are some of the very virtues ascribed to eloquence by Gower and Lydgate:

> It causith love, it maketh men gracious
> And favorabil in euery mannys siht, *man's sight*
> It makith accord attween folk envious,
> Comfortith sorweful, makyth hevy hertis liht.
> (246–9)

The irony of the fable so far turns on the fact that the churl has unknowingly exchanged a jacinth of immeasurable worth for three lousy proverbs ('wisdoms'). The bird mocks the churl accordingly, saying that in desiring 'wisdam' he is like 'an asse that listeth on [*listens, heeds*] a harpe' (274–5). But the proverb is applied eccentrically. Instead of signifying insensibility towards wisdom, bizarrely the proverb is used to mock seduction *by* proverbial wisdom. Or is the stone an emblem of a higher wisdom that has been neglected for a lower? The bird's moral rhetoric is equivocal and epitomizes the recursive complexity of the fable where it touches the theme of covert meaning. It turns out that the jacinth is not what it seems (neither stone nor wisdom), for the bird reveals that there is no such magical substance hidden in her body. She was telling a fable! She chides the churl for mourning the loss of the imaginary stone, forgetting her original 'wisdomes': he should not have believed every tale he is told, nor should he have desired the impossible, nor lamented his lost treasure. The bird speaks of the futility of teaching such 'proverbis of substaunce' (310) to a churl, and reinvokes the proverbial ass to the harp, but this time in its traditional association with neglected wisdom (339–40). She complains again that everything returns to its natural order and semblance, for there is no escaping the inevitability of (churlish) human habits. The poet restates the bird's wisdoms in a final *verba auctoris*, applying them relatively straightforwardly to the fable.

Lydgate's ironic fable seems to erode the credibility of its own moral rhetoric, and indeed the *Churl and the Bird* plainly generates a crisis of belief. For one thing, the fable shows that the rhetoric is not always effectual, for proverbial wisdom does nothing to change the churl's behaviour. Moral rhetoric is wasted on fools, just the sort of people who need it most. And if so, then perhaps the *auctor* should be considered just as foolish for thinking the fable has any great consequence or moral substance. Has he not failed to learn from his own exemplum – about moral and rhetorical failure, after all – when he endorses the bird's three wisdoms? Maybe the fable should be read as nothing more than an amusing tale about a churl and a bird, to recall one description of Chaucer's Nun's Priest's Tale. The enchanting but absent stone figures the difficulty of whether the fable has a moral core or is void. Just as the bird's words lack substance, so the fable may have nothing concealed (*covert*) under its attractive plumage. What the bird finds particularly ridiculous is the churl's failure to notice that her body could never have contained a stone such as the one she described weighing one ounce: 'Al my body weieth nat an vnce [*not one ounce*], / How myth I than have in me a stoon, / That peisith [*weighs*] more than doth a grett iagounce [*jacinth*]?' (316–18). As is still the case today the language of weight and weighing – *peis* (noun) and *peisen* (verb) in Middle English – functions metaphorically to signify heavy or ponderous speech, giving weight or credence, or weighing in the balance and pondering. Due to the absence of the stone at the centre of the bird, should we not say the tale is similarly lightweight? Should readers beware of being tricked into thinking the fable has substance?

These are rhetorical questions that already suggest practical solutions. All the figurative senses of *peis* are relevant to the fable and point to its main concern with the application of moral rhetoric, but only because of the primacy of the literal sense: the original problem for the churl is a practical one of failing to recall the bird's bodyweight. Never mind the insides of the bird, he should have known by experience that she was telling a lie; the truth of the bird could have been accessed from the outside. Experience and exteriority point to the real locus of meaning in this fable, even for the audience of the *Churl and the Bird*. Meaning is conveyed through the *experience* of reading. To illustrate, consider the ironic way the bird restates the first proverb – 'Thou shuldist nat, aftir my sentence, / To euery tale yeue to [*give too*] hasty credence' (322). The bird's 'sentence' is a species of the self-referential statement (popularly known as the 'liar paradox') that medieval philosophers called *insolubilia*.[10] If we give credence to her rhetoric, we should doubt her; if we doubt her, we cannot help but give credence to her rhetoric. There is no way of accessing the *real* (or putative core) meaning. One way to look at the paradox is to say it is circular and self-consuming, as already suggested, emptying the bird's rhetoric of significance. But a more interesting and accurate account is that there is nothing more instructive: for whether you believe the bird or (perhaps especially) you do not, you cannot help but confirm her wisdom about the need for circumspection. In an analogous way, the fable is self-confirming despite – or rather, because – it is self-consuming. The *Churl and the Bird* is no straightforward negative exemplum instructing readers in how to avoid deception. The audience is in a much more precarious situation, weighed in the balance, tempted by sweet rhetoric, and subject to the play of exterior surfaces and semblances. Our credulity, tricked and tested, is exercised by insoluble circumstances. If that is a desirable practical result, then the fable may fulfil its rhetorical function.

The poem has a lapidary conceptual complexity that defies easy explanation or moralization, but it does not on that account cease to function exemplarily. Its meaning is not found 'inside'; it is rather derived, as it were, from the exterior surface of the tale. Equally, the tale resides at the edges of Lydgate's corpus. The *Churl and the Bird* has been called a 'parergon', an exception to the rule, lying outside the ordinary literary practices of the poet (Schirmer 1961: 37). The fable is an extraordinary and peripheral case. But it is also a *parergon* (Greek for 'outside the work') in the more important sense of being the rule of the exception, an example of exemplary rhetoric, something extra that comes to 'intervene in the inside only to the extent that the inside is lacking'.[11] Lydgate's inclusion of this exceptional example within his *oeuvre* is instructive: the fable is one of his most significant poems because it marks out the limits of his body of work.

See also: 8 Translation and Society, 14 England's Antiquities, 18 Images, 33 The *Canterbury Tales*, 35 Thomas Hoccleve, 36 The Poetry of Robert Henryson.

Notes

1 Gower's *Vox Clamantis* (c.1378–82) takes its title from the gospel description of John the Baptist ('the one who cries out'). The Latin *Vox* is the second of Gower's three principal works, composed after his French *Mirour de l'omme* (1360s) and before his mostly English *Confessio Amantis* (c.1390–3).

2 Gower's *Confessio Amantis* was originally dedicated to Richard II, but the poet would eventually rededicate the work to Henry of Lancaster. Lydgate's canon consists of over 145,000 lines of English verse written on various occasions and numerous subjects, some of it under municipal or royal patronage, earning for him something like the status of a national poet laureate. For instance, Lydgate's *Troy Book*, 1412–20, was made for Henry V. In this essay I will be discussing Lydgate's *Fall of Princes*, 1431–9, commissioned for Henry, Duke of Gloucester.

3 *Life of St Anne,* line 1403 (p. 38), in *Legendys of Hooly Wummen*, ed. M. S. Serjeantson, EETS os 206 (1938). I have preferred 'fyrst' to 'fyrsh' (fresh), an emendation made by an earlier editor of the work.

4 Brunetto Latini, *The Book of the Treasure (Li Livres dou Tresor)*, trans. Paul Barrette and Spurgeon Baldwin (New York: Garland, 1993), p. 5.

5 *The English Works of John Gower,* vols. 1 and 2, ed. G. C. Macaulay, EETS es 81–2 (1900; repr. 1979). Citations are taken from this edition throughout, with parenthetical references given in the text. Translations from the Latin are assisted by those of Andrew Galloway in the edition of Russell Peck, *John Gower: Confessio Amantis*, vols. 1 and 2 (Kalamazoo, Mich.: Medieval Institute Publications for TEAMS, 2000–3).

6 John of Salisbury, *Metalogicon* 3.10; trans. Daniel D. McGarry (Berkeley: University of California Press, 1962), p. 193.

7 *The Siege of Thebes,* ed. Robert R. Edwards (Kalamazoo, Mich.: Medieval Institute Publications for TEAMS, 2001); references to this edition are given in parentheses.

8 *Fall of Princes,* ed. Henry Bergen, EETS es 121–4 (1924–7; repr. 1967); parenthetical citations will be given in the text throughout.

9 *The Minor Poems of John Lydgate: Part II, Secular Poems,* ed. Henry Noble MacCracken, EETS os 92 (1934; repr. 1961); parenthetical citations will be given according to line numbers in the respective poems.

10 Fourteenth-century examples include Pierre d'Ailly's *Conceptus et insolubilia* (1372) and John Wyclif's *Summa insolubilium* (c.1350). See the article on *insolubilia* in *The Cambridge History of Later Medieval Philosophy: From the Rediscovery of Aristotle to the Disintegration of Scholasticism, 1100–1600*, ed. Norman Kretzmann, Anthony Kenny and Jan Pinborg; assoc. ed., Eleonore Stump (New York: Cambridge University Press, 1982), pp. 246–53.

11 Jacques Derrida, *The Truth in Painting*, trans. Geoff Bennington and Ian McLeod (Chicago: University of Chicago Press, 1987), p. 56.

References and Further Reading

Copeland, Rita 1991. *Rhetoric, Hermeneutics, and Translation in the Middle Ages: Academic Traditions and Vernacular Texts.* Cambridge: Cambridge University Press. Refers to forms of rhetorical invention in the works of Chaucer and Gower.

—— 1992. 'Lydgate, Hawes, and the Science of Rhetoric in the Late Middle Ages.' *Modern Language Quarterly* 53, 57–82. About the evolution of rhetorical theory in the fourteenth and fifteenth centuries, paralleling a transition from civic ideology to stylistics, exemplified in the works of Gower and Lydgate.

Ebin, Lois A. 1988. *Illuminator, Makar, Vates: Visions of Poetry in the Fifteenth Century.* Lincoln: University of Nebraska Press. Includes a chapter on the importance of eloquence and other rhetorical terms in Lydgate.

Echard, Siân (ed.) 2004. *A Companion to Gower.* Cambridge: Brewer. Essays on the life, legacy and literary output of the poet; has a bibliography of Gower scholarship.

Ferster, Judith 1996. *Fictions of Advice: The Literature and Politics of Counsel in Late Medieval England.* Philadelphia: University of Pennsylvania Press. Explores the theory and practices of advice-giving, with a particular focus on the slippage between morals and stories; see especially the chapter 'O Political Gower'.

Fisher, John H. 1964. *John Gower: Moral Philosopher and Friend of Chaucer.* New York: New York University Press. A comprehensive biographical and literary study.

Middleton, Anne 1978. 'The Idea of Public Poetry in the Reign of Richard II.' *Speculum* 53, 94–114. A landmark essay setting out the original idea of public poetry and the 'ideal of literary eloquence implicit in it'.

Mitchell, J. Allan 2004. *Ethics and Exemplary Narrative in Chaucer and Gower.* Cambridge: Brewer. Argues that exemplary rhetoric for these fourteenth-century poets expresses a flexible and improvisatory approach towards moral deliberation.

Olsson, Kurt 1992. *John Gower and the Structures of Conversion: A Reading of the Confessio Amantis.* Cambridge: Brewer. Interprets the poem as compilation of disparate material that defies moralization but acts as a moral stimulus.

Pearsall, Derek 1970. *John Lydgate.* London: Routledge and Kegan Paul. An influential early reassessment of the poetical and rhetorical competence of Lydgate.

—— 1992. 'Lydgate as Innovator.' *Modern Language Quarterly* 53, 5–22. Claims that the poet's stylistic innovations are coherent with his role as apologist for the Lancastrian regime.

Peck, Russell 1978. *Kingship and Common Profit in Gower's 'Confessio Amantis'.* Carbondale: Southern Illinois University Press. Progresses through each book of the poem, arguing that they are held together by the poet's preoccupation with good governance.

Scanlon, Larry 1994. *Narrative, Authority, and Power: The Medieval Exemplum and the Chaucerian Tradition.* Cambridge: Cambridge University Press. Includes a chapter on exemplary morality and so-called 'bad examples' in Gower's *Confessio Amantis*, and another on the idea of poetry in Lydgate's *Fall of Princes.*

Schirmer, Walter F. 1961. *John Lydgate: A Study in the Culture of the XVth Century.* London: Methuen. Originally published in German in 1952, this is the earliest general study and remains a useful account of the life and works of Lydgate.

Simpson, James 1997. '"Dysemol daies and fatal houres": Lydgate's *Destruction of Thebes* and Chaucer's *Knight's Tale.*' In *The Long Fifteenth Century: Essays for Douglas Gray*, ed. Helen Cooper and Sally Mapstone (Oxford: Oxford University Press), pp. 15–33. Sets idealistic notions of prudence and political rhetoric against their vulnerability in Theban history.

Strohm, Paul 1998. *England's Empty Throne: Usurpation and the Language of Legitimation, 1399–1422.* New Haven, Conn.: Yale University Press. Includes a chapter on Lydgate as an emergent and only partially successful Lancastrian propagandist.

Watt, Diane 2003. *Amoral Gower: Language, Sex, and Politics.* Minneapolis: University of Minnesota Press. Considers a variety of questions relating to rhetoric, erotic desire and politics in *Confessio Amantis.*

Yeager, R. F. 1990. *John Gower's Poetic: The Search for a New Arion.* Cambridge: Brewer. A wide-ranging study of the poetic styles and sensibility of Gower.

35
Thomas Hoccleve, *La Male Regle*

Nicholas Perkins

La Male Regle de T. Hoccleue (written sometime between late September 1405 and late March 1406) opens with a formal invocation to a god – or perhaps *the* God, we might think as we begin:

O precious tresor inconparable!
O ground and roote of prosperitee!
O excellent richesse commendable
Abouen all þat in eerthe be!
Who may susteene thyn aduersitee? *withstand*
What wight may him auante of worldly welthe, *man; boast*
But if he fully stande in grace of thee,
Eerthely god, piler of lyf, thow helthe?

(1–8)[1]

The final word of the stanza makes us reassess this prayer to an 'eerthely god'. Is 'helthe' an external agent or an inherent part of us? This ambiguity over how solid Hoccleve's imagined protagonists are – a slippage between the bodily and the figural – is one striking feature of his writing. The next stanza demands further readjustments:

Whil thy power and excellent vigour,
As was plesant vnto thy worthynesse,
Regned in me, and was my gouernour,
Than was I wel, tho felte I no duresse.
Tho farsid was I with hertes gladnesse. *stuffed*
And now my body empty is, and bare
Of ioie and ful of seekly heuynesse,
Al poore of ese and ryche of euel fare. *misfortune*

(9–16)

The first stanza's Latinate register ('inconparable', 'commendable', 'excellent', 'precious') is sustained, while the speaker remembers those good old days, but as the focus narrows

– from timeless apostrophe (stanza one) to the recent past ('Than') – and reality bites ('And now'), Hoccleve's verbal richness also drains away; the last line's elisions turn it into a series of monosyllables. We also learn something about the speaker: once 'wel', now sick. His 'empty' body and the contrast of 'poore' and 'ryche' cast the previous references to 'worldly welthe', 'precious tresor' and 'prosperitee' in a less innocent light: only one letter divides 'helthe' from 'welthe'. As a late medieval poem addressing a powerful lord from a situation of lack, this prayer to a god is also a petition (Burrow 1981; Perkins 2001: 34–8). The two genres are intimately connected, and Hoccleve is especially alert here to the vocabulary resonating in both arenas: 'grace', 'power', 'vigour', 'worthynesse', 'Regned', 'gouernour'. The roles of regulation and governance are indeed to be major themes here, transferable across religious, political and personal boundaries.

After the invocation, Hoccleve's *alter ego* describes the afflictions that he has suffered as a result of his wild youth. He was a regular in Westminster taverns, spending too much and flirting with girls, before catching a drunken (and ruinously expensive) ferryboat down the Thames to his lodgings near the Strand. He laments the malign influence of flattery, which deceived him and blinds those in authority to their failings. He then renews his appeal to 'helthe', asking him to give the Treasurer, Lord Furnival (the poem's real target), the wherewithal to pay Hoccleve his overdue annuity.

Hoccleve's *Male Regle* is only 448 lines long, and was written early in his poetic career, but crystallizes many of the problems, styles, genres and pleasures with which his poetry presents us. Hoccleve himself copied the poem into one of two manuscripts compiled towards the end of his life (now San Marino, Huntington Library MS HM 111; the other is MS HM 744). These collections contain begging poems to royalty and courtiers, religious lyrics, 'official' poems on public events, short ballades and rondels, and a reworking of the *Epistre de Cupide* by Christine de Pizan. Hoccleve's so-called *Series* (c.1420–1) appears in his distinctive handwriting in Durham, University Library MS Cosin V. iii. 9.[2] The *Series* is a collection of exemplary narratives framed by a conversation between the poet's *alter ego* and a friend, who argues with, criticizes and helps Hoccleve by fetching material for the project. Hoccleve's other major poem, *The Regiment of Princes* (1410–11), does not survive in his own hand, but two early presentation manuscripts are extant, along with over forty other copies, a few of which include the *Series* too. The *Regiment* is a 'mirror for princes' – an advice book for the future King Henry V – but is also a petition for payment and, along with obligatory flattery, contains warnings to the prince about the state of the realm.[3]

Hoccleve left one other substantial document: a collection of letters and rhetorical excerpts known as the Formulary (London, British Library MS Additional 24062). He compiled this while working as a clerk in the Privy Seal, a government office based in Westminster Hall dealing with royal correspondence, including petitions to the court. Hoccleve was born in 1366 or 1367, joined the Privy Seal in about 1387, and worked there until shortly before his death in 1426 (Burrow 1994). We know a good deal about his life and work, partly through references in bureaucratic documents (such as payment for ink, wax and parchment, and the much-delayed annuity), but also because he talks about himself in his poetry, especially his debilitating anxiety and lack of money.

External evidence mostly supports these revelations, but as interesting as their accuracy is the way that Hoccleve 'stages' his life in his writing. Hoccleve's life writing is not, to use J. L. Austin's influential terminology, merely 'constative' or descriptive of a fact, but 'performative' – designed to make something happen.[4] Petitionary writing, of course, is an especially acute example of performative language, but its success relies on the wit that it uses to mask or sweeten its uncomfortable message. Hoccleve's own persona is one of his principal resources in this poetry of display and diversion.

The Self Speaking and Writing

Hoccleve's poetry crackles with the spoken vernacular. His speakers are not rounded 'characters' – like Chaucer's, they act more as rhetorical devices or masks – but they talk in a vital and believably colloquial style. Their speech is peppered with proverbs, questions and sly word-play, and usually inhabits Hoccleve's regular ten-syllable metre with an easy fluency. Take this passage from the *Male Regle*, where Hoccleve describes the end of a heavy drinking session and the morning after:

> But whan the cuppe had thus my neede sped, *answered*
> And sumdel more than necessitee,
> With repleet spirit wente I to my bed,
> And bathid ther in superfluitee. *excess*
> But on the morn was wight of no degree
> So looth as I to twynne fro my cowche, *get up*
> By aght I woot. Abyde; let me see. *For anything*
> Of two as looth I am seur kowde I towche.
> (313–20)

Hoccleve's speaker-persona animates the objects around him – here the 'cuppe' becomes the grammatical subject of Hoccleve's drinking, pointedly answering his 'neede' for a drink with 'more than necessitee'. Lines 315–16 combine a sense of drunken elation with its physical and moral outcome. He bathes in 'superfluitee' – literally the excess liquid in his body (ME 'spirit' (315) can mean a vaporous substance, for example the pure alchohol used in alchemy) and metaphorically the sinful excess that caused his fall into poverty. As often in Hoccleve's verse, Latinate polysyllables – here 'necessitee' and 'superfluitee' – are balanced by the plain English 'sped' and 'bed'. The second half of the stanza slides into the familiar self-pity of a hangover morning, until Hoccleve suddenly stops, looks round ('Abyde; let me see'), and diverts his own shame towards two other late risers. These are 'Prentys and Arondel' (321), Hoccleve's fellow clerks. He implies that they escape poverty because of the services they render to lords: 'For they, in mirthe and vertuous gladnesse, / Lordes recomforten in sundry wyse' (335–6). After the joke against his colleagues, Hoccleve returns to his apparent theme: 'But to my purpos' (337).

This passage, where the speaker shapes verse from his own folly, and ideas spin out control, is characteristic of Hoccleve. Elsewhere in the *Male Regle* he draws attention to his inability to regulate his thoughts: 'no more of this as now, / But to my misreule wole I refeere' (289–90); 'No force of al this' (305); 'Ey, what is me, þat to myself thus longe / Clappid [*chattered*] haue I? I trowe þat I raue' (393–4). Here Hoccleve recalls himself to the 'proper' subject of his poem – his confession, contrition and plea for a remedy – but he is also recalling his *self* to the reader's attention, reminding us that his subjectivity is intrinsic to the *Male Regle.* One effect of writing 'against' himself is to reveal the fissures in identity that accompany the staging of the self, either in a written document or in the social 'performance' of one's identity. Hoccleve's concerns with identity are now much discussed (Burrow 1984; Goldie 1999; Knapp 2001: 17–43; Patterson 2001; Simpson 1991), and his complex literary selfhood can help us to rethink artificial distinctions between the 'medieval' and 'modern'.[5] I shall briefly discuss how Hoccleve's selfhood seems threatened in the *Male Regle* and elsewhere, and then indicate ways in which conventional formulations, and the activities of reading and writing, help to reform (and re-form) his identity.

In the *Male Regle*'s first stanza we came across the difficulty of assigning 'helthe' to a position inside or outside the body or psyche. The problem of boundaries and of the coherence of the body/self recurs throughout Hoccleve's work. Addressing 'helthe' in stanza three, Hoccleve says:

> If þat thy fauour twynne from a wight, *separate*
> Smal is his ese and greet is his greuance.
> Thy loue is lyf. Thyn hate sleeth doun right.
> Who may conpleyne thy disseuerance *departure*
> Bettre than I þat, of myn ignorance,
> Vnto seeknesse am knyt, thy mortel fo?
> (17–22)

Images of division dominate ('twynne', 'disseuerance'), while conversely sickness is 'knyt' to him. Hoccleve says in the next stanza that had he realized how much power 'helthe' possessed, sickness would not have clung on: 'Nat sholde his lym han cleued to my gore [*clothing*]' (31). In this characteristically tangible, dynamic image, 'lym' is sticky birdlime (used proverbially by Chaucer in *Troilus and Criseyde*, 1.353), but its evocation of an unwanted substance or person clinging to a garment – with a possible pun on *lim* (limb or hand) – also parallels the operation of the *Male Regle* itself. Hoccleve uses commonplace expressions – 'Prosperitee is blynd' (34), 'And now my smert [*hurt*] accusith my folie' (40) – but in this environment they become nascent allegorical entities, vying for control over his mind and body.[6] Hoccleve blames his excesses on 'myn vnwar yowthe' (41), this time splitting his self on a temporal axis. Imaginary or proverbial entities with this fleeting agency make the poem a crowded arena: 'reson' (66, 105), 'Excesse' (112), 'riot' (199), 'flaterie' (206), 'Glotonye' (301), 'Malencolie' (302), 'Stryf' (303) all hover between figure of thought and figure of action. Meanwhile,

Hoccleve's physical integrity is threatened by the actions or failures of parts of his body and mind, including 'wit' (93), 'herte' (94), 'yen' (97), 'tonge' (164), 'spirit' (315, 424).

Hoccleve's *Series* provides a larger setting for this confessional, fragmented autobiography. In its 'Complaint' he describes a 'wyld infirmite . . . whiche me oute of mysilfe caste and threwe' (40, 42). Now recovered, he is nevertheless ostracized by his erstwhile friends, who doubt that he is really cured. He hears (or imagines?) their whispering accusations, and scrutinizes himself in a mirror:

And in my chaumbre at home whanne þat I was
Mysilfe aloone I in þis wise wrouȝt:
I streite vnto my mirrour and my glas,
To loke how þat me of my chere þouȝt, *my expression seemed to me*
If any othir were it than it ouȝt,
For fain wolde I, if it not had bene riȝt, *gladly*
Amendid it to my kunnynge and myȝt. *corrected*
('Complaint', 155–61)

This moment of being 'Mysilfe aloone' (the mid-line rhyme with 'home' reinforces its claustrophobic separation) also becomes a moment of doubling, as Hoccleve's *alter ego* attempts to see himself from the outside – to read his own face (Mills 1996: 96–7). 'Amendid' here shares the vocabulary of the medieval scribe, whose job is indeed to copy meaningful characters onto skin in the form of parchment. He eventually realizes that this is impossible: 'Men in her owne cas bene blinde alday' ('Complaint', 170). The unreadability of this other face (some would read it as the psychoanalytic Other) is a haunting feature of Hoccleve's struggle to represent his self, just as the subsequent discussion with his friend (who is, in effect, another self-projection) shows how audiences often misread the words and intentions of the writer (Simpson 1991: 21–2).[7]

The *Male Regle* acutely delineates the alienation of the individual amidst a group, especially in the brittle social environment of the city (Patterson 2001; Strohm 2000: 3–19). Concern about social placement is central to that identity, in a period where fears of economic decline, social flux and religious division were a nagging presence. Hoccleve seems poised on the margins of various, sometimes competing spheres: London and Westminster; 'clerkly' and secular; extremes of wealth and poverty; feudal service and the money economy. This pressurizes his language: the word 'conpaignie', for example, used by Chaucer of the Canterbury pilgrims (GP 24) and there evoking an associational bond based on 'felaweshipe' (26), is in the *Male Regle* reduced to a financial transaction:

Fy! Lak of coyn departith conpaignie,
And heuy purs, with herte liberal,
Qwenchith the thristy hete of hertes drie,
Wher chynchy herte hath therof but smal. *stingy*
(133–6)

In another bitter use of the vocabulary of social grouping, Hoccleve describes the feigned respect shown by his 'meynee' – a term used of lords' personal entourages, who were frequently accused of extravagance and dangerous violence: 'Othir than maistir callid was I neuere / Among this meynee, in myn audience' (201–2; see Strohm 2000: 14, for 'maistir'). These fair-weather friends fall silent once the money dries up:

Despenses large enhaunce a mannes loos	*reputation*
Whil they endure, and whan they be forbore	*dispensed with*
His name is deed. Men keepe hir mowthes cloos,	
As nat a peny had he spent tofore.	
My thank is qweynt, my purs his stuf hath lore,	*quenched; lost*
And my carkeis repleet with heuynesse.	*body*
(345–52)	

Identity, as so often in medieval texts, is tied to reputation, to 'name'. In the *Male Regle*, this is a precarious existence at the mercy of the uncontrollable voices of others, and their 'thank', in the form of verbal expenditure, is intimately linked to one's own cash-flow: money talks. As Robert Meyer-Lee notes (2001: 182–3), the process Hoccleve describes is self-defeating: to keep his reputation he must spend the very money that gave it to him. Hoccleve's stark language ('deed', 'qweynt', 'carkeis') underlines the dangerous power that other people's words possess in this unstable world.

The *Male Regle*, then, captures that sense of not-belonging that is often cited as a marker of 'modern' identity, and which Hoccleve extends in the *Regiment* and *Series*. Despite (post)structuralist assaults on the centrality of the author, it is this insistent autobiographical presence that still intrigues Hoccleve's readers. But these poems are also a performance – a staging of sickness, confession and recovery that draws on long-established literary, medical and moral traditions (Burrow 1982, 1984; Goldie 1999; Simpson 1991). Furthermore, the performance is designed to achieve an effect: pity, disgust, amusement, shame. Hoccleve's individualism is inseparable from traditional and rhetorical formulations.

One such tradition is the dialogue, a long-established form in which a teacher, friend, adviser or opponent comforts, instructs or castigates the main protagonist. Boethius' *Consolation of Philosophy* is an especially influential example, and one thinks also of *Pearl*, Gower's *Confessio Amantis* and, later, Thomas More's *Utopia* and *Dialogue of Comfort*. The *Male Regle* is not, strictly speaking, a dialogue. Hoccleve instead creates different voices and identities within one speaker: reprobate, moralist, penitent, petitioner. In one passage he even warns himself publicly – 'Bewaar, Hoccleue' (351, continuing to 392). Later poems develop this incipient dialogism. The 'Dialogue with a Friend' in the *Series* gives Hoccleve an outlet that his self-scrutiny in the mirror failed to provide. The friend tries to dissuade him from writing, but in fact provokes Hoccleve to defend his psychological and authorial integrity, and allows a transition from isolated complaint to public composition (Simpson 1991: 24–6). Likewise, the Old Man whom Hoccleve meets in the *Regiment*'s opening Dialogue is a double or mirror of the poet's persona, a former dissolute turned adviser, who provides the impetus for Hoccleve to write an advice book for Prince Henry: 'Sharpe thy penne and wryte on lustyly' (*Regiment*, 1905). Dialogues, then, allow Hoccleve both to raise and to counter troubling questions about his motivations, anxieties and selfhood. They also enable advice and complaint to be voiced indirectly, so as to be 'overheard' by powerful readers (Perkins 2001: 103–14; Simpson 1995: 169–72), like the calculated indirection in the *Male Regle*'s address to 'helthe'.

Another set of traditional formulations that Hoccleve manipulates in the *Male Regle* are those that connect the petitioner, the penitent and the diseased. Since sickness and poverty were commonly viewed as punishments for sin, so prayer, confession and petition were overlapping forms. Hoccleve begins MS HM 111 with an accomplished translation of a French 'conpleynte', addressed by the Virgin Mary to God. This, like the *Male Regle*, can be read as an appeal to a God who is withholding relief from the sick or needy suppliant. The question of identity also emerges, since Mary's pain at the passion is figured as self-division:

> No wight for thee [*Christ*] swich cause hath for to pleyne
> As þat haue I. Shalt thow fro me disseuere *separate*
> Þat aart al hoolly myn? My sorwes deepe
> Han al myn hertes ioie leid to sleepe.
> (*Conpleynte Paramont*, 107–10)

In an elaborate verbal play, Mary (Maria) says that she has become bitter (Latin *amara*) with the removal from her name of the 'i', 'which is Ihesus' (186). This complaint provides a powerful additional context for Hoccleve's exploration of divided selfhood and unstable governance (Bryan 2002; Knapp 2001: 151–2). Likewise, the *Male Regle*'s confessional frame playfully appropriates religious forms, but its undertow of moral narrative cannot be ignored. Lurking behind any begging poem is the suspicion of avarice, but Hoccleve's confession also involves pride, lechery, gluttony and sloth:

> Excesse of mete and drynke is glotonye;
> Glotonye awakith malencolie;
> Malencolie engendrith werre and stryf;
> Stryf causith mortel hurt thurgh hir folie.
> Thus may excesse reue a soule hir lyf. *take from*
> (300–4)

Melancholy was, of course, one of the four 'humours' (along with the sanguine, the choleric and the phlegmatic). Medieval medical theories viewed them as an inherent part of one's physical and psychological make-up. Melancholy as a disease was, however, also associated with the sin of sloth, whose symptoms included idleness (or even despair) and unregulated or aimless words and deeds. Dangerous melancholy underlies Hoccleve's 'encombrous thoght' (185) in the *Regiment*, 'wilde infirmite' (40) in the *Series*, and the recurring 'excesse' of the *Male Regle*. Hoccleve's mental health has been the subject of modern medical speculation, but he reads his symptoms through a moral lens. That Hoccleve's *Male Regle* does not initially seem a straightforwardly 'moral' poem is because it also reminds us that sinning can be fun, and that talking about it afterwards can be even better. The turbulent energy of his writing throws us into the 'Poules Heed' tavern along with the drunkards, prostitutes and boatmen of fifteenth-century London. Confession operates here not simply as an antidote to sin, but as itself the generator of dangerous and excessive narrative.[8]

In Hoccleve's poetry, then, traditional models of morality or personality are made visible, but are nevertheless part of one's selfhood. One of the strongest aspects of Hoccleve's 'textual self' is precisely its nature as *textual*: perhaps more than any other Middle English writer, Hoccleve makes us aware of the material conditions of writing and ties his own identity to his role as scribe and clerk. In the *Male Regle*, this emerges in the carefully graded petitionary language and use of bureaucratic formulations, and in the tension between the apparently spontaneous, spoken appeals of the poem, and the literary form in which it is recorded:

Ey, what is me, þat to myself thus longe
Clappid haue I? I trowe þat I raue. — *chattered; am raving*
A, nay, my poore purs and peynes stronge
Han artid me speke as I spoken haue. — *compelled*
Whoso him shapith mercy for to craue — *whoever prepares*
His lesson moot recorde in sundry wyse,
And whil my breeth may in my body waue, — *move*
To recorde it vnnethe I may souffyse. — *scarcely; suffice*
(393–400)

The word 'recorde' (to remember or declare, but also to set down in writing or substantiate) leaves the stanza poised between the voice and the page. Hoccleve did 'recorde' the *Male Regle* himself in MS HM 111, and so we might feel that we have access to the 'real' text of the poem. We can learn much from Hoccleve's own writing practice, his consistent spelling and punctuation, the layout of the text and so on. But before thinking that this allows an unmediated connection with the text and author, we must remember that Hoccleve's copy is also just that: a copy of a poem composed over fifteen years previously, and placed in the context of a personal anthology, another 'performance' of Hoccleve's poetic identity which mingles his roles as author, compiler, scribe, penitent and petitioner.

It seems perverse to say that Hoccleve's poetry is full of speaking yet bookish, but it is precisely this friction that he exploits. The *Regiment*'s opening Dialogue disguises its writtenness partly by discussing the origins and intentions of the 'real' document that follows (Perkins 2001: 115). The *Series* is a self-conscious act of compilation, whose editorial decisions are likewise staged in the dialogues between Hoccleve and his friend (Burrow 1984). Appeals to patrons, addresses to the book and professions of dullness are all motifs that imagine a community of readers, deflect criticism by anticipating it, and implicitly warn readers not to shirk their own responsibility for the text's shared meaning.

Hoccleve does not take the act of writing for granted. Indeed, his job at the Privy Seal made him acutely aware of the consequences and power of words. His poetry reveals language to be fractured and difficult, but also generative and necessary. In the *Male Regle,* this means forming his divided spirit and body into a document that has an exchange value. In the *Regiment*'s Dialogue, Hoccleve describes writing as just such a knitting together of mental and physical – a communal act on the part of the body:

A wryter moot thre thynges to him knytte,
And in tho may be no disseverance:
Mynde, ye, and hand – noon may from othir flitte,
But in hem moot be joynt continuance. *united persistence*
(995–8)

The Dialogue then works to establish a role for the writer as royal adviser which can be fulfilled in the *Regiment* proper, forming a therapeutic or purgative text for the Prince and nation. The *Series* likewise aspires to this model of therapeutic reading. Hoccleve is comforted by reading –

This othir day a lamentacioun
Of a wooful man in a book I sy,
To whom wordis of consolacioun
Resoun ȝaf spekynge effectuelly
('Complaint', 309–12)

– and then uses writing as a marker of his own integrity. The subsequent parts of the *Series* act as exemplary narratives that stage crises of identity or division and their eventual resolutions, through suffering, revenge, death or forgiveness.

Hoccleve's angling of medical, moral and literary traditions to refract his autobiographical identity returns us to the functions of his marginal selfhood for the *Male Regle.* His lack of 'mesure', once taken at face value by critics, is a strategic waywardness intended to ambush his audience into pity for the speaker's naivety, and to accept his problematic claim that his diseased body and purse can be cured by the 'medecyne' (446) of money. Through the voices and personas that speak his poetry, Hoccleve makes his own self available for public scrutiny. This type of revelation encourages us to believe that we can reach to some core in his identity, but in fact displays the ways in which Hoccleve's literary identity, and more generally the formation of the self, are subject to fracture under the pressure of social mores, literary genres, religious beliefs and medical traditions. Hoccleve's identity, then, is both subject of and subject to the texts he writes.

Inheritance

Where does Hoccleve's poetry come from? I have already mentioned the genre of therapeutic or educative dialogue, while confessional autobiography has a pedigree stretching back to St Augustine's *Confessions*, and is strikingly deployed in the *Canterbury Tales* and the *Book of Margery Kempe*. The *Male Regle* certainly belongs to a medieval tradition of begging poetry, and of satiric 'goliardic' writing in Latin and French. One comparable French poet is Eustache Deschamps (c.1346–c.1406), who wrote numerous ballades complaining about poverty, winter, or the rotten food in Bohemia, or simply cursing his bad luck. This tradition of comic autobiography and satiric complaint was taken up in France by François Villon (c.1431–63) and in Scotland by William Dunbar (c.1460–1513). Chaucer too wrote a 'Complaint to his Purse', which he imagines as his 'lady dere', appealing to her to 'beth hevy agen, or elles moot I dye' (2, 21), before redirecting his petition to the new king, Henry IV.[9] It is, indeed, Chaucer that Hoccleve explicitly acknowledges in the *Regiment* as his mentor and model. But this is not a petitionary Chaucer, more a literary father and guarantor of vernacular authority:

O maistir deere and fadir reverent,
My maistir Chaucer, flour of eloquence,
Mirour of fructous entendement, *fertile intellect*
O universal fadir in science!
(1961–4)

Chaucer's name holds such resonance that no sooner is Hoccleve himself named in the *Regiment*'s Dialogue than Chaucer appears, as if to shore up Hoccleve's own presence:

'What shal I calle thee, what is thy name?'
'Hoccleve, fadir myn, men clepen me.'
'Hoccleve, sone?' 'Ywis, fadir, that same.'
'Sone, I have herd or this men speke of thee;
Thow were aqweyntid with Chaucer, pardee –
God have his soule, best of any wight!'
(1863–9)

Later, Hoccleve has a picture of Chaucer placed in the margin, again binding the survival of Chaucer's memory to that of his self-styled literary son (figure 35.1):

Althogh his lyf be qweynt, the resemblance
Of him hath in me so fressh lyflynesse
That to putte othir men in remembrance
Of his persone, I have heere his liknesse

Figure 35.1 Portrait of Geoffrey Chaucer, from *The Regiment of Princes* by Thomas Hoccleve. London, British Library, MS Harley 4866, folio 88. (By permission of the British Library.)

> Do make, to this ende, in soothfastnesse,
> That they that han of him lost thoght and mynde
> By this peynture may ageyn him fynde.
>
> (4992–8)

This is a remarkable moment, combining boldness and effacement (Knapp 2001: 119–24; Perkins 2001: 114–21), reminiscent of Chaucer's own knowing command that his 'litel book' should 'kis the steppes' where Virgil, Ovid, Homer, Lucan and Statius pass by (*TC* 5.1789–92). Making his picture such an integral part of the poem's design shows once again Hoccleve's alertness to the interplay of word and image, text and outside-text, with the aim of reinforcing the 'soothfastnesse' (truthfulness or fidelity) of his project. With his sober academic garb, pen hanging round his neck, and rosary in his hand, Chaucer becomes joint patron of the poem along with Prince Henry, who would have been pictured receiving Hoccleve's book earlier in the manuscript.[10] Reading these and other passages in the work of Chaucer, Hoccleve and also John Lydgate (1371–1449) gives the impression that a vernacular canon is being generated before one's eyes.[11] Indeed, one of the fascinations of late medieval writing in English is the variety of response and challenge to Chaucer; Hoccleve is among the first and most sensitive of these Chaucer readers.

Such explicit *hommages* are not the only places where Chaucer's presence is felt in Hoccleve's writing. Hoccleve's style and literary persona develop Chaucer's in a distinctive way, through quotation and allusion, tone and technique. As A. C. Spearing has shown in a perceptive reading of the poem (Spearing 1985: 110–20), the *Male Regle* glints with Chaucerian allusion and echo, without being overshadowed by them. For example, Hoccleve's opening invocation recalls the apostrophe to Venus in *Troilus and Criseyde*:

O blisful light of which the bemes clere
Adorneth al the thridde heven faire!
O sonnes lief, O Joves doughter deere, *beloved of the sun*
Plesance of love, O goodly debonaire,
In gentil hertes ay redy to repaire! *go, visit*
O veray cause of heele and of gladnesse,
Iheryed be thy myght and thi goodnesse! *praised*
(*TC* 3.1–7)

Hoccleve also learnt from Chaucer's deft changes of stylistic register. After Book 3's lengthy 'prohemium', which combines rhetorical grandeur with troubling and violent imagery, Chaucer returns us to Troilus, who is waiting in suspense (as is the reader) across the boundary of Books 2 and 3:

Lay al this mene while Troilus,
Recordyng his lesson in this manere:
'Mafay,' thoughte he, 'thus wol I sey, and thus; *by my faith*
Thus wol I pleyne unto my lady dere.'
(3.50–1)

Hoccleve shares Chaucer's ability to move quickly from the formal to the colloquial, to use high style without gilding the lily, and to represent natural speech patterns in metrical verse. Hoccleve's decasyllabic line and his verse forms (eight-line 'Monk's Tale' stanzas in the *Male Regle*; rhyme royal in the *Regiment* and *Series*) are certainly indebted to Chaucer, while as a small example of verbal borrowing and (perhaps unconscious) allusion, we might note that the *Male Regle*'s line 'His lesson moot recorde in sundry wyse' (398) echoes Troilus 'Recordyng his lesson in this manere' quoted above. Spearing suggests that Hoccleve's apparently natural, confessional mode is an extension of the way Chaucer 'allows his Canterbury pilgrims to reveal and expose themselves unguardedly' (1985: 114), with Hoccleve transferring this comedy, confession and revelation from the pilgrims to himself. Perhaps the closest match for Hoccleve's persona in Chaucer is to be found in the *Book of the Duchess*, itself indebted to French traditions, where the melancholy narrator is 'Alway in poynt to falle a-doun; / For sorwful ymaginacioun / Ys alway hooly in my mynde' (13–15), before picking up a bedtime book – Ovid's *Metamorphoses* – to 'rede and drive the night away' (49).

An equally prominent, teasingly autobiographical and vulnerable 'I' in Middle English writing is that of Langland's Will in *Piers Plowman*. Hoccleve's more open self-interest matches his petitionary mode in the *Male Regle* and elsewhere, but his explorations of writerly identity are closely affiliated to Langland's portrayal of Will as dreamer, writer, reader, clerk and sinner. Langland's capacity to animate moral abstractions, to slide quickly from politics to religion to the tavern, and to use contemporary London as an arena for moral action, spawned an energetic tradition of politically engaged poetry in the early fifteenth century – including *Richard the Redeless* and *Mum and the Soothsegger* – and provided Hoccleve with vital stylistic and thematic precedents. Hoccleve never acknowledges *Piers Plowman* directly, but does eulogize one other Ricardian poet, 'my maistir Gower' (*Regiment*, 1975). Gower's *Confessio Amantis* (c.1386–90; revised 1393) was a major influence on political writing in late medieval England, combining confessional morality, love, politics and submerged autobiography. Hoccleve helped to copy a manuscript of the *Confessio* as a freelance scribe, but he certainly also read it, absorbing its concerns with self- and public governance, and the balance between individual desire and ethical imperatives, topics to which I shall return shortly.

Hoccleve, then, portrays himself as poetic latecomer, struggling to come to terms with the legacy of his great predecessors. His mask of dullness – itself evolving from Chaucer's poetic persona – ironically helped to form literary history's subsequent picture of Chaucer's works as a 'premature renaissance', misunderstood by his fifteenth-century followers. Fortunately, this myth is now being challenged, allowing their varied individual voices to be heard (Cannon 1998: 179–220; Lawton 1981). Hoccleve's self-conscious play with literary tradition and his interest in poetic inheritance provide him with powerful motifs to explore the place and 'value' of his own poetry. Equally, his distinctive use of styles and genres can be seen in the context of contemporary attempts to develop the range and resonance of vernacular writing – in devotional texts, poetry, historical and scientific works and theology.

Regulating the Poet and Realm

In the Huntington manuscript, Hoccleve prefaces his poem with 'Cy ensuyt la male regle de T. Hoccleue'. We derive the poem's modern title from this colophon, implicitly reading the words as 'Here follows the *Male Regle* by Thomas Hoccleve'. But they can equally be descriptive: 'Here follows the bad governance of Thomas Hoccleve'. We have already encountered Hoccleve's habit of making text from 'staging' his life, and the colophon initiates that move in the *Male Regle* as it now exists. But in addition, Hoccleve's wording foregrounds a vocabulary of regulation that connects the body of the poet with public governance.

The language of ruling and governance, introduced as we saw from the outset of the poem, is developed throughout. Hoccleve makes a resolution that 'I for ay misreule wole exyle' (56) and imagines an inner battle for control between health and sickness/poverty, a *psychomachia* that interlaces confession, violence and petition:

But thy mercy excede myn offense, *unless*
The keene assautes of thyn aduersarie
Me wole oppresse with hir violence.
(57–9)

For 'mercy' in these lines, we can read 'money' – and not only because the Latin *merces* itself means 'pay', 'wages'. Here excess is a necessary condition of Hoccleve's cure, and indeed excess is the idea that (un)governs the poem. Hoccleve's self-portrait as the very embodiment of dangerous 'riot' (199) quickly shifts to an attack on flattery – an excess of verbal expenditure that bankrupts the governance of the country. Flattery can 'glose in contenance and cheere', and is thus 'preferred . . . thogh ther be no dissert' (266, 272):

> But whan the sobre, treewe, and weel auysid *prudent*
> With sad visage his lord enfourmeth pleyn *serious*
> How þat his gouernance is despysid
> Among the peple, and seith him as they seyn,
> As man treewe oghte vnto his souereyn,
> Conseillynge him amende his gouernance,
> The lordes herte swellith for desdeyn,
> And bit him voide blyue with meschance. *bids; depart at once*
> (273–80)

Here, at the heart of the poem, is the bitter political message that England's governance is badly in need of reform. The rhyme words in this stanza – *auysid/despysid*, *souereyn/desdeyn*, *gouernance/meschance* – articulate that misapprehension between loyal speech and the contempt of the powerful that is a recurring feature of political and 'protest' poetry in the later Middle Ages (Simpson 1995: 149–59).

Hoccleve goes on to lament the loss of 'trouthe' (echoing the sentiment of Chaucer's own balade *Truth*):

> Men setten nat by trouthe nowadayes.
> Men loue it nat. Men wole it nat cherice.
> And yit is trouthe best at all assayes.
> (281–3)

The 'trouthe' of Hoccleve's own poem has to lie in its insistence that the marginal poet, the apparently idle fool, is inextricably part of a political and social body whose excesses and lacks are in clear need of healing and 'mesure'. Such concerns were pressing in 1405–6. The reign of Henry IV (1399–1413) was rocked by rebellions, financial crises and anxiety over the king's health, quite apart from continual unease about his usurpation of Richard II's throne. In June 1405, Henry condemned to death Richard Scrope, the Archbishop of York, for his involvement in a northern uprising. The king was rumoured to have been struck down by a disfiguring disease at the very time of Scrope's execution – a reflection of the shock felt at Henry's sacrilegious disregard for Church privilege. March 1406 saw the opening of the reformist 'Long Parliament', which called for 'good and abundant governance' and, in return for granting taxes that Henry desperately needed, demanded that the king be guided by a 'continual council' to limit his personal powers and reform his profligate household. In April, illness forced the king to miss the start of the Parliament's second session, adding to fears of malaise both in the king's physical body and in the 'body politic' of which he was head. Written in the midst of this unease, the *Male Regle*'s pervasive imagery of excess, ill-governance and sickness has a force beyond the individual petition of a lone clerk. Indeed, images of cost and expenditure so frequently inhabit Hoccleve's language that they form a discourse of their own, a 'poetry of money' (Meyer-Lee 2001: 190) which makes the reader see everything through its evaluative prism. In this passage, the figures of Excesse and Seeknesse occupy and distort the economy of Hoccleve's own body:

Nat two yeer or three,	
But xxti wyntir past continuelly,	*twenty*
Excesse at borde hath leyd his knyf with me.	
The custume of my repleet abstinence,	*abstaining only when full*
My greedy mowth, receite of swich outrage,	*receiver; excess*
And hondes two, as woot my negligence,	*knows*
Thus han me gyded and broght in seruage	
Of hir þat werreieth euery age,	*attacks*
Seeknesse, Y meene, riotoures whippe,	*scourge of the riotous man*
Habundantly þat paieth me my wage,	
So þat me neithir daunce list, ne skippe.	
(110–20)	

Hoccleve's discussion of excess is matched by an overflow of punning word-play. The Langlandian image of Excesse as a greedy dinner companion flows into the imagined body as a state whose mouth, as 'receiver', should help to regulate the import of costly goods. The 'custume' of stopping only when replete is thus also a lax customs post at the border of the vulnerable body. The metaphor then slips to one of political betrayal as, instead of fulfilling their proper function, the mouth and hands bring the body under the yoke of 'Seeknesse', whose ironic wages are poverty and despair. As in the second stanza's 'poore of ese and ryche of euel fare' (16), Hoccleve here makes economic contradiction a characteristic of his own textual body (see also 'my carkeis repleet with heuynesse', 350), while the final appeal of the poem imagines the hoped-for injection of 'coyn' as paradoxically an emptying out, a way to 'voide me of pyne' (448).

Medieval English society operated through an intricate system of actual and symbolic exchanges, many of which were sublimated by the language of free gift, duty or grace. The Latin word *gratia* literally means something that is freely given, and Hoccleve makes a nice play on the word when he reminds 'helthe' that 'It sit a god been of his grace free' (407). Grace that is not 'free' (Middle English *free* means both 'generous' and 'free') is by definition not grace, and therefore unbecoming in a god. Hoccleve, then, literalizes the vocabulary of gift and grace to suggest that with power comes the responsibility to match rhetoric with action. By the poem's conclusion, the always tenuous concealment of Hoccleve's need for money under the cloak of sickness can no longer be sustained, and the two ailing bodies are prominently merged: 'My body and purs been at ones seeke' (409). Hoccleve turns to a proverb to show how 'neede' compels him to speak:

> The prouerbe is, the doumb man no lond getith.
> Whoso nat spekith and with neede is bete, *afflicted*
> And thurgh arghnesse his owne self forgetith, *cowardice*
> No wondir, thogh anothir him forgete.
> Neede hath no lawe, as þat the clerkes trete,
> And thus to craue artith me my neede. *compels*
> (433–8)

The insistence that his payment is 'due' (420, 440, 441) tolls through the final lines, reminding Furnival that the health of the subject's body is intimately linked to the good management of the political body. Here Hoccleve gets down to the details of his petition. As any child writing to Santa Claus knows, the petitioner needs to let the giver know exactly what is wanted and who is asking (Burrow 1981: 62). 'Helthe' is to give Furnival 'a tokne or tweye' (419) to pay Hoccleve his annuity of £10 from the previous Michaelmas. In the margin of MS HM 111, folio 25v, Hoccleve wrote next to these lines 'Annus ille fuit annus restrictionis annuitatum' (That was the year of the restriction of annuities). This reminder of the historical conditions under which the *Male Regle* was written also forces us to attend to the poem's alignment of personal, moral and political regulation. Just as the narrator's advice to keep to a 'mene reule' (352) is addressed apparently to himself, but clearly speaks to the royal finances and nation as a whole, so Hoccleve's self-portrayal as 'mirour . . . of riot and excesse' (330) forms a troubling reflection on the state of Lancastrian England.

Conclusion

The experience of reading Hoccleve's poetry is centrifugal – spinning off into apparently discrepant styles, discourses, identities and poetic traditions. His poetic persona is insistently real, yet also involves masking, impersonation and convention. He is fascinated but also repelled by social engagement. All these effects are achieved in the face of claims that as a petitioner and propagandist he is focused on the centre and complicit with dominant ideologies. Hoccleve's roles as public, apparently celebratory, poet and private, anxious individual are in fact impossible to separate, since both are porous, allowing layers of reference and resonance to soak through. Despite straining for the ideal of a coherent, stable world, Hoccleve is faced with the fracturing of personal, religious and political structures. Rather than retreating to safe ground, though, he stages these dilemmas in his poetry, making his own body and identity their testing ground. In a manuscript in Canterbury Cathedral archive, stanzas from the *Male Regle* have been excerpted and edited to form a short didactic balade.[12] This text uses Hoccleve's moral exhortations, but excludes the dangerous, autobiographical body of the poet himself.

The Canterbury poem demonstrates in negative how Hoccleve's insistent tugging at the sleeve of the reader – to confess, nudge or complain – gives his writing an edge that critics have traditionally found lacking in fifteenth-century poetry. The *Male Regle*, though avowedly marginal, even parasitic, nevertheless makes from its excessive language a complex speech-act which still challenges us to pay it its due.

See also 7 From Manuscript to Modern Text, 11 The Forms of Verse, 18 Images, 26 Accounts of Lives, 30 The *Book of Margery Kempe*, 32 *Piers Plowman*, 33 The *Canterbury Tales*, 34 John Gower and John Lydgate.

Notes

1 I quote Hoccleve's *Male Regle*, *Series* and *Compleynte paramont* from *Thomas Hoccleve, 'My Compleinte' and Other Poems*, ed. Roger Ellis (Exeter: University of Exeter Press, 2001). They also appear in *Hoccleve's Works: The Minor Poems*, ed. Frederick J. Furnivall and I. Gollancz, rev. Jerome Mitchell and A. I. Doyle, EETS es 61 and 73 (1970). I quote Hoccleve's *Regiment* from Thomas Hoccleve, *The Regiment of Princes*, ed. Charles R. Blyth (Kalamazoo, Mich.: Medieval Institute Publications for TEAMS, 1999).

2 See J. A. Burrow and A. I. Doyle, *Thomas Hoccleve: A Facsimile of the Autograph Verse Manuscripts*, EETS ss 19 (2002).

3 On Hoccleve's relation to royal power, see Pearsall 1994, Perkins 2001, Strohm 1998: 173–95, and James Simpson, *The Oxford English Literary History. Vol. 2: 1350–1547: Reform and Cultural Revolution* (Oxford: Oxford University Press, 2002), pp. 191–254.

4 J. L. Austin, *How to Do Things with Words*, 2nd edn (Oxford: Oxford University Press, 1976).

5 On the whole question of subjectivity and periodization, see David Aers, 'A Whisper in the Ear of Early Modernists: Or Reflections on Literary Critics Writing the "History of the Subject"', in *Culture and History 1350–1600: Essays on English Communities, Identities, and Writing*, ed. David Aers (New York: Harvester Wheatsheaf, 1992), pp. 177–202.

6 See Hasler 1990 for this effect in the *Regiment*.

7 This scene might be read with reference to Lacan's theory of the 'mirror stage', if we recognize its force here as theatrical 'staging' rather than case study. For the mirror stage as 'suggestive allegory' and Hoccleve's *Regiment*, see Strohm 2000: 253, n. 8.

8 For confession and narrative, and confession as narrative, see Michel Foucault, *The History of Sexuality. Vol. 1: An Introduction*, trans. Robert Hurley (Harmondsworth: Penguin, 1990), pp. 58–63. I am indebted here to Paul Strohm, for a lecture which discussed *Piers Plowman* and Chaucer's Wife of Bath and Pardoner in this context.

9 It was attributed to Hoccleve in Speght's 1602 Chaucer edition, perhaps because begging was thought to be beneath the great man.

10 The presentation portrait has been removed from MS Harley 4866, but survives in London, British Library MS Arundel 38, folio 37r (Perkins 2001: plate 1).

11 See Pearsall 1994: 397–403. Hoccleve may also have known Chaucer's actual son, Thomas: see Derek Pearsall, *The Life of Chaucer: A Critical Biography* (Oxford: Blackwell, 1992), p. 289.

12 Stanzas 5, 6, 9, 10, 12, 14, 45, 44 and 51. See Marian Trudgill and J. A. Burrow, 'A Hoccleveau Balade', *Notes and Queries* 243 (1998), 178–80.

References and Further Reading

Bryan, Jennifer E. (2002). 'Hoccleve, the Virgin, and the Politics of Complaint.' *Publications of the Modern Language Association* 117, 1172–87. Examines connections between devotional complaint, interiority and petitionary revelation.

Burrow, J. A. 1981. 'The Poet as Petitioner.' *Studies in the Age of Chaucer* 3, 61–75. Wide-ranging survey of the distinctive manoeuvres of petitionary poetry.

—— 1982. 'Autobiographical Poetry in the Middle Ages: The Case of Thomas Hoccleve.' *Proceedings of the British Academy* 68, 389–412. Pioneering study of the complexity and significance of Hoccleve's self-revelations.

—— 1984. 'Hoccleve's *Series*: Experience and Books.' In *Fifteenth-Century Studies: Recent Essays*, ed. Robert F. Yeager (Hamden, Conn.: Archon Books), pp. 259–73. Focuses on the self-conscious textuality of the *Series*.

—— 1994. *Thomas Hoccleve.* Aldershot: Variorum. Indispensable guide, including biography, life records and full bibliography.

Cannon, Christopher 1998. *The Making of Chaucer's English: A Study of Words.* Cambridge: Cambridge University Press. Excellent study of Chaucer's language; the final chapter investigates the myth of Chaucer as founding father of English poetry.

Goldie, Matthew Boyd 1999. 'Psychosomatic Illness and Identity in London, 1416–1421: Hoccleve's *Complaint* and *Dialogue with a Friend*.' *Exemplaria* 11, 23–52. Examines the context of medical discourses and the environment of the city.

Hasler, Anthony J. 1990. 'Hoccleve's Unregimented Body.' *Paragraph* 13, 164–83. Provocative study linking Hoccleve's wayward body with that of the Prince and the realm.

Knapp, Ethan 2001. *The Bureaucratic Muse: Thomas Hoccleve and the Literature of Late Medieval England.* University Park: Pennsylvania State University Press. Engaging analysis of a variety of Hoccleve's writings, placing him in the context of Lancastrian bureaucratic culture.

Lawton, David 1981. 'Dullness and the Fifteenth Century.' *ELH: A Journal of English Literature and History* 54, 761–99. Influentially argues that fifteenth-century writers hide uncomfortable political messages beneath a cloak of dullness.

Meyer-Lee, Robert J. 2001. 'Thomas Hoccleve and the Apprehension of Money.' *Exemplaria* 13, 173–214. Exploration of Hoccleve's monetary concerns and language in the context of the late medieval urban economy.

Mills, David 1996. 'The Voices of Thomas Hoccleve.' In *Essays on Thomas Hoccleve*, ed. Catherine Batt (London: Centre for Medieval and Renaissance Studies, Queen Mary and Westfield College; Turnhout: Brepols), pp. 85–107. Discussion of genre, register, and the roles of writer and audience (especially in Hoccleve's *Series*).

Patterson, Lee 2001. '"What is Me?": Self and Society in the Poetry of Thomas Hoccleve.' *Studies in the Age of Chaucer* 23, 437–70. Examination of Hoccleve's selfhood and representation of social relationships, especially in the context of urban culture.

Pearsall, Derek 1994. 'Thomas Hoccleve's *Regement of Princes*: The Poetics of Royal Self-Representation.' *Speculum* 69, 386–410. Places the *Regiment* in the context of Lancastrian politics, arguing that Hoccleve is a mouthpiece for Prince Henry's self-representation.

Perkins, Nicholas 2001. *Hoccleve's 'Regiment of Princes': Counsel and Constraint.* Cambridge: Brewer. Studies the poem's discursive contexts, genre, sources, politics and manuscripts, arguing that Hoccleve both dramatizes and overcomes constraints on giving advice to princes.

Simpson, James 1991. 'Madness and Texts: Hoccleve's *Series*.' In *Chaucer and Fifteenth-Century Poetry*, ed. Julia Boffey and Janet Cowen (London: Centre for Late Antique and Medieval Studies, King's College), pp. 15–29. Extends the insights of Burrow 1984, showing how Hoccleve resists readings of his life and poetry based narrowly on autobiography or literary convention.

—— 1995. 'Nobody's Man: Thomas Hoccleve's *Regement of Princes*.' In *London and Europe in the Later Middle Ages*, ed. Julia Boffey and Pamela King (London: Centre for Medieval and Renaissance Studies, Queen Mary and Westfield College), pp. 149–80. Argues persuasively that

Hoccleve rejects Boethian consolation in favour of Aristotelian political engagement, enabling him to voice troubling complaints in the *Regiment*.

Spearing, A. C. 1985. *Medieval to Renaissance in English Poetry*. Cambridge: Cambridge University Press. Valuable readings of poetry after Chaucer, including the *Male Regle* (110–20).

Strohm, Paul 1998. *England's Empty Throne: Usurpation and the Language of Legitimation, 1399–1422*. New Haven, Conn.: Yale University Press. Examines the relationships of Lancastrian texts to royal and religious ideologies; ch. 7 and the 'Coda' read Hoccleve as a propagandist inevitably undone by the unmanageable task of 'forgetting' the Lancastrian usurpation.

—— 2000. *Theory and the Premodern Text*. Minneapolis: University of Minnesota Press. Provocative experiments in reading medieval texts alongside critical theory and history.

36

Discipline and Relaxation in the Poetry of Robert Henryson[1]

R. James Goldstein

Although Robert Henryson is a traditionalist whose poetry suggests ties to some of the most conservative moral and religious ideologies of his day, his work reveals an intriguing (if limited) commitment to the values of secular life and its distinctive forms of worldly enjoyment, which has suggested to some critics his possible affinities with early humanism. An important measure of Henryson's broadly humanist agenda lies in his aspirations to achieve the status of a vernacular author – his ambition to work within literary traditions begun by the classical *auctores* and modified by recent vernacular poets such as Chaucer and Lydgate. What has been said of late medieval innovators in vernacular literature applies equally to Henryson, who both acknowledges the 'prestige of Latin texts and *auctores*' and seeks 'to assimilate that prestige, in an endless shuttling between gestures of deference and gestures of displacement' (Wogan-Browne, Watson, Taylor and Evans 1999: 322).

Although Henryson certainly makes frequent 'gestures of deference' to culturally powerful institutions, it is less often noted how his work also voices fictional resistance to the reigning structures of authority – cultural, political and religious – in his 'gestures of displacement', however partial or tentative. Interwoven with culturally powerful discourses and institutions, his writing contributes to the work of disciplining bodies and producing subjects, yet it is also worth recognizing the extent to which his poetry imagines possible sites of resistance, even if only in play. Focusing on tensions in his work between older ascetic ideologies that hold the world in contempt, and his more this-worldly acknowledgement of the need for pleasurable release from the severe discipline of the body, the present essay will read his two major works, *The Morall Fabillis* and *The Testament of Cresseid*, as meditations on the function of vernacular authorship and the discursive regimes that authors serve. In carving out an imaginative space of freedom in which the pleasures and relaxations of literary play may be enjoyed without a sense of guilt, Henryson engages in practices of discipline for himself and his readers that place his poetry at a crossroads between the medieval and early modern worlds in ways that ensured that his model of authorship continued to resonate for audiences and writers well into the sixteenth century.

The Morall Fabillis

In aspiring to the kind of cultural authority that Latin authors had previously monopolized, Henryson engages in an audacious act of literary self-canonization. His poetry bases its vernacular authority on a wide range of fifteenth-century discourses and their powerful institutions (the classroom, the confessional, the pulpit, the monastery, the law court, the burgh and so on). Although not a great deal is known for certain about his life, he was a trained notary and seems to have been the same Robert Henryson who held two degrees from another university and was incorporated into the University of Glasgow in 1462. Sixteenth-century evidence plausibly claims that the poet was a master of the grammar school in the royal burgh of Dunfermline (Fox 1981: xiii–xxv). The fragmentary biographical evidence thus suggests that his authority as vernacular poet was to some extent derived from his specific location within fifteenth-century institutions of education and documentary culture. His *auctoritas* resembles that of John Ireland, another fifteenth-century Scottish author and preacher much concerned with moral discipline and governance, whose *Meroure of Wyssdome*, begun for James III, was dedicated to James IV (Ireland 1490). Not only does the work of these two contemporary writers offer numerous ideological parallels, but Ireland clearly admired the kind of poetry that Henryson wrote, as we may infer from his praise of Chaucer, Gower, Lydgate 'and mony wthire' vernacular poets whose books of 'tragedy' induce their readers 'to lefe [*leave*] vicis and folow wertuis' by showing the true nature of 'waurdly plesaunce – in the begynnyng, gret plesaunce and dilectacioune, and in the ende, all manere of sorow and displesaunce' (Ireland 1490: I, 164; text modified). Ireland, who takes some pride in his regnal nationality (III, 165), would doubtless have included Henryson in his list of canonical vernacular poets had he known his work.

If Ireland constantly cites his credentials as the author of Latin theological works in a prestigious university setting, Henryson's connection with pedagogical institutions at a more primary level would be clear from *The Morall Fabillis* even if his association with the grammar school of Dunfermline turned out to be spurious. The medieval classroom inherited from the classical world the pedagogic method of paraphrasing Aesopic fables, the *progymnasmata* exercises described by Quintilian and developed by the fourth-century grammarian Priscian (Wheatley 2000: 34–8). *The Morall Fabillis* depends closely on this classroom training ground while greatly transcending the limitations of that discursive setting. Comprising a prologue and thirteen rhyme-royal tales, each followed by a verse *moralitas*, *The Morall Fabillis* is Henryson's most ambitious work and forms the largest compendium of Aesopic fables in an English vernacular. For his main source, Henryson turned to the most widely circulating Aesopic collection in the later Middle Ages, the sixty fables in Latin elegiac verses compiled by the late twelfth-century Gualterus Anglicus (Walter the Englishman), a collection also known as the 'elegiac Romulus'. For some tales, however, Henryson draws on the non-Aesopic tradition of beast tales stemming from a version of the *Roman de Renart*, although he casts these tales in a form that would be instantly recognized by his educated readers as modelled on the same procedures of scholastic commentary as his properly Aesopic fables. Since it is not possible here to consider each of the fables, we will focus on a selection to show how Henryson's construction of vernacular authority explores the polarities and tensions between obeying and resisting the disciplinary regimes of his day.

The poet takes great pains to create literary authority for himself in the prologue, drawing on the standard classroom text of the elegiac Romulus and the body of scholastic introductions or *accessus* that typically circulated with manuscripts and early prints of the Latin fables (Wheatley 2000: 151). In a prologue that 'appeal[s] to almost all the topoi ever used to justify fiction' (Wogan-Browne, Watson, Taylor and Evans 1999: 211), Henryson argues that even if 'feinȝeit [*invented*] fabils of ald poetre / Be not al grunded vpon truth' (1–2),[2] the seductive pleasures of poetic fiction offer an attractive venue for moral discipline. Just as the string of a bow that is always bent grows dull, so does the mind that never relaxes from studying. While the poet introduces his work as a pleasant way to instil wholesome morality into his audience, he alludes in a syntactically tortured stanza (29–35) to the multiple nexus of discipline and authority to which he is subject: his audience of 'maisteris', to whose classroom authority he submits for 'correctioun' (Wheatley 2000: 152); the poet Aesop, the Latin *auctor* from whose work he proposes to 'mak ane maner of translatioun'; and the unnamed lord who serves as literary patron. Moreover, when Henryson explains that the translation was made not 'of my self, for vane presumptioun' but at the 'requeist and precept' of the lord (33–4), he implicitly submits to ecclesiastical authority, drawing on penitential discourse in identifying the potential sin of presumption.

The prologue defines the mode of the book's truth as a kind of figurative discourse that shows by 'exempill and similitude' (47) how men resemble lower animals. Educated readers would have learned in their early elementary classroom exercises to produce Latin verse and prose paraphrases of this kind, and to write commentaries that interpreted beast fables according to the exegetical protocols developed and controlled by the Church (Wheatley 2000: 52–96). Yet the apparatus of education not only provides the author and his readers with a disciplined training in the arts; it also produces docile bodies by promoting moral values that overlap with those urged from the pulpit. Beast fables provide a relaxing way to pass the time, but such reading helps control the lower carnal impulses before satisfaction of appetite becomes habitually rooted in the soul. In short, the fusion of penitential and pedagogical discourses in the prologue bears witness to a larger cultural development in which 'classroom and confession are linked through the idea of *disciplina*, the regulation of knowledge and the regulation of the self' (Woods and Copeland 1999: 376–7). Again, the parallel with Ireland is instructive, whose lengthy peroration on the value of penance includes an apostrophe to his reader, 'O bestlie man' (Ireland 1490: III, 71).

Henryson's first fable, the Cock and the Jasp, serves as both an exemplum of the kind of moral vigilance espoused in the prologue and a kind of meta-fable about the poet's own discursive mode. The rooster recognizes the value humans place on the jewel he discovers on the dung heap, but the only value pertinent to his own daily struggle for existence is satisfaction of bodily need, a literal 'corne' (94) that contrasts with the nourishing grain in the prologue. In a literal sense, the bird's reasoning is impeccable: he cannot eat the jewel, and the vigour with which he defends his actions encourages the reader to sympathize. Yet the *moralitas* turns this logic on its head by reading the jewel as a figure for transcendent meaning: 'perfite prudence and cunning, / Ornate with mony deidis of vertew, / Mair [*more*] excellent than ony eirthly thing' (128–30). The playful disjunction between the sound reasoning of the bird and the high-minded wisdom of the narrator in the *moralitas* is typical of the genre as a whole. The disciplinary mechanisms correcting the fiction are calculated to thwart the enjoyment incited by the fable. Yet as creatures who know hunger and need, readers cannot entirely abandon the rooster's perspective so long as we occupy our bodies.

The Cock and the Fox, an adaptation of the Nun's Priest's Tale, submits the fable to the discipline of moral and biblical truth to a greater degree than Geoffrey Chaucer's highly ambiguous and ironic version. The narrative portion of the tale includes moments of disciplining commentary. Yet the pleasures of fiction exceed the disciplinary control over its meaning, carving out spaces of resistance to the transcendent values of Christian morality. When the fox runs off the with rooster, the hen Pertok, in a lament for her lost lover, celebrates the erotic life and momentarily escapes the impulse to chasten and correct (504–7) until Coppok argues in the stern voice of a 'curate' (530) that the lecherous Chantecleir has been punished by God's vengeance. Yet the mock-serious tone of the fable deliberately undermines it own moral authority, since the accusation of adultery must seem ludicrous in the case of chickens.

In the Fox and the Wolf, Henryson traces subsequent events in the life of the fox from the previous tale, who becomes subject to the disciplinary apparatuses of canon law and the secular state. Submitting his conscience to the demands of penitential theology, the fox wishes to amend his life and seeks a confessor. But he also worries about justice in the present world, fearing the penalties of criminal law. When he turns to the university-trained wolf for shrift, however, the sacrament of penance goes comically awry. The post-1215 conjunction of classroom and confessional discourse clearly emerges as the confessor questions and teaches the fox, who is unable quite to bring himself to contrition for his past sins, haunted as he is by the sweet memory of hens and lambs. When the wolf assigns the penitential regime of avoiding meat until Easter to 'tame' the flesh (724), the poet comically expresses desires subversive of church discipline: the fox asks for licence to eat whatever tasty morsel of his prey he pleases (727–9). Even the wolf's permissive penance is too much for the fox, however, who soon christens a stolen kid his 'new-maid salmond' (753). But pleasure must be paid for: mortally wounded by the keeper, the fox recognizes that he has subverted language by misusing its power to name things truthfully (confession after all depends on accurately naming one's sins). The parallel with the defensive poetics of the playful fables is clear as the fox bitterly complains that 'na man may speik ane word in play, / Bot now on dayis in ernist it is tane' (770–1).

In contrast to the previous fable, the next two fables, the Trial of the Fox and the Sheep and the Dog, focus on the administration of justice by institutions of secular government and law. The first tale portrays the fifteenth-century parliament in its capacity as the highest criminal court. The mare, the fox and the wolf become enmeshed in legal proceedings as the fable explores the relations among institutions of higher learning, documentary legal culture and the administration of justice. The *moralitas* subjects the fable to the discipline of scholastic hermeneutics in surprising ways, allegorically reading the just lion as a figure for the world, the fox as temptation. The fox's comical resistance to clerical and political discipline is thus subsumed by the transcendent meaning of the tale, which purports to be about divine justice. The next tale satirizes the corruption of legal justice by rapacious officers of the court, both church and civil. In a tale dense with legal jargon, the ability to manipulate the language of law is revealed to be a form of social power easy to abuse. The social allegory in the *moralitas* pits the integrity of the wrongfully accused sheep, a figure for the 'pure commounis' (1259), against the corruption of law and justice. The voice of the poet becomes indistinguishable from that of the shorn sheep who takes shelter from the cold as the beast heroically uses eloquence, his last resource, to protest injustice. Yet such gestures of resistance are limited, and the voice of complaint finally assimilates the meaning of the fable to the larger pattern of the suffering that God inflicts to discipline bodies.

The centrally placed fable, the Lion and the Mouse, contains its own prologue, a dream-vision in which the author encounters the venerable authority of Aesop himself, who questions the disciplining of knowledge and the self in the discourses of classroom and pulpit as he wonders what use it is 'to tell ane fenȝeit taill, / Quhen haly preiching may na thing auaill' (1389–90). Despite his reservations, Aesop tells the fable of the lion and the mouse, illustrating a successful use of persuasion. Language in this fable exceeds that rhetorical purpose, however, as the repeated verb 'dance' (1410, 1416, 1442; cf. 1605) tracks the innocent pleasures of the mouse. Indeed, the dance at first appears to be a realm of spontaneous enjoyment beyond the reach of discipline, and it seems good. As the apologetic mouse explains to the offended lion: 'The sweit sesoun prouokit vs to dance / And mak sic mirth as nature to vs leird [*taught*]' (1442–3). Yet the joyous freedom of the mouse celebrated in the fable proper is again subjected to the *moralitas* in surprising ways, which reads the mice as the rebellious commons in the forest of 'warldlie lust and vane plesance' (1602), to which even great lords succumb.

The Preaching of the Swallow stretches the bounds of the Aesopic genre with a complex framing device that draws on traditional philosophical and theological ideas to contrast the perfect intellect of God with finite human understanding. Drawing on Christian neoplatonism, the frame argues that the soul is fettered in a corporeal prison of sensuality (1629–30), although the natural creation offers finite reason a means of approaching divine wisdom. The narrator participates as a silent observer, an ambiguous figure who maintains attachments to the very world of sensuality that the opening calls into question. Like Chaucer's persona in the Prologue to the *Legend of Good Women* he steps outdoors 'blyth' (1714), but like William Langland's wandering figure of Will, he rambles aimlessly, like a secular pilgrim with staff in hand, passing 'to and fro'

(1717). He takes great pleasure in observing agricultural workers from a distance, not participating in their activities. The wandering narrator's unselfconscious enjoyment of the life of the body is described without locating its meaning within the cosmic order, although the natural world serves as a mirror of wisdom as the swallow offers lessons in prudence, warning the other birds not to allow the flax seeds to mature. Although they resist his counsel with 'exuberantly larky irresponsibility' (Burrow 1975: 26), the fable clearly establishes that the birds are compelled by necessity to ignore his advice: nearly famished for hunger, they have little choice except by 'scraipand [*scraping*] for to seik thair fude' (1868). By dispensing with the fable's recognitions of bodily need, the *moralitas* imposes an especially heavy burden of 'morall edificatioun' (1893) on the tale, which becomes an exemplum of reason 'blindit with affectioun' (1906). Drawing on an Augustinian analysis of the three stages of sin (1902–5; cf. Ireland 1490: III, 26), the moral reworks the agricultural imagery in such a way that the seeds' natural growth is no longer viewed as a sign of divine goodness but is refigured as the ripening of sin.

With the eleventh fable, the Wolf and the Wether, Henryson begins a series of disturbingly abrupt narrative resolutions; the disjunction between the morality and the fable adds to the growing sense of urgent questions about the disciplinary force of the poem. The sheep advises his shepherd to cheer up after the guard dog's death, heroically offering to wear its skin to keep watch. The plan proceeds well until the sheep foolishly continues his pursuit, giving the wolf an opportunity to discover his real identity. The sheep desperately attempts to persuade the wolf that his chase was not in earnest, since he only intended 'to haue playit with ȝow' (2558). The wolf appropriates the sheep's comic language but turns it to tragedy as he abruptly snaps his victim's neck. The ponderous Latinisms and tortured syntax of the first stanza of the *moralitas*, which contains some of the worst poetry in all of Henryson, raise questions about how seriously we should take the interpretation of the sheep as representing poor men who fail to know their place; indeed, it is difficult to imagine a reader who would find this conservative voice of moral discipline more attractive than that of the misguided sheep who is brutally crushed in the fable.

The brutality continues in the Wolf and the Lamb, when the lamb attempts to use reason to persuade the wolf to drop his unjust accusation of fouling his water. The lamb's academic discipline, with his learned allusions, fails miserably, as does his insistence that the wolf follow correct legal procedure. Ironically, the appeal to reasonable constraints on natural appetite that forms the argument of the entire book falls on deaf ears in this particular instance. In the *moralitas* Henryson provides his most sustained defence of the rights of the poor against their oppressors, although the general sentiments are commonplace in medieval sermons and social satire (Fox 1981: 315). Indeed, the poet diagnoses the oppression of the poor in terms of the moral failings of corrupt individuals who lack 'conscience' (2727) without challenging the system of land tenure and law that allows the propertied classes to exploit the poor tenants. Little room is imagined for effective resistance to the social and legal disciplinary mechanisms that could lead to structural reform of the oppressive system itself. Although Henryson keeps one eye on fifteenth-century legal and political institutions, the other eye looks to heaven for the only plausible solution, divine punishment of injustice. The poet abandons reasonable persuasion and prays directly to God, imploring him to punish transgressors with help from the king (2770–6).

In the last fable, the Paddock and the Mouse, bodily necessity compels the mouse to cross the river for nourishment because, as she tells the frog, 'I am hungrie' (2793). Once again the power of rhetoric and academic learning to serve malicious purposes is demonstrated in the debate between the frog and the mouse over the significance of the ugly appearance of the frog, who draws on a variety of learned discourses to persuade the mouse to ride on his back. The mouse quickly finds herself in a struggle for life until the kite abruptly swoops down and disembowels them both. The first three stanzas of the *moralitas* warn the reader of the dangers posed by 'silkin toung' (the rhetorical skill on which poets must depend), since it may be subverted by 'ane hart of crueltie' (2922). Acknowledging that no amount of learning or ingenuity in the playful discipline of fiction is adequate in itself, Henryson finally abandons poetry for prayer. His final gesture seems emblematic of tensions in the work as a whole: on the one hand Henryson affirms the value of poetry to delight and instruct; on the other, he registers considerable anxiety about its moral efficacy. A different anxiety is registered by the Protestant reviser of the Bassandyne print, which disciplines the theological implications of the poet's final admonition to the reader by correcting 'gud deidis' to read 'faith in Christ' (2967). With only minor adjustments to his language, Henryson's austere but playful voice continued to resonate with authority for later sixteenth-century Scottish readers.

The Testament of Cresseid

At first glance, Henryson might seem to relieve his other great work from the overtly Christian moralizing so evident in the *Fables*. Indeed, it seems likely that Chaucer's *Troilus and Criseyde* helped reveal to his Scottish successor how the creation of an autonomous, fictional pagan world might open a space for exploring moral and philosophical issues while liberating the poet from the need to formulate his concerns within the narrow boundaries of Christian truth. No less than Chaucer's adaptations of *trecento* poetry, Henryson's poem, with its recreation of classical antiquity, learned attention to pagan deities, assertion of human dignity and celebration of earthly love, represents a kind of humanism, although not necessarily one that was influenced by contemporary Italian humanistic learning (Gray 1979: 25). Although some critics read Henryson's meaning as fundamentally Christian, the poet deliberately quarantines his poem from any unambiguous reference to specifically Christian beliefs or practices. Despite Henryson's conspicuous refusal to imitate Chaucer's closing strategy of correcting pagan history by explicitly evoking Christian doctrine, however, other disciplinary strategies and techniques operate in and on the poem (and indeed on its author) to defuse any questioning of the divine order, or women's subservient role in patriarchal society, or any potentially subversive effects implied by an author's freedom to invent new fictions to displace old ones.

The *Testament* audaciously requires its readers to revise much of what they know from Chaucer's *Troilus*. Henryson traces the declining fortune of Cresseid, abandoned by Diomeid and forced to return in disgrace to her father's home, where after a nightmare vision of the planetary deities she contracts leprosy as punishment for blasphemy and is reduced to beggary. The emotional climax of the poem occurs during her final encounter with Troilus, eerily revivified in a sharply imagined scene where the former lovers fail to recognize each other. Yet something in her appearance reminds Troilus of his old love, inducing him to offer her alms. When a fellow leper identifies him, Troilus's act of charity sparks in Cresseid a recognition of her moral culpability, whereupon she writes her testament and dies.

Little about this deliberately ambiguous poem remains uncontroversial, starting from Henryson's creation of an elaborate opening frame that introduces the problem of embodiment by creating a first-person subjectivity: an old man suffering the residual effects of sexual desire, who passes time on a frigid spring evening by examining Chaucer's *Troilus* before taking up 'ane vther quair [*another book*]' (61) that recounts the final destiny of Cresseid. The narrator grapples with a harsh natural world that sets limits and disciplines the will; he reports how the cold 'causit me remufe [*to depart*] aganis my will' (21). Stepping from his oratory into his 'chalmer' (28) to warm himself by the fire, the narrator, who confesses his faith in the power of Venus to work miracles in an old man's body, appears to be a modern devotee of the old pagan religion of love. Taking down Chaucer's book as part of a medicinal regime (along with strong drink and the fire) to restore vital heat, the narrator seems to grasp how the life of the body is inseparable from the desiring subject's history of reading and writing.

At the end of the *Troilus*, Chaucer appeals to Gower and Strode to 'correct' the book where necessary (*TC* 5.1856–9). Henryson in effect makes such a correction by inventing the fiction of an alternative version of the ending:

> Quha wait gif all that Chauceir wrait was trew? *Who knows if; wrote*
> Nor I wait nocht gif this narratioun
> Be authoreist, or fenȝeit of the new
> Be sum poeit, throw his inuentioun
> Maid to report the lamentatioun
> And wofull end of this lustie Creisseid,
> And quhat distres scho thoillit, and quhat deid. *what; suffered; death*
> (64–70)

This contrast implies that a narration is *authorized* only if it corresponds to historical reality, only if (in the language of the *Fables*) it is 'al grunded vpon truth'. Henryson thus disciplines Chaucerian poetic fiction, extending its project while submitting it to correction. The process is by implication interminable: Henryson expects his own readers to discipline and correct his wayward text and their own bodies. That Henryson felt the need to present the narrator as 'a figure of ridicule' (Pearsall 2000: 174) before he could subject the female protagonist to the terrifying power of the deities for her wayward sexuality and speech (Cox 1996) suggests that author and poem are subject to disciplinary regimes that parallel those he imposes on Cresseid. The uses of pleasure, literary and otherwise, must be carefully managed.

Although the other quire reduces 'lustie Creisseid' (69) to a wretched end, Diomeid is hardly presented in flattering terms: he fulfils 'all his appetyte, / And mair [*more*]' on her before he chooses another woman on whom to 'set his haill [*whole*] delyte' (71–3). The unmistakable moral disapprobation in these lines clashes with the image of the narrator as would-be Venerian sensualist in the prologue. Such contradictions provide evidence for the conflicting pressures exerted by different disciplinary regimes. Recognizing the presence of such gaps in the text allows us to discard the view that the poem enforces the 'ostensibly monolithic patriarchal order' (Pearsall 2000: 181).

Yet masculine regimes of power, which in part depend on the instrumentality of writing, alter Cresseid's life when Diomeid sends his 'lybell of repudie' (74). The consequences of her repudiation are as devastating as they are morally ambiguous: 'Than desolait scho walkit vp and doun, / And sum men sayis, into the court, commoun' (76–7). Although some critics continue to read the line as implying prostitution, others insist that it signals no more than her promiscuity. The inconsistencies and contradictions in the text's treatment of Cresseid are perhaps best captured in this frequently quoted stanza:

O fair Creisseid, the flour and A per se — *paragon*
Of Troy and Grece, how was thow fortunait
To change in filth all thy feminitie,
And be with fleschelie lust sa maculait, — *corrupted*
And go amang the Greikis air and lait, — *early and late*
Sa giglotlike takand thy foull plesance! — *like a wanton woman, taking*
I haue pietie thow suld fall sic mischance! — *you should have such bad luck*
(78–84)

The 'pity' or sympathetic response to her plight conveyed in the final verse clashes with the moral outrage of the rest of the stanza, yet to read the apparent contradictions in psychological terms as betraying 'an impotent old man's disgust with female sexuality' (Nitecki 1985: 126) would be to read the passage too narrowly, elevating the personality of the narrator 'into a hermeneutical principle' (Pearsall 2000: 175). Larger discursive processes are at work here: the Virgin/whore dichotomy often present in misogynistic discourse clearly exerts pressure on the line describing Cresseid in terms that reverse commonplace descriptions of Mary's purity (cf. Henryson's lyric 'The Annunciation', esp. line 64). Yet these misogynistic aspects of the text should not be read in isolation from its insistence that bodily pleasures in general must be controlled by the exercise of discipline. The moral disapprobation here echoes the language describing the satisfaction of Diomeid's appetite; some very old ideological currents indeed run through the poem. The next stanza (85–91) further registers the complexities of attributing guilt as even the syntax begins to break down. If the gesture of making additional allowances owing to her sex's putative weakness reminds us of Chaucer's excusing of Criseyde (*TC* 5.1097–9), it remains unclear how the same verb ('excuse') may govern her 'wisdome' (88) except ironically, since it is her *lack* of it that needs excusing. The stanza's syntax is further stretched in the final verse, which 'breaks out into an exclamatory infinitive' (Fox 1981: 346 n.). These syntactic stutters register the conflicting pressures exerted by the disciplinary mechanisms that produce bodies and texts, forces that exceed the individual's intentions or agency. We would do well to avoid attributing these conflicts to a single author or narrator as origin, since there is no stable subject-position from which to voice these contrary movements.

Cresseid surreptitiously returns to her father's house an isolated figure who encloses herself in a 'secreit orature' (120), which parallels the 'oratur' (8) in the outer frame. When Cresseid angrily complains to Venus and Cupid that she is 'clene excludit, as abiect [*outcast*] odious' (133), she falls into her nightmare vision in which her personal disaster assumes cosmic proportions as the seven planetary deities descend from their spheres to assert their power over her body. If this section of the poem marks a turning-point in the zeal with which the flesh is disciplined, however, it also marks the place where Henryson most conspicuously asserts his right to the prestige of vernacular authorship. The balanced symmetries of the gods' formal portraits (151–263) create a learned *tour de force*. Yet the poem's fictional dalliance with pagan deities is not entirely liberated from pressures to add moralizing details. Venus's face, for example, is unstable and shifting, like the iconography of Fortune; one eye laughs while another weeps as a sign 'that all fleschelie paramour' is subject to change and decay (232–8), a *moralitas* that coincides with the final stanza of the poem, with Chaucer's rejection of earthly love at the end of the *Troilus*, and with Ireland's assessment of the moral value of tragedy.

Cupid levels the charge of blasphemy against Cresseid (274), but his concern with her 'leuing [*living*] vnclene and lecherous' (285) registers further ideological tension; the exact charge is less important than the inexorable need to punish her. In a horrifying scene, Cresseid is never even given a chance to respond to the accusation. Like the trial scenes of the satirically motivated fables, the judicial process seems dysfunctional here. With Saturn and the Moon serving as arbiters, it is a foregone conclusion that Cresseid can expect no mercy: since her crime is 'oppin and manifest' (305) she must suffer a life of incurable sickness (306–7). The theatrical spectacle of judicial cruelty towards the vulnerable body nearly rises to the level of Michel Foucault's famous account of the offended sovereign's spectacle of torture used to reassert his power. As Saturn pronounces and enacts the 'duleful [*dismal*] sentence' (309), laying his 'frostie wand' (311) on her head, the balanced antitheses of the stanza (313–15) suggest that Henryson wields his rhetorical mastery like a trenchant sword. The slow-motion punishment is interrupted by an apostrophe that captures the contradictory forces working on poem and author alike:

O cruell Saturne, fraward and angrie, *ill-humoured*
Hard is thy dome and to malitious!
On fair Cresseid quhy hes thow na mercie, *why*
Quhilk was sa sweit, gentill and amorous? *Who*
Withdraw thy sentence and be gracious –
As thow was neuer; sa schawis through thy deid, *deed*
Ane wraikful sentence geuin on fair Cresseid. *vengeful; given*
(323–9)

It does not serve Henryson's immediate rhetorical purpose to acknowledge the extent to which the poem has already participated in injuring her with its own 'scornefull langage' (86). Indeed, the complex play of deixis, in which the spoken time 'now' of the discourse briefly merges with the historical time 'then' of the judicial process, creates the effect of 'subjectivization, the encoding of subjectivity in the very texture of the story', although the first-person subject 'has no single position; it is not a point of origin from which a voice emerges' (Spearing 2001: 734–5). The criticism of the disproportionately severe sentence subjectively inscribed in the stanza clashes with the vindictive punishment; the shifting deictics of the stanza take us very far indeed from any consistent illusion of the presence of a sexually frustrated old man reading and writing in his study.

The punishment of Cresseid's 'play and wantones' (319), whether we are meant to understand the offence as sexual, verbal, or both, is the result of a disciplinary apparatus that exceeds the control of any individual agent. Henryson may be the author who invents this particular exemplum, but he is subject to similar disciplinary techniques, including those of advisory literature like Ireland's *Meroure*. When Cynthia takes over from her co-adjudicator to read the sentence, the description of symptoms makes the diagnosis of leprosy clear. We should understand that well beyond the Middle Ages, leprosy was perceived as a direct affliction by the hand of God, a disciplining of the soul as well as the body. Although Cynthia prophesied that Cresseid would end her days as a leper 'begging fra hous to hous' (342), lepers in medieval Scotland were generally not so mobile. Segregating the infected body from society, the leper laws of medieval and early modern Europe provided one of the most drastic means of disciplining bodies. Lepers were not exactly prisoners, although their movements were highly restricted. (They were permitted to enter a burgh for a few daylight hours, if at all; they could not go door to door or enter public places; they must step aside if meeting a passer-by on a road and so on.) There was a seclusion ritual in which the priest performed the last rites, declared the leper to be dead to the world and symbolically buried the afflicted (Richards 1977: 123–24). Lepers in the medieval and early modern period who refused to enter into isolation would be forcibly moved. Wishing to avoid public recognition, Cresseid asks her father to send her surreptitiously to the hospital outside town; although her 'almost obsessive secrecy' is based on her desire to avoid shame (Patterson 1973: 704), we need not interpret her behaviour at this stage as shallow, merely a prelude to her later capacity for authentic self-reflection and a sense of personal guilt. Instead, what seems most remarkable is how she has sufficiently internalized the prohibitions of her culture so as not to require anyone from her community, no civic or religious authority, to enforce her seclusion. By portraying Cresseid's separation as self-initiated, Henryson erases one site of possible resistance in her docile body.

Cresseid asks her father to support her by sending 'sum meit for cheritie' (383); once she is there, her father daily sends her 'part of his almous' (392). Yet her familial support system, with its ambiguous echoes of Christian charity, is insufficient to meet her needs, and so she must beg. The same kind of double support is evident in a statute in the Burgh Laws of Scotland, which on the one hand requires the leper to be placed 'in the spytaile [*hospital*] of the burgh' if 'he hafe gudis of his awne thruch the whilk [*through which*] he may be sustenyt and cled [*clothed*]', and on the other hand restricts him to the 'toune end and thar ask almous' from passers-by (quoted Fox 1981: lxxxviii n.). Although local practices varied, the typical medieval leper hospital as an institution was a highly regulated, hierarchal, disciplinary apparatus. Houses were often modelled on or subject to a monastic house and overseen by a prior, and required strict observance of rules, even a profession of vows.

When she arrives at the 'spittail hous' Cresseid rejoins a community for the first time since her return to her father's house (391). Withdrawing to a dark corner, Cresseid utters a formal complaint that has been read as evidence of her continuing moral blindness for not yet accepting personal responsibility (Patterson 1973: 705–10). Yet with the *ubi sunt* typical of the complaint genre, the reader is invited at least in part to take up multiple subject positions: as 'the wise man, meditating on the presence of death', and 'the voice of memory', which 'recalls the joyous moments of the past' (Gray 1979: 198). The complaint expresses a passionate commitment to the world in describing the costly fabrics of a luxurious bedroom, the delicacies and precious gold and silver plate of the noble hall (416–24), the world of aristocratic pleasure, of 'ladyis fair in carrolling' and 'garmentis gay' (431, 433). But the momentary glorification of the sensuous life is severely disciplined by the implicit call for readers to renounce their commitment to the world, as the *contemptus mundi* tradition and Chaucer's *Troilus* palinode explicitly demand. Cresseid finds moral lessons in her experience, admonishing the 'ladyis fair of Troy and Grece' (452) to prepare for the same miserable fate. Yet her acceptance of the exemplary status of her suffering is complicated by her 'chydand with [*chiding against*] hir drerie destenye' (470). The futility of her resistance is suggested by a 'lipper lady' (474) who counsels her to stop mourning what cannot be altered. This voice of counsel persuades Cresseid to learn the disciplinary rule of leper law: 'Go leir to clap thy clapper to and fro, / And leif efter [*live according to*] the law of lipper leid [*leper folk*]' (479–80). Like the beasts of the *Fables* relentlessly driven by bodily need, Cresseid is compelled by cold and hunger to do whatever it takes to survive; unlike them, however, she finds her way amid human company.

Having reluctantly accepted her subjection as a member of the infected mendicant community, Cresseid encounters Troilus for the last time according to a chronology that blatantly clashes with Chaucer's. Once more ambiguously echoing the language of Christian charity, the lepers call 'for Goddis lufe of heuin' to a group of knights to give 'almous' (493–4). Cresseid's disfigured face recalls the image of his former lover to Troilus's mind, yet the 'spark of lufe' (512) that her memory kindles is evidently not the fire of love kindled in his soul by the Holy Spirit but the residual effect of carnal passion. The imperfection of his 'knichlie pietie [*pity/piety*]' (519) is registered in the ambiguity of his gesture, when he takes a purse of gold and jewels and 'in the skirt of Cresseid doun can swak [*fling*]' (522). However much the jarring final verb registers Henryson's ironic distance from this emotionally powerful scene, from Cresseid's perspective the knight has performed an act of 'greit humanitie' (534). Only when her fellow leper identifies him as Troilus 'gentill and fre' (536) does she experience 'ane bitter stound [*pain*] / Throwout hir hart' (538–9), echoing the language of penitential remorse (cf. Ireland 1490: III, 46). But her prolonged swooning and self-accusations arise for offending not the divinity but her former lover, whom she idealizes in wholly positive terms even as she loads her self-description with the vocabulary of medieval misogyny, decrying her 'wantones', her 'fickill and friuolous' behaviour (549, 552).

Those who read this as marking the turning-point in a coherent fictional character's moral growth (Gray 1979: 207; Patterson 1973: 712–13) may in fact be responding to the 'discontinuous subject positions' offered for Cresseid (Riddy 1997: 244). Her apparent moral epiphany could be viewed as one specific discursive effect implicated in the poem's terminal narrowing of agency, a final release of any residual attempts to cling to the joys and pleasures of this life, whether through the heroine's tenacious memory or in the narrator's desperate attempt in the opening frame to recapture lost erotic pleasures. Such doors are now closed for good as Cresseid's subject position becomes indistinguishable from that of the more ascetical version of the narrator, as she exercises discipline over her unruly desires by adopting a familiar abhorrence of bodily pleasures: 'My mynd in fleschelie foull affectioun / Was inclynit to lustis lecherous' (558–9; cf. Ireland 1490: III, 121). When Cresseid addresses herself to (male) lovers who must beware of unfaithful partners, it is as though she has reached the same point of renunciation as Chaucer's palinode does without her arriving at a correcting alternative – Christ, the only object of love who 'nyl falsen no wight' (*TC* 5.1845). Paradoxically, then, the poem both demands obedience to moral absolutes and falls short of naming the theological ground of its truth. We are only a short step away from the savage irony and hollow world of Shakespeare's *Troilus and Cressida*.

In writing her testament, Cresseid severs her remaining links to the world. Before death reduces her to terminal silence, her final words plaintively voice her recognition of Troilus's 'trew lufe' (590). Without a word of forgiveness, Troilus erects a marble tomb above her pauper's grave. His epitaph, inscribed in golden letters, contrasts her final days as a leper with her earlier state as 'the flour of womanheid' (608), creating an effect similar to that of a transom tomb, where an image of worldly splendour is juxtaposed with one of rotting flesh. Both inscription and final stanza prominently feature the word 'deid [*dead*]'. Yet the closing stanza, although written in the first person, refuses to return us to the same discursive space as the opening frame, raising once more the question of who is speaking. Is this final voice that of the flawed old man or the disciplined fifteenth-century moralist? Or does the stanza provide further evidence of the 'subjectivation' effect of late medieval narrative, requiring us to abandon the assumption that we are in the presence of a stable origin? One thing is clear: in providing what scholastic commentators would identify as the *intentio auctoris*, the first-person subject of the stanza deictically encodes a specifically gendered mode of address:

> Now, worthie wemen, in this ballet schort, *poem*
> Maid for ȝour worschip and instructioun, *honour*
> Of cheritie, I monische and exhort,
> Ming not ȝour lufe with fals deceptioun. . . . *Mix*
> (610–13)

If the stanza presents death itself as the ultimate disciplinary force by holding up Cresseid's 'sore conclusioun' (614) as a 'charitable' moral lesson for the putative female audience, Henryson remains enmeshed in disciplinary webs as powerful as those within his poem. Indeed, her death reduces the poet to silence: 'Sen [*since*] scho is deid I speik of hir no moir' (616). Perhaps he implies that falling silent at the end-time 'now' of his discourse presages his own inevitable death, that he too will soon lie buried under a funeral marble for future readers. If Henryson expected his work to endure as a poetic monument after his death, the document inscribed in 'goldin letteris' (606) and the 'tomb of merbell gray' (603) on which it is placed may stand as an emblem of the poem itself, at times drearily monochrome, at times glistening brilliantly. At the crossroads between medieval and early modern culture, the work of this northern humanist author lives on as a memorial celebrating the hard discipline of a poetic act of 'greit humanitie', one that registers both the beauty and the horror of earthly joys.

See also: 5 Women's Voices and Roles, 14 England's Antiquities, 17 Literature and Law, 19 Love, 22 Dream Poems, 32 *Piers Plowman*, 33 The *Canterbury Tales*, 34 John Gower and John Lydgate, 35 Thomas Hoccleve.

Notes

1 The author wishes to thank A. C. Spearing for helpful comments, Roderick J. Lyall for biographical information, and the College of Liberal Arts, Auburn University for a Humanities Development Fund Summer Grant that helped support research for this essay.

2 Line references are to Fox 1981.

References and Further Reading

Burrow, J. A. 1975. 'Henryson: *The Preaching of the Swallow*.' *Essays in Criticism* 25, 25–37. Reads the fable as structurally unified by the theme of prudence.

Cox, Catherine S. 1996. 'Froward Language and Wanton Play: The "Commoun" Text of Henryson's *Testament of Cresseid*.' *Studies in Scottish Literature* 29, 58–72. A feminist analysis of errant sexuality and language.

Fox, Denton (ed.) 1981. *The Poems of Robert Henryson*. Oxford: Clarendon Press. Monumental standard edition, with excellent introduction and commentary.

Fradenburg, Louise O. 1984. 'Henryson Scholarship: The Recent Decades.' In *Fifteenth-Century*

Studies: Recent Essays, ed. Robert F. Yeager (Hamden, Conn.: Archon Books), pp. 65–92. An excellent overview of scholarship up to 1982.

Gray, Douglas 1979. *Robert Henryson*. Leiden: Brill. Remains the most stimulating and comprehensive general study of the poetry.

Ireland, John 1490. *The Meroure of Wyssdome, Composed for the Use of James IV, King of Scots, A. D. 1490 by Johannes de Irlandia*, ed. Charles Macpherson, F. Quinn and Craig MacDonald. 3 vols. Scottish Text Society, 2nd ser., 19; 4th ser., 2, 19. Edinburgh and London: Blackwood, 1926, 1965; Aberdeen: Aberdeen University Press, 1990. Book of theological and political 'advice to the prince' by eminent Scottish professor of theology, royal chaplain and confessor.

Mathews, Jana 2002. 'Land, Lepers, and the Law in *The Testament of Cresseid*.' In *The Letter of the Law: Legal Practice and Literary Production in Medieval England*, ed. Emily Steiner and Candace Barrington (Ithaca, N.Y.: Cornell University Press), pp. 40–66. New historicist reading of the construction of 'legal personhood' in the poem.

Nitecki, Alicia K. 1985. '"Fenȝeit of the new": Authority in *The Testament of Cresseid*'. *Journal of Narrative Technique* 15, 120–32. Studies narrative method, arguing that the lack of a stable narrative voice deliberately undermines the poem's own authority.

Patterson, Lee W. 1973. 'Christian and Pagan in *The Testament of Cresseid*.' *Philological Quarterly* 52, 696–714. Argues that in moving from superficial pagan sense of shame to internalized guilt, Cresseid experiences the moral growth of a Christian penitent.

Pearsall, Derek 2000. '"Quha wait gif all that Chauceir wrait was trew?": Henryson's *Testament of Cresseid*.' In *New Perspectives on Middle English Texts: A Festschrift for R. A. Waldron*, ed. Susan Powell and Jeremy J. Smith (Cambridge: Brewer), pp. 169–82. Insists on the need for interpretations of the poem to acknowledge its aesthetic value; includes response to feminist critics.

Richards, Peter 1977. *The Medieval Leper and his Northern Heirs*. Cambridge: Brewer; Totowa, NJ: Rowman and Littlefield. Detailed historical account of leprosy in northern Europe from Middle Ages through the early modern period.

Riddy, Felicity 1997. '"Abject odious": Feminine and Masculine in Henryson's *Testament of Cresseid*.' In *The Long Fifteenth Century: Essays for Douglas Gray*, ed. Helen Cooper and Sally Mapstone (Oxford: Clarendon Press; New York: Oxford University Press), pp. 228–48. Draws on postmodern feminist theory to oppose 'liberal humanist' interpretations.

Spearing, A. C. 2001. 'Narrative Voice: The Case of Chaucer's *Man of Law's Tale*.' *New Literary History* 32, 715–46. Surveys the critical impasse created by the widespread assumption of a stable narrative voice in a Chaucerian fiction; drawing on linguistic analysis of deixis and poststructuralist theory, offers alternative methodology to identify discursive effect of late medieval subjectivity.

Wheatley, Edward 2000. *Mastering Aesop: Medieval Education, Chaucer, and his Followers*. Gainesville: University Press of Florida. A study of the vernacular fables in the context of the medieval system of education; the Henryson chapter draws on extensive knowledge of Latin traditions.

Wogan-Browne, Jocelyn, Watson, Nicholas, Taylor, Andrew and Evans, Ruth (eds) 1999. *The Idea of the Vernacular: An Anthology of Middle English Literary Theory, 1280–1520*. University Park: Pennsylvania State University Press. Well-annotated prologues and other excerpts from Middle English writings as sources of theorizing about literary authority, the construction of audiences and the process of reading; includes important essays on the theory and politics of vernacular writing.

Woods, Marjorie Curry and Copeland, Rita 1999. 'Classroom and Confession.' In *The Cambridge History of Medieval English Literature*, ed. David Wallace (Cambridge: Cambridge University Press), pp. 376–406. Surveys closely related institutions of pedagogy and penitential practice in post-1215 England.

37
Sir Gawain and the Green Knight

Kevin Gustafson

Sir Gawain and the Green Knight is generally considered the best Middle English romance. This is potentially a dubious distinction, because 'romance' is a notoriously slippery term that has been used to categorize a quite diverse body of medieval writings. For present purposes, however, it can be seen as a fictional or pseudo-historical narrative that reflects, celebrates or even criticizes the ideals and social practices of aristocratic life. The general term for these values and practices is chivalry, a code of knighthood that has been characterized as 'an ethos in which martial, aristocratic and Christian elements are fused together' (Keen 1984: 1–2). Romances tend to explore this code by means of adventure, a narrative unit that emphasizes crisis and development. And to the extent that knights and lords were the audience as well as the subject of romance, these stories of adventure were a key means of constructing and perpetuating aristocratic masculinity in the later Middle Ages – although of course there is good reason to believe that romance promoted the ideology of chivalry, and the interests of the landowning classes more generally, to a diverse public, including women as well as non-aristocratic men (Knight 1986; Meale 1994).

Chivalric Identity

Gawain conforms to this rough definition in obvious ways. The poet shows a keen interest in and knowledge of the values and details of aristocratic life. And as the epitome of Arthurian chivalry, Gawain is tested several times in the course of the poem. Yet *Gawain* is also far more complex than most romances. It is so for numerous reasons, but not least because it persistently reminds us that chivalry, the subject of romance texts, is also the product of texts. This story, which the poet claims is recorded in the 'þe best boke of romaunce', draws on a range of writings: other Arthurian romances, to be sure, as well as traditions of love discourse, penance, clerical antifeminism, legal contracts and possibly economic theory. But even the characters within this poem seem familiar with romances and the literary traditions on which such works are based. The most obvious examples concern Gawain, as he encounters his reputation and the expectations of knighthood more generally. The lady who attempts to seduce Gawain betrays a keen knowledge of chivalry and romance texts when she claims that love is, for knights, 'þe tytelet [*inscribed*] token and tyxt of her werrkez' (1515),[1] and when she jokes that Gawain cannot really be who he says he is, since *that* knight would try to steal a kiss. Gawain, for his part, deftly if reluctantly plays this game, speaking of himself in the third person even as he worries about how to conform to the 'Gawain' that the lady seems to have encountered in books. Such self-consciousness has two quite different implications for the poet's notion of character. One is to make Gawain seem particularly rounded, to give him the interiority and psychological depth for which the poet has been justly praised. Another, quite different, effect is to make any notion of Gawain seem distinctly provisional and performative. Even he seems to recognize that to be Gawain is to play a role, and that to be a perfect knight is to adopt a number of different parts, some of them potentially in conflict.

Gawain's struggle with chivalric codes and his own literary reputation is both a major source of humour and, I would suggest, part of the poet's larger concern with the place of texts, including romance texts, in the formation and perpetuation of masculine aristocratic identity. Indeed, *Gawain* continues to appeal to contemporary readers in part because its treatment of knighthood resonates with recent discussions of gender and discourse (Fisher 1987; Heng 1991, 1992; Kinney 1994). Drawing on earlier feminist work, contemporary masculinity studies maintains that manhood is not innate or unchanging, but a socially and historically constructed role; that manhood, far from being a self-evident first principle, is instead a product of difference, so that being a 'man' depends on identifying and often castigating various 'others', most notably 'woman'; and that, to the extent that masculinity relies on such dichotomies, it can be seen as a product of discourse rather than an entity external to language (Butler 1990). These premises, though rooted in contemporary philosophy, provide valuable insight into the structure of the poem and its treatment of chivalry. The poet in basic ways remains committed to romance as a fiction of aristocratic masculine identity. But, as I will suggest, *Gawain* also challenges the assumptions about gender on which such identity is based. This challenge is most notable in the third and fourth fitts (or parts) of the poem, where a previously repressed female agency becomes increasingly central to Gawain's chivalric identity, and the weaknesses traditionally ascribed to women are shown to be thoroughly male as well.

The all-male genealogy that opens *Gawain* exemplifies the way in which masculine aristocratic identity is initially defined in the poem by selectively including but primarily excluding women. In tracing Arthur's court to the destruction of Troy, the poem articulates two patriarchal ideals. One is the fantasy that men appear to beget men. (There is no mention, for example, of Aeneas's marriage to Lavinia, a crucial element in Virgil's legendary history of Rome.) The other is that lands derive their names from, and thus are an extension of, various 'patrounes' (6): Rome from Romulus – who 'neuenes [*names*] hit his aune [*own*] nome, as hit now hat [*is called*]' (10) – Lombard from Langaberde, and of course Britain from Felix Brutus. Women attain a superficially greater role as the poem shifts from epic migration to Arthur's Christmas feast. The poet, for example, calls Gawain and Agravayn 'kynges sistersunes' (111), thus reinserting women in the genealogy. Yet Arthur's court is foremost a fraternity of the 'rich breþer' (39) of the Round Table, and women are mentioned primarily in passing and generally in addition to men. Male experience is even privileged in the entertainment of the court. Before he will eat dinner, Arthur demands a highly self-regarding kind of 'marvel': a masculine tale 'of alderes [*princes*], of armes, of oþer auenturus' (95) that corresponds fairly closely to the features of chivalric romance. Guinevere, the only woman named in this part of the poem, appears to be an exception to the pattern, because she is described in some detail. Yet she is probably best understood as an icon of courtliness and sensitivity, a role that seems implicit on the two occasions on which she is addressed, first by Gawain (in a mere concessionary clause) and later by Arthur, who tries to console her after the spectacle of the Green Knight has left everyone confused and ill at ease. We have little sense of what she thinks or feels – a fact that seems all the more significant in a poem that so carefully reflects on the emotions of male characters.

Guinevere's mute presence at the centre of Arthur's court points to a paradox of chivalry: women are key to defining the code yet excluded from actively participating in it. Indeed, the aspects of chivalry most associated with women – manners, courtesy – can also be seen as a distinct threat to masculinity. The fear that court life may emasculate the knight is exemplified in the description and subsequent challenge of the Green Knight. An 'aghlich [*terrible*] mayster' (136), this live response to Arthur's demand for a fictional marvel is introduced by means of *effictio*, an elaborate rhetorical device that is typically used to catalogue female beauty but here serves to underscore the physical prowess of the male challenger. Indeed, the Green Knight wears his manhood on his torso, with its strong back and chest yet attractively small stomach and waist; and his bushy beard is surely intended to indicate virility, particularly since he later taunts Arthur's court as a collection of beardless youths. The Green Knight has been variously interpreted – the court suspects that he is a 'fantoume or fairyȝe' (240) and critics have variously identified him as a holdover from a vegetation myth, the devil, a mummer, or a messenger from a disapproving God – but he seems significant in the scene primarily because he quite literally embodies the single greatest threat to Arthurian masculinity: a manifestly stronger man who is equally well appointed. And while the Green Knight's brusqueness may mark him as distinctly discourteous, and thus masculine but perhaps not fully chivalric, his withering laugh suggests that the courtesy of Arthur's silent knights may simply be masking cowardice – a criticism already hinted at by the poet:

'What, is þis Arþures hous,' quoþ þe haþel þenne, *knight*
'Þat al þe rous rennes of þurȝ ryalmes so mony? *fame*
Where is now your sourquydrye and your conquestes, *pride*
Your gryndellayk and your greme, and your grete wordes? *fierceness; wrath*
Now is þe reuel and þe renoun of þe Rounde Table

Ouerwalt wyth a worde of on wyȝes speche, *man's*
For al dares for drede withoute dynt schewed!' *cowers; blow*

(309–15)

The king's shame implicitly acknowledges the hit. Either the Round Table has no right to its published reputation (the poet notes that the court is young), or it has become 'soft' and needs to defend its honour. In this context Gawain's initial speech is a triumph of chivalry, for the knight manages to combine courtesy and bravery as he takes up the challenge without offending Arthur (who has already seized the axe) or humiliating his peers. The Green Knight's challenge and Gawain's acceptance of that challenge also reinforce our sense that Arthur's court is a world of men. The first fitt, which begins with an all-male epic genealogy, concludes with Arthurian masculinity at stake in a distinctly martial beheading 'game'. The public exchanges – of vows, of names, of blows – in this culture of honour take place between men who must prove to one another that they are, in fact, real men.

Trawþe and Love

In Fitt 2 the focus shifts more decisively to Gawain, who as 'tulk [*knight*] of tale most trwe' (638) represents the various dimensions of chivalric masculinity through an arming scene, his initial quest for the Green Chapel, and his introduction at the castle later identified as Hautdesert. The arming scene offers a counterpart to the *effictio* of the Green Knight in Fitt 1, but it is also notably different, at once more social and more conspicuously learned. Gawain may be the best of men, but he is also an image of the court (or how it would like to see itself). And his manliness, unlike that of the Green Knight, is expressed less through physical form – we learn very little about the contours of his body – than through a set of values, the most important of which is *trawþe*. This term, which is semantically much richer than its modern counterpart, can refer to simple veracity, fidelity or even one's pledged word. It is the last two meanings that are most important to various games in *Gawain* as well as the feudal world it rather nostalgically depicts. The court expresses the complexity and quasi-religious significance of *trawþe* by means of the pentangle, or five-pointed star, that adorns Gawain's shield. Like that device, in which 'vche lyne vmbelappez [*overlaps*] and loukez [*fastens*] in oþer' (628) in order to form 'þe endeles knot' (630), *trawþe* involves a mysterious fusion, in this case of body and spirit, of secular and religious values. Gawain's five senses are joined to his five fingers, the five wounds of Christ and the five joys of the Virgin. But most attention is devoted to the fifth five, a collection of chivalric terms that refer to the abstract ideals as well as concrete practices of knighthood: *pité*, *clannesse*, *cortaysye*, *felaȝschip* and *fraunchise*. Their inclusion underscores the sense that chivalry must be performed, enacted and otherwise earned. Yet the pentangle, and by implication Arthurian masculinity, is also decidedly bookish. Called the 'pure pentangle' by people 'with lore' (665), the sign originates with no less an authority than Solomon, the wisest of Old Testament kings, and the poet correspondingly treats the device as a sacred text, to be divided into its constituent parts and carefully explicated. The poet's emphasis on the perfection of the pentangle and his conspicuously learned presentation of it offer a hint that *trawþe* may be an attractive but unattainable ideal, even for the 'gentlyst kny3t' (639). Yet it is only as Fitts 3 and 4 unfold that we see tensions within this particular version of aristocratic masculinity and limitations in Gawain's capacity to perform it.

Gawain's journey north is another distinctly masculine act (women are always indoors in this poem; men alone venture out), and here too chivalric identity is defined through differentiation, in this case with the non-courtly 'other': untamed animals and the quasi-human 'wodwos' (721). But Gawain is most troubled by solitude and the harshness of a winter outside the charmed sphere of court, and such deprivation forms the backdrop for his introduction to Hautdesert, a court that offers the comfort of Camelot yet is characterized in quite different ways. Whereas Arthur's castle is dominated by a great hall, the chimneys dotting the rooftop of Hautdesert indicate a number of smaller chambers, and it is in these that a great deal of the action, much of it private and even secretive, will take place. There is also a difference in the role of women in these two settings, and in a way that throws into relief another dimension of chivalry and Gawain's literary reputation: love. We have already been exposed to Gawain's *cortaysye* in his graciously self-effacing speech and the description of the pentangle. Now, as the term takes on decidedly amorous connotations, *cortaysye* is associated with desire and his interactions with women are correspondingly more pronounced. The courtiers at Hautdesert believe that Gawain, 'þat fyne fader of nurture' (919), will teach them of 'luf-talkyng' (927), and the knight lives up to his reputation. Upon seeing two noble women – a brilliantly interlacing double *effictio* distinguishes one as young and beautiful, the other as old and ugly, so that together they form an emblem of temporality, even mortality – he approaches and pledges his service to them both. Later he and the younger lady innocently flirt, finding entertainment 'Þur3 her dere dalayaunce of her derne [*private*] wordez' as they engage in 'clene *cortays* carp [*talk*] closed fro fylþe' (1012–13; emphasis mine). Meanwhile, the lord of the castle introduces a game that implicitly identifies chivalric masculinity with amatory play: he offers to exchange what he kills the next day while hunting for whatever Gawain manages to 'catch' while staying behind at the castle. Gift-giving is a key ritual of nobility in the Middle Ages (Harwood 1991: 484). In this case, it is a ritual with a distinct sexual politics. Like the earlier contract with the Green Knight, this merry bond is an expression of *trawþe* between men, but now it is established and mediated through a kind of trafficking in women, the implication being that women, much like beasts in the forest, belong to the lord. Gawain does not question this assignment of gender roles, either here or when he actually exchanges winnings on three successive evenings. Women, or at least the young and pretty ones, are readily assumed to be tokens in a male game and objects of 'ese'.

Female Agency and *Cortaysye*

Fitt 3 is the most structurally elaborate and linguistically rich part of *Gawain.* And it is here that the poet begins to complicate gender roles, as female agency becomes an increasingly crucial element in the poem. On three days the lord hunts – for does, then a boar, finally a fox – and on each morning the lady seeks out Gawain in his chamber. The persistent juxtaposition of hunting and seduction invites comparison between the two acts. Each is an aristocratic pastime, each a highly formalized expression of desire – a point that is brought home by the poet's vivid and highly technical description of how to dismember a deer (1130–52). And each is, traditionally at least, a means by which the aristocratic male defines himself through the pursuit of an 'other'. But despite the pact with the lord, it is Gawain who seems most like the quarry in these scenes. More specifically, the humour of Fitt 3 depends on recognizing that the lady pursues him by manipulating a textual tradition of love discourse in which men are sexual predators. The tradition is exemplified by Andreas Capellanus's Latin *De amore*, which presents a series of hypothetical dialogues in which men of various social stations use logic, flattery and shame to seduce women. But the poet and his audience could have encountered the conventions of seduction from a number of vernacular sources, most notably the highly popular *Roman de la rose*, a work that is actually referred to in *Cleanness*, another poem in the same manuscript as *Gawain.* At Hautdesert the lady goads Gawain by suggesting that he fails to live up to either the textual ideal of the aristocratic male as seducer or his own reputation, from French romance, as a womanizer (Putter 1995).

The complex dynamics and ambiguous tone of the seduction scenes are quickly established on the first morning. Since the exchange-of-winnings game tacitly objectifies women, it is only appropriate that we see the lady through Gawain's decidedly male gaze, as it focuses on the laughter that comes from a small red mouth that is at once appealing and frightening. For even as the ensuing exchange about imprisonment and servitude picks up on the love language of Fitt 2, here the violence of the metaphors is more threatening, despite the laughter on both sides. The two of them are now in private – the door is locked, she notes, and all the servants are asleep – and she reinforces her playful speech with an ambiguous invitation to her 'cors' (1237), a term that may refer either to her person or to her body more plain and simple. Yet speech is her main tool, particularly once she begins to manipulate him, praising him as the man 'þat al lykez' (1234) and appealing to his reputation for *cortaysye.* One of the qualities that makes up the last of the five fives on Gawain's shield, *cortaysye* is also one of the most ambiguous, 'a single, immensely rich complex of ideas and feelings, which is capable of specialization in any of a number of directions' (Spearing 1970: 200). The lady chooses to emphasize the erotic and even rakish connotations of the term, because these, she claims, fit the reputation of her companion:

> 'So god as Gawayn gaynly is halden, *fitly*
> And cortaysye is closed so clene in hymseluen, *completely*

Couth not ly3tly haf lenged so long wyth a lady, *stayed*
Bot he had craued a cosse, bi his cortaysye, *kiss*
Bi sum towch of summe tryfle at sum talez ende.
(1297–1301)

Gawain does not deny this account of himself, and it would be naive to see him merely as a victim of either female entrapment or his own ignorance, his protestations aside. He is sufficiently skilful – sufficiently courteous – to acknowledge and deflect the lady's compliment by coyly denying that he has any right to it; and in an attempt to turn the tables in this game of praise, he claims that *he* should instead be showing reverence to a lady of such obvious worth. Yet the focus continues to be on Gawain's *prys*, his character as well as his reputation (Mann 1986). Like the women in Andreas's dialogues, he is primarily on the verbal defensive, seeking to maintain his *trawþe* and *clannesse* even as he worries about failing in the forms of his speech. And when she accuses him of lacking *cortaysye*, the lady employs exactly the kind of rhetorical stratagem that a man might use against a woman in one of Andreas's dialogues: if you are really noble, you would give a kiss, which is a sign of good breeding. She even manipulates *cortaysye* in precisely the way that she claims Gawain the seducer of romance fame would use it, as a means to win a kiss at the end of some clever speech.

The playful struggle of the first morning reveals tensions within the supposedly harmonious pentangle. These conflicts within chivalry arise in part because aristocratic masculine identity is based on a diverse and ambiguous textual tradition. But the lady can shame Gawain only because he achieves his chivalric identity by consciously adhering to such codes, whatever their contradictions. Gawain is an interpreter as well as a fighter. Indeed, he manages to succeed on the first day primarily by means of canny interpretation. He satisfies *cortaysye* by kissing the lady, and *trawþe* by turning that kiss over to the lord, but stays out of trouble only by refusing to reveal the source of his winnings, correctly if somewhat legalistically claiming that he is not contractually bound to do so. Gawain is perfectly adept at playing verbal games, and the lady appeals explicitly to Gawain's literacy on the second morning. She again jokes that he must be an imposter – 'Sir, 3if 3e be Wawen, wonder me þynkkez' (1481) – because he still seems hopelessly inept at her form of *cortaysye*. Now she also expresses her disappointment by means of textual metaphors, claiming that such a courteous man should 'teche sum tokenez of trweluf craftes' (1527), unless he is 'lewed' (1528; see also lines 1515 and 1541). This charge is somewhat ironic, because in medieval England it was generally assumed that knights would in fact be *lewed*, or Latin-illiterate. But her use of the term is significant and perhaps not completely figurative. The implication is that Gawain should in fact be fluent in *cortaysye* as found in texts, and that his failure to learn lessons about kissing makes him the chivalric equivalent of a Latin-illiterate clerk. Her criticism is effective because, whatever she desires, Gawain clearly prides himself on knowing and following the rules of chivalry. His commitment is even evident on the one occasion on which he rejects her conception of *cortaysye*: when she suggests that he is strong enough to take her by force, and that it would be 'vilanous' for anyone to resist such a man (1496–7). He politely turns down her offer of rape not because it is inherently discourteous – ' "ȝe, be God," quoþ Gawayn, "good is your speche" ' (1498) – but because force is against the rule of his land. It seems that he can counter one interpretation of chivalry only by appealing to another.

Dawn of the third day finds Gawain troubled by dreams of the Green Chapel, but the poet notes that he is in 'gret perile' of a different sort with the lady. That danger at first appears to be sexual, as she enters wearing a particularly revealing gown (1738–45) and uttering 'spechez of specialité' (1778), and as he looks at her ardently. Her increasingly forward manner renders the tensions within the pentangle explicit, at least in Gawain's mind: 'He cared for his cortaysye, lest craþayn [*a churl*] he were, / And more for his meschef ȝif he schulde make synne, / And be traytor to ȝat tolke [*knight*] þat þat telde [*house*] aȝt [*owned*]' (1773–5). Gawain nevertheless manages to preserve all his virtues, remaining courteous even as he rejects her advances and successive offers of a ring and then her girdle (or sash) as love tokens. It is only when she mentions the power of the latter to protect its wearer against harm that he begins to weaken. In one of the poem's characteristically fine depictions of Gawain's calculation, the knight recognizes that he will break his bond with the lord if he keeps the girdle but imagines that 'þe sleȝt [*device*] were noble' (1858) if he can save his life. It would be easy to judge Gawain too harshly at this point. This is, after all, a romance rather than a saint's life. Yet the ironic conjunction of 'noble' and 'sleȝt' suggests that, however much we may sympathize with Gawain, his decision to keep the girdle represents a fall from the ideal of the pentangle. The debasement of his *trawþe* is ironically indicated by the lady's request that he should not report the garment, but instead 'lelly layne' (1863), or faithfully conceal, it from her husband. Nor it is accidental that Gawain breaks his *trawþe* by wearing the lady's garment. For this scene only completes a process of feminization that began when he entered Hautdesert at the end of Fitt 2. Stripped of the armour that marks him as a man and dressed in a fine robe, he pledged himself to ladies and, on the following days, remained 'at ese' with them while the lord and his men hunted. He even took on traditionally female roles by striving to preserve his *clannesse* against seduction and recreating her kisses with the lord, 'as comyly as he cowþe awyse' (1389). Now Gawain enters an agreement with the lady that compels him to break his pact with the lord. Gawain's chivalric identity, initially expressed through same-sex bonds and the exclusion or objectification of women, is now fractured through his interaction with a woman who has her own agency and desire.

Beyond Stereotypes

Gawain initially manages to suppress such complications, first when he confesses to a priest at Hautdesert and then as he sets out to fulfil his contract with the Green Knight. Yet his second preparation to seek the Green Chapel, which in many ways echoes the earlier arming scene in Fitt 2, also contains a notable difference: the addition of the lady's girdle – now looped twice around his waist – to his armour and symbolic system.

It is explicitly noted that Gawain wears the garment not for pride but to save himself. And in a phrase that ironically echoes the earlier description of the pentangle, the poet claims that the garment 'wel bisemed' (2035) the knight. Gawain's 'sleȝt' makes his subsequent expressions of bravery seem a bit hollow. His guide reiterates the strength and cruelty of the Green Knight – he is bigger than the four largest men in Arthur's court and mercilessly kills knights as well as (presumably unarmed) churls, clerks and monks (2107–8). But Gawain indignantly dismisses an offer to sneak away, protesting that he would be a 'knyȝt kowarde' (2131) to leave without fulfilling his oath, and that he should in any case trust in Providence. Besides giving Gawain a chance to assert his honour and bravery, the guide's rehearsal of the Green Knight's cruelty feeds another self-serving chivalric fantasy: that the enemy is evil, a diabolical 'other'. Gawain imagines the chapel, which is really no more than an overgrown cave, as the 'corsedest kyrk' (2196) and a 'chapel of meschaunce' (2195), a place where this 'Fende' (2193) may make 'deuocioun on þe Devuelez wyse' (2192). Such demonizing is the height of chivalric pride. For while the pentangle combines religious and secular values, it is only after Gawain's *trawþe* is compromised that he fancies himself not simply a knight defending the court's honour, but a Christian hero engaged in a monumental battle against evil.

Such demonizing is deeply ironic, because religious language informs the subsequent criticism of Gawain's own *vntrawþe* in the scene that follows. The Green Knight actually turns out to be less a devil than a provocateur, and ultimately a kind of chivalric father confessor. He initially praises Gawain for coming to fulfil his contract 'as truee men schulde' (2241). But when Gawain flinches at the first blow, the Green Knight shames him for failing to live up to his chivalric ideals and literary reputation, and in much the same terms that he used to chide the entire court in the first fitt:

> 'Þou art not Gawayn,' quoþ þe gome, 'þat is so goud halden, *man*
> Þat neuer arȝed for no here by hylle ne be vale, *quailed; warriors*
> And now þou fles for ferde er þou fele harmez! *in fear*
> Such cowardise of þat knyȝt cowþe I neuer here.'
>
> (2270–3)

This challenge to Gawain's masculinity forms a backdrop to the Green Knight's triumphant claim that he is the better man because he calmly withstood a blow (2278–9). More serious, if less mocking, is his accusation of Gawain's *vntrawþe* for keeping the girdle. In a revelation that collapses two seemingly distinct plots, it turns out that the Green Knight is in fact Bertilak of Hautdesert, the lord who initiated the exchange-of-winnings game. He praises Gawain for withstanding both sexual temptation and the threat of the axe, and claims that the knight is better than other men 'as perle bi þe quite pese [*white pea*] is of prys [*value*] more' (2364). But in the end Gawain's *prys* is only comparative, not the absolute faultlessness signified by the pentangle. For in keeping the girdle, he 'lakked a lyttel' (2366), a fault that the Green Knight finds understandable because the knight merely wanted to save his life. Like the Green Knight's accusation, Gawain's subsequent confession draws on penitential language in a way that redefines chivalric masculinity, so that it includes imperfection and fear, as well as a sense of humility that arises from recognition of one's own weakness rather than from mere politeness. For the Green Knight at least, Gawain is 'confessed so clene' (2397), and, having endured a nick on the neck by way of penance, the knight is 'polyshed of þat ply3t' (2393). The Green Knight concludes his act of forgiveness by offering the girdle as a sign of a new chivalric identity brought about by 'þe chaunce of þe Grene Chapel at cheualrous kny3tez' (2399).

Gawain's reaction to this disclosure is more complex, and in ways that underscore the poet's overarching concern with gender, identity and texts. Despite the Green Knight's forgiveness, he remains fixated on his dishonour, accepting the girdle not as a souvenir of adventure, but as a sign of 'surfet' (2433) and a reminder of 'Þe faut and þe fayntyse [*frailty*] of þe flesche crabbed [*perverse*]' (2435). Then, in what seems to be a complete about-face, he immediately launches into an antifeminist diatribe, claiming that he should be excused for being beguiled by a lady, since he is in the company of Adam, Solomon, Samson and David. This controversial speech is perhaps best understood dramatically, as the self-serving product of Gawain's wounded ego. The Green Knight has already noted that Gawain failed not because of lust but out of a desire, quite literally, to save his neck; perhaps the most one can say to exculpate Gawain is that the lady presented an opportunity for him to act upon his weakness. It is, I would suggest, a residual unwillingness to acknowledge such weakness *as* his own that motivates the antifeminism. He noted in his earlier confession that fear of the blow caused him to forsake his 'kynde', or nature, 'Þat is larges [*generosity*] and lewte [*loyalty*], þat longez to kny3tez' (2381). 'Now am I fauty and falce' (2382), he claimed, as if he had never been that way before. Here, faced with the prospect that 'larges and lewte' are not his nature, he turns to a textual tradition that blames women for male weakness. In Fitt 3, the lady suggested that men use stories out of self-interest (in her example, erotic self-interest, as they try to steal a kiss at the end of some tale). Gawain's antifeminism is just such a textual reflex. Rooted in teachings of the church fathers but also available in a variety of antimatrimonial treatises, the speech is a weak attempt to re-establish an idealized aristocratic masculine identity by locating *vntrawþe* in the female 'other'. A similar dynamic seems to govern Gawain's decision to accept and rename the girdle. Like the lady, the girdle is external to the knight, an object out there that allows him to stabilize and control what he would like to think is uncharacteristic behaviour. This is not to say that Gawain has no regret, or that his confession before the Green Knight is not sincere. Rather, the poet is making another fine psychological insight, suggesting the limits of the knight's ability or willingness to embrace weakness as intrinsically his. Faced with a crisis of chivalric identity, Gawain falls back on a familiar tradition that conveniently supports a model in which men are strong, women are weak and male cowardice is a result of association, even contamination.

Because Gawain's antifeminist speech is particularly virulent and self-serving, there is good reason to be sceptical about how seriously we are meant to take it. Less clear is the extent to which the poet manages to stand outside the more general antifeminism of his culture. On the one hand, Gawain's speech is part of a larger shift in which women, so often marginalized in romance, become increasingly important in this one. The Old Testament exempla offer a striking contrast to the all-male secular genealogy that opens the poem. And while it is true that the lady was seducing Gawain with the full knowledge and encouragement of her husband, this plot was in turn initiated by another woman: Morgan La Fee, the revered older lady at Hautdesert, who was trying to test the pride of Arthur's brotherhood and frighten Guenevere to death. This reference to Morgan is often seen as a gesture to romance conventions, specifically the need for supernatural plot elements. More recent critics, however, have no doubt been right to see significance in her central role in the plot (if not the narrative) of *Gawain*. Not only is this 'goddess' (2452) the origin of an adventure that challenges and ultimately redefines chivalric identity; she is also, as Arthur's half-sister and Gawain's aunt, central to a final genealogy in which aristocratic masculine identity is intertwined with female desire. Gawain clearly takes pride in being Arthur's nephew, but Morgan's blood runs through his veins as well, and in the course of the poem he exhibits guile as well as bravery, vengeance as well as courtesy. Yet for all the emphasis on female agency, it may be a mistake to see the poem as feminist in any modern sense. Female characters still largely conform to medieval stereotypes – the silent icon of courtesy, the beautiful seductress, the vengeful old witch, the Virgin Mary – and very rarely are we privy to their inner thoughts. The latter fact alone would suggest that the poet is, like so many writers of romance, interested in female figures primarily as a way to develop masculine identity, rather than as independent subjects of analysis.

What the poet arguably does offer through his fiction of gender is insight into the politics of such stereotyping, as well as fantasies of male exclusiveness more generally. As we have seen, chivalry is based on exclusiveness. And one important way aristocratic men define themselves as a group is by suppressing or stigmatizing 'woman', whether by omitting her from genealogies, engaging in stereotypes about weakness and guile, treating her as a token or mere object of desire, or (perhaps most subtly) praising her for passive virtues unfitting for a warrior. Gawain's adventures on the way to the Green Chapel challenge the validity of such strategies. The readiness with which he falls into traditionally female roles in Fitt 3 indicates that gender boundaries are much more fluid than the first two fitts of the poem would suggest. The culmination of this transformation – his decision to wear the girdle – indicates that he also embodies the vices of cowardice and guile stereotypically associated with the 'other'. His subsequent attempt to blame female guile for his own weakness is not only humorous; it also reveals the self-serving way in which men use women – and texts about women – to mask their own faults. The poet's treatment of antifeminism is thus analogous to Chaucer's handling of it in the Wife of Bath's Prologue, where the Wife of Bath confesses to and exemplifies every fault that clerks associate with women; yet the Prologue amply demonstrates that men, including clerks, have those faults as well.

One could imagine the poet making a broader criticism, in which both tensions within the pentangle and Gawain's failure to live up to it would indicate the limitations of chivalry and precipitate its replacement by another code, one that focuses more explicitly on heavenly values. The poet is certainly capable of such a shift in perspective if he is also, as most critics assume, the author of the three explicitly religious poems that precede *Gawain* in a unique fourteenth-century manuscript. The penitential language at the Green Chapel even hints at such a resolution. But Gawain points his horse towards Camelot, not a monastery, and his return to Arthur's court indicates that the poet remains committed to aristocratic rituals and values. Indeed, the poem concludes with just such an aristocratic ritual, as the court laughs and adopts the girdle – a 'token of *vntrawþe*' – in Gawain's honour. There is little direct evidence that would allow us to assess the significance of this final act, either to the court or to the poet. The gesture can plausibly be seen as a kind of capitulation, in which both the court and, by extension, the poet castigate the feminine as vice and thus argue for the need to suppress a dangerous female agency (Fisher 1987: 72). The final ritual can also be seen, however, as the poet's attempt, through a quintessentially chivalric ritual, to move beyond gender distinctions in order to make a point about humanity more generally. As various critics have suggested in various ways, the girdle is a remarkably flexible symbol, especially when compared to the static complexity of the pentangle. It is also an increasingly androgynous one. Gawain initially adopts it as a token of the frailty of his flesh, which he associates specifically with female guile. The court, by contrast, wears the garment in honour of male adventure. And while the Green Knight claims that Gawain should wear it as an example for other knights, now both men and women wear the sash:

> Þe kyng comfortez þe knyȝt, and alle þe court als
> Laȝen loude þerat, and luflyly acorden *laughed; graciously*
> Þat lordes and ladis þat longed to þe Table,
> Vche burne of þe broþerhede, a bauderyk schulde haue. *man; baldric*
> (2513–16)

Editors often amend 'ladis' (ladies) to 'ledes' (men) in line 2515, partly because the rest of the passage mentions only men and partly because military orders in medieval Europe excluded women. But given the focus of this poem, the manuscript reading also makes sense as a gender-inclusive statement that acknowledges the frailty of all people. Gawain's main lesson at the Green Chapel is that even the most perfect of men is imperfect, a confession that he makes with great resistance and immediately tries to qualify. The communal laughter of the court, by contrast, shows a ready acceptance of human frailty. Real men – and real women – require laughter and forgiveness.

Modern readers may understandably remain dissatisfied with a ritual that relies on a female garment to symbolize universal human weakness. And to the extent that knights of the Round Table must cross-dress to denote their imperfection, the poem does perpetuate antifeminist stereotypes. A more generous view would emphasize the poet's awareness of the politics of such stereotyping. *Gawain* begins as a romance that celebrates masculine aristocratic identity. But even as the poet draws on familiar conventions for defining masculinity, he also offers complications, blurring gender roles and showing that the texts underlying chivalric identity are multiple, contradictory and open to divergent and self-interested interpretations. Gawain's antifeminism is a particularly keen example of such self-interest, and may indicate the limited ability of the code to confront its own contradictions – of the Christian knight to accept his inherent imperfection. Such criticism can be taken as an invitation to redefine aristocratic masculinity. The analysis of gender in *Gawain* may also be the poet's attempt to transform chivalry and romance into vehicles for exploring secular identity more generally. The court's adoption of the girdle would indicate that this identity is extemporaneous and full of contradictions, an ever-changing role ritualistically created and performed by an ever-changing humanity.

See also: 5 Women's Voices and Roles, 12 England and France, 16 War and Chivalry, 19 Love, 20 Middle English Romance, 21 Writing Nation, 38 Malory's *Morte Darthur*.

Note

1 All quotations are from the standard text edited by J. R. R. Tolkien and E. V. Gordon, *Sir Gawain and the Green Knight*, 2nd edn, ed. Norman Davis (Oxford: Clarendon Press, 1967).

References and Further Reading

Aers, David 1988. '"In Arthurus Day": Community, Virtue, and Individual Identity in *Sir Gawain and the Green Knight*.' In his *Community, Gender, and Individual Identity: English Writing 1360–1430* (London: Routledge), pp. 153–78. Sees the juxtaposition of public and private worlds as an attempt to explore tensions between the individual moral agent and a communal code of honour.

Auerbach, Erich 1953. 'The Knight Sets Forth'. In his *Mimesis: The Representation of Reality in Western Literature* (Princeton, N.J.: Princeton University Press), pp. 123–42. Characterizes French chivalric romance as an aristocratic mode that treats the ideals as well as the realities of court life, even as it covers its ideological bases and biases.

Barron, W. R. J. 1987. *English Medieval Romance.* London: Longman. General survey that treats romance as a mode and organizes various Middle English examples according to traditional 'matters'.

Burrow, J. A. 1965. *A Reading of Sir Gawain and the Green Knight.* London: Routledge and Kegan Paul. A detailed reading that focuses on Gawain's fidelity to his formal agreements, his *trawþe*.

Butler, Judith 1990. *Gender Trouble: Feminism and the Subversion of Identity.* New York and London: Routledge. Key psychoanalytic and poststructuralist study that uses the category of gender to analyse and criticize essentialist conceptions of identity.

Dinshaw, Carolyn 1992. 'A Kiss Is Just a Kiss: Heterosexuality and its Consolations in *Sir Gawain and the Green Knight*'. *Diacritics* 24, 205–26. Argues that the poem promotes heterosexual identity and heteronormative modes of reading by staging – and then rendering unintelligible – the kisses between Gawain and Bertilak.

Fewster, Carol 1987. *Traditionality and Genre in Middle English Romance.* Cambridge: Brewer. A study of stylization, self-consciousness and self-referentiality in Middle English romance: the tendency of these works to refer to other romances or even an archetypal romance style.

Fisher, Sheila 1987. 'Taken Men and Token Women in *Sir Gawain and the Green Knight*.' In *Seeking the*

Woman in Late Medieval and Renaissance Writings: Essays in Feminist Contextual Criticism, ed. Sheila Fisher and Janet E. Halley (Knoxville: University of Tennessee Press), pp. 71–105. Argues that the poet puts the lady and Morgan la Fee at the centre of the poem in order to demonstrate the threat women pose to Christian chivalry and thus the need to marginalize them.

Harwood, Britton J. 1991. '*Gawain* and the Gift.' *Publications of the Modern Language Association of America* 106, 483–99. Argues that gift-giving, initially associated in *Gawain* with nobility and aristocratic largesse, is ultimately subsumed by the Christian notion of forgiveness as a gift that requires knightly humility and cannot be repaid.

Heng, Geraldine 1991. 'Feminine Knots and the Other *Sir Gawain and the Green Knight*.' *Publications of the Modern Language Association of America* 106, 500–14. Rejecting the assumption that Gawain is the centre of the poem, locates a 'feminine text' in *Gawain*, in which the conjunction and identification of female characters undermines any fixed sense of identity.

—— 1992. 'What a Woman Wants: The Lady, *Gawain*, and the Forms of Seduction.' *Yale Journal of Criticism* 5.3, 101–35. A feminist and psychoanalytic study that sees discourse as its own end, so that the seduction scenes of Fitt 3 are less a matter of temptation than an elaboration of desire, specifically of a protean female desire that undermines the gender construction of the courtly subject.

Hopkins, Andrea 1990. *The Sinful Knights: A Study of Middle English Penitential Romance*. Oxford: Clarendon Press. An examination of the penitential romance that notes important ways in which *Gawain* does not fit into the subgenre.

Keen, Maurice 1984. *Chivalry*. New Haven, Conn.: Yale University Press. An authoritative study that examines handbooks as a basis to examine chivalry as a literary and social phenomenon.

Kinney, Clare R. 1994. 'The (Dis)embodied Hero and the Signs of Manhood in *Sir Gawain and the Green Knight*.' In Lees 1994, pp. 47–57. Examines the fluctuations of masculine identity within the poem.

Knight, Stephen 1986. 'The Social Function of the Middle English Romances.' In *Medieval Literature: Criticism, Ideology and History*, ed. David Aers (Brighton: Harvester), pp. 99–122. A materialist account of romances as works that raise and then resolve threats to the interests of landowners in medieval England.

Lees, Clare A. (ed.) 1994. *Medieval Masculinities: Regarding Men in the Middle Ages*. Minneapolis: University of Minnesota Press. Application of contemporary understandings of gender as a social and historical construct to a range of medieval texts.

Mann, Jill 1986. 'Price and Value in *Sir Gawain and the Green Knight*.' *Essays in Criticism* 36, 294–318. Reading the commercial language of the poem in the context of medieval economic theory, emphasizes the primary role of exchange in determining a value of Gawain that is neither intrinsic nor completely extrinsic.

Meale, Carol M. (ed.) 1994. *Readings in Medieval English Romance*. Cambridge: Brewer. Collection of scholarship that tends to focus on the audience and manuscript contexts of romance.

Moi, Toril 1985. *Sexual/Textual Politics: Feminist Literary Theory*. London: Routledge. Introductory survey of French and Anglo-American feminist literary theory, with an emphasis on gender identity as an expression of power relations and on woman as 'other', at once alien and necessary to defining man.

Potkay, Monica Brzezinski 2001. 'The Violence of Courtly Exegesis in *Sir Gawain and the Green Knight*'. In *Representing Rape in Medieval and Early Modern Literature*, ed. Elizabeth Robertson and Christine M. Rose (New York: Palgrave), pp. 97–124. Locating Fitt 3 of the poem in a tradition that associates reading with rape, argues that the Lady's appropriation of seduction strategies shows how the reader-as-rapist can potentially become the object of rape.

Putter, Ad 1995. *Sir Gawain and the Green Knight and French Arthurian Romance*. Oxford: Clarendon Press. A source study that sees *Gawain* as a fully conventional romance that embraces the values, concerns and attitudes of the French *roman courtois*.

Scaglione, Aldo 1991. *Knights at Court: Courtliness, Chivalry, and Courtesy from Ottonian Germany to the Italian Renaissance*. Berkeley and Los Angeles: University of California Press. Surveys the interrelation of social and literary dimensions of courtliness and chivalry as cultural models of behaviour.

Shoaf, R. A. 1984. *The Poem as Green Girdle:* Commercium *in* Sir Gawain and the Green Knight. Gainesville: University of Florida Press. Argues that the poem is about the conflict between chivalry and commerce, systems of value that are embodied in the pentangle and the girdle respectively.

Spearing, A. C. 1970. *The Gawain-Poet: A Critical Study.* Cambridge: Cambridge University Press, pp. 171–236. Sees Gawain's pledge as an opportunity to examine conflicts within the pentangle – notably between *cortaysye* and *clannesse*, but also within *cortaysye*.

38
Blood and Love in Malory's *Morte Darthur*

Catherine La Farge

Blood and love are the two great good things in Malory's *Morte Darthur.* Noble blood and love in many forms command the story's plot and its moments of greatest elation and compunction. The 'worshyp' due to good blood is inestimable, and yet in the form of shared blood the intense affection it inspires is shadowed by its opposite: the drive to kill. Brotherly embraces hover on the brink of murder. Love between brother and sister is crucially represented by fatal incest. The mutual admiration of men of noble blood frequently suggests religious fervour, the erotic, or both; meanwhile, in a period generally known for its quasi-religious handling of love, sexual interest between men and women is comparatively free from intimations of divinity. Love and blood are intertwined, and their precise roles in the story are complicated further by the text's desire not to know. The narrative shares its characters' endemic reluctance to recognize how and why things happen, especially where blood and love are implicated. With Gawain, the text might as well say: 'Jesu defende me . . . that I never se hit nor know hit' (683.3–4).[1]

It is not surprising that *Le Morte Darthur* has a difficult time with causation. I say this roughly in the way one speaks of a person having problems with a particular issue which represents for her unwelcome truths or submerged, troubling memories. Texts do not behave or come into being in precisely the same way that people do, but it is nevertheless useful to speak of a text having an unconscious and a pattern of behaviour stemming from repressions and unwitting admissions analogous to those which feature in the lives of individuals. Textual patterns of this kind may record engagements with the psychic patterns of their writers, scribes and editors, but are not identical to them. Part of the job of the critic is to trace the structures of silence and revelation, allowing the text a certain coherence apart from its writer and sources while at the same time inviting that background to illuminate the problems where it can.[2]

We readily speak of a 'knowing' style. Is it valid to speak of one text as being more *self*-knowing than another? If so, sheer chronology is by no means a good indicator. The reader of many works preceding Malory, such as Chrétien's *Yvain*, Chaucer's *Troilus* or

Sir Gawain and the Green Knight, might well feel that these texts have more of a handle on their own repetitions, evasions and circumlocutions than Malory's work can muster. Certainly, there would seem to be a greater gap between what Malory's text explicitly aims to show and what it actually betrays in its less guarded moments. The degree to which *Le Morte Darthur* fails to contain its own contradictions must stem, as Felicity Riddy has so convincingly observed, in no small measure from its desperate desire to sustain fifteenth-century English ideologies of empire and gentility in the face of contemporary events: the loss of French territories conquered by Henry V and the consequent blow to the sense of identity and entitlement of the knightly class. Riddy reads the civil war occasioned by Lancelot's and Guinevere's adultery as 'issu[ing] from the intervention of the feminine into the world of homosocial ambition', the plot thereby providing an alternative to any blame or weakness which might otherwise be attached to the business of masculine empire-building (Riddy 1996: 65). The fall of the Round Table and the death of Arthur have to happen somehow, and an attack from within gives the story a satisfying explanation as to how his limitlessly victorious reign can have come to an end. As Riddy suggests, however, Malory's adoption of this approach is problematic since he wants to have his cake and eat it too. Not only is Guinevere eventually to be saved, but she is to be so *because* of her way of loving, not despite it: 'whyle she lyved she was a trew lover, and therefore she had a good ende' (649.34–5). The text undertakes to enshrine more than it can, and tell-tale slips are bound to occur.

For the purposes of this chapter I am chiefly going to consider examples of these issues as they affect two of Malory's tales, *The Tale of Sir Lancelot and Queen Guinevere* and *The Tale of Sir Gareth. Lancelot and Guinevere*, while marked by its own internal symmetries, is far more affected than *Gareth* by the urgencies of the larger plot, a fact which accounts for the greater energy it expends in attempting to stuff the evidence under the carpet. *Gareth*, appearing much earlier in the text, is something of a happy plateau within the overall shape of the narrative: Arthur's kingship has been established, and *Gareth* provides an example of how things happened in love and blood in those better times.

The Tale of Sir Lancelot and Queen Guinevere

Even a first reading of the penultimate tale, alongside the final débâcle, allows for a diffuse sense that 'things keep going wrong at Camelot these days', a pattern most comically represented by a local huntress's wounding Lancelot by mistake in the buttock, and most tragically by the surfacing of the corpse of Elayne (La Farge 1992). The desire-engendered myopia of characters and text alike is such that one's sense of these difficulties may at first resemble Bors's when he rightly if vaguely claims that Guinevere had 'none evyll wyll' towards any of the twenty-four knights at the dinner (a technically accurate claim symmetrical to Lancelot's in the episode of the Knight of the Cart regarding the ten wounded knights with whom she did not sleep), and that 'howsomever the game goth there was treson amonge us' (617.25, 28–9). Malory's narrative, whether he or it would like it or not, gives us the material to trace a bit more precisely how the game goes.

In the first episode of *The Tale of Lancelot and Guinevere* the queen is accused of treason because Sir Patryse dies from eating a poisoned apple at her private dinner party. By the combined forces of trial by combat and the Lady of the Lake – the text seems to want both, perhaps feeling that the former needs the reinforcement of direct revelation – the truth comes out: Guinevere is not guilty. She did not put the poison in the apple. And yet, as we all know, Guinevere *is* guilty. Not only has she been sleeping with Lancelot again, but she held the dinner specifically to display what is not true: 'that she had as grete joy in all other knyghtes of the Rounde Table as she had in Sir Launcelot' (613.15–17). The alibi itself, as in an Iris Murdoch plot, causes the problem. It is not just that Guinevere happens to be guilty, although not of what she has been accused; it is that her actual guilt, which some might call treason (not yet the subject of public 'sclawndir and noyse'), brought about the dinner party disaster. In other words, although she was of 'good entente' and was 'never purposed' to murder anybody, she is treasonous and without her treason Patryse would not have died (615.3, 5).

In averting its gaze from this unpalatable fact, the text focuses instead on family feud. It is Sir Pynell who inadvertently killed Patryse, having meant to poison Gawain – and there a classic spiral of blood-based revenge awaits the persistent enquirer: Pynell wanted to kill Gawain because Gawain had killed his cousin Lamerok, who – although the text at this point does not remind us of these further details – had slept with Gawain's mother and was the son of Pellinore, who killed Lot, Gawain's father. All this is without mentioning that, even before Arthur slept with Lot's wife, Lot opposed Arthur's kingship – a fact that, in a culture very aware of familial inheritance of power, might be assumed to arise from Arthur's father killing Lot's wife's father and marrying her mother. Gawain's mother and her sisters are the step-daughters of Uther whose birth son triumphs. Morgause's and Morgan's baleful forays against their brother can only have some connection to this familial background. For the Poisoned Apple sequence, even without plumbing these depths, the bottomless pit of blood feud offers the path of least resistance where a scapegoat is required.

In the text's desire to have this dizzying regression be the whipping-boy instead of the love of Lancelot and Guinevere, which is somehow other than what we moderns can understand, we can see romance's disdain for the machinery of epic. In many ways, Malory's work is something of a throwback to the earlier genre. But in this instance and elsewhere, the text wants to argue that blood is the regrettable and less worthy, albeit mighty, cause of things, and that the sublimities of love are innocent. In fact, as we have seen, love is quite evidently implicated.

The patterning of Guinevere's guilt in loving is matched by the similar patterning of Lancelot's alleged guilt in not loving enough. Guinevere has accused Lancelot of caring less about her and of being 'a common lechourer' (612.20). Lancelot has been espousing the causes of other ladies precisely because of his affair with Guinevere. As in her case, it is the smokescreen itself which gets him into trouble. This much is clear.

What is somewhat less clear in both cases is whose benefit the alibis are for. Did Guinevere arrange the dinner to show Lancelot, or the world at large, that she cherished him no more than other knights? Was she miming his earlier attempts at discretion or parodying them on purpose to upset him? A more complex tangle of motivations surrounds Lancelot's recent activities: what is the balance between his wish 'to do for the pleasure of our Lorde Jesu Cryst', given his muted achievements in the Grail Quest (along with a measure of irritation with Guinevere for being the reason for his failure) and his desire, mentioned in the same sentence, to 'eschew the sclawndir and noyse' (612.23–5)? His own speech to her is redolent of this uncertainty, giving her reaction a degree of psychological realism as well as of textual accuracy: he is not so innocent after all.[3] He is not sleeping with his new needy damsels any more than she will sleep with her ten wounded knights three episodes later, but as Paul Strohm says of Mellyagaunce on that occasion, in her accusations she is 'on to something' (Strohm 2000: 207).

Lancelot's words on the subject of why 'thys batayle ought to be myne' (618.44) would seem in some particulars to run against the grain of his or the narrative's purposes. Readers of Arthurian romances are accustomed to a high degree of arbitrariness where the assignment or taking of adventures is concerned. Whatever one makes of the appropriateness of other cases, such as Gawain's in *Sir Gawain and the Green Knight* or Balyn's hundreds of pages earlier in *Le Morte Darthur*, the Poisoned Apple combat ought to be Lancelot's according to a far more sequential logic.[4] Lancelot is Guinevere's lover and she got into this scrape because they are lovers. And yet, since Lancelot's words before the battle do not exceed the usual formulations for adventure-claiming, the text can present adventure and claimant as being related in the more opaque manner of other takings, an opacity which allows for shades of everything from the arbitrariness of turn-taking, to the aesthetically appropriate, to the numinous. Normal fair play between lovers need not come into it.

But there is irresistible pressure upon this textual mystification from the material it seeks to conceal. When the battle is over and Arthur has thanked Lancelot on his and the queen's behalf, Lancelot replies decorously that his actions have been only fitting given that Arthur knighted him. He then adds:

> and that day my lady, your quene, ded me worshyp. And ellis had I bene shamed, for that same day that ye made me knyght, thorow my hastynes I loste my swerde, and my lady, youre quene, founde hit, and lapped hit in her trayne, and gave me my swerde whan I had nede thereto; and ells had I bene shamed amonge all knyghtes. And therefore, my lorde Arthure, I promysed her at that day ever to be her knyght in ryght other in wronge. (620.21–30)

To the modern reader, the Freudian implications of this incident might be felt to be considerably more embarrassing than any shame occasioned by missing military gear. It is significant that the episode, roughly drawn from the opening section of the French prose *Lancelot*, turns up at this late stage in Malory where the narrative strain to repress is reaching breaking-point, both in this particular story and in *Le Morte Darthur* as a whole. The French text had it that Arthur, hassled by this young knight in a hurry, forgot to give him the sword – a memory lapse with its own psychoanalytic potential. But it is Malory's text which adds the lapping of the sword in Guinevere's train by way of restoration.[5]

This arresting moment is on one level typical of *Le Morte Darthur*'s texture, where a ruthlessly plot-driven plain style erupts rarely and briefly into a sensuous detail of thematic import, for instance Lyonesse's 'mantell furred with ermyne' (205.39) or Lancelot's soon-to-be wounded naked hand (656.13), both in the context of lovers' secret meetings. But Lancelot's lapped sword, evinced as a rationale for his coming to Guinevere's rescue, goes beyond these examples, giving the lie to the niceties Lancelot articulated earlier. One might feel that, short of burlesque, or at least narrative irony, only a pre-Freudian text could allow itself such a brazenly symbolic slip.

Revealing slips occur in the text in a number of forms. Malory's conversations, as we have seen, display a localized dramatic understanding of a given psychological predicament. We might speculate as to whether there is any connection between this tendency towards dramatic exploration and the emergence of drama as a dominant form in the coming century. Just as Malory's dialogue is interested in situation rather than individuality, beyond the most obvious distinctions between virtue and evil the plot sequences in *Le Morte Darthur* are similarly not designed to imitate naturalistically how different people really act. Surrounding Lancelot's unintended *double entendre* are structural patterns which likewise trace submerged issues. One can see the renamings, disguises, wounds and increasingly uncertain geographical location of Lancelot in the whole penultimate tale as a playing out of self-formulation translated into a procession of rather placard-like emblems; they investigate identity, but without the individualizing agenda of novelistic developments of character.

Looking specifically at the plot of the Knight of the Cart episode, a reader might ask why it is that in the first narrative sequence, to Lancelot's irritation, Guinevere demands a peaceful treatment of her abductor, Sir Mellyagaunt, and then in the second so decisively demands his death, 'wagg[ing] hir hede uppon sir Launcelot, as ho seyth "sle hym"' (662.25). The treatment of Sir Mellyagaunt has little to do with either Guinevere's or Lancelot's particular psyche. The plot sequence can be read as offering instead an opportunity to evade what Strohm calls 'the text's own self-serving simplifications' (Strohm 2000: 213–14). Sir Mellyagaunt is Sir Lancelot's double. He serves a purpose which the text can ill afford to foreshorten by killing him off half-way through but, as a scandalous double, he has to be killed off eventually. Mellyagaunt does not simply reflect Lancelot's own illicit desire for Guinevere, albeit in debased form; the point is reinforced by unflattering comedy which equates Lancelot's injured masculinity with Mellyagaunt's wimpish cowering. Both are to some extent infantilized, and the queen turns from one to the other like a mother caring for two whingeing boys. 'What ayles you now?' she says to Lancelot, and to Mellyagaunt less than a page later, 'Why be ye so amoved?' (655.8, 28).[6] Needless to say, the more explicit activities of the text counter this sense of Mellyagaunt as a Lancelot by emphasizing the extent to which he is Lancelot's foil: hence Lancelot's somewhat loquacious assurance that he is not the treasonous type and the sententious passage a few lines later on the theme that 'ever a man of worshyp and of proues dredis but lytyll of perels, for they wene that every man be as they bene' (659.27–30, 37–41). But Mellyagaunt *is* much as Lancelot is. Despite his 'I wote nat what ye meane' when chided for his indecorum, both Mellyagaunt and Lancelot understand full well the desire to open the curtains to Guinevere's bed and lie down by her, and they would not be in the same room having that conversation if this were not the case. While protesting their difference at one level, the narrative seems to need to let off steam, to flirt with the extent of symmetry between Lancelot and the ill-mannered abductor. But in the end, Mellyagaunt has to go, and the unusual aggression of Guinevere's head-wagging may betray the text's anxiety about that symmetry.

There is another reason why Mellyagaunt needs to be killed off. The penultimate tale as a whole functions as a series of near-misses, or, thinking of it another way, rehearsals of the showdown in the final tale. Mellyagaunt's fumbling attempt to out Guinevere's adultery is a comic precursor of Aggravayne's more sinister and effective machinations, with Lavayne as understudy to Bors in voicing his misgivings to the unheeding Lancelot (657.6–658.24; 675.21–676.31). The decisive slicing up of Mellyagaunt is in this regard pure wish-fulfilment; as in a dream, the text affords itself the satisfaction of cleansing the scene of the villain. But neither Mellyagaunt nor Aggravayne is really the problem. Since Mellyagaunt has not quite got the story straight, and will fail and die, the comic dream version can afford to be quite open about what went on in the bedroom:

> sir Launcelot wente to bedde with the quene and toke no force of hys hurte honde, but toke his plesaunce and hys lykynge untyll hit was the dawning of the day; for wyte you well he slept nat, but wacched. (657.33–5)

In the second version, however, where the villain cannot be killed off – the main plot needs him, and he deflects attention from the bedroom activities – the narrative famously draws the curtains:

> For, as the Freynshhe booke seyth, the quene and sir Launcelot were togydyrs. And whether they were abed other at other maner of disportis, me lyste nat therof make no mencion, for love that tyme was nat as love ys nowadays. (676.1–4)

This transparent attempt to obfuscate is a last-ditch effort, faced with a villain who, however much one plays up the impurities of his motivation or his family traits, is in fact articulating the truth.

Alongside the conversational slips and structural traces of concealed issues in Malory is another habit which also reveals what has been repressed. A feature of Malory's style is the repetition of a thematic word or concept within a particular episode which at times can seem to become a mindless echo, as if the record has got stuck and the same word is being pointlessly applied to everything in sight. Examples in this part of the narrative include the vocabulary of 'hete', attached not only to Lancelot's and Guinevere's love (611.16), Gawain's 'nature' (613.35), Mador's anger (616.40) and, implicitly, the fire in which the queen might burn (615.13) but also, more trivially, to the effect of alcohol on the hapless Patryse (613.41). While one can, somewhat awkwardly, create patterns of a conventional, thematic sort out of these repetitions – the heat of love or anger leads to the heat of the fire and so on – the sense one has is of the idea leaking rather messily into the entire episode, creating the effect of a sort of haze infusing the whole picture rather than delineating precise correspondences and causes. Speaking of the 'saturation' of the text with the idea of treason, and Mellyagaunt's usefulness as a 'beacon' attracting treason to himself and away from the main players, Strohm understands such clusters as examples of Freudian 'overdetermination', whereby a narrative refers repeatedly to its own matters of anxiety, excessively and not necessarily in places where they make most sense (Strohm 2000: 208).[7] In fact, a certain stubborn inaccuracy is likely to characterize the location of such references, the narrative at once revealing and concealing its apprehensions. The effect of the 'hete' cluster is to lose the inflammable potency of love in a general atmosphere where even its causal connection with anger is somewhat blurred. It is an anti-analytical move. Things are hotting up but the narrative would rather not know exactly how.

Interestingly, given that the twin purposes of this habit, according to Freud, are revelation and concealment, one of the most noticeable subjects of overdetermination in this section of the text is precisely that: the opposition between openness and privacy itself. The introductory passage of the post-Quest tale maps out the difficulty: the contradiction between Lancelot's 'outward' righteousness and 'inward' devotion to the queen. The opposition then resounds in Guinevere's 'privy' party (613.14) and outward bravura after throwing Lancelot out of the court (613.14–17), in the open shaming threatening her (617.8), and in the open disclosing of the truth – rather long-windedly stated and near-sightedly defined – at the end of the episode (621.3, 5, 7). The text has no intention of facing into the task of reconciling the public with the private, since it has invested heavily both in the public sphere of Arthur's realm and in the sacrosanctity of the private life, and one of them would have to give. It is as if, by intoning the opposition like a refrain, the text vainly hopes the problem – itself an open and shut case, as the saying goes – will be deflated and disappear, or even that it can be adequately rationalized by somewhat randomly nailing Aggravayne, 'for he was ever opynne-mowthed' (611.19). The contradiction between public and private is a matter of anxiety in the text, just as treason and heat are, and the text is similarly evasive, while loquacious, on the subject. But on a meta-level, the opposition of openness and concealment itself betrays the very form of the text's defence mechanism.

I noted earlier the way blood feud was brought into the Poisoned Apple episode as a red herring, distracting attention from the heat of adultery to focus instead on enmity surrounding Gawain, who is hot 'of nature'. While noble deeds in Malory will always eventually turn out to be explained by noble birth, in a certain sense the text favours culture over nature, the symbolic brotherhood of knights over literal brotherhood of blood. Gawain was kind to the unpromisingly attired Bewmaynes because of a gut reaction based, unbeknown to him, on genetic connection, whereas Lancelot acted out of his 'grete jantylnesse and curtesy' (179.3–6). Needless to say, Lancelot is not indiscriminate in his good manners; he clearly suspects that the lad will reveal himself to be well born, but the text is explicitly proud of Lancelot's rising above the merely familial. Conversely, it is a sign of how far the unsettling of Lancelot's identity has gone in the episode of the Fair Maid of Astolat that even he sets in motion a scene where he nearly dies 'of my cousyne jermaynes hondys' (628.2–3) and, if it had not been for the sight of their 'visages' he could have killed his cousins himself (626.35–9). The primal catastrophe of spilling family blood would seem to be a spectral possibility lying in wait for anyone pressed to the limit by the business of self-making – a possibility which Lancelot glimpses in horror and from which he retreats.

A relevant early example of overdetermination characterizes the tale of Balyn, a story which launches a number of bafflingly doom-laden causative issues for the narrative as a whole. The narrative is virtually sodden in blood. It circles around the idea of blood which heals, with Christ's as exemplar, but it culminates in the irony that Balan, who identifies himself by reference to blood brotherhood and is dressed, horse and man, all in red, and fights until 'alle the place they foght was blood red', cannot recognize his blood brother because his face is so covered in the stuff (56.32–3; 57.7, 12, 18, 21–3). The thrusting off of helmets and consequent seeing 'in the visage' is for Malory the *locus classicus* of affective recognition, but in this case the moment is helplessly anticlimactic; it is only when Balyn wakes up from his swoon that he is able to reveal his identity. Knights in Malory treat each other's bodies and blood as the dwelling-place of the most urgent and powerful mystery in the text,[8] but noble blood in itself is one thing, familial noble blood another. When affinity in blood reaches a certain point it tips over into its opposite: unrecognition.

The Tale of Sir Gareth

Familial blood ties represent the excesses of affinity based on blood, or at least the dangers occasioned by such an affinity if pressed to an extreme. The incestuous engendering of Mordred gives this peril an iconic status in the text. The other end of the spectrum is affinity or reward based on merit, an idea with which *The Tale of Sir Gareth* flirts, as do many romances and novels before and since, but with no intention of endorsing it. The Fair Unknown Bewmaynes, like Chrétien's *Chevalier au lion*, has an adolescent relationship with his origins. He wants to make his name before his name is revealed. It is significant that he allows Lancelot to know who he is before his immediate family knows, as it is that his further intimacy by battle with Lancelot does not reach the bloody extreme of his battle with Gawain. Love and blood are continually yoked in the text, but familial love is unstable, ever ready to turn into hate.

What I am arguing is that while the Poisoned Apple episode and others seem to fall back upon issues of kinship as a way of avoiding talking about love, Malory's text is by no means comfortable with the topic of blood either. The text honours blood, as it honours love, but it is uneasy about both. It seeks to contain the subtler difficulties of both issues by way of simplified encapsulations: bad love can be seen, even laughed at, and dispatched in the form of Mellyagaunt; bad blood can be depicted in the blabber-mouthed Aggravayne and, more tragically, in the person of Gawain, where the text hopes to simplify further by making out that it is his 'nature' which is at fault. Just as the text avoids facing what it is that love can cause, it is also loath to notice the extent to which that spiral of family loyalties, touched upon briefly in the Poisoned Apple where it was convenient, commands the deep structure of the plot. On the one hand, blood is sacred; on the other it represents a primitive atavism which the civilities of the text cannot countenance.

Surprisingly, Malory's text is fleetingly able to imagine points of view with no interest at all in knightliness and nobility of blood. Torre's supposed father, Aryes the cowherd, rather than being impressed by the boy's obsession with jousts, considers him the ugly duckling of his brood, a child who was no help at all around the farm (61.24–9). While one might read Aryes as comically blind to the merits of blood, nevertheless he is allowed to articulate his position in a way which makes the activities of a knight sound rather effete. More assertive than his counterpart in the source, he phrases Torre's difference not as a lack in himself, but as a lack in Torre: 'he never had no tacchys of me' (62.26).[9] Aryes is one of the very rare exceptions which prove the rule, though one might wonder whether he is not yet another sign that sustaining the rule has become something of a strain by Malory's lifetime.[10]

We have traced examples of the way Malory's text juggles love and blood. But we have also noticed that the two are not simply alternative explanations for why things happen between which the text moves as suits it; they are intricately and mutually enmeshed. Unavoidably, distinctions need to be made in this regard with reference to gender. The immediate, quasi-chemical sensing in the text that one is in the presence of special blood typifies men's affective relationships with each other rather than the contact of men with women. Men in Malory fall under each other's spell by blood seemingly speaking to blood, by their hearts' impulsive apprehension of greatness, and by the confirmation of these vibrations in armed combat.[11] As Gareth says to Lancelot, 'hit doth me good to fele your myght' (181.19–20). The impression given is one of knights apprehending in each other a third element, a mystery embodied in both but ultimately beyond either. The peculiarly charged quality of homosocial relations in Malory's *Gareth* does not reach the erotic heights or the blatant sidelining of the female partner which occurs in Tennyson's version: Gareth's elated submission at the touch of the disguised Lancelot's 'skilled spear, the wonder of the world', his ecstatic 'Thou – Lancelot! . . . O Lancelot – thou!' once identities are revealed, and Lancelot's own apparent inability to concentrate during his reply to the 'harsh' and 'petulant' interjections of the puzzled maiden, so much more urgent is his desire to talk to Gareth: 'not less I felt / Thy manhood through that wearied lance of thine'.[12] But the Victorian remake is instructive as an exaggeration of elements which are suggested in Malory.

Women in *Le Morte Darthur* do not generally seem to have the right antennae for this quasi-sacramental communion. Lyonesse has to resort to kidnapping Gareth's dwarf and interrogating him for his master's pedigree; while she already thinks well of him, she is not sensitive to the adumbrations which affect Lancelot. Elayne, admittedly, rhymes with her brother Lavayne in love as in name, but her description of her overwhelming feelings for Lancelot is not characterized by either mystery or mystification. On the contrary, while departing from earthly life and while claiming that this 'good love' emanates from God, she insists upon her own and Lancelot's earthliness (639.31–7). Of course he is noble, but her attraction to him has none of the sacral quality of men's mutual admiration.

This numinous aura does not typify men's love for women in the text either. Often the received design of romance *aventure* dictates that a knight be in love with a particular woman. Having taken on a series of adventures, Chrétien's Yvain, already committed to one woman, finds himself in the awkward position of being expected to marry several more, each of whom is part of the package of a particular task. This *aventure* logic is palpable in the case of Gareth and Lyonesse:

> 'Sir,' seyde the damesell Lynet unto Sir Bewmaynes, 'loke ye be glad and light, for yonder is your dedly enemy, and at yonder window is my lady, my sister dame Lyones.'
>
> 'Where?' seyde Bewmaynes.
>
> 'Yondir,' seyde the damesell, and pointed with her fyngir.
>
> 'That is trouth,' seyde Bewmaynes, 'she besemyth afarre the fayryst lady that ever I loked upon, and truly,' he seyde, 'I aske no better quarrel than now for to do batayle, for truly she shall be my lady and for hir woll I fight.'
>
> And ever he loked up to the window with glad countenaunce, and this lady dame Lyones made curtesy to hym downe to the erth, holdynge up both her hondys. (197.19–30)

The freeze-framing of Gareth's first sight of his lady, focused by the pointing and followed by the stately dance gesture of the curtsy and raising of her hands, removes it from the flow of narrative. Framed by her window she is instead a paradigm suspended above the story, and Bewmaynes follows the argument to its conclusion: 'she shall be my lady'. Tellingly, his 'beholdyng' is bifocal: his commitment to love her is sealed by looking at the Red Knight and countering his claims to her.

Why is it that Gareth falls in love with Lyonesse a second time? On the face of it, having sadly taken up her assignment of another year's worship-winning before he can have her love, his fancying of this apparently new lady – actually Lyonesse in disguise – a couple of days later might seem to Lyonesse, the reader and, upon reflection, to Gareth himself, to amount to inconstancy. Far from being so knocked sideways by his infatuation that, in the manner of Tristram, he forgets Lyonesse, Gareth compares her unfavourably to the new lady and remarks upon the convenient geographical location of this dalliance, given his commitment to the old one (204.20–1, 205.5–8). And yet there seems to be no invitation for us to frown upon him. One rationale for the repetition might be that the narrative, having delineated love as duty, wants to play it again with love freed from the binding force of adventure. Just as the text flirts with the idea of earning a name, so it flirts with the idea of love and marriage arising, as Lancelot puts it in the case of Elayne, 'of the harte selffe, and nat by none constraynte' (641.37–8). Lyonesse's words to Arthur reinforce this textual agenda: 'yf ye woll suffir hym to have his wyll and fre choyse, I dare say he woll have me' (223.37–8).[13]

One could argue then that the commitment to Lyonesse is actually threefold: in step one, she becomes his lady because the adventure 'belongs' to him and she belongs to the adventure; in step two her beauty urges him to embrace his duty with new zeal; and the final step confirms the first two by experimenting with the lady separated from duty and finds that he chooses her anyway. But the affective power of beauty does not approach the odd sense of epiphany palpable in the relationship of two men.

If the second falling in love with Lyonesse suggests the text's wistfulness for a love match, the person of Lynet represents, *inter alia*, its submerged coveting of the idea of the beloved as companion – another inference extended by Tennyson.[14] Modern readers of medieval romances are struck by the distancing of the heroes' ladies from the action of the stories, but in Malory Arthur himself is puzzled by it: why is Gareth's lady so out of touch? It is left to Lynet to point out that her sister does not even know where Gareth is, and to go and tell her (223.9–17). By Gareth's having, in a sense, not one but two ladies, or, to think of the doubling another way, two versions of one lady, the text can retain the ideal of the distant beloved, and can at the same time covertly entertain the possibility of another model of love in her similarly named but less remote sister. Companions in Malory are generally men – Lavayne, not Elayne. But in Lynet the text, like Chrétien's *Yvain*, plays with the possibility that on this score things could be different.

The big flirtation of Gareth's story, however, is between the hero and Arthur's fellowship. It is with them that he plays hard to get: he is hiding from them, confident that they will come looking for him. Whereas one might have expected the court to be curious about the woman to whom this youngest son has given his love, all the talk is of Gareth himself, and she stage-manages a tournament at which, while she is the prize, it is Gareth's shimmering iridescence which excites the wonder of the company. The tournament takes the form of a contest between her knights and Arthur's, and as such pits Gareth's role as the knight of the lady of the castle against his identity as Arthur's nephew; but the two interests are fused by the fact that Lyonesse is at this point more administrator of the show than its *prima donna*, and Arthur asserts his paternalism by throwing a very big wedding party. *Yvain* leaves the tension much more artificially resolved. More importantly for our purposes, *The Tale of Sir Gareth* contrasts with *The Tale of Lancelot and Guinevere* where Elayne displays what happens when the freedom to love is not mutual and where Lancelot's self-exploration cannot finally be subsumed in matrimony. Liberated from the exigencies of the received plot, in *Gareth* the narrative can make things work out which it cannot put right in the last tales.

In *Gareth* as in *Lancelot and Guinevere*, the investigation of self reaches a certain extreme when the hero fights against his own blood. Gareth's initial smiting of Gawain clearly arises from having been identified precipitately (218.5–7). It is as if blood brotherhood represents the excessive fixing of identity which his colour-shifting so gratifyingly erased, and as such it must be attacked. The unknowing battle of the brothers, in which 'the bloode trayled downe to the grounde' (221.38–9), is a nursery version of Lancelot's later skirmish with Bors. Lynet, ever the governess, puts an end to the contest:

surely they have had enough, their horses are bruised, and it is time for them to turn in. The perils of blood are transmuted into the positive warmth of homecoming. But during the episode Gareth subtly registers the awfulness of what he has done in his somewhat manic 'thrang[ing] here and there' (218.10) and his flight into the woods, and later Gawain betrays a flicker of awareness of the inferiority of blood kinship: 'Alas! My fayre brother . . . I ought of ryght to worshyp you, and ye were nat my brother, for ye have worshipt kynge Arthure and all his courte' (222.12–14). Gawain may be read as saying that, even setting blood brotherhood aside, he should have honoured Gareth. One might equally understand him to be making the opposite point: were it not for blood brotherhood, he would have honoured him; the fight, representing as it does Gareth's need to push family aside in the culminating gesture of his self-making, and Gawain's need to assert the demands of blood, would not have arisen. The fact that the point is made ambiguously is itself informative, expressing at once the twin structure of familial love: 'What ar ye,' seyde sir Gareth, 'that ryght now were so stronge and so mighty, and now so sodeynly is yelde to me?'(222.3–4).

While *The Tale of Sir Lancelot and Queen Guinevere* is comic only by the skin of its teeth, *The Tale of Sir Gareth*, not without its own forebodings about Gawain's 'conducions' and the infuriating tendency of top knights to depart suddenly, represents less precariously the good times of the past (224.20–3, 226.1–3). And yet the text's ambivalence about familial ties endangers the cosy ending of even this less troubled tale.

Readers of Malory are familiar with the idea that *Le Morte Darthur*, with King Arthur summing up the position, cares less about love than about fellowship. It is always possible to get another queen (685.29–32). And yet heterosexual love in the text refreshingly escapes the mystification which colours homosocial bonds among men of good blood. When those more numinous affective ties are considered in their manifestations within the family, their full malignant potential is revealed. The blood family nurtures, comforts and confirms, but the self-making knight has to fly past its nets, has to wound and be wounded by this first love. Nothing matters more in the text than blood, and yet, to borrow Elayne's description of her love for Lancelot, brotherly bonds are blood 'out of measure'. Elayne's earthly feelings for an earthly man were at the expense of her life on earth, but her love was not alloyed by its opposite. That distinction is left to the more central love of blood.

See also: 12 England and France, 16 War and Chivalry, 19 Love, 20 Middle English Romance, 21 Writing Nation, 37 *Sir Gawain and the Green Knight*.

Notes

1 Quotations are from Malory 1971.

2 See Strohm 2000. 165–81 for lucid discussion of these issues.

3 For further discussion of conversational patterns, see La Farge 1987.

4 For a study of these issues in *Balyn*, see Mann 1981.

5 See Sommer 1908–16: III, 131, 137 for the source, and *Malory* 1990: III, 1599, n. 1058.21–32. Heng 1996: 98–9 and 109 n. 9

reads the incident in the context of other female sword-suppliers, and sees it as establishing primary allegiance to the queen.

6 In his brilliant discussion, Strohm 2000: 204–11 associates Mellyagaunt with the infant of Freud's 'primal scene' in his inept, voyeuristic reaction to Guinevere's bloody sheets.

7 On overdetermination, see Freud 1953: v, 408–9 and Wright 1984: 21.

8 For the religious aspects of this issue see Mann 1996.

9 For Malory's deletions from and additions to his source for this episode, see Malory 1990: III, 1325–7.

10 See La Farge 1992 for a reading of the huntress of the Great Tournament episode as a further example.

11 For the symmetry of sex and fighting, see Lynch 1997: 60, 98.

12 A. Tennyson, 'Gareth and Lynette', in *The Idylls of the King* in *The Poems of Tennyson*, ed. C. Ricks, 3 vols (Harlow: Longman, 1987), III, 281–323, lines 1192, 1196, 1210, 1214, 1215, 1233–4.

13 For the influence of the *fée amante* topos on this doubling, see Nolan 1996: 161.

14 Tennyson, 'Gareth and Lynette', lines 393–4.

References and Further Reading

Archibald, E. and Edwards, A. S. G. (eds) 1996. *A Companion to Malory* (Cambridge: Brewer). An excellent volume of essays. See below under Edwards 1996, Mann 1996, Nolan 1996, Riddy 1996.

Chrétien de Troyes 1971. *Le Chevalier au Lion (Yvain)*, ed. M. Roques. Paris: Champion. Far more self-conscious and ironic in style, this twelfth-century romance deals with many of the same issues as Malory's *Gareth*.

Edwards, E. 1996. 'The Place of Women in the *Morte Darthur*.' In Archibald and Edwards 1996: 37–54. This article provides interesting discussion of how the location of Malory's women – for instance, in forests and castles – reveals them as signs of fear of the feminine.

—— 2000. *The Genesis of Narrative in Malory's Morte Darthur*. Cambridge: Boydell and Brewer. A perceptive and intricate study of how things occur in Malory's text approached by way of its various narrative structures.

Freud, S. 1953. *The Interpretation of Dreams* and *On Dreams*, trans. and ed. J. Strachey. *The Standard Edition of the Complete Psychological Works of Sigmund Freud*, vols 4 and 5. London: Hogarth Press and the Institute of Psycho-Analysis. One of Freud's most stimulating analyses of how repression gives rise to narratives.

Heng, G. 1996. 'Enchanted Ground: The Feminine Subtext in Malory.' In *Arthurian Women*, ed. T. S. Fenster (New York: Routledge), pp. 97–13. Argues for a feminine subtext in Malory which grants women a powerful and enabling role.

La Farge, C. 1987. 'Conversation in Malory's *Morte Darthur*.' *Medium Ævum* 56, 225–38. A study of dialogue which emphasizes the tendency of speakers not to hear and to speak at cross-purposes, especially where differing obsessions or self-delusions are at stake.

—— 1992. 'The Hand of the Huntress: Repetition and Malory's *Morte Darthur*.' In *New Feminist Discourses: Critical Essays on Theories and Texts*, ed. I. Armstrong (London: Routledge), pp. 263–79. A reading of one brief comic episode as a sign of submerged issues in *The Tale of Sir Lancelot and Queen Guinevere*.

Lambert, M. 1975. *Malory: Style and Vision in* Le Morte Darthur. New Haven, Conn.: Yale University Press. A lively seminal discussion of issues such as shame and guilt, narratorial mannerisms and the handling of causes.

Lynch, A. 1997. *Malory's Book of Arms: The Narrative of Combat in* Le Morte Darthur. Cambridge: Brewer. A stimulating study which comments on the meaning of noble blood and on the intense relationships of knight and knight expressed through battle.

Malory, T. 1971. *Works*, ed. E. Vinaver, 2nd edn. London: Oxford University Press. The affordable single-volume edition of the standard text based primarily on the one surviving manuscript.

—— 1990. *The Works of Sir Thomas Malory*, ed. E. Vinaver, 3rd edn, rev. P. J. C. Field, 3 vols. London: Oxford University Press. A revised version of the standard text including Vinaver's massive annotations which are especially useful for signalling departures from the French sources.

Mann, J. 1981. 'Taking the Adventure: Malory and the *Suite du Merlin*.' In *Aspects of Malory*, ed. T. Takamiya and D. Brewer (Cambridge: Brewer), pp. 71–91. An important study of the logic of narrative.

—— 1996. 'Malory and the Grail Legend.' In Archibald and Edwards 1996: 203–20. An essay delineating the eucharistic theme which informs the topic of body and blood in Malory's text.

Nolan, B. 1996. '*The Tale of Sir Gareth* and *The Tale of Sir Lancelot*.' In Archibald and Edwards 1996: 153–81. A comparative essay which includes helpful comment on generic issues and on Malory's use of the *bel inconnu*, *fée-amante* and younger brother story structures in *Sir Gareth*.

Riddy, F. 1987. *Sir Thomas Malory*. Leiden: Brill. A study which places the text in its cultural context alongside other examples of fifteenth-century anxieties about manners and right conduct, and argues convincingly for the 'fissile' tendencies of Malory's work.

—— 1996. 'Contextualizing *Le Morte Darthur*: Empire and Civil War.' In Archibald and Edwards 1996: 55–73. A deft example of historical criticism at its very best.

Sommer, H. O. (ed.) 1908–16. *The Vulgate Version of the Arthurian Romances*, 8 vols. Carnegie Institution of Washington Publications, 74. Washington, D.C.: Carnegie Institution. Provides a large proportion of Malory's thirteenth-century French source material.

Strohm, P. 2000. 'Psychoanalysis and Medieval Studies.' In his *Theory and the Premodern Text*. Medieval Cultures, 26 (Minneapolis: University of Minnesota Press), pp. 165–214. While 'Mellyagaunt's Primal Scene' (pp. 201–14) is of most direct relevance, the other essays in this section also provide lively defences and illustrations of the psychoanalytic analyses of early texts.

Wright, E. 1984. *Psychoanalytic Criticism: Theory in Practice*. London: Methuen. A very helpful guide to the psychoanalytic approach to literature.

Index

Illustrations are denoted by page numbers in italics.